76% of instructors state that student reading of text chapters is very or extremely important for success in their courses.

> *Essentials of Understanding Psychology* supports student reading and comprehension of material through its modular organization; introductory *Making the Grade* section; listing of key concepts for each module; engaging *Prologue, Looking Ahead,* and *Looking Back* sections; and *Study Alerts.*

> *Essentials of Understanding Psychology* provides an adaptive diagnostic tool that ensures students understand the key concepts in the chapter. Whether they use this dynamic resource before or after class, your students will read more material more effectively. Students who use this adaptive diagnostic tool are seeing their grades improve by a letter grade or more.

> An optional e-book format is available for students "on the go" or who prefer reading in small chunks.

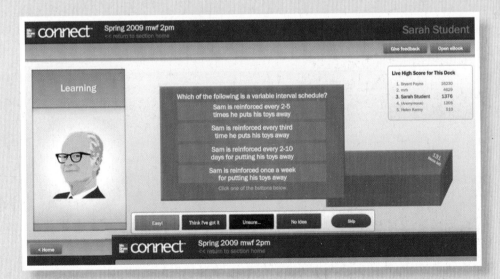

If you would like to participate in any of the McGraw-Hill research initiatives please contact us at **research@mcgraw-hill.com**

NINTH EDIT

Essentials of Understanding Psychology

Robert S. Feldman
University of Massachusetts, Amherst

McGraw Hill

Connect
Learn
Succeed™

Published by McGraw-Hill, a business unit of The McGraw-Hill Companies, Inc., 1221 Avenue of the Americas, New York, NY 10020. Copyright © 2011, 2009, 2008, 2005, 2002, 1999, 1996, 1993, 1990, 1987 by The McGraw-Hill Companies, Inc. All rights reserved. No part of this publication may be reproduced or distributed in any form or by any means, or stored in a database or retrieval system, without the prior written consent of The McGraw-Hill Companies, Inc., including, but not limited to, any network or other electronic storage or transmission, or broadcast for distance learning. Some ancillaries, including electronic and print components, may not be available to customers outside the United States.

2 3 4 5 6 7 8 9 0 DOW/DOW 1

ISBN: 978-0-07-338280-7
MHID: 0-07-338280-9

Vice President, Editorial: *Michael Ryan*
Director, Editorial: *Beth Mejia*
Publisher: *Michael Sugarman*
Executive Editor: *Krista Bettino*
Development Editors: *Cara Labell and*
    Sue Ewing
Editorial Coordinator: *Megan Stotts*
Executive Marketing Manager: *Julia Flohr*
Marketing Manager: *Yasuko Okada*
Digital Product Manager: *Jay Gubernick*
Media Project Manager: *Thomas Brierly*
Production Editor: *Anne Fuzellier*
Text Permission Coordinator: *Marty Moga*

Art Manager: *Robin Mouat*
Art Director: *Preston Thomas*
Interior Designer: *Ellen Pettengel*
Cover Designer: *Laurie Entringer*
Photo Manager: *Brian J.Pecko*
Photo Researcher: *Toni Michaels*
Buyer II: *Tandra Jorgensen*
Production Service: *The Left Coast Group, Inc.*
Composition: *9.5/12 Palatino by Aptara, Inc.*
Printing: *45# New Era Thin by RR Donnelley*
    & Sons
Cover image: *©Stockbyte/PunchStock*

Credits: The credits section for this book begins on page C-1 and is considered an extension of the copyright page.

Library of Congress Cataloging-in-Publication Data

Feldman, Robert S. (Robert Stephen), 1947–
  Essentials of understanding psychology / Robert S. Feldman.—9th ed.
     p. cm.
  An abbreviated version of the author's Understanding psychology. 10th ed. c2011.
  Includes bibliographical references and index.
  ISBN-13: 978-0-07-338280-7 (alk. paper)
  ISBN-10: 0-07-338280-9 (mhid : alk. paper)
  1. Psychology—Textbooks. I. Feldman, Robert S. (Robert Stephen), 1947–
  Understanding psychology. II. Title.
  BF121.F34 2011b
  150—dc22
                    2010031467

The Internet addresses listed in the text were accurate at the time of publication. The inclusion of a website does not indicate an endorsement by the authors or McGraw-Hill, and McGraw-Hill does not guarantee the accuracy of the information presented at these sites.

www.mhhe.com

To
Jon, Leigh, Alex, Josh,
Julie, Sarah, and Kathy

About the Author

ROBERT S. FELDMAN is Professor of Psychology and Dean of the College of Social and Behavioral Sciences at the University of Massachusetts, Amherst. A recipient of the College Distinguished Teacher Award, he teaches psychology classes ranging in size from 15 to nearly 500 students. During the course of more than two decades as a college instructor, he has taught undergraduate and graduate courses at Mount Holyoke College, Wesleyan University, and Virginia Commonwealth University in addition to the University of Massachusetts.

Professor Feldman, who initiated the Minority Mentoring Program at the University of Massachusetts, also has served as a Hewlett Teaching Fellow and Senior Online Teaching Fellow. He initiated distance learning courses in psychology at the University of Massachusetts.

A Fellow of both the American Psychological Association and the Association for Psychological Science, Professor Feldman received a BA with High Honors from Wesleyan University and an MS and PhD from the University of Wisconsin-Madison. He is a winner of a Fulbright Senior Research Scholar and Lecturer Award and the Distinguished Alumnus Award from Wesleyan. He is on the Boards of the Federation of Associations in Behavioral and Brain Sciences (FABBS) and the FABBS Foundation, which advocate for the field of psychology.

He has written and edited more than 150 books, book chapters, and scientific articles. He has edited *Development of Nonverbal Behavior in Children, Applications of Nonverbal Behavioral Theory and Research, Improving the First Year of College: Research and Practice,* and co-edited *Fundamentals of Nonverbal Behavior.* He is also author of *Development Across the Life Span, Child Development,* and *P.O.W.E.R. Learning: Strategies for Success in College and Life.* His books have been translated into many languages, including Spanish, French, Portuguese, Dutch, Chinese, Korean, and Japanese. His research interests include deception and honesty in everyday life, work that he described in *The Liar in Your Life,* a trade book published in 2009. His research has been supported by grants from the National Institute of Mental Health and the National Institute on Disabilities and Rehabilitation Research.

Professor Feldman loves music, is an enthusiastic pianist, and enjoys cooking and traveling. He has three children and a young grandson. He and his wife, a psychologist, live in western Massachusetts in a home overlooking the Holyoke mountain range.

Brief Contents

Contents

CHAPTER 4

States of Consciousness 128

CHAPTER 10

Personality 376

CHAPTER 14

Social Psychology 516

Preface

Students first.

If I were to use only a few words to summarize my goal for this book, as well as my teaching philosophy, that's what I would say. Students first. I believe that an effective textbook must be oriented to students—informing them, engaging them, and exciting them about the field and helping them connect it to their worlds. When students are engaged and challenged, they understand psychology at a deep and meaningful level.

Luckily, psychology is a science that is inherently interesting to students. It is a discipline that speaks with many voices, offering a personal message to each student. To some, psychology provides a better understanding of others' behavior. Others view psychology as a pathway to self-understanding. Still others see the potential for a future career, and some are drawn to psychology by the opportunity for intellectual discovery that its study provides.

No matter what brings students into the introductory course and regardless of their initial motivation, *Essentials of Understanding Psychology*, Ninth Edition, is designed to draw students into the field and stimulate their thinking. By focusing on students first, and connecting with them, the text promotes student success by *engaging* their attention in order to *inform* them, which results in students learning the course content and becoming *excited* about the field of psychology.

Ways of Connecting with Today's Students

Today's students are as different from the learners of the last generation as today's discipline of psychology is different from the field 30 years ago. Students now learn in multiple modalities; rather than sitting down and reading traditional printed chapters in linear fashion from beginning to end, their work preferences tend to be more visual and more interactive, and their reading and study often occur in short bursts. For many students, a traditionally formatted printed textbook is no longer enough when they have instant, 24/7 access to news and information from around the globe.

Connect Psychology is our response to today's student. The groundbreaking adaptive diagnostic tool helps students "know what they know" while helping them learn what they don't know through engaging interactivities, exercises, videos, and readings. Instructors using Connect are reporting their students' performance is improving by a letter grade or more.

Through this unique tool, *Essentials of Understanding Psychology* gives instructors the ability to identify struggling students quickly and easily *before* the first exam. Connect Psychology's adaptive diagnostic tool develops an individualized learning plan for every student. Confidence levels tailor the next question to each individual, helping students to know what they don't know. If your student is doing well, the adaptive diagnostic tool will challenge the student with more applied and conceptual questions. If your student is struggling, the system identifies problem areas and directs the student to the exact page they need to read. In doing so, it works like a GPS, helping students master key concepts efficiently and effectively. Regardless of individual study habits, preparation, and approaches to the course, students will find *Essentials of Understanding Psychology,* coupled with Connect Psychology, adapts to them individually and provides a road map for success.

Ways of Engaging Students

PROLOGUE Each chapter starts with an account of a real-life situation that demonstrates the relevance of basic principles and concepts of psychology to pertinent issues and problems. These prologues depict well-known people and events.

LOOKING AHEAD The prologue situation is then tied to key themes and issues discussed in the subsequent modules.

Prologue *Trapped in a Male's Body*

The images are iconic TV moments: precious little Chastity Bono, with her blonde hair and chubby cheeks, gracing her parents' 1970s variety show *The Sonny and Cher Comedy Hour* with a family song or the sweet sign-off, "Goodnight everybody and God bless!" While girls at home may have been envious of Cher's glittery outfits, Chastity, who always wore costumes to complement either that of her Mom's and Dad's, later admitted, "I especially liked it when they put me in clothes that matched my father's."

In fact, when Chastity came out as a lesbian to *The Advocate* in 1995, she said, "As a kid I thought I was a little boy." (Bartolomeo et al., 2009, p. 54)

Chastity Bono never actually stopped thinking of herself as male. In spring 2009, at the age of 40, Chastity announced to the world that she was transitioning from female to male and would henceforth be known as Chaz.

 Looking **Ahead**

Chaz's story illustrates the emotion and confusion that often characterize one of the most universal behaviors: sexuality. Exemplifying major personal as well as societal concerns, sex and the interrelated topic of gender are also key topics for psychologists in a variety of specialties. For instance, psychologists interested in motivation view sexuality in terms of sexual needs, drives, and gratification. Neuroscientists consider sexuality from the perspective of the relationship of the brain and nervous system to the functioning of the sexual organs. Social psychologists and psychologists who specialize in the study of women focus on society's rules of sexual conduct and the role sexual behavior plays in interpersonal behavior.

In this set of modules, we consider human sexuality from several of these vantage points. We begin by examining gender and discussing differences in societal expectations about how men and women should behave and the impact of those expectations on behavior and attitudes. Next we turn to sexual behavior. We describe the biological aspects of sexual excitement and arousal and then examine the variety of sexual activities in which people engage. We conclude with a discussion of nonconsenting sex, sexually transmitted infections, and the psychological aspects of sexual difficulties.

Classical Conditioning   START OVER

Do you remember Pavlov's dog experiments? Pavlov repeatedly paired a bell with the delivery of meat until finally dogs salivated at the sound of the bell alone.

Advertisers use this same principle to sell products to consumers. Many advertising campaigns associate products with either negative or positive unconditioned stimuli such as emotional arousal, hunger, or fear. The advertisers hope that viewers will learn to be aroused by the sight of their product, to become hungry for their product, or to become afraid of their competitors' products.

NEXT

VIDEO CLIPS AND INTERACTIVE EXERCISES Students can see what key concepts look like in the real world and apply what they are learning through video clips and interactive exercises you assign through Connect. The clips and exercises are keyed to learning objectives and levels of Bloom's taxonomy.

Attention-Deficit Hyperactivity Disorder

00:08/03:56

LOOKING BACK AND EPILOGUE Found at the end of every set of modules, *Looking Back* contains critical thinking questions involving the use of Web resources and the interactivities that go with those modules. Critical thinking questions in the *Epilogue* that follows *Looking Back* relate to the *Prologue* at the opening of the set of modules. The thought-provoking questions in these sections provide a way of tying together a set of modules on one topic and illustrating how the concepts addressed in each module apply to the real-world situation described in the *Prologue*.

Looking Back

Psychology on the Web

1. Find at least two recent news articles or discussions on the web dealing with the issue of gender equality in school or the workplace, especially unequal treatment of individuals because of their gender. Summarize in writing what you found, and discuss your own attitudes toward this issue.
2. Find information on the web about date rape, including guidelines or suggestions published by other colleges for preventing rape among students. Summarize your findings, including recommendations for behavioral or policy changes that might be effective at your college. If your college's policies toward or publications about this topic could benefit from your findings, bring them to the attention of the appropriate office at your institution and suggest specific changes.

Epilogue

We have seen how psychologists are dealing with the topics of gender and sex, first with regard to gender roles, gender stereotyping, gender schemas, and sexism. Society's expectations regarding male and female characteristics and behaviors lead to inequities in the treatment of men and women in school, the workplace, and the rest of society—inequities that largely favor men.

With regard to sexuality, we discussed the nature of the physical processes that surround sexuality and addressed the controversial issue of "normality" in sexual behavior. We saw the broad diversity of sexual behavior, and we discussed premarital sex and marital sex, as well as heterosexuality, homosexuality, and bisexuality. We also examined rape and other forms of nonconsenting sex, including childhood sexual abuse.

Finally, we looked at the sexual problems that people may have, including STIs and sexual dysfunctions. We explored the nature of these problems and discussed ways to treat and deal with them.

Before we turn to the subject of human development in the next few modules, return to the prologue of this chapter concerning Chaz Bono's sense that she is a male trapped in a female's body. Using your knowledge of gender and sex, consider the following questions.

1. Why might Bono's family, friends, and fans react negatively to her decision to become a man?
2. How is Bono's transsexualism different from lesbianism?
3. Why do you think Bono believed herself to be a lesbian before deciding that she was really a man?
4. What difficulties might Bono encounter in her journey to become male?

Ways of Informing Students

COMPREHENSIVE CONTENT COVERAGE *Essentials of Understanding Psychology* provides broad coverage of the field of psychology, including the theories, research, and applications that permeate the discipline. Along with the traditional areas of psychology (neuroscience, sensation and perception, states of consciousness, learning, memory, cognition, human development, personality, abnormal behavior and treatment, and social psychology), the applied topic of health psychology (Chapter 11) receives extensive attention.

MODULAR ORGANIZATION The text is organized into modules in which each of the 14 chapters is divided into three or four manageable, self-contained sections that include learning objectives and assessment opportunities. Each module ends with questions that assess learning on both an objective and more conceptual, higher-order level.

Rather than facing a long and potentially daunting chapter, students can study material in smaller chunks, which psychological research long ago found to be the optimal way to learn. Moreover, instructors can customize assignments for their students by asking them to read only those modules that fit their course outline and in the sequence that matches their syllabus. Alternatively, instructors who prefer to assign whole chapters can do so.

CONNECTION TO APA STUDENT COMPETENCIES Conforming to recommendations of an American Psychological Association (APA) task force report on undergraduate student competencies (Board of Educational Affairs, 2002), *every* component of the text and its package is tied to specific psychological concepts and their application in everyday life. A chart indicating how the features of the textbook directly address the APA student competencies is provided in Figure 1 on page xxvii. Equally important, every one of the thousands of test items in the Test Banks available to instructors is keyed to its corresponding APA competency in a document that is available on the Online Learning Center.

KEY CONCEPTS Each major section of a module begins with questions about the key concepts addressed in that section. These questions provide a framework for understanding and organizing the material that follows, as well as providing assessment benchmarks.

EXPLORING DIVERSITY In addition to substantial coverage of material relevant to diversity throughout, every set of modules also includes at least one special section devoted to an aspect of racial, ethnic, gender, or cultural diversity. These sections highlight the way in which psychology informs (and is informed by) issues relating to the increasing multiculturalism of our global society.

Exploring DIVERSITY
Does Culture Influence How We Learn?

When a member of the Chilcotin Indian tribe teaches her daughter to prepare salmon, at first she allows the daughter only to observe the entire process. A little later, she permits her child to try out some basic parts of the task. Her response to questions is noteworthy. For example, when the daughter asks about how to do "the backbone part," the mother's response is to repeat the entire process with another salmon. The reason? The mother feels that one cannot learn the individual parts of the task apart from the context of preparing the whole fish. (Tharp, 1989)

It should not be surprising that children raised in the Chilcotin tradition, which stresses instruction that starts by communicating the entire task, may have difficulty with traditional Western schooling. In the approach to teaching most characteristic of Western culture, tasks are broken down into their component parts. Only after each small step is learned is it thought possible to master the complete task.

Do the differences in teaching approaches between cultures affect how people learn? Some psychologists, taking a cognitive perspective on learning, suggest that people develop particular *learning styles*, characteristic ways of approaching material, based on their cultural background and unique pattern of abilities (Anderson & Adams, 1992; Barmeyer, 2004; Wilkinson & Olliver-Gray, 2006).

Book Feature	APA Learning Goals									
	Knowledge Base of Psychology	Research Methods in Psychology	Critical Thinking Skills in Psychology	Application of Psychology	Values in Psychology	Information and Technological Literacy	Communication Skills	Sociocultural and International Awareness	Personal Development	Career Planning and Development
Chapter Content	X	X	X	X	X	X	X	X	X	X
Prologue	X		X	X				X		
Looking Ahead	X	X	X		X					
Key Concepts	X		X	X				X		
Applying Psychology in the 21st Century	X	X		X				X	X	X
Exploring Diversity	X				X		X	X	X	
Neuroscience in Your Life	X	X	X	X						
PsychWork	X			X					X	X
Video Clips	X			X						
Interactive Exercises	X									
Running Glossary	X			X		X				
Becoming an Informed Consumer of Psychology	X	X		X	X		X		X	X
Study Alerts	X	X		X						
Recap/Evaluate/Rethink	X		X	X						
Looking Back	X		X	X		X	X			
Epilogue	X		X	X				X		
Adaptive Diagnostic Tool	X									

FIGURE 1 This grid shows the relationship between the broad learning goals devised by the American Psychological Association and specific types of content in *Essentials of Understanding Psychology*. In addition, each of the test items in the Test Bank for the book, consisting of nearly 4,000 individual, scorable items, is keyed to specific learning outcomes.

STUDY ALERTS Throughout the modules, marginal notes point out especially important and difficult concepts and topics. These Study Alerts offer suggestions for learning the material effectively and for studying for tests. In Chapter 4, Module 12, for example, a Study Alert emphasizes the importance of differentiating the five stages of sleep; the feature in Module 13 makes clear the key issue about hypnosis—whether it represents a different state of consciousness or is similar to normal waking consciousness; and in Module 14 it highlights Figure 2 for its clear view of the different ways that drugs produce their effects at a neurological level.

> **Study Alert**
> Differentiate the five stages of sleep (stage 1, stage 2, stage 3, stage 4, and REM sleep), which produce different brain-wave patterns.

RECAP/EVALUATE/RETHINK Each module concludes with a Recap/Evaluate/Rethink section. The *Recap* sections review the concept questions found at the beginning of each module. *Evaluate* sections test recall of the material, assessing the degree of initial learning. The *Rethink* sections provide thought-provoking questions designed to provoke critical thinking about the material.

RUNNING GLOSSARY Key terms are highlighted in boldface type within the text where they are introduced, and definitions are given in the margin of the page, along with pronunciation guides for difficult words. To facilitate study, at the end of each module there is a list of the key terms and concepts introduced in that module. There is also a glossary of all key terms and concepts at the end of the book.

PRE- AND POST-TESTS Students can practice with key concepts with pre- and post-tests you assign through Connect. The test items are keyed to learning objectives and levels of Bloom's taxonomy.

Ways of Exciting Students and Helping Them Relate Psychology to Their World

APPLYING PSYCHOLOGY IN THE 21st CENTURY These boxes highlight the relevance of psychology by presenting current and potential applications of psychological theory and research findings to real-world problems. For example, one box discusses the psychological principles that explain the dangers of texting while driving, while another highlights how artificial intelligence researchers are building "smarter" robots that have the potential to transform our daily lives.

Applying Psychology in the 21st Century

Driven to Distraction

Twenty-four year old Aiden Quinn couldn't believe his good fortune. At his young age, he had beaten the competition to land his dream job of conducting trolleys through the streets of Boston. But in just one moment his world came crashing down around him: It was the moment when he took his eyes off the tracks to send a text message to his girlfriend and the trolley he was driving crashed into the one ahead of it.

Increasing research shows that texting while driving is extremely dangerous.

If you've ever texted while driving, you're not alone. A recent survey conducted by the AAA Foundation for Traffic Safety shows that nearly half of drivers aged 18 to 24 admit to doing so, even though the majority of them were aware that they were increasing their risk of having an accident. In fact, nearly 90% of survey respondents rated texting while driving as a very serious threat to safety (AAA Foundation for Traffic Safety, 2008, 2009).

Researchers are now confirming what intuition suggests is true: The distraction caused by texting while driving is extremely dangerous. One study used video cameras to monitor truckers on long hauls and found that they were 23 times more [likely to have a collisio]n while texting than [normally. Collisions caused by drivers typically taken his [...] about 5 seconds—a

seemingly short period of time until you realize that a vehicle at highway speed travels about 150 yards in those few seconds (Virginia Tech Transportation Institute, 2009).

Another study using college students and a driving simulator showed that texting produced the same duration of about 5 seconds of distraction and that the students were 8 times more likely to have a collision while texting. Although those may seem like better odds, they're still

much worse than the risk presented by other distractors such as changing the station on a car's radio. Even though the study used students, who are likely skillful at texting and multitasking, and light vehicles that are more maneuverable than trucks, the results clearly show that texting while driving poses a terrific risk (Cooper & Strayer, 2008).

Multitasking in general is difficult. For instance, in one study, researchers divided a group of college students into two groups, one composed of students who multitasked online regularly and a second that did not. The frequent multitaskers were more easily distracted, and they were unable to filter out stimuli that were irrelevant to tasks that they were trying to complete (Ophir, Nass, & Wagner, 2009).

If you, like many of the respondents to the AAA Foundation for Traffic Safety survey, believe that you're the exception to the rule, just keep one thing in mind: that's what Aiden Quinn thought, too. He lost his job and is facing civil lawsuits and criminal prosecution.

RETHINK
- Most people assume that they are able to text and drive at the same time without declines in their driving ability. Why do you think that is the case, and how accurate is their assumption?
- Why would frequent multitaskers be more distractible than those who multitask less frequently?

Neuroscience in Your Life: When Brain and Socialization Meet

FIGURE 6 Differences in how men and women process information reflect differences in learning and experience with those objects. In an fMRI study, (a) women showed greater activation in certain areas of the brain when they processed names for tools and (b) men showed greater activation in other areas of the brain when they processed names of plants. (Source: Garn et al., 2009.)

(a) Areas more strongly activated in females to tools

(b) Areas more strongly activated in males to plants

NEUROSCIENCE IN YOUR LIFE This feature, which appears in each chapter, emphasizes the importance of neuroscientific research within the various subfields of the discipline and in students' lives. Compelling brain scans, with both caption and textual explanation, illustrate significant neuroscientific findings that are increasingly influencing the field of psychology. For example, one *Neuroscience in Your Life* feature shows MRI techniques that illustrate how our brains process information coming from each eye separately. Another shows how the brains of smokers—even those who have quit—are activated when they see images related to smoking. Yet another discusses the effects of sleep on memory.

BECOMING AN INFORMED CONSUMER OF PSYCHOLOGY Every set of modules includes material designed to make readers more informed consumers of psychological information by giving them the ability to evaluate critically what the field of psychology offers. These discussions also provide sound, useful guidance concerning common problems.

PsychWork
SEEING EYE GUIDE DOG TRAINER

Name: Lea Johnson

Position: Seeing Eye Guide Dog Trainer

Education: BS, Geography, Dartmouth College, Hanover, NH

For decades, guide dogs have provided a set of eyes to the visually impaired, expanding the opportunities open to them and increasing their independence. But it takes a great deal of training to make a dog an effective seeing eye guide dog, according to Lea Johnson, who works with The Seeing Eye agency in Morristown, New Jersey. Johnson teaches apprentice instructors to carry out the demanding, but rewarding, process of training dogs.

"We hire college graduates, and while we don't require a specific major, a background in psychology or animal science allows employees to more easily connect with different aspects of the job," she said.

An apprentice instructor needs to have self-motivation in order to complete all aspects of the dog's training. In addition, they need to be able to work in a team setting, according to Johnson. But that's only part of it.

"The process of training the dogs is complex," says Johnson. "For example, the dog must be obedient and respond to their visually-impaired owner. But they also get praised for sometimes refusing their owner's commands, if it would put their owner in danger."

Once a dog learns the skills it needs, the trainer must then teach a visually-impaired person how to work with the dog.

"After training dogs for four months, the trainers must be able to teach blind people the skills to care for and travel with their Seeing Eye dog safely," Johnson said. Not only must trainers relate well to dogs, but they also must interact well with blind people. She adds, "The training of people is intense and emotionally challenging in a very different way from the dog training portion. Without a good heart to start with, trainers would never be successful."

PSYCHWORK New in this edition, *PsychWork* introduces students to different career paths to which an understanding of psychology leads. Each *PsychWork* profile illustrates people in a variety of occupations whose knowledge of psychology informs and enhances their work. Among the individuals profiled are a social worker, a nutritionist, a physical rehabilitation counselor, and an advertising executive, showing that psychology is all around us and important to many occupations.

What's New and Updated in the Ninth Edition

The Ninth Edition of *Essentials of Understanding Psychology* contains a significant amount of new and updated features and content reflecting the advances in the field and the suggestions of reviewers. Chapter 3 (Sensation and Perception), Chapter 4 (States of Consciousness), and Chapter 7 (Thinking, Language, and Intelligence) have undergone especially heavy revisions. More than 1,000 new citations have been added, and most of them refer to articles and books published since 2008.

In addition, this edition incorporates a wide range of new topics. The following sample of new and revised topics provides a good indication of the book's currency.

Chapter 1—Introduction to Psychology
- Gender ratios in the field
- Distinction between psychiatrists and psychologists
- Psychologist work sites
- Replication
- Random sampling in surveys
- Correlation and causality
- Self-affirmations

Chapter 2—Neuroscience and Behavior
- Neurogenesis
- Hemispheric specialization emergence
- Brain wave-controlled devices
- Optogenetics

Chapter 3—Sensation and Perception
- Culture and susceptibility to visual illusions
- Divided attention and texting
- Multimodal perception
- Balance and the vestibular system
- Moon illusion (specialist)
- Ewald Hering
- Thomas Young
- Hermann von Helmholtz
- Rarity of complete color blindness
- Pheromones and humans
- Change order of perceptual constancy and depth perception
- Psychophysics still an active field
- Pheromones
- Otoliths and hair cells
- Pain theories
- Absolute threshold
- Flowers reflecting ultraviolet light
- Primacy of cornea in focusing light
- Aging and auditory perception
- Ring tones and students/teachers
- Apparent motion
- Vomeronasal organ
- Speech perception

Chapter 4—States of Consciousness
- Biological dependence
- Oxycodone

- Psychological dependence
- activation information modulation (AIM) theory
- Added Red Bull to chart on caffeine
- Added new prologue and Applying Psychology in the 21st century
- Consciousness versus unconsciousness
- Night terrors
- Insomnia #1
- Role of sleep in learning and memory
- Process of hypnosis
- Hypnosis and divided consciousness
- Daydreaming and brain activation
- Release of growth hormones and sleep

Chapter 5—Learning
- Description of habituation
- Spontaneous recovery definition
- Stimulus generalization definition
- Biological constraints on learning
- Reinforcment for parenting and academic success
- Conditioning of emotions

Chapter 6—Memory
- Hyperthymestic syndrome
- Neural basis of memory consolidation
- PKM-zeta and traumatic memories

Chapter 7—Thinking, Language, and Intelligence
- Algorithm
- Concepts
- Language in animals
- Cognition and hunches regarding danger
- Language acquisition in bilingual infants
- Creativity in different domains
- Language definition
- Confirmation bias
- G-factor

- Mental age
- Down syndrome
- Artificial intelligence
- Adaptive testing
- Flynn effect
- Fetal alcohol syndrome statistics

Chapter 8—Motivation and Emotion
- Facial expressions across cultures
- Ghrelin and hunger
- Insulin
- Self-determination theory
- High fiber foods and weight loss

Chapter 9—Development
- Midlife crisis myth
- Video game play and cognitive declines in late adulthood
- Disengagement theory lack of support
- Emerging adulthood

Chapter 10—Personality
- Biological basis of personality
- Situationism
- Cognitive-affective processing system (CAPS)
- Quick judgments of personality

Chapter 11—Health Psychology: Stress, Coping, and Well-Being
- General Adaptation Model and cortisol secretion
- Cancer and quality of life
- Smoking and loss of autonomy
- Smoking cessation and social support
- Smoking in developing countries
- Gender differences in happiness

Chapter 12—Psychological Disorders
- College student stress and depression
- Autism prevalence increase
- Formal thought disorder
- Definition of obsessive-compulsive disorder
- Type I and II schizophrenia treatment outcomes

Chapter 13—Treatment of Psychological Disorders

- Prescription drugs prescribed by clinical psychologists
- Self-actualization and humanistic therapy
- Interventions for prevention of psychological disorders

- Cingulotomy
- Gamma knife surgery
- Ketamine in the treatment of depression
- PsychWork on halfway house

Chapter 14—Social Psychology

- PsychWork on advertising agency owner

- Behavioral economics
- Social networking sites and friendship
- Milgram replication
- Roots of morality

Students First: The Bottom Line

Based on extensive student feedback, systematic research involving a wide range of instructors, and endorsements received from reviewers at a variety of schools, I am confident that this edition reflects what instructors want and need: a book that motivates students to understand and apply psychology to their own lives. *Essentials of Understanding Psychology*, Ninth Edition, is designed to expose readers to the content—and promise—of psychology, and to do so in a way that will nurture students' excitement about psychology and keep their enthusiasm alive for a lifetime.

Integrated Learning System

Whether traditional text-based instruction or a blend of traditional and digital media is favored, Ninth Edition integrated learning system provides complementary experiences for instructors and students. All of the components of the integrated learning system are built around the core concepts articulated in the text to promote a deeper understanding of psychology. This type of integration gives instructors the flexibility to use any of the text-specific digital or print materials knowing they are completely compatible with one another. Please contact your McGraw-Hill sales representative for information on policy, price, and availability of the following materials.

FOR THE INSTRUCTOR

What if…

- You could recreate the one-on-one experience of working through difficult concepts in office hours with every one of your students without having to invest any office-hour time to do so?
- You could see at a glance how well each of your students (or sections) was performing in each segment of your course?
- You had all of the assignments and resources for your course preorganized by learning objective and with point-and-click flexibility?

Over the course of developing *Essentials of Understanding Psychology*, we asked these questions and many more. But we did not stop at simply asking questions. We visited with faculty across the country and also observed you doing what you do to prepare and deliver your courses. We observed students as they worked through assignments and studied for exams. The result of these thousands of hours of research and development is a state of the art learning environment tool that bolsters student performance at the same time as it makes instructor's lives easier and more efficient. To experience this environment for yourself, please visit www.mcgraw-hillconnect.com.

Online Learning Center for Instructors. The password-protected instructor side of the Online Learning Center (www.mhhe.com/feldmaness9e) contains the Instructor's Manual, Test Bank files, PowerPoint slides, Classroom Performance System (CPS) Questions, Image Gallery, and other valuable material to help you design and enhance your course. See more information about specific assets below. Ask your local McGraw-Hill representative for password information.

Instructor's Manual by Susan Krauss Whitbourne, University of Massachusetts, Amherst. This comprehensive guide provides all the tools and resources instructors need to present and enhance their introductory psychology course. The Instructor's Manual contains detailed lecture launchers, learning objectives, interesting lecture and media presentation ideas, student assignments and handouts. The many tips and activities in this manual can be used with any class, regardless of size or teaching approach.

Test Banks revised by Michelle Merwin, University of Tennessee at Martin, and Matthew Isaak, University of Louisiana at Lafayette. Both test banks incorporate the new content in *Essentials of Understanding Psychology*, Ninth Edition. Each test bank contains more than 2,000 multiple-choice items, classified by cognitive type and level of difficulty and keyed to the appropriate key concept and page in the textbook. Fill-in-the-blank, matching, and short-answer questions are provided for all modules. Moreover, each of the thousands of test items is keyed to the APA core psychology competencies. All questions are compatible with EZ Test, McGraw-Hill's Computerized Test Bank program.

PowerPoint Presentations by Cathy Hunt of Pennsylvania State University. These presentations cover the key points of each chapter and include charts and graphs from the text. They can be used as is, or you may modify them to meet your specific needs.

Classroom Performance System Content by Robert Moore of Iowa Valley Community College District. The Classroom Performance System (CPS) from eInstruction allows instructors to gauge immediately what students are learning during lectures. Instructors can draw on the quiz and poll questions provided to get instant feedback, even from students who are reluctant to speak out in class. In addition, CPS facilitates taking attendance, giving and grading pop quizzes, and giving formal, printed class tests with multiple versions of the test using CPS for immediate grading.

Image Gallery. More than 100 figures from the text can be downloaded from the Image Gallery on the Instructor's Online Learning Center.

Create Craft your teaching resources to match the way you teach! With McGraw-Hill Create, www.mcgrawhillcreate.com, you can easily rearrange chapters, combine material from other content sources, and quickly upload content you have written like your course syllabus or teaching notes. Find the content you need in Create by searching through thousands of leading McGraw-Hill textbooks. Arrange your book to fit your teaching style. Create even allows you to personalize your book's appearance by selecting the cover and adding your name, school, and course information. Order a Create book and you'll receive a complimentary print review copy in three to five business days or a complimentary electronic review copy (eComp) via email in about one hour. Go to www.mcgrawhillcreate.com today and register. Experience how McGraw-Hill Create empowers you to teach your students your way.

CourseSmart e-Textbook This text is available as an eTextbook at www.CourseSmart.com. At CourseSmart your students can take advantage of significant savings off the cost of a print textbook, reduce their impact on the environment, and gain access to powerful web tools for learning. CourseSmart eTextbooks can be viewed online or downloaded to a computer. The eTextbooks allow students to do full text searches, add highlighting and notes, and share notes with classmates. CourseSmart has the largest selection of eTextbooks available anywhere. Visit www.CourseSmart.com to learn more and to try a sample chapter.

Tegrity Tegrity Campus is a service that makes class time available all the time by automatically capturing every lecture in a searchable format for students to review when they study and complete assignments. With a simple one-click start and stop process, you capture all computer screens and corresponding audio. Students replay any part of any class with easy-to-use browser-based viewing on a PC or Mac.

Educators know that the more students can see, hear, and experience class resources, the better they learn. With Tegrity Campus, students quickly recall key moments by using Tegrity Campus's unique search feature. This search helps students efficiently find what they need, when they need it across an entire semester of class recordings. Help turn all your students' study time into learning moments immediately supported by your lecture.

FOR THE STUDENT

Adaptive Diagnostic Tool. This diagnostic tool is an unparalleled, intelligent learning system based on cognitive mapping that *diagnoses* your students' knowledge of a particular subject and then creates an individualized learning path geared toward student success in your course. It offers individualized assessment by delivering appropriate learning material in the form of questions at the right time, helping students attain mastery of the content. Whether the system is assigned by you or used independently by students as a study tool, the results can be recorded in an easy-to-use grade report that allows you to measure student progress at all times and coach your students to success.

As an added benefit, all content covered in this adaptive diagnostic is tied to learning objectives for your course so that you can use the results as evidence of subject mastery. This tool also provides a personal study plan that allows the student to estimate the time it will take and number of questions required to learn the subject matter. Your students will learn faster, study more efficiently, and retain more knowledge when using *Essentials of Understanding Psychology*.

Optional Modules on Diversity and I/O Psychology. For instructors who like to incorporate lectures on diversity or industrial/organizational issues in their introductory psychology course, optional full-color modules on these topics can be packaged with students' copies of *Essentials of Understanding Psychology*, Ninth Edition. The Diversity module, written by Mark H. Chae of William Paterson University, discusses the roots of diversity and addresses related issues, such as conflict and cooperation. The module on Industrial-Organizational Psychology, written by Carnot Nelson and Russell Johnson of the University of South Florida, broadly introduces this growing area of interest. Instructors may request these modules through their McGraw-Hill sales representative.

Annual Editions: Psychology 10/11 (edited by William Buskist, Auburn University). This annually updated reader provides convenient, inexpensive access to current articles selected from the best of the public press. Organizational features include an annotated listing of selected Worldwide Web sites; an annotated table of contents; a topic guide; a general introduction; brief overviews for each section; a topical index; and an instructor's resource guide with testing materials.

Classic Edition Sources: Psychology, 4e (edited by Terry Pettijohn of Ohio State University—Marion). This reader provides more than 40 selections of enduring intellectual value—classic articles, book excerpts, and research studies—that have shaped the study of psychology and our contemporary understanding of it.

Taking Sides: Clashing Views on Psychological Issues, 16e (edited by Brent Slife of Brigham Young University). This reader presents current controversial issues in a debate-style format designed to stimulate student interest and develop critical thinking skills. Each issue is thoughtfully framed with an issue summary, an issue introduction, and a postscript. An instructor's manual with testing material is available for each volume.

Acknowledgments

One of the central features of *Essentials of Understanding Psychology* is the involvement of both professionals and students in the review process. The ninth edition of *Essentials of Understanding Psychology* has relied heavily—and benefited substantially—from the advice of instructors and students from a wide range of backgrounds.

I am extraordinarily grateful to the following reviewers, who provided their time and expertise to help insure that *Essentials of Understanding Psychology*, Ninth Edition, reflects the best that psychology has to offer.

MANUSCRIPT REVIEWERS

Bernard J. Baars
The Neurosciences Institute

Susan Barnett
Northwestern State University

John Begeny
North Carolina State University

Alan Beauchamp
Northern Michigan University

Conna Bral
Kirkwood Community College

Liz Clark
Kaplan University

Dara Cox
Harrison College

Brenda Dubuc
Wytheville Community College

Michael Firmin
Cedarville University

Jeff Green
Virginia Commonwealth University

Jonathan Grimes
The Community College of Baltimore County, Essex

Marlene Groomes
Miami Dade College, Homestead

Rob Guttentag
University of North Carolina, Greensboro

Nicole Korzetz
Lee College

Shirley P. Kuhn
Pittsburgh Community College

Eta Lin
Foothill College

Tanya MacNeil
American Intercontinental University

Cheryl McDowell
Keiser University

Giovanni Misceo
Benedictine College

Pat Nation
Bluegrass Community and Technical College

Peter Phipps
SUNY Dutchess Community College

Mark Rittman
Cuyahoga Community College, Metro

Victoria V. Roark
Troy University

Sylvia Robb
Hudson County Community College

Krista Rumage
St. Catharine College

Nancy Simpson
Trident Technical College

Cyd Skinner
Northampton Community College

Sherry Span
California State University, Long Beach

John E. Sparrow
University of New Hampshire at Manchester

Teresa Tempelmeyer
Kaplan University

Jay Wenger
Central Pennsylvania Community College, Lancaster

Chad Worthington
Glen Oaks Community College

In addition, Jane W. Couperus of Hampshire College provided exceptional support in helping identify appropriate neuroscientific research to include in the Neuroscience in Your Life features. I thank her for her superb work.

Many teachers along my educational path have shaped my thinking. I was introduced to psychology at Wesleyan University, where several committed and inspiring teachers—and in particular Karl Scheibe—conveyed their sense of excitement about the field and made its relevance clear to me. Karl epitomizes the teacher-scholar combination to which I aspire, and I continue to marvel at my good fortune in having such a role model.

By the time I left Wesleyan I could envision no other career but that of psychologist. Although the nature of the University of Wisconsin, where I did my graduate work, could not have been more different from the much smaller Wesleyan, the excitement and inspiration were similar. Once again, a cadre of excellent teachers—led, especially, by the late Vernon Allen—molded my thinking and taught me to appreciate the beauty and science of the discipline of psychology.

My colleagues and students at the University of Massachusetts, Amherst, provide ongoing intellectual stimulation, and I thank them for making the university a fine place to work. Several people also provided extraordinary research and editorial help. In particular, I am grateful to my superb students, past and present, including Erik Coats, Sara Levine, Jim Tyler, Chris Poirier, and Matt Zimbler. John Bickford, in particular, provided editorial input that has enhanced the book considerably. Finally, I am grateful to John Graiff, whose hard work and dedication helped immeasurably on just about everything involving this book.

I also offer great thanks to the McGraw-Hill editorial team that participated in this edition of the book. Steve Debow's hands-on interest, as well as his friendship, helped support the book through the last decade. Editorial Vice President Mike Ryan and Editorial Director Beth Mejia created a creative, energetic, and supportive environment, and I am in awe of their enthusiasm, commitment, and never-ending good ideas. I also thank Cara Labell and Sue Ewing, Developmental Editors on this edition. They did a superb job of managing a myriad of details (as well as me). I'm also pleased that Sponsoring Editor Krista Bettino worked on this edition of *Essentials of Understanding Psychology*. She brought motivation, intelligence, and good ideas to the project. Finally, every reader of this book owes a debt to Rhona Robbin and Judith Kromm, developmental editors on earlier editions of *Essentials of Understanding Psychology*. Their relentless pursuit of excellence helped form the core of this book, and they taught me a great deal about the craft and art of writing.

Central to the design, production, and marketing process were the Production Service Manager Chris Schabow, Lead Production Editor Anne Fuzellier, Buyer II Tandra Jorgensen, and Designer Ellen Pettengel. Photo editor Toni Michaels did her usual superb job in identifying photos and, as always, was a pleasure to work with. I would also like to thank marketing managers Julia Flohr and Yasuko Okada for their enthusiasm and commitment to this project. I am proud to be a part of this world-class team.

Finally, I remain completely indebted to my family. My parents, Leah Brochstein and the late Saul D. Feldman, provided a lifetime foundation of love and support, and I continue to see their influence in every corner of my life. I am grateful, too, to the late Harry Brochstein, who enriched my life and thinking in many ways.

My extended family also plays a central role in my life. They include, more or less in order of age, my nieces and nephews, my terrific brother, and my brothers- and sisters-in-law, and the late Ethel Radler. Finally, my mother-in-law, the late Mary Evans Vorwerk, had an important influence on this book, and I remain ever grateful to her.

Ultimately, my children, Jonathan, Joshua, and Sarah; my daughters-in-law Leigh and Julie; my grandson Alex; and my wife, Katherine, remain the focal point of my life. I thank them, with immense love.

Robert S. Feldman
Amherst, Massachusetts

Making the Grade: A Practical Guide

No matter why you are taking introductory psychology, it's a safe bet you're interested in maximizing your understanding of the material and getting a good grade. And you want to accomplish these goals as quickly and efficiently as possible.

Good news: You're taking the right course, and you're learning the right material. Several subfields of psychology have identified a variety of guidelines and techniques that will help you learn and remember material not only related to psychology, but also relevant to every other discipline that you will study.

We'll consider a variety of guidelines relating to doing well in your psychology class—and every other class you'll take in your college career. Here's my guarantee to you: If you learn and follow the guidelines in each of these areas, you'll become a better student and get better grades. Always remember that *good students are made, not born,* and these suggestions will help you become an all-around better student.

Adopt a General Study Strategy

Let's begin with a brief consideration of a general study strategy, applicable to all of your courses, including introductory psychology. Psychologists have devised several excellent (and proven) techniques for improving study skills, two of which are described here: "P.O.W.E.R.," or *Prepare, Organize, Work, Evaluate,* and *Rethink;* and "SQ3R," or *Survey, Question, Read, Recite,* and *Review.* By employing one of these two procedures, you can increase your ability to learn and retain information and to think critically.

P.O.W.E.R. The *P.O.W.E.R.* learning strategy systematizes the acquisition of new material by providing a learning and critical thinking framework. It stresses the importance of learning objectives and appropriate preparation before you begin to study as well as the significance of self-evaluation and the incorporation of critical thinking into the learning process. Specifically, use of the P.O.W.E.R. learning system entails the following steps:

- **Prepare.** Before starting any journey, we need to know where we are headed. Academic journeys are no different; we need to know what our goals are. The *Prepare* stage consists of thinking about what we hope to gain from reading a specific section of the text by identifying specific goals that we seek to accomplish. In *Understanding Psychology,* Tenth Edition, these goals are presented as broad questions at the start of each chapter and again at the beginning of each module.

- **Organize.** Once we know what our goals are, we can develop a route to accomplish those goals. The *Organize* stage involves developing a mental road-map of where we are headed. *Understanding*

Psychology highlights the organization of each upcoming chapter. Read the outline at the beginning of each chapter to get an idea of what topics are covered and how they are organized.

- **Work.** The key to the P.O.W.E.R. learning system is actually reading and studying the material presented in the book. In some ways *Work* is the easy part because, if you have carried out the steps in the preparation and organization stages, you'll know where you're headed and how you'll get there. Remember, the main text isn't the only material that you need to read and think about. It's also important to read the boxes and the material in the margins in order to gain a full understanding of the material.

- **Evaluate.** The fourth step, *Evaluate*, provides the opportunity to determine how effectively you have mastered the material. In *Understanding Psychology*, a series of questions at the end of each module permits a rapid check of your understanding of the material. Quizzes on the book's website, or Online Learning Center, provide additional opportunities to test yourself. Evaluating your progress is essential to assessing your degree of mastery of the material.

- **Rethink.** The final step in the *P.O.W.E.R.* learning system requires that you think critically about the content. Critical thinking entails re-analyzing, reviewing, questioning, and challenging assumptions. It affords you the opportunity to consider how the material fits with other information you have already learned. Every major section of *Understanding Psychology* ends with a *Rethink* section. Answering its thought-provoking questions will help you understand the material more fully and at a deeper level.

SQ3R. Use of the SQ3R learning system entails the following specific steps:

- **Survey.** The first step of the SQ3R method is to *survey* the material by reading the outlines that open each module, the headings, figure captions, recaps, and Looking Ahead and Looking Back sections, providing yourself with an overview of the major points of the chapter.

- **Question.** The next step—the "Q"—is to *question*. Formulate questions about the material, either aloud or in writing, prior to actually reading a section of text. The questions posed at the beginning of each module and the *Evaluate* and *Rethink* questions that end each part of the chapter are examples.

- **Read.** Read carefully and, even more importantly, read actively and critically. While you are reading, answer the questions you have asked yourself. Critically evaluate material by considering the implications of what you are reading, thinking about possible exceptions and contradictions, and examining underlying assumptions.

- **Recite.** This step involves describing and explaining to yourself (or to a friend) the material you have just read and answering the questions you have posed earlier. Recite aloud; the recitation process helps to identify your degree of understanding of the material you have just read.

- **Review.** In this final step, review the material, looking it over, reading the Looking Back summaries, and answering the in-text review questions.

Manage Your Time

Without looking up from the page, answer this question: What time is it?

Most people are pretty accurate in their answer. And if you don't know for sure, it's very likely that you can find out. There may be a cell phone in your pocket; there may be a clock on the wall, desk, or computer screen; or maybe you're riding in a car that shows the time. Even if you don't have a timepiece of some sort nearby, your body keeps its own beat. Humans have an internal clock that regulates the beating of our heart, the pace of our breathing, the discharge of chemicals within our bloodstream, and myriad other bodily functions.

Managing your time as you study is a central aspect of academic success. But remember: The goal of time management is not to schedule every moment so we become pawns of a timetable that governs every waking moment of the day. Instead, the goal is to permit us to make informed choices about how we use our time. Rather than letting the day slip by, largely without our awareness, the time management procedures we'll discuss can make us better able to harness time for our own ends.

We'll consider a number of steps to help you improve your time management skills.

Set Your Priorities. To figure out the best use of your time, you need to determine your priorities. *Priorities* are the tasks and activities you need and want to do, rank-ordered from most important to least important. There are no right or wrong priorities; maybe spending time on your studies is most important to you, or maybe your top priority is spending time with your family. Only you can decide. Furthermore, what's important to you now may be less of a priority to you next month, next year, or in five years.

The best procedure is to start off by identifying priorities for an entire term. What do you need to accomplish? Don't just choose obvious, general goals, such as "passing all my classes." Instead, think in terms of specific, measurable activities, such as "studying 10 hours before each chemistry exam."

Identify Your Prime Time. Do you enthusiastically bound out of bed in the morning, ready to start the day and take on the world? Or is the alarm clock a hated and unwelcome sound that jars you out of pleasant slumber? Are you zombie-like by 10 at night, or are you a person who is just beginning to rev up at midnight? Each of us has his or her own style based on some inborn body clock. Being aware of the time or times of day when you can do your best work will help you plan and schedule your time most effectively.

Master the Moment. Here's what you'll need to organize your time:

- A *master calendar* that shows all the weeks of the term on one page. It should include every week of the term and seven days per week. Using your class syllabi, write on the master calendar every assignment and test you will have, noting the date that it is due. Pencil in tentative assignments on the appropriate date. Also include on the master calendar important activities from your personal life, drawn from your list of priorities. And don't forget to schedule some free time for yourself.

- *A weekly timetable,* a master grid with the days of the week across the top and the hours, from 6:00 A.M. to midnight, along the side. Fill in the times of all your fixed, prescheduled activities—the times that your classes meet, when you have to be at work, the times you have to pick up your child at day care, and any other recurring appointments. Add assignment due dates, tests, and any other activities on the appropriate days of the week. Then pencil in blocks of time necessary to prepare for those events.

- *A daily to-do list.* Your daily to-do list can be written on a small, portable calendar that includes a separate page for each day of the week, or you can maintain a calendar electronically in a cell phone or a device such as a Treo, iPhone, or Blackberry. List all the things that you intend to do during the next day and their priority. Start with the things you know you *must* do and that have fixed times, such as classes, work schedules, and appointments. Then add in the other things that you *should* accomplish, such as an hour of study for an upcoming test, work on research for an upcoming paper, or finishing up a lab report. Finally, list things that are a low priority but enjoyable, like a run or a walk.

Control Your Time. If you follow the schedules that you've prepared, you've taken the most important steps in time management. However, our lives are filled with surprises: Things always seem to take longer than we've planned. A crisis occurs, buses are late, computers break down, kids get sick.

The difference between effective time management and time management that doesn't work lies in how well you deal with the inevitable surprises. There are several ways to take control of your days and permit yourself to follow your intended schedule:

- **Just say no.** You don't have to agree to every request and every favor that others ask of you.

- **Get away from it all.** Go to the library. Lock yourself in your bedroom. Find an out-of-the-way unused classroom. Adopt a specific spot as your own, such as a corner desk in a secluded nook in the library. If you use it enough, your body and mind will automatically get into study mode as soon as you seat yourself at it.

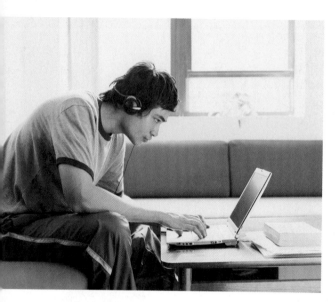

- **Enjoy the sounds of silence.** Although many students insist they accomplish most while a television, radio, or CD is playing, scientific studies suggest otherwise—we are able to concentrate most when our environment is silent. Experiment and work in silence for a few days. You may find that you get more done in less time than you would in a more distracting environment.
- **Take an e-break.** We may not control when communications arrive, but we can make the messages wait until we are ready to receive them. Take an e-break and shut down your communication sources for some period of time. Phone calls can be stored on voice-mail systems; text messages, IMs, and e-mail can be saved on a phone or computer. They'll wait.
- **Expect the unexpected.** You'll never be able to escape from unexpected interruptions and surprises that require your attention. But by trying to anticipate them in advance and thinking about how you'll react to them, you'll be positioning yourself to react more effectively when they do occur.

Read Your Textbook Effectively

Reading a textbook is different from reading for pleasure. With textbooks, you have specific goals: understanding, learning, and ultimately recalling the information. There are several steps you can take to achieve these goals:

- **Read the front matter.** If you'll be using a text extensively throughout the term, start by reading the preface and/or introduction and scanning the table of contents—what publishers call the *front matter*. It is there that the author has a chance to explain, often more personally than elsewhere in the text, what he or she considers important. Knowing this will give you a sense of what to expect as you read. (Note: You're reading part of the front matter at this very moment!)
- **Identify your personal objectives.** Before you begin an assignment, think about what your specific objectives are. Will you be reading a textbook on which you'll be thoroughly tested? Or, will your reading provide background information for future learning that won't itself be tested? Is the material going to be useful to you personally? Your objectives for reading will help you determine which reading strategy to adopt and how much time you can devote to the reading assignment. You aren't expected to read everything with the same degree of intensity. You may feel comfortable skimming some material. You'll want to put in the maximum effort into other material.
- **Identify and use the advance organizers.** The next step in reading a textbook is to become familiar with the *advance organizers*—outlines, overviews, section objectives, or other clues to the meaning and organization of new material—provided in the material you are reading. Look at

the start of every chapter in this book, which includes a chapter outline plus a set of questions at the end of the "Looking Ahead" section. You can also create your own advance organizers by skimming material to be read and sketching out the general outline of the material you'll be reading. These steps can help you recall material better after you've read it.

- **Stay focused as you read.** There are a million and one possible distractions that can invade your thoughts as you read. Your job is to keep distracting thoughts at bay and focus on the material you are supposed to be reading. Here are some things you can do to help yourself stay focused:

  - **Read in small bites.** If you think it is going to take you 4 hours to read an entire chapter, break up the 4 hours into more manageable time periods. Promise yourself that you'll read for 1 hour in the afternoon, another hour in the evening, and the next 2 hours spaced out during the following day.

  - **Take a break.** Actually plan to take several short breaks to reward yourself while you're reading. During your break, do something enjoyable—eat a snack, watch a bit of a ball game on television, play a video game, or the like. Just try not to get drawn into your break activity to the point that it takes over your reading time.

- **Highlight and take notes as you read.** Highlighting and taking notes as you read a textbook are essential activities. Good annotations can help you learn and review the information prior to tests as well as help you to stay focused as you read. There are several things you can do to maximize the effectiveness of your notes:

  - **Rephrase key points.** Make notes to yourself, in your own words, about what the author is trying to get across. Don't just copy what's been said. Think about the material, and rewrite it in words that are your own. The very act of writing engages an additional type of perception that involves the physical sense of moving a pen or pressing a keyboard.

  - **Highlight or underline key points.** Often the first or last sentence in a paragraph, or the first or last paragraph in a section, will present a key point. Before you highlight anything, though, read the whole paragraph through. Then you'll be sure that what you highlight is, in fact, the key information. You should find yourself highlighting only one or two sentences or phrases per page. *In highlighting and underlining, less is more.* One guideline: No more than 10 percent of the material should be highlighted or underlined.

- **Use arrows, diagrams, outlines, tables, timelines, charts, and other visuals to help you understand and later recall what you are reading.** If three examples are given for a specific point, number them. If a sequence of steps is presented, number each step. If a paragraph discusses a situation in which an earlier point does not hold, link the original point to the exception by an arrow. Representing the material graphically will get you thinking about it in new and different ways. The act of creating visual annotations will not only help you to understand the material better, but will also ease its later recall.
- **Look up unfamiliar words.** Even though you may be able to figure out the meaning of an unfamiliar word from its context, look up unfamiliar words in a dictionary or online. You'll also find out what the word sounds like, which will be important if your instructor uses the word in class.

Take Good Notes in Class

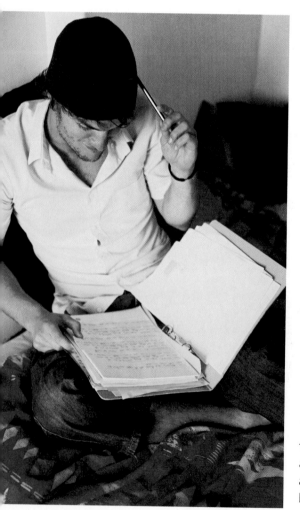

Perhaps you know students who manage to write down nearly everything their instructors say in class. And perhaps you have thought to yourself, "If only I took such painstaking notes, I'd do much better in my classes." Contrary to what many students think, however, good notetaking does not mean writing down every word that an instructor utters. With notetaking, less is often more. Let's consider some of the basic principles of notetaking:

- **Identify the instructor's—and your—goals for the course.** On the first day of class, most instructors talk about their objectives for the course. Most review the information on the class syllabus, the written document that explains the assignments for the semester. The information you get during that first session and through the syllabus is critical. In addition to the instructor's goals, you should have your own. What is it you want to learn from the course? How will the information from the course help you to enhance your knowledge, improve yourself as a person, achieve your goals?
- **Complete assignments before coming to class.** Your instructor enthusiastically describes the structure of the neuron, recounting excitedly how electrons flow across neurons, changing their electrical charge. One problem: You have only the vaguest idea what a neuron is. And the reason you don't know is that you haven't read the assignment.

Chances are you have found yourself in this situation at least a few times, so you know firsthand that sinking feeling as you become more and more confused. The moral: Always go to class prepared. Instructors assume that their students have done what they've assigned, and their lectures are based on that assumption.

- **Choose a notebook that assists in notetaking.** Loose-leaf notebooks are especially good for taking notes because they permit you to go back later and change the order of the pages or add additional material. Whatever kind of notebook you use, *use only one side of the page for writing; keep one side free of notes.* There may be times that you'll want to spread out your notes in front of you, and it's much easier if no material is written on the back of the pages.

  Walter Pauk devised what is sometimes called the Cornell Method of Notetaking. Using this method, draw a line down the left side of your notebook page, about 2½ inches from the left-hand margin. Keep the notes you write in class to the right of the line. Indent major supporting details beneath each main idea, trying to use no more than one line for each item, and leave space between topics to add information. When it comes time to review your notes later, you'll be able to jot down a keyword, catch phrase, or major idea on the left side of the page (Pauk, 2007).

- **Listen for the key ideas.** Not every sentence in a lecture is equally important. One of the most useful skills you can develop is separating the key ideas from supporting information. Good lecturers strive to make just a few main points. The rest of what they say consists of explanation, examples, and other supportive material that expand upon the key ideas. To distinguish the key ideas from their support, you need to be alert and always searching for the *meta-message* of your instructor's words—that is, the underlying main ideas that a speaker is seeking to convey.

  How can you discern the meta-message? One way is to *listen for key words.* Phrases like "you need to know...," "the most important thing that must be considered...," "there are four problems with this approach ...," and—a big one—"this will be on the test..." should cause you to sit up and take notice. Also, if an instructor says the same thing in several ways, it's a clear sign that the material being discussed is important.

- **Use short, abbreviated phrases—not full sentences when taking notes.** Forget everything you've ever heard about always writing in full sentences. In fact, it's often useful to take notes in the form of an outline. An outline summarizes ideas in short phrases and indicates the relationship among concepts through the use of indentations.

- **Pay attention to what is written on the board or projected from overheads and PowerPoint slides. Remember these tips:**

  - **Listening is more important than seeing.** The information that your instructor projects on screen, while important, ultimately is less critical than what he or she is saying. Pay primary attention to the spoken word and secondary attention to the screen.

  - **Don't copy everything that is on every slide.** Instructors can present far more information on their slides than they would if they were writing on a blackboard. Oftentimes there is so much information that it's impossible to copy it all down. Don't even try. Instead, concentrate on taking down the key points.

- **Remember that key points on slides are . . . key points.** The key points (often indicated by bullets) often relate to central concepts. Use these points to help organize your studying for tests, and don't be surprised if test questions directly assess the bulleted items on slides.
- **Check to see if the presentation slides are available online.** Some instructors make their class presentations available to their students on the Web, either before or after class time. If they do this before class, print them out and bring them to class. Then you can make notes on your copy, clarifying important points. If they are not available until after a class is over, you can still make good use of them when it comes time to study the material for tests.
- **Remember that presentation slides are not the same as good notes for a class.** If you miss a class, don't assume that getting a copy of the slides is sufficient. Studying the notes of a classmate who is a good notetaker will be far more beneficial than studying only the slides.

Memorize Efficiently: Use Proven Strategies to Memorize New Materials

Here's a key principle of effective memorization: Memorize what you need to memorize. *Forget about the rest.*

The average textbook chapter has some 20,000 words. But, within those 20,000 words, there may be only 30 to 40 specific concepts that you need to learn. And perhaps there are only 25 key words. *Those* are the pieces of information on which you should focus in your efforts to memorize. By extracting what is important from what is less crucial, you'll be able to limit the amount of the material that you need to recall. You'll be able to focus on what you need to remember.

You have your choice of dozens of techniques of memorization. As we discuss the options, keep in mind that no one strategy works by itself. Also, feel free to devise your own strategies or add those that have worked for you in the past.

Rehearsal. Say it aloud: rehearsal. Think of this word in terms of its three syllables: re—hear—sal. If you're scratching your head about why you should do this, it's to illustrate the point of *rehearsal:* to transfer material that you encounter into long-term memory.

To test if you've succeeded in transferring the word "rehearsal" into your memory, put down this book and go off for a few minutes. Do something entirely unrelated to reading this book. Have a snack, catch up on the latest sports scores on ESPN, or read the front page of a newspaper. If the word "rehearsal" popped into your head when you picked up this book again, you've passed your first memory test—the word "rehearsal" has been transferred into your memory.

Rehearsal is the key strategy in remembering information. If you don't rehearse material, it will never make it into your memory. Repeating the information, summarizing it, associating it with other memories, and above all thinking about it when you first come across it will ensure that rehearsal will be effective in placing the material into your memory.

Mnemonics. This odd word (pronounced with the "m" silent—"neh MON ix") describes formal techniques used to make material more readily remembered. *Mnemonics* are the tricks-of-the-trade that professional memory experts use, and you too can use them to nail down the information you will need to recall for tests.

Among the most common mnemonics are the following:

- **Acronyms.** *Acronyms* are words or phrases formed by the first letters of a series of terms. The word "laser" is an acronym for "light amplification by stimulated emissions of radiation," and "radar" is an acronym for "radio detection and ranging."

  Acronyms can be a big help in remembering things. For example, Roy G. Biv is a favorite of physics students who must remember the colors of the spectrum (red, orange, yellow, green, blue, indigo, and violet.) The benefit of acronyms is that they help us to recall a complete list of steps or items.
- **Acrostics.** *Acrostics* are sentences in which the first letters spell out something that needs to be recalled. The benefits—as well as the drawbacks—of acrostics are similar to those of acronyms.
- **Rhymes and jingles.** "Thirty days hath September, April, June, and November." If you know the rest of the rhyme, you're familiar with one of the most commonly used mnemonic jingles in the English language.

Use of Multiple Senses. The more senses you can involve when you're trying to learn new material, the better you'll be able to remember. Here's why: Every time we encounter new information, all of our senses are potentially at work. Each piece of sensory information is stored in a separate location in the brain, and yet all the pieces are linked together in extraordinarily intricate ways.

What this means is that when we seek to remember the details of a specific event, recalling a memory of one of the sensory experiences can trigger recall of the other types of memories. You can make use of the fact that memories are stored in multiple ways by applying the following techniques:

- **When you learn something, use your body.** Don't sit passively at your desk. Instead, move around. Stand up; sit down. Touch the page. Trace figures with your fingers. Talk to yourself. Think out loud. By involving every part of your body, you've increased the number of potential ways to trigger a relevant memory later, when you need to recall it. And when one memory is triggered, other related memories may come tumbling back.

- **Draw and diagram the material.** Structuring written material by graphically grouping and connecting key ideas and themes is a powerful technique. When we draw and diagram material, one of the things we're doing is expanding the modalities in which information can be stored in our minds. Other types of drawing can be useful in aiding later recall. Creating drawings, sketches, and even cartoons can help us remember better.
- **Visualize.** You already know that memory requires three basic steps: the initial recording of information, the storage of that information, and, ultimately, the retrieval of the stored information. *Visualization* is a technique by which images are formed to ensure that material is recalled. Don't stop at visualizing images just in your mind's eye. Actually drawing what you visualize will help you to remember the material even better. Visualization is effective because it serves several purposes. It helps make abstract ideas concrete; it engages multiple senses; it permits us to link different bits of information together; and it provides us with a context for storing information.
- **Overlearning.** Lasting learning doesn't come until you have overlearned the material. *Overlearning* consists of studying and rehearsing material past the point of initial mastery. Through overlearning, recall becomes automatic. Rather than searching for a fact, going through mental contortions until perhaps the information surfaces, overlearning permits us to recall the information without even thinking about it.

Test-Taking Strategies

Preparing for tests is a long-term proposition. It's not a matter of "giving your all" the night *before* the test. Instead, it's a matter of giving your all to every aspect of the course.

Here are some guidelines that can help you do your best on tests:

Know What You Are Preparing For. Determine as much as you can about the test *before* you begin to study for it. The more you know about a test beforehand, the more efficient your studying will be.

To find out about an upcoming test, ask this question:

- Is the test called a "test," an "exam," a "quiz," or something else? The names imply different things.
  - **Essay:** Requires a fairly extended, on-the-spot composition about some topic. Examples include questions that call on you to describe a person, process, or event, or those that ask you to compare or contrast two separate sets of material.
  - **Multiple-choice:** Usually contains a question or statement, followed by a number of possible answers (usually 4 or 5 of them). You are supposed to choose the best response from the choices offered.
  - **True–false:** Presents statements about a topic that are either accurate or inaccurate. You are to indicate whether each statement is accurate (true) or inaccurate (false).

- **Matching:** Presents two lists of related information, arranged in column form. Typically, you are asked to pair up the items that go together (for example, a scientific term and its definition, or a writer and the title of a book he or she wrote).
- **Short-answer:** Requires brief responses (usually a few sentences at most) in a kind of mini-essay.
- **Fill-in:** Requires you to add one or more missing words to a sentence or series of sentences.

Match Test Preparation to Question Types. Each kind of test question requires a somewhat different style of preparation.

- **Essay questions.** Essay tests focus on the big picture—ways in which the various pieces of information being tested fit together. You'll need to know not just a series of facts, but also the connections between them, and you will have to be able to discuss these ideas in an organized and logical way. The best approach to studying for an essay test involves four steps:

  1. Carefully reread your class notes and any notes you've made on assigned readings that will be covered on the upcoming exam. Also go through the readings themselves, reviewing underlined or high-lighted material and marginal notes.
  2. Think of likely exam questions. For example, use the key words, phrases, concepts, and questions that come up in your class notes or in your text. Some instructors give out lists of possible essay topics; if yours does, focus on this list, but don't ignore other possibilities.
  3. Without looking at your notes or your readings, answer each potential essay question—aloud. Don't feel embarrassed about doing this. Talking aloud is often more useful than answering the question in your head. You can also write down the main points that any answer should cover. (Don't write out *complete* answers to the questions unless your instructor tells you in advance exactly what is going to be on the test. Your time is probably better spent learning the material than rehearsing precisely formulated responses.)
  4. After you've answered the questions, check yourself by looking at the notes and readings once again. If you feel confident that you've answered specific questions adequately, check them off. You can go back later for a quick review. But if there are questions that you had trouble with, review that material immediately. Then repeat the third step above, answering the questions again.

- **Multiple-choice, true–false, and matching questions.** While the focus of review for essay questions should be on major issues and controversies, studying for multiple-choice, true–false, and matching questions requires more attention to the details. Almost anything is fair game for multiple-choice, true–false, and matching questions, so you can't afford to overlook anything when studying. It's a good idea to write down important facts on index cards: They're portable and available all the time, and the act of creating them helps drive the material into your memory. Furthermore, you can shuffle them and test yourself repeatedly until you've mastered the material.

- **Short-answer and fill-in questions.** Short-answer and fill-in questions are similar to essays in that they require you to recall key pieces of information rather than finding it on the page in front of you, as is the case with multiple-choice, true–false, and matching questions. However, short-answer and fill-in questions typically don't demand that you integrate or compare different types of information. Consequently, the focus of your study should be on the recall of specific, detailed information.

Test Yourself. Once you feel you've mastered the material, test yourself on it. There are several ways to do this. Often textbooks are accompanied by websites that offer automatically scored practice tests and quizzes. (*Understanding Psychology* does: go to www.mhhe.com/feldman/up10 to try one!) You can also create a test for yourself, in writing, making its form as close as possible to what you expect the actual test to be. For instance, if your instructor has told you the classroom test will be primarily made up of short-answer questions, your test should reflect that.

You might also construct a test and administer it to a classmate or a member of your study group. In turn, you could take a test that someone else has constructed. Constructing and taking practice tests are excellent ways of studying the material and cementing it into memory.

Deal with Test Anxiety. What does the anticipation of a test do to you? Do you feel shaky? Is there a knot in your stomach? Do you grit your teeth? *Test anxiety* is a temporary condition characterized by fears and concerns about test-taking. Almost everyone experiences it to some degree, although for some people it's more of a problem than for others. You'll never eliminate test anxiety completely, nor do you want to. A little bit of nervousness can energize us, making us more attentive and vigilant. Like any competitive event, testing can motivate us to do our best.

On the other hand, for some students, anxiety can spiral into the kind of paralyzing fear that makes their minds go blank. There are several ways to keep this from happening to you:

1. *Prepare thoroughly.* The more you prepare, the less test anxiety you'll feel. Good preparation can give you a sense of control and mastery, and it will prevent test anxiety from overwhelming you.
2. *Take a realistic view of the test.* Remember that your future success does not hinge on your performance on any single exam. Think of the big picture: Put the task ahead in context, and remind yourself of all the hurdles you've passed so far.
3. *Learn relaxation techniques.* These techniques are covered in the text's chapter on health psychology, but the basic process is straightforward: Breathe evenly, gently inhaling and exhaling. Focus your mind on a

pleasant, relaxing scene such as a beautiful forest or a peaceful farm or on a restful sound such as that of ocean waves breaking on the beach.

4. *Visualize success.* Think of an image of your instructor handing back your test marked with a big "A." Or imagine your instructor congratulating you on your fine performance the day after the test. Positive visualizations that highlight your potential success can help replace images of failure that may fuel test anxiety.

What if these strategies don't work? If your test anxiety is so great that it's getting in the way of your success, make use of your college's resources. Most provide a learning resource center or a counseling center that can provide you with personalized help.

Form a Study Group. *Study groups* are small, informal groups of students who work together to learn course material and study for a test. Forming such a group can be an excellent way to prepare for any kind of test. Some study groups are formed for particular tests, while others meet consistently throughout the term. The typical study group meets a week or two before a test and plans a strategy for studying. Members share their understanding of what will be on the test, based on what an instructor has said in class and on their review of notes and text material. Together, they develop a list of review questions to guide their individual study. The group then breaks up, and the members study on their own.

A few days before the test, members of the study group meet again. They discuss answers to review questions, go over the material, and share any new insights they may have about the upcoming test. They may also quiz one another about the material to identify any weaknesses or gaps in their knowledge.

Study groups can be extremely powerful tools because they help accomplish several things:

- They help members organize and structure the material to approach their studying in a systematic and logical way.
- They allow students to share different perspectives on the material.
- They make it more likely that students will not overlook any potentially important information.
- They force members to rethink the course material, explaining it in words that other group members will understand. As we will discuss in Chapter 14, this helps both understanding and recall of the information when it is needed on the test.
- Finally, they help motivate members to do their best. When you're part of a study group, you're no longer working just for yourself; your studying also benefits the other study group members. Not wanting to let down your classmates in a study group may encourage you to put in your best effort.

Some Final Comments

We have discussed numerous techniques for increasing your study, classroom, and test effectiveness. But you need not feel tied to a specific strategy. You might want to combine other elements to create your own study system. Additional learning tips and strategies for critical thinking are presented throughout *Understanding Psychology*.

Whatever learning strategies you use, you will maximize your understanding of the material in this book and master techniques that will help you learn and think critically in all of your academic endeavors. More important, you will optimize your understanding of the field of psychology. It is worth the effort: The excitement, challenges, and promise that psychology holds for you are significant.

Subfield	Description
Behavioral genetics	*Behavioral genetics* studies the inheritance of traits related to behavior.
Behavioral neuroscience	*Behavioral neuroscience* examines the biological basis of behavior.
Clinical psychology	*Clinical psychology* deals with the study, diagnosis, and treatment of psychological disorders.
Clinical neuropsychology	*Clinical neuropsychology* unites the areas of biopsychology and clinical psychology, focusing on the relationship between biological factors and psychological disorders.
Cognitive psychology	*Cognitive psychology* focuses on the study of higher mental processes.
Counseling psychology	*Counseling psychology* focuses primarily on educational, social, and career adjustment problems.
Cross-cultural psychology	*Cross-cultural psychology* investigates the similarities and differences in psychological functioning in and across various cultures and ethnic groups.
Developmental psychology	*Developmental psychology* examines how people grow and change from the moment of conception through death.
Educational psychology	*Educational psychology* is concerned with teaching and learning processes, such as the relationship between motivation and school performance.
Environmental psychology	*Environmental psychology* considers the relationship between people and their physical environment.
Evolutionary psychology	*Evolutionary psychology* considers how behavior is influenced by our genetic inheritance from our ancestors.
Experimental psychology	*Experimental psychology* studies the processes of sensing, perceiving, learning, and thinking about the world.
Forensic psychology	*Forensic psychology* focuses on legal issues, such as determining the accuracy of witness memories.
Health psychology	*Health psychology* explores the relationship between psychological factors and physical ailments or disease.
Industrial/organizational psychology	*Industrial/organizational psychology* is concerned with the psychology of the workplace.
Personality psychology	*Personality psychology* focuses on the consistency in people's behavior over time and the traits that differentiate one person from another.
Program evaluation	*Program evaluation* focuses on assessing large-scale programs, such as the Head Start preschool program, to determine whether they are effective in meeting their goals.
Psychology of women	*Psychology of women* focuses on issues such as discrimination against women and the causes of violence against women.
School psychology	*School psychology* is devoted to counseling children in elementary and secondary schools who have academic or emotional problems.
Social psychology	*Social psychology* is the study of how people's thoughts, feelings, and actions are affected by others.
Sport psychology	*Sport psychology* applies psychology to athletic activity and exercise.

FIGURE 2 The major subfields of psychology.

HOW DO PSYCHOLOGICAL FACTORS AFFECT PHYSICAL AND MENTAL HEALTH?

Frequent depression, stress, and fears that prevent people from carrying out their normal activities are topics that would interest a health psychologist, a clinical psychologist, and a counseling psychologist. *Health psychology* explores the relationship between psychological factors and physical ailments or disease. For example, health psychologists are interested in assessing how long-term stress (a psychological factor) can affect physical health and in identifying ways to promote behavior that brings about good health (Belar, 2008; Yardley & Moss-Morris, 2009).

Clinical psychology deals with the study, diagnosis, and treatment of psychological disorders. Clinical psychologists are trained to diagnose and treat problems that range from the crises of everyday life, such as unhappiness over the breakup of a relationship, to more extreme conditions, such as profound, lingering depression. Some clinical psychologists also research and investigate issues that vary from identifying the early signs of psychological disturbance to studying the relationship between family communication patterns and psychological disorders.

Like clinical psychologists, counseling psychologists deal with people's psychological problems, but the problems they deal with are more specific. *Counseling psychology* focuses primarily on educational, social, and career adjustment problems. Almost every college has a center staffed with counseling psychologists. This is where students can get advice on the kinds of jobs they might be best suited for, on methods of studying effectively, and on strategies for resolving everyday difficulties, such as problems with roommates and concerns about a specific professor's grading practices. Many large business organizations also employ counseling psychologists to help employees with work-related problems.

HOW DO OUR SOCIAL NETWORKS AFFECT BEHAVIOR?

Our complex networks of social interrelationships are the focus for many subfields of psychology. For example, *social psychology* is the study of how people's thoughts, feelings, and actions are affected by others. Social psychologists concentrate on such diverse topics as human aggression, liking and loving, persuasion, and conformity.

Cross-cultural psychology investigates the similarities and differences in psychological functioning in and across various cultures and ethnic groups. For example, cross-cultural psychologists examine how cultures differ in their use of punishment during child rearing.

EXPANDING PSYCHOLOGY'S FRONTIERS

The boundaries of the science of psychology are constantly growing. Three newer members of the field's family tree—evolutionary psychology, behavioral genetics, and clinical neuropsychology—have sparked particular excitement, and debate, within psychology.

Evolutionary Psychology *Evolutionary psychology* considers how behavior is influenced by our genetic inheritance from our ancestors. The evolutionary approach suggests that the chemical coding of information in our cells not only determines traits such as hair color and race but also holds the key to understanding a broad variety of behaviors that helped our ancestors survive and reproduce.

Evolutionary psychology stems from Charles Darwin's arguments in his groundbreaking 1859 book, *On the Origin of Species.* Darwin suggested that a process of natural selection leads to the survival of the fittest and the development of traits that enable a species to adapt to its environment.

Evolutionary psychologists take Darwin's arguments a step further. They argue that our genetic inheritance determines not only physical traits such as skin and eye color but certain personality traits and social behaviors as well. For example, evolutionary psychologists suggest that behavior such as shyness, jealousy, and cross-cultural similarities in qualities desired in potential mates are at least partially determined by genetics, presumably because such behavior helped increase the survival rate of humans' ancient relatives (Buss, 2003; Sefcek, Brumbach, & Vasquez, 2007).

Although they are increasingly popular, evolutionary explanations of behavior have stirred controversy. By suggesting that many significant behaviors unfold automatically, because they are wired into the human species, evolutionary approaches minimize the role of environmental and social forces. Still, the evolutionary approach has stimulated a significant amount of research on how our biological inheritance influences our traits and behaviors (Begley, 2005; Buss, 2004; Neher, 2006).

Behavioral Genetics Another rapidly growing area in psychology focuses on the biological mechanisms, such as genes and chromosomes, that enable inherited behavior to unfold. *Behavioral genetics* seeks to understand how we might inherit certain behavioral traits and how the environment influences whether we actually display such traits (Bjorklund & Ellis, 2005; Moffitt & Caspi, 2007; Rende, 2007).

Clinical Neuropsychology *Clinical neuropsychology* unites the areas of neuroscience and clinical psychology: It focuses on the origin of psychological disorders in biological factors. Building on advances in our understanding of the structure and chemistry of the brain, this specialty has already led to promising new treatments for psychological disorders as well as debates over the use of medication to control behavior (Boake, 2008).

Working at Psychology

Help Wanted: Assistant professor at a small liberal arts college. Teach undergraduate courses in introductory psychology and courses in specialty areas of cognitive psychology, perception, and learning. Strong commitment to quality teaching, as well as evidence of scholarship and research productivity, necessary.

Help Wanted: Industrial-organizational consulting psychologist. International firm seeks psychologists for full-time career positions as consultants to management. Candidates must have the ability to establish a rapport with senior business executives and help them find innovative and practical solutions to problems concerning people and organizations.

Help Wanted: Clinical psychologist. PhD, internship experience, and license required. Comprehensive clinic seeks psychologist to work with children and adults providing individual and group therapy, psychological evaluations, crisis intervention, and development of behavior treatment plans on multidisciplinary team.

As these job ads suggest, psychologists are employed in a variety of settings. Many doctoral-level psychologists are employed by institutions of higher learning (universities and colleges) or are self-employed, usually working as private practitioners treating clients (see Figure 3). Other work sites include hospitals, clinics, mental health centers, counseling centers, government human-services organizations, businesses, schools, and even prisons. Psychologists are employed in the military, working with soldiers, veterans, and their families, and they work for the federal government Department of Homeland Security, fighting terrorism (American Psychological Association, 2007; DeAngelis & Monahan, 2008).

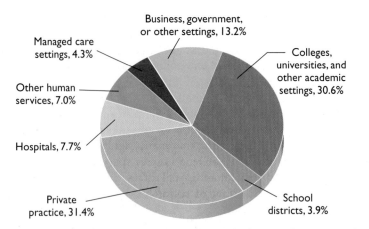

FIGURE 3 The breakdown of where U.S. psychologists (who have a PhD or PsyD degree) work. Why do you think so many psychologists work in college and university settings? (Source: American Psychological Association, 2007.)

Most psychologists, though, work in academic settings, allowing them to combine the three major roles played by psychologists in society: teacher, scientist, and clinical practitioner. Many psychology professors are also actively involved in research or in serving clients. Whatever the particular job site, however, psychologists share a commitment to improving individual lives as well as society in general.

Keep in mind that many professionals from a variety of professions use the findings of psychologists. As you can see in each *PsychWork* box here and throughout the text, we focus on how a non-psychologist uses psychology.

PsychWork

LICENSED SOCIAL WORKER

Name: Christin Poirier, LICSW

Position: Social Worker

Education: BA in Psychology, Stonehill College; MA in Social Work, University of New Hampshire

For Christin Poirier, psychology is central to her occupation as a social worker, a field dedicated to enhancing the well-being of individuals, families, groups, and communities. As a social worker, Poirier works at a community mental health center where she helps children and adolescents who are experiencing emotional or behavioral difficulties or both. Says Poirier, "The strategies I employ in counseling sessions are derived from basic psychological concepts and theories. In addition, in order to know what strategies are age-appropriate for a particular client, I need to consider their stage of psychological development. Finally, it is necessary to consider how culture and ethnicity affect clients, so I incorporate these aspects into my clients' treatment plans."

PSYCHOLOGISTS: A PORTRAIT

Although there is no "average" psychologist in terms of personal characteristics, we can draw a statistical portrait of the field. There are close to 300,000 psychologists working today in the United States, but they are outnumbered by psychologists in other countries. Europe has more than 290,000 psychologists, and in Brazil alone there are 140,000 licensed psychologists. Although most research is conducted in the United States, psychologists in other countries are increasingly influential in adding to the knowledge base and practices of psychology (Nelson, 2007; Peiro & Lunt, 2003; Stevens & Gielen, 2007).

In the United States, women outnumber men in the field, a big change from earlier years when women faced bias and were actively discouraged from becoming psychologists. Today, around three-fourths of new psychology doctorate degrees are earned by women. There is an active debate about whether, and how, to seek balance in the percentage of men and women in the field (Cynkar, 2007; Frincke & Pate, 2004).

The vast majority of psychologists in the United States are white, limiting the diversity of the field. Only 6% of all psychologists are members of racial minority groups. Although the number of minority individuals entering the field is higher than a decade ago—around 20% of new master's degrees and 16% of new doctorate degrees are awarded to people of color—the numbers have not kept up with the dramatic growth of the minority population at large (Hoffer et al., 2005; Maton et al., 2006).

The underrepresentation of racial and ethnic minorities among psychologists is significant for several reasons. First, the field of psychology is diminished by a lack of the diverse perspectives and talents that minority-group members can provide. Furthermore, minority-group psychologists serve as role models for members of minority communities, and their underrepresentation in the profession might deter other minority-group members from entering the field. Finally, because members of minority groups often prefer to receive psychological therapy from treatment providers of their own race or ethnic group, the rarity of minority psychologists can discourage some members of minority groups from seeking treatment (Bernal et al., 2002; Bryant et al., 2005; Jenkins et al., 2003).

THE EDUCATION OF A PSYCHOLOGIST

How do people become psychologists? The most common route is a long one. Most psychologists have a doctorate, either a *PhD* (doctor of philosophy) or, less frequently, a *PsyD* (doctor of psychology). The PhD is a research degree that requires a dissertation based on an original investigation. The PsyD is obtained by psychologists who wish to focus on the treatment of psychological disorders. (Psychologists are distinct from psychiatrists, who have a medical degree and specialize in the diagnosis and treatment of psychological disorders, often using treatments that involve the prescription of drugs.)

Both the PhD and the PsyD typically take four or five years of work past the bachelor's level. Some fields of psychology involve education beyond the doctorate. For instance, doctoral-level clinical psychologists, who deal with people with psychological disorders, typically spend an additional year doing an internship.

About a third of people working in the field of psychology have a master's degree as their highest degree, which they earn after two or three years of graduate work. These psychologists teach, provide therapy, conduct research, or work in specialized programs dealing with drug abuse or crisis intervention. Some work in universities, government, and business, collecting and analyzing data.

> **Study Alert**
>
> Be sure you can differentiate between a PhD (doctor of philosophy) and a PsyD (doctor of psychology), as well as between psychologists and psychiatrists.

CAREERS FOR PSYCHOLOGY MAJORS

Although some psychology majors head for graduate school in psychology or an unrelated field, the majority join the workforce immediately after graduation. Most report that the jobs they take after graduation are related to their psychology background.

An undergraduate major in psychology provides excellent preparation for a variety of occupations. Because undergraduates who specialize in psychology develop good analytical skills, are trained to think critically, and are able to synthesize and evaluate information well, employers in business, industry, and the government value their preparation (Kuther, 2003).

The most common areas of employment for psychology majors are in the social services, including working as an administrator, serving as a counselor, and providing

Positions Obtained by Psychology Majors		
Business Field	**Education/Academic Field**	**Social Field**
Administrative assistant	Administration	Activities coordinator
Affirmative action officer	Child-care provider	Behavioral specialist
Advertising trainee	Child-care worker/	Career counselor
Benefits manager	supervisor	Case worker
Claims specialist	Data management	Child protection worker
Community relations officer	Laboratory assistant	Clinical coordinator
Customer relations	Parent/family education	Community outreach worker
Data management	Preschool teacher	Corrections officer
Employee recruitment	Public opinion surveyor	Counselor assistant
Employee counselor	Research assistant	Crisis intervention counselor
Human resources coordinator/	Teaching assistant	Employment counselor
manager/specialist		Group home attendant
Labor relations manager/specialist		Occupational therapist
Loan officer		Probation officer
Management trainee		Program manager
Marketing		Rehabilitation counselor
Personnel manager/officer		Residence counselor
Product and services research		Mental health assistant
Programs/events coordination		Social service assistant
Public relations		Social worker
Retail sales management		Substance abuse counselor
Sales representative		Youth counselor
Special features writing/reporting		
Staff training and development		
Trainer/training office		

FIGURE 4 Although many psychology majors pursue employment in social services, a background in psychology can prepare one for many professions outside the social services field. What is it about the science and art of psychology that makes it such a versatile field? (Source: From Tara L. Kuther, *The Psychology Major's Handbook*, 1st ed., p. 114. © 2003 Wadsworth, a part of Cengage Learning, Inc. Reproduced by permission. www.cengage.com/permissions.)

direct care. Some 20% of recipients of bachelor's degrees in psychology work in the social services or in some other form of public affairs. In addition, psychology majors often enter the fields of education or business or work for federal, state, and local governments (see Figure 4; American Psychological Association, 2000; Murray, 2002).

RECAP/EVALUATE/RETHINK

RECAP

What is the science of psychology?

- Psychology is the scientific study of behavior and mental processes, encompassing not just what people do but also their biological activities, feelings, perceptions, memory, reasoning, and thoughts. (p. 5)

What are the major specialties in the field of psychology?

- Behavioral neuroscientists focus on the biological basis of behavior, and experimental psychologists study the processes of sensing, perceiving, learning, and thinking about the world. (p. 6)
- Cognitive psychology, an outgrowth of experimental psychology, studies higher mental processes, including memory, knowing, thinking, reasoning, problem solving, judging, decision making, and language. (p. 6)
- Developmental psychologists study how people grow and change throughout the life span. (p. 6)
- Personality psychologists consider the consistency and change in an individual's behavior, as well as the individual differences that distinguish one person's behavior from another's. (p. 6)

- Health psychologists study psychological factors that affect physical disease, whereas clinical psychologists consider the study, diagnosis, and treatment of abnormal behavior. Counseling psychologists focus on educational, social, and career adjustment problems. (p. 8)
- Social psychology is the study of how people's thoughts, feelings, and actions are affected by others. (p. 8)
- Cross-cultural psychology examines the similarities and differences in psychological functioning among various cultures. (p. 8)
- Other increasingly important fields are evolutionary psychology, behavioral genetics, and clinical neuropsychology. (p. 8)

Where do psychologists work?

- Psychologists are employed in a variety of settings. Although the primary sites of employment are private practice and colleges, many psychologists are found in hospitals, clinics, community mental health centers, and counseling centers. (p. 9)

EVALUATE

Match each subfield of psychology with the issues or questions posed below.

a. behavioral neuroscience
b. experimental psychology
c. cognitive psychology
d. developmental psychology
e. personality psychology
f. health psychology
g. clinical psychology
h. counseling psychology
i. educational psychology
j. school psychology
k. social psychology
l. industrial psychology

1. Joan, a college freshman, is worried about her grades. She needs to learn better organizational skills and study habits to cope with the demands of college.
2. At what age do children generally begin to acquire an emotional attachment to their fathers?
3. It is thought that pornographic films that depict violence against women may prompt aggressive behavior in some men.
4. What chemicals are released in the human body as a result of a stressful event? What are their effects on behavior?
5. Luis is unique in his manner of responding to crisis situations, with an even temperament and a positive outlook.
6. The teachers of 8-year-old Jack are concerned that he has recently begun to withdraw socially and to show little interest in schoolwork.
7. Janetta's job is demanding and stressful. She wonders if her lifestyle is making her more prone to certain illnesses, such as cancer and heart disease.
8. A psychologist is intrigued by the fact that some people are much more sensitive to painful stimuli than others are.
9. A strong fear of crowds leads a young man to seek treatment for his problem.
10. What mental strategies are involved in solving complex word problems?
11. What teaching methods most effectively motivate elementary school students to successfully accomplish academic tasks?
12. Jessica is asked to develop a management strategy that will encourage safer work practices in an assembly plant.

RETHINK

1. Do you think intuition and common sense are sufficient for understanding why people act the way they do? In what ways is a scientific approach appropriate for studying human behavior?

2. *From an educator's perspective:* Suppose you are a teacher who has a 7-year-old child in your class who is having unusual difficulty learning to read. Imagine that you could consult as many psychologists with different specialties as you wanted. What are the different types of psychologists that you might approach to address the problem?

Answers to Evaluate Questions

1. a-4; b-8; c-10; d-2; e-5; f-7; g-9; h-1; i-11; j-6; k-3; l-12

KEY TERM

psychology p. 5

A Science Evolves: The Past, the Present, and the Future

Seven thousand years ago, people assumed that psychological problems were caused by evil spirits. To allow those spirits to escape from a person's body, ancient healers chipped a hole in a patient's skull with crude instruments—a procedure called trephining.

According to the 17th-century philosopher Descartes, nerves were hollow tubes through which "animal spirits" conducted impulses in the same way that water is transmitted through a pipe. So when a person got too close to a fire, heat was transmitted to the brain through the tubes.

Franz Josef Gall, an 18th-century physician, argued that a trained observer could discern intelligence, moral character, and other basic personality characteristics from the shape and number of bumps on a person's skull. His theory gave rise to the field of phrenology, employed by hundreds of practitioners in the 19th century.

Although these explanations might sound far-fetched, in their own times they represented the most advanced thinking about what might be called the psychology of the era. Our understanding of behavior has progressed tremendously since the 18th century, but most of the advances have been recent. As sciences go, psychology is one of the new kids on the block. (For highlights in the development of the field, see Figure 1 on page 16.)

Key Concepts

What are the origins of psychology?

What are the major approaches in contemporary psychology?

What are psychology's key issues and controversies?

What is the future of psychology likely to hold?

The Roots of Psychology

We can trace psychology's roots back to the ancient Greeks, who considered the mind a suitable topic for scholarly contemplation. Later philosophers argued for hundreds of years about some of the questions psychologists still grapple with today. For example, the 17th-century British philosopher John Locke believed that children were born into the world with minds like "blank slates" (*tabula rasa* in Latin) and that their experiences determined what kind of adults they would become. His views contrasted with those of Plato and the 17th-century French philosopher René Descartes, who argued that some knowledge was inborn in humans.

However, the formal beginning of psychology as a scientific discipline is generally considered to be in the late 19th century when, in Leipzig, Germany, Wilhelm Wundt established the first experimental laboratory devoted to psychological phenomena. At about the same time, William James was setting up his laboratory in Cambridge, Massachusetts.

When Wundt set up his laboratory in 1879, his aim was to study the building blocks of the mind. He considered psychology to be the study of conscious experience. His perspective, which came to be known as **structuralism,** focused on uncovering the fundamental mental components of perception, consciousness, thinking, emotions, and other kinds of mental states and activities.

To determine how basic sensory processes shape our understanding of the world, Wundt and other structuralists used a procedure called **introspection,** in which they

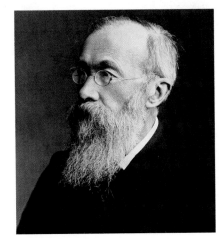

Wilhelm Wundt

structuralism Wundt's approach, which focuses on uncovering the fundamental mental components of consciousness, thinking, and other types of mental states and activities.

introspection This procedure to study the structure of the mind has subjects describe in detail what they are experiencing when they are exposed to a stimulus.

15

1690 John Locke introduces idea of *tabula rasa*

◄ **5,000 BCE** Trephining used to allow the escape of evil spirits

◄ **430 BCE** Hippocrates argues for four temperaments of personality

1879 Wilhelm Wundt inaugurates first psychology laboratory in Leipzig, Germany

1905 Mary Calkins works on memory

1915 Strong emphasis on intelligence testing

Forerunners of Psychology   1800

1900   **First Psychologists**

1637 Descartes describes animal spirits

1807 Franz Josef Gall proposes phrenology

1895 Functionalist model formulated

1320 Gestalt psychology becomes influential

1890 *Principles of Psychology* published by William James

1900 Sigmund Freud develops the psychodynamic perspective

1904 Ivan Pavlov wins Nobel Prize for work on digestion that led to fundamental principles of learning

FIGURE 1 This time line illustrates major milestones in the development of psychology.

presented people with a stimulus—such as a bright green object or a sentence printed on a card—and asked them to describe, in their own words and in as much detail as they could, what they were experiencing. Wundt argued that by analyzing their replies, psychologists could come to a better understanding of the structure of the mind.

Over time, psychologists challenged Wundt's approach. They became increasingly dissatisfied with the assumption that introspection could reveal the structure of the mind. Because there were few ways an outside observer could confirm the accuracy of others' introspections, introspection was not a truly scientific technique, they argued. Moreover, people had difficulty describing some kinds of inner experiences, such as emotional responses. Those drawbacks led to the development of new approaches that largely replaced structuralism.

The perspective that replaced structuralism is known as functionalism. Rather than focusing on the mind's structure, **functionalism** concentrated on what the mind *does* and how behavior *functions*. Functionalists, whose perspective became prominent in the early 1900s, asked what role behavior plays in helping people adapt to their environments. For example, a functionalist might examine the function of the emotion of fear in preparing us to deal with emergency situations.

Led by the American psychologist William James, the functionalists examined how behavior enables people to satisfy their needs and how our "stream of consciousness"

functionalism An early approach to psychology that concentrated on what the mind does—the functions of mental activity—and the role of behavior in allowing people to adapt to their environments.

1924
John B. Watson, an early behaviorist, publishes *Behaviorism*

1980
Jean Piaget, an influential developmental psychologist, dies

2010
New subfields develop such as clinical neuropsychology and evolutionary psychology

1957 Leon Festinger publishes *A Theory of Cognitive Dissonance*, producing a major impact on social psychology

1951
Carl Rogers publishes *Client-Centered Therapy*, helping to establish the humanistic perspective

1990 Greater emphasis on multiculturalism and diversity

Modern Psychology

2000

1953
B. F. Skinner publishes *Science and Human Behavior*, advocating the behavioral perspective

1969
Arguments regarding the genetic basis of IQ fuel lingering controversies

1985 Increasing emphasis on cognitive perspective

1928
Leta Stetter Hollingworth publishes work on adolescence

1954
Abraham Maslow publishes *Motivation and Personality*, developing the concept of self-actualization

1981 David Hubel and Torsten Wiesel win Nobel Prize for work on vision cells in the brain

2000
Elizabeth Loftus does pioneering work on false memory and eyewitness testimony

thinking permits us to adapt to our environment. The American educator John Dewey drew on functionalism to develop the field of school psychology, proposing ways to best meet students' educational needs.

Another important reaction to structuralism was the development of gestalt psychology in the early 1900s. **Gestalt psychology** emphasizes how perception is organized. Instead of considering the individual parts that make up thinking, gestalt psychologists took the opposite tack, studying how people consider individual elements together as units or wholes. Led by German scientists such as Hermann Ebbinghaus and Max Wertheimer, gestalt psychologists proposed that "The whole is different from the sum of its parts," meaning that our perception (or understanding) of objects is greater and more meaningful than the individual elements that make up our perceptions. Gestalt psychologists have made substantial contributions to our understanding of perception.

gestalt (geh SHTALLT) psychology An approach to psychology that focuses on the organization of perception and thinking in a "whole" sense rather than on the individual elements of perception.

WOMEN IN PSYCHOLOGY: FOUNDING MOTHERS

As in many scientific fields, social prejudices hindered women's participation in the early development of psychology. For example, many universities would not even admit women to their graduate psychology programs in the early 1900s.

▶ **Study Alert**
Knowing the basic outlines of the history of the field will help you understand how today's major persp have evolved.

Despite the hurdles they faced, women made notable contributions to psychology, although their impact on the field was largely overlooked until recently. For example, Margaret Floy Washburn (1871–1939) was the first woman to receive a doctorate in psychology, and she did important work in animal behavior. Leta Stetter Hollingworth (1886–1939) was one of the first psychologists to focus on child development and on women's issues. She collected data to refute the view popular in the early 1900s that women's abilities periodically declined during certain phases of the menstrual cycle (Hollingworth, 1943/1990; Denmark & Fernandez, 1993; Furumoto & Scarborough, 2002).

Mary Calkins (1863–1930), who studied memory in the early part of the 20th century, became the first female president of the American Psychological Association. Karen Horney (pronounced "HORN-eye") (1885–1952) focused on the social and cultural factors behind personality, and June Etta Downey (1875–1932) spearheaded the study of personality traits and became the first woman to head a psychology department at a state university. Anna Freud (1895–1982), the daughter of Sigmund Freud, also made notable contributions to the treatment of abnormal behavior, and Mamie Phipps Clark (1917–1983) carried out pioneering work on how children of color grew to recognize racial differences (Horney, 1937; Stevens & Gardner, 1982; Lal, 2002).

Today's Perspectives

The men and women who laid the foundations of psychology shared a common goal: to explain and understand behavior using scientific methods. Seeking to achieve the same goal, the tens of thousands of psychologists who followed those early pioneers embraced—and often rejected—a variety of broad perspectives.

The perspectives of psychology offer distinct outlooks and emphasize different factors. Just as we can use more than one map to find our way around a particular region—for instance, a map that shows roads and highways and another map that shows major landmarks—psychologists developed a variety of approaches to understanding behavior. When considered jointly, the different perspectives provide a means to explain behavior in its amazing variety.

Today, the field of psychology includes five major perspectives (summarized in Figure 2). These broad perspectives emphasize different aspects of behavior and mental processes, and each takes our understanding of behavior in a somewhat different direction.

Study Alert

Use Figure 2 to differentiate the five perspectives. These are important because they provide a foundation for every topic covered throughout the text.

Neuroscience

Views behavior from the perspective of biological functioning

Psychodynamic

Believes behavior is motivated by inner, unconscious forces over which a person has little control

Behavioral

Focuses on observable behavior

Cognitive

Examines how people understand and think about the world

Humanistic

Contends that people can control their behavior and that they naturally try to reach their full potential

FIGURE 2 The major perspectives of psychology.

THE NEUROSCIENCE PERSPECTIVE: BLOOD, SWEAT, AND FEARS

When we get down to the basics, humans are animals made of skin and bones. The **neuroscience perspective** considers how people and nonhumans function biologically: how individual nerve cells are joined together, how the inheritance of certain characteristics from parents and other ancestors influences behavior, how the functioning of the body affects hopes and fears, which behaviors are instinctual, and so forth. Even more complex kinds of behaviors, such as a baby's response to strangers, are viewed as having critical biological components by psychologists who embrace the neuroscience perspective. This perspective includes the study of heredity and evolution, which considers how heredity may influence behavior; and behavioral neuroscience, which examines how the brain and the nervous system affect behavior.

Because every behavior can be broken down ultimately into its biological components, the neuroscience perspective has broad appeal. Psychologists who subscribe to this perspective have made major contributions to the understanding and betterment of human life, ranging from cures for certain types of deafness to drug treatments for people with severe mental disorders. Furthermore, advances in methods for examining the anatomy and functioning of the brain have permitted the neuroscientific perspective to extend its influence across a broad range of subfields in psychology. (We'll see examples of these methods throughout this book in *Neuroscience and Life*.)

> **neuroscience perspective** The approach that studies behavior from the perspective of the biological functions of the brain, the nervous system, and other body systems.

THE PSYCHODYNAMIC PERSPECTIVE: UNDERSTANDING THE INNER PERSON

To many people who have never taken a psychology course, psychology begins and ends with the psychodynamic perspective. Proponents of the **psychodynamic perspective** argue that behavior is motivated by inner forces and conflicts about which we have little awareness or control. They view dreams and slips of the tongue as indications of what a person is truly feeling within a seething cauldron of unconscious psychic activity.

The origins of the psychodynamic view are linked to one person: Sigmund Freud. Freud was a Viennese physician in the early 1900s whose ideas about unconscious determinants of behavior had a revolutionary effect on 20th-century thinking, not just in psychology but in related fields as well. Although some original Freudian principles have been roundly criticized, the contemporary psychodynamic perspective provides a means not only to understand and treat some kinds of psychological disorders but also to understand everyday phenomena such as prejudice and aggression.

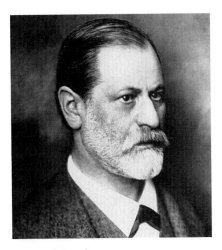

Sigmund Freud

THE BEHAVIORAL PERSPECTIVE: OBSERVING THE OUTER PERSON

Whereas the neuroscience and psychodynamic approaches look inside the organism to determine the causes of its behavior, the behavioral perspective takes a very different approach. The **behavioral perspective** grew out of a rejection of psychology's early emphasis on the inner workings of the mind. Instead, early behaviorists suggested that the field should focus on observable behavior that can be measured objectively.

John B. Watson was the first major American psychologist to advocate a behavioral approach. Working in the 1920s, Watson was adamant in his view that one could gain a complete understanding of behavior by studying and modifying the environment in which people operate.

In fact, Watson believed rather optimistically that it was possible to elicit any desired type of behavior by controlling a person's environment. This philosophy is clear from his own words: "Give me a dozen healthy infants, well-formed, and my own specified world to bring them up in and I'll guarantee to take any one at random and train him to become any type of specialist I might select—doctor,

> **psychodynamic perspective** The approach based on the view that behavior is motivated by unconscious inner forces over which the individual has little control.

> **behavioral perspective** The approach that suggests that observable, measurable behavior should be the focus of study.

lawyer, artist, merchant-chief, and yes, even beggar-man and thief, regardless of his talents, penchants, tendencies, abilities, vocations, and race of his ancestors" (Watson, 1924).

The behavioral perspective was championed by B. F. Skinner, a pioneer in the field. A great deal of our understanding about how people learn new behaviors is based on the behavioral perspective. As we will see, the behavioral perspective crops up along every byway of psychology. Along with its influence in the area of learning processes, this perspective has made contributions in such diverse areas as treating mental disorders, curbing aggression, resolving sexual problems, and ending drug addiction (Silverman, Roll, & Higgins, 2008).

THE COGNITIVE PERSPECTIVE: IDENTIFYING THE ROOTS OF UNDERSTANDING

cognitive perspective The approach that focuses on how people think, understand, and know about the world.

Efforts to understand behavior led some psychologists straight into the mind. Evolving in part from structuralism and in part as a reaction to behaviorism, which focused so heavily on observable behavior and the environment, the **cognitive perspective** focuses on how people think, understand, and know about the world. Its emphasis is on learning how people comprehend and represent the outside world within themselves and how our ways of thinking about the world influence our behavior.

Many psychologists who adhere to the cognitive perspective compare human thinking to the workings of a computer that takes in information and transforms, stores, and retrieves it. In their view, thinking is *information processing*.

Psychologists who rely on the cognitive perspective ask questions ranging from how people make decisions to whether a person can watch television and study at the same time. Common elements that link cognitive approaches are an emphasis on how people understand and think about the world, and an interest in describing the patterns and irregularities in the operation of our minds.

THE HUMANISTIC PERSPECTIVE: THE UNIQUE QUALITIES OF THE HUMAN SPECIES

humanistic perspective The approach that suggests that all individuals naturally strive to grow, develop, and be in control of their lives and behavior.

Rejecting the view that behavior is determined largely by automatically unfolding biological forces, unconscious processes, or the environment, the **humanistic perspective** instead suggests that all individuals naturally strive to grow, develop, and be in control of their lives and behavior. Humanistic psychologists maintain that each of us has the capacity to seek and reach fulfillment.

According to Carl Rogers and Abraham Maslow, who were central figures in the development of the humanistic perspective, people will strive to reach their full potential when given the opportunity. The emphasis of the humanistic perspective is *free will*, the ability to freely make decisions about one's own behavior and life. The notion of free will stands in contrast to *determinism*, which sees behavior as caused or determined by things beyond a person's control.

The humanistic perspective assumes that people are able to make their own choices about their behavior rather than relying on societal standards. More than any other approach, it stresses the role of psychology in enriching people's lives and helping them achieve self-fulfillment. By reminding psychologists of their commitment to the individual person in society, the humanistic perspective has been an important influence (Dillon, 2008; Robbins, 2008).

It's important not to let the abstract qualities of the broad approaches we have discussed lull you into thinking that they are purely theoretical: These perspectives underlie ongoing work of a practical nature, as we will discuss throughout this book. To start seeing how psychology can improve everyday life, read *Applying Psychology in the 21st Century.*

Psychology Matters

"Investigators search for clues at site of suicide bombing."

"Deepest recession in decades produces huge rates of unemployment."

"Eyewitness to killing proves unable to provide reliable clues."

"Texting while driving blamed for rise in traffic fatalities."

"Childhood obesity rates surge."

A quick review of any day's news headlines reminds us that the world is beset by a variety of stubborn problems that resist easy solutions. At the same time, a considerable number of psychologists are devoting their energies and expertise to addressing these problems and improving the human condition. Let's consider some of the ways that psychology has addressed and helped work toward solutions of society's major problems:

Terrorism and its causes are among the world's most pressing issues. What can psychologists add to our understanding of the problem?

- **What are the causes of terrorism?** What motivates suicide bombers? Are they psychologically disordered, or can their behavior be seen as a rational response to a particular system of beliefs? As we'll see in Module 39 when we discuss psychological disorders, psychologists are gaining an understanding of the factors that lead people to embrace suicide and to engage in terrorism to further a cause in which they deeply believe (Stronink, 2007; Locicero & Sinclair, 2008; Post et al., 2009; Mintz & Brule, 2009).

- **How can people best cope with an economic crisis?** When the economy sours, financial loss and the hovering threat of unemployment create a great deal of stress. Psychologists study how these stressors affect family relations and produce psychological harm—particularly to children of stressed and depressed parents—that can long outlast the economic crisis. They can then help people use coping strategies that are effective at preventing long-term harm (Conger and Donnellan, 2007; Ünal-Karagüven, 2009).

- **Why do eyewitnesses to crimes often remember the events inaccurately, and how can we increase the precision of eyewitness accounts?** Psychologists' research has come to an important conclusion: Eyewitness testimony in criminal cases is often inaccurate and biased. Memories of crimes are often clouded by emotion, and the questions asked by police investigators often elicit inaccurate responses. Work by psychologists has been used to provide national guidelines for obtaining more accurate memories during criminal investigations (Loftus & Bernstein, 2005; Kassin, 2005; Busey & Loftus, 2007).

- **Does texting while driving impair people's driving ability?** Several states have enacted controversial laws banning cell phone use and texting while driving. Although many people believe that they are perfectly able to talk and drive at the same time, psychological research on attention tells a different story: Merely talking on a cellphone, whether hands-free or not, impairs people's driving about as much as if they were legally drunk (Strayer et al., 2005; Taggi et al., 2007; Drews, Pasupathi, & Strayer, 2008; Charlton, 2009).

- **What are the roots of obesity, and how can healthier eating and better physical fitness be encouraged?** Why are some people more predisposed to obesity than others? What social factors might be at play in the rising rate of obesity in childhood? As we'll discuss in Module 25, obesity is a complex problem with biological, psychological, and social underpinnings. Approaches to treating obesity therefore must take many factors into account in order to be successful. There is no magic bullet providing a quick fix, but psychologists recommend a number of strategies that help make weight-loss goals more achievable (Puhl & Latner, 2007; MacLean et al., 2009; Neumark-Sztainer, 2009).

These topics represent just a few of the issues that psychologists address on a daily basis. To further explore the many ways that psychology has an impact on everyday life, check out the American Psychological Association (APA) website, which features psychological applications in everyday life, at www.apa.org.

RETHINK

- What do *you* think are the major problems affecting society today?
- What are the psychological issues involved in these problems, and how might psychologists help find solutions to them?

Psychology's Key Issues and Controversies

As you consider the many topics and perspectives that make up psychology, ranging from a narrow focus on minute biochemical influences on behavior to a broad focus on social behaviors, you might find yourself thinking that the discipline lacks cohesion. However, the field is more unified than a first glimpse might suggest. For one thing, no matter what topical area a psychologist specializes in, he or she will rely primarily on one of the five major perspectives. For example, a developmental psychologist who specializes in the study of children is likely to make use of the cognitive perspective or the psychodynamic perspective more than the other major perspectives.

Psychologists also agree on what the key issues of the field are (see Figure 3). Despite major arguments regarding how best to address and resolve these key issues, psychology is a unified science because psychologists of all perspectives agree that the issues must be addressed if the field is going to advance. As you contemplate these key issues, try not to think of them in "either/or" terms. Instead, consider the opposing viewpoints on each issue as the opposite ends of a continuum, with the positions of individual psychologists typically falling somewhere between the two ends.

Nature (heredity) versus nurture (environment) is one of the major issues that psychologists grapple with. How much of individual behavior is due to one's genetically determined nature (heredity), and how much is due to nurture (the influences of the physical and social environment in which a child is raised)? Furthermore, what is the interplay between heredity and environment? These questions have deep philosophical and historical roots, and they are involved in many topics in psychology.

> ### ◣ Study Alert
>
> Use Figure 3 to learn the key issues that underlie every subfield of psychology.

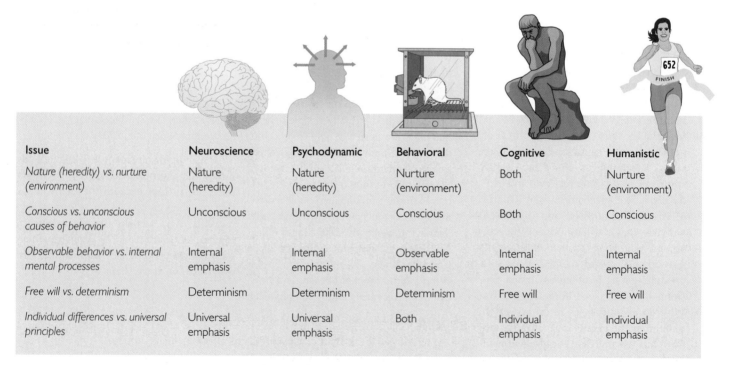

Issue	Neuroscience	Psychodynamic	Behavioral	Cognitive	Humanistic
Nature (heredity) vs. nurture (environment)	Nature (heredity)	Nature (heredity)	Nurture (environment)	Both	Nurture (environment)
Conscious vs. unconscious causes of behavior	Unconscious	Unconscious	Conscious	Both	Conscious
Observable behavior vs. internal mental processes	Internal emphasis	Internal emphasis	Observable emphasis	Internal emphasis	Internal emphasis
Free will vs. determinism	Determinism	Determinism	Determinism	Free will	Free will
Individual differences vs. universal principles	Universal emphasis	Universal emphasis	Both	Individual emphasis	Individual emphasis

FIGURE 3 Key issues in psychology and the positions taken by psychologists subscribing to the five major perspectives of psychology.

A psychologist's take on this issue depends partly on which major perspective he or she subscribes to. For example, developmental psychologists who follow a neuroscience perspective and focus on how people grow and change throughout the course of their lives may be most interested in learning more about hereditary influences. In contrast, developmental psychologists who are proponents of the behavioral perspective would be more likely to focus on environment (Rutter, 2002, 2006).

However, every psychologist would agree that neither nature nor nurture alone is the sole determinant of behavior; rather, it is a combination of the two. In a sense, then, the real controversy involves how much of our behavior is caused by heredity and how much is caused by environmental influences.

A second major question addressed by psychologists concerns *conscious versus unconscious causes of behavior*. How much of our behavior is produced by forces of which we are fully aware, and how much is due to unconscious activity—mental processes that are not accessible to the conscious mind? This question represents one of the great controversies in the field of psychology. For example, clinical psychologists adopting a psychodynamic perspective argue that psychological disorders are brought about by unconscious factors, whereas psychologists employing the cognitive perspective suggest that psychological disorders largely are the result of faulty thinking processes.

The next issue is *observable behavior versus internal mental processes*. Should psychology concentrate solely on behavior that can be seen by outside observers, or should it focus on unseen thinking processes? Some psychologists, particularly those relying on the behavioral perspective, contend that the only legitimate source of information for psychologists is behavior that can be observed directly. Other psychologists, building on the cognitive perspective, argue that what goes on inside a person's mind is critical to understanding behavior, and so we must concern ourselves with mental processes.

Free will versus determinism is another key issue. How much of our behavior is a matter of **free will** (choices made freely by an individual), and how much is subject to **determinism,** the notion that behavior is largely produced by factors beyond one's willful control? An issue long debated by philosophers, the free will/determinism argument is also central to the field of psychology (Dennett, 2003; Cary, 2007).

For example, some psychologists who specialize in psychological disorders argue that people make intentional choices and that those who display so-called abnormal behavior should be considered responsible for their actions. Other psychologists disagree and contend that such individuals are the victims of forces beyond their control. The position psychologists take on this issue has important implications for the way they treat psychological disorders, especially when deciding whether treatment should be forced on people who don't want it.

The last of the key issues concerns *individual differences versus universal principles*. How much of our behavior is a consequence of our unique and special qualities, and how much reflects the culture and society in which we live? How much of our behavior is universally human? Psychologists who rely on the neuroscience perspective tend to look for universal principles of behavior, such as how the nervous system operates or the way certain hormones automatically prime us for sexual activity. Such psychologists concentrate on the similarities in our behavioral destinies despite vast differences in our upbringing. In contrast, psychologists who employ the humanistic perspective focus more on the uniqueness of every individual. They consider every person's behavior a reflection of distinct and special individual qualities.

The question of the degree to which psychologists can identify universal principles that apply to all people has taken on new significance in light of the tremendous demographic changes now occurring in the United States and around the world. As we discuss next, these changes raise new and critical issues for the discipline of psychology in the 21st century.

free will The idea that behavior is caused primarily by choices that are made freely by the individual.

determinism The idea that people's behavior is produced primarily by factors outside their willful control.

Psychology's Future

We have examined psychology's foundations, but what does the future hold for the discipline? Although the course of scientific development is notoriously difficult to predict, several trends seem likely:

- As its knowledge base grows, psychology will become increasingly specialized and new perspectives will evolve. For example, our growing understanding of the brain and the nervous system, combined with scientific advances in genetics and gene therapy, will allow psychologists to focus on *prevention* of psychological disorders rather than only on their treatment (Cuijpers et al., 2008).
- The evolving sophistication of neuroscientific approaches is likely to have an increasing influence over other branches of psychology. For instance, social psychologists already are increasing their understanding of social behaviors such as persuasion by using brain scans as part of an evolving field known as *social neuroscience* (Bunge & Wallis, 2008; Cacioppo et al., 2009).
- Psychology's influence on issues of public interest also will grow. The major problems of our time—such as violence, terrorism, racial and ethnic prejudice, poverty, and environmental and technological disasters—have important psychological aspects (Zimbardo, 2004; Marshall et al., 2007; Hobfoll et al., 2007).
- Finally, as the population becomes more diverse, issues of diversity—embodied in the study of racial, ethnic, linguistic, and cultural factors—will become more important to psychologists providing services and doing research. The result will be a field that can provide an understanding of *human* behavior in its broadest sense (Leung & Blustein, 2000; Chang & Sue, 2005; Quintana et al., 2006).

RECAP/EVALUATE/RETHINK

RECAP

What are the origins of psychology?
- Wilhelm Wundt laid the foundation of psychology in 1879, when he opened his laboratory in Germany. (p. 15)
- Early perspectives that guided the work of psychologists were structuralism, functionalism, and gestalt psychology. (p. 15)

What are the major approaches in contemporary psychology?
- The neuroscience perspective focuses on the biological components of the behavior of people and animals. (p. 19)
- The psychodynamic perspective suggests that powerful, unconscious inner forces and conflicts about which people have little or no awareness are the primary determinants of behavior. (p. 19)
- The behavioral perspective de-emphasizes internal processes and concentrates instead on observable, measurable behavior, suggesting that understanding and control of a person's environment are sufficient to fully explain and modify behavior. (p. 19)

- The cognitive perspective to behavior considers how people know, understand, and think about the world. (p. 20)
- The humanistic perspective emphasizes that people are uniquely inclined toward psychological growth and higher levels of functioning and that they will strive to reach their full potential. (p. 20)

What are psychology's key issues and controversies?
- Psychology's key issues and controversies center on how much human behavior is a product of nature or nurture, conscious or unconscious thoughts, observable actions or internal mental processes, free will or determinism, and individual differences or universal principles. (p. 22)

What is the future of psychology likely to hold?
- Psychology will become increasingly specialized, will pay greater attention to prevention instead of just treatment, will become more and more concerned with the public interest, and will take the growing diversity of the country's population into account more fully. (p. 24)

EVALUATE

1. Wundt described psychology as the study of conscious experience, a perspective he called _____.

2. Early psychologists studied the mind by asking people to describe what they were experiencing when exposed to various stimuli. This procedure was known as _____.

3. The statement "In order to study human behavior, we must consider the whole of perception rather than its component parts" might be made by a person subscribing to which perspective of psychology?

4. Jeanne's therapist asks her to recount a violent dream she recently experienced in order to gain insight into the unconscious forces affecting her behavior. Jeanne's therapist is working from a _____ perspective.

5. "It is behavior that can be observed that should be studied, not the suspected inner workings of the mind." This statement was most likely made by someone with which perspective?
   a. Cognitive perspective
   b. Neuroscience perspective
   c. Humanistic perspective
   d. Behavioral perspective

6. "My therapist is wonderful! He always points out my positive traits. He dwells on my uniqueness and strength as an individual. I feel much more confident about myself—as if I'm really growing and reaching my potential." The therapist being described most likely follows a _____ perspective.

7. In the nature–nurture issue, nature refers to heredity, and nurture refers to the _____.

8. Race is a biological concept rather than a psychological one. True or false?

RETHINK

1. Focusing on one of the five major perspectives in use today (i.e., neuroscience, psychodynamic, behavioral, cognitive, and humanistic), describe the kinds of research questions and studies that researchers using that perspective might pursue.

2. *From a journalist's perspective:* Choose a current major political controversy. What psychological approaches or perspectives can be applied to that issue?

Answers to Evaluate Questions

1. structuralism; 2. introspection; 3. gestalt; 4. psychodynamic; 5. d; 6. humanistic; 7. environment; 8. true

KEY TERMS

structuralism p. 15
introspection p. 15
functionalism p. 16
gestalt (geh SHTALLT) psychology p. 17

neuroscience perspective p. 19
psychodynamic perspective p. 19

behavioral perspective p. 19
cognitive perspective p. 20

humanistic perspective p. 20
free will p. 23
determinism p. 23

Research in Psychology

scientific method The approach through which psychologists systematically acquire knowledge and understanding about behavior and other phenomena of interest.

theories Broad explanations and predictions concerning phenomena of interest.

The Scientific Method

"Birds of a feather flock together" . . . or "Opposites attract"? "Two heads are better than one" . . . or "If you want a thing done well, do it yourself"? "The more the merrier" . . . or "Two's company, three's a crowd"?

If we were to rely on common sense to understand behavior, we'd have considerable difficulty—especially because commonsense views are often contradictory. In fact, one of the major undertakings for the field of psychology is to develop suppositions about behavior and to determine which of those suppositions are accurate.

Psychologists—as well as scientists in other disciplines—meet the challenge of posing appropriate questions and properly answering them by relying on the scientific method. The **scientific method** is the approach used by psychologists to systematically acquire knowledge and increase understanding about behavior and other phenomena of interest. As illustrated in Figure 1, it consists of four main steps: (1) identifying questions of interest, (2) formulating an explanation, (3) carrying out research designed to support or refute the explanation, and (4) communicating the findings.

THEORIES: SPECIFYING BROAD EXPLANATIONS

When using the scientific method, psychologists start by identifying questions of interest. We've all been curious at some time about our observations of everyday behavior. If you have ever asked yourself why a particular teacher is so easily annoyed, why a friend is always late for appointments, or how your dog understands your commands, you have been formulating questions about behavior.

Psychologists, too, ask questions about the nature and causes of behavior. They may explore explanations for everyday behaviors or for various phenomena. They may also pose questions that build on findings from their own previous research or from research carried out by other psychologists. Or they may produce new questions based on curiosity, creativity, or insight.

Once a question has been identified, the next step in the scientific method is to develop a theory to explain the observed phenomenon. **Theories** are broad explanations and predictions concerning phenomena of interest. They provide a framework for understanding the relationships among a set of otherwise unorganized facts or principles.

All of us have developed our own informal theories of human behavior, such as "People are basically good" or "People's behavior is usually motivated by

THEORIES OF EVERYTHING

self-interest." However, psychologists' theories are more formal and focused. They are established on the basis of a careful study of the psychological literature to identify earlier relevant research and previously formulated theories, as well as on psychologists' general knowledge of the field (Sternberg & Beall, 1991; McGuire, 1997).

Growing out of the diverse approaches employed by different psychologists, theories vary both in their breadth and in their level of detail. For example, one theory might seek to explain and predict a phenomenon as broad as emotional experience. A narrower theory might attempt to explain why people display the emotion of fear nonverbally after receiving a threat (Guerrero, La Valley, & Farinelli, 2008; Waller, Cray, & Burrows, 2008).

Theories can help us understand otherwise perplexing behavior. For example, consider the famous case of a woman named Kitty Genovese, who was attacked by a man near a crowded apartment building in New York City. At one point during the assault, which lasted 30 minutes, she managed to free herself and screamed, "Oh, my God, he stabbed me. Please help me!" But not one person helped, and Genovese was stabbed to death and sexually molested (Rogers & Eftimiades, 1995; Rosenthal, 2008).

Responding to the failure of bystanders to intervene while Kitty Genovese was murdered in New York, psychologists Bibb Latané and John Darley developed what they called a theory of *diffusion of responsibility* (Latané & Darley, 1970). According to their theory, the greater the number of bystanders or witnesses to an event that calls for helping behavior, the more the responsibility for helping is perceived to be shared by all the bystanders. Thus, the greater the number of bystanders in an emergency situation, the smaller the share of the responsibility each person feels—and the less likely it is that any single person will come forward to help.

HYPOTHESES: CRAFTING TESTABLE PREDICTIONS

Although the diffusion of responsibility theory seems to make sense, it represented only the beginning of Latané and Darley's investigative process. Their next step was to devise a way to test their theory. To do this, they needed to create a hypothesis. A **hypothesis** is a prediction stated in a way that allows it to be tested. Hypotheses stem from theories; they help test the underlying soundness of theories.

In the same way that we develop our own broad theories about the world, we also construct hypotheses about events and behavior in our lives. Those hypotheses can range from trivialities (such as why our English teacher wears those weird shirts) to more meaningful matters (such as what is the best way to study for a test). Although we rarely test these hypotheses systematically, we do try to determine whether they are right. Perhaps we try comparing two strategies: cramming the night before an exam versus spreading out our study over several nights. By assessing which approach yields better test performance, we have created a way to compare and even measure the two strategies.

A hypothesis must be restated in a way that will allow it to be tested, which involves creating an operational definition. An **operational definition** is the translation of a hypothesis into specific, testable procedures that can be measured and observed.

There is no single way to go about devising an operational definition for a hypothesis; it depends on logic, the equipment and facilities available, the psychological perspective being employed, and ultimately, the creativity of the researcher. For example, one researcher might develop a hypothesis that uses "an increase in heart rate" as an operational definition of "fear." In contrast, another psychologist's an operational definition of "fear" might be written responses to the question "How much fear are you experiencing at this moment?"

Latané and Darley's hypothesis was a straightforward prediction from their more general theory of diffusion of responsibility: The more people who witness an emergency situation, the less likely it is that help will be given to a victim. They could,

FIGURE 1 The scientific method, which encompasses the process of identifying, asking, and answering questions, is used by psychologists, and by researchers from every other scientific discipline, to come to an understanding about the world. What do you think are the advantages of this method?

hypothesis A prediction stemming from a theory that's stated in a way that allows it to be tested.

operational definition The translation of a hypothesis into specific, testable procedures that can be measured and observed.

Study Alert

Use Figure 1 to remember the four steps of the scientific method: identifying questions, formulating an explanation, carrying out research, and communicating the findings.

of course, have chosen another hypothesis (try to think of one!), but their initial formulation seemed to offer the most direct explanation of the theory.

Psychologists rely on formal theories and hypotheses for many reasons. For one thing, theories and hypotheses allow them to make sense of unorganized, separate observations and bits of information by permitting them to place the pieces within a coherent framework. In addition, theories and hypotheses offer psychologists the opportunity to move beyond known facts and make deductions about unexplained phenomena and develop ideas for future investigation (Howitt & Cramer, 2000; Cohen, 2003; Gurin, 2006).

In short, the scientific method, with its emphasis on theories and hypotheses, helps psychologists pose appropriate questions. With properly stated questions in hand, psychologists then can choose from a variety of research methods to find answers.

Study Alert

Remember that a theory is a broad explanation, while a hypothesis is a more narrow prediction.

Psychological Research

Research—or systematic inquiry aimed at the discovery of new knowledge—is a central ingredient of the scientific method in psychology. It provides the key to understanding the degree to which hypotheses (and the theories behind them) are accurate.

Just as we can apply different theories and hypotheses to explain the same phenomena, we can use a number of alternative methods to conduct research. As we consider the major tools psychologists use to conduct research, keep in mind that their relevance extends beyond testing and evaluating abstract hypotheses in psychology. All of us carry out elementary forms of practical research on our own. For instance, a supervisor might evaluate an employee's performance; a physician may systematically test the effects of different doses of a drug on a patient; a salesperson can compare different persuasive strategies. Each of these situations draws on the research practices we are about to discuss.

Descriptive Research

Let's begin by considering several types of *descriptive research* designed to systematically investigate a person, group, or patterns of behavior. These methods include archival research, naturalistic observation, survey research, and case studies.

ARCHIVAL RESEARCH

Suppose that, like the psychologists Latané and Darley (1970), you were interested in finding out more about emergency situations in which bystanders did not provide help. One of the first places you might look would be historical accounts. By searching newspaper records, for example, you might find historic support for the notion that a decrease in helping behavior has accompanied an increase in the number of bystanders.

archival research Research in which existing data, such as census documents, college records, and newspaper clippings, are examined to test a hypothesis.

Using newspaper articles is an example of archival research. In **archival research,** existing data, such as census documents, college records, and newspaper clippings, are examined to test a hypothesis. For example, college records may be used to determine if there are gender differences in academic performance (Sullivan, Riccio, & Reynolds, 2008).

Archival research is a relatively inexpensive means of testing a hypothesis because someone else has already collected the basic data. Of course, the use of existing data has several drawbacks. For one thing, the data may not be in a form that allows the researcher to test a hypothesis fully. The information could be incomplete, or it could have been collected haphazardly (Simonton, 2000; Riniolo et al., 2003; Vega, 2006).

Most attempts at archival research are hampered by the simple fact that records with the necessary information often do not exist. In these instances, researchers often turn to another research method: naturalistic observation.

NATURALISTIC OBSERVATION

During **naturalistic observation,** the investigator observes some naturally occurring behavior and doesn't make a change in the situation. For example, a researcher investigating helping behavior might observe the kind of help given to victims in a high-crime area of a city. The important point to remember about naturalistic observation is that the researcher simply records what occurs, making no modification to the situation that's being observed (Schutt, 2001; Moore, 2002; Rustin, 2006).

Although the advantage of naturalistic observation is obvious—we get a sample of what people do in their "natural habitat"—there is also an important drawback: the inability to control any of the factors of interest. For example, we might find so few naturally occurring instances of helping behavior that we would be unable to draw any conclusions. Because naturalistic observation prevents researchers from making changes in a situation, they must wait until the appropriate conditions occur. Furthermore, if people know they are being watched, they may alter their reactions and produce behavior that is not truly representative.

SURVEY RESEARCH

There is no more straightforward way of finding out what people think, feel, and do than asking them directly. For this reason, surveys are an important research method. In **survey research,** a *sample* of people chosen to represent a larger group of interest (a *population*) is asked a series of questions about their behavior, thoughts, or attitudes. Survey methods have become so sophisticated that even with a very small sample researchers are able to infer with great accuracy how a larger group would respond. For instance, a sample of just a few thousand voters is sufficient to predict within one or two percentage points who will win a presidential election—if the representative sample is chosen with care (Sommer & Sommer, 2001; Groves et al., 2004; Igo, 2006).

Researchers investigating helping behavior might conduct a survey that asks people to indicate their reluctance about giving aid to someone. Similarly, researchers interested in learning about sexual practices have carried out surveys to learn which practices are common and which are not and to chart changing notions of sexual morality over several decades (Reece et al., 2009; Santelli et al., 2009).

However, survey research has several potential pitfalls. For one thing, if the sample of people who are surveyed is not representative of the broader population of interest, the results of the survey will have little meaning. For instance, if a sample of voters in a town only includes Republicans, it would hardly be useful for predicting the results of an election in which both Republicans and Democrats are voting. Consequently, researchers using surveys strive to obtain a *random sample* of the population in question, in which every member of the population—in this case, every voter—has an equal chance of being included in the sample receiving the survey (Daley, 2003; Dale, 2006).

In addition, survey respondents may not want to admit to holding socially undesirable attitudes. (Most racists know they are racists but might not want to admit it.) And in some cases, people may not even be consciously aware of what their true attitudes are or why they hold them.

Dian Fossey, a pioneer in the study of endangered mountain gorillas in their native habitat, relied on naturalistic observation for her research. What are the advantages of this approach?

naturalistic observation Research in which an investigator simply observes some naturally occurring behavior and does not make a change in the situation.

survey research Research in which people chosen to represent a larger population are asked a series of questions about their behavior, thoughts, or attitudes.

"This is the New York Times' Business Poll again, Mr. Landau. Do you feel better or worse about the economy than you did twenty minutes ago?"

THE CASE STUDY

When they read about a suicide bomber in the Middle East, many people wonder what it is about the terrorist's personality or background that leads to such behavior. To answer this question, psychologists might conduct a case study. In contrast to a survey, in which many people are studied, a **case study** is an in-depth, intensive investigation of a single individual or a small group. Case studies often include *psychological testing*, a procedure in which a carefully designed set of questions is used to gain insight into the personality of the individual or group (Gass et al., 2000; Addus, Chen, & Khan, 2007).

When case studies are used as a research technique, the goal is often not only to learn about the few individuals being examined but also to use insights gained from the study to improve our understanding of people in general. Sigmund Freud developed his theories through case studies of individual patients. Similarly, case studies of terrorists might help identify others who are prone to violence.

The drawback to case studies? If the individuals examined are unique in certain ways, it is impossible to make valid generalizations to a larger population. Still, they sometimes lead the way to new theories and treatments for psychological disorders.

CORRELATIONAL RESEARCH

When using the descriptive research methods we have discussed above, researchers often wish to determine the relationship between two variables. **Variables** are behaviors, events, or other characteristics that can change or vary in some way. For example, in a study to determine whether the amount of time spent studying makes a difference in test scores, the variables would be study time and test scores.

In **correlational research,** two sets of variables are examined to determine whether they are associated or "correlated." The strength and direction of the relationship between the two variables are represented by a mathematical statistic known as a *correlation* (or, more formally, a *correlation coefficient*) that can range from +1.0 to −1.0.

A *positive correlation* indicates that as the value of one variable increases, we can predict that the value of the other variable will also increase. For example, if we predict that the more time students spend studying for a test, the higher their grades on the test will be, and that the less they study, the lower their test scores will be, we are expecting to find a positive correlation. In other words, higher values of the variable "amount of study time" is associated with higher values of the variable "test score," and lower values of "amount of study time" is associated with lower values of "test score." The correlation, then, would be indicated by a positive number, and the stronger the association was between studying and test scores, the closer the number would be to +1.0. For example, we might find a correlation of +.85 between test scores and amount of study time, indicating a strong positive association.

In contrast, a *negative correlation* tells us that as the value of one variable increases, the value of the other decreases. For instance, we might predict that as the number of hours spent studying increases, the number of hours spent partying decreases. Here we are expecting a negative correlation, ranging between 0 and −1.0. More studying is associated with less partying, and less studying is associated with more partying. The stronger the association between studying and partying, the closer the correlation will be to −1.0. For instance, a correlation of −.85 would indicate a strong negative association between partying and studying.

Of course, it's quite possible that little or no relationship exists between any two variables. For instance, we would probably not expect to find a relationship between number of study hours and height. Lack of a relationship would be indicated by a correlation close to 0. For example, if we found a correlation of −.02 or +.03, it's a weak correlation indicating that there is virtually no association between the two variables; knowing how much someone studies does not tell us anything about how tall he or she is.

case study An in-depth, intensive investigation of an individual or small group of people.

variables Behaviors, events, or other characteristics that can change or vary in some way.

correlational research Research in which the relationship between two sets of variables is examined to determine whether they are associated or "correlated."

Possible Cause

Potential Result

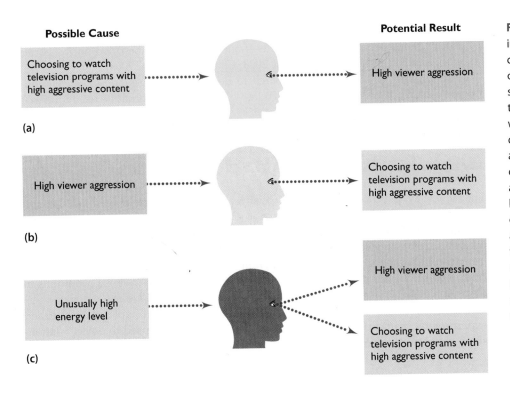

Choosing to watch television programs with high aggressive content

High viewer aggression

(a)

High viewer aggression

Choosing to watch television programs with high aggressive content

(b)

Unusually high energy level

High viewer aggression

Choosing to watch television programs with high aggressive content

(c)

FIGURE 2 If we find that frequent viewing of television programs with aggressive content is associated with high levels of aggressive behavior, we might cite several plausible causes, as suggested in this figure. For example, (a) choosing to watch shows with aggressive content could produce aggression; or (b) being a highly aggressive person might cause one to choose to watch televised aggression; or (c) having a high energy level might cause a person to both choose to watch aggressive shows and act aggressively. Correlational findings, then, do not permit us to determine causality. Can you think of a way to study the effects of televised aggression on aggressive behavior that is not correlational?

When two variables are strongly correlated with each other, it is tempting to assume that one variable causes the other. For example, if we find that more study time is associated with higher grades, we might guess that more studying *causes* higher grades. Although this is not a bad guess, it remains just a guess—because finding that two variables are correlated does not mean that there is a causal relationship between them. The strong correlation suggests that knowing how much a person studies can help us predict how that person will do on a test, but it does not mean that the studying causes the test performance. It might be, for instance, that people who are more interested in the subject matter tend to study more than do those who are less interested, and that the amount of interest, not the number of hours spent studying, predicts test performance. The mere fact that two variables occur together does not mean that one causes the other.

Similarly, suppose you learned that the number of houses of worship in a large sample of cities was positively correlated with the number of people arrested, meaning that the more houses of worship, the more arrests there were in a city. Does this mean that the presence of more houses of worship *caused* the greater number of arrests? Almost surely not, of course. In this case, the underlying cause is probably the size of the city: In bigger cities, there are both more houses of worship *and* more arrests.

One more example illustrates the critical point that correlations tell us nothing about cause and effect but instead provide a measure of the strength of a relationship between two variables. We might find that children who watch a lot of television programs featuring high levels of aggression are likely to demonstrate a relatively high degree of aggressive behavior and that those who watch few television shows that portray aggression are apt to exhibit a relatively low degree of such behavior (see Figure 2). But we cannot say that the aggression is *caused* by the TV viewing, because many other explanations are possible.

For instance, it could be that children who have an unusually high level of energy seek out programs with aggressive content *and* are more aggressive. The children's energy level, then, could be the true cause of the children's higher incidence of aggression. It is also possible that people who are already highly aggressive choose to watch

Many studies show that the observation of violence in the media is associated with aggression in viewers. Can we conclude that the observation of violence causes aggression?

experiment The investigation of the relationship between two (or more) variables by deliberately producing a change in one variable in a situation and observing the effects of that change on other aspects of the situation.

experimental manipulation The change that an experimenter deliberately produces in a situation.

shows with a high aggressive content *because* they are aggressive. Clearly, then, any number of causal sequences are possible—none of which can be ruled out by correlational research (Feshbach & Tangney, 2008; Grimes & Bergen, 2008).

The inability of correlational research to demonstrate cause-and-effect relationships is a crucial drawback to its use. There is, however, an alternative technique that does establish causality: the experiment.

Experimental Research

The *only* way psychologists can establish cause-and-effect relationships through research is by carrying out an experiment. In a formal **experiment,** the researcher investigates the relationship between two (or more) variables by deliberately changing one variable in a controlled situation and observing the effects of that change on other aspects of the situation. In an experiment, then, the conditions are created and controlled by the researcher, who deliberately makes a change in those conditions to observe the effects of that change.

The change that the researcher deliberately makes in an experiment is called **experimental manipulation.** Experimental manipulations are used to detect relationships between different variables.

Several steps are involved in carrying out an experiment, but the process typically begins with the development of one or more hypotheses for the experiment to test. For example, in testing their theory of the diffusion of responsibility in bystander behavior, Latané and Darley developed this hypothesis: The higher the number of people who witness an emergency situation, the less likely it is that any will help the victim. They then designed an experiment to test this hypothesis.

Their first step was to formulate an operational definition of the hypothesis by conceptualizing it in a way that could be tested. Latané and Darley had to take into account the fundamental principle of experimental research mentioned earlier: Experimenters must manipulate at least one variable in order to observe the effects of the manipulation on another variable while keeping other factors in the situation constant. However, the manipulation cannot be viewed by itself, in isolation; if a cause-and-effect relationship is to be established, the effects of the manipulation must be compared with the effects of no manipulation or a different kind of manipulation.

"What if these guys in white coats who bring us food are, like, studying us and we're part of some kind of big experiment?"

EXPERIMENTAL GROUPS AND CONTROL GROUPS

Experimental research requires, then, that the responses of at least two groups be compared. One group will receive some special **treatment**—the manipulation implemented by the experimenter—and the other group will receive either no treatment or a different treatment. Any group that receives a treatment is called an **experimental group;** a group that receives no treatment is called a **control group.** (In some experiments there are multiple experimental and control groups, each of which is compared with another group.)

By employing both experimental and control groups in an experiment, researchers are able to rule out the possibility that something other than the experimental manipulation produced the results observed in the experiment. Without a control group, we couldn't be sure that some other variable, such as the temperature at the time of the experiment, the color of the experimenter's hair, or even the mere passage of time, wasn't causing the changes observed.

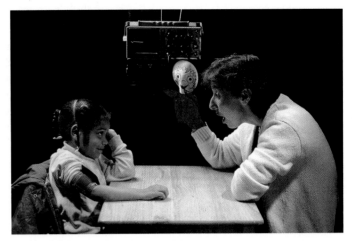

In this experiment, preschoolers' reactions to the puppet are monitored. Can you think of a hypothesis that might be tested in this way?

For example, consider a medical researcher who thinks he has invented a medicine that cures the common cold. To test his claim, he gives the medicine one day to a group of 20 people who have colds and finds that 10 days later all of them are cured.

Eureka? Not so fast. An observer viewing this flawed study might reasonably argue that the people would have gotten better even without the medicine. What the researcher obviously needed was a control group consisting of people with colds who *don't* get the medicine and whose health is also checked 10 days later. Only if there is a significant difference between experimental and control groups can the effectiveness of the medicine be assessed. Through the use of control groups, then, researchers can isolate specific causes for their findings—and draw cause-and-effect inferences.

Returning to Latané and Darley's experiment, we see that the researchers needed to translate their hypothesis into something testable. To do this, they decided to create a false emergency situation that would appear to require the aid of a bystander. As their experimental manipulation, they decided to vary the number of bystanders present. They could have had just one experimental group with, say, two people present, and a control group for comparison purposes with just one person present. Instead, they settled on a more complex procedure involving groups of three sizes—consisting of two, three, and six people—that could be compared with one another.

Independent and Dependent Variables. Latané and Darley's experimental design now included an operational definition of what is called the **independent variable.** The independent variable is the condition that is manipulated by an experimenter. (You can think of the independent variable as being independent of the actions of those taking part in an experiment; it is controlled by the experimenter.) In the case of the Latané and Darley experiment, the independent variable was the number of people present as manipulated by the experimenters.

The next step was to decide how they were going to determine the effect that varying the number of bystanders had on the behavior of those in the experiment. Crucial to every experiment is the **dependent variable,** the variable that is measured and is expected to change as a result of changes caused by the experimenter's manipulation of the independent variable. The dependent variable is dependent on the actions of the *participants* or *subjects*—the people taking part in the experiment.

treatment The manipulation implemented by the experimenter.

experimental group Any group participating in an experiment that receives a treatment.

control group A group participating in an experiment that receives no treatment.

independent variable The variable that is manipulated by an experimenter.

dependent variable The variable that is measured and is expected to change as a result of changes caused by the experimenter's manipulation of the independent variable.

Latané and Darley had several possible choices for their dependent measure. One might have been a simple yes/no measure of the participants' helping behavior. But the investigators also wanted a more precise analysis of helping behavior. Consequently, they also measured the amount of time it took for a participant to provide help.

Latané and Darley now had all the necessary components of an experiment. The independent variable, manipulated by them, was the number of bystanders present in an emergency situation. The dependent variable was the measure of whether bystanders in each of the groups provided help and the amount of time it took them to do so. Consequently, like all experiments, this one had both an independent variable and a dependent variable. *All* true experiments in psychology fit this straightforward model.

RANDOM ASSIGNMENT OF PARTICIPANTS

To make the experiment a valid test of the hypothesis, Latané and Darley needed to add a final step to the design: properly assigning participants to a particular experimental group.

The significance of this step is clear when we examine various alternative procedures. For example, the experimenters might have assigned just males to the group with two bystanders, just females to the group with three bystanders, and both males and females to the group with six bystanders. If they had done this, however, any differences they found in helping behavior could not be attributed with any certainty solely to group size, because the differences might just as well have been due to the composition of the group. A more reasonable procedure would be to ensure that each group had the same composition in terms of gender; then the researchers would be able to make comparisons across groups with considerably more accuracy.

Participants in each of the experimental groups ought to be comparable, and it's easy enough to create groups that are similar in terms of gender. The problem becomes a bit more tricky, though, when we consider other participant characteristics. How can we ensure that participants in each experimental group will be equally intelligent, extroverted, cooperative, and so forth, when the list of characteristics— any one of which could be important—is potentially endless?

random assignment to condition
A procedure in which participants are assigned to different experimental groups or "conditions" on the basis of chance and chance alone.

The solution is a simple but elegant procedure called **random assignment to condition:** Participants are assigned to different experimental groups or "conditions" on the basis of chance and chance alone. The experimenter might, for instance, flip a coin for each participant and assign a participant to one group when "heads" came up, and to the other group when "tails" came up. The advantage of this technique is that there is an equal chance that participant characteristics will be distributed across the various groups. When a researcher uses random assignment—which in practice is usually carried out using computer-generated random numbers— chances are that each of the groups will have approximately the same proportion of intelligent people, cooperative people, extroverted people, males and females, and so on.

Figure 3 provides another example of an experiment. Like all experiments, it includes the following set of key elements, which are important to keep in mind as you consider whether a research study is truly an experiment:

- An independent variable, the variable that is manipulated by the experimenter.
- A dependent variable, the variable measured by the experimenter that's expected to change as a result of the manipulation of the independent variable.
- A procedure that randomly assigns participants to different experimental groups or "conditions" of the independent variable.
- A hypothesis that predicts the effect the independent variable will have on the dependent variable.

1 Identify participants

2 Randomly assign participants to a condition

3 Manipulate the independent variable

4 Measure the dependent variable

5 Compare the results of the two groups

Group 1: Treatment group

Receive-drug condition

Group 2: Control group

No-drug condition

FIGURE 3 In this depiction of a study investigating the effects of the drug propranolol on stress, we can see the basic elements of all true experiments. The participants in the experiment were monkeys who were randomly assigned to one of two groups. Monkeys assigned to the treatment group were given propranolol, hypothesized to prevent heart disease, whereas those in the control group were not given the drug. Administration of the drug, then, was the independent variable.

All the monkeys were fed a high-fat diet that was the human equivalent of two eggs with bacon every morning, and they occasionally were reassigned to different cages to provide a source of stress. To determine the effects of the drug, the monkeys' heart rates and other measures of heart disease were assessed after 26 months. These measures constituted the dependent variable. (The results? As hypothesized, monkeys who received the drug showed lower heart rates and fewer symptoms of heart disease than those who did not.) (Source: Based on a study by Kaplan & Manuck, 1989.)

Only if each of these elements is present can a research study be considered a true experiment in which cause-and-effect relationships can be determined. (For a summary of the different types of research that we've discussed, see Figure 4.)

WERE LATANÉ AND DARLEY RIGHT?

To test their hypothesis that increasing the number of bystanders in an emergency situation would lower the degree of helping behavior, Latané and Darley placed the participants in a room and told them that the purpose of the experiment was to talk about personal problems associated with college. The discussion was to be held over an intercom, supposedly to avoid the potential embarrassment of face-to-face contact. Chatting about personal problems was not, of course, the true purpose of the experiment, but telling the participants that it was provided a way of keeping their expectations from biasing their behavior. (Consider how they would have been affected if they had been told that their helping behavior in emergencies was being tested. The experimenters could never have gotten an accurate assessment of what the participants would actually do in an emergency. By definition, emergencies are rarely announced in advance.)

Research Method	Description	Advantages	Shortcomings
Descriptive and correlational research	Researcher observes a previously existing situation but does not make a change in the situation	Offers insight into relationships between variables	Cannot determine causality
Archival research	Examines existing data to confirm hypothesis	Ease of data collection because data already exist	Dependent on availability of data
Naturalistic observation	Observation of naturally occurring behavior, without making a change in the situation	Provides a sample of people in their natural environment	Cannot control the "natural habitat" being observed
Survey research	A sample is chosen to represent a larger population and asked a series of questions	A small sample can be used to infer attitudes and behavior of a larger population	Sample may not be representative of the larger population; participants may not provide accurate responses to survey questions
Case study	Intensive investigation of an individual or small group	Provides a thorough, in-depth understanding of participants	Results may not be generalizable beyond the sample
Experimental research	Investigator produces a change in one variable to observe the effects of that change on other variables	Experiments offer the only way to determine cause-and-effect relationships	To be valid, experiments require random assignment of participants to conditions, well-conceptualized independent and dependent variables, and other careful controls

FIGURE 4 Research strategies.

The sizes of the discussion groups were two, three, and six people, which constituted the manipulation of the independent variable of group size. Participants were randomly assigned to these groups upon their arrival at the laboratory. Each group included a trained *confederate*, or employee, of the experimenters. In each two-person group, then, there was only one real "bystander."

As the participants in each group were holding their discussion, they suddenly heard through the intercom one of the other participants—the confederate—having what sounded like an epileptic seizure and calling for help.

The participants' behavior was now what counted. The dependent variable was the time that elapsed from the start of the "seizure" to the time a participant began trying to help the "victim." If six minutes went by without a participant's offering help, the experiment was ended.

As predicted by the hypothesis, the size of the group had a significant effect on whether a participant provided help. The more people who were present, the less likely it was that someone would supply help, as you can see in Figure 5 (Latané & Darley, 1970).

Because these results are so straightforward, it seems clear that the experiment confirmed the original hypothesis. However, Latané and Darley could not be sure that the results were truly meaningful until they determined whether the results represented a **significant outcome.** Using statistical analysis, researchers can determine

significant outcome Meaningful results that make it possible for researchers to feel confident that they have confirmed their hypotheses.

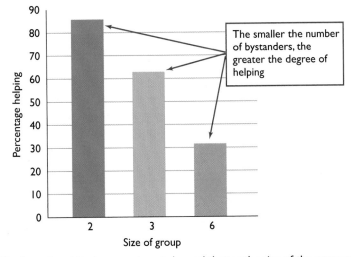

FIGURE 5 The Latané and Darley experiment showed that as the size of the group witnessing an emergency increased (the independent variable in the experiment), helping behavior decreased (the dependent variable in the experiment). (Source: Darley & Latané, 1968.)

whether a numeric difference is a real difference or is due merely to chance. Only when differences between groups are large enough that statistical tests show them to be significant is it possible for researchers to confirm a hypothesis (Cwikel, Behar, & Rabson-Hare, 2000; Cohen, 2002).

Moving Beyond the Study. The Latané and Darley study contains all the elements of an experiment: an independent variable, a dependent variable, random assignment to conditions, and multiple experimental groups. Consequently, we can say with some confidence that group size *caused* changes in the degree of helping behavior.

Of course, one experiment alone does not forever resolve the question of bystander intervention in emergencies. Psychologists—like other scientists—require that findings be **replicated** or repeated, sometimes using other procedures in other settings with other groups of participants, before full confidence can be placed in the results of any single experiment. A procedure called *meta-analysis* permits psychologists to combine the results of many separate studies into one overall conclusion (Tenenbaum & Ruck, 2007; Cooper & Patall, 2009).

In addition to replicating experimental results, psychologists need to test the limitations of their theories and hypotheses to determine under which specific circumstances they do and do not apply. It seems unlikely, for instance, that increasing the number of bystanders *always* results in less helping. Therefore, it is critical to continue carrying out experiments to understand the conditions in which exceptions to this general rule occur and other circumstances in which the rule holds (Garcia et al., 2002).

Before leaving the Latané and Darley study, it's important to note that it represents a good illustration of the basic principles of the scientific method we considered earlier (as outlined in Figure 1 of Module 3). The two psychologists began with a *question of interest,* in this case stemming from a real-world incident in which bystanders in an emergency did not offer help. They then *formulated an explanation* by specifying a theory of diffusion of responsibility, and from that formulated the specific hypothesis that increasing the number of bystanders in an emergency situation would lower the degree of helping behavior. Finally, they *carried out research* to confirm their hypothesis and they eventually *communicated their findings* by publishing their results. This four-step process embodied in the scientific method underlies all scientific inquiry, allowing us to develop a valid understanding of others'—and our own—behavior.

replicated research Research that is repeated, sometimes using other procedures, settings, and groups of participants, to increase confidence in prior findings.

RECAP/EVALUATE/RETHINK

RECAP

What is the scientific method?
- The scientific method is the approach psychologists use to understand behavior. It consists of four steps: identifying questions of interest, formulating an explanation, carrying out research that is designed to support or refute the explanation, and communicating the findings. (p. 26)
- To test a hypothesis, researchers must formulate an operational definition that translates the abstract concepts of the hypothesis into the actual procedures used in the study. (p. 27)

What role do theories and hypotheses play in psychological research?
- Research in psychology is guided by theories (broad explanations and predictions regarding phenomena of interest) and hypotheses (theory-based predictions stated in a way that allows them to be tested). (p. 28)

What research methods do psychologists use?
- Archival research uses existing records, such as old newspapers or other documents, to test a hypothesis. In naturalistic observation, the investigator acts mainly as an observer, making no change in a naturally occurring situation. For survey research, people are asked a series of questions about their behavior, thoughts, or attitudes. The case study is an in-depth interview and examination of one person or group. (p. 28)
- These descriptive research methods rely on correlational techniques, which describe associations between variables but cannot determine cause-and-effect relationships. (p. 30)

How do psychologists establish cause-and-effect relationships using experiments?
- During a formal experiment, the relationship between variables is investigated by deliberately producing a change—called the experimental manipulation—in one variable and observing changes in the other variable. (p. 32)
- In an experiment, at least two groups must be compared to assess cause-and-effect relationships. The group receiving the treatment (the special procedure devised by the experimenter) is the experimental group; the second group (which receives no treatment) is the control group. There also may be multiple experimental groups, each of which is subjected to a different procedure and then is compared with the others. (p. 33)
- The variable that experimenters manipulate is the independent variable. The variable that they measure and expect to change as a result of manipulation of the independent variable is called the dependent variable. (p. 33)

- During a formal experiment, participants must be assigned randomly to treatment conditions so that participant characteristics are distributed evenly across the different conditions. (p. 34)
- Psychologists use statistical tests to determine whether research findings are significant. (p. 36)

EVALUATE

1. An explanation for a phenomenon of interest is known as a _____.
2. To test this explanation, a researcher must state it in terms of a testable question known as a _____.
3. An experimenter is interested in studying the relationship between hunger and aggression. She decides that she will measure aggression by counting the number of times a participant hits a punching bag. In this case, her _____ definition of aggression is the number of times the participant hits the bag.
4. Match the following forms of research to their definitions:
   1. Archival research
   2. Naturalistic observation
   3. Survey research
   4. Case study

   a. Directly asking a sample of people questions about their behavior
   b. Examining existing records to test a hypothesis
   c. Looking at behavior in its true setting without intervening in the setting
   d. Doing an in-depth investigation of a person or small group
5. Match each of the following research methods with its primary disadvantage:
   1. Archival research
   2. Naturalistic observation
   3. Survey research
   4. Case study

   a. The researcher may not be able to generalize to the population at large.
   b. People's behavior can change if they know they are being watched.
   c. The data may not exist or may be unusable.
   d. People may lie in order to present an acceptable image.
6. A psychologist wants to study the effect of attractiveness on willingness to help a person with a math problem. Attractiveness would be the _____ variable, and the amount of helping would be the _____ variable.
7. The group in an experiment that receives no treatment is called the _____ group.

RETHINK

1. Starting with the theory that diffusion of responsibility causes responsibility for helping to be shared among bystanders, Latané and Darley derived the hypothesis that the more people who witness an emergency situation, the less likely it is that help will be given to a victim. How many other hypotheses can you think of that are based on the same theory of diffusion of responsibility.

2. Can you describe how a researcher might use naturalistic observation, case studies, and survey research to investigate gender differences in aggressive behavior at the workplace? First state a hypothesis, then describe your

research approaches. What positive and negative features does each method have?

3. *From a health-care worker's perspective*: Tobacco companies have asserted that no experiment has ever proved that tobacco use causes cancer. Can you explain this claim in terms of the research procedures and designs discussed in this module? What sort of research would establish a cause-and-effect relationship between tobacco use and cancer?

Answers to Evaluate Questions

1. theory; 2. hypothesis; 3. operational; 4. 1-b, 2-c, 3-a, 4-d; 5. 1-c, 2-b, 3-d, 4-a; 6. independent, dependent; 7. control

KEY TERMS

scientific method p. 26
theories p. 26
hypothesis p. 27
operational
  definition p. 27
archival research p. 28

naturalistic
  observation p. 29
survey research p. 29
case study p. 30
variable p. 30
correlational research p. 30

experiment p. 32
experimental
  manipulation p. 32
treatment p. 33
experimental group p. 33
control group p. 33

independent variable p. 33
dependent variable p. 33
random assignment to
  condition p. 34
significant outcome p. 36
replicated research p. 37

Research Challenges: Exploring the Process

You probably realize by now that there are few simple formulas for psychological research. Psychologists must make choices about the type of study to conduct, the measures to take, and the most effective way to analyze the results. Even after they've made these essential decisions, they must still consider several critical issues. We turn first to the most fundamental of these issues: ethics.

The Ethics of Research

Put yourself in the place of one of the participants in the experiment conducted by Latané and Darley to examine the helping behavior of bystanders, during which another "bystander" simulating a seizure turned out to be a confederate of the experimenters (Latané & Darley, 1970). How would you feel when you learned that the supposed victim was in reality a paid accomplice?

Although you might at first experience relief that there had been no real emergency, you might also feel some resentment that you had been deceived by the experimenter. You might also experience concern that you had been placed in an embarrassing or compromising situation—one that might have dealt a blow to your self-esteem, depending on how you had behaved.

Most psychologists argue that deception is sometimes necessary to prevent participants from being influenced by what they think a study's true purpose is. (If you knew that Latané and Darley were actually studying your helping behavior, wouldn't you automatically have been prompted to intervene in the emergency?) To avoid such outcomes, a small proportion of research involves deception.

Nonetheless, because research has the potential to violate the rights of participants, psychologists are expected to adhere to a strict set of ethical guidelines aimed at protecting participants (American Psychological Association, 2002). Those guidelines involve the following safeguards:

Study Alert

Because protecting participants is so essential, it is important to understand the key ethical guideline of informed consent.

- Protection of participants from physical and mental harm.
- The right of participants to privacy regarding their behavior.
- The assurance that participation in research is completely voluntary.
- The necessity of informing participants about the nature of the procedures before their participation in the experiment.

All experiments must be reviewed by an independent panel before being conducted, including the minority of studies that involve deception (Smith, 2003; Fisher et al., 2002, 2003).

One of psychologists' key ethical principles is **informed consent.** Before participating in an experiment, all participants must sign a document affirming that they have been told the basic outlines of the study and are aware of what their participation will involve, what risks the experiment may hold, that their participation is purely voluntary, and that they may terminate it at any time. Furthermore, after participation in a study, they must be given a debriefing in which they receive an explanation of the study and the procedures that were involved. The only time

informed consent A document signed by participants affirming that they have been told the basic outlines of the study and are aware of what their participation will involve.

Although readily available and widely used as research subjects, college students may not represent the population at large. What are some advantages and drawbacks of using college students as subjects?

informed consent and a debriefing can be eliminated is for experiments in which the risks are minimal, as in a purely observational study in a public place (Koocher, Norcross, & Hill, 2005; Fallon, 2006; Barnett et al., 2007).

Exploring DIVERSITY

Choosing Participants Who Represent the Scope of Human Behavior

When Latané and Darley, both college professors, decided who would participate in their experiment, they turned to the people most available to them: college students. Using college students as participants has both advantages and drawbacks. The biggest benefit is that because most research occurs in university settings, college students are readily available. Typically, they cost the researcher very little: They often participate for either extra course credit or a relatively small payment.

The problem is that college students may not represent the general population adequately. They tend to be younger and better educated than a significant percentage of the rest of the population of the United States. Compared with older adults, their attitudes are likely to be less formed, and they are more apt to be influenced by authority figures and peers (Sears, 1986).

College students are also disproportionately white and middle class. However, even in research that doesn't involve college students, participants are often white and middle class; the use of African Americans, Latinos, Asians, and other minorities as participants is relatively low (Graham, 1992; Guthrie, 1998). Because psychology is a science with the goal to explain human behavior generally, it is critical to use participants who are fully representative of the general population in terms of gender, age, race, ethnicity, socioeconomic status, and educational level (also see Figure 1). To encourage a wider range of participants, the National Institute of Mental Health and the National Science Foundation—the primary U.S. funding sources for psychological research—now require that experiments address issues that apply to diverse populations (Carpenter, 2002; Lindley, 2006).

Neuroscience in Your Life: The Importance of Using Representative Participants

FIGURE 1 In this study, scientists recorded electrical brain activity to gauge attention in children. The results demonstrated that the level of education a child's mother has influences her child's ability to pay attention. Children whose mothers had a higher level of education show greater brain activation when listening to a story than when they were ignoring the story, compared with children whose mothers had a lower level of education. (Source: Stevens et al., 2009.)

High Maternal Education

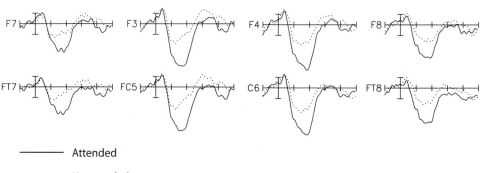

——— Attended

············ Unattended

Low Maternal Education

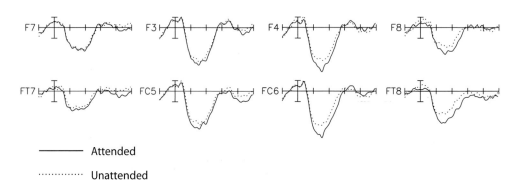

——— Attended

············ Unattended

Should Animals Be Used in Research?

Like those who work with humans, researchers who use nonhuman animals in experiments have their own set of exacting guidelines to ensure that the animals do not suffer. Specifically, researchers must make every effort to minimize discomfort, illness, and pain. Procedures that subject animals to distress are permitted only when an alternative procedure is unavailable and when the research is justified by its prospective value. Moreover, researchers strive to avoid causing physical discomfort, but they are also required to promote the *psychological* well-being of some species of research animals, such as primates (Rusche, 2003; Lutz & Novak, 2005; Auer et al., 2007).

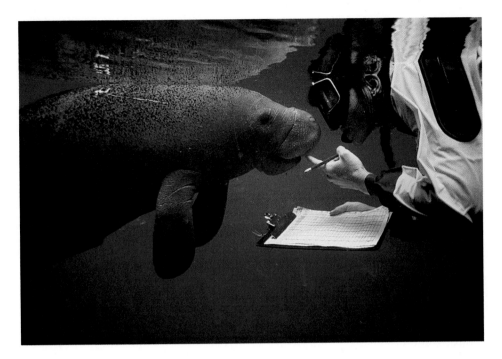

Research involving animals is controversial but, when conducted within ethical guidelines, yields significant benefits for humans.

But why should animals be used for research in the first place? Is it really possible to learn about human behavior from the results of research employing rats, gerbils, and pigeons?

The answer is that psychological research that employs nonhumans is designed to answer questions that are different from those posed in research with humans. For example, the shorter life span of animals (rats live an average of 2 years) allows researchers to learn about the effects of aging in a relatively short time frame. It is also possible to provide greater experimental control over nonhumans and to carry out procedures that might not be possible with people. For example, some studies require large numbers of participants that share similar backgrounds or have been exposed to particular environments—conditions that could not practically be met with human beings.

Research with animals has provided psychologists with information that has profoundly benefited humans. For instance, it furnished the keys to detecting eye disorders in children early enough to prevent permanent damage; to communicating more effectively with severely retarded children; and to reducing chronic pain in people. Still, the use of research using nonhumans is controversial, involving complex moral and philosophical concerns. Consequently, all research involving nonhumans must be carefully reviewed beforehand to ensure that it is conducted ethically (Saucier & Cain, 2006; Hackam, 2007; Shankar & Simmons, 2009).

Threats to Experimental Validity: Avoiding Experimental Bias

Even the best-laid experimental plans are susceptible to **experimental bias**—factors that distort the way the independent variable affects the dependent variable in an experiment. One of the most common forms of experimental bias is *experimenter expectations:* An experimenter unintentionally transmits cues to participants about the way they are expected to behave in a given experimental condition. The danger is

experimental bias Factors that distort how the independent variable affects the dependent variable in an experiment.

that those expectations will bring about an "appropriate" behavior—one that otherwise might not have occurred (Rosenthal, 2002, 2003).

A related problem is *participant expectations* about appropriate behavior. If you have ever been a participant in an experiment, you know that you quickly develop guesses about what is expected of you. In fact, it's typical for people to develop their own hypotheses about what the experimenter hopes to learn from the study. If participants form their own hypotheses, it may the participant's expectations rather than the experimental manipulation that produce an effect (Rutherford et al., 2009).

To guard against participant expectations biasing the results of an experiment, the experimenter may try to disguise the true purpose of the experiment. Participants who do not know that helping behavior is being studied, for example, are more apt to act in a "natural" way than they would if they knew.

Sometimes it's impossible to hide the actual purpose of research; when that's the case, other techniques are available to prevent bias. Suppose you were interested in testing the ability of a new drug to alleviate the symptoms of severe depression. If you simply gave the drug to half your participants and not to the other half, the participants who were given the drug might report feeling less depressed merely because they knew they were getting a drug. Similarly, participants who got nothing might report feeling no better because they knew that they were in a no-treatment control group.

To solve this problem, psychologists typically use a procedure so that all participants receive a treatment, but those in the control group receive only a **placebo** or false treatment such as a pill, "drug," or other substance that has no significant chemical properties or active ingredient. Because members of both groups are kept in the dark about whether they are getting a real or a false treatment, any differences in outcome can be attributed to the quality of the drug and not to the possible psychological effects of being administered a pill or other substance (Rajagopal, 2006; Crum & Langer, 2007).

However, there is one more safeguard that a careful researcher must apply in an experiment such as this one. To offset the possibility that experimenter expectations will affect the participant, the person who administers the drug shouldn't know whether it's actually the true drug or the placebo. By keeping both the participant and the experimenter who interacts with the participant "blind" to the nature of the drug that is being administered, researchers can more accurately assess the effects of the drug. This method is known as the *double-blind procedure*.

placebo A false treatment, such as a pill, "drug," or other substance without any significant chemical properties or active ingredient.

If you were about to purchase an automobile, it's unlikely that you would stop at the nearest dealership and drive off with the first car a salesperson recommended. Instead, you would probably mull over the purchase, read about automobiles, consider the alternatives, talk to others about their experiences, and ultimately put in a fair amount of thought before you made such a major purchase.

In contrast, many of us are considerably less conscientious when we expend our intellectual rather than financial assets. People often jump to conclusions on the basis of incomplete and inaccurate information, and only rarely do they take the time to critically evaluate the research and data to which they are exposed.

Because the field of psychology is based on an accumulated body of research, it's crucial to scrutinize thoroughly the methods, results, and claims of researchers. Several basic questions can help us sort through what is valid and what is not. Among the most important questions to ask are the following:

- *What was the purpose of the research?* Research studies should evolve from a clearly specified theory. Furthermore, we must take into account the specific hypothesis that is being tested. Unless we know what hypothesis is being examined, it is not possible to judge how successful a study has been.

- *How well was the study conducted?* Consider who the participants were, how many were involved, what methods were employed, and what problems the researcher encountered in collecting the data. There are important differences, for example, between a case study that reports the anecdotes of a handful of respondents and a survey that collects data from several thousand people.

- *Are the results presented fairly?* It is necessary to assess statements on the basis of the actual data they reflect and their logic. For instance, when the manufacturer of car X boasts that "no other car has a better safety record than car X," this does not mean that car X is safer than every other car. It just means that no other car has been proved safer, though many other cars could be just as safe as car X. Expressed in the latter fashion, the finding doesn't seem as worth bragging about.

These three basic questions can help you assess the validity of research findings you come across—both within and outside the field of psychology. The more you know how to evaluate research in general, the better you'll be able to assess what the field of psychology has to offer.

RECAP/EVALUATE/RETHINK

RECAP

What major issues confront psychologists conducting research?

- One of the key ethical principles followed by psychologists is that of informed consent. Before participation, participants must be informed about the basic outline of the experiment and the risks and potential benefits of their participation. (p. 40)
- Although using college students as participants has the advantage of easy availability, there are drawbacks too. For instance, students do not necessarily represent the population as a whole. The use of nonhuman animals as participants may also have costs in terms of the ability to generalize study results to humans; nonetheless, the benefits of using animals in research have been profound. (p. 41)
- Experiments are subject to a number of biases or threats. Experimenter expectations can produce bias when an experimenter unintentionally transmits cues to participants about her or his expectations regarding their behavior in a given experimental condition. Participant expectations can also bias an experiment. Among the tools experimenters use to help eliminate bias are placebos and double-blind procedures. (p. 43)

EVALUATE

1. Ethical research begins with the concept of informed consent. Before signing up to participate in an experiment, participants should be informed of
   a. the procedure of the study, stated generally.
   b. the risks that may be involved.
   c. their right to withdraw at any time.
   d. all of the above.

2. List three benefits of using animals in psychological research.
3. Deception is one means experimenters can use to try to eliminate participant expectations. True or false?
4. A false treatment, such as a pill that has no significant chemical properties or active ingredient, is known as a _____.
5. According to a report, a study has shown that men differ from women in their preference for ice cream flavors. This study was based on a sample of two men and three women. What might be wrong with this study?

RETHINK

1. A researcher strongly believes that college professors tend to show female students less attention and respect in the classroom than they show male students. He sets up an experimental study involving observations of classrooms in different conditions. In explaining the study to the professors and students who will participate, what steps should the researcher take to eliminate experimental bias based on both experimenter and participant expectations?
2. *From a research analyst's perspective*: You are hired to study people's attitudes toward welfare programs by developing and circulating a questionnaire via the Internet. Is this study likely to accurately reflect the views of the general population? Why or why not?

Answers to Evaluate Questions

1. d; 2. (1) We can study some phenomena in animals more easily than we can in people, because with animal subjects we have greater control over environmental and genetic factors. (2) Large numbers of similar participants can be easily obtained. (3) We can look at generational effects much more easily in animals, because of their shorter life span, than we can with people; 3. true; 4. placebo; 5. There are far too few participants. Without a larger sample, no valid conclusions can be drawn about ice cream preferences based on gender.

KEY TERMS

informed consent p. 40
experimental bias p. 43
placebo p. 44

Neurons: The Basic Elements of Behavior

Watching Serena Williams hit a stinging backhand, Dario Vaccaro dance a complex ballet routine, or Derek Jeter swing at a baseball, you may have marveled at the complexity—and wondrous abilities—of the human body. But even the most everyday tasks, such as pouring a cup of coffee or humming a tune, depend on a sophisticated sequence of events in the body that is itself truly impressive.

The nervous system is the pathway for the instructions that permit our bodies to carry out such precise activities. Here we look at the structure and function of neurons, the cells that make up the nervous system, including the brain.

The Structure of the Neuron

Playing the piano, driving a car, or hitting a tennis ball depends, at one level, on exact muscle coordination. But if we consider *how* the muscles can be activated so precisely, we see that more fundamental processes are involved. For the muscles to produce the complex movements that make up any meaningful physical activity, the brain has to provide the right messages to them and coordinate those messages.

Such messages—as well as those which enable us to think, remember, and experience emotion—are passed through specialized cells called neurons. **Neurons, or nerve cells, are the basic elements of the nervous system.** Their quantity is staggering—perhaps as many as 1 *trillion* neurons throughout the body are involved in the control of behavior (Boahen, 2005).

Although there are several types of neurons, they all have a similar structure, as illustrated in Figure 1. Like most cells in the body, neurons have a cell body that contains a nucleus. The nucleus incorporates the hereditary material that determines how a cell will function. Neurons are physically held in place by *glial cells*. Glial cells provide nourishment to neurons, insulate them, help repair damage, and generally support neural functioning (Bassotti et al., 2007; Fields, 2004; Kettenmann & Ransom, 2005).

In contrast to most other cells, however, neurons have a distinctive feature: the ability to communicate with other cells and transmit information across relatively long distances. Many of the body's neurons receive signals from the environment or relay the nervous system's messages to muscles and other target cells, but the vast majority of neurons communicate only with other neurons in the elaborate information system that regulates behavior.

As shown in Figure 1, a neuron has a cell body with a cluster of fibers called **dendrites** at one end. Those fibers, which look like the twisted branches of a tree, receive messages from other neurons. On the opposite side of the cell body is a long, slim, tubelike extension called an **axon.** The axon carries messages received by the dendrites to other neurons. The axon is considerably longer than the rest of the neuron. Although most axons are several millimeters in length, some are as long as 3 feet. Axons end in small bulges called **terminal buttons,** which send messages to other neurons.

The messages that travel through a neuron are electrical in nature. Although there are exceptions, those electrical messages, or *impulses,* generally move across neurons in one direction only, as if they were traveling on a one-way street. Impulses

Key Concepts

Why do psychologists study the brain and the nervous system?

What are the basic elements of the nervous system?

How does the nervous system communicate electrical and chemical messages from one part to another?

neurons Nerve cells, the basic elements of the nervous system.

dendrite A cluster of fibers at one end of a neuron that receives messages from other neurons.

axon The part of the neuron that carries messages destined for other neurons.

terminal buttons Small bulges at the end of axons that send messages to other neurons.

51

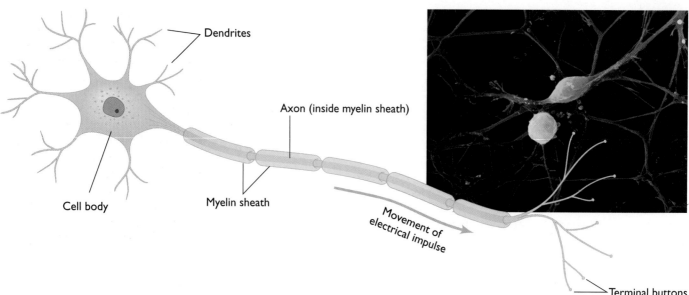

FIGURE 1 The primary components of the specialized cell called the neuron, the basic element of the nervous system. A neuron, like most types of cells in the body, has a cell body, but it also contains structures that carry messages: the dendrites, which receive messages from other neurons, and the axon, which carries messages to other neurons or body cells. In this neuron, as in most neurons, the axon is protected by the sausage-like myelin sheath. What advantages does the treelike structure of the neuron provide?

Study Alert

Remember that *dendrites* *d*etect messages from other neurons; *axons* carry signals *away* from the cell body.

myelin sheath A protective coat of fat and protein that wraps around the axon.

all-or-none law The rule that neurons are either on or off.

resting state The state in which there is a negative electrical charge of about –70 millivolts within a neuron.

follow a route that begins with the dendrites, continues into the cell body, and leads ultimately along the tubelike extension, the axon, to adjacent neurons.

To prevent messages from short-circuiting one another, axons must be insulated in some fashion (just as electrical wires must be insulated). Most axons are insulated by a **myelin sheath,** a protective coating of fat and protein that wraps around the axon like the casing on links of sausage.

The myelin sheath also serves to increase the velocity with which electrical impulses travel through axons. Those axons that carry the most important and most urgently required information have the greatest concentrations of myelin. If your hand touches a painfully hot stove, for example, the information regarding the pain is passed through axons in the hand and arm that have a relatively thick coating of myelin, speeding the message of pain to the brain so that you can react instantly.

How Neurons Fire

Like a gun, neurons either fire—that is, transmit an electrical impulse along the axon—or don't fire. There is no in-between stage, just as pulling harder on a gun trigger doesn't make the bullet travel faster. Similarly, neurons follow an **all-or-none law:** They are either on or off, with nothing in between the on state and the off state. Once there is enough force to pull the trigger, a neuron fires.

Before a neuron is triggered—that is, when it is in a **resting state**—it has a negative electrical charge of about –70 millivolts (a millivolt is one $\frac{1}{1,000}$ of a volt). This charge is caused by the presence of more negatively charged ions within the neuron than outside it. (An ion is an atom that is electrically charged.) You might think of the neuron as a miniature battery in which the inside of the neuron represents the negative pole and the outside represents the positive pole.

Time 1

Voltage

Time 2

Voltage

Time 3

Voltage

■ Positive charge

■ Negative charge

→ Direction of impulse

FIGURE 2 Movement of an action potential along an axon. Just before Time 1, positively charged ions enter the cell membrane, changing the charge in the nearby part of the axon from negative to positive and triggering an action potential. The action potential travels along the axon, as illustrated in the changes occurring from Time 1 to Time 3 (from top to bottom in this drawing). Immediately after the action potential has passed through a section of the axon, positive ions are pumped out, restoring the charge in that section to negative. The change in voltage illustrated at the top of the axon can be seen in greater detail in Figure 3. (Source: Stevens, 1979.)

When a message arrives at a neuron, gates along the cell membrane open briefly to allow positively charged ions to rush in at rates as high as 100 million ions per second. The sudden arrival of these positive ions causes the charge within the nearby part of the cell to change momentarily from negative to positive. When the positive charge reaches a critical level, the "trigger" is pulled, and an electrical impulse, known as an *action potential,* travels along the axon of the neuron (see Figure 2).

The **action potential** moves from one end of the axon to the other like a flame moving along a fuse. As the impulse travels along the axon, the movement of ions causes a change in charge from negative to positive in successive sections of the axon (see Figure 3) on page 54. After the impulse has passed through a particular section of the axon, positive ions are pumped out of that section, and its charge returns to negative while the action potential continues to move along the axon.

Just after an action potential has passed through a section of the axon, the cell membrane in that region cannot admit positive ions again for a few milliseconds, and so a neuron cannot fire again immediately no matter how much stimulation it receives. It is as if the gun has to be reloaded after each shot. There then follows a period in which, though it is possible for the neuron to fire, a stronger stimulus is needed than would be if the neuron had reached its normal resting state. Eventually, though, the neuron is ready to fire once again.

These complex events can occur at dizzying speeds, although there is great variation among different neurons. The particular speed at which an action potential travels along an axon is determined by the axon's size and the thickness of its myelin sheath. Axons with small diameters carry impulses at about 2 miles per hour; longer and thicker ones can average speeds of more than 225 miles per hour.

Neurons differ not only in terms of how quickly an impulse moves along the axon but also in their potential rate of firing. Some neurons are capable of firing as many as 1,000 times per second; others fire at much slower rates. The intensity of a stimulus determines how much of a neuron's potential firing rate is reached. A strong stimulus, such as a bright light or a loud sound, leads to a higher rate of firing than a less intense stimulus does. Thus, even though all impulses move at the same strength or speed through a particular axon—because of the all-or-none

action potential An electric nerve impulse that travels through a neuron's axon when it is set off by a "trigger," changing the neuron's charge from negative to positive.

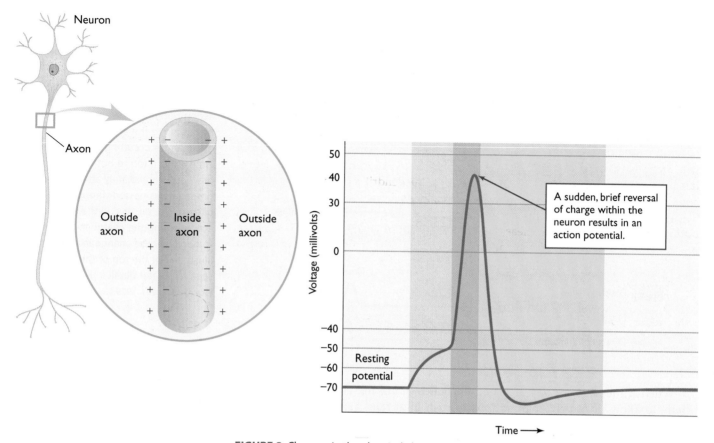

FIGURE 3 Changes in the electrical charge in a neuron during the passage of an action potential. In its normal resting state, a neuron has a negative charge of about −70 millivolts. When an action potential is triggered, however, the charge becomes positive, increasing from around −70 millivolts to about +40 millivolts. Following the passage of the action potential, the charge becomes even more negative than it is in its typical resting state. It is not until the charge returns to its normal resting state that the neuron will be fully ready to be triggered once again.

law—there is variation in the frequency of impulses, providing a mechanism by which we can distinguish the tickle of a feather from the weight of someone standing on our toes.

MIRROR NEURONS

Although all neurons operate through the firing of action potentials, there is significant specialization among different types of neurons. For example, in the last decade, neuroscientists have discovered the existence of **mirror neurons,** neurons that fire not only when a person enacts a particular behavior but also when a person simply observes *another* individual carrying out the same behavior (Falck-Ytter, 2006; Lepage & Theoret, 2007; Schulte-Ruther et al., 2007).

Mirror neurons may help explain how (and why) humans have the capacity to understand others' intentions. Specifically, mirror neurons may fire when we view someone doing something, helping us to predict what their goals are and what they may do next.

The discovery of mirror neurons suggests that the capacity of even young children to imitate others may be an inborn behavior. Furthermore, mirror neurons may be at the root of empathy—those feelings of concern, compassion, and sympathy for others—and even the development of language in humans (Iacoboni, 2009; Ramachandra, 2009; Triesch, Jasso, & Deák, 2007).

mirror neurons Specialized neurons that fire not only when a person enacts a particular behavior, but also when a person simply observes *another* individual carrying out the same behavior.

Where Neurons Meet: Bridging the Gap

If you have looked inside a computer, you've seen that each part is physically connected to another part. In contrast, evolution has produced a neural transmission system that at some points has no need for a structural connection between its components. Instead, a chemical connection bridges the gap, known as a synapse, between two neurons (see Figure 4). The **synapse** is the space between two neurons where the axon of a sending neuron communicates with the dendrites of a receiving neuron by using chemical messages (Dean & Dresbach, 2006; Fanselow & Poulos, 2005).

When a nerve impulse comes to the end of the axon and reaches a terminal button, the terminal button releases a chemical courier called a neurotransmitter. **Neurotransmitters** are chemicals that carry messages across the synapse to a dendrite

synapse The space between two neurons where the axon of a sending neuron communicates with the dendrites of a receiving neuron by using chemical messages.

neurotransmitters Chemicals that carry messages across the synapse to the dendrite (and sometimes the cell body) of a receiver neuron.

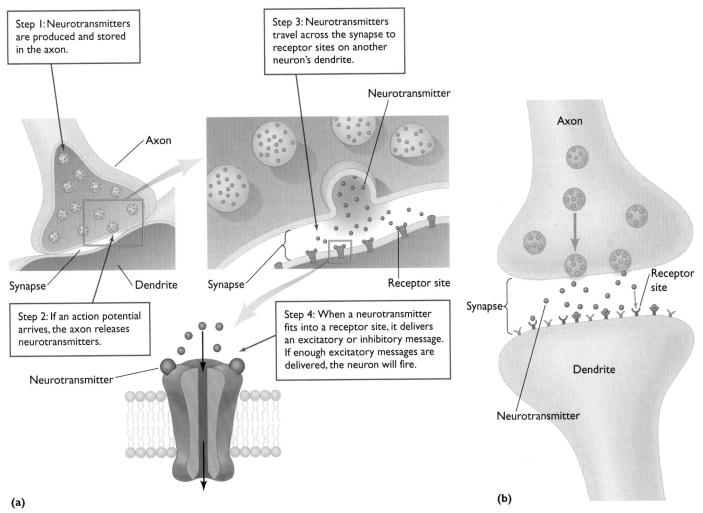

Step 1: Neurotransmitters are produced and stored in the axon.

Step 3: Neurotransmitters travel across the synapse to receptor sites on another neuron's dendrite.

Neurotransmitter

Axon

Synapse

Dendrite

Synapse

Receptor site

Step 2: If an action potential arrives, the axon releases neurotransmitters.

Step 4: When a neurotransmitter fits into a receptor site, it delivers an excitatory or inhibitory message. If enough excitatory messages are delivered, the neuron will fire.

Neurotransmitter

(a)

Axon

Receptor site

Synapse

Dendrite

Neurotransmitter

(b)

FIGURE 4 A synapse is the junction between an axon and a dendrite. The gap between the axon and the dendrite is bridged by chemicals called neurotransmitters (Mader, 2000). In (a) read Step 1 through Step 4 to follow this process. (b) Just as the pieces of a jigsaw puzzle can fit in only one specific location in a puzzle, each kind of neurotransmitter has a distinctive configuration that allows it to fit into a specific type of receptor cell (Johnson, 2000). Why is it advantageous for axons and dendrites to be linked by temporary chemical bridges rather than by the hard wiring typical of a radio connection or telephone hookup?

▶ **Study Alert**
Remember this key fact: Messages inside neurons are transmitted in electrical form, whereas messages traveling between neurons travel via chemical means.

(and sometimes the cell body) of a receiving neuron. Like a boat that ferries passengers across a river, these chemical messengers move toward the shorelines of other neurons. The chemical mode of message transmission that occurs between neurons is strikingly different from the means by which communication occurs inside neurons: Although messages travel in electrical form *within* a neuron, they move *between* neurons through a chemical transmission system.

There are several types of neurotransmitters, and not all neurons are capable of receiving the chemical message carried by a particular neurotransmitter. In the same way that a jigsaw puzzle piece can fit in only one specific location in a puzzle, each kind of neurotransmitter has a distinctive configuration that allows it to fit into a specific type of receptor site on the receiving neuron (see Figure 4b). It is only when a neurotransmitter fits precisely into a receptor site that successful chemical communication is possible.

If a neurotransmitter does fit into a site on the receiving neuron, the chemical message it delivers is basically one of two types: excitatory or inhibitory. **Excitatory messages** make it more likely that a receiving neuron will fire and an action potential will travel down its axon. **Inhibitory messages,** in contrast, do just the opposite; they provide chemical information that prevents or decreases the likelihood that the receiving neuron will fire.

excitatory message A chemical message that makes it more likely that a receiving neuron will fire and an action potential will travel down its axon.

inhibitory message A chemical message that prevents or decreases the likelihood that a receiving neuron will fire.

Because the dendrites of a neuron receive both excitatory and inhibitory messages simultaneously, the neuron must integrate the messages by using a kind of chemical calculator. Put simply, if the excitatory messages ("Fire!") outnumber the inhibitory ones ("Don't fire!"), the neuron fires. In contrast, if the inhibitory messages outnumber the excitatory ones, nothing happens, and the neuron remains in its resting state (Flavell et al., 2006; Mel, 2002; Rapport, 2005).

If neurotransmitters remained at the site of the synapse, receiving neurons would be awash in a continual chemical bath, producing constant stimulation or constant inhibition of the receiving neurons—and effective communication across the synapse would no longer be possible. To solve this problem, neurotransmitters are either deactivated by enzymes or—more commonly—reabsorbed by the terminal button in an example of chemical recycling called **reuptake.** Like a vacuum cleaner sucking up dust, neurons reabsorb the neurotransmitters that are now clogging the synapse. All this activity occurs at lightning speed, with the process taking just several milliseconds (Helmuth, 2000; Holt & Jahn, 2004).

reuptake The reabsorption of neurotransmitters by a terminal button.

Our understanding of the process of reuptake has permitted the development of a number of drugs used in the treatment of psychological disorders. As we discuss later in the book, some antidepressant drugs, called *SSRIs,* or *selective serotonin reuptake inhibitors,* permit certain neurotransmitters to remain active for a longer period at certain synapses in the brain, thereby reducing the symptoms of depression (Montgomery, 2006; Ramos, 2006).

Neurotransmitters: Multitalented Chemical Couriers

Neurotransmitters are a particularly important link between the nervous system and behavior. Not only are they important for maintaining vital brain and body functions, a deficiency or an excess of a neurotransmitter can produce severe behavior disorders. More than a hundred chemicals have been found to act as neurotransmitters, and neuroscientists believe that more may ultimately be identified (Penney, 2000; Schmidt, 2006).

Neurotransmitters vary significantly in terms of how strong their concentration must be to trigger a neuron to fire. Furthermore, the effects of a particular neurotransmitter vary, depending on the area of the nervous system in which it is produced.

Neurotransmitter Name	Location	Effect	Function
Acetylcholine (ACh)	Brain, spinal cord, peripheral nervous system, especially some organs of the parasympathetic nervous system	Excitatory in brain and autonomic nervous system; inhibitory elsewhere	Muscle movement, cognitive functioning
Glutamate	Brain, spinal cord	Excitatory	Memory
Gamma-amino butyric acid (GABA)	Brain, spinal cord	Main inhibitory neurotransmitter	Eating, aggression, sleeping
Dopamine (DA)	Brain	Inhibitory or excitatory	Movement control, pleasure and reward, attention
Serotonin	Brain, spinal cord	Inhibitory	Sleeping, eating, mood, pain, depression
Endorphins	Brain, spinal cord	Primarily inhibitory, except in hippocampus	Pain suppression, pleasurable feelings, appetites, placebos

Dopamine pathways

Serotonin pathways

FIGURE 5 Major neurotransmitters.

The same neurotransmitter, then, can act as an excitatory message to a neuron located in one part of the brain and can inhibit firing in neurons located in another part. (The major neurotransmitters and their effects are described in Figure 5.)

One of the most common neurotransmitters is *acetylcholine* (or *ACh*, its chemical symbol), which is found throughout the nervous system. ACh is involved in our every move, because—among other things—it transmits messages relating to our skeletal muscles. ACh is also involved in memory capabilities, and diminished production of ACh may be related to Alzheimer's disease (Bazalakova et al., 2007; Mohapel et al., 2005).

Another common excitatory neurotransmitter, *glutamate,* plays a role in memory. Memories appear to be produced by specific biochemical changes at particular synapses, and glutamate, along with other neurotransmitters, plays an important role in this process (Carvalho, 2006; Riedel, Platt, & Micheau, 2003; Winters & Bussey, 2005).

Gamma-amino butyric acid (GABA), which is found in both the brain and the spinal cord, appears to be the nervous system's primary inhibitory neurotransmitter. It moderates a variety of behaviors, ranging from eating to aggression. Several common substances, such as the tranquilizer Valium and alcohol, are effective because they permit GABA to operate more efficiently (Akirav, Raizel, & Maroun, 2006; Ball, 2004; Criswell et al., 2008; Lobo & Harris, 2008).

Another major neurotransmitter is *dopamine (DA),* which is involved in movement, attention, and learning. The discovery that certain drugs can have a significant effect on dopamine release has led to the development of effective treatments for a wide variety of physical and mental ailments. For instance, Parkinson's disease, from which actor Michael J. Fox suffers, is caused by a deficiency of dopamine in the brain. Techniques for increasing the production of dopamine in Parkinson's patients are proving effective (Antonini & Barone, 2008; Iversen & Iversen, 2007; Willis, 2005).

Michael J. Fox suffers from Parkinson's disease, and has become a strong advocate for research into the disorder.

In other instances, *over*production of dopamine produces negative consequences. For example, researchers have hypothesized that schizophrenia and some other severe mental disturbances are affected or perhaps even caused by the presence of unusually high levels of dopamine. Drugs that block the reception of dopamine reduce the symptoms displayed by some people diagnosed with schizophrenia (Di Forti, Lappin, & Murray, 2007; Howes & Kapur, 2009; Murray, Lappin, & Di Forti, 2008).

Another neurotransmitter, *serotonin,* is associated with the regulation of sleep, eating, mood, and pain. A growing body of research points toward a broader role for serotonin, suggesting its involvement in such diverse behaviors as alcoholism, depression, suicide, impulsivity, aggression, and coping with stress (Carillo et al., 2009; Murphy, Lappin, & Di Forti, 2008; Popa et al., 2008).

Endorphins, another class of neurotransmitters, are a family of chemicals produced by the brain that are similar in structure to painkilling drugs such as morphine. The production of endorphins reflects the brain's effort to deal with pain as well as to elevate mood.

Endorphins also may produce the euphoric feelings that runners sometimes experience after long runs. The exertion and perhaps the pain involved in a long run may stimulate the production of endorphins, ultimately resulting in what has been called "runner's high" (Kolata, 2002; Pert, 2002; Stanojevic, Mitic, & Vujic, 2007).

Endorphin release might also explain other phenomena that have long puzzled psychologists. For example, the act of taking placebos (pills or other substances that contain no actual drugs but that patients *believe* will make them better) may induce the release of endorphins, leading to the reduction of pain (Crum & Langer, 2007; Rajagopal, 2006; Wager, 2005).

RECAP/EVALUATE/RETHINK

RECAP

Why do psychologists study the brain and nervous system?

- A full understanding of human behavior requires knowledge of the biological influences underlying that behavior, especially those originating in the nervous system. Psychologists who specialize in studying the effects of biological structures and functions on behavior are known as behavioral neuroscientists. (p. 50)

What are the basic elements of the nervous system?

- Neurons, the most basic elements of the nervous system, carry nerve impulses from one part of the body to another. Information in a neuron generally follows a route that begins with the dendrites, continues into the cell body, and leads ultimately down the tubelike extension, the axon. (p. 51)

How does the nervous system communicate electrical and chemical messages from one part to another?

- Most axons are insulated by a coating called the myelin sheath. When a neuron receives a message to fire, it releases an action potential, an electric charge that travels through the axon. Neurons operate according to an all-or-none law: Either they are at rest, or an action potential is moving through them. There is no in-between state. (p. 52)
- Once a neuron fires, nerve impulses are carried to other neurons through the production of chemical substances, neurotransmitters, that actually bridge the gaps—known as synapses—between neurons. Neurotransmitters may be either excitatory, telling other neurons to fire, or inhibitory, preventing or decreasing the likelihood of other neurons firing. (p. 55)

- Endorphins, another type of neurotransmitter, are related to the reduction of pain. Endorphins aid in the production of a natural painkiller and are probably responsible for creating the kind of euphoria that joggers sometimes experience after running. (p. 58)

EVALUATE

1. The _____ is the fundamental element of the nervous system.
2. Neurons receive information through their _____ and send messages through their _____.
3. Just as electrical wires have an outer coating, axons are insulated by a coating called the _____ _____ .
4. The gap between two neurons is bridged by a chemical connection called a _____.
5. Endorphins are one kind of _____, the chemical "messengers" between neurons.

RETHINK

1. How might psychologists use drugs that mimic the effects of neurotransmitters to treat psychological disorders?
2. *From the perspective of a health care provider:* How would you explain the placebo effect and the role of endorphins to patients who wish to try unproven treatment methods that they find on the Web?

Answers to Evaluate Questions

1. neuron; 2. dendrites, axons; 3. myelin sheath; 4. synapse; 5. neurotransmitter

KEY TERMS

behavioral neuroscientists (or biopsychologists) p. 50	axon p. 51	resting state p. 52	neurotransmitters p. 55
neurons p. 51	terminal buttons p. 51	action potential p. 53	excitatory message p. 56
dendrite p. 51	myelin sheath p. 52	mirror neurons p. 54	inhibitory message p. 56
	all-or-none law p. 52	synapse p. 55	reuptake p. 56

The Nervous System and the Endocrine System: Communicating Within the Body

Key Concepts

How are the structures of the nervous system linked?

How does the endocrine system affect behavior?

In light of the complexity of individual neurons and the neurotransmission process, it should come as no surprise that the connections and structures formed by the neurons are complicated. Because each neuron can be connected to 80,000 other neurons, the total number of possible connections is astonishing. For instance, estimates of the number of neural connections within the brain fall in the neighborhood of 10 quadrillion—a 1 followed by 16 zeros—and some experts put the number even higher. However, connections among neurons are not the only means of communication within the body; as we'll see, the endocrine system, which secretes chemical messages that circulate through the blood, also communicates messages that influence behavior and many aspects of biological functioning (Kandel, Schwartz, & Jessell, 2000; Forlenza & Baum, 2004; Boahen, 2005).

The Nervous System: Linking Neurons

Whatever the actual number of neural connections, the human nervous system has both logic and elegance. We turn now to a discussion of its basic structures.

CENTRAL AND PERIPHERAL NERVOUS SYSTEMS

As you can see from the schematic representation in Figure 1, the nervous system is divided into two main parts: the central nervous system and the peripheral nervous system. The **central nervous system (CNS)** is composed of the brain and spinal cord. The **spinal cord,** which is about the thickness of a pencil, contains a bundle of neurons that leaves the brain and runs down the length of the back (see Figure 2). As you can see in Figure 1, the spinal cord is the primary means for transmitting messages between the brain and the rest of the body.

However, the spinal cord is not just a communication channel. It also controls some simple behaviors on its own, without any help from the brain. An example is the way the knee jerks forward when it is tapped with a rubber hammer. This behavior is a type of **reflex,** an automatic, involuntary response to an incoming stimulus. A reflex is also at work when you touch a hot stove and immediately withdraw your hand. Although the brain eventually analyzes and reacts to the situation ("Ouch—hot stove—pull away!"), the initial withdrawal is directed only by neurons in the spinal cord.

central nervous system (CNS) The part of the nervous system that includes the brain and spinal cord.

spinal cord A bundle of neurons that leaves the brain and runs down the length of the back and is the main means for transmitting messages between the brain and the body.

reflex An automatic, involuntary response to an incoming stimulus.

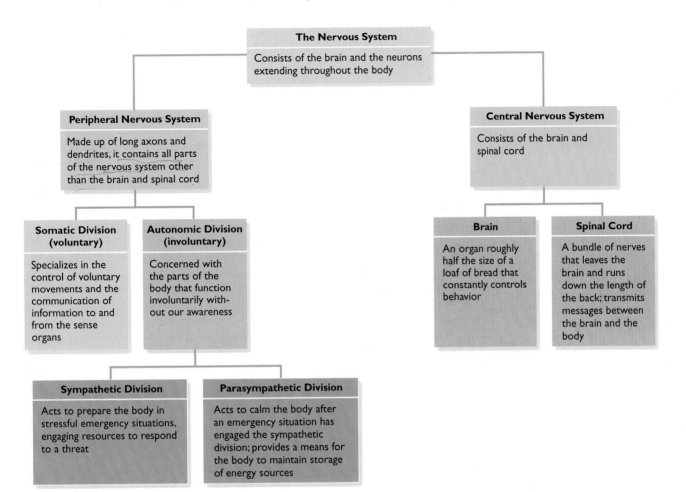

The Nervous System

Consists of the brain and the neurons extending throughout the body

Peripheral Nervous System

Made up of long axons and dendrites, it contains all parts of the nervous system other than the brain and spinal cord

Central Nervous System

Consists of the brain and spinal cord

Somatic Division (voluntary)

Specializes in the control of voluntary movements and the communication of information to and from the sense organs

Autonomic Division (involuntary)

Concerned with the parts of the body that function involuntarily without our awareness

Brain

An organ roughly half the size of a loaf of bread that constantly controls behavior

Spinal Cord

A bundle of nerves that leaves the brain and runs down the length of the back; transmits messages between the brain and the body

Sympathetic Division

Acts to prepare the body in stressful emergency situations, engaging resources to respond to a threat

Parasympathetic Division

Acts to calm the body after an emergency situation has engaged the sympathetic division; provides a means for the body to maintain storage of energy sources

FIGURE 1 A schematic diagram of the relationship of the parts of the nervous system.

Central nervous system

Brain

Spinal cord

Peripheral nervous system

Spinal nerves

FIGURE 2 The central nervous system consists of the brain and spinal cord, and the peripheral nervous system encompasses the network of nerves connecting the brain and spinal cord to other parts of the body.

Study Alert

Use Figures 1 and 2 to learn the components of the central and peripheral nervous systems.

sensory (afferent) neurons Neurons that transmit information from the perimeter of the body to the central nervous system.

motor (efferent) neurons Neurons that communicate information from the nervous system to muscles and glands.

interneurons Neurons that connect sensory and motor neurons, carrying messages between the two.

peripheral nervous system The part of the nervous system that includes the autonomic and somatic subdivisions; made up of neurons with long axons and dendrites, it branches out from the spinal cord and brain and reaches the extremities of the body.

somatic division The part of the peripheral nervous system that specializes in the control of voluntary movements and the communication of information to and from the sense organs.

autonomic division The part of the peripheral nervous system that controls involuntary movement of the heart, glands, lungs, and other organs.

sympathetic division The part of the autonomic division of the nervous system that acts to prepare the body for action in stressful situations, engaging all the organism's resources to respond to a threat.

parasympathetic division The part of the autonomic division of the nervous system that acts to calm the body after an emergency has ended.

Three kinds of neurons are involved in reflexes. **Sensory (afferent) neurons** transmit information from the perimeter of the body to the central nervous system. **Motor (efferent) neurons** communicate information from the nervous system to muscles and glands. **Interneurons** connect sensory and motor neurons, carrying messages between the two.

The importance of the spinal cord and reflexes is illustrated by the outcome of accidents in which the cord is injured or severed. In some cases, injury results in *quadriplegia*, a condition in which voluntary muscle movement below the neck is lost. In a less severe but still debilitating condition, *paraplegia*, people are unable to voluntarily move any muscles in the lower half of the body.

As suggested by its name, the **peripheral nervous system** branches out from the spinal cord and brain and reaches the extremities of the body. Made up of neurons with long axons and dendrites, the peripheral nervous system encompasses all the parts of the nervous system other than the brain and spinal cord. There are two major divisions—the somatic division and the autonomic division—both of which connect the central nervous system with the sense organs, muscles, glands, and other organs. The **somatic division** specializes in the control of voluntary movements—such as the motion of the eyes to read this sentence or those of the hand to turn this page—and the communication of information to and from the sense organs. The **autonomic division** controls the parts of the body that keep us alive—the heart, blood vessels, glands, lungs, and other organs that function involuntarily without our awareness. As you are reading at this moment, the autonomic division of the peripheral nervous system is pumping blood through your body, pushing your lungs in and out, and overseeing the digestion of your last meal.

ACTIVATING THE DIVISIONS OF THE AUTONOMIC NERVOUS SYSTEM

The autonomic division plays a particularly crucial role during emergencies. Suppose that as you are reading you suddenly sense that a stranger is watching you through the window. As you look up, you see the glint of something that might be a knife. As confusion clouds your mind and fear overcomes your attempts to think rationally, what happens to your body? If you are like most people, you react immediately on a physiological level. Your heart rate increases, you begin to sweat, and you develop goose bumps all over your body.

The physiological changes that occur during a crisis result from the activation of one of the two parts of the autonomic nervous system: the **sympathetic division.** The sympathetic division acts to prepare the body for action in stressful situations by engaging all of the organism's resources to run away or to confront the threat. This is often called the "fight or flight" response.

In contrast, the **parasympathetic division** acts to calm the body after the emergency has ended. When you find, for instance, that the stranger at the window is actually your roommate, who has lost his keys and is climbing in the window to avoid waking you, your parasympathetic division begins to take over, lowering your heart rate, stopping your sweating, and returning your body to the state it was in before you became alarmed. The parasympathetic division also directs the body to store energy for use in emergencies.

The sympathetic and parasympathetic divisions work together to regulate many functions of the body (see Figure 3). For instance, sexual arousal is controlled by the parasympathetic division, but sexual orgasm is a function of the sympathetic division. The sympathetic and parasympathetic divisions also are involved in a number of disorders. For example, one explanation of documented examples of "voodoo death"—in which a person is literally scared to death resulting from a voodoo curse—may be produced by overstimulation of the sympathetic division due to extreme fear (Sternberg, 2002).

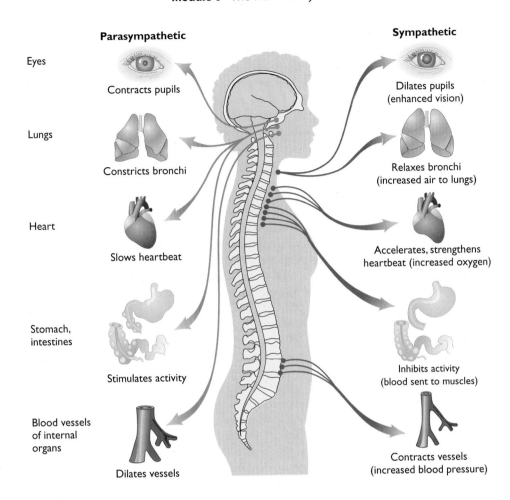

Parasympathetic

Eyes
Contracts pupils

Lungs
Constricts bronchi

Heart
Slows heartbeat

Stomach, intestines
Stimulates activity

Blood vessels of internal organs
Dilates vessels

Sympathetic

Dilates pupils (enhanced vision)

Relaxes bronchi (increased air to lungs)

Accelerates, strengthens heartbeat (increased oxygen)

Inhibits activity (blood sent to muscles)

Contracts vessels (increased blood pressure)

FIGURE 3 The major functions of the autonomic nervous system. The sympathetic division acts to prepare certain organs of the body for stressful situations, and the parasympathetic division acts to calm the body after the emergency has been passed. Can you explain why each response of the sympathetic division might be useful in an emergency?

The Evolutionary Foundations of the Nervous System

The complexities of the nervous system can be better understood if we take the course of evolution into consideration. The forerunner of the human nervous system is found in the earliest simple organisms to have a spinal cord. Basically, those organisms were simple input-output devices: When the upper side of the spinal cord was stimulated by, for instance, being touched, the organism reacted with a simple response, such as jerking away. Such responses were completely a consequence of the organism's genetic makeup.

Over millions of years, the spinal cord became more specialized, and organisms became capable of distinguishing between different kinds of stimuli and responding appropriately to them. Ultimately, a portion of the spinal cord evolved into what we would consider a primitive brain.

Today, the nervous system is *hierarchically organized,* meaning that relatively newer (from an evolutionary point of view) and more sophisticated regions of the brain regulate the older, and more primitive, parts of the nervous system. As we move up along the spinal cord and continue upward into the brain, then, the functions controlled by the various regions become progressively more advanced.

Why should we care about the evolutionary background of the human nervous system? The answer comes from researchers working in the area of **evolutionary psychology,** the branch of psychology that seeks to identify how behavior is influenced and produced by our genetic inheritance from our ancestors.

evolutionary psychology The branch of psychology that seeks to identify behavior patterns that are a result of our genetic inheritance from our ancestors.

Evolutionary psychologists argue that the course of evolution is reflected in the structure and functioning of the nervous system and that evolutionary factors consequently have a significant influence on our everyday behavior. Their work, in conjunction with the research of scientists studying genetics, biochemistry, and medicine, has led to an understanding of how our behavior is affected by heredity, our genetically determined heritage. In fact, evolutionary psychologists have spawned a new and increasingly influential field: behavioral genetics.

BEHAVIORAL GENETICS

behavioral genetics The study of the effects of heredity on behavior.

Our evolutionary heritage manifests itself not only through the structure and functioning of the nervous system but through our behavior as well. In the view of a growing area of study, people's personality and behavioral habits are affected in part by their genetic heritage. **Behavioral genetics** is the study of the effects of heredity on behavior. Behavioral genetics researchers are finding increasing evidence that cognitive abilities, personality traits, sexual orientation, and psychological disorders are determined to some extent by genetic factors (Ilies, Arvey, & Bouchard, 2006; Livesley & Jang, 2008; Vernon et al., 2008).

Behavioral genetics lies at the heart of the nature-nurture question, one of the key issues in the study of psychology. Although no one would argue that our behavior is determined *solely* by inherited factors, evidence collected by behavioral geneticists does suggest that our genetic inheritance predisposes us to respond in particular ways to our environment, and even to seek out particular kinds of environments. For instance, research indicates that genetic factors may be related to such diverse behaviors as level of family conflict, schizophrenia, learning disabilities, and general sociability (Ball et al., 2008; Davis, Haworth, & Plomin, 2009; Lakhan & Vieira, 2009).

Furthermore, important human characteristics and behaviors are related to the presence (or absence) of particular *genes,* the inherited material that controls the transmission of traits. For example, researchers have found evidence that novelty-seeking behavior is determined, at least in part, by a certain gene (Golimbet et al., 2007).

As we consider later in the book when we discuss human development, researchers have identified some 25,000 individual genes, each of which appears in a specific sequence on a particular *chromosome,* a rod-shaped structure that transmits genetic information across generations. In 2003, after a decade of effort, researchers identified the sequence of the 3 billion chemical pairs that make up human *DNA,* the basic component of genes. Understanding the basic structure of the human *genome*—the "map" of humans' total genetic makeup—brings scientists a giant step closer to understanding the contributions of individual genes to specific human structures and functioning (Andreasen, 2005; Dale & von Schantz, 2007; Plomin & Davis, 2009).

Molecular Genetics and Psychological Disorders Despite its relative infancy, the field of behavioral genetics has already made substantial contributions to our understanding of behavior. One branch of behavioral genetics, *molecular genetics,* seeks to identify specific genes that are associated with behavior and, in particular, psychological disorders. Genes that are physically close to one another on a particular chromosome tend to be linked and inherited together. By finding *genetic markers*—genes with a known location—that are linked to a disorder, scientists are beginning to learn how disorders such as schizophrenia and depression develop and can potentially be treated.

Molecular geneticists have already found that the risk of developing autism (a disorder that influences the development of language and effective social functioning) is increased in the presence of a gene related to early brain development. Children with this gene, a variation of the gene called *HOXA1,* are twice as likely to develop the disorder as children who do not have this variant (Hyman, 2003; Gregg et al., 2007).

Yet having the variant gene does not always lead to autism. More than 99.5% of people with the variant do not develop the disorder, and 60% of those with autism do not have the variant. It is probable that autism, like other disorders with a genetic basis, is not triggered by the presence or absence of a single, particular gene. More likely, it is produced by several genes in combination, as well as perhaps requiring the presence of certain environmental influences, such as infection or brain injury. The challenge for behavior geneticists, then, is not only to determine what genes are responsible for particular behaviors but also to identify the environmental triggers that activate those genes (Sen et al., 2007).

In examining the genetic roots of various behaviors, the study of behavior genetics has stirred controversy. For instance, questions about the existence of genetic influences on criminality, intelligence, and homosexuality raise considerable emotion. Furthermore, it is unclear what the social and political consequences of discoveries in behavioral genetics would be. Would finding a strong genetic basis for criminal behavior lead to genetic screening and restricted civil rights for individuals having "criminal" genes? Clearly, behavioral genetic discoveries could have an impact on a number of important social issues (Wensley & King, 2008).

Behavioral Genetics, Gene Therapy, and Genetic Counseling Behavioral genetics also holds the promise of developing new diagnostic and treatment techniques for genetic deficiencies that can lead to physical and psychological difficulties. In *gene therapy*, scientists inject into a patient's bloodstream genes meant to cure a particular disease. When the genes arrive at the site of defective genes that are producing the illness, they trigger the production of chemicals that can treat the disease (Jaffé, Prasad, & Larcher, 2006; Eberling et al., 2008; Isacson & Kordower, 2008).

The number of diseases that can be treated through gene therapy is growing, as we will see when we discuss human development. For example, gene therapy is now being used in experimental trials involving people with certain forms of cancer and blindness (Hirschler, 2007; Nakamura, 2004; Wagner et al., 2004).

Advances in behavioral genetics also have led to the development of a profession that did not exist several decades ago: genetic counseling. Genetic counselors help people deal with issues related to inherited disorders. For example, genetic counselors provide advice to prospective parents about the potential risks in a future pregnancy, based on their family history of birth defects and hereditary illnesses. In addition, the counselor considers the parents' age and problems with children they already have. They also can take blood, skin, and urine samples to examine specific chromosomes.

Scientists have already developed genetic tests to determine whether someone is susceptible to certain types of cancer or heart disease, and it may not be long before analysis of a drop of blood can indicate whether a child—or potentially an unborn fetus—is susceptible to certain psychological disorders. How such knowledge will be used is a source of considerable speculation and controversy, controversy that is certain to grow as genetic testing becomes more common (Etchegary, 2004; Malpas, 2008).

The Endocrine System:
Of Chemicals and Glands

Another of the body's communication systems, the **endocrine system** is a chemical communication network that sends messages throughout the body via the bloodstream. Its job is to secrete **hormones**, chemicals that circulate through the blood and regulate the functioning or growth of the body. It also influences—and is influenced by—the functioning of the nervous system. Although the endocrine system is not part of the brain, it is closely linked to the hypothalamus.

As chemical messengers, hormones are like neurotransmitters, although their speed and mode of transmission are quite different. Whereas neural messages are measured in thousandths of a second, hormonal communications may take minutes to reach their destination. Furthermore, neural messages move through neurons in

endocrine system A chemical communication network that sends messages throughout the body via the bloodstream.

hormones Chemicals that circulate through the blood and regulate the functioning or growth of the body.

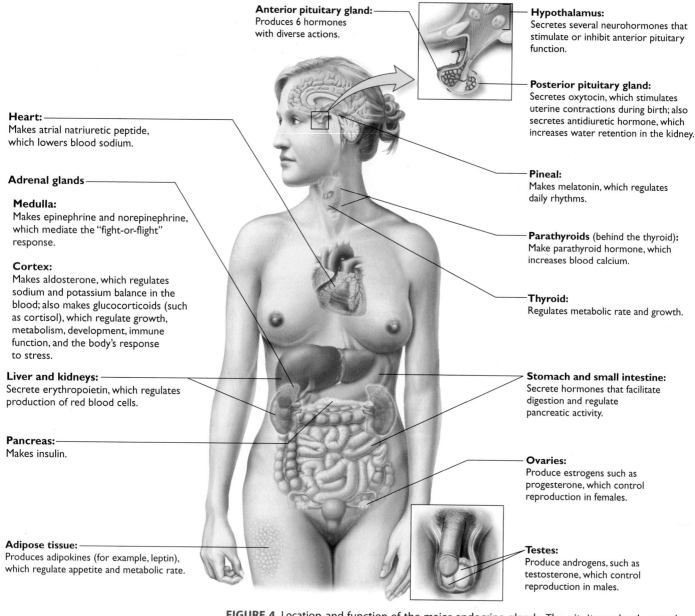

Anterior pituitary gland: Produces 6 hormones with diverse actions.

Hypothalamus: Secretes several neurohormones that stimulate or inhibit anterior pituitary function.

Posterior pituitary gland: Secretes oxytocin, which stimulates uterine contractions during birth; also secretes antidiuretic hormone, which increases water retention in the kidney.

Heart: Makes atrial natriuretic peptide, which lowers blood sodium.

Pineal: Makes melatonin, which regulates daily rhythms.

Adrenal glands

Medulla: Makes epinephrine and norepinephrine, which mediate the "fight-or-flight" response.

Parathyroids (behind the thyroid): Make parathyroid hormone, which increases blood calcium.

Cortex: Makes aldosterone, which regulates sodium and potassium balance in the blood; also makes glucocorticoids (such as cortisol), which regulate growth, metabolism, development, immune function, and the body's response to stress.

Thyroid: Regulates metabolic rate and growth.

Liver and kidneys: Secrete erythropoietin, which regulates production of red blood cells.

Stomach and small intestine: Secrete hormones that facilitate digestion and regulate pancreatic activity.

Pancreas: Makes insulin.

Ovaries: Produce estrogens such as progesterone, which control reproduction in females.

Adipose tissue: Produces adipokines (for example, leptin), which regulate appetite and metabolic rate.

Testes: Produce androgens, such as testosterone, which control reproduction in males.

FIGURE 4 Location and function of the major endocrine glands. The pituitary gland controls the functioning of the other endocrine glands and, in turn, is regulated by the hypothalamus.

specific lines (like a signal carried by wires strung along telephone poles), whereas hormones travel throughout the body, similar to the way radio waves are transmitted across the entire landscape. Just as radio waves evoke a response only when a radio is tuned to the correct station, hormones flowing through the bloodstream activate only those cells that are receptive and "tuned" to the appropriate hormonal message.

A key component of the endocrine system is the tiny **pituitary gland,** which is found near—and regulated by—the hypothalamus. The pituitary gland has sometimes been called the "master gland" because it controls the functioning of the rest of the endocrine system. But the pituitary gland is more than just the taskmaster of other glands; it has important functions in its own right. For instance, hormones secreted by the pituitary gland control growth. Extremely short people and unusually tall ones usually have pituitary gland abnormalities. Other endocrine glands, shown in Figure 4, affect emotional reactions, sexual urges, and energy levels.

pituitary gland The major component of the endocrine system, or "master gland," which secretes hormones that control growth and other parts of the endocrine system.

Steroids can provide added muscle and strength, but they have dangerous side effects. A number of well-known athletes in a variety of sports have been accused of using the drugs illegally.

Despite its designation as the "master gland," the pituitary is actually a servant of the brain, because the brain is ultimately responsible for the endocrine system's functioning. The brain maintains the internal balance of the body through the hypothalamus.

Individual hormones can wear many hats, depending on circumstances. For example, the hormone oxytocin is at the root of many of life's satisfactions and pleasures. In new mothers, oxytocin produces an urge to nurse newborn offspring. The same hormone also seems to stimulate cuddling between species members. And—at least in rats—it encourages sexually active males to seek out females more passionately, and females to be more receptive to males' sexual advances. There's even evidence that oxytocin is related to the development of trust in others, helping to grease the wheels of effective social interaction (Kosfeld et al., 2005; Meinlschmidt & Heim, 2007; Guastella, Mitchell, & Dadds, 2008).

Although hormones are produced naturally by the endocrine system, the ingestion of artificial hormones has proved to be both beneficial and potentially dangerous. For example, before the early 2000s, physicians frequently prescribed hormone replacement therapy (HRT) to treat symptoms of menopause in older women. However, because recent research suggests that the treatment has potentially dangerous side effects, health experts now warn that the dangers outweigh the benefits (Herrington & Howard, 2003).

The use of testosterone, a male hormone, and drugs known as *steroids*, which act like testosterone, is increasingly common. For athletes and others who want to bulk up their appearance, steroids provide a way to add muscle weight and increase strength. However, these drugs can lead to heart attacks, strokes, cancer, and even violent behavior, making them extremely dangerous. For example, in one infamous case, professional wrestler Chris Benoit strangled his wife, suffocated his son, and later hanged himself—acts that were attributed to his use of steroids (Klötz, 2006; Pagonis, Angelopoulos, & Koukoulis, 2006; Sandomir, 2007).

Study Alert

The endocrine system produces hormones, chemicals that circulate through the body via the bloodstream.

RECAP/EVALUATE/RETHINK

RECAP

How are the structures of the nervous system linked?

- The nervous system is made up of the central nervous system (the brain and spinal cord) and the peripheral nervous system. The peripheral nervous system is made up of the somatic division, which controls voluntary movements and the communication of information to and from the sense organs, and the autonomic division, which controls involuntary functions such as those of the heart, blood vessels, and lungs. (p. 60)
- The autonomic division of the peripheral nervous system is further subdivided into the sympathetic and parasympathetic divisions. The sympathetic division prepares the body in emergency situations, and the parasympathetic division helps the body return to its typical resting state. (p. 62)
- Evolutionary psychology, the branch of psychology that seeks to identify behavior patterns that are a result of our genetic inheritance, has led to increased understanding of the evolutionary basis of the structure and organization of the human nervous system. Behavioral genetics extends this study to include the evolutionary and hereditary basis of human personality traits and behavior. (p. 63)

How does the endocrine system affect behavior?

- The endocrine system secretes hormones, chemicals that regulate the functioning of the body, via the bloodstream. The pituitary gland secretes growth hormones and influences the release of hormones by other endocrine glands, and in turn is regulated by the hypothalamus. (p. 65)

EVALUATE

1. If you put your hand on a red-hot piece of metal, the immediate response of pulling it away would be an example of a(n) _____.
2. The central nervous system is composed of the _____ and the _____.
3. In the peripheral nervous system, the _____ division controls voluntary movements, whereas the _____ division controls organs that keep us alive and function without our awareness.
4. Maria saw a young boy run into the street and get hit by a car. When she got to the fallen child, she was in a state of panic. She was sweating, and her heart was racing. Her biological state resulted from the activation of what division of the nervous system?
   a. parasympathetic
   b. central
   c. sympathetic
5. The emerging field of _____ studies ways in which our genetic inheritance predisposes us to behave in certain ways.

RETHINK

1. In what ways is the "fight-or-flight" response helpful to humans in emergency situations?
2. *From the perspective of a genetic counselor:* How would you explain the pros and cons of genetic counseling to someone who was interested in receiving genetic screening for various diseases and disorders?

Answers to Evaluate Questions

1. reflex; 2. brain, spinal cord; 3. somatic, autonomic; 4. c. sympathetic; 5. behavioral genetics

KEY TERMS

central nervous system (CNS) p. 60
spinal cord p. 60
reflex p. 60
sensory (afferent) neurons p. 62

motor (efferent) neurons p. 62
interneurons p. 62
peripheral nervous system p. 62
somatic division p. 62

autonomic division p. 62
sympathetic division p. 62
parasympathetic division p. 62
evolutionary psychology p. 63

behavioral genetics p. 64
endocrine system p. 65
hormones p. 65
pituitary gland p. 66

The Brain

It is not much to look at. Soft, spongy, mottled, and pinkish-gray in color, it hardly can be said to possess much in the way of physical beauty. Despite its physical appearance, however, it ranks as the greatest natural marvel that we know and has a beauty and sophistication all its own.

The object to which this description applies: the brain. The brain is responsible for our loftiest thoughts—and our most primitive urges. It is the overseer of the intricate workings of the human body. If one were to attempt to design a computer to mimic the range of capabilities of the brain, the task would be nearly impossible; in fact, it has proved difficult even to come close. The sheer quantity of nerve cells in the brain is enough to daunt even the most ambitious computer engineer. Many billions of neurons make up a structure weighing just 3 pounds in the average adult. However, it is not the number of cells that is the most astounding thing about the brain but its ability to allow the human intellect to flourish by guiding our behavior and thoughts.

We turn now to a consideration of the particular structures of the brain and the primary functions to which they are related. However, a caution is in order. Although we'll discuss specific areas of the brain in relation to specific behaviors, this approach is an oversimplification. No straightforward one-to-one correspondence exists between a distinct part of the brain and a particular behavior. Instead, behavior is produced by complex interconnections among sets of neurons in many areas of the brain: Our behavior, emotions, thoughts, hopes, and dreams are produced by a variety of neurons throughout the nervous system working in concert.

Key Concepts

How do researchers identify the major parts and functions of the brain?

What are the major parts of the brain, and for what behaviors is each part responsible?

How do the two halves of the brain operate inter-dependently?

How can an understanding of the nervous system help us find ways to alleviate disease and pain?

Studying the Brain's Structure and Functions: Spying on the Brain

The brain has posed a continual challenge to those who would study it. For most of history, its examination was possible only after an individual had died. Only then could the skull be opened and the brain cut into without serious injury. Although informative, this procedure could hardly tell us much about the functioning of the healthy brain.

Today, however, brain-scanning techniques provide a window into the living brain. Using these techniques, investigators can take a "snapshot" of the internal workings of the brain without having to cut open a person's skull. The most important scanning techniques, illustrated in Figure 1 on page 70, are the electroencephalogram (EEG), positron emission tomography (PET), functional magnetic resonance imaging (fMRI), and transcranial magnetic stimulation imaging (TMS).

The *electroencephalogram (EEG)* records electrical activity in the brain through electrodes placed on the outside of the skull. Although traditionally the EEG could produce only a graph of electrical wave

The brain (shown here in cross-section) may not be much to look at, but it represents one of the great marvels of human development. Why do most scientists believe that it will be difficult, if not impossible, to duplicate the brain's abilities?

69

(a) EEG

(b) fMRI

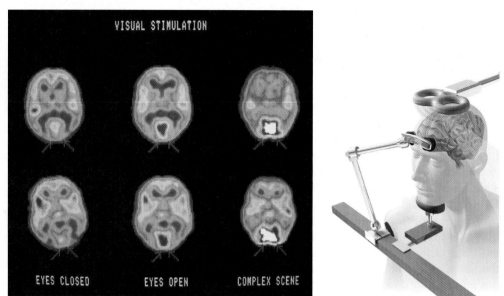
(c) PET scan

(d) TMS Apparatus

FIGURE 1 Brain scans produced by different techniques. (a) A computer-produced EEG image. (b) The fMRI scan uses a magnetic field to provide a detailed view of brain activity on a moment-by-moment basis. (c) The PET scan displays the functioning of the brain at a given moment. (d) Transcranial magnetic stimulation (TMS), the newest type of scan, produces a momentary disruption in an area of the brain, allowing researchers to see what activities are controlled by that area. TMS also has the potential to treat some psychological disorders.

patterns, new techniques are now used to transform the brain's electrical activity into a pictorial representation of the brain that allows more precise diagnosis of disorders such as epilepsy and learning disabilities.

Functional magnetic resonance imaging (fMRI) scans provide a detailed, three-dimensional computer-generated image of brain structures and activity by aiming a powerful magnetic field at the body. With fMRI scanning, it is possible to produce vivid, detailed images of the functioning of the brain.

Using fMRI scans, researchers are able to view features of less than a millimeter in size and view changes occurring in intervals of ¹⁄₁₀ of a second. For example, fMRI scans can show the operation of individual bundles of nerves by tracing the flow of blood, opening the way for improved diagnosis of ailments ranging from chronic back pain to nervous system disorders such as strokes, multiple sclerosis, and Alzheimer's. Scans using fMRI are routinely used in planning brain surgery, because they can help surgeons distinguish areas of the brain involved in normal and disturbed functioning (Mazard et al., 2005; Quenot et al., 2005; D'Arcy et al., 2007).

Positron emission tomography (PET) scans show biochemical activity within the brain at a given moment. PET scans begin with the injection of a radioactive (but safe) liquid into the bloodstream, which makes its way to the brain. By locating radiation within the brain, a computer can determine which are the more active regions, providing a striking picture of the brain at work. For example, PET scans may be used in cases of memory problems, seeking to identify the presence of brain tumors (Gronholm et al., 2005; McMurtray et al., 2007).

Transcranial magnetic stimulation (TMS) is one of the newest types of scan. By exposing a tiny region of the brain to a strong magnetic field, TMS causes a momentary interruption of electrical activity. Researchers then are able to note the effects of this interruption on normal brain functioning. The procedure is sometimes called a

> **Study Alert**
>
> Remember that EEG, fMRI, PET, and TMS differ in terms of whether they examine brain *structures* or brain *functioning*.

"virtual lesion," because it produces effects analogous to what would occur if areas of the brain were physically cut. The enormous advantage of TMS, of course, is that the virtual cut is only temporary. In addition to identifying areas of the brain that are responsible for particular functions, TMS has the potential to treat certain kinds of psychological disorders, such as depression and schizophrenia, by shooting brief magnetic pulses through the brain (Fitzgerald & Daskalakis, 2008; Rado, Dowd, & Janicak, 2008; Pallanti & Bernardi, 2009).

Future discoveries may yield even more sophisticated methods of examining the brain. For example, the emerging field of *optogenetics* involves genetic engineering and the use of special types of light to view individual circuits of neurons (Gradinaru et al., 2009; Miesenbock, 2008).

Advances in our understanding of the brain also are paving the way for the development of new methods for harnessing the brain's neural signals. We consider some of these intriguing findings in *Applying Psychology in the 21st Century.*

The Central Core:
Our "Old Brain"

Although the capabilities of the human brain far exceed those of the brain of any other species, humans share some basic functions, such as breathing, eating, and sleeping, with more primitive animals. Not surprisingly, those activities are directed by a relatively primitive part of the brain. A portion of the brain known as the **central core** (see Figure 2) is quite similar in all vertebrates (species with backbones). The central core is sometimes referred to as the "old brain," because its evolution can be traced back some 500 million years to primitive structures found in nonhuman species.

If we were to move up the spinal cord from the base of the skull to locate the structures of the central core of the brain, the first part we would come to would be the *hindbrain,* which contains the medulla, pons, and cerebellum (see Figure 3 on page 73). The *medulla* controls a number of critical body functions, the most important of which are breathing and heartbeat. The *pons* comes next, joining the two halves of the cerebellum, which lies adjacent to it. Containing large bundles of nerves, the pons acts as a transmitter of motor information, coordinating muscles and integrating movement between the right and left halves of the body. It is also involved in regulating sleep.

The **cerebellum** is found just above the medulla and behind the pons. Without the help of the cerebellum we would be unable to walk a straight line without staggering and lurching forward, for it is the job of the cerebellum to control bodily balance. It constantly monitors feedback from the muscles to coordinate their placement, movement, and tension. In fact, drinking too much alcohol seems to depress the activity of the cerebellum, leading to the unsteady gait and movement characteristic of drunkenness. The cerebellum is also involved in several intellectual functions, ranging from the analysis and coordination of sensory information to problem solving (Bower & Parsons, 2003; Paquier & Mariën, 2005; Vandervert, Schimpf, & Liu, 2007).

The **reticular formation** extends from the medulla through the pons, passing through the middle section of the brain—or *midbrain*—and into the front-most part of the brain, called the *forebrain.* Like an ever-vigilant guard, the reticular formation is made up of groups of nerve cells that can activate other parts of the brain immediately to produce general bodily arousal. If, for example, we are startled by a loud noise, the reticular formation can prompt a heightened state of awareness to determine whether a response is necessary. The reticular formation serves a different function when we are sleeping, seeming to filter out background stimuli to allow us to sleep undisturbed.

Cerebral cortex
(the "new brain")

Central core
(the "old brain")

FIGURE 2 The major divisions of the brain: the cerebral cortex and the central core. (Source: Seeley, Stephens, & Tate, 2000.)

central core The "old brain," which controls basic functions such as eating and sleeping and is common to all vertebrates.

cerebellum (ser-uh-BELL-um) The part of the brain that controls bodily balance.

reticular formation The part of the brain extending from the medulla through the pons and made up of groups of nerve cells that can immediately activate other parts of the brain to produce general bodily arousal.

Mind over Cursor: Harnessing Brainpower to Improve Lives

Hans-Peter Salzmann, a lawyer suffering from Lou Gehrig's disease, was locked within his own body. Paralyzed by the disease and unable to eat, speak, or even breathe on his own, he had to rely on a respirator and a feeding tube to survive. Although his mind functioned normally, he was unable to communicate with the outside world.

All that changed, however, after Salzmann obtained an experimental device that allows brain waves to be translated into written communication. Using EEG scanning techniques that react to the pattern of brain waves originating in the brain, Salzmann learned to boost and curtail certain types of brain waves. After hundreds of hours of practice, he was able to select letters that appear on a video screen. By stringing letters together, he could spell out messages. The process, which makes use of brain waves called "slow cortical potentials," permitted Salzmann to communicate effectively for the first time in years. Although the method is slow and tedious—Salzmann can produce only about two characters per minute—it holds great promise for people with spinal cord injuries and diseases that have left them paralyzed (Neumann & Birbaumer, 2004; Pollack, 2006; Hatsopoulos & Donoghue, 2009).

Neuroscience researchers are making remarkable progress at developing this technology of thought-based interfaces. It's not ready to be put into widespread use, but recent discoveries show how rapidly the technology is developing. In one extraordinary experiment, researchers implanted freckle-sized electrodes onto the brains of two monkeys at the motor cortex—the region of the brain responsible for voluntary muscle movement. Each electrode connected with 100 individual neurons in this region. A computer wired to the electrodes interpreted the signals coming from these neurons and used the information to direct the movement of a mechanical arm while the monkeys' own arms were restrained (Velliste et al., 2008).

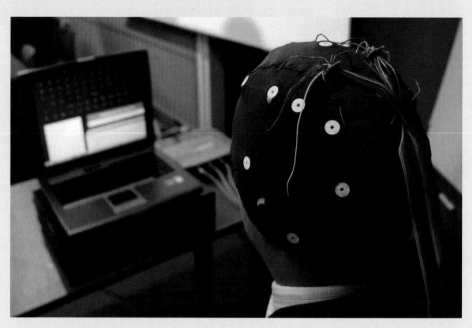

Brain scanning techniques allow people to communicate via brain waves alone.

The monkeys were initially "trained" in the manipulation of the arm, using joysticks at first and then using the brain interface with additional computer guidance (somewhat like using training wheels while learning to ride a bicycle). Within days, the monkeys were operating the arm using just their thoughts with no additional help. They sat in a chair and used the arm to reach out and grab treats such as grapes and marshmallows and bring them to their mouths. This task required them not only to move the arm through space but also to manipulate the grip on its end to seize the food and then to release it into their mouths.

While this much of a successful accomplishment was extraordinary by itself, the progress didn't stop there. The monkeys actually proceeded to show the scientists a new trick or two by becoming adept enough with the brain interface to improvise entirely unanticipated manipulations of the mechanical arm, such as using it to push food into their mouths as if it were their own hand. This ability is an important step forward, as any practical device for assisting the disabled would have to be able to be used in inventive ways in order to provide for their unique needs in a natural way. No computer program alone can anticipate every possible movement that might be necessary, but the monkeys showed that they could adapt the device to serve their own goals (Carey, 2008; Velliste et al., 2008).

Many hurdles remain before paralyzed people will be using thought-controlled devices routinely, particularly in terms of the need for stable electrodes, wireless communication, and portable translating computers. But achievements such as this give researchers hope that they are close to overcoming the remaining challenges such that one day—perhaps sooner than one might expect—their seemingly wild dream of giving new mobility to paralyzed people will be realized (Stix, 2008).

RETHINK

- Why is it so important to develop a complex and very expensive means of communication for the relatively small number of people who are living with locked-in syndrome?

Cerebral cortex

Corpus callosum
Bridge of fibers passing
information between the
two cerebral hemispheres

Hippocampus

Amygdala

Cerebellum
Controls bodily balance

Spinal cord
Responsible for communication
between brain and rest of body;
involved in simple reflexes

Thalamus
Relay center for cortex;
handles incoming and
outgoing signals

Midbrain

Hypothalamus
Responsible for regulating basic
biological needs: hunger, thirst,
temperature control

Olfactory bulb

Pituitary gland
"Master" gland that regulates
other endocrine glands

Pons
Involved in sleep and arousal

Medulla
Responsible for regulating largely
unconscious functions such as
breathing and circulation

FIGURE 3 The major structures in the brain. (Source: Brooker, Widmaier, Graham, & Stiling, 2008.)

Hidden within the forebrain, the **thalamus** acts primarily as a relay station for information about the senses. Messages from the eyes, ears, and skin travel to the thalamus to be communicated upward to higher parts of the brain. The thalamus also integrates information from higher parts of the brain, sorting it out so that it can be sent to the cerebellum and medulla.

The **hypothalamus** is located just below the thalamus. Although tiny—about the size of a fingertip—the hypothalamus plays an extremely important role. One of its major functions is to maintain *homeostasis,* a steady internal environment for the body. The hypothalamus helps provide a constant body temperature and monitors the amount of nutrients stored in the cells. A second major function is equally important: the hypothalamus produces and regulates behavior that is critical to the basic survival of the species, such as eating, self-protection, and sex.

thalamus The part of the brain located in the middle of the central core that acts primarily to relay information about the senses.

hypothalamus A tiny part of the brain, located below the thalamus, that maintains homeostasis and produces and regulates vital behavior, such as eating, drinking, and sexual behavior.

The Limbic System:
Beyond the Central Core

In an eerie view of the future, science fiction writers have suggested that people someday will routinely have electrodes implanted in their brains. Those electrodes will permit them to receive tiny shocks that will produce the sensation of pleasure by stimulating certain centers of the brain. When they feel upset, people will simply activate their electrodes to achieve an immediate high.

Although far-fetched—and ultimately improbable—such a futuristic fantasy is based on fact. The brain does have pleasure centers in several areas, including some in the **limbic system.** Consisting of a series of doughnut-shaped structures that

limbic system The part of the brain that controls eating, aggression, and reproduction.

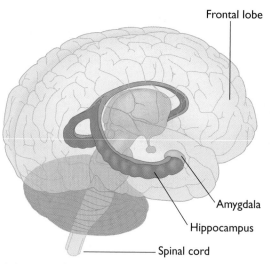

Frontal lobe

Amygdala

Hippocampus

Spinal cord

FIGURE 4 The limbic system is involved in self-preservation, learning, memory, and the experience of pleasure.

include the *amygdala* and *hippocampus*, the limbic system borders the top of the central core and has connections with the cerebral cortex (see Figure 4).

The structures of the limbic system jointly control a variety of basic functions relating to emotions and self-preservation, such as eating, aggression, and reproduction. Injury to the limbic system can produce striking changes in behavior. For example, injury to the amygdala, which is involved in fear and aggression, can turn animals that are usually docile and tame into belligerent savages. Conversely, animals that are usually wild and uncontrollable may become meek and obedient following injury to the amygdala (Bedard & Persinger, 1995; Gontkovsky, 2005).

Research examining the effects of mild electric shocks to parts of the limbic system and other parts of the brain has produced some thought-provoking findings. In one experiment, rats that pressed a bar received mild electric stimulation through an electrode implanted in their brains, which produced pleasurable feelings. Even starving rats on their way to food would stop to press the bar as many times as they could. Some rats would actually stimulate themselves literally thousands of times an hour—until they collapsed with fatigue (Routtenberg & Lindy, 1965; Olds & Fobes, 1981; Fountas & Smith, 2007).

The extraordinarily pleasurable quality of certain kinds of stimulation has also been experienced by humans, who, as part of the treatment for certain kinds of brain disorders, have received electrical stimulation to certain areas of the limbic system. Although at a loss to describe just what it feels like, these people report the experience to be intensely pleasurable, similar in some respects to sexual orgasm.

The limbic system and hippocampus in particular play an important role in learning and memory, a finding demonstrated in patients with epilepsy. In an attempt to stop their seizures, such patients have had portions of the limbic system removed. One unintended consequence of the surgery is that individuals sometimes have difficulty learning and remembering new information. In one case, a patient who had undergone surgery was unable to remember where he lived, although he had resided at the same address for eight years. Further, even though the patient was able to carry on animated conversations, he was unable, a few minutes later, to recall what had been discussed (Milner, 1966; Rich & Shapiro, 2007).

The limbic system, then, is involved in several important functions, including self-preservation, learning, memory, and the experience of pleasure. These functions are hardly unique to humans; in fact, the limbic system is sometimes referred to as the "animal brain," because its structures and functions are so similar to those of other mammals. To identify the part of the brain that provides the complex and subtle capabilities that are uniquely human, we need to turn to another structure—the cerebral cortex.

The Cerebral Cortex: Our "New Brain"

As we have proceeded up the spinal cord and into the brain, our discussion has centered on areas of the brain that control functions similar to those found in less sophisticated organisms. But where, you may be asking, are the portions of the brain that enable humans to do what they do best and that distinguish humans from all other animals? Those unique features of the human brain—indeed, the very capabilities that allow you to come up with such a question in the first place—are embodied in the ability to think, evaluate, and make complex judgments. The principal location of these abilities, along with many others, is the **cerebral cortex**.

cerebral cortex The "new brain," responsible for the most sophisticated information processing in the brain; contains four lobes.

Frontal lobe
- Motor area
- Broca's area

Somatosensory area
Somatosensory association area
} **Parietal lobe**

Primary auditory area
Wernicke's area
Auditory association area
} **Temporal lobe**

Visual area
Visual association area
} **Occipital lobe**

FIGURE 5 The cerebral cortex of the brain. The major physical structures of the cerebral cortex are called lobes. This figure also illustrates the functions associated with particular areas of the cerebral cortex. Are any areas of the cerebral cortex present in nonhuman animals?

The cerebral cortex is referred to as the "new brain" because of its relatively recent evolution. It consists of a mass of deeply folded, rippled, convoluted tissue. Although only about $\frac{1}{12}$ of an inch thick, it would, if flattened out, cover an area more than 2 feet square. This configuration allows the surface area of the cortex to be considerably greater than it would be if it were smoother and more uniformly packed into the skull. The uneven shape also permits a high level of integration of neurons, allowing sophisticated information processing.

The cortex has four major sections called **lobes.** If we take a side view of the brain, the *frontal lobes* lie at the front center of the cortex and the *parietal lobes* lie behind them. The *temporal lobes* are found in the lower-center portion of the cortex, with the *occipital lobes* lying behind them. These four sets of lobes are physically separated by deep grooves called sulci. Figure 5 shows the four areas.

Another way to describe the brain is in terms of the functions associated with a particular area. Figure 5 also shows the specialized regions within the lobes related to specific functions and areas of the body. Three major areas are known: the motor areas, the sensory areas, and the association areas. Although we will discuss these areas as though they were separate and independent, keep in mind that this is an oversimplification. In most instances, behavior is influenced simultaneously by several structures and areas within the brain, operating interdependently. To give one example, people use different areas of the brain when they create sentences (a verbal task) compared with when they improvise musical tunes. Furthermore, when people suffer brain injury, uninjured portions of the brain can sometimes take over the functions that were previously handled by the damaged area. (Also see *PsychWork.*) In short, the brain is extraordinarily adaptable (Sacks, 2003; Boller, 2004; Brown, Martinez, & Parsons, 2006).

lobes The four major sections of the cerebral cortex: frontal, parietal, temporal, and occipital.

PsychWork

REHABILITATION COUNSELOR

Name: Monique J. Tremaine

Position: Rehabilitation Counselor

Education: BS in Psychology & Natural Sciences, Ball State University; MA in Clinical Psychology, California School of Professional Psychology; PhD in Clinical Neuropsychology, California School of Professional Psychology

Rehabilitation counselor Monique Tremaine helps individuals who have suffered severe brain injury regain as much normal functioning as possible. She does this by systematically assessing patients' problems, providing psychological and behavioral treatment, and ensuring that the treatment is state-of-the-art and is grounded in evidence gleaned from research.

According to Tremaine, her work requires an understanding of the structure of the brain and nervous system as well as expertise in clinical psychology in order to understand how brain injury effects emotion, function, and behavior.

"Sudden acquired or traumatic brain injury can impact many aspects of an individual's life, including their personality, cognition, sense of physical well-being, family roles, and occupational functioning," she noted. "It is my role to communicate such changes to a multidisciplinary staff, to the patient, and to the family to develop a comprehensive treatment plan."

THE MOTOR AREA OF THE CORTEX

motor area The part of the cortex that is largely responsible for the body's voluntary movement.

If you look at the frontal lobe in Figure 5, you will see a shaded portion labeled **motor area.** This part of the cortex is largely responsible for the body's voluntary movement. Every portion of the motor area corresponds to a specific locale within the body. If we were to insert an electrode into a particular part of the motor area of the cortex and apply mild electrical stimulation, there would be involuntary movement in the corresponding part of the body. If we moved to another part of the motor area and stimulated it, a different part of the body would move.

The motor area is so well mapped that researchers have identified the amount and relative location of cortical tissue used to produce movement in specific parts of the human body. For example, the control of movements that are relatively large scale and require little precision, such as the movement of a knee or a hip, is centered in a very small space in the motor area. In contrast, movements that must be precise and delicate, such as facial expressions and finger movements, are controlled by a considerably larger portion of the motor area (Schwenkreis et al., 2007).

In short, the motor area of the cortex provides a guide to the degree of complexity and the importance of the motor capabilities of specific parts of the body. In fact, it may do even more: Increasing evidence shows that not only does the motor cortex control different parts of the body, but it may also direct body parts into complex postures, such as the stance of a football center just before the ball is snapped to the quarterback or a swimmer standing at the edge of a diving board (Graziano, Taylor, & Moore, 2002; Dessing et al., 2005).

Ultimately, movement, like other behavior, is produced through the coordinated firing of a complex variety of neurons in the nervous system. The neurons that produce movement are linked in elaborate ways and work closely together.

THE SENSORY AREA OF THE CORTEX

sensory area The site in the brain of the tissue that corresponds to each of the senses, with the degree of sensitivity related to the amount of tissue.

Given the one-to-one correspondence between the motor area and body location, it is not surprising to find a similar relationship between specific portions of the cortex and the senses. The **sensory area** of the cortex includes three regions: one that corresponds primarily to body sensations (including touch and pressure), one relating to sight, and a third relating to sound. For instance, the *somatosensory area* in the parietal lobe encompasses specific locations associated with the ability to perceive touch and pressure in a particular area of the body. As with the motor area, the amount of brain tissue related to a particular location on the body determines the degree of sensitivity of that location: The greater the area devoted to a specific area of the body within the cortex, the more sensitive is that area of the body. As you can see from the weird-looking individual in Figure 6, parts such as the fingers are related to a larger portion of the somatosensory area and are the most sensitive.

The senses of sound and sight are also represented in specific areas of the cerebral cortex. An *auditory area* located in the temporal lobe is responsible for the sense of hearing. If the auditory area is stimulated electrically, a person will hear sounds such as clicks or hums. It also appears that particular locations within the auditory area respond to specific pitches (Hudspeth, 2000; Brown & Martinez, 2007; Hyde, Peretz, & Zatorre, 2008; Bizley et al., 2009).

The visual area in the cortex, located in the occipital lobe, responds in the same way to electrical stimulation. Stimulation by electrodes produces the experience of flashes of light or colors, suggesting that the raw sensory input of images from the eyes is received in this area of the brain and transformed into meaningful stimuli. The visual area provides another example of how areas of the brain are intimately related to specific areas of the body: Specific structures in the eye are related to a particular part of the cortex—with, as you might guess, more area of the brain given to the most sensitive portions of the retina (Wurtz & Kandel, 2000; Stenbacka & Vanni, 2007).

FIGURE 6 The greater the amount of tissue in the somatosensory area of the brain that is related to a specific body part, the more sensitive is that body part. If the size of our body parts reflected the corresponding amount of brain tissue, we would look like this strange creature.

THE ASSOCIATION AREAS OF THE CORTEX

In a freak accident in 1848, an explosion drove a 3-feet-long iron bar completely through the skull of railroad worker Phineas Gage, where it remained after the accident. Amazingly, Gage survived and, despite the rod lodged through his head, a few minutes later seemed to be fine.

But he wasn't. Before the accident, Gage was hard-working and cautious. Afterward, he became irresponsible, drank heavily, and drifted from one wild scheme to another. In the words of one of his physicians, "he was 'no longer Gage'" (Harlow, 1869, p. 14).

What had happened to the old Gage? Although there is no way of knowing for sure, we can speculate that the accident injured the region of Gage's cerebral cortex known as the **association areas**, which generally are considered to be the site of higher mental processes such as thinking, language, memory, and speech (Rowe et al., 2000).

The association areas make up a large portion of the cerebral cortex and consist of the sections that are not directly involved in either sensory processing or directing movement. The association areas control *executive functions*, which abilities are relating to planning, goal setting, judgment, and impulse control.

Much of our understanding of the association areas comes from patients who, like Phineas Gage, have suffered some type of brain injury. For example, when parts of the association areas are damaged, people undergo personality changes that affect their ability to make moral judgments and process emotions. At the same time, people with damage in those areas can still be capable of reasoning logically, performing calculations, and recalling information (Bechara et al., 1994).

Injuries to the association areas of the brain can produce *aphasia*, problems with language. In *Broca's aphasia*, speech becomes halting, laborious, and often ungrammatical, and a speaker is unable to find the right words. In contrast, *Wernicke's aphasia* produces difficulties both in understanding others' speech and in the production of language. The disorder is characterized by speech that sounds fluent but

association areas One of the major regions of the cerebral cortex; the site of the higher mental processes, such as thought, language, memory, and speech.

makes no sense, as in this example from a Wernicke's patient: "Boy, I'm sweating, I'm awful nervous, you know, once in a while I get caught up, I can't mention the tarripoi, a month ago, quite a little . . ." (Gardner, 1975: Kearns, 2005; Caplan, Waters, & Dede, 2007).

Neuroplasticity and the Brain

Shortly after he was born, Jacob Stark's arms and legs started jerking every 20 minutes. Weeks later he could not focus his eyes on his mother's face. The diagnosis: uncontrollable epileptic seizures involving his entire brain.

His mother, Sally Stark, recalled: "When Jacob was 2½ months old, they said he would never learn to sit up, would never be able to feed himself. . . . They told us to take him home, love him, and find an institution. (Blakeslee, 1992: C3)

Instead, Jacob had brain surgery when he was 5 months old in which physicians removed 20% of his brain. The operation was a complete success. Three years later Jacob seemed normal in every way, with no sign of seizures.

The surgery that helped Jacob was based on the premise that the diseased part of his brain was producing seizures throughout the brain. Surgeons reasoned that if they removed the misfiring portion, the remaining parts of the brain, which appeared intact in PET scans, would take over. They correctly bet that Jacob could still lead a normal life after surgery, particularly because the surgery was being done at so young an age.

The success of Jacob's surgery illustrates that the brain has the ability to shift functions to different locations after injury to a specific area or in cases of surgery. But equally encouraging are some new findings about the *regenerative* powers of the brain and nervous system.

Scientists have learned in recent years that the brain continually reorganizes itself in a process termed **neuroplasticity.** Although for many years conventional wisdom held that no new brain cells are created after childhood, new research finds otherwise. Not only do the interconnections between neurons become more complex throughout life, but it now appears that new neurons are also created in certain areas of the brain during adulthood—a process called **neurogenesis.** Each day, thousands of new neurons are created, especially in areas of the brain related to learning and memory (Jang, You, & Ahn, 2007; Poo & Isaacson, 2007; Shors, 2009).

The ability of neurons to renew themselves during adulthood has significant implications for the potential treatment of disorders of the nervous system (see Figure 7). For example, drugs that trigger the development of new neurons might be used to counter such diseases as Alzheimer's, which are produced when neurons die (Tsai, Tsai, & Shen, 2007; Eisch et al., 2008; Waddell & Shors, 2008).

Furthermore, specific experiences can modify the way in which information is processed. For example, if you learn to read Braille, the amount of tissue in your cortex related to sensation in the fingertips will expand. Similarly, if you take up the violin, the area of the brain that receives messages from your fingers will grow—but only relating to the fingers that actually move across the violin's strings (Kolb, Gibb, & Robinson, 2003; Schwartz & Begley, 2002).

The future also holds promise for people who suffer from the tremors and loss of motor control produced by Parkinson's disease, although the research is mired in controversy. Because Parkinson's disease is caused by a gradual loss of cells that stimulate the production of dopamine in the brain, many investigators have reasoned that a procedure that would increase the supply of dopamine might be effective. They seem to be on the right track. When stem cells—immature cells from human fetuses that have the potential to develop into a variety of specialized cell types, depending on where they are implanted—are injected directly into the brains of Parkinson's sufferers, they take root and stimulate dopamine production. Preliminary

neuroplasticity Changes in the brain that occur throughout the life span relating to the addition of new neurons, new interconnections between neurons, and the reorganization of information-processing areas.

neurogenesis The creation of new neurons.

Study Alert

Remember that *neuroplasticity* is the reorganization of existing neuronal connections, whereas *neurogenesis* is the creation of new neurons.

Neuroscience in Your Life: The Plastic Brain

FIGURE 7 The brain is incredibly plastic, meaning that it can change structurally (through changing connections between neurons) and chemically (through changing levels of neurotransmitters and hormones) throughout our lifetime. This plasticity can also be used to adapt to new situations. For example, it can reorganize how it represents the motor system when limbs are lost. (a) Here we see how the brain learns to respond and control a new artificial robotic hand. In the brain scans in (b) and (c), we see the areas responsible for hand movement. They appear in red and yellow. The first scan (b) shows the activation in the motor and parietal cortex before the person has used the robotic hand. The second scan (c) shows greater activation after the person has used it for a month, demonstrating the brain's ability to alter its functioning to better utilize the new prosthetic hand. (Source: Kato et al., 2009.)

(a)

(b)   (c)

results have been promising, with some patients showing great improvement (Korecka, Verhaagen, & Hol, 2007; Parish & Arenas, 2007; Newman & Bakay, 2008).

Stem cells thus hold great promise. When a stem cell divides, each newly created cell has the potential to be transformed into more specialized cells that have the potential to repair damaged cells. Because many of the most disabling diseases, ranging from cancer to stroke, result from cell damage, the potential of stem cells to revolutionize medicine is significant.

However, because the source of implanted stem cells typically is aborted fetuses, their use is controversial. Some critics have argued that the use of stem cells in research and treatment should be prohibited, while supporters argue that the potential benefits of the research are so great that stem cell research should be unrestricted. The issue has been politicized, and the question of whether and how stem cell research should be regulated is not clear (Rosen, 2005; Giacomini, Baylis, & Robert, 2007; Holden, 2007).

The Specialization of the Hemispheres: Two Brains or One?

The most recent development, at least in evolutionary terms, in the organization and operation of the human brain probably occurred in the last several million years: a specialization of the functions controlled by the left and right sides of the brain (Hopkins & Cantalupo, 2008; MacNeilage, Rogers, & Vallortigara, 2009; Tommasi, 2009).

The brain is divided into two roughly mirror-image halves. Just as we have two arms, two legs, and two lungs, we have a left brain and a right brain. Because of the way nerves in the brain are connected to the rest of the body, these symmetrical left and right halves, called **hemispheres,** control motion in—and receive sensation

hemispheres Symmetrical left and right halves of the brain that control the side of the body opposite to their location.

from—the side of the body opposite their location. The left hemisphere of the brain, then, generally controls the right side of the body, and the right hemisphere controls the left side of the body. Thus, damage to the right side of the brain is typically indicated by functional difficulties in the left side of the body.

Despite the appearance of similarity between the two hemispheres of the brain, they are somewhat different in the functions they control and in the ways they control them. Certain behaviors are more likely to reflect activity in one hemisphere than in the other, or are **lateralized.**

For example, for most people, language processing occurs more in the left side of the brain. In general, the left hemisphere concentrates more on tasks that require verbal competence, such as speaking, reading, thinking, and reasoning. In addition, the left hemisphere tends to process information sequentially, one bit at a time (Turkewitz, 1993; Banich & Heller, 1998; Hines, 2004).

The right hemisphere has its own strengths, particularly in nonverbal areas such as the understanding of spatial relationships, recognition of patterns and drawings, music, and emotional expression. The right hemisphere tends to process information globally, considering it as a whole (Ansaldo, Arguin, & Roch-Locours, 2002; Holowka & Petitto, 2002).

Keep in mind that the differences in specialization between the hemispheres are not great, and the degree and nature of lateralization vary from one person to another. If, like most people, you are right-handed, the control of language is probably concentrated more in your left hemisphere. By contrast, if you are among the 10% of people who are left-handed or are ambidextrous (you use both hands interchangeably), it is much more likely that the language centers of your brain are located more in the right hemisphere or are divided equally between the left and right hemispheres.

Furthermore, the two hemispheres of the brain function in tandem. It is a mistake to think of particular kinds of information as being processed solely in the right or the left hemisphere. The hemispheres work interdependently in deciphering, interpreting, and reacting to the world.

In addition, people who suffer injury to the left side of the brain and lose linguistic capabilities often recover the ability to speak: The right side of the brain often takes over some of the functions of the left side, especially in young children; the extent of recovery increases the earlier the injury occurs (Gould et al., 1999; Kempermann & Gage, 1999; Johnston, 2004).

Researchers also have unearthed evidence that there may be subtle differences in brain lateralization patterns between males and females and members of different cultures, as we see next.

lateralization The dominance of one hemisphere of the brain in specific functions, such as language.

Study Alert

Although the hemispheres of the brain specialize in particular kinds of functions, the degree of specialization is not great, and the two hemispheres work interdependently.

Exploring DIVERSITY
Human Diversity and the Brain

The interplay of biology and environment in behavior is especially clear when we consider evidence suggesting that even in brain structure and function there are both sex and cultural differences. Let's consider sex differences first. Accumulating evidence seems to show intriguing differences in males' and females' brain lateralization and weight (Kosslyn et al., 2002; Boles, 2005; Clements, Rimvodt, & Abel, 2006).

For instance, most males tend to show greater lateralization of language in the left hemisphere. For them, language is clearly relegated largely to the left side of the brain. In contrast, women display less lateralization, with language abilities apt to be more evenly divided between the two hemispheres. Such differences in brain lateralization may account, in part, for the superiority often displayed by females on certain measures of verbal skills, such as the onset and fluency of speech (Frings et al., 2006; Petersson et al., 2007).

Other research suggests that men's brains are somewhat bigger than women's brains even after taking differences in body size into account. In contrast, part of the *corpus callosum*, a bundle of fibers that connects the hemispheres of the brain, is proportionally larger in women than in men (Cahill, 2005; Luders et al., 2006; Smith et al., 2007).

Men and women also may process information differently. For example, in one study, fMRI brain scans of men making judgments discriminating real from false words showed activation of the left hemisphere of the brain, whereas women used areas on both sides of the brain (Rossell et al., 2002).

The meaning of such sex differences is far from clear. Consider one possibility related to differences in the proportional size of the corpus callosum. Its greater size in women may permit stronger connections to develop between the parts of the brain that control speech. In turn, this would explain why speech tends to emerge slightly earlier in girls than in boys.

Before we rush to such a conclusion, though, we must consider an alternative hypothesis: The reason verbal abilities emerge earlier in girls may be that infant girls receive greater encouragement to talk than do infant boys. In turn, this greater early experience may foster the growth of certain parts of the brain. Hence, physical brain differences may be a *reflection* of social and environmental influences rather than a *cause* of the differences in men's and women's behavior. At this point, it is impossible to know which of these alternative hypotheses is correct.

Culture also gives rise to differences in brain lateralization. Native speakers of Japanese seem to process information regarding vowel sounds primarily in the brain's left hemisphere. In contrast, North and South Americans, Europeans, and individuals of Japanese ancestry who learn Japanese later in life handle vowel sounds principally in the right hemisphere. One explanation for this difference is that certain characteristics of the Japanese language, such as the ability to express complex ideas by using only vowel sounds, result in the development of a specific type of brain lateralization in native speakers (Tsunoda, 1985; Kess & Miyamoto, 1994; Lin et al., 2005).

The Split Brain: Exploring the Two Hemispheres

The patient, V. J., had suffered severe seizures. By cutting her corpus callosum, the fibrous portion of the brain that carries messages between the hemispheres, surgeons hoped to create a firebreak to prevent the seizures from spreading. The operation did decrease the frequency and severity of V. J.'s attacks. But V. J. developed an unexpected side effect: She lost the ability to write at will, although she could read and spell words aloud. (Strauss, 1998, p. 287)

People like V. J., whose corpus callosum has been surgically cut to stop seizures and who are called *split-brain patients*, offer a rare opportunity for researchers investigating the independent functioning of the two hemispheres of the brain. For example, psychologist Roger Sperry—who won the Nobel Prize for his work—developed a number of ingenious techniques for studying how each hemisphere operates (Sperry, 1982; Gazzaniga, 1998; Savazzi et al., 2007).

In one experimental procedure, blindfolded patients touched an object with their right hand and were asked to name it (see Figure 8). Because the right side of the body corresponds to the language-oriented left side of the brain, split-brain patients were able to name it. However, if blindfolded patients touched the object with their left hand, they were unable to name it aloud, even though the information had registered in their brains: When the blindfold was removed, patients could identify the object they had touched. Information can be learned and remembered, then, using only the right side of the brain. (By the way, unless you've had split-brain surgery, this experiment won't work with you, because the bundle of fibers connecting the two hemispheres of a normal brain immediately transfers the information from one hemisphere to the other.)

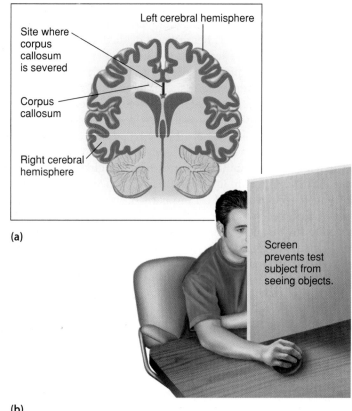

(a)

(b)

FIGURE 8 Hemispheres of the brain. (a) The corpus callosum connects the cerebral hemispheres of the brain as shown in this cross-section. (b) A split-brain patient is tested by touching objects behind a screen. Patients could name objects when they touched it with their right hand, but couldn't if they touched with their left hand. If a split-brain patient with her eyes closed was given a pencil to hold and called it a pencil, what hand was the pencil in? (Source: Brooker et al., 2008, p. 943.)

It is clear from experiments like this one that the right and left hemispheres of the brain specialize in handling different sorts of information. At the same time, it is important to realize that both hemispheres are capable of understanding, knowing, and being aware of the world, in somewhat different ways. The two hemispheres, then, should be regarded as different in terms of the efficiency with which they process certain kinds of information, rather than as two entirely separate brains. The hemispheres work interdependently to allow the full range and richness of thought of which humans are capable.

BECOMING AN INFORMED CONSUMER

of Psychology

Learning to Control Your Heart —and Mind—Through Biofeedback

When Tammy DeMichael was involved in a horrific car accident that broke her neck and crushed her spinal cord, experts told her that she was doomed to be a quadriplegic for the rest of her life, unable to move from the neck down. But they were wrong. Not only did she regain the use of her arms, but she was able to walk 60 feet with a cane (Hess, Houg, & Tammaro, 2007 Morrow & Wolf, 1991).

The key to DeMichael's astounding recovery: biofeedback. **Biofeedback** is a procedure in which a person learns to control through conscious thought internal physiological processes such as blood pressure, heart and respiration rate, skin temperature, sweating, and the constriction of particular muscles. Although it traditionally had been thought that the heart rate, respiration rate, blood pressure, and other bodily functions are under the control of parts of the brain over which we have no influence, psychologists have discovered that these responses are actually susceptible to voluntary control (Nagai et al., 2004; Cho, Holyoak, & Cannon, 2007).

In biofeedback, a person is hooked up to electronic devices that provide continuous feedback relating to the physiological response in question. For instance, a person interested in controlling headaches through biofeedback might have electronic sensors placed on certain muscles on her head and learn to control the constriction and relaxation of those muscles. Later, when she felt a headache starting, she could relax the relevant muscles and abort the pain (Andrasik, 2007; Nestoriuc et al., 2008).

In DeMichael's case, biofeedback was effective because not all of the nervous system's connections between the brain and her legs were severed. Through biofeedback, she learned how to send messages to specific muscles, "ordering" them to move. Although it took more than a year, DeMichael was successful in restoring a large degree of her mobility.

Although the control of physiological processes through the use of biofeedback is not easy to learn, it has been employed with success in a variety of ailments, including emotional problems (such as anxiety, depression, phobias, tension headaches, insomnia, and hyperactivity), physical illnesses with a psychological component (such as asthma, high blood pressure, ulcers, muscle spasms, and migraine headaches), and physical problems (such as DeMichael's injuries, strokes, cerebral palsy, and curvature of the spine) (Cho, Holyoak, & Cannon, 2007; Morone & Greco, 2007; Reiner, 2008).

biofeedback A procedure in which a person learns to control through conscious thought internal physiological processes such as blood pressure, heart and respiration rate, skin temperature, sweating, and the constriction of particular muscles.

RECAP/EVALUATE/RETHINK

RECAP

How do researchers identify the major parts and functions of the brain?
- Brain scans take a "snapshot" of the internal workings of the brain without having to cut surgically into a person's skull. Major brain-scanning techniques include the electroencephalogram (EEG), positron emission tomography (PET), functional magnetic resonance imaging (fMRI), and transcranial magnetic stimulation imaging (TMS). (p. 69)

What are the major parts of the brain, and for what behaviors is each part responsible?
- The central core of the brain is made up of the medulla (which controls functions such as breathing and the heartbeat), the pons (which coordinates the muscles and the two sides of the body), the cerebellum (which controls balance), the reticular formation (which acts to heighten awareness in emergencies), the thalamus (which communicates sensory messages to and from the brain), and the hypothalamus (which maintains homeo-

stasis, or body equilibrium, and regulates behavior related to basic survival). The functions of the central core structures are similar to those found in other vertebrates. This central core is sometimes referred to as the "old brain." (p. 71)
- The cerebral cortex—the "new brain"—has areas that control voluntary movement (the motor area); the senses (the sensory area); and thinking, reasoning, speech, and memory (the association areas). The limbic system, found on the border of the "old" and "new" brains, is associated with eating, aggression, reproduction, and the experiences of pleasure and pain. (p. 74)

How do the two halves of the brain operate interdependently?
- The brain is divided into left and right halves, or hemispheres, each of which generally controls the opposite side of the body. Each hemisphere can be thought of as being specialized in the functions it carries out: The left specializes in verbal tasks, such as logical reasoning, speaking, and reading; the right specializes in nonverbal tasks, such as spatial perception, pattern recognition, and emotional expression. (p. 79)

How can an understanding of the nervous system help us to find ways to alleviate disease and pain?

- Biofeedback is a procedure by which a person learns to control internal physiological processes. By controlling involuntary responses, people are able to relieve anxiety, tension, migraine headaches, and a wide range of other psychological and physical problems. (p. 82)

EVALUATE

1. Match the name of each brain scan with the appropriate description:

   a. EEG
   b. fMRI
   c. PET

   1. By locating radiation within the brain, a computer can provide a striking picture of brain activity.
   2. Electrodes placed around the skull record the electrical signals transmitted through the brain.
   3. This technique provides a three-dimensional view of the brain by aiming a magnetic field at the body.

2. Match the portion of the brain with its function:

   a. medulla
   b. pons
   c. cerebellum
   d. reticular formation

   1. Maintains breathing and heartbeat.
   2. Controls bodily balance.
   3. Coordinates and integrates muscle movements.
   4. Activates other parts of the brain to produce general bodily arousal.

3. A surgeon places an electrode on a portion of your brain and stimulates it. Immediately, your right wrist involuntarily twitches. The doctor has most likely stimulated a portion of the _____ area of your brain.
4. Each hemisphere controls the _____ side of the body.
5. Nonverbal realms, such as emotions and music, are controlled primarily by the _____ hemisphere of the brain, whereas the _____ hemisphere is more responsible for speaking and reading.

RETHINK

1. Before sophisticated brain-scanning techniques were developed, behavioral neuroscientists' understanding of the brain was based largely on the brains of people who had died. What limitations would this pose, and in what areas would you expect the most significant advances once brain-scanning techniques became possible?
2. Could personal differences in people's specialization of right and left hemispheres be related to occupational success? For example, might an architect who relies on spatial skills have a pattern of hemispheric specialization different from that of a writer?
3. *From the perspective of an educator:* How might you use different techniques to teach reading to boys and girls based on the brain evidence?

Answers to Evaluate Questions

1. a-2, b-3, c-1; 2. a-1, b-3, c-2, d-4; 3. motor; 4. opposite; 5. right, left

KEY TERMS

central core p. 71
cerebellum
   (ser-uh-BELL-um) p. 71
reticular formation p. 71
thalamus p. 73

hypothalamus p. 73
limbic system p. 73
cerebral cortex p. 74
lobes p. 75

motor area p. 76
sensory area p. 76
association areas p. 77
neuroplasticity p. 78

neurogenesis p. 78
hemispheres p. 79
lateralization p. 80
biofeedback p. 83

Key Concepts for Chapter 3

Prologue *Never Forgetting a Face*

She never forgets a face. Literally.

For a woman known as C. S., remembering people is not a problem. In fact, she—like a very few other individuals—can remember faces of people she met years ago, sometimes only in passing. These "super-recognizers," as they are called, excel at recalling faces.

One super-recognizer said she had identified another woman on the street who served her as a waitress five years earlier in a different city. Critically, she was able to confirm that the other woman had, in fact, been a waitress in the different city. Often, super-recognizers are able to recognize another person despite significant changes in appearance, such as aging or a different hair color.

But being a super-recognizer is a mixed blessing. As one woman with this ability says, "It doesn't matter how many years pass, if I've seen your face before I will be able to recall it." In fact, she sometimes pretends she doesn't remember a person, "because it seems like I stalk them, or that they mean more to me than they do when I recall that we saw each other once walking on campus four years ago in front of the quad!" (Munger, 2009; Russell, Duchaine, & Nakayma, 2009)

Looking Ahead

Most of us are reasonably good at recognizing people's faces, thanks in part to regions of the brain that specialize in detecting facial patterns. Super-recognizers represent a small minority of people who happen to be exceptionally good at facial recognition. At the other extreme are people with "faceblindness," a rare disorder that makes it extremely difficult for them to recognize faces at all—even those of friends and family.

Disorders such as super-recognition and faceblindness illustrate how much we depend on our senses to function normally. Our senses offer a window to the world, not only providing us with an awareness, understanding, and appreciation of the world's beauty, but alerting us to its dangers. Our senses enable us to feel the gentlest of breezes, see flickering lights miles away, and hear the soft murmuring of distant songbirds.

In the next four modules, we focus on the field of psychology that is concerned with the ways our bodies take in information through the senses and the ways we interpret that information. We explore both sensation and perception. *Sensation* encompasses the processes by which our sense organs receive information from the environment. *Perception* is the brain's and the sense organs' sorting out, interpretation, analysis, and integration of stimuli.

Although perception clearly represents a step beyond sensation, in practice it is sometimes difficult to find the precise boundary between the two. Indeed, psychologists—and philosophers as well—have argued for years over the distinction. The primary difference is that sensation can be thought of as an organism's first encounter with a raw sensory stimulus, whereas perception is the process by which it interprets, analyzes, and integrates that stimulus with other sensory information.

For example, if we were considering sensation, we might ask about the loudness of a ringing fire alarm. If we were considering perception, we might ask whether someone recognizes the ringing sound as an alarm and identifies its meaning.

To a psychologist interested in understanding the causes of behavior, sensation and perception are fundamental topics, because so much of our behavior is a reflection of how we react to and interpret stimuli from the world around us. The areas of sensation and perception deal with a wide range of questions—among them, how we respond to the characteristics of physical stimuli; what processes enable us to see, hear, and experience pain; why visual illusions fool us; and how we distinguish one person from another. As we explore these issues, we'll see how the senses work together to provide us with an integrated view and understanding of the world.

Sensing the World Around Us

As Isabel sat down to Thanksgiving dinner, her father carried the turkey in on a tray and placed it squarely in the center of the table. The noise level, already high from the talking and laughter of family members, grew louder still. As Isabel picked up her fork, the smell of the turkey reached her and she felt her stomach growl hungrily. The sight and sound of her family around the table, along with the smells and tastes of the holiday meal, made Isabel feel more relaxed than she had since starting school in the fall.

Put yourself in this setting and consider how different it might be if any one of your senses were not functioning. What if you were blind and unable to see the faces of your family members or the welcome shape of the golden-brown turkey? What if you had no sense of hearing and could not listen to the conversations of family members or were unable to feel your stomach growl, smell the dinner, or taste the food? Clearly, you would experience the dinner very differently from someone whose sensory apparatus was intact.

Moreover, the sensations mentioned above barely scratch the surface of sensory experience. Although perhaps you were taught, as I was, that there are just five senses—sight, sound, taste, smell, and touch—that enumeration is too modest. Human sensory capabilities go well beyond the basic five senses. For example, we are sensitive not merely to touch but to a considerably wider set of stimuli—pain, pressure, temperature, and vibration, to name a few. In addition, vision has two subsystems—relating to day and night vision—and the ear is responsive to information that allows us not only to hear but also to keep our balance.

To consider how psychologists understand the senses and, more broadly, sensation and perception, we first need a basic working vocabulary. In formal terms, **sensation** is the activation of the sense organs by a source of physical energy. **Perception** is the sorting out, interpretation, analysis, and integration of stimuli carried out by the sense organs and brain. A **stimulus** is any passing source of physical energy that produces a response in a sense organ.

Stimuli vary in both type and intensity. Different types of stimuli activate different sense organs. For instance, we can differentiate light stimuli (which activate the sense of sight and allow us to see the colors of a tree in autumn) from sound stimuli (which, through the sense of hearing, permit us to hear the sounds of an orchestra). In addition, stimuli differ in intensity, relating to how strong a stimulus needs to be before it can be detected.

Questions of stimulus type and intensity are considered in a branch of psychology known as psychophysics. **Psychophysics** is the study of the relationship between the physical aspects of stimuli and our psychological experience of them. Psychophysics played a central role in the development of the field of psychology. Many of the first psychologists studied issues related to psychophysics, and there is still an active group of psychophysics researchers (Chechile, 2003; Gardner, 2005; Hock & Ploeger, 2006).

Key Concepts

What is sensation, and how do psychologists study it?

What is the relationship between a physical stimulus and the kinds of sensory responses that result from it?

Study Alert

Remember that *sensation* refers to the activation of the sense organs (a physical response), whereas *perception* refers to how stimuli are interpreted (a psychological response).

sensation The activation of the sense organs by a source of physical energy.

perception The sorting out, interpretation, analysis, and integration of stimuli by the sense organs and brain.

stimulus Energy that produces a response in a sense organ.

psychophysics The study of the relationship between the physical aspects of stimuli and our psychological experience of them.

Crowded conditions, sounds, and sights can all be considered as noise that interferes with sensation. Can you think of other examples of noise that is not auditory in nature?

absolute threshold The smallest intensity of a stimulus that must be present for the stimulus to be detected.

Absolute Thresholds: Detecting What's Out There

Just when does a stimulus become strong enough to be detected by our sense organs? The answer to this question requires an understanding of the concept of absolute threshold. An **absolute threshold** is the smallest intensity of a stimulus that must be present for it to be detected (Aazh & Moore, 2007).

Despite the "absolute" in absolute threshold, things are not so cut and dried. As the strength of a stimulus increases, the likelihood that it will be detected increases gradually. Technically, then, an absolute threshold is the stimulus intensity that is detected 50% of the time.

It often takes a very small stimulus to produce a response in our senses. For example, the sense of touch is so sensitive that we can feel a bee's wing falling on our cheeks when it is dropped from a distance of 1 centimeter. Test your knowledge of the absolute thresholds of other senses by completing the questionnaire in Figure 1.

In fact, our senses are so fine-tuned that we might have problems if they were any more sensitive. For instance, if our ears were slightly more acute, we would be able to hear the sound of air molecules in our ears knocking into the eardrum—a phenomenon that would surely prove distracting and might even prevent us from hearing sounds outside our bodies.

Of course, the absolute thresholds we have been discussing are measured under ideal conditions. Normally our senses cannot detect stimulation quite as well because of the presence of noise. *Noise,* as defined by psychophysicists, is background stimulation that interferes with the perception of other stimuli. Hence, noise refers not just to auditory stimuli, as the word suggests, but also to unwanted stimuli that interfere with other senses.

For example, picture a talkative group of people crammed into a small, crowded, smoke-filled room at a party. The din of the crowd makes it hard to hear individual voices, and the smoke makes it difficult to see, or even taste, the food. In this case, the smoke and the crowded conditions would both be considered "noise," because

FIGURE 1 This test can shed some light on how sensitive the human senses are. (Source: Galanter, 1962.)

How Sensitive Are You?

To test your awareness of the capabilities of your senses, answer the following questions:

1. How far can a candle flame be seen on a clear, dark night:
   a. From a distance of 10 miles _____
   b. From a distance of 30 miles _____
2. How far can the ticking of a watch be heard under quiet conditions?
   a. From 5 feet away _____
   b. From 20 feet away _____
3. How much sugar is needed to allow it to be detected when dissolved in 2 gallons of water?
   a. 2 tablespoons _____
   b. 1 teaspoon _____
4. Over what area can a drop of perfume be detected?
   a. A 5-foot by 5-foot area _____
   b. A 3-room apartment _____

Scoring: In each case, the answer is b, illustrating the tremendous sensitivity of our senses.

Driven to Distraction

Twenty-four year old Aiden Quinn couldn't believe his good fortune. At his young age, he had beaten the competition to land his dream job of conducting trolleys through the streets of Boston. But in just one moment his world came crashing down around him: It was the moment when he took his eyes off the tracks to send a text message to his girlfriend and the trolley he was driving crashed into the one ahead of it.

Increasing research shows that texting while driving is extremely dangerous.

If you've ever texted while driving, you're not alone. A recent survey conducted by the AAA Foundation for Traffic Safety shows that nearly half of drivers aged 18 to 24 admit to doing so, even though the majority of them were aware that they were increasing their risk of having an accident. In fact, nearly 90% of survey respondents rated texting while driving as a very serious threat to safety (AAA Foundation for Traffic Safety, 2008, 2009).

Researchers are now confirming what intuition suggests is true: The distraction caused by texting while driving is extremely dangerous. One study used video cameras to monitor truckers on long hauls and found that they were 23 times more likely to be in a collision while texting than while not texting. In collisions caused by texting, the driver had typically taken his eyes off the road for about 5 seconds—a

seemingly short period of time until you realize that a vehicle at highway speed travels about 150 yards in those few seconds (Virginia Tech Transportation Institute, 2009).

Another study using college students and a driving simulator showed that texting produced the same duration of about 5 seconds of distraction and that the students were 8 times more likely to have a collision while texting. Although those may seem like better odds, they're still

much worse than the risk presented by other distractors such as changing the station on a car's radio. Even though the study used students, who are likely skillful at texting and multitasking, and light vehicles that are more maneuverable than trucks, the results clearly show that texting while driving poses a terrific risk (Cooper & Strayer, 2008).

Multitasking in general is difficult. For instance, in one study, researchers divided a group of college students into two groups, one composed of students who multitasked online regularly and a second that did not. The frequent multitaskers were more easily distracted, and they were unable to filter out stimuli that were irrelevant to tasks that they were trying to complete (Ophir, Nass, & Wagner, 2009)

If you, like many of the respondents to the AAA Foundation for Traffic Safety survey, believe that you're the exception to the rule, just keep one thing in mind: that's what Aiden Quinn thought, too. He lost his job and is facing civil lawsuits and criminal prosecution.

RETHINK

- Most people assume that they are able to text and drive at the same time without declines in their driving ability. Why do you think that is the case, and how accurate is their assumption?
- Why would frequent multitaskers be more distractible than those who multitask less frequently?

they are preventing sensation at more discriminating levels. Similarly, we have limited ability to concentrate on several stimuli simultaneously, as we discuss in *Applying Psychology in the 21st Century*.

Difference Thresholds: Noticing Distinctions Between Stimuli

Suppose you wanted to choose the six best apples from a supermarket display—the biggest, reddest, and sweetest apples. One approach would be to compare one apple with another systematically until you were left with a few so similar that you could not tell the difference between them. At that point, it wouldn't matter which ones you chose.

Psychologists have discussed this comparison problem in terms of the **difference threshold,** the smallest level of added (or reduced) stimulation required to sense that

difference threshold (just noticeable difference) The smallest level of added or reduced stimulation required to sense that a change in stimulation has occurred.

a *change* in stimulation has occurred. Thus, the difference threshold is the minimum change in stimulation required to detect the difference between two stimuli, and so it also is called a **just noticeable difference** (Nittrouer & Lowenstein, 2007).

The size of a stimulus that constitutes a just noticeable difference depends on the initial intensity of the stimulus. The relationship between changes in the original size of a stimulus and the degree to which a change will be noticed forms one of the basic laws of psychophysics: Weber's law. **Weber's law** (*Weber* is pronounced "VAY-ber") states that a just noticeable difference is a *constant proportion* of the intensity of an initial stimulus (rather than a constant amount).

For example, Weber found that the just noticeable difference for weight is 1:50. Consequently, it takes a 1-ounce increase in a 50-ounce weight to produce a noticeable difference, and it would take a 10-ounce increase to produce a noticeable difference if the initial weight were 500 ounces. In both cases, the same proportional increase is necessary to produce a just noticeable difference—1:5 = 10:500. Similarly, the just noticeable difference distinguishing changes in loudness between sounds is larger for sounds that are initially loud than it is for sounds that are initially soft, but the *proportional* increase remains the same.

Weber's law helps explain why a person in a quiet room is more startled by the ringing of a telephone than is a person in an already noisy room. To produce the same amount of reaction in a noisy room, a telephone ring might have to approximate the loudness of cathedral bells. Similarly, when the moon is visible during the late afternoon, it appears relatively dim—yet against a dark night sky, it seems quite bright.

Weber's law A basic law of psychophysics stating that a just noticeable difference is a constant proportion to the intensity of an initial stimulus (rather than a constant amount).

Study Alert

Remember that Weber's law holds for every type of sensory stimuli: vision, sound, taste, and so on.

Sensory Adaptation: Turning Down Our Responses

You enter a movie theater, and the smell of popcorn is everywhere. A few minutes later, though, you barely notice the smell. The reason you become accustomed to the odor is sensory adaptation. **Adaptation** is an adjustment in sensory capacity after prolonged exposure to unchanging stimuli. Adaptation occurs as people become accustomed to a stimulus and change their frame of reference. In a sense, our brain mentally turns down the volume of the stimulation that it's experiencing (Calin-Jageman & Fischer, 2007).

One example of adaptation is the decrease in sensitivity that occurs after repeated exposure to a strong stimulus. If you were to hear a loud tone over and over again, eventually it would begin to sound softer. Similarly, although jumping into a cold lake may be temporarily unpleasant, eventually you probably will get used to the temperature.

This apparent decline in sensitivity to sensory stimuli is due to the inability of the sensory nerve receptors to fire off messages to the brain indefinitely. Because these receptor cells are most responsive to *changes* in stimulation, constant stimulation is not effective in producing a sustained reaction (Wark, Lundstrom, & Fairhall, 2007).

Judgments of sensory stimuli are also affected by the context in which the judgments are made. This is the case because judgments are made not in isolation from other stimuli but in terms of preceding sensory experience. You can demonstrate this for yourself by trying a simple experiment:

Take two envelopes, one large and one small, and put 15 nickels in each one. Now lift the large envelope, put it down, and lift the small one. Which seems to weigh more? Most people report that the small one is heavier, although, as you know, the weights are nearly identical. The reason for this misconception is that the visual context of the envelope interferes with the sensory experience of weight. Adaptation to the context of one stimulus (the size of the envelope) alters responses to another stimulus (the weight of the envelope) (Coren, 2004).

adaptation An adjustment in sensory capacity after prolonged exposure to unchanging stimuli.

RECAP/EVALUATE/RETHINK

RECAP

What is sensation, and how do psychologists study it?

- Sensation is the activation of the sense organs by any source of physical energy. In contrast, perception is the process by which we sort out, interpret, analyze, and integrate stimuli to which our senses are exposed. (p. 89)

What is the relationship between a physical stimulus and the kinds of sensory responses that result from it?

- Psychophysics studies the relationship between the physical nature of stimuli and the sensory responses they evoke. (p. 89)
- The absolute threshold is the smallest amount of physical intensity at which a stimulus can be detected. Under ideal conditions absolute thresholds are extraordinarily sensitive, but the presence of noise (background stimuli that interfere with other stimuli) reduces detection capabilities. (p. 90)
- The difference threshold, or just noticeable difference, is the smallest change in the level of stimulation required to sense that a change has occurred. According to Weber's law, a just noticeable difference is a constant proportion of the intensity of an initial stimulus. (p. 91)
- Sensory adaptation occurs when we become accustomed to a constant stimulus and change our evaluation of it. Repeated exposure to a stimulus results in an apparent decline in sensitivity to it. (p. 92)

EVALUATE

1. _____ is the stimulation of the sense organs; _____ is the sorting out, interpretation, analysis, and integration of stimuli by the sense organs and the brain.
2. The term *absolute threshold* refers to the _____ intensity of a stimulus that must be present for the stimulus to be detected.
3. Weber discovered that for a difference between two stimuli to be perceptible, the stimuli must differ by at least a _____ proportion.
4. After completing a very difficult rock climb in the morning, Carmella found the afternoon climb unexpectedly easy. This example illustrates the phenomenon of _____.

RETHINK

1. Do you think it is possible to have sensation without perception? Is it possible to have perception without sensation?
2. *From the perspective of a manufacturer:* How might you need to take psychophysics into account when developing new products or modifying existing ones?

Answers to Evaluate Questions

1. Sensation; perception; 2. smallest; 3. constant; 4. adaptation

KEY TERMS

sensation p. 89
perception p. 89
stimulus p. 89
psychophysics p. 89

absolute threshold p. 90
difference threshold (just
   noticeable difference) p. 91

Weber's law p. 92
adaptation p. 92

Vision: Shedding Light on the Eye

Key Concepts

What basic processes underlie the sense of vision?

How do we see colors?

If, as poets say, the eyes provide a window to the soul, they also provide us with a window to the world. Our visual capabilities permit us to admire and to react to scenes ranging from the beauty of a sunset, to the configuration of a lover's face, to the words written on the pages of a book.

Vision starts with light, the physical energy that stimulates the eye. Light is a form of electromagnetic radiation waves, which, as shown in Figure 1, are measured in wavelengths. The sizes of wavelengths correspond to different types of energy. The range of wavelengths that humans are sensitive to—called the *visual spectrum*—is relatively small. Many nonhuman species have different capabilities. For instance, some reptiles and fish sense energies of longer wavelengths than humans do, and certain insects sense energies of shorter wavelengths than humans do. For example, bees are attracted to flowers that reflect ultraviolet rays that humans can't detect.

Light waves coming from some object outside the body (such as the tree in Figure 2) are sensed by the only organ that is capable of responding to the visible spectrum: the eye. Our eyes convert light to a form that can be used by the neurons that serve as messengers to the brain. The neurons themselves take up a relatively small percentage of the total eye. Most of the eye is a mechanical device that is similar in many respects to a nonelectronic camera that uses film, as you can see in Figure 2.

Despite the similarities between the eye and a camera, vision involves processes that are far more complex and sophisticated than those of any camera. Furthermore, once an image reaches the neuronal receptors of the eye, the eye/camera analogy ends, for the processing of the visual image in the brain is more reflective of a computer than it is of a camera.

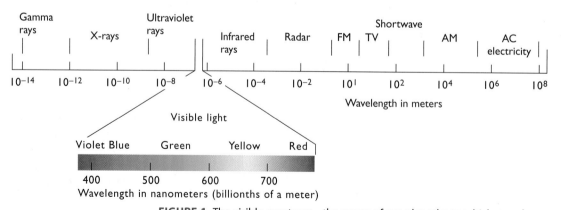

FIGURE 1 The visible spectrum—the range of wavelengths to which people are sensitive—is only a small part of the kinds of wavelengths present in our environment. Is it a benefit or disadvantage to our everyday lives that we aren't more sensitive to a broader range of visual stimuli? Why?

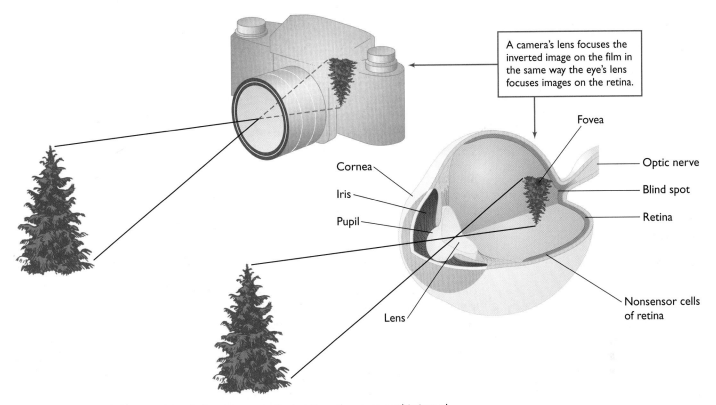

A camera's lens focuses the inverted image on the film in the same way the eye's lens focuses images on the retina.

FIGURE 2 Although human vision is far more complicated than the most sophisticated camera, in some ways basic visual processes are analogous to those used in photography. Like the automatic lighting system on a traditional, nondigital camera, the human eye dilates to let in more light and contracts to block out light.

Illuminating the Structure of the Eye

The ray of light being reflected off the tree in Figure 2 first travels through the *cornea*, a transparent, protective window. The cornea, because of its curvature, bends (or *refracts*) light as it passes through, playing a primary role in focusing the light more sharply. After moving through the cornea, the light traverses the pupil. The *pupil* is a dark hole in the center of the *iris*, the colored part of the eye, which in humans ranges from a light blue to a dark brown. The size of the pupil opening depends on the amount of light in the environment. The dimmer the surroundings are, the more the pupil opens to allow more light to enter.

Like the automatic lighting system on a camera, the pupil in the human eye expands to let in more light (left) and contracts to block out light (right). Can humans adjust their ears to let in more or less sound in a similar manner?

Why shouldn't the pupil be open completely all the time, allowing the greatest amount of light into the eye? The answer relates to the basic physics of light. A small pupil greatly increases the range of distances at which objects are in focus. With a wide-open pupil, the range is relatively small, and details are harder to discern. The eye takes advantage of bright light by decreasing the size of the pupil and thereby becoming more discriminating. In dim light the pupil expands to enable us to view the situation better—but at the expense of visual detail. (Perhaps one reason candle-light dinners are thought of as romantic is that the dim light prevents one from seeing a partner's physical flaws.)

Once light passes through the pupil, it enters the *lens,* which is directly behind the pupil. The lens acts to bend the rays of light so that they are properly focused on the rear of the eye. The lens focuses light by changing its own thickness, a process called *accommodation*: It becomes flatter when viewing distant objects and rounder when looking at closer objects.

REACHING THE RETINA

retina The part of the eye that converts the electromagnetic energy of light to electrical impulses for transmission to the brain.

rods Thin, cylindrical receptor cells in the retina that are highly sensitive to light.

cones Cone-shaped, light-sensitive receptor cells in the retina that are responsible for sharp focus and color perception, particularly in bright light.

Having traveled through the pupil and lens, the image of the tree finally reaches its ultimate destination in the eye—the **retina.** It is within the retina that the electromagnetic energy of light is converted to electrical impulses for transmission to the brain. Note that, because of the physical properties of light, the image has reversed itself in traveling through the lens, and it reaches the retina upside down (relative to its original position). Although it might seem that this reversal would cause difficulties in understanding and moving about the world, this is not the case. The brain interprets the image in terms of its original position.

The retina consists of a thin layer of nerve cells at the back of the eyeball (see Figure 3). There are two kinds of light-sensitive receptor cells in the retina. The names they have been given describe their shapes: rods and cones. **Rods** are thin, cylindrical receptor cells that are highly sensitive to light. **Cones** are typically cone-shaped, light-sensitive receptor cells that are responsible for sharp focus and color perception, particularly in bright light. The rods and cones are distributed unevenly throughout the retina. Cones are concentrated on the part of the retina called the *fovea.* The fovea is a particularly sensitive region of the retina. If you want to focus on something of particular interest, you will automatically try to center the image on the fovea to see it more sharply.

The rods and cones not only are structurally dissimilar but they also play distinctly different roles in vision. Cones are primarily responsible for the sharply focused perception of color, particularly in brightly lit situations; rods are related to vision in dimly lit situations and are largely insensitive to color and to details as sharp as those the cones are capable of recognizing. The rods play a key role in *peripheral vision*—seeing objects that are outside the main center of focus—and in night vision.

Rods and cones also are involved in *dark adaptation,* the phenomenon of adjusting to dim light after being in brighter light. (Think of the experience of walking into a dark movie theater and groping your way to a seat but a few minutes later seeing the seats quite clearly.) The speed at which dark adaptation occurs is a result of the rate of change in the chemical composition of the rods and cones. Although the cones reach their greatest level of adaptation in just a few minutes, the rods take 20 to 30 minutes to reach the maximum level. The opposite phenomenon—*light adaptation,* or the process of adjusting to bright light after exposure to dim light—occurs much faster, taking only a minute or so.

> **Study Alert**
>
> Remember that cones relate to color vision.

SENDING THE MESSAGE FROM THE EYE TO THE BRAIN

When light energy strikes the rods and cones, it starts a chain of events that transforms light into neural impulses that can be communicated to the brain. Even before

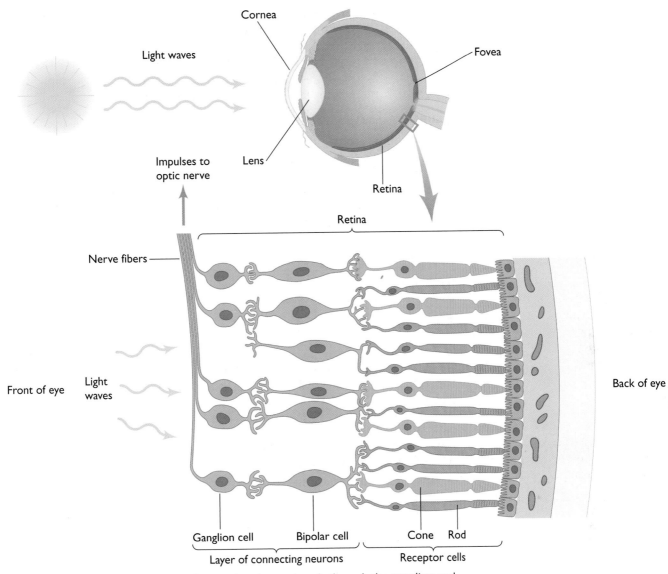

FIGURE 3 The basic cells of the eye. Light entering the eye travels through the ganglion and bipolar cells and strikes the light-sensitive rods and cones located at the back of the eye. The rods and cones then transmit nerve impulses to the brain via the bipolar and ganglion cells. (Source: Shier, Butler, & Lewis, 2000.)

the neural message reaches the brain, however, some initial coding of the visual information takes place.

What happens when light energy strikes the retina depends in part on whether it encounters a rod or a cone. Rods contain *rhodopsin*, a complex reddish-purple substance whose composition changes chemically when energized by light. The substance in cone receptors is different, but the principles are similar. Stimulation of the nerve cells in the eye triggers a neural response that is transmitted to other nerve cells in the retina called *bipolar cells* and *ganglion cells*.

Bipolar cells receive information directly from the rods and cones and communicate that information to the ganglion cells. The ganglion cells collect and summarize visual information, which is then moved out the back of the eyeball and sent to the brain through a bundle of ganglion axons called the **optic nerve.**

Because the opening for the optic nerve passes through the retina, there are no rods or cones in the area, and that creates a blind spot. Normally, however, this

optic nerve A bundle of ganglion axons that carry visual information to the brain.

FIGURE 4 To find your blind spot, close your right eye and look at the haunted house with your left eye. You will see the ghost on the periphery of your vision. Now, while staring at the house, move the page toward you. When the book is about a foot from your eye, the ghost will disappear. At this moment, the image of the ghost is falling on your blind spot.

But also notice how, when the page is at that distance, not only does the ghost seem to disappear, but the line seems to run continuously through the area where the ghost used to be. This simple experiment shows how we automatically compensate for missing information by using nearby material to complete what is unseen. That's the reason you never notice the blind spot. What is missing is replaced by what is seen next to the blind spot. Can you think of any advantages that this tendency to provide missing information gives humans as a species?

absence of nerve cells does not interfere with vision because you automatically compensate for the missing part of your field of vision. (To find your blind spot, see Figure 4.)

Once beyond the eye itself, the neural impulses relating to the image move through the optic nerve. As the optic nerve leaves the eyeball, its path does not take the most direct route to the part of the brain right behind the eye. Instead, the optic nerves from each eye meet at a point roughly between the two eyes—called the *optic chiasm* (pronounced KI-asm)—where each optic nerve then splits.

When the optic nerves split, the nerve impulses coming from the right half of each retina are sent to the right side of the brain, and the impulses arriving from the left half of each retina are sent to the left side of the brain. Because the image on the retinas is reversed and upside down, however, those images coming from the right half of each retina actually originated in the field of vision to the person's left, and the images coming from the left half of each retina originated in the field of vision to the person's right (see Figure 5).

PROCESSING THE VISUAL MESSAGE

By the time a visual message reaches the brain, it has passed through several stages of processing. One of the initial sites is the ganglion cells. Each ganglion cell gathers information from a group of rods and cones in a particular area of the eye and compares the amount of light entering the center of that area with the amount of light in the area around it. Some ganglion cells are activated by light in the center (and darkness in the surrounding area). Other ganglion cells are activated when there is darkness in the center and light in the surrounding areas. The outcome of this process is to maximize the detection of variations in light and darkness. The image that is passed on to the brain, then, is an enhanced version of the actual visual stimulus outside the body (Kubovy, Epstein, & Gepshtein, 2003; Pearson & Clifford, 2005; Lascaratos, Ji, & Wood, 2007).

The ultimate processing of visual images takes place in the visual cortex of the brain, and it is here that the most complex kinds of processing occur. Psychologists David Hubel and Torsten Wiesel won the Nobel Prize in 1981 for their discovery that many neurons in the cortex are extraordinarily specialized, being activated only by

Primary visual area
of cerebral cortex

Optic tract

Optic chiasm

Optic nerve

Right
visual field

Left visual field

FIGURE 5 Because the optic nerve coming from the eye splits at the optic chiasm, the image to a person's right eye is sent to the left side of the brain and the image to the person's left is transmitted to the right side of the brain. (Source: Mader, 2000.)

visual stimuli of a particular shape or pattern—a process known as **feature detection.** They found that some cells are activated only by lines of a particular width, shape, or orientation. Other cells are activated only by moving, as opposed to stationary, stimuli (Hubel & Wiesel, 2004; Pelli, Burns, & Farell, 2006).

More recent work has added to our knowledge of the complex ways in which visual information coming from individual neurons is combined and processed. Different parts of the brain process nerve impulses in several individual systems simultaneously. For instance, one system relates to shapes, one to colors, and others to movement, location, and depth. Furthermore, different parts of the brain are involved in the perception of specific *kinds* of stimuli, showing distinctions, for example, between the perception of human faces, animals, and inanimate stimuli (Bindemann et al., 2008; Platek & Kemp, 2009; Werblin & Roska, 2007; Winston, O'Doherty, & Kilner, 2006).

If separate neural systems exist for processing information about specific aspects of the visual world, how are all these data integrated by the brain? The brain makes use of information regarding the frequency, rhythm, and timing of the firing of particular sets of neural cells. Furthermore, the brain's integration of visual information does not occur in any single step or location in the brain but rather is a process that occurs on several levels simultaneously. The ultimate outcome, though, is indisputable: a vision of the world around us (de Gelder, 2000; Macaluso, Frith, & Driver, 2000; Werner, Pinna, & Spillmann, 2007; also see Figure 6 on page 100).

feature detection The activation of neurons in the cortex by visual stimuli of specific shapes or patterns.

Neuroscience in Your Life: Seeing Vision in the Brain

FIGURE 6 In addition to having specialized neurons that respond more strongly to particular shapes, orientations, and widths, our brains process information coming from each eye separately, creating what are called ocular dominance columns. With new MRI techniques, researchers can note the activity of the each eye more precisely. In these scans we can see the variation in ocular dominance columns for three individuals. The red areas show the response of one eye, and blue areas show the response of the other. (Source: Shmuel et al., 2010.)

Participant 1

Participant 2

Participant 3

Color Vision and Color Blindness: The 7-Million-Color Spectrum

Although the range of wavelengths to which humans are sensitive is relatively narrow, at least in comparison with the entire electromagnetic spectrum, the portion to which we are capable of responding allows us great flexibility in sensing the world. Nowhere is this clearer than in terms of the number of colors we can discern. A person with normal color vision is capable of distinguishing no less than 7 million different colors (Bruce, Green, & Georgeson, 1997; Rabin, 2004).

Although the variety of colors that people are generally able to distinguish is vast, there are certain individuals whose ability to perceive color is quite limited—the color-blind. Interestingly, the condition of these individuals has provided some of the most important clues to understanding how color vision operates (Bonnardel, 2006; Neitz, Neitz, & Kainz, 1996).

Approximately 7% of men and .4% of women are color-blind. For most people with color-blindness, the world looks quite dull (see Figure 7). Red fire engines appear yellow, green grass seems yellow, and the three colors of a traffic light all

(a)   (b)   (c)

FIGURE 7 To someone with normal vision, the hot-air balloon in the foreground appears with regions of very pure red, orange, yellow, green, blue, and violet, as well as off-white; and the balloon in the rear is a bright shade of red-orange. (b) A person with red-green color blindness would see the scene in part (a) like this, in hues of blue and yellow. (c) A person who is blue-yellow blind, conversely, would see it in hues of red and green.

look yellow. In fact, in the most common form of color-blindness, all red and green objects are seen as yellow. In other forms of color-blindness, people are unable to tell the difference between yellow and blue. In the most extreme cases of color-blindness, which are quite rare, people perceive no color at all. To such individuals, the world looks something like the picture on an old black-and-white television set.

EXPLAINING COLOR VISION

To understand why some people are color-blind, we need to consider the basics of color vision. Two processes are involved. The first process is explained by the **trichromatic theory of color vision,** which was first proposed by Thomas Young and extended by Hermann von Helmholtz in the first half of the 1800s. This theory suggests that there are three kinds of cones in the retina, each of which responds primarily to a specific range of wavelengths. One is most responsive to blue-violet colors, one to green, and the third to yellow-red (Brown & Wald, 1964). According to trichromatic theory, perception of color is influenced by the relative strength with which each of the three kinds of cones is activated. If we see a blue sky, the blue-violet cones are primarily triggered, and the others show less activity.

However, there are aspects of color vision that the trichromatic theory is less successful at explaining. For example, the theory does not explain what happens after you stare at something like the flag shown in Figure 8 on page 102 for about a minute. Try this yourself and then look at a blank white page: You'll see an image of the traditional red, white, and blue U.S. flag. Where there was yellow, you'll see blue, and where there were green and black, you'll see red and white.

The phenomenon you have just experienced is called an *afterimage*. It occurs because activity in the retina continues even when you are no longer staring at the original picture. However, it also demonstrates that the trichromatic theory does not explain color vision completely. Why should the colors in the afterimage be different from those in the original?

trichromatic theory of color vision
The theory that there are three kinds of cones in the retina, each of which responds primarily to a specific range of wavelengths.

FIGURE 8 Stare at the dot in this flag for about a minute and then look at a piece of plain white paper. What do you see? Most people see an afterimage that converts the colors in the figure into the traditional red, white, and blue U.S. flag. If you have trouble seeing it the first time, blink once and try again.

opponent-process theory of color vision The theory that receptor cells for color are linked in pairs, working in opposition to each other.

Study Alert

Keep in mind that there are two explanations for color vision: trichromatic and opponent-process theories.

Because trichromatic processes do not provide a full explanation of color vision, alternative explanations have been proposed. According to the **opponent-process theory of color vision,** first proposed by German physiologist Ewald Hering in the 19th century, receptor cells are linked in pairs, working in opposition to each other. Specifically, there are a blue-yellow pairing, a red-green pairing, and a black-white pairing. If an object reflects light that contains more blue than yellow, it will stimulate the firing of the cells sensitive to blue, simultaneously discouraging or inhibiting the firing of receptor cells sensitive to yellow—and the object will appear blue. If, in contrast, a light contains more yellow than blue, the cells that respond to yellow will be stimulated to fire while the blue ones are inhibited, and the object will appear yellow (D. N. Robinson, 2007).

The opponent-process theory provides a good explanation for afterimages. When we stare at the yellow in the figure, for instance, our receptor cells for the yellow component of the yellow-blue pairing become fatigued and are less able to respond to yellow stimuli. In contrast, the receptor cells for the blue part of the pair are not tired, because they are not being stimulated. When we look at a white surface, the light reflected off it would normally stimulate both the yellow and the blue receptors equally. But the fatigue of the yellow receptors prevents this from happening. They temporarily do not respond to the yellow, which makes the white light appear to be blue. Because the other colors in the figure do the same thing relative to their specific opponents, the afterimage produces the opponent colors—for a while. The afterimage lasts only a short time, because the fatigue of the yellow receptors is soon overcome, and the white light begins to be perceived more accurately.

We now know that both opponent processes and trichromatic mechanisms are at work in producing the perception of color vision, but in different parts of the visual sensing system. Trichromatic processes work within the retina itself, whereas opponent mechanisms operate both in the retina and at later stages of neuronal processing (Baraas, Foster, & Amano, 2006; Chen, Zhou, & Gong, 2004; Gegenfurtner, 2003).

RECAP/EVALUATE/RETHINK

RECAP

What basic processes underlie the sense of vision?

- Vision depends on sensitivity to light, electromagnetic waves in the visible part of the spectrum that are either reflected off objects or produced by an energy source. The eye shapes the light into an image that is transformed into nerve impulses and interpreted by the brain. (p. 94)
- As light enters the eye, it passes through the cornea, pupil, and lens and ultimately reaches the retina, where the electromagnetic energy of light is converted to nerve impulses for transmission to the brain. These impulses leave the eye via the optic nerve. (p. 95)
- The visual information gathered by the rods and cones is transferred via bipolar and ganglion cells through the optic nerve, which leads to the optic chiasm—the point where the optic nerve splits. (p. 96)

How do we see colors?

- Color vision seems to be based on two processes described by the trichromatic theory and the opponent-process theory. (p. 101)
- The trichromatic theory suggests that there are three kinds of cones in the retina, each of which is responsive to a certain range of colors. The opponent-process theory presumes pairs of different types of cells in the eye that work in opposition to each other. (p. 101)

EVALUATE

1. Light entering the eye first passes through the _____, a protective window.

2. The structure that converts light into usable neural messages is called the _____.
3. A woman with blue eyes could be described as having blue pigment in her _____.
4. What is the process by which the thickness of the lens is changed in order to focus light properly?
5. The proper sequence of structures that light passes through in the eye is the _____, _____, _____, and _____.
6. Match each type of visual receptor with its function.
   - a. rods
   - b. cones
   1. used for dim light, largely insensitive to color
   2. detect color, good in bright light
7. _____ theory states that there are three types of cones in the retina, each of which responds primarily to a different color.

RETHINK

1. If the eye had a second lens that "unreversed" the image hitting the retina, do you think there would be changes in the way people perceive the world?
2. *From the perspective of an advertising specialist:* How might you market your products similarly or differently to those who are color-blind versus those who have normal color vision?

Answers to Evaluate Questions

1. cornea; 2. retina; 3. iris; 4. accommodation; 5. cornea, pupil, lens, retina; 6. a-1, b-2; 7. Trichromatic

KEY TERMS

retina p. 96
rods p. 96
cones p. 96

optic nerve p. 97
feature detection p. 99

trichromatic theory of color vision p. 101

opponent-process theory of color vision p. 102

MODULE 10

Hearing and the Other Senses

The blast-off was easy compared with what the astronaut was experiencing now: space sickness. The constant nausea and vomiting were enough to make him wonder why he had worked so hard to become an astronaut. Even though he had been warned that there was a two-thirds chance that his first experience in space would cause these symptoms, he wasn't prepared for how terribly sick he really felt.

Whether or not the astronaut wishes he could head right back to earth, his experience, a major problem for space travelers, is related to a basic sensory process: the sense of motion and balance. This sense allows people to navigate their bodies through the world and keep themselves upright without falling. Along with hearing—the process by which sound waves are translated into understandable and meaningful forms—the sense of motion and balance resides in the ear.

Sensing Sound

Although many of us think primarily of the outer ear when we speak of the ear, that structure is only one simple part of the whole. The outer ear acts as a reverse megaphone, designed to collect and bring sounds into the internal portions of the ear (see Figure 1). The location of the outer ears on different sides of the head helps with *sound localization,* the process by which we identify the direction from which a sound is coming. Wave patterns in the air enter each ear at a slightly different time, and the brain uses the discrepancy as a clue to the sound's point of origin. In addition, the two outer ears delay or amplify sounds of particular frequencies to different degrees.

Sound is the movement of air molecules brought about by a source of vibration. Sounds travel through the air in wave patterns similar in shape to those made in water when a stone is thrown into a still pond. Sounds, arriving at the outer ear in the form of wavelike vibrations, are funneled into the *auditory canal,* a tubelike passage that leads to the eardrum. The **eardrum** is aptly named because it operates as a miniature drum, vibrating when sound waves hit it. The more intense the sound, the more the eardrum vibrates. These vibrations are then transferred into the *middle ear,* a tiny chamber containing three bones (the *hammer,* the *anvil,* and the *stirrup*) that transmit vibrations to the oval window, a thin membrane leading to the inner ear. Because the hammer, anvil, and stirrup act as a set of levers, they not only transmit vibrations but also increase their strength. Moreover, because the opening into the middle ear (the eardrum) is considerably larger than the opening out of it (the *oval window*), the force of sound waves on the oval window becomes amplified. The middle ear, then, acts as a tiny mechanical amplifier.

The *inner ear* is the portion of the ear that changes the sound vibrations into a form in which they can be transmitted to the brain. (As you will see, it also contains the organs that allow us to locate our position and determine how we are moving through space.) When sound enters the inner ear through the oval window, it moves into the **cochlea,** a coiled tube that looks something like a snail and is filled with fluid that vibrates in response to sound. Inside the cochlea is the **basilar membrane,**

sound The movement of air molecules brought about by a source of vibration.

eardrum The part of the ear that vibrates when sound waves hit it.

cochlea (KOKE-lee-uh) A coiled tube in the ear filled with fluid that vibrates in response to sound.

basilar membrane A vibrating structure that runs through the center of the cochlea, dividing it into an upper chamber and a lower chamber and containing sense receptors for sound.

FIGURE 1 The major parts of the ear. (Source: Brooker et al., 2008, Figure 45.6.)

a structure that runs through the center of the cochlea, dividing it into an upper chamber and a lower chamber. The basilar membrane is covered with **hair cells.** When the hair cells are bent by the vibrations entering the cochlea, the cells send a neural message to the brain (Cho, 2000; Zhou, Liu, & Davis, 2005).

hair cells Tiny cells covering the basilar membrane that, when bent by vibrations entering the cochlea, transmit neural messages to the brain.

THE PHYSICAL ASPECTS OF SOUND

As we mentioned earlier, what we refer to as sound is actually the physical movement of air molecules in regular, wavelike patterns caused by a vibrating source. Sometimes it is even possible to see these vibrations: If you have ever seen an audio speaker that has no enclosure, you know that, at least when the lowest notes are playing, you can see the speaker moving in and out. Less obvious is what happens next: The speaker pushes air molecules into waves with the same pattern as its movement. Those wave patterns soon reach your ear, although their strength has been weakened considerably during their travels. All other sources that produce sound work in essentially the same fashion, setting off wave patterns that move through the air to the ear. Air—or some other medium, such as water—is necessary to make the vibrations of objects reach us. This explains why there can be no sound in a vacuum.

We are able to see the audio speaker moving when low notes are played because of a primary characteristic of sound called frequency. *Frequency* is the number of wave cycles that occur in a second. At very low frequencies there are relatively few wave cycles per second (see Figure 2). These cycles are visible to the naked eye as vibrations in the speaker. Low frequencies are translated into a sound that is very low in pitch. (*Pitch* is the characteristic that makes sound seem "high" or "low.") For

FIGURE 2 The sound waves produced by different stimuli are transmitted—usually through the air—in different patterns, with lower frequencies indicated by fewer peaks and valleys per second. (Source: Seeley, Stephens, & Tate, 2000.)

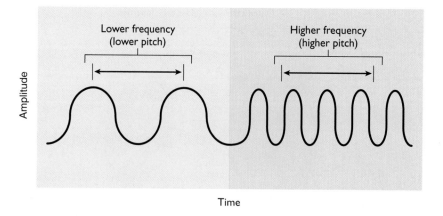

example, the lowest frequency that humans are capable of hearing is 20 cycles per second. Higher frequencies are heard as sounds of higher pitch. At the upper end of the sound spectrum, people can detect sounds with frequencies as high as 20,000 cycles per second.

Amplitude is a feature of wave patterns that allows us to distinguish between loud and soft sounds. Amplitude is the spread between the up-and-down peaks and valleys of air pressure in a sound wave as it travels through the air. Waves with small peaks and valleys produce soft sounds; those with relatively large peaks and valleys produce loud sounds.

We are sensitive to broad variations in sound amplitudes. The strongest sounds we are capable of hearing are over a trillion times as intense as the very weakest sound we can hear. This range is measured in *decibels*. When sounds get higher than 120 decibels, they become painful to the human ear.

Our sensitivity to different frequencies changes as we age. For instance, as we get older, the range of frequencies we can detect declines, particularly for high-pitched sounds. This is why high school students sometimes choose high-pitched ring tones for their cell phones in settings where cell phone use is forbidden: the ringing sound goes undetected by their aging teachers (Vitello, 2006) (see Figure 3).

Sorting Out Theories of Sound How are our brains able to sort out wavelengths of different frequencies and intensities? One clue comes from studies of the basilar membrane, the area in the cochlea that translates physical vibrations into neural impulses. It turns out that sounds affect different areas of the basilar membrane, depending on the frequency of the sound wave. The part of the basilar membrane nearest to the oval window is most sensitive to high-frequency sounds, and the part nearest to the cochlea's inner end is most sensitive to low-frequency sounds. This finding has led to the **place theory of hearing,** which states that different areas of the basilar membrane respond to different frequencies.

However, place theory does not tell the full story of hearing, because very low frequency sounds trigger neurons across such a wide area of the basilar membrane that no single site is involved. Consequently, an additional explanation for hearing has been proposed: frequency theory. The **frequency theory of hearing** suggests that the entire basilar membrane acts as a microphone, vibrating as a whole in response to a sound. According to this explanation, the nerve receptors send out signals that are tied directly to the frequency (the number of wave crests per second) of the sounds to which we are exposed, with the number of nerve impulses being a direct function of a sound's frequency. Thus, the higher the pitch of a sound (and therefore the greater the frequency of its wave crests), the greater the number of nerve impulses that are transmitted up the auditory nerve to the brain.

Neither place theory nor frequency theory provides the full explanation for hearing. Place theory provides a better explanation for the sensing of high-frequency

place theory of hearing The theory that different areas of the basilar membrane respond to different frequencies.

frequency theory of hearing The theory that the entire basilar membrane acts like a microphone, vibrating as a whole in response to a sound.

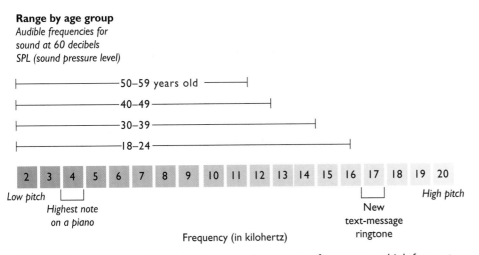

Range by age group
*Audible frequencies for
sound at 60 decibels
SPL (sound pressure level)*

FIGURE 3 Some teenagers set their text-message ring tone to a frequency too high for most adults to hear, allowing them to use cell phones where they are prohibited. (Source: Vitello, 2006.)

sounds, whereas frequency theory explains what happens when low-frequency sounds are encountered. Medium-frequency sounds incorporate both processes (Hirsh & Watson, 1996; Hudspeth, 2000).

After an auditory message leaves the ear, it is transmitted to the auditory cortex of the brain through a complex series of neural interconnections. As the message is transmitted, it is communicated through neurons that respond to specific types of sounds. Within the auditory cortex itself, there are neurons that respond selectively to very specific sorts of sound features, such as clicks and whistles. Some neurons respond only to a specific pattern of sounds, such as a steady tone but not an intermittent one. Furthermore, specific neurons transfer information about a sound's location through their particular pattern of firing (Middlebrooks et al., 2005; Alho et al., 2006; Wang et al., 2005).

If we were to analyze the configuration of the cells in the auditory cortex, we would find that neighboring cells are responsive to similar frequencies. The auditory cortex, then, provides us with a "map" of sound frequencies, just as the visual cortex furnishes a representation of the visual field. In addition, because of the asymmetry in the two hemispheres of the brain (which we discussed in the last chapter), the left and right ears process sound differently. The right ear reacts more to speech, while the left ear responds more to music (Sininger & Cone-Wesson, 2004, 2006).

Speech perception requires that we make fine discriminations among sounds that are quite similar in terms of their physical properties. Furthermore, not only are we able to understand *what* is being said from speech, we can use vocal cues to determine who is speaking, if they have an accent and where they may be from, and even their emotional state. Such capabilities illustrate the sophistication of our sense of hearing (Fowler & Galantucci, 2008; Massaro & Chen, 2008; Pell et al., 2009).

Balance: The Ups and Downs of Life Several structures of the ear are related more to our sense of balance than to our hearing. Collectively, these structures are known as the *vestibular system,* which responds to the pull of gravity and allows us to maintain our balance, even when standing in a bus in stop-and-go traffic.

The main structure of the vestibular system is formed by the **semicircular canals** of the inner ear (refer to Figure 1 on page 105), which consist of three tubes containing fluid that sloshes through them when the head moves, signaling rotational or angular movement to the brain. The pull on our bodies caused by the acceleration of forward, backward, or up-and-down motion, as well as the constant pull of gravity, is sensed by the *otoliths,* tiny, motion-sensitive crystals in the semicircular canals. When we move, these crystals shift as sands do on a windy beach, contacting the

Study Alert
Be sure to understand the differences between the place and frequency theories of hearing.

semicircular canals Three tubelike structures of the inner ear containing fluid that sloshes through them when the head moves, signaling rotational or angular movement to the brain.

The weightlessness of the ear's otoliths produces space sickness in most astronauts.

specialized receptor *hair cells* in the semicircular canals. The brain's inexperience in interpreting messages from the weightless otoliths is the cause of the space sickness commonly experienced by two-thirds of all space travelers, mentioned at the start of this module (Flam, 1991; Stern & Koch, 1996).

Smell and Taste

> Until he bit into a piece of raw cabbage on that February evening . . . , Raymond Fowler had not thought much about the sense of taste. The cabbage, part of a pasta dish he was preparing for his family's dinner, had an odd, burning taste, but he did not pay it much attention. Then a few minutes later, his daughter handed him a glass of cola, and he took a swallow. "It was like sulfuric acid," he said. "It was like the hottest thing you could imagine boring into your mouth." (Goode, 1999, pp. D1–D2)

It was evident that something was very wrong with Fowler's sense of taste. After extensive testing, it became clear that he had damaged the nerves involved in his sense of taste, probably because of a viral infection or a medicine he was taking. (Luckily for him, a few months later his sense of taste returned to normal.)

Even without disruptions in our ability to perceive the world such as those experienced by Fowler, we all know the important roles that taste and smell play. We'll consider these two senses next.

SMELL

Although many animals have keener abilities to detect odors than we do, the human sense of smell (*olfaction*) permits us to detect more than 10,000 separate smells. We also have a good memory for smells, and long-forgotten events and memories—good and bad—can be brought back with the mere whiff of an odor associated with a memory (Schroers, Prigot, & Fagen, 2007; Stevenson & Case, 2005; Willander & Larsson, 2006).

Results of "sniff tests" have shown that women generally have a better sense of smell than men do (Engen, 1987). People also have the ability to distinguish males from females on the basis of smell alone. In one experiment, blindfolded students who were asked to sniff the breath of a female or male volunteer who was hidden

More than 1,000 receptor cells, known as olfactory cells, are spread across the nasal cavity. The cells are specialized to react to particular odors. Do you think it is possible to "train" the nose to pick up a greater number of odors?

from view were able to distinguish the sex of the donor at better than chance levels. People can also distinguish happy from sad emotions by sniffing under-arm smells, and women are able to identify their babies solely on the basis of smell just a few hours after birth (Doty et al., 1982; Fusari & Ballesteros, 2008; Haviland-Jones & Chen, 1999).

The sense of smell is sparked when the molecules of a substance enter the nasal passages and meet *olfactory cells*, the receptor neurons of the nose, which are spread across the nasal cavity. More than 1,000 separate types of receptors have been identified on those cells so far. Each of these receptors is so specialized that it responds only to a small band of different odors. The responses of the separate olfactory cells are then transmitted to the brain, where they are combined into recognition of a particular smell (Marshall, Laing, & Jinks, 2006; Murphy et al., 2004; Zhou & Buck, 2006).

Smell may also act as a hidden means of communication for humans. It has long been known that nonhumans release *pheromones*, chemicals they secrete into the environment that produce a reaction in other members of the same species, permitting the transmission of messages such as sexual availability. For instance, the vaginal secretions of female monkeys contain pheromones that stimulate the sexual interest of male monkeys (Hawkes & Doty, 2009; Holy, Dulac, & Meister, 2000; Touhara, 2007).

The degree to which pheromones are part of the human experience remains an open question. Some psychologists believe that human pheromones affect emotional responses, although the evidence is inconclusive. For one thing, it is not clear what specific sense organ is receptive to pheromones. In non-humans, it is the *vomeronasal organ* in the nose, but in humans the organ appears to recede during fetal development (Haviland-Jones & Wilson, 2008; Hummer & McClintock, 2009).

TASTE

The sense of taste (*gustation*) involves receptor cells that respond to four basic stimulus qualities: sweet, sour, salty, and bitter. A fifth category also exists, a flavor called *umami*, although there is controversy about whether it qualifies as a fundamental taste. Umami is a hard-to-translate Japanese word, although the English "meaty" or "savory" comes close. Chemically, umami involves food stimuli that contain amino acids (the substances that make up proteins) (McCabe & Rolls, 2007; Erickson, 2008).

Although the specialization of the receptor cells leads them to respond most strongly to a particular type of taste, they also are capable of responding to other tastes as well. Ultimately, every taste is simply a combination of the basic flavor qualities, in the same way that the primary colors blend into a vast variety of shades and hues (Dilorenzo & Youngentob, 2003; Yeomans, Tepper, & Ritezschel, 2007).

The receptor cells for taste are located in roughly 10,000 *taste buds*, which are distributed across the tongue and other parts of the mouth and throat. The taste buds wear out and are replaced every 10 days or so. That's a good thing, because if our taste buds weren't constantly reproducing, we'd lose the ability to taste after we'd accidentally burned our tongues.

The sense of taste differs significantly from one person to another, largely as a result of genetic factors. Some people, dubbed "supertasters," are highly sensitive to taste; they have twice as many taste receptors as "nontasters," who are relatively insensitive to taste. Supertasters (who, for unknown reasons, are more likely to be female than male) find sweets sweeter, cream creamier, and spicy dishes spicier, and weaker concentrations of flavor are enough to satisfy any cravings they may have. In contrast, because they aren't so sensitive to taste, nontasters may seek out relatively sweeter and fattier foods in order to maximize the taste. As a consequence, they may be prone to obesity (Bartoshuk, 2000; Pickering & Gordon, 2006; Snyder, Fast, & Bartoshuk, 2004).

Are you a supertaster? To find out, complete the questionnaire in Figure 4 on page 110.

There are 10,000 taste buds on the tongue and other parts of the mouth. Taste buds wear out and are replaced every 10 days. What would happen if taste buds were not regenerated?

FIGURE 4 All tongues are not created equal, according to taste researchers Linda Bartoshuk and Laurie Lucchina. Instead they suggest that the intensity of a flavor experienced by a given person is determined by that person's genetic background. This taste test can help determine if you are a nontaster, average taster, or supertaster. (Source: Bartoshuk & Lucchina, 1997.)

Take a Taste Test

1. Taste Bud Count
   Punch a hole with a standard hole punch in a square of wax paper. Paint the front of your tongue with a cotton swab dipped in blue food coloring. Put wax paper on the tip of your tongue, just to the right of center. With a flashlight and magnifying glass, count the number of pink, unstained circles. They contain taste buds.
2. Sweet Taste
   Rinse your mouth with water before tasting each sample. Put ½ cup sugar in a measuring cup, and then add enough water to make I cup. Mix. Coat front half of your tongue, including the tip, with a cotton swab dipped in the solution. Wait a few moments. Rate the sweetness according to the scale shown below.
3. Salt Taste
   Put 2 teaspoons of salt in a measuring cup and add enough water to make I cup. Repeat the steps listed above, rating how salty the solution is.
4. Spicy Taste
   Add I teaspoon of Tabasco sauce to I cup of water. Apply with a cotton swab to first ½ inch of the tongue, including the tip. Keep your tongue out of your mouth until the burn reaches a peak, then rate the burn according to the scale.

TASTE SCALE

Barely Detectable — Weak — Moderate — Strong — Very Strong — Strongest Imaginable Sensation

0   10   20   30   40   50   60   70   80   90   100

	SUPERTASTERS	NONTASTERS
Number of taste buds	25 on Average	10
Sweet rating	56 on Average	32
Tabasco	64 on Average	31

Average tasters lie in between supertasters and nontasters. Bartoshuk and Lucchina lack the data at this time to rate salt reliably, but you can compare your results with others taking the test.

The Skin Senses: Touch, Pressure, Temperature, and Pain

It started innocently when Jennifer Darling hurt her right wrist during gym class. At first it seemed like a simple sprain. But even though the initial injury healed, the excruciating, burning pain accompanying it did not go away. Instead, it spread to her other arm and then to her legs. The pain, which Jennifer described as similar to "a hot iron on your arm," was unbearable—and never stopped.

The source of Darling's pain turned out to be a rare condition known as "reflex sympathetic dystrophy syndrome," or RSDS. For a victim of RSDS, a stimulus as mild as a gentle breeze or the touch of a feather can produce agony. Even bright sunlight or a loud noise can trigger intense pain.

Pain such as Darling's can be devastating, yet a lack of pain can be equally bad. If you never experienced pain, for instance, you might not notice that your arm had brushed against a hot pan, and you would suffer a severe burn. Similarly, without

(a) Closure

(b) Proximity

(c) Similarity

(d) Simplicity

FIGURE 2 Organizing these various bits and pieces of information into meaningful wholes constitutes some of the most basic processes of perception, which are summed up in the gestalt laws of organization. Do you think any other species share this organizational tendency? How might we find out?

concentrate on the overall form. Figure 2b demonstrates the principle of *proximity*: We perceive elements that are closer together as grouped together. As a result, we tend to see pairs of dots rather than a row of single dots in Figure 2b.

Elements that are *similar* in appearance we perceive as grouped together. We see, then, horizontal rows of circles and squares in Figure 2c rather than vertical mixed columns. Finally, in a general sense, the overriding gestalt principle is *simplicity*: When we observe a pattern, we perceive it in the most basic, straightforward manner that we can. For example, most of us see Figure 2d as a square with lines on two sides, rather than as the block letter *W* on top of the letter *M*. If we have a choice of interpretations, we generally opt for the simpler one.

Although gestalt psychology no longer plays a prominent role in contemporary psychology, its legacy endures. One fundamental gestalt principle that remains influential is that two objects considered together form a whole that is different from the simple combination of the objects. Gestalt psychologists argued that the perception of stimuli in our environment goes well beyond the individual elements that we sense. Instead, it represents an active, constructive process carried out within the brain (Humphreys & Müller, 2000; Lehar, 2003; van der Helm, 2006) (see Figure 3).

"I'm turning into my mother."

Understanding this cartoon involves the separation of the figure and ground. If you're having trouble appreciating the humor, stare at the woman on the right, who eventually will be transformed.

Top-Down and Bottom-Up Processing

Ca- yo- re-d t-is -en-en-e, w-ic- ha- ev-ry -hi-d l-tt-r m-ss-ng? It probably won't take you too long to figure out that it says, "Can you read this sentence, which has every third letter missing?"

If perception were based primarily on breaking down a stimulus into its most basic elements, understanding the sentence, as well as other ambiguous stimuli, would not be possible. The fact that you were probably able to recognize such an imprecise stimulus illustrates that perception proceeds along two different avenues, called top-down processing and bottom-up processing.

In **top-down processing,** perception is guided by higher-level knowledge, experience, expectations, and motivations. You were able to figure out the meaning of the sentence with the missing letters because of your prior reading experience and because written English contains redundancies. Not every letter of each word is

top-down processing Perception that is guided by higher-level knowledge, experience, expectations, and motivations.

FIGURE 3 Although at first it is difficult to distinguish anything in this drawing, keep looking, and eventually you'll probably be able to see the figure of a dog. The dog represents a gestalt, or perceptual, whole, which is something greater than the sum or the individual elements.

necessary to decode its meaning. Moreover, your expectations played a role in your being able to read the sentence. You were probably expecting a statement that had *something* to do with psychology, not the lyrics to a Lady Gaga song.

Top-down processing is illustrated by the importance of context in determining how we perceive objects. Look, for example, at Figure 4. Most of us perceive that the first row consists of the letters *A* through *F*, while the second contains the numbers 10 through 14. But take a more careful look and you'll see that the "B" and the "13" are identical. Clearly, our perception is affected by our expectations about the two sequences—even though the two stimuli are exactly the same.

However, top-down processing cannot occur on its own. Even though top-down processing allows us to fill in the gaps in ambiguous and out-of-context stimuli, we would be unable to perceive the meaning of such stimuli without bottom-up processing. **Bottom-up processing** consists of the progression of recognizing and processing information from individual components of a stimuli and moving to the perception of the whole. We would make no headway in our recognition of the sentence without being able to perceive the individual shapes that make up the letters. Some perception, then, occurs at the level of the patterns and features of each of the separate letters.

Top-down and bottom-up processing occur simultaneously, and interact with each other, in our perception of the world around us. Bottom-up processing permits us to process the fundamental characteristics of stimuli, whereas top-down processing allows us to bring our experience to bear on perception. As we learn more about the complex processes involved in perception, we are developing a better understanding of how the brain continually interprets information from the senses and permits us to make responses appropriate to the environment (Folk & Remington, 2008; Sobel et al., 2007; Westerhausen et al., 2009).

bottom-up processing Perception that consists of the progression of recognizing and processing information from individual components of a stimuli and moving to the perception of the whole.

FIGURE 4 The power of context is shown in this figure. Note how the B and the 13 are identical. (Source: Coren & Ward, 1989.)

Depth Perception: Translating 2-D to 3-D

As sophisticated as the retina is, the images projected onto it are flat and two-dimensional. Yet the world around us is three-dimensional, and we perceive it that way. How do we make the transformation from 2-D to 3-D?

The ability to view the world in three dimensions and to perceive distance—a skill known as **depth perception**—is due largely to the fact that we have two eyes. Because there is a certain distance between the eyes, a slightly different image reaches each retina. The brain integrates the two images into one view, but it also recognizes the difference in images and uses this difference to estimate the distance of an object from us. The difference in the images seen by the left eye and the right eye is known as *binocular disparity* (Hibbard, 2007; Kara & Boyd, 2009).

To get a sense of binocular disparity, hold a pencil at arm's length and look at it first with one eye and then with the other. There is little difference between the two views relative to the background. Now bring the pencil just 6 inches away from your face, and try the same thing. This time you will perceive a greater difference between the two views.

The fact that the discrepancy between the images in the two eyes varies according to the distance of objects that we view provides us with a means of determining distance. If we view two objects and one is considerably closer to us than the other is, the retinal disparity will be relatively large and we will have a greater sense of depth between the two. However, if the two objects are a similar distance from us, the retinal disparity will be minor, and we will perceive them as being a similar distance from us.

In some cases, certain cues permit us to obtain a sense of depth and distance with just one eye. These cues are known as *monocular cues*. One monocular cue—*motion parallax*—is the change in position of an object on the retina caused by movement of your body relative to the object. For example, suppose you are a passenger in a moving car, and you focus your eye on a stable object such as a tree. Objects that are closer than the tree will appear to move backward, and the nearer the object

depth perception The ability to view the world in three dimensions and to perceive distance.

Railroad tracks that seem to join together in the distance are an example of linear perspective.

When the moon is near the horizon, we do not see it by itself, and perceptual constancy leads us to take into account a misleading sense of distance.

is, the more quickly it will appear to move. In contrast, objects beyond the tree will seem to move at a slower speed, but in the same direction as you are. Your brain is able to use these cues to calculate the relative distances of the tree and other objects.

Similarly, experience has taught us that if two objects are the same size, the one that makes a smaller image on the retina is farther away than is the one that provides a larger image—an example of the monocular cue of *relative size*. But it's not just size of an object that provides information about distance; the quality of the image on the retina helps us judge distance. The monocular cue of *texture gradient* provides information about distance, because the details of things that are far away are less distinct (Proffitt, 2006).

Finally, anyone who has ever seen railroad tracks that seem to come together in the distance knows that distant objects appear to be closer together than are nearer ones, a phenomenon called linear perspective. People use *linear perspective* as a monocular cue in estimating distance, allowing the two-dimensional image on the retina to record the three-dimensional world (Bruce, Green, & Georgeson, 1997; Bruggeman, Yonas, & Konczak, 2007; Dobbins et al., 1998; Shimono & Wade, 2002).

Perceptual Constancy

Consider what happens as you finish a conversation with a friend and he begins to walk away from you. As you watch him walk down the street, the image on your retina becomes smaller and smaller. Do you wonder why he is shrinking?

Of course not. Despite the very real change in the size of the retinal image, because of perceptual constancy you factor into your thinking the knowledge that your friend is moving farther away from you. **Perceptual constancy** is a phenomenon in which physical objects are perceived as unvarying and consistent despite changes in their appearance or in the physical environment. Perceptual constancy leads us to view objects as having an unvarying size, shape, color, and brightness, even if the image on our retina varies. For example, despite the varying images on the retina as an airplane approaches, flies overhead, and disappears, we do not perceive the airplane as changing shape (Garrigan & Kellman, 2008; Redding, 2002; Wickelgren, 2004).

In some cases, though, our application of perceptual constancy can mislead us. One good example of this involves the rising moon. When the moon first appears at night, close to the horizon, it seems to be huge—much larger than when it is high

perceptual constancy The phenomenon in which physical objects are perceived as unvarying and consistent despite changes in their appearance or in the physical environment.

in the sky later in the evening. You may have thought that the apparent change in the size of the moon was caused by the moon's being physically closer to the earth when it first appears. In fact, though, this is not the case at all: the actual image of the moon on our retina is the same, whether it is low or high in the sky.

There are several explanations for the moon illusion. One suggests that the moon appears to be larger when it is close to the horizon primarily because of perceptual constancy. When the moon is near the horizon, the perceptual cues of intervening terrain and objects such as trees on the horizon produce a misleading sense of distance, leading us to misperceive the moon as relatively large.

In contrast, when the moon is high in the sky, we see it by itself, and we don't try to compensate for its distance from us. In this case, then, perceptual constancy leads us to perceive it as relatively small. To experience perceptual constancy, try looking at the moon when it is relatively low on the horizon through a paper-towel tube; the moon suddenly will appear to "shrink" back to normal size (Coren, 1992; Imamura & Nakamizo, 2006; Kaufman, Johnson, & Liu, 2008; Ross & Plug, 2002).

Perceptual constancy is not the only explanation for the moon illusion, and it remains a puzzle to psychologists. It may be that several different perceptual processes are involved in the illusion (Gregory, 2008; Kim, 2008).

Motion Perception: As the World Turns

When a batter tries to hit a pitched ball, the most important factor is the motion of the ball. How is a batter able to judge the speed and location of a target that is moving at some 90 miles per hour?

The answer rests in part on several cues that provide us with relevant information about the perception of motion. For one thing, the movement of an object across the retina is typically perceived relative to some stable, unmoving background. Moreover, if the stimulus is heading toward us, the image on the retina expands in size, filling more and more of the visual field. In such cases, we assume that the stimulus is approaching—not that it is an expanding stimulus viewed at a constant distance.

It is not, however, just the movement of images across the retina that brings about the perception of motion. If it were, we would perceive the world as moving every time we moved our heads. Instead, one of the critical things we learn about perception is to factor information about our own head and eye movements along with information about changes in the retinal image.

Sometimes we perceive motion when it doesn't occur. Have you ever been on a stationary train that feels as if it is moving, because a train on an adjacent track begins to slowly move past? Or have you been in an IMAX movie theater, in which you feel as if you were falling as a huge image of plane moves across the screen? In both cases, the experience of motion is convincing. *Apparent movement* is the perception that a stationary object is moving. It occurs when different areas of the retina are quickly stimulated, leading us to interpret motion (Ekroll & Scherzer, 2009; Lindemann & Bekkering, 2009).

Perceptual Illusions: The Deceptions of Perceptions

If you look carefully at the Parthenon, one of the most famous buildings of ancient Greece, still standing at the top of an Athens hill, you'll see that it was built with a bulge on one side. If it didn't have that bulge—and quite a few other architectural "tricks" like it, such as columns that incline inward—it would look as if it were

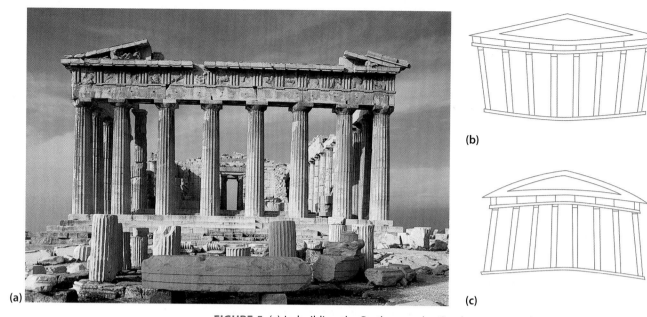

(a)

(b)

(c)

FIGURE 5 (a) In building the Parthenon, the Greeks constructed an architectural wonder that looks perfectly straight, with right angles at every corner as in. (b) However, if it had been built with completely true right angles, it would have looked as it does here. (c) To compensate for this illusion, the Parthenon was designed to have a slight upward curvature, as shown here. (Source: Coren & Ward, 1989, p. 5.)

visual illusions Physical stimuli that consistently produce errors in perception.

Study Alert

The explanation for the Müller-Lyer illusion is complicated. Figure 6 will help you master it.

crooked and about to fall down. Instead, it appears to stand completely straight, at right angles to the ground.

The fact that the Parthenon appears to be completely upright is the result of a series of visual illusions. **Visual illusions** are physical stimuli that consistently produce errors in perception. In the case of the Parthenon, the building appears to be completely square, as illustrated in Figure 5a. However, if it had been built that way, it would look to us as it does in Figure 5b. The reason for this is an illusion that makes right angles placed above a line appear as if they were bent. To offset the illusion, the Parthenon was constructed as in Figure 5c, with a slight upward curvature.

The *Müller-Lyer illusion* (illustrated in Figure 6) has fascinated psychologists for decades. Although the two lines are the same length, the one with the arrow tips pointing outward, away from the vertical line (Figure 6a, left) appears to be shorter than the one with the arrow tips pointing inward (Figure 6a, right).

Although all kinds of explanations for visual illusions have been suggested, most concentrate either on the physical operation of the eye or on our misinterpretation of the visual stimulus. For example, one explanation for the Müller-Lyer illusion is that eye movements are greater when the arrow tips point inward, making us perceive the line as longer than it is when the arrow tips face outward. In contrast, a different explanation for the illusion suggests that we unconsciously attribute particular significance to each of the lines (Gregory, 1978; Redding & Hawley, 1993). When we see the left line in Figure 6a we tend to perceive it as if it were the relatively close outside corner of a rectangular object, such as the outside corner of the room illustrated in Figure 6b. In contrast, when we view the line on the right in Figure 6a, we perceive it as the relatively more distant inside corner of a rectangular object, such as the inside room corner in Figure 6c. Because previous experience leads us to assume that the outside corner is closer than the inside corner, we make the further assumption that the inside corner must therefore be longer.

Despite the complexity of the latter explanation, a good deal of evidence supports it. For instance, cross-cultural studies show that people raised in areas where there are few right angles—such as the Zulu in Africa—are much less susceptible to

(a)   (b)   (c)

FIGURE 6 In the Müller-Lyer illusion (a), the vertical line on the left appears shorter than the one on the right, even though they are identical in length. One explanation for the Müller-Lyer illusion suggests that the line on the left (with arrow points directed outward) is perceived as the relatively close corner of a rectangular object, such as the building corner in (b), and the line on the right (with the arrow points directed inward) is interpreted as the inside corner of a rectangular object, such as the room extending away from us (c). Our previous experience with distance cues leads us to assume that the outside corner is closer than the inside corner and, consequently, that the inside corner must therefore be longer.

the illusion than are people who grow up where most structures are built using right angles and rectangles (Segall, Campbell, & Herskovits, 1966).

As the example of the Zulu indicates, the culture in which we are raised has clear consequences for how we perceive the world. Consider the drawing in Figure 7. Sometimes called the "devil's tuning fork," it is likely to produce a mind-boggling effect, as the center tine of the fork alternates between appearing and disappearing.

Exploring DIVERSITY

Culture and Perception

Now try to reproduce the drawing on a piece of paper. Chances are that the task is nearly impossible for you—unless you are a member of an African tribe with little exposure to Western cultures. For such individuals, the task is simple; they have no trouble reproducing the figure. The reason is that Westerners automatically interpret the drawing as something that cannot exist in three dimensions, and they therefore are inhibited from reproducing it. The African tribal members, in contrast, do not make the assumption that the figure is "impossible" and instead view it in two dimensions, a perception that enables them to copy the figure with ease (Deregowski, 1973).

Cultural differences are also reflected in depth perception. A Western viewer of Figure 8 would interpret the hunter in the drawing as aiming for the antelope in the foreground, while an elephant stands under the tree in the background. A member of an isolated African tribe, however, interprets the scene very differently by assuming that the hunter is aiming at the elephant. Westerners use the difference in sizes between the two animals as a cue that the elephant is farther away than the antelope (Hudson, 1960).

Does this mean that basic perceptual processes differ among people of different cultures? No. Variations in learning and experience produce cross-cultural differences in perception, and the underlying psychological processes involved in perception are similar (McCauley & Henrich, 2006).

Although visual illusions may seem like mere psychological curiosities, they actually illustrate something fundamental about perception. There is a basic connection between our prior knowledge, needs, motivations, and expectations about how

FIGURE 7 The "devil's tuning fork" has three prongs . . . or does it have two?

FIGURE 8 Is the man aiming for the elephant or the antelope? Westerners assume that the difference in size between the two animals indicates that the elephant is farther away, and therefore the man is aiming for the antelope. In contrast, members of some African tribes, not used to depth cues in two-dimensional drawings, assume that the man is aiming for the elephant. (The drawing is based on Deregowski, 1973.) Do you think Westerners, who view the picture in three dimensions, could explain what they see to someone who views the scene in two dimensions and eventually get that person to view it in three dimensions?

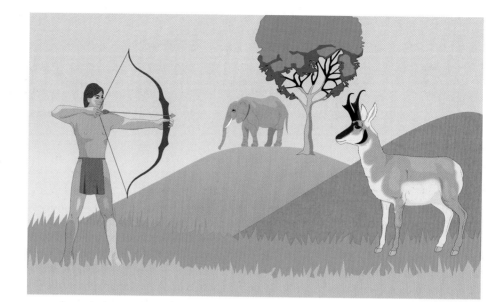

the world is put together and the way we perceive it. Our view of the world is very much an outcome, then, of fundamental psychological factors. Furthermore, each person perceives the environment in a way that is unique and special (Knoblich & Sebanz, 2006; Repp & Knoblich, 2007).

SUBLIMINAL PERCEPTION

Can stimuli that we're not consciously aware of change our behavior? In some ways, yes.

Subliminal perception refers to the perception of messages about which we have no awareness. The stimulus could be a written word, a sound, or even a smell that activates the sensory system but that is not intense enough for a person to report having experienced it. For example, in some studies people are exposed to a descriptive label—called a *prime*—about a person (such as the word *smart* or *happy*) so briefly that they cannot report seeing the label. Later, however, they form impressions that are influenced by the content of the prime. Somehow, they have been influenced by the prime that they say they couldn't see, providing some evidence for subliminal perception (Greenwald, Draine, & Abrams, 1996; Key, 2003).

Although subliminal messages (which social psychologists refer to as *priming*) can influence behavior in subtle ways, there's little evidence that it can lead to *major* changes in attitudes or behavior. Most research suggests that they cannot. For example, people who are subliminally exposed to an image of a Coke can and the word "thirst" do later rate themselves as thirstier, and they actually do drink more when given the opportunity. However, they don't particularly care if they drink Coke or some other liquid to quench their thirst (Dijksterhuis, Chartrand, & Aarts, 2007).

In short, although we are able to perceive at least some kinds of information of which we are unaware, there's little evidence that subliminal messages can change our attitudes or behavior in substantial ways. At the same time, subliminal perception does have at least some consequences. If our motivation to carry out a behavior is already high and the appropriate stimuli are presented subliminally, subliminal perception may have at least some effect on our behavior (Abrams, Klinger, & Greenwald, 2002; Pratkanis, Epley, & Savitsky, 2007; Randolph-Seng & Nielsen, 2009).

EXTRASENSORY PERCEPTION (ESP)

Given the lack of evidence that subliminal perception can alter our behavior in substantial ways, psychologists are particularly skeptical of reports of *extrasensory perception*, or ESP—perception that does not involve our known senses. Although half of the general population of the United States believes it exists, most psychologists reject the existence of ESP, asserting that there is no sound documentation of the phenomenon (Gallup Poll, 2001; Hyman, 1994; Swets & Bjork, 1990).

However, a debate in one of the most prestigious psychology journals, *Psychological Bulletin*, heightened interest in ESP. According to proponents of ESP, reliable evidence exists for an "anomalous process of information transfer," or *psi*. These researchers, who painstakingly reviewed considerable evidence, argue that a cumulative body of research shows reliable support for the existence of psi (Bem & Honorton, 1994; Parra & Argibay, 2007; Storm & Ertel, 2001).

Their conclusion has been challenged on several counts. For example, critics suggest that the research methodology was inadequate and that the experiments supporting psi are flawed (Hyman, 1994; Kennedy, 2004; Milton & Wiseman, 1999).

Because of questions about the quality of the research, as well as a lack of any credible theoretical explanation for how extrasensory perception might take place, the vast majority of psychologists continue to believe that there is no reliable scientific support for ESP (Rose & Blackmore, 2002; Wiseman & Greening, 2002). Still, the exchanges in *Psychological Bulletin* are likely to heighten the debate. More important, the renewed interest in ESP among psychologists is likely to inspire more research, which is the only way the issue can be resolved.

RECAP/EVALUATE/RETHINK

RECAP

What principles underlie our organization of the visual world and allow us to make sense of our environment?

- Perception is a constructive process in which people go beyond the stimuli that are physically present and try to construct a meaningful interpretation. (p. 116)
- The gestalt laws of organization are used to describe the way in which we organize bits and pieces of information into meaningful wholes, known as gestalts, through closure, proximity, similarity, and simplicity. (p. 116)
- In top-down processing, perception is guided by higher-level knowledge, experience, expectations, and motivations. In bottom-up processing, perception consists of the progression of recognizing and processing information from individual components of a stimuli and moving to the perception of the whole. (p. 117)

How are we able to perceive the world in three dimensions when our retinas are capable of sensing only two-dimensional images?

- Depth perception is the ability to perceive distance and view the world in three dimensions even though the images projected on our retinas are two-dimensional. We are able to judge depth and distance as a result of binocular disparity and monocular cues, such as motion

parallax, the relative size of images on the retina, and linear perspective. (p. 119)
- Perceptual constancy permits us to perceive stimuli as unvarying in size, shape, and color despite changes in the environment or the appearance of the objects being perceived. (p. 120)
- Motion perception depends on cues such as the perceived movement of an object across the retina and information about how the head and eyes are moving. (p. 121)

What clues do visual illusions give us about our understanding of general perceptual mechanisms?

- Visual illusions are physical stimuli that consistently produce errors in perception, causing judgments that do not reflect the physical reality of a stimulus accurately. One of the best-known illusions is the Müller-Lyer illusion. (p. 122)
- Visual illusions are usually the result of errors in the brain's interpretation of visual stimuli. Furthermore, culture clearly affects how we perceive the world. (p. 122)
- Subliminal perception refers to the perception of messages about which we have no awareness. The reality of the phenomenon, as well as of ESP, is open to question and debate. (p. 124)

EVALUATE

1. Match each of the following organizational laws with its meaning:
   - **a.** closure
   - **b.** proximity
   - **c.** similarity
   - **d.** simplicity

   1. Elements close together are grouped together.
   2. Patterns are perceived in the most basic, direct manner possible.
   3. Groupings are made in terms of complete figures.
   4. Elements similar in appearance are grouped together.

2. _____ analysis deals with the way in which we break an object down into its component pieces in order to understand it.

3. Processing that involves higher functions such as expectations and motivations is known as _____, whereas processing that recognizes the individual components of a stimulus is known as _____.

4. When a car passes you on the road and appears to shrink as it gets farther away, the phenomenon of _____ _____ permits you to realize that the car is not in fact getting smaller.

5. _____ _____ is the ability to view the world in three dimensions instead of two.

6. The brain makes use of a phenomenon known as _____ _____, or the difference in the images the two eyes see, to give three dimensions to sight.

RETHINK

1. In what ways do painters represent three-dimensional scenes in two dimensions on a canvas? Do you think artists in non-Western cultures use the same or different principles to represent three-dimensionality? Why?

2. *From the perspective of a corporate executive:* What arguments might you make if a member of your staff proposed a subliminal advertising campaign? Do you think your explanation would be enough to convince them? Why?

Answers to Evaluate Questions

1. a-3, b-1, c-4, d-2; 2. Feature; 3. top-down, bottom-up; 4. perceptual constancy; 5. Depth perception; 6. binocular disparity

KEY TERMS

gestalt laws of organization p. 116

top-down processing p. 117
bottom-up processing p. 118

depth perception p. 119
perceptual constancy p. 120

visual illusions p. 122

Psychology on the Web

1. Select one topic of personal interest to you that was mentioned in this set of modules (for instance, cochlear implants, visual illusions, psi). Find one "serious" or scientific website and one "popular" or commercial website with information about the chosen topic. Compare the type, level, and reliability of the information that you find on each site. Write a summary of your findings.
2. Are there more gestalt laws of organization than the four we've considered (closure, proximity, similarity, and simplicity)? Find the answer to this question on the Internet and write a summary of any additional gestalt laws you find.

Epilogue

We have noted the important distinction between sensation and perception, and we have examined the processes that underlie both of them. We've seen how external stimuli evoke sensory responses and how our different senses process the information contained in those responses. We also have focused on the physical structure and internal workings of the individual senses, including vision, hearing, balance, smell, taste, and the skin senses, and we've explored how our brains organize and process sensory information to construct a consistent, integrated picture of the world around us.

To complete our investigation of sensation and perception, let's reconsider super-recognizers like C. S., who are able to recognize faces years after they have met people, often only in passing. Using your knowledge of sensation and perception, answer these questions:

1. Why might some people be extremely capable at recognizing faces?
2. Is having extremely sensitive perception always a good thing? What might be some drawbacks to being a super-recognizer?
3. Does the ability of super-recognizers seem to be a matter of sensation or of perception? Why do you think so?

States of Consciousness

Key Concepts for Chapter 4

What are the different states of consciousness? ● What happens when we sleep, and what are the meaning and function of dreams? ● What are the major sleep disorders, and how can they be treated? ● How much do we daydream?

What is hypnosis, and are hypnotized people in a different state of consciousness? ● What are the effects of meditation?

What are the major classifications of drugs, and what are their effects?

Prologue *Out of Control*

Annie Fuller knew she was in trouble a year ago, when in the space of a few hours she managed to drink a male co-worker more than twice her size under the table. Of course, she'd been practicing for a quarter of her life by then; at 47, she was pouring a pint of bourbon, a 12-pack of beer, and a couple of bottles of wine into her 115-pound body each day. She had come to prefer alcohol to food, sex, or the company of friends and loved ones. Her marriage had ended; she had virtually stopped leaving the house, except to work and to drink. Fuller had tried and failed enough times over the years to know that she would not be able to sober up on her own. (Interlandi, 2008, p. 36)

Looking Ahead

Annie Fuller was an alcoholic—a person who abuses alcohol to the point where it causes serious life problems. A common experience of alcoholics is that they develop a resistance to alcohol, having to consume ever greater quantities of it to achieve the same effects, as Annie Fuller experienced. What those effects are, why people find them so pleasurable, and why some people become alcoholics are some of the questions we will address as we turn our attention to the study of consciousness.

Consciousness is the awareness of the sensations, thoughts, and feelings we experience at a given moment. Consciousness is our subjective understanding of both the environment around us and our private internal world, unobservable to outsiders.

In *waking consciousness*, we are awake and aware of our thoughts, emotions, and perceptions. All other states of consciousness are considered *altered states of consciousness*. Among these, sleeping and dreaming occur naturally; drug use and hypnosis, in contrast, are methods of deliberately altering one's state of consciousness.

In the past, because consciousness is so personal a phenomenon, psychologists were sometimes reluctant to study it. After all, who can say that your consciousness is similar to or, for that matter, different from anyone else's? Although the earliest psychologists, including William James (1890), saw the study of consciousness as central to the field, later psychologists suggested that it was out of bounds for the discipline. They argued that consciousness could be understood only by relying "unscientifically" on what experimental participants said they were experiencing. In this view, it was philosophers—not psychologists—who should speculate on such knotty issues as whether consciousness is separate from the physical body, how people know they exist, and how the body and mind are related to each other (Barresi, 2007; Gennaro, 2004; Rychlak, 1997).

Contemporary psychologists reject the view that the study of consciousness is unsuitable for the field of psychology. Instead, they argue that several approaches permit the scientific study of consciousness. For example, behavioral neuroscientists can measure brain-wave patterns under conditions of consciousness ranging from sleep to waking to hypnotic trances. And new understanding of the chemistry of drugs such as marijuana and alcohol has provided insights into the way they produce their pleasurable—as well as adverse—effects (Baars & Seth, 2009; Damasio, 2003; Mosher & Akins, 2007).

Yet how humans experience consciousness remains an open question. Some psychologists believe that the experience of consciousness is produced by a quantitative increase in neuronal activity that occurs throughout the brain. For example, an alarm clock moves us from sleep to waking consciousness by its loud ringing, which stimulates neurons throughout the brain as a whole (Greenfield, 2002; Koch & Greenfield, 2007).

In contrast, others believe that states of consciousness are produced by particular sets of neurons and neuronal pathways that are activated in specific ways. In this view, an alarm clock wakes us from sleep into consciousness, because specific neurons related to the auditory nerve are activated; the auditory nerve then sends a message to other neurons to release particular neurotransmitters that produce awareness of the alarm (Tononi & Koch, 2008).

Although we don't know yet which of these views is correct, it is clear that whatever state of consciousness we are in—be it waking, sleeping, hypnotic, or drug-induced—the complexities of consciousness are profound.

consciousness The awareness of the sensations, thoughts, and feelings being experienced at a given moment.

Sleep and Dreams

Mike Trevino, 29, slept nine hours in nine days in his quest to win a 3,000-mile, cross-country bike race. For the first 38 hrs. and 646 miles, he skipped sleep entirely. Later he napped—with no dreams he can remember—for no more than 90 minutes a night. Soon he began to imagine that his support crew was part of a bomb plot. "It was almost like riding in a movie. I thought it was a complex dream, even though I was conscious," says Trevino, who finished second. (Springen, 2004, p. 47)

Trevino's case is unusual—in part because he was able to function with so little sleep for so long—and it raises a host of questions about sleep and dreams. Can we live without sleep? What is the meaning of dreams? More generally, what is sleep?

Although sleeping is a state that we all experience, there are still many unanswered questions about sleep that remain, along with a considerable number of myths. Test your knowledge of sleep and dreams by answering the questionnaire in Figure 1.

Key Concepts

What are the different states of consciousness?

What happens when we sleep, and what are the meaning and function of dreams?

What are the major sleep disorders, and how can they be treated?

How much do we daydream?

FIGURE 1 There are many unanswered questions about sleep. Taking this quiz can help you clear up some of the myths.

Sleep Quiz

Although sleeping is something we all do for a significant part of our lives, myths and misconceptions about the topic abound. To test your own knowledge of sleep and dreams, try answering the following questions before reading further.

_____ 1. Some people never dream _True or false?_	_____ 6. If we lose some sleep we will eventually make up all the lost sleep the next night or another night. _True or false?_
_____ 2. Most dreams are caused by bodily sensations such as an upset stomach. _True or false?_	_____ 7. No one has been able to go for more than 48 hours without sleep. _True or false?_
_____ 3. It has been proved that people need eight hours of sleep to maintain mental health. _True or false?_	_____ 8. Our muscles are the most relaxed of the night when we are dreaming. _True or false?_
_____ 4. When people do not recall their dreams, it is probably because they are secretly trying to forget them. _True or false?_	_____ 9. Sleep enables the brain to rest because little brain activity takes place during sleep. _True or false?_
_____ 5. Depriving someone of sleep will invariably cause the individual to become mentally imbalanced. _True or false?_	_____10. Drugs have been proved to provide a long term cure for sleeplessness. _True or false?_

Scoring: This is an easy set of questions to score for every item is false. But don't lose any sleep if you missed them; they were chosen to represent the most common myths regarding sleep.

The Stages of Sleep

Most of us consider sleep a time of tranquility when we set aside the tensions of the day and spend the night in uneventful slumber. However, a closer look at sleep shows that a good deal of activity occurs throughout the night.

Measures of electrical activity in the brain show that the brain is quite active during the night. It produces electrical discharges with systematic, wavelike patterns that change in height (or amplitude) and speed (or frequency) in regular sequences. There is also significant physical activity in muscle and eye movements.

People progress through a series of distinct stages of sleep during a night's rest—known as *stage 1* through *stage 4* and *REM sleep*—moving through the stages in cycles lasting about 90 minutes. Each of these sleep stages is associated with a unique pattern of brain waves, which you can see in Figure 2.

When people first go to sleep, they move from a waking state in which they are relaxed with their eyes closed into **stage 1 sleep,** which is characterized by relatively rapid, low-amplitude brain waves. This is actually a stage of transition between wakefulness and sleep and lasts only a few minutes. During stage 1, images sometimes appear, as if we were viewing still photos, although this is not true dreaming, which occurs later in the night.

As sleep becomes deeper, people enter **stage 2 sleep,** which makes up about half of the total sleep of those in their early 20s and is characterized by a slower, more regular wave pattern. However, there are also momentary interruptions of sharply pointed, spiky waves that are called, because of their configuration, *sleep spindles.* It becomes increasingly difficult to awaken a person from sleep as stage 2 progresses.

As people drift into **stage 3 sleep,** the brain waves become slower, with higher peaks and lower valleys in the wave pattern. By the time sleepers arrive at **stage 4 sleep,** the pattern is even slower and more regular, and people are least responsive to outside stimulation.

stage 1 sleep The state of transition between wakefulness and sleep, characterized by relatively rapid, low-amplitude brain waves.

stage 2 sleep A sleep deeper than that of stage 1, characterized by a slower, more regular wave pattern, along with momentary interruptions of "sleep spindles."

stage 3 sleep A sleep characterized by slow brain waves, with greater peaks and valleys in the wave pattern than in stage 2 sleep.

stage 4 sleep The deepest stage of sleep, during which we are least responsive to outside stimulation.

FIGURE 2 Brain-wave patterns (measured by an EEG apparatus) vary significantly during the different stages of sleep (Hobson, 1989). As sleep moves from stage 1 through stage 4, brain waves become slower. During REM sleep, however, the fast wave patterns are similar to relaxed wakefulness.

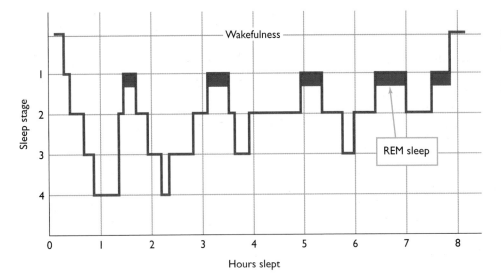

FIGURE 3 During the night, the typical sleeper passes through all four stages of sleep and several REM periods. (Source: From Ernest Hartmann, *The Biology of Dreaming* (1967), p. 6. Courtesy of Charles C Thomas Publisher, Ltd., Springfield, Illinois.)

As you can see in Figure 3, stage 4 sleep is most likely to occur during the early part of the night. In the first half of the night, sleep is dominated by stages 3 and 4. The second half is characterized by stages 1 and 2—as well as a fifth stage during which dreams occur.

REM Sleep: The Paradox of Sleep

Several times a night, when sleepers have cycled back to a shallower state of sleep, something curious happens. Their heart rate increases and becomes irregular, their blood pressure rises, and their breathing rate increases. Most characteristic of this period is the back-and-forth movement of their eyes, as if they were watching an action-filled movie. This period of sleep is called **rapid eye movement,** or **REM sleep,** and it contrasts with stages 1 through 4, which are collectively labeled *non-REM* (or *NREM*) sleep. REM sleep occupies a little more than 20% of adults' total sleeping time.

rapid eye movement (REM) sleep Sleep occupying 20% of an adult's sleeping time, characterized by increased heart rate, blood pressure, and breathing rate; erections; eye movements; and the experience of dreaming.

People progress through four distinct stages of sleep during a night's rest spread over cycles lasting about 90 minutes. REM sleep, which occupies only 20% of adults' sleeping time, occurs in stage 1 sleep. These photos, taken at different times of night, show the synchronized patterns of a couple accustomed to sleeping in the same bed.

Let Me Sleep on It: The Role of Sleep in Memory and Thinking

"Let me sleep on it. And I'll give you an answer in the morning."

As the popular song lyric suggests, laypeople and scientists alike have long suspected that sleep plays an important role in thinking and memory—but what that role might be has been less than clear. One idea is that a process called memory consolidation occurs during sleep. While we're awake, our brains store information from our experiences throughout the day in the hippocampus region. But for long term storage, those memories need to be relocated to the cortex, where connections are made between the new information and what we already know. This process helps us to make better sense of the new information and to retain it—and it may be facilitated by sleep, when the influx of new information slows to a trickle (Cai et al., 2009; Gilestro, Tononi, & Cirelli, 2009).

Recent studies are shedding light on how memory consolidation works. In one, participants memorized a long list of word pairs immediately before they went to sleep. As soon as they reached the deepest stages of sleep, researchers used electrodes to stimulate very slow brain waves in some of the participants. The participants whose brain waves were altered in this way showed better recall for the word

Does sleeping help us to remember more effectively?

pairs the next morning. The researchers theorize that these slow brain waves improved memory storage by strengthening the connections between neurons (Verleger et al., 2008).

Another study showed how sleep is involved in thinking as well as memory. The researchers gave participants a puzzle that involved performing a set of seven operations on a set of numbers, with the outcome

of the seventh operation as the final answer. The participants were given a series of these puzzles using different number sets, and they were instructed to find the answers quickly. What the participants didn't know was that there was a "trick" to the puzzles: the final answer was always the same as the outcome of the second operation. If they realized this trick, they could skip most of the work and give the final answer much more quickly.

The question was whether "sleeping on it" would help participants achieve this insight—and it did. Participants who worked a set of puzzles before sleeping and then worked another set the next morning were almost three times more likely to discover the trick than were participants who took a long break between puzzle sessions but did not sleep (Stickgold & Wehrwein, 2009; Yordanova et al., 2008).

This, and other findings like it, suggest that sleep plays an important role in helping us to analyze and make meaning of our waking experiences. "Sleeping on it," then, may turn out to be a reasonable strategy for coming to solutions for our problems.

RETHINK

- Why do you think memory and thinking may be improved by sleeping?
- How could students make use of memory consolidation while sleeping to improve their test performance?

Paradoxically, while all this activity is occurring, the major muscles of the body appear to be paralyzed. In addition, and most important, REM sleep is usually accompanied by dreams, which—whether or not people remember them—are experienced by *everyone* during some part of their night's sleep. Although some dreaming occurs in non-REM stages of sleep, dreams are most likely to occur in the REM period, where they are the most vivid and easily remembered (Conduit, Crewther, & Coleman, 2004; Lu et al., 2006; Titone, 2002).

There is good reason to believe that REM sleep plays a critical role in everyday human functioning. People deprived of REM sleep—by being awakened every time they begin to display the physiological signs of that stage—show a *rebound effect* when allowed to rest undisturbed. With this rebound effect, REM-deprived sleepers spend significantly more time in REM sleep than they normally would. In addition, REM sleep may play a role in learning and memory, allowing us to rethink and restore information and emotional experiences that we've had during the day (Nishida et al., 2009; Walker & van der Helm, 2009). (Also see *Applying Psychology in the 21st Century*.)

Study Alert

Differentiate the five stages of sleep (stage 1, stage 2, stage 3, stage 4, and REM sleep), which produce different brain-wave patterns.

Why Do We Sleep, and How Much Sleep Is Necessary?

Sleep is a requirement for normal human functioning, although, surprisingly, we don't know exactly why. It is reasonable to expect that our bodies would require a tranquil "rest and relaxation" period to revitalize themselves, and experiments with rats show that total sleep deprivation results in death. But why?

One explanation, based on an evolutionary perspective, suggests that sleep permitted our ancestors to conserve energy at night, a time when food was relatively hard to come by. Consequently, they were better able to forage for food when the sun is up.

A second explanation for why we sleep is that sleep restores and replenishes our brains and bodies. For instance, the reduced activity of the brain during non-REM sleep may give neurons in the brain a chance to repair themselves. Furthermore, the onset of REM sleep stops the release of neurotransmitters called *monoamines* and so permits receptor cells to get some necessary rest and to increase their sensitivity during periods of wakefulness (McNamara, 2004; Siegel, 2003; Steiger, 2007).

Finally, sleep may be essential, because it assists physical growth and brain development in children. For example, the release of growth hormones is associated with deep sleep (Peterfi et al., 2010).

Still, these explanations remain speculative, and there is no definitive answer as to why sleep is essential. Furthermore, scientists have been unable to establish just how much sleep is absolutely required. Most people today sleep between seven and eight hours each night, which is three hours a night *less* than people slept a hundred years ago. In addition, there is wide variability among individuals, with some people needing as little as three hours of sleep (see Figure 4). Sleep requirements also vary over the course of a lifetime: As they age, people generally need less and less sleep.

People who participate in sleep deprivation experiments, in which they are kept awake for stretches as long as 200 hours, show no lasting effects. It's no fun—they feel weary and irritable, can't concentrate, and show a loss of creativity, even after only minor deprivation. They also show a decline in logical reasoning ability. However, after being allowed to sleep normally, they bounce back quickly and are able to perform at predeprivation levels after just a few days (Babson et al., 2009; Mograss et al., 2009).

In short, as far as we know, most people suffer no permanent consequences of such temporary sleep deprivation. But—and this is an important but—a lack of sleep

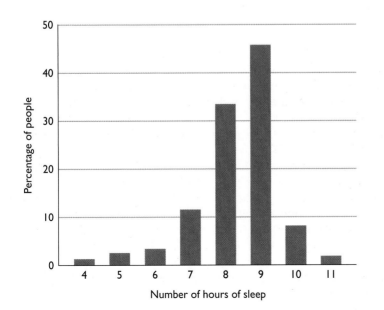

FIGURE 4 Although most people report sleeping between eight and nine hours per night, the amount that individuals needs varies a great deal (Borbely, 1986). Where would you place yourself on this graph, and why do you think you need more or less sleep than others?

Neuroscience in Your Life: Why Are You Cranky? Your Brain Is Too Awake

FIGURE 5 One explanation about why we need sleep is that we need to restore and repair various systems in our brains. One such system is the one that regulates our emotions. In the MRI scan, the amygdala, which helps process emotions, shows less activation (seen in reds and oranges) when viewing emotional pictures when participants had enough sleep compared to when they were sleep deprived, suggesting that participants responded more emotionally when they had less sleep. (Source: Walker and van der Helm 2009.)

can make us feel edgy, slow our reaction time, and lower our performance on academic and physical tasks. In addition, we put ourselves, and others, at risk when we carry out routine activities, such as driving, when we're very sleepy (Anderson & Home, 2006; Morad et al., 2009; Philip et al., 2005) (also see Figure 5).

The Function and Meaning of Dreaming

I was sitting at my desk when I remembered that this was the day of my chemistry final! I was terrified, because I hadn't studied a bit for it. In fact, I had missed every lecture all semester. In a panic, I began running across campus desperately searching for the classroom, to which I'd never been. It was hopeless; I knew I was going to fail and flunk out of college.

FIGURE 6 Although dreams tend to be subjective to the person having them, there are common elements that frequently occur in everyone's dreams. Why do you think so many common dreams are unpleasant and so few are pleasant? Do you think this tells us anything about the function of dreams? (Source: Schneider & Domhoff, 2002.)

Thematic Event	Percentage of Dreams Reporting at Least One Event	
	Males	Females
Aggression	47%	44%
Friendliness	38	42
Sexuality	12	04
Misfortune	36	33
Success	15	08
Failure	15	10

Theory	Basic Explanation	Meaning of Dreams	Is Meaning of Dream Disguised?
Unconscious wish fulfillment theory (Freud)	Psychoanalytical explanation where dreams represent unconscious wishes the dreamer wants to fulfill	Latent content reveals unconscious wishes	Yes, by manifest content of dreams
Dreams-for-survival theory	Evolutionary explanation where information relevant to daily survival is reconsidered and reprocessed	Clues to everyday concerns about survival	Not necessarily
Activation-synthesis theory	Neuroscience explanation where dreams are the result of random activation of various memories, which are tied together in a logical story line	Dream scenario that is constructed is related to dreamer's concerns	Not necessarily

FIGURE 7 Three theories of dreams. As researchers have yet to agree on the fundamental meaning of dreams, several theories about dreaming have emerged.

If you have had a similar dream—a surprisingly common dream among people involved in academic pursuits—you know how utterly convincing are the panic and fear that the events in the dream can bring about. *Nightmares*, unusually frightening dreams, occur fairly often. In one survey, almost half of a group of college students who kept records of their dreams over a two-week period reported having at least one nightmare. This works out to some 24 nightmares per person each year, on average (Levin & Nielsen, 2009; Nielson, Stenstrom, & Levin, 2006; Schredl et al., 2009).

However, most of the 150,000 dreams the average person experiences by the age of 70 are much less dramatic. They typically encompass everyday events such as going to the supermarket, working at the office, and preparing a meal. Students dream about going to class; professors dream about lecturing. Dental patients dream of getting their teeth drilled; dentists dream of drilling the wrong tooth. The English have tea with the queen in their dreams; in the United States, people go to a bar with the president (Domhoff, 1996; Schredl & Piel, 2005; Taylor & Bryant, 2007). Figure 6 shows the most common themes found in people's dreams.

But what, if anything, do all these dreams mean? Whether dreams have a specific significance and function is a question that scientists have considered for many years, and they have developed the three alternative theories we discuss below (and summarized in Figure 7).

PSYCHOANALYTIC EXPLANATIONS OF DREAMS: DO DREAMS REPRESENT UNCONSCIOUS WISH FULFILLMENT?

Using psychoanalytic theory, Sigmund Freud viewed dreams as a guide to the unconscious (Freud, 1900). In his **unconscious wish fulfillment theory**, he proposed that dreams represent unconscious wishes that dreamers desire to see fulfilled. However, because these wishes are threatening to the dreamer's conscious awareness, the actual wishes—called the **latent content of dreams**—are disguised. The true subject and meaning of a dream, then, may have little to do with its apparent story line, which Freud called the **manifest content of dreams**.

To Freud, it was important to pierce the armor of a dream's manifest content to understand its true meaning. To do this, Freud tried to get people to discuss their dreams, associating symbols in the dreams with events in the past. He also suggested that certain common symbols with universal meanings appear in dreams. For example, to Freud, dreams in which a person is flying symbolize a wish for sexual intercourse. (See Figure 8 for other common symbols.)

Many psychologists reject Freud's view that dreams typically represent unconscious wishes and that particular objects and events in a dream are symbolic. Rather,

Study Alert

Use Figure 7 to learn the differences between the three main explanations of dreaming.

unconscious wish fulfillment theory Sigmund Freud's theory that dreams represent unconscious wishes that dreamers desire to see fulfilled.

latent content of dreams According to Freud, the "disguised" meanings of dreams, hidden by more obvious subjects.

manifest content of dreams According to Freud, the apparent story line of dreams.

Symbol (Manifest Content of Dream)	Interpretation (Latent Content)
Climbing up a stairway, crossing a bridge, riding an elevator, flying in an airplane, walking down a long hallway, entering a room, train traveling through a tunnel	Sexual intercourse
Apples , peaches grapefruits	Breasts
Bullets, fire, snakes, sticks, umbrellas, guns, hoses, knives	Male sex organs
Ovens, boxes, tunnels, closets, caves, bottles, ship	Female sex organs

FIGURE 8 According to Freud, dreams contain common symbols with universal meanings.

they believe that the direct, overt action of a dream is the focal point of its meaning. For example, a dream in which we are walking down a long hallway to take an exam for which we haven't studied does not relate to unconscious, unacceptable wishes. Instead, it simply may mean that we are concerned about an impending test. Even more complex dreams can often be interpreted in terms of everyday concerns and stress (Picchioni et al., 2002; Cartwright, Agargum, & Kirkby, 2006).

Moreover, some dreams reflect events occurring in the dreamer's environment as he or she is sleeping. For example, sleeping participants in one experiment were sprayed with water while they were dreaming. Those unlucky volunteers reported more dreams involving water than did a comparison group of participants who were left to sleep undisturbed (Dement & Wolpert, 1958). Similarly, it is not unusual to wake up to find that the doorbell that was heard ringing in a dream is actually an alarm clock telling us it is time to get up.

However, PET brain scan research does lend a degree of support for the wish fulfillment view. For instance, the limbic and paralimbic regions of the brain, which are associated with emotion and motivation, are particularly active during REM sleep. At the same time, the association areas of the prefrontal cortex, which control logical analysis and attention, are inactive during REM sleep. The high activation of emotional and motivational centers of the brain during dreaming makes it more plausible that dreams may reflect unconscious wishes and instinctual needs, as Freud suggested (Braun et al., 1998; Occhionero, 2004; Wehrle et al., 2007).

EVOLUTIONARY EXPLANATIONS OF DREAMS: DREAMS-FOR-SURVIVAL THEORY

dreams-for-survival theory The theory suggesting that dreams permit information that is critical for our daily survival to be reconsidered and reprocessed during sleep.

According to the **dreams-for-survival theory,** which is based in the evolutionary perspective, dreams permit us to reconsider and reprocess during sleep information that is critical for our daily survival. Dreaming is considered an inheritance from our animal ancestors, whose small brains were unable to sift sufficient information during waking hours. Consequently, dreaming provided a mechanism that permitted the processing of information 24 hours a day.

According to this theory, dreams represent concerns about our daily lives, illustrating our uncertainties, indecisions, ideas, and desires. Dreams are seen, then, as consistent with everyday living. Rather than being disguised wishes, as Freud suggested, they represent key concerns growing out of our daily experiences (Ross, 2006; Winson, 1990).

Research supports the dreams-for-survival theory, suggesting that certain dreams permit people to focus on and to consolidate memories, particularly dreams that pertain to "how-to-do-it" memories related to motor skills. For example, rats seem to dream about mazes that they learned to run through during the day, at least according to the patterns of brain activity that appear while they are sleeping (Kenway & Wilson, 2001; Kuriyama, Stickgold, & Walker, 2004; Smith, 2006; Stickgold et al., 2001).

A similar phenomenon appears to work in humans. For instance, in one experiment, participants learned a visual memory task late in the day. They were then sent to bed, but awakened at certain times during the night. When they were awakened at times that did not interrupt dreaming, their performance on the memory task typically improved the next day. But when they were awakened during rapid eye movement (REM) sleep—the stage of sleep when people dream—their performance declined. The implication is that dreaming, at least when it is uninterrupted, can play a role in helping us remember material to which we have been previously exposed (Karni et al., 1994; Marshall & Born, 2007; Nishida et al., 2009).

NEUROSCIENCE EXPLANATIONS OF DREAMS: ACTIVATION-SYNTHESIS THEORY

Using the neuroscience perspective, psychiatrist J. Allan Hobson has proposed the activation-synthesis theory of dreams. The **activation-synthesis theory** focuses on the random electrical energy that the brain produces during REM sleep, possibly as a result of changes in the production of particular neurotransmitters. This electrical energy randomly stimulates memories stored in the brain. Because we have a need to make sense of our world even while asleep, the brain takes these chaotic memories and weaves them into a logical story line, filling in the gaps to produce a rational scenario (Hobson, 2005; Porte & Hobson, 1996).

Activation-synthesis theory has been refined by the *activation information modulation (AIM)* theory. According to AIM, dreams are initiated in the brain's pons, which sends random signals to the cortex. Areas of the cortex that are involved in particular waking behaviors are related to the content of dreams. For example, areas of the brain related to vision are involved in the visual aspects of the dream, while areas of the brain related to movement are involved in aspects of the dream related to motion (Hobson, 2007).

Activation-synthesis and AIM theories do not entirely reject the view that dreams reflect unconscious wishes. They suggest that the particular scenario a dreamer produces is not random but instead is a clue to the dreamer's fears, emotions, and concerns. Hence, what starts out as a random process culminates in something meaningful.

THE FAR SIDE By GARY LARSON

"I've got it again, Larry ... an eerie feeling like there's something on top of the bed."

activation-synthesis theory Hobson's theory that the brain produces random electrical energy during REM sleep that stimulates memories stored in the brain.

Sleep Disturbances: Slumbering Problems

At one time or another, almost all of us have difficulty sleeping—a condition known as insomnia. It could be due to a particular situation, such as the breakup of a relationship, concern about a test score, or the loss of a job. Some cases of insomnia, however, have no obvious cause. Some people are simply unable to fall asleep easily, or they go to sleep readily but wake up frequently during the night. Insomnia is a problem that afflicts as many as one-third of all people. Women and older adults are more likely to suffer from insomnia, as well as people who are unusually thin or are depressed (Bains, 2006; Cooke & Ancoli-Israel, 2006; Henry et al., 2008).

Some people who *think* they have sleeping problems actually are mistaken. For example, researchers in sleep laboratories have found that some people who report being up all night actually fall asleep in 30 minutes and stay asleep all night. Furthermore, some people with insomnia accurately recall sounds that they heard while they were asleep, which gives them the impression that they were awake during the night (Semler & Harvey, 2005; Yapko, 2006). (Also see *PsychWork*.)

PsychWork

SLEEP TECHNOLOGIST

Name: Brandon Liebig

Position: Sleep Technologist, Central Sleep Diagnostics, Northbrook, IL

Education: BFA, Studio Art, University of Nebraska at Omaha; Graduate of Accredited Sleep Technology Education Program, University of Massachusetts Memorial Hospital Sleep Center, Worcester, MA; Certified by the Board of Registered Polysomnographic Technologists

Although each of us spends the majority of our time sleeping, sleep—or rather a lack of it—is a state that is problematic for many people. For those seeking treatment for sleep disorders, sleep technologist Brandon Liebig is on the front lines, assisting in clinical assessments, helping to monitor and test patients, and participating in the development of treatment procedures.

As Liebig notes, "Patients seen in the sleep lab often have complicated medical backgrounds and health needs, and some may have cognitive limitations/disabilities or coexisting psychological conditions in addition to their sleep symptoms."

"Sleep technologists must recognize the particular needs of a patient and adjust their style of providing care to best suit the patient and promote the best possible outcomes, both for the patient's experience in the sleep lab and the data collected in research studies," he added.

"Often, patients may find it stressful, unfamiliar, and sometimes uncomfortable to sleep in a lab setting with the sensors and other equipment attached to their bodies. Sleep technologists use their knowledge of psychology to provide the patient with understanding, reassurance, respect, and patience," said Liebig.

Other sleep problems are less common than insomnia, although they are still widespread. For instance, some 20 million people suffer from sleep apnea. *Sleep apnea* is a condition in which a person has difficulty breathing while sleeping. The result is disturbed, fitful sleep, and a significant loss of REM sleep, as the person is constantly reawakened when the lack of oxygen becomes great enough to trigger a waking response. Some people with apnea wake as many as 500 times during the course of a night, although they may not even be aware that they have wakened. Not surprisingly, such disturbed sleep results in extreme fatigue the next day. Sleep apnea also may play a role in *sudden infant death syndrome (SIDS)*, a mysterious killer of seemingly normal infants who die while sleeping (Aloia, Smith, & Arnedt, 2007; Gami et al., 2005; Tippin, Sparks, & Rizzo, 2009).

Night terrors are sudden awakenings from non-REM sleep that are accompanied by extreme fear, panic, and strong physiological arousal. Usually occurring in stage 4 sleep, night terrors may be so frightening that a sleeper awakens with a shriek. Although night terrors initially produce great agitation, victims usually can get back to sleep fairly quickly. They are far less frequent than nightmares, and, unlike nightmares, they typically occur during slow-wave, non-REM sleep. They occur most frequently in children between the ages of 3 and 8 (Lowe, Humphreys, & Williams, 2007).

Narcolepsy is uncontrollable sleeping that occurs for short periods while a person is awake. No matter what the activity—holding a heated conversation, exercising, or driving—a narcoleptic will suddenly fall asleep. People with narcolepsy go directly from wakefulness to REM sleep, skipping the other stages. The causes of narcolepsy are not known, although there could be a genetic component, because narcolepsy runs in families (Billiard, 2008; Ervik, Abdelnoor, & Heier, 2006; Mahmood & Black, 2005; Nishino, 2007).

We know relatively little about sleeptalking and sleepwalking, two sleep disturbances that are usually harmless. Both occur during stage 4 sleep and are more common in children than in adults. Sleeptalkers and sleepwalkers usually have a vague consciousness of the world around them, and a sleepwalker may be able to walk with agility around obstructions in a crowded room. Unless a sleepwalker wanders into a dangerous environment, sleepwalking typically poses little risk. And the common idea that it's dangerous to wake a sleepwalker? It's just superstition (Baruss, 2003; Guilleminault et al., 2005; Lee-Chiong, 2006).

Sleepwalking (along with sleeptalking) are more common in children than adults, and they both occur during stage 4 of sleep.

Circadian Rhythms: Life Cycles

The fact that we cycle back and forth between wakefulness and sleep is one example of the body's circadian rhythms. **Circadian rhythms** (from the Latin *circa diem*, or "about a day") are biological processes that occur regularly on approximately a 24-hour cycle. Sleeping and waking, for instance, occur naturally to the beat of an internal pacemaker that works on a cycle of about 24 hours. Several other bodily functions, such as body temperature, hormone production, and blood pressure, also follow circadian rhythms (Beersma & Gordijn, 2007; Blatter & Cajochen, 2007; Saper et al., 2005).

Circadian cycles are complex, and they involve a variety of behaviors. For instance, sleepiness occurs not just in the evening but throughout the day in regular patterns, with most of us getting drowsy in mid-afternoon—regardless of whether we have eaten a heavy lunch. By making an afternoon siesta part of their everyday habit, people in several cultures take advantage of the body's natural inclination to sleep at this time (Reilly & Waterhouse, 2007; Takahashi et al., 2004; Wright, 2002).

The brain's *suprachiasmatic nucleus (SCN)* controls circadian rhythms. However, the relative amount of light and darkness, which varies with the seasons of the year, also plays a role in regulating circadian rhythms. In fact, some people experience *seasonal affective disorder*, a form of severe depression in which feelings of despair and hopelessness increase during the winter and lift during the rest of the year. The disorder appears to be a result of the brevity and gloom of winter days. Daily exposure to bright lights is sometimes sufficient to improve the mood of those with this disorder (Golden et al., 2005; Kasof, 2009; Rohan, Roecklein, & Tierney Lindsey, 2007).

Circadian rhythms produce jet lag.

circadian rhythms Biological processes that occur regularly on approximately a 24-hour cycle.

daydreams Fantasies that people construct while awake.

Daydreams: Dreams Without Sleep

It is the stuff of magic: Our past mistakes can be wiped out and the future filled with noteworthy accomplishments. Fame, happiness, and wealth can be ours. In the next moment, though, the most horrible tragedies can occur, leaving us devastated, alone, and penniless.

The source of these scenarios is **daydreams,** fantasies that people construct while awake. Unlike dreaming that occurs during sleep, daydreams are more under people's control. Therefore, their content is often more closely related to immediate events in the environment than is the content of the dreams that occur during sleep. Although they may include sexual content, daydreams also pertain to other activities or events that are relevant to a person's life.

Daydreams are a typical part of waking consciousness, even though our awareness of the environment around us declines while we are daydreaming. People vary considerably in the amount of daydreaming they do. For example, around 2% to 4% of the population spend at least half their free time fantasizing. Although most people daydream much less frequently, almost everyone fantasizes to some degree. Studies that ask people to identify what they are doing at random times during the day have shown that they are daydreaming about 10% of the time (Holler, 2006; Lynn et al., 1996; Singer, 2006).

The brain is surprisingly active during daydreaming. For example, several areas of the brain that are associated with complex problem solving become activated during daydreaming. In fact, daydreaming may be the only time these areas are activated simultaneously, suggesting that daydreaming may lead to insights about problems that we are grappling with (Fleck et al., 2008; Kounios et al., 2008).

Daydreams are fantasies that people construct while they are awake. What are the similarities and differences between daydreams and night dreams?

© Drew Dernavich/The New Yorker Collection/www.cartoonbank.com.

"When I can't sleep, I find that it sometimes helps to get up and jot down my anxieties."

BECOMING AN INFORMED CONSUMER

of Psychology

Sleeping Better

Do you have trouble sleeping? You're not alone—70 million people in the United States have sleep problems. For those of us who spend hours tossing and turning in bed, psychologists studying sleep disturbances have a number of suggestions for overcoming insomnia (Benca, 2005; Edinger et al., 2001; Finley & Cowley, 2005). Here are some ideas.

- *Exercise during the day (at least six hours before bedtime) and avoid naps.* Not surprisingly, it helps to be tired before going to sleep! Moreover, learning systematic relaxation techniques and biofeedback can help you unwind from the day's stresses and tensions.
- *Choose a regular bedtime and stick to it.* Adhering to a habitual schedule helps your internal timing mechanisms regulate your body more effectively.
- *Avoid drinks with caffeine after lunch.* The effects of beverages such as coffee, tea, and some soft drinks can linger for as long as 8 to 12 hours after they are consumed.
- *Drink a glass of warm milk at bedtime.* Your grandparents were right when they dispensed this advice: Milk contains the chemical tryptophan, which helps people fall asleep.
- *Avoid sleeping pills.* Even though 25% of U.S. adults report having taken medication for sleep in the previous year, in the long run sleep medications can do more harm than good, because they disrupt the normal sleep cycle.
- *Try* not *to sleep.* This approach works because people often have difficulty falling asleep, because they are trying so hard. A better strategy is to go to bed only when you feel tired. If you don't get to sleep within 10 minutes, leave the bedroom and do something else, returning to bed only when you feel sleepy. Continue this process all night if necessary. But get up at your usual hour in the morning, and don't take any naps during the day. After three or four weeks, most people become conditioned to associate their beds with sleep—and fall asleep rapidly at night (Sloan et al., 1993; Smith, 2001; Ubell, 1993).

For long-term problems with sleep, you might consider visiting a sleep disorders center. For information on accredited clinics, consult the American Academy of Sleep Medicine at www.aasmnet.org.

RECAP/EVALUATE/RETHINK

RECAP

What are the different states of consciousness?

- Consciousness is a person's awareness of the sensations, thoughts, and feelings at a given moment. Waking consciousness can vary from more active to more passive states. (p. 130)
- Altered states of consciousness include naturally occurring sleep and dreaming, as well as hypnotic and drug-induced states. (p. 130)

What happens when we sleep, and what are the meaning and function of dreams?

- The brain is active throughout the night, and sleep proceeds through a series of stages identified by unique patterns of brain waves. (p. 132)
- REM (rapid eye movement) sleep is characterized by an increase in heart rate, a rise in blood pressure, an increase in the rate of breathing, and, in males, erections. Dreams most often occur during this stage. (p. 133)
- According to Freud's psychoanalytic approach, dreams have both a manifest content (an apparent story line) and a latent content (a true meaning). He suggested that the latent content provides a guide to a dreamer's unconscious, revealing unfulfilled wishes or desires. (p. 137)
- The dreams-for-survival theory, grounded in an evolutionary perspective, suggests that information relevant to daily survival is reconsidered and reprocessed in dreams. Taking a neuroscience approach, the activation-synthesis theory proposes that dreams are a result of random electrical energy that stimulates different memories, which then are woven into a coherent story line. (p. 138)

What are the major sleep disorders, and how can they be treated?

- Insomnia is a sleep disorder characterized by difficulty sleeping. Sleep apnea is a condition in which people have difficulty sleeping and breathing at the same time. People with narcolepsy have an uncontrollable urge to sleep. Sleepwalking and sleeptalking are relatively harmless. (p. 139)

How much do we daydream?

- Wide individual differences exist in the amount of time devoted to daydreaming. Almost everyone daydreams or fantasizes to some degree. (p. 141)

EVALUATE

1. _____ is the term used to describe our understanding of the world external to us, as well as our own internal world.
2. A great deal of neural activity goes on during sleep. True or false?
3. Dreams most often occur in _____ sleep.
4. _____ _____ are internal bodily processes that occur on a daily cycle.
5. Freud's theory of unconscious _____ _____ states that the actual wishes an individual expresses in dreams are disguised, because they are threatening to the person's conscious awareness.
6. Match the theory of dreaming with its definition.
   1. activation-synthesis theory
   2. dreams-for-survival theory
   3. dreams as wish fulfillment
   a. Dreams permit important information to be reprocessed during sleep.
   b. The manifest content of dreams disguises the latent content of the dreams.
   c. Electrical energy stimulates random memories, which are woven together to produce dreams.

RETHINK

1. Suppose that a new "miracle pill" allows a person to function with only one hour of sleep per night. However, because a night's sleep is so short, a person who takes the pill will never dream again. Knowing what you do about the functions of sleep and dreaming, what would be some advantages and drawbacks of such a pill from a personal standpoint? Would you take such a pill?
2. *From the perspective of an educator:* How might you use the findings in sleep research to maximize student learning?

Answers to Evaluate Questions

1. Consciousness; 2. true; 3. REM; 4. Circadian rhythms; 5. wish fulfillment; 6. 1-c, 2-a, 3-b

KEY TERMS

consciousness p. 130
stage 1 sleep p. 132
stage 2 sleep p. 132
stage 3 sleep p. 132
stage 4 sleep p. 132

rapid eye movement (REM) sleep p. 133
unconscious wish fulfillment theory p. 137
latent content of dreams p. 137

manifest content of dreams p. 137
dreams-for-survival theory p. 138

activation-synthesis theory p. 139
circadian rhythms p. 141
daydreams p. 141

Hypnosis and Meditation

Key Concepts

What is hypnosis, and are hypnotized people in a different state of consciousness?

What are the effects of meditation?

You are feeling relaxed and drowsy. You are getting sleepier. Your body is becoming limp. Your eyelids are feeling heavier. Your eyes are closing; you can't keep them open anymore. You are totally relaxed. Now, place your hands above your head. But you will find they are getting heavier and heavier—so heavy you can barely keep them up. In fact, although you are straining as hard as you can, you will be unable to hold them up any longer.

An observer watching this scene would notice a curious phenomenon. Many of the people listening to the voice are dropping their arms to their sides. The reason for this strange behavior? Those people have been hypnotized.

Hypnosis: A Trance-Forming Experience?

hypnosis A trancelike state of heightened susceptibility to the suggestions of others.

People under **hypnosis** are in a trancelike state of heightened susceptibility to the suggestions of others. In some respects, it appears that they are asleep. Yet other aspects of their behavior contradict this notion, for people are attentive to the hypnotist's suggestions and may carry out bizarre or silly suggestions.

How is someone hypnotized? Typically, the process follows a series of four steps. First, a person is made comfortable in a quiet environment. Second, the hypnotist explains what is going to happen, such as telling the person that he or she will experience a pleasant, relaxed state. Third, the hypnotist tells the person to concentrate on a specific object or image, such as the hypnotist's moving finger or an image of a calm lake. The hypnotist may have the person concentrate on relaxing different parts of the body, such as the arms, legs, and chest. Fourth, once the subject is in a highly relaxed state, the hypnotist may make suggestions that the person interprets as being produced by hypnosis, such as "Your arms are getting heavy" and "Your eyelids are more difficult to open." Because the person begins to experience these sensations, he or she believes they are caused by the hypnotist and becomes susceptible to the suggestions of the hypnotist.

Despite their compliance when hypnotized, people do not lose all will of their own. They will not perform antisocial behaviors, and they will not carry out self-destructive acts. People will not reveal hidden truths about themselves, and they are capable of lying. Moreover, people cannot be hypnotized against their will—despite popular misconceptions (Gwynn & Spanos, 1996; Raz, 2007).

There are wide variations in people's susceptibility to hypnosis. About 5% to 20% of the population cannot be hypnotized at all, and some 15% are very easily hypnotized. Most people fall somewhere in between. Moreover, the ease with which a person is hypnotized is related to a number of other characteristics. People who are readily hypnotized are also easily absorbed while reading books or listening to music, becoming unaware of what is happening around them, and they often spend an unusual amount of time daydreaming. In sum, then, they show a high ability to concentrate and to become completely absorbed in what

Despite common misconceptions, people cannot be hypnotized against their will, nor do they lose all will of their own when they are hypnotized. Why, then, do people sometimes behave so unusually when asked to by a hypnotist?

they are doing (Benham, Woody, & Wilson, 2006; Kirsch & Braffman, 2001; Rubichi et al., 2005).

A DIFFERENT STATE OF CONSCIOUSNESS?

The question of whether hypnosis is a state of consciousness that is qualitatively different from normal waking consciousness is controversial. Some psychologists believe that hypnosis represents a state of consciousness that differs significantly from other states. In this view, high suggestibility, increased ability to recall and construct images, and acceptance of suggestions that clearly contradict reality suggest it is a different state. Moreover, changes in electrical activity in the brain are associated with hypnosis, supporting the position that hypnosis is a state of consciousness different from normal waking (Fingelkurts, Fingelkurts, & Kallio, 2007; Hilgard, 1992; Kallio & Revonsuo, 2003).

In this view, hypnosis represents a state of *divided consciousness*. According to famed hypnosis researcher Ernest Hilgard, hypnosis brings about a *dissociation*, or division, of consciousness into two simultaneous components. In one stream of consciousness, hypnotized people are following the commands of the hypnotist. Yet on another level of consciousness, they are acting as "hidden observers," aware of what is happening to them. For instance, hypnotic subjects may appear to be following the hypnotist's suggestion about feeling no pain, yet in another stream of consciousness they may be actually aware of the pain.

On the other side of the controversy are psychologists who reject the notion that hypnosis is a state significantly different from normal waking consciousness. They argue that altered brain-wave patterns are not sufficient to demonstrate a qualitative difference, because no other specific physiological changes occur when people are in trances. Furthermore, little support exists for the contention that adults can recall memories of childhood events accurately while hypnotized. That lack of evidence suggests that there is nothing qualitatively special about the hypnotic trance (Hongchun & Ming, 2006; Lynn et al., 2003; Lynn, Fassler, & Knox, 2005; Wagstaff, 2009).

There is increasing agreement that the controversy over the nature of hypnosis has led to extreme positions on both sides of the issue. More recent approaches suggest that the hypnotic state may best be viewed as lying along a continuum in which hypnosis is neither a totally different state of consciousness nor totally similar to normal waking consciousness (Jamieson, 2007; Lynn et al., 2000; Kihlstrom, 2005b).

Study Alert

The question of whether hypnosis represents a different state of consciousness or is similar to normal waking consciousness is a key issue.

As arguments about the true nature of hypnosis continue, though, one thing is clear: Hypnosis has been used successfully to solve practical human problems. In fact, psychologists working in many different areas have found hypnosis to be a reliable, effective tool. It has been applied to a number of areas, including the following:

- *Controlling pain.* Patients suffering from chronic pain may be given the suggestion, while hypnotized, that their pain is gone or reduced. They also may be taught to hypnotize themselves to relieve pain or gain a sense of control over their symptoms. Hypnosis has proved to be particularly useful during childbirth and dental procedures (Accardi & Milling, 2009; Hammond, 2007; Mehl-Madrona, 2004).

- *Reducing smoking.* Although it hasn't been successful in stopping drug and alcohol abuse, hypnosis sometimes helps people stop smoking through hypnotic suggestions that the taste and smell of cigarettes are unpleasant (Elkins et al., 2006; Fuller, 2006; Green, Lynn, & Montgomery, 2008).

- *Treating psychological disorders.* Hypnosis sometimes is used during treatment for psychological disorders. For example, it may be employed to heighten relaxation, reduce anxiety, increase expectations of success, or modify self-defeating thoughts (Golden, 2006; Iglesias, 2005; Zarren & Eimer, 2002).

- *Assisting in law enforcement.* Witnesses and victims are sometimes better able to recall the details of a crime when hypnotized. In one often-cited case, a witness to the kidnapping of a group of California schoolchildren was placed under hypnosis and was able to recall all but one digit of the license number on the kidnapper's vehicle. However, hypnotic recollections may also be inaccurate, just as other recollections are often inaccurate. Consequently, the legal status of hypnosis is unresolved (Kazar, 2006; Knight & Meyer, 2007; Whitehouse et al., 2005).

- *Improving athletic performance.* Athletes sometimes turn to hypnosis to improve their performance. For example, some baseball players have used hypnotism to increase their concentration when batting, with considerable success (Barker & Jones, 2008; Grindstaff & Fisher, 2006; Lindsay, Maynard, & Thomas, 2005).

Meditation: Regulating Our Own State of Consciousness

meditation A learned technique for refocusing attention that brings about an altered state of consciousness.

When traditional practitioners of the ancient Eastern religion of Zen Buddhism want to achieve greater spiritual insight, they turn to a technique that has been used for centuries to alter their state of consciousness. This technique is called meditation.

Meditation is a learned technique for refocusing attention that brings about an altered state of consciousness. Meditation typically consists of the repetition of a *mantra*—a sound, word, or syllable—over and over. In some forms of meditation, the focus is on a picture, flame, or specific part of the body. Regardless of the nature of the particular initial stimulus, the key to the procedure is concentrating on it so thoroughly that the meditator becomes unaware of any outside stimulation and reaches a different state of consciousness.

After meditation, people report feeling thoroughly relaxed. They sometimes relate that they have gained new insights into themselves and the problems they are facing. The long-term practice of meditation may even improve health because of the biological changes it produces. For example, during meditation, oxygen usage decreases, heart rate and blood pressure decline, and brain-wave patterns change (Barnes et al., 2004; Lee, Kleinman, & Kleinman, 2007; Travis et al., 2009).

Anyone can meditate by following a few simple procedures. The fundamentals include sitting in a quiet room with the eyes closed, breathing deeply and rhythmically, and repeating a word or sound—such as the word *one*—over and over. Practiced twice a day for 20 minutes, the technique is effective in bringing about relaxation (Aftanas & Golosheykin, 2005; Benson et al., 1994).

Meditation is a means of altering consciousness that is practiced in many different cultures, though it can take different forms and serve different purposes across cultures. In fact, one impetus for the study of consciousness is the realization that people in many different cultures routinely seek ways to alter their states of consciousness (Walsh & Shapiro, 2006).

Exploring DIVERSITY

Cross-Cultural Routes to Altered States of Consciousness

A group of Native-American Sioux men sit naked in a steaming sweat lodge as a medicine man throws water on sizzling rocks to send billows of scalding steam into the air.

Aztec priests smear themselves with a mixture of crushed poisonous herbs, hairy black worms, scorpions, and lizards. Sometimes they drink the potion.

During the 16th century, a devout Hasidic Jew lies across the tombstone of a celebrated scholar. As he murmurs the name of God repeatedly, he seeks to be possessed by the soul of the dead wise man's spirit. If successful, he will attain a mystical state, and the deceased's words will flow out of his mouth.

Each of these rituals has a common goal: suspension from the bonds of everyday awareness and access to an altered state of consciousness. Although they may seem exotic from the vantage point of many Western cultures, these rituals represent an apparently universal effort to alter consciousness (Bartocci, 2004; Irwin, 2006).

StudyAlert

Remember that although there are alternate techniques used in meditation, they are all designed to bring about an altered state of consciousness in which attention is refocused.

Some scholars suggest that the quest to alter consciousness represents a basic human desire (Siegel, 1989). Whether or not we accept such an extreme view, variations in states of consciousness clearly share some basic characteristics across a variety of cultures. One is an alteration in thinking, which may become shallow, illogical, or otherwise different from normal. In addition, people's sense of time can become disturbed, and their perceptions of the physical world and of themselves may change. They may lose self-control, doing things that they would never otherwise do. Finally, they may feel a sense of *ineffability*—the inability to understand an experience rationally or describe it in words (Finkler, 2004; Martindale, 1981; Travis, 2006).

Of course, realizing that efforts to produce altered states of consciousness are widespread throughout the world's societies does not answer a fundamental question: Is the experience of unaltered states of consciousness similar across different cultures?

Because humans share basic biological commonalties in the ways their brains and bodies are wired, we might assume that the fundamental experience of consciousness is similar across cultures. As a result, we could suppose that consciousness shows some basic similarities across cultures. However, the ways in which certain aspects of consciousness are interpreted and viewed show substantial differences from culture to culture. For example, people in disparate cultures view the experience of the passage of time in varying ways. For instance, Arabs appear to perceive the passage of time more slowly than North Americans (Alon & Brett, 2007; Haynes, Nixon, & West, 2007).

RECAP/EVALUATE/RETHINK

RECAP

What is hypnosis, and are hypnotized people in a different state of consciousness?

- Hypnosis produces a state of heightened susceptibility to the suggestions of the hypnotist. Under hypnosis, significant behavioral changes occur, including increased concentration and suggestibility, heightened ability to recall and construct images, lack of initiative, and acceptance of suggestions that clearly contradict reality. (p. 144)

What are the effects of meditation?

- Meditation is a learned technique for refocusing attention that brings about an altered state of consciousness. (p. 146)
- Different cultures have developed their own unique ways to alter states of consciousness. (p. 147)

EVALUATE

1. _____ is a state of heightened susceptibility to the suggestions of others.
2. A friend tells you, "I once heard of a person who was murdered by being hypnotized and then told to jump from the Golden Gate Bridge!" Could such a thing have happened? Why or why not?
3. _____ is a learned technique for refocusing attention to bring about an altered state of consciousness.
4. Leslie repeats a unique sound, known as a _____, when she engages in meditation.

RETHINK

1. Why do you think people in almost every culture seek ways of altering their states of consciousness?
2. *From the perspective of a human resources specialist*: Would you allow (or even encourage) employees to engage in meditation during the workday? Why or why not?

Answers to Evaluate Questions

1. Hypnosis; 2. no; people who are hypnotized cannot be made to perform self-destructive acts; 3. Meditation; 4. mantra

KEY TERMS

hypnosis p. 144
meditation p. 146

Drug Use: The Highs and Lows of Consciousness

John Brodhead's bio reads like a script for an episode of VH1's *Behind the Music.* A young rebel from the New Jersey suburbs falls in with a fast crowd, gets hooked on parties and booze and, with intensive counseling and a bit of tough love, manages to get his life back together. What makes his story different? Just one thing: his age. John is 13. (Rogers, 2002)

John Brodhead was lucky. Now in recovery, John had begun to drink when he was in the sixth grade. He is not alone: The number of kids who start drinking by the eighth grade has increased by almost a third since the 1970s, even though alcohol consumption overall has stayed fairly steady among the general population.

Drugs of one sort or another are a part of almost everyone's life. From infancy on, most people take vitamins, aspirin, cold-relief medicine, and the like, and surveys find that 80% of adults in the United States have taken an over-the-counter pain reliever in the last six months. However, these drugs rarely produce an altered state of consciousness (Dortch, 1996).

In contrast, some substances, known as psychoactive drugs, lead to an altered state of consciousness. **Psychoactive drugs** influence a person's emotions, perceptions, and behavior. Yet even this category of drugs is common in most of our lives. If you have ever had a cup of coffee or sipped a beer, you have taken a psychoactive drug. A large number of individuals have used more potent—and more dangerous—psychoactive drugs than coffee and beer (see Figure 1 on page 150); for instance, surveys find that 41% of high school seniors have used an illegal drug in the last year. In addition, 30% report having been drunk on alcohol. The figures for the adult population are even higher (Johnston et al., 2009).

Of course, drugs vary widely in the effects they have on users, in part because they affect the nervous system in very different ways. Some drugs alter the limbic system, and others affect the operation of specific neurotransmitters across the synapses of neurons. For example, some drugs block or enhance the release of neurotransmitters, others block the receipt or the removal of a neurotransmitter, and still others mimic the effects of a particular neurotransmitter (see Figure 2 on page 150).

Addictive drugs produce a physiological or psychological dependence (or both) in the user, and withdrawal from them leads to a craving for the drug that, in some cases, may be nearly irresistible. In *physiological dependence,* the body becomes so accustomed to functioning in the presence of a drug that it cannot function without it. In *psychological dependence,* people believe that they need the drug to respond to the stresses of daily living. Although we generally associate addiction with drugs such as heroin, everyday sorts of drugs, such as caffeine (found in coffee) and nicotine (found in cigarettes), have addictive aspects as well (Li, Volkow, & Balu, 2007).

We know surprisingly little about the underlying causes of addiction. One of the problems in identifying those causes is that different drugs (such as alcohol and cocaine) affect the brain in very different ways—yet they may be equally addicting. Furthermore, it takes longer to become addicted to some drugs than to others, even though the ultimate consequences of addiction may be equally grave (Crombag & Robinson, 2004; Nestler & Malenka, 2004; Smart, 2007).

Why do people take drugs in the first place? There are many reasons, ranging from the perceived pleasure of the experience itself, to the escape that a drug-induced

Key Concept

What are the major classifications of drugs, and what are their effects?

John Brodhead began to drink heavily when he was in the sixth grade.

psychoactive drugs Drugs that influence a person's emotions, perceptions, and behavior.

addictive drugs Drugs that produce a biological or psychological dependence in the user so that withdrawal from them leads to a craving for the drug that, in some cases, may be nearly irresistible.

FIGURE 1 How many teenagers use drugs? The results of the most recent comprehensive survey of 14,000 high school seniors across the United States show the percentage of respondents who have used various substances for nonmedical purposes at least once. Can you think of any reasons why teenagers—as opposed to older people—might be particularly likely to use drugs? (Source: Johnston et al., 2009.)

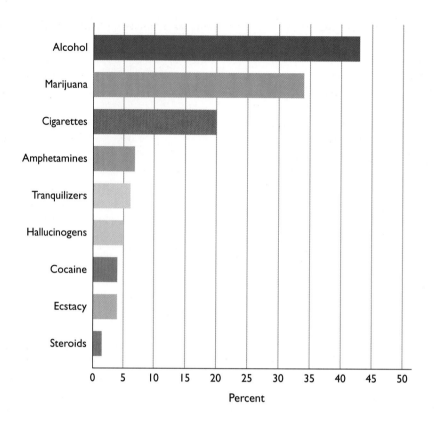

high affords from the everyday pressures of life, to an attempt to achieve a religious or spiritual state. However, other factors having little to do with the nature of the experience itself, also lead people to try drugs (McDowell & Spitz, 1999).

For instance, the highly publicized drug use of role models such as movie stars and professional athletes, the easy availability of some illegal drugs, and peer pressure all play a role in the decision to use drugs. In some cases, the motive is simply the thrill of trying something new. Finally, genetic factors may predispose some people to be more susceptible to drugs and to become addicted to them. Regardless of the forces that lead a person to begin using drugs, drug addiction is among the

FIGURE 2 Different drugs affect different parts of the nervous system and brain and each drug functions in one of these specific ways.

StudyAlert

Use Figure 2 to learn the different ways that drugs produce their effects on a neurological level.

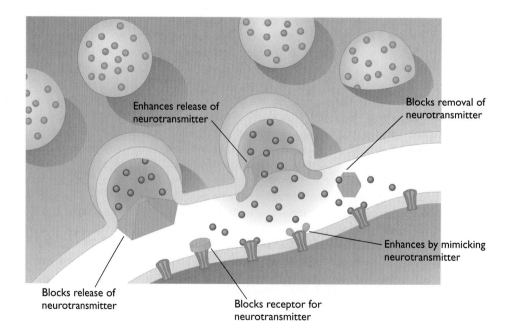

most difficult of all behaviors to modify, even with extensive treatment (Lemonick, 2000; Mosher & Akins, 2007; Ray & Hutchison, 2007).

Because of the difficulty in treating drug problems, there is little disagreement that the best hope for dealing with the overall societal problem of substance abuse is to prevent people from becoming involved with drugs in the first place. However, there is little accord on how to accomplish this goal.

Even drug reduction programs widely publicized for their effectiveness—such as DARE (Drug Abuse Resistance Education)—are of questionable effectiveness. Used in more than 80% of school districts in the United States, DARE consists of a series of 17 lessons on the dangers of drugs, alcohol, and gangs taught to fifth- and sixth-graders by a police officer. The program is highly popular with school officials, parents, and politicians. The problem? Repeated careful evaluations have been unable to demonstrate that the DARE program is effective in reducing drug use over the long term. In fact, one study even showed that DARE graduates were more likely to use marijuana than was a comparison group of nongraduates (Des Jarlais et al., 2006; Kalb, 2001b; Lucas, 2008; West & O'Neal, 2004).

Stimulants: Drug Highs

It's 1:00 a.m., and you still haven't finished reading the last chapter of the text on which you will be tested later in the morning. Feeling exhausted, you turn to the one thing that may help you stay awake for the next two hours: a cup of strong black coffee.

If you have ever found yourself in such a position, you have resorted to a major *stimulant,* caffeine, to stay awake. *Caffeine* is one of a number of **stimulants,** drugs whose effect on the central nervous system causes a rise in heart rate, blood pressure, and muscular tension. Caffeine is present not only in coffee; it is an important ingredient in tea, soft drinks, and chocolate as well (see Figure 3).

Caffeine produces several reactions. The major behavioral effects are an increase in attentiveness and a decrease in reaction time. Caffeine can also bring about an improvement in mood, most likely by mimicking the effects of a natural brain chemical, adenosine. Too much caffeine, however, can result in nervousness and insomnia. People can build up a biological dependence on the drug. Regular users who

stimulants Drugs that have an arousal effect on the central nervous system, causing a rise in heart rate, blood pressure, and muscular tension.

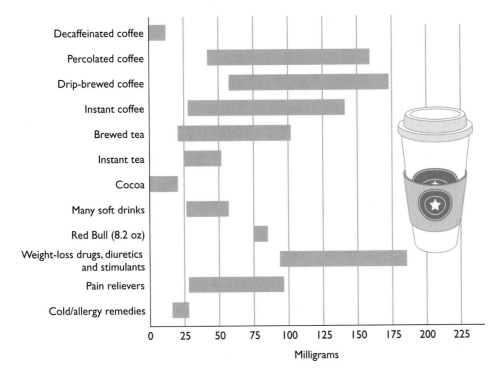

FIGURE 3 How much caffeine do you consume? This chart shows the range of caffeine found in common foods and drinks. The average coffee drinker in the United States consumes about 200 milligrams of caffeine each day, or around three cups of coffee. (Blakeslee, 1991.)

Drugs	Street Name	Effects	Withdrawal Symptoms	Adverse/Overdose Reactions
Stimulants				
Amphetamines		Increased confidence, mood elevation, sense of energy and alertness, decreased appetite, anxiety, irritability, insomnia, transient drowsiness, delayed orgasm	Apathy, general fatigue, prolonged sleep, depression, disorientation, suicidal thoughts, agitated motor activity, irritability, bizarre dreams	Elevated blood pressure, increase in body temperature, face picking, suspiciousness, bizarre and repetitive behavior, vivid hallucinations, convulsions, possible death
Benzedrine	Speed			
Dexedrine	Speed			
Cocaine	Coke, blow, snow, lady, crack			
Depressants				
Alcohol	Booze	Anxiety reduction, impulsiveness, dramatic mood swings, bizarre thoughts, suicidal behavior, slurred speech, disorientation, slowed mental and physical functioning, limited attention span	Weakness, restlessness, nausea and vomiting, headaches, nightmares, irritability, depression, acute anxiety, hallucinations, seizures, possible death	Confusion, decreased response to pain, shallow respiration, dilated pupils, weak and rapid pulse, coma, possible death
Barbiturates				
Nembutal	Yellowjackets, yellows			
Seconal				
Phenobarbital	Reds			
Rohypnol	Roofies, rope, "date-rape drug"	Muscle relaxation, amnesia, sleep	Seizures	Seizures, coma, incapacitation, inability to resist sexual assault
Narcotics				
Heroin	H, hombre, junk, smack, dope, crap, horse	Anxiety and pain reduction, apathy, difficulty in concentration, slowed speech, decreased physical activity, drooling, itching, euphoria, nausea	Anxiety, vomiting, sneezing, diarrhea, lower back pain, watery eyes, runny nose, yawning, irritability, tremors, panic, chills and sweating, cramps	Depressed levels of consciousness, low blood pressure, rapid heart rate, shallow breathing, convulsions, coma, possible death
Morphine	Drugstore dope, cube, first line, mud			

FIGURE 4 Drugs and their effects. A comprehensive breakdown of effects of the most commonly used drugs.

suddenly stop drinking coffee may experience headaches or depression. Many people who drink large amounts of coffee on weekdays have headaches on weekends because of the sudden drop in the amount of caffeine they are consuming (Clayton & Lundberg-Love, 2009; Hammond & Gold, 2008; Kendler, Myers, & Gardner, 2006).

Nicotine, found in cigarettes, is another common stimulant. The soothing effects of nicotine help explain why cigarette smoking is addictive. Smokers develop a dependence on nicotine, and those who suddenly stop smoking develop a strong craving for the drug. This is not surprising: Nicotine activates neural mechanisms similar to those activated by cocaine, which, as we see next, is also highly addictive (Haberstick et al., 2007; Ray et al., 2008).

AMPHETAMINES

Amphetamines such as dexedrine and benzedrine, popularly known as speed, are strong stimulants. In small quantities, amphetamines—which stimulate the central nervous system—bring about a sense of energy and alertness, talkativeness, heightened confidence, and a mood "high." They increase concentration and reduce fatigue. Amphetamines also cause a loss of appetite, increased anxiety, and irritability. When

> ### StudyAlert
>
> Figure 4, which summarizes the different categories of drugs (stimulants, depressants, narcotics, and hallucinogens), will help you learn the effects of particular drugs.

Drugs	Street Name	Effects	Withdrawal Symptoms	Adverse/Overdose Reactions
Oxycodone	Oxy, OC, Percs	Pain reduction, shallow breathing, slow heartbeat, seizure (convulsions); cold, clammy skin; confusion	Sweating, chills, abdominal cramps, insomnia, vomiting, diarrhea	Extreme drowsiness, muscle weakness, confusion, cold and clammy skin, pinpoint pupils, shallow breathing, slow heart rate, fainting, or coma
Hallucinogens				
Cannabis Marijuana Hashish Hash oil	Bhang, kif, ganja, dope, grass, pot, hemp, joint, weed, bone, Mary Jane, reefer	Euphoria, relaxed inhibitions, increased appetite, disoriented behavior	Hyperactivity, insomnia, decreased appetite, anxiety	Severe reactions rare but include panic, paranoia, fatigue, bizarre and dangerous behavior, decreased testosterone over long-term; immune-system effects
MDMA	Ecstasy	Heightened sense of oneself and insight, feelings of peace, empathy, energy	Depression, anxiety, sleeplessness	Increase in body temperature, memory difficulties
LSD	Acid, quasey, microdot, white lightning	Heightened aesthetic responses; vision and depth distortion; heightened sensitivity to faces and gestures; magnified feelings; paranoia, panic, euphoria	Not reported	Nausea and chills; increased pulse, temperature, and blood pressure; slow, deep breathing; loss of appetite; insomnia; bizarre, dangerous behavior
Steroids				
	Rhoids, juice	Aggression, depression, acne, mood swings, masculine traits in women and feminine traits in men	Symptoms can mimic other medical problems and include weakness, fatigue, decreased appetite, weight loss; women may note menstrual changes	Long-term, high-dose effects of steroid use are largely unknown, but can lead to swelling and weight gain

taken over long periods of time, amphetamines can cause feelings of being persecuted by others, as well as a general sense of suspiciousness. People taking amphetamines may lose interest in sex. If taken in too large a quantity, amphetamines overstimulate the central nervous system to such an extent that convulsions and death can occur (Carhart-Harris, 2007).

Methamphetamine is a white, crystalline drug that U.S. police now say is the most dangerous street drug. "Meth" is highly addictive and relatively cheap, and it produces a strong, lingering high. It has made addicts of people across the social spectrum, ranging from soccer moms to urban professionals to poverty-stricken inner-city residents. After becoming addicted, users take it more and more frequently and in increasing doses. Long-term use of the drug can lead to brain damage (Halkitis, 2009; Kish et al., 2009; Sharma, Sjoquist, & Ali, 2007).

More than 1.5 million people in the United States are regular methamphetamine users. Because it can be made from nonprescription cold pills, retailers such as Wal-Mart and Target have removed these medications from their shelves. Illicit labs devoted to the manufacture of methamphetamine have sprung up in many locations around the United States (Jefferson, 2005). Figure 4 provides a summary of the effects of amphetamines and other illegal drugs.

COCAINE

Although its use has declined over the last decade, the stimulant cocaine and its derivative, crack, still represent a serious concern. Cocaine is inhaled or "snorted" through the nose, smoked, or injected directly into the bloodstream. It is rapidly absorbed into the body and takes effect almost immediately.

When used in relatively small quantities, cocaine produces feelings of profound psychological well-being, increased confidence, and alertness. Cocaine produces this "high" through the neurotransmitter dopamine. Dopamine is one of the chemicals that transmit between neurons messages that are related to ordinary feelings of pleasure. Normally when dopamine is released, excess amounts of the neurotransmitter are reabsorbed by the releasing neuron. However, when cocaine enters the brain, it blocks reabsorption of leftover dopamine. As a result, the brain is flooded with dopamine-produced pleasurable sensations (Jarlais, Arasteh, & Perlis, 2007; Redish, 2004).

However, there is a steep price to be paid for the pleasurable effects of cocaine. The brain may become permanently rewired, triggering a psychological and physical addiction in which users grow obsessed with obtaining the drug. Over time, users deteriorate mentally and physically. In extreme cases, cocaine can cause hallucinations—a common one is of insects crawling over one's body. Ultimately, an overdose of cocaine can lead to death (George & Moselhy, 2005; Little et al., 2009; Paulozzi, 2006).

Almost 2.5 million people in the United States are occasional cocaine users, and as many as 1.8 million people use the drug regularly. Given the strength of cocaine, withdrawal from the drug is difficult. Although the use of cocaine among high school students has declined in recent years, the drug still represents a major problem (Johnston et al., 2009).

Depressants: Drug Lows

depressants Drugs that slow down the nervous system.

In contrast to the initial effect of stimulants, which is an increase in arousal of the central nervous system, the effect of **depressants** is to impede the nervous system by causing neurons to fire more slowly. Small doses result in at least temporary feelings of *intoxication*—drunkenness—along with a sense of euphoria and joy. When large amounts are taken, however, speech becomes slurred and muscle control becomes disjointed, making motion difficult. Ultimately, heavy users may lose consciousness entirely.

ALCOHOL

The most common depressant is alcohol, which is used by more people than is any other drug. Based on liquor sales, the average person over the age of 14 drinks 2½ gallons of pure alcohol over the course of a year. This works out to more than 200 drinks per person. Although alcohol consumption has declined steadily over the last decade, surveys show that more than three-fourths of college students indicate that they have had a drink within the last 30 days (Jung, 2002; Midanik, Tam, & Weisner, 2007).

One of the more disturbing trends is the high frequency of binge drinking among college students. For men, *binge drinking* is defined as having five or more drinks in one sitting; for women, who generally weigh less than men and whose bodies absorb alcohol less efficiently, binge drinking is defined as having four or more drinks at one sitting (Mokdad, Brewer, & Naimi, 2007).

Around 50% of male college students and 40% of female college students say they engaged in binge drinking at least once within the previous two weeks (see Figure 5). Some 17% of female students and 31% of male students admitted drinking on 10 or more occasions during the previous 30 days. Furthermore, even light drinkers were affected by the high rate of alcohol use: Two-thirds of lighter drinkers said that they

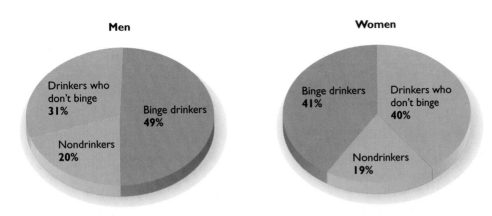

Men

Drinkers who don't binge 31%

Binge drinkers 49%

Nondrinkers 20%

Women

Binge drinkers 41%

Drinkers who don't binge 40%

Nondrinkers 19%

FIGURE 5 Drinking habits of college students (Wechsler et al., 2003). For men, binge drinking was defined as consuming five or more drinks in one sitting; for women, the total was four or more.

had had their studying or sleep disturbed by drunk students, and a quarter of the women said they had been the target of an unwanted sexual advance by a drunk class-mate (Grucza, Norberg, & Beirut, 2009; Read et al., 2008; Wechsler et al., 2000, 2002).

Women are typically somewhat lighter drinkers than men—although the gap between the sexes is narrowing for older women and has closed completely for teenagers. Women are more susceptible to the effects of alcohol, and alcohol abuse may harm the brains of women more than men (Mancinelli, Binetti, & Ceccanti, 2007; Mann et al., 2005; Wuethrich, 2001).

There are also cultural and ethnic differences in alcohol consumption. For example, teenagers in Europe drink more than teenagers in the United States do. Further-more, people of East Asian backgrounds who live in the United States tend to drink significantly less than do Caucasians and African Americans, and their incidence of alcohol-related problems is lower. It may be that physical reactions to drinking, which may include sweating, a quickened heartbeat, and flushing, are more unpleas-ant for East Asians than for other groups (Garcia-Andrade, Wall, & Ehlers, 1997; Garlow, Purselle, & Heninger, 2007; Kantrowitz & Underwood, 2007).

Although alcohol is a depressant, most people claim that it increases their sense of sociability and well-being. The discrepancy between the actual and the perceived effects of alcohol lies in the initial effects it produces in the majority of individuals who use it: release of tension and stress, feelings of happiness, and loss of inhibitions (Sayette, 1993; Steele & Josephs, 1990).

Although most alcohol consumers are casual users, there are more than 14 million alcoholics in the United States. The effects of alcohol vary significantly, depending on who is drinking it and the setting in which people drink. If alcohol were a newly discovered drug, do you think its sale would be legal?

Number of drinks consumed in two hours		Alcohol in blood (percentage)	Typical effects
	2	0.05	Judgment, thought, and restraint weakened; tension released, giving carefree sensation
	3	0.08	Tensions and inhibitions of everyday life lessened; cheerfulness
	4	0.10	Voluntary motor action affected, making hand and arm movements, walk, and speech clumsy
	7	0.20	Severe impairment—staggering, loud, incoherent, emotionally unstable, 100 times greater traffic risk; exuberance and aggressive inclinations magnified
	9	0.30	Deeper areas of brain affected, with stimulus-response and understanding confused; stuporous; blurred vision
	12	0.40	Incapable of voluntary action; sleepy, difficult to arouse; equivalent of surgical anesthesia
	15	0.50	Comatose; centers controlling breathing and heartbeat anesthetized; death increasingly probable

Note: A drink refers to a typical 12-ounce bottle of beer, a 1.5-ounce shot of hard liquor, or a 5-ounce glass of wine.

FIGURE 6 The effects of alcohol. The quantities represent only rough benchmarks; the effects vary significantly depending on an individual's weight, height, recent food intake, genetic factors, and even psychological state.

As the dose of alcohol increases, however, the depressive effects become more pronounced (see Figure 6). People may feel emotionally and physically unstable. They also show poor judgment and may act aggressively. Moreover, memory is impaired, brain processing of spatial information is diminished, and speech becomes slurred and incoherent. Eventually they may fall into a stupor and pass out. If they drink enough alcohol in a short time, they may die of alcohol poisoning (Murphy et al., 1998; Thatcher & Clark, 2006; Zeigler et al., 2005).

Although most people fall into the category of casual users, 14 million people in the United States—1 in every 13 adults—have a drinking problem. *Alcoholics,* people with alcohol-abuse problems, come to rely on alcohol and continue to drink even though it causes serious difficulties. In addition, they become increasingly immune to the effects of alcohol. Consequently, alcoholics must drink progressively more to experience the initial positive feelings that alcohol produces.

In some cases of alcoholism, people must drink constantly in order to feel well enough to function in their daily lives. In other cases, though, people drink inconsistently but occasionally go on binges in which they consume large quantities of alcohol.

It is not clear why certain people become alcoholics and develop a tolerance for alcohol, whereas others do not. There may be a genetic cause, although the question of whether there is a specific inherited gene that produces alcoholism is controversial. What is clear is that the chances of becoming an alcoholic are considerably higher if alcoholics are present in earlier generations of a person's family. However, not all alcoholics have close relatives who are alcoholics. In these cases, environmental stressors are suspected of playing a larger role (Nurnberger & Bierut, 2007; Whitfield et al., 2004; Zimmermann, Blomeyer, & Laucht, 2007).

BARBITURATES

Barbiturates, which include drugs such as Nembutal, Seconal, and phenobarbital, are another form of depressant. Frequently prescribed by physicians to induce sleep or reduce stress, barbiturates produce a sense of relaxation. Yet they, too, are psychologically and physically addictive and, when combined with alcohol, can be deadly, since such a combination relaxes the muscles of the diaphragm to such an extent that the user stops breathing.

ROHYPNOL

Rohypnol is sometimes called the "date rape drug," because, when it is mixed with alcohol, it can prevent victims from resisting sexual assault. Sometimes people who are unknowingly given the drug are so incapacitated that they have no memory of the assault.

Even legal drugs, when used improperly, lead to addiction.

Narcotics: Relieving Pain and Anxiety

Narcotics are drugs that increase relaxation and relieve pain and anxiety. Two of the most powerful narcotics, *morphine* and *heroin,* are derived from the poppy seed pod. Although morphine is used medically to control severe pain, heroin is illegal in the United States. This status has not prevented its widespread use.

narcotics Drugs that increase relaxation and relieve pain and anxiety.

Heroin users usually inject the drug directly into their veins with a hypodermic needle. The immediate effect has been described as a "rush" of positive feeling, similar in some respects to a sexual orgasm—and just as difficult to describe. After the rush, a heroin user experiences a sense of well-being and peacefulness that lasts three to five hours. When the effects of the drug wear off, however, the user feels extreme anxiety and a desperate desire to repeat the experience. Moreover, larger amounts of heroin are needed each time to produce the same pleasurable effect. These last two properties are all the ingredients necessary for physiological and psychological dependence: The user is constantly either shooting up or attempting to obtain ever-increasing amounts of the drug. Eventually, the life of the addict revolves around heroin.

Because of the powerful positive feelings the drug produces, heroin addiction is particularly difficult to cure. One treatment that has shown some success is the use of methadone. *Methadone* is a synthetic chemical that satisfies a heroin user's physiological cravings for the drug without providing the "high" that accompanies heroin. When heroin users are placed on regular doses of methadone, they may be able to function relatively normally. The use of methadone has one substantial drawback, however: Although it removes the psychological dependence on heroin, it replaces the physiological dependence on heroin with a physiological dependence on methadone. Researchers are attempting to identify nonaddictive chemical

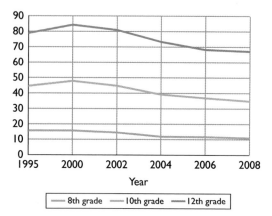

FIGURE 7 Although the level of marijuana use has declined slightly in recent years, overall the absolute number of teenagers who have used the drug in the last year remains relatively high. (Source: Johnston et al., 2009.)

hallucinogen A drug that is capable of producing hallucinations, or changes in the perceptual process.

This drawing, made by someone taking LSD, suggests the effects of hallucinogens on thinking.

substitutes for heroin as well as substitutes for other addictive drugs that do not replace one addiction with another (Amato et al., 2005; Joe, Flynn, & Broome, 2007; Oviedo-Joekes et al., 2009; Verdejo, Toribio, & Orozco, 2005).

Oxycodone (sold as the prescription drug *OxyContin*) is a type of pain reliever that has led to a significant amount of abuse. Many well-known people (including Courtney Love and Rush Limbaugh) have become dependent on it.

HALLUCINOGENS: PSYCHEDELIC DRUGS

What do mushrooms, jimsonweed, and morning glories have in common? Besides being fairly common plants, each can be a source of a powerful hallucinogen, a drug that is capable of producing **hallucinations,** or changes in the perceptual process.

The most common hallucinogen in widespread use today is *marijuana,* whose active ingredient—tetrahydrocannabinol (THC)—is found in a common weed, cannabis. Marijuana is typically smoked in cigarettes or pipes, although it can be cooked and eaten. Just over 32% of high school seniors and 11% of eighth-graders report having used marijuana in the last year (Johnston et al., 2009) (see Figure 7).

The effects of marijuana vary from person to person, but they typically consist of feelings of euphoria and general well-being. Sensory experiences seem more vivid and intense, and a person's sense of self-importance seems to grow. Memory may be impaired, causing users to feel pleasantly "spaced out." However, the effects are not universally positive. Individuals who use marijuana when they feel depressed can end up even more depressed, because the drug tends to magnify both good and bad feelings.

There are clear risks associated with long-term, heavy marijuana use. Although marijuana does not seem to produce addiction by itself, some evidence suggests that there are similarities in the way marijuana and drugs such as cocaine and heroin affect the brain. Furthermore, there is some evidence that heavy use at least temporarily decreases the production of the male sex hormone testosterone, potentially affecting sexual activity and sperm count (Iverson, 2000; Lane, Cherek, & Tcheremissine, 2007; Rossato, Pagano, & Vettor, 2008).

In addition, marijuana smoked during pregnancy may have lasting effects on children who are exposed prenatally, although the results are inconsistent. Heavy use also affects the ability of the immune system to fight off germs and increases stress on the heart, although it is unclear how strong these effects are. There is one unquestionably negative consequence of smoking marijuana: The smoke damages the lungs much the way cigarette smoke does, producing an increased likelihood of developing cancer and other lung diseases (Cornelius et al., 1995; Julien, 2001).

Despite the possible dangers of marijuana use, there is little scientific evidence for the popular belief that users "graduate" from marijuana to more dangerous drugs. Furthermore, the use of marijuana is routine in certain cultures. For instance, some people in Jamaica habitually drink a marijuana-based tea related to religious practices. In addition, marijuana has several medical uses; it can be used to prevent nausea from chemotherapy, treat some AIDS symptoms, and relieve muscle spasms for people with spinal cord injuries. In a controversial move, several states have made the use of the drug legal if it is prescribed by a physician—although it remains illegal under U.S. federal law (Chapkis & Webb, 2008; Cohen, 2009; Iverson, 2000; Seamon et al., 2007).

MDMA (ECSTASY) AND LSD

MDMA ("Ecstasy") and *lysergic acid diethylamide (LSD, or "acid")* fall into the category of hallucinogens. Both drugs affect the operation of the neurotransmitter serotonin in the brain, causing an alteration in brain-cell activity and perception (Buchert et al., 2004; Cloud, 2000).

Ecstasy users report a sense of peacefulness and calm. People on the drug report experiencing increased empathy and connection with others, as well as feeling more relaxed, yet energetic. Although the data are not conclusive, some researchers have found declines in memory and performance on intellectual tasks, and such findings suggest that there may be long-term changes in serotonin receptors in the brain (El-Mallakh & Abraham, 2007; Jones et al., 2008; Montgomery et al., 2005).

LSD, which is structurally similar to serotonin, produces vivid hallucinations. Perceptions of colors, sounds, and shapes are altered so much that even the most mundane experience—such as looking at the knots in a wooden table—can seem moving and exciting. Time perception is distorted, and objects and people may be viewed in a new way, with some users reporting that LSD increases their understanding of the world. For others, however, the experience brought on by LSD can be terrifying, particularly if users have had emotional difficulties in the past. Furthermore, people occasionally experience flashbacks, in which they hallucinate long after they initially used the drug (Baruss, 2003; Wu, Schlenger, & Galvin, 2006).

BECOMING AN INFORMED CONSUMER
of Psychology
Identifying Drug and Alcohol Problems

In a society bombarded with commercials for drugs that are guaranteed to do everything from curing restless leg syndrome to erectile dysfunction, it is no wonder that drug-related problems are a major social issue. Yet many people with drug and alcohol problems deny that they have them, and even close friends and family members may fail to realize when occasional social use of drugs or alcohol has turned into abuse.

Certain signs, however, indicate when use becomes abuse (National Institute on Drug Abuse, 2000). Among them are the following:

- Always getting high to have a good time.
- Being high more often than not.
- Getting high to get oneself going.
- Going to work or class while high.
- Missing or being unprepared for class or work because you were high.
- Feeling badly later about something you said or did while high.
- Driving a car while high.
- Coming in conflict with the law because of drugs.
- Doing something while high that you wouldn't do otherwise.
- Being high in nonsocial, solitary situations.
- Being unable to stop getting high.
- Feeling a need for a drink or a drug to get through the day.
- Becoming physically unhealthy.
- Failing at school or on the job.
- Thinking about liquor or drugs all the time.
- Avoiding family or friends while using liquor or drugs.

Any combination of these symptoms should be sufficient to alert you to the potential of a serious drug problem. Because drug and alcohol dependence are almost impossible to cure on one's own, people who suspect that they have a problem should seek immediate attention from a psychologist, physician, or counselor.

You can also get help from national hotlines. For alcohol difficulties, call the National Council on Alcoholism at (800) 622-2255. For drug problems, call the National Institute on Drug Abuse at (800) 662-4357. You can also check your telephone book for a local listing of Alcoholics Anonymous or Narcotics Anonymous. Finally, check out the websites of the National Institute on Alcohol Abuse and Alcoholism (www.niaaa.nih.gov) and the National Institute on Drug Abuse (www.nida.nih.gov).

RECAP/EVALUATE/RETHINK

RECAP

What are the major classifications of drugs, and what are their effects?

- Drugs can produce an altered state of consciousness. However, they vary in how dangerous they are and in whether they are addictive. (p. 149)
- Stimulants cause arousal in the central nervous system. Two common stimulants are caffeine and nicotine. More dangerous are cocaine and amphetamines, which in large quantities can lead to convulsions and death. (p. 151)
- Depressants decrease arousal in the central nervous system. They can cause intoxication along with feelings of euphoria. The most common depressants are alcohol and barbiturates. (p. 154)
- Alcohol is the most frequently used depressant. Its initial effects of released tension and positive feelings yield to depressive effects as the dose of alcohol increases. Both heredity and environmental stressors can lead to alcoholism. (p. 154)
- Morphine and heroin are narcotics, drugs that produce relaxation and relieve pain and anxiety. Because of their addictive qualities, morphine and heroin are particularly dangerous. (p. 157)
- Hallucinogens are drugs that produce hallucinations or other changes in perception. The most frequently used hallucinogen is marijuana, which has several long-term risks. Two other hallucinogens are LSD and Ecstasy. (p. 158)
- A number of signals indicate when drug use becomes drug abuse. A person who suspects that he or she has a drug problem should get professional help. People are almost never capable of solving drug problems on their own. (p. 159)

EVALUATE

1. Drugs that affect a person's consciousness are referred to as _____.
2. Match the type of drug to an example of that type.
   1. narcotic—a pain reliever
   2. amphetamine—a strong stimulant
   3. hallucinogen—capable of producing hallucinations
   a. LSD
   b. heroin
   c. dexedrine, or speed
3. Classify each drug listed as a stimulant (S), depressant (D), hallucinogen (H), or narcotic (N).
   1. nicotine
   2. cocaine
   3. alcohol
   4. morphine
   5. marijuana
4. The effects of LSD can recur long after the drug has been taken. True or false?
5. _____ is a drug that has been used to treat people with heroin addiction.

RETHINK

1. Why have drug education campaigns largely been ineffective in stemming the use of illegal drugs? Should the use of certain now-illegal drugs be made legal? Would it be more effective to stress reduction of drug use rather than a complete prohibition of drug use?
2. *From the perspective of a substance abuse counselor:* How would you explain why people start using drugs to the family members of someone who was addicted? What types of drug prevention programs would you advocate?

Answers to Evaluate Questions

1. psychoactive; 2. 1-b, 2-c, 3-a; 3. 1-S, 2-S, 3-D, 4-N, 5-H; 4. true; 5. Methadone

KEY TERMS

psychoactive drugs p. 149   stimulants p. 151   narcotics p. 157
addictive drugs p. 149   depressants p. 154   hallucinogen p. 158

Classical Conditioning

Does the mere sight of the golden arches in front of McDonald's make you feel pangs of hunger and think about hamburgers? If it does, you are displaying an elementary form of learning called classical conditioning. *Classical conditioning* helps explain such diverse phenomena as crying at the sight of a bride walking down the aisle, fearing the dark, and falling in love.

Classical conditioning is one of a number of different types of learning that psychologists have identified, but a general definition encompasses them all: **Learning** is a relatively permanent change in behavior that is brought about by experience.

How do we know when a behavior has been influenced by learning—or even is a result of learning? Part of the answer relates to the nature-nurture question, one of the fundamental issues underlying the field of psychology. In the acquisition of behaviors, experience—which is essential to the definition of learning—is the "nurture" part of the nature-nurture question.

However, it's not always easy to identify whether a change in behavior is due to nature or nurture, because some changes in behavior or performance come about through maturation alone and don't involve experience. For instance, children become better tennis players as they grow older partly because their strength increases with their size—a maturational phenomenon. To understand when learning has occurred, we must differentiate maturational changes from improvements resulting from practice, which indicate that learning actually has occurred.

Similarly, short-term changes in behavior that are due to factors other than learning, such as declines in performance resulting from fatigue or lack of effort, are different from performance changes that are due to actual learning. If Serena Williams has a bad day on the tennis court because of tension or fatigue, this does not mean that she has not learned to play correctly or has "unlearned" how to play well. Because there is not always a one-to-one correspondence between learning and performance, understanding when true learning has occurred is difficult.

It is clear that we are primed for learning from the beginning of life. Infants exhibit a simple type of learning called habituation. *Habituation* is the decrease in response to a stimulus that occurs after repeated presentations of the same stimulus. For example, young infants may initially show interest in a novel stimulus, such as a brightly colored toy, but they will soon lose interest if they see the same toy over and over. (Adults exhibit habituation, too: Newlyweds soon stop noticing that they are wearing a wedding ring.) Habituation permits us to ignore things that have stopped providing new information.

Most learning is considerably more complex than habituation, and the study of learning has been at the core of the field of psychology. Although philosophers since the time of Aristotle have speculated on the foundations of learning, the first systematic research on learning was done at the beginning of the 20th century, when Ivan Pavlov (does the name ring a bell?) developed the framework for learning called classical conditioning.

Key Concepts

What is learning?

How do we learn to form associations between stimuli and responses?

learning A relatively permanent change in behavior brought about by experience.

Ivan Pavlov (center) developed the principles of classical conditioning.

Quiz   Friday

classical conditioning A type of learning in which a neutral stimulus comes to bring about a response after it is paired with a stimulus that naturally brings about that response.

neutral stimulus A stimulus that, before conditioning, does not naturally bring about the response of interest.

unconditioned stimulus (UCS) A stimulus that naturally brings about a particular response without having been learned.

unconditioned response (UCR) A response that is natural and needs no training (e.g., salivation at the smell of food).

conditioned stimulus (CS) A once-neutral stimulus that has been paired with an unconditioned stimulus to bring about a response formerly caused only by the unconditioned stimulus.

conditioned response (CR) A response that, after conditioning, follows a previously neutral stimulus (e.g., salivation at the ringing of a bell).

The Basics of Classical Conditioning

Ivan Pavlov, a Russian physiologist, never intended to do psychological research. In 1904 he won the Nobel Prize for his work on digestion, testimony to his contribution to that field. Yet Pavlov is remembered not for his physiological research but for his experiments on basic learning processes—work that he began quite accidentally (Marks, 2004; Samoilov & Zayas, 2007).

Pavlov had been studying the secretion of stomach acids and salivation in dogs in response to the ingestion of varying amounts and kinds of food. While doing that, he observed a curious phenomenon: Sometimes stomach secretions and salivation would begin in the dogs when they had not yet eaten any food. The mere sight of the experimenter who normally brought the food, or even the sound of the experimenter's footsteps, was enough to produce salivation in the dogs. Pavlov's genius lay in his ability to recognize the implications of this discovery. He saw that the dogs were responding not only on the basis of a biological need (hunger) but also as a result of learning—or, as it came to be called, classical conditioning. **Classical conditioning** is a type of learning in which a neutral stimulus (such as the experimenter's footsteps) comes to elicit a response after being paired with a stimulus (such as food) that naturally brings about that response.

To demonstrate classical conditioning, Pavlov (1927) attached a tube to the salivary gland of a dog, allowing him to measure precisely the dog's salivation. He then rang a bell and, just a few seconds later, presented the dog with meat. This pairing occurred repeatedly and was carefully planned so that, each time, exactly the same amount of time elapsed between the presentation of the bell and the meat. At first the dog would salivate only when the meat was presented, but soon it began to salivate at the sound of the bell. In fact, even when Pavlov stopped presenting the meat, the dog still salivated after hearing the sound. The dog had been classically conditioned to salivate to the bell.

As you can see in Figure 1, the basic processes of classical conditioning that underlie Pavlov's discovery are straightforward, although the terminology he chose is not simple. Consider first the diagram in Figure 1a. Before conditioning, there are two unrelated stimuli: the ringing of a bell and meat. We know that normally the ringing of a bell does not lead to salivation but to some irrelevant response, such as pricking up the ears or perhaps a startle reaction. The bell is therefore called the **neutral stimulus,** because it is a stimulus that, before conditioning, does not naturally bring about the response in which we are interested. We also have meat, which naturally causes a dog to salivate—the response we are interested in conditioning. The meat is considered an **unconditioned stimulus** (**UCS**) because food placed in a dog's mouth automatically causes salivation to occur. The response that the meat elicits (salivation) is called an **unconditioned response** (**UCR**)—a natural, innate, reflexive response that is not associated with previous learning. Unconditioned responses are always brought about by the presence of unconditioned stimuli.

Figure 1b illustrates what happens during conditioning. The bell is rung just before each presentation of the meat. The goal of conditioning is for the dog to associate the bell with the unconditioned stimulus (meat) and therefore to bring about the same sort of response as the unconditioned stimulus. After a number of pairings of the bell and meat, the bell alone causes the dog to salivate.

When conditioning is complete, the bell has evolved from a neutral stimulus to a **conditioned stimulus** (**CS**). At this time, salivation that occurs as a response to the conditioned stimulus (bell) is considered a **conditioned response** (**CR**). This situation

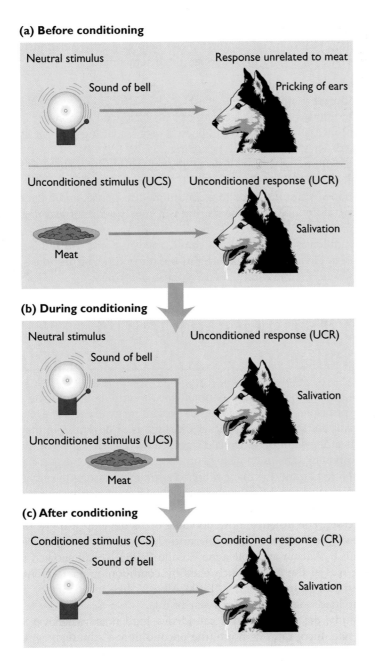

(a) Before conditioning

Neutral stimulus

Sound of bell

Response unrelated to meat

Pricking of ears

Unconditioned stimulus (UCS)

Meat

Unconditioned response (UCR)

Salivation

(b) During conditioning

Neutral stimulus

Sound of bell

Unconditioned response (UCR)

Salivation

Unconditioned stimulus (UCS)

Meat

(c) After conditioning

Conditioned stimulus (CS)

Sound of bell

Conditioned response (CR)

Salivation

FIGURE 1 The basic process of classical conditioning. (a) Before conditioning, the ringing of a bell does not bring about salivation—making the bell a neutral stimulus. In contrast, meat naturally brings about salivation, making the meat an unconditioned stimulus and salivation an unconditioned response. (b) During conditioning, the bell is rung just before the presentation of the meat. (c) Eventually, the ringing of the bell alone brings about salivation. We now can say that conditioning has been accomplished: The previously neutral stimulus of the bell is now considered a conditioned stimulus that brings about the conditioned response of salivation.

StudyAlert

Figure 1 can help you to learn and understand the process (and terminology) of classical conditioning, which can be confusing.

is depicted in Figure 1c. After conditioning, then, the conditioned stimulus evokes the conditioned response.

The sequence and timing of the presentation of the unconditioned stimulus and the conditioned stimulus are particularly important. Like a malfunctioning warning light at a railroad crossing that goes on after the train has passed by, a neutral stimulus that *follows* an unconditioned stimulus has little chance of becoming a conditioned stimulus. However, just as a warning light works best if it goes on right before a train passes, a neutral stimulus that is presented *just before* the unconditioned stimulus is most apt to result in successful conditioning. Research has shown that conditioning is most effective if the neutral stimulus (which will become a conditioned stimulus) precedes the unconditioned stimulus by between a half second and several seconds, depending on what kind of response is being conditioned (Bitterman, 2006; Wasserman & Miller, 1997).

Although the terminology Pavlov used to describe classical conditioning may seem confusing, the following summary can help make the relationships between stimuli and responses easier to understand and remember:

- Conditioned = learned.
- Unconditioned = not learned.
- An *un*conditioned stimulus leads to an *un*conditioned response.
- *Un*conditioned stimulus–*un*conditioned response pairings are *not* learned and *not* trained: They are naturally occurring.
- During conditioning, a previously neutral stimulus is transformed into the conditioned stimulus.
- A conditioned stimulus leads to a conditioned response, and a conditioned stimulus–conditioned response pairing is a consequence of learning and training.
- An unconditioned response and a conditioned response are similar (such as salivation in Pavlov's experiment), but the unconditioned response occurs naturally, whereas the conditioned response is learned.

Applying Conditioning Principles to Human Behavior

Although the initial conditioning experiments were carried out with animals, classical conditioning principles were soon found to explain many aspects of everyday human behavior. Recall, for instance, the earlier illustration of how people may experience hunger pangs at the sight of McDonald's golden arches. The cause of this reaction is classical conditioning: The previously neutral arches have become associated with the food inside the restaurant (the unconditioned stimulus), causing the arches to become a conditioned stimulus that brings about the conditioned response of hunger.

Emotional responses are especially likely to be learned through classical conditioning processes. For instance, how do some of us develop fears of mice, spiders, and other creatures that are typically harmless? In a now infamous case study, psychologist John B. Watson and colleague Rosalie Rayner (1920) showed that classical conditioning was at the root of such fears by conditioning an 11-month-old infant named Albert to be afraid of rats. "Little Albert," like most infants, initially was frightened by loud noises but had no fear of rats.

In the study, the experimenters sounded a loud noise whenever Little Albert touched a white, furry rat. The noise (the unconditioned stimulus) evoked fear (the unconditioned response). After just a few pairings of noise and rat, Albert began to show fear of the rat by itself, bursting into tears when he saw it. The rat, then, had become a CS that brought about the CR, fear. Furthermore, the effects of the conditioning lingered: five days later, Albert reacted with some degree of fear not only when shown a rat, but when shown objects that looked similar to the white, furry rat, including a white rabbit, a white seal-skin coat, and even a white Santa Claus mask. (By the way, although we don't know for certain what happened to the unfortunate Little Albert, it appears he was a sickly child who died at the age of 5. In any case, Watson, the experimenter, has been condemned for using ethically questionable procedures that could never be conducted today; Beck, Levinson, & Irons, 2009.)

Learning by means of classical conditioning also occurs during adulthood. For example, you may not go to a dentist as often as you should because of previous associations of dentists with pain. In more extreme cases, classical conditioning can lead to the development of *phobias,* which are intense, irrational fears that we will consider later in the book. For example, an insect phobia might develop in someone who is stung by a bee. The insect phobia might be so severe that the person refrains from leaving home. *Posttraumatic stress disorder (PTSD),* suffered by some war veterans

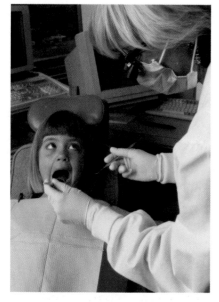

Because of a previous unpleasant experience, a person may expect a similar occurrence when faced with a comparable situation in the future, a process known as stimulus generalization. Can you think of ways that this process occurs in everyday life?

and others who have had traumatic experiences, can also be produced by classical conditioning. Even years after their battlefield experiences, veterans may feel a rush of fear and anxiety at a stimulus such as a loud noise (Kaštelan et al., 2007; Kozaric-Kovacic, & Borovecki, 2005; Roberts, Moore, & Beckham, 2007).

However, classical conditioning also accounts for pleasant experiences. For instance, you may have a particular fondness for the smell of a certain perfume or aftershave lotion because thoughts of an early love come rushing back whenever you encounter it. Or hearing a certain song can bring back happy or bittersweet emotions due to associations that you have developed in the past. Classical conditioning, then, explains many of the reactions we have to stimuli in the world around us.

Extinction

What do you think would happen if a dog that had become classically conditioned to salivate at the ringing of a bell never again received food when the bell was rung? The answer lies in one of the basic phenomena of learning: extinction. **Extinction** occurs when a previously conditioned response decreases in frequency and eventually disappears.

To produce extinction, one needs to end the association between conditioned stimuli and unconditioned stimuli. For instance, if we had trained a dog to salivate (the conditioned response) at the ringing of a bell (the conditioned stimulus), we could produce extinction by repeatedly ringing the bell but *not* providing meat. At first the dog would continue to salivate when it heard the bell, but after a few such instances, the amount of salivation would probably decline, and the dog would eventually stop responding to the bell altogether. At that point, we could say that the response had been extinguished. In sum, extinction occurs when the conditioned stimulus is presented repeatedly without the unconditioned stimulus (see Figure 2).

We should keep in mind that extinction can be a helpful phenomenon. Consider, for instance, what it would be like if the fear you experienced while watching the shower murder scene in the classic movie *Psycho* never was extinguished. You might well tremble with fright every time you took a shower.

Once a conditioned response has been extinguished, has it vanished forever? Not necessarily. Pavlov discovered this phenomenon when he returned to his dog a few days after the conditioned behavior had seemingly been extinguished. If he rang a bell, the dog once again salivated—an effect known as **spontaneous recovery,** or the

Quiz

extinction A basic phenomenon of learning that occurs when a previously conditioned response decreases in frequency and eventually disappears.

Quiz

spontaneous recovery The reemergence of an extinguished conditioned response after a period of rest and with no further conditioning.

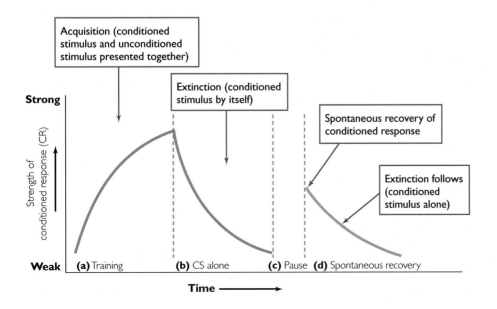

FIGURE 2 Acquisition, extinction, and spontaneous recovery of a classically conditioned response. (a) A conditioned response (CR) gradually increases in strength during training. (b) However, if the conditioned stimulus (CS) is presented by itself enough times, the conditioned response gradually fades, and extinction occurs. (c) After a pause (d) in which the conditioned stimulus is not presented, spontaneous recovery can occur. However, extinction typically reoccurs soon after.

reemergence of an extinguished conditioned response after a period of time and with no further conditioning.

Spontaneous recovery helps explain why it is so hard to overcome drug addictions. For example, cocaine addicts who are thought to be "cured" can experience an irresistible impulse to use the drug again if they are subsequently confronted by a stimulus with strong connections to the drug, such as a white powder (DiCano & Everitt, 2002; Plowright, Simonds, & Butler, 2006; Rodd et al., 2004).

Generalization and Discrimination

stimulus generalization A process in which, after a stimulus has been conditioned to produce a particular response, stimuli that are similar to the original stimulus produce the same response

Despite differences in color and shape, to most of us a rose is a rose is a rose. The pleasure we experience at the beauty, smell, and grace of the flower is similar for different types of roses. Pavlov noticed a similar phenomenon. His dogs often salivated not only at the ringing of the bell that was used during their original conditioning but at the sound of a buzzer as well.

Such behavior is the result of stimulus generalization. **Stimulus generalization** is a process in which, after a stimulus has been conditioned to produce a particular response, stimuli that are similar to the original stimulus produce the same response. The greater the similarity between two stimuli, the greater the likelihood of stimulus generalization. Little Albert, who, as we mentioned earlier, was conditioned to be fearful of white rats, grew afraid of other furry white things as well. However, according to the principle of stimulus generalization, it is unlikely that he would have been afraid of a black dog, because its color would have differentiated it sufficiently from the original fear-evoking stimulus.

The conditioned response elicited by the new stimulus is usually not as intense as the original conditioned response, although the more similar the new stimulus is to the old one, the more similar the new response will be. It is unlikely, then, that Little Albert's fear of the Santa Claus mask was as great as his learned fear of a rat. Still, stimulus generalization permits us to know, for example, that we ought to brake at all red lights, even if there are minor variations in size, shape, and shade.

stimulus discrimination The process that occurs if two stimuli are sufficiently distinct from one another that one evokes a conditioned response but the other does not; the ability to differentiate between stimuli.

Stimulus discrimination, in contrast, occurs if two stimuli are sufficiently distinct from each other that one evokes a conditioned response but the other does not. Stimulus discrimination provides the ability to differentiate between stimuli. For example, my dog Cleo comes running into the kitchen when she hears the sound of the electric can opener, which she has learned is used to open her dog food when her dinner is about to be served. She does not bound into the kitchen at the sound of the food processor, although it sounds similar. In other words, she discriminates between the stimuli of can opener and food processor. Similarly, our ability to discriminate between the behavior of a growling dog and that of one whose tail is wagging can lead to adaptive behavior—avoiding the growling dog and petting the friendly one.

Beyond Traditional Classical Conditioning: Challenging Basic Assumptions

Although Pavlov hypothesized that all learning is nothing more than long strings of conditioned responses, this notion has not been supported by subsequent research. It turns out that classical conditioning provides us with only a partial explanation of how people and animals learn; indeed, Pavlov was wrong in some of his basic assumptions (Hollis, 1997).

For example, according to Pavlov, the process of linking stimuli and responses occurs in a mechanistic, unthinking way. In contrast to this perspective, learning theorists influenced by cognitive psychology have argued that learners actively develop an understanding and expectancy about which particular unconditioned stimuli are matched with specific conditioned stimuli. A ringing bell, for instance, gives a dog something to think about: the impending arrival of food (Kirsch et al., 2004; Rescorla, 198).

Traditional explanations of how classical conditioning operates have also been challenged by John Garcia, a learning psychologist. He found that some organisms— including humans—were *biologically prepared* to quickly learn to avoid foods that smelled or tasted like something that made them sick. For instance, a dog quickly learns to avoid rotting food that in the past made it sick. Similarly, if every time you ate peanuts you had an upset stomach several hours later, eventually you would learn to avoid peanuts. In fact, you might develop a *learned taste aversion*, so that peanuts no longer even taste good to you (Garcia, 1990, 2003).

The surprising part of Garcia's discovery was his demonstration that conditioning could occur even when the interval between exposure to the conditioned stimulus of tainted food and the response of sickness was as long as eight hours. Furthermore, the conditioning persisted over very long periods and sometimes occurred after just one exposure.

These findings have had important practical implications. For example, to keep crows from stealing eggs, dairy farmers may lace an egg with a chemical and leave it in a place where crows will find it. The drug temporarily makes the crows ill, but it does not harm them permanently. After exposure to a chemical-laden egg, crows no longer finds them appetizing (Baker, Johnson, & Slater, 2007; Cox et al., 2004; Green, Henderson, & Collinge, 2003).

RECAP/EVALUATE/RETHINK

RECAP

What is learning?
- Learning is a relatively permanent change in behavior resulting from experience. (p. 165)

How do we learn to form associations between stimuli and responses?
- One major form of learning is classical conditioning, which occurs when a neutral stimulus—one that normally brings about no relevant response—is repeatedly paired with a stimulus (called an unconditioned stimulus) that brings about a natural, untrained response. (p. 166)
- Conditioning occurs when the neutral stimulus is repeatedly presented just before the unconditioned stimulus. After repeated pairings, the neutral stimulus elicits the same response that the unconditioned stimulus brings about. When this occurs, the neutral stimulus has become a conditioned stimulus, and the response a conditioned response. (p. 166)

- Learning is not always permanent. Extinction occurs when a previously learned response decreases in frequency and eventually disappears. (p. 169)
- Stimulus generalization is the tendency for a conditioned response to follow a stimulus that is similar to, but not the same as, the original conditioned stimulus. The converse phenomenon, stimulus discrimination, occurs when an organism learns to distinguish between stimuli. (p. 170)

EVALUATE

1. _____ involves changes brought about by experience, whereas maturation describes changes resulting from biological development.

2. _____ is the name of the scientist responsible for discovering the learning phenomenon known as _____ conditioning, whereby an organism learns a response to a stimulus to which it normally would not respond.

Refer to the passage below to answer questions 3 through 5:

The last three times little Theresa visited Dr. Lopez for checkups, he administered a painful preventive immunization shot that left her in tears. Today, when her mother takes her for another checkup, Theresa begins to sob as soon as she comes face to face with Dr. Lopez, even before he has had a chance to say hello.

3. The painful shot that Theresa received during each visit was a(n) _____ _____ that elicited the _____ _____, her tears.

4. Dr. Lopez is upset because his presence has become a _____ _____ for Theresa's crying.

5. Fortunately, Dr. Lopez gave Theresa no more shots for quite some time. Over that period she gradually stopped crying and even came to like him. _____ had occurred.

1. How likely is it that Little Albert, Watson's experimental subject, went through life afraid of Santa Claus? Describe what could have happened to prevent his continual dread of Santa.

2. *From the perspective of an advertising executive:* How might knowledge of classical conditioning be useful in creating an advertising campaign? What, if any, ethical issues arise from this use?

Answers to Evaluate Questions

1. Learning; 2. Pavlov, classical; 3. unconditioned stimulus, unconditioned response; 4. conditioned stimulus; 5. Extinction

KEY TERMS

learning p. 165
classical
 conditioning p. 166
neutral stimulus p. 166
unconditioned stimulus
 (UCS) p. 166

unconditioned response
 (UCR) p. 166
conditioned stimulus
 (CS) p. 166

conditioned response
 (CR) p. 166
extinction p. 169
spontaneous
 recovery p. 169

stimulus
 generalization p. 170
stimulus
 discrimination p. 170

Operant Conditioning

Very good . . . What a clever idea . . . Fantastic . . . I agree . . . Thank you . . . Excellent . . . Super . . . Right on . . . This is the best paper you've ever written; you get an A . . . You are really getting the hang of it . . . I'm impressed . . . You're getting a raise . . . Have a cookie . . . You look great . . . I love you . . .

Few of us mind being the recipient of any of these comments. But what is especially noteworthy about them is that each of these simple statements can be used, through a process known as operant conditioning, to bring about powerful changes in behavior and to teach the most complex tasks. Operant conditioning is the basis for many of the most important kinds of human, and animal, learning.

Operant conditioning is learning in which a voluntary response is strengthened or weakened, depending on its favorable or unfavorable consequences. When we say that a response has been strengthened or weakened, we mean that it has been made more or less likely to recur regularly.

Unlike classical conditioning, in which the original behaviors are the natural, biological responses to the presence of a stimulus such as food, water, or pain, operant conditioning applies to voluntary responses, which an organism performs deliberately to produce a desirable outcome. The term *operant* emphasizes this point: The organism *operates* on its environment to produce a desirable result. Operant conditioning is at work when we learn that toiling industriously can bring about a raise or that studying hard results in good grades.

As with classical conditioning, the basis for understanding operant conditioning was laid by work with animals. We turn now to some of that early research, which began with a simple inquiry into the behavior of cats.

Key Concepts

What is the role of reward and punishment in learning?

What are some practical methods for bringing about behavior change, both in ourselves and in others?

operant conditioning Learning in which a voluntary response is strengthened or weakened, depending on its favorable or unfavorable consequences.

Thorndike's Law of Effect

If you placed a hungry cat in a cage and then put a small piece of food outside the cage, just beyond the cat's reach, chances are that the cat would eagerly search for a way out of the cage. The cat might first claw at the sides or push against an opening. Suppose, though, you had rigged things so that the cat could escape by stepping on a small paddle that released the latch to the door of the cage (see Figure 1). Eventually, as it moved around the cage, the cat would happen to step on the paddle, the door would open, and the cat would eat the food.

What would happen if you then returned the cat to the box? The next time, it would probably take a little less time for the cat to step on the paddle and escape. After a few trials, the cat would deliberately step on the paddle as soon as it was placed in the cage. What would have occurred, according to Edward L. Thorndike (1932), who studied this situation extensively, was that the cat would have learned that pressing the paddle was associated with the desirable consequence of getting food. Thorndike summarized that relationship by formulating the *law of effect*: Responses that lead to satisfying consequences are more likely to be repeated.

Thorndike believed that the law of effect operates as automatically as leaves fall off a tree in autumn. It was not necessary for an organism to understand that there

FIGURE 1 Edward L. Thorndike devised this puzzle box to study the process by which a cat learns to press a paddle to escape from the box and receive food. Do you think Thorndike's work has relevance to the question of why humans voluntarily solve puzzles, such as crossword puzzles and jigsaw puzzles? Do they receive any rewards?

was a link between a response and a reward. Instead, Thorndike believed, over time and through experience the organism would make a direct connection between the stimulus and the response without any awareness that the connection existed.

The Basics of Operant Conditioning

Thorndike's early research served as the foundation for the work of one of the 20th century's most influential psychologists, B. F. Skinner (1904–1990). You may have heard of the Skinner box (shown in Figure 2), a chamber with a highly controlled environment that was used to study operant conditioning processes with laboratory animals. Whereas Thorndike's goal was to get his cats to learn to obtain food by leaving the box, animals in a Skinner box learn to obtain food by operating on their environment within the box. Skinner became interested in specifying how behavior varies as a result of alterations in the environment.

Skinner, whose work went far beyond perfecting Thorndike's earlier apparatus, is considered the inspiration for a whole generation of psychologists studying operant conditioning. To illustrate Skinner's contribution, let's consider what happens to a rat in the typical Skinner box (Keehn, 1996; Pascual & Rodríguez, 2006).

Suppose you want to teach a hungry rat to press a lever that is in its box. At first the rat will wander around the box, exploring the environment in a relatively random fashion. At some point, however, it will probably press the lever by chance, and when it does, it will receive a food pellet. The first time this happens, the rat will not learn the connection between pressing a lever and receiving food and will continue to explore the box. Sooner or later the rat will press the lever again and receive a pellet, and in time the frequency of the pressing response will increase. Eventually, the rat will press the lever continually until it satisfies its hunger, thereby demonstrating that it has learned that the receipt of food is contingent on pressing the lever.

REINFORCEMENT: THE CENTRAL CONCEPT OF OPERANT CONDITIONING

reinforcement The process by which a stimulus increases the probability that a preceding behavior will be repeated.

Skinner called the process that leads the rat to continue pressing the key "reinforcement." **Reinforcement** is the process by which a stimulus increases the probability that a preceding behavior will be repeated. In other words, pressing the lever is more likely to occur again because of the stimulus of food.

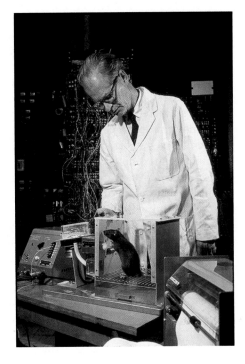

FIGURE 2 B. F. Skinner with a Skinner box used to study operant conditioning. Laboratory rats learn to press the lever in order to obtain food, which is delivered in the tray.

In a situation such as this one, the food is called a reinforcer. A **reinforcer** is any stimulus that increases the probability that a preceding behavior will occur again. Hence, food is a reinforcer, because it increases the probability that the behavior of pressing (formally referred to as the *response* of pressing) will take place.

What kind of stimuli can act as reinforcers? Bonuses, toys, and good grades can serve as reinforcers—if they strengthen the probability of the response that occurred before their introduction. What makes something a reinforcer depends on individual preferences. Although a Hershey bar can act as a reinforcer for one person, an individual who dislikes chocolate may find one dollar more desirable. The only way we can know if a stimulus is a reinforcer for a particular organism is to observe whether the frequency of a previously occurring behavior increases after the presentation of the stimulus.

Of course, we are not born knowing that one dollar can buy us a candy bar. Rather, through experience we learn that money is a valuable commodity because of its association with stimuli, such as food and drink, that are naturally reinforcing. This fact suggests a distinction between primary reinforcers and secondary reinforcers. A *primary reinforcer* satisfies some biological need and works naturally, regardless of a person's previous experience. Food for a hungry person, warmth for a cold person, and relief for a person in pain all would be classified as primary reinforcers. A *secondary reinforcer*, in contrast, is a stimulus that becomes reinforcing because of its association with a primary reinforcer. For instance, we know that money is valuable, because we have learned that it allows us to obtain other desirable objects, including primary reinforcers such as food and shelter. Money thus becomes a secondary reinforcer (Moher et al., 2008).

reinforcer Any stimulus that increases the probability that a preceding behavior will occur again.

StudyAlert

Remember that primary reinforcers satisfy a biological need; secondary reinforcers are effective due to previous association with a primary reinforcer.

POSITIVE REINFORCERS, NEGATIVE REINFORCERS, AND PUNISHMENT

In many respects, reinforcers can be thought of in terms of rewards; both a reinforcer and a reward increase the probability that a preceding response will occur again. But the term *reward* is limited to *positive* occurrences, and this is where it differs from a reinforcer—for it turns out that reinforcers can be positive or negative.

positive reinforcer A stimulus added to the environment that brings about an increase in a preceding response.

negative reinforcer An unpleasant stimulus whose removal leads to an increase in the probability that a preceding response will be repeated in the future.

punishment A stimulus that decreases the probability that a previous behavior will occur again.

A **positive reinforcer** is a stimulus *added* to the environment that brings about an increase in a preceding response. If food, water, money, or praise is provided after a response, it is more likely that that response will occur again in the future. The paychecks that workers get at the end of the week, for example, increase the likelihood that they will return to their jobs the following week.

In contrast, a **negative reinforcer** refers to an unpleasant stimulus whose removal leads to an increase in the probability that a preceding response will be repeated in the future. For example, if you have an itchy rash (an unpleasant stimulus) that is relieved when you apply a certain brand of ointment, you are more likely to use that ointment the next time you have an itchy rash. Using the ointment, then, is negatively reinforcing, because it removes the unpleasant itch. Similarly, if your iPod volume is so loud that it hurts your ears when you first turn it on, you are likely to reduce the volume level. Lowering the volume is negatively reinforcing, and you are more apt to repeat the action in the future when you first turn it on. Negative reinforcement, then, teaches the individual that taking an action removes a negative condition that exists in the environment. Like positive reinforcers, negative reinforcers increase the likelihood that preceding behaviors will be repeated (Magoon & Critchfield, 2008).

Note that negative reinforcement is not the same as punishment. **Punishment** refers to a stimulus that *decreases* the probability that a prior behavior will occur again. Unlike negative reinforcement, which produces an *increase* in behavior, punishment reduces the likelihood of a prior response. If we receive a shock that is meant to decrease a certain behavior, then we are receiving punishment, but if we are already receiving a shock and do something to stop that shock, the behavior that stops the shock is considered to be negatively reinforced. In the first case, the specific behavior is apt to decrease because of the punishment; in the second, it is likely to increase because of the negative reinforcement.

There are two types of punishment: positive punishment and negative punishment, just as there are positive reinforcement and negative reinforcement. (In both cases, "positive" means adding something, and "negative" means removing something.) *Positive punishment* weakens a response through the application of an unpleasant stimulus. For instance, spanking a child for misbehaving or spending ten years in jail for committing a crime is positive punishment. In contrast, *negative punishment* consists of the removal of something pleasant. For instance, when a teenager is told she is "grounded" and will no longer be able to use the family car because of her poor grades, or when an employee is informed that he has been demoted with a cut in pay because of a poor job evaluation, negative punishment is being administered. Both positive and negative punishment result in a decrease in the likelihood that a prior behavior will be repeated.

The following rules (and the summary in Figure 3) can help you distinguish these concepts from one another:

- Reinforcement *increases* the frequency of the behavior preceding it; punishment *decreases* the frequency of the behavior preceding it.
- The *application* of a *positive* stimulus brings about an increase in the frequency of behavior and is referred to as positive reinforcement; the *application* of a *negative* stimulus decreases or reduces the frequency of behavior and is called punishment.
- The *removal* of a *negative* stimulus that results in an increase in the frequency of behavior is negative reinforcement; the *removal* of a *positive* stimulus that decreases the frequency of behavior is negative punishment.

THE PROS AND CONS OF PUNISHMENT: WHY REINFORCEMENT BEATS PUNISHMENT

Is punishment an effective way to modify behavior? Punishment often presents the quickest route to changing behavior that, if allowed to continue, might be dangerous

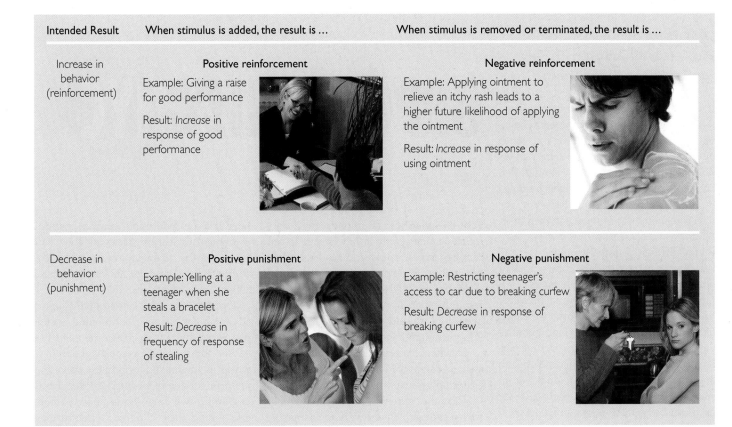

Intended Result	When stimulus is added, the result is ...	When stimulus is removed or terminated, the result is ...
Increase in behavior (reinforcement)	**Positive reinforcement** Example: Giving a raise for good performance Result: *Increase* in response of good performance	**Negative reinforcement** Example: Applying ointment to relieve an itchy rash leads to a higher future likelihood of applying the ointment Result: *Increase* in response of using ointment
Decrease in behavior (punishment)	**Positive punishment** Example: Yelling at a teenager when she steals a bracelet Result: *Decrease* in frequency of response of stealing	**Negative punishment** Example: Restricting teenager's access to car due to breaking curfew Result: *Decrease* in response of breaking curfew

FIGURE 3 Types of reinforcement and punishment.

to an individual. For instance, a parent may not have a second chance to warn a child not to run into a busy street, and so punishing the first incidence of this behavior may prove to be wise. Moreover, the use of punishment to suppress behavior, even temporarily, provides an opportunity to reinforce a person for subsequently behaving in a more desirable way.

There are some rare instances in which punishment can be the most humane approach to treating certain severe disorders. For example, some children suffer from *autism,* a psychological disorder that can lead them to abuse themselves by tearing at their skin or banging their heads against the wall, injuring themselves severely in the process. In such cases—and when all other treatments have failed—punishment in the form of a quick but intense electric shock has been used to prevent self-injurious behavior. Such punishment, however, is used only to keep the child safe and to buy time until positive reinforcement procedures can be initiated (Ducharme, Sanjuan, & Drain, 2007; Matson & LoVullo, 2008; Toole et al., 2004).

Punishment has several disadvantages that make its routine questionable. For one thing, punishment is frequently ineffective, particularly if it is not delivered shortly after the undesired behavior or if the individual is able to leave the setting in which the punishment is being given. An employee who is reprimanded by the boss may quit; a teenager who loses the use of the family car may borrow a friend's car instead. In such instances, the initial behavior that is being punished may be replaced by one that is even less desirable.

Even worse, physical punishment can convey to the recipient the idea that physical aggression is permissible and perhaps even desirable. A father who yells at and hits his son for misbehaving teaches the son that aggression is an appropriate, adult response. The son soon may copy his father's behavior by acting aggressively toward others. In addition, physical punishment is often administered by people who are

Dollars for Scholars: Should Parents and Children Be Paid for Doing the Right Thing?

OPPORTUNITY NYC

It's one of the basic rules of parenting: Good fathers and mothers are supposed to be involved in their children's lives and watch out for their best interests. Yet some parents don't do this as much as they should. Perhaps these behaviors were never modeled by their own parents, or perhaps they are overwhelmed by the stressors in their lives. But for whatever reason, they don't do such things for their children as taking them to the dentist, getting them a library card, or attending parent-teacher conferences.

To deal with the problem, a privately funded program in New York city called Opportunity NYC is testing a highly controversial solution for getting low-income parents more involved in their children's health and education: It pays them to do it. For instance, the program pays parents $200 for each child who receives an annual medical checkup. It pays $50 every two months for each child who attends school regularly during that period. It even makes some payments to the children themselves if they are in high school, and, for instance, they take precollege standardized tests or accumulate sufficient credits toward graduation.

Opportunity NYC has the goal of lessening economic hardship in low-income families through these direct payments and encouraging families to take the initiative to invest in their children and to improve their futures. This seems noble enough—families get money they very much need, but only if they engage in certain behaviors to advance the health and education of their children. In operant conditioning terms, the payment is a positive reinforcement. In principle, the beneficial behaviors should become well learned (OpportunityNYC.org, 2009).

So what objections could people have to such a program? For one thing, it has been criticized as insulting and patronizing to low-income parents. But also, whether such a program would work to change behavior for the better over the long term is an open question. People might be motivated by the rewards to learn to engage in the appropriate behaviors, but it's unclear that those behaviors would persist without the rewards. Furthermore, some critics believe it may undermine students' natural enjoyment of learning; instead, they will focus on the financial rewards (Kelley, 2007; Sebire, Standage, & Vansteenkiste, 2009; Vansteenkiste et al., 2005).

Opportunity NYC intentionally takes advantage of operant conditioning principles in an attempt to change people's behavior for the greater social good. If it works as intended, it will help relieve the financial strains of poverty-stricken families, and it will have coaxed those parents into giving their children better futures than they might otherwise have had. Still, the idea of paying people to be socially responsible and meet their parental obligations strikes many people as the wrong approach to take, and it remains to be seen whether the program is effective.

RETHINK

- Do you believe that rewarding students financially for doing well in school reduces their motivation to learn for learning's sake? Why or why not?
- How might you determine if Opportunity NYC is an effective program?

themselves angry or enraged. It is unlikely that individuals in such an emotional state will be able to think through what they are doing or control carefully the degree of punishment they are inflicting. Ultimately, those who resort to physical punishment run the risk that they will grow to be feared. Punishment can also reduce the self-esteem of recipients unless they can understand the reasons for it (Leary et al., 2008; Miller-Perrin, Perrin, & Kocur, 2009; Zolotor et al., 2008).

Finally, punishment does not convey any information about what an alternative, more appropriate behavior might be. To be useful in bringing about more desirable behavior in the future, punishment must be accompanied by specific information about the behavior that is being punished, along with specific suggestions concerning a more desirable behavior. Punishing a child for staring out the window in school could merely lead her to stare at the floor instead. Unless we teach her appropriate ways to respond, we have merely managed to substitute one undesirable behavior for another. If punishment is not followed up with reinforcement for subsequent behavior that is more appropriate, little will be accomplished.

In short, reinforcing desired behavior is a more appropriate technique for modifying behavior than using punishment. Both in and out of the scientific arena, then, reinforcement usually beats punishment (Hiby, Rooney, & Bradshaw, 2004; Pogarsky & Piquero, 2003; Sidman, 2006). (Also see *Applying Psychology in the 21st Century*.)

SCHEDULES OF REINFORCEMENT: TIMING LIFE'S REWARDS

The world would be a different place if poker players never played cards again after the first losing hand, fishermen returned to shore as soon as they missed a catch, or telemarketers never made another phone call after their first hang-up. The fact that such unreinforced behaviors continue, often with great frequency and persistence, illustrates that reinforcement need not be received continually for behavior to be learned and maintained. In fact, behavior that is reinforced only occasionally can ultimately be learned better than can behavior that is always reinforced.

When we refer to the frequency and timing of reinforcement that follows desired behavior, we are talking about **schedules of reinforcement.** Behavior that is reinforced every time it occurs is said to be on a **continuous reinforcement schedule;** if it is reinforced some but not all of the time, it is on a **partial** (or **intermittent**) **reinforcement schedule.** Although learning occurs more rapidly under a continuous reinforcement schedule, behavior lasts longer after reinforcement stops when it is learned under a partial reinforcement schedule (Casey, Cooper-Brown, & Wacher, 2006; Gottlieb, 2004; Reed, 2007; Staddon & Cerutti, 2003).

Why should intermittent reinforcement result in stronger, longer-lasting learning than continuous reinforcement? We can answer the question by examining how we might behave when using a candy vending machine compared with a Las Vegas slot machine. When we use a vending machine, previous experience has taught us that every time we put in the appropriate amount of money, the reinforcement, a candy bar, ought to be delivered. In other words, the schedule of reinforcement is continuous. In comparison, a slot machine offers intermittent reinforcement. We have learned that after putting in our cash, most of the time we will not receive anything in return. At the same time, though, we know that we will occasionally win something.

Now suppose that, unknown to us, both the candy vending machine and the slot machine are broken, and so neither one is able to dispense anything. It would not be very long before we stopped depositing coins into the broken candy machine. Probably at most we would try only two or three times before leaving the machine in disgust. But the story would be quite different with the broken slot machine. Here, we would drop in money for a considerably longer time, even though there would be no payoff.

In formal terms, we can see the difference between the two reinforcement schedules: Partial reinforcement schedules (such as those provided by slot machines) maintain performance longer than do continuous reinforcement schedules (such as those established in candy vending machines) before *extinction*—the disappearance of the conditioned response—occurs.

Certain kinds of partial reinforcement schedules produce stronger and lengthier responding before extinction than do others. Although many different partial reinforcement schedules have been examined, they can most readily be put into two categories: schedules that consider the *number of responses* made before reinforcement is given, called fixed-ratio and variable-ratio schedules, and those that consider the *amount of time* that elapses before reinforcement is provided, called fixed-interval and variable-interval schedules (Gottlieb, 2006; Pellegrini et al., 2004; Reed & Morgan, 2008; Svartdal, 2003).

Fixed- and Variable-Ratio Schedules In a **fixed-ratio schedule,** reinforcement is given only after a specific number of responses.

schedules of reinforcement Different patterns of frequency and timing of reinforcement following desired behavior.

continuous reinforcement schedule Reinforcing of a behavior every time it occurs.

partial (or intermittent) reinforcement schedule Reinforcing of a behavior some but not all of the time.

fixed-ratio schedule A schedule by which reinforcement is given only after a specific number of responses are made.

FIGURE 4 Typical outcomes of different reinforcement schedules. (a) In a fixed-ratio schedule, reinforcement is provided after a specific number of responses are made. Because the more responses, the more reinforcement, fixed-ratio schedules produce a high rate of responding. (b) In a variable-ratio schedule, responding also occurs at a high rate. (c) A fixed-interval schedule produces lower rates of responding, especially just after reinforcement has been presented, because the organism learns that a specified time period must elapse between reinforcements. (d) A variable-interval schedule produces a fairly steady stream of responses.

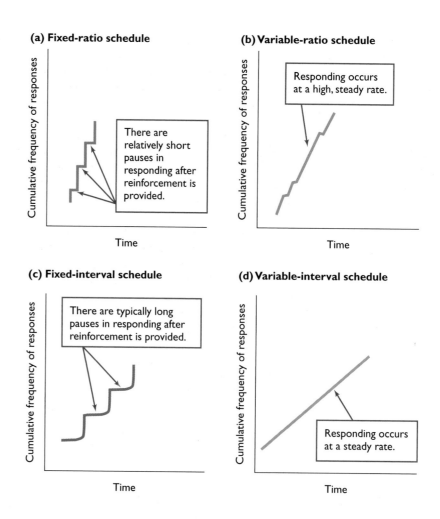

(a) Fixed-ratio schedule

There are relatively short pauses in responding after reinforcement is provided.

(b) Variable-ratio schedule

Responding occurs at a high, steady rate.

(c) Fixed-interval schedule

There are typically long pauses in responding after reinforcement is provided.

(d) Variable-interval schedule

Responding occurs at a steady rate.

variable-ratio schedule A schedule by which reinforcement occurs after a varying number of responses rather than after a fixed number.

StudyAlert

Remember that the different schedules of reinforcement affect the rapidity with which a response is learned and how long it lasts after reinforcement is no longer provided.

For instance, a rat might receive a food pellet every tenth time it pressed a lever; here, the ratio would be 1:10. Similarly, garment workers are generally paid on fixed-ratio schedules: They receive a specific number of dollars for every blouse they sew. Because a greater rate of production means more reinforcement, people on fixed-ratio schedules are apt to work as quickly as possible (see Figure 4).

In a **variable-ratio schedule,** reinforcement occurs after a varying number of responses rather than after a fixed number. Although the specific number of responses necessary to receive reinforcement varies, the number of responses usually hovers around a specific average. A good example of a variable-ratio schedule is a telephone salesperson's job. He might make a sale during the 3rd, 8th, 9th, and 20th calls without being successful during any call in between. Although the number of responses he must make before making a sale varies, it averages out to a 20% success rate. Under these circumstances, you might expect that the salesperson would try to make as many calls as possible in as short a time as possible. This is the case with all variable-ratio schedules, which lead to a high rate of response and resistance to extinction.

Fixed- and Variable-Interval Schedules: The Passage of Time In contrast to fixed- and variable-ratio schedules, in which the crucial factor is the number of responses, fixed-*interval* and variable-*interval* schedules focus on the amount of time that has elapsed since a person or animal was rewarded. One example of a fixed-interval schedule is a weekly paycheck. For people who receive regular, weekly paychecks, it typically makes relatively little difference exactly how much they produce in a given week.

Because a **fixed-interval schedule** provides reinforcement for a response only if a fixed time period has elapsed, overall rates of response are relatively low. This is especially true in the period just after reinforcement, when the time before another reinforcement is relatively great. Students' study habits often exemplify this reality. If the periods between exams are relatively long (meaning that the opportunity for reinforcement for good performance is given fairly infrequently), students often study minimally or not at all until the day of the exam draws near. Just before the exam, however, students begin to cram for it, signaling a rapid increase in the rate of their studying response. As you might expect, immediately after the exam there is a rapid decline in the rate of responding, with few people opening a book the day after a test. Fixed-interval schedules produce the kind of "scalloping effect" shown in Figure 4 (Saville, 2009).

One way to decrease the delay in responding that occurs just after reinforcement, and to maintain the desired behavior more consistently throughout an interval, is to use a variable-interval schedule. In a **variable-interval schedule,** the time between reinforcements varies around some average rather than being fixed. For example, a professor who gives surprise quizzes that vary from one every three days to one every three weeks, averaging one every two weeks, is using a variable-interval schedule. Compared to the study habits we observed with a fixed-interval schedule, students' study habits under such a variable-interval schedule would most likely be very different. Students would be apt to study more regularly because they would never know when the next surprise quiz was coming. Variable-interval schedules, in general, are more likely to produce relatively steady rates of responding than are fixed-interval schedules, with responses that take longer to extinguish after reinforcement ends.

DISCRIMINATION AND GENERALIZATION IN OPERANT CONDITIONING

It does not take a child long to learn that a red light at an intersection means stop and a green light indicates that it is permissible to continue, in the same way that a pigeon can learn to peck a key when a green light goes on but not when a red light appears. Just as in classical conditioning, then, operant learning involves the phenomena of discrimination and generalization.

The process by which people learn to discriminate stimuli is known as stimulus control training. In *stimulus control training,* a behavior is reinforced in the presence of a specific stimulus, but not in its absence. For example, one of the most difficult discriminations many people face is determining when someone's friendliness is not mere friendliness, but a signal of romantic interest. People learn to make the discrimination by observing the presence of certain nonverbal cues—such as increased eye contact and touching—that indicate romantic interest. When such cues are absent, people learn that no romantic interest is indicated. In this case, the nonverbal cue acts as a discriminative stimulus, one to which an organism learns to respond during stimulus control training. A *discriminative stimulus* signals the likelihood that reinforcement will follow a response. For example, if you wait until your roommate is in a good mood before you ask to borrow her favorite CD, your behavior can be said to be under stimulus control because you can discriminate between her moods.

Just as in classical conditioning, the phenomenon of stimulus generalization, in which an organism learns a response to one stimulus and then exhibits the same response to slightly different stimuli, occurs in operant conditioning. If you have learned that being polite helps you to get your way in a certain situation (reinforcing your politeness), you are likely to generalize your response to other situations. Sometimes, though, generalization can have unfortunate consequences, as when people behave negatively toward all members of a racial group because they have had an unpleasant experience with one member of that group.

fixed-interval schedule A schedule that provides reinforcement for a response only if a fixed time period has elapsed, making overall rates of response relatively low.

variable-interval schedule A schedule by which the time between reinforcements varies around some average rather than being fixed.

SHAPING: REINFORCING WHAT DOESN'T COME NATURALLY

Consider the difficulty of using operant conditioning to teach people to repair an automobile transmission. If you had to wait until they chanced to fix a transmission perfectly before you provided them with reinforcement, the Model T Ford might be back in style long before they mastered the repair process.

There are many complex behaviors, ranging from auto repair to zoo management, that we would not expect to occur naturally as part of anyone's spontaneous behavior. For such behaviors, for which there might otherwise be no opportunity to provide reinforcement (because the behavior would never occur in the first place), a procedure known as shaping is used. **Shaping** is the process of teaching a complex behavior by rewarding closer and closer approximations of the desired behavior. In shaping, you start by reinforcing any behavior that is at all similar to the behavior you want the person to learn. Later, you reinforce only responses that are closer to the behavior you ultimately want to teach. Finally, you reinforce only the desired response. Each step in shaping, then, moves only slightly beyond the previously learned behavior, permitting the person to link the new step to the behavior learned earlier (Krueger & Dayan, 2009).

Shaping allows even lower animals to learn complex responses that would never occur naturally, ranging from lions jumping through hoops, dolphins rescuing divers lost at sea, or rodents finding hidden land mines. Shaping also underlies the learning of many complex human skills. For instance, the organization of most textbooks is based on the principles of shaping. Typically, information is presented so that new material builds on previously learned concepts or skills. Thus, the concept of shaping could not be presented until we had discussed the more basic principles of operant learning (Meyer & Ladewig, 2008). (Also see *PsychWork*.)

shaping The process of teaching a complex behavior by rewarding closer and closer approximations of the desired behavior.

PsychWork
SEEING EYE GUIDE DOG TRAINER

Name: Lea Johnson

Position: Seeing Eye Guide Dog Trainer

Education: BS, Geography, Dartmouth College, Hanover, NH

For decades, guide dogs have provided a set of eyes to the visually impaired, expanding the opportunities open to them and increasing their independence. But it takes a great deal of training to make a dog an effective seeing eye guide dog, according to Lea Johnson, who works with The Seeing Eye agency in Morristown, New Jersey. Johnson teaches apprentice instructors to carry out the demanding, but rewarding, process of training dogs.

"We hire college graduates, and while we don't require a specific major, a background in psychology or animal science allows employees to more easily connect with different aspects of the job," she said.

An apprentice instructor needs to have self-motivation in order to complete all aspects of the dog's training. In addition, they need to be able to work in a team setting, according to Johnson. But that's only part of it.

"The process of training the dogs is complex," says Johnson. "For example, the dog must be obedient and respond to their visually-impaired owner. But they also get praised for sometimes refusing their owner's commands, if it would put their owner in danger."

Once a dog learns the skills it needs, the trainer must then teach a visually-impaired person how to work with the dog.

"After training dogs for four months, the trainers must be able to teach blind people the skills to care for and travel with their Seeing Eye dog safely," Johnson said. Not only must trainers relate well to dogs, but they also must interact well with blind people. She adds, "The training of people is intense and emotionally challenging in a very different way from the dog training portion. Without a good heart to start with, trainers would never be successful."

BIOLOGICAL CONSTRAINTS ON LEARNING: YOU CAN'T TEACH AN OLD DOG JUST ANY TRICK

Not all behaviors can be trained in all species equally well. Instead, there are *biological constraints*, built-in limitations in the ability of animals to learn particular behaviors. In some cases, an organism has a special predisposition that will aid in its learning a behavior (such as pecking behaviors in pigeons). In other cases, biological constraints act to prevent or inhibit an organism from learning a behavior. For example, it's impossible to train pigs to pick up a disk, because they are biologically programmed to push objects like it along the ground. Similarly, although a raccoon can be conditioned to drop a single coin into a piggy bank, it will do so only after rubbing the coin against the outside of the bank. The reason? After catching a fish, raccoons instinctually rub them against the ground to remove their outer covering (Breland & Breland, 1966; Stevens & Pashler, 2002).

Biological constraints make it nearly impossible for animals to learn certain behaviors. Here, psychologist Marian Breland attempts to overcome the natural limitations that inhibit the success of conditioning this rooster.

The existence of biological constraints is consistent with evolutionary explanations of behavior. Clearly, there are adaptive benefits that promote survival for organisms that quickly learn—or avoid—certain behaviors. For example, our ability to rapidly learn to avoid touching hot surfaces increases our chances of survival. Additional support for the evolutionary interpretation of biological constraints lies in the fact the associations that animals learn most readily involve stimuli that are most relevant to the specific environment in which they live (Cosmides & Tooby, 2004; Davis, 2007; Terry, 2003).

Furthermore, psychologists taking an evolutionary perspective have suggested that we may be genetically predisposed to be fearful of certain stimuli, such as snakes or even threatening faces. For example, people in experiments learn associations relatively quickly between photos of faces with threatening expressions and neutral stimuli (such as an umbrella). In contrast, they are slower to learn associations between faces that have pleasant expressions and neutral stimuli. Stimuli that pose potential threats, like snakes or people with hostile facial expressions, posed a potential danger to early humans, and there may be an evolved "fear module" in the brain that is sensitized to such threats (DeLoache & LoBue, 2009; Endres & Fendt, 2007; Georgiou et al., 2005; Gerdes, Uhl, & Alpers, 2009; Oehman & Mineka, 2003).

COMPARING CLASSICAL AND OPERANT CONDITIONING

We've considered classical conditioning and operant conditioning as two completely different processes. And, as summarized in Figure 5, there are a number of key distinctions between the two forms of learning. For example, the key concept in classical conditioning is the association between stimuli, whereas in operant conditioning it is reinforcement. Furthermore, classical conditioning involves an involuntary, natural, innate behavior, but operant conditioning is based on voluntary responses made by an organism.

Some researchers are asking if, in fact, the two types of learning are so different after all. Some learning psychologists have suggested that classical and operant conditioning might share some underlying processes. Arguing from an evolutionary viewpoint, they contend that it is unlikely that two completely separate basic processes would evolve. Instead, one process—albeit with considerable complexity in the way it operates—might better explain behavior. Although it's too early to know if this point of view will be supported, it is clear that there are a number of processes that operate both in classical and operant conditioning, including extinction, stimulus generalization, and stimulus discrimination (Donahoe, 2003; Donahoe & Vergas, 2004; Silva, Goncalves, & Garcia-Mijares, 2007).

Concept	Classical Conditioning	Operant Conditioning
Basic principle	Building associations between a conditioned stimulus and conditioned response.	Reinforcement *increases* the frequency of the behavior preceding it; punishment *decreases* the frequency of the behavior preceding it.
Nature of behavior	Based on involuntary, natural, innate behavior. Behavior is elicited by the unconditioned or conditioned stimulus.	Organism voluntarily operates on its environment to produce a desirable result. After behavior occurs, the likelihood of the behavior occurring again is increased or decreased by the behavior's consequences.
Order of events	Before conditioning, an unconditioned stimulus leads to an unconditioned response. After conditioning, a conditioned stimulus leads to a conditioned response.	Reinforcement leads to an increase in behavior; punishment leads to a decrease in behavior.
Example	After a physician gives a child a series of painful injections (an unconditioned stimulus) that produce an emotional reaction (an unconditioned response), the child develops an emotional reaction (a conditioned response) whenever he sees the physician (the conditioned stimulus).	A student who, after studying hard for a test, earns an A (the positive reinforcer), is more likely to study hard in the future. A student who, after going out drinking the night before a test, fails the test (punishment) is less likely to go out drinking the night before the next test.

FIGURE 5 Comparing key concepts in classical conditioning and operant conditioning.

BECOMING AN INFORMED CONSUMER

of Psychology

Using Behavior Analysis and Behavior Modification

A couple who had been living together for three years began to fight frequently. The issues of disagreement ranged from who was going to do the dishes to the quality of their love life.

Disturbed, the couple went to a *behavior analyst,* a psychologist who specialized in behavior-modification techniques. He asked them to keep a detailed written record of their interactions over the next two weeks.

When they returned with the data, he carefully reviewed the records with them. In doing so, he noticed a pattern: Each of their arguments had occurred just after one or the other had left a household chore undone, such as leaving dirty dishes in the sink or draping clothes on the only chair in the bedroom.

Using the data the couple had collected, the behavior analyst asked them to list all the chores that could possibly arise and assign each one a point value depending on how long it took to complete. Then he had them divide the chores equally and agree in a written contract to fulfill the ones assigned to them. If either failed to carry out one of the assigned chores, he or she would have to place $1 per point in a fund for the other to spend. They also agreed to a program of verbal praise, promising to reward each other verbally for completing a chore.

The couple agreed to try it for a month and to keep careful records of the number of arguments they had during that period. To their surprise, the number declined rapidly.

behavior modification A formalized technique for promoting the frequency of desirable behaviors and decreasing the incidence of unwanted ones.

This case provides an illustration of **behavior modification,** a formalized technique for promoting the frequency of desirable behaviors and decreasing the incidence of unwanted ones. Using the basic principles of learning theory, behavior-modification techniques have proved to be helpful in a variety of situations. People with severe mental retardation have, for the first time in their lives, started dressing and feeding themselves. Behavior modification has also helped people lose weight, give up smoking, and behave more safely (Delinsky, Latner, & Wilson, 2006; Ntinas, 2007; Wadden, Crerand, & Brock, 2005).

The techniques used by behavior analysts are as varied as the list of processes that modify behavior. They include reinforcement scheduling, shaping, generalization training, discrimination training, and extinction. Participants in a behavior-change program do, however, typically follow a series of similar basic steps that include the following:

- *Identifying goals and target behaviors.* The first step is to define *desired behavior*. Is it an increase in time spent studying? A decrease in weight? An increase in the use of language? A reduction in the amount of aggression displayed by a child? The goals must be stated in observable terms and must lead to specific targets. For instance, a goal might be "to increase study time," whereas the target behavior would be "to study at least two hours per day on weekdays and an hour on Saturdays."

- *Designing a data-recording system and recording preliminary data.* To determine whether behavior has changed, it is necessary to collect data before any changes are made in the situation. This information provides a baseline against which future changes can be measured.

- *Selecting a behavior-change strategy.* The crucial step is to select an appropriate strategy. Because all the principles of learning can be employed to bring about behavior change, a "package" of treatments is normally used. This might include the systematic use of positive reinforcement for desired behavior (verbal praise or something more tangible, such as food), as well as a program of extinction for undesirable behavior (ignoring a child who throws a tantrum). Selecting the right reinforcers is critical, and it may be necessary to experiment a bit to find out what is important to a particular individual.

- *Implementing the program.* Probably the most important aspect of program implementation is consistency. It is also important to reinforce the intended behavior. For example, suppose a mother wants her son to spend more time on his homework, but as soon as he sits down to study, he asks for a snack. If the mother gets a snack for him, she is likely to be reinforcing her son's delaying tactic, not his studying.

- *Keeping careful records after the program is implemented.* Another crucial task is record keeping. If the target behaviors are not monitored, there is no way of knowing whether the program has actually been successful.

- *Evaluating and altering the ongoing program.* Finally, the results of the program should be compared with baseline, pre-implementation data to determine its effectiveness. If the program has been successful, the procedures employed can be phased out gradually. For instance, if the program called for reinforcing every instance of picking up one's clothes from the bedroom floor, the reinforcement schedule could be modified to a fixed-ratio schedule in which every third instance was reinforced. However, if the program has not been successful in bringing about the desired behavior change, consideration of other approaches might be advisable.

Behavior-change techniques based on these general principles have enjoyed wide success and have proved to be one of the most powerful means of modifying behavior. Clearly, it is possible to employ the basic notions of learning theory to improve our lives.

RECAP/EVALUATE/RETHINK

RECAP

What is the role of reward and punishment in learning?

- Operant conditioning is a form of learning in which a voluntary behavior is strengthened or weakened. According to B. F. Skinner, the major mechanism underlying learning is reinforcement, the process by which a stimulus increases the probability that a preceding behavior will be repeated. (p. 173)
- Primary reinforcers are rewards that are naturally effective without previous experience, because they satisfy a biological need. Secondary reinforcers begin to act as if they were primary reinforcers through association with a primary reinforcer. (p. 174)
- Positive reinforcers are stimuli that are added to the environment and lead to an increase in a preceding response. Negative reinforcers are stimuli that remove something unpleasant from the environment, also leading to an increase in the preceding response. (p. 175)
- Punishment decreases the probability that a prior behavior will occur. Positive punishment weakens a response through the application of an unpleasant stimulus, whereas negative punishment weakens a response by the removal of something positive. In contrast to reinforcement, in which the goal is to increase the incidence of behavior, punishment is meant to decrease or suppress behavior. (p. 176)
- Schedules and patterns of reinforcement affect the strength and duration of learning. Generally, partial reinforcement schedules—in which reinforcers are not delivered on every trial—produce stronger and longer-lasting learning than do continuous reinforcement schedules. (p. 179)
- Among the major categories of reinforcement schedules are fixed- and variable-ratio schedules, which are based on the number of responses made, and fixed- and variable-interval schedules, which are based on the time interval that elapses before reinforcement is provided. (p. 179)
- Stimulus control training (similar to stimulus discrimination in classical conditioning) is reinforcement of a behavior in the presence of a specific stimulus but not in its absence. In stimulus generalization, an organism learns a response to one stimulus and then exhibits the same response to slightly different stimuli. (p. 181)
- Shaping is a process for teaching complex behaviors by rewarding closer and closer approximations of the desired final behavior. (p. 182)
- There are biological constraints, or built-in limitations, on the ability of an organism to learn: Certain behaviors will be relatively easy for individuals of a species to learn, whereas other behaviors will be either difficult or impossible for them to learn. (p. 183)

What are some practical methods for bringing about behavior change, both in ourselves and in others?

- Behavior modification is a method for formally using the principles of learning theory to promote the frequency of desired behaviors and to decrease or eliminate unwanted ones. (p. 184)

EVALUATE

1. _____ conditioning describes learning that occurs as a result of reinforcement.
2. Match the type of operant learning with its definition:
   1. An unpleasant stimulus is presented to decrease behavior.
   2. An unpleasant stimulus is removed to increase behavior.
   3. A pleasant stimulus is presented to increase behavior.
   4. A pleasant stimulus is removed to decrease behavior.

   a. positive reinforcement
   b. negative reinforcement
   c. positive punishment
   d. negative punishment
3. Sandy had had a rough day, and his son's noisemaking was not helping him relax. Not wanting to resort to scolding, Sandy told his son in a serious manner that he was very tired and would like the boy to play quietly for an hour. This approach worked. For Sandy, the change in his son's behavior was
   a. positively reinforcing.
   b. negatively reinforcing.
4. In a _____ reinforcement schedule, behavior is reinforced some of the time, whereas in a _____ reinforcement schedule, behavior is reinforced all the time.
5. Match the type of reinforcement schedule with its definition.
   1. Reinforcement occurs after a set time period.
   2. Reinforcement occurs after a set number of responses.
   3. Reinforcement occurs after a varying time period.
   4. Reinforcement occurs after a varying number of responses.

   a. fixed-ratio
   b. variable-interval
   c. fixed-interval
   d. variable-ratio

RETHINK

1. Using the scientific literature as a guide, what would you tell parents who wish to know if the routine use of physical punishment is a necessary and acceptable form of child rearing?

2. *From the perspective of an educator:* How would you use your knowledge of operant conditioning in the classroom to set up a program to increase the likelihood that children will complete their homework more frequently?

Answers to Evaluate Questions

1. Operant; 2. 1-c; 2-b; 3-a; 4-d 3. b 4. partial (or intermittent), continuous; 5. 1-c, 2-a, 3-b, 4-d

KEY TERMS

operant conditioning p. 173
reinforcement p. 174
reinforcer p. 175
positive reinforcer p. 176
negative reinforcer p. 176
punishment p. 176

schedules of reinforcement p. 179
continuous reinforcement schedule p. 179
partial (or intermittent) reinforcement schedule p. 179

fixed-ratio schedule p. 179
variable-ratio schedule p. 180
fixed-interval schedule p. 181

variable-interval schedule p. 181
shaping p. 182
behavior modification p. 184

Cognitive Approaches to Learning

What is the role of cognition and thought in learning?

cognitive learning theory An approach to the study of learning that focuses on the thought processes that underlie learning.

StudyAlert

Remember that the cognitive learning approach focuses on the *internal* thoughts and expectations of learners, whereas classical and operant conditioning approaches focus on *external* stimuli, responses, and reinforcement.

latent learning Learning in which a new behavior is acquired but is not demonstrated until some incentive is provided for displaying it.

Consider what happens when people learn to drive a car. They don't just get behind the wheel and stumble around until they randomly put the key into the ignition and, later, after many false starts, accidentally manage to get the car to move forward, thereby receiving positive reinforcement. Rather, they already know the basic elements of driving from previous experience as passengers, when they more than likely noticed how the key was inserted into the ignition, the car was put in drive, and the gas pedal was pressed to make the car go forward.

Clearly, not all learning is due to operant and classical conditioning. In fact, such activities as learning to drive a car imply that some kinds of learning must involve higher-order processes in which people's thoughts and memories and the way they process information account for their responses. Such situations argue against regarding learning as the unthinking, mechanical, and automatic acquisition of associations between stimuli and responses, as in classical conditioning, or the presentation of reinforcement, as in operant conditioning.

Some psychologists view learning in terms of the thought processes, or cognitions, that underlie it—an approach known as **cognitive learning theory.** Although psychologists working from the cognitive learning perspective do not deny the importance of classical and operant conditioning, they have developed approaches that focus on the unseen mental processes that occur during learning, rather than concentrating solely on external stimuli, responses, and reinforcements.

In its most basic formulation, cognitive learning theory suggests that it is not enough to say that people make responses because there is an assumed link between a stimulus and a response—a link that is the result of a past history of reinforcement for a response. Instead, according to this point of view, people, and even lower animals, develop an *expectation* that they will receive a reinforcer after making a response. Two types of learning in which no obvious prior reinforcement is present are latent learning and observational learning.

Latent Learning

Evidence for the importance of cognitive processes comes from a series of animal experiments that revealed a type of cognitive learning called latent learning. In **latent learning,** a new behavior is learned but not demonstrated until some incentive is provided for displaying it (Tolman & Honzik, 1930). In short, latent learning occurs without reinforcement.

In the studies demonstrating latent learning, psychologists examined the behavior of rats in a maze such as the one shown in Figure 1a. In one experiment, a group of rats was allowed to wander around the maze once a day for 17 days without ever receiving a reward. Understandably, those rats made many errors and spent a relatively long time reaching the end of the maze. A second group, however, was always given food at the end of the maze. Not surprisingly, those rats learned to run quickly and directly to the food box, making few errors.

A third group of rats started out in the same situation as the unrewarded rats, but only for the first 10 days. On the 11th day, a critical experimental manipulation

(a)   (b)

FIGURE 1 (a) In an attempt to demonstrate latent learning, rats were allowed to roam through a maze of this sort once a day for 17 days. (b) The rats that were never rewarded (the unrewarded control condition) consistently made the most errors, whereas those that received food at the finish every day (the rewarded control condition) consistently made far fewer errors. But the results also showed latent learning: Rats that were initially unrewarded but began to be rewarded only after the 10th day (the experimental group) showed an immediate reduction in errors and soon became similar in error rate to the rats that had been rewarded consistently. According to cognitive learning theorists, the reduction in errors indicates that the rats had developed a cognitive map—a mental representation—of the maze. Can you think of other examples of latent learning?

was introduced: From that point on, the rats in this group were given food for completing the maze. The results of this manipulation were dramatic, as you can see from the graph in Figure 1b. The previously unrewarded rats, which had earlier seemed to wander about aimlessly, showed such reductions in running time and declines in error rates that their performance almost immediately matched that of the group that had received rewards from the start.

To cognitive theorists, it seemed clear that the unrewarded rats had learned the layout of the maze early in their explorations; they just never displayed their latent learning until the reinforcement was offered. Instead, those rats seemed to develop a *cognitive map* of the maze—a mental representation of spatial locations and directions.

People, too, develop cognitive maps of their surroundings. For example, latent learning may permit you to know the location of a kitchenware store at a local mall you've frequently visited, even though you've never entered the store and don't even like to cook.

The possibility that we develop our cognitive maps through latent learning presents something of a problem for strict operant

Albert Bandura examined the principles of observational learning.

observational learning Learning by observing the behavior of another person, or model.

StudyAlert

A key point of observational learning approaches is that the behavior of models who are rewarded for a given behavior is more likely to be imitated than behavior in which the model is punished for the behavior.

This boy is displaying observational learning based on previous observation of his father. How does observational learning contribute to learning gender roles?

conditioning theorists. If we consider the results of the maze-learning experiment, for instance, it is unclear what reinforcement permitted the rats that initially received no reward to learn the layout of the maze, because there was no obvious reinforcer present. Instead, the results support a cognitive view of learning, in which changes occurred in unobservable mental processes (Frensch & Rünger, 2003; Iaria et al., 2009; Stouffer & White, 2006).

Observational Learning: Learning Through Imitation

Let's return for a moment to the case of a person learning to drive. How can we account for instances in which an individual with no direct experience in carrying out a particular behavior learns the behavior and then performs it? To answer this question, psychologists have focused on another aspect of cognitive learning: observational learning.

According to psychologist Albert Bandura and colleagues, a major part of human learning consists of **observational learning,** which is learning by watching the behavior of another person, or *model*. Because of its reliance on observation of others—a social phenomenon—the perspective taken by Bandura is often referred to as a *social cognitive* approach to learning (Bandura, 1999, 2004).

Bandura dramatically demonstrated the ability of models to stimulate learning in a classic experiment. In the study, young children saw a film of an adult wildly hitting a 5-feet-tall inflatable punching toy called a Bobo doll (Bandura, Ross, & Ross, 1963a, 1963b). Later the children were given the opportunity to play with the Bobo doll themselves, and, sure enough, most displayed the same kind of behavior, in some cases mimicking the aggressive behavior almost identically.

Not only negative behaviors are acquired through observational learning. In one experiment, for example, children who were afraid of dogs were exposed to a model—dubbed the Fearless Peer—playing with a dog (Bandura, Grusec, & Menlove, 1967). After exposure, observers were considerably more likely to approach a strange dog than were children who had not viewed the Fearless Peer.

Observational learning is particularly important in acquiring skills in which the operant conditioning technique of shaping is inappropriate. Piloting an airplane and performing brain surgery, for example, are behaviors that could hardly be learned by using trial-and-error methods without grave cost—literally—to those involved in the learning process.

Observational learning may have a genetic basis. For example, we find observational learning at work with mother animals teaching their young such activities as hunting. In addition, the discovery of *mirror neurons* that fire when we observe another person carrying out a behavior (discussed in the chapter on neuroscience) suggests that the capacity to imitate others may be innate (Lepage & Theoret, 2007; Thornton & McAuliffe, 2006; Schulte-Ruther et al., 2007) (see Figure 2).

Not all behavior that we witness is learned or carried out, of course. One crucial factor that determines whether we later imitate a model is whether the model is rewarded for his or her behavior. If we observe a friend being rewarded for putting more time into his studies by receiving higher grades, we are more likely to imitate his behavior than we would if his behavior resulted only in being stressed and tired. Models who are rewarded for behaving in a particular way are more apt to be mimicked than are models who receive punishment. Observing the punishment of a model, however, does not necessarily stop observers from learning the behavior. Observers can still describe the model's behavior—they are just less apt to perform it (Bandura, 1977, 1986, 1994).

Observational learning is central to a number of important issues relating to the extent to which people learn simply by watching the behavior of others. For

Psychology on the Web

1. B. F. Skinner had an impact on society and on thought that is only hinted at in our discussion of learning. Find additional information on the web about Skinner's life and influence. See what you can find out about his ideas for an ideal, utopian society based on the principles of conditioning and behaviorism. Write a summary of your findings.

2. Select a topic discussed in this set of modules that is of interest to you—for example, reinforcement versus punishment, teaching complex behaviors by shaping, violence in video games, relational versus analytical learning styles, behavior modification, and so on. Find at least two sources of information on the web about your topic and summarize the results of your quest. It may be most helpful to find two different approaches to your topic and compare them.

Epilogue

Here we have discussed several kinds of learning, ranging from classical conditioning, which depends on the existence of natural stimulus–response pairings, to operant conditioning, in which reinforcement is used to increase desired behavior. These approaches to learning focus on outward, behavioral learning processes. Cognitive approaches to learning focus on mental processes that enable learning.

We have also noted that learning is affected by culture and individual differences, with individual learning styles potentially affecting the ways in which people learn most effectively. And we saw some ways in which our learning about learning can be put to practical use, through such means as behavior-modification programs designed to decrease negative behaviors and increase positive ones.

Return to the prologue of this set of modules and consider the following questions about the very-well-learned response to cellphones and other handheld devices:

1. When people check their messages as soon as their device beeps, is that an example of classical conditioning, operant conditioning, or cognitive learning? Why?

2. In the example of people checking their messages, what is the stimulus and what is the response?

3. What is the reinforcement that keeps the message-checking behavior strong? Is it positive or negative reinforcement? Is the behavior ever punished? How so?

4. If the message-checking behavior is so frequent that it becomes a problem, as Senator Cochran described, what strategies could be used to stop or control the behavior?

Memory

Key Concepts for Chapter 6

Prologue *Remembering It All*

Meet Jill Price at one of her favorite Los Angeles restaurants, and she'll scoot into a booth and start to reminisce. "On Wednesday, December 11, 1996, my friend and I came here hunting for the perfect crab cake," she says. She also remembers Saturday, November 4, 1995 (she saw on TV that Israeli Prime Minister Yitzhak Rabin was killed) and Friday, September 20, 1985 (her first visit to the eatery; she wore a large hat). "It's all flashing through my head," she says matter-of-factly. "I'm totally in the moment. I just have a split screen of my past, too."

What Price, 42, has is the first-ever diagnosed case of highly superior autobiographical memory, which forces her to recall every day of her life from the age of 14. Given a date, she can tell you on what day of the week it fell, what she did and any historical event she heard of that day. "It's like I walk around with a video camera," says Price. "My memories are nonstop and involuntary." (Perry, 2008, p. 143)

Looking **Ahead**

While we might think that having perfect recall for all the events in our lives would be a blessing, Jill Price's experience suggests otherwise. Her extremely rare condition (called *hyperthymestic syndrome*) affects the part of her memory that stores experiences related to life events. She has perfect, vivid memories of virtually every day of her life, memories both good and bad. And while it's pleasant for her to relive her fond memories, she can't escape the pain of the bad ones (Parker, Cahill, & McGaugh, 2006; Price, 2008).

Price's condition illustrates the complexity and the mystery of the phenomenon we call memory. Memory allows us to retrieve a vast amount of information. We are able to remember the name of a friend we haven't talked with for years and recall the details of a picture that hung in our bedroom as a child. At the same time, though, memory failures are common. We forget where we left the keys to the car and fail to answer an exam question about material we studied only a few hours earlier. Why?

We turn now to the nature of memory, considering the ways in which information is stored and retrieved. We examine the problems of retrieving information from memory, the accuracy of memories, and the reasons information is sometimes forgotten. We also consider the biological foundations of memory and discuss some practical means of increasing memory capacity.

The Foundations of Memory

You are playing a game of Trivial Pursuit, and winning the game comes down to one question: On what body of water is Mumbai located? As you rack your brain for the answer, several fundamental processes relating to memory come into play. You may never, for instance, have been exposed to information regarding Mumbai's location. Or if you have been exposed to it, it may simply not have registered in a meaningful way. In other words, the information might not have been recorded properly in your memory. The initial process of recording information in a form usable to memory, a process called *encoding*, is the first stage in remembering something.

Even if you had been exposed to the information and originally knew the name of the body of water, you may still be unable to recall it during the game because of a failure to retain it. Memory specialists speak of *storage*, the maintenance of material saved in memory. If the material is not stored adequately, it cannot be recalled later.

Memory also depends on one last process—*retrieval*: Material in memory storage has to be located and brought into awareness to be useful. Your failure to recall Mumbai's location, then, may rest on your inability to retrieve information that you learned earlier.

In sum, psychologists consider **memory** to be the process by which we encode, store, and retrieve information (see Figure 1). Each of the three parts of this definition—encoding, storage, and retrieval—represents a different process. You can think of these processes as being analogous to a computer's keyboard (encoding), hard drive (storage), and software that accesses the information for display on the screen (retrieval). Only if all three processes have operated will you experience success and be able to recall the body of water on which Mumbai is located: the Arabian Sea.

Recognizing that memory involves encoding, storage, and retrieval gives us a start in understanding the concept. But how does memory actually function? How do we explain what information is initially encoded, what gets stored, and how it is retrieved?

According to the *three-system approach to memory* that dominated memory research for several decades, there are different memory storage systems or stages through which information must travel if it is to be remembered (Atkinson & Shiffrin, 1968, 1971). Historically, the approach has been extremely influential in the development of our understanding of memory, and—although new theories have augmented it— it still provides a useful framework for understanding how information is recalled.

Key Concepts

What is memory?

Are there different kinds of memory?

What are the biological bases of memory?

memory The process by which we encode, store, and retrieve information.

Encoding
(Initial recording of information)

Storage
(Information saved for future use)

Retrieval
(Recovery of stored information)

FIGURE 1 Memory is built on three basic processes—encoding, storage, and retrieval—that are analogous to a computer's keyboard, hard drive, and software to access the information for display on the screen. The analogy is not perfect, however, because human memory is less precise than a computer. How might you modify the analogy to make it more accurate?

FIGURE 2 In this three-stage model of memory, information initially recorded by the person's sensory system enters sensory memory, which momentarily holds the information. The information then moves to short-term memory, which stores it for 15 to 25 seconds. Finally, the information can move into long-term memory, which is relatively permanent. Whether the information moves from short-term to long-term memory depends on the kind and amount of rehearsal of the material that is carried out. (Source: Atkinson & Shifrin, 1968.)

sensory memory The initial, momentary storage of information, lasting only an instant.

short-term memory Memory that holds information for 15 to 25 seconds.

long-term memory Memory that stores information on a relatively permanent basis, although it may be difficult to retrieve.

The three-system memory theory proposes the existence of the three separate memory stores shown in Figure 2. **Sensory memory** refers to the initial, momentary storage of information that lasts only an instant. Here an exact replica of the stimulus recorded by a person's sensory system is stored very briefly. In a second stage, **short-term memory** holds information for 15 to 25 seconds and stores it according to its meaning rather than as mere sensory stimulation. The third type of storage system is **long-term memory.** Information is stored in long-term memory on a relatively permanent basis, although it may be difficult to retrieve.

Sensory Memory

A momentary flash of lightning, the sound of a twig snapping, and the sting of a pinprick all represent stimulation of exceedingly brief duration, but they may nonetheless provide important information that can require a response. Such stimuli are initially—and fleetingly—stored in sensory memory, the first repository of the information the world presents to us. Actually, there are several types of sensory memories, each related to a different source of sensory information. For instance, *iconic memory* reflects information from the visual system. *Echoic memory* stores auditory information coming from the ears. In addition, there are corresponding memories for each of the other senses.

Sensory memory can store information for only a very short time. If information does not pass into short-term memory, it is lost for good. For instance, iconic memory seems to last less than a second, and echoic memory typically fades within two or three seconds. However, despite the brief duration of sensory memory, its precision is high: Sensory memory can store an almost exact replica of each stimulus to which it is exposed (Darwin, Turvey, & Crowder, 1972; Long & Beaton, 1982; Sams et al., 1993; Deouell, Parnes, & Pickard, 2006).

Psychologist George Sperling (1960) demonstrated the existence of sensory memory in a series of clever and now-classic studies. He briefly exposed people to a series of 12 letters arranged in the following pattern:

$$
\begin{array}{cccc}
F & T & Y & C \\
K & D & N & L \\
Y & W & B & M \\
\end{array}
$$

Study Alert

Although the three types of memory are discussed as separate memory stores, these are not mini-warehouses located in specific areas of the brain. Instead, they represent three different types of memory systems with different characteristics.

When exposed to this pattern of letters for just one twentieth of a second, most people could recall only four or five of the letters accurately. Although they knew that they had seen more, the memory of those letters had faded by the time they reported the first few letters. It was possible, then, that the information had initially been accurately stored in sensory memory. But during the time it took to verbalize the first four or five letters, the memory of the other letters faded.

To test that possibility, Sperling conducted an experiment in which a high, medium, or low tone sounded just after a person had been exposed to the full pattern of letters. People were told to report the letters in the highest line if a high tone was sounded, the middle line if the medium tone occurred, or the lowest line at the sound of the low tone. Because the tone occurred after the exposure, people had to rely on their memories to report the correct row.

The results of the study clearly showed that people had been storing the complete pattern in memory. They accurately recalled the letters in the line that had been indicated by the tone regardless of whether it was the top, middle, or bottom line. Obviously, *all* the lines they had seen had been stored in sensory memory. Despite its rapid loss, then, the information in sensory memory was an accurate representation of what people had seen.

By gradually lengthening the time between the presentation of the visual pattern and the tone, Sperling was able to determine with some accuracy the length of time that information was stored in sensory memory. The ability to recall a particular row of the pattern when a tone was sounded declined progressively as the period between the visual exposure and the tone increased. This decline continued until the period reached about one second in duration, at which point the row could not be recalled accurately at all. Sperling concluded that the entire visual image was stored in sensory memory for less than a second.

In sum, sensory memory operates as a kind of snapshot that stores information—which may be of a visual, auditory, or other sensory nature—for a brief moment in time. But it is as if each snapshot, immediately after being taken, is destroyed and replaced with a new one. Unless the information in the snapshot is transferred to some other type of memory, it is lost.

A momentary flash of lightning leaves a sensory visual memory, a fleeting but exact replica of the stimulus that fades away.

Short-Term Memory

Because the information that is stored briefly in sensory memory consists of representations of raw sensory stimuli, it is not meaningful to us. If we are to make sense of it and possibly retain it, the information must be transferred to the next stage of memory: short-term memory. Short-term memory is the memory store in which information first has meaning, although the maximum length of retention there is relatively short (Hamilton & Martin, 2007).

The specific process by which sensory memories are transformed into short-term memories is not clear. Some theorists suggest that the information is first translated into graphical representations or images, and others hypothesize that the transfer occurs when the sensory stimuli are changed to words (Baddeley & Wilson, 1985). What is clear, however, is that unlike sensory memory, which holds a relatively full and detailed—if short-lived—representation of the world, short-term memory has incomplete representational capabilities.

In fact, the specific amount of information that can be held in short-term memory has been identified as seven items, or "chunks," of information, with variations up to plus or minus two chunks. A **chunk** is a meaningful grouping of stimuli that can be stored as a unit in short-term memory. According to George Miller (1956), a chunk can be individual letters or numbers, permitting us to hold a seven-digit phone number (such as 226-4610) in short-term memory.

But a chunk also may consist of larger categories, such as words or other meaningful units. For example, consider the following list of 21 letters:

P B S F O X C N N A B C C B S M T V N B C

chunk A meaningful grouping of stimuli that can be stored as a unit in short-term memory.

FIGURE 3 Examine the chessboard on the left for about five seconds. Then cover up the board and draw the position of the pieces on the blank chessboard. (You could also use a chessboard of your own and place the pieces in the same positions.) Unless you are an experienced chess player, you are likely to have great difficulty carrying out such a task. Yet chess masters—those who win tournaments—do this quite well (deGroot, 1966). They are able to reproduce correctly 90% of the pieces on the board. In comparison, inexperienced chess players are typically able to reproduce only 40% of the board properly. The chess masters do not have superior memories in other respects; they generally test normally on other measures of memory. What they can do better than others is see the board in terms of chunks or meaningful units and reproduce the position of the chess pieces by using those units.

Because the list exceeds seven chunks, it is difficult to recall the letters after one exposure. But suppose they were presented as follows:

PBS FOX CNN ABC CBS MTV NBC

In this case, even though there are still 21 letters, you'd be able to store them in short-term memory since they represent only seven chunks.

Chunks can vary in size from single letters or numbers to categories that are far more complicated. The specific nature of what constitutes a chunk varies according to one's past experience. You can see this for yourself by trying an experiment that was first carried out as a comparison between expert and inexperienced chess players and is illustrated in Figure 3 (deGroot, 1978; Oberauer, 2007; Gilchrist, Cowan, & Naveh-Benjamin, 2009).

Although it is possible to remember seven or so relatively complicated sets of information entering short-term memory, the information cannot be held there very long. Just how brief is short-term memory? If you've ever looked up a telephone number in a phone directory, repeated the number to yourself, put away the directory, and then forgotten the number after you've tapped the first three numbers into your phone, you know that information does not remain in short-term memory very long. Most psychologists believe that information in short-term memory is lost after 15 to 25 seconds—unless it is transferred to long-term memory.

REHEARSAL

The transfer of material from short- to long-term memory proceeds largely on the basis of **rehearsal,** the repetition of information that has entered short-term memory. Rehearsal accomplishes two things. First, as long as the information is repeated, it is maintained in short-term memory. More important, however, rehearsal allows us to transfer the information into long-term memory (Kvavilashvili & Fisher, 2007).

Whether the transfer is made from short- to long-term memory seems to depend largely on the kind of rehearsal that is carried out. If the information is simply repeated over and over again—as we might do with a telephone number while we rush from the phone book to the phone—it is kept current in short-term memory, but it will not necessarily be placed in long-term memory. Instead, as soon as we stop punching in the phone numbers, the number is likely to be replaced by other information and will be completely forgotten.

In contrast, if the information in short-term memory is rehearsed using a process called elaborative rehearsal, it is much more likely to be transferred into long-term memory. *Elaborative rehearsal* occurs when the information is considered and organized in some fashion. The organization might include expanding the information to make it fit into a logical framework, linking it to another memory, turning it into an image, or transforming it in some other way. For example, a list of vegetables to be purchased at a store could be woven together in memory as items being used to prepare an elaborate salad, could be linked to the items bought on an earlier shopping trip, or could be thought of in terms of the image of a farm with rows of each item.

By using organizational strategies such as these—called *mnemonics*—we can vastly improve our retention of information. Mnemonics (pronounced "neh MON ix") are formal techniques for organizing information in a way that makes it more likely to be remembered. For instance, when a beginning musician learns that the spaces on the music staff spell the word *FACE,* or when we learn the rhyme "Thirty days hath September, April, June, and November . . . ," we are using mnemonics (Bellezza, 2000; Carney & Levin, 2003; Sprenger, 2007).

rehearsal The repetition of information that has entered short-term memory.

Working Memory

Rather than seeing short-term memory as an independent way station into which memories arrive, either to fade or to be passed on to long-term memory, many contemporary memory theorists conceive of short-term memory as far more active. In this view, short-term memory is like an information-processing system that manages both new material gathered from sensory memory and older material that has been pulled from long-term storage. In this increasingly influential view, short-term memory is referred to as **working memory** and defined as a set of temporary memory stores that actively manipulate and rehearse information (Bayliss et al., 2005a, 2005b; Unsworth & Engle, 2005).

Working memory is thought to contain a *central executive* processor that is involved in reasoning and decision making. The central executive coordinates three distinct storage-and-rehearsal systems: the *visual store,* the *verbal store,* and the *episodic buffer.* The visual store specializes in visual and spatial information, whereas the verbal store holds and manipulates material relating to speech, words, and numbers. The episodic buffer contains information that represents episodes or

working memory A set of active, temporary memory stores that actively manipulate and rehearse information.

FIGURE 4 Working memory is an active "workspace" in which information is retrieved and manipulated and in which information is held through rehearsal (Gathercole & Baddeley, 1993). It consists of a "central executive" that coordinates the visual store (which concentrates on visual and spatial information), the verbal store (which concentrates on speech, words, and numbers), and the episodic buffer (which represents episodes or occurrences that are encountered). (Source: Adapted from Baddeley, Chincotta, & Adlam, 2001.)

events (Baddeley, 2001; Bröder & Schiffer, 2006; Rudner & Rönnberg, 2008; see Figure 4).

Working memory permits us to keep information in an active state briefly so that we can do something with the information. For instance, we use working memory when we're doing a multistep arithmetic problem in our heads, storing the result of one calculation while getting ready to move to the next stage. (I make use of my working memory when I figure a 20% tip in a restaurant by first calculating 10% of the total bill and then doubling it.)

Although working memory aids in the recall of information, it uses a significant amount of cognitive resources during its operation. In turn, this can make us less aware of our surroundings—something that has implications for the debate about the use of cell telephones in automobiles. If a phone conversation requires thinking, it will burden working memory and leave drivers less aware of their surroundings, an obviously dangerous state of affairs (Sifrit, 2006; Strayer & Drews, 2007).

Furthermore, stress can reduce the effectiveness of working memory by reducing its capacity. In fact, one study found that students with the highest working memory capacity and greatest math ability were the ones who were most vulnerable to pressure to perform well. Those who should have performed best, then, were the ones most apt to choke on the test because their working memory capacities were reduced by the stress (Beilock & Carr, 2005; Carey, 2004).

Long-Term Memory

Material that makes its way from short-term memory to long-term memory enters a storehouse of almost unlimited capacity. Like a new file we save on a hard drive, the information in long-term memory is filed and coded so that we can retrieve it when we need it.

Evidence of the existence of long-term memory, as distinct from short-term memory, comes from a number of sources. For example, people with certain kinds of brain damage have no lasting recall of new information received after the damage occurred, although people and events stored in memory before the injury remain intact (Milner, 1966). Because information that was encoded and stored before the injury can be recalled and because short-term memory after the injury appears to be operational—new material can be recalled for a very brief period—we can infer that there are two distinct types of memory: one for short-term and one for long-term storage.

Results from laboratory experiments are also consistent with the notion of separate short-term and long-term memory. For example, in one set of studies, people were asked to recall a relatively small amount of information (such as a set of three letters). Then, to prevent practice of the initial information, participants were required to recite some extraneous material aloud, such as counting backward by threes (Brown, 1958; Peterson & Peterson, 1959). By varying the amount of time between the presentation of the initial material and the need for its recall, investigators found that recall was quite good when the interval was very short but declined rapidly thereafter. After 15 seconds had gone by, recall hovered at around 10% of the material initially presented.

Apparently, the distraction of counting backward prevented almost all the initial material from reaching long-term memory. Initial recall was good because it was coming from short-term memory, but those memories were lost at a rapid rate. Eventually, all that could be recalled was the small amount of material that had made its way into long-term storage despite the distraction of counting backward.

The distinction between short- and long-term memory is also supported by the *serial position effect*, in which the ability to recall information in a list depends on where in the list an item appears. For instance, often a *primacy effect* occurs, in which items presented early in a list are remembered better. There is also a *recency effect*, in which items presented late in a list are remembered best (Bonanni et al., 2007; Tan & Ward, 2008; Tydgat & Grainger, 2009).

LONG-TERM MEMORY MODULES

Just as short-term memory is often conceptualized in terms of working memory, many contemporary researchers now regard long-term memory as having several different components, or *memory modules*. Each of these modules represents a separate memory system in the brain.

One major distinction within long-term memory is that between declarative memory and procedural memory. **Declarative memory** is memory for factual information: names, faces, dates, and facts, such as "a bike has two wheels." In contrast, **procedural memory** (or *nondeclarative memory*) refers to memory for skills and habits, such as how to ride a bike or hit a baseball. Information about *things* is stored in declarative memory; information about *how to do things* is stored in procedural memory (Feldhusen, 2006; Brown & Robertson, 2007; Bauer, 2008).

Declarative memory can be subdivided into semantic memory and episodic memory. **Semantic memory** is memory for general knowledge and facts about the world, as well as memory for the rules of logic that are used to deduce other facts. Because of semantic memory, we remember that the ZIP code for Beverly Hills is 90210, that Mumbai is on the Arabian Sea, and that *memoree* is the incorrect spelling of *memory*. Thus, semantic memory is somewhat like a mental almanac of facts (Nyberg & Tulving, 1996; Tulving, 2002).

In contrast, **episodic memory** is memory for events that occur in a particular time, place, or context. For example, recall of learning to ride a bike, our first kiss, or arranging a surprise 21st birthday party for our brother is based on episodic memories. Episodic memories relate to particular contexts. For example, remembering *when* and *how* we learned that 2 × 2 = 4 would be an episodic memory; the fact itself (that 2 × 2 = 4) is a semantic memory. (Also see Figure 5.)

Episodic memories can be surprisingly detailed. Consider, for instance, how you'd respond if you were asked to identify what you were doing on a specific day two years ago. Impossible? You may think otherwise as you read the following exchange between

declarative memory Memory for factual information: names, faces, dates, and the like.

procedural memory Memory for skills and habits, such as riding a bike or hitting a baseball; sometimes referred to as *nondeclarative memory*.

semantic memory Memory for general knowledge and facts about the world, as well as memory for the rules of logic that are used to deduce other facts.

episodic memory Memory for events that occur in a particular time, place, or context.

FIGURE 5 Long-term memory can be subdivided into several different types. What type of long-term memory is involved in your recollection of the moment you first arrived on your campus at the start of college? What type of long-term memory is involved in remembering the lyrics to a song, compared with the tune of a song?

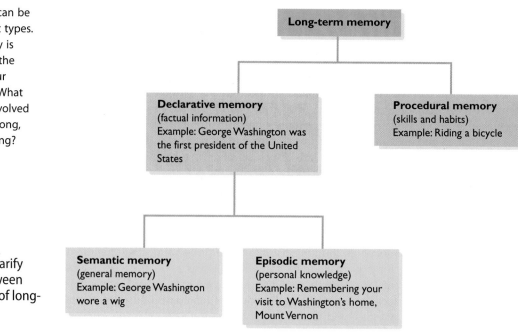

Study Alert

Use Figure 5 to help clarify the distinctions between the different types of long-term memory.

a researcher and a participant in a study who was asked, in a memory experiment, what he was doing "on Monday afternoon in the third week of September two years ago."

PARTICIPANT: Come on. How should I know?

EXPERIMENTER: Just try it anyhow.

PARTICIPANT: OK. Let's see: Two years ago . . . I would be in high school in Pittsburgh . . . . That would be my senior year. Third week in September—that's just after summer—that would be the fall term . . . . Let me see. I think I had chemistry lab on Mondays. I don't know. I was probably in chemistry lab. Wait a minute—that would be the second week of school. I remember he started off with the atomic table—a big fancy chart. I thought he was crazy trying to make us memorize that thing. You know, I think I can remember sitting . . . . (Lindsay & Norman, 1977).

Episodic memory, then, can provide information about events that happened long in the past (Reynolds & Takooshian, 1988). But semantic memory is no less impressive, permitting us to dredge up tens of thousands of facts ranging from the date of our birthday to the knowledge that $1 is less than $5.

SEMANTIC NETWORKS

Try to recall, for a moment, as many things as you can think of that are the color red. Now pull from your memory the names of as many fruits as you can recall.

Did the same item appear when you did both tasks? For many people, an apple comes to mind in both cases since it fits equally well in each category. And the fact that you might have thought of an apple when doing the first task makes it even more likely that you'll think of it when doing the second task.

It's actually quite amazing that we're able to retrieve specific material from the vast store of information in our long-term memories. According to some memory researchers, one key organizational tool that allows us to recall detailed information from long-term memory is the associations that we build between different pieces of information. In this view, knowledge is stored in **semantic networks,** mental representations of clusters of interconnected information (Collins & Quillian, 1969; Collins & Loftus, 1975; Cummings, Ceponiene, & Koyama, 2006).

semantic networks Mental representations of clusters of interconnected information.

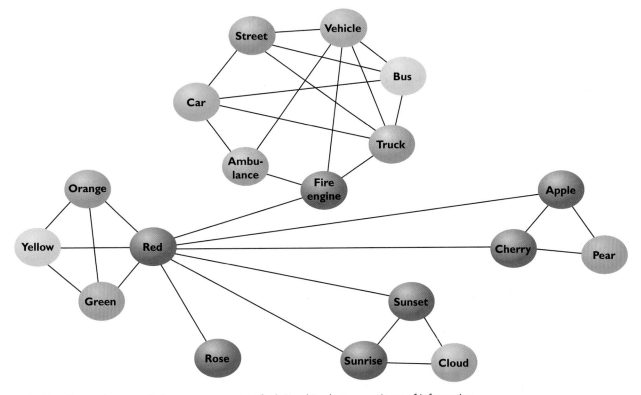

FIGURE 6 Semantic networks in memory consist of relationships between pieces of information, such as those relating to the concept of a fire engine. The lines suggest the connections that indicate how the information is organized within memory. The closer together two concepts are, the greater the strength of the association. (Source: Collins & Loftus, 1975.)

Consider, for example, Figure 6, which shows some of the relationships in memory relating to fire engines, the color red, and a variety of other semantic concepts. Thinking about a particular concept leads to recall of related concepts. For example, seeing a fire engine may activate our recollections of other kinds of emergency vehicles, such as an ambulance, which in turn may activate recall of the related concept of a vehicle. And thinking of a vehicle may lead us to think about a bus that we've seen in the past. Activating one memory triggers the activation of related memories in a process known as *spreading activation* (Foster et al., 2008; Kreher et al, 2008).

THE NEUROSCIENCE OF MEMORY

Can we pinpoint a location in the brain where long-term memories reside? Is there a single site that corresponds to a particular memory, or is memory distributed in different regions across the brain? Do memories leave an actual physical trace that scientists can view?

The search for the *engram,* the term for the physical memory trace that corresponds to a memory, has proved to be a major puzzle to psychologists and other neuroscientists interested in memory. Using advanced brain scanning procedures in their efforts to determine the neuroscientific basis of memory formation, investigators have learned that certain areas and structures of the brain specialize in different types of memory-related activities. The *hippocampus,* a part of the brain's limbic system (see Figure 7), plays a central role in the consolidation of memories. Located within the brain's *medial temporal lobes* just behind the eyes, the hippocampus aids in the initial encoding of information, acting as a kind of neurological e-mail system. That information is

FIGURE 7 The hippocampus and amygdala, parts of the brain's limbic system, play a central role in the consolidation of memories. (Source: Van De Graff, 2000.)

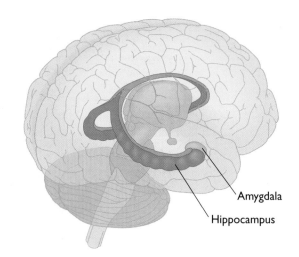

subsequently passed along to the cerebral cortex of the brain, where it is actually stored (Govindarajan, Kelleher, & Tonegawa, 2006; J. Peters et al., 2007; Lavenex & Lavenex, 2009).

The significance of the hippocampus is exemplified by studies of individuals who have particularly good, yet specialized, types of memories. For instance, taxi drivers in London, England, must have accurate, complete recall of the location of the maze of streets and alleys within a six-mile radius of the center of the city. It takes years of study to memorize the material. MRI brain scans of taxi drivers show that, relative to non–taxi drivers with fewer navigational skills, the back of the hippocampus is larger while the front is smaller. The findings are consistent with the idea that particular areas of the hippocampus are involved in the consolidation of

"The matters about which I'm being questioned, Your Honor, are all things I should have included in my long-term memory but which I mistakenly inserted in my short-term memory."

Neuroscience in Your Life: Experience, Memory, and the Brain

FIGURE 8 Illustrating how experience can shape how our brain processes memories, these fMRI scans show how the number of years spent driving a taxi relates to the size of particular areas of the hippocampus as participants become spatial and navigational memory experts. In (a) we see areas of the posterior (back) hippocampus that increase in activity (in yellow) with the number of years spent driving a taxi. We also see the relationship illustrated graphically in the graph to the right of the figure. In contrast, in (b) we see areas of the anterior (front) hippocampus that show reduced activity (also in yellow) after many years of driving a taxi and the relationship portrayed graphically. The changes in the areas activated during memory tasks show how practice can shape the brain and how this allows us to develop specialized skills such as memory for spatial locations. (Source: Maguire et al., 2006.)

(a) Posterior hippocampus (HC)

Posterior HC grey matter volume

(b) Anterior hippocampus (HC)

Anterior HC grey matter volume

spatial memories (see Figure 8; Maguire, Woollett, & Spiers, 2006; Spiers & Maguire, 2007; Woollett & Maguire, 2009).

The *amygdala*, another part of the limbic system, also plays an important role in memory. The amygdala is especially involved with memories involving emotion. For example, if you are frightened by a large Doberman, you're likely to remember the event vividly—an outcome related to the functioning of the amygdala. Encountering the Doberman or any large dog in the future is likely to reactivate the amygdala and bring back the unpleasant memory (Hamann, 2001; Buchanan & Adolphs, 2004; Talmi et al., 2008).

Memory at the Level of Neurons. Although it is clear that the hippocampus and amygdala play a central role in memory formation, how is the transformation of information into a memory reflected at the level of neurons?

One answer is *long-term potentiation,* which shows that certain neural pathways become easily excited while a new response is being learned. At the same time, the

In Pursuit of a Memory Eraser

Most of us would welcome a way to improve our memories. Wouldn't it be helpful to retain more information in textbooks, or to remember the names of people we meet at a party, or just to recall where we left our car keys?

But would it also be important to devise a method to be able to *forget* information in memory?

Some researchers believe so, and they are trying to identify ways to allow people to forget traumatic events, persistent fears, or even annoying habits. Researchers recently took an important step in the direction of being able to erase unwanted memories by discovering an intriguing substance that seems to be a key player in the formation of memories. The substance, called *PKM-zeta*, seems to be present whenever a connection between neurons is strengthened. So researchers put PKM-zeta to a test in lab rats. The rats were trained to associate a certain tone with receiving a mild electric shock, such that they became fearful of the tone—a learning experience that was stored in their memories. However, when the rats' brains were injected later with a drug that stops production of PKM-zeta, a strange thing happened: The tone no longer produced a fear response. The rats forgot what they had originally learned (Pastalkova et al., 2006; Yao et al., 2008).

The study supports the hypothesis that memory, far from being a rigid and durable phenomenon, is actually fluid and malleable.

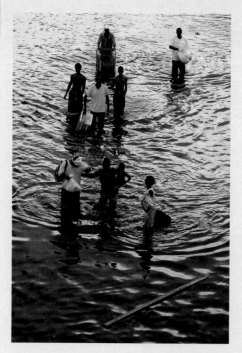

New treatments erase intrusive traumatic memories.

The inhibition of PKM-zeta did not induce the rats to forget what they learned as much as it stopped the memory from being re-encoded in the brain after it was activated.

A treatment that can stop the encoding of memories has the potential to help people who are suffering from intrusive traumatic memories. For example, the blood-pressure drug propranolol affects areas of the brain that are responsible for memory storage. In one study, researchers gave a small group of hospital patients who had just suffered an accident or a rape a course of treatment with either propranolol or a placebo. Three months later, when the patients were exposed to reminders of their traumatic experiences, those who had received the propranolol had a less stressful reaction than those who had received the placebo (Jha, 2006; Brunet et al., 2007; Brunet et al., 2008).

Ultimately, the goal of researchers is to use substances such as PKM-zeta and propranolol to interfere with the reconsolidation of traumatic memories that have been reawakened. The idea is not to block the memory entirely but to reduce its intensity upon reconsolidation so that the victim will remember what happened but not be tortured by the memory. If that happens, victims may be treated more successfully (Pitman & Delahanty, 2005; Carey, 2009a).

RETHINK

- Why might researchers want only to reduce the intensity of a traumatic memory rather than erase it altogether?
- What might be some of the practical or ethical issues involved with erasing unwanted memories?

number of synapses between neurons increase as the dendrites branch out to receive messages. These changes reflect a process called *consolidation*, in which memories become fixed and stable in long-term memory. Long-term memories take some time to stabilize; this explains why events and other stimuli are not suddenly fixed in memory. Instead, consolidation may continue for days and even years (McGaugh, 2003; Meeter & Murre, 2004; Kawashima, Izaki, & Grace, 2006).

Because a stimulus may contain different sensory aspects, visual, auditory, and other areas of the brain may be simultaneously processing information about that stimulus. Information storage appears to be linked to the sites where this processing occurs, and it is therefore located in the particular areas that initially processed the information in terms of its visual, auditory, and other sensory stimuli. For this reason, memory traces are distributed throughout the brain. For example, when you recall a beautiful beach sunset, your recollection draws on memory stores located in visual areas of the brain (the view of the sunset), auditory areas (the sounds of the ocean), and tactile areas (the feel of the wind) (Desimone, 1992; Brewer et al., 1998; Squire, Clark, & Bayley, 2004).

In short, the physical stuff of memory—the engram—is produced by a complex of biochemical and neural processes. Scientists are just beginning to understand how the brain compiles the individual neural components into a single, coherent memory. It may be that the same neurons that fire when we are initially exposed to material are reactivated during efforts to recall that information. Still, although memory researchers have made considerable strides in understanding the neuroscience behind memory, more remains to be learned—and remembered (Gelbard-Sagiv et al., 2008). (For more on the biological basis of memory, see *Applying Psychology in the 21st Century*.)

RECAP/EVALUATE/RETHINK

RECAP

What is memory?
- Memory is the process by which we encode, store, and retrieve information. (p. 199)

Are there different kinds of memory?
- Sensory memory, corresponding to each of the sensory systems, is the first place where information is saved. Sensory memories are very brief, but they are precise, storing a nearly exact replica of a stimulus. (p. 200)
- Roughly seven (plus or minus two) chunks of information can be transferred and held in short-term memory. Information in short-term memory is held from 15 to 25 seconds and, if not transferred to long-term memory, is lost. (p. 201)
- Memories are transferred into long-term storage through rehearsal. If memories are transferred into long-term memory, they become relatively permanent. (p. 203)
- Some theorists view short-term memory as a working memory in which information is retrieved and manipulated and held through rehearsal. In this view, it is a central executive processor involved in reasoning and decision making; it coordinates a visual store, a verbal store, and an episodic buffer. (p. 203)
- Long-term memory can be viewed in terms of memory modules, each of which is related to separate memory systems in the brain. For instance, we can distinguish between declarative memory and procedural memory. Declarative memory is further divided into episodic memory and semantic memory. (p. 204)
- Semantic networks suggest that knowledge is stored in long-term memory as mental representations of clusters of interconnected information. (p. 206)

What are the biological bases of memory?
- The hippocampus and amygdala are especially important in the establishment of memory. (p. 207)

- Memories are distributed across the brain, relating to the different sensory information-processing systems involved during the initial exposure to a stimulus. (p. 218)

EVALUATE

1. Match the type of memory with its definition:
   1. long-term memory
   2. short-term memory
   3. sensory memory

   a. holds information 15 to 25 seconds
   b. stores information on a relatively permanent basis
   c. direct representation of a stimulus

2. A(n)_____ is a meaningful group of stimuli that can be stored together in short-term memory.
3. There appear to be two types of declarative memory: _____ memory for knowledge and facts and _____ memory for personal experiences.
4. Some memory researchers believe that long-term memory is stored as associations between pieces of information in _____ networks.

RETHINK

1. It is a truism that "you never forget how to ride a bicycle." Why might this be so? In what type of memory is information about bicycle riding stored?
2. *From a marketing specialist's perspective:* How might advertisers and others use ways of enhancing memory to promote their products? What ethical principles are involved? Can you think of a way to protect yourself from unethical advertising?

Answers to Evaluate Questions

1. 1-b, 2-a, 3-c; 2. chunk; 3. semantic, episodic; 4. semantic

KEY TERMS

memory p. 199	long-term memory p. 200	working memory p. 203	semantic memory p. 205
sensory memory p. 200	chunk p. 201	declarative memory p. 205	episodic memory p. 205
short-term memory p. 200	rehearsal p. 203	procedural memory p. 205	semantic networks p. 206

Recalling Long-Term Memories

What causes difficulties and failures in remembering?

An hour after his job interview, Ricardo was sitting in a coffee shop, telling his friend Laura how well it had gone, when the woman who had interviewed him walked in. "Well, hello, Ricardo. How are you doing?" Trying to make a good impression, Ricardo began to make introductions, but suddenly realized he could not remember the interviewer's name. Stammering, he desperately searched his memory but to no avail. "I *know* her name," he thought to himself, "but here I am, looking like a fool. I can kiss this job good-bye."

tip-of-the-tongue phenomenon The inability to recall information that one realizes one knows—a result of the difficulty of retrieving information from long-term memory.

Have you ever tried to remember someone's name, convinced that you knew it but unable to recall it no matter how hard you tried? This common occurrence—known as the **tip-of-the-tongue phenomenon**—exemplifies how difficult it can be to retrieve information stored in long-term memory (Schwartz, 2001, 2002, 2008; Cleary, 2006; Brennen, Vikan, & Dybdahl, 2007).

Retrieval Clues

recall Memory task in which specific information must be retrieved.

recognition Memory task in which individuals are presented with a stimulus and asked whether they have been exposed to it in the past or to identify it from a list of alternatives.

Perhaps recall of names and other memories is not perfect because there is so much information stored in long-term memory. Because the material that makes its way to long-term memory is relatively permanent, the capacity of long-term memory is vast. For instance, if you are like the average college student, your vocabulary includes some 50,000 words, you know hundreds of mathematical "facts," and you are able to conjure up images—such as the way your childhood home looked—with no trouble at all. In fact, simply cataloging all your memories would probably take years of work.

How do we sort through this vast array of material and retrieve specific information at the appropriate time? One way is through retrieval cues. A *retrieval cue* is a stimulus that allows us to recall more easily information that is in long-term memory. It may be a word, an emotion, or a sound; whatever the specific cue, a memory will suddenly come to mind when the retrieval cue is present. For example, the smell of roasting turkey may evoke memories of Thanksgiving or family gatherings.

Retrieval cues guide people through the information stored in long-term memory in much the same way that a search engine such as Google guides people through the Internet. They are particularly important when we are making an effort to *recall* information, as opposed to being asked to *recognize* material stored in memory. In **recall,** a specific piece of information must be retrieved—such as that needed to answer a fill-in-the-blank question or to write an essay on a test. In contrast, **recognition** occurs when people are presented with a stimulus and asked whether they have been exposed to it previously or are asked to identify it from a list of alternatives.

FIGURE 1 Try to recall the names of these characters. Because this is a recall task, it is relatively difficult.

As you might guess, recognition is generally a much easier task than recall (see Figures 1 and 2). Recall is more difficult

Answer this recognition question:
Which of the following are the names of the seven dwarfs in the Disney movie
Snow White and the Seven Dwarfs?

Goofy	Bashful
Sleepy	Meanie
Smarty	Doc
Scaredy	Happy
Dopey	Angry
Grumpy	Sneezy
Wheezy	Crazy

(The correct answers are Bashful, Doc, Dopey, Grumpy, Happy, Sleepy, and Sneezy.)

FIGURE 2 Naming the characters in Figure 1 (a recall task) is more difficult than solving the recognition problem posed in this list.

because it consists of a series of processes: a search through memory, retrieval of potentially relevant information, and then a decision regarding whether the information you have found is accurate. If the information appears to be correct, the search is over, but if it is not, the search must continue. In contrast, recognition is simpler because it involves fewer steps (Miserando, 1991; Leigh, Zinkhan, & Swaminathan, 2006).

Levels of Processing

One determinant of how well memories are recalled is the way in which material is first perceived, processed, and understood. The **levels-of-processing theory** emphasizes the degree to which new material is mentally analyzed. It suggests that the amount of information processing that occurs when material is initially encountered is central in determining how much of the information is ultimately remembered. According to this approach, the depth of information processing during exposure to material—meaning the degree to which it is analyzed and considered—is critical; the greater the intensity of its initial processing, the more likely we are to remember it (Craik, 1990; Troyer, Häfliger, & Cadieux, 2006; Craik & Lockhart, 2008).

Because we do not pay close attention to much of the information to which we are exposed, very little mental processing typically takes place, and we forget new material almost immediately. However, information to which we pay greater attention is processed more thoroughly. Therefore, it enters memory at a deeper level—and is less apt to be forgotten than is information processed at shallower levels.

The theory goes on to suggest that there are considerable differences in the ways in which information is processed at various levels of memory. At shallow levels, information is processed merely in terms of its physical and sensory aspects. For example, we may pay attention only to the shapes that make up the letters in the word *dog*. At an intermediate level of processing, the shapes are translated into meaningful units—in this case, letters of the alphabet. Those letters are considered in the context of words, and specific phonetic sounds may be attached to the letters.

At the deepest level of processing, information is analyzed in terms of its meaning. We may see it in a wider context and draw associations between the meaning of the information and broader networks of knowledge. For instance, we may think of dogs not merely as animals with four legs and a tail, but also in terms of their relationship to cats and other mammals. We may form an image of our own dog, thereby relating the concept to our own lives. According to the levels-of-processing approach, the deeper the initial level of processing of specific information, the longer the information will be retained.

There are considerable practical implications to the notion that recall depends on the degree to which information is initially processed. For example, the depth of information processing is critical when learning and studying course material. Rote

Study Alert

Remember the distinction between recall (in which specific information must be retrieved) and recognition (in which information is presented and must be identified or distinguished from other material).

levels-of-processing theory The theory of memory that emphasizes the degree to which new material is mentally analyzed.

memorization of a list of key terms for a test is unlikely to produce long-term recollection of information because processing occurs at a shallow level. In contrast, thinking about the meaning of the terms and reflecting on how they relate to information that one currently knows results in far more effective long-term retention (Conway, 2002; Wenzel, Zetocha, & Ferraro, 2007).

Explicit and Implicit Memory

If you've ever had surgery, you probably hoped that the surgeons were focused completely on the surgery and gave you their undivided attention while slicing into your body. The reality in most operating rooms is quite different, though. Surgeons may be chatting with nurses about a new restaurant as soon as they sew you up.

If you are like most patients, you are left with no recollection of the conversation that occurred while you were under anesthesia. However, it is very possible that although you had no conscious memories of the discussions on the merits of the restaurant, on some level you probably did recall at least some information. In fact, careful studies have found that people who are anesthetized during surgery can sometimes recall snippets of conversations they heard during surgery—even though they have no conscious recollection of the information (Kihlstrom et al., 1990; Sebel, Bonke, & Winogard, 1993).

The discovery that people have memories about which they are unaware has been an important one. It has led to speculation that two forms of memory, explicit and implicit, may exist side by side. **Explicit memory** refers to intentional or conscious recollection of information. When we try to remember a name or date we have encountered or learned about previously, we are searching our explicit memory.

In contrast, **implicit memory** refers to memories of which people are not consciously aware but that can affect subsequent performance and behavior. Skills that operate automatically and without thinking, such as jumping out of the path of an automobile coming toward us as we walk down the side of a road, are stored in implicit memory. Similarly, a feeling of vague dislike for an acquaintance, without knowing why we have that feeling, may be a reflection of implicit memories. Perhaps the person reminds us of someone else in our past that we didn't like, even though we are not aware of the memory of that other individual (Tulving, 2000; Uttl, Graf, & Consentino, 2003; Coates, Butler, & Berry, 2006; Voss & Paller, 2008).

Implicit memory is closely related to the prejudice and discrimination people exhibit toward members of minority groups. As we first discussed in the module on conducting psychological research, even though people may say and even believe they harbor no prejudice, assessment of their implicit memories may reveal that they have negative associations about members of minority groups. Such associations can influence people's behavior without their being aware of their underlying beliefs (Greenwald, Nosek, & Banaji, 2003; Greenwald, Nosek, & Sriram, 2006; Hofmann et al., 2008).

One way that memory specialists study implicit memory is through experiments that use priming. **Priming** is a phenomenon in which exposure to a word or concept (called a *prime*) later makes it easier to recall related information. Priming effects occur even when people have no conscious memory of the original word or concept (Schacter & Badgaiyan, 2001; Toth & Daniels, 2002; Schacter, Dobbins, & Schnyer, 2004).

The typical experiment designed to illustrate priming helps clarify the phenomenon. In priming experiments, participants are rapidly exposed to a stimulus such as a word, an object, or perhaps a drawing of a face. The second phase of the experiment is done after an interval ranging from several seconds to several months. At that point, participants are exposed to incomplete perceptual information that is related to the first stimulus, and they are asked whether they recognize it. For example, the new material may consist of the first letter of a word that had been presented earlier or a part of a face that had been shown earlier. If participants are able to identify the stimulus more readily than they identify stimuli that have not been

explicit memory Intentional or conscious recollection of information.

implicit memory Memories of which people are not consciously aware but that can affect subsequent performance and behavior.

priming A phenomenon in which exposure to a word or concept (called a prime) later makes it easier to recall related information, even when there is no conscious memory of the word or concept.

presented earlier, priming has taken place. Clearly, the earlier stimulus has been remembered—although the material resides in implicit memory, not explicit memory.

The same thing happens to us in our everyday lives. Suppose several months ago you watched a documentary on the planets, and the narrator described the moons of Mars, focusing on its moon named Phobos. You promptly forget the name of the moon, at least consciously. Then, several months later, you're completing a crossword puzzle that you have partially filled in, and it includes the letters *obos*. As soon as you look at the set of letters, you think of Phobos, and suddenly you recall for the first time since your initial exposure to the information that it is one of the moons of Mars. The sudden recollection occurred because your memory was primed by the letters *obos*.

In short, when information that we are unable to consciously recall affects our behavior, implicit memory is at work. Our behavior may be influenced by experiences of which we are unaware—an example of what has been called "retention without remembering" (Horton et al., 2005).

Flashbulb Memories

Where were you on February 1, 2003? You will most likely draw a blank until this piece of information is added: February 1, 2003, was the date the Space Shuttle *Columbia* broke up in space and fell to Earth.

You probably have little trouble recalling your exact location and a variety of other trivial details that occurred when you heard about the shuttle disaster, even though the incident happened a few years ago. Your ability to remember details about this fatal event illustrates a phenomenon known as flashbulb memory. **Flashbulb memories** are memories related to a specific, important, or surprising event that are so vivid they represent a virtual snapshot of the event.

Several types of flashbulb memories are common among college students. For example, involvement in a car accident, meeting one's roommate for the first time, and the night of high school graduation are all typical flashbulb memories (Romeu, 2006; Bohn & Berntsen, 2007; Talarico, 2009; see Figure 3).

Of course, flashbulb memories do not contain every detail of an original scene. I remember vividly that more than four decades ago I was sitting in Mr. Sharp's 10th-grade geometry class when I heard that President John Kennedy had been shot. However, although I recall where I was sitting and how my classmates reacted to the news, I do not recollect what I was wearing or what I had for lunch that day.

Furthermore, the details recalled in flashbulb memories are often inaccurate. For example, think back to the tragic day when the World Trade Center in New York was attacked by suicidal terrorists. Do you remember watching television that morning and seeing images of the first plane, and then the second plane, striking the towers?

If you do, you are among the 73% of Americans who recall viewing the initial television images of both planes on September 11, 2001. However, that recollection is wrong: In fact, television broadcasts showed images only of the second plane on September 11. No video of the first plane was available until early the following morning, September 12, when it was shown on television (Begley, 2002).

Flashbulb memories illustrate a more general phenomenon about memory: Memories that are exceptional are more easily retrieved (although not necessarily accurately) than are those relating to events that are commonplace. The more distinctive a stimulus is, and the more personal relevance the event has, the more likely we are to recall it later (Berntsen & Thomsen, 2005; Shapiro, 2006; Talarico & Rubin, 2007).

Even with a distinctive stimulus, however, we may not remember where the information came from. *Source amnesia* occurs when an individual has a memory for some material but cannot recall where he or she encountered it. For example, source amnesia can explain situations in which you meet someone you know but can't remember where you'd met that person initially.

flashbulb memories Memories centered on a specific, important, or surprising event that are so vivid it is as if they represented a snapshot of the event.

Percentage of sample reporting that event resulted
in "flashbulb memories"

FIGURE 3 These are the most common flashbulb memory events, based on a survey of college students. What are some of your flashbulb memories? (Source: From David C. Rubin, "The Subtle Deceiver: Recalling Our Past," *Psychology Today*, September 1985, pp. 39–46. Reprinted with permission from *Psychology Today* magazine. (Copyright © 1985 Sussex Publishers, LLC.))

Similarly, our motivation to remember material when we are exposed to it initially affects how well we can later recall it. If we know we are going to need to recall material later, we are going to be more attentive to it. In contrast, if we don't expect to need to recall material later, then we are less likely to remember it (Naveh-Benjamin et al., 2000; Kassam et al., 2009).

Constructive Processes in Memory: Rebuilding the Past

As we have seen, although it is clear that we can have detailed recollections of significant and distinctive events, it is difficult to gauge the accuracy of such memories. In fact, it is apparent that our memories reflect, at least in part, **constructive processes,** processes in which memories are influenced by the meaning we give to events. When we retrieve information, then, the memory that is produced is affected not just by the direct prior experience we have had with the stimulus, but also by our guesses and inferences about its meaning.

The notion that memory is based on constructive processes was first put forward by Frederic Bartlett, a British psychologist. He suggested that people tend to remember information in terms of **schemas,** organized bodies of information stored in

constructive processes Processes in which memories are influenced by the meaning we give to events.

schemas Organized bodies of information stored in memory that bias the way new information is interpreted, stored, and recalled.

memory that bias the way new information is interpreted, stored, and recalled (Bartlett, 1932). Our reliance on schemas means that memories often consist of a general reconstruction of previous experience. Bartlett argued that schemas are based not only on the specific material to which people are exposed, but also on their understanding of the situation, their expectations about the situation, and their awareness of the motivations underlying the behavior of others.

One of the earliest demonstrations of schemas came from a classic study that involved a procedure similar to the children's game of "telephone," in which information from memory is passed sequentially from one person to another. In the study, a participant viewed a drawing in which there were a variety of people of differing racial and ethnic backgrounds on a subway car, one of whom—a white person—was shown with a razor in his hand (Allport & Postman, 1958). The first participant was asked to describe the drawing to someone else without looking back at it. Then that person was asked to describe it to another person (without looking at the drawing), and then the process was repeated with still one more participant.

The report of the last person differed in significant, yet systematic, ways from the initial drawing. Specifically, many people described the drawing as depicting an African American with a knife—an incorrect recollection, given that the drawing showed a razor in the hand of a Caucasian person. The transformation of the Caucasian's razor into an African American's knife clearly indicates that the participants held a schema that included the unwarranted prejudice that African Americans are more violent than Caucasians and thus more apt to be holding a knife. In short, our expectations and knowledge—and prejudices—affect the reliability of our memories (McDonald & Hirt, 1997; Newby-Clark & Ross, 2003).

MEMORY IN THE COURTROOM: THE EYEWITNESS OF TRIAL

For Calvin Willis, the inadequate memories of two people cost him more than two decades of his life. Willis was the victim of mistaken identity when a young rape victim picked out his photo as the perpetrator of the rape. On that basis, he was tried, convicted, and sentenced to life in prison. Twenty-one years later, DNA testing showed that Willis was innocent, and the victim's identification wrong (Corsello, 2005).

Unfortunately, Willis is not the only victim to whom apologies have had to be made; many cases of mistaken identity have led to unjustified legal actions. Research on eyewitness identification of suspects, as well as on memory for other details of crimes, has shown that eyewitnesses are apt to make significant errors when they try to recall details of criminal activity—even if they are highly confident about their recollections (Thompson, 2000; Wells, Olson, & Charman, 2002; Zaragoza, Belli, & Payment, 2007).

One reason is the impact of the weapons used in crimes. When a criminal perpetrator displays a gun or knife, it acts like a perceptual magnet, attracting the eyes of the witnesses. As a consequence, witnesses pay less attention to other details of the crime and are less able to recall what actually occurred (Steblay et al., 2003; Zaitsu, 2007; Pickel, 2009).

One reason eyewitnesses are prone to memory-related errors is that the specific wording of questions posed to them by police officers or attorneys can affect the way they recall information, as a number of experiments illustrate. For example, in one experiment the participants were shown a film of two cars crashing into each other. Some were then asked the question, "About how fast were the cars going when they *smashed* into each other?" On average, they estimated the speed to be 40.8 miles per hour. In contrast, when another group of participants was asked, "About how fast were the cars going when they *contacted* each other?" the average estimated speed was only 31.8 miles per hour (Loftus & Palmer, 1974; see Figure 4).

Study Alert

A key fact about memory is that it is a constructive process in which memories are influenced by the meaning given to what is being recalled.

FIGURE 4 After viewing an accident involving two cars, the participants in a study were asked to estimate the speed of the two cars involved in the collision. Estimates varied substantially, depending on the way the question was worded. (Source: Loftus & Palmer, 1974.)

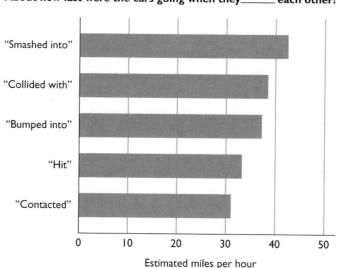

About how fast were the cars going when they_____ each other?

"Smashed into"

"Collided with"

"Bumped into"

"Hit"

"Contacted"

0   10   20   30   40   50

Estimated miles per hour

Six years after being convicted of murder based on a so-called repressed memory of his daughter, George Franklin Sr.'s conviction was overturned.

Children's Reliability. The problem of memory reliability becomes even more acute when children are witnesses because increasing evidence suggests that children's memories are highly vulnerable to the influence of others (Loftus, 1993; Douglas, Goldstein, & Bjorklund, 2000). For instance, in one experiment, 5- to 7-year-old girls who had just had a routine physical examination were shown an anatomically explicit doll. The girls were shown the doll's genital area and asked, "Did the doctor touch you here?" Three of the girls who did not have a vaginal or anal exam said that the doctor had in fact touched them in the genital area, and one of those three made up the detail "The doctor did it with a stick" (Saywitz & Goodman, 1990).

Children's memories are especially susceptible to influence when the situation is highly emotional or stressful. For example, in trials in which there is significant pretrial publicity or in which alleged victims are questioned repeatedly, often by untrained interviewers, the memories of the alleged victims may be influenced by the types of questions they are asked (Scullin, Kanaya, & Ceci, 2002; Lamb & Garretson, 2003; Quas, Malloy, & Melinder, 2007; Goodman & Quas, 2008).

Repressed and False Memories: Separating Truth from Fiction. Consider the case of George Franklin Sr., a man charged with murdering his daughter's playmate. The entire case was based on memories of Franklin's daughter, who claimed that she had repressed them until she began to have flashbacks of the event two decades later. Gradually, the memories became clearer until she recalled her father lifting a rock over his head and then seeing her friend covered with blood. On the basis of her memories, her father was convicted—but later was cleared of the crime after an appeal of the conviction.

There is good reason to question the validity of *repressed memories,* recollections of events that are initially so shocking that the mind responds by pushing them into the unconscious. Supporters of the notion of repressed memory (based on Freud's psychoanalytic theory) suggest that such memories may remain hidden, possibly throughout a person's lifetime, unless they are triggered by some current circumstance, such as the probing that occurs during psychological therapy.

However, memory researcher Elizabeth Loftus maintains that so-called repressed memories may well be inaccurate or even wholly false—representing *false memory.* For example, false memories develop when people are unable to recall the source of a memory of a particular event about which they have only vague recollections. When the source of the memory becomes unclear or ambiguous, people may become confused about whether they actually experienced the event or whether it was imagined. Ultimately, people come to believe that the event actually occurred (Loftus, 2004; Wade, Sharman, & Garry, 2007; Bernstein & Loftus, 2009a).

There is great controversy regarding the legitimacy of repressed memories. Many therapists give great weight to authenticity of repressed memories, and their views are supported by research showing that there are specific regions of the brain that help keep unwanted memories out of awareness. On the other side of the issue are researchers who maintain that there is insufficient scientific support for the existence of such memories. There is also a middle ground: memory researchers who suggest that false memories are a result of normal information processing. The challenge for those on all sides of the issue is to distinguish truth from fiction (Brown & Pope, 1996; Strange, Clifasefi, & Garry, 2007; Bernstein & Loftus, 2009b).

AUTOBIOGRAPHICAL MEMORY: WHERE PAST MEETS PRESENT

Your memory of experiences in your own past may well be a fiction—or at least a distortion of what actually occurred. The same constructive processes that make us inaccurately recall the behavior of others also reduce the accuracy of autobiographical memories. **Autobiographical memories** are our recollections of circumstances and episodes from our own lives. Autobiographical memories encompass the episodic memories we hold about ourselves (Rubin, 1999; Sutin & Robins, 2007).

For example, we tend to forget information about our past that is incompatible with the way in which we currently see ourselves. One study found that adults who were well adjusted but who had been treated for emotional problems during the early years of their lives tended to forget important but troubling childhood events, such as being in foster care. College students misremember their bad grades—but remember their good ones (see Figure 5; Walker, Skowronski, & Thompson, 2003; Kemps & Tiggemann, 2007).

Similarly, when a group of 48-year-olds were asked to recall how they had responded on a questionnaire they had completed when they were high school freshman, their accuracy was no better than chance. For example, although 61% of the questionnaire respondents said that playing sports and other physical activities was their favorite pastime, only 23% of the adults recalled it accurately (Offer et al., 2000).

It is not just certain kinds of events that are distorted; particular periods of life are remembered more easily than others. For example, when people reach late adulthood, they remember periods of life in which they experienced major transitions, such as attending college and working at their first job, better than they remember their middle-age years. Similarly, although most adults' earliest memories of their own lives are of events that occurred when they were toddlers, toddlers show evidence of recall of events that occurred when they were as young as 6 months old (Simcock & Hayne, 2002; Wang, 2003; Cordnoldi, De Beni, & Helstrup, 2007).

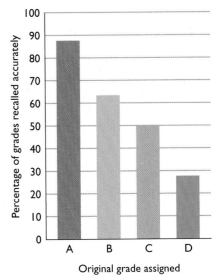

FIGURE 5 We tend to distort memories of unpleasant events. For example, college students are much more likely to accurately recall their good grades while inaccurately recalling their poor ones (Bahrick et al., 1996). Now that you know this, how well do you think you can recall your high school grades?

autobiographical memories Our recollections of circumstances and episodes from our own lives.

Travelers who have visited areas of the world in which there is no written language often have returned with tales of people with phenomenal memories. For instance, storytellers in some preliterate cultures can recount long chronicles that recall the names and activities of people over many generations. Those feats led experts to argue initially that people in preliterate societies develop a different, and perhaps better, type of memory than do those in cultures that employ a written language. They suggested that in a society that lacks writing, people are motivated to recall information with accuracy, especially information relating to tribal histories and traditions that would be lost if they were not passed down orally from one generation to another (Daftary & Meri, 2002; Berntsen & Rubin, 2004).

Exploring DIVERSITY

Are There Cross-Cultural Differences in Memory?

Storytellers in many cultures can recount hundreds of years of history in vivid detail. Research has found that this amazing ability is due less to basic memory processes than to the ways in which they acquire and retain information.

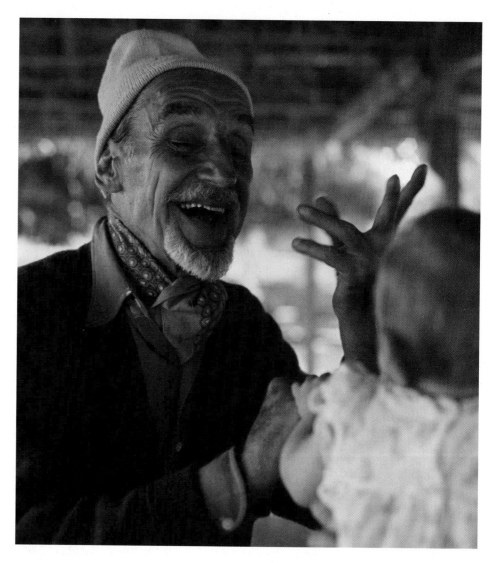

Today, memory researchers dismiss that view. For one thing, preliterate peoples don't have an exclusive claim to amazing memory feats. Some Hebrew scholars memorize thousands of pages of text and can recall the locations of particular words on the page. Similarly, poetry singers in the Balkans can recall thousands of lines of poetry. Even in cultures in which written language exists, then, astounding feats of memory are possible (Strathern & Stewart, 2003; Rubin et al., 2007).

Memory researchers now suggest that there are both similarities and differences in memory across cultures. Basic memory processes such as short-term memory capacity and the structure of long-term memory—the "hardware" of memory—are universal and operate similarly in people in all cultures. In contrast, cultural differences can be seen in the way information is acquired and rehearsed—the "software" of memory. Culture determines how people frame information initially, how much they practice learning and recalling it, and the strategies they use to try to recall it (Mack, 2003; Wang & Conway, 2006; Rubin et al., 2007).

RECAP/EVALUATE/RETHINK

RECAP

What causes difficulties and failures in remembering?

- The tip-of-the-tongue phenomenon is the temporary inability to remember information that one is certain one knows. Retrieval cues are a major strategy for recalling information successfully. (p. 212)
- The levels-of-processing approach to memory suggests that the way in which information is initially perceived and analyzed determines the success with which it is recalled. The deeper the initial processing, the greater the recall. (p. 213)
- Explicit memory refers to intentional or conscious recollection of information. In contrast, implicit memory refers to memories of which people are not consciously aware but that can affect subsequent performance and behavior. (p. 214)
- Flashbulb memories are memories centered on a specific, important event. The more distinctive a memory is, the more easily it can be retrieved. (p. 215)
- Memory is a constructive process: We relate memories to the meaning, guesses, and expectations we give to events. Specific information is recalled in terms of schemas, organized bodies of information stored in memory that bias the way new information is interpreted, stored, and recalled. (p. 216)
- Eyewitnesses are apt to make substantial errors when they try to recall the details of crimes. The problem of memory reliability becomes even more acute when the witnesses are children. (p. 217)
- Autobiographical memory is influenced by constructive processes. (p. 219)

EVALUATE

1. While with a group of friends at a dance, Eva bumps into a man she dated last month. But when she tries to introduce him to her friends, she cannot remember his name. What is the term for this occurrence?
2. _____ is the process of retrieving a specific item from memory.
3. A friend tells you, "I know exactly where I was and what I was doing when I heard that Michael Jackson died." What is this type of memory phenomenon called?
4. _____ _____ _____ theory states that the more a person analyzes a statement, the more likely he or she is to remember it later.

RETHINK

1. Research shows that an eyewitness's memory for details of crimes can contain significant errors. How might a lawyer use this information when evaluating an eyewitness's testimony? Should eyewitness accounts be permissible in a court of law?
2. *From a social worker's perspective:* Should a child victim of sexual abuse be allowed to testify in court, based on what you've learned about children's memories under stress?

Answers to Evaluate Questions

1. tip-of-the-tongue phenomenon; 2. recall; 3. flashbulb memory; 4. levels-of-processing

KEY TERMS

tip-of-the-tongue
  phenomenon p. 212
recall p. 212
recognition p. 212

levels-of-processing
  theory p. 213
explicit memory p. 214
implicit memory p. 214

priming p. 214
flashbulb memories p. 215
constructive
  processes p. 216

schemas p. 216
autobiographical
  memories p. 219

Forgetting: When Memory Fails

Key Concepts

Why do we forget information?

What are the major memory impairments?

Known in the scientific literature by the alias of H.M., he could remember, quite literally, nothing—nothing, that is, that had happened since the loss of his brain's temporal lobes and hippocampus during experimental surgery to reduce epileptic seizures. Until that time, H.M.'s memory had been quite normal. But after the operation he was unable to recall anything for more than a few minutes, and then the memory was seemingly lost forever. He did not remember his address, or the name of the person to whom he was talking. H.M. would read the same magazine over and over again. According to his own description, his life was like waking from a dream and being unable to know where he was or how he got there. (Milner, 1966, 2005)

As the case of H.M. illustrates, a person without a normal memory faces severe difficulties. All of us who have experienced even routine instances of forgetting—such as not remembering an acquaintance's name or a fact on a test—understand the very real consequences of memory failure.

Of course, memory failure is also essential to remembering important information. The ability to forget inconsequential details about experiences, people, and objects helps us avoid being burdened and distracted by trivial stores of meaningless data. Forgetting permits us to form general impressions and recollections. For example, the reason our friends consistently look familiar to us is because we're able to forget their clothing, facial blemishes, and other transient features that change from one occasion to the next. Instead, our memories are based on a summary of various critical features—a far more economical use of our memory capabilities.

The first attempts to study forgetting were made by German psychologist Hermann Ebbinghaus about a hundred years ago. Using himself as the only participant in his study, Ebbinghaus memorized lists of three-letter nonsense syllables—meaningless sets of two consonants with a vowel in between, such as FIW and BOZ. By measuring how easy it was to relearn a given list of words after varying periods of time had passed since the initial learning, he found that forgetting occurred systematically, as shown in Figure 1. As the figure indicates, the most

FIGURE 1 In his classic work, Ebbinghaus found that the most rapid forgetting occurs in the first nine hours after exposure to new material. However, the rate of forgetting then slows down and declines very little even after many days have passed (Ebbinghaus, 1885, 1913). Check your own memory: What were you doing exactly two hours ago? What were you doing last Tuesday at 5 p.m.? Which information is easier to retrieve?

rapid forgetting occurs in the first nine hours, particularly in the first hour. After nine hours, the rate of forgetting slows and declines little, even after the passage of many days.

Despite his primitive methods, Ebbinghaus's study had an important influence on subsequent research, and his basic conclusions have been upheld. There is almost always a strong initial decline in memory, followed by a more gradual drop over time. Furthermore, relearning of previously mastered material is almost always faster than starting from scratch, whether the material is academic information or a motor skill such as serving a tennis ball (Wixted & Carpenter, 2007).

Why We Forget

Why do we forget? One reason is that we may not have paid attention to the material in the first place—a failure of *encoding*. For example, if you live in the United States, you probably have been exposed to thousands of pennies during your life. Despite this experience, you probably don't have a clear sense of the details of the coin. (See this for yourself by looking at Figure 2.) Consequently, the reason for your memory failure is that you probably never encoded the information into long-term memory initially. Obviously, if information was not placed in memory to start with, there is no way the information can be recalled.

But what about material that has been encoded into memory and that can't later be remembered? Several processes account for memory failures, including decay, interference, and cue-dependent forgetting.

Decay is the loss of information through nonuse. This explanation for forgetting assumes that *memory traces,* the physical changes that take place in the brain when new material is learned, simply fade away over time (Grann, 2007).

decay The loss of information in memory through its nonuse.

Although there is evidence that decay does occur, this does not seem to be the complete explanation for forgetting. Often there is no relationship between how long ago a person was exposed to information and how well that information is recalled. If decay explained all forgetting, we would expect that the more time that has elapsed between the initial learning of information and our attempt to recall it, the harder it would be to remember it because there would be more time for the memory trace to decay. Yet people who take several consecutive tests on the same

FIGURE 2 One of these pennies is the real thing. Can you find it? Why is this task harder than it seems at first?
(Source: Nickerson & Adams, 1979.)

If you don't have a penny handy, the correct answer is "A."

"He must have forgotten something."

interference The phenomenon by which information in memory disrupts the recall of other information.

cue-dependent forgetting Forgetting that occurs when there are insufficient retrieval cues to rekindle information that is in memory.

Study Alert

Memory loss through decay comes from nonuse of the memory; memory loss through interference is due to the presence of other information in memory.

proactive interference Interference in which information learned earlier disrupts the recall of newer material.

retroactive interference Interference in which there is difficulty in the recall of information learned earlier because of later exposure to different material.

material often recall more of the initial information when taking later tests than they did on earlier tests. If decay were operating, we would expect the opposite to occur (Payne, 1986).

Because decay does not fully account for forgetting, memory specialists have proposed an additional mechanism: **interference.** In interference, information in memory disrupts the recall of other information (Naveh-Benjamin, Guez, & Sorek, 2007; Pilotti, Chodorow, & Shono, 2009).

To distinguish between decay and interference, think of the two processes in terms of a row of books on a library shelf. In decay, the old books are constantly crumbling and rotting away, leaving room for new arrivals. Interference processes suggest that new books knock the old ones off the shelf, where they become inaccessible.

Finally, forgetting may occur because of **cue-dependent forgetting,** forgetting that occurs when there are insufficient retrieval cues to rekindle information that is in memory (Tulving & Thompson, 1983). For example, you may not be able to remember where you lost a set of keys until you mentally walk through your day, thinking of each place you visited. When you think of the place where you lost the keys—say, the library—the retrieval cue of the library may be sufficient to help you recall that you left them on the desk in the library. Without that retrieval cue, you may be unable to recall the location of the keys.

Most research suggests that interference and cue-dependent forgetting are key processes in forgetting (Mel'nikov, 1993; Bower, Thompson, & Tulving, 1994). We forget things mainly because new memories interfere with the retrieval of old ones or because appropriate retrieval cues are unavailable, not because the memory trace has decayed.

Proactive and Retroactive Interference: The Before and After of Forgetting

There are actually two sorts of interference that influence forgetting: proactive and retroactive. In **proactive interference,** information learned earlier disrupts the recall of newer material. Suppose, as a student of foreign languages, you first learned French in the 10th grade, and then in the 11th grade you took Spanish. When in the 12th grade you take a college achievement test in Spanish, you may find you have difficulty recalling the Spanish translation of a word because all you can think of is its French equivalent (Bunting, 2006).

In contrast, **retroactive interference** refers to difficulty in the recall of information because of later exposure to different material. If, for example, you have difficulty on a French achievement test because of your more recent exposure to Spanish, retroactive interference is the culprit (see Figure 3). One way to remember the difference between proactive and retroactive interference is to keep in mind that *pro*active interference progresses in time—the past interferes with the present—whereas *retro*active interference retrogresses in time, working backward as the present interferes with the past (Jacoby et al., 2007).

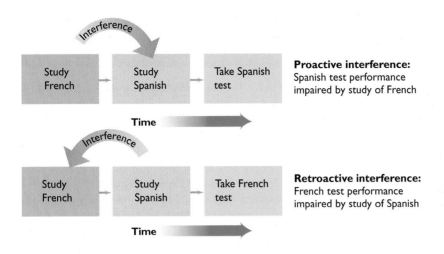

Although the concepts of proactive and retroactive interference illustrate how material may be forgotten, they still do not explain whether forgetting is caused by the actual loss or modification of information or by problems in the retrieval of information. Most research suggests that material that has apparently been lost because of interference can eventually be recalled if appropriate stimuli are presented (Tulving & Psotka, 1971; Anderson, 1981), but the question has not been fully answered.

Memory Dysfunctions: Afflictions of Forgetting

First you notice that you're always misplacing things or that common nouns are evading you as stubbornly as the names of new acquaintances. Pretty soon you're forgetting appointments and getting flustered when you drive in traffic. On bad days you find you can't hold numbers in your mind long enough to dial the phone. You try valiantly to conceal your lapses, but they become ever more glaring. You crash your car. You spend whole mornings struggling to dress yourself properly. And even as you lose the ability to read or play the piano, you're painfully aware of what's happening to you. (Cowley, 2000, p. 46)

These memory problems are symptomatic of **Alzheimer's disease,** an illness characterized in part by severe memory problems. Alzheimer's is the fourth leading cause of death among adults in the United States, affecting an estimated 5 million people.

In the beginning, Alzheimer's symptoms appear as simple forgetfulness of things such as appointments and birthdays. As the disease progresses, memory loss becomes more profound, and even the simplest tasks—such as using a telephone—are forgotten. Ultimately, victims may lose their ability to speak or comprehend language, and physical deterioration sets in, leading to death.

The causes of Alzheimer's disease are not fully understood. Increasing evidence suggests that Alzheimer's results from an inherited susceptibility to a defect in the production of the protein beta amyloid, which is necessary for the maintenance of nerve cell connections. When the synthesis of beta amyloid goes awry, large clumps of cells form, triggering inflammation and the deterioration of nerve cells in the brain (Selkoe, 2002; Detoledo-Morrell, Stoub, & Wang, 2007; Horínek, Varjassyová, & Hort, 2007; Selkoe, 2008; see Figure 4).

Alzheimer's disease An illness characterized in part by severe memory problems.

Neuroscience in Your Life: Alzheimer's Disease and Brain Deterioration

FIGURE 4 Alzheimer's disease, which is the fourth leading cause of death among adults in the United States, is characterized by significant memory declines. Here a man with Alzheimer's was followed for three years to learn how his brain processed autobiographical memories as the disease progressed. (a) While in the first year, the areas of the brain used for long-term memory, such as the hippocampus and surrounding temporal lobe (shown in yellow, orange, and red), are activated similarly to healthy adults. (b) In the second year, as his abilities began to decline, other areas of the brain began to compensate by increasing the levels of activity in surrounding areas. Finally, in the third year when his abilities decreased substantially, other areas of the brain were no longer able to compensate and activity decreased overall. On the other hand, some areas of the brain—such as those involved in visual processing—did not change over the three-year period, illustrating that not all areas of the brain are affected by the disease. (Source: Maguire et al., 2010.)

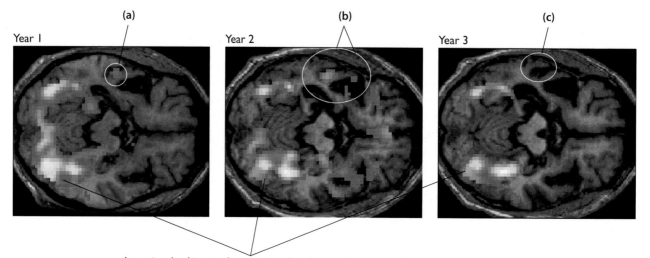

(a)   (b)   (c)

Year 1   Year 2   Year 3

Areas involved in visual processing that do not change over time

amnesia Memory loss that occurs without other mental difficulties.

retrograde amnesia Amnesia in which memory is lost for occurrences prior to a certain event.

anterograde amnesia Amnesia in which memory is lost for events that follow an injury.

Korsakoff's syndrome A disease that afflicts long-term alcoholics, leaving some abilities intact but including hallucinations and a tendency to repeat the same story.

Alzheimer's disease is one of a number of memory dysfunctions. Another is **amnesia,** memory loss that occurs without other mental difficulties. The type of amnesia immortalized in countless Hollywood films involves a victim who receives a blow to the head and is unable to remember anything from his or her past. In reality, amnesia of this type, known as retrograde amnesia, is quite rare. In **retrograde amnesia,** memory is lost for occurrences prior to a certain event. Usually, lost memories gradually reappear, although full restoration may take as long as several years. In certain cases, some memories are lost forever. But even in cases of severe memory loss, the loss is generally selective. For example, although people suffering from retrograde amnesia may be unable to recall friends and family members, they still may be able to play complicated card games or knit a sweater quite well (Verfaellie & Keane, 2002; Bright, Buckman, & Fradera, 2006).

A second type of amnesia is exemplified by people who remember nothing of their current activities. In **anterograde amnesia** loss of memory occurs for events that follow an injury. Information cannot be transferred from short-term to long-term memory, resulting in the inability to remember anything other than what was in long-term storage before the accident (Gilboa, Winocur, & Rosenbaum, 2006).

Amnesia is also a result of **Korsakoff's syndrome,** a disease that afflicts long-term alcoholics. Although many of their intellectual abilities may be intact, Korsakoff's sufferers display a strange array of symptoms, including hallucinations and a tendency to repeat the same story over and over (van Oort & Kessels, 2009).

Fortunately, most of us have intact memory, and the occasional failures we suffer may actually be preferable to having a perfect memory. Consider, for instance, the case of a man who had total recall. After reading passages of Dante's *The Divine Comedy* in Italian—a language he did not speak—he was able to repeat them from memory some 15 years later. He could memorize lists of 50 unrelated words and recall them at will more than a decade later. He could even repeat the same list of words backward, if asked (Luria, 1968).

Such a skill at first may seem to be enviable, but it actually presented quite a problem. The man's memory became a jumble of lists of words, numbers, and names; when he tried to relax, his mind was filled with images. Even reading was difficult since every word evoked a flood of thoughts from the past that interfered with his ability to understand the meaning of what he was reading. Partially as a consequence of the man's unusual memory, psychologist A. R. Luria, who studied his case, found him to be a "disorganized and rather dull-witted person" (Luria, 1968, p. 65). We might be grateful, then, that forgetfulness plays a role in our lives.

Study Alert

Except for Alzheimer's disease, memory disorders are relatively rare.

Apart from the advantages of forgetting, say, a bad date, most of us would like to find ways to improve our memories. Among the effective strategies for studying and remembering course material:

BECOMING AN INFORMED CONSUMER of Psychology

Improving Your Memory

- *Use the keyword technique.* If you are studying a foreign language, try the *keyword technique* of pairing a foreign word with a common English word that has a similar sound. This English word is known as the *keyword*. For example, to learn the Spanish word for duck (*pato*, pronounced *pot-o*), you might choose the keyword *pot*; for the Spanish word for horse (*caballo*, pronounced *cob-eye-yo*), the keyword might be *eye*. Once you have thought of a keyword, imagine the Spanish word "interacting" with the English keyword. You might envision a duck taking a bath in a pot to remember the word *pato* or a horse with a large, bulging eye in the center of its head to recall *caballo* (Carney & Levin, 1998; Wyra, Lawson, & Hungi, 2007).

- *Rely on organization cues.* Recall material you read in textbooks by organizing the material in memory the first time you read it. Organize your reading on the basis of any advance information you have about the content and about its arrangement. You will then be able to make connections and see relationships among the various facts and process the material at a deeper level, which in turn will later aid recall.

- *Take effective notes.* "Less is more" is perhaps the best advice for taking lecture notes that facilitate recall. Rather than trying to jot down every detail of a lecture, it is better to listen and think about the material, and take down the main points. In effective note taking, thinking about the material when you first hear it is more important than writing it down. This is one reason that borrowing someone else's notes is a bad idea; you will have no framework in memory that you can use to understand them (Feldman, 2010).

- *Practice and rehearse.* Although practice does not necessarily make perfect, it helps. By studying and rehearsing material past initial mastery—a process called *overlearning*—people are able to show better long-term recall than they show if they stop practicing after their initial learning of the material.

- *Don't believe claims about drugs that improve memory.* Advertisements for One-a-Day vitamins with ginkgo biloba or Quanterra Mental Sharpness Product would have you believe that taking a drug or supplement can improve your memory. Not so, according to the results of numerous studies. No research has shown that commercial memory enhancers are effective (Gold, Cahill, & Wenk, 2002; McDaniel, Maier, & Einstein, 2002; Burns, Bryan, & Nettelbeck, 2006).

RECAP/EVALUATE/RETHINK

RECAP

Why do we forget information?
- Several processes account for memory failure, including decay, interference (both proactive and retroactive), and cue-dependent forgetting. (p. 223)

What are the major memory impairments?
- Among the memory dysfunctions are Alzheimer's disease, which leads to a progressive loss of memory, and amnesia, a memory loss that occurs without other mental difficulties and can take the forms of retrograde amnesia and anterograde amnesia. Korsakoff's syndrome is a disease that afflicts long-term alcoholics, resulting in memory impairment. (p. 225)
- Among the techniques for improving memory are the keyword technique to memorize foreign language vocabulary; using the encoding specificity phenomenon; organizing text material and lecture notes; and practice and rehearsal, leading to overlearning. (p. 227)

EVALUATE

1. If, after learning the history of the Middle East for a class two years ago, you now find yourself unable to recall what you learned, you are experiencing memory _____, caused by nonuse.
2. Difficulty in accessing a memory because of the presence of other information is known as _____.
3. _____ interference occurs when material is difficult to retrieve because of subsequent exposure to other material; _____ interference refers to difficulty in retrieving material as a result of the interference of previously learned material.
4. Match the following memory disorders with the correct information:
   1. Affects alcoholics; may result in hallucinations.
   2. Memory loss occurring without other mental problems.
   3. Beta amyloid defect; progressive forgetting and physical deterioration.

   a. Alzheimer's disease
   b. Korsakoff's syndrome
   c. Amnesia

RETHINK

1. What are the implications of proactive and retroactive interference for learning multiple foreign languages? Would earlier language training in a different language help or hinder learning a new language?
2. *From a healthcare provider's perspective:* Alzheimer's disease and amnesia are two of the most pervasive memory dysfunctions that threaten many individuals. What sorts of activities might health care providers offer their patients to help them combat their memory loss?

Answers to Evaluate Questions

1. decay; 2. interference; 3. retroactive, proactive; 4. 1-b, 2-c, 3-a

KEY TERMS

decay p. 223
interference p. 224
cue-dependent
  forgetting p. 224

proactive
  interference p. 224
retroactive
  interference p. 224

Alzheimer's disease p. 225
amnesia p. 226
retrograde amnesia p. 226

anterograde amnesia p. 226
Korsakoff's
  syndrome p. 226

"robin" is a prototype of the concept "bird." Similarly, when we think of the concept of a table, we're likely to think of a coffee table before we think of a drafting table, making a coffee table closer to our prototype of a table.

Relatively high agreement exists among people in a particular culture about which examples of a concept are prototypes, as well as which examples are not. For instance, most people in Western cultures consider cars and trucks good examples of vehicles, whereas elevators and wheelbarrows are not. Consequently, cars and trucks are prototypes of the concept of a vehicle.

Concepts enable us to think about and understand more readily the complex world in which we live. For example, the suppositions we make about the reasons for other people's behavior are based on the ways in which we classify behavior. Hence, our conclusion about a person who washes her hands 20 times a day could vary depending on whether we place her behavior within the conceptual framework of a health-care worker or a mental patient. Similarly, physicians make diagnoses by drawing on concepts and prototypes of symptoms that they learned about in medical school. Finally, concepts and prototypes facilitate our efforts to draw suitable conclusions through the cognitive process of reasoning.

Algorithms and Heuristics

When making a decision, we often turn to various kinds of cognitive shortcuts known as algorithms and heuristics to help us. An **algorithm** is a rule that, if applied appropriately, guarantees a solution to a problem. We can use an algorithm even if we can't understand why it works. For example, you may know that you can find the length of the third side of a right triangle by using the formula $a^2 + b^2 = c^2$, although you may not have the foggiest notion of the mathematical principles behind the formula.

For many problems and decisions, however, no algorithm is available. In those instances, we may be able to use heuristics to help us. A **heuristic** is a thinking strategy that may lead us to a solution to a problem or decision, but—unlike algorithms—it may sometimes lead to errors. Heuristics increase the likelihood of success for coming to a solution but, unlike algorithms, they cannot ensure it. For example, when I play tic-tac-toe, I follow the heuristic of placing an X in the center square when I start the game. This tactic doesn't guarantee that I'll win, but experience has taught me that it will increase my chances of success. Similarly, some students follow the heuristic of preparing for a test by ignoring the assigned textbook reading and only studying their lecture notes—a strategy that may or may not pay off.

Although heuristics often help people solve problems and make decisions, certain kinds of heuristics may lead to inaccurate conclusions. For example, we sometimes use the *representativeness heuristic* when we judge people by the degree to which they represent a certain category or group of people. Suppose, for instance, you are the owner of a fast-food store that has been robbed many times by teenagers. The representativeness heuristic would lead you to raise your guard each time someone from this age group enters your store even though, statistically, it is unlikely that any given teenager will rob the store (Fisk, Bury, & Holden, 2006; Nilsson, Juslin, & Olsson, 2008).

The *availability heuristic* involves judging the probability of an event on the basis of how easily the event can be recalled from memory. According to this heuristic, we assume that events we remember easily are likely to have occurred more frequently in the past—and are more likely to occur in the future—than events that are harder to remember.

For instance, the availability heuristic makes us more afraid of dying in a plane crash than in an auto accident, despite statistics clearly showing that airplane travel is much safer than travel by car. Similarly, although 10 times as many people die from falling out of bed than from lightning strikes, we're more afraid of being hit by lightning. The reason is that plane crashes and lightning strikes receive far more publicity, and they are therefore more easily remembered (Oppenheimer, 2004; Fox, 2006; Kluger, 2006; Caruso, 2008).

algorithm A rule that, if applied appropriately, guarantees a solution to a problem.

heuristic A thinking strategy that may lead us to a solution to a problem or decision, but—unlike algorithms— may sometimes lead to errors.

Study Alert

Remember that algorithms are rules that *always* provide a solution, while heuristics are shortcuts or strategies that *may* provide a solution.

Solving Problems

According to an old legend, a group of Vietnamese monks guard three towers on which sit 64 golden rings. The monks believe that if they succeed in moving the rings from the first tower to the third according to a series of rigid rules, the world as we know it will come to an end. (Should you prefer that the world remain in its present state, there's no need for immediate concern: The puzzle is so complex that it will take the monks about a trillion years to solve it.)

In the Tower of Hanoi puzzle—a simpler version of the task facing the monks—three disks are placed on three posts in the order shown in Figure 2. The goal of the puzzle is to move all three disks to the third post, arranged in the same order, by making as few moves as possible. There are two restrictions: Only one disk can be moved at a time, and no disk can ever cover a smaller one during a move.

Why are cognitive psychologists interested in the Tower of Hanoi problem? Because the way people go about solving such puzzles helps illuminate how people solve complex, real-life problems. Psychologists have found that problem solving typically involves the three steps illustrated in Figure 3: preparing to create solutions, producing solutions, and evaluating the solutions that are generated.

PREPARATION: UNDERSTANDING AND DIAGNOSING PROBLEMS

When approaching a problem like the Tower of Hanoi, most people begin by trying to understand the problem thoroughly. If the problem is a novel one, they probably will pay particular attention to any restrictions placed on coming up with a solution—such as the rule for moving only one disk at a time in the Tower of Hanoi problem. If, by contrast, the problem is a familiar one, they are apt to spend considerably less time in this preparation stage.

Problems vary from well defined to ill defined. In a *well-defined problem*—such as a mathematical equation or the solution to a jigsaw puzzle—both the nature of the problem itself and the information needed to solve it are available and clear. Thus, we can make straightforward judgments about whether a potential solution is appropriate. With an *ill-defined problem,* such as how to increase morale on an assembly line or bring peace to the Middle East, not only may the specific nature of the problem be unclear, but the information required to solve the problem may be even less obvious (Evans, 2004; Vartanian, 2009).

Kinds of Problems. Typically, a problem falls into one of the three categories shown in Figure 4: arrangement, inducing structure, and transformation. Solving each type

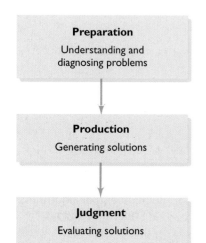
Preparation
Understanding and diagnosing problems

↓

Production
Generating solutions

↓

Judgment
Evaluating solutions

FIGURE 3 Steps in problem solving.

FIGURE 2 The goal of the Tower of Hanoi puzzle is to move all three disks from the first post to the third and still preserve the original order of the disks, using the fewest number of moves possible while following the rules that only one disk at a time can be moved and no disk can cover a smaller one during a move. Try it yourself before you look at the solution, which is listed according to the sequence of moves.

(Solution: Move C to 3, B to 2, C to 2, A to 3, C to 1, B to 3, and C to 3.)

a. Arrangement problems

1. Anagrams: Rearrange the letters in each set to make an English word:

2. Two strings hang from a ceiling but are too far apart to allow a person to hold one and walk to the other. On the floor are a book of matches, a screwdriver, and a few pieces of cotton. How could the strings be tied together?

b. Problems of inducing structure

1. What number comes next in the series?

   1 4 2 4 3 4 4 4 5 4 6 4

2. Complete these analogies:

   baseball is to bat as tennis is to_____

   merchant is to sell as customer is to_____

c. Transformation problems

1. Water jars: A person has three jars with the following capacities:

 Jar A: 28 ounces   Jar B: 7 ounces   Jar C: 5 ounces

   How can the person measure exactly 11 ounces of water?

2. Ten coins are arranged in the following way. By moving only *two* of the coins, make two rows that each contains six coins.

FIGURE 4 The three major categories of problems: (a) arrangement, (b) inducing structure, and (c) transformation. Solutions appear in Figure 5. (Sources: Bourne & Dominowski, *Cognitive Processes,* 1st ed., © 1979. Reproduced in print and electronic formats by permission of Pearson Education, Inc., Upper Saddle River, New Jersey; Aschcraft, 1994.)

FIGURE 5 Solutions to the problems in Figure 4 on the previous page.

a. Arrangement problems

1. FACET, DOUBT, THICK, NAIVE, ANVIL

2. The screwdriver is tied to one of the strings. This makes a pendulum that can be swung to reach the other string.

b. Problems of inducing structure

1. 7

2. racket; buy

c. Transformation problems

1. Fill jar A; empty into jar B once and into jar C twice. What remains in jar A is 11 ounces

2.

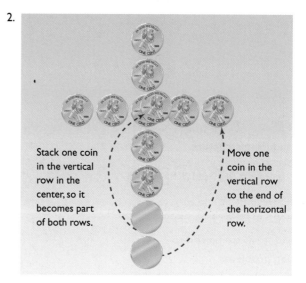

Stack one coin in the vertical row in the center, so it becomes part of both rows.

Move one coin in the vertical row to the end of the horizontal row.

requires somewhat different kinds of psychological skills and knowledge (Spitz, 1987; Chronicle, MacGregor, & Ormerod, 2004).

Arrangement problems require the problem solver to rearrange or recombine elements in a way that will satisfy a certain criterion. Usually, several different arrangements can be made, but only one or a few of the arrangements will produce a solution. Anagrams and jigsaw puzzles are examples of arrangement problems (Coventry, Venn, Smith, & Morley, 2003).

In *problems of inducing structure,* a person must identify the existing relationships among the elements presented and then construct a new relationship among them. In such a problem, the problem solver must determine not only the relationships among the elements but also the structure and size of the elements involved. In the example shown in Figure 4, a person must first determine that the solution requires that numbers be considered in pairs (14-24-34-44-54-64). Only after identifying that part of the problem can a person determine the solution or pattern (the first number of each pair increases by one, while the second number remains the same).

The Tower of Hanoi puzzle represents the third kind of problem—*transformation problems*—which consist of an initial state, a goal state, and a method for changing the initial state into the goal state. In the Tower of Hanoi problem, the initial state is the original configuration, the goal state is to have the three disks on the third peg, and the method is the rules for moving the disks (Mataix-Cols & Bartres-Faz, 2002; Emick & Welsh, 2005; Majeres, 2007).

Problem: Surgery or radiation?

Survival Frame

Surgery: Of 100 people having surgery, 90 live through the post-operative period, 68 are alive at the end of the first year, and 34 are alive at the end of five years.

Radiation: Of 100 people having radiation therapy, all live through the treatment, 77 are alive at the end of one year, and 22 are alive at the end of five years.

Far more patients choose surgery

Mortality Frame

Surgery: Of 100 people having surgery, 10 die during surgery, 32 die by the end of the first year, and 66 die by the end of five years.

Radiation: Of 100 people having radiation therapy, none die during the treatment, 23 die by the end of one year, and 78 die by the end of five years.

Far more patients choose radiation

FIGURE 6 A decision often is affected by the way a problem is framed. In this case, most would choose radiation over surgery, despite similar results.

Whether the problem is one of arrangement, inducing structure, or transformation, the preparation stage of understanding and diagnosing is critical in problem solving because it allows us to develop our own cognitive representation of the problem and to place it within a personal framework. We may divide the problem into subparts or ignore some information as we try to simplify the task. Winnowing out nonessential information is often a critical step in the preparation stage of problem solving.

Our ability to comprehend a problem—and the kind of solution we eventually come to—depends on the way a problem is phrased or framed. Consider, for example, if you were a cancer patient having to choose between surgery and radiation and were given the two sets of treatment options shown in Figure 6 (Tversky & Kahneman, 1987; Chandran & Menon, 2004). When the options are framed in terms of the likelihood of survival, only 18% of participants in a study chose radiation over surgery. However, when the choice was framed in terms of the likelihood of dying, 44% chose radiation over surgery—even though the outcomes are identical in both sets of framing conditions.

PRODUCTION: GENERATING SOLUTIONS

After preparation, the next stage in problem solving is producing possible solutions. If a problem is relatively simple, we may already have a direct solution stored in long-term memory, and all we need to do is retrieve the appropriate information. If we cannot retrieve or don't know the solution, we must generate possible solutions and compare them with information in our long- and short-term memory.

At the most basic level, we can solve problems through trial and error. Thomas Edison invented the lightbulb only because he tried thousands of different kinds of materials for a filament before he found one that worked (carbon). The difficulty with trial and error, of course, is that some problems are so complicated that it would take a lifetime to try out every possibility. For example, according to some estimates, there are some 10^{120} possible sequences of chess moves (Fine & Fine, 2003).

means-ends analysis Involves repeated tests for differences between the desired outcome and what currently exists.

In place of trial and error, complex problem solving often involves the use of heuristics, cognitive shortcuts that can generate solutions. Probably the most frequently applied heuristic in problem solving is a **means-ends analysis,** which involves repeated tests for differences between the desired outcome and what currently exists (Newell & Simon, 1972; Huber, Beckmann, & Herrmann, 2004; Chrysikou, 2006). Consider this simple example:

> I want to take my son to preschool. What's the difference between what I have and what I want? One of distance. What changes distance? My automobile. My automobile won't work. What is needed to make it work? A new battery. What has new batteries? An auto repair shop. . . .

In a means-end analysis, each step brings the problem solver closer to a resolution. Although this approach is often effective, if the problem requires indirect steps that temporarily *increase* the discrepancy between a current state and the solution, means-ends analysis can be counterproductive. For example, sometimes the fastest route to the summit of a mountain requires a mountain climber to backtrack temporarily; a means-end approach—which implies that the mountain climber should always forge ahead and upward—will be ineffective in such instances.

For other problems, the best approach is to work backward by focusing on the goal, rather than the starting point, of the problem. Consider, for example, the water lily problem:

> Water lilies are growing on Blue Lake. The water lilies grow rapidly, so that the amount of water surface covered by lilies doubles every 24 hours.

> On the first day of summer, there was just one water lily. On the 90th day of the summer, the lake was entirely covered. On what day was the lake half covered? (Reisberg, 1997)

THE FAR SIDE® BY GARY LARSON

© 1981 FarWorks, Inc. All Rights Reserved/Dist. by Creators Syndicate

PRIMATE RESEARCH LAB

If you start searching for a solution to the problem by thinking about the initial state on day 1 (one water lily) and move forward from there, you're facing a daunting task of trial-and-error estimation. But try taking a different approach: Start with day 90, when the entire lake was covered with lilies. Given that the lilies double their coverage daily, on the prior day only half the lake was covered. The answer, then, is day 89, a solution found by working backward (Bourne et al., 1986; Hunt, 1994).

Forming Subgoals: Dividing Problems into Their Parts. Another heuristic commonly used to generate solutions is to divide a problem into intermediate steps, or *subgoals,* and solve each of those steps. For instance, in our modified Tower of Hanoi problem, we could choose several obvious subgoals, such as moving the largest disk to the third post.

If solving a subgoal is a step toward the ultimate solution to a problem, identifying subgoals is an appropriate strategy. In some cases, however, forming subgoals is not all that helpful and may actually increase the time needed to find a solution. For example, some problems cannot be subdivided. Others—like some complicated mathematical problems—are so complex that it takes longer to identify the appropriate subdivisions than to solve the problem by other means (Reed, 1996; Kaller et al., 2004; Fishbach, Dhar, & Zhang, 2006).

Insight: Sudden Awareness. Some approaches to generating possible solutions focus less on step-by-step heuristics than on

(a)

(b)

(c)

FIGURE 7 (a) In an impressive display of insight, Sultan, one of the chimpanzees in Köhler's experiments in problem solving, sees a bunch of bananas that is out of reach. (b) He then carries over several crates, stacks them, and (c) stands on them to reach the bananas.

the sudden bursts of comprehension that one may experience during efforts to solve a problem. In a classic study the German psychologist Wolfgang Köhler examined learning and problem-solving processes in chimpanzees (Köhler, 1927). In his studies, Köhler exposed chimps to challenging situations where the elements of the solution were all present; all the chimps needed to do was put them together.

In one of Köhler's studies, chimps were kept in a cage in which boxes and sticks were strewn about, and a bunch of tantalizing bananas hung from the ceiling out of reach. Initially, the chimps made trial-and-error attempts to get to the bananas: They would throw sticks at the bananas, jump from one of the boxes, or leap wildly from the ground. Frequently, they would seem to give up in frustration, leaving the bananas dangling temptingly overhead. But then, in what seemed like a sudden revelation, they would stop whatever they were doing and stand on a box to reach the bananas with a stick (Figure 7). Köhler called the cognitive process underlying the chimps' new behavior **insight,** a sudden awareness of the relationships among various elements that had previously appeared unrelated.

Although Köhler emphasized the apparent suddenness of insightful solutions, subsequent research has shown that prior experience and trial-and-error practice in problem solving must precede "insight." Consequently, the chimps' behavior may simply represent the chaining together of previously learned responses, which is no different from the way a pigeon learns by trial and error to peck a key (Epstein, 1996; Windholz & Lamal, 2002).

insight A sudden awareness of the relationships among various elements that had previously appeared independent of one another.

JUDGMENT: EVALUATING SOLUTIONS

The final stage in problem solving is judging the adequacy of a solution. Often this is a simple matter: If the solution is clear—as in the Tower of Hanoi problem—we will know immediately whether we have been successful (Varma, 2007).

The Thoughts Behind Avoiding Danger: When Hunches Save Lives

The sight was not that unusual, at least not for Mosul, Iraq: a car parked on the sidewalk, facing opposite traffic, its windows rolled up tight. Two young boys stared out the back window, their faces leaning together as if to share a whisper. The soldier patrolling closest to the car stopped. He had an urge to move back before he knew why: "My body suddenly got cooler, you know, that danger feeling" (Carey, 2009).

That "danger feeling" saved the soldier's life: Moments after he turned to retreat, an improvised explosive device—a home-made bomb—detonated the car, throwing the soldier to the ground.

U.S. troops patrolling Iraq have expensive military equipment to avoid the threat of hidden bombs, but it turns out that even the best equipment is not as effective as soldiers' own hunches. Researchers are studying soldiers' thought and decision-making processes to determine how exactly they sense imminent danger, and the initial answers are surprising.

We might expect that training plays a part in this ability, and it does: Elite soldiers are highly trained in what to look for. But they also seem to manage their anxiety, process visual imagery, and interpret their own emotional reactions in ways that make them more sensitive to danger (Rachman, 1990; Li et al., 2007).

Keeping anxiety at bay helps soldiers stay focused on the task of spotting bombs, and some ways they keep their emotions in check are by thinking of themselves as being on the offensive rather than on the defensive and by identifying strongly with their units. Studies also show that well-trained troops tend to recover more quickly than others from the cortisol rush produced by a threat (Haslam et al., 2005).

Heightened visual ability also plays a part. Highly trained soldiers seem to be particularly sensitized to relevant visual images—they sometimes have an uncanny knack for picking up on subtle features or changes in the environment that may be clues to a threatening situation, and they tend to process this information faster than other people do (Carey, 2009).

In fact, the visual signals can be so subtle and the soldiers process them so quickly that they may sense danger without consciously knowing what tells them it exists. Studies of people who respond to threats in this manner show that the brain regions involved in decision making and in interpreting bodily sensations to produce an emotion are particularly active. This heightened ability to process emotions is evident in trained soldiers (Clark et al., 2008).

Consequently, when faced with the task of detecting stimuli that are nearly undetectable, trained soldiers are able to make use of information that most of us would miss, and they do so quickly. The hunches that result often make the difference between life and death (Gigerenzer, 2007; Carey, 2009).

RETHINK

- How might you train soldiers to make better use of their cognitive processes to respond effectively to dangerous situations?
- What relevance do the findings about soldiers' hunches and their ability to avoid danger have to other areas of life?

If the solution is less concrete or if there is no single correct solution, evaluating solutions becomes more difficult. In such instances, we must decide which solution among alternates is best. Unfortunately, we often quite inaccurately estimate the quality of our own ideas. For instance, a team of drug researchers working for a particular company may consider their remedy for an illness superior to all others, overestimating the likelihood of their success and downplaying the remedies of competing drug companies (Eizenberg & Zaslavsky, 2004).

Theoretically, if we apply appropriate heuristics and valid information to make decisions, we can make accurate choices among alternative solutions. However, as we see next, several kinds of obstacles to and biases in problem solving affect the quality of the decisions and judgments we make. (Also see the *Applying Psychology in the 21st Century* box.)

IMPEDIMENTS TO SOLUTIONS: WHY IS PROBLEM SOLVING SUCH A PROBLEM?

Consider the following problem-solving test (Duncker, 1945):

> You are given a set of tacks, candles, and matches, each in a small box, and told your goal is to place three candles at eye level on a nearby door so that wax will not drip on the floor as the candles burn (see Figure 8). How would you approach this challenge?

If you have difficulty solving the problem, you're not alone. Most people can't solve it when it's presented in the manner illustrated in the figure, in which the objects are *inside* the boxes. However, if the objects were presented *beside* the boxes, just resting on the table, chances are that you would solve the problem much more readily—which, in case you are wondering, requires tacking the boxes to the door and then placing the candles inside them (see Figure 9 on the next page).

The difficulty you probably encountered in solving this problem stems from its presentation, which misled you at the initial preparation stage. Actually, significant obstacles to problem solving can exist at each of the three major stages. Although cognitive approaches to problem solving suggest that thinking proceeds along rational, logical lines as a person confronts a problem and considers various solutions, several factors can hinder the development of creative, appropriate, and accurate solutions.

Functional Fixedness and Mental Set. The difficulty most people experience with the candle problem is caused by **functional fixedness,** the tendency to think of an object only in terms of its typical use. For instance, functional fixedness probably leads you to think of this book as something to read, instead of its potential use as a doorstop or as kindling for a fire. In the candle problem, because the objects are first presented inside the boxes, functional fixedness leads most people to see the boxes simply as containers for the objects they hold rather than as a potential part of the solution. They can't envision another function for the boxes.

Functional fixedness is an example of a broader phenomenon known as **mental set,** the tendency for old patterns of problem solving to persist. A classic experiment (Luchins, 1946) demonstrated this phenomenon. As you can see in Figure 10, the object of the task is to use the jars in each row to measure out the designated amount of liquid. (Try it yourself to get a sense of the power of mental set before moving on.)

If you have tried to solve the problem, you know that the first five rows are all solved in the same way: First fill the largest jar (B) and then from it fill the middle-size jar (A) once and the smallest jar (C) two times. What is left in B is the designated amount. (Stated as a formula, the designated amount is $B - A - 2C$.) The demonstration of mental set comes in the sixth row of the problem, a point at which you probably encountered some difficulty. If you are like most people, you tried the formula and were perplexed when it failed. Chances are, in fact, that you missed the simple (but different) solution to the problem, which involves merely subtracting C from A. Interestingly, people who were given the problem in row 6 *first* had no difficulty with it at all.

functional fixedness The tendency to think of an object only in terms of its typical use.

mental set The tendency for old patterns of problem solving to persist.

FIGURE 8 The problem here is to place three candles at eye level on a nearby door so that the wax will not drip on the floor as the candles burn—using only material in the figure. For a solution, see Figure 9.

FIGURE 9 A solution to the problem in Figure 7 involves tacking the boxes to the door and placing the candles in the boxes.

Inaccurate Evaluation of Solutions. When the United States invaded Iraq, it did so because government leaders believed that Saddam Hussein possessed weapons of mass destruction that posed a threat to the security of the Middle East. The belief proved false, and a bipartisan U.S. Senate committee later found that the belief was based on a flawed interpretation of intelligence information. According to the Senate committee, government leaders had made up their minds early on about the presence of weapons of mass destruction, and they ignored contradictory evidence and focused more on information that supported their view (U.S. Senate Select Committee on Intelligence, 2004).

Given jars with these capacities (in ounces):

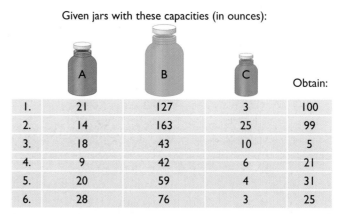

	A	B	C	Obtain:
1.	21	127	3	100
2.	14	163	25	99
3.	18	43	10	5
4.	9	42	6	21
5.	20	59	4	31
6.	28	76	3	25

FIGURE 10 Try this classic demonstration, which illustrates the importance of mental set in problem solving. The object is to use the jars in each row to measure out the designated amount of liquid. After you figure out the solution for the first five rows, you'll probably have trouble with the sixth row—even though the solution is actually easier. In fact, if you had tried to solve the problem in the sixth row first, you probably would have had no difficulty at all.

The mistake made by government leaders exemplifies **confirmation bias,** in which problem solvers favor initial hypotheses and ignore contradictory information that supports alternative hypotheses or solutions. Even when we find evidence that contradicts a solution we have chosen, we are apt to stick with our original hypothesis.

Confirmation bias occurs for several reasons. For one thing, because rethinking a problem that appears to be solved already takes extra cognitive effort, we are apt to stick with our first solution. For another, we give greater weight to subsequent information that supports our initial position than to information that is not supportive of it (Evans & Feeney, 2004; Parmley, 2007; Rassin, 2008).

confirmation bias The tendency to seek out and weight more heavily information that supports one's initial hypotheses, and to ignore contradictory information that supports alternative hypotheses or solutions.

Creativity and Problem Solving

Despite obstacles to problem solving, many people adeptly discover creative solutions to problems. One enduring question that cognitive psychologists have sought to answer is what factors underlie **creativity,** the ability to generate original ideas or solve problems in novel ways.

Although identifying the stages of problem solving helps us understand how people approach and solve problems, it does little to explain why some people come up with better solutions than others do. Even possible solutions to a simple problem often show wide discrepancies. Consider, for example, your response to the question "How many uses can you think of for a newspaper?"

Now compare your solutions with this list proposed by a 10-year-old boy:

creativity The ability to generate original ideas or solve problems in novel ways.

> You can read it, write on it, lay it down and paint a picture on it. . . . You could put it in your door for decoration, put it in the garbage can, put it on a chair if the chair is messy. If you have a puppy, you put newspaper in its box or put it in your backyard for the dog to play with. When you build something and you don't want anyone to see it, put newspaper around it. Put newspaper on the floor if you have no mattress, use it to pick up something hot, use it to stop bleeding, or to catch the drips from drying clothes. You can use a newspaper for curtains, put it in your shoe to cover what is hurting your foot, make a kite out of it, shade a light that is too bright. You can wrap fish in it, wipe windows, or wrap money in it. . . . You put washed shoes in newspaper, wipe eyeglasses with it, put it under a dripping sink, put a plant on it, make a paper bowl out of it, use it for a hat if it is raining, tie it on your feet for slippers. You can put it on the sand if you had no towel, use it for bases in baseball, make paper airplanes with it, use it as a dustpan when you sweep, ball it up for the cat to play with, wrap your hands in it if it is cold. (Ward, Kogan, & Pankove, 1972)

"I'll be happy to give you innovative thinking. What are the guidelines?"

© Leo Cullum/The New Yorker Collection/www. cartoonbank.com.

This list shows extraordinary creativity. Unfortunately, it's much easier to identify *examples* of creativity than to determine its causes. Similarly, it's not clear that the kind of creativity shown by highly creative people in the arts, such as Pablo Picasso, is the same kind of creativity shown by highly creative people like Albert Einstein in the sciences (Simonton, 2009).

However, we do know that several characteristics are associated with creativity. For one thing, highly creative individuals show **divergent thinking,** the ability to generate unusual, yet appropriate, responses to problems or questions. This type of thinking contrasts with **convergent thinking,** which produces responses that are based primarily on knowledge and logic. For instance, someone relying on convergent thinking would answer "You can read it" to the query "What can you do with a newspaper?" In contrast, "You can use it as a dustpan" is a more divergent—and creative—response (Runco, 2006; Cropley, 2006; Schepers & van den Berg, 2007).

divergent thinking The ability to generate unusual, yet nonetheless appropriate, responses to problems or questions.

convergent thinking The ability to produce responses that are based primarily on knowledge and logic.

Pablo Picasso is considered one of the greatest artists of the 20th century. Do you think he relied more on convergent or divergent thinking in his art?

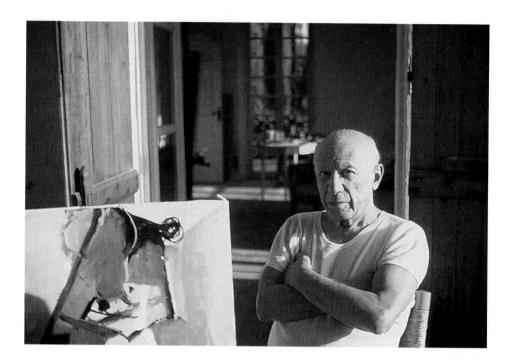

Another aspect of creativity is its *cognitive complexity*, or preference for elaborate, intricate, and complex stimuli and thinking patterns. For instance, creative people often have a wider range of interests and are more independent and more interested in philosophical or abstract problems than are less creative individuals (Barron, 1990; Richards, 2006).

One factor that is *not* closely related to creativity is intelligence. Traditional intelligence tests—which ask focused questions that have only one acceptable answer—test convergent thinking skills. Highly creative people may therefore find that traditional tests penalize their divergent thinking. This may explain why researchers consistently find that creativity is only slightly related to school grades and intelligence when intelligence is measured using traditional intelligence tests (Sternberg & O'Hara, 2000; Heilman, 2005).

Study Alert

Remember *divergent* thinking produces *different* and *diverse* kinds of responses, while *convergent* thinking produces more *commonsense* kinds of responses.

BECOMING AN INFORMED CONSUMER

of Psychology

Thinking Critically and Creatively

Can we learn to be better thinkers?

Cognitive researchers have found that people can learn the abstract rules of logic and reasoning and that such knowledge can improve our reasoning about the underlying causes of everyday events in our lives. Research suggests that critical and creative thinkers are made, not born. Consider, for instance, these suggestions for increasing critical thinking and creativity (Burbach, Matkin, & Fritz, 2004; Kaufman & Baer, 2006):

- *Redefine problems.* We can modify boundaries and assumptions by rephrasing a problem at either a more abstract or a more concrete level.
- *Use subgoals.* By developing subgoals, we can divide a problem into intermediate steps. This process, known as *fractionation*, allows us to examine each part for new possibilities and approaches, leading to a novel solution for the problem as a whole.
- *Adopt a critical perspective.* Rather than passively accepting assumptions or arguments, we can evaluate material critically, consider its implications, and think about possible exceptions and contradictions.
- *Consider the opposite.* By considering the opposite of a concept we're seeking to understand, we can sometimes make progress. For example, to define "good mental health," it may be useful to consider what "bad mental health" means.

- *Use analogies.* Analogies provide alternative frameworks for the interpretation of facts and help us uncover new understanding. One particularly effective means of coming up with analogies is to look for examples in the animal world. For instance, architects discovered how to construct the earliest sky-scrapers by noting how lily pads on a pond could support the weight of a person (Getner & Holyoak, 1997; Bearman, Ball, & Omerod, 2007; Cho, Holy-oak, & Cannon, 2007).

- *Think divergently.* Instead of the most logical or common use for an object, consider how you might use the object if you were forbidden to use it in the usual way.

- *Use heuristics.* Heuristics are cognitive shortcuts that can help bring about a solution to a problem. If the problem has a single correct answer and you can use or construct a heuristic, you can often find the solution more rapidly and effectively.

- *Experiment with various solutions.* Don't be afraid to use different routes to find solutions for problems (verbal, mathematical, graphic, even dramatic). For instance, try to come up with every conceivable idea you can, no matter how wild or bizarre it may seem at first. After you've come up with a list of solutions, review each one and try to think of ways to make what at first appeared imprac-tical seem more feasible.

RECAP/EVALUATE/RETHINK

RECAP

What is thinking?

- Cognitive psychology encompasses the higher mental processes, including the way people know and under-stand the world, process information, make decisions and judgments, and describe their knowledge and understanding to others. (p. 233)

- Thinking is the manipulation of mental representations of information. Thinking transforms such representa-tions into novel and different forms, permitting people to answer questions, solve problems, and reach goals. (p. 233)

- Mental images are representations in the mind of an object or event. (p. 233)

- Concepts are categorizations of objects, events, or people that share common properties. Prototypes are the most representative examples of concepts. (p. 234)

What processes underlie reasoning and decision making?

- Decisions sometimes (but not always) may be improved through the use of algorithms and heuristics. An algo-rithm is a rule that, if applied appropriately, guarantees a solution; a heuristic is a cognitive shortcut that may lead to a solution but is not guaranteed to do so. (p. 235)

How do people approach and solve problems?

- Problem solving typically involves three major stages: preparation, production of solutions, and evaluation of solutions that have been generated. (p. 236)

- In the preparation stage, how the problem is framed determines the kind of solution we choose. (p. 236)

- Preparation involves placing the problem in one of three categories. In arrangement problems, a group of elements must be rearranged or recombined in a way that will sat-isfy a certain criterion. In problems of inducing structure, a person first must identify the existing relationships among the elements presented and then construct a new relationship among them. Finally, transformation prob-lems consist of an initial state, a goal state, and a method for changing the initial state into the goal state. (p. 236)

- In the production stage, people try to generate solutions. They may find solutions to some problems in long-term memory. Alternatively, they may solve some problems through simple trial and error and use algorithms and heuristics to solve more complex problems. (p. 239)

- Using the heuristic of a means-ends analysis, a person will repeatedly test for differences between the desired outcome and what currently exists, trying each time to come closer to the goal. (p. 240)

- Köhler's research with chimpanzees illustrates insight, a sudden awareness of the relationships among elements that had previously seemed unrelated. (p. 241)

What are the major obstacles to problem solving?

- Several factors hinder effective problem solving. Mental set, of which functional fixedness is an example, is the tendency for old patterns of problem solving to persist. Inappropriate use of algorithms and heuristics can also act as an obstacle to the production of solutions. Confirmation bias, in which initial hypotheses are favored, can hinder the accurate evaluation of solutions to problems. (p. 242)
- Creativity is an ability to combine responses or ideas in novel ways. Creativity is related to divergent thinking (the ability to generate unusual, but still appropriate, responses to problems or questions) and cognitive complexity. (p. 245)

EVALUATE

1. _____ _____ are representations in the mind of an object or event.
2. _____ are categorizations of objects that share common properties.

3. Solving a problem by trying to reduce the difference between the current state and the goal state is known as a _____.
4. _____ is the term used to describe the sudden "flash" of revelation that often accompanies the solution to a problem.
5. Thinking of an object only in terms of its typical use is known as _____ _____. A broader, related tendency for old problem-solving patterns to persist is known as a _____ _____.
6. Generating unusual but appropriate approaches to a question is known as _____ _____.

RETHINK

1. How might the availability heuristic contribute to prejudices based on race, age, and gender? Can awareness of this heuristic prevent this from happening?
2. *From the perspective of a manufacturer:* How might you encourage your employees to develop creative ways to improve the products that you produce?

Answers to Evaluate Questions

1. mental images; 2. concepts; 3. means-end analysis; 4. insight; 5. functional fixedness, mental set; 6. divergent thinking

KEY TERMS

cognitive psychology p. 232
thinking p. 233
mental images p. 233
concepts p. 234

prototypes p. 234
algorithm p. 235
heuristic p. 235
means-ends analysis p. 240

insight p. 241
functional fixedness p. 243
mental set p. 243
confirmation bias p. 245

creativity p. 245
divergent thinking p. 245
convergent thinking p. 245

Language

> 'Twas brillig, and the slithy toves
> Did gyre and gimble in the wabe:
> All mimsy were the borogoves,
> And the mome raths outgrabe.

Key Concepts

How do people use language?

How does language develop?

Although few of us have ever come face to face with a tove, we have little difficulty in discerning that in Lewis Carroll's (1872) poem "Jabberwocky," the expression *slithy toves* contains an adjective, *slithy*, and the noun it modifies, *toves*.

Our ability to make sense out of nonsense, if the nonsense follows typical rules of language, illustrates the complexity of both human language and the cognitive processes that underlie its development and use. The use of **language**—the communication of information through symbols arranged according to systematic rules—is a central cognitive ability, one that is indispensable for us to communicate with one another. Not only is language central to communication, it is also closely tied to the very way in which we think about and understand the world. Without language, our ability to transmit information, acquire knowledge, and cooperate with others would be tremendously hindered. No wonder psychologists have devoted considerable attention to studying language (Stapel & Semin, 2007; Hoff, 2008; Resiberg, 2009).

language The communication of information through symbols arranged according to systematic rules.

Grammar: Language's Language

To understand how language develops and relates to thought, we first need to review some of the formal elements of language. The basic structure of language rests on **grammar,** the system of rules that determine how our thoughts can be expressed.

Grammar deals with three major components of language: phonology, syntax, and semantics. **Phonology** is the study of the smallest basic units of speech that affect meaning, called **phonemes,** and of the way we use those sounds to form words and produce meaning. For instance, the *a* sound in *fat* and the *a* sound in *fate* represent two different phonemes in English (Hardison, 2006).

Linguists have identified more than 800 different phonemes among all the world's languages. Although English speakers use just 52 phonemes to produce words, other languages use from as few as 15 to as many as 141. Differences in phonemes are one reason people have difficulty learning other languages. For example, to a Japanese speaker, whose native language does not have an *r* phoneme, pronouncing such English words as *roar* present some difficulty (Gibbs, 2002; Iverson et al., 2003).

Syntax refers to the rules that indicate how words and phrases can be combined to form sentences. Every language has intricate rules that guide the order in which words must be strung together to communicate meaning. English speakers have no difficulty recognizing that "TV down the turn" is not a meaningful sequence, whereas "Turn down the TV" is. To understand the effect of syntax in English, consider the changes in meaning caused by the different word orders in the following three utterances: "John kidnapped the boy," "John, the kidnapped boy," and "The boy kidnapped John" (Eberhard, Cutting, & Bock, 2005; Robert, 2006).

grammar The system of rules that determine how our thoughts can be expressed.

phonology The study of the smallest units of speech, called phonemes.

phonemes The smallest units of speech.

syntax Ways in which words and phrases can be combined to form sentences.

semantics The rules governing the meaning of words and sentences.

The third major component of language is **semantics,** the meanings of words and sentences. Semantic rules allow us to use words to convey the subtle nuances in meaning. For instance, we are able to make the distinction between "The truck hit Laura"—which we might say if we had just seen a truck crashing into Laura—versus "Laura was hit by a truck"—which we might say to explain why Laura didn't show up for a party (Richgels, 2004; Pietarinen, 2006).

Despite the complexities of language, most of us acquire the basics of grammar without even being aware that we have learned its rules. Moreover, even though we may have difficulty explicitly stating the rules of grammar, our linguistic abilities are so sophisticated that we can utter an infinite number of different statements. How do we acquire such abilities?

Language Development: Developing a Way with Words

To parents, the sounds of their infant babbling and cooing are music to their ears (except, perhaps, at 3 o'clock in the morning). These sounds also serve an important function. They mark the first step on the road to the development of language.

BABBLING

babble Meaningless speechlike sounds made by children from around the age of 3 months through 1 year.

Children **babble**—make speechlike but meaningless sounds—from around the age of 3 months through 1 year. While babbling, they may produce, at one time or another, any of the sounds found in all languages, not just the one to which they are exposed. Even deaf children display their own form of babbling, for infants who are unable to hear, yet who are exposed to sign language from birth, "babble" with their hands (Pettito, 1993; Locke, 2006).

An infant's babbling increasingly reflects the specific language being spoken in the infant's environment, initially in terms of pitch and tone and eventually in terms of specific sounds. Young infants can distinguish among all 869 phonemes that have been identified across the world's languages. However, after the age of 6 to 8 months, that ability begins to decline. Infants begin to "specialize" in the language to which they are exposed as neurons in their brains reorganize to respond to the particular phonemes infants routinely hear.

Some theorists argue that a *critical period* exists for language development early in life, during which a child is particularly sensitive to language cues and most easily acquires language. In fact, if children are not exposed to language during this critical period, later they will have great difficulty overcoming this deficit (Bates, 2005; Shafer & Garrido-Nag, 2007). Cases in which abused children have been isolated from contact with others support the theory of such critical periods. In one case, for example, a girl named Genie was exposed to virtually no language from the age of 20 months until she was rescued at age 13. She was unable to speak at all. Despite intensive instruction, she learned only some words and was never able to master the complexities of language (Rymer, 1994; Veltman & Browne, 2001).

A syllable in signed language, similar to the ones seen in the manual babbling of deaf infants and in the spoken babbling of hearing infants. The similarities in language structure suggest that language has biological roots.

PRODUCTION OF LANGUAGE

By the time children are approximately 1 year old, they stop producing sounds that are not in the language to which they've been exposed. It's then a short step to the production of actual words. In English, these are typically short words that start with a consonant sound such as *b, d, m, p,* and *t*—this helps explain why *mama* and *dada* are so often among babies' first words. Of course, even before they produce their first words, children can understand a fair amount of the language they hear. Language comprehension precedes language production.

After the age of 1, children begin to learn more complicated forms of language. They produce two-word combinations, the building blocks of sentences, and sharply increase the number of different words they are able to use. By age 2, the average child has a vocabulary of more than 50 words. Just 6 months later, that vocabulary has grown to several hundred words. At that time, children can produce short sentences, although they use **telegraphic speech**—sentences that sound as if they were part of a telegram, in which words not critical to the message are left out. Rather than saying, "I showed you the book," a child using telegraphic speech may say, "I show book," and "I am drawing a dog" may become "Drawing dog." As children get older, of course, they use less telegraphic speech and produce increasingly complex sentences (Volterra et al., 2003).

By age 3, children learn to make plurals by adding *s* to nouns and to form the past tense by adding *-ed* to verbs. This skill also leads to errors, since children tend to apply rules inflexibly. In such **overgeneralization,** children employ rules even when doing so results in an error. Thus, although it is correct to say "he walked" for the past tense of *walk*, the *-ed* rule doesn't work quite so well when children say "he runned" for the past tense of *run* (Howe, 2002; Rice et al., 2004; Gershkoff-Stowe, Connell, & Smith, 2006; Kidd & Lum, 2008).

By age 5, children have acquired the basic rules of language. However, they do not attain a full vocabulary and the ability to comprehend and use subtle grammatical rules until later. For example, a 5-year-old boy who sees a blindfolded doll and is asked, "Is the doll easy or hard to see?" would have great trouble answering the question. In fact, if he were asked to make the doll easier to see, he would probably try to remove the doll's blindfold. By the time they are 8 years old, however, children have little difficulty understanding this question, because they realize that the doll's blindfold has nothing to do with an observer's ability to see the doll (Chomsky, 1969; Hoff, 2003).

telegraphic speech Sentences in which words not critical to the message are left out.

overgeneralization The phenomenon by which children apply language rules even when the application results in an error.

Understanding Language Acquisition: Identifying the Roots of Language

Anyone who spends even a little time with children will notice the enormous strides that they make in language development throughout childhood. However, the reasons for this rapid growth are far from obvious. Psychologists have offered two major explanations, one based on learning theory and the other based on innate processes.

LEARNING-THEORY APPROACHES: LANGUAGE AS A LEARNED SKILL

The **learning-theory approach** suggests that language acquisition follows the principles of reinforcement and conditioning discovered by psychologists who study learning. For example, a child who says "mama" receives hugs and praise from her mother, which reinforce the behavior of saying "mama" and make its repetition more likely. This view suggests that children first learn to speak by being rewarded for making sounds that approximate speech. Ultimately, through a process of shaping, language becomes more and more like adult speech (Skinner, 1957; Ornat & Gallo, 2004).

In support of the learning-theory approach to language acquisition, the more that parents speak to their young children, the more proficient the children become in language use. In addition, by the time they are 3 years old, children who hear higher levels of linguistic sophistication in their parents' speech show a greater rate of vocabulary growth, vocabulary use, and even general intellectual achievement than do children whose parents' speech is more simple (Hart & Risley, 1997).

learning-theory approach (to language development) The theory suggesting that language acquisition follows the principles of reinforcement and conditioning.

Noam Chomsky argues that all languages share a universal grammar.

The learning-theory approach is less successful in explaining how children acquire language rules. Children are reinforced not only when they use language correctly, but also when they use it incorrectly. For example, parents answer a child's "Why the dog won't eat?" as readily as they do the correctly phrased question, "Why won't the dog eat?" Listeners understand both sentences equally well. Learning theory, then, has difficulty fully explaining language acquisition.

NATIVIST APPROACHES: LANGUAGE AS AN INNATE SKILL

Pointing to such problems with learning-theory approaches to language acquisition, linguist Noam Chomsky (1968, 1978, 1991) provided a groundbreaking alternative. Chomsky argued that humans are born with an innate linguistic capability that emerges primarily as a function of maturation. According to his **nativist approach** to language, all the world's languages share a common underlying structure called a **universal grammar.** Chomsky suggested that the human brain has a neural system, the **language-acquisition device,** that not only lets us understand the structure language provides but also gives us strategies and techniques for learning the unique characteristics of our native language (McGilvray, 2004; Lidz & Gleitman, 2004; White, 2007).

Chomsky used the concept of the language-acquisition device as a metaphor, and he did not identify a specific area of the brain in which it resides. However, evidence collected by neuroscientists suggests that the ability to use language, which was a significant evolutionary advance in human beings, is tied to specific neurological developments (Sakai, 2005; Sahin, Pinker, & Halgren, 2007; Willems & Hagoort, 2007).

For example, scientists have discovered a gene related to the development of language abilities that may have emerged as recently—in evolutionary terms—as 100,000 years ago. Furthermore, it is clear that there are specific sites within the brain that are closely tied to language, and that the shape of the human mouth and throat are tailored to the production of speech. And there is evidence that features of specific types of languages are tied to particular genes, such as in "tonal" languages in which pitch is used to convey meaning (Hauser, Chomsky, & Fitch, 2002; Chandra, 2007; Dediu & Ladd, 2007; Gontier, 2008; Grigorenko, 2009).

Still, Chomsky's view has its critics. For instance, learning theorists contend that the apparent ability of certain animals, such as chimpanzees, to learn the fundamentals of human language contradicts the innate linguistic capability view.

nativist approach (to language development) The theory that a genetically determined, innate mechanism directs language development.

universal grammar Noam Chomsky's theory that all the world's languages share a common underlying structure.

language-acquisition device A neural system of the brain hypothesized by Noam Chomsky to permit understanding of language.

INTERACTIONIST APPROACHES

To reconcile the differing views, many theorists take an **interactionist approach** to language development. The interactionist approach suggests that language development is produced through a combination of genetically determined predispositions and environmental circumstances that help teach language.

Specifically, proponents of the interactionist approach suggest that the brain's hardwired language-acquisition device that Chomsky and geneticists point to provides the hardware for our acquisition of language, whereas the exposure to language in our environment that learning theorists observe allows us to develop the appropriate software. But the issue of how language is acquired remains hotly contested (Pinker & Jackendoff, 2005; Hoff, 2008; Waxman, 2009).

The Influence of Language on Thinking: Do Eskimos Have More Words for Snow Than Texans Do?

Do Eskimos living in the frigid Arctic have a more expansive vocabulary for discussing snow than people living in warmer climates?

It makes sense, and arguments that the Eskimo language has many more words than English for snow have been made since the early 1900s. At that time, linguist Benjamin Lee Whorf contended that because snow is so relevant to Eskimos' lives, their language provides a particularly rich vocabulary to describe it—considerably larger than what we find in other languages such as English (Martin & Pullum, 1991; Pinker, 1994).

The contention that the Eskimo language is especially abundant in snow-related terms led to the **linguistic-relativity hypothesis,** the notion that language shapes and, in fact, may determine the way people in a specific culture perceive and understand the world. According to this view, language provides us with categories that we use to construct our view of people and events in the world around us. Consequently, language shapes and produces thought (Whorf, 1956; Casasanto, 2008; Tan et al., 2008).

Let's consider another possibility, however. Suppose that instead of language being the *cause* of certain ways of thinking, thought *produces* language. The only reason to expect that Eskimo language might have more words for snow than English does is that they think about it more. Snow is considerably more relevant to Eskimos than it is to people in other cultures.

Which view is correct? Most recent research refutes the linguistic-relativity hypothesis and suggests, instead, that thinking produces language. In fact, new analyses of the Eskimo language suggest that Eskimos have no more words for snow than English speakers, for if one examines the English language closely, one sees that it is hardly impoverished when it comes to describing snow (consider, for example, *sleet*, *slush*, *blizzard*, *dusting*, and *avalanche*).

Still, the linguistic-relativity hypothesis has not been entirely discarded. A newer version of the hypothesis suggests that speech patterns may influence certain aspects of thinking. For example, in some languages such as English, speakers distinguish between nouns that can be counted (as in "five chairs") and nouns that require a measurement unit to be quantified (as in "a liter of water"). However, in some other languages, such as the Mayan language called Yucatec, all nouns require a measurement unit. In such cultures, people appear to think more closely about what things are made of than do people in cultures where English is spoken. In contrast, English

---

interactionist approach (to language development) The view that language development is produced through a combination of genetically determined predispositions and environmental circumstances that help teach language.

 Study Alert

It's important to be able to compare and contrast the major approaches to language development: learning theory, nativist, and interactionist approaches.

linguistic-relativity hypothesis The notion that language shapes and may determine the way people in a particular culture perceive and understand the world.

 Study Alert

The *l*inguistic-relativity hypothesis suggests *l*anguage *l*eads to thought.

"He's pretty good at rote categorization and single-object relational tasks but he's not so hot at differentiating between representational and associational signs, and he's very weak on syntax."

speakers focus more on the shape of objects (Gentner, Goldin, & Goldin-Meadow, 2003; Tsukasaki & Ishii, 2004).

In short, although research does not support the linguistic-relativity hypothesis that language *causes* thought, it is clear that language influences how we think. And, of course, it certainly is the case that thought influences language, suggesting that language and thinking interact in complex ways (Ross, 2004; Thorkildsen, 2006; Proudfoot, 2009).

Do Animals Use Language?

One question that has long puzzled psychologists is whether language is uniquely human or if other animals are able to acquire it as well. Many animals communicate with one another in rudimentary forms. For instance, fiddler crabs wave their claws to signal, bees dance to indicate the direction in which food will be found, and certain birds call *"zick, zick"* during courtship and *"kia"* when they are about to fly away. However, researchers have yet to demonstrate conclusively that these animals use true language, which is characterized in part by the ability to produce and communicate new and unique meanings by following a formal grammar.

Psychologists have, however, been able to teach chimps to communicate at surprisingly high levels. For instance, after 4 years of training, a chimp named Washoe learned to make signs for 132 words and combine those signs into simple sentences. Even more impressively, Kanzi, a pygmy chimpanzee, has linguistic skills that some psychologists claim are close to those of a 2-year-old human being. Kanzi's trainers

Sue Savage-Rumbaugh with a primate friend, Panbanisha. Does the use of sign language by primates indicate true mastery of language?

suggest that he can create grammatically sophisticated sentences and can even invent new rules of syntax (Raffaele, 2006; Savage-Rumbaugh, Toth, & Schick, 2007).

Despite the skills displayed by primates such as Kanzi, critics contend that the language such animals use still lacks the grammar and the complex and novel constructions of human language. Instead, they maintain that the chimps are displaying a skill no different from that of a dog that learns to lie down on command to get a reward. Furthermore, we lack firm evidence that animals can recognize and respond to the mental states of others of their species, an important aspect of human communication. Consequently, the issue of whether other animals can use language in a way that humans do remains controversial (Aboitiz et al., 2006; Hillix, 2007; Liszkowski et al., 2009).

Exploring DIVERSITY

Teaching with Linguistic Variety: Bilingual Education

In New York City, 1 in 6 of the city's 1.1 million students are enrolled in some form of bilingual or English as a Second Language (ESL) instruction. And New York City is far from being the only school district with a significant population of nonnative English speakers. From the biggest cities to our most rural areas, the face—and voice—of education in the United States is changing. More and more schoolchildren today have last names like Kim, Valdez, and Karachnicoff. In seven states, including Texas and Colorado, more than one-quarter of the students are not native English speakers. For some 47 million Americans, English is their second language (Holloway, 2000; see Figure 1).

How to appropriately and effectively teach the increasing number of children who do not speak English is not always clear. Many educators maintain that *bilingual education* is best. With a bilingual approach, students learn some subjects in their native language while simultaneously learning English. Proponents of bilingualism believe that students must develop a sound footing in basic subject areas and that, initially at least, teaching those subjects in their native language is the only way to provide them with that foundation. During the same period, they learn English with the eventual goal of shifting all instruction into English.

In contrast, other educators insist that all instruction ought to be in English from the moment students, including those who speak no English at all, enroll in school. In

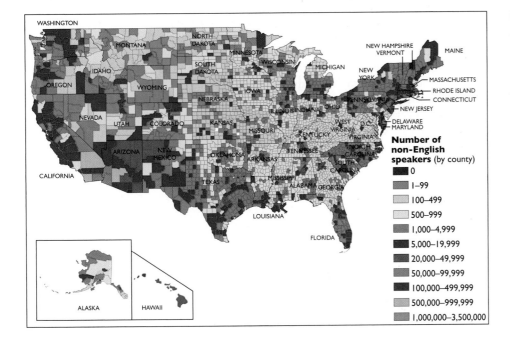

FIGURE 1 The language of diversity. Some 22% of the people in the United States speak a language other than English at home. Most of them speak Spanish; the rest speak an astounding variety of different languages. Where are the largest clusters of non-English speakers in the United States, and what do you think explains these concentrations? (Source: MLA Language Map, 2005, based on 2000 Census.)

Neuroscience in Your Life: Bilingualism and the Brain

FIGURE 2 Researchers studying bilinguals (individuals fluent in two languages) and monolinguals (individuals fluent in one language) found differences in the way in which language was processed between the two groups. For example, this fMRI scan shows that bilinguals process information differently according to whether they are speaking in only one language or are switching between languages. The results show that there may be distinct patterns of activity for each language used. (Source: Kovelman et al., 2008.)

immersion programs, students are immediately plunged into English instruction in all subjects. The reasoning—endorsed by voters in California in a referendum designed to end bilingual education—is that teaching students in a language other than English simply hinders nonnative English speakers' integration into society and ultimately does them a disservice. Proponents of English immersion programs point as evidence to improvements in standardized test scores that followed the end of bilingual education programs (Wildavsky, 2000).

Although the controversial issue of bilingual education versus immersion has strong political undercurrents, evidence shows that the ability to speak two languages provides significant cognitive benefits over speaking only one language. For example, bilingual speakers show more cognitive flexibility and may understand concepts more easily than those who speak only one language. They have more linguistic tools for thinking because of their multiple-language abilities. In turn, this makes them more creative and flexible in solving problems (Heyman & Diesendruck, 2002; Bialystok & Martin, 2004; Kuo, 2007).

Furthermore, speaking several languages changes the organization of the brain. For example, bilingual speakers who learn their second language as adults show different areas of brain activation compared with those who learn their second language in childhood. In addition, brain scans show that people who speak multiple languages have distinct patterns of brain activity according to the language that they are using (see Figure 2). (Kim et al., 1997; Kovelman, Baker, & Petitto, 2008; Kovacs & Mehler, 2009).

Related to questions about bilingual education is the matter of *biculturalism,* that is, being a member of two cultures and its psychological impact. Some psychologists argue that society should promote an *alternation model* of bicultural competence. Such a model supports members of a culture in their efforts to maintain their original cultural identity, as well as in their integration into the adopted culture. In this view, a person can belong to two cultures and have two cultural identities without having to choose between them. Whether society will adopt the alternation model remains to be seen (Carter, 2003; Benet-Martínez, Lee, & Leu, 2006; Tadmor, 2007).

RECAP/EVALUATE/RETHINK

RECAP

How do people use language?
- Language is the communication of information through symbols arranged according to systematic rules. All languages have a grammar—a system of rules that determines how thoughts can be expressed—that encompasses the three major components of language: phonology, syntax, and semantics. (p. 249)

How does language develop?
- Language production, which follows language comprehension, develops out of babbling, which then leads to the production of actual words. After age 1, children use two-word combinations, increase their vocabulary, and use telegraphic speech, which drops words not critical to the message. By age 5, acquisition of language rules is relatively complete. (p. 250)
- Learning theorists suggest that language is acquired through reinforcement and conditioning. In contrast, the nativist approach suggests that an innate language-acquisition device guides the development of language. The interactionist approach argues that language development is produced through a combination of genetically determined predispositions and environmental circumstances that help teach language. (p. 251)
- The linguistic-relativity hypothesis suggests that language shapes and may determine the way people think about the world. Most evidence suggests that although language does not determine thought, it does affect the way people store information in their memory and how well they can retrieve it. (p. 253)
- The degree to which language is a uniquely human skill remains an open question. Some psychologists contend that even though certain primates communicate at a high level, those animals do not use language; other psychologists suggest that those primates truly understand and produce language in much the same way as humans. (p. 254)
- People who speak more than one language may have a cognitive advantage over those who speak only one. (p. 256)

EVALUATE

1. Match the component of grammar with its definition:
   1. Syntax
   2. Phonology
   3. Semantics
   a. Rules showing how words can be combined into sentences
   b. Rules governing the meaning of words and sentences
   c. The study of the sound units that affect speech

2. Language production and language comprehension develop in infants at about the same time. True or false?

3. _____ _____ refers to when young children omit nonessential portions of sentences.

4. A child knows that adding *-ed* to certain words puts them in the past tense. As a result, instead of saying "He came," the child says "He comed." This is an example of _____.

5. _____ theory assumes that language acquisition is based on principles of operant conditioning and shaping.

6. In his theory of language acquisition, Chomsky argues that language acquisition is an innate ability tied to the structure of the brain. True or false?

RETHINK

1. Do people who use two languages—for example, one at home and one at school—automatically have two cultures? Why might people who speak two languages have cognitive advantages over those who speak only one?

2. *From the perspective of a child-care provider:* How would you encourage children's language abilities at the different stages of development?

Answers to Evaluate Questions

1. 1-a, 2-c, 3-b; 2. false; Language comprehension precedes language production; 3. telegraphic speech; 4. overgeneralization; 5. learning; 6. true

KEY TERMS

language p. 249
grammar p. 249
phonology p. 249
phonemes p. 249
syntax p. 249
semantics p. 250

babble p. 250
telegraphic speech p. 251
overgeneralization p. 251
learning-theory approach
    (to language
    development) p. 251

nativist approach
    (to language
    development) p. 252
universal grammar p. 252
language-acquisition
device p. 252

interactionist approach
    (to language
    development) p. 253
linguistic-relativity
    hypothesis p. 253

Intelligence

Members of the Trukese tribe in the South Pacific often sail a hundred miles in open ocean waters. Although their destination may be just a small dot of land less than a mile wide, the Trukese are able to navigate precisely toward it without the aid of a compass, chronometer, sextant, or any of the other sailing tools that are used by Western navigators. They are able to sail accurately, even when the winds do not allow a direct approach to the island and they must take a zigzag course. (Gladwin, 1964; Mytinger, 2001)

How are the Trukese able to navigate so effectively? If you asked them, they couldn't explain it. They might tell you that they use a process that takes into account the rising and setting of the stars and the appearance, sound, and feel of the waves against the side of the boat. But at any given moment as they are sailing along, they could not identify their position or say why they are doing what they are doing. Nor could they explain the navigational theory underlying their sailing technique.

Some people might say that the inability of the Trukese to explain in Western terms how their sailing technique works is a sign of primitive or even unintelligent behavior. In fact, if we gave Trukese sailors a Western standardized test of navigational knowledge and theory or, for that matter, a traditional test of intelligence, they might do poorly on it. Yet, as a practical matter, it isn't possible to accuse the Trukese of being unintelligent: Despite their inability to explain how they do it, they are able to navigate successfully on the open ocean.

Trukese navigation points out the difficulty in coming to grips with what is meant by intelligence. To a Westerner, traveling in a straight line along the most direct and quickest route by using a sextant and other navigational tools is likely to represent the most "intelligent" kind of behavior; in contrast, a zigzag course, based on the "feel" of the waves, would not seem very reasonable. To the Trukese, who are used to their own system of navigation, however, the use of complicated navigational tools might seem so overly complex and unnecessary that they might think of Western navigators as lacking intelligence.

It's clear from this example that the term *intelligence* can have many different meanings. If, for instance, you lived in a remote part of the Australian outback, the way you would differentiate between more intelligent and less intelligent people might have to do with successfully mastering hunting skills, whereas to someone living in the heart of urban Miami, intelligence might be exemplified by being "streetwise" or by achieving success in business.

Each of these views of intelligence is reasonable. Each represents an instance in which more intelligent people are better able to use the resources of their environment than are less intelligent people, a distinction that is presumably basic to any definition of intelligence. Yet it is also clear that these views represent very different views of intelligence.

That two such different sets of behavior can exemplify the same psychological concept has long posed a challenge

Key Concepts

What are the different definitions and conceptions of intelligence?

What are the major approaches to measuring intelligence, and what do intelligence tests measure?

How are the extremes of intelligence characterized?

Are traditional IQ tests culturally biased?

To what degree is intelligence influenced by the environment, and to what degree by heredity?

What does the Trukese people's method of navigation—which is done without maps or instruments—tell us about the nature of intelligence?

to psychologists. For years they have grappled with the issue of devising a general definition of intelligence. Ironically, laypersons have fairly clear ideas of what intelligence is, although the nature of their ideas is related to their culture. Westerners view intelligence as the ability to establish categories and debate rationally. In contrast, people in Eastern cultures and some African communities view intelligence more in terms of understanding and relating to one another (Nisbett, 2003; Brislin, Worthley, & MacNab, 2006; Sternberg, 2005, 2007).

The definition of intelligence that psychologists employ contains some of the same elements found in the layperson's conception. To psychologists, **intelligence** is the capacity to understand the world, think rationally, and use resources effectively when faced with challenges.

This definition does not lay to rest a key question asked by psychologists: Is intelligence a unitary attribute, or are there different kinds of intelligence? We turn now to various theories of intelligence that address the issue.

intelligence The capacity to understand the world, think rationally, and use resources effectively when faced with challenges.

Theories of Intelligence: Are There Different Kinds of Intelligence?

Perhaps you see yourself as a good writer but as someone who lacks ability in math. Or maybe you're a "science" person who easily masters physics but has few strengths in interpreting literature. Perhaps you view yourself as fairly smart in general, with intelligence that permits you to excel across several domains.

The different ways people view their own talents mirror a question that psychologists have grappled with: Is intelligence a single, general ability, or is it multifaceted and related to specific abilities? Early psychologists interested in intelligence assumed that there was a single, general factor for mental ability that they called g, or the **g-factor.** This assumption was based on the fact that different measures of intelligence, whether they focused on, say, mathematical expertise, verbal competency, or spatial visualization skills, all ranked test-takers in roughly the same order. People who were good on one test generally were good on others; those who did poorly on one test tended to do poorly on others.

Given that there was a correlation between performance on the different types of tests, the assumption was that there was a general, global intellectual ability underlying performance on the various measures—the g-factor. This general intelligence factor was thought to underlie performance in every aspect of intelligence, and it was the g-factor that was presumably being measured on tests of intelligence (Spearman, 1927; Colom, Jung, & Haier, 2006; Haier et al., 2009).

More recent theories explain intelligence in a different light. Rather than viewing intelligence as a unitary ability, some psychologists consider it to be a multidimensional concept that includes different types of intelligence (Tenopyr, 2002; Stankov, 2003; Sternberg & Pretz, 2005).

g or g-factor The single, general factor for mental ability assumed to underlie intelligence in some early theories of intelligence.

fluid intelligence Intelligence that reflects information-processing capabilities, reasoning, and memory.

Piloting a helicopter requires the use of both fluid intelligence and crystallized intelligence. Which of the two kinds of intelligence do you believe is more important for such a task?

FLUID AND CRYSTALLIZED INTELLIGENCE

Some psychologists suggest that there are two different kinds of intelligence: fluid intelligence and crystallized intelligence. **Fluid intelligence** reflects information-processing capabilities, reasoning, and memory. Fluid intelligence encompasses the ability to reason abstractly. If we were asked to solve an analogy, group a series of letters according to some criterion, or remember a set of numbers, we would be using fluid intelligence. We use fluid intelligence when we're trying to rapidly solve a puzzle (Kane & Engle, 2002; Saggino et al., 2006; Di Fabio & Palazzeschi, 2009).

In contrast, **crystallized intelligence** is the accumulation of information, skills, and strategies that people have learned through experience and that they can apply in problem-solving situations. It reflects our ability to call up information from long-term memory. We would be likely to rely on crystallized intelligence for instance, if we were asked to participate in a discussion about the solution to the causes of poverty, a task that allows us to draw on our own past experiences and knowledge of the world. In contrast to fluid intelligence, which reflects a more general kind of intelligence, crystallized intelligence is more a reflection of the culture in which a person is raised. The differences between fluid intelligence and crystallized intelligence become especially evident in late adulthood, when people show declines in fluid, but not crystallized, intelligence (Aartsen, Martin, & Zimprich, 2002; Buehner et al., 2006; Tranter & Koutstaal, 2008).

crystallized intelligence The accumulation of information, skills, and strategies that are learned through experience and can be applied in problem-solving situations.

GARDNER'S MULTIPLE INTELLIGENCES: THE MANY WAYS OF SHOWING INTELLIGENCE

Psychologist Howard Gardner differs from traditional thinking about intelligence. Gardner argues that rather than asking, "How smart are you?" we should be asking a different question: "How are you smart?" To answer the latter question, Gardner has developed a **theory of multiple intelligences** that has become quite influential (Gardner, 2000).

Gardner argues that we have at a minimum eight different forms of intelligence, each relatively independent of the others: musical, bodily kinesthetic, logical-mathematical, linguistic, spatial, interpersonal, intrapersonal, and naturalist. (Figure 1 describes the eight types of intelligence with some of Gardner's examples of people who excel in each type.) In Gardner's view, each of the multiple intelligences is linked to an independent system in the brain. Furthermore, he suggests that there may be even more types of intelligence, such as *existential intelligence,* which involves identifying and thinking about the fundamental questions of human existence. For example, the Dalai Lama might exemplify this type of intelligence (Gardner, 1999, 2000).

Although Gardner illustrates his concept of the specific types of intelligence with descriptions of well-known people, each person has the same eight kinds of intelligence—to different degrees. Moreover, although the eight basic types of intelligence are presented individually, Gardner suggests that these separate intelligences do not operate in isolation. Any normal activity encompasses several kinds of intelligence working together.

theory of multiple intelligences Gardner's intelligence theory proposing that there are eight distinct spheres of intelligence.

Study Alert

Remember that Gardner's theory suggests that each individual has every kind of intelligence, but in different degrees.

The concept of multiple intelligences has led to the development of intelligence tests that include questions for which more than one answer can be correct; these provide an opportunity for test-takers to demonstrate creative thinking. In addition, many educators who've embraced the concept of multiple intelligences have designed classroom curricula that are meant to draw on different aspects of intelligence (Kelly & Tangney, 2006; Douglas, Burton, & Reese-Durham, 2008; Tirri & Nokelainen, 2008).

INFORMATION PROCESSING AS INTELLIGENCE

One of the newer contributions to understanding intelligence comes from the work of cognitive psychologists who take an *information-processing approach.* They assert that the

"To be perfectly frank, I'm not nearly as smart as you seem to think I am."

1. Musical intelligence (skills in tasks involving music). Case example:

When he was 3, Yehudi Menuhin was smuggled into San Francisco Orchestra concerts by his parents. By the time he was 10 years old, Menuhin was an international performer.

2. Bodily kinesthetic intelligence (skills in using the whole body or various portions of it in the solution of problems or in the construction of products or displays, exemplified by dancers, athletes, actors, and surgeons). Case example:

Fifteen-year-old Babe Ruth played third base. During one game, his team's pitcher was doing very poorly and Babe loudly criticized him from third base. Brother Matthias, the coach, called out, "Ruth, if you know so much about it, *you* pitch!" Ruth said later that at the very moment he took the pitcher's mound, he *knew* he was supposed to be a pitcher.

3. Logical-mathematical intelligence (skills in problem solving and scientific thinking). Case example:

Barbara McClintock, who won the Nobel Prize in medicine, describes one of her breakthroughs, which came after thinking about a problem for half an hour . . . : "Suddenly I jumped and ran back to the (corn) field. At the top of the field (the others were still at the bottom) I shouted, 'Eureka, I have it!'"

4. Linguistic intelligence (skills involved in the production and use of language). Case example:

At the age of 10, T. S. Eliot created a magazine called *Fireside*, to which he was the sole contributor.

5. Spatial intelligence (skills involving spatial configurations, such as those used by artists and architects). Case example:

Natives of the Truk Islands navigate at sea without instruments. During the actual trip, the navigator must envision mentally a reference island as it passes under a particular star and from that he computes the number of segments completed, the proportion of the trip remaining, and any corrections in heading.

6. Interpersonal intelligence (skills in interacting with others, such as sensitivity to the moods, temperaments, motivations, and intentions of others). Case example:

When Anne Sullivan began instructing the deaf and blind Helen Keller, her task was one that had eluded others for years. Yet, just two weeks after beginning her work with Keller, Sullivan achieved great success.

7. Intrapersonal intelligence (knowledge of the internal aspects of oneself; access to one's own feelings and emotions). Case example:

In her essay "A Sketch of the Past," Virginia Woolf displays deep insight into her own inner life through these lines, describing her reaction to several specific memories from her childhood that still, in adulthood, shock her: "Though I still have the peculiarity that I receive these sudden shocks, they are now always welcome; after the first surprise, I always feel instantly that they are particularly valuable. And so I go on to suppose that the shock-receiving capacity is what makes me a writer."

8. Naturalist intelligence (ability to identify and classify patterns in nature). Case example:

During prehistoric times, hunter/gatherers would rely on naturalist intelligence to identify what flora and fauna were edible. People who are adept at distinguishing nuances between large numbers of similar objects may be expressing naturalist intelligence abilities.

FIGURE 1 Howard Gardner believes that there are eight major types of intelligences, corresponding to abilities in different domains. In what area does your greatest intelligence reside, and why do you think you have particular strengths in that area? (Source: Adapted from Gardner, 2000.)

way people store information in memory and use that information to solve intellectual tasks provides the most accurate measure of intelligence. Consequently, rather than focusing on the structure of intelligence or its underlying content or dimensions, information-processing approaches examine the *processes* involved in producing intelligent behavior (Hunt, 2005; Neubauer & Fink, 2005; Pressley & Harris, 2006).

For example, research shows that people with high scores on intelligence tests spend more time on the initial encoding stages of the problems, identifying the parts of a problem and retrieving relevant information from long-term memory, than do people with lower scores. This initial emphasis on recalling relevant information pays off in the end; those who use this approach are more successful in finding solutions than are those who spend relatively less time on the initial stages (Sternberg, 1990; Deary & Der, 2005; Hunt, 2005).

Other information-processing approaches examine the sheer speed of processing. For example, research shows that the speed with which people are able to retrieve information from memory is related to verbal intelligence. In general, people with high scores on measures of intelligence react more quickly on a variety of information-processing tasks ranging from reactions to flashing lights to distinguishing between letters. The speed of information processing, then, may underlie differences in intelligence (Jensen, 2005; Gontkovsky & Beatty, 2006; Helmbold, Troche, & Rammsayer, 2007; Sheppard & Vernon, 2008).

PRACTICAL INTELLIGENCE AND EMOTIONAL INTELLIGENCE

Consider the following situation:

> An employee who reports to one of your subordinates has asked to talk with you about waste, poor management practices, and possible violations of both company policy and the law on the part of your subordinate. You have been in your present position only a year, but in that time you have had no indications of trouble about the subordinate in question. Neither you nor your company has an "open door" policy, so it is expected that employees should take their concerns to their immediate supervisors before bringing a matter to the attention of anyone else. The employee who wishes to meet with you has not discussed this matter with her supervisors because of its delicate nature (Sternberg, 1998, p. 17).

Your response to this situation has a lot to do with your future success in a business career, according to psychologist Robert Sternberg. The question is one of a series designed to help give an indication of your intelligence. However, it is not traditional intelligence that the question is designed to tap, but rather intelligence of a specific kind: practical intelligence. **Practical intelligence** is intelligence related to overall success in living (Sternberg, 2000, 2002; Sternberg & Hedlund, 2002; Wagner, 2002; Muammar, 2007).

Noting that traditional tests pertain to academic success, Sternberg points to evidence showing that most traditional measures of intelligence do not relate especially well to *career* success (McClelland, 1993). Specifically, although successful business executives usually score at least moderately well on intelligence tests, the rate at which they advance and their ultimate business achievements are only minimally associated with traditional measures of their intelligence.

Sternberg argues that career success requires a very different type of intelligence from that required for academic success. Whereas academic success is based on knowledge of a specific information base obtained from reading and listening, practical intelligence is learned mainly through observation of others' behavior. People who are high in practical intelligence are able to learn general norms and principles and apply them appropriately. Consequently, practical intelligence tests, like the one shown in Figure 2, measure an ability to employ broad principles in solving everyday problems (Sternberg & Pretz, 2005; Stemler & Sternberg, 2006; Stemler et al., 2009).

practical intelligence According to Sternberg, intelligence related to overall success in living.

FIGURE 2 Most standard tests of intelligence primarily measure analytical skills; more comprehensive tests measure creative and practical abilities as well. (Source: From Sternberg, R. J. (2000). The Holy Grail of general intelligence. *Science, 289,* no. 5478, 399-401. Reprinted with permission from AAAS.)

You are given a map of an entertainment park. You walk from the lemonade stand to the computer games arcade. Your friend walks from the shooting gallery to the roller coaster. Which of these are you BOTH most likely to pass? (a) the merry-go-round, (b) the music hall, (c) the pizza stand, or (d) the dog show.

In addition to practical intelligence, Sternberg argues there are two other basic, interrelated types of intelligence related to life success: analytical and creative. Analytical intelligence focuses on abstract but traditional types of problems measured on IQ tests, and creative intelligence involves the generation of novel ideas and products (Benderly, 2004; Sternberg et al., 2004; Sternberg et al., 2005).

Some psychologists broaden the concept of intelligence even further beyond the intellectual realm to include emotions. **Emotional intelligence** is the set of skills that underlie the accurate assessment, evaluation, expression, and regulation of emotions (Mayer, Salovey, & Caruso, 2004; Humphrey et al., 2007; Mayer, Salovey, & Caruso, 2008).

Emotional intelligence is the basis of empathy for others, self-awareness, and social skills. It encompasses the ability to get along well with others. It provides us with an understanding of what other people are feeling and experiencing, which permits us to respond appropriately to others' needs. This ability may help explain why people with only modest scores on traditional intelligence tests can be quite successful: The basis of their success may be a high emotional intelligence that allows them to respond appropriately and quickly to others' feelings.

Although the notion of emotional intelligence makes sense, it has yet to be quantified in a rigorous manner. Furthermore, the view that emotional intelligence is so important that skills related to it should be taught in school has raised concerns among some educators. They suggest that the nurturance of emotional intelligence is best left to students' families, especially because there is no well-specified set of criteria for what constitutes emotional intelligence (Sleek, 1997; Becker, 2003).

emotional intelligence The set of skills that underlie the accurate assessment, evaluation, expression, and regulation of emotions.

Study Alert

Traditional intelligence relates to academic performance; practical intelligence relates to success in life; and emotional intelligence relates to emotional skills.

Major Approaches to Intelligence	
Approach	**Characteristics**
Fluid and crystallized intelligence	Fluid intelligence relates to reasoning, memory, and information-processing capabilities; crystallized intelligence relates to information, skills, and strategies learned through experience
Gardner's multiple intelligences	Eight independent forms of intelligence
Information-processing approaches	Intelligence is reflected in the ways people store and use material to solve intellectual tasks
Practical intelligence	Intelligence in terms of nonacademic, career, and personal success
Emotional intelligence	Intelligence that provides an understanding of what other people are feeling and experiencing and permits us to respond appropriately to others' needs

FIGURE 3 Just as there are many views of the nature of intelligence, there are also numerous ways to demonstrate intelligent behavior. This summary provides an overview of the various approaches used by psychologists.

Still, the notion of emotional intelligence reminds us that there are many ways to demonstrate intelligent behavior—just as there are many views of the nature of intelligence (Fox & Spector, 2000; Barrett & Salovey, 2002). Figure 3 summarizes the different approaches used by psychologists.

Assessing Intelligence

Given the variety of approaches to the many components of intelligence, it's not surprising that measuring intelligence has proved challenging. Psychologists who study intelligence have focused a great deal of their attention on the development of **intelligence tests** and have relied on such tests to quantify a person's level of intelligence. These tests have proved to be of great benefit in identifying students in need of special attention in school, diagnosing cognitive difficulties, and helping people make optimal educational and vocational choices. At the same time, their use has proved controversial, raising important social and educational issues.

intelligence tests Tests devised to quantify a person's level of intelligence.

Historically, the first effort at intelligence testing was based on an uncomplicated but completely wrong assumption: that the size and shape of a person's head could be used as an objective measure of intelligence. The idea was put forward by Sir Francis Galton (1822–1911), an eminent English scientist whose ideas about other topics proved to be considerably more valid than his notions about intelligence.

Galton's motivation to identify people of high intelligence stemmed from personal prejudices. He sought to demonstrate the natural superiority of people of high social class (including himself) by showing that intelligence is inherited. He hypothesized that head configuration, being genetically determined, is related to brain size and therefore is related to intelligence.

Galton's theories were proved wrong on virtually every count. Head size and shape are not related to intellectual performance at all, and subsequent research has found little relationship between brain size and intelligence. However, Galton's work did have at least one desirable result: He was the first person to suggest that intelligence could be quantified and measured in an objective manner (Jensen, 2002).

Alfred Binet

mental age The age for which a given level of performance is average or typical.

intelligence quotient (IQ) A score that takes into account an individual's mental and chronological ages.

BINET AND THE DEVELOPMENT OF IQ TESTS

The first real intelligence tests were developed by the French psychologist Alfred Binet (1857–1911). His tests followed from a simple premise: If performance on certain tasks or test items improved with *chronological* or physical age, performance could be used to distinguish more intelligent people from less intelligent ones within a particular age group. On the basis of this principle, Binet devised the first formal intelligence test, which was designed to identify the "dullest" students in the Paris school system in order to provide them with remedial aid.

Binet began by presenting tasks to same-age students who had been labeled "bright" or "dull" by their teachers. If a task could be completed by the bright students but not by the dull ones, he retained that task as a proper test item; otherwise it was discarded. In the end he came up with a test that distinguished between the bright and dull groups and—with further work—one that distinguished among children in different age groups (Binet & Simon, 1916; Sternberg & Jarvin, 2003).

On the basis of the Binet test, children were assigned a score relating to their **mental age,** the age for which a given level of performance is average or typical. For example, if the average 8-year-old answered, say, 45 items correctly on a test, anyone who answered 45 items correctly would be assigned a mental age of 8 years. Consequently, whether the person taking the test was 20 years old or 5, he or she would have the same mental age of 8 years (Cornell, 2006).

Assigning a mental age to students gave an indication of their general level of performance. However, it didn't allow for adequate comparisons among people of different chronological ages. By using mental age alone, for instance, we might assume that an 18-year-old responding at a 20-year-old's level would be demonstrating the same degree of intelligence as a 5-year-old answering at a 7-year-old's level, when actually the 5-year-old would be displaying a much greater *relative* degree of intelligence.

A solution to the problem came in the form of the **intelligence quotient** or **IQ,** a score that takes into account an individual's mental *and* chronological ages. Historically, the first IQ scores employed the following formula, in which *MA* stands for mental age and *CA* for chronological age:

$$\text{IQ score} = \frac{\text{MA}}{\text{CA}} \times 100$$

Using this formula, we can return to the earlier example of an 18-year-old performing at a mental age of 20 and calculate an IQ score of (20/18) × 100 = 111. In contrast, the 5-year-old performing at a mental age of 7 comes out with a considerably higher IQ score: (7/5) × 100 = 140.

As a bit of trial and error with the formula will show you, anyone who has a mental age equal to his or her chronological age will have an IQ equal to 100. Moreover, people with a mental age that is lower than their chronological age will have IQs that fall below 100.

Although the basic principles behind the calculation of an IQ score still hold, today IQ scores are determined in a different manner and are known as *deviation IQ scores*. First, the average test score for everyone of the same age who takes the test is determined, and that average score is assigned an IQ of 100. Then, with the aid of statistical techniques that calculate the differences (or "deviations") between each score and the average, IQ scores are assigned.

As you can see in Figure 4, when IQ scores from large numbers of people are plotted on a graph, they form a *bell-shaped distribution* (called "bell-shaped" because it looks like a bell when plotted). Approximately two-thirds of all individuals fall within 15 IQ points of the average score of 100. As scores increase or fall beyond that range, the percentage of people in a category falls considerably.

CONTEMPORARY IQ TESTS: GAUGING INTELLIGENCE

Remnants of Binet's original intelligence test are still with us, although the test has been revised in significant ways. Now in its fifth edition and called the *Stanford-Binet Intelligence Scale,* the test consists of a series of items that vary according to the age of the person being tested (Roid, 2003). For example, young children are asked to copy figures or answer questions about everyday activities. Older people are asked to solve analogies, explain proverbs, and describe similarities that underlie sets of words.

The test is administered orally and includes both verbal and nonverbal assessments. An examiner begins by finding a mental age level at which a person is able to answer all the questions correctly, and then moves on to successively more difficult problems. When the test-taker can't answer any of the questions at a given mental age level, the test is over. By studying the pattern of correct and incorrect responses, the examiner is able to compute an IQ score for the person being tested. In addition,

> **Study Alert**
>
> It's important to know the traditional formula for IQ scores in which IQ is the ratio of mental age divided by chronological age, then multiplied by 100. Remember, though, that the actual calculation of IQ scores today is done in a more sophisticated manner.

The average IQ score is 100, and 68% of people score between 85 and 115.

FIGURE 4 The average and most common IQ score is 100, and 68% of all people are within a 30-point range centered on 100. Some 95% of the population have scores that are within 30 points above or below 100, and 99.8% have scores that are between 55 and 145.

Types of Items on WAIS-IV		
Name	**Goal of Item**	**Example**
Information	Assess general information	Who wrote *Tom Sawyer?*
Comprehension	Assess understanding and evaluation of social norms and past experience	Why is copper often used for electrical wires?
Arithmetic	Assess math reasoning through verbal problems	Three women divided 18 golf balls equally among themselves. How many golf balls did each person receive?
Similarities	Test understanding of how objects or concepts are alike, tapping abstract reasoning	In what way are a circle and a triangle alike?
Figure weights	Test Perceptual Reasoning	Problems require test-taker to determine which possibility balances the final scale. 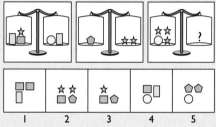
Matrix reasoning	Test spatial reasoning	Test-taker must decide which of the five possibilities replaces the question mark and completes the sequence.
Block design item	Test understanding of relationship of parts to whole	Problems require test-takers to reproduce a design in fixed amount of time.

FIGURE 5 Typical kinds of items found on the Wechsler Adult Intelligence Scales (WAIS-IV). (Simulated items similar to those in the *Wechsler Adult Intelligence Scale, Fourth Edition (WAIS-IV).* Copyright © 2003 NCS Pearson, Inc. Reproduced with permission. All rights reserved. "Wechsler Adult Intelligence Scale," "WAIS," and "Weschler," are trademarks, in the US and/or other countries, of Pearson Education, Inc. or its affiliates.)

the Stanford-Binet test yields separate subscores that provide clues to a test-taker's particular strengths and weaknesses.

The IQ tests most frequently used in the United States were devised by psychologist David Wechsler and are known as the *Wechsler Adult Intelligence Scale–IV* or, more commonly, the *WAIS-IV* (for adults) and a children's version, the *Wechsler Intelligence Scale for Children–IV* or *WISC-IV*. Both the WAIS-IV and the WISC-IV measure verbal comprehension, perceptual reasoning, working memory, and processing speed. (See sample WAIS-IV items in Figure 5.)

Because the Stanford-Binet, WAIS-IV, and WISC-IV all require individualized, one-on-one interaction, they are relatively difficult to administer and score on a large-scale basis. Consequently, there are now a number of IQ tests that allow group

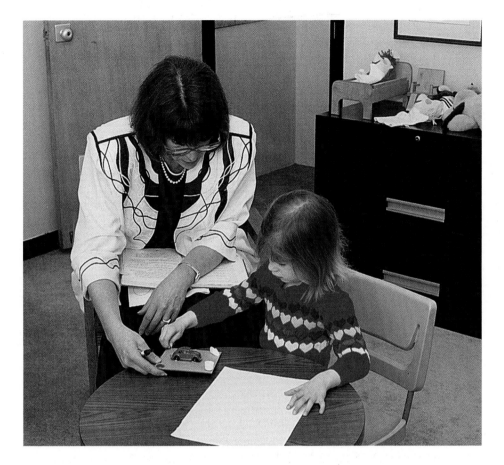

administration. Rather than have one examiner ask one person at a time to respond to individual items, group IQ tests are strictly paper-and-pencil tests. The primary advantage of group tests is their ease of administration (Anastasi & Urbina, 1997).

However, sacrifices are made in group testing that in some cases may outweigh the benefits. For instance, group tests generally offer fewer kinds of questions than tests administered individually do. Furthermore, people may be more motivated to perform at their highest ability level when working one-to-one with a test administrator than they are in a group. Finally, in some cases it's simply impossible to employ group tests, particularly with young children or people with unusually low IQs (Aiken, 1996).

RELIABILITY AND VALIDITY: TAKING THE MEASURE OF TESTS

When we use a ruler, we expect it to measure an inch in the same way every time we use it. When we weigh ourselves on a bathroom scale, we hope that the variations we see on the scale are due to changes in our weight and not to errors on the part of the scale (unless the change in weight is in an unwanted direction!).

In the same way, we hope that psychological tests have **reliability**—that they measure consistently what we're trying to measure. We need to be sure that each time we administer the test, a test-taker will achieve the same results—assuming that nothing about the person has changed relevant to what is being measured.

Suppose, for instance, that when you first took the SAT exams, you scored 400 on the verbal section of the test. Then, after re-taking the test a few months later without studying to improve your results, you scored 700. You might well stop celebrating for a moment to question whether the test is reliable, for it's unlikely that your abilities could have changed enough to raise your score by 300 points (Coyle, 2006).

reliability The property by which tests measure consistently what they are trying to measure.

validity The property by which tests actually measure what they are supposed to measure.

But suppose your score changed hardly at all—both times you received a score of about 400. You couldn't complain about a lack of reliability. However, if you knew your verbal skills were above average, you might be concerned that the test did not adequately measure what it was supposed to measure. In sum, the question has now become one of *validity* rather than reliability. A test has **validity** when it actually measures what it's supposed to measure.

Knowing that a test is reliable is no guarantee that it is also valid. For instance, Sir Francis Galton assumed that skull size is related to intelligence, and he was able to measure skull size with great reliability. However, the measure of skull size was not valid—it had nothing to do with intelligence. In his case, we have reliability without validity.

Clearly, if a test is unreliable it can't be valid. Assuming that all other factors—motivation to score well, knowledge of the material, health, and so forth—are similar, if a person scores high the first time he or she takes a specific test and low the second time, the test cannot be measuring what it is supposed to measure. Therefore, the test is both unreliable and not valid.

Test validity and reliability are prerequisites for accurate assessment of intelligence—as well as for any other measurement carried out by psychologists. Consequently, the measures of personality carried out by personality psychologists, of assessments of psychological disorders by clinical psychologists, and of attitudes by social psychologists must meet the tests of validity and reliability for the results to be meaningful (Feldt, 2005; Phelps, 2005; Yao et al., 2006).

Assuming that a test is both valid and reliable, one further step is necessary in order to interpret the meaning of a particular test-taker's score: the establishment of norms. **Norms** are standards of test performance that permit the comparison of one person's score on a test to the scores of others who have taken the same test. For example, a norm permits test-takers to know that they have scored, say, in the top 15% of those who have taken the test previously. Tests for which norms have been developed are known as *standardized tests*.

norms Standards of test performance that permit the comparison of one person's score on a test with the scores of other individuals who have taken the same test.

Test designers establish norms by calculating the average score achieved by a specific group of people for whom the test has been designed. Then the test designers can determine the extent to which each person's score differs from the scores of the other individuals who have taken the test in the past and provide future test-takers with a qualitative sense of their performance.

Obviously, the samples of test-takers used to establish norms are critical to the norming process. The people used to determine norms must be representative of the individuals to whom the test is directed.

ADAPTIVE TESTING: USING COMPUTERS TO ASSESS PERFORMANCE

Ensuring that tests are reliable, valid, and based on appropriate norms has become more critical with computer-administered testing. In computerized versions of tests such as the Graduate Record Exam (GRE), a test used for entrance to graduate school, not only are test questions viewed and answered on a computer, the test itself is individualized. Every test-taker does not receive identical sets of test questions. Instead, the computer programmed for *adaptive testing* first presents a randomly selected question of moderate difficulty. If the test-taker answers it correctly, the computer then presents a randomly chosen item of slightly greater difficulty. If the test-taker answers it incorrectly, the computer presents a slightly easier item. Each question becomes slightly harder or easier than the question preceding it, depending on whether the previous response is correct. Ultimately, the greater the number of difficult questions answered correctly, the higher the score (Chang & Ansley, 2003; Marszalek, 2007; Belov & Armstrong, 2009).

Variations in Intellectual Ability

More than 7 million people in the United States, including around 11 per 1,000 children, have been identified as far enough below average in intelligence to be regarded as having a serious intellectual deficit. Individuals with low IQs (people with mental retardation or intellectual disabilities) as well as those with unusually high IQs (the intellectually gifted) require special attention if they are to reach their full potential.

MENTAL RETARDATION (INTELLECTUAL DISABILITIES)

Although sometimes thought of as a rare phenomenon, mental retardation (or, as it is increasingly being called, intellectual disabilities) occurs in 1 to 3% of the population. There is wide variation among those labeled as mentally retarded or "mentally challenged," in large part because of the inclusiveness of the definition developed by the American Association on Intellectual and Developmental Disabilities. The association suggests that **mental retardation** (or **intellectual disability**) is a disability characterized by significant limitations both in intellectual functioning and in conceptual, social, and practical adaptive skills (AAMR, 2002). (Although experts are increasingly using the term "intellectual disability" instead of "mental retardation," our discussion will use the original term because it continues to be more widespread.)

mental retardation (or intellectual disability) A condition characterized by significant limitations both in intellectual functioning and in conceptual, social, and practical adaptive skills.

Although below-average intellectual functioning can be measured in a relatively straightforward manner—using standard IQ tests—it is more difficult to determine how to gauge limitations in adaptive behavior. Consequently, there is a lack of uniformity in how experts apply the labels *mental retardation* and *intellectual disabilities*. People labeled mentally retarded vary—from those who can be taught to work and function with little special attention to those who cannot be trained and are institutionalized throughout their lives (Detterman, Gabriel, & Ruthsatz, 2000; Greenspan, 2006).

Most people with mental retardation have relatively minor deficits and are classified as having *mild retardation*. These individuals, who have IQ scores ranging from 55 to 69, constitute approximately 90% of all people with mental retardation. Although their development is typically slower than that of their peers, they can function quite independently by adulthood and are able to hold jobs and have families of their own (Bates, Cuvo, Miner, & Korabeck, 2001; Smith, 2006).

With greater degrees of intellectual deficit—*moderate retardation* (IQs of 40 to 54), *severe retardation* (IQs of 25 to 39), and *profound retardation* (IQs below 25)—the difficulties are more pronounced. For people with moderate retardation, deficits are obvious early, with language and motor skills lagging behind those of peers. Although these individuals can hold simple jobs, they need to have a moderate degree of supervision throughout their lives. Individuals with severe and profound mental retardation are generally unable to function independently and typically require care their entire lives (Garwick, 2007).

Identifying the Roots of Mental Retardation. What produces mental retardation? In nearly one-third of the cases there is an identifiable cause related to biological or environmental factors. The most common preventable cause of retardation is **fetal alcohol syndrome,** caused by a mother's use of alcohol while pregnant. Increasing evidence shows that even small amounts of alcohol intake can produce intellectual deficits. One in every 750 infants is born with fetal alcohol syndrome in the United States (West & Blake, 2005; Manning & Hoyme, 2007; Murthy et al., 2009).

fetal alcohol syndrome The most common cause of mental retardation in newborns occurring when the mother uses alcohol during pregnancy.

familial retardation Mental retardation in which no apparent biological defect exists but there is a history of retardation in the family.

Down syndrome represents another major cause of mental retardation. *Down syndrome* results when a person is born with 47 chromosomes instead of the usual 46. In most cases, there is an extra copy of the 21st chromosome that leads to problems in how the brain and body develop (Sherman et al., 2007).

In other cases of mental retardation, the structure of particular chromosomes is abnormal. Birth complications, such as a temporary lack of oxygen, may also cause retardation. In some cases, mental retardation occurs after birth, following a head injury, a stroke, or infections such as meningitis (Plomin, 2005; Bittles et al., 2007).

However, the majority of cases of mental retardation are classified as **familial retardation,** in which no apparent biological defect exists other than a history of retardation in the family. Whether the family history of retardation is caused by environmental factors, such as extreme continuous poverty leading to malnutrition, or by underlying genetic factors is usually impossible to determine (Zigler et al., 2002).

Integrating Individuals with Mental Retardation. Important advances in the care and treatment of those with retardation have been made since Congress passed the Education for All Handicapped Children Act (Public Law 94-142) in the mid-1970s. This federal law stipulates that people with retardation are entitled to a full education and that they must be educated and trained in the least restrictive environment. The law increases the educational opportunities for individuals with mental retardation, facilitating their integration into regular classrooms as much as possible—a process known as *mainstreaming* (Katsiyannis, et al., 2005; Aussilloux & Baghdadli, 2006; Gibb et al., 2007).

The philosophy behind mainstreaming suggests that students with and without mental retardation interacting together in regular classrooms will improve educational opportunities for those with retardation as it increases their social acceptance and facilitates their integration into society as a whole. Of course, special education classes still exist; some mentally challenged individuals function at too low a level to benefit from placement in regular classrooms. Moreover, children with mental retardation who are mainstreamed into regular classes typically attend special classes for at least part of the day (Hastings & Oakford, 2003; Williamson et al., 2006; also see *PsychWork*).

PsychWork

DIRECTOR OF SPECIAL EDUCATION

Name: Shannon Lynch

Position: Director of Special Education

Education: BA, Liberal Studies, Northern Arizona University, Flagstaff, AZ; MA, Special Education, Northern Arizona University, Flagstaff, AZ; State of Arizona Teaching certificate in Elementary and Special Education

For Shannon Lynch, Director of Special Education at The Willow Creek Charter School in Prescott, Arizona, being a special education teacher means providing ways for every student to achieve success. Each child presents different needs, and Lynch approaches her teaching accordingly.

"For children with specific learning disabilities, I have found it is helpful to utilize repetition, hands-on activities, music, movements with information, and rhymes to get the information to stick," she explained.

"Children on the autism spectrum have challenges with social skills. Great programs exist that provide models and scripts of appropriate social interactions," Lynch said. "Emotional disabilities require a very different approach and involve providing counseling to cope with the difficult emotions students face.

"The biggest factor for students with special needs is providing ways for them to achieve success. They have spent much of their academic career feeling incapable and inadequate, so just giving them small opportunities for success can make a huge difference in their confidence," Lynch noted.

THE INTELLECTUALLY GIFTED

Another group of people—the intellectually gifted—differ from those with average intelligence as much as do individuals with mental retardation, although in a different manner. Accounting for 2% to 4% of the population, the **intellectually gifted** have IQ scores greater than 130.

Although the stereotype associated with the gifted suggests that they are awkward, shy social misfits who are unable to get along well with peers, most research indicates that just the opposite is true. The intellectually gifted are most often outgoing, well adjusted, healthy, popular people who are able to do most things better than the average person can (Lubinski et al., 2006; Guldemond et al., 2007; Mueller, 2009).

For example, in a famous study by psychologist Lewis Terman that started in the early 1920s, 1,500 children who had IQ scores above 140 were followed for the rest of their lives. From the start, the members of this group were more physically, academically, and socially capable than their nongifted peers. In addition to doing better in school, they also showed better social adjustment than average. All these advantages paid off in terms of career success: As a group, the gifted received more awards and distinctions, earned higher incomes, and made more contributions in art and literature than typical individuals. Perhaps most important, they reported greater satisfaction in life than the nongifted (Hegarty, 2007).

Of course, not every member of the group Terman studied was successful. Furthermore, high intelligence is not a homogeneous quality; a person with a high overall IQ is not necessarily gifted in every academic subject, but may excel in just one or two. A high IQ is not a universal guarantee of success (Shurkin, 1992; Winner, 2003; Clemons, 2006).

intellectually gifted The 2% to 4% of the population who have IQ scores greater than 130.

Group Differences in Intelligence: Genetic and Environmental Determinants

Kwang is often washed with a pleck tied to a:

   a. rundel
   b. flink
   c. pove
   d. quirj

If you found this kind of item on an intelligence test, you would probably complain that the test was totally absurd and had nothing to do with your intelligence or anyone else's—and rightly so. How could anyone be expected to respond to items presented in a language that was so unfamiliar?

Yet to some people, even more reasonable questions may appear just as nonsensical. Consider the example of a child raised in a city who is asked about procedures for milking cows, or someone raised in a rural area who is asked about subway ticketing procedures. Obviously, the previous experience of the test-takers would affect their ability to answer correctly. And if such types of questions were included on an IQ test, a critic could rightly contend that the test had more to do with prior experience than with intelligence.

Although IQ tests do not include questions that are so clearly dependent on prior knowledge as questions about cows and subways, the background and experiences of test-takers do have the potential to affect results. In fact, the issue of devising fair intelligence tests that measure knowledge unrelated to culture, family background, and experience is central to explaining an important and persistent finding: Members of certain racial and cultural groups consistently score lower on traditional intelligence tests than do members of other groups. For example, as a group, blacks tend to average 10 to 15 IQ points lower than whites. Does this variation reflect a true difference in intelligence, or are the questions biased in regard to the kinds of knowledge they test? Clearly, if whites perform better because of their greater familiarity with the kind of information that is being tested, their higher IQ scores are not an indication that they are more intelligent than members of other groups (Templer & Arikawa, 2006; Fagan & Holland, 2007; Morgan, Marsiske, & Whitfield, 2008).

There's good reason to believe that some standardized IQ tests contain elements that discriminate against minority-group members whose experiences differ from those of the white majority. Consider the question "What should you do if another child grabbed your hat and ran off with it?" Most white middle-class children answer that they would tell an adult, and this response is scored as correct. However, a reasonable response might be to chase the person and fight to get the hat back, the answer that's chosen by many urban black children—but one that's scored as incorrect (Miller-Jones, 1991; Aiken, 1997; Reynolds & Ramsay, 2003).

culture-fair IQ test A test that does not discriminate against the members of any minority group.

Exploring DIVERSITY

The Relative Influence of Genetics and Environment: Nature, Nurture, and IQ

In an attempt to produce a **culture-fair IQ test,** one that does not discriminate against the members of any minority group, psychologists have tried to devise test items that assess experiences common to all cultures or emphasize questions that do not require language usage. However, test-makers have found this difficult to do because past experiences, attitudes, and values almost always have an impact on respondents' answers (Fagan & Holland, 2009).

For example, children raised in Western cultures group things on the basis of what they *are* (such as putting *dog* and *fish* into the category of *animal*). In contrast, members of the Kpelle tribe in Africa see intelligence demonstrated by grouping things according to what they *do* (grouping *fish* with *swim*). Similarly, children in the United States asked to memorize the position of objects on a chessboard perform better than do African children living in remote villages when household objects familiar to the American children are used. But if rocks are used instead of household objects, the African children do better. In short, it's difficult to produce a test that is truly culture-fair (Sandoval et al., 1998; Serpell, 2000; Valencia & Suzuki, 2003).

The efforts of psychologists to produce culture-fair measures of intelligence relate to a lingering controversy over differences in intelligence between members of different racial and ethnic groups. In attempting to identify whether there are differences between such groups, psychologists have had to confront the broader issue of the relative contribution to intelligence of genetic factors (heredity) and experience (environment)—the nature-nurture issue that is one of the basic issues of psychology.

Richard Herrnstein, a psychologist, and Charles Murray, a sociologist, fanned the flames of the debate with the publication of their book *The Bell Curve* in the mid-1990s (Herrnstein & Murray, 1994). They argued that an analysis of IQ differences between whites and blacks demonstrated that although environmental factors played a role, there were also basic genetic differences between the two races. They based their argument on a number of findings. For instance, on average whites score 15 points

Study Alert

Remember that the differences in IQ scores are much greater when comparing individuals than when comparing groups.

Relationship	Genetic overlap	Rearing	Correlation
Monozygotic (identical) twins	100%	Together	.86
Dizygotic (fraternal) twins	50%	Together	.62
Siblings	50%	Together	.41
Siblings	50%	Apart	.24
Parent-child	50%	Together	.35
Parent-child	50%	Apart	.31
Adoptive parent-child	0%	Together	.16
Unrelated children	0%	Together	.25
Spouses	0%	Apart	.29

The difference between these two correlations shows the impact of the environment

The relatively low correlation for unrelated children raised together shows the importance of genetic factors

FIGURE 6 The relationship between IQ and closeness of genetic relationship. In general, the more similar the genetic and environmental background of two people, the greater the correlation. Note, for example, that the correlation for spouses, who are genetically unrelated and have been reared apart, is relatively low, whereas the correlation for identical twins reared together is substantial. (Source: Adapted from Henderson, 1982.)

higher than do blacks on traditional IQ tests even when socioeconomic status (SES) is taken into account. According to Herrnstein and Murray, middle- and upper-SES blacks score lower than do middle- and upper-SES whites, just as lower-SES blacks score lower on average than do lower-SES whites. Intelligence differences between blacks and whites, they concluded, could not be attributed to environmental differences alone.

IQ AND HERITABILITY

It's clear that intelligence in general shows a high degree of **heritability,** a measure of the degree to which a characteristic can be attributed to genetic, inherited factors (e.g., Petrill, 2005; Miller & Penke, 2007; Plomin, 2009). As can be seen in Figure 6, the closer the genetic link between two related people, the greater the correspondence of IQ scores. Using data such as these, Herrnstein and Murray argued that differences between races in IQ scores were largely caused by genetically based differences in intelligence.

However, many psychologists reacted strongly to the arguments laid out in *The Bell Curve,* refuting several of the book's basic arguments. One criticism is that even when attempts are made to hold socioeconomic conditions constant, wide variations remain among individual households. Furthermore, no one can convincingly assert that the living conditions of blacks and whites are identical even when their socioeconomic status is similar. In addition, as we discussed earlier, there is reason to believe that traditional IQ tests may discriminate against lower-SES urban blacks by asking for information pertaining to experiences they are unlikely to have had (American Psychological Association Task Force on Intelligence, 1996; Hall, 2002; Horn, 2002; Nisbett, 2007).

Moreover, blacks who are raised in economically enriched environments have similar IQ scores to whites in comparable environments. For example, in a study of black children who had been adopted at an early age by white middle-class

heritability A measure of the degree to which a characteristic is related to genetic, inherited factors.

families of above-average intelligence, the IQ scores of those children averaged 106—about 15 points above the average IQ scores of unadopted black children in the study. Other research shows that the racial gap in IQ narrows considerably after a college education, and cross-cultural data demonstrate that when racial gaps exist in other cultures, it's the economically disadvantaged groups that typically have lower scores. In short, the evidence that genetic factors play the major role in determining racial differences in IQ is not compelling (Scarr & Weinberg, 1976; Sternberg, Grigorenko, & Kidd, 2005; Fagan & Holland, 2007; Nisbett, 2009).

Furthermore, drawing comparisons between different races on any dimension, including IQ scores, is an imprecise, potentially misleading, and often fruitless venture. By far, the greatest discrepancies in IQ scores occur when comparing *individuals,* not when comparing mean IQ scores of different *groups.* There are blacks who score high on IQ tests and whites who score low, just as there are whites who score high and blacks who score low. For the concept of intelligence to aid in the betterment of society, we must examine how *individuals* perform, not the groups to which they belong (Angoff, 1988; Fagan & Holland, 2002, 2007).

The more critical question to ask, then, is not whether hereditary or environmental factors primarily underlie intelligence, but whether there is anything we can do to maximize the intellectual development of each individual. If we can find ways to do this, we will be able to make changes in the environment—which may take the form of enriched home and school environments—that can lead each person to reach his or her potential.

RECAP/EVALUATE/RETHINK

RECAP

What are the different definitions and conceptions of intelligence?

- Because intelligence can take many forms, defining it is challenging. One commonly accepted view is that intelligence is the capacity to understand the world, think rationally, and use resources effectively when faced with challenges. (p. 259)
- The earliest psychologists assumed that there is a general factor for mental ability called *g*. However, later psychologists disputed the view that intelligence is unidimensional. (p. 260)
- Some researchers suggest that intelligence can be broken down into fluid intelligence and crystallized intelligence. Gardner's theory of multiple intelligences proposes that there are eight spheres of intelligence. (p. 260)
- Information-processing approaches examine the processes underlying intelligent behavior rather than focusing on the structure of intelligence. (p. 261)
- Practical intelligence is intelligence related to overall success in living; emotional intelligence is the set of skills that underlie the accurate assessment, evaluation, expression, and regulation of emotions. (p. 263)

What are the major approaches to measuring intelligence, and what do intelligence tests measure?

- Intelligence tests have traditionally compared a person's mental age and chronological age to yield an IQ, or intelligence quotient, score. (p. 265)
- Specific tests of intelligence include the Stanford-Binet test, the Wechsler Adult Intelligence Scale–IV (WAIS-IV), and the Wechsler Intelligence Scale for Children–IV (WISC-IV). (p. 267)
- Tests are expected to be both reliable and valid. Reliability refers to the consistency with which a test measures what it is trying to measure. A test has validity when it actually measures what it is supposed to measure. (p. 269)

How are the extremes of intelligence characterized?

- The levels of mental retardation or intellectual disability include mild, moderate, severe, and profound retardation. (p. 271)
- About one-third of the cases of retardation have a known biological cause; fetal alcohol syndrome is the most common. Most cases, however, are classified as familial retardation, for which there is no known biological cause. (p. 271)
- The intellectually gifted are people with IQ scores greater than 130. Intellectually gifted people tend to be healthier and more successful than are the nongifted. (p. 273)

Are traditional IQ tests culturally biased?

- Traditional intelligence tests have frequently been criticized for being biased in favor of the white middle-class population. This controversy has led to attempts to devise culture-fair tests, IQ measures that avoid questions that depend on a particular cultural background. (p. 273)

To what degree is intelligence influenced by the environment, and to what degree by heredity?

- Attempting to distinguish environmental from hereditary factors in intelligence is probably futile and certainly misguided. Because individual IQ scores vary far more than do group IQ scores, it is more critical to ask what can be done to maximize the intellectual development of each individual. (p. 274)

EVALUATE

1. _____ is a measure of intelligence that takes into account a person's chronological and mental ages.
2. Some psychologists make the distinction between _____ intelligence, which reflects reasoning, memory, and information-processing capabilities, and _____ intelligence, which is the information, skills, and strategies that people have learned through experience.
3. _____ _____ _____ is the most common biological cause of mental retardation.
4. People with high intelligence are generally shy and socially withdraw. True or False?
5. A(n) _____ _____ test tries to use only questions appropriate to all the people taking the test.

RETHINK

1. What is the role of emotional intelligence in the classroom? How might emotional intelligence be tested? Should emotional intelligence be a factor in determining academic promotion to the next grade?
2. *From the human resource specialist's perspective:* Job interviews are really a kind of test, but they rely on interviewers' judgments and have no formal validity or reliability. Do you think job interviews can be made to have greater validity and reliability?

Answers to Evaluate Questions

1. IQ; 2. fluid, crystallized; 3. fetal alcohol syndrome; 4. false; The gifted are generally more socially adept than those with lower IQ; 5. culture-fair

KEY TERMS

intelligence p. 260
g or *g*-factor p. 260
fluid intelligence p. 260
crystallized
  intelligence p. 261
theory of multiple
  intelligences p. 261

practical intelligence p. 263
emotional
  intelligence p. 264
intelligence tests p. 265
mental age p. 266
intelligence quotient
  (IQ) p. 266

reliability p. 269
validity p. 270
norms p. 270
mental retardation
  (or intellectual
  disability) p. 271

fetal alcohol
  syndrome p. 271
familial retardation p. 272
intellectually gifted p. 273
culture-fair IQ test p. 274
heritability p. 274

Psychology on the Web

1. Do animals think? What evidence is there to support either side of this question? Search the Web for at least one example of research and/or argument for each stance. Summarize your findings and use your knowledge of cognitive psychology to state your own position on this question.

2. Many sites on the Web permit you to assess your IQ. Take at least two such tests and (a) compare your results, (b) indicate what mental qualities seemed to be tested on the tests, and (c) discuss your impression of the reliability and validity of the tests. Write up your conclusions.

Epilogue

The topics in this chapter occupy a central place in the field of psychology, encompassing a variety of areas—including thinking, problem solving, decision making, creativity, language, memory, and intelligence. First, we examined thinking and problem solving, focusing on the importance of mental images and concepts and identifying the steps commonly involved in solving problems. We then discussed language by describing the components of grammar and tracing language development in children. Finally, we considered intelligence. Some of the most heated discussions in all of psychology focus on this topic, engaging educators, policymakers, politicians, and psychologists alike. The issues include the very meaning of intelligence, its measurement, individual extremes of intelligence, and finally, the heredity/environment question.

Before proceeding, turn back to the prologue about Clifford Matson's "Eureka!" moment. Answer the following questions in light of what you have learned about reasoning, problem solving, and creativity:

1. What factors led to Matson's invention of Cork-EZ?
2. How do the concepts of functional fixedness and mental set relate to Matson's inventiveness? Are they related to the notion of prototypes?
3. How do you think insight is involved in Matson's inventiveness?
4. In what ways do you think divergent and convergent thinking are involved in the processes of invention? Do they play different roles during the various stages of the act of invention, including identifying the need for an invention, devising possible solutions, and creating a practical invention?

CHAPTER 8

Motivation and Emotion

Key Concepts for Chapter 8

When Kirstie Alley stepped on the scale for the first time in 15 months, she had a hunch that it wouldn't be pretty. "I thought I weighed 190, but I got on the scale and started screaming," recalls Alley. "It said 228 lbs., which is my highest weight ever."

But looking back, Alley, 58, is hardly shocked that her body. . . had ballooned beyond 200 lbs. yet again. . . . She had not worked out and even banished her gym equipment to the garage. As for her diet, her small, low-calorie portions gave way to Chinese takeout and pasta drenched in butter.

"I fell off the horse," says the 5'8" star. . . . "I just sort of went wild." (Leonard, 2009, p. 50)

Looking **Ahead**

Actress Kirstie Alley's notorious up-and-down battle with obesity—at one point she dieted down to 145 pounds, only to gain back the weight—is just one very public example of the struggles that hundreds of millions of people have maintaining an appropriate weight. But why is it so difficult to maintain an appropriate weight? Why do the natural mechanisms that regulate our other bodily functions often fail when it comes to regulating our eating behavior? These questions and many others are addressed by psychologists who study the topics of motivation and emotion. These psychologists seek to discover the particular desired goals or motives that underlie behavior—behaviors as basic as drinking to satisfy thirst and as inconsequential as taking a stroll to get exercise exemplify motives. Psychologists specializing in the study of motivation assume that such underlying motives steer our choices of activities.

Whereas motivation concerns the forces that direct future behavior, emotion pertains to the feelings we experience throughout our lives. The study of emotions focuses on our internal experiences at any given moment. All of us feel a variety of emotions: happiness at succeeding at a difficult task, sadness over the death of a loved one, anger at being treated unfairly. Because emotions not only play a role in motivating our behavior but also act as a reflection of our underlying motivation, they play an important role in our lives.

We begin this set of modules by focusing on the major conceptions of motivation, discussing how different motives and needs jointly affect behavior. We consider motives that are biologically based and universal within the animal kingdom, such as hunger, as well as motives that are unique to humans, such as the need for achievement.

We then turn to emotions, considering the roles and functions that emotions play in people's lives and discussing several approaches that explain how people understand their emotions. Finally, we look at how nonverbal behavior communicates emotions.

Explaining Motivation

In just a moment, 27-year-old Aron Ralston's life changed. An 800-pound boulder dislodged in a narrow canyon where Ralston was hiking in an isolated Utah canyon, pinning his lower arm to the ground.

For the next five days, Ralston lay in the dense, lonely forest, unable to escape. An experienced climber who had search-and-rescue training, he had ample time to consider his options. He tried unsuccessfully to chip away at the rock, and he rigged up ropes and pulleys around the boulder in a vain effort to move it.

Finally, out of water and nearly dehydrated, Ralston reasoned there was only one option left short of dying. In acts of incredible bravery, Ralston broke two bones in his wrist, applied a tourniquet, and used a dull pen knife to amputate his arm beneath the elbow.

Freed from his entrapment, Ralston climbed down from where he had been pinned, and then hiked five miles to safety (Cox, 2003; Lofholm, 2003).

What motivation lay behind Ralston's resolve?

To answer this question, psychologists consider the concept of **motivation**, the factors that direct and energize the behavior of humans and other organisms. Motivation has biological, cognitive, and social aspects, and its complexity has led psychologists to develop a variety of approaches. All seek to explain the energy or impetus that guides people's behavior in specific directions.

Instinct Approaches: Born to Be Motivated

When psychologists first tried to explain motivation, they turned to **instincts**, inborn patterns of behavior that are biologically determined rather than learned. According to instinct approaches to motivation, people and animals are born preprogrammed with sets of behaviors essential to their survival. Those instincts provide the energy that guides behavior in appropriate directions. Hence, sexual behavior may be a response to an instinct to reproduce, and someone exhibiting exploratory behavior may be motivated by an instinct to examine one's territory.

This concept presents several difficulties, however. For one thing, psychologists don't agree on what or even how many primary instincts exist. One early psychologist, William McDougall (1908), suggested that there are 18 instincts. Other theorists came up with even more, with one sociologist (Bernard, 1924) claiming that there are exactly 5,759 distinct instincts!

Furthermore, explanations based on the concept of instincts don't go very far toward explaining why one specific pattern of behavior and not others has appeared in a given species. In addition, although it's clear that a great deal of animal behavior is based on instincts, because much of the variety and complexity of human behavior is learned, that behavior cannot be seen as instinctual.

As a result of these shortcomings, newer explanations have replaced conceptions of motivation based on instincts. Nonetheless, instinct approaches still play a role in

Key Concept

How does motivation direct and energize behavior?

Aron Ralston

motivation The factors that direct and energize the behavior of humans and other organisms.

instincts Inborn patterns of behavior that are biologically determined rather than learned.

certain theories, especially those based on evolutionary approaches that focus on our genetic inheritance. Furthermore, Freud's work suggests that instinctual drives of sex and aggression motivate behavior (Katz, 2001).

Drive-Reduction Approaches: Satisfying Our Needs

drive-reduction approaches to motivation Theories suggesting that a lack of a basic biological requirement such as water produces a drive to obtain that requirement (in this case, the thirst drive).

drive Motivational tension or arousal that energizes behavior to fulfill a need.

After rejecting instinct theory, psychologists first proposed simple drive-reduction theories of motivation to take its place (Hull, 1943). **Drive-reduction approaches** suggest that the lack of a basic biological requirement like water produces a drive to obtain that requirement (in this case, the thirst drive).

To understand this approach, we begin with the concept of drive. A **drive** is motivational tension or arousal that energizes behavior to fulfill a need. Many basic drives, such as hunger, thirst, sleep, and sex, are related to biological needs of the body or of the species as a whole. These are called *primary drives*. Primary drives contrast with secondary drives, for which behavior fulfills no obvious biological need. In *secondary drives*, prior experience and learning bring about needs that can be highly individual by their nature. For instance, some people have a strong need to achieve academically and professionally. Applying the drive concept, we would say that their achievement need is reflected in a secondary drive that's motivating the behavior (McKinley et al., 2004; Seli, 2007).

We usually try to satisfy a primary drive by reducing the need underlying it. For example, we become hungry after not eating for a few hours and may raid the refrigerator, especially if the next scheduled meal isn't imminent. If the weather turns cold, we put on extra clothing or raise the thermostat to keep warm. If our bodies need liquids to function properly, we are thirsty and seek out water.

HOMEOSTASIS

homeostasis The body's tendency to maintain a steady internal state.

Homeostasis—the body's tendency to maintain a steady internal state—underlies primary drives. Using feedback loops, homeostasis brings deviations in body functioning back to an optimal state, similar to the way a thermostat and a furnace work in a home heating system to maintain a steady temperature. Receptor cells throughout the body constantly monitor factors such as temperature and nutrient levels. When deviations from the ideal state occur, the body adjusts to return to an optimal state. Many fundamental needs, including the needs for food, water, stable body temperature, and sleep, operate via homeostasis (Black, 2006; Shin, Zheng, & Berthoud, 2009; Vassalli & Dijk, 2009).

Although drive-reduction theories are a good explanation of how primary drives motivate behavior, they cannot fully explain a behavior for which the goal is not to reduce a drive, but rather to maintain or even increase one's level of excitement or arousal. An example of a behavior motivated by nothing more than curiosity is rushing to check an incoming text message. Similarly, many people pursue thrills like riding a roller coaster or steering a raft through river rapids. Such behaviors certainly don't fit the drive-reduction approach (Begg & Langley, 2001; Rosenbloom & Wolf, 2002).

Both curiosity and thrill-seeking behavior, then, shed doubt on the drive-reduction approach as a complete explanation for motivation. In both cases, rather than seeking to reduce an underlying drive, people and animals appear to be motivated to increase their overall level of stimulation and activity. To explain this phenomenon, psychologists have devised an alternative: arousal approaches to motivation.

Study Alert

To remember the concept of homeostasis, keep in mind the analogy of a thermostat that regulates the temperature in a house.

Arousal Approaches: Beyond Drive Reduction

Arousal approaches seek to explain behavior for which the goal is to maintain or increase excitement. According to **arousal approaches** to motivation, each person tries to maintain a certain level of stimulation and activity. As with the drive-reduction model, this model suggests that if our stimulation and activity levels become too high, we try to reduce them. But, in contrast to the drive-reduction model, the arousal model also addresses that if levels of stimulation and activity are too low, we will try to increase them by seeking stimulation.

People vary widely in the optimal level of arousal they seek out, with some people looking for especially high levels of arousal. For example, people who participate in daredevil sports, high-stakes gamblers, and criminals who pull off high-risk robberies may be exhibiting a particularly high need for arousal (see Figure 1 on the next page; Zuckerman & Kuhlman, 2000; Zuckerman, 2002; Cavenett & Nixon, 2006).

arousal approaches to motivation The belief that we try to maintain certain levels of stimulation and activity, increasing or reducing them as necessary.

Incentive Approaches: Motivation's Pull

When a luscious dessert appears on the table after a filling meal, its appeal has little or nothing to do with internal hunger drives or the maintenance of arousal. Rather, if we choose to eat the dessert, such behavior is motivated by the external stimulus of the dessert itself, which acts as an anticipated reward. This reward, in motivational terms, is an *incentive*.

Incentive approaches to motivation suggest that motivation stems from the desire to obtain valued external goals or incentives. In this view, the desirable properties of external stimuli—whether grades, money, affection, food, or sex—account for a person's motivation (Festinger et al., 2009).

Although the theory explains why we may succumb to an incentive (such as a mouthwatering dessert) even though we lack internal cues (such as hunger), it doesn't provide a complete explanation of motivation because organisms sometimes seek to fulfill needs even when incentives aren't there. Consequently, many psychologists believe that the internal drives proposed by drive-reduction theory work in tandem with the external incentives of incentive theory to "push" and "pull" behavior, respectively. Thus, at the same time that we seek to satisfy our underlying hunger needs (the push of drive-reduction theory), we are drawn to food that appears very appetizing (the pull of incentive theory). Rather than contradicting each other, then, drives and incentives may work together in motivating behavior (Pinel, Assanand, & Lehman, 2000; Lowery, Fillingim, & Wright, 2003; Berridge, 2004).

incentive approaches to motivation Theories suggesting that motivation stems from the desire to obtain valued external goals or incentives.

Cognitive Approaches: The Thoughts Behind Motivation

Cognitive approaches to motivation suggest that motivation is a result of people's thoughts, expectations, and goals—their cognitions. For instance, the degree to which people are motivated to study for a test is based on their expectation of how well studying will pay off in terms of a good grade.

Cognitive theories of motivation draw a key distinction between intrinsic and extrinsic motivation. *Intrinsic motivation* causes us to participate in an activity for our

cognitive approaches to motivation Theories suggesting that motivation is a product of people's thoughts and expectations—their cognitions.

FIGURE 1 Some people seek high levels of arousal, while others are more easygoing. You can get a sense of your own preferred level of stimulation by completing this questionnaire. (Source: "Do You Seek Out Sensation?" questionnaire from Marvin Zuckerman, "The Search for High Sensation," *Psychology Today,* February 1978, pp. 30-46. Reprinted with permission from *Psychology Today* magazine [Copyright © 1978 Sussex Publishers, LLC].)

Do You Seek Out Sensation?

How much stimulation do you crave in your everyday life? You will have an idea after you complete the following questionnaire, which lists some items from a scale designed to assess your sensation-seeking tendencies. Circle either A or B in each pair or statements.

1. A I would like a job that requires a lot of travelling.
    B I would prefer a job in one location.
2. A I am invigorated by a brisk, cold day.
    B I can't wait to get indoors on a cold day.
3. A I get bored seeing the same old faces.
    B I like the comfortable familiarity of everyday friends.
4. A I would prefer living in an ideal society in which everyone was safe, secure, and happy.
    B I would have preferred living in the unsettled days of our history.
5. A I sometimes like to do things that are a little frightening.
    B A sensible person avoids activities that are dangerous.
6. A I would not like to be hypnotized.
    B I would like to have the experience of being hypnotized.
7. A The most important goal of life is to live it to the fullest and to experience as much as possible.
    B The most important goal of life is to find peace and happiness.
8. A I would like to try parachute jumping.
    B I would never want to try jumping out of a plane, with or without a parachute.
9. A I enter cold water gradually, giving myself time to get used to it.
    B I like to dive or jump right into the ocean or a cold pool.
10. A When I go on a vacation, I prefer the comfort of a good room and bed.
    B When I go on a vacation, I prefer the change of camping out.
11. A I prefer people who are emotionally expressive, even if they are a bit unstable.
    B I prefer people who are calm and even-tempered.
12. A A good painting should shock or jolt the senses.
    B A good painting should give one a feeling of peace and security.
13. A People who ride motorcycles must have some kind of unconscious need to hurt themselves.
    B I would like to drive or ride a motorcycle.

Scoring: Give yourself one point for each of the following responses: 1*A*, 2*A*, 3*A*, 4*B*, 5*A*, 6*B*, 7*A*, 8*A*, 9*B*, 10*B*, 11*A*, 12*A*, 13*B*. Find your total score by adding up the number of points and then use the following scoring key.

0–3 very low sensation seeking

4–5 low

6–9 average

10–11 high

12–13 very high

Keep in mind, of course, that this short questionnaire, for which the scoring is based on the results of college students who have taken it, provides only a rough estimate of your sensation-seeking tendencies. Moreover, as people get older, their sensation-seeking scores tend to decrease. Still, the questionnaire will at least give you an indication of how your sensation-seeking tendencies compare with those of others.

own enjoyment rather than for any concrete, tangible reward that it will bring us. In contrast, *extrinsic motivation* causes us to do something to obtain money, a grade, or some other concrete, tangible reward. For example, when a physician works long hours because she loves medicine, intrinsic motivation is prompting her; if she works hard to make a lot of money, extrinsic motivation underlies her efforts (Lepper, Corpus, & Iyengar, 2005; Shaikholeslami & Khayyer, 2006; Finkelstien, 2009).

We are more apt to persevere, work harder, and do better work when our motivation for a task is intrinsic rather than extrinsic. In fact, in some cases providing rewards for desirable behavior (thereby increasing extrinsic motivation) actually may decrease intrinsic motivation (Henderlong & Lepper, 2002; James, 2005; Grant, 2008).

Maslow's Hierarchy: Ordering Motivational Needs

What do Eleanor Roosevelt, Abraham Lincoln, and Albert Einstein have in common? The common thread, according to the approach to motivation devised by psychologist Abraham Maslow, is that each of them fulfilled the highest levels of motivational needs underlying human behavior.

Maslow's approach places motivational needs in a hierarchy requiring that, before more sophisticated higher-order needs can be met, certain primary needs must be satisfied first (Maslow, 1970, 1987). A pyramid graphically represents his approach, with the more basic needs at the bottom and the higher-level needs at the top (see Figure 2). A person must first fulfill the more basic needs in the hierarchy in order to activate higher-order needs.

The basic needs are primary drives: needs for water, food, sleep, sex, and the like. To move up the hierarchy, a person must first meet these basic *physiological needs*. *Safety needs* come next in the hierarchy; Maslow suggests that people need a safe, secure environment in order to function effectively. Physiological and safety needs compose the lower-order needs.

Only after meeting these basic lower-order needs can a person consider fulfilling higher-order needs, such as the needs for love and a sense of belonging, esteem, and self-actualization. *Love and belongingness needs* include the needs to obtain and give

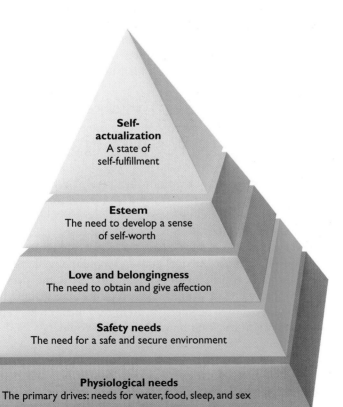

Self-actualization
A state of self-fulfillment

Esteem
The need to develop a sense of self-worth

Love and belongingness
The need to obtain and give affection

Safety needs
The need for a safe and secure environment

Physiological needs
The primary drives: needs for water, food, sleep, and sex

FIGURE 2 Maslow's hierarchy shows how our motivation progresses up the pyramid from the broadest, most fundamental biological needs to higher-order ones. Do you agree that lower-order needs must be satisfied before higher-order needs? Do hermits and monks who attempt to fulfill spiritual needs while denying basic physical needs contradict Maslow's hierarchy? (After Maslow, 1970.)

affection and to be a contributing member of some group such as a family or society. After fulfilling these needs, a person strives for *esteem*. According to Maslow's thinking, esteem pertains to the need to develop a sense of self-worth from recognizing that others know and value one's competence.

Once these four sets of needs are fulfilled—no easy task—a person is able to strive for the highest-level need, *self-actualization*. By his definition, **self-actualization** is a state of self-fulfillment in which people achieve their highest potentials, each in his or her own unique way. Although Maslow first suggested that self-actualization occurred in only a few famous individuals, he later expanded the concept to encompass everyday people. For example, a parent with excellent nurturing skills who raises a family; a teacher who year after year creates an environment that maximizes students' opportunities for success; and an artist who realizes his creative potential all may be self-actualized. The important thing is that people feel at ease with themselves and satisfied that they're using their talents to the fullest. In a sense, achieving self-actualization reduces one's striving and yearning for greater fulfillment that mark most people's lives and instead provides a sense of satisfaction with one's current state of affairs (Piechowski, 2003; Reiss & Havercamp, 2005; Laas, 2006).

Although research has been unable to validate the specific ordering of Maslow's stages, and it's difficult to measure self-actualization objectively, Maslow's heirarchy of needs is important for two reasons: It highlights the complexity of human needs, and it emphasizes the idea that until more basic biological needs are met, people will be relatively unconcerned with higher-order needs. For example, if people are hungry, their first interest will be in obtaining food; they won't be concerned with needs such as love and self-esteem (Hanley & Abell, 2002; Samantaray, Srivastava, & Misbra, 2002; Ojha & Pramanick, 2009).

Maslow's hierarchy of needs has spawned more recent approaches to motivation. For example, Edward Deci and Richard Ryan (2008) have considered human needs in light of psychological well-being. In their *self-determination theory*, they suggest that people have the three basic needs: competence, autonomy, and relatedness. Competence is the need to produce desired outcomes, while autonomy is the perception that we have control over our own lives. Relatedness is the need to be involved in close, warm relationships. According to self-determination theory, these three psychological needs are innate and universal across cultures, and they are essential as basic biological needs (Jang et al., 2009; Nansteenkiste et al., 2009).

Applying the Different Approaches to Motivation

The various approaches to motivation offer several different perspectives. Which provides the fullest account of motivation? Actually, many of the approaches are complementary rather than contradictory. In fact, employing more than one approach can help us understand motivation in a particular case.

Consider, for example, Aron Ralston's accident while hiking (described earlier). His interest in climbing in an isolated and potentially dangerous area may be explained by arousal approaches to motivation. From the perspective of instinct approaches, we can see that Aron had an overwhelming instinct to preserve his life at all costs. From a cognitive perspective, we would focus on his careful consideration of various strategies to extricate himself from the boulder.

In short, applying multiple approaches to motivation in a given situation provides a broader understanding than we might obtain by employing only a single approach. We'll see this again when we consider specific motives—such as the needs for food, achievement, affiliation, and power—and draw on several of the approaches for the fullest account of what motivates our behavior.

self-actualization A state of self-fulfillment in which people realize their highest potential, each in his or her own unique way.

Study Alert

Review distinctions between the different explanations for motivation (instinct, drive reduction, arousal, incentive, cognitive, and Maslow's hierarchy of needs).

RECAP/EVALUATE/RETHINK

RECAP

How does motivation direct and energize behavior?

- Motivation relates to the factors that direct and energize behavior. (p. 283)
- Drive is the motivational tension that energizes behavior to fulfill a need. (p. 284)
- Homeostasis, the maintenance of a steady internal state, often underlies motivational drives. (p. 284)
- Arousal approaches suggest that we try to maintain a particular level of stimulation and activity. (p. 285)
- Incentive approaches focus on the positive aspects of the environment that direct and energize behavior. (p. 285)
- Cognitive approaches focus on the role of thoughts, expectations, and one's understanding of the world in producing motivation. (p. 285)
- Maslow's hierarchy identifies five basic needs: physiological, safety, love and belongingness, esteem, and self-actualization. Only after the more basic needs are fulfilled can a person move toward meeting higher-order needs. (p. 287)

EVALUATE

1. _____ are forces that guide a person's behavior in a certain direction.
2. Biologically determined, inborn patterns of behavior are known as _____.

3. Your psychology professor tells you, "Explaining behavior is easy! When we lack something, we are motivated to get it." Which approach to motivation does your professor subscribe to?
4. By drinking water after running a marathon, a runner tries to keep his or her body at an optimal level of functioning. This process is called _____.
5. I help an elderly person cross the street because doing a good deed makes me feel good. What type of motivation is at work here? What type of motivation would be at work if I were to help an elderly man across the street because he paid me $20?
6. According to Maslow, a person with no job, no home, and no friends can become self-actualized. True or false?

RETHINK

1. Which approaches to motivation are more commonly used in the workplace? How might each approach be used to design employment policies that can sustain or increase motivation?
2. *From the perspective of an educator:* Do you think that giving students grades serves as an external reward that could decrease their intrinsic motivation for the subject matter? Why or why not?

Answers to Evaluate Questions

1. motives; 2. instincts; 3. drive reduction; 4. homeostasis; 5. intrinsic, extrinsic; 6. false; Lower-order needs must be fulfilled before self-actualization can occur.

KEY TERMS

motivation p. 283
instincts p. 283
drive-reduction approaches to motivation p. 284
drive p. 284

homeostasis p. 284
arousal approaches to motivation p. 285
incentive approaches to motivation p. 285

cognitive approaches to motivation p. 285
self-actualization p. 288

Human Needs and Motivation: Eat, Drink, and Be Daring

As a sophomore at the University of California, Santa Cruz, Lisa Arndt followed a menu of her own making: For breakfast she ate cereal or fruit, with 10 diet pills and 50 chocolate-flavored laxatives. Lunch was a salad or sandwich; dinner: chicken and rice. But it was the feast that followed that Arndt relished most. Almost every night at about 9 p.m., she would retreat to her room and eat an entire small pizza and a whole batch of cookies. Then she'd wait for the day's laxatives to take effect. "It was extremely painful," says Arndt of those days. . . . "But I was that desperate to make up for my bingeing. I was terrified of fat the way other people are afraid of lions or guns." (Hubbard, O'Neill, & Cheakalos, 1999, p. 59)

Lisa was one of the estimated 10 million women (and 1 million men) who suffer from an eating disorder. These disorders, which usually appear during adolescence, can bring about extraordinary weight loss and other forms of physical deterioration. Extremely dangerous, they sometimes result in death.

Why are Lisa and others like her subject to such disordered eating that revolves around the motivation to avoid weight gain at all costs? And why do so many other people engage in overeating, which often leads to obesity?

To answer these questions, we must consider some of the specific needs that underlie behavior. In this module, we examine several of the most important human needs. We begin with hunger, the primary drive that has received the most attention from researchers, and then turn to secondary drives—those uniquely human endeavors, based on learned needs and past experience that help explain why people strive to achieve, to affiliate with others, and to seek power over others.

The Motivation Behind Hunger and Eating

obesity Body weight that is more than 20% above the average weight for a person of a particular height.

Two hundred million people in the United States—some two-thirds of the population—are overweight, and almost a quarter are so heavy that they have **obesity;** a body weight that's more than 20% above the average weight for a person of a particular height. And the rest of the world is not far behind: A billion people around the globe are overweight or obese. The World Health Organization has said that worldwide obesity has reached epidemic proportions, producing increases in heart disease, diabetes, cancer, and premature deaths (Hill, Catenacci, & Wyatt, 2005; Stephenson & Banet-Weiser, 2007).

The most widely used measure of obesity is *body mass index (BMI)*, which is based on a ratio of weight to height. People with a BMI greater than 30 are considered obese, whereas those with a BMI between 25 and 30 are overweight. (Use the formulas in Figure 1 to determine your own BMI.)

Although the definition of obesity is clear from a scientific point of view, people's perceptions of what an ideal body looks like vary significantly across different cultures and, within Western cultures, from one time period to another. For instance, many contemporary Western cultures stress the importance of slimness in women—

FIGURE 1 Use this procedure to find your body mass index.

To calculate your body mass index, follow these steps:

1. Indicate your weight in pounds: _____ pounds
2. Indicate your height in inches: _____ inches
3. Divide your weight (item 1) by your height (item 2), and write the outcome here:
   _____
4. Divide the result above (item 3) by your height (item 2), and write the outcome here:
   _____
5. Multiply the number above by 703, and write the product here: _____. This is your body mass index.

Example:
   For a person who weights 210 pounds and who is 6 feet tall, divide 210 pounds by 72 inches, which equals 2.917. Then divide 2.917 by 72 inches (item 3), which yields .041. Multiplying .041 (from item 4) by 703 yields a BMI of 28.5.

Interpretation:
- Underweight = less than 18.5
- Normal weight = 18.5–24.9
- Overweight = 25–29.9
- Obesity = BMI of 30 or greater

Keep in mind that a BMI greater than 25 may or may not be due to excess body fat. For example, professional athletes may have little fat but weigh more than the average person because they have greater muscle mass.

a relatively recent view. In 19th-century Hawaii, women considered the most attractive were those who were the heaviest. Furthermore, for most of the 20th century, the ideal female figure was relatively full. Even today, weight standards differ among different cultural groups. For instance, in some traditional Arab cultures, obese women are so prized as wives, parents force-feed their female children to make them more desirable (Naik, 2004; Blixen et al., 2006; Marsh et al., 2007).

Regardless of cultural standards for appearance and weight, no one doubts that being overweight represents a major health risk. However, controlling weight is complicated, because eating behavior involves a variety of factors. For our discussion of what motivates people to eat, we'll start with its biological aspect.

BIOLOGICAL FACTORS IN THE REGULATION OF HUNGER

In contrast to human beings, other species are unlikely to become obese. Their internal mechanisms regulate not only the quantity of food they consume but also the kind of food they desire. For example, rats deprived of particular foods seek out alternatives that contain the specific nutrients their diet is lacking, and many species, given the choice of a wide variety of foods, select a well-balanced diet (Bouchard & Bray, 1996; Woods et al., 2000; Jones & Corp, 2003).

Complex biological mechanisms signal organisms whether they require food or should stop eating. It's not just a matter of an empty stomach causing hunger pangs and a full one alleviating those pangs. (Even

"Gee, I had no idea you were married to a supermodel."

individuals who've had their stomachs removed still experience the sensation of hunger.) One important factor is changes in the chemical composition of the blood. For instance, changes in levels of glucose, a kind of sugar, regulate feelings of hunger. In addition, the hormone *insulin* causes the body to store excess sugar in the blood as fats and carbohydrates. Finally, the hormone *ghrelin* communicates to the brain feelings of hunger. Production of ghrelin increases according to meal schedules, as well as the sight or smell of food, producing the feeling that tells us we're hungry and should eat (Teff, 2007; Wren & Bloom, 2007; Kojima & Kangawa, 2008).

The brain's *hypothalamus* monitors glucose levels. Increasing evidence suggests that the hypothalamus is primarily responsible for monitoring food intake. Injury to the hypothalamus has radical consequences for eating behavior depending on the site of the injury. For example, rats whose *lateral hypothalamus* is damaged may literally starve to death. They refuse food when it's offered, and unless they're force-fed, they eventually die. Rats with an injury to the *ventromedial hypothalamus* display the opposite problem: extreme overeating. Rats with this injury can increase in weight by as much as 400%. Similar phenomena occur in humans who have tumors of the hypothalamus (Woods & Seeley, 2002; Seymour, 2006; Fedeli et al., 2009).

weight set point The particular level of weight that the body strives to maintain.

Although the important role the hypothalamus plays in regulating food intake is clear, the exact way this organ operates is still unclear. One hypothesis suggests that injury to the hypothalamus affects the **weight set point,** or the particular level of weight that the body strives to maintain, which in turn regulates food intake. Acting as a kind of internal weight thermostat, the hypothalamus calls for either greater or less food intake (Capaldi, 1996; Woods et al., 2000; Berthoud, 2002).

In most cases, the hypothalamus does a good job. Even people who aren't deliberately monitoring their weight show only minor weight fluctuations in spite of substantial day-to-day variations in how much they eat and exercise. However, injury to the hypothalamus can alter the weight set point, following which a person struggles to meet the altered internal goal by changing food consumption. Even temporary exposure to certain drugs can alter the weight set point (Cabanac & Frankhan, 2002; Hallschmid et al., 2004; Khazaal et al., 2008).

metabolism The rate at which food is converted to energy and expended by the body.

Genetic factors determine the weight set point, at least in part. People seem destined through heredity to have a particular **metabolism,** the rate at which food is converted to energy and expended by the body. People with a high metabolic rate can eat virtually as much as they want without gaining weight, whereas others with low metabolism may eat literally half as much yet gain weight readily (Jequier, 2002; Westerterp, 2006).

SOCIAL FACTORS IN EATING

Study Alert

A key point: Eating and hunger are influenced by both biological and social factors.

You've just finished a full meal and feel completely stuffed. Suddenly your host announces with great fanfare that he'll be serving his "house specialty" dessert, bananas flambé, and that he's spent the better part of the afternoon preparing it. Even though you are full and don't even like bananas, you accept a serving of his dessert and eat it all.

Clearly, internal biological factors do not fully explain such eating behavior. External social factors based on societal rules and on what we've learned about appropriate eating behavior also play an important role. Take, for example, the simple fact that people customarily eat breakfast, lunch, and dinner at approximately the same times every day. Because we tend to eat on schedule every day, we feel hungry as the usual hour approaches, sometimes quite independently of what our internal cues are telling us.

Similarly, we put roughly the same amount of food on our plates every day, even though the amount of exercise we may have had and, consequently, our need for energy replenishment, varies from day to day. We also tend to prefer particular foods over others. Rats and dogs may be a delicacy in certain Asian cultures, but few in Western cultures find them appealing despite their potentially high nutritional value.

Even the amount of food we eat varies according to cultural norms. For instance, people in the United States eat bigger portions than people in France. In sum, cultural influences and our individual habits play important roles in determining when, what, and how much we eat (Miller & Pumariega, 2001; Rozin et al., 2003).

Other social factors relate to our eating behavior as well. Some of us head toward the refrigerator after a difficult day, seeking solace in a pint of Heath Bar Crunch ice cream. Why? Perhaps when we were children, our parents gave us food when we were upset. Eventually, we may have learned, through the basic mechanisms of classical and operant conditioning, to associate food with comfort and consolation. Similarly, we may learn that eating, which focuses our attention on immediate pleasures, provides an escape from unpleasant thoughts. Consequently, we may eat when we feel distressed (Bulik et al., 2003; O'Connor & O'Connor, 2004; Elfhag, Tynelius, & Rasmussen, 2007; also see PsychWork).

Obesity has become a serious health issue for many Americans, who struggle to maintain a healthy diet and weight. For Gail Rupert, a nutritionist with The Weight Loss Clinic in Harrisburg, PA, motivation is a key ingredient in losing weight.

In her approach to getting people motivated, Rupert says, "It's important to empathize with the patient so they don't feel like they're on their own with no support. I tell them I understand that the weight loss process can be frustrating and emotional, and it may take a lot of persistence and consistency before seeing any reduction in weight.

"Each client is different. Some patients have absolutely no knowledge of nutrition, while others have at least some familiarity," she explained. "For those with little knowledge, I have to break down more difficult concepts to help them better understand the procedure.

"For all patients, I make sure to give a reason why I'm suggesting a change. Most patients wouldn't change eating or exercise habits if I didn't explain the positive consequences of their actions. For example, exercising three times per week will improve their metabolism and increase their weight loss," she added.

PsychWork
NUTRITIONIST

Name: Gail K. Rupert

Position: Nutritionist

Education: BS in Nutrition and Dietetics, University of Pennsylvania, West Chester, PA

THE ROOTS OF OBESITY

Given that both biological and social factors influence eating behavior, determining the causes of obesity has proved to be a challenging task. Researchers have followed several paths.

Some psychologists suggest that oversensitivity to external eating cues based on social factors, coupled with insensitivity to internal hunger cues, produces obesity. Others argue that overweight people have higher weight set points than other people do. Because their set points are unusually high, their attempts to lose weight by eating less may make them especially sensitive to external, food-related cues and therefore more apt to overeat, perpetuating their obesity (Tremblay, 2004; West, Harvey-Berino, & Raczynski, 2004).

But why may some people's weight set points be higher than those of others? One biological explanation is that obese individuals have a higher level of the hormone *leptin*, which appears to be designed from an evolutionary standpoint to "protect" the body against weight loss. The body's weight-regulation system thus appears to be designed more to protect against losing weight than to protect against gaining it. Therefore, it's easier to gain weight than to lose it (Ahiima & Osei, 2004; Zhang et al., 2005; Levin, 2006).

Another biologically based explanation for obesity pertains to fat cells in the body. Starting at birth, the body stores fat either by increasing the number of fat cells

Obesity is reaching epidemic proportions in the United States.

Despite looking skeleton-like to others, people with the weight disorder anorexia nervosa see themselves as overweight.

anorexia nervosa A severe eating disorder in which people may refuse to eat while denying that their behavior and appearance—which can become skeleton-like—are unusual.

bulimia A disorder in which a person binges on large quantities of food, followed by efforts to purge the food through vomiting or other means.

or by increasing the size of existing fat cells. Furthermore, any loss of weight past infancy does not decrease the number of fat cells; it only affects their size. Consequently, people are stuck with the number of fat cells they inherit from an early age, and the rate of weight gain during the first four months of life is related to being overweight during later childhood (Stettler et al, 2002).

According to the weight-set-point hypothesis, the presence of too many fat cells from earliest weight gain may result in the set point's becoming "stuck" at a higher level than is desirable. In such circumstances, losing weight becomes a difficult proposition because one is constantly at odds with one's own internal set point when dieting (Freedman, 1995; Leibel, Rosenbaum & Hirsch, 1995).

Not everyone agrees with the set-point explanation for obesity. Pointing to the rapid rise in obesity over the last several decades in the United States, some researchers suggest that the body does not try to maintain a fixed weight set point. Instead, they suggest, the body has a *settling point* determined by a combination of our genetic heritage and the nature of the environment in which we live. If high-fat foods are prevalent in our environment and we're genetically predisposed to obesity, we settle into an equilibrium that maintains a relatively high weight. In contrast, if our environment is nutritionally healthier, a genetic predisposition to obesity will not be triggered and we'll settle into an equilibrium in which our weight is lower (Comuzzie & Allison, 1998; Pi-Sunyer, 2003).

EATING DISORDERS

Eating disorders are among the 10 most frequent causes of disability in young women. One devastating weight-related disorder is **anorexia nervosa.** In this severe eating disorder, people may refuse to eat while denying that their behavior and appearance—which can become skeleton-like—are unusual. Some 10% of people with anorexia literally starve themselves to death (Striegel-Moore & Bulik, 2007).

Anorexia nervosa mainly afflicts females between the ages of 12 and 40, although both men and women of any age may develop it. People with the disorder are often successful, attractive, and relatively affluent. The disorder often begins after serious dieting that somehow gets out of control. Life begins to revolve around food: Although people with the disorder eat little, they may cook for others, go shopping for food frequently, or collect cookbooks (Polivy, Herman, & Boivin, 2005; Myers, 2007; Jacobs et al., 2009).

A related problem, **bulimia,** from which Lisa Arndt (described earlier) suffered, is a disorder that leads people to binge on large quantities of food. For instance, they may consume an entire gallon of ice cream and a whole pie in a single sitting. After bingeing, sufferers feel guilt and depression and often induce vomiting or take laxatives to rid themselves of the food—behavior known as purging. Constant bingeing-and-purging cycles and the use of drugs to induce vomiting or diarrhea can lead to heart failure. Often, though, the weight of a person with bulimia remains normal (Mora-Giral et al., 2004; Couturier & Lock, 2006).

Eating disorders represent a growing problem: Estimates show that between 1 and 4% of high school–age and college-age women have either anorexia nervosa or bulimia. As many as 10% of women suffer from bulimia at some point in their lives. Furthermore, an increasing number of men are diagnosed with eating disorders; an estimated 10 to 13% of all cases occur in males (Kaminski et al, 2005; Swain, 2006; Park, 2007).

What are the causes of anorexia nervosa and bulimia? Some researchers suspect a biological cause such as a chemical imbalance in the hypothalamus or pituitary gland, perhaps brought on by genetic factors. Furthermore, scans of the brains of people with eating disorders show that they process information about food differently

Neuroscience in Your Life:
Cognitive Processing in Anorexic Patients

FIGURE 2 In this study, participants—either patients with anorexia or healthy individuals—viewed images of different foods when hungry or full to examine their cognitive processing. Comparison of fMRI scans of patients with anorexia (left column a) and healthy participants (right column b) showed significant differences in their reactions to the food stimuli. The figures show that people with anorexia generate little additional brain activity when hungry (green) as compared to when full (red), whereas those without anorexia show additional green activity when hungry as compared to when full (red). The differences suggest that patients with anorexia differ from non-anorexics when it comes to their attention to food stimuli, which in turn may be related to restrictions in the eating behavior of the anorexics. (Source: Santel et al., 2006, Figure 4.)

(a)   (b)

from healthy individuals (see Figure 2; Polivy & Herman, 2002; Santel et al., 2006; Klump & Culbert, 2007).

Others believe that the cause has its roots in society's valuation of slenderness and the parallel notion that obesity is undesirable. These researchers maintain that people with anorexia nervosa and bulimia become preoccupied with their weight and take to heart the cliché that "one can never be too thin." This may explain why, as countries become more developed and Westernized, and dieting becomes more popular, eating disorders increase. Finally, some psychologists suggest that the disorders result from overly demanding parents or other family problems (Grilo et al., 2003; Couturier & Lock, 2006; Kluck, 2008).

Complete explanations for anorexia nervosa and bulimia remain elusive. These disorders most likely stem from both biological and social causes, and successful treatment probably encompasses several strategies, including therapy and dietary changes (Wilson, Grilo, & Vitousek, 2007; O'Brien & LeBow, 2007; Cooper & Shafran, 2008).

If you or a family member needs advice or help with an eating problem, contact the American Anorexia Bulimia Association at www.aabainc.org or call 212-575-6200. You can also get more information at www.nlm.nih.gov/medlineplus/eatingdisorders .html.

Although 60% of people in the United States say they want to lose weight, it's a losing battle for the majority of them. Most people who diet eventually regain the weight they've lost, and so they try again and get caught in a seemingly endless cycle of weight loss and gain (Newport & Carroll, 2002; Parker-Pope, 2003; Cachelin & Regan, 2006).

You should keep several things in mind when trying to lose weight (Gatchel & Oordt, 2003; Heshka et al., 2003):

- *There is no easy route to weight control.* You will have to make permanent changes in your life to lose weight without gaining it back. The most obvious strategy—cutting down on the amount of food you eat—is just the first step toward a lifetime commitment to changing your eating habits.
- *Keep track of what you eat and what you weigh.* Unless you keep careful records, you won't really know how much you're eating and whether any diet is working.
- *Eat "big" foods.* Eat fiber–rich foods that are bulky and heavy but low in calories, such as grapes and soup. Such foods trick your body into thinking you've eaten more and thus decrease hunger.
- *Cut out television.* One reason for the epidemic of obesity is the number of hours spent viewing television by people in the United States. Not only does watching television preclude other activities that burn calories (even walking around the house is helpful), but people often gorge on junk food while watching (Hu et al., 2003).
- *Exercise.* Exercise at least 30 consecutive minutes three times each week. When you exercise, you use up fat stored in your body as fuel for your muscles, which is measured in calories. As you use up this fat, you'll probably lose weight. Almost any activity helps burn calories.
- *Decrease the influence of external, social stimuli on your eating behavior.* Serve yourself smaller portions of food, and leave the table before you see what's being served for dessert. Don't even buy snack foods such as nachos and potato chips; if they're not readily available in the kitchen cupboard, you're not as apt to eat them. Wrap refrigerated foods in aluminum foil so you can't see the contents and be tempted every time you open the refrigerator.
- *Avoid fad diets.* No matter how popular they are at a particular time, extreme diets (including liquid diets) usually don't work in the long run and can be dangerous to your health.
- *Avoid taking any of the numerous diet pills promising quick and easy results.*
- *Maintain good eating habits.* When you've reached your desired weight, maintain the new habits you learned while dieting to avoid gaining back the weight you've lost.
- *Set reasonable goals.* Know how much weight you want to lose before you start to diet. Don't try to lose too much weight too quickly or you may doom yourself to failure. Even small changes in behavior—such as walking 15 minutes a day or eating a few less bites at each meal—can prevent weight gain (Hill et al., 2003).

Sexual Motivation

Anyone who's seen two dogs mating knows that sexual behavior has a biological basis. Their sexual behavior appears to occur naturally and without much prompting. A number of genetically controlled factors influence the sexual behavior of non-human animals. For instance, animal behavior is affected by the presence of certain hormones in the blood. Moreover, female animals are receptive to sexual advances only during certain relatively limited periods of the year.

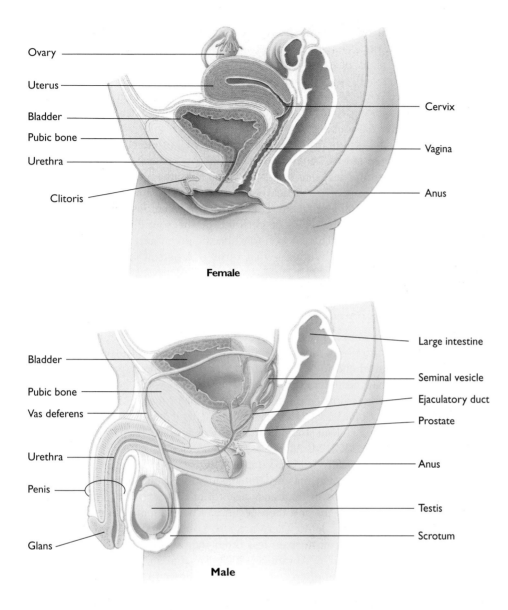

Ovary

Uterus

Bladder

Pubic bone

Urethra

Clitoris

Cervix

Vagina

Anus

Female

Bladder

Pubic bone

Vas deferens

Urethra

Penis

Glans

Large intestine

Seminal vesicle

Ejaculatory duct

Prostate

Anus

Testis

Scrotum

Male

FIGURE 3 Cutaway side views of the female and male sex organs.

Human sexual behavior, by comparison, is more complex, although the underlying biology is not all that different from related species. In males, for example, the *testes* begin to secrete **androgens**, or male sex hormones, at puberty. (See Figure 3 for the basic anatomy of the male and female **genitals** or sex organs.) Not only do androgens produce secondary sexual characteristics, such as the growth of body hair and a deepening of the voice, they also increase the sex drive. Because the level of androgen production by the testes is fairly constant, men are capable of (and interested in) sexual activities without any regard to biological cycles. Given the proper arousal stimuli, male sexual behavior can occur at any time (Goldstein, 2000).

Women show a different pattern. When they reach maturity at puberty, the two *ovaries* begin to produce **estrogens** and **progesterone,** the female sex hormones. However, those hormones aren't produced consistently; instead, their production follows a cyclical pattern. The greatest output occurs during **ovulation,** when an egg is released from the ovaries to increase the chances of fertilization by a sperm cell. Whereas in nonhumans the period around ovulation is the only time the female is receptive to sex, humans are different; although there are reported variations in sex drive, women are receptive to sex throughout their cycles (Leiblum & Chivers, 2007).

androgens Male sex hormones secreted by the testes.

genitals The male and female sex organs.

estrogens Class of female sex hormones.

progesterone A female sex hormone secreted by the ovaries.

ovulation The point at which an egg is released from the ovaries.

Looking at sex drive or receptivity to sex apart from hormone levels, some evidence suggests that males have a stronger sex drive than females, although the difference may be the result of society's discouragement of female sexuality rather than of innate differences between men and women. It is clear that men think about sex more than women: While 54% of men report thinking about sex every day, only 19% of women report thinking about it on a daily basis (Mendelsohn, 2003; Gangestad et al., 2004; Baumeister & Stillman, 2006).

Though biological factors prime people for sex, it takes more than hormones to motivate and produce sexual behavior. In animals the presence of a partner who provides arousing stimuli leads to sexual activity. Humans are considerably more versatile; not only other people but nearly any object, sight, smell, sound, or other stimulus can lead to sexual excitement. Due to prior associations, then, people may be turned on sexually by the smell of perfume or the sound of a favorite song hummed softly in their ears. The reaction to a specific potentially arousing stimulus, as we shall see, is highly individual—what turns one person on may do just the opposite for another (Benson, 2003).

MASTURBATION: SOLITARY SEX

masturbation Sexual self-stimulation.

If you listened to physicians 75 years ago, you would've been told that **masturbation** or sexual self-stimulation—often using the hand to rub the genitals—would lead to a wide variety of physical and mental disorders ranging from hairy palms to insanity. If those physicians had been correct, however, most of us would be wearing gloves to hide our hair-covered palms—for masturbation is one of the most frequently practiced sexual activities. Some 94% of all males and 63% of all females have masturbated at least once, and among college students, the frequency ranges from "never" to "several times a day" (Hunt, 1974; Michael et al., 1994; Laqueur, 2003, Polonsky, 2006).

Men and women typically begin to masturbate for the first time at a different average age. Furthermore, men masturbate considerably more often than women, although there are differences in frequency according to age. Male masturbation is most common in the early teens and then declines, whereas females both begin and reach a maximum frequency later. There are also some racial differences: African American men and women masturbate less often than whites do (Oliver & Hyde, 1993; Pinkerton, Bogart, Cecil, & Abramson, 2002; Das, Parish, & Laumann, 2009).

Although masturbation is often considered an activity to engage in only if no other sexual outlets are available, this view bears little relationship to reality. Close to three-quarters of married men (age 20 to 40) report masturbating an average of 24 times a year, and 68% of married women in the same age group masturbate an average of 10 times a year (Hunt, 1974; Michael et al., 1994; Das, 2007).

Despite the high incidence of masturbation, attitudes toward it still reflect some of the negative views of the past. For instance, one survey found that around 10% of people who masturbate experience feelings of guilt, and 5% of males and 1% of females consider their behavior perverted (Arafat & Cotton, 1974). Despite these negative attitudes, however, most experts on sex view masturbation as a healthy, legitimate, and harmless sexual activity. In addition, masturbation is seen as providing a means of learning about one's own sexuality and a way of discovering changes in one's body such as the emergence of precancerous lumps (Coleman, 2002; Levin, 2007; Herbenick et al., 2009).

HETEROSEXUALITY

heterosexuality Sexual attraction and behavior directed to the other sex.

People often believe that the first time they have sexual intercourse they've achieved one of life's major milestones. However, **heterosexuality**—sexual attraction and behavior directed to the other sex—consists of far more than male-female intercourse. Kissing, fondling, caressing, massaging, and other forms of sexual play are all components of heterosexual behavior. Still, sex researchers tend to focus on the act of intercourse, especially its first occurrence and its frequency.

PREMARITAL SEX

Sex before marriage—at least for women—was once considered a major taboo in our society. In prior generations, women were warned that "nice girls don't"; men were told that although premarital sex is okay for them, they should marry virgins. This view that premarital sex is permissible for males but not for females is called a **double standard** (Liang, 2007).

Although as recently as the 1960s the majority of adult Americans believed that premarital sex was always wrong, since that time there has been a dramatic change in public opinion. For example, the percentage of middle-age people who say sex before marriage is "not wrong at all" has increased considerably in the 21st century, and overall 60% of Americans say premarital sex is okay. More than half say that living together before marriage is morally acceptable (C&F Report, 2001; Thornton & Young-DeMarco, 2001).

Changes in attitudes toward premarital sex have been matched by changes in actual rates of premarital sexual activity. For instance, the most recent figures show that just over one-half of women between the ages of 15 and 19 have had premarital sexual intercourse. These figures are close to double the number of women in the same age range who reported having intercourse in 1970. Clearly, the trend over the last several decades has been toward more women engaging in premarital sex (Jones, Darroch, & Singh, 2005).

Males, too, have shown an increase in the incidence of premarital sexual intercourse, although the increase hasn't been as dramatic as it has been for females—probably because the rates for males were higher to begin with. For instance, the first surveys of premarital intercourse carried out in the 1940s showed an incidence of 84% across males of all ages; recent figures put the figure at closer to 95%. Moreover, the average age of males' first sexual experience has been declining steadily. Almost half of males have had sexual intercourse by the age of 18, and by the time they reach age 20, 88% have had intercourse. There also are race and ethnicity differences: African Americans tend to have sex for the first time earlier than do Puerto Ricans, who have sex earlier than whites do. Racial and ethnic differences probably reflect differences in socioeconomic opportunities and family structure (Arena, 1984; Singh et al., 2000; Hyde, 2008).

MARITAL SEX

Judging by the number of articles about sex in heterosexual marriages, one would think that sexual behavior was the number one standard by which marital bliss is measured. Married couples are often concerned that they are having too little sex, too much sex, or the wrong kind of sex (Harvey, Wenzel, & Sprecher, 2005).

Although there are many different dimensions along which sex in marriage is measured, one is certainly the frequency of sexual intercourse. What is typical? As with most other types of sexual activities, there is no easy answer to the question because there are such wide variations in patterns between individuals. We do know that 43% of married couples have sexual intercourse a few times a month and 36% of couples have it two or three times a week. With increasing age and length of marriage, the frequency of intercourse declines. Still, sex continues into late adulthood, with almost half of people reporting that they engage in sexual activity at least once a month and that its quality is high (Michael et al., 1994; Powell, 2006).

Although early research found **extramarital sex** to be widespread, the current reality appears to be otherwise. According to surveys, 85% of married women and more than 75% of married men are faithful to their spouses. Furthermore, the median number of sex partners inside and outside of marriage since age 18 for men was six, and for women, two. Accompanying these numbers is a high, consistent degree of disapproval of extramarital sex, with 9 of 10 people saying that it is "always" or "almost always" wrong (Michael et al., 1994; Daines, 2006; Whisman & Snyder, 2007).

double standard The view that premarital sex is permissible for males but not for females.

extramarital sex Sexual activity between a married person and someone who is not his or her spouse.

Extensive research has found that bisexuals and homosexuals enjoy the same overall degree of mental and physical health as heterosexuals.

HOMOSEXUALITY AND BISEXUALITY

homosexuals Persons who are sexually attracted to members of their own sex.

bisexuals Persons who are sexually attracted to people of the same sex and the other sex.

Homosexuals are sexually attracted to members of their own sex, whereas **bisexuals** are sexually attracted to people both of the same sex and the other sex. Many male homosexuals prefer the term *gay* and female homosexuals the label *lesbian* because they refer to a broader array of attitudes and lifestyles than the term *homosexual*, which focuses on the sexual act.

The number of people who choose same-sex sexual partners at one time or another is considerable. Estimates suggest that around 20 to 25% of males and about 15% of females have had at least one gay or lesbian experience during adulthood. The exact number of people who identify themselves as exclusively homosexual has proved difficult to gauge, with some estimates as low as 1.1% and some as high as 10%. Most experts suggest that between 5 and 10% of both men and women are exclusively gay or lesbian during extended periods of their lives (Hunt, 1974; Sells, 1994; Firestein, 1996).

Although people often view homosexuality and heterosexuality as two completely distinct sexual orientations, the issue is not that simple. Pioneering sex researcher Alfred Kinsey acknowledged this when he considered sexual orientation along a scale or continuum, with "exclusively homosexual" at one end and "exclusively heterosexual" at the other. In the middle were people who showed both homosexual and heterosexual behavior. Kinsey's approach suggests that sexual orientation is dependent on a person's sexual feelings and behaviors and romantic feelings (Weinberg, Williams, & Pryor, 1991).

What determines whether people become homosexual or heterosexual? Although there are a number of theories, none has proved completely satisfactory.

Some explanations for sexual orientation are biological, suggesting that there are genetic causes. Evidence for a genetic origin to sexual orientation comes from studies of identical twins, which found that when one twin identified himself or herself as homosexual, the occurrence of homosexuality in the other twin was higher than it was in the general population. Such results occur even for twins who have been separated early in life and who therefore are not necessarily raised in similar social environments (Hamer et al., 1993; Turner, 1995; Kirk, Bailey, & Martin, 2000; Gooren, 2006).

Hormones also may play a role in determining sexual orientation. For example, research shows that women exposed to DES or diethylstilbestrol before birth (when their mothers took the drug to avoid miscarriage) were more likely to be homosexual or bisexual (Meyer-Bahlburg, 1997).

Some evidence suggests that differences in brain structures may be related to sexual orientation. For instance, the structure of the anterior hypothalamus, an area of the brain that governs sexual behavior, differs in male homosexuals and heterosexuals. Similarly, other research shows that, compared with heterosexual men or women, gay men have a larger anterior commissure, which is a bundle of neurons connecting the right and left hemispheres of the brain (LeVay, 1993; Byne, 1996; Witelson et al., 2008).

However, research suggesting that biological causes are at the root of homosexuality is not conclusive because most findings are based on only small samples of individuals. Still, it seems clear that some inherited or biological factor exists that predisposes people toward homosexuality if certain environmental conditions are met (Veniegas, 2000; Teodorov et al., 2002; Rahman, Kumari, & Wilson, 2003).

"Frankly, I've repressed my sexuality so long I've actually forgotten what my orientation is."

Little evidence supports that sexual orientation is brought about by child-rearing practices or family dynamics. Although proponents of psychoanalytic theories once argued that the nature of the parent-child relationship can produce homosexuality (e.g., Freud, 1922/1959), research evidence does not support such explanations (Isay, 1994; Roughton, 2002).

Another explanation for sexual orientation rests on learning theory (Masters & Johnson, 1979). According to this view, sexual orientation is learned through rewards and punishments in much the same way that we may learn to prefer swimming over tennis. For example, a young adolescent who had an unpleasant heterosexual experience might develop disagreeable associations with the other sex. If the same person had a rewarding and pleasant gay or lesbian experience, homosexuality might be incorporated into his or her sexual fantasies. If such fantasies are used during later sexual activities—such as masturbation—they may be positively reinforced through orgasm, and the association of homosexual behavior and sexual pleasure eventually may cause homosexuality to become the preferred form of sexual behavior.

Although the learning-theory explanation is plausible, several difficulties rule it out as a definitive explanation. Because our society has traditionally held homosexuality in low esteem, one ought to expect that the negative treatment of homosexual behavior would outweigh the rewards attached to it. Furthermore, children growing up with a gay or lesbian parent are statistically unlikely to become homosexual, thus contradicting the notion that homosexual behavior may be learned from others (Golombok, 1995; Victor & Fish, 1995; Tasker, 2005).

Because it's difficult to find a consistent explanation, we can't answer the question of what determines sexual orientation. It does seem unlikely that any single factor orients a person toward homosexuality or heterosexuality. Instead, it seems reasonable to assume that a combination of biological and environmental factors is involved (Bem, 1996; Hyde, 2008).

Although we don't know at this point exactly why people develop a certain sexual orientation, one thing is clear: There is no relationship between sexual orientation and psychological adjustment. Gays, lesbians, and bisexuals generally enjoy the same quality of mental and physical health that heterosexuals do, although the discrimination they experience may produce higher rates of some disorders such as depression (Poteat & Espelage, 2007). Bisexuals and homosexuals also hold equivalent ranges and types of attitudes about themselves, independent of sexual orientation. For these reasons, the American Psychological Association and other mental health organizations have endorsed efforts to eliminate discrimination against gays and lesbians by, for example, revoking the ban against homosexuals in the military (Cochran, 2000; Perez, DeBord, & Bieschke, 2000; Morris, Waldo, & Rothblum, 2001).

Study Alert

The determinants of sexual orientation have proven difficult to pinpoint. It is important to know the variety of explanations that have been put forward.

TRANSSEXUALISM

transsexuals Persons who believe they were born with the body of the other gender.

Transsexuals are people who believe they were born with the body of the other gender. In fundamental ways, transsexualism represents less a sexual difficulty than a gender issue involving one's sexual identity (Meyerowitz, 2004; Heath, 2006).

Transsexuals sometimes seek sex-change operations to surgically remove their existing genitals and have the genitals of the desired sex fashioned. Several steps, including intensive counseling, hormone injections, and living as a member of the desired sex for several years, precede surgery that is, not surprisingly, very complicated. The outcome, though, can be quite positive (O'Keefe & Fox, 2003; Stegerwald & Janson, 2003; Lobato et al., 2006).

Transsexualism is part of a broader category known as transgenderism. The term *transgenderism* encompasses not only transsexuals but also people who view themselves as a third gender called transvestites (who dress in the clothes of the other gender), or others who believe that traditional male-female gender classifications inadequately characterize them (Prince, 2005; Hyde, 2008).

Transsexuals are distinct from individuals who are known as *intersex* or by the older term *hermaphrodite*. An intersex person is someone who is born with an atypical combination of sexual organs or of chromosomal or gene patterns. In some cases, they are born with both male and female sex organs, or the organs are ambiguous. It's an extremely rare condition found in only 1 in 4,500 births. Intersexism involves a complex mix of physiological and psychological issues (Lehrman, 2007; Diamond, 2009).

The Needs for Achievement, Affiliation, and Power

Although hunger may be one of the more potent primary drives in our day-to-day lives, powerful secondary drives that have no clear biological basis also motivate us. Among the more prominent of these is the need for achievement.

THE NEED FOR ACHIEVEMENT: STRIVING FOR EXCELLENCE

need for achievement A stable, learned characteristic in which a person obtains satisfaction by striving for and attaining a level of excellence.

The **need for achievement** is a stable, learned characteristic that brings a person satisfaction by striving for and attaining a level of excellence (McClelland et al., 1953). People with a high need for achievement seek out situations in which they can compete against some standard—be it grades, money, or winning at a game—and prove themselves successful. But they are not indiscriminate when it comes to picking their challenges: They tend to avoid situations in which success will come too easily (which wouldn't be challenging) and situations where success is unlikely. Instead, people high in achievement motivation generally choose tasks that are of intermediate difficulty (Speirs & Finch, 2006).

In contrast, people with low achievement motivation tend to be motivated primarily by a desire to avoid failure. As a result, they seek out easy tasks, being sure to avoid failure, or seek out very difficult tasks for which failure has no negative implications, because almost anyone would fail at them. People with a high fear of failure will stay away from tasks of intermediate difficulty because they may fail where others have been successful (Martin & Marsh, 2002; Puca, 2005; Morrone & Pintrich, 2006).

A high need for achievement generally produces positive outcomes, at least in a success-oriented culture such as Western society. For instance, people motivated by a high need for achievement are more likely to attend college than are their low-achievement counterparts; and once they are in college, they tend to receive higher

Study Alert

A key feature of people with a high need for achievement is that they prefer tasks of *moderate* difficulty.

grades in classes related to their future careers. Furthermore, high achievement motivation indicates future economic and occupational success (McClelland, 1985; Thrash & Elliot, 2002).

MEASURING ACHIEVEMENT MOTIVATION

How can we measure a person's need for achievement? The measuring instrument used most frequently is the *Thematic Apperception Test (TAT)* (Spangler, 1992). To administer the TAT, an examiner shows a series of ambiguous pictures such as the one in Figure 4, then tells participants to write a story that describes what is happening, who the people are, what led to the situation, what the people are thinking or wanting, and what will happen next. Researchers then use a standard scoring system to determine the amount of achievement imagery in people's stories. For example, someone who writes a story in which the main character strives to beat an opponent, studies in order to do well at some task, or works hard to get a promotion shows clear signs of an achievement orientation. The inclusion of such achievement-related imagery in the participants' stories is assumed to indicate an unusually high degree of concern with—and therefore a relatively strong need for—achievement (Tuerlinckx, DeBoeck, & Lens, 2002).

THE NEED FOR AFFILIATION: STRIVING FOR FRIENDSHIP

Few of us choose to lead our lives as hermits. Why?

One main reason is that most people have a **need for affiliation,** an interest in establishing and maintaining relationships with other people. Individuals with a high need for affiliation write TAT stories that emphasize the desire to maintain or reinstate friendships and show concern over being rejected by friends.

People who have higher affiliation needs are particularly sensitive to relationships with others. They desire to be with their friends more of the time and alone less often, compared with people who are lower in their need for affiliation. However, gender is a greater determinant of how much time is actually spent with friends: Regardless of their affiliative orientation, female students spend significantly more time with their friends and less time alone than male students do (Cantwell & Andrews, 2002; Johnson, 2004; Semykina & Linz, 2007).

THE NEED FOR POWER: STRIVING FOR IMPACT ON OTHERS

If your fantasies include becoming president of the United States or running Microsoft, your dreams may reflect a high need for power. The **need for power**—a tendency to seek impact, control, or influence over others and to be seen as a powerful individual—is an additional type of motivation (Lee-Chai & Bargh, 2001; Winter, 2007; Zians, 2007).

As you might expect, people with strong needs for power are more apt to belong to organizations and seek office than are those low in the need for power. They also tend to work in professions in which their power needs may be fulfilled, such as business management and—you may or may not be surprised—teaching (Jenkins, 1994). In addition, they seek to display the trappings of power. Even in college, they are more likely to collect prestigious possessions such as electronic equipment and sports cars.

Some significant gender differences exist in the display of need for power. Men with high power needs tend to show unusually high levels of aggression, drink heavily, act in a sexually exploitative manner, and participate more frequently in competitive sports—behaviors that collectively represent somewhat extravagant, flamboyant behavior. In contrast, women display their power needs with more restraint; this is congruent with traditional societal constraints on women's behavior. Women with high power needs are more apt than men to channel those needs in a socially responsible manner, such as by showing concern for others or displaying highly nurturing behavior (Maroda, 2004; Winter, 1988, 1995, 2007; Schubert & Koole, 2009).

FIGURE 4 This ambiguous picture is similar to those used in the Thematic Apperception Test to determine people's underlying motivation. What do you see? Do you think your response is related to your motivation? (Source: © 1943 by the President and Fellows of Harvard College; 1971 by Henry A. Murray.)

need for affiliation An interest in establishing and maintaining relationships with other people.

need for power A tendency to seek impact, control, or influence over others, and to be seen as a powerful individual.

RECAP/EVALUATE/RETHINK

RECAP

What biological and social factors underlie hunger?
- Eating behavior is subject to homeostasis, as most people's weight stays within a relatively stable range. The hypothalamus in the brain is central to the regulation of food intake. (p. 290)
- Social factors, such as mealtimes, cultural food preferences, and other learned habits, also play a role in the regulation of eating, determining when, what, and how much one eats. An oversensitivity to social cues and an insensitivity to internal cues may also be related to obesity. In addition, obesity may be caused by an unusually high weight set point—the weight the body attempts to maintain—and genetic factors. (p. 292)

What are the varieties of sexual behavior?
- Although biological factors, such as the presence of androgens (male sex hormones) and estrogens and progesterone (female sex hormones), prime people for sex, almost any kind of stimulus can produce sexual arousal depending on a person's prior experience. (p. 297)
- The frequency of masturbation is high, particularly for males. Although increasingly liberal, attitudes toward masturbation have traditionally been negative even though no negative biological consequences have been detected. (p. 298)
- Heterosexuality, or sexual attraction to members of the other sex, is the most common sexual orientation. (p. 298)
- The double standard that says premarital sex is more permissible for men than for women has declined, particularly among young people. For many, the double standard has been replaced by endorsement of "permissiveness with affection," the view that premarital intercourse is permissible if it occurs in the context of a loving and committed relationship. (p. 299)
- Homosexuals are sexually attracted to members of their own sex; bisexuals are sexually attracted to people of the same sex and the other sex. No explanation for why people are homosexual has been confirmed; among the possibilities are genetic or biological factors, childhood and family influences, and prior learning experiences and conditioning. However, no relationship exists between sexual orientation and psychological adjustment. (p. 300)

How are needs relating to achievement, affiliation, and power motivation exhibited?
- Need for achievement refers to the stable, learned characteristic in which a person strives to attain a level of excellence. Need for achievement is usually measured through the Thematic Apperception Test (TAT), a series of pictures about which a person writes a story. (p. 302)
- The need for affiliation is a concern with establishing and maintaining relationships with others, whereas the need for power is a tendency to seek to exert an impact on others. (p. 303)

EVALUATE

1. Match the following terms with their definitions:
   1. Hypothalamus
   2. Lateral hypothalamic damage
   3. Ventromedial hypothalamic damage

   a. Leads to refusal of food and starvation
   b. Responsible for monitoring food intake
   c. Causes extreme overeating

2. The _____ _____ _____ is the specific level of weight the body strives to maintain.
3. _____ is the rate at which energy is produced and expended by the body.
4. Although the incidence of masturbation among young adults is high, once men and women become involved in intimate relationships, they typically cease masturbating. True or false?
5. The increase in premarital sex in recent years has been greater for women than for men. True or false?
6. Julio is the type of person who constantly strives for excellence. He feels intense satisfaction when he is able to master a new task. Julio most likely has a high need for _____.
7. Debbie's Thematic Apperception Test (TAT) story depicts a young girl who is rejected by one of her peers and seeks to regain her friendship. What major type of motivation is Debbie displaying in her story?

   a. Need for achievement
   b. Need for motivation
   c. Need for affiliation
   d. Need for power

RETHINK

a. In what ways do societal expectations as expressed by TV shows, commercials, and other forms of advertisement contribute to both obesity and excessive concern about weight loss? How could the media contribute to better eating habits and attitudes toward weight? Should it be required to do so?

b. *From the perspective of a human resources specialist:* How might you use characteristics such as need for achievement, need for power, and need for affiliation to select workers for jobs? What additional criteria would you have to consider?

Answers to Evaluate Questions

1. 1-b, 2-a, 3-c; 2. weight set point; 3. metabolism; 4. false; 5. true; 6. achievement; 7. c.

KEY TERMS

obesity p. 290
weight set point p. 292
metabolism p. 292
anorexia nervosa p. 294
bulimia p. 294
androgens p. 297

genitals p. 297
estrogens p. 297
progesterone p. 297
ovulation p. 297
masturbation p. 298
heterosexuality p. 298

double standard p. 299
extramarital sex p. 299
homosexuals p. 300
bisexuals p. 300
transsexuals p. 302

need for
  achievement p. 302
need for affiliation p. 303
need for power p. 303

Understanding Emotional Experiences

Key Concepts

What are emotions, and how do we experience them?

What are the functions of emotions?

What are the explanations for emotions?

How does nonverbal behavior relate to the expression of emotions?

emotions Feelings that generally have both physiological and cognitive elements and that influence behavior.

Karl Andrews held in his hands the envelope he had been waiting for. It could be the ticket to his future: an offer of admission to his first-choice college. But what was it going to say? He knew it could go either way; his grades were pretty good and he had been involved in some extracurricular activities, but his SAT scores had not been so terrific. He felt so nervous that his hands shook as he opened the thin envelope. (Not a good sign, he thought.) Here it comes. "Dear Mr. Andrews," it read. "The Trustees of the University are pleased to admit you. . . ." That was all he needed to see. With a whoop of excitement, Karl found himself jumping up and down gleefully. A rush of emotion overcame him as it sank in that he had, in fact, been accepted. He was on his way.

At one time or another, all of us have experienced the strong feelings that accompany both very pleasant and very negative experiences. Perhaps we've felt the thrill of getting a sought-after job, the joy of being in love, the sorrow over someone's death, or the anguish of inadvertently hurting someone. Moreover, we experience similar reactions on a less intense level throughout our day: the pleasure of a friendship, the enjoyment of a movie, and the embarrassment of breaking a borrowed item.

Despite the varied nature of these feelings, they all represent emotions. Although everyone has an idea of what an emotion is, formally defining the concept has proved to be elusive. Here, we'll use a general definition: **Emotions** are feelings that generally have both physiological and cognitive elements and that influence behavior.

Think, for example, about how it feels to be happy. First, we obviously experience a feeling that we can differentiate from other emotions. It's likely we also experience some identifiable physical changes in our bodies: Perhaps our heart rate increases or—as in the example of Karl Andrews—we find ourselves "jumping for joy." Finally, the emotion probably encompasses cognitive elements: Our understanding and evaluation of the meaning of what is happening prompts our feelings of happiness.

It is also possible, however, to experience an emotion without the presence of cognitive elements. For instance, we may react with fear to an unusual or novel situation (such as coming into contact with an erratic, unpredictable individual), or we may experience pleasure over sexual arousal without having cognitive awareness or understanding of just what it is about the situation that's exciting.

Some psychologists argue that entirely separate systems govern cognitive and emotional responses. A current controversy focuses on whether the emotional response predominates over the cognitive one or vice versa. Some theorists suggest that we first respond to a situation with an emotional reaction and later try to understand it. For example, we may enjoy a symphony without at first understanding it or knowing why we like it. In contrast, other theorists propose that people first develop cognitions about a situation and *then* react emotionally. This school of thought suggests that we must think about and understand a stimulus or situation by relating it to what we already know before we can react on an emotional level (Murphy & Zajonc, 1993; Lazarus, 1995; Oatley, Keltner, & Jenkins, 2006).

Because proponents of both sides of this debate can cite research to support their viewpoints, the question is far from resolved. Perhaps the sequence varies from situation to situation, with emotions predominating in some instances and cognitive processes occurring first in others. Both sides agree that we can experience emotions that involve little or no conscious thought. We may not know why we're afraid of mice, understanding objectively that they represent no danger, but we may still be frightened when we see them. Neuroimaging studies of the brain may help resolve this debate as well as others about the nature of emotions (Barrett & Wager, 2006; Niedenthal, 2007; Karaszewski, 2008).

The Functions of Emotions

Imagine what it'd be like if we didn't experience emotion—no depths of despair, no depression, no remorse, but at the same time no happiness, joy, or love. Obviously, life would be considerably less satisfying and even dull if we lacked the capacity to sense and express emotion.

But do emotions serve any purpose beyond making life interesting? Indeed they do. Psychologists have identified several important functions that emotions play in our daily lives (Frederickson & Branigan, 2005; Frijda, 2005; Gross, 2006; Siemer, Mauss, & Gross, 2007). Among the most important are the following:

- *Preparing us for action.* Emotions act as a link between events in our environment and our responses. For example, if you saw an angry dog charging toward you, your emotional reaction (fear) would be associated with physiological arousal of the sympathetic division of the autonomic nervous system to activate the "fight-or-flight" response.
- *Shaping our future behavior.* Emotions promote learning that will help us make appropriate responses in the future. For instance, your emotional response to unpleasant events teaches you to avoid similar circumstances in the future.
- *Helping us interact more effectively with others.* We often communicate the emotions we experience through our verbal and nonverbal behaviors, making our emotions obvious to observers. These behaviors can signal to observers, allowing them to understand better what we're experiencing and to help them predict our future behavior.

Determining the Range of Emotions: Labeling Our Feelings

If we were to list the words in the English language that have been used to describe emotions, we would end up with at least 500 examples (Averill, 1975). The list would range from such obvious emotions as *happiness* and *fear* to less common ones, such as *adventurousness* and *pensiveness*.

One challenge for psychologists has been to sort through this list to identify the most important fundamental emotions. Theorists have hotly contested the issue of cataloging emotions and have come up with different lists depending on how they define the concept of emotion. In fact, some reject the question entirely, saying that *no* set of emotions should be singled out as most basic and that emotions are best understood by breaking them down into their component parts. Other researchers argue for looking at emotions in terms of a hierarchy, dividing them into positive and negative categories, and then organizing them into increasingly narrower subcategories (see Figure 1; Manstead, Frijda, & Fischer, 2003; Dillard & Shen, 2007).

Still, most researchers agree that a list of basic emotions would include, at a minimum, happiness, anger, fear, sadness, and disgust. Other lists are broader, including emotions such as surprise, contempt, guilt, and joy (Ekman, 1994a; Shweder, 1994; Tracy & Robins, 2004).

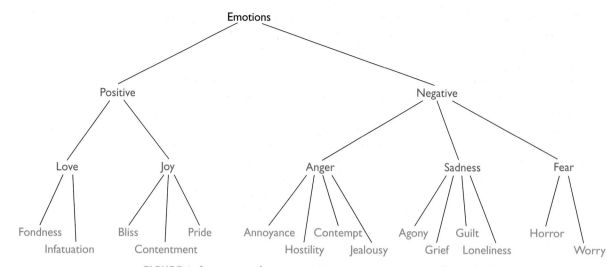

FIGURE 1 One approach to organizing emotions is to use a hierarchy that divides emotions into increasingly narrow subcategories. (Source: Adapted from Fischer, Shaver, & Carnochan, 1990.)

One difficulty when defining a basic set of emotions is that substantial differences exist in how emotions are described among various cultures. For instance, Germans report experiencing *schadenfreude,* a feeling of pleasure over another person's difficulties, and the Japanese experience *hagaii,* a mood of vulnerable heartache colored by frustration. In Tahiti, people experience *musu,* a feeling of reluctance to yield to unreasonable demands made by one's parents.

Finding *schadenfreude, hagaii,* or *musu* within a particular culture doesn't mean that members of other cultures are incapable of experiencing the same emotions, of course. It does suggest, though, that fitting a particular emotion into a linguistic category to describe it may make it easier to discuss, contemplate, and perhaps experience (Russell & Sato, 1995; Li, Wang, & Fischer, 2004; Kuppens et al., 2006).

The Roots of Emotions

> I've never been so angry before; I feel my heart pounding, and I'm trembling all over. . . . I don't know how I'll get through the performance. I feel like my stomach is filled with butterflies. . . . That was quite a mistake! My face must be incredibly red. . . . When I heard the footsteps in the night, I was so frightened I couldn't catch my breath.

If you examine our language, you'll find that there are literally dozens of ways to describe how we feel when we experience an emotion, and the language we use to describe emotions is, for the most part, based on the physical symptoms associated with a particular emotional experience (Kobayashi, Schallert, & Ogren, 2003; Manstead & Wagner, 2004; Spackman, Fujiki, & Brinton, 2006).

Consider, for instance, the experience of fear. Pretend that it's late on New Year's Eve. You're walking down a dark road, and you hear a stranger approaching behind you. It's clear that he's not trying to hurry by but is coming directly toward you. You think about what you'll do if the stranger attempts to rob you or, worse, hurt you in some way.

While these thoughts are running through your head, something dramatic will be happening to your body. The most likely reactions, which are associated with activation of the autonomic nervous system, include an increase in your rate of breathing, an acceleration of your heart rate, a widening of your pupils (to increase visual sensitivity), and a dryness in your mouth as the functioning of your salivary glands, and in fact of your entire digestive system, ceases. At the same time, though, your sweat glands probably will increase their activity, because increased sweating will help you rid yourself of the excess heat developed by any emergency activity in which you engage.

Of course, all these physiological changes are likely to occur without your awareness. At the same time, though, the emotional experience accompanying them will be obvious to you: You most surely would report being fearful.

Although it's easy to describe the general physical reactions that accompany emotions, defining the specific role that those physiological responses play in the experience of emotions has proved to be a major puzzle for psychologists. As we shall see, some theorists suggest that specific bodily reactions *cause* us to experience a particular emotion—we experience fear, for instance, *because* the heart is pounding and we are breathing deeply. In contrast, other theorists suggest that the physiological reaction results from the experience of an emotion. In this view, we experience fear and, as a result, the heart pounds and our breathing deepens.

THE JAMES-LANGE THEORY: DO GUT REACTIONS EQUAL EMOTIONS?

To William James and Carl Lange, who were among the first researchers to explore the nature of emotions, emotional experience is, very simply, a reaction to instinctive bodily events that occur as a response to some situation or event in the environment. This view is summarized in James's statement, "We feel sorry because we cry, angry because we strike, afraid because we tremble" (James, 1890).

James and Lange took the view that the instinctive response of crying at a loss leads us to feel sorrow, that striking out at someone who frustrates us results in our feeling anger, that trembling at a menacing threat causes us to feel fear. They suggested that for every major emotion there is an accompanying physiological or "gut" reaction of internal organs—called a *visceral experience*. It is this specific pattern of visceral response that leads us to label the emotional experience.

In sum, James and Lange proposed that we experience emotions as a result of physiological changes that produce specific sensations. The brain interprets these sensations as specific kinds of emotional experiences (see the first part of Figure 2). This view has come to be called the **James-Lange theory of emotion** (Laird & Bresler, 1990; Cobo et al., 2002).

The James-Lange theory has some serious drawbacks, however. For the theory to be valid, visceral changes would have to occur relatively quickly because we experience some emotions—such as fear upon hearing a stranger rapidly approaching on a dark night—almost instantaneously. Yet emotional experiences frequently occur even before there's time for certain physiological changes to be set into motion. Because of the slowness with which some visceral changes take place, it's hard to see how they could be the source of immediate emotional experience.

The James-Lange theory poses another difficulty: Physiological arousal does not invariably produce emotional experience. For example, a person who is jogging has an increased heartbeat and respiration rate as well as many of the other physiological changes associated with certain emotions. Yet joggers typically don't feel a response on an emotional level. There can't be a one-to-one correspondence, then, between visceral changes and emotional experience. Visceral changes by themselves may not be sufficient to produce emotion.

Finally, our internal organs produce a relatively limited range of sensations. Although some types of physiological changes are associated with specific emotional experiences, it's difficult to imagine how each of the myriad emotions that people are capable of could be the result of a unique visceral change. Many emotions actually are associated with relatively similar sorts of visceral changes, a fact that contradicts the James-Lange theory (Davidson et al., 1994; Cameron, 2002).

James-Lange theory of emotion The belief that emotional experience is a reaction to bodily events occurring as a result of an external situation ("I feel sad because I'm crying").

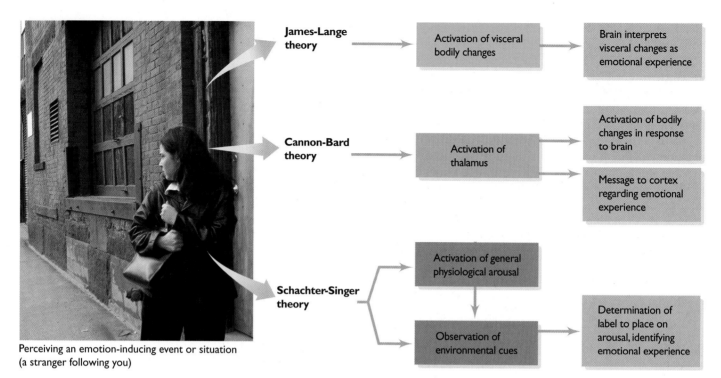

Perceiving an emotion-inducing event or situation
(a stranger following you)

FIGURE 2 A comparison of three models of emotion.

THE CANNON-BARD THEORY: PHYSIOLOGICAL REACTIONS AS THE RESULT OF EMOTIONS

In response to the difficulties inherent in the James-Lange theory, Walter Cannon, and later Philip Bard, suggested an alternative view. In what has come to be known as the **Cannon-Bard theory of emotion,** they proposed the model illustrated in the second part of Figure 2 (Cannon, 1929). This theory rejects the view that physiological arousal alone leads to the perception of emotion. Instead, the theory assumes that both physiological arousal *and* emotional experience are produced simultaneously by the same nerve stimulus, which Cannon and Bard suggested emanates from the thalamus in the brain.

The theory states that after we perceive an emotion-producing stimulus, the thalamus is the initial site of the emotional response. Next, the thalamus sends a signal to the autonomic nervous system, thereby producing a visceral response. At the same time, the thalamus also communicates a message to the cerebral cortex about the nature of the emotion being experienced. Hence, it's not necessary for different emotions to have unique physiological patterns associated with them—as long as the message sent to the cerebral cortex differs according to the specific emotion.

In rejecting the view that physiological arousal alone accounts for emotions, the Cannon-Bard theory seems to have been accurate. However, more recent research has led to some important modifications of the theory. For one thing, we now understand that the hypothalamus and the limbic system, not the thalamus, play a major role in emotional experience. In addition, the simultaneous occurrence of the physiological and emotional responses—a fundamental assumption of the Cannon-Bard theory—has yet to be demonstrated conclusively. This ambiguity has allowed room for yet another theory of emotions: the Schachter-Singer theory.

THE SCHACHTER-SINGER THEORY: EMOTIONS AS LABELS

Suppose that, as you're being followed down that dark street on New Year's Eve, you notice a man being followed by another shady figure on the other side of the

Cannon-Bard theory of emotion
The belief that both physiological arousal and emotional experience are produced simultaneously by the same nerve stimulus.

Study Alert
Use Figure 2 to distinguish the three classic theories of emotion (James-Lange, Cannon-Bard, and Schachter-Singer).

street. Now assume that instead of reacting with fear, the man begins to laugh and act gleeful. Would the reactions of this other individual be sufficient to lay your fears to rest? Might you, in fact, decide there's nothing to fear and get into the spirit of the evening by beginning to feel happiness and glee yourself?

According to an explanation that focuses on the role of cognition, the **Schachter-Singer theory of emotion,** this might very well happen. This approach to explaining emotions emphasizes that we identify the emotion we are experiencing by observing our environment and comparing ourselves with others (Schachter & Singer, 1962).

Schachter and Singer's classic experiment found evidence for this hypothesis. In the study, participants were told that they would receive an injection of a vitamin. In reality, they were given epinephrine, a drug that causes an increase in physiological arousal, including higher heart and respiration rates and a reddening of the face, responses that typically occur during strong emotional reactions. The members of both groups were then placed individually in a situation where a confederate of the experimenter acted in one of two ways. In one condition he acted angry and hostile, and in the other he behaved as if he were exuberantly happy.

The purpose of the experiment was to determine how the participants would react emotionally to the confederate's behavior. When they were asked to describe their own emotional state at the end of the experiment, the participants exposed to the angry confederate reported that they felt angry, while those exposed to the happy confederate reported feeling happy. In sum, the results suggest that participants turned to the environment and the behavior of others for an explanation of the physiological arousal they were experiencing.

The results of the Schachter-Singer experiment, then, supported a cognitive view of emotions that posits emotions are determined jointly by a relatively nonspecific kind of physiological arousal *and* the labeling of that arousal on the basis of cues from the environment (refer to the third part of Figure 2). Later research has found that arousal isn't as nonspecific as Schachter and Singer assumed. When the source of physiological arousal is unclear, however, we may look to our surroundings to determine just what we are experiencing.

Schachter-Singer theory of emotion The belief that emotions are determined jointly by a nonspecific kind of physiological arousal and its interpretation based on environmental cues.

CONTEMPORARY PERSPECTIVES ON THE NEUROSCIENCE OF EMOTIONS

When Schachter and Singer carried out their groundbreaking experiment in the early 1960s, the ways in which they could evaluate the physiology that accompanies emotion were relatively limited. However, advances in measuring the nervous system and other parts of the body have allowed researchers to examine more closely the biological responses involved in emotion. As a result, contemporary research on emotion indicates a revision of earlier views that physiological responses associated with emotions are undifferentiated. Instead, evidence is growing that specific patterns of biological arousal are associated with individual emotions (Franks & Smith, 2000; Vaitl, Schienle, & Stark, 2005; Woodson, 2006).

For instance, researchers have found that specific emotions activate very different portions of the brain. In one study, participants undergoing positron emission tomography (PET) brain scans were asked to recall events that made them feel sad, such as deaths and funerals, or events that made them feel happy, such as weddings and births. They also looked at photos of faces that appeared happy or sad. The results of the PET scans were clear: Happiness was related to a decrease in activity in certain areas of the cerebral cortex, whereas sadness was associated with increases in activity in particular portions of the cortex (George et al., 1995; Hamann, Ely, Hoffman, & Kilts, 2002; Prohovnik, Skudlarski, Fulbright, Gore, & Wexler, 2004).

In addition, the *amygdala* in the brain's temporal lobe is important in the experience of emotions, for it provides a link between the perception of an emotion-producing stimulus and the recall of that stimulus later. For example, if we've been attacked once by a vicious pit bull, the amygdala processes that information and

FIGURE 3 Connections from the amygdala, seen here in red, allow it to mediate many of the autonomic expressions of emotional states through the hippocampus (purple) and visual cortex (orange). (Source: From Dolan, R. J. (2002). Emotion, cognition, and behavior. *Science, 298,* no. 5596, 1191–1194 (Figure 1, p. 1192). Drawing of brain reprinted with permission from AAAS.)

Study Alert

It's important to understand the basic neuroscience of emotional experience.

leads us to react with fear when we see a pit bull later—an example of a classically conditioned fear response (Miller et al., 2005; Berntson et al., 2007; Kensinger, 2007; LaBar, 2007).

Because neural pathways connect the amygdala, the visual cortex, and the *hippocampus* (which plays an important role in the consolidation of memories), some scientists speculate that emotion-related stimuli can be processed and responded to almost instantaneously (see Figure 3). This immediate response occurs so rapidly that higher-order, more rational thinking (which takes more time) seems not to be involved initially. In a slower but more thoughtful response to emotion-evoking stimuli, emotion-related sensory information is first evaluated and then sent on to the amygdala. It appears that the quicker system offers an immediate response to emotion-evoking stimuli, whereas the slower system helps confirm a threat and prepare a more thoughtful response (Dolan, 2002).

MAKING SENSE OF THE MULTIPLE PERSPECTIVES ON EMOTION

As new approaches to emotion continue to develop, it's reasonable to ask why so many theories of emotion exist and, perhaps more important, which one provides the most complete explanation. Actually, we've only scratched the surface. There are almost as many explanatory theories of emotion as there are individual emotions (e.g., Manstead, Frijda, & Fischer, 2003; Frijda, 2005; Prinz, 2007; Herzberg, 2009).

Why are theories of emotion so plentiful? For one thing, emotions are not a simple phenomenon but are intertwined closely with motivation, cognition, neuroscience, and a host of related branches of psychology. For example, evidence from brain imaging studies shows that even when people come to supposedly rational, nonemotional decisions—such as making moral, philosophical judgments—emotions come into play (Greene et al., 2001).

In short, emotions are such complex phenomena encompassing both biological and cognitive aspects that no single theory has been able to explain fully all the facets of emotional experience. Furthermore, contradictory evidence of one sort or another challenges each approach, and therefore no theory has proved invariably accurate in its predictions.

This abundance of perspectives on emotion is not a cause for despair—or unhappiness, fear, or any other negative emotion. It simply reflects the fact that psychology is an evolving, developing science. As we gather more evidence, the specific answers to questions about the nature of emotions will become clearer.

Consider, for a moment, the six photos displayed in Figure 4. Can you identify the emotions being expressed by the person in each of the photos?

Exploring DIVERSITY

Do People in All Cultures Express Emotion Similarly?

If you're a good judge of facial expressions, you'll conclude that these expressions display six of the basic emotions: happiness, anger, sadness, surprise, disgust, and fear. Hundreds of studies of nonverbal behavior show that these emotions are consistently distinct and identifiable, even by untrained observers (Ekman & O'Sullivan, 1991).

Interestingly, these six emotions are not unique to members of Western cultures; rather, they constitute the basic emotions expressed universally by members of the human race, regardless of where individuals have been raised and what learning experiences they have had. Psychologist Paul Ekman convincingly demonstrated this when he studied the members of an isolated New Guinea jungle tribe who had had almost no contact with Westerners (Ekman, 1972). The people of the tribe didn't speak or understand English, had never seen a movie, and had had very limited experience with Caucasians before Ekman's arrival. Yet their nonverbal responses to emotion-evoking stories, as well as their ability to identify basic emotions, were quite similar to those of Westerners.

FIGURE 4 These photos demonstrate six of the primary emotions: happiness, anger, sadness, surprise, disgust, and fear.

© Gahan Wilson/The New Yorker Collection/www.cartoonbank.com.

"And just exactly what is that expression intended to convey?"

facial-affect program Activation of a set of nerve impulses that make the face display the appropriate expression.

facial-feedback hypothesis The hypothesis that facial expressions not only reflect emotional experience but also help determine how people experience and label emotions.

Being so isolated, the New Guineans could not have learned from Westerners to recognize or produce similar facial expressions. Instead, their similar abilities and manner of responding emotionally appear to have been present innately. Although one could argue that similar experiences in both cultures led the members of each to learn similar types of nonverbal behavior, this appears unlikely because the two cultures are so very different. The expression of basic emotions, thus, seems to be universal (Ekman, 1994b; Izard, 1994; Matsumoto, 2002).

Why do people across cultures express emotions similarly? A hypothesis known as the **facial-affect program** gives one explanation. The facial-affect program—which is assumed to be universally present at birth—is analogous to a computer program that is turned on when a particular emotion is experienced. When set in motion, the "program" activates a set of nerve impulses that make the face display an appropriate expression. Each primary emotion produces a unique set of muscular movements forming the kinds of expressions shown in Figure 4. For example, the emotion of happiness is universally displayed by movement of the zygomatic major, a muscle that raises the corners of the mouth—forming what we would call a smile (Ekman, 2003; Kohler et al., 2004; Kim et al., 2007; Kendler et al., 2008).

The importance of facial expressions is illustrated by an intriguing notion known as the **facial-feedback hypothesis.** According to this hypothesis, facial expressions not only *reflect* emotional experience, they also help *determine* how people experience and label emotions. Basically put, "wearing" an emotional expression provides muscular feedback to the brain that helps produce an emotion congruent with that expression (Izard, 1990; Davis, Senghas, & Ochsner, 2009).

For instance, the muscles activated when we smile may send a message to the brain indicating the experience of happiness—even if there is nothing in the environment that would produce that particular emotion. Some theoreticians have gone further, suggesting that facial expressions are *necessary* for an emotion to be experienced (Rinn, 1984, 1991). In this view, if no facial expression is present, the emotion can't be felt.

Support for the facial-feedback hypothesis comes from a classic experiment carried out by psychologist Paul Ekman and colleagues (Ekman, Levenson, & Friesen, 1983). In the study, professional actors were asked to follow very explicit instructions to move muscles in their faces. You might try this example yourself:

- Raise your brows and pull them together.
- Raise your upper eyelids.
- Now stretch your lips horizontally back toward your ears.

After carrying out these directions—which, as you may have guessed, are meant to produce an expression of fear—the actors' heart rates rose and their body temperatures declined, physiological reactions that characterize fear. Overall, facial expressions representing the primary emotions produced physiological effects similar to those accompanying the genuine emotions in other circumstances (Keillor et al., 2002; Soussignan, 2002). (Also see *Applying Psychology in the 21st Century*.)

Smiling Athletes: Do Their Facial Expressions Come Naturally?

There's no more stirring sight than medal-winning Olympic athletes standing on the podium as their national anthem is played. Have you ever wondered why—no matter which country winners are from—their facial expressions are so readily understandable?

The question of whether the similarity of basic facial expressions are due to innate, inborn factors or if people learn them in similar ways across cultures, has fascinated psychologists for decades. A new study sheds light on this issue, adding to the evidence that basic facial expressions are inborn rather than learned.

The researchers used a clever tactic to approach this question: They examined the facial expressions of people blind from birth who, of course, couldn't have learned these behaviors by observing them in others. Judo athletes who won medals in the Olympics were photographed when they completed their matches, during the awards ceremony, and when they were on the medalists' podium. Their facial expressions were compared with blind judo athletes—some blind from birth—who won medals in a similar competition for athletes with disabilities called the Paralympic Games. The blind medalists were photographed at times corresponding to the sighted ones. Comparisons of the photographs revealed that the blind athletes expressed anger, contempt, disgust, sadness, surprise, and smiling behavior in the same ways as the sighted athletes (Ekman, 2003; Matsumoto & Willingham, 2009).

Most of the blind athletes smiled when they finished their matches and were standing on the podium, and nearly all produced genuine smiles when they were receiving their medals. The sighted athletes showed comparable frequency of smiling across these different contexts. More interestingly, of the blind athletes who won silver medals (in other words, who had lost the match and the gold), none smiled following the match but most smiled politely while on the podium and while receiving their medals. This is also what the sighted

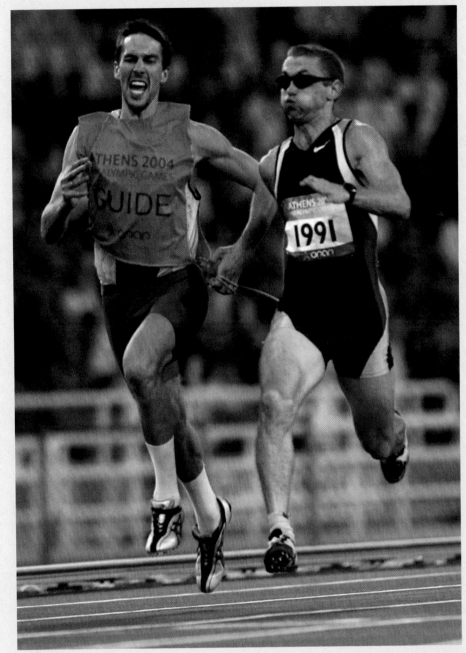

Are the facial expressions of competitive athletes due to innate, inborn factors, or are they learned?

silver medalists did, showing that all the athletes knew to put on a pleased expression at the appropriate time.

The athletes who were blind from birth showed no differences from the athletes who became blind later in life. These findings col-

lectively show that blind and sighted people express emotion on their faces in the same ways across different contexts, suggesting that observation of others is not a precondition for learning facial expression of emotion (Matsumoto and Willingham, 2009).

RETHINK

- How could blind athletes have learned when they would be expected to "smile politely" even if they did not feel happiness?
- Although it seems like basic emotions are expressed similarly across cultures, can you think of examples of nonverbal behaviors that differ across cultures?

RECAP/EVALUATE/RETHINK

RECAP

What are emotions, and how do we experience them?

- Emotions are broadly defined as feelings that may affect behavior and generally have both a physiological and a cognitive component. Debate continues over whether separate systems govern cognitive and emotional responses and whether one has primacy over the other. (p. 306)

What are the functions of emotions?

- Emotions prepare us for action, shape future behavior through learning, and help us interact more effectively with others. (p. 307)

What are the explanations for emotions?

- Several theories explain emotions. The James-Lange theory suggests that emotional experience is a reaction to bodily or visceral changes that occur as a response to an environmental event and are interpreted as an emotional response. (p. 309)
- In contrast, the Cannon-Bard theory contends that both physiological arousal and an emotional experience are produced simultaneously by the same nerve stimulus and that the visceral experience does not necessarily differ among differing emotions. (p. 310)
- The Schachter-Singer theory suggests that emotions are determined jointly by a relatively nonspecific physiological arousal and the subsequent labeling of that arousal by using cues from the environment to determine how others are behaving in the same situation. (p. 310)
- The most recent approaches to emotions focus on their biological origins. For instance, it now seems that specific patterns of biological arousal are associated with individual emotions. Furthermore, new scanning techniques have identified the specific parts of the brain that are activated during the experience of particular emotions. (p. 311)

How does nonverbal behavior relate to the expression of emotions?

- A person's facial expressions can reveal emotions. In fact, members of different cultures understand the emotional expressions of others in similar ways. One explanation for this similarity is that an innate facial-affect program activates a set of muscle movements representing the emotion being experienced. (p. 314)
- The facial-feedback hypothesis suggests that facial expressions not only reflect, but also produce, emotional experiences. (p. 314)

EVALUATE

1. Emotions are always accompanied by a cognitive response. True or false?
2. The _____ _____ theory of emotion states that emotions are a response to instinctive bodily events.
3. According to the _____ _____ theory of emotion, both an emotional response and physiological arousal are produced simultaneously by the same nerve stimulus.
4. Your friend—a psychology major—tells you, "I was at a party last night. During the course of the evening, my general level of arousal increased. Since I was at a party where people were enjoying themselves, I assume I must have felt happy." What theory of emotion does your friend subscribe to?
5. What are the six primary emotions that can be identified from facial expressions?

RETHINK

1. If researchers learned how to control emotional responses so that targeted emotions could be caused or prevented, what ethical concerns might arise? Under what circumstances, if any, should such techniques be used?
2. *From the perspective of an advertising executive:* How might you use the findings by Schachter and Singer on the labeling of arousal to create interest in a product? Can you think of other examples whereby people's arousal could be manipulated, which would lead to different emotional responses?

Answers to Evaluate Questions

1. false; emotions may occur without a cognitive response; 2. James-Lange; 3. Cannon-Bard; 4. Schachter-Singer; 5. surprise, sadness, happiness, anger, disgust, and fear

KEY TERMS

emotions p. 306
James-Lange theory of emotion p. 309

Cannon-Bard theory of emotion p. 310
Schachter-Singer theory of emotion p. 310

facial-affect program p. 314
facial-feedback hypothesis p. 314

Nature and Nurture, and Prenatal Development

How many bald, six-foot-six, 250-pound volunteer firefighters in New Jersey wear droopy mustaches, aviator eyeglasses, and a key ring on the right side of their belts? The answer is two: Gerald Levey and Mark Newman. As it happens, they're twins who were separated at birth. Neither knew the other existed until they were reunited—in a fire station—by a fellow firefighter who knew Newman and was startled to see his double, Levey, at a firefighters' convention.

The lives of the twins, though separate, followed remarkably similar paths. Levey went to college, studying forestry; Newman planned to study forestry in college but instead took a job trimming trees. Both had worked in supermarkets. One had had a job installing sprinkler systems; the other installed fire alarms.

Both men are unmarried and find the same kind of woman attractive: "tall, slender, long hair." They share similar hobbies, enjoying hunting, fishing, going to the beach, and watching old John Wayne movies and professional wrestling. Both like Chinese food and drink the same brand of beer. Their mannerisms are also similar—for example, each one throws his head back when he laughs. And of course, there's one more thing: They share a passion for fighting fires.

The similarities we see in twins Gerald Levey and Mark Newman vividly raise one of the fundamental questions posed by **developmental psychology,** the study of the patterns of growth and change that occur throughout life. The question is this: How can we distinguish between the *environmental* causes of behavior (the influence of parents, siblings, family, friends, schooling, nutrition, and all the other experiences a child is exposed to) and *hereditary* causes (those based on the genetic makeup of an individual that influence growth and development throughout life)? This question embodies the **nature–nurture issue.** In this context, nature refers to hereditary factors, and nurture to environmental influences.

Although the question was first posed as a nature-*versus*-nurture issue, developmental psychologists today agree that *both* nature and nurture interact to produce specific developmental patterns and outcomes. Consequently, the question has evolved into *How and to what degree* do environment and heredity both produce their effects? No one grows up free of environmental influences, nor does anyone develop without being affected by his or her inherited *genetic makeup.* However, the debate over the comparative influence of the two factors remains active, with different approaches and different theories of development emphasizing the environment or heredity to a greater or lesser degree (Gottesman & Hanson, 2005; Rutter, 2006; Belsky & Pluess, 2009).

For example, some developmental theories rely on basic psychological principles of learning and stress the role learning plays in producing changes in behavior in a developing child. Such theories emphasize the role of the environment in development. In contrast, other developmental theories

Key Concepts

How do psychologists study the degree to which development is an interaction of hereditary and environmental factors?

What is the nature of development before birth?

What factors affect a child during the mother's pregnancy?

developmental psychology
The branch of psychology that studies the patterns of growth and change that occur throughout life.

nature–nurture issue The viewpoint that weighs the degree to which environment and heredity influence behavior.

Gerald Levey and Mark Newman

FIGURE 1 Characteristics influenced significantly by genetic factors. Although these characteristics have strong genetic components, they are also affected by environmental factors.

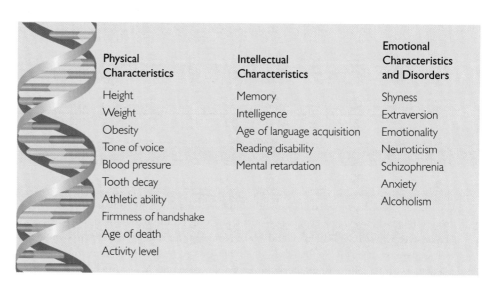

Physical Characteristics	Intellectual Characteristics	Emotional Characteristics and Disorders
Height	Memory	Shyness
Weight	Intelligence	Extraversion
Obesity	Age of language acquisition	Emotionality
Tone of voice	Reading disability	Neuroticism
Blood pressure	Mental retardation	Schizophrenia
Tooth decay		Anxiety
Athletic ability		Alcoholism
Firmness of handshake		
Age of death		
Activity level		

emphasize the influence of one's physiological makeup and functioning on development. Such theories stress the role of heredity and *maturation*—the unfolding of biologically predetermined patterns of behavior—in producing developmental change. Maturation is demonstrated, for instance, by the development of sex characteristics (such as breasts and body hair) at the start of adolescence. Furthermore, the work of behavioral geneticists (who study the effects of heredity on behavior) and the theories of evolutionary psychologists (who identify behavior patterns that result from our genetic inheritance) have influenced developmental psychologists. Both behavioral geneticists and evolutionary psychologists have highlighted the importance of heredity in influencing human behavior (Buss, 2003; Reif & Lesch, 2003; Ilies, Arvey, & Bouchard, 2006).

Despite their differences over theory, developmental psychologists concur on some points. They agree that genetic factors not only provide the potential for specific behaviors or traits to emerge, but also place limitations on the emergence of such behavior or traits. For instance, heredity defines people's general level of intelligence, setting an upper limit that—regardless of the quality of the environment—people cannot exceed. Heredity also places limits on physical abilities; humans simply cannot run at a speed of 60 miles an hour, nor will they grow as tall as 10 feet, no matter what the quality of their environment (Pinker, 2004; Dodge, 2004).

Figure 1 lists some of the characteristics most affected by heredity. As you consider these items, it's important to keep in mind that these characteristics aren't *entirely* determined by heredity; environmental factors also play a role.

Developmental psychologists also agree that in most instances environmental factors play a critical role in enabling people to reach the potential capabilities that their genetic background makes possible. If Albert Einstein had received no intellectual stimulation as a child and hadn't been sent to school, it's unlikely that he would have reached his genetic potential. Similarly, a great athlete such as baseball star Derek Jeter would have been unlikely to display much physical skill if he hadn't been raised in an environment that nurtured his innate talent and gave him the opportunity to train and perfect his natural abilities.

Clearly, the relationship between heredity and environment is far from simple. As a consequence, developmental psychologists typically take an *interactionist* position on the nature–nurture issue, suggesting that a combination of hereditary and environmental factors influences development. Developmental psychologists face the challenge of identifying the relative strength of each of these influences on the individual, as well as that of identifying the specific changes that occur over the course of development (McGregor & Capone, 2004; Moffitt, Caspi, & Rutter, 2006).

Study Alert

The nature–nurture issue is a key question that is pervasive throughout the field of psychology, asking how and to what degree do environment and heredity produce their joint effects.

Determining the Relative Influence of Nature and Nurture

Developmental psychologists use several approaches to determine the relative influence of genetic and environmental factors on behavior. In one approach, researchers can experimentally control the genetic makeup of laboratory animals by carefully breeding them for specific traits. For instance, by placing and observing animals with identical genetic backgrounds in varied environments, researchers can learn the effects of specific kinds of environmental stimulation. Although researchers must be careful when generalizing the findings of nonhuman research to a human population, findings from animal research provide important information that cannot be obtained, often for ethical reasons, by using human participants.

Human twins serve as another important source of information about the relative effects of genetic and environmental factors. If **identical twins** (those who are genetically identical) display different patterns of development, those differences must be attributed to variations in the environment in which the twins were raised. The most useful data come from identical twins (such as Gerald Levey and Mark Newman) adopted at birth by different sets of adoptive parents and raised apart in differing environments. Studies of nontwin siblings raised in totally different environments also shed some light on the issue. Because they have relatively similar genetic backgrounds, siblings who show similarities as adults provide strong evidence for the importance of heredity (Sternberg, 2002a; Vitaro, Brendgen, & Arseneault, 2009).

Researchers can also take the opposite tack. Instead of concentrating on people with similar genetic backgrounds who are raised in different environments, they may consider people raised in similar environments who have totally dissimilar genetic backgrounds. If they find, for example, similar courses of development in two adopted children who have different genetic backgrounds yet have been raised in the same family, they have evidence for the importance of environmental influences on development. Moreover, psychologists can carry out research with animals with dissimilar genetic backgrounds; by experimentally varying the environment in which they're raised, researchers can determine the influence of environmental factors (independent of heredity) on development (Petrill & Deater-Deckard, 2004).

identical twins Twins who are genetically identical.

Developmental Research Techniques

Due to the demands of measuring behavioral change across different ages, developmental researchers use several unique methods. The most frequently used, **cross-sectional research,** compares people of different ages at the same point in time. Cross-sectional studies reveal information about differences in development between different age groups (Creasey, 2005; Huijie, 2006).

Suppose, for instance, we're interested in the development of intellectual ability in adulthood. To carry out a cross-sectional study, we might compare a sample of 25-, 45-, and 65-year-olds who all take the same IQ test. We then can determine whether average IQ test scores differ for each age group.

Cross-sectional research has limitations, however. For instance, we can't be sure that the differences in IQ scores we might find in our sample are due to age differences alone. Instead, the scores may reflect differences in the educational attainment of the cohorts represented. A cohort is a group of people who grow up at similar times, in similar places, and in similar conditions. In the case of IQ differences, any age differences we find in a cross-sectional study may reflect educational differences

cross-sectional research A research method that compares people of different ages at the same point in time.

among the cohorts studied: People in the older age group may belong to a cohort that was less likely to attend college than were those in the younger groups.

A longitudinal study, the second major research strategy used by developmental psychologists, provides one way around this problem. **Longitudinal research** traces the behavior of one or more participants as the participants age. Longitudinal studies assess *change* in behavior over time, whereas cross-sectional studies assess *differences* among groups of people.

For instance, consider how we might investigate intellectual development during adulthood by using a longitudinal research strategy. First, we might give an IQ test to a group of 25-year-olds. We'd then come back to the same people 20 years later and retest them at age 45. Finally, we'd return to them once more when they're 65 years old and test them again.

By examining changes at several points in time, we can clearly see how individuals develop. Unfortunately, longitudinal research requires an enormous amount of time (as the researcher waits for the participants to get older), and participants who begin a study at an early age may drop out, move away, or even die as the research continues. Moreover, participants who take the same test at several points in time may become "test-wise" and perform better each time they take it by having become more familiar with the test.

To make up for the limitations in both cross-sectional and longitudinal research, investigators have devised an alternative strategy. Known as **sequential research,** it combines cross-sectional and longitudinal approaches by taking a number of different age groups and examining them at several points in time. For example, investigators might use a group of 3-, 5-, and 7-year-olds, examining them every 6 months for a period of several years. This technique allows a developmental psychologist to tease out the specific effects of age changes from other possibly influential factors.

longitudinal research A research method that investigates behavior as participants age.

Study Alert

Be sure you can distinguish the three different types of developmental research: cross-sectional (comparing people of different ages at the same time); longitudinal (studying participants as they age); and sequential (a combination of cross-sectional and longitudinal).

sequential research A research method that combines cross-sectional and longitudinal research by considering a number of different age groups and examining them at several points in time.

Prenatal Development: Conception to Birth

When the Morrisons were expecting their second child, the young couple faced an anguishing dilemma.

Their first child, a girl born in 2002, had a condition known as congential adrenal hyperplasia, or CAH, which can sometimes result in male-like genitals in female newborns. So when Mrs. Morrison became pregnant again, the couple was well aware the baby had a 1-in-8 chance of being born with the same disorder.

There were choices. They could treat the fetus with a powerful steroid that would most likely avert the possibility of the genitals becoming malformed. But the couple worried about doing this. There was little research on the long-term effects of treating a fetus with steroids, and statistically, there was a much greater chance that the baby wouldn't have the genital problem at all....

The couple decided to forgo the steroid treatment. "It was touch-and-go, but in the end I couldn't expose the baby to the drugs," says Mrs. Morrison. When the baby arrived, it was a girl [who], like her older sister, was born with swollen genitalia (Naik, 2009, p. D1).

The Morrisons will never know if they made the right choice. But their case shows the difficult choices that parents may encounter due to our increasing understanding of life spent inside a mother's womb.

Yet our knowledge of the biology of *conception*—when a male's sperm cell penetrates a female's egg cell—and its aftermath makes the start of life no less a miracle. Let's consider how an individual is created by looking first at the genetic endowment that a child receives at the moment of conception.

(a) Conception   **(b)** 23 pairs of chromosomes   **(c)** DNA sequence   **(d)** Genes

FIGURE 2 Every individual's characteristics are determined by the individual's specific genetic information. (a) At the moment of conception, (b) humans receive 23 pairs of chromosomes, half from the mother and half from the father. (c) These chromosomes are made up of coils of DNA. (d) Each chromosome contains thousands of genes that "program" the future development of the body.

THE BASICS OF GENETICS

The one-cell entity established at conception contains 23 pairs of **chromosomes,** rod-shaped structures that contain all basic hereditary information. One member of each pair is from the mother, and the other is from the father.

Each chromosome contains thousands of **genes**—smaller units through which genetic information is transmitted. Either individually or in combination, genes produce the particular characteristics of each person. Composed of sequences of *DNA (deoxyribonucleic acid)* molecules, genes are the biological equivalent of software that programs the future development of all parts of the body's hardware. Humans have some 25,000 different genes (see Figure 2).

Some genes control the development of systems common to all members of the human species—the heart, circulatory system, brain, lungs, and so forth; others shape the characteristics that make each human unique, such as facial configuration, height, and eye color. The child's sex is also determined by a particular combination of genes. Specifically, a child inherits an X chromosome from its mother and either an X or a Y chromosome from its father. When it receives an XX combination, it's a female; with an XY combination, it develops as a male. Male development is triggered by a single gene on the Y chromosome, and without the presence of that specific gene, the individual will develop as a female.

As behavioral geneticists have discovered, genes are also at least partially responsible for a wide variety of personal characteristics, including cognitive abilities, personality traits, and psychological disorders. Of course, few of these characteristics are determined by a single gene. Instead, most traits result from a combination of multiple genes that operate together with environmental influences (Plomin & McGuffin, 2003; Haberstick et al., 2005; Ramus, 2006).

THE HUMAN GENOME PROJECT

Our understanding of genetics took a giant leap forward in 2001, when scientists were able to map the specific location and sequence of every human gene as part of the massive *Human Genome Project*. This accomplishment was one of the most important in the history of biology (International Human Genome Sequencing Consortium, 2001).

chromosomes Rod-shaped structures that contain all basic hereditary information.

genes The parts of chromosomes through which genetic information is transmitted.

Study Alert

It's important to understand the basic building blocks of genetics: chromosomes that contain genes, which in turn are composed of sequences of DNA.

Identification of genes and their sequences opens the possibilities of gene therapy.

The success of the *Human Genome Project* started a revolution in health care by enabling scientists to identify particular genes responsible for genetically caused disorders. It's already leading not only to the identification of risk factors in children, but also to the development of new treatments for physical and psychological disorders.

For example, in *gene therapy*, health-care providers inject genes to correct particular diseases directly into a patient's bloodstream. When the gene arrives at the location of a problem (or potential problem), it leads the body to produce chemicals to alleviate the danger. In other cases, additional genes are inserted that replace missing or defective cells. Eventually, it also may be possible to "harvest" defective cells from a child prior to birth. These cells could be treated with gene therapy and reintroduced into the unborn child, thereby repairing the defect (Lymberis et al., 2004; Sato et al., 2007; Naldini, 2009).

Although the promise of gene therapy is real, the number of diseases that can be treated today is actually fairly limited. Furthermore, the long-term success of gene therapy remains unknown. In fact, after a seeming initial cure, some recipients of gene therapy have relapsed, and others have suffered from unpleasant side effects. Still, the potential uses of gene therapy are growing rapidly. For example, disorders such as AIDS, cancer, rheumatoid arthritis, and macular degeneration are strong candidates for the procedure (Feret et al., 2007; Rossi, June, & Kohn, 2007; Miller et al., 2008).

EARLIEST DEVELOPMENT

When an egg becomes fertilized by a sperm, the resulting one-celled entity, called a **zygote**, immediately begins to develop. The zygote starts out as a microscopic speck. Three days after fertilization, though, the zygote increases to approximately 32 cells, and within a week it has grown to 100–150 cells. These first two weeks are known as the *germinal period*.

Two weeks after conception, the developing individual enters the *embryonic period*, which lasts from week 2 through week 8, and he or she is now called an **embryo.** As an embryo develops through an intricate preprogrammed process of cell

zygote The new cell formed by the union of an egg and a sperm.

embryo A developed zygote that has a heart, a brain, and other organs.

These remarkable photos of live fetuses display the degree of physical development at prenatal ages 4 and 15 weeks.

division, it grows 10,000 times larger by 4 weeks of age, attaining a length of about one-fifth of an inch. At this point it's developed a rudimentary beating heart, a brain, an intestinal tract, and a number of other organs. Although all these organs are at a primitive stage of development, they are clearly recognizable. Moreover, by week 8 the embryo is about an inch long and has discernible arms, legs, and a face.

From week 8 and continuing until birth, the developing individual enters the *fetal period* and is called a **fetus.** At the start of this period, it begins responding to touch, bending its fingers when touched on the hand. At 16 to 18 weeks, its movements become strong enough for the mother to feel them. At the same time, hair may begin to grow on the fetus's head, and the facial features become similar to those the child will display at birth. The major organs begin functioning, although the fetus could not be kept alive outside its mother. In addition, a lifetime's worth of brain neurons are produced—although it's unclear whether the brain is capable of thinking at this early stage.

By week 24, a fetus has many of the characteristics it will display as a newborn. In fact, when an infant is born prematurely at this age, it can open and close its eyes; suck; cry; look up, down, and around; and even grasp objects placed in its hands.

Within the womb, the fetus continues to develop before birth. It begins to grow fatty deposits under the skin and gains weight. The fetus reaches the **age of viability,** the point at which it can survive if born prematurely, at about prenatal age 22 weeks.

fetus A developing individual, from eight weeks after conception until birth.

age of viability The point at which a fetus can survive if born prematurely.

At prenatal age 28 weeks, the fetus weighs less than 3 pounds and is about 16 inches long. It may be capable of learning: One study found that the infants of mothers who had repeatedly read aloud the Dr. Seuss story *The Cat in the Hat* before the infants' birth preferred the sound of that particular story to other stories after they were born (Spence & DeCasper, 1982; Schenone et al., 2010).

Before birth, a fetus passes through several *sensitive periods*. A sensitive period is the time when organisms are particularly susceptible to certain kinds of stimuli. For example, fetuses are especially affected by their mothers' use of drugs during certain sensitive periods before birth. If they are exposed to a particular drug before or after the sensitive period, it may have relatively little impact, but if exposure comes during a critical period, the impact will be significant (Konig, 2005; Werker & Tees, 2005; Uylings, 2006).

Sensitive periods can also occur after birth. Some language specialists suggest, for instance, that there is a period during which children are particularly receptive to developing language. If children are not exposed to appropriate linguistic stimuli, however, their language development may be impaired (Innocenti, 2007; Sohr-Preston & Scaramella, 2007).

During the final weeks of pregnancy, the fetus continues to gain weight and grow. At the end of the normal term—38 weeks of pregnancy—the fetus typically weighs 7 pounds and is about 20 inches in length. However, the story is different for *preterm infants*, who are born before week 38. Because they haven't been able to develop fully, these infants are at higher risk for illness, future problems, and even death. For infants who have been in the womb for more than 30 weeks, the prospects are relatively good. However, for those born before week 30, the story is often less positive. Such newborns, who may weigh as little as 2 pounds at birth, are in grave danger because they have immature organs; they have less than a 50-50 chance of survival. If they do survive—and it takes extraordinarily heroic (and expensive) medical intervention to assure this—they may later experience significant developmental delays.

Genetic Influences on the Fetus. The process of fetal growth that we've just described reflects normal development as occurs in 95 to 98% of all pregnancies. Some individuals are less fortunate, for in the remaining 2 to 5% of cases, children are born with serious birth defects. A major cause of such defects is faulty genes or chromosomes. Here are some of the more common genetic and chromosomal difficulties.

- *Phenylketonuria (PKU).* A child born with the inherited disease phenylketonuria can't produce an enzyme required for normal development. This deficiency results in an accumulation of poisons that eventually cause profound mental retardation. The disease is treatable, however, if it's caught early. Most infants today are routinely tested for PKU, and children with the disorder can be placed on a special diet that allows them to develop normally (Ievers-Landis et al., 2005; Christ et al., 2006; Widaman, 2009).
- *Sickle-cell anemia.* About 10% of the African-American population has the possibility of passing on sickle-cell anemia, a disease that gets its name from the abnormally shaped red blood cells it causes. Children with the disease may have episodes of pain, yellowish eyes, stunted growth, and vision problems (Taras & Potts-Datema, 2005; Selove, 2007).
- *Tay-Sachs disease.* Children born with Tay-Sachs disease, a disorder most often found in Jews of Eastern European ancestry, usually die by age 3 or 4 due to their body's inability to break down fat. If both parents carry the genetic defect that produces the fatal illness, their child has a one in four chance of being born with the disease (Leib et al., 2005; Weinstein, 2007).
- *Down syndrome.* Down syndrome, one of the causes of mental retardation, occurs when the zygote receives an extra chromosome at the moment of conception. Down syndrome is often related to the mother's age; mothers

Study Alert

Critical or sensitive periods, which can occur before or after birth, are important because they indicate a specific time that organisms are particularly susceptible to damage that may affect them for the rest of their lives.

more than age 35 and younger than age 18 stand a higher risk of having a child with the syndrome than other women (Roizen & Patterson, 2003; Sherman et al., 2007).

Prenatal Environmental Influences. Genetic factors are not the only causes of difficulties in fetal development. Environmental influences—the *nurture* part of the nature–nurture equation—also affect the fetus. Some of the more profound consequences are brought about by **teratogens,** environmental agents such as a drug, chemical, virus, or other factor that produce a birth defect. Among the major prenatal environmental influences on the fetus are the following:

teratogens Environmental agents such as a drug, chemical, virus, or other factor that produce a birth defect.

- *Mother's nutrition.* What a mother eats during her pregnancy can have important implications for the health of her baby. Seriously undernourished mothers can't provide adequate nutrition to a growing fetus, and they're likely to give birth to underweight babies. Poorly nourished babies are also more susceptible to disease, and a lack of nourishment may have an adverse impact on their mental development (Zigler, Finn-Stevenson, & Hall, 2002; Najman et al., 2004; Everette, 2008).

- *Mother's illness.* Several diseases that have a relatively minor effect on the health of a mother can have devastating consequences for a developing fetus if they are contracted during the early part of a pregnancy. For example, rubella (German measles), syphilis, diabetes, and high blood pressure may each produce a permanent effect on the fetus. The virus that causes AIDS can also be passed from mother to child before birth, as well as through breast-feeding after birth (Nesheim et al., 2004; Magoni et al., 2005).

- *Mother's emotional state.* A mother's emotional state affects her baby. Mothers who are anxious and tense during the last months of their pregnancies are more apt to have irritable infants who sleep and eat poorly. The reason? The autonomic nervous system of the fetus becomes especially sensitive as a result of chemical changes produced by the mother's emotional state (Relier, 2001; Hollins, 2007).

- *Mother's use of drugs.* Mothers who take illegal, physically addictive drugs such as cocaine run the risk of giving birth to babies who are similarly addicted. Their newborns suffer painful withdrawal symptoms and sometimes show permanent physical and mental impairment as well. Even legal drugs taken by a pregnant woman who may not know yet that she's pregnant can have a tragic effect (Ikonomidou et al, 2000; Schecter, Finkelstein, & Koren, 2005).

- *Alcohol.* Alcohol is extremely dangerous to fetal development. For example, 1 out of every 750 infants is born with *fetal alcohol syndrome (FAS)*, a condition resulting in below-average intelligence, growth delays, and facial deformities. FAS is now the primary preventable cause of mental retardation. Even mothers who use small amounts of alcohol during pregnancy place their child at risk. *Fetal alcohol effects (FAE)* is a condition in which children display some, although not all, of the problems of FAS due to their mother's consumption of alcohol during pregnancy (Henderson, Kesmodel, & Gray, 2007; Niccools, 2007; Murthy et al., 2009).

- *Nicotine use.* Pregnant mothers who smoke put their children at considerable risk. Smoking while pregnant can lead to miscarriage and infant death. For children who do survive, the harm from a mother's tobacco use can last a lifetime (Haslam & Lawrence, 2004; Shea & Steiner, 2008; Rogers, 2009).

FIGURE 3 A variety of environmental factors can play a role in prenatal development.

Environmental Factor	Possible Effect on Prenatal Development
Rubella (German measles)	Blindness, deafness, heart abnormalities, stillbirth
Syphilis	Mental retardation, physical deformities, maternal miscarriage
Addictive drugs	Low birth weight, addiction of infant to drug, with possible death after birth from withdrawal
Nicotine	Premature birth, low birth weight and length
Alcohol	Mental retardation, lower-than-average birth weight, small head, limb deformities
Radiation from X-rays	Physical deformities, mental retardation
Inadequate diet	Reduction in growth of brain, smaller-than-average weight and length at birth
Mother's age—younger than 18 at birth of child	Premature birth, increased incidence of Down syndrome
Mother's age—older than 35 at birth of child	Increased incidence of Down syndrome
DES (diethylstilbestrol)	Reproductive difficulties and increased incidence of genital cancer in children of mothers who were given DES during pregnancy to prevent miscarriage
AIDS	Possible spread of AIDS virus to infant; facial deformities; growth failure
Accutane	Mental retardation and physical deformities

Several other environmental factors have an impact on the child before and during birth (see Figure 3). Keep in mind, however, that although we've been discussing the influences of genetics and environment separately, neither factor works alone. Furthermore, despite the emphasis here on some of the ways in which development can go wrong, the vast majority of births occur without difficulty. And in most instances, subsequent development also proceeds normally.

RECAP/EVALUATE/RETHINK

RECAP

How do psychologists study the degree to which development is an interaction of hereditary and environmental factors?

- Developmental psychology studies growth and change throughout life. One fundamental question is how much developmental change is due to heredity and how much is due to environment—the nature–nurture issue. Heredity seems to define the upper limits of our growth and change, whereas the environment affects the degree to which the upper limits are reached. (p. 321)
- Cross-sectional research compares people of different ages with one another at the same point in time. In contrast, longitudinal research traces the behavior of one or more participants as the participants become older. Finally, sequential research combines the two methods by taking several different age groups and examining them at several points in time. (p. 323)

What is the nature of development before birth?

- At the moment of conception, a male's sperm cell and a female's egg cell unite, with each contributing to the new individual's genetic makeup. The union of sperm and egg produces a zygote, which contains 23 pairs of chromosomes—with one member of each pair coming from the father and the other coming from the mother. (p. 324)
- Each chromosome contains genes through which genetic information is transmitted. Genes, which are composed of DNA sequences, are the "software" that programs the future development of the body's "hardware." (p. 325)
- Genes affect not only physical attributes but also a wide array of personal characteristics such as cognitive abilities, personality traits, and psychological disorders. (p. 325)

- After 2 weeks the zygote becomes an embryo. By week 8, the embryo is called a fetus and is responsive to touch and other stimulation. At about week 22 it reaches the age of viability, which means it may survive if born prematurely. A fetus is normally born after 38 weeks of pregnancy, weighing around 7 pounds and measuring about 20 inches. (p. 326)

What factors affect a child during the mother's pregnancy?
- Genetic abnormalities produce birth defects such as phenylketonuria (PKU), sickle-cell anemia, Tay-Sachs disease, and Down syndrome. (p. 328)
- Among the environmental influences on fetal growth are the mother's nutrition, illnesses, and drug intake. (p. 329)

EVALUATE

1. Developmental psychologists are interested in the effects of both _____ and _____ on development.
2. Environment and heredity both influence development, with genetic potentials generally establishing limits on environmental influences. True or false?
3. By observing genetically similar animals in differing environments, we can increase our understanding of the influences of hereditary and environmental factors in humans. True or false?
4. _____ research studies the same individuals over a period of time, whereas _____-_____ research studies people of different ages at the same time.

5. Match each of the following terms with its definition:
   1. Zygote
   2. Gene
   3. Chromosome
   a. Smallest unit through which genetic information is passed
   b. Fertilized egg
   c. Rod-shaped structure containing genetic information
6. Specific kinds of growth must take place during a _____ period if the embryo is to develop normally.

RETHINK

1. When researchers find similarities in development between very different cultures, what implications might such findings have for the nature–nurture issue?
2. *From the perspective of a child-care provider:* Consider what factors might determine why a child is not learning to walk at the same pace as his peers. What kinds of environmental influences might be involved? What kinds of genetic influences might be involved? What recommendations might you make to the child's parents about the situation?

Answers to Evaluate Questions

1. heredity (or nature), environment (or nurture); 2. true; 3. true; 4. longitudinal, cross-sectional 5. 1-b, 2-a, 3-c; 6. sensitive (or critical)

KEY TERMS

developmental
  psychology p. 321
nature–nurture issue p. 323
identical twins p. 323

cross-sectional
  research p. 323
longitudinal research p. 324
sequential research p. 324

chromosomes p. 325
genes p. 325
zygote p. 326
embryo p. 326

fetus p. 327
age of viability p. 327
teratogens p. 329

Infancy and Childhood

Key Concepts

What are the major competencies of newborns?

What are the milestones of physical and social development during childhood?

How does cognitive development proceed during childhood?

neonate A newborn child.

His head was molded into a long melon shape and came to a point at the back. . . . He was covered with a thick greasy white material known as "vernix," which made him slippery to hold, and also allowed him to slip easily through the birth canal. In addition to a shock of black hair on his head, his body was covered with dark, fine hair known as "lanugo." His ears, his back, his shoulders, and even his cheeks were furry. . . . His skin was wrinkled and quite loose, ready to scale in creased places such as his feet and hands. . . . His ears were pressed to his head in unusual positions—one ear was matted firmly forward on his cheek. His nose was flattened and pushed to one side by the squeeze as he came through the pelvis. (Brazelton, 1969, p. 3)

What kind of creature is this? Although the description hardly fits that of the adorable babies seen in ads for baby food, we are in fact talking about a normal, completely developed child just after the moment of its birth. Called a **neonate,** a newborn arrives in the world in a form that hardly meets the standards of beauty against which we typically measure babies. Yet ask any parents: Nothing is more beautiful or exciting than the first glimpse of their newborn.

The Extraordinary Newborn

Several factors cause a neonate's strange appearance. The trip through the mother's birth canal may have squeezed the incompletely formed bones of the skull together and squashed the nose into the head. The skin secretes *vernix,* a white, greasy covering, for protection before birth, and the baby may have *lanugo,* a soft fuzz, over the entire body for a similar purpose. The infant's eyelids may be puffy due to an accumulation of fluids because of its upside-down position during birth.

All these features change during the first two weeks of life as the neonate takes on a more familiar appearance. Even more impressive are the capabilities a neonate begins to display from the moment of birth—capabilities that grow at an astounding rate over the ensuing months.

REFLEXES

reflexes Unlearned, involuntary responses that occur automatically in the presence of certain stimuli.

A neonate is born with a number of **reflexes**—unlearned, involuntary responses that occur automatically in the presence of certain stimuli. Critical for survival, many of those reflexes unfold naturally as part of an infant's ongoing maturation. The *rooting reflex,* for instance, causes neonates to turn their heads toward things that touch their cheeks—such as the mother's nipple or a bottle. Similarly, a *sucking reflex* prompts infants to suck at things that touch their lips. Among other reflexes are a *gag reflex* (to clear the throat), the *startle reflex* (a series of movements in which an infant flings out the arms, fans the fingers, and arches the back in response to a

Many of the reflexes that a neonate is born with are critical for survival and unfold naturally as a part of an infant's ongoing maturation. Do you think humans have more or fewer reflexes than other animals?

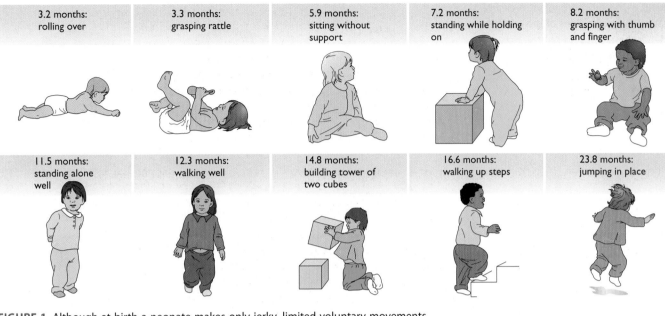

FIGURE 1 Although at birth a neonate makes only jerky, limited voluntary movements, during the first year of life the ability to move independently grows enormously. Ages indicate the time when 50% of children are able to perform each skill. Remember, however, that the time when each skill appears can vary considerably. For example, 25% of children are able to walk well at age 11 months, and by 15 months 90% of children are walking well. (Source: Frankenburg et al., 1992.)

sudden noise), and the *Babinski reflex* (a baby's toes fan out when the outer edge of the sole of the foot is stroked).

Infants lose these primitive reflexes after the first few months of life, replacing them with more complex and organized behaviors. Although at birth a neonate is capable of only jerky, limited voluntary movements, during the first year of life his or her ability to move independently grows enormously. The typical baby rolls over by the age of about 3 months, sits without support at about 6 months, stands alone at about 11 months, and walks at just over a year old. Not only does the ability to make large-scale movements improve during this time, fine-muscle movements become increasingly sophisticated (see Figure 1).

DEVELOPMENT OF THE SENSES: TAKING IN THE WORLD

When proud parents peer into the eyes of their neonate, is the child able to return their gaze? Although it was thought for some time that newborns can see only a hazy blur, most current findings indicate that the capabilities of neonates are far more impressive. Although their eyes have a limited capacity to focus on objects that aren't within a 7- to 8-inches from the face, neonates can follow objects moving within their field of vision. They also show the rudiments of depth perception by raising their hands when an object appears to be moving rapidly toward their face (Gelman & Kit-Fong Au, 1996; Maurer et al., 1999).

You might think that it would be hard to figure out just how well neonates see because they lack both language and reading ability, so they can't identify what direction the E on a vision chart is facing. However, researchers have devised a number of ingenious methods relying on the newborn's biological responses and innate reflexes to test perceptual skills.

For instance, infants who see a novel stimulus typically pay close attention to it and, as a consequence, their heart rates increase. But if they repeatedly see the same stimulus, their attention to it decreases, as indicated by a return to a slower heart rate. This phenomenon is known as **habituation,** the decrease in response to a

Study Alert

The basic neonatal reflexes—unlearned, involuntary responses—include the rooting reflex, the sucking reflex, the gag reflex, the startle reflex, and the Babinski reflex.

habituation The decrease in response to a stimulus that occurs after repeated presentations of the same stimulus.

FIGURE 2 This newborn infant is clearly imitating the expressions of the adult model in these amazing photos. How does this ability contribute to social development? (Courtesy of Dr. Tiffany Field.)

FIGURE 2 This newborn infant is clearly imitating the expressions of the adult model in these amazing photos. How does this ability contribute to social development? (Courtesy of Dr. Tiffany Field.)

stimulus that occurs after repeated presentations of the same stimulus. By studying habituation, developmental psychologists can tell when a child who is too young to speak can detect and discriminate a stimulus (Grunwald et al., 2003; Hannon & Johnson, 2005; del Rosal et al., 2006).

Researchers have developed many other methods for measuring neonate and infant perception. One technique, for instance, involves babies sucking on a nipple attached to a computer. A change in the rate and vigor with which the babies suck allows researchers to infer that babies can perceive variations in stimuli. Other approaches include examining babies' eye movements and observing which way babies move their heads in response to a visual stimulus (George, 1999; Franklin, Pilling, & Davies, 2005).

Through these research techniques, we now know that infants' visual perception is remarkably sophisticated from the start of life. At birth, babies prefer patterns with contours and edges over less distinct patterns, indicating that they can respond to the configuration of stimuli. Furthermore, even newborns are aware when the size of an object changes, because they appear sensitive to when an image on the retina changes size as the distance between the object and the retina varies (Norcia et al., 2005; Moore et al., 2007).

In fact, neonates can discriminate facial expressions—and even imitate them. As you can see in Figure 2, newborns can imitate an adult's expressions. Even very young infants, then, can respond to the emotions and moods that their caregivers' facial expressions reveal. This capability provides the foundation for social interaction skills in children (Meltzoff, 1996; Lavelli & Fogel, 2005; Grossman, Striano, & Friederici, 2007).

Other visual abilities grow rapidly after birth. By the end of their first month, babies can distinguish some colors from others, and after 4 months they can focus on near or far objects. By 4 or 5 months they're able to recognize two- and three-dimensional objects, and they can perceive the gestalt organizing principles discovered by psychologists who study perception. By 7 months, neural systems that process information about facial expressions are highly sophisticated, causing babies to respond differently to specific facial expressions (see Figure 3). Overall, their perceptual abilities rapidly

Neuroscience in Your Life: Young Infants Recognize Emotions Early in Life

FIGURE 3 Using a method that measures electrophysiological responses in the brain (event related potentials), researchers have found that by 7 months of age, infants show distinct responses to happy, fearful, and neutral facial expressions using different regions of their brain (specifically, the medial, semi-medial, and lateral regions). For example, approximately 400 milliseconds after seeing a fearful face (see arrow), infants show greater brain activity than when seeing either a neutral or happy face. This demonstrates that infants recognize differences between these facial expressions. (Source: Leppanen et al., 2007, Figure 2.)

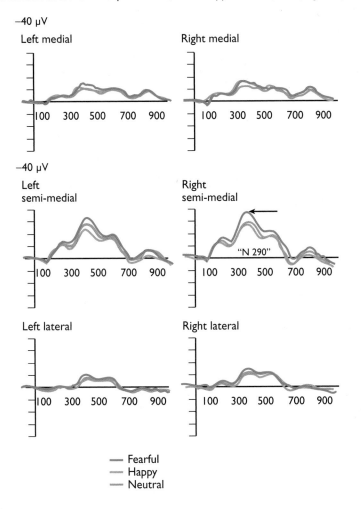

improve: Sensitivity to visual stimuli, for instance, becomes 3 to 4 times greater at age 1 than it was at birth (Johnson, 2004; Striano & Vaish, 2006; Leppanen et al., 2007).

In addition to vision, infants display other impressive sensory capabilities. Newborns can distinguish different sounds to the point of being able to recognize their own mothers' voices at 3 days old. They can also make the subtle perceptual distinctions that underlie language abilities. For example, at 2 days of age, infants can distinguish between their native tongue and foreign languages, and they can discriminate between such closely related sounds as *ba* and *pa* when they are 4 days old. By 6 months of age, they can discriminate virtually any difference in sound that is relevant to the production of language. Moreover, they can recognize different tastes and smells at a very early age. There even seems to be something of a built-in sweet tooth: Neonates prefer liquids that have been sweetened with sugar over their unsweetened counterparts (Cohen & Cashon, 2003; Rivera-Gaxiola et al., 2005).

The Growing Child: Infancy Through Middle Childhood

It was during the windy days of March that the problem in the day care center first arose. Its source: 10-month-old Russell Ruud. Otherwise a model of decorum, Russell had somehow learned how to unzip the Velcro chin strap to his winter hat. He would remove the hat whenever he got the urge, seemingly oblivious to the potential health problems that might follow.

But that was just the start of the real difficulty. To the chagrin of the teachers in the day care center, not to speak of the children's parents, soon other children were following his lead, removing their own caps at will. Russell's mother, made aware of the anarchy at the day care center—and the other parents' distress over Russell's behavior—pleaded innocent. "I never showed Russell how to unzip the Velcro," claimed his mother, Judith Ruud, an economist with the Congressional Budget Office in Washington, D.C. "He learned by trial and error, and the other kids saw him do it one day when they were getting dressed for an outing." (Goleman, 1993a, C10)

At the age of 10 months, Russell asserted his personality, illustrating the tremendous growth that occurs in a variety of domains during the first year of life. Throughout the remainder of childhood, moving from infancy into middle childhood and the start of adolescence around age 11 or 12, children develop physically, socially, and cognitively in extraordinary ways. In the remainder of this module, we'll consider this development.

PHYSICAL DEVELOPMENT

Children's physical growth provides the most obvious sign of development. During the first year of life, children typically triple their birthweight, and their height increases by about half. This rapid growth slows down as the child gets older—think how gigantic adults would be if that rate of growth were constant—and from age 3 to the beginning of adolescence at around age 13, growth averages a gain of about 5 pounds and 3 inches a year (see Figure 4).

The physical changes that occur as children develop are not just a matter of increasing growth; the relationship of the size of the various body parts to one another changes dramatically as children age. As you can see in Figure 5, the head of a fetus (and a newborn) is disproportionately large. However, the head soon becomes more proportional to the rest of the body as growth occurs mainly in the trunk and legs.

DEVELOPMENT OF SOCIAL BEHAVIOR: TAKING ON THE WORLD

As anyone who has seen an infant smiling at the sight of his or her mother can guess, at the same time that infants grow physically and hone their perceptual abilities, they also develop socially. The nature of a child's early social development provides the foundation for social relationships that will last a lifetime.

Attachment, the positive emotional bond that develops between a child and a particular individual, is the most important form of social development that occurs during infancy. The earliest studies of attachment were carried out by animal ethologist Konrad Lorenz (1966). Lorenz focused on newborn goslings, which under normal circumstances instinctively follow their mother, the first moving object they perceive after birth. Lorenz found that goslings whose eggs were raised in an incubator and viewed him immediately after hatching would follow his every movement, as if he were their mother. He labeled this process *imprinting*, a behavior that takes place during a critical period and involves attachment to the first moving object that's observed.

attachment The positive emotional bond that develops between a child and a particular individual.

Study Alert

Attachment—the positive emotional bond that develops between a child and a particular individual—is a key concept in understanding the social development of children.

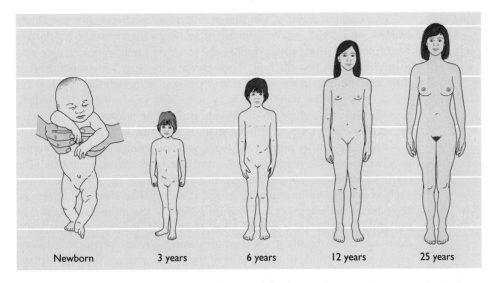

Newborn   3 years   6 years   12 years   25 years

FIGURE 5 As development progresses, the size of the head relative to the rest of the body decreases until the individual reaches adulthood. Why do you think the head starts out so large? (Source: Adapted from Figure 5 from W. J. Robbins, *Growth*. Copyright © 1928 Yale University Press. Used by permission of Yale University Press.)

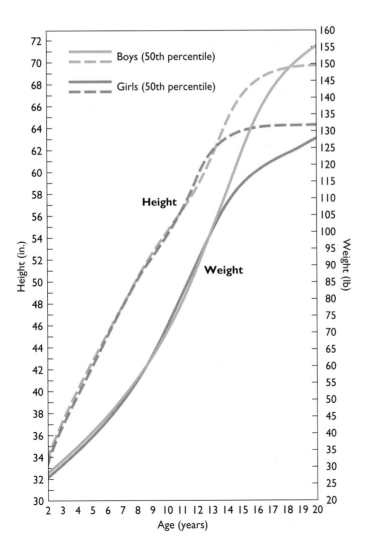

FIGURE 4 The average heights and weights of males and females in the United States from birth through age 20. At what ages are girls typically heavier and taller than boys? (Source: National Center for Health Statistics, 2000.)

FIGURE 6 Although the wire "mother" dispensed milk to the hungry infant monkey, the infant preferred the soft, terry-cloth "mother." Do you think human babies would react the same way? What does this experiment tell us about attachment? (Source: Harry Harlow Primate Laboratory/University of Wisconsin.)

Our understanding of attachment progressed when psychologist Harry Harlow, in a classic study, gave infant monkeys the choice of cuddling a wire "monkey" that provided milk, or a soft terry-cloth "monkey" that was warm but didn't provide milk. Their choice was clear: They spent most of their time clinging to the warm cloth "monkey," although they made occasional forays to the wire monkey to nurse. Obviously, the cloth monkey provided greater comfort to the infants; milk alone was insufficient to create attachment (Harlow & Zimmerman, 1959; Blum, 2002; see Figure 6).

Building on this pioneering work with nonhumans, developmental psychologists have suggested that human attachment grows through the responsiveness of infants' caregivers to the signals the babies provide, such as crying, smiling, reaching, and clinging. The greater the responsiveness of the caregiver to the child's signals, the more likely it is that the child will become securely attached. Full attachment eventually develops as a result of the complex series of interactions between caregiver and child. In the course of these interactions, the infant plays as critical and active a role as the caregiver in the formation of the bond. Infants who respond positively to a caregiver produce more positive behavior on the part of the caregiver, which in turn produces an even stronger degree of attachment in the child.

Assessing Attachment. Developmental psychologists have devised a quick and direct way to measure attachment. Developed by Mary Ainsworth, the *Ainsworth strange situation* consists of a sequence of events involving a child and (typically) his or her mother. Initially, the mother and baby enter an unfamiliar room, and the mother permits the baby to explore while she sits down. An adult stranger then enters the room, after which the mother leaves. The mother returns, and the stranger leaves. The mother once again leaves the baby alone, and the stranger returns. Finally, the stranger leaves, and the mother returns (Ainsworth et al., 1978; Izard & Abe, 2004; Combrink-Graham & McKenna, 2006).

Babies' reactions to the experimental situation vary drastically, depending, according to Ainsworth, on their degree of attachment to the mother. One-year-old children who are *securely attached* employ the mother as a kind of home base, exploring independently but returning to her occasionally. When she leaves, they exhibit distress and go to her when she returns. *Avoidant* children don't cry when the mother leaves and they seem to avoid her when she returns, as if they're indifferent to her. *Ambivalent* children display anxiety before they're separated and are upset when the mother leaves, but they may show ambivalent reactions to her return, such as seeking close contact but simultaneously hitting and kicking her. A fourth reaction is *disorganized-disoriented*; these children show inconsistent, often contradictory behavior.

The nature of attachment between children and their mothers has far-reaching consequences for later development. For example, children who are securely attached to their mothers tend to be more socially and emotionally competent than are their less securely attached peers, and others find them more cooperative, capable, and playful. Furthermore, children who are securely attached at age 1 show fewer psychological difficulties when they grow older compared with avoidant and ambivalent youngsters. As adults, children who are securely attached tend to have more successful romantic relationships. On the other hand, being securely attached at an early age doesn't guarantee healthy adjustment later, and, conversely, children who lack secure attachment don't always have difficulties later in life (Mikulincer & Shaver, 2005; Roisman et al., 2005; Hardy, 2007).

The Father's Role. Although early developmental research focused largely on the mother-child relationship, more recent research has highlighted the father's role in parenting, and with good reason: The number of fathers who are primary caregivers

Although each crisis is never resolved entirely—and life becomes increasingly complicated as we grow older—it has to be resolved sufficiently to equip us to deal with demands made during the following stage of development.

In Erikson's first stage of psychosocial development, the **trust-versus-mistrust stage** (from birth to 18 months), infants develop feelings of trust if their physical requirements and psychological needs for attachment are consistently met and their interactions with the world are generally positive. In contrast, inconsistent care and unpleasant interactions with others can lead to mistrust and leave an infant unable to meet the challenges required in the next stage of development.

In the second stage, the **autonomy-versus-shame-and-doubt stage** (ages 1½ to 3 years), toddlers develop independence and autonomy if exploration and freedom are encouraged, or they experience shame, self-doubt, and unhappiness if they're overly restricted and protected. According to Erikson, the key to the development of autonomy during this period is that the child's caregivers provide the appropriate amount of control. If parents provide too much control, children can't assert themselves and develop their own sense of control over their environment; if parents provide too little control, the children become overly demanding and controlling.

Next, children face the crises of the **initiative-versus-guilt stage** (ages 3 to 6). During this stage, children's desire to act independently conflicts with the guilt that comes from the unintended and unexpected consequences of such behavior. Children in this period come to understand that they are persons in their own right, and they begin to make decisions about their behavior. If parents react positively to children's attempts at independence, they'll help their children resolve the initiative-versus-guilt crisis positively.

The fourth and last stage of childhood is the **industry-versus-inferiority stage** (ages 6 to 12). During this period, increasing competency in all areas from social interactions to academic skills, characterizes successful psychosocial development. In contrast, difficulties during this stage lead to feelings of failure and inadequacy.

Erikson's theory suggests that psychosocial development continues throughout life, and he proposes four more crises that are faced after childhood (described in the next module). Although his theory has been criticized on several grounds—such as the imprecision of the concepts he employs and his greater emphasis on male development than female development—it remains influential and is one of the few theories that encompass the entire life span.

COGNITIVE DEVELOPMENT: CHILDREN'S THINKING ABOUT THE WORLD

Suppose you had two drinking glasses of different shapes—one short and broad and the other tall and thin. Now imagine that you fill the short broad one with soda (filling it to about halfway) and then poured the liquid from that glass into the tall one. The soda in the second glass would appear to fill it to about three-quarters. Because of this difference between the two fill-lines, is there more soda in the second glass than in the first?

You might think that such a simple question hardly deserves an answer; of course there's no difference in the amount of soda in the two glasses. However, most 4-year-olds are likely to respond that there's more soda in the second glass. Even if you then poured the soda back into the short glass, the 4-year-old would say there's now less soda than there'd been in the taller glass.

Why are young children confused by this problem? The reason isn't immediately obvious. Anyone who's observed preschoolers should be impressed by how far they've progressed from the early stages of development. Preschoolers speak with ease, know the alphabet, count, play complex games, use computers, tell stories, and communicate ably. Yet despite this seeming sophistication, there are deep gaps in their understanding of the

trust-versus-mistrust stage According to Erikson, the first stage of psychosocial development that occurs from birth to age 1½ years, during which time infants develop feelings of trust or a lack of trust.

autonomy-versus-shame-and-doubt stage The period during which, according to Erikson, toddlers (ages 1½ to 3) develop independence and autonomy if exploration and freedom are encouraged, or shame and self-doubt if they are restricted and overprotected.

initiative-versus-guilt stage According to Erikson, the period during which children ages 3 to 6 experience conflict between independence of action and the sometimes negative results of that action.

industry-versus-inferiority stage According to Erikson, the last stage of childhood during which children ages 6 to 12 may develop positive social interactions with others or may feel inadequate and become less sociable.

> **Study Alert**
> Four of Erikson's stages of psychosocial development occur during childhood: trust-versus-mistrust, autonomy-versus-shame-and-doubt, initiative-versus-guilt, and industry-versus inferiority.

"Please, Jason. Don't you want to grow up to be an autonomous peson?"

important

Cognitive Stage	Approximate Age Range	Major Characteristics
Sensorimotor	Birth–2 years	Development of object permanence, development of motor skills, little or no capacity for symbolic representation
Preoperational	2–7 years	Development of language and symbolic thinking, egocentric thinking
Concrete operational	7–12 years	Development of conservation, mastery of concept of reversibility
Formal operational	12 years–adulthood	Development of logical and abstract thinking

FIGURE 9 According to Piaget, all children pass through four stages of cognitive development.

cognitive development The process by which a child's understanding of the world changes as a function of age and experience.

world. Some theorists have suggested that children can't understand certain ideas and concepts until they reach a particular stage of **cognitive development**—the process by which a child's understanding of the world changes with age and experience. In contrast to the theories of physical and social development discussed earlier (such as those of Erikson), theories of cognitive development explain the quantitative and qualitative intellectual advances that occur during development.

Piaget's Theory of Cognitive Development. No theory of cognitive development has had more impact than that of Swiss psychologist Jean Piaget. Piaget (1970) suggested that children around the world proceed through a series of stages of intellectual development in a fixed order. He maintained that these stages differ not only in the *quantity* of information acquired at each stage but in the *quality* of the knowledge and understanding as well. Taking an interactionist point of view, he suggested that movement from one stage to the next occurs when a child reaches an appropriate level of maturation *and* is exposed to relevant types of experiences. Piaget assumed that, without having such experiences, children can't reach their highest level of cognitive growth.

Study Alert

Use Figure 9 to help remember Piaget's stages of cognitive development.

sensorimotor stage According to Piaget, the stage from birth to age 2, during which a child has little competence in communicating about the environment by using images, language, or other symbols.

object permanence The awareness that objects—and people—continue to exist even if they're out of sight.

preoperational stage According to Piaget, the period from ages 2 to 7 that's characterized by language development.

Piaget proposed four stages: the sensorimotor, preoperational, concrete operational, and formal operational (see Figure 9). Let's examine each and the approximate ages that they span.

Sensorimotor Stage: Birth to 2 Years. During the **sensorimotor stage,** children base their understanding of the world primarily on touching, sucking, chewing, shaking, and manipulating objects. At the initial part of the stage, children have relatively little competence in representing the environment by using images, language, or other kinds of symbols. Consequently, infants lack what Piaget calls **object permanence,** the awareness that objects—and people—continue to exist even if they're out of sight.

How can we know that children lack object permanence? Although we can't ask infants, we can observe their reactions when a toy they're playing with is hidden from their sight. Until approximately 9 months of age, children will make no attempt to locate the hidden toy no matter how obvious its hiding place. However, soon after that age they'll begin an active search for the missing object, indicating that they've developed a mental representation of the toy. This object permanence signals a critical development during the sensorimotor stage.

Preoperational Stage: 2 to 7 Years. The most important development during the **preoperational stage** is the use of language. Children develop internal representational systems that allow them to describe people, events, and feelings. They even use symbols in play, pretending, for example, that a book pushed across the floor is a car.

Although children use more advanced thinking in this stage than they did in the earlier sensorimotor stage, their thinking is still qualitatively inferior to that of adults. We see this when we observe a preoperational child using **egocentric thought,** or thinking that the world operates entirely from his or her own perspective. A preoperational child thinks that everyone shares his or her perspective and knowledge. Thus, children's stories and explanations to adults can be maddeningly uninformative because they're delivered without context. For example, a preoperational child may start a story saying, "He wouldn't let me go," neglecting to mention who "he" is or where the narrator intends to go. We also see egocentric thinking when children at the preoperational stage play hiding games. For instance, 3-year-olds frequently hide with their faces against a wall by covering their eyes—although they're still in plain view. It seems to them that if *they* can't see you, then no one else is able to see *them*, because they assume that others share their unseeing view of the world.

In addition, preoperational children don't yet understand the **principle of conservation**—the knowledge that quantity is unrelated to the arrangement and physical appearance of objects. Children who haven't mastered this concept don't know that the amount, volume, or length of an object doesn't change when its shape or configuration changes. The question about the two glasses—one short and broad and the other tall and thin—with which we began our discussion of cognitive development illustrates this point clearly. Children who do not understand the principle of conservation invariably state that the amount of liquid changes as it is poured back and forth. They cannot comprehend that a transformation in appearance does not imply a transformation in amount. Instead, it seems as reasonable to the child that there is a change in quantity as it does to the adult that there is no change.

In a number of other ways, some quite startling, this failure to understand the principle of conservation affects children's responses. Research demonstrates that principles that are obvious to and unquestioned by adults may be completely misunderstood by children during the preoperational period, and that it's not until the next stage of cognitive development that children grasp the concept of conservation (see Figure 10).

Concrete Operational Stage: 7 to 12 Years. Mastery of the principle of conservation marks the beginning of the **concrete operational stage.** However, children do not fully understand some aspects of conservation—such as conservation of weight and volume—for a number of years.

During the concrete operational stage, children can think in a more logical manner and begin to overcome some of the egocentrism characteristic of the preoperational period. One of the major principles children learn during this stage is reversibility, the idea that some changes can be undone by reversing an earlier action. For example, they can understand that when someone rolls a ball of clay into a long sausage shape, that person can re-create the original ball by reversing the action. Eventually children can even conceptualize this principle in their heads without having to see the action performed before them.

Although children make important advances in their logical capabilities during the concrete operational stage, their thinking still displays one major limitation: They are largely bound to the concrete, physical reality of the world. For the most part, they have difficulty understanding questions of an abstract or hypothetical nature.

Formal Operational Stage: 12 Years to Adulthood. The **formal operational stage** produces a new kind of thinking that is abstract, formal, and logical. Thinking is no longer tied to events that individuals observe in the environment but makes use of logical techniques to resolve problems.

The way in which children approach the "pendulum problem" devised by Piaget (Piaget & Inhelder, 1958) illustrates the emergence of formal operational thinking. The problem solver is asked to figure out what determines how fast a pendulum swings.

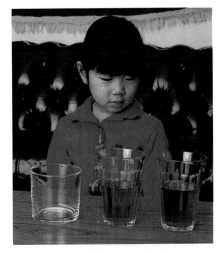

Children who have not mastered the principle of conservation assume that the volume of a liquid increases when it is poured from a short, wide container to a tall, thin one. What other tasks might a child under age 7 have difficulty comprehending?

egocentric thought A way of thinking such that a child views the world entirely from his or her own perspective.

principle of conservation The knowledge that quantity is unrelated to the arrangement and physical appearance of objects.

concrete operational stage According to Piaget, the period from ages 7 to 12 characterized by logical thought and a loss of egocentrism.

formal operational stage According to Piaget, the period from age 12 to adulthood that's characterized by abstract thought.

FIGURE 10 These tests are frequently used to assess whether children have learned the principle of conservation across a variety of dimensions. Do you think children in the preoperational stage can be taught to avoid conservation mistakes before the typical age of mastery?

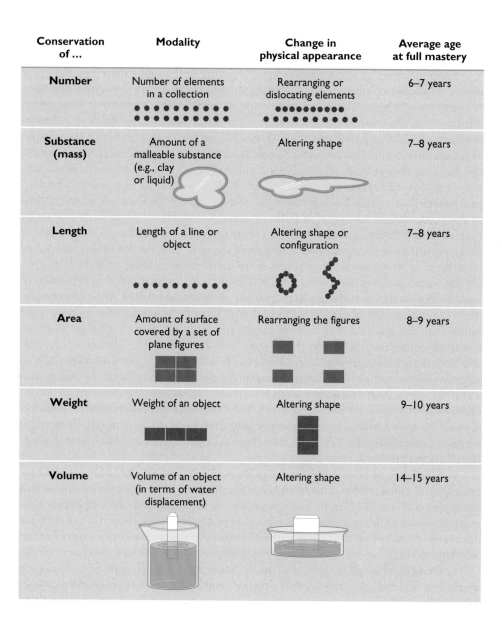

Conservation of …	Modality	Change in physical appearance	Average age at full mastery
Number	Number of elements in a collection	Rearranging or dislocating elements	6–7 years
Substance (mass)	Amount of a malleable substance (e.g., clay or liquid)	Altering shape	7–8 years
Length	Length of a line or object	Altering shape or configuration	7–8 years
Area	Amount of surface covered by a set of plane figures	Rearranging the figures	8–9 years
Weight	Weight of an object	Altering shape	9–10 years
Volume	Volume of an object (in terms of water displacement)	Altering shape	14–15 years

Is it the length of the string, the weight of the pendulum, or the force with which the pendulum is pushed? (For the record, the answer is the length of the string.)

Children in the concrete operational stage approach the problem haphazardly, without a logical or rational plan of action. For example, they may simultaneously change the length of the string and the weight on the string and the force with which they push the pendulum. Because they're varying all the factors at once, they can't tell which factor is the critical one. In contrast, people in the formal operational stage approach the problem systematically. Acting as if they're scientists conducting an experiment, they examine the effects of changes one variable at a time. This ability to rule out competing possibilities characterizes formal operational thought.

Although formal operational thought emerges during the teenage years, some individuals use this type of thinking only infrequently. Moreover, it appears that many individuals never reach this stage at all; most studies show that only 40–60% of college students and adults fully reach it, with some estimates running as low as 25% of the general population. In addition, in certain cultures—particularly those that are less technologically oriented than Western societies—almost no one reaches the formal operational stage (Keating & Clark, 1980; Super, 1980; Genovese, 2006).

Stages versus Continuous Development: Is Piaget Right? No other theorist has given us as comprehensive a theory of cognitive development as Piaget. Still, many contemporary theorists suggest that a better explanation of how children develop cognitively can be provided by theories that don't involve a stage approach. For instance, children aren't always consistent in their performance of tasks that—if Piaget's theory is accurate—they ought to perform equally well once they've reached a particular stage (Feldman, 2003, 2004).

Furthermore, some developmental psychologists suspect that cognitive development proceeds in a more continuous fashion than Piaget's stage theory allows. They propose that cognitive development is primarily quantitative in nature rather than qualitative. They argue that although there are differences in when, how, and to what extent a child can use specific cognitive abilities—reflecting quantitative changes—the underlying cognitive processes change relatively little with age (Gelman & Baillargeon, 1983; Case & Okamoto, 1996).

Piaget also underestimated the age at which infants and children can understand specific concepts and principles; in fact, they seem to be more sophisticated in their cognitive abilities than Piaget believed. For instance, some evidence suggests that infants as young as 5 months have rudimentary mathematical skills (Wynn, Bloom, & Chiang, 2002; McCrink & Wynn, 2007; van Marle & Wynn, 2009).

Despite such criticisms, most developmental psychologists agree that although the processes that underlie changes in cognitive abilities may not unfold in the manner suggested by his theory, Piaget has generally provided us with an accurate account of age-related changes in cognitive development. Moreover, his theory has had an enormous influence in education. For example, by suggesting that individuals cannot increase their cognitive performance unless both cognitive readiness brought about by maturation and appropriate environmental stimulation are present. This view has inspired the nature and structure of educational curricula and teaching methods. Researchers have also used Piaget's theory and methods to investigate issues surrounding animal cognition, such as whether primates show object permanence, which they seem to (Hauser, 2000; Egan, 2005; Cunningham, 2006).

Information-Processing Approaches: Charting Children's Mental Programs. If cognitive development doesn't proceed as a series of stages as Piaget suggested, what does underlie the enormous growth in children's cognitive abilities that even the untutored eye can observe? To many developmental psychologists, changes in **information processing**—the way in which people take in, use, and store information—account for cognitive development (Lacerda, von Hofsten, & Heimann, 2001; Cashon & Cohen, 2004; Munakata, 2006).

information processing The way that people take in, use, and store information.

According to this approach, quantitative changes occur in children's ability to organize and manipulate information. From this perspective, children become increasingly adept at information processing, much as a computer program may become more sophisticated as a programmer modifies it on the basis of experience. Information-processing approaches consider the kinds of "mental programs" that children invoke when approaching problems.

Several significant changes occur in children's information-processing capabilities. For one thing, the speed of processing increases with age as some abilities become more automatic. For example, the speed at which children can scan, recognize, and compare stimuli increases with age. As they grow older, children also can pay attention to stimuli longer and discriminate between different stimuli more readily, and they're less easily distracted (Myerson et al., 2003; Van den Wildenberg & Van der Molen, 2004).

Memory also improves dramatically with age. Preschoolers can hold only two or three chunks of information in their short-term memory, 5-year-olds can hold four, and 7-year-olds can hold five. (Adults are able to keep seven, plus or minus two, chunks in short-term memory.) The size of chunks also grows with age, as does the

FIGURE 11 Memory span increases with age for both numbers and letters. (Source: Adapted from Dempster, 1981.)

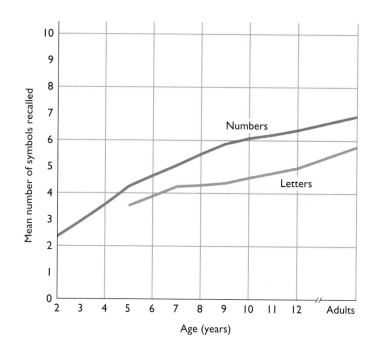

metacognition An awareness and understanding of one's own cognitive processes.

sophistication and organization of knowledge stored in one's memory (see Figure 11). Still, memory capabilities are impressive at a very early age: Even before they can speak, infants can remember for months events in which they actively participated (Cowan et al., 2003; Bayliss et al., 2005).

Finally, improvement in information processing relates to advances in **metacognition,** an awareness and understanding of one's own cognitive processes. Metacognition involves the planning, monitoring, and revising of cognitive strategies. Younger children who lack an awareness of their own cognitive processes often don't realize how they are incapable. Thus, when they misunderstand others, they may fail to recognize their own errors. It's only later, when metacognitive abilities become more sophisticated, that children are able to know when they *don't* understand. Such increasing sophistication reflects a change in children's *theory of mind,* their knowledge and beliefs about the way the mind operates (Bernstein, Loftus, & Meltzoff, 2005; Matthews & Funke, 2006; Lockl & Schneider, 2007).

Vygotsky's View of Cognitive Development: Considering Culture. According to Russian developmental psychologist Lev Vygotsky, the culture in which we're raised significantly affects our cognitive development. In an increasingly influential view, Vygotsky suggests that the focus on individual performance of both Piagetian and information-processing approaches is misplaced. Instead, he holds that we can't understand cognitive development without taking into account the social aspects of learning (Vygotsky, 1926/1997; Maynard & Martini, 2005; Rieber & Robinson, 2006).

Vygotsky argues that cognitive development occurs as a consequence of how much children work with others through social interaction to jointly solve problems. Through such interactions, children's cognitive skills increase and their ability to function better intellectually on their own is enhanced. More specifically, he suggests that children's cognitive abilities increase when they encounter information that falls within their zone of proximal development. The **zone of proximal development,** or **ZPD,** is the level at which a child can almost, but not fully, comprehend or perform a task on his or her own. When children receive information that falls within the ZPD, they can increase their understanding or master a new task. In contrast, if the information lies outside children's ZPD, they will not be able to master it (see Figure 12).

zone of proximal development (ZPD) According to Vygotsky, the level at which a child can almost, but not fully, comprehend or perform a task on his or her own.

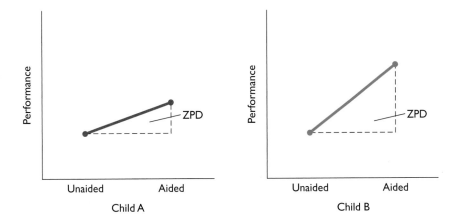

In short, cognitive development occurs when parents, teachers, or skilled peers assist a child by presenting information that is both new and within the ZPD. This type of assistance, called *scaffolding*, provides support for learning and problem solving that encourages independence and growth. Vygotsky claims that scaffolding not only promotes solving specific problems, but also aids in the development of overall cognitive abilities (Schaller & Crandall, 2004).

More than other approaches to cognitive development, Vygotsky's theory considers how an individual's specific cultural and social context affects his or her intellectual growth. The way in which children understand the world grows out of interactions with parents, peers, and other members of a specific culture (John-Steiner & Mahn, 2003; Kozulin et al., 2003).

RECAP/EVALUATE/RETHINK

RECAP

What are the major competencies of newborns?

- Newborns, or neonates, have reflexes—unlearned, involuntary responses that occur automatically in the presence of certain stimuli. (p. 332)
- Sensory abilities also develop rapidly; infants can distinguish color, depth, sound, tastes, and smells relatively soon after birth. (p. 333)
- After birth, physical development is rapid; children typically triple their birthweight in a year. (p. 336)

What are the milestones of physical and social development during childhood?

- Attachment—the positive emotional bond between a child and a particular individual—marks social development in infancy. Measured in the laboratory by means of the Ainsworth strange situation, attachment relates to later social and emotional adjustment. (p. 336)
- As children become older, the nature of their social interactions with peers changes. Initially play occurs relatively independently, but it becomes increasingly cooperative. (p. 339)
- The different child-rearing styles include authoritarian, permissive, authoritative, and uninvolved. (p. 340)
- According to Erikson, people's changing interactions and understanding of themselves and others occur in

eight stages of psychosocial development. During childhood, the four stages are trust-versus-mistrust (birth to 1½ years), autonomy-versus-shame-and-doubt (1½ to 3 years), initiative-versus-guilt (3 to 6 years), and industry-versus-inferiority (6 to 12 years). (p. 342)

How does cognitive development proceed during childhood?

- Piaget's theory posits that cognitive development proceeds through four stages during which qualitative changes occur in thinking: the sensorimotor stage (birth to 2 years), the preoperational stage (2 to 7 years), the concrete operational stage (7 to 12 years), and the formal operational stage (12 years to adulthood). (p. 344)
- Information-processing approaches suggest that quantitative changes occur in children's ability to organize and manipulate information about the world, as pertain to significant increases in one's speed of processing, attention span, and memory. In addition, children advance in metacognition, the awareness and understanding of one's own cognitive processes. (p. 347)
- Vygotsky argued that children's cognitive development occurs as a consequence of social interactions during which children and others work together to solve problems. (p. 348)

EVALUATE

1. Researchers studying newborns use _____, or the decrease in the response to a stimulus that occurs after repeated presentations of the same stimulus, as an indicator of a baby's interest.
2. The emotional bond that develops between a child and its caregiver is known as _____.
3. Match the parenting style with its definition:

   1. Permissive   **a.** Rigid; highly punitive; demanding
   2. Authoritative   obedience
   3. Authoritarian   **b.** Gives little direction; lax on
   4. Uninvolved   obedience
                   c. Firm but fair; tries to explain
                     parental decisions
                   d. Emotionally detached and unloving
4. Erikson's theory of _____ development involves a series of eight stages, each of which must be resolved for a person to develop optimally.
5. Match the stage of development with the thinking style characteristic of that stage:

   1. Egocentric thought   **a.** Sensorimotor
   2. Object permanence   **b.** Formal operational
   3. Abstract reasoning   **c.** Preoperational
   4. Conservation; reversibility   **d.** Concrete operational

6. _____ _____ theories of development suggest that the way a child handles information is critical to his or her development.
7. According to Vygotsky, information that's within a child's _____ _____ _____ _____ is most likely to result in cognitive development.

RETHINK

1. Do you think the widespread use of IQ testing in the United States contributes to parents' views that their children's academic success is due largely to the children's innate intelligence? Why? Would it be possible (or desirable) to change this view?
2. *From the perspective of a child-care provider:* If a parent were not sure whether to enroll his or her child in your program, what advice would you give about the possible positive and negative consequences about day care?

Answers to Evaluate Questions

1. habituation; 2. attachment; 3. 1-b, 2-c, 3-a, 4-d; 4. psychosocial; 5. 1-c, 2-a, 3-b, 4-d; 6. information-processing; 7. zone of proximal development

KEY TERMS

neonate p. 332
reflexes p. 332
habituation p. 333
attachment p. 336
authoritarian parents p. 340
permissive parents p. 341
authoritative
    parents p. 341
uninvolved parents p. 341
temperament p. 341

psychosocial
    development p. 342
trust-versus-mistrust
    stage p. 343
autonomy-versus-shame-
    and-doubt stage p. 343
initiative-versus-guilt
    stage p. 343
industry-versus-inferiority
    stage p. 343

cognitive
    development p. 344
sensorimotor stage p. 344
object permanence p. 344
preoperational stage p. 344
egocentric thought p. 345
principle of
    conservation p. 345
concrete operational
    stage p. 345

formal operational
    stage p. 345
information
    processing p. 347
metacognition p. 348
zone of proximal
    development (ZPD) p. 348

Adolescence: Becoming an Adult

Joseph Charles, Age 13: Being 13 is very hard at school. I have to be bad in order to be considered cool. I sometimes do things that aren't good. I have talked back to my teachers and been disrespectful to them. I do want to be good, but it's just too hard. (Gibbs, 2005, p. 51)

Trevor Kelson, Age 15: "Keep the Hell Out of my Room!" says a sign on Trevor's bedroom wall, just above an unmade bed, a desk littered with dirty T-shirts and candy wrappers, and a floor covered with clothes. Is there a carpet? "Somewhere," he says with a grin. "I think it's gold." (Fields-Meyer, 1995, p. 53)

Lauren Barry, Age 18: "I went to a National Honor Society induction. The parents were just staring at me. I think they couldn't believe someone with pink hair could be smart. I want to be a high-school teacher, but I'm afraid that, based on my appearance, they won't hire me." (Gordon et al., 1999, p. 47)

Although Joseph, Trevor, and Lauren have never met, they share anxieties that are common to adolescence—concerns about friends, parents, appearance, independence, and their futures. **Adolescence,** the developmental stage between childhood and adulthood, is a crucial period. It's a time of profound changes and, occasionally, turmoil. Considerable biological change occurs as adolescents attain sexual and physical maturity. At the same time, and rivaling these physiological changes, important social, emotional, and cognitive changes occur as adolescents strive for independence and move toward adulthood.

Because many years of schooling precede most people's entry into the workforce in Western societies, our stage of adolescence is fairly long, beginning just before the teenage years and ending just after them. No longer children but considered by society to be not quite adults, adolescents face a period of rapid physical, cognitive, and social change that affects them for the rest of their lives.

Dramatic changes in society also affect adolescents' development. More than half of all children in the United States will spend all or some of their childhood and adolescence in single-parent families. Furthermore, adolescents spend considerably less time with their parents and more with their peers than they did in the past. Finally, the ethnic and cultural diversity of adolescents as a group is increasing dramatically. A third of all adolescents today are of non-European descent, and by the year 2050 the number of adolescents of Hispanic, African American, Native American, and Asian origin collectively will surpass that of whites (National Adolescent Health Information Center, 2003).

Physical Development: The Changing Adolescent

If you think back to the start of your own adolescence, the most dramatic changes you probably remember are physical ones. A spurt in height, the growth of breasts in girls, deepening voices in boys, the development of body hair, and intense sexual feelings cause curiosity, interest, and often embarrassment for individuals entering adolescence.

Key Concept

What major physical, social, and cognitive transitions characterize adolescence?

adolescence The developmental stage between childhood and adulthood.

FIGURE 1 The range of ages during which major sexual changes occur during adolescence is shown by the colored bars. (Source: Based on Tanner, 1978.)

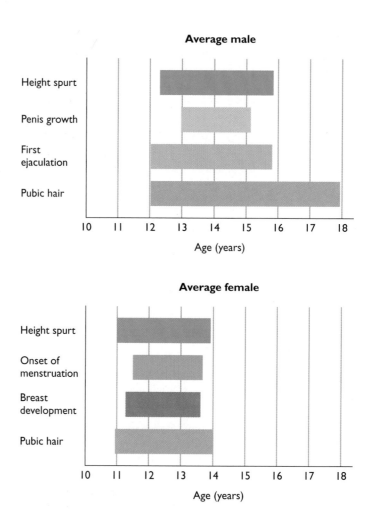

puberty The period at which maturation of the sexual organs occurs, usually beginning at approximately age 11 or 12 for girls and age 13 or 14 for boys.

The physical changes that occur at the start of adolescence result largely from the secretion of various sex hormones, and they affect virtually every aspect of an adolescent's life. Not since infancy has development been so dramatic. Weight and height increase rapidly because of a growth spurt that typically begins around age 10 for girls and age 12 for boys. Adolescents may grow as much as 5 inches in one year.

Puberty, the period at which maturation of the sexual organs occurs, begins at about age 11 or 12 for girls, when menstruation starts. However, there are wide variations (see Figure 1). For example, some girls begin to menstruate as early as age 8 or 9 or as late as age 16. Furthermore, in Western cultures the average age at which adolescents reach sexual maturity has been steadily decreasing over the last century, most likely as a result of improved nutrition and medical care. Sexual *attraction* to others begins even before the maturation of the sexual organs, at around age 10 (see Figure 1; Tanner, 1990; Finlay, Jones, & Coleman, 2002).

For boys, the onset of puberty is marked by their first ejaculation, known as *spermarche*. Spermarche usually occurs around the age of 13 (see Figure 1). At first, relatively few sperm are produced during an ejaculation, but the amount increases significantly within a few years.

The age at which puberty begins has implications for the way adolescents feel about themselves—as well as the way others treat them. Boys who mature early have a distinct advantage over later-maturing boys. They do better in athletics, are generally more popular with peers, and have more positive self-concepts (Ge et al., 2003; Becker & Luthar, 2007).

The picture differs for girls. Although early-maturing girls are more sought after as dates and have better self-esteem than do later-maturing girls, some consequences of early physical maturation may be less positive. For example, early

Although puberty begins around age 11 or 12 for girls and 13 or 14 for boys, there are wide variations. What are some advantages and disadvantages of early puberty?

breast development may set them apart from their peers and be a source of ridicule (Franko & Striegel-Moore, 2002; Olivardia & Pope, 2002; Nadeem & Graham, 2005).

Late physical maturation may produce certain psychological difficulties for both boys and girls. Boys who are smaller and less coordinated than their more mature peers tend to feel ridiculed and less attractive. Similarly, late-maturing girls are at a disadvantage in middle school and early high school. They hold relatively low social status and may be overlooked in dating (Lanza & Collins, 2002).

Clearly, the rate at which physical changes occur during adolescence can affect the way people are viewed by others and the way they view themselves. Just as important as physical changes, however, are the psychological and social changes that unfold during adolescence.

Moral and Cognitive Development: Distinguishing Right from Wrong

In a European country, a woman is near death from a special kind of cancer. The one drug that the doctors think might save her is a medicine that a medical researcher has recently discovered. The drug is expensive to make, and the researcher is charging ten times the cost, or $5,000, for a small dose. The sick woman's husband, Henry, approaches everyone he knows in hopes of borrowing money, but he can raise only about $2,500. He tells the researcher that his wife is dying and asks him to lower the price of the drug or let him pay later. The researcher says, "No, I discovered the drug, and I'm going to make money from it." Henry is desperate and considers stealing the drug for his wife.

What would you tell Henry to do?

KOHLBERG'S THEORY OF MORAL DEVELOPMENT

In the view of psychologist Lawrence Kohlberg, the advice you give Henry reflects your level of moral development. According to Kohlberg, people pass through a series of

	Sample Moral Reasoning of Subjects	
Level	**In Favor of Stealing the Drug**	**Against Stealing the Drug**
Level 1 Preconventional morality: At this level, the concrete interests of the individual are considered in terms of rewards and punishments.	"If you let your wife die, you will get in trouble. You'll be blamed for not spending the money to save her, and there'll be an investigation of you and the druggist for your wife's death."	"You shouldn't steal the drug because you'll be caught and sent to jail if you do. If you do get away, your conscience will bother you thinking how the police will catch up with you at any minute."
Level 2 Conventional morality: At this level, people approach moral problems as members of society. They are interested in pleasing others by acting as good members of society.	"If you let your wife die, you'll never be able to look anybody in the face again."	"After you steal the drug, you'll feel bad thinking how you've brought dishonor on your family and yourself; you won't be able to face anyone again."
Level 3 Postconventional morality: At this level, people use moral principles which are seen as broader than those of any particular society.	"If you don't steal the drug, and if you let your wife die, you'll always condemn yourself for it afterward. You won't be blamed and you'll have lived up to the outside rule of the law, but you won't have lived up to your own conscience and standards of honesty."	"If you steal the drug, you won't be blamed by other people, but you'll condemn yourself because you won't have lived up to your own conscience and standards of honesty."

FIGURE 2 Developmental psychologist Lawrence Kohlberg theorized that people move through a three-level sequence of moral reasoning in a fixed order. However, he contended that few people ever reach the highest level of moral reasoning.

stages in the evolution of their sense of justice and in the kind of reasoning they use to make moral judgments (Kohlberg, 1984). Largely because of the various cognitive limitations that Piaget described, preadolescent children tend to think either in terms of concrete, unvarying rules ("It's always wrong to steal" or "I'll be punished if I steal") or in terms of the rules of society ("Good people don't steal" or "What if everyone stole?").

Adolescents, however, can reason on a higher plane, having typically reached Piaget's formal operational stage of cognitive development. Because they're able to comprehend broad moral principles, they can understand that morality is not always black and white and that conflict can exist between two sets of socially accepted standards.

Kohlberg (1984) suggests that the changes in moral reasoning can be understood best as a three-level sequence (see Figure 2). His theory assumes that people move through the levels in a fixed order, and that they cannot reach the highest level until about age 13—primarily because of limitations in cognitive development before that age. However, many people never reach the highest level of moral reasoning. In fact, Kohlberg found that only a relatively small percentage of adults rise above the second level of his model (Kohlberg & Ryncarz, 1990; Hedgepeth, 2005; Powers, 2006).

Although Kohlberg's theory has had a substantial influence on our understanding of moral development, the research support is mixed. One difficulty with the theory is that it pertains to moral *judgments*, not moral *behavior*. Knowing right from wrong doesn't mean that we'll always act in accordance with our judgments. In addition, the theory applies primarily to Western society and its moral code; cross-cultural research conducted in cultures with different moral systems suggests that Kohlberg's theory is not necessarily applicable (Coles, 1997; Damon, 1999; Nucci, 2002; Barandiaran, Pascual, & Samaniego, 2006).

MORAL DEVELOPMENT IN WOMEN

One glaring shortcoming of Kohlberg's research is that he primarily used male participants. Furthermore, psychologist Carol Gilligan (1996) argues that because of men's and women's distinctive socialization experiences, a fundamental difference exists in the way each gender views moral behavior. According to Gilligan, men view morality primarily in terms of broad principles, such as justice and fairness. In contrast, women see it in terms of responsibility toward individuals and willingness to make sacrifices to help a specific individual within the context of a particular relationship. Compassion for individuals is a more salient factor in moral behavior for women than it is for men.

Because Kohlberg's model defines moral behavior largely in terms of abstract principles such as justice, Gilligan finds that it inadequately describes the moral development of females. She suggests that women's morality centers on individual well-being and social relationships—a morality of *caring*. In her view, compassionate concern for the welfare of others represents the highest level of morality.

The fact that Gilligan's conception of morality differs greatly from Kohlberg's suggests that gender plays an important role in determining what a person sees as moral. Although the research evidence is not definitive, it seems plausible that their differing conceptions of what constitutes moral behavior may lead men and women to regard the morality of a specific behavior in different ways (Jorgensen, 2006; Sherblom, 2008; Walker & Frimer, 2009).

Social Development: Finding One's Self in a Social World

"Who am I?" "How do I fit into the world?" "What's life all about?"

Questions such as these assume special significance during the teenage years as adolescents seek to find their place in the broader social world. As we'll see, this quest takes adolescents along several routes.

ERIKSON'S THEORY OF PSYCHOSOCIAL DEVELOPMENT: THE SEARCH FOR IDENTITY

Erikson's theory of psychosocial development emphasizes the search for identity during the adolescent years. As was noted earlier, psychosocial development encompasses the way people's understanding of themselves, one another, and the world around them changes during the course of human development (Erikson, 1963).

The fifth stage of Erikson's theory (summarized, with the other stages, in Figure 3), the **identity-versus-role-confusion stage,** encompasses adolescence. During this stage, a time of major testing, people try to determine what's unique about themselves. They attempt to discover who they are, what their strengths are, and what kinds of roles they're best suited to play for the rest of their lives—in short, their **identity.** A person confused about his or her most appropriate role to play in life may lack a stable identity, adopt an unacceptable role such as that of a social deviant, or have difficulty maintaining close personal relationships later in life (Updegraff et al., 2004; Vleioras & Bosma, 2005; Goldstein, 2006).

During the identity-versus-role-confusion period, an adolescent feels pressure to identify what to do with his or her life. Because these pressures come at a time of major physical changes as well as important changes in what society expects of them, adolescents can find the period an especially difficult one. The identity-versus-role-confusion stage has another important characteristic: declining reliance on adults for information, with a shift toward using the peer group as a source of social judgments. The peer group becomes increasingly important, enabling adolescents to form close, adultlike relationships and helping them clarify their personal identities. According to Erikson, the identity-versus-role-confusion stage marks a pivotal point in psychosocial development, paving the way for continued growth and the future development of personal relationships.

identity-versus-role-confusion stage According to Erikson, a time in adolescence of major testing to determine one's unique qualities.

identity The distinguishing character of the individual: Who each of us is, what our roles are, and what we are capable of.

Stage	Approximate Age	Positive Outcomes	Negative Outcomes
1. Trust-vs.-mistrust	Birth–1½ years	Feelings of trust from environmental support	Fear and concern regarding others
2. Autonomy-vs.-shame-and-doubt	1½–3 years	Self-sufficiency if exploration is encouraged	Doubts about self, lack of independence
3. Initiative-vs.-guilt	3–6 years	Discovery of ways to initiate actions	Guilt from actions and thoughts
4. Industry-vs.-inferiority	6–12 years	Development of sense of competence	Feelings of inferiority, no sense of mastery
5. Identity-vs.-role-confusion	Adolescence	Awareness of uniqueness of self, knowledge of role to be followed	Inability to identify appropriate roles in life
6. Intimacy-vs.-isolation	Early adulthood	Development of loving, sexual relationships and close friendships	Fear of relationships with others
7. Generativity-vs.-stagnation	Middle adulthood	Sense of contribution to continuity of life	Trivialization of one's activities
8. Ego-integrity-vs.-despair	Late adulthood	Sense of unity in life's accomplishments	Regret over lost opportunities of life

FIGURE 3 Erikson's stages of psychosocial development. According to Erikson, people proceed through eight stages of psychosocial development across their lives. He suggested that each stage requires the resolution of a crisis or conflict and may produce both positive and negative outcomes.

intimacy-versus-isolation stage According to Erikson, a period during early adulthood that focuses on developing close relationships.

During early adulthood, people enter the **intimacy-versus-isolation stage.** Spanning the period of early adulthood (from post-adolescence to the early 30s), this stage focuses on developing close relationships with others. Difficulties during this stage result in feelings of loneliness and a fear of such relationships, whereas successful resolution of the crises of the stage results in the possibility of forming relationships that are intimate on a physical, intellectual, and emotional level.

generativity-versus-stagnation stage According to Erikson, a period in middle adulthood during which we take stock of our contributions to family and society.

Development continues during middle adulthood as people enter the **generativity-versus-stagnation stage.** Generativity is the ability to contribute to one's family, community, work, and society, and to assist the development of the younger generation. Success in this stage results in a person's feeling positive about the continuity of life, whereas difficulties lead a person to feel that his or her activities are trivial or stagnant and have done nothing for upcoming generations. In fact, if a person has not successfully resolved the identity crisis of adolescence, he or she may still be foundering in identifying an appropriate career, for example.

ego-integrity-versus-despair stage According to Erikson, a period from late adulthood until death when we review life's accomplishments and failures.

Finally, the last stage of psychosocial development, the **ego-integrity-versus-despair stage,** spans later adulthood and continues until death. Now a sense of overall accomplishment and satisfaction with one's life signifies success in resolving the difficulties presented by this stage of life; failure to resolve the difficulties results in regret over what might've been achieved but wasn't.

Notably, Erikson's theory suggests that development does not stop at adolescence but continues throughout adulthood, a view that a substantial amount of research now confirms. For instance, a 22-year study by psychologist Susan Whitbourne found considerable support for the fundamentals of Erikson's theory, determining that psychosocial development continues through adolescence and adulthood. In sum, adolescence is not an end point but rather a way station on the path of psychosocial development (Whitbourne et al., 1992; McAdams et al., 1997).

Although Erikson's theory provides a broad outline of identity development, critics have pointed out that his approach is anchored in male-oriented concepts of individuality and competitiveness. In an alternative schema, psychologist Carol

Gilligan suggests that women may develop identity through the establishment of relationships. In her view, a primary component of women's identity is the construction of caring networks among themselves and others (Gilligan, 2004).

STORMY ADOLESCENCE: MYTH OR REALITY?

Does puberty invariably foreshadow a stormy, rebellious period of adolescence?

At one time, psychologists thought that most children entering adolescence were beginning a period fraught with stress and unhappiness. However, research now shows that this characterization is largely a myth, that most young people pass through adolescence without appreciable turmoil in their lives, and that parents speak easily—and fairly often—with their children about a variety of topics (van Wel, Linssen, & Abma, 2000; Granic, Hollenstein, & Dishion, 2003).

Not that adolescence is completely calm! In most families with adolescents, the amount of arguing and bickering clearly rises. As part of their search for identity, most young teenagers experience tension between their attempts to become independent from their parents and their actual dependence on them. They may experiment with a range of behaviors, flirting with a variety of activities that their parents and even society as a whole find objectionable. Happily, though, for most families such tensions stabilize during middle adolescence—around age 15 or 16—and eventually decline around age 18 (Smetana, Daddis, & Chuang, 2003; Smetana, 2005).

One reason for the increase in discord during adolescence appears to be the now-typical protracted period that children stay at home with their parents. In prior historical periods—and in some non-Western cultures today—children leave home immediately after puberty and are considered adults. Today, however, sexually mature adolescents may spend as many as 7 or 8 years with their parents. Current social trends even hint at an extension of the conflicts of adolescence beyond the teenage years. Typically for economic reasons, a significant number of young adults— known as *boomerang children*—return to live with their parents after leaving home for some period. Although some parents welcome the return of their children, others are less sympathetic, opening the way to conflict (Bianchi & Casper, 2000; Lewin, 2003).

Another source of strife with parents lies in the way adolescents think. Adolescence fosters *adolescent egocentrism*, a state of self-absorption that causes a teenager to view the world from his or her own point of view. Egocentrism leads adolescents to be highly critical of authority figures, unwilling to accept criticism, and quick to fault others. It also makes them believe that they're the center of everyone else's attention, leading to self-consciousness. Furthermore, they develop *personal fables*—beliefs that their experience is unique, exceptional, and shared by no one else. Such personal fables may make adolescents feel invulnerable to the risks that threaten others (Tucker Blackwell, 2006; Alberts, Elkind, & Ginsberg, 2007; Schwartz, Maynard, & Uzelac, 2008).

Finally, parent-adolescent discord occurs because adolescents are much more apt to engage in risky behavior than is likely later in life. In large part, this riskiness is due to immature brain systems that regulate impulse control, some of which don't fully develop until people are in their 20s (Steinberg, 2007).

ADOLESCENT SUICIDE

Although the vast majority of teenagers pass through adolescence without major psychological difficulties, some experience unusually severe psychological problems. Sometimes those problems are so extreme, adolescents take their own lives. Suicide is the third leading cause of death for adolescents (after accidents and homicide) in

> ▸ **Study Alert**
> The characterization of a stormy adolescence is a myth for most adolescents.

THE WORLD'S FIRST GENETICALLY ENGINEERED HUMAN HITS ADOLESCENCE

We buy you the best genes in the world— FOR THIS?

So, I got my nose pierced. So what, man.

I remember checking "genius" on the order form— AND NOW LOOK!

© Roz Chast/The New Yorker Collection/www.cartoonbank.com.

These students are mourning the deaths of two classmates who committed suicide. The rate of suicide among teenagers has risen significantly over the last few decades. Can you think of any reasons for this phenomenon?

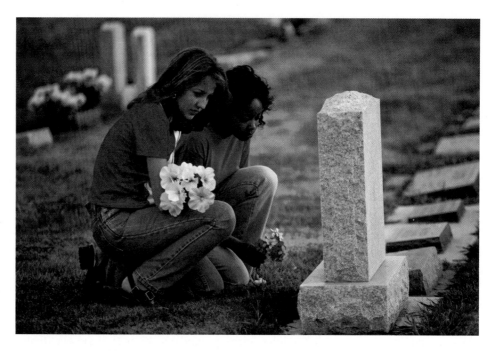

the United States. More teenagers and young adults die from suicide than from cancer, heart disease, AIDS, birth defects, stroke, pneumonia and influenza, and chronic lung disease combined (CDC, 2004).

A teenager commits suicide every 90 minutes. Furthermore, the reported rate of suicide may actually be understated because medical personnel hesitate to report suicide as a cause of death. Instead, they frequently label a death as an accident to protect the survivors. In addition, as many as 200 adolescents may attempt suicide for every 1 who actually takes his or her own life (CDC, 2000; Brausch & Gutierrez, 2009).

Male adolescents are five times more likely to commit suicide than are females, although females *attempt* suicide more often than males do. The rate of adolescent suicide is significantly greater among whites than nonwhites. However, the suicide rate of African-American males has increased much more rapidly than has that of white males over the last two decades. Native Americans have the highest suicide rate of any ethnic group in the United States, and Asian Americans have the lowest (CDC, 2004; Gutierrez et al., 2005; Boden, Fergusson, & Horwood, 2007).

Although the overall rates of suicide have slowly declined, rates are still higher for adolescents than any other age group except the elderly. Some psychologists suggest that the sharp rise in stress that teenagers experience—due to academic and social pressure, alcoholism, drug abuse, and family difficulties—provokes the most troubled adolescents to take their own lives. However, that's not the whole story, for the suicide rate for other age groups has remained fairly stable in the last few decades. It's unlikely that stress has increased only for adolescents and not for the rest of the population (Lubell et al., 2004).

Although the question of why adolescent suicide rates are so high remains unanswered, several factors put adolescents at risk. One factor is depression, characterized by unhappiness, extreme fatigue, and—a variable that seems especially important—a profound sense of hopelessness. In other cases, adolescents who commit suicide are perfectionists who are inhibited socially and prone to extreme anxiety when they face any social or academic challenge (see Figure 4; CDC, 2004; Richardson et al., 2005; Caelian, 2006).

Family background and adjustment difficulties are also related to suicide. A long-standing history of conflicts between parents and children may lead to adolescent behavior problems like delinquency, dropping out of school, and aggressive tendencies.

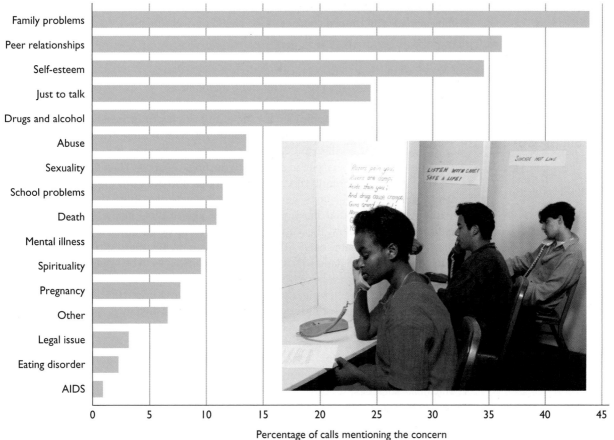

FIGURE 4 According to a review of phone calls to one telephone help line, adolescents who were considering suicide most often mentioned family, peer relationships, and self-esteem problems. (Source: Boehm & Campbell, 1995.)

In addition, teenage alcoholics and abusers of other drugs have a relatively high rate of suicide (Winstead & Sanchez, 2005; Bagge & Sher, 2008; Hardt et al., 2008).

Several warning signs indicate when a teenager's problems may be severe enough to warrant concern about the possibility of a suicide attempt. They include the following:

- School problems, such as missing classes, truancy, and a sudden change in grades
- Frequent incidents of self-destructive behavior, such as careless accidents
- Loss of appetite or excessive eating
- Withdrawal from friends and peers
- Sleeping problems
- Signs of depression, tearfulness, or overt indications of psychological difficulties, such as hallucinations
- A preoccupation with death, an afterlife, or what would happen "if I died"
- Putting his or her affairs in order, such as giving away prized possessions or making arrangements for the care of a pet
- An explicit announcement of thoughts of suicide

If you know someone who shows signs that he or she is suicidal, urge that person to seek professional help. You may need to take assertive action, such as enlisting the assistance of family members or friends. Talk of suicide is a serious signal for help, not a secret to be kept.

For immediate help with a suicide-related problem, call 1-800-273-8255, a national hotline staffed with trained counselors, or visit their website at www.suicideprevention-lifeline.org.

Exploring DIVERSITY

Rites of Passage: Coming of Age Around the World

It's not easy for male members of the Awa tribe in New Guinea to make the transition from childhood to adulthood. First come whippings with sticks and prickly branches, both for the boys' own past misdeeds and in honor of those tribesmen who were killed in warfare. During the next phase of the ritual, adults jab sharpened sticks into the boys' nostrils. Then they force a 5-foot length of vine into the boys' throats until they gag and vomit. Finally, tribesmen cut the boys' genitals, causing severe bleeding.

Although the rites that mark the coming of age of boys in the Awa tribe sound horrifying to Westerners, they are comparable to those in other cultures. In some, youths must kneel on hot coals without displaying pain. In others, girls must toss wads of burning cotton from hand to hand and allow themselves to be bitten by hundreds of ants (Selsky, 1997).

Other cultures have less fearsome, although no less important, ceremonies that mark the passage from childhood to adulthood. For instance, when a girl first menstruates in traditional Apache tribes, the event is marked by dawn-to-dusk chanting. Western religions, too, have several types of celebrations, including bar and bat mitzvahs at age 13 for Jewish boys and girls and confirmation ceremonies for children in many Christian denominations (Magida, 2006).

In most societies, males—but not females—are the focus of coming-of-age ceremonies. The renowned anthropologist Margaret Mead remarked, only partly in jest, that the preponderance of male ceremonies might reflect that "the worry that boys will not grow up to be men is much more widespread than that girls will not grow up to be women" (1949, p. 195). Said another way, it may be that in most cultures men traditionally have higher status than women, and therefore those cultures regard boys' transition into adulthood as more important.

However, another fact may explain why most cultures place greater emphasis on male rites than on female ones. For females, the transition from childhood is marked by a definite biological event: menstruation. For males, in contrast, no single event can be used to pinpoint entry into adulthood. Thus, men are forced to rely on culturally determined rituals to acknowledge their arrival into adulthood.

RECAP/EVALUATE/RETHINK

RECAP

What major physical, social, and cognitive transitions characterize adolescence?

- Adolescence, the developmental stage between childhood and adulthood, is marked by the onset of puberty, the point at which sexual maturity occurs. The age at which puberty begins has implications for the way people view themselves and the way others see them. (p. 351)
- Moral judgments during adolescence increase in sophistication, according to Kohlberg's three-level model. Although Kohlberg's levels provide an adequate description of males' moral judgments, Gilligan suggests that women view morality in terms of caring for individuals rather than in terms of broad, general principles of justice. (p. 353)
- According to Erikson's model of psychosocial development, adolescence may be accompanied by an identity crisis. Adolescence is followed by three more stages of psychosocial development that cover the remainder of the life span. (p. 355)
- Suicide is the third leading cause of death in adolescents. (p. 357)

EVALUATE

1. _____ is the period during which the sexual organs begin to mature.
2. Delayed maturation typically provides both males and females with a social advantage. True or false?

3. _____ proposed a set of three levels of moral development ranging from reasoning based on rewards and punishments to abstract thinking involving concepts of justice.
4. Erikson believed that during adolescence, people must search for _____, whereas during the early adulthood, the major task is _____.

RETHINK

1. In what ways do school cultures help or hurt teenage students who are going through adolescence? What school policies might benefit early-maturing girls and late-maturing boys? Explain how same-sex schools could help, as some have argued.
2. *From the perspective of a social worker:* How might you determine if an adolescent is at risk for suicide? What strategies would you use to prevent the teen from committing suicide? Would you use different strategies depending on the teenager's gender?

Answers to Evaluate Questions

1. puberty; 2. false; both male and female adolescents suffer if they mature late; 3. Kohlberg; 4. identity, intimacy

KEY TERMS

adolescence p. 351
puberty p. 352
identity-versus-role-
   confusion stage p. 355

identity p. 355
intimacy-versus-isolation
   stage p. 356

generativity-versus-
   stagnation stage p. 356

ego-integrity-versus-despair
   stage p. 356

Adulthood

Key Concepts

What are the principal physical, social, and intellectual changes that occur in early and middle adulthood, and what are their causes?

How does the reality of late adulthood differ from the stereotypes about that period?

How can we adjust to death?

emerging adulthood The period beginning in the late teenage years and extending into the mid-twenties.

I thought I got better as I got older. I found out that wasn't the case in a real hurry last year. After going 12 years in professional football and 12 years before that in amateur football without ever having surgery performed on me, the last two seasons of my career I went under the knife three times. It happened very quickly and without warning, and I began to ask myself, "Is this age? Is this what's happening?" Because up until that moment, I'd never realized that I was getting older. (Kotre & Hall, 1990, pp. 257, 259–260)

As a former professional football player, Brian Sipes intensely felt the changes in his body brought about by aging. But the challenges he experienced are part of a normal process that affects all people as they move through adulthood.

Psychologists generally agree that early adulthood begins around age 20 and lasts until about age 40 to 45, with middle adulthood beginning then and continuing until approximately age 65. Despite the enormous importance of these periods of life—both their accomplishments and their overall length (together they span some 44 years)—they've been studied less than has any other life stage. For one reason, the physical changes that occur during these periods are less apparent and more gradual than at other times during the life span. In addition, the diversity of social changes that arise during this period defy simple categorization.

The self-exploration that occurs in early adulthood has led many developmental psychologists to view the start of the period as a transitional phase called emerging adulthood. **Emerging adulthood** is the period beginning in the late teenage years and extending into the mid-20s. During emerging adulthood, people are no longer adolescents, but they haven't fully taken on the responsibilities of adulthood either. Instead, they're still engaged in determining who they are and what their life and career paths should be (Schwartz, Côté, & Arnett, 2005; Bukobza, 2009; Lamborn & Groh, 2009).

The view that adulthood is preceded by an extended period of emerging adulthood is a response to the fact that the economies of industrialized countries have shifted away from manufacturing to technology and information, which require more time for education and training. Furthermore, the age at which most people marry and have children has risen significantly (Arnett, 2007).

There's also an increasing ambivalence about reaching adulthood. When people in their late teens and early twenties are asked if they feel they've reached adulthood, most say "yes and no" (see Figure 1). In short, emerging adulthood is an age of identity exploration during which individuals are more self-focused and uncertain than they will be at a later stage in early adulthood (Arnett, 2000, 2006).

As we discuss the changes that occur during emerging adulthood, early adulthood, middle adulthood, and ultimately late adulthood, keep in mind that demarcations between the periods are fuzzy. However, the changes are certainly no less profound than they were in earlier periods of development.

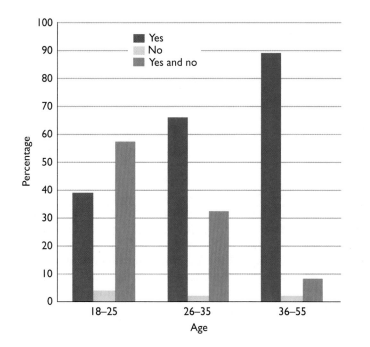

FIGURE 1 Evidence of a period of emerging adulthood is provided by the responses to a questionnaire asking "Do you feel that you have reached adulthood?" Most people between the ages of 18–25 were ambivalent, responding "yes and no." Later, this ambivalence disappeared, with most people 26–35 saying "yes." (Source: Arnett, 2000.)

Physical Development: The Peak of Health

For most, early adulthood marks the peak of one's physical health. From about ages 18 to 25, physical strength is greatest, reflexes are quickest, and the chances of dying from disease are quite slim. Moreover, reproductive capabilities are at their highest.

Near age 25, the body becomes slightly less efficient and more susceptible to disease. Overall, however, ill health remains the exception; most people stay remarkably healthy during early adulthood. (Can you think of any machine other than the human body that can operate without pause for so long a period?)

During middle adulthood people gradually become aware of changes in their bodies. Many gain weight (although diet and exercise can help offset this tendency). Furthermore, the sense organs gradually become less sensitive, and reactions to stimuli are slower. But generally, the physical declines that occur during middle adulthood are minor and often unnoticeable (DiGiovanna, 1994; Forzanna et al., 1994).

The major biological change that does occur during middle adulthood pertains to reproductive capabilities. On average, during their late 40s or early 50s, women begin **menopause,** during which they stop menstruating and are no longer fertile. Because menopause is accompanied by a significant reduction in estrogen production (a female hormone), women sometimes experience symptoms such as hot flashes or sudden surges of heat. Many symptoms can be treated with *hormone therapy (HT)* to adjust levels of the hormones estrogen and progesterone.

However, hormone therapy poses several dangers, such as an increase in the risk of breast cancer, blood clots, and coronary heart disease. These uncertainties make routine use of HT controversial. Currently, the medical consensus seems to be that younger women with severe menopausal symptoms ought to consider HT on a short-term basis, whereas HT is less appropriate for older women after menopause (Rossouw et al., 2007; Lindh-Åstrand et al., 2007; MacLennan, 2009).

menopause The period during which women stop menstruating and are no longer fertile.

Women's reactions to menopause vary significantly across cultures, and according to one study, the more a society values old age, the less difficulty its women have during menopause. Why do you think this would be the case?

Menopause was once blamed for a variety of psychological symptoms, including depression and memory loss. However, such difficulties, if they do occur, may be caused by women's expectations about reaching "old age" in a society that highly values youth. For this reason, women's reactions to menopause vary significantly across cultures; the more a society values old age, the less difficulty its women have during menopause (Elliot, Berman, & Kim, 2002; Beyene, Gilliss, & Lee, 2007).

For men, the aging process during middle adulthood is somewhat subtler. There are no physiological signals of increasing age equivalent to the end of menstruation in women; that is, no male menopause exists. In fact, men remain fertile and capable of fathering children until well into late adulthood. However, some gradual biological reproductive decline occurs: Sperm production decreases, and the frequency of orgasm tends to diminish. Once again, though, any psychological difficulties associated with these changes are usually brought about not so much by physical deterioration as by the inability of an aging individual to meet the exaggerated standards of youthfulness in our culture.

Social Development: Working at Life

Whereas physical changes during adulthood reflect developments of a quantitative nature, social developmental transitions are qualitative and more profound. During this period, people typically launch themselves into careers, marriage, and families.

The entry into early adulthood is usually marked by leaving one's childhood home and entering the work world. People envision their life goals and make career choices. During this time, lives and identities often center on building careers (Vaillant & Vaillant, 1990; Levinson, 1990, 1992).

In their early 40s, however, many begin to question their lives as they enter a period called the *midlife transition*. The realization that life will eventually end often influences their thinking more, leading them to question their past accomplishments (Gould, 1978).

Although popular opinion suggests that physical aging and dissatisfaction with one's life marks a so-called "midlife crisis," there is little evidence for such a "crisis." In fact, for most people the passage into middle age is relatively calm. Most 40-year-olds view their lives and accomplishments positively enough to proceed smoothly through midlife, and the 40s and 50s are often a particularly rewarding period. Rather than looking too far into the future, many concentrate on the present, with their involvement with families, friends, and other social groups taking on new importance. A major developmental thrust of this period is coming to terms with one's circumstances (Whitbourne, 2000, 2010).

Finally, during the last stages of adulthood people tend to become more accepting of others and of their own lives and are less concerned about issues or problems that once bothered them. Most come to accept that death is inevitable, and they try to understand their accomplishments in terms of the broader meaning of life. Although some may begin for the first time to label themselves as "old," many also feel a sense of wisdom and greater freedom to enjoy life (Baltes & Kunzmann, 2003; Miner-Rubino, Winter, & Stewart, 2004; Ward-Baker, 2007).

Marriage, Children, and Divorce: Family Ties

In the typical fairy tale, a dashing young man and a beautiful young woman marry, have children, and live happily ever after. However, that scenario doesn't match the realities of love and marriage in the 21st century. Today, it's just as likely that the man and woman would first live together, then get married and have children, but ultimately get divorced.

The percentage of U.S. households made up of unmarried couples has increased dramatically over the last two decades. At the same time, the average age at which marriage takes place is higher than at any time since the turn of the last century. These changes are dramatic, and they suggest that the institution of modern marriage has evolved considerably from earlier historical periods.

When people do marry, the probability of divorce is high, especially for younger couples. Even though divorce rates have been declining since peaking in 1981, about half of all first marriages end in divorce. Before age 18, two-fifths of children will see their parents' marriages end. Moreover, the rise in divorce is not just a U.S. phenomenon: The divorce rate has accelerated over the last several decades in most industrialized countries. For some countries, this increase has been enormous. In South Korea, for example, the divorce rate quadrupled, from 11% to 47% in the 12-year period ending in 2002 (Schaefer, 2000; Lankov, 2004; Olson & DeFrain, 2005).

Changes in marriage together with divorce trends have doubled the number of single-parent households in the United States over the last two decades. Almost 25% of all family households are now headed by one parent, compared with 13% in 1970. If present trends continue, almost three-fourths of American children will spend some portion of their lives in a single-parent family before they turn 18. For children in minority households, these numbers are even higher. Almost 60% of all black children and more than one-third of Hispanic children live in homes with only one parent. Furthermore, in most single-parent families, it's the mother

Single-parent families have doubled within the past decade, with the mother usually as head of the household. What are some of the challenges facing children in single-parent families?

rather than the father with whom the children reside—a phenomenon consistent across racial and ethnic groups throughout the industrialized world (U.S. Bureau of the Census, 2000).

What are the economic and emotional consequences for children living in homes with only one parent? Single-parent families are often economically less well off, and this economic disadvantage has an impact on children's opportunities. Over one-third of single-mothers with children have incomes below the poverty line. In addition, quality child care at an affordable price is often hard to find. Furthermore, for children of divorce, the parents' separation is often a painful experience that may create obstacles later in life for children establishing close relationships. In addition, children may blame themselves for the breakup or feel pressure to take sides (U.S. Bureau of the Census, 2000; Wallerstein et al., 2000; Liu, He, & Wu, 2007).

Most evidence, however, suggests that children from single-parent families are no less well adjusted than are those from two-parent families. In fact, children growing up in a harmonious single-parent family may be more successful than others in a two-parent family that engages in continuous conflict (Harold et al., 1997; Clarke-Stewart et al., 2000; Kelly, 2000; Olson & DeFrain, 2006).

CHANGING ROLES OF MEN AND WOMEN: THE TIME OF THEIR LIVES

One of the major changes in family life during the last two decades has been the evolution of men's and women's roles. More women than ever before juggle being wives, mothers, and wage earners—in contrast to women in traditional marriages where the husband is the sole wage earner and the wife's primary responsibility is care of the home and children.

Close to 75% of all married women with school-age children are now employed outside the home, and 55% of mothers with children under age 6 are working. In the mid-1960s, only 17% of mothers of 1-year-olds worked full-time; now, more than half are in the labor force (U.S, Bureau of the Census, 2001; Halpern, 2005).

Unfortunately, most married working women aren't free of household responsibilities. Even in marriages where spouses hold jobs of similar status and similar workday hours, the distribution of household tasks between husbands and wives hasn't changed substantially. Working wives are still more likely than husbands to feel responsible for traditional homemaking tasks such as cooking and cleaning. By contrast, husbands still view their primary responsibility for household tasks like repairing broken appliances and doing outside yard work (Ganong & Coleman, 1999; Juster, Ono, & Stafford, 2002).

Women's "Second Shift." The number of hours put in by working mothers can be staggering. One survey, for instance, found that if we add the number of hours they work on the job and in the home, employed mothers of children under age 3 log an average of 90 hours per week! This additional work performed by women is sometimes called the "second shift." National surveys show women who are both employed and mothers put in an extra month of 24-hour days during the course of a year. Researchers see similar patterns in many developing societies throughout the world, with women working at full-time jobs and also retaining primary responsibility for child care (Hochschild, 2001; Jacobs & Gerson, 2004; Bureau of Labor Statistics, 2007).

Consequently, rather than having careers become a substitute for what women do at home, they often simply add onto the role of homemaker. It's not surprising that some wives resent it when husbands spend less time on child care and housework than wives expected before the birth of their children (Kiecolt, 2003; Gerstel, 2005; Fagan & Press, 2008).

The Later Years of Life: Growing Old

I've always enjoyed doing things in the mountains—hiking or, more recently, active cliff-climbing. The more difficult the climb, the more absorbing it is. The climbs I really remember are the ones I had to work on. Maybe a particular section where it took two or three tries before I found the right combination of moves that got me up easily—and, preferably, elegantly. It's a wonderful exhilaration to get to the top and sit down and perhaps have lunch and look out over the landscape and be so grateful that it's still possible for me to do that sort of thing. (Lyman Spitzer, age 74, quoted in Kotre & Hall, 1990, pp. 358–359)

If you can't quite picture a 74-year-old rock climbing, some rethinking of your view of late adulthood may be in order. In spite of the societal stereotype of "old age" as a time of inactivity and physical and mental decline, gerontologists (specialists who study aging) are beginning to paint a very different portrait of late adulthood.

By focusing on the period of life that starts at approximately age 65, gerontologists are clarifying the capabilities of older adults. Their work is demonstrating that significant developmental processes continue even during so-called old age. And as life expectancy increases, the number of people who reach older adulthood will continue to grow substantially. Consequently, developing an understanding of late adulthood has become a critical priority for psychologists (Birren, 1996; Moody, 2000; Schaie, 2005).

PHYSICAL CHANGES IN LATE ADULTHOOD: THE AGING BODY

Napping, eating, walking, conversing. It probably doesn't surprise you that these relatively nonstrenuous activities represent the typical pastimes of late adulthood. But it *is* striking that these activities are identical to the most common leisure activities reported in a survey of college students as well (Harper, 1978). Although the students cited more active pursuits—such as sailing and playing basketball—as their favorite activities, in actuality they engaged in such sports relatively infrequently, spending most of their free time napping, eating, walking, and conversing.

Although the leisure activities that older adults engage in may not differ all that much from those younger people pursue, many physical changes are, of course, brought about by the aging process. The most obvious pertain to appearance—hair that thins and turns gray, skin that wrinkles and folds, and sometimes a slight loss of height as the thickness of the disks between vertebrae in the spine decreases—but subtler changes also occur in the body's biological functioning. For example, sensory capabilities decrease as a result of aging: Vision, hearing, smell, and taste become less sensitive. Reaction time slows, and physical stamina changes (Stenklev & Laukli, 2004; Schieber, 2006; Madden, 2007).

What are the reasons for these physical declines? **Genetic preprogramming theories of aging** suggest that human cells have a built-in time limit to their ability to reproduce. These theories suggest that after a certain time, cells stop dividing or become harmful to the body—as if a kind of automatic self-destruct button had been pushed. In contrast, **wear-and-tear theories of aging** suggest that the mechanical functions of the body simply work less efficiently as people age. Waste by-products of energy production eventually accumulate, and mistakes are made when cells divide. Eventually the body, in effect, wears out, just like an old automobile does (Ly et al., 2000; Miquel, 2006; Hayflick, 2007).

Evidence supports both the genetic preprogramming and the wear-and-tear views, and it may be that both processes contribute to natural aging. However, it's clear that physical aging is not a disease but a natural biological process. Many physical functions don't decline with age. For example, sex remains pleasurable well

> **Study Alert**
>
> Two major theories of aging—the genetic preprogramming and the wear-and-tear views—explain some of the physical changes that happen in older adults.

genetic preprogramming theories of aging Theories that suggest that human cells have a built-in limit to their ability to reproduce, and that after a certain time they're no longer able to divide.

wear-and-tear theories of aging Theories that suggest that the mechanical functions of the body simply stop working efficiently.

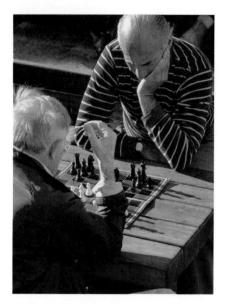

Although there are declines in fluid intelligence in late adulthood, skills relating to crystallized intelligence remain steady and may actually improve.

into old age (although the frequency of sexual activity tends to decrease), and some even report that the pleasure they derive from sex increases during late adulthood (Gelfand, 2000; DeLamater & Sill, 2005).

COGNITIVE CHANGES: THINKING ABOUT— AND DURING—LATE ADULTHOOD

At one time, many gerontologists would have agreed with the prevailing notion that older adults are forgetful and confused. Today, however, most research indicates that this assessment is far from accurate about older people's actual capabilities.

One reason for the change in view is that more sophisticated research techniques exist for studying the cognitive changes of late adulthood. For example, if we were to give a group of older adults an IQ test, we might find that the average score was lower than the score achieved by a same-sized group of younger people. We might conclude that this signifies a decline in intelligence. Yet if we looked a little more closely at the specific test, we might find that that conclusion was unwarranted. For instance, many IQ tests base tasks on speed or on physical performance (such as arranging a group of blocks). In such cases, a lower test score may be due to decreased reaction time—a physical decline that accompanies late adulthood and has little or nothing to do with the intellectual capability of older adults.

Other difficulties hamper research into cognitive functioning during late adulthood. For example, seniors are often less healthy than younger adults; when only *healthy* older adults are compared to healthy younger adults, intellectual differences are far less evident. Furthermore, for current generations, the average number of years in school is often lower in older adults (for historical reasons) than in younger ones, and older adults may be less motivated to perform well on intelligence tests than their younger counterparts. Finally, traditional IQ tests may not be the best measures of intelligence in late adulthood; older adults sometimes perform better on tests of practical intelligence than do younger individuals (Willis & Schaie, 1994; Dixon & Cohen, 2003).

Still, some declines in intellectual functioning during late adulthood do occur, although the pattern of age differences is not uniform for all types of cognitive abilities (see Figure 2). In general, skills relating to *fluid intelligence* (that involves

FIGURE 2 Age-related changes in intellectual skills vary according to the specific cognitive ability in question. (Source: Schaie, K. W. (2005). Longitudinal studies. In *Developmental influences on adult intelligence: The Seattle Longitudinal Study*, Figure 5.7a (p. 127). Copyright © 2005 by Oxford University Press, Inc. By permission of Oxford University Press, Inc. www.oup.co.uk)

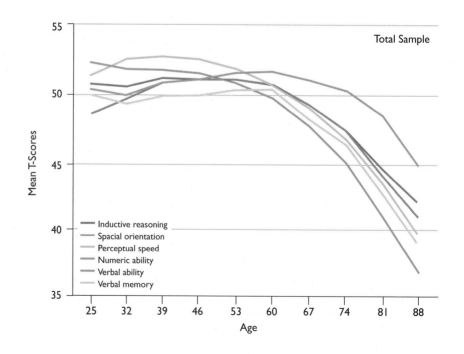

information-processing skills such as memory, calculations, and analogy solving) show declines in late adulthood. In contrast, skills relating to *crystallized intelligence* (intelligence based on the accumulation of information, skills, and strategies learned through experience) remain steady and in some cases actually improve (Rozencwajg et al., 2005; van Hooren et al., 2007; Kaufman, Johnson, & Liu, 2008).

Even when changes in intellectual functioning do occur during late adulthood, people often are able to compensate for any decline. They can still learn new things; it may just take more time. Furthermore, when the elderly are taught strategies for dealing with new problems, this can prevent declines in performance (Saczynski, Willis, & Schaie, 2002; Cavallini, Pagnin, & Vecchi, 2003; Peters et al., 2007; also see *Applying Psychology in the 21st Century*).

MEMORY CHANGES IN LATE ADULTHOOD: ARE OLDER ADULTS FORGETFUL?

One of the characteristics most frequently attributed to aging during late adulthood is forgetfulness. How accurate is this assumption?

Most evidence suggests that memory change is not an inevitable part of the aging process. For instance, research shows that older people in cultures in which older adults are held in high esteem, such as China, are less likely to show memory losses than are those living in cultures where there's an expectation that memory will decline. Similarly, when older people in Western societies are reminded of the advantages of age (for example, "age brings wisdom"), they tend to do better on tests of memory (Levy, 1996; Hess, Hinson, & Statham, 2004; Dixon et al., 2007).

Even when people show memory declines during late adulthood, these deficits are limited to certain types of memory. For instance, losses tend to be limited to episodic memories that relate to specific experiences in people's lives. Other types of memories, such as semantic memories (general knowledge and facts) and implicit memories (memories that we're not consciously aware of), are largely unaffected by age (Fleischman et al., 2004; Mitchell & Schmitt, 2006; St. Jacques & Levine, 2007).

Declines in episodic memories can often be traced to changes in the lives of older adults. For instance, it's not surprising that a retired person who no longer faces the same consistent intellectual challenges from a job, may get less practice using memory or even be less motivated to remember things, leading to an apparent decline in memory. Even in cases in which long-term memory declines, older adults can profit from training that targets memory skills (Fritsch et al., 2007; West, Bagwell, & Dark-Freudeman, 2007).

In the past, older adults with severe cases of memory decline accompanied by other cognitive difficulties were said to suffer from senility. *Senility* is a broad, imprecise term typically applied to older adults who experience progressive deterioration of mental abilities, including memory loss, disorientation to time and place, and general confusion. Once thought to be an inevitable state that accompanies aging, most gerontologists now view senility as a label that's outlived its usefulness. Rather than seeing senility as the vague cause of certain symptoms, symptoms are now linked to other physical or biological factors.

Some cases of memory loss, however, are produced by actual disease. For instance, **Alzheimer's disease** is a progressive brain disorder that leads to a gradual and irreversible decline in cognitive abilities. Nineteen percent of people age 75 to 84 have Alzheimer's, and almost 50% of those over age 85 are affected by the disease. Unless a cure is found, approximately 14 million people are projected to have Alzheimer's by 2050—a rate more than three times the current number (Cowley, 2000b; Feinberg, 2002; Lovestone, 2005; Rogers, 2007).

Alzheimer's occurs when production of the *beta amyloid precursor protein* goes awry, producing large clumps of cells that trigger inflammation and deterioration of nerve cells. The brain shrinks, neurons die, and areas of the hippocampus and frontal and temporal lobes deteriorate. So far, there's no effective treatment (Wolfe, 2006; Medeiros et al., 2007; Behrens, Lendon, & Roe, 2009).

Alzheimer's disease A progressive brain disorder that leads to a gradual and irreversible decline in one's cognitive abilities.

Gaming in Late Adulthood: How Video Games May Improve Cognitive Functioning in Older Adults

Have you ever frittered away an afternoon—or maybe even an entire day—playing a video game like *World of Warcraft* or *Grand Theft Auto?* A lot of people do. Perhaps you've told yourself that you're doing something to improve yourself, such as increasing your eye-hand coordination or honing your mental skills beyond just whiling away the time.

Turns out you may have been right, according to recent research that looked at the benefits of playing video games. And that may be especially true if you're an older adult playing video games.

Claims that playing video games can enhance skills and even improve cognitive ability are not new. There are even games marketed specifically as "mental workouts" that supposedly sharpen brain skills. But it's only recently that researchers have become interested in the possible use of video games to help slow the normal declines of cognitive functioning in late adulthood. Although research has found that activities that involve cognitive stimulation are generally helpful, up to now it hasn't been clear if video games provide the right kind of stimulation in the right amounts to do the trick (Tsai et al., 2008; Nunes & Kramer, 2009).

Recent studies are encouraging, however. In one study, older adults played a real-time strategic video game called *Rise of Nations* that had them managing and defending an empire of cities for almost 24 hours over several sessions. Not only did their skill at playing the game improve over time, but they also improved at real-world skills such as task

Maintaining interests and activities one had during middle age can contribute to a more successful late adulthood, according to the activity theory of aging.

switching, short-term memory, and reasoning (Basak et al., 2008).

In another study, groups of older and younger adults received 5 weeks of computerized cognitive skills training that became progressively more challenging. After the training, both groups showed noticeable increases in cognitive functioning, both in tests and in their daily lives. What's more, the effects tended to last and could be measured several months after the training had concluded (Westerberg et al., 2008).

The potential cognitive-improvement benefits of video games to those in late adulthood are so promising that the

National Science Foundation recently awarded a team of researchers at North Carolina State University and Georgia Tech a 4-year, million dollar grant to study the effects of playing selected Nintendo Wii games on older adults. Researchers will investigate not only what cognitive improvements can be realized from gaming, but also what aspects of game playing (such as the novelty of the games or the social interaction they require) are responsible for cognitive improvements. Ultimately they hope to create new games based on the research that maximizes the cognitive benefit to those in late adulthood (Hamilton, 2009).

RETHINK

- What aspects of video games do you think would most help prevent cognitive decline in late adulthood?
- What other activities do you think would be helpful to avert cognitive deterioration?

In other cases, cognitive decline may be caused by overmedication or short-term anxiety and depression, which can be treated successfully. The danger is that people with such symptoms may be left untreated, thereby continuing their decline (Selkoe, 1997; Sachs-Ericsson et al., 2005).

In sum, declines in cognitive functioning in late adulthood for the most part aren't inevitable. The key to maintaining cognitive skills may lie in continued intellectual stimulation. Like the rest of us, older adults need a stimulating environment to hone and maintain their skills (Bosma et al., 2003; Glisky, 2007; Hertzog et al., 2008).

Study Alert

It's important to be able to describe the nature of intellectual changes during late adulthood.

THE SOCIAL WORLD OF LATE ADULTHOOD: OLD BUT NOT ALONE

Just as the view that old age predictably means mental decline has proved to be wrong, so has the view that late adulthood inevitably brings loneliness. People in late adulthood most often see themselves as functioning members of society with only a small number of them reporting that loneliness is a serious problem (Binstock & George, 1996; Jylha, 2004).

Certainly, late adulthood brings significant challenges. People who have spent their adult lives working undergo a major shift in their role when they retire. More-over, many must face the death of a spouse. Especially if the marriage has been a long and happy one, the death of a partner means the loss of a companion, confidante, and lover. These losses can likewise bring about changes in economic well being.

There's no single way to age successfully. According to one early theory, the **disengagement theory of aging,** aging produces a gradual withdrawal from the world on physical, psychological, and social levels. This disengagement serves the purpose of providing an opportunity for increased reflectiveness and decreased emotional investment in others at a time of life when social relationships will inevitably be ended by death (Adams, 2004; Wrosch, Bauer, & Scheier, 2005).

However, little research supports disengagement theory. Consequently, alternative theories have arisen. According to the **activity theory of aging,** people who age most successfully are those who maintain the interests, activities, and level of social interaction they experienced during middle adulthood. Activity theory argues that late adulthood should reflect a continuation, as much as possible, of the activities that people participated in during earlier times of their lives (Crosnoe & Elder, 2002; Nimrod & Kleiber, 2007).

Although most research is supportive of activity theory, not everyone in late adulthood needs a life filled with activities and social interaction to be happy; as in every stage of life, some older adults are just as satisfied leading a relatively inactive solitary existence.

What may be more important is how people view the aging process: Evidence shows that positive self-perceptions of aging are associated with increased longevity (Levy et al., 2002; Levy & Myers, 2004).

disengagement theory of aging A largely discredited theory that suggests that aging produces a gradual withdrawal from the world on physical, psychological, and social levels.

activity theory of aging A theory that suggests that the elderly who are most successful while aging are those who maintain the interests and activities they had during middle age.

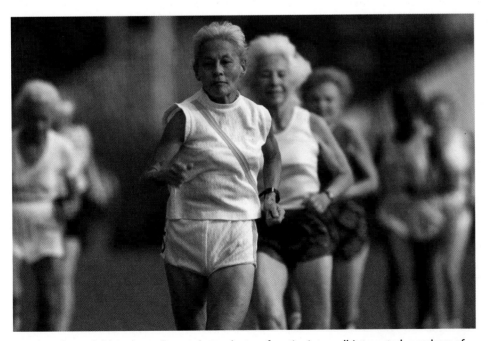

People in late adulthood usually see themselves as functioning, well-integrated members of society, and many maintain activities in which they participated earlier in life.

life review The process by which people examine and evaluate their lives.

Regardless of how they age, most people engage in a process of **life review,** during which they examine and evaluate their lives. By remembering and reconsidering what has occurred in the past, people in late adulthood often reach a better understanding of themselves, sometimes resolving lingering problems and conflicts, and face their lives with greater wisdom and serenity.

Clearly, people in late adulthood are not just marking time until death. Rather, old age is a time of continued growth and development, as important as any other period of life.

BECOMING AN INFORMED CONSUMER
of Psychology
Adjusting to Death

At some time in our lives, we all face death—certainly our own, as well as the deaths of friends, loved ones, and even strangers. Although there's nothing more inevitable in life, death remains a frightening, emotion-laden topic. Little is more stressful than the death of a loved one or the contemplation of our own imminent death, and preparing for death is one of our most crucial developmental tasks (Aiken, 2000).

A few generations ago, talk of death was taboo. The topic was simply never mentioned, including with those who were dying, and gerontologists had little to say about it. That changed, however, with the pioneering work of Elisabeth Kübler-Ross (1969), who brought the subject of death into the open with her observation that those facing impending death tend to move through five broad stages:

- *Denial.* In this stage, people resist the idea that they're dying. Even if told that their chances for survival are small, most refuse to admit that they're facing death.
- *Anger.* After moving beyond the denial stage, dying people become angry—angry at people around them who are in good health, angry at medical professionals for being ineffective, angry at God.
- *Bargaining.* Anger leads to bargaining, as the dying try to think of ways to postpone death. They may decide to dedicate their lives to religion, for example, if God spares them; they may say, "If only I can live to see my son married, I'll accept death then."
- *Depression.* When dying people conclude that bargaining is of no use, they move to the next stage: depression. They realize that their lives really are coming to an end, leading to what Kübler-Ross calls "preparatory grief" for their own deaths.
- *Acceptance.* In this stage, people accept impending death. Usually they're unemotional and uncommunicative; it's as if they've made peace with themselves and are expecting death with no bitterness.

It's important to keep in mind that not everyone experiences each of these stages or in the same way. In fact, Kübler-Ross's stages pertain only to individuals who are fully aware that they're dying and have the time to evaluate their impending death. Furthermore, vast differences occur in the way individuals react to impending death. The specific cause and duration of dying, as well as the person's sex, age, and personality and the extent of support received from family and friends, all have an impact on how people respond to death (Carver & Scheier, 2002; Coyle, 2006).

Few of us enjoy contemplating death. Yet awareness of its psychological aspects and consequences can make its inevitable arrival less anxiety-producing and perhaps more understandable.

RECAP/EVALUATE/RETHINK

RECAP

What are the principal physical, social, and intellectual changes that occur in early and middle adulthood, and what are their causes?

- Early adulthood marks the peak of physical health. Physical changes usually occur gradually in men and women during adulthood. (p. 362)
- One major physical change occurs at the end of middle adulthood for women: They begin menopause, after which they're no longer fertile. (p. 363)
- During middle adulthood, people typically experience a midlife transition in which the notion that life will end becomes more important. In some cases this may lead to a midlife crisis, although the passage into middle age is typically relatively calm. (p. 364)
- As aging continues during middle adulthood, people realize in their 50s that their lives and accomplishments are fairly set, and they try to come to terms with them. (p. 364)
- Among the important developmental milestones during adulthood are marriage, family changes, and divorce. Another important determinant of adult development is work or career. (p. 365)

How does the reality of late adulthood differ from stereotypes about that period?

- Old age may bring marked physical declines caused by genetic preprogramming or physical wear and tear. Although the activities of those in late adulthood are not all that different from those of younger people, older adults experience declines in reaction time, sensory abilities, and physical stamina. (p. 367)
- Intellectual declines are not an inevitable part of aging. Fluid intelligence does decline with age, and long-term memory abilities are sometimes impaired. In contrast, crystallized intelligence shows slight increases with age, and short-term memory remains at about the same level. (p. 368)

- Although disengagement theory sees successful aging as a process of gradual withdrawal from the physical, psychological, and social worlds, there is little research supporting this view. Instead, activity theory—the view that maintaining interests and activities from earlier years leads to successful aging—is a more accurate explanation. (p. 371)

How can we adjust to death?

- According to Kübler-Ross, dying people commonly move through five stages as they face death: denial, anger, bargaining, depression, and acceptance. (p. 372)

EVALUATE

1. Rob recently turned age 40 and surveyed his goals and accomplishments to date. Although he's accomplished a lot, he realized that many of his goals won't be met during his lifetime. This stage is called a _____ _____.
2. In households where both partners have similar jobs, the division of labor that generally occurs is the same as in "traditional" households where the husband works and the wife stays at home. True or false?
3. _____ _____ theories suggest that there is a maximum time span in which cells are able to reproduce. This time limit explains the eventual breakdown of the body.
4. Lower IQ test scores during late adulthood don't necessarily mean a decrease in intelligence. True or false?
5. During old age, a person's _____ intelligence continues to increase, whereas _____ intelligence may decline.
6. In Kübler-Ross's _____ stage, people resist the idea of death. In the _____ stage, they attempt to make deals to avoid death, and in the _____ stage, they passively await death.

RETHINK

1. Is the possibility that life may be extended for several decades a mixed blessing? What societal consequences might an extended life span bring?
2. *From the perspective of a health-care provider:* What sorts of recommendations would you make to older patients

about how to deal with aging? How would you handle someone who believed that getting older had only negative consequences?

Answers to Evaluate Questions

1. midlife transition; 2. true; 3. genetic preprogramming; 4. true; 5. crystallized, fluid; 6. denial, bargaining, acceptance

KEY TERMS

emerging adulthood p. 362

menopause p. 363

genetic preprogramming
   theories of aging p. 367

wear-and-tear theories
   of aging p. 367

Alzheimer's disease p. 369

disengagement theory of aging p. 371

activity theory of aging p. 371

life review p. 372

Psychology on the Web

1. Find information on the Web about gene therapy. What recent advances in gene therapy have been made by researchers? What developments appear to be on the horizon? What ethical issues have been raised regarding the use of gene therapy to produce children with characteristics specified by their parents?
2. Find different answers to the question "Why do people die?" Search the Web for scientific, philosophical, and spiritual or religious answers. Write a summary comparing the different approaches to this question. How does the thinking in any one realm influence the thinking in others?

Epilogue

We have traced major events in the development of physical, social, and cognitive growth throughout the life span. Clearly, people change throughout their lives.

As we explored each area of development, we encountered anew the nature–nurture issue, concluding in every significant instance that both nature and nurture contribute to a person's development of skills, personality, and interactions. Specifically, our genetic inheritance—nature—lays down general boundaries within which we can advance and grow, and our environment—nurture—helps determine the extent to which we take advantage of our potential.

Before proceeding to the next set of modules, turn once again to the prologue that introduced this one about Marcie McCartney's parents' decision to remove her tumor prior to birth. Using your knowledge of human development, consider the following questions.

1. Why was Marcie McCartney returned to her mother's womb after the tumor was removed?
2. Describe the stages of development that Marcie progressed through from conception to birth.
3. What genetic influences might have acted on Marcie in the womb?
4. What environmental influences might have acted on Marcie in the womb?

CHAPTER 10

Personality

Key Concepts for Chapter 10

Prologue *Who Is the Real Madoff?*

To some, Bernard L. Madoff was an affable, charismatic man who moved comfortably among power brokers on Wall Street and in Washington. He secured a long-standing role as an elder statesman on Wall Street, allowing him to land on important boards and commissions where his opinions helped shape securities regulations. And his employees say he treated them like family.

There was, of course, another side to Mr. Madoff. Reclusive, at times standoffish and aloof, this Bernard rarely rubbed elbows in Manhattan's cocktail circuit or at Palm Beach balls. This Bernard was quiet, controlled, and closely attuned to his image down to the most minute details. (Creswell & Landon, 2009, p. 1)

Looking **Ahead**

Which was the real Bernard Madoff? Was he the powerful, charismatic Wall Street businessman? Or was he the self-conscious, detail-oriented recluse? And perhaps most important, were there any signs that Madoff was secretly operating a fraudulent investment scheme that ultimately cheated thousands of people out of billions of dollars?

Many people, like Madoff, have different sides to their personalities, appearing one way to some and quite differently to others. Determining who a person truly is falls to a branch of psychology that seeks to understand the characteristic ways people behave—personality psychology.

Personality is the pattern of enduring characteristics that produce consistency and individuality in a given person. Personality encompasses the behaviors that make each of us unique and that differentiate us from others. Personality also leads us to act consistently in different situations and over extended periods of time.

We will consider a number of approaches to personality. For historical reasons, we begin with psychodynamic theories of personality, which emphasize the importance of the unconscious. Next, we consider approaches that concentrate on identifying the most fundamental personality traits; theories that view personality as a set of learned behaviors; biological and evolutionary perspectives on personality; and approaches, known as humanistic theories, that highlight the uniquely human aspects of personality. We end our discussion by focusing on how personality is measured and how personality tests can be used.

personality The pattern of enduring characteristics that produce consistency and individuality in a given person.

Psychodynamic Approaches to Personality

The college student was intent on making a good first impression on an attractive woman he had spotted across a crowded room at a party. As he walked toward her, he mulled over a line he had heard in an old movie the night before: "I don't believe we've been properly introduced yet." To his horror, what came out was a bit different. After threading his way through the crowded room, he finally reached the woman and blurted out, "I don't believe we've been properly seduced yet."

Although this student's error may seem to be merely an embarrassing slip of the tongue, according to some personality theorists such a mistake is not an error at all (Motley, 1987). Instead, *psychodynamic personality theorists* might argue that the error illustrates one way in which behavior is triggered by inner forces that are beyond our awareness. These hidden drives, shaped by childhood experiences, play an important role in energizing and directing everyday behavior.

Psychodynamic approaches to personality are based on the idea that personality is motivated by inner forces and conflicts about which people have little awareness and over which they have no control. The most important pioneer of the psychodynamic approach was Sigmund Freud. A number of Freud's followers, including Carl Jung, Karen Horney, and Alfred Adler, refined Freud's theory and developed their own psychodynamic approaches.

Key Concepts

How do psychologists define and use the concept of personality?

What do the theories of Freud and his successors tell us about the structure and development of personality?

psychodynamic approaches to personality Approaches that assume that personality is motivated by inner forces and conflicts about which people have little awareness and over which they have no control.

Freud's Psychoanalytic Theory: Mapping the Unconscious Mind

Sigmund Freud, an Austrian physician, developed **psychoanalytic theory** in the early 1900s. According to Freud's theory, conscious experience is only a small part of our psychological makeup and experience. He argued that much of our behavior is motivated by the **unconscious,** a part of the personality that contains the memories, knowledge, beliefs, feelings, urges, drives, and instincts of which the individual is not aware.

Like the unseen mass of a floating iceberg, the contents of the unconscious far surpass in quantity the information in our conscious awareness. Freud maintained that to understand personality, it is necessary to expose what is in the unconscious. But because the unconscious disguises the meaning of the material it holds, the content of the unconscious cannot be observed directly. It is therefore necessary to interpret clues to the unconscious—slips of the tongue, fantasies, and dreams—to understand the unconscious processes that direct behavior. A slip of the tongue such as the one quoted earlier (sometimes termed a *Freudian slip*) may be interpreted as revealing the speaker's unconscious sexual desires.

To Freud, much of our personality is determined by our unconscious. Some of the unconscious is made up of the *preconscious*, which contains material that is not threatening and is easily brought to mind, such as the knowledge that 2 + 2 = 4. But deeper in the unconscious are instinctual drives—the wishes, desires, demands, and needs that are hidden from conscious awareness because of the conflicts and

psychoanalytic theory Freud's theory that unconscious forces act as determinants of personality.

unconscious A part of the personality that contains the memories, knowledge, beliefs, feelings, urges, drives, and instincts of which the individual is not aware.

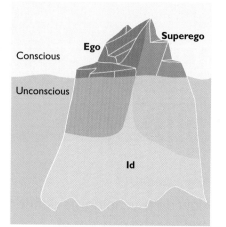

FIGURE 1 In Freud's personality model, there are three major components: the id, the ego, and the superego. As the iceberg analogy shows, only a small portion of personality is conscious. Why do you think that only the ego and superego have conscious components?

 Study Alert

Remember that the three parts of personality in Freud's theory—the id, the ego, and the superego—are abstract conceptions that don't exist as physical structures in the brain.

id The raw, unorganized, inborn part of personality whose sole purpose is to reduce tension created by primitive drives related to hunger, sex, aggression, and irrational impulses.

ego The part of the personality that provides a buffer between the id and the outside world.

pain they would cause if they were part of our everyday lives. The unconscious provides a "safe haven" for our recollections of threatening events.

STRUCTURING PERSONALITY: ID, EGO, AND SUPEREGO

To describe the structure of personality, Freud developed a comprehensive theory that held that personality consists of three separate but interacting components: the id, the ego, and the superego. Freud suggested that the three structures can be diagrammed to show how they relate to the conscious and the unconscious (see Figure 1).

Although the three components of personality Freud described may appear to be actual physical structures in the nervous system, they are not. Instead, they represent abstract conceptions of a general *model* of personality that describes the interaction of forces that motivate behavior.

If personality consisted only of primitive, instinctual cravings and longings, it would have just one component: the id. The **id** is the raw, unorganized, inborn part of personality. From the time of birth, the id attempts to reduce tension created by primitive drives related to hunger, sex, aggression, and irrational impulses. Those drives are fueled by "psychic energy," which we can think of as a limitless energy source constantly putting pressure on the various parts of the personality.

The id operates according to the *pleasure principle* in which the goal is the immediate reduction of tension and the maximization of satisfaction. However, in most cases, reality prevents the fulfillment of the demands of the pleasure principle: We cannot always eat when we are hungry, and we can discharge our sexual drives only when the time and place are appropriate. To account for this fact of life, Freud suggested a second component of personality, which he called the ego.

The **ego**, which begins to develop soon after birth, strives to balance the desires of the id and the realities of the objective, outside world. In contrast to the pleasure-seeking id, the ego operates according to the *reality principle* in which instinctual energy is restrained to maintain the individual's safety and to help integrate the person into society. In a sense, then, the ego is the "executive" of personality: It makes decisions, controls actions, and allows thinking and problem solving of a higher order than the id's capabilities permit.

Freud suggests that the superego, the part of personality that represents the rights and wrongs of society, develops from direct teaching from parents, teachers, and other significant individuals.

Stage	Age	Major Characteristics
Oral	Birth to 12–18 months	Interest in oral gratification from sucking, eating, mouthing, biting
Anal	12–18 months to 3 years	Gratification from expelling and withholding feces; coming to terms with society's controls relating to toilet training
Phallic	3 to 5–6 years	Interest in the genitals, coming to terms with Oedipal conflict leading to identification with same-sex parent
Latency	5–6 years to adolescence	Sexual concerns largely unimportant
Genital	Adolescence to adulthood	Reemergence of sexual interests and establishment of mature sexual relationships

FIGURE 2 Freud's theory of personality development suggests that there are several distinct stages.

The **superego,** the final personality structure to develop in childhood, represents the rights and wrongs of society as taught and modeled by a person's parents, teachers, and other significant individuals. The superego includes the *conscience,* which prevents us from behaving in a morally improper way by making us feel guilty if we do wrong. The superego helps us control impulses coming from the id, making our behavior less selfish and more virtuous.

Both the superego and the id are unrealistic in that they do not consider the practical realities imposed by society. The superego, if left to operate without restraint, would create perfectionists unable to make the compromises that life requires. An unrestrained id would create a primitive, pleasure-seeking, thoughtless individual seeking to fulfill every desire without delay. As a result, the ego must mediate between the demands of the superego and the demands of the id.

DEVELOPING PERSONALITY: PSYCHOSEXUAL STAGES

Freud also provided us with a view of how personality develops through a series of five **psychosexual stages** during which children encounter conflicts between the demands of society and their own sexual urges (in which sexuality is more about experiencing pleasure and less about lust). According to Freud, failure to resolve the conflicts at a particular stage can result in **fixations,** conflicts or concerns that persist beyond the developmental period in which they first occur. Such conflicts may be due to having needs ignored or (conversely) being overindulged during the earlier period.

The sequence Freud proposed is noteworthy because it explains how experiences and difficulties during a particular childhood stage may predict specific characteristics in the adult personality. This theory is also unique in associating each stage with a major biological function, which Freud assumed to be the focus of pleasure in a given period. (See Figure 2 for a summary of the stages.)

In the first psychosexual stage of development, called the **oral stage,** the baby's mouth is the focal point of pleasure. During the first 12 to 18 months of life, children suck, eat, mouth, and bite anything they can put into their mouths. To Freud, this behavior suggested that the mouth is the primary site of a kind of sexual pleasure and that weaning (withdrawing the breast or bottle) represents the main conflict during the oral stage. If infants are either overindulged (perhaps by being fed every time they cry) or frustrated in their search for oral gratification, they may become fixated at this stage. For example, fixation might occur if an infant's oral needs were

superego According to Freud, the final personality structure to develop; it represents the rights and wrongs of society as handed down by a person's parents, teachers, and other important figures.

psychosexual stages Developmental periods that children pass through during which they encounter conflicts between the demands of society and their own sexual urges.

fixations Conflicts or concerns that persist beyond the developmental period in which they first occur.

Study Alert

The five psychosexual stages of personality development in Freud's theory—oral, anal, phallic, latency, and genital— indicate how personality develops as people age.

oral stage According to Freud, a stage from birth to age 12 to 18 months, in which an infant's center of pleasure is the mouth.

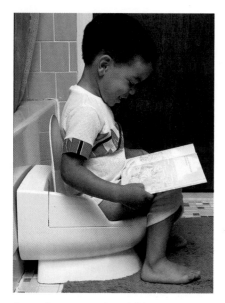

According to Freud, a child goes through the anal stage from age 12 to 18 months until 3 years of age. Toilet training is a crucial event at this stage—one that psychoanalytic theory claims directly influences the formation of an individual's personality.

anal stage According to Freud, a stage from age 12 to 18 months to 3 years of age, in which a child's pleasure is centered on the anus.

phallic stage According to Freud, a period beginning around age 3 during which a child's pleasure focuses on the genitals.

Oedipal conflict A child's sexual interest in his or her opposite-sex parent, typically resolved through identification with the same-sex parent.

identification The process of wanting to be like another person as much as possible, imitating that person's behavior and adopting similar beliefs and values.

latency period According to Freud, the period between the phallic stage and puberty during which children's sexual concerns are temporarily put aside.

genital stage According to Freud, the period from puberty until death, marked by mature sexual behavior (that is, sexual intercourse).

constantly gratified immediately at the first sign of hunger rather than if the infant learned that feeding takes place on a schedule because eating whenever an infant wants to eat is not always realistic. Fixation at the oral stage might produce an adult who was unusually interested in oral activities—eating, talking, smoking—or who showed symbolic sorts of oral interests such as being "bitingly" sarcastic or very gullible ("swallowing" anything).

From around age 12 to 18 months until 3 years of age—a period when the emphasis in Western cultures is on toilet training—a child enters the **anal stage.** At this point, the major source of pleasure changes from the mouth to the anal region, and children obtain considerable pleasure from both retention and expulsion of feces. If toilet training is particularly demanding, fixation might occur. Fixation during the anal stage might result in unusual rigidity, orderliness, punctuality—or extreme disorderliness or sloppiness—in adulthood.

At about age 3, the **phallic stage** begins. At this point there is another major shift in the child's primary source of pleasure. Now interest focuses on the genitals and the pleasures derived from fondling them. During this stage the child must also negotiate one of the most important hurdles of personality development: the **Oedipal conflict.** According to Freudian theory, as children focus attention on their genitals, the differences between male and female anatomy become more salient. Furthermore, according to Freud, at this time the male unconsciously begins to develop a sexual interest in his mother, starts to see his father as a rival, and harbors a wish to kill his father—as Oedipus did in the ancient Greek tragedy. But because he views his father as too powerful, he develops a fear that his father may retaliate drastically by removing the source of the threat: the son's penis. The fear of losing one's penis leads to *castration anxiety,* which ultimately becomes so powerful that the child represses his desires for his mother and identifies with his father. **Identification** is the process of wanting to be like another person as much as possible, imitating that person's behavior and adopting similar beliefs and values. By identifying with his father, a son seeks to obtain a woman like his unattainable mother.

For girls, the process is different. Freud reasoned that girls begin to experience sexual arousal toward their fathers and begin to experience penis envy. They wish they had the anatomical part that, at least to Freud, seemed most clearly "missing" in girls. Blaming their mothers for their lack of a penis, girls come to believe that their mothers are responsible for their "castration." (This aspect of Freud's theory later provoked accusations that he considered women to be inferior to men.) Like males, though, they find that they can resolve such unacceptable feelings by identifying with the same-sex parent, behaving like her, and adopting her attitudes and values. In this way, a girl's identification with her mother is completed.

At this point, the Oedipal conflict is said to be resolved, and Freudian theory assumes that both males and females move on to the next stage of development. If difficulties arise during this period, however, all sorts of problems are thought to occur, including improper sex-role behavior and the failure to develop a conscience.

After the resolution of the Oedipal conflict, typically around age 5 or 6, children move into the **latency period,** which lasts until puberty. During this period, sexual interests become dormant, even in the unconscious. Then, during adolescence, sexual feelings re-emerge, which marks the start of the final period, the **genital stage,** which extends until death. The focus during the genital stage is on mature, adult sexuality, which Freud defined as sexual intercourse.

DEFENSE MECHANISMS

Freud's efforts to describe and theorize about the underlying dynamics of personality and its development were motivated by very practical problems that his patients faced in dealing with *anxiety,* an intense, negative emotional experience. According to Freud, anxiety is a danger signal to the ego. Although anxiety can arise from realistic fears—such as seeing a poisonous snake about to strike—it can also occur

Freud's Defense Mechanisms		
Defense Mechanism	**Explanation**	**Example**
Repression	Unacceptable or unpleasant impulses are pushed back into the unconscious.	A woman is unable to recall that she was raped.
Regression	People behave as if they were at an earlier stage of development.	A boss has a temper tantrum when an employee makes a mistake.
Displacement	The expression of an unwanted feeling or thought is redirected from a more threatening powerful person to a weaker one.	A brother yells at his younger sister after a teacher gives him a bad grade.
Rationalization	People provide self-justifying explanations in place of the actual, but threatening, reason for their behavior.	A student who goes out drinking the night before a big test rationalizes his behavior by saying the test isn't all that important.
Denial	People refuse to accept or acknowledge an anxiety-producing piece of information.	A student refuses to believe that he has flunked a course.
Projection	People attribute unwanted impulses and feelings to someone else.	A man who is unfaithful to his wife and feels guilty suspects that his wife is unfaithful.
Sublimation	People divert unwanted impulses into socially approved thoughts, feelings, or behaviors.	A person with strong feelings of aggression becomes a soldier.
Reaction formation	Unconscious impulses are expressed as their opposite in consciousness.	A mother who unconsciously resents her child acts in an overly loving way toward the child.

FIGURE 3 According to Freud, people are able to use a wide range of defense mechanisms to cope with anxieties.

in the form of *neurotic anxiety* in which irrational impulses emanating from the id threaten to burst through and become uncontrollable.

Because anxiety is obviously unpleasant, Freud believed that people develop a range of defense mechanisms to deal with it. **Defense mechanisms** are unconscious strategies that people use to reduce anxiety by concealing its source from themselves and others.

The primary defense mechanism is **repression** in which unacceptable or unpleasant id impulses are pushed back into the unconscious. Repression is the most direct method of dealing with anxiety; instead of handling an anxiety-producing impulse on a conscious level, we simply ignore it. For example, a college student who feels hatred for his mother may repress those personally and socially unacceptable feelings. The feelings remain lodged within the unconscious because acknowledging them would provoke anxiety. Similarly, memories of childhood abuse may be repressed. Although such memories may not be consciously recalled, according to Freud they can affect later behavior, and they may be revealed through dreams or slips of the tongue or symbolically in some other fashion.

If repression is ineffective in keeping anxiety at bay, we might use other defense mechanisms. Freud and later his daughter Anna Freud (who became a well-known psychoanalyst) formulated an extensive list of potential defense mechanisms. The major defense mechanisms are summarized in Figure 3 (Conte, Plutchik & Draguns, 2004; Hentschel et al., 2004; Cramer, 2007).

All of us employ defense mechanisms to some degree, according to Freudian theory, and they can serve a useful purpose by protecting us from unpleasant

defense mechanisms In Freudian theory, unconscious strategies that people use to reduce anxiety by concealing the source of it from themselves and others.

repression The primary defense mechanism in which unacceptable or unpleasant id impulses are pushed back into the unconscious.

Study Alert

Use Figure 3 to remember the most common defense mechanisms (unconscious strategies used to reduce anxiety by concealing its source from ourselves and others).

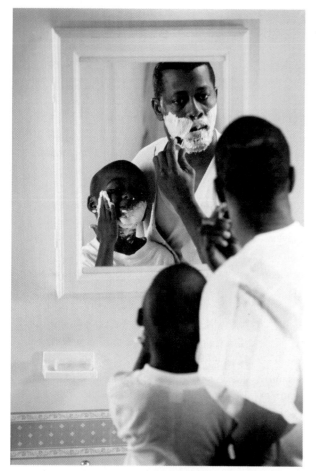

Imitating a person's behavior and adopting similar beliefs and values are part of Freud's concept of identification. How can this concept be applied to the definition of gender roles? Is identification similar in all cultures?

information. Yet some people fall prey to them to such an extent that they must constantly direct a large amount of psychic energy toward hiding and rechanneling unacceptable impulses. When this occurs, everyday living becomes difficult. In such cases, the result is a mental disorder produced by anxiety—what Freud called "neurosis." (Psychologists rarely use this term today, although it endures in everyday conversation.)

EVALUATING FREUD'S LEGACY

Freud's theory has had a significant impact on the field of psychology—and even more broadly on Western philosophy and literature. Many people have accepted the ideas of the unconscious, defense mechanisms, and childhood roots of adult psychological difficulties.

However, many contemporary personality psychologists have leveled significant criticisms against psychoanalytic theory. Among the most important is the lack of compelling scientific data to support it. Although individual case studies *seem* supportive, we lack conclusive evidence that shows the personality is structured and operates along the lines Freud laid out. The lack of evidence is due, in part, to the fact that Freud's conception of personality is built on unobservable abstract concepts. Moreover, it is not clear that the stages of personality Freud laid out provide an accurate description of personality development. We also know now that important changes in personality can occur in adolescence and adulthood—something that Freud did not believe happened. Instead, he argued that personality largely is set by adolescence.

The vague nature of Freud's theory also makes it difficult to predict how an adult will display certain developmental difficulties. For instance, if a person is fixated at the anal stage, according to Freud, he or she may be unusually messy—or unusually neat. Freud's theory offers no way to predict how the difficulty will be exhibited (Macmillan, 1996; Crews, 1996). Furthermore, Freud can be faulted for seeming to view women as inferior to men because he argued that women have weaker superegos than men and in some ways unconsciously yearn to be men (the concept of penis envy).

Finally, Freud made his observations and derived his theory from a limited population. His theory was based almost entirely on upper-class Austrian women living in the strict, puritanical era of the early 1900s, who had come to him seeking treatment for psychological and physical problems. How far one can generalize beyond this population is a matter of considerable debate. For instance, in some Pacific Island societies, the mother's oldest brother and not the father plays the role of disciplinarian. In such a culture, it is unreasonable to argue that the Oedipal conflict will progress in the same way that it did in Austrian society in which the father typically was the major disciplinarian. In short, a cross-cultural perspective raises questions about the universality of Freud's view of personality development (Doi, 1990; Altman, 1996; Spielberger, 2006).

Still, Freud generated an important method of treating psychological disturbances called *psychoanalysis*. As we will see when we discuss treatment approaches to psychological disorders, psychoanalysis remains in use today (Messer & McWilliams, 2003; Heller, 2005; Riolo, 2007).

Moreover, Freud's emphasis on the unconscious has been partially supported by current research on dreams and implicit memory. As we first noted when we discussed dreaming, advances in neuroscience are consistent with some of Freud's arguments. For example, the fact that some behavior is motivated by occurrences that apparently have been forgotten, as well as the discovery of neural pathways relating to emotional memories, supports the notion of repression. Furthermore, cognitive and social psychologists have found increasing evidence that unconscious processes help us think about and evaluate our world, set goals, and choose a course of action. The degree to which future neuroscientific advances will support the criticisms leveled against Freud's psychoanalytic theory remains to be seen (Derryberry, 2006; Litowitz, 2007; Turnbull & Solms, 2007).

The Neo-Freudian Psychoanalysts: Building on Freud

Freud laid the foundation for important work done by a series of successors who were trained in traditional Freudian theory but later rejected some of its major points. These theorists are known as **neo-Freudian psychoanalysts.**

The neo-Freudians placed greater emphasis than Freud on the functions of the ego by suggesting that it has more control than the id over day-to-day activities. They focused more on the social environment and minimized the importance of sex as a driving force in people's lives. They also paid greater attention to the effects of society and culture on personality development.

neo-Freudian psychoanalysts Psychoanalysts who were trained in traditional Freudian theory but who later rejected some of its major points.

JUNG'S COLLECTIVE UNCONSCIOUS

Carl Jung (pronounced "yoong"), one of the most influential neo-Freudians, rejected Freud's view of the primary importance of unconscious sexual urges. Instead, he looked at the primitive urges of the unconscious more positively and argued that they represented a more general and positive life force that encompasses an inborn drive motivating creativity and more positive resolution of conflict (Lothane, 2005; Cassells, 2007).

Jung suggested that we have a universal **collective unconscious,** a common set of ideas, feelings, images, and symbols that we inherit from our relatives, the whole human race, and even nonhuman animal ancestors from the distant past. This collective unconscious is shared by everyone and is displayed in behavior that is common across diverse cultures—such as love of mother, belief in a supreme being, and even behavior as specific as fear of snakes (Oehman & Mineka, 2003; Drob, 2005; Hauke, 2006).

Jung went on to propose that the collective unconscious contains **archetypes,** universal symbolic representations of a particular person, object, or experience. For

collective unconscious According to Jung, a common set of ideas, feelings, images, and symbols that we inherit from our ancestors, the whole human race, and even animal ancestors from the distant past.

archetypes According to Jung, universal symbolic representations of a particular person, object, or experience (such as good and evil).

In terms of Jung's theory, Harry Potter and Voldemort represent the archetypes, or universally recognizable symbols, of good and evil.

Karen Horney was one of the earliest proponents of women's issues.

instance, a mother archetype, which contains reflections of our ancestors' relationships with mother figures, is suggested by the prevalence of mothers in art, religion, literature, and mythology. (Think of the Virgin Mary, Earth Mother, wicked stepmothers in fairy tales, Mother's Day, and so forth!) Jung also suggested that men possess an unconscious feminine archetype that affects how they behave, whereas women have an unconscious male archetype that colors their behavior (Jung, 1961; Bair, 2003; Smetana, 2007).

To Jung, archetypes play an important role in determining our day-to-day reactions, attitudes, and values. For example, Jung might explain the popularity of the *Star Wars* movies as being due to their use of broad archetypes of good (Luke Skywalker) and evil (Darth Vader).

Although no reliable research evidence confirms the existence of the collective unconscious—and even Jung acknowledged that such evidence would be difficult to produce—Jung's theory has had significant influence in areas beyond psychology. For example, personality types derived from Jung's personality approach form the basis for the Myers-Briggs personality test, which is widely used in business and industry to provide insights into how employees make decisions and perform on the job (Gladwell, 2004; Bayne, 2005; Furnham & Crump, 2005).

HORNEY'S NEO-FREUDIAN PERSPECTIVE

Karen Horney (pronounced "HORN-eye") was one of the earliest psychologists to champion women's issues and is sometimes called the first feminist psychologist. Horney suggested that personality develops in the context of social relationships and depends particularly on the relationship between parents and child and how well the child's needs are met. She rejected Freud's suggestion that women have penis envy; she asserted that what women envy most in men is not their anatomy but the independence, success, and freedom women often are denied (Horney, 1937; Miletic, 2002; Smith, 2007).

Horney was also one of the first to stress the importance of cultural factors in the determination of personality. For example, she suggested that society's rigid gender roles for women lead them to experience ambivalence about success because they fear they will make enemies if they are too successful. Her conceptualizations, developed in the 1930s and 1940s, laid the groundwork for many of the central ideas of feminism that emerged decades later (Eckardt, 2005; Jones, 2006).

ADLER AND THE OTHER NEO-FREUDIANS

Alfred Adler, another important neo-Freudian psychoanalyst, also considered Freudian theory's emphasis on sexual needs misplaced. Instead, Adler proposed that the primary human motivation is a striving for superiority, not in terms of superiority over others but in a quest for self-improvement and perfection.

inferiority complex According to Adler, a problem affecting adults who have not been able to overcome the feelings of inferiority that they developed as children, when they were small and limited in their knowledge about the world.

Adler used the term **inferiority complex** to describe situations in which adults have not been able to overcome the feelings of inferiority they developed as children, when they were small and limited in their knowledge about the world. Early social relationships with parents have an important effect on children's ability to outgrow feelings of personal inferiority and instead to orient themselves toward attaining more socially useful goals, such as improving society.

Other neo-Freudians included Erik Erikson, whose theory of psychosocial development we discussed in earlier modules, and Freud's daughter, Anna Freud. Like Adler and Horney, they focused less than Freud on inborn sexual and aggressive drives and more on the social and cultural factors behind personality.

RECAP/EVALUATE/RETHINK

RECAP

How do psychologists define and use the concept of personality?

- Personality is the pattern of enduring characteristics that produce consistency and individuality in a given person. (p. 378)

What do the theories of Freud and his successors tell us about the structure and development of personality?

- According to psychodynamic approaches to personality, much behavior is caused by parts of personality that are found in the unconscious and of which we are unaware. (p. 379)
- Freud's psychoanalytic theory, one of the psychodynamic approaches, suggests that personality is composed of the id, the ego, and the superego. The id is the unorganized, inborn part of personality whose purpose is to immediately reduce tensions relating to hunger, sex, aggression, and other primitive impulses. The ego restrains instinctual energy to maintain the individual's safety and to help the person be a member of society. The superego represents society's rights and wrongs and includes the conscience. (p. 380)
- Freud's psychoanalytic theory suggests that personality develops through a series of psychosexual stages (oral, anal, phallic, latency, and genital), each of which is associated with a primary biological function. (p. 381)
- Defense mechanisms, according to Freudian theory, are unconscious strategies with which people reduce anxieties relating to impulses from the id. (p. 382)
- Freud's psychoanalytic theory has provoked a number of criticisms, including a lack of supportive scientific data, the theory's inadequacy in making predictions, and its reliance on a highly restricted population. On the other hand, recent neuroscience research has offered some support for the concept of the unconscious. (p. 384)
- Neo-Freudian psychoanalytic theorists built on Freud's work, although they placed greater emphasis on the role of the ego and paid more attention to the role of social factors in determining behavior. (p. 385)

EVALUATE

1. _____ approaches state that behavior is motivated primarily by unconscious forces.
2. Match each section of the personality (according to Freud) with its description:
   1. Ego
   2. Id
   3. Superego

   a. Determines right from wrong on the basis of cultural standards.
   b. Operates according to the "reality principle"; energy is redirected to integrate the person into society.
   c. Seeks to reduce tension brought on by primitive drives.
3. Which of the following represents the proper order of personality development, according to Freud?
   a. Oral, phallic, latency, anal, genital
   b. Anal, oral, phallic, genital, latency
   c. Oral, anal, phallic, latency, genital
   d. Latency, phallic, anal, genital, oral
4. _____ _____ is the term Freud used to describe unconscious strategies used to reduce anxiety.

RETHINK

1. Can you think of ways in which Freud's theories of unconscious motivations are commonly used in popular culture? How accurately do you think such popular uses of Freudian theories reflect Freud's ideas?
2. *From the perspective of an advertising executive:* How might you use Jung's concept of archetypes in designing your advertisements? Which of the archetypes would you use?

Answers to Evaluate Questions

1. psychodynamic; 2. 1-b, 2-c, 3-a; 3. c; 4. defense mechanisms

KEY TERMS

personality p. 378
psychodynamic approaches to personality p. 379
psychoanalytic theory p. 379
unconscious p. 379
id p. 380

ego p. 380
superego p. 381
psychosexual stages p. 381
fixations p. 381
oral stage p. 381
anal stage p. 382

phallic stage p. 382
Oedipal conflict p. 382
identification p. 382
latency period p. 382
genital stage p. 382
defense mechanisms p. 383
repression p. 383

neo-Freudian psychoanalysts p. 385
collective unconscious p. 385
archetypes p. 385
inferiority complex p. 386

Trait, Learning, Biological and Evolutionary, and Humanistic Approaches to Personality

Key Concept

What are the major aspects of trait, learning, biological and evolutionary, and humanistic approaches to personality?

"Tell me about Nelson," said Johnetta.

"Oh, he's just terrific. He's the friendliest guy I know—goes out of his way to be nice to everyone. He hardly ever gets mad. He's just so even-tempered, no matter what's happening. And he's really smart, too. About the only thing I don't like is that he's always in such a hurry to get things done. He seems to have boundless energy, much more than I have."

"He sounds great to me, especially in comparison to Rico," replied Johnetta. "He is so self-centered and arrogant that it drives me crazy. I sometimes wonder why I ever started going out with him."

Friendly. Even-tempered. Smart. Energetic. Self-centered. Arrogant.

The above exchange is made up of a series of trait characterizations of the speakers' friends. In fact, much of our own understanding of others' behavior is based on the premise that people possess certain traits that are consistent across different situations. For example, we generally assume that if someone is outgoing and sociable in one situation, he or she is outgoing and sociable in other situations (Gilbert et al., 1992; Gilbert, Miller, & Ross, 1998; Mischel, 2004).

Dissatisfaction with the emphasis in psychoanalytic theory on unconscious—and difficult to demonstrate—processes in explaining a person's behavior led to the development of alternative approaches to personality, including a number of trait-based approaches. Other theories reflect established psychological perspectives, such as learning theory, biological and evolutionary approaches, and the humanistic approach.

Trait Approaches: Placing Labels on Personality

If someone asked you to characterize another person, like Johnetta and her friend you probably would come up with a list of that individual's personal qualities as you see them. But how would you know which of those qualities are most important to an understanding of that person's behavior?

Personality psychologists have asked similar questions. To answer them, they have developed a model of personality known as trait theory. **Trait theory** seeks to explain in a straightforward way the consistencies in individuals' behavior. **Traits** are consistent personality characteristics and behaviors displayed in different situations.

Trait theorists do not assume that some people have a trait and others do not; rather, they propose that all people possess certain traits but the degree to which a particular trait applies to a specific person varies and can be quantified. For instance, you may be relatively friendly, whereas I may be relatively unfriendly. But we both have a "friendliness" trait, although your degree of "friendliness" is higher than

trait theory A model of personality that seeks to identify the basic traits necessary to describe personality.

traits Consistent personality characteristics and behaviors displayed in different situations.

mine. The major challenge for trait theorists taking this approach has been to identify the specific primary traits necessary to describe personality. As we shall see, different theorists have come up with surprisingly different sets of traits.

ALLPORT'S TRAIT THEORY: IDENTIFYING BASIC CHARACTERISTICS

When personality psychologist Gordon Allport systematically pored over an unabridged dictionary in the 1930s, he came up with some 18,000 separate terms that could be used to describe personality. Although he was able to pare down the list to a mere 4,500 descriptors after eliminating words with the same meaning, he was left with a problem crucial to all trait approaches: Which of those traits were the most basic?

Allport eventually answered this question by suggesting that there are three fundamental categories of traits: cardinal, central, and secondary (Allport, 1961, 1966). A *cardinal trait* is a single characteristic that directs most of a person's activities. For example, a totally selfless woman may direct all her energy toward humanitarian activities; an intensely power-hungry person may be driven by an all-consuming need for control.

Most people, however, do not develop a single, comprehensive cardinal trait. Instead, they possess a handful of central traits that make up the core of personality. *Central traits,* such as honesty and sociability, are an individual's major characteristics; they usually number from five to ten in any one person. Finally, *secondary traits* are characteristics that affect behavior in fewer situations and are less influential than central or cardinal traits. For instance, a reluctance to eat meat and a love of modern art would be considered secondary traits (Nicholson, 2003; Glicksohn & Nahari, 2007).

CATTELL AND EYSENCK: FACTORING OUT PERSONALITY

Later attempts to identify primary personality traits have centered on a statistical technique known as factor analysis. *Factor analysis* is a statistical method of identifying associations among a large number of variables to reveal more general patterns. For example, a personality researcher might administer a questionnaire to many participants that asks them to describe themselves by referring to an extensive list of traits. By statistically combining responses and computing which traits are associated with one another in the same person, a researcher can identify the most fundamental patterns or combinations of traits—called *factors*—that underlie participants' responses.

Using factor analysis, personality psychologist Raymond Cattell (1965) suggested that 16 pairs of *source traits* represent the basic dimensions of personality. Using those source traits, he developed the Sixteen Personality Factor Questionnaire, or 16 PF, a measure that provides scores for each of the source traits (Cattell, Cattell, & Cattell, 1993; 2000).

Another trait theorist, psychologist Hans Eysenck (1995), also used factor analysis to identify patterns of traits, but he came to a very different conclusion about the nature of personality. He found that personality could best be described in terms of just three major dimensions: *extraversion, neuroticism,* and *psychoticism.* The extraversion dimension relates to the degree of sociability, whereas the neurotic dimension encompasses emotional stability. Finally, psychoticism refers to the degree to which reality is distorted. By evaluating people along these three dimensions, Eysenck was able to predict behavior accurately in a variety of situations. Figure 1 lists specific traits associated with each of the dimensions.

THE BIG FIVE PERSONALITY TRAITS

For the last two decades, the most influential trait approach contends that five traits or factors—called the "Big Five"—lie at the core of personality. Using modern factor analytic statistical techniques, a host of researchers have identified a similar set of five factors

Study Alert

All trait theories explain personality in terms of traits (consistent personality characteristics and behaviors), but they differ in terms of which and how many traits are seen as fundamental.

Extraversion
• Sociable
• Lively
• Active
• Assertive
• Sensation-seeking

Neuroticism
• Anxious
• Depressed
• Guilt feelings
• Low self-esteem
• Tense

Psychoticism
• Aggressive
• Cold
• Egocentric
• Impersonal
• Impulsive

FIGURE 1 According to Eysenck, personality could best be described in terms of just three major dimensions: extraversion, neuroticism, and psychoticism. Eysenck was able to predict behavior accurately in a variety of types of situations by evaluating people along these three dimensions. (Source: Eysenck, 1990).

FIGURE 2 Five broad trait factors, referred to as the "Big Five," are considered to be the core of personality. (Source: Adapted from Pervin, 1990, Chapter 3, and McCrae & Costa, 1986, p. 1002.)

The Big Five Personality Factors and Dimensions of Sample Traits

Openness to experience
Independent—Conforming
Imaginative—Practical
Preference for variety—Preference for routine

Conscientiousness
Careful—Careless
Disciplined—Impulsive
Organized—Disorganized

Extraversion
Talkative—Quiet
Fun-loving—Sober
Sociable—Retiring

Agreeableness
Sympathetic—Fault-finding
Kind—Cold
Appreciative—Unfriendly

Neuroticism (Emotional Stability)
Stable—Tense
Calm—Anxious
Secure—Insecure

Study Alert

You can remember the "Big Five" set of personality traits by using the acronym OCEAN (*o*penness to experience, *c*onscientiousness, *e*xtraversion, *a*greeableness, and *n*euroticism).

that underlie personality. The five factors, described in Figure 2, are *openness to experience, conscientiousness, extraversion, agreeableness,* and *neuroticism* (emotional stability).

The Big Five emerge consistently across a number of domains. For example, factor analyses of major personality inventories, self-report measures made by observers of others' personality traits, and checklists of self-descriptions yield similar factors. In addition, the Big Five emerge consistently in different populations of individuals, including children, college students, older adults, and speakers of different languages. Cross-cultural research conducted in areas ranging from Europe to the Middle East to Africa also has been supportive. Finally, studies of brain functioning show that Big Five personality traits are related to the way the brain processes information (McCrae et al., 2005; Schmitt, Allik, & McCrae, 2007; Schmitt et al., 2008).

In short, a growing consensus exists that the Big Five represent the best description of personality traits we have today. Still, the debate over the specific number and kinds of traits—and even the usefulness of trait approaches in general—remains a lively one.

EVALUATING TRAIT APPROACHES TO PERSONALITY

Trait approaches have several virtues. They provide a clear, straightforward explanation of people's behavioral consistencies. Furthermore, traits allow us to readily compare one person with another. Because of these advantages, trait approaches to personality have had an important influence on the development of several useful personality measures (Funder, 1991; Wiggins, 2003; Larsen & Buss, 2006).

However, trait approaches also have some drawbacks. For example, we have seen that various trait theories describing personality come to very different conclusions about which traits are the most fundamental and descriptive. The difficulty in determining which of the theories is the most accurate has led some personality psychologists to question the validity of trait conceptions of personality in general.

Actually, there is an even more fundamental difficulty with trait approaches. Even if we are able to identify a set of primary traits, we are left with little more than a label or description of personality—rather than an explanation of behavior. If we say that someone who donates money to charity has the trait of generosity, we

Judged at First Sight

Imagine that you've just showed up to an important job interview dressed in your best business attire, and the personnel director greets you and ushers you into her office. Or perhaps you've arrived at a party where there are many other students from your campus that you'd like to get to know. In either case, you might be focused on how well you're coming across and thinking that you have only a few minutes to make a good first impression—and that's where you're wrong. Whatever impression you were going to make, you did so already.

At least that's the surprising finding of recent research on how people make judgments of others' personality. For instance, in one study, participants were shown photographs of faces of unfamiliar people and asked to rate those people on a number of characteristics, such as attractiveness, trustworthiness, and competence. These participants showed high agreement in their judgments of these characteristics. Then another group of participants were shown the same photographs, but they were asked to make the same judgments under time constraints. In some cases the judgment had to be made in 1 second, in others in ½ of a second, and in still others in just $\frac{1}{10}$ of a second (Willis & Todorov, 2006; Oosterhof & Todorov, 2008).

When the time-constrained judgments were compared to the judgments made

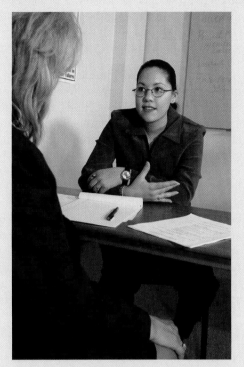

Research has found that first impressions are made almost instantaneously.

with no time constraints, the researchers found that the judgments were extremely similar. Moreover, the length of the time

constraint made no difference—the judgments made in $\frac{1}{10}$ of a second were just as accurate as those made in a ½ or 1 second.

What these findings suggest is that people make virtually instantaneous judgments about others essentially the moment that they lay eyes on them. This may be particularly true of judgments about attractiveness and trustworthiness, which the participants were able to assess most quickly. But even other types of judgments—such as a person's sexual orientation—are made extremely quickly; sometimes such quick judgments are more accurate than those made more thoughtfully and deliberately (Rule, Amabady, & Hallett, 2009).

Researchers have theorized that the ability to judge characteristics quickly and accurately may have evolved in humans because it once had survival value. Today it means, for better or for worse, that we accurately size each other up at just a glance (Todorov & Duchaine, 2008; Oveis et al., 2009).

RETHINK

- Do you think people should attempt to override their first judgments about others' personalities and make more thoughtful judgments? Why or why not?
- Why would the ability to judge personality characteristics quickly be valuable from an evolutionary perspective?

still do not know *why* that person became generous in the first place or the reasons for displaying generosity in a specific situation. In the view of some critics, then, traits do not provide explanations for behavior; they merely describe it. On the other hand, laypersons certainly use traits to make judgments of others, as we can see in *Applying Psychology in the 21st Century.*

Learning Approaches:
We Are What We've Learned

The psychodynamic and trait approaches we've discussed concentrate on the "inner" person—the fury of an unobservable but powerful id or a hypothetical but critical set of traits. In contrast, learning approaches to personality focus on the "outer" person. To a strict learning theorist, personality is simply the sum of learned responses to the external environment. Internal events such as thoughts, feelings, and motivations are ignored. Although the existence of personality is not denied, learning theorists say that it is best understood by looking at features of a person's environment.

SKINNER'S BEHAVIORIST APPROACH

According to the most influential learning theorist, B. F. Skinner (who carried out pioneering work on operant conditioning), personality is a collection of learned behavior patterns (Skinner, 1975). Similarities in responses across different situations are caused by similar patterns of reinforcement that have been received in such situations in the past. If I am sociable both at parties and at meetings, it is because I have been reinforced for displaying social behaviors—not because I am fulfilling an unconscious wish based on experiences during my childhood or because I have an internal trait of sociability.

Strict learning theorists such as Skinner are less interested in the consistencies in behavior across situations than in ways of modifying behavior. Their view is that humans are infinitely changeable through the process of learning new behavior patterns. If we are able to control and modify the patterns of reinforcers in a situation, behavior that other theorists would view as stable and unyielding can be changed and ultimately improved. Learning theorists are optimistic in their attitudes about the potential for resolving personal and societal problems through treatment strategies based on learning theory.

SOCIAL COGNITIVE APPROACHES TO PERSONALITY

social cognitive approaches to personality Theories that emphasize the influence of a person's cognitions—thoughts, feelings, expectations, and values—as well as observation of others' behavior, in determining personality.

Not all learning theories of personality take such a strict view in rejecting the importance of what is "inside" a person by focusing solely on the "outside." Unlike other learning approaches to personality, **social cognitive approaches to personality** emphasize the influence of cognition—thoughts, feelings, expectations, and values—as well as observation of others' behavior, on personality. According to Albert Bandura, one of the main proponents of this point of view, people can foresee the possible outcomes of certain behaviors in a specific setting without actually having to carry them out. This understanding comes primarily through *observational learning*—viewing the actions of others and observing the consequences (Bandura, 1986, 1999).

For instance, children who view a model behaving in, say, an aggressive manner tend to copy the behavior if the consequences of the model's behavior are seen as positive. If, in contrast, the model's aggressive behavior has resulted in no consequences or negative consequences, children are considerably less likely to act aggressively. According to social cognitive approaches, then, personality develops through repeated observation of others' behavior.

self-efficacy Belief in one's personal capabilities. Self-efficacy underlies people's faith in their ability to carry out a particular behavior or produce a desired outcome.

SELF-EFFICACY

Bandura places particular emphasis on the role played by **self-efficacy,** belief in one's personal capabilities. Self-efficacy underlies people's faith in their ability to carry out a specific task or produce a desired outcome. People with high self-efficacy have higher aspirations and greater persistence in working to attain goals and ultimately achieve greater success than those with lower self-efficacy (Bandura & Locke, 2003; Glickler, 2006; Betz, 2007).

How do we develop self-efficacy? One way is by paying close attention to our prior successes and failures. If we try snowboarding and experience little success, we'll be less likely to try it again. However, if our initial efforts appear promising, we'll be more likely to attempt it again. Direct reinforcement and encouragement from others also play a role in developing self-efficacy (Devonport & Lane, 2006; Buchanan & Selmon, 2008).

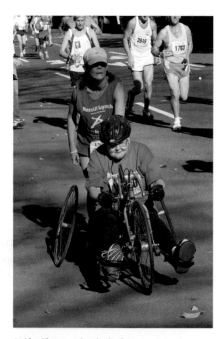

Self-efficacy, the belief in one's own capabilities, leads to higher aspirations and greater persistence.

Compared with other learning theories of personality, social cognitive approaches are distinctive in their emphasis on the reciprocity between individuals and their environment. Not only is the environment assumed to affect personality, but people's behavior and personalities are also assumed to "feed back" and modify the environment (Bandura, 1999, 2000).

HOW MUCH CONSISTENCY EXISTS IN PERSONALITY?

Another social cognitive theorist, Walter Mischel, takes a different approach to personality from that of Albert Bandura. He rejects the view that personality consists of broad traits that lead to substantial consistencies in behavior across different situations. Instead, he sees personality as considerably more variable from one situation to another (Mischel, 2009).

In this view, particular situations give rise to particular kinds of behavior. Some situations are especially influential (think of a movie theater, where everyone displays pretty much the same behavior by sitting quietly and watching the film). Other situations permit much variability in behavior (think of a party, for example, where some people may be dancing, while others are eating and drinking).

From this perspective, personality cannot be considered without taking the particular context of the situation into account—a view known as *situationism*. In his *cognitive-affective processing system (CAPS)* theory, Mischel argues that people's thoughts and emotions about themselves and the world determine how they view, and then react, in particular situations. Personality is thus seen as a reflection of how people's prior experiences in different situations affect their behavior (Shoda & Mischel, 2006; Mischel & Shoda, 2008).

SELF-ESTEEM

Our behavior also reflects the view we have of ourselves and the way we value the various parts of our personalities. **Self-esteem** is the component of personality that encompasses our positive and negative self-evaluations. Unlike self-efficacy, which focuses on our views of whether we are able to carry out a task, self-esteem relates to how we feel about ourselves.

Although people have a general level of self-esteem, it is not unidimensional. We may see ourselves positively in one domain but negatively in others. For example, a good student may have high self-esteem in academic domains but lower self-esteem in sports (Swann, Chang-Schneider, & Larsen McClarty, 2007; Salmela-Aro & Nurmi, 2007; Gentile et al., 2009).

Self-esteem has strong cultural components. For example, having high *relationship harmony*—a sense of success in forming close bonds with other people—is more important to self-esteem in Asian cultures than it is in more individualistic Western societies (Spencer-Rodgers et al., 2004; Lun & Bond, 2006; Cheng & Kwan, 2008).

Although almost everyone goes through periods of low self-esteem (for instance, after an undeniable failure), some people are chronically low in self-esteem. For them, failure seems to be an inevitable part of life. In fact, low self-esteem may lead to a cycle of failure in which past failure breeds future failure.

For example, consider students with low self-esteem who are studying for a test. Because of their low self-esteem, they expect to do poorly on the test. In turn, this belief raises their anxiety level, which makes it increasingly difficult to study and perhaps even leading them not to work as hard. Because of these attitudes, they do, in fact, ultimately perform badly on the test. Ultimately, the failure reinforces their low self-esteem, and the cycle is perpetuated as illustrated in Figure 3. In short, low self-esteem can lead to a self-destructive cycle of failure.

self-esteem The component of personality that encompasses our positive and negative self-evaluations.

FIGURE 3 The cycle of low self-esteem begins with an individual already having low self-esteem. As a consequence, the person will have low performance expectations and expect to fail a test, thereby producing anxiety and reduced effort. As a result, the person will actually fail, and failure in turn reinforces low self-esteem.

EVALUATING LEARNING APPROACHES TO PERSONALITY

Because they ignore the internal processes that are uniquely human, traditional learning theorists such as Skinner have been accused of oversimplifying personality to such an extent that the concept becomes meaningless. Their critics think that reducing behavior to a series of stimuli and responses and excluding thoughts and feelings from the realm of personality leaves behaviorists practicing an unrealistic and inadequate form of science.

Of course, some of these criticisms are blunted by social cognitive approaches, which explicitly consider the role of cognitive processes in personality. Still, learning approaches tend to share a highly *deterministic* view of human behavior, which maintains that behavior is shaped primarily by forces beyond the individual's control. As in psychoanalytic theory (which suggests that personality is determined by the unconscious forces) and trait approaches (which views personality in part as a mixture of genetically determined traits), learning theory's reliance on deterministic principles de-emphasizes people's ability to pilot their own course through life.

Nonetheless, learning approaches have had a major impact on the study of personality. For one thing, they have helped make personality psychology an objective, scientific venture by focusing on observable behavior and the effects of their environments. In addition, they have produced important, successful means of treating a variety of psychological disorders. The degree of success of these treatments is a testimony to the merits of learning theory approaches to personality.

Biological and Evolutionary Approaches: Are We Born with Personality?

Approaching the question of what determines personality from a different direction, **biological and evolutionary approaches to personality** suggest that important components of personality are inherited. Building on the work of behavioral geneticists,

biological and evolutionary approaches to personality Theories that suggest that important components of personality are inherited.

Biological and evolutionary approaches to personality seek to explain the consistencies in personality that are found in some families.

researchers using biological and evolutionary approaches argue that personality is determined at least in part by our genes in much the same way that our height is largely a result of genetic contributions from our ancestors. The evolutionary perspective assumes that personality traits that led to our ancestors' survival and reproductive success are more likely to be preserved and passed on to subsequent generations (Buss, 2001, 2009).

Twin studies illustrate the importance of genetic factors in personality. For instance, personality psychologists Auke Tellegen and colleagues at the University of Minnesota examined the personality traits of pairs of twins who were genetically identical but were raised apart from each other (Tellegen et al., 1988; Bouchard, et al., 2004). In the study, each twin was given a battery of personality tests, including one that measured 11 key personality characteristics.

The results of the personality tests indicated that in major respects the twins were quite similar in personality, despite having separated at an early age. Moreover, certain traits were more heavily influenced by heredity than others. For example, social potency (the degree to which a person assumes mastery and leadership roles in social situations) and traditionalism (the tendency to follow authority) had particularly strong genetic components, whereas achievement and social closeness had relatively weak genetic components (see Figure 4).

Furthermore, it is increasingly clear that the roots of adult personality emerge in the earliest periods of life. Infants are born with a specific **temperament,** an innate disposition. Temperament encompasses several dimensions, including general activity level and mood. For instance, some individuals are quite active, while others are relatively calm. Similarly, some are relatively easygoing, while others are irritable,

Study Alert

Remember that biological and evolutionary approaches focus on the way in which people's genetic heritage affects personality.

temperament The innate disposition that emerges early in life.

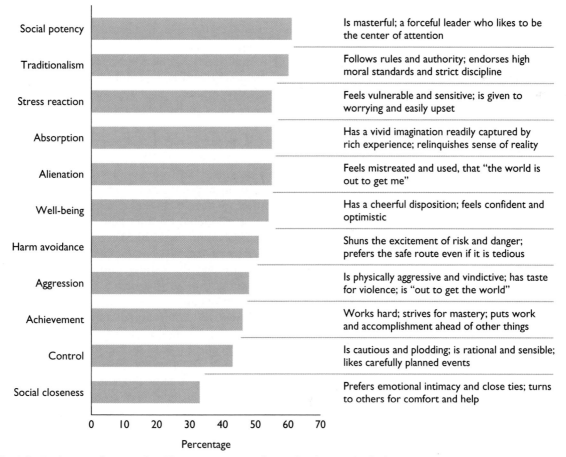

FIGURE 4 The inherited roots of personality. The percentages indicate the degree to which 11 personality characteristics reflect the influence of heredity. (Source: Tellegen et al., 1988.)

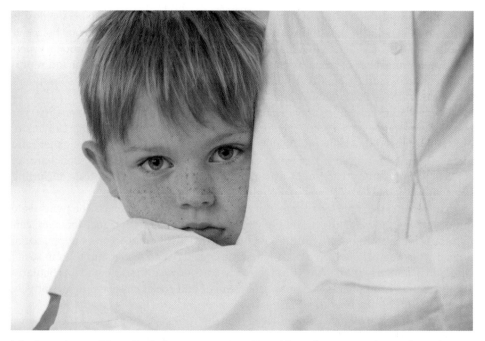

Infants are born with particular temperaments—dispositions that are consistent throughout childhood.

easily upset, and difficult to soothe. Temperament is quite consistent, with significant stability from infancy well into adolescence (Wachs et al., 2004; Kagan et al., 2007; Evans & Rothbart, 2007, 2009).

Some researchers contend that specific genes are related to personality. For example, people with a longer dopamine-4 receptor gene are more likely to be thrill-seekers than those without such a gene. These thrill-seekers tend to be extroverted, impulsive, quick-tempered, and always in search of excitement and novel situations. Furthermore, the structure of their brains may reflect their thrill-seeking tendencies (see *Neuroscience in Your Life*, Figure 5; Robins, 2005; Golimbet et al., 2007; Ray et al., 2009).

Does the identification of specific genes linked to personality, coupled with the existence of temperaments from the time of birth, mean that we are destined to have certain types of personalities? Hardly. First, it is unlikely that any single gene is linked to a specific trait. For instance, the dopamine-4 receptor accounts for only around 10% of the variation in novelty seeking between different individuals. The rest of the variation is attributable to other genes and environmental factors (Keltikangas-Järvinen et al., 2004; Lahti et al., 2005).

More important, genes interact with the environment. As we see in discussions of the heritability of intelligence and the nature–nurture issue, it is impossible to completely divorce genetic factors from environmental factors. Although studies of identical twins raised in different environments are helpful, they are not definitive because it is impossible to assess and control environmental factors fully. Furthermore, estimates of the influence of genetics are just that—estimates—and apply to groups, not individuals. Consequently, findings such as those shown in Figure 4 must be regarded as approximations.

Finally, even if more genes are found to be linked to specific personality characteristics, genes still cannot be viewed as the sole cause of personality. For one thing, genetically determined characteristics may not be expressed if they are not "turned on" by particular environmental experiences. Furthermore, behaviors produced by genes may help to create a specific environment. For instance, a cheerful, smiley baby may lead her parents to smile more and be more responsive, thereby creating a supportive, pleasant environment. In contrast, the parents of a cranky, fussy baby

Neuroscience in Your Life: Wired for Thrills— The Biological Underpinnings of Personality

FIGURE 5 Research suggests that personality characteristics may be related to differences in brain structure. Scientists used magnetic resonance imaging (MRI) to look for relationships between personality traits such as novelty-seeking and differences in the number of neurons in various parts of the brain. In this MRI, the red areas of the frontal and posterior cingulate are related to novelty-seeking. This MRI helps us understand that those who are more likely to seek novel experiences have a greater number of neurons in the highlighted areas of the brain. (Source: Gardini et al., 2009, Figure 1.)

may be less inclined to smile at the child; in turn, the environment in which that child is raised will be less supportive and pleasant. In a sense, then, genes not only influence a person's behavior—they also help produce the environment in which a person develops (Scarr, 1998; Plomin & Caspi, 1999; Kim-Cohen, Caspi, & Moffitt, 2003; Kim-Cohen et al., 2005).

Although an increasing number of personality theorists are taking biological and evolutionary factors into account, no comprehensive, unified theory that considers biological and evolutionary factors is widely accepted. Still, it is clear that certain personality traits have substantial genetic components and that heredity and environment interact to determine personality (Ebstein, Benjamin, & Belmaker, 2003; Bouchard, 2004; South & Krueger, 2008).

Humanistic Approaches: The Uniqueness of You

In all the approaches to personality that we have discussed, where is an explanation for the saintliness of a Mother Teresa, the creativity of a Michelangelo, and the brilliance and perseverance of an Einstein? An understanding of such unique individuals—as well as more ordinary sorts of people who have some of the same attributes—comes from humanistic theory.

According to humanistic theorists, all the approaches to personality we have discussed share a fundamental misperception in their views of human nature. Instead of seeing people as controlled by unconscious, unseen forces (psychodynamic approaches), a set of stable traits (trait approaches), situational reinforcements and punishments (learning theory), or inherited factors (biological and evolutionary approaches), **humanistic approaches to personality** emphasize people's inherent goodness and their tendency to move toward higher levels of functioning. It is this

humanistic approaches to personality Theories that emphasize people's innate goodness and desire to achieve higher levels of functioning.

"So, while extortion, racketeering, and murder may be bad acts, they don't make you a bad person."

conscious, self-motivated ability to change and improve, along with people's unique creative impulses, that humanistic theorists argue make up the core of personality.

ROGERS AND THE NEED FOR SELF-ACTUALIZATION

The major proponent of the humanistic point of view is Carl Rogers (1971). Along with other humanistic theorists, such as Abraham Maslow, Rogers maintains that all people have a fundamental need for **self-actualization,** a state of self-fulfillment in which people realize their highest potential, each in a unique way. He further suggests that people develop a need for positive regard that reflects the desire to be loved and respected. Because others provide this positive regard, we grow dependent on them. We begin to see and judge ourselves through the eyes of other people, relying on their values and being preoccupied with what they think of us.

According to Rogers, one outgrowth of placing importance on others' opinions is that a conflict may grow between people's experiences and their *self-concepts,* the set of beliefs they hold about what they are like as individuals. If the discrepancies are minor, so are the consequences. But if the discrepancies are great, they will lead to psychological disturbances in daily functioning, such as the experience of frequent anxiety.

Rogers suggests that one way of overcoming the discrepancy between experience and self-concept is through the receipt of unconditional positive regard from another person—a friend, a spouse, or a therapist. **Unconditional positive regard** refers to an attitude of acceptance and respect on the observer's part, no matter what a person says or does. This acceptance, says Rogers, gives people the opportunity to evolve and grow both cognitively and emotionally and to develop more realistic self-concepts. You may have experienced the power of unconditional positive regard when you confided in someone, revealing embarrassing secrets because you knew the listener would still love and respect you even after hearing the worst about you (Snyder, 2002; Marshall, 2007).

In contrast, *conditional positive regard* depends on your behavior. In such cases, others withdraw their love and acceptance if you do something of which they don't approve. The result is a discrepancy between your true self and what others wish you would be, which leads to anxiety and frustration (see Figure 6).

self-actualization A state of self-fulfillment in which people realize their highest potential, each in a unique way.

unconditional positive regard An attitude of acceptance and respect on the part of an observer, no matter what a person says or does.

EVALUATING HUMANISTIC APPROACHES

Although humanistic theories suggest the value of providing unconditional positive regard toward people, unconditional positive regard toward humanistic theories has been less forthcoming. The criticisms have centered on the difficulty of verifying the basic assumptions of the approach as well as on the question of whether unconditional positive regard does, in fact, lead to greater personality adjustment.

FIGURE 6 According to the humanistic view of Carl Rogers, people have a basic need to be loved and respected. If you receive unconditional positive regard from others, you will develop a more realistic self-concept; but if the response is conditional, it may lead to anxiety and frustration.

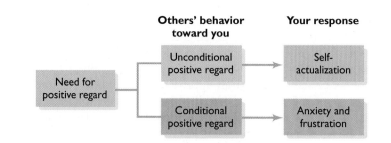

Humanistic approaches have also been criticized for making the assumption that people are basically "good"—a notion that is unverifiable—and, equally important, for using nonscientific values to build supposedly scientific theories. Still, humanistic theories have been important in highlighting the uniqueness of human beings and guiding the development of a significant form of therapy designed to alleviate psychological difficulties (Cain, 2002; Bauman & Kopp, 2006; Elkins, 2009).

Comparing Approaches to Personality

In light of the multiple approaches we have discussed, you may be wondering which of the theories provides the most accurate description of personality. That question cannot be answered precisely. Each theory is built on different assumptions and focuses on somewhat different aspects of personality (see Figure 7). Furthermore, there is no clear way to scientifically test the various approaches and their assumptions against one another. Given the complexity of every individual, it seems reasonable that personality can be viewed from a number of perspectives simultaneously (Pervin, 2003).

Theoretical Approach and Major Theorists	Conscious Versus Unconscious Determinants of Personality	Nature (Hereditary Factors) Versus Nurture (Environmental Factors)	Free Will Versus Determinism	Stability Versus Modifiability
Psychodynamic (Freud, Jung, Horney, Adler)	Emphasizes the unconscious	Stresses innate, inherited structure of personality while emphasizing importance of childhood experience	Stresses determinism, the view that behavior is directed and caused by factors outside one's control	Emphasizes the stability of characteristics throughout a person's life
Trait (Allport, Cattell, Eysenck)	Disregards both conscious and unconscious	Approaches vary	Stresses determinism, the view that behavior is directed and caused by factors outside one's control	Emphasizes the stability of characteristics throughout a person's life
Learning (Skinner, Bandura)	Disregards both conscious and unconscious	Focuses on the environment	Stresses determinism, the view that behavior is directed and caused by factors outside one's control	Stresses that personality remains flexible and resilient throughout one's life
Biological and Evolutionary (Tellegen)	Disregards both conscious and unconscious	Stresses the innate, inherited determinants of personality	Stresses determinism, the view that behavior is directed and caused by factors outside one's control	Emphasizes the stability of characteristics throughout a person's life
Humanistic (Rogers, Maslow)	Stresses the conscious more than unconscious	Stresses the interaction between both nature and nurture	Stresses the freedom of individuals to make their own choices	Stresses that personality remains flexible and resilient throughout one's life

FIGURE 7 The multiple perspectives of personality.

RECAP/EVALUATE/RETHINK

RECAP

What are the major aspects of trait, learning, biological and evolutionary, and humanistic approaches to personality?

- Trait approaches have been used to identify relatively enduring dimensions along which people differ from one another—dimensions known as traits. (p. 388)
- Learning approaches to personality concentrate on observable behavior. To a strict learning theorist, personality is the sum of learned responses to the external environment. (p. 391)
- Social cognitive approaches concentrate on the role of cognition in determining personality. Those approaches pay particular attention to self-efficacy and self-esteem in determining behavior. (p. 392)
- Biological and evolutionary approaches to personality focus on the way in which personality characteristics are inherited. (p. 394)
- Humanistic approaches emphasize people's inherent goodness. They consider the core of personality in terms of a person's ability to change and improve. (p. 397)
- The major personality approaches differ substantially from one another; the differences may reflect both their focus on different aspects of personality and the overall complexity of personality. (p. 399)

EVALUATE

1. Carl's determination to succeed is the dominant force in all his activities and relationships. According to Gordon Allport's theory, this is an example of a _____ trait. In contrast, Cindy's fondness for old western movies is an example of a _____ trait.

2. Eysenck might describe a person who enjoys activities such as parties and hang-gliding as high on what trait?

3. Proponents of which approach to personality would be most likely to agree with the statement, "Personality can be thought of as learned responses to a person's upbringing and environment"?
   a. Humanistic
   b. Biological and evolutionary
   c. Learning
   d. Trait

4. Bandura would rate a person who would make the statement, "I know I can't do it" as low on _____ _____.

5. Which approach to personality emphasizes the innate goodness of people and their desire to grow?
   a. Humanistic
   b. Psychodynamic
   c. Learning
   d. Biological and evolutionary

RETHINK

1. If personality traits are merely descriptive and not explanatory, what use are they? Can assigning a trait to a person be harmful—or helpful? Why or why not?

2. *From the perspective of an educator:* How might you encourage your students' development of self-esteem and self-efficacy? What steps would you take to ensure that their self-esteem did not become over-inflated?

Answers to Evaluate Questions

1. cardinal, secondary; 2. extraversion; 3. c; 4. self-efficacy; 5. a

KEY TERMS

trait theory p. 388
traits p. 388
social cognitive approaches to personality p. 392

self-efficacy p. 392
self-esteem p. 393
biological and evolutionary approaches to personality p. 394

temperament p. 395
humanistic approaches to personality p. 397

self-actualization p. 398
unconditional positive regard p. 398

Assessing Personality: Determining What Makes Us Distinctive

You have a need for other people to like and admire you.

You have a tendency to be critical of yourself.

You have a great deal of unused potential that you have not turned to your advantage.

Although you have some personality weaknesses, you generally are able to compensate for them.

Relating to members of the opposite sex has presented problems for you.

Although you appear to be disciplined and self-controlled to others, you tend to be anxious and insecure inside.

At times you have serious doubts about whether you have made the right decision or done the right thing.

You prefer a certain amount of change and variety and become dissatisfied when hemmed in by restrictions and limitations.

You do not accept others' statements without satisfactory proof.

You have found it unwise to be too frank in revealing yourself to others.

If you think these statements provide a surprisingly accurate account of your personality, you are not alone: Most college students think that these descriptions are tailored just to them. In fact, the statements were designed intentionally to be so vague that they apply to just about anyone (Forer, 1949; Russo, 1981).

The ease with which we can agree with such imprecise statements underscores the difficulty in coming up with accurate and meaningful assessments of people's personalities. Psychologists interested in assessing personality must be able to define the most meaningful ways of discriminating between one person's personality and another's. To do this, they use **psychological tests,** standard measures devised to assess behavior objectively. With the results of such tests, psychologists can help people better understand themselves and make decisions about their lives. Researchers interested in the causes and consequences of personality also employ psychological tests (Aiken, 2000; Kaplan & Saccuzzo, 2001; Hambleton, 2006).

Like the assessments that seek to measure intelligence, all psychological tests must have reliability and validity. *Reliability* refers to a test's measurement consistency. If a test is reliable, it yields the same result each time it is administered to a specific person or group. In contrast, unreliable tests give different results each time they are administered.

For meaningful conclusions to be drawn, tests also must be valid. Tests have *validity* when they actually measure what they are designed to measure. If a test is constructed to measure sociability, for instance, we need to know that it actually measures sociability and not some other trait.

Key Concepts

How can we most accurately assess personality?

What are the major types of personality measures?

psychological tests Standard measures devised to assess behavior objectively; used by psychologists to help people make decisions about their lives and understand more about themselves.

Study Alert

The distinction between reliability and validity is important. For instance, a test that measures trustfulness is reliable if it yields the same results each time it is administered, while it would be valid if it measures trustfulness accurately.

Finally, psychological tests are based on *norms,* standards of test performance that permit the comparison of one person's score on a test with the scores of others who have taken the same test. For example, a norm permits test-takers who have received a certain score on a test to know that they have scored in the top 10% of all those who have taken the test.

Norms are established by administering a specific test to a large number of people and determining the typical scores. It is then possible to compare a single person's score with the scores of the group, which provides a comparative measure of test performance against the performance of others who have taken the test.

The establishment of appropriate norms is not a simple endeavor. For instance, the specific group that is employed to determine norms for a test has a profound effect on the way an individual's performance is evaluated. In fact, as we discuss next, the process of establishing norms can take on political overtones.

Exploring DIVERSITY

Should Race and Ethnicity Be Used to Establish Norms?

The passions of politics may confront the objectivity of science when test norms are established, at least in the realm of standardized tests that are meant to predict future job performance. In fact, a national controversy has developed around the question of whether different norms should be established for members of various racial and ethnic groups (Manly, 2005, 2006; Manly & Echemendia, 2007; Pedraza & Mungas, 2008).

The test that sparked the controversy was the U.S. government's General Aptitude Test Battery, a test that measures a broad range of abilities from eye-hand coordination to reading proficiency. The problem was that African Americans and Hispanics tend to score lower on the test, on average, than members of other groups. The lower scores often are due to a lack of prior relevant experience and job opportunities, which in turn has been due to prejudice and discrimination.

To promote the employment of minority racial groups, the government developed a separate set of norms for African Americans and Hispanics. Rather than using the pool of all people who took the tests, the scores of African-American and Hispanic applicants were compared only with the scores of other African Americans and Hispanics. Consequently, a Hispanic who scored in the top 20% of the Hispanics taking the test was considered to have performed equivalently to a white job applicant who scored in the top 20% of the whites who took the test, even though the absolute score of the Hispanic might be lower than that of the white.

Critics of the adjusted norming system suggested that such a procedure discriminates in favor of certain racial and ethnic groups at the expense of others, thereby fanning the flames of racial bigotry. The practice was challenged legally; with the passage of the Civil Rights Act in 1991, race norming on the General Aptitude Test Battery was discontinued (Galef, 2001).

However, proponents of race norming continue to argue that norming procedures that take race into account are an affirmative action tool that simply permits minority job-seekers to be placed on an equal footing with white job-seekers. Furthermore, a panel of the National Academy of Sciences supported the practice of adjusting test norms. It suggested that the unadjusted test norms are not very useful in predicting job performance and that they would tend to screen out otherwise qualified minority group members (Fleming, 2000).

Job testing is not the only area in which issues arise regarding norms and the meaning of test scores. The issue of how to treat racial differences in IQ scores is also controversial and divisive. Clearly, race norming raises profound and intense feelings that may come into conflict with scientific objectivity (Leiter & Leiter, 2003; Rushton & Jensen, 2006; Davis, 2009).

Psychology on the Web

1. Sigmund Freud is one of the towering figures in psychology. His influence extends far beyond his psychoanalytic work. Find information about Freud on the web. Pick one aspect of his work or influence (for example, on therapy, medicine, literature, film, or culture and society) and summarize in writing what you have found, including your attitude toward your findings.
2. Find a website that links to personality tests and take one or two tests. Remember to take them with skepticism. For each test, summarize in writing the aspects of personality that were tested, the theoretical approach the test appeared to be based on, and your assessment of the trustworthiness of the results.

Epilogue

We have discussed the different ways in which psychologists have interpreted the development and structure of personality. The perspectives we examined ranged from Freud's analysis of personality based primarily on internal, unconscious factors to the externally based view championed by learning theorists of personality as a learned set of traits and actions. We also noted that there are many ways to interpret personality; by no means does a consensus exist on what the key traits are that are central to personality.

Return to the prologue and consider the case of convicted swindler Bernie Madoff. Use your understanding of personality to consider the following questions.

1. How typical is it for people to have different sides to their personalities as Madoff does?
2. How do you think Madoff would score on a test of extraversion? On a test of conscientiousness?
3. How could you explain Madoff's personality from a biological approach? From a learning approach?
4. Might a personality test have indicated Madoff's criminal intentions? Why or why not?

CHAPTER 11

Health Psychology: Stress, Coping, and Well-Being

Key Concepts for Chapter 11

Prologue *Never a Moment's Rest*

Louisa Denby's day began badly: She slept through her alarm and had to skip breakfast to catch the bus to campus. Then, when she went to the library to catch up on the reading she had to do before taking a test the next day, the one article she needed was missing. The librarian told her that replacing it would take 24 hours. Feeling frustrated, she walked to the computer lab to print out the paper she had completed at home the night before.

The computer wouldn't read her disk. She searched for someone to help her, but she was unable to find anyone who knew any more about computers than she did.

It was only 9:42 a.m., and Louisa had a wracking headache. Apart from that pain, she was conscious of only one feeling: stress (Feldman, 2010).

Looking Ahead

It's not hard to understand why Louisa Denby was experiencing stress. For people like her—and that probably includes most of us—the intensity of juggling multiple roles leads to feelings of never having sufficient time and, in some cases, takes a toll on both physical and psychological well-being.

Stress and how we cope with it have long been central topics of interest for psychologists. However, in recent years the focus has broadened as psychology has come to view stress in the broader context of one of psychology's newer subfields: health psychology. **Health psychology** investigates the psychological factors related to wellness and illness, including the prevention, diagnosis, and treatment of medical problems. Health psychologists investigate the effects of psychological factors such as stress on illness. They examine the psychological principles underlying treatments for disease and illness. They also study prevention: how healthier behavior can help people avoid and reduce health problems such as stress and heart disease.

Health psychologists take a decisive stand on the enduring mind–body issue that philosophers, and later psychologists, have debated since the time of the ancient Greeks. In their view, the mind and the body are clearly linked rather than representing two distinct systems (Sternberg, 2000; Dalal & Misra, 2006).

Health psychologists recognize that good health and the ability to cope with illness are affected by psychological factors such as thoughts, emotions, and the ability to manage stress. They have paid particular attention to the *immune system,* the complex system of organs, glands, and cells that constitute our bodies' natural line of defense in fighting disease.

In fact, health psychologists are among the primary investigators in a growing field called **psychoneuroimmunology, or PNI,** the study of the relationship among psychological factors, the immune system, and the brain. PNI has led to discoveries such as the existence of an association between a person's emotional state and the success of the immune system in fighting disease (Dickerson et al., 2004; Kemeny, 2007; Byrne-Davis & Vedhara, 2008).

In sum, health psychologists view the mind and the body as two parts of a whole human being that cannot be considered independently. This more recent view marks a sharp departure from earlier thinking. Previously, disease was seen as a purely biological phenomenon, and psychological factors were of little interest to most health-care workers. In the early 20th century, the primary causes of death were short-term infections from which one either rapidly recovered—or died. Now, however, the major causes of death, such as heart disease, cancer, and diabetes, are chronic illnesses that pose significant psychological issues because they often cannot be cured and may linger for years (Bishop, 2005; Rotan & Ospina-Kammerer, 2007).

Advances in health psychology have had an impact across a variety of disciplines and professions. For instance, health-care professionals such as physicians and nurses, social workers, dieticians, pharmacists, occupational therapists, and even clergy are increasingly likely to receive training in health psychology.

In the three modules that follow, we discuss the ways in which psychological factors affect health. We first focus on the causes and consequences of stress as well as on the means of coping with it. Next, we explore the psychological aspects of several major health problems, including heart disease, cancer, and ailments resulting from smoking. Finally, we examine the ways in which patient-physician interactions influence our health and offer suggestions for increasing people's compliance with recommendations about behavior that will improve their well-being.

health psychology The branch of psychology that investigates the psychological factors related to wellness and illness, including the prevention, diagnosis, and treatment of medical problems.

psychoneuroimmunology (PNI) The study of the relationship among psychological factors, the immune system, and the brain.

Stress and Coping

Anthony Lepre started feeling awful almost as soon as Tom Ridge [U.S. Homeland Security Secretary] put the nation on high alert for a terrorist attack. . . . He awoke in the middle of the night short of breath, his heart pounding. And the sound of his telephone seemed a sure sign of bad news. By midweek, he was rushing off to Costco to stock up on fruit juice, bottled water, peanut butter, canned tuna, "and extra food for my cats Monster, Monkey and Spike." He also picked up a first-aid kit, six rolls of duct tape, and a bulk package of plastic wrap to seal his windows. "The biggest problem was that I felt helpless," he says, "completely powerless over the situation." (Cowley, 2003, pp. 43–44)

Stress: Reacting to Threat and Challenge

Most of us need little introduction to the phenomenon of **stress,** people's response to events that threaten or challenge them. Whether it is a paper or an exam deadline, a family problem, or even the ongoing threat of a terrorist attack, life is full of circumstances and events known as *stressors* that produce threats to our well-being. Even pleasant events—such as planning a party or beginning a sought-after job—can produce stress, although negative events result in greater detrimental consequences than positive ones.

All of us face stress in our lives. Some health psychologists believe that daily life actually involves a series of repeated sequences of perceiving a threat, considering ways to cope with it, and ultimately adapting to the threat with greater or lesser success. Although adaptation is often minor and occurs without our awareness, adaptation requires a major effort when stress is more severe or long lasting. Ultimately, our attempts to overcome stress may produce biological and psychological responses that result in health problems (Boyce & Ellis, 2005; Dolbier, Smith, & Steinhardt, 2007).

THE NATURE OF STRESSORS: MY STRESS IS YOUR PLEASURE

Stress is a very personal thing. Although certain kinds of events, such as the death of a loved one or participation in military combat, are universally stressful, other situations may or may not be stressful to a specific person.

Consider, for instance, bungee jumping. Some people would find jumping off a bridge while attached to a slender rubber tether extremely stressful. However, there are individuals who see such an activity as challenging and fun filled. Whether bungee jumping is stressful depends in part, then, on a person's perception of the activity.

For people to consider an event stressful, they must perceive it as threatening or challenging and must lack all the resources to deal with it effectively. Consequently, the same event may at some times be stressful and at other times provoke no stressful reaction at all. A young man may experience stress when he is turned down for a date—if he attributes the refusal to his unattractiveness or unworthiness. But if

Key Concepts

How is health psychology a union between medicine and psychology?

What is stress, how does it affect us, and how can we best cope with it?

stress A person's response to events that are threatening or challenging.

> ### Study Alert
> Remember the distinction between stressors and stress, which can be tricky: stressors (like an exam) *cause* stress (the physiological and psychological reaction that comes from the exam).

Even positive events can produce significant stress.

Posttraumatic stress disorder (PTSD) in 20 percent of residents south of Canal Street, close to World Trade Center.

PTSD in 7.5 percent of residents north of Canal Street and south of 110th Street, the northernmost point surveyed

THE BRONX

N
W   E
S

110th Street

NEW JERSEY

Hudson River

QUEENS

East River

Canal Street   BROOKLYN

World Trade Center Site
(Ground Zero)

FIGURE 1 The closer people lived to the site of the World Trade Center terrorist attack, the greater the rate of posttraumatic stress disorder. (Source: Susser, Herman, & Aaron, 2002.)

cataclysmic events Strong stressors that occur suddenly and typically affect many people at once (e.g., natural disasters).

personal stressors Major life events, such as the death of a family member, that have immediate negative consequences that generally fade with time.

posttraumatic stress disorder (PTSD) A phenomenon in which victims of major catastrophes or strong personal stressors feel long-lasting effects that may include re-experiencing the event in vivid flashbacks or dreams.

he attributes it to some factor unrelated to his self-esteem, such as a previous commitment of the woman he asked, the experience of being refused may create no stress at all. Hence, a person's interpretation of events plays an important role in the determination of what is stressful (Folkman & Moskowitz, 2000; Giacobbi Jr., et al., 2004; Friborg et al., 2006).

CATEGORIZING STRESSORS

What kinds of events tend to be seen as stressful? There are three general types of stressors: cataclysmic events, personal stressors, and background stressors.

Cataclysmic events are strong stressors that occur suddenly and typically affect many people simultaneously. Disasters such as tornadoes and plane crashes as well as terrorist attacks are examples of cataclysmic events that can affect hundreds or thousands of people simultaneously.

Although it might seem that cataclysmic events would produce potent, lingering stress, in many cases they do not. In fact, cataclysmic events involving natural disasters may produce less stress in the long run than events that initially are not as devastating. One reason is that natural disasters have a clear resolution. Once they are over, people can look to the future knowing that the worst is behind them. Moreover, others who also experienced the disaster share the stress induced by cataclysmic events. Such sharing permits people to offer one another social support and a firsthand understanding of the difficulties others are going through (Hobfoll et al., 1996; Benight, 2004; Yesilyaprak, Kisac, & Sanlier, 2007).

In contrast, terrorist attacks like the one on the World Trade Center in 2001 are cataclysmic events that produce considerable stress. Terrorist attacks are deliberate, and victims (and observers) know that future attacks are likely. Government warnings in the form of heightened terror alerts may further increase the stress (Murphy, Wismar, & Freeman, 2003; Laugharne, Janca, & Widiger, 2007).

The second major category of stressor is the personal stressor. **Personal stressors** include major life events such as the death of a parent or spouse, the loss of one's job, a major personal failure, or even something positive such as getting married. Typically, personal stressors produce an immediate major reaction that soon tapers off. For example, stress arising from the death of a loved one tends to be greatest just after the time of death, but people begin to feel less stress and are better able to cope with the loss after the passage of time.

Some victims of major catastrophes and severe personal stressors experience **posttraumatic stress disorder,** or **PTSD,** in which a person has experienced a significantly stressful event that has long-lasting effects that may include re-experiencing the event in vivid flashbacks or dreams. An episode of PTSD may be triggered by an otherwise innocent stimulus, such as the sound of a honking horn, that leads a person to re-experience a past event that produced considerable stress.

Symptoms of posttraumatic stress disorder also include emotional numbing, sleep difficulties, interpersonal problems, alcohol and drug abuse, and in some cases suicide. For instance, the suicide rate for military veterans, many of whom participated in the Iraq and Afghanistan wars, is twice as high as for nonveterans (Pole, 2007; Kaplan et al., 2007; Magruder & Yeager, 2009).

Around 16% of soldiers returning from Iraq show symptoms of PTSD. Furthermore, those who have experienced child abuse or rape, rescue workers facing overwhelming situations, and victims of sudden natural disasters or accidents that produce feelings of helplessness and shock may suffer from the same disorder (Hoge & Castro, 2006; Friedman, 2006; Marmar, 2009).

Terrorist attacks produce high incidences of PTSD. For example, 11% of people in New York City had some form of PTSD in the months after the September 11 terrorist attacks. But the responses varied significantly with a resident's proximity to the attacks, as illustrated in Figure 1; the closer someone lived to the World Trade Center, the greater the likelihood of PTSD (Susser, Herman, & Aaron, 2002; Lee, Isaac, & Janca, 2007; Marshall et al., 2007).

Background stressors, or more informally, *daily hassles,* are the third major category of stressors. Exemplified by standing in a long line at a bank and getting stuck in a traffic jam, daily hassles are the minor irritations of life that we all face time and time again. Another type of background stressor is a long-term, chronic problem, such as experiencing dissatisfaction with school or a job, being in an unhappy relationship, or living in crowded quarters without privacy (Weinstein et al., 2004; McIntyre, Korn, & Matsuo, 2008).

Everyone confronts daily hassles, or background stressors, at some point. At what point do daily hassles become more than mere irritants?

By themselves, daily hassles do not require much coping or even a response on the individual's part, although they certainly produce unpleasant emotions and moods. Yet, daily hassles add up—and ultimately they may take as great of a toll as a single, more stressful incident. In fact, the *number* of daily hassles people face is associated with psychological symptoms and health problems such as flu, sore throat, and backaches.

The flip side of hassles is *uplifts,* the minor positive events that make us feel good—even if only temporarily. As indicated in Figure 2 on the next page, uplifts range from relating well to a companion to finding one's surroundings pleasing. What is especially intriguing about uplifts is that they are associated with people's psychological health in just the opposite way that hassles are: The greater the number of uplifts we experience, the fewer the psychological symptoms we report later (Chamberlain & Zika, 1990; Ravindran et al., 2002; Jain, Mills, & Von Känel, 2007).

background stressors ("daily hassles") Everyday annoyances, such as being stuck in traffic, that cause minor irritations and may have long-term ill effects if they continue or are compounded by other stressful events.

The High Cost of Stress

Stress can produce both biological and psychological consequences. Often the most immediate reaction to stress is biological. Exposure to stressors generates a rise in hormone secretions by the adrenal glands, an increase in heart rate and blood pressure, and changes in how well the skin conducts electrical impulses. On a short-term basis, these responses may be adaptive because they produce an "emergency reaction" in which the body prepares to defend itself through activation of the sympathetic nervous system. Those responses may allow more effective coping with the stressful situation (Akil & Morano, 1996; McEwen, 1998).

FIGURE 2 The most common everyday hassles and uplifts. How many of these are part of your life, and how do you cope with them? (Source: Hassles—Chamberlain & Zika, 1990; Uplifts—Kanner et al., 1981.)

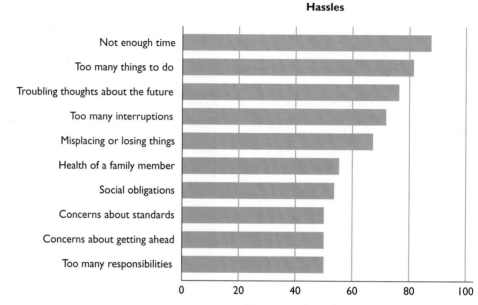

Hassles

Not enough time
Too many things to do
Troubling thoughts about the future
Too many interruptions
Misplacing or losing things
Health of a family member
Social obligations
Concerns about standards
Concerns about getting ahead
Too many responsibilities

Percentage of people experiencing

Study Alert

Remember the three categories of stressors—cataclysmic events, personal stressors, and background stressors—and that they produce different levels of stress.

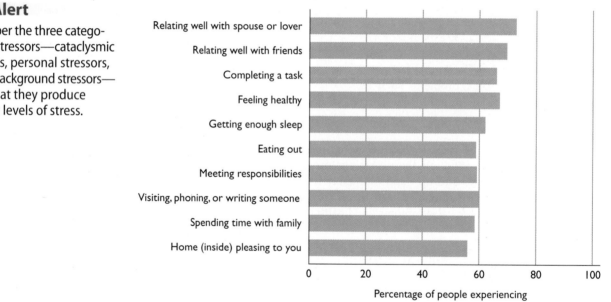

Uplifts

Relating well with spouse or lover
Relating well with friends
Completing a task
Feeling healthy
Getting enough sleep
Eating out
Meeting responsibilities
Visiting, phoning, or writing someone
Spending time with family
Home (inside) pleasing to you

Percentage of people experiencing

However, continued exposure to stress results in a decline in the body's overall level of biological functioning because of the constant secretion of stress-related hormones. Over time, stressful reactions can promote deterioration of body tissues such as blood vessels and the heart. Ultimately, we become more susceptible to disease as our ability to fight off infection is lowered (Brydon et al., 2004; Dean-Borenstein, 2007; Ellins et al., 2008).

Furthermore, an entire class of physical problems known as **psychophysiological disorders** often result from or are worsened by stress. Once referred to as *psychosomatic disorders* (a term dropped because people assumed that the disorders were somehow unreal), psychophysiological disorders are actual medical problems that are influenced by an interaction of psychological, emotional, and physical difficulties. The more common

psychophysiological disorders
Medical problems influenced by an interaction of psychological, emotional, and physical difficulties.

psychophysiological disorders range from major problems, such as high blood pressure, to usually less serious conditions, such as headaches, backaches, skin rashes, indigestion, fatigue, and constipation. Stress has even been linked to the common cold (Cohen et al., 2003; Andrasik, 2006).

On a psychological level, high levels of stress prevent people from adequately coping with life. Their view of the environment can become clouded (for example, a minor criticism made by a friend is blown out of proportion). Moreover, at the highest levels of stress, emotional responses may be so extreme that people are unable to act at all. People under a lot of stress also become less able to deal with new stressors.

In short, stress affects us in multiple ways. It may increase the risk that we will become ill, it may directly cause illness, it may make us less able to recover from a disease, and it may reduce our ability to cope with future stress. (See Figure 3 to get a measure of your own level of stress.)

How Stressful Is Your Life?

Test your level of stress by answering these questions, and adding the score from each box. Questions apply to the last month only. A key below will help you determine the extent of your stress.

1. How often have you been upset because of something that happened unexpectedly?
   [2] 0=never, 1=almost never, 2=sometimes, 3=fairly often, 4=very often

2. How often have you felt that you were unable to control the important things in your life?
   [1] 0=never, 1=almost never, 2=sometimes, 3=fairly often, 4=very often

3. How often have you felt nervous and "stressed"?
   [2] 0=never, 1=almost never, 2=sometimes, 3=fairly often, 4=very often

4. How often have you felt confident about your ability to handle your personal problems?
   [0] 4=never, 3=almost never, 2=sometimes, 1=fairly often, 0=very often

5. How often have you felt that things were going your way?
   [1] 4=never, 3=almost never, 2=sometimes, 1=fairly often, 0=very often

6. How often have you been able to control irritations in your life?
   [2] 4=never, 3=almost never, 2=sometimes, 1=fairly often, 0=very often

7. How often have you found that you could not cope with all the things that you had to do?
   [2] 0=never, 1=almost never, 2=sometimes, 3=fairly often, 4=very often

8. How often have you felt that you were on top of things?
   [2] 4=never, 3=almost never, 2=sometimes, 1=fairly often, 0=very often

9. How often have you been angered because of things that were outside your control?
   [1] 0=never, 1=almost never, 2=sometimes, 3=fairly often, 4=very often

10. How often have you felt difficulties were piling up so high that you could not overcome them?
    [2] 0=never, 1=almost never, 2=sometimes, 3=fairly often, 4=very often

How You Measure Up

Stress levels vary among individuals—compare your total score to the averages below:

AGE		GENDER	
18–29	14.2	Men	12.1
30–44	13.0	Women	13.7
45–54	12.6		
55–64	11.9		
65 & over	12.0		

MARITAL STATUS

Widowed	12.6
Married or living with a partner	12.4
Single or never wed	14.1
Divorced	14.7
Separated	16.6

FIGURE 3 To get a sense of the level of stress in your life, complete this questionnaire.
(Source: Cohen, Kamarck, & Mermelstein, 1983.)

THE GENERAL ADAPTATION SYNDROME MODEL: THE COURSE OF STRESS

general adaptation syndrome (GAS) A theory developed by Selye that suggests that a person's response to a stressor consists of three stages: alarm and mobilization, resistance, and exhaustion.

The effects of long-term stress are illustrated in a series of stages proposed by Hans Selye (pronounced "sell-yay"), a pioneering stress theorist (Selye, 1976, 1993). This model, the **general adaptation syndrome (GAS),** suggests that the physiological response to stress follows the same set pattern regardless of the cause of stress.

As shown in Figure 4, the GAS has three phases. The first stage—*alarm and mobilization*—occurs when people become aware of the presence of a stressor. On a biological level, the sympathetic nervous system becomes energized, which helps a person cope initially with the stressor.

However, if the stressor persists, people move into the second response stage: *resistance*. During this stage, the body is actively fighting the stressor on a biological level. During resistance, people use a variety of means to cope with the stressor— sometimes successfully but at a cost of some degree of physical or psychological well-being. For example, a student who faces the stress of failing several courses might spend long hours studying seeking to cope with the stress.

If resistance is inadequate, people enter the last stage of the GAS: *exhaustion*. During the exhaustion stage, a person's ability to fight the stressor declines to the point where negative consequences of stress appear: physical illness and psychological symptoms in the form of an inability to concentrate, heightened irritability, or, in severe cases, disorientation and a loss of touch with reality. In a sense, people wear out, and their physiological resources to fight the stressor are used up.

How do people move out of the third stage after they have entered it? In some cases, exhaustion allows people to escape a stressor. For example, people who become

Stressor

1. Alarm and mobilization
Meeting and
resisting stressor.

2. Resistance
Coping with stress and
resistance to stressor.

3. Exhaustion
Negative consequences of
stress (such as illness) occur
when coping is inadequate.

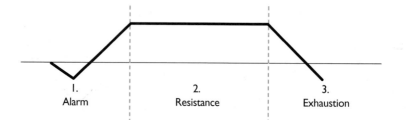

1.
Alarm

2.
Resistance

3.
Exhaustion

FIGURE 4 According to the general adaptation syndrome (GAS) model there are three major stages to stress responses: alarm and mobilization; resistance; and exhaustion. The graph below the illustration shows the degree of effort expended to cope with stressors at each of the three stages. (Source: Selye, 1976.)

FIGURE 5 Three major types of consequences result from stress: direct physiological effects, harmful behaviors, and indirect health-related behaviors. (Source: Adapted from Baum, 1994.)

ill from overwork may be excused from their duties for a time, which gives them a temporary respite from their responsibilities. At least for a time, then, the immediate stress is reduced.

Although the GAS has had a substantial impact on our understanding of stress, Selye's theory has not gone unchallenged. For example, the theory suggests that the biological reaction is similar regardless of the stressor, but some health psychologists disagree. They believe that people's biological responses are specific to the way they appraise a stressful event. If a stressor is seen as unpleasant but not unusual, then the biological response may be different than if the stressor is seen as unpleasant, out of the ordinary, and unanticipated. This perspective has led to an increased focus on psychoneuroimmunology (Taylor et al., 2000; Gaab, Rohleder, Nater, & Ehlert, 2005; Irwin, 2008).

PSYCHONEUROIMMUNOLOGY AND STRESS

Contemporary health psychologists specializing in PNI have taken a broader approach to stress. Focusing on the outcomes of stress, they have identified three main consequences of it (see Figure 5).

First, stress has direct physiological results, including an increase in blood pressure, an increase in hormonal activity, and an overall decline in the functioning of the immune system. Second, stress leads people to engage in behaviors that are harmful to their health, including increased nicotine, drug, and alcohol use; poor eating habits; and decreased sleep. Finally, stress produces indirect consequences that result in declines in health: a reduction in the likelihood of obtaining health care and decreased compliance with medical advice when it is sought (Sapolsky, 2003; Broman, 2005; Lindblad, Lindahl, & Theorell, 2006).

Why is stress so damaging to the immune system? One reason is that stress may overstimulate it. Rather than fighting invading bacteria, viruses, and other foreign invaders, it may begin to attack the body itself and damage healthy tissue. When that happens, it can lead to disorders such as arthritis and allergic reactions.

The ability to fight off disease is related to psychological factors. Here a cell from the body's immune system engulfs and destroys disease-producing bacteria.

coping The efforts to control, reduce, or learn to tolerate the threats that lead to stress.

Stress can also decrease the immune system response, permitting germs that produce colds to reproduce more easily or allowing cancer cells to spread more rapidly. In normal circumstances, our bodies produce *lymphocytes,* specialized white blood cells that fight disease at an extraordinary rate—some 10 million every few seconds. It is possible that stress can alter this level of production (Cohen, Hamrick, N., & Rodriguez, 2002; Segerstrom & Miller, 2004; Dougall & Baum, 2004).

Coping with Stress

Stress is a normal part of life—and not necessarily a completely bad part. For example, without stress, we might not be sufficiently motivated to complete the activities we need to accomplish. However, it is also clear that too much stress can take a toll on physical and psychological health. How do people deal with stress? Is there a way to reduce its negative effects?

Efforts to control, reduce, or learn to tolerate the threats that lead to stress are known as **coping.** We habitually use certain coping responses to deal with stress. Most of the time, we're not aware of these responses—just as we may be unaware of the minor stressors of life until they build up to harmful levels (Wrzesniewski & Chylinska, 2007).

We also have other, more direct and potentially more positive ways of coping with stress, which fall into two main categories (Folkman & Moskowitz, 2000, 2004; Baker & Berenbaum, 2007):

- **Emotion-focused coping.** In *emotion-focused coping,* people try to manage their emotions in the face of stress by seeking to change the way they feel about or perceive a problem. Examples of emotion-focused coping include strategies such as accepting sympathy from others and looking at the bright side of a situation.
- **Problem-focused coping.** *Problem-focused coping* attempts to modify the stressful problem or source of stress. Problem-focused strategies lead to changes in behavior or to the development of a plan of action to deal with stress. Starting a study group to improve poor classroom performance is an example of problem-focused coping. In addition, one might take a time-out from stress by creating positive events. For example, taking a day off from caring for a relative with a serious, chronic illness to go a health club or spa can bring significant relief from stress.

People often employ several types of coping strategies simultaneously. Furthermore, they use emotion-focused strategies more frequently when they perceive circumstances as being unchangeable and problem-focused strategies more often in situations they see as relatively modifiable (Stanton et al., 2000; Penley, Tomaka, & Wiebe, 2002).

Some forms of coping are less successful. One of the least effective forms of coping is avoidant coping. In *avoidant coping,* a person may use wishful thinking to reduce stress or use more direct escape routes, such as drug use, alcohol use, and overeating. An example of wishful thinking to avoid a test would be to say to oneself, "Maybe it will snow so hard tomorrow that the test will be canceled." Alternatively, a person might get drunk to avoid a problem. Either way, avoidant coping usually results in a postponement of dealing with a stressful situation, and this often makes the problem even worse (Roesch et al., 2005; Hutchinson, Baldwin, & Oh, 2006; Glass et al., 2009).

Another way of dealing with stress occurs unconsciously through the use of defense mechanisms. As we discussed in Chapter 13, Personality, *defense mechanisms* are unconscious strategies that people use to reduce anxiety by concealing the source from themselves and others. Defense mechanisms permit people to avoid stress by acting as if the stress were not even there. For example, one study examined California college students who lived in dormitories close to a geological fault (Lehman & Taylor, 1988). Those who lived in dorms that were known to be unlikely to withstand an earthquake were significantly *more* likely to doubt experts' predictions of an impending earthquake than were those who lived in safer structures.

Another defense mechanism used to cope with stress is *emotional insulation* in which a person stops experiencing any emotions at all and thereby remains unaffected and unmoved by both positive and negative experiences. The problem with defense mechanisms, of course, is that they merely hide the problem and do not deal with reality.

LEARNED HELPLESSNESS

Have you ever faced an intolerable situation that you just couldn't resolve, and you finally simply gave up and accepted things the way they were? This example illustrates one of the possible consequences of being in an environment in which control over a situation is not possible—a state that produces learned helplessness. **Learned helplessness** occurs when people conclude that unpleasant or aversive stimuli cannot be controlled—a view of the world that becomes so ingrained that they cease trying to remedy the aversive circumstances even if they actually can exert some influence on the situation (Seligman, 1975, 2007; Aujoulat, Luminet, & Deccache, 2007).

Victims of learned helplessness have concluded that there is no link between the responses they make and the outcomes that occur. People experience more physical symptoms and depression when they perceive that they have little or no control than they do when they feel a sense of control over a situation (Chou, 2005; Bjornstad, 2006).

learned helplessness A state in which people conclude that unpleasant or aversive stimuli cannot be controlled— a view of the world that becomes so ingrained that they cease trying to remedy the aversive circumstances even if they actually can exert some influence on the situation.

COPING STYLES: THE HARDY PERSONALITY

Most of us characteristically cope with stress by employing a *coping style* that represents our general tendency to deal with stress in a specific way. For example, you may know people who habitually react to even the smallest amount of stress with hysteria and others who calmly confront even the greatest stress in an unflappable manner. These kinds of people clearly have very different coping styles (Taylor, 2003; Kato & Pedersen, 2005).

Among those who cope with stress most successfully are people who are equipped with **hardiness,** a personality characteristic associated with a lower rate of stress-related illness. Hardiness consists of three components (Baumgartner, 2002; Maddi, 2007):

hardiness A personality characteristic that is associated with a lower rate of stress-related illness and consists of three components: commitment, challenge, and control.

- *Commitment.* Commitment is a tendency to throw ourselves into whatever we are doing with a sense that our activities are important and meaningful.
- *Challenge.* Hardy people believe that change rather than stability is the standard condition of life. To them, the anticipation of change serves as an incentive rather than a threat to their security.
- *Control.* Hardiness is marked by a sense of control—the perception that people can influence the events in their lives.

Hardy individuals approach stress optimistically and take direct action to learn about and deal with stressors; they thereby change stressful events into less threatening ones. As

"Today, we examined our life style, we evaluated our diet and our exercise program, and we also assessed our behavioral pattern. Then we needed a drink."

Neuroscience in Your Life:
Stress and Social Support

FIGURE 6 Participants in a study were threatened by being told they would be receiving a shock. When they were provided social support, areas of the brain that become activated during stress showed reduced activation. Specifically, social support in this study was having either a stranger or the participant's spouse hold his or her hand. In the figure, the color green highlights brain areas that showed reductions in activity when a spouse held the participant's hand, and the color blue highlights reductions in activity when either a spouse or a stranger held the participant's hand. (Source: Coan, Schaefer, & Davidson, 2006, Figure 3.)

a consequence, hardiness acts as a defense against stress-related illness (Andrew et al., 2008; Bartone et al., 2008; Vogt et al., 2008).

For those who confront the most profound difficulties, such as the death of a loved one or a permanent injury such as paralysis after an accident, a key ingredient in their psychological recovery is their degree of resilience. *Resilience* is the ability to withstand, overcome, and actually thrive after profound adversity (Bonanno, 2004; Norlander, Von Schedvin, & Archer, 2005; Jackson, 2006).

Resilient people are generally easygoing, good-natured, and have good social skills. They are usually independent, and they have a sense of control over their own destiny—even if fate has dealt them a devastating blow. In short, they work with what they have and make the best of whatever situation they find themselves in (Spencer et al., 2003; Deshields et al., 2006; Friborg et al., 2005).

SOCIAL SUPPORT: TURNING TO OTHERS

social support A mutual network of caring, interested others.

Our relationships with others also help us cope with stress. Researchers have found that **social support,** the knowledge that we are part of a mutual network of caring, interested others, enables us to experience lower levels of stress and better cope with the stress we do undergo (Cohen, 2004; Martin & Brantley, 2004; Bolger & Amarel, 2007).

The social and emotional support people provide each other helps in dealing with stress in several ways. For instance, such support demonstrates that a person is an important and valued member of a social network. Similarly, other people can provide information and advice about appropriate ways of dealing with stress (Day & Livingstone, 2003; Lindorff, 2005).

Finally, people who are part of a social support network can provide actual goods and services to help others in stressful situations. For instance, they can supply temporary living quarters to a person whose house has burned down, or they can offer study help to a student who is experiencing stress because of poor academic performance (Natvig, Albrektsen, & Ovamstrom, 2003; Takizawa, Kondo, & Sakihara, 2007).

Findings that attendance at religious services (as well as spirituality in general) provides health-related benefits also illustrate the importance of social support. For example, healthy people who regularly attend religious services live longer than those who do not attend regularly (Miller & Thoresen, 2003; Powell, Shahabi, & Thoresen, 2003; Gilbert, 2007).

Recent research is also beginning to identify how social support affects brain processing. For instance, one experiment found that activation of the areas of the brain reflecting stress was reduced when social support—simply being able to hold the hand of another person—was available (see *Neuroscience in Your Life*, Figure 6; Coan, Schaefer, & Davidson, 2006).

How can we deal with the stress in our lives? Although there is no universal solution because effective coping depends on the nature of the stressor and the degree to which it can be controlled, here are some general guidelines (Aspinwall & Taylor, 1997; Folkman & Moskowitz, 2000):

BECOMING AN INFORMED CONSUMER

of Psychology

Effective Coping Strategies

- *Turn a threat into a challenge.* When a stressful situation might be controllable, the best coping strategy is to treat the situation as a challenge and focus on ways to control it. For instance, if you experience stress because your car is always breaking down, you might take a course in auto mechanics and learn to deal directly with the car's problems.
- *Make a threatening situation less threatening.* When a stressful situation seems to be uncontrollable, you need to take a different approach. It is possible to change your appraisal of the situation, view it in a different light, and modify your attitude toward it. Research supports the old truism, "Look for the silver lining in every cloud" (Smith & Lazarus, 2001; Cheng & Cheung, 2005).
- *Change your goals.* If you are faced with an uncontrollable situation, a reasonable strategy is to adopt new goals that are practical in view of the particular situation. For example, a dancer who has been in an automobile accident and has lost full use of her legs may no longer aspire to a career in dance but might modify her goals and try to become a choreographer.
- *Take physical action.* Changing your physiological reaction to stress can help with coping. For example, biofeedback (in which a person learns to control internal physiological processes through conscious thought) can alter basic physiological processes and allow people to reduce blood pressure, heart rate, and other consequences of heightened stress. Exercise can also be effective in reducing stress (Langreth, 2000; Spencer et al., 2003; Hamer, Taylor, & Steptoe, 2006).
- *Prepare for stress before it happens.* A final strategy for coping with stress is *proactive coping*, anticipating and preparing for stress *before* it is encountered. For example, if you're expecting to go through a one-week period in which you must take a number of major tests, you can try to arrange your schedule so you have more time to study (Aspinwall & Taylor, 1997; Bode et al., 2007).

RECAP/EVALUATE/RETHINK

RECAP

How is health psychology a union between medicine and psychology?

- The field of health psychology considers how psychology can be applied to the prevention, diagnosis, and treatment of medical problems. (p. 412)

What is stress, how does it affect us, and how can we best cope with it?

- Stress is a response to threatening or challenging environmental conditions. People encounter stressors—the circumstances that produce stress—of both a positive and a negative nature. (p. 413)
- The way an environmental circumstance is interpreted affects whether it will be considered stressful. Still, there are general classes of events that provoke stress: cataclysmic events, personal stressors, and background stressors (daily hassles). (p. 414)
- Stress produces immediate physiological reactions. In the short term those reactions may be adaptive, but in the long term they may have negative consequences, including the development of psychophysiological disorders. (p. 415)
- The consequences of stress can be explained in part by Selye's general adaptation syndrome (GAS), which suggests that there are three stages in stress responses: alarm and mobilization, resistance, and exhaustion. (p. 418)
- Coping with stress can take a number of forms, including the unconscious use of defense mechanisms and the use of emotion-focused or problem-focused coping strategies. (p. 420)
- Stress can be reduced by developing a sense of control over one's circumstances. In some cases, however, people develop a state of learned helplessness. (p. 421)

EVALUATE

1. _____ is defined as a response to challenging or threatening events.
2. Match each portion of the GAS with its definition.
   1. Alarm and mobilization
   2. Exhaustion
   3. Resistance

   a. Ability to adapt to stress diminishes; symptoms appear.
   b. Activation of sympathetic nervous system.
   c. Various strategies are used to cope with a stressor.
3. Stressors that affect a single person and produce an immediate major reaction are known as
   a. Personal stressors
   b. Psychic stressors
   c. Cataclysmic stressors
   d. Daily stressors
4. People with the personality characteristic of _____ seem to be better able to successfully combat stressors.

RETHINK

1. Why are cataclysmic stressors less stressful in the long run than other types of stressors? Does the reason relate to the coping phenomenon known as social support? How?
2. *From the perspective of a social worker:* How would you help people deal with and avoid stress in their everyday lives? How might you encourage people to create social support networks?

Answers to Evaluate Questions

1. stress; 2. 1-b; 2-a; 3-c; 3. a; 4. hardiness

KEY TERMS

health psychology p. 412
psychoneuroimmunology (PNI) p. 412
stress p. 413
cataclysmic events p. 414

personal stressors p. 414
posttraumatic stress disorder (PTSD) p. 414
background stressors ("daily hassles") p. 415

psychophysiological disorders p. 416
general adaptation syndrome (GAS) p. 418
coping p. 420

learned helplessness p. 421
hardiness p. 421
social support p. 422

Psychological Aspects of Illness and Well-Being

I feel that it is absolutely necessary to be my own best advocate, and the best place to learn how to do that is in a group of other well-educated patients and their caregivers. We know what life post-diagnosis is like, and we help each other in ways that no docs, nurses, clergy, well-meaning friends and family possibly can. We laugh, we cry, we bitch, and we push and pull each other! We mourn the losses, celebrate small and large victories, and we educate ourselves and others. But most importantly—we embrace each other and our lives. (Anonymous blogpost, 2010)

Key Concept

How do psychological factors affect health-related problems such as coronary heart disease, cancer, and smoking?

As recently as three decades ago, most psychologists and health-care providers would have scoffed at the notion that a discussion group could improve a cancer patient's chances of survival. Today, however, such methods have gained increasing acceptance.

Growing evidence suggests that psychological factors have a substantial impact both on major health problems that were once seen in purely physiological terms and on our everyday sense of health, well-being, and happiness. We'll consider the psychological components of three major health problems—heart disease, cancer, and smoking—and then consider the nature of people's well-being and happiness.

The As, Bs, and Ds of Coronary Heart Disease

Tim knew it wasn't going to be his day when he got stuck in traffic behind a slow-moving farm truck. How could the driver dawdle like that? Didn't he have anything of any importance to do? Things didn't get any better when Tim arrived on campus and discovered the library didn't have the books he needed. He could almost feel the tension rising.

"I need that material to finish my paper," he thought to himself.

He knew that meant he wouldn't be able to get his paper done early, and that meant he wouldn't have the time he wanted to revise the paper. He wanted it to be a first-class paper. This time Tim wanted to get a better grade than his roommate, Luis. Although Luis didn't know it, Tim felt they were in competition and that Luis was always trying to better him whether academically or just playing cards.

"In fact," Tim mused to himself, "I feel like I'm in competition with everyone, no matter what I'm doing."

Have you, like Tim, ever seethed impatiently at being caught behind a slow-moving vehicle, felt anger and frustration at not finding material you needed at the library, or experienced a sense of competitiveness with your classmates?

Many of us experience these sorts of feelings at one time or another, but for some people they represent a pervasive, characteristic set of personality traits known as the Type A behavior pattern. The **Type A behavior pattern** is a cluster of behaviors involving hostility, competitiveness, time urgency, and feeling driven. In contrast, the

Type A behavior pattern A cluster of behaviors involving hostility, competitiveness, time urgency, and feeling driven.

Type B behavior pattern is characterized by a patient, cooperative, noncompetitive, and nonaggressive manner. It's important to keep in mind that Type A and Type B represent the ends of a continuum, and most people fall somewhere in between the two endpoints. Few people are purely a Type A or a Type B.

The importance of the Type A behavior pattern lies in its links to coronary heart disease. Men who display the Type A pattern develop coronary heart disease twice as often and suffer significantly more fatal heart attacks than those classified as having the Type B pattern. Moreover, the Type A pattern predicts who is going to develop heart disease at least as well as—and independently of—any other single factor, including age, blood pressure, smoking habits, and cholesterol levels in the body (Rosenman et al., 1994; Wielgosz & Nolan, 2000; Beresnevaité, Taylor, & Bagby, 2007).

Hostility is the key component of the Type A behavior pattern that is related to heart disease. Although competition, time urgency, and feelings of being driven may produce stress and potentially other health and emotional problems, they aren't linked to coronary heart disease the way that hostility is (Williams et al., 2000; Boyle et al., 2005; Ohira et al., 2007).

Why is hostility so toxic? The key reason is that hostility produces excessive physiological arousal in stressful situations. That arousal, in turn, results in increased production of the hormones epinephrine and norepinephrine as well as increases in heart rate and blood pressure. Such an exaggerated physiological response ultimately produces an increased incidence of coronary heart disease (Eaker et al., 2004; Demaree & Everhart, 2004; Myrtek, 2007).

It's important to keep in mind that not everyone who displays Type A behaviors is destined to have coronary heart disease. For one thing, a firm association between Type A behaviors and coronary heart disease has not been established for women; most findings pertain to males partly because until recently most research was done on men. In addition, other types of negative emotions besides the hostility found in Type A behavior appear to be related to heart attacks. For example, psychologist Johan Denollet has found evidence that what he calls *Type D*—for "distressed"—behavior is linked to coronary heart disease. In this view, insecurity, anxiety, and the negative outlook Type Ds display puts them at risk for repeated heart attacks (Denollet, 2005; Schiffer et al., 2005; Spindler et al., 2009).

> **Study Alert**
>
> It's important to distinguish among Type A (hostility, competitiveness), Type B (patience, cooperativeness), and Type D (distressed) behaviors.

Psychological Aspects of Cancer

Hardly any disease is feared more than cancer. Most people think of cancer in terms of lingering pain, and being diagnosed with the disease is typically viewed as receiving a death sentence.

Although a diagnosis of cancer is not as grim as it once was—several kinds of cancer have a high cure rate if detected early enough—cancer remains the second leading cause of death after coronary heart disease. The precise trigger for the disease is not well understood, but the process by which cancer spreads is straightforward. Certain cells in the body become altered and multiply rapidly in an uncontrolled fashion. As those cells grow, they form tumors; if left unchecked, the tumors suck nutrients from healthy cells and body tissue and ultimately destroy the body's ability to function properly.

Although the processes involved in the spread of cancer are basically physiological, some research suggests that the emotional responses of cancer patients to their disease may affect its course. For example, some findings show that a "fighting spirit" leads to better coping. On the other hand, there is little evidence that long-term survival rates are better than for patients with a less positive attitude (Watson et al., 1999; Rom, Miller, & Peluso, 2009).

Despite conflicting evidence, health psychologists believe that patients' emotions may at least partially determine the course of their disease. In the case of cancer, it is possible that positive emotional responses may help generate specialized "killer" cells that help control the size and spread of cancerous tumors. Conversely, negative emotions may suppress the ability of those cells to fight tumors (Schedlowski & Tewes, 1999; Noy, 2006).

Is a particular personality type linked to cancer? Some researchers suggest that cancer patients are less emotionally reactive, suppress anger, and lack outlets for emotional release. However, the data are too tentative and inconsistent to suggest firm conclusions about a link between personality characteristics and cancer. Certainly no conclusive evidence suggests that people who develop cancer would not have done so if their personality had been of a different sort or if their attitudes had been more positive (Smith, 1988; Zevon & Corn, 1990; Holland & Lewis, 2001).

What is increasingly clear, however, is that certain types of psychological therapy have the potential for improving quality of life and even extending the lives of cancer patients. For example, the results of one study showed that women with breast cancer who received psychological treatment lived at least a year and a half longer and experienced less anxiety and pain than women who did not participate in therapy. Research on patients with other health problems, such as heart disease, also has found that therapy can be both psychologically and medically beneficial (Spiegel, 1996; Frasure-Smith, Lesperance, & Talajic, 2000; Butler et al., 2009).

Smoking

Would you walk into a convenience store and buy an item with a label warning you that its use could kill you? Although most people would probably answer no, millions make such a purchase everyday: a pack of cigarettes. Furthermore, they do this despite clear, well-publicized evidence that smoking is linked to cancer, heart attacks, strokes, bronchitis, emphysema, and a host of other serious illnesses. Smoking is the greatest preventable cause of death in the United States; one in five U.S. deaths is caused by smoking. Worldwide, close to 5 million people die each year from the effects of smoking (Danaei et al., 2005).

WHY PEOPLE SMOKE

Why do people smoke despite all the evidence showing that it is bad for their health? It is not that they are somehow unaware of the link between smoking and disease; surveys show that most *smokers* agree with the statement, "Cigarette smoking frequently causes disease and death." And almost three-quarters of the 48 million smokers in the United States say they would like to quit. Still, 700,000 people a year take up the habit (Wetter et al., 1998; Price, 2008).

Heredity seems to determine, in part, whether people will become smokers, how much they will smoke, and how easily they can quit. Genetics also influences how susceptible people are to the harmful effects of smoking. For instance, there is an almost 50% higher rate of lung cancer in African-American smokers than in white smokers. This difference may be due to genetically produced variations in the efficiency with which enzymes are able to reduce the effects of the cancer-causing chemicals in tobacco smoke (Pomerlau, 1995; Li et al., 2003; Li et al., 2008).

However, although genetics plays a role in smoking, most research suggests that environmental factors are the primary cause of the habit. Smoking at first may be seen as "cool" or sophisticated, as a rebellious act, or as facilitating calm performance in stressful situations. Greater exposure to smoking in media such as film also leads to a higher risk of becoming an established smoker. In addition, smoking a cigarette is sometimes viewed as a "rite of passage" for adolescents undertaken at the urging of friends and viewed as a sign of growing up (Sargent et al., 2007; Wills et al., 2008; Heatherton & Sargent, 2009).

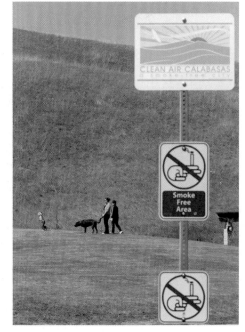

Although smoking is prohibited in an increasing number of places, it remains a substantial social problem.

Neuroscience in Your Life: Smoking— Why It's So Difficult to Quit

FIGURE 1 Even with the use of treatments such as nicotine replacement therapies, relapse for exsmokers is common. One potential reason smokers relapse is that media, such as cigarette ads, can trigger cravings in exsmokers even when they are no longer addicted to nicotine. These MRI scans show the brain of a person after quitting smoking. Some areas of the brain, shown in red, relate to habit learning, action planning, and craving. These areas show greater activation when viewing smoking-related images after quitting as compared to before quitting smoking. In addition, some areas of the brain, shown in blue, relate to memory formation and show reduced activity while viewing smoking-related images after quitting. Differences in how an exsmoker's brain responds to these images may explain why the desire to smoke persists long after quitting smoking. (Source: Janes et al., 2009, Figure 1.)

Ultimately, smoking becomes a habit. And it's an easy habit to pick up: Smoking even a single cigarette leads to a loss of autonomy, when a smoker finds that not smoking requires an effort or involves discomfort. Subsequently, people begin to label themselves smokers, and smoking becomes part of their self-concept. Moreover, they become dependent physiologically as a result of smoking because nicotine, a primary ingredient of tobacco, is highly addictive. A complex relationship develops among smoking, nicotine levels, and a smoker's emotions in which a certain nicotine level becomes associated with a positive emotional state. As a result, people smoke in an effort to regulate *both* emotional states and nicotine levels in the blood (Amos, Wiltshire, & Haw, 2006; Kassel et al., 2007; Ursprung, Sanouri, & DiFranza, 2009).

QUITTING SMOKING

Because smoking has both psychological and biological components, few habits are as difficult to break. Long-term successful treatment typically occurs in just 15% of those who try to stop smoking; once smoking becomes a habit, it is as hard to stop as an addiction to cocaine or heroin. In fact, some of the biochemical reactions to nicotine are similar to those to cocaine, amphetamines, and morphine. Furthermore, changes in brain chemistry brought about by smoking may make smokers more resistant to antismoking messages see also Figure 1; (Vanasse, Niyonsenga, & Courteau, 2004; Foulds et al., 2006; Dani & Montague, 2007).

Many people try to quit smoking but fail. The average smoker tries to quit 8 to 10 times before being successful, and even then many relapse. Even long-time

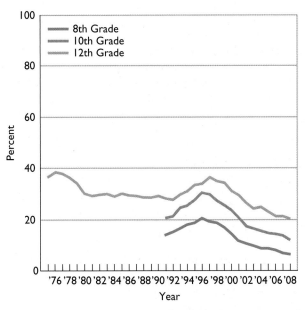

FIGURE 2 Although smoking among teenagers is lower than it was 20 years ago, a significant number still report smoking regularly. What factors might account for the continued high use of tobacco by teenagers despite the increase in antismoking advertising? (Source: Johnston et al., 2009.)

quitters can fall off the wagon: About 10% relapse after more than year of avoiding cigarettes (Grady & Altman, 2008).

Among the most effective tools for ending the smoking habit are drugs that replace the nicotine found in cigarettes. Whether in the form of gum, patches, nasal sprays, or inhalers, these products provide a dose of nicotine that reduces dependence on cigarettes. Another approach is exemplified by the drugs Zyban and Chantrix; rather than replacing nicotine, they reduce the pleasure from smoking and suppress withdrawal symptoms that smokers experience when they try to stop (Garwood & Potts, 2007; Shiffman, 2007; Brody, 2008).

Behavioral strategies, which view smoking as a learned habit and concentrate on changing the smoking response, can also be effective. Initial "cure" rates of 60% have been reported, and one year after treatment more than half of those who quit have not resumed smoking. Individual or group counseling also increases the rate of success in breaking the habit. The best treatment seems to be a combination of nicotine replacement and counseling. What doesn't work? Going it alone: Only 5% of smokers who quit cold-turkey on their own are successful (Noble, 1999; Rock, 1999; Woodruff, Conway, & Edwards, 2007).

In the long term, the most effective means of reducing smoking may be changes in societal norms and attitudes toward the habit. For instance, many cities and towns have made smoking in public places illegal; legislation based on strong popular sentiment that bans smoking in places such as college classrooms and buildings is being passed with increasing frequency. In addition, smokers are more likely to quit when their friends are quitting, so the social support of others quitting is helpful (Hamilton, Biener, & Brennan, 2007; Christakis & Fowler, 2008).

The long-term effect of the barrage of information regarding the negative consequences of smoking on people's health has been substantial; overall, smoking has declined over the last two decades, particularly among males. Still, more than one-fourth of students enrolled in high school are active smokers by the time they graduate, and there is evidence that the decline in smoking is leveling off. Among these students, around 10% become active smokers as early as the eighth grade (see Figure 2; Johnston, O'Malley, & Bachman, 2009; Fichtenberg & Glantz, 2006).

Exploring DIVERSITY

Hucksters of Death: Promoting Smoking Throughout the World

A Jeep decorated with the Camel logo pulls up to a high school in Buenos Aires. A woman begins handing out free cigarettes to 15- and 16-year-olds during their lunch recess. At a video arcade in Taipei, free American cigarettes are strewn atop each game. At a disco filled with high school students, free packs of Salems are on each table. (Ecenbarger, 1993, p. 50)

Because the number of smokers has steadily declined in the United States, cigarette manufacturers have turned their sights to other parts of the world, where they see a fertile market for their product. Although they must often sell cigarettes more cheaply than they do in the United States, the huge number of potential smokers still makes it financially worthwhile for the tobacco companies. The United States is now the world's largest exporter of cigarettes (Bartecchi, MacKenzie, & Schrier, 1995; Brown, 2001).

Clearly, the push into worldwide markets has been successful. In some Latin American cities, as many as 50% of teenagers smoke. Children as young as age 7 smoke in Hong Kong; 30% of children smoked their first whole cigarette before the age of 10 in India, Ghana, Jamaica, and Poland. The World Health Organization predicts that smoking will prematurely kill some 200 million of the world's children and that ultimately 10% of the world's population will die as a result of smoking. Of everyone alive today, 500 million will eventually die from tobacco use (Mackay & Eriksen, 2002).

One reason for the increase in smoking in developing countries is that their governments make little effort to discourage it. In fact, many governments are in the tobacco business themselves and rely on revenues from tobacco. For example, the world's largest manufacturer of cigarettes is the China National Tobacco Corporation, which is owned by the Chinese government (Marsh, 2008).

In some countries, children as young as 6 smoke regularly.

RECAP/EVALUATE/RETHINK

RECAP

How do psychological factors affect health-related problems such as coronary heart disease, cancer, and smoking?

- Hostility, a key component of the Type A behavior pattern, is linked to coronary heart disease. The Type A behavior pattern is a cluster of behaviors involving hostility, competitiveness, time urgency, and feeling driven. (p. 425)
- People's attitudes and emotional responses may affect the course of cancer through links to the immune system. (p. 426)
- Smoking, the leading preventable cause of health problems, has proved to be difficult to quit, even though most smokers are aware of the dangerous consequences of the behavior. (p. 427)

EVALUATE

1. Type _____ behavior is characterized by cooperativeness and by being easygoing; Type _____ behavior is characterized by hostility and competitiveness.
2. The Type A behavior pattern is known to directly cause heart attacks. True or false?

3. A cancer patient's attitude and emotions may affect that person's _____ system and thus help or hinder the patient's fight against the disease.
4. Smoking is used to regulate both nicotine levels and emotional states in smokers. True or false?

RETHINK

1. Is there a danger of "blaming the victim" when we argue that the course of cancer can be improved if a person with the disease holds positive attitudes or beliefs, particularly when we consider people with cancer who are not recovering? Explain your answer.
2. *From the perspective of a health-care provider:* What type of advice would you give to your patients about the connections between personality and disease? For example, would you encourage Type A people to become "less Type A" in order to decrease their risk of heart disease?

Answers to Evaluate Questions

1. B, A; 2. false; Type A behavior is related to a higher incidence of coronary heart disease but does not necessarily cause it directly; 3. immune; 4. true

KEY TERMS

Type A behavior pattern p. 425   Type B behavior pattern p. 426

Promoting Health and Wellness

How do our interactions with physicians affect our health and compliance with medical treatment?

How does a sense of well-being develop?

When Stuart Grinspoon first noticed the small lump in his arm, he assumed it was just a bruise from the touch football game he had played the previous week. But as he thought about it more, he considered more serious possibilities and decided that he'd better get it checked out at the university health service. But the visit was less than satisfactory. A shy person, Stuart felt embarrassed talking about his medical condition. Even worse, after answering a string of questions, he couldn't even understand the physician's diagnosis and was too embarrassed to ask for clarification.

Many of us share Stuart Grinspoon's attitudes toward health care. We approach physicians the same way we approach auto mechanics. When something goes wrong with the car, we want the mechanic to figure out the problem and then fix it. In the same way, when something isn't working right with our bodies, we want a diagnosis of the problem and then a (we hope, quick) repair.

Yet such an approach ignores the fact that—unlike auto repair—good health care requires taking psychological factors into account. Health psychologists have sought to determine the factors involved in the promotion of good health and, more broadly, a sense of well-being and happiness. Let's take a closer look at two areas they have tackled: producing compliance with health-related advice and identifying the determinants of well-being and happiness.

Following Medical Advice

We're not very good at taking medical advice. Consider these figures:

- As many as 85% of patients do not fully comply with a physician's recommendations.
- Between 14–21% of patients don't ever fill their drug prescriptions.
- Some 10% of adolescent pregnancies result from noncompliance with birth control practices.
- Sixty percent of all patients cannot identify their own medicines.
- From 30–50% of all patients ignore instructions or make errors in taking medication (Christensen & Johnson, 2002; Health Pages, 2003; Colland et al., 2004).

Noncompliance with medical advice can take many forms. For example, patients may fail to show up for scheduled appointments, not follow diets or not give up smoking, or discontinue medication during treatment. In some cases, they fail to take prescribed medicine at all.

Patients also may practice *creative nonadherence* in which they adjust a treatment prescribed by a physician by relying on their own medical judgment and experience. In many cases patients' lack of medical knowledge may be harmful (Taylor, 1995; Hamani et al., 2007).

Noncompliance is sometimes a result of psychological reactance. **Reactance** is a negative emotional and cognitive reaction that results from the restriction of one's freedom. People who experience reactance feel hostility and anger. Because of such

reactance A negative emotional and cognitive reaction that results from the restriction of one's freedom.

emotions, they may seek to restore their sense of freedom but in a self-destructive manner by refusing to accept medical advice and perhaps acting in a way that worsens their medical condition. For instance, a man who is placed on a strict diet may experience reactance and tend to eat even more than he did before his diet was restricted (Fogarty & Young, 2000; Dillard & Shen, 2004; Woller, Buboltz, & Loveland, 2007).

COMMUNICATING EFFECTIVELY WITH HEALTH-CARE PROVIDERS

> I was lying on a gurney, trying to prepare myself for a six-hour breast-reconstruction surgery. A few months earlier, I'd had a mastectomy for breast cancer. Because I'm small-boned, my doctor told me I needed to have a muscle sliced from my back and moved to my chest to create a proper foundation for an implant. I knew the operation would slow me down—bad news for someone who swims, runs, and chases three young kids. But as the surgeon diagrammed incision points on my chest with a felt-tip pen, my husband asked a question: "Is it really necessary to transfer this back muscle?" (Halpert, 2003, p. 63)

The surgeon's answer shocked the patient: No, it wasn't necessary. And if she didn't have the procedure, her recovery time would be cut in half. The surgeon had simply assumed, without asking the patient, that she would prefer the more complicated procedure because it would be preferable cosmetically. But after a hurried consultation with her husband, the patient opted for the less invasive procedure.

Lack of communication between medical care providers and patients can be a major obstacle to good medical care. Such communication failures occur for several reasons. One is that physicians make assumptions about what patients prefer, or they push a specific treatment that they prefer without consulting patients. Furthermore, the relatively high prestige of physicians may intimidate patients. Patients may also be reluctant to volunteer information that might cast them in a bad light, and physicians may have difficulties encouraging their patients to provide information. In many cases, physicians dominate an interview with questions of a technical nature, whereas patients attempt to communicate a personal sense of their illness and the impact it is having on their lives, as illustrated in Figure 1 (Ihler, 2003; Schillinger et al., 2004; Wain, Grammer, & Stasinos, 2006).

Furthermore, the view many patients hold that physicians are "all knowing" can result in serious communication problems. Many patients do not understand their treatments yet fail to ask their physicians for clear explanations of a prescribed course of action. About half of all patients are unable to report accurately how long they are to continue taking a medication prescribed for them, and about a quarter do not even know the purpose of the drug. In fact, some patients are not even sure as they are about to be rolled into the operating room, why they are having surgery (Svarstad, 1976; Atkinson, 1997; Halpert, 2003)!

Sometimes patient–physician communication difficulties occur because the material that must be communicated is too technical for patients, who may lack fundamental knowledge about the body and basic medical practices. In response to this problem, some health-care providers routinely use baby talking (calling patients "honey" or telling them to go "night-night") and assume that patients are unable to understand even simple information (Whitbourne & Wills, 1993; Mika et al., 2007).

The amount of physician–patient communication also is related to the sex of a physician and patient. Overall, female primary care physicians provide more patient-centered communications than do male primary care physicians. Furthermore, patients often prefer same-sex physicians (Roter, Hall, & Aoki, 2002; Kiss, 2004; Schnatz et al., 2007; Bertakis, 2009; Bertakis, Franks, & Epstein, 2009).

"There's no easy way I can tell you this, so I'm sending you to someone who can."

A Patient Talks to Her Physician

The following excerpt from a case study used at the Harvard Medical School is an example of poor interviewing technique on the part of the physician.

Patient: I can hardly drink water.
Doctor: Um hum.
Patient: Remember when it started? . . . It was pains in my head. It must have been then.
Doctor: Um-hum.
Patient: I don't know what it is. The doctor looked at it . . . said something about glands.
Doctor: Ok. Um-hum, aside from this, how have you been feeling?
Patient: Terrible.
Doctor: Yeah.
Patient: Tired . . . there's pains . . . I don't know what it is.
Doctor: Ok. . . . Fever or chills?
Patient: No.
Doctor: Ok. . . . Have you been sick to your stomach or anything?
Patient: (Sniffles, crying) I don't know what's going on. I get up in the morning tired. The only time I feel good . . . maybe like around suppertime . . . and everything (crying) and still the same thing.
Doctor: Um-hum. You're getting the nausea before you eat or after? (Goleman, 1988, p. B16)

Although the frequent "um-hums" suggest that the physician is listening to the patient, in fact he does not encourage the patient to disclose more pertinent details. Even more, late in the interview, the physician ignores the patient's emotional distress and coldly continues through the list of questions.

Cultural values and expectations also contribute to communication barriers between patients and their physicians. Providing medical advice to a patient whose native language is not English may be problematic. Furthermore, medical practices differ between cultures, and medical practitioners need to be familiar with a patient's culture in order to produce compliance with medical recommendations (Whaley, 2000; Ho et al., 2004; Culhane-Pera, Borkan, & Patten, 2007).

What can patients do to improve communication with health-care providers? Here are some tips provided by physician Holly Atkinson (Atkinson, 2003):

- Make a list of health-related concerns before you visit a health-care provider.
- Before a visit, write down the names and dosages of every drug you are currently taking.
- Determine if your provider will communicate with you via e-mail and under what circumstances.
- If you find yourself intimidated, take along an advocate—a friend or relative—who can help you communicate more effectively.
- Take notes during the visit.

INCREASING COMPLIANCE WITH MEDICAL ADVICE

Although compliance with medical advice does not guarantee that a patient's medical problems will go away, it does optimize the possibility that the patient's condition will improve. What, then, can health-care providers do to produce greater compliance on the part of their patients? One strategy is to provide clear instructions to patients regarding drug regimens. Maintaining good, warm relations with patients also leads to increased compliance (Cheney, 1996; Arbuthnott & Sharpe, 2009).

In addition, honesty helps. Patients generally prefer to be well informed—even if the news is bad; their degree of satisfaction with their medical care is linked to

Psychology on the Web

1. Find three or more websites that deal with stress reduction. Gather at least five techniques for reducing stress and summarize them. Write a critique and evaluation of those techniques using the information you have learned about stress. Which ones seem to have a sound basis in psychological theory and/or research?

2. Are you closer to a Type A or a Type B personality? Find two websites offering tests that claim to provide the answer. Summarize the quality of the tests from a scientific point of view and compare the results you received from each one.

Epilogue

In this set of modules, we have explored the intersection of psychology and biology. We have seen how the emotional and psychological experience of stress can lead to physical symptoms of illness, how personality factors may be related to major health problems, and how psychological factors can interfere with effective communication between physician and patient. We have also looked at the other side of the coin noting that some relatively simple strategies can help us control stress, affect illness, and improve our interactions with physicians.

Turn back to the prologue of this set of modules about Louisa Denby and her hectic schedule. Use your understanding of health psychology and stress to consider these questions.

1. Based on the description of Denby's day, which are personal stressors and which are background stressors? What might happen to "elevate" the stress level of a background stressor to a more serious level?

2. Are there likely to be any uplifts in her day?

3. How does the GAS apply to Denby's situation? How might events in her life move her along the three stages of the model?

4. What steps would you advise Denby to take to keep her level of stress under control? How might others in her life be involved in such an effort?

CHAPTER 12

Psychological Disorders

Key Concepts for Chapter 12

441

Prologue *Lily*

To have coffee with Lily (a pseudonym), you wouldn't get much sense of how she has suffered. She is 50 but could pass for 30. . . . She was friendly but not terribly expressive, and she carried an aura of self-protection. . . .

As a teenager, Lily felt little self-confidence. "Junior high and high school just sucks, right?" she said, laughing. "But I had a propensity to take it a little more seriously." With the help of therapy, she made it through high school and college, but in her late 20s, she became dissatisfied with her job selling specialty equipment. One October day, as she headed out for a mountain-biking trip, she looked at the sky and had the feeling that something was wrong. Bleakness massed around her quickly, much faster than it had when she was younger. Soon, nothing gave Lily much joy.

She recalled a talk show in which girls had discussed cutting themselves as a release, a way to relieve depression. "I was so numb," she said. "I just wanted to feel something—anything." So she took a knife from the kitchen and cut deeply into her left arm. (Cloud, 2009, p. 45)

Looking Ahead

Lily suffered from borderline personality disorder, a psychological disorder that afflicts an estimated 6% of the population. As we'll discuss later in the chapter, it is characterized by difficulties in forming a clear sense of self-identity, relationship problems, mood swings, and high rates of self-injury.

Lily's difficulties raise many questions. What triggered her disorder? Were genetic factors involved, or were stressors in her life responsible? Could the disorder have been prevented? And, more generally, how do we distinguish normal from abnormal behavior, and how can Lily's behavior be categorized and classified in such a way as to pinpoint the specific nature of her problem?

We address the issues raised by Lily's case in this chapter. We begin by discussing the difference between normal and abnormal behavior, which can be surprisingly indistinct. We then turn to a consideration of the most significant kinds of psychological disorders. Finally, we'll consider ways of evaluating behavior—one's own and that of others—to determine whether seeking help from a mental health professional is warranted.

Normal Versus Abnormal: Making the Distinction

Universally that person's acumen is esteemed very little perceptive concerning what-soever matters are being held as most profitable by mortals with sapience endowed to be studied who is ignorant of that which the most in doctrine erudite and certainly by reason of that in them high mind's ornament deserving of veneration constantly maintain when by general consent they affirm that other circumstances being equal by no exterior splendour is the prosperity of a nation. . .

It would be easy to conclude that these words are the musings of a madman. To most people, the passage does not seem to make any sense at all. But literary schol-ars would disagree. Actually, this passage is from James Joyce's classic *Ulysses*, hailed as one of the major works of 20th-century literature (Joyce, 1934, p. 377).

As this example illustrates, casually examining a person's writing is insufficient to determine the degree to which that person is "normal." But even when we con-sider more extensive samples of a person's behavior, we will find that there may be only a fine line between behavior that is considered normal and behavior that is considered abnormal.

How can we distinguish normal from abnormal behavior?

What are the major perspec-tives on psychological dis-orders used by mental health professionals?

What are the major categories of psychological disorders?

Defining Abnormality

Because of the difficulty in distinguishing normal from abnormal behavior, psychol-ogists have struggled to devise a precise, scientific definition of "abnormal behavior." For instance, consider the following definitions, each of which has advantages and disadvantages:

- *Abnormality as deviation from the average.* To employ this statistically based approach, we simply observe what behaviors are rare or occur infrequently in a specific society or culture and label those deviations from the norm "abnormal."

   The difficulty with this definition is that some statistically rare behav-iors clearly do not lend themselves to classification as abnormal. If most people prefer to have cornflakes for breakfast but you prefer raisin bran, this deviation hardly makes your behavior abnormal. Similarly, such a concept of abnormality would unreasonably label a person who has an unusually high IQ as abnormal simply because a high IQ is statistically rare. In short, a definition of abnormality that rests on deviation from the average is insufficient.

- *Abnormality as deviation from the ideal.* An alternative approach considers abnormality in relation to the standard toward which most people are striv-ing—the ideal. This sort of definition considers behavior abnormal if it devi-ates enough from some kind of ideal or cultural standard. However, society has few standards on which people universally agree. (For example, we would be hard pressed to find agreement on whether the New Testament, the Koran, the Talmud, or the Book of Mormon provides the most reasonable standards.)

Andrea Yates

abnormal behavior Behavior that causes people to experience distress and prevents them from functioning in their daily lives.

Furthermore, standards that do arise change over time and vary across cultures. Thus, the deviation-from-the-ideal approach is also inadequate.

- *Abnormality as a sense of personal discomfort.* A more useful definition concentrates on the psychological consequences of the behavior for the individual. In this approach, behavior is considered abnormal if it produces a sense of personal distress, anxiety, or guilt in an individual—or if it is harmful to others in some way.

  Even a definition that relies on personal discomfort has drawbacks, though, because in some especially severe forms of mental disturbance, people report feeling wonderful even though their behavior seems bizarre to others. In such cases, a personal state of well-being exists, yet most people would consider the behavior abnormal. For example, most of us would think that a woman who says she is hearing uplifting messages from Martians would be displaying abnormal behavior even though she may say that the messages make her feel happy.

- *Abnormality as the inability to function effectively.* Most people are able to feed themselves, hold a job, get along with others, and in general live as productive members of society. Yet there are those who are unable to adjust to the demands of society or function effectively.

  According to this view of abnormality, people who are unable to function effectively and to adapt to the demands of society are considered abnormal. For example, an unemployed, homeless woman living on the street may be considered unable to function effectively. Therefore, her behavior can be viewed as abnormal even if she has chosen to live this way. Her inability to adapt to the requirements of society is what makes her "abnormal," according to this approach.

- *Abnormality as a legal concept.* According to the jury that first heard her case, Andrea Yates, a woman who drowned her five children in a bathtub, was sane. She was sentenced to life in prison for her act.

  Although you might question this view (and a later appeals jury overturned the conviction), the initial verdict reflected the way in which the law defines abnormal behavior. To the judicial system, the distinction between normal and abnormal behavior rests on the definition of insanity, which is a legal but not a psychological term. The definition of insanity varies from one jurisdiction to another. In some states, insanity simply means that defendants cannot understand the difference between right and wrong at the time they commit a criminal act. Other states consider whether defendants are substantially incapable of understanding the criminality of their behavior or unable to control themselves. And in some jurisdictions, pleas of insanity are not allowed at all. (Weiner & Wettstein, 1993; Frost & Bonnie, 2001; Sokolove, 2003)

Clearly, none of the previous definitions is broad enough to cover all instances of abnormal behavior. Consequently, the distinction between normal and abnormal behavior often remains ambiguous even to trained professionals. Furthermore, to a large extent, cultural expectations for "normal" behavior in a particular society influence the understanding of "abnormal behavior" (Scheff, 1998; Sanderson, 2007). Given the difficulties in precisely defining the construct, psychologists typically define **abnormal behavior** broadly as behavior that causes people to experience distress and prevents them from functioning in their daily lives (Nolen-Hoeksema, 2007). Because of the imprecision of this definition, it's best to view abnormal behavior and normal behavior as marking two ends of a continuum rather than as absolute states. Behavior should be evaluated in terms of gradations that range from fully normal functioning to extremely abnormal behavior. Behavior typically falls somewhere between those extremes.

Perspectives on Abnormality: From Superstition to Science

Throughout much of human history, people linked abnormal behavior to superstition and witchcraft. Individuals who displayed abnormal behavior were accused of being possessed by the devil or some sort of demonic god. Authorities felt justified in "treating" abnormal behavior by attempting to drive out the source of the problem. This typically involved whipping, immersion in hot water, starvation, or other forms of torture in which the cure was often worse than the affliction (Berrios, 1996).

Contemporary approaches take a more enlightened view. Today, six major perspectives are used to understand psychological disorders. These perspectives suggest not only different causes of abnormal behavior but different treatment approaches as well. Furthermore, some perspectives are more applicable to specific disorders than are others. Figure 1 summarizes the perspectives and the way in which they can be applied to the experience of Lily, the person discussed in the chapter prologue.

Study Alert

Use Figure 1 to review the six major perspectives on abnormality and consider how they relate to the major perspectives on the field of psychology that we discussed in Chapter 1.

MEDICAL PERSPECTIVE

When people display the symptoms of tuberculosis, medical professionals can generally find tubercular bacteria in their body tissue. Similarly, the **medical perspective** suggests that when an individual displays symptoms of abnormal behavior, the fundamental cause will be found through a physical examination of the individual, which may reveal a hormonal imbalance, a chemical deficiency, or a brain injury. Indeed, when we speak of mental "illness," "symptoms" of abnormal behavior, and mental "hospitals," we are using terminology associated with the medical perspective.

Because many abnormal behaviors have been linked to biological causes, the medical perspective is a reasonable approach, yet serious criticisms have been leveled against it. For one thing, no biological cause has been identified for many forms of abnormal behavior. In addition, some critics have argued that the use of the term *illness* implies that people who display abnormal behavior have no responsibility for their actions (Szasz, 1994, 2006, Laing & Szasz, 2004).

medical perspective The perspective that suggests that when an individual displays symptoms of abnormal behavior, the root cause will be found in a physical examination of the individual, which may reveal a hormonal imbalance, a chemical deficiency, or a brain injury.

Perspectives on Psychological Disorders		
Perspective	**Description**	**Possible Application of Perspective to Lily's Case**
Medical	Assumes that physiological causes are at the root of psychological disorders	Examine Lily for medical problems, such as brain tumor, chemical imbalance in the brain, or disease
Psychoanalytic	Argues that psychological disorders stem from childhood conflicts	Seek out information about Lily's past, considering possible childhood conflicts
Behavioral	Assumes that abnormal behaviors are learned responses	Concentrate on rewards and punishments for Lily's behavior, and identify environmental stimuli that reinforce her behavior
Cognitive	Assumes that cognitions (people's thoughts and beliefs) are central to psychological disorders	Focus on Lily's perceptions of self and her environment
Humanistic	Emphasizes people's responsibility for their own behavior and the need to self-actualize	Consider Lily's behavior in terms of her choices and efforts to reach her potential
Sociocultural	Assumes that behavior is shaped by family, society, and culture	Focus on how societal demands contributed to Lily's disorder

FIGURE 1 In considering Lily's case discussed in the prologue, we can employ each of the different perspectives on abnormal behavior. Note, however, that because of the nature of her psychological disorder, some of the perspectives are more applicable than others.

Still, recent advances in our understanding of the biological bases of behavior underscore the importance of considering physiological factors in abnormal behavior. For instance, some of the more severe forms of psychological disturbance, such as major depression and schizophrenia, are influenced by genetic factors and malfunctions in neurotransmitter signals (Plomin & McGuffin, 2003; Iversen & Iversen, 2007; Howes & Kapur, 2009).

PSYCHOANALYTIC PERSPECTIVE

psychoanalytic perspective
The perspective that suggests that abnormal behavior stems from childhood conflicts over opposing wishes regarding sex and aggression.

Whereas the medical perspective suggests that biological causes are at the root of abnormal behavior, the **psychoanalytic perspective** holds that abnormal behavior stems from childhood conflicts over opposing wishes regarding sex and aggression. According to Freud, children pass through a series of stages in which sexual and aggressive impulses take different forms and produce conflicts that require resolution. If these childhood conflicts are not dealt with successfully, they remain unresolved in the unconscious and eventually bring about abnormal behavior during adulthood.

To uncover the roots of people's disordered behavior, the psychoanalytic perspective scrutinizes their early life history. However, because there is no conclusive way to link people's childhood experiences with the abnormal behaviors they display as adults, we can never be sure that the causes suggested by psychoanalytic theory are accurate. Moreover, psychoanalytic theory paints a picture of people as having relatively little control over their behavior because much of it is guided by unconscious impulses. In the eyes of some critics, this perspective suggests that people have little responsibility for their own behavior.

On the other hand, the contributions of psychoanalytic theory have been significant. More than any other approach to abnormal behavior, this perspective highlights the fact that people can have a rich, involved inner life and that prior experiences can have a profound effect on current psychological functioning (Bornstein, 2003; Elliott, 2002; Rangell, 2007).

BEHAVIORAL PERSPECTIVE

behavioral perspective The perspective that looks at the behavior itself as the problem.

Both the medical and psychoanalytic perspectives look at abnormal behaviors as *symptoms* of an underlying problem. In contrast, the **behavioral perspective** views the behavior itself as the problem. Using the basic principles of learning, behavioral theorists see both normal and abnormal behaviors as responses to various stimuli—responses that have been learned through past experience and are guided in the present by stimuli in the individual's environment. To explain why abnormal behavior occurs, we must analyze how an individual has learned it and observe the circumstances in which it is displayed.

The emphasis on observable behavior represents both the greatest strength and the greatest weakness of the behavioral approach to abnormal behavior. This perspective provides the most precise and objective approach for examining behavioral symptoms of specific disorders, such as attention-deficit hyperactivity disorder (ADHD), which we will discuss in a later module. At the same time, though, critics charge that the perspective ignores the rich inner world of thoughts, attitudes, and emotions that may contribute to abnormal behavior.

COGNITIVE PERSPECTIVE

cognitive perspective The perspective that suggests that people's thoughts and beliefs are a central component of abnormal behavior.

The medical, psychoanalytic, and behavioral perspectives view people's behavior as the result of factors largely beyond their control. To many critics of these views, however, people's thoughts cannot be ignored.

In response to such concerns, some psychologists employ a **cognitive perspective.** Rather than considering only external behavior, as in traditional behavioral approaches, the cognitive approach assumes that *cognitions* (people's thoughts and beliefs) are central to a person's abnormal behavior. A primary goal of treatment using the cognitive perspective is to explicitly teach new, more adaptive ways of thinking.

For instance, suppose that you develop the erroneous belief that "doing well on this exam is crucial to my entire future" whenever you take an exam. Through therapy, you might learn to hold the more realistic and less anxiety-producing thought, "my entire future is not dependent on this one exam." By changing cognitions in this way, psychologists working within a cognitive framework help people free themselves from thoughts and behaviors that are potentially maladaptive (Clark, 2004; Everly & Lating, 2007).

The cognitive perspective is not without critics. For example, it is possible that maladaptive cognitions are the symptoms or consequences of disorders rather than their cause. Furthermore, there are circumstances in which negative beliefs may not be irrational at all but simply reflect the unpleasant environments in which people live—after all, there are times when a single exam may be extremely important. Still, cognitive theorists would argue that one can find a more adaptive way of framing beliefs even in the most negative circumstances.

HUMANISTIC PERSPECTIVE

Psychologists who subscribe to the **humanistic perspective** emphasize the responsibility people have for their own behavior even when their behavior is considered abnormal. The humanistic perspective—growing out of the work of Carl Rogers and Abraham Maslow—concentrates on what is uniquely human—that is, it views people as basically rational, oriented toward a social world, and motivated to seek self-actualization (Rogers, 1995).

humanistic perspective The perspective that emphasizes the responsibility people have for their own behavior, even when such behavior is abnormal.

Humanistic approaches focus on the relationship of the individual to society; it considers the ways in which people view themselves in relation to others and see their place in the world. The humanistic perspective views people as having an awareness of life and of themselves that leads them to search for meaning and self-worth. Rather than assuming that individuals require a "cure," the humanistic perspective suggests that they can, by and large, set their own limits of what is acceptable behavior. As long as they are not hurting others and do not feel personal distress, people should be free to choose the behaviors in which they engage.

Although the humanistic perspective has been criticized for its reliance on unscientific, unverifiable information and its vague, almost philosophical formulations, it offers a distinctive view of abnormal behavior. It stresses the unique aspects of being human and provides a number of important suggestions for helping those with psychological problems.

SOCIOCULTURAL PERSPECTIVE

The **sociocultural perspective** assumes that people's behavior—both normal and abnormal—is shaped by the kind of family group, society, and culture in which they live. According to this view, the nature of one's relationships with others may support abnormal behaviors and even cause them. Consequently the kinds of stresses and conflicts people experience in their daily interactions with others can promote and maintain abnormal behavior.

sociocultural perspective The perspective that assumes that people's behavior—both normal and abnormal—is shaped by the kind of family group, society, and culture in which they live.

This perspective finds statistical support for the position that sociocultural factors shape abnormal behavior given the fact that some kinds of abnormal behavior are far more prevalent among certain social classes than they are in others. For instance, diagnoses of schizophrenia tend to be higher among members of lower socioeconomic groups than among members of more affluent groups. Proportionally more African-American individuals are hospitalized involuntarily for psychological disorders than are whites. Furthermore, poor economic times seem to be linked to general declines in psychological functioning, and social problems such as homelessness are associated

"First off, you're not a nut. You're a legume."

with psychological disorders (López & Guarnaccia, 2005; Conger et al., 2002; Nasir & Hand, 2006; Greenberg & Rosenheck, 2008).

On the other hand, alternative explanations abound for the association between abnormal behavior and social factors. For example, people from lower socioeconomic levels may be less likely than those from higher levels to seek help, gradually reaching a point where their symptoms become severe and warrant a serious diagnosis. Furthermore, sociocultural explanations provide relatively little specific guidance for the treatment of individuals showing mental disturbance because the focus is on broader societal factors (Paniagua, 2000).

Classifying Abnormal Behavior: The ABCs of *DSM*

Crazy. Whacked. Mental. Loony. Insane. Neurotic. Psycho. Strange. Demented. Odd. Possessed.

Society has long placed labels on people who display abnormal behavior. Unfortunately, most of the time these labels have reflected intolerance and have been used with little thought as to what each label signifies.

Providing appropriate and specific names and classifications for abnormal behavior has presented a major challenge to psychologists. It is not hard to understand why, given the difficulties discussed earlier in simply distinguishing normal from abnormal behavior. Yet psychologists and other careproviders need to classify abnormal behavior in order to diagnose it and ultimately treat it.

DSM-IV-TR: DETERMINING DIAGNOSTIC DISTINCTIONS

Over the years, mental health professionals have developed many different classification systems that vary in terms of their utility and the degree to which they have been accepted. However, one standard system, devised by the American Psychiatric Association, has emerged in the United States. Most professionals today use this classification system, known as the ***Diagnostic and Statistical Manual of Mental Disorders*, Fourth Edition, Text Revision (*DSM-IV-TR*)** to diagnose and classify abnormal behavior.

DSM-IV-TR presents comprehensive and relatively precise definitions for more than 200 disorders divided into 17 major categories. It also includes five types of information, known as axes, which have to be considered in assessing a patient:

- **Axis I: Clinical Disorders.** Disorders that produce distress and impair functioning.
- **Axis II: Personality Disorders and Mental Retardation.** Enduring, rigid behavior patterns.
- **Axis III: General Medical Conditions.** Physical disorders that may be related to psychological disorders.
- **Axis IV: Psychosocial and Environmental Problems.** Problems in a person's life such as stressors or life events that may affect the diagnosis, treatment, and outcome of psychological disorders.
- **Axis V: Global Assessment of Functioning.** Overall level of mental, social, occupational, and leisure functioning.

Diagnostic and Statistical Manual of Mental Disorders, Fourth Edition, Text Revision (*DSM-IV-TR*) A system, devised by the American Psychiatric Association, used by most professionals to diagnose and classify abnormal behavior.

Categories of Disorders	Examples
Anxiety (problems in which anxiety impedes daily functioning)	Generalized anxiety disorder, panic disorder, phobic disorder, obsessive-compulsive disorder, posttraumatic stress disorder
Somatoform (psychological difficulties displayed through physical problems)	Hypochondriasis, conversion disorder
Dissociative (the splitting apart of crucial parts of personality that are usually integrated)	Dissociative identity disorder (multiple personality), dissociative amnesia, dissociative fugue
Mood (emotions of depression or euphoria that are so strong they intrude on everyday living)	Major depression, bipolar disorder
Schizophrenia and psychotic disorders (declines in functioning, thought and language disturbances, perception disorders, emotional disturbances, and withdrawal from others)	Disorganized, paranoid, catatonic, undifferentiated, residual
Personality (problems that create little personal distress but that lead to an inability to function as a normal member of society)	Antisocial (sociopathic) personality disorder, narcissistic personality disorder
Sexual (problems related to sexual arousal from unusual objects or problems related to functioning)	Paraphilia, sexual dysfunction
Substance-related (problems related to drug dependence and abuse)	Alcohol, cocaine, hallucinogens, marijuana
Dementia, amnesia, and other cognitive disorders	

DIAGNOSTIC AND STATISTICAL MANUAL OF MENTAL DISORDERS

FOURTH EDITION

TEXT REVISION

DSM-IV-TR

AMERICAN PSYCHIATRIC ASSOCIATION

FIGURE 2 This list of disorders represents the major categories from the *DSM-IV-TR*. It is only a partial list of the more than 200 disorders included there.

By following the criteria presented in the *DSM-IV-TR* classification system, diagnosticians can identify the specific problem an individual is experiencing. (Figure 2 provides a brief outline of the major diagnostic categories.)

DSM-IV-TR is primarily descriptive and avoids suggesting an underlying cause for an individual's behavior and problems. For instance, the term *neurotic*—a label that is commonly used by people in their everyday descriptions of abnormal behavior—is not listed as a *DSM-IV-TR* category. Because the term *neurosis* refers to problems associated with a specific cause based in Freud's theory of personality, it is not included in *DSM-IV-TR*.

DSM-IV-TR has the advantage, then, of providing a descriptive system that does not specify the cause of or reason for a problem. Rather, it paints a picture of the behavior that is being displayed. Why should this approach be important? For one thing, it allows communication between mental health professionals of diverse backgrounds and theoretical approaches. In addition, precise classification enables researchers to explore the causes of a problem. Without reliable descriptions of abnormal behavior, researchers would be hard pressed to find ways to investigate the disorder. Finally, *DSM-IV-TR* provides a kind of conceptual shorthand through which professionals can describe the behaviors that tend to occur together in an individual (Widiger & Clark, 2000; First, Frances, & Pincus, 2002).

CONNING THE CLASSIFIERS: THE SHORTCOMINGS OF *DSM-IV-TR*

When clinical psychologist David Rosenhan and eight colleagues sought admission to separate mental hospitals across the United States in the 1970s, each stated that he or she was hearing voices—"unclear voices" that said "empty," "hollow," and "thud"—and each was immediately admitted to the hospital. However, the truth was that they actually were conducting a study, and none of them was really hearing voices. Aside from these misrepresentations, *everything* else they did and said represented their true behavior, including the responses they gave during extensive admission interviews and their answers to the battery of tests they were asked to complete. In fact, as soon as they were admitted, they said they no longer heard any voices. In short, each of the pseudo-patients acted in a "normal" way (Rosenhan, 1973).

We might assume that Rosenhan and his colleagues would have been quickly discovered as the impostors they were, but this was not the case. Instead, each of them was diagnosed as severely abnormal on the basis of observed behavior. Mental health professionals labeled most as suffering from schizophrenia and kept them in the hospital 3–52 days, with the average stay of 19 days. Even when they were discharged, most of the "patients" left with the label *schizophrenia—in remission,* implying that the abnormal behavior had only temporarily subsided and could recur at any time. Most disturbing, no one on the hospital staff identified any of the pseudo-patients as impostors—although some of the actual patients figured out the ruse.

The results of Rosenhan's classic study illustrate that placing labels on individuals powerfully influences the way mental health workers perceive and interpret their actions. It also points out that determining who is psychologically disordered is not always a clear-cut or accurate process.

Although *DSM-IV-TR* was developed to provide more accurate and consistent diagnoses of psychological disorders, it has not been entirely successful. For instance, critics charge that it relies too much on the medical perspective. Because it was drawn up by psychiatrists—who are physicians—some condemn it for viewing psychological disorders primarily in terms of the symptoms of an underlying physiological disorder. It also does not fully take into account the advances in behavioral neuroscience that have identified the genetic underpinnings of some psychological disorders. Moreover, critics suggest that *DSM-IV-TR* compartmentalizes people into inflexible, all-or-none categories rather than considering the degree to which a person displays psychologically disordered behavior (Schmidt, Kotov, & Joiner, 2004; Samuel & Widiger, 2006).

Other concerns with *DSM-IV-TR* are more subtle but equally important. For instance, some critics argue that labeling an individual as abnormal provides a dehumanizing, lifelong stigma. (Think, for example, of political contenders whose candidacies have been terminated by the disclosure that they received treatment for severe psychological disorders.) Furthermore, after an initial diagnosis has been made, mental health professionals, who may concentrate on the initial diagnostic category, could overlook other diagnostic possibilities (Szasz, 1994; Duffy et al., 2002; Quinn, Kahng, & Crocker, 2004).

Still, despite the drawbacks inherent in any labeling system, *DSM-IV-TR* has had an important influence on the way in which mental health professionals view psychological disorders. It has increased both the reliability and the validity of diagnostic categorization. In addition, it offers a logical way to organize examination of the major types of mental disturbance.

> ### ⬥ Study Alert
> It is important to understand the advantages and weaknesses of the *DSM* classification system.

RECAP/EVALUATE/RETHINK

RECAP

How can we distinguish normal from abnormal behavior?

- Definitions of abnormality include deviation from the average, deviation from the ideal, a sense of personal discomfort, the inability to function effectively, and legal conceptions. (p. 443)
- Although no single definition is adequate, abnormal behavior can be considered to be behavior that causes people to experience distress and prevents them from functioning in their daily lives. Most psychologists believe that abnormal and normal behavior should be considered in terms of a continuum. (p. 444)

What are the major perspectives on psychological disorders used by mental health professionals?

- The medical perspective views abnormality as a symptom of an underlying disease. (p. 445)
- Psychoanalytic perspectives suggest that abnormal behavior stems from childhood conflicts in the unconscious. (p. 446)
- Behavioral approaches view abnormal behavior not as a symptom of an underlying problem but as the problem itself. (p. 446)
- The cognitive approach suggests that abnormal behavior is the result of faulty cognitions (thoughts and beliefs). In this view, abnormal behavior can be remedied by changing one's flawed thoughts and beliefs. (p. 446)
- Humanistic approaches emphasize the responsibility people have for their own behavior even when such behavior is seen as abnormal. (p. 447)
- Sociocultural approaches view abnormal behavior in terms of difficulties arising from family and other social relationships. (p. 447)

What are the major categories of psychological disorders?

- The most widely used system for classifying psychological disorders is *DSM-IV-TR—Diagnostic and Statistical Manual of Mental Disorders, Fourth Edition, Text Revision.* (p. 448)

EVALUATE

1. One problem in defining abnormal behavior is that
   a. Statistically rare behavior may not be abnormal.
   b. Not all abnormalities are accompanied by feelings of discomfort.
   c. Cultural standards are too general to use as a measuring tool.
   d. All of the above.

2. If abnormality is defined as behavior that causes personal discomfort or harms others, which of the following people is most likely to need treatment?
   a. An executive is afraid to accept a promotion because it would require moving from his ground-floor office to the top floor of a tall office building.
   b. A woman decides to quit her job and chooses to live on the street in order to live a "simpler life."
   c. A man believes that friendly spacemen visit his house every Thursday.
   d. A photographer lives with 19 cats in a small apartment lovingly caring for them.

3. Virginia's mother thinks that her daughter's behavior is clearly abnormal because, despite being offered admission to medical school, Virginia decides to become a waitress. What approach is Virginia's mother using to define abnormal behavior?

4. Which of the following is a strong argument against the medical perspective on abnormality?
   a. Physiological abnormalities are almost always impossible to identify.
   b. There is no conclusive way to link past experience and behavior.
   c. The medical perspective rests too heavily on the effects of nutrition.
   d. Assigning behavior to a physical problem takes responsibility away from the individual for changing his or her behavior.

5. Cheryl is painfully shy. According to the behavioral perspective, the best way to deal with her "abnormal" behavior is to
   a. Treat the underlying physical problem.
   b. Use the principles of learning theory to modify her shy behavior.
   c. Express a great deal of caring.
   d. Uncover her negative past experiences through hypnosis.

RETHINK

1. Do you agree or disagree that *DSM* should be updated every several years? Why? What makes abnormal behavior so variable?

2. *From the perspective of an employer:* Imagine that a well-paid employee was arrested for shoplifting a sweater that costs $15. What sort of explanation for this behavior would the proponents of *each* perspective on abnormality provide:

the medical perspective, the psychoanalytic perspective, the behavioral perspective, the cognitive perspective, the humanistic perspective, and the sociocultural perspective? Based on the potential causes of the shoplifting, would you fire the employee? Why or why not?

Answers to Evaluate Questions

1. d; 2. a; 3. deviation from the ideal; 4. d; 5. b

KEY TERMS

abnormal behavior p. 444
medical perspective p. 445
psychoanalytic perspective p. 446
behavioral perspective p. 446

cognitive perspective p. 446
humanistic perspective p. 447
sociocultural perspective p. 447

Diagnostic and Statistical Manual of Mental Disorders, Fourth Edition, Text Revision (*DSM-IV-TR*) p. 448

The Major Psychological Disorders

Sally experienced her first panic attack out of the blue, 3 weeks after completing her senior year in college. She had just finished a job interview and was meeting some friends for dinner. In the restaurant, she began to feel dizzy. Within a few seconds, her heart was pounding, and she was feeling breathless, as though she might pass out. Her friends noticed that she did not look well and offered to drive her home. Sally suggested they stop at the hospital emergency room instead. Although she felt better by the time they arrived at the hospital, and tests indicated nothing wrong, Sally experienced a similar episode a week later while at a movie. . . .

Her attacks became more and more frequent. Before long, she was having several attacks per week. In addition, she constantly worried about having attacks. She began to avoid exercise and other activities that produced physical sensations. She also noticed the attacks were worse when she was alone. She began to avoid driving, shopping in large stores, and eating in all restaurants. Some weeks she avoided leaving the house completely. (Antony, Brown, & Barlow, 1992, p. 79)

Sally suffered from panic disorder, one of the specific psychological disorders we'll consider in this module. Keep in mind that although we'll be discussing these disorders objectively, each represents a very human set of difficulties that influence and in some cases considerably disrupt people's lives.

Key Concept

What are the major psychological disorders?

Anxiety Disorders

All of us at one time or another experience *anxiety,* a feeling of apprehension or tension, in reaction to stressful situations. There is nothing "wrong" with such anxiety. It is a normal reaction to stress that often helps rather than hinders our daily functioning. Without some anxiety, for instance, most of us probably would not have much motivation to study hard, undergo physical exams, or spend long hours at our jobs.

But some people experience anxiety in situations in which there is no external reason or cause for such distress. When anxiety occurs without external justification and begins to affect people's daily functioning, mental health professionals consider it a psychological problem known as **anxiety disorder.** We'll discuss the four major types of anxiety disorders: phobic disorder, panic disorder, generalized anxiety disorder, and obsessive-compulsive disorder.

anxiety disorder The occurrence of anxiety without an obvious external cause that affects daily functioning.

PHOBIC DISORDER

It's not easy moving through the world when you're terrified of electricity. "Donna," 45, a writer, knows that better than most. Get her in the vicinity of an appliance or a light switch or—all but unthinkable—a thunderstorm, and she is overcome by a terror so blinding she can think of nothing but fleeing. That, of course, is not always possible, so over time, Donna has come up with other answers. When she opens the refrigerator door, rubber-sole shoes are a must. If a light bulb blows, she will tolerate the dark until someone else changes it for her. Clothes shopping is done only when necessary, lest static on garments send her running from the store. And swimming at night is absolutely out of the question, lest underwater lights electrocute her. (Kluger, 2001, p. 51)

Phobic Disorder	Description	Example	
Agoraphobia	Fear of places, such as unfamiliar or crowded spaces, where help might not be available in case of emergency	Person becomes housebound because any place other than the person's home arouses extreme anxiety symptoms.	
Specific phobias	Fear of specific objects, places, or situations		
Animal type	Specific animals or insects	Person has extreme fear of dogs, cats, or spiders.	
Natural environment type	Events or situations in the natural environment	Person has extreme fear of storms, heights, or water.	
Situational type	Public transportation, tunnels, bridges, elevators, flying, driving	Person becomes extremely claustrophobic in elevators.	
Blood injection-injury type	Blood, injury, injections	Person panics when viewing a child's scraped knee.	
Social phobia	Fear of being judged or embarrassed by others	Person avoids all social situations and becomes a recluse for fear of encountering others' judgment.	

FIGURE 1 Phobic disorders differ from generalized anxiety and panic disorders because a specific stimulus can be identified. Listed here are a number of types of phobias and their triggers. (Source: Adapted from Nolen-Hoeksema, 2007).

phobias Intense, irrational fears of specific objects or situations.

Donna suffers from a **phobia,** an intense, irrational fear of a specific object or situation. For example, claustrophobia is a fear of enclosed places, acrophobia is a fear of high places, xenophobia is a fear of strangers, social phobia is the fear of being judged or embarrassed by others, and—as in Donna's case—electrophobia is a fear of electricity.

The objective danger posed by an anxiety-producing stimulus (which can be just about anything, as you can see in Figure 1) is typically small or nonexistent. However, to someone suffering from the phobia, the danger is great, and a full-blown panic attack may follow exposure to the stimulus. Phobic disorders differ from generalized anxiety disorders and panic disorders in that there is a specific, identifiable stimulus that sets off the anxiety reaction.

Phobias may have only a minor impact on people's lives if those who suffer from them can avoid the stimuli that trigger fear. For example, a fear of heights may have little impact on people's everyday lives (although it may prevent them from living in a high floor in an apartment)—unless they are firefighters or window-washers. On the other hand, a *social phobia,* or a fear of strangers, presents a more serious problem. In one extreme case, a Washington woman left her home just three times in 30 years—once to visit her family, once for an operation, and once to purchase ice cream for a dying companion (Adler, 1984; Kimbrel, 2007).

PANIC DISORDER

panic disorder Anxiety disorder that takes the form of panic attacks lasting from a few seconds to several hours.

In another type of anxiety disorder, **panic disorder,** *panic attacks* occur that last from a few seconds to several hours. Unlike phobias, which are stimulated by specific objects or situations, panic disorders do not have any identifiable stimuli. Instead, during an attack such as those Sally experienced in the case described earlier, anxiety suddenly—and often without warning—rises to a peak, and an individual feels a sense of impending, unavoidable doom. Although the physical symptoms differ from person to person, they may include heart palpitations, shortness of breath, unusual amounts of sweating, faintness and dizziness, gastric sensations, and sometimes a sense of imminent death. After such an attack, it is no wonder that people tend to feel exhausted (Rachman & deSilva, 2004; Laederach-Hofmann & Messerli-Buergy, 2007).

Panic attacks seemingly come out of nowhere and are unconnected to any specific stimulus. Because they don't know what triggers their feelings of panic, victims of panic attacks may become fearful of going places. In fact, some people with panic disorder develop a complication called *agoraphobia,* the fear of being in a situation in which escape is difficult and in which help for a possible panic attack would not be available. In extreme cases, people with agoraphobia never leave their homes (Marcaurelle, Belanger, & Marchand, 2005; Herrán, Carrera, & Sierra-Biddle, 2006; Wittchen et al., 2008).

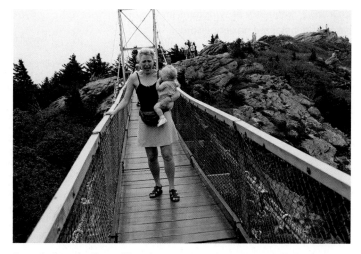

Acrophobia, the fear of heights, is not an uncommon phobia. What sort of behavior-modification approaches might be used to deal with acrophobia?

In addition to the physical symptoms, panic disorder affects how the brain processes information. For instance, people with panic disorder have reduced reactions in the anterior cingulate cortex to stimuli (such as viewing a fearful face) that normally produce a strong reaction in those without the disorder. It may be that recurring high levels of emotional arousal that patients with panic disorder experience desensitizes them to emotional stimuli (Pillay et al., 2006; Pillay et al., 2007).

GENERALIZED ANXIETY DISORDER

People with **generalized anxiety disorder** experience long-term, persistent anxiety and uncontrollable worry. Sometimes their concerns are about identifiable issues involving family, money, work, or health. In other cases, though, people with the disorder feel that something dreadful is about to happen but can't identify the reason and thus experience "free-floating" anxiety.

generalized anxiety disorder
The experience of long-term, persistent anxiety and worry.

Because of persistent anxiety, people with generalized anxiety disorder cannot concentrate or set their worry and fears aside; their lives become centered on their worry. Furthermore, their anxiety is often accompanied by physiological symptoms such as muscle tension, headaches, dizziness, heart palpitations, or insomnia (Starcevic et al., 2007). Figure 2 shows the most common symptoms of generalized anxiety disorder.

Obsessive-Compulsive Disorder. In **obsessive-compulsive disorder (OCD),** people are plagued by unwanted thoughts, called obsessions, or feel that they must carry out behaviors, termed compulsions, which they feel driven to perform.

obsessive-compulsive disorder (OCD)
A disorder characterized by obsessions or compulsions.

An **obsession** is a persistent, unwanted thought or idea that keeps recurring. For example, a student may be unable to stop thinking that she has neglected to put her name on a test and may think about it constantly for the two weeks it takes to get the paper back. A man may go on vacation and wonder the whole time whether he locked his house. A woman may hear the same tune running through her head over and over. In each case, the thought or idea is unwanted and difficult to put out of mind. Of course, many people suffer from mild obsessions from time to time, but usually such thoughts persist only for a short period. For people with serious obsessions, however, the thoughts persist for days or months and may consist of bizarre, troubling images (Lee & Kwon, 2003, Lee et al., 2005; Rassin & Muris, 2007).

obsession A persistent, unwanted thought or idea that keeps recurring.

FIGURE 2 Frequency of symptoms in cases of generalized anxiety disorder. (Source: Adapted from Beck & Emery, 1985, pp. 87–88.)

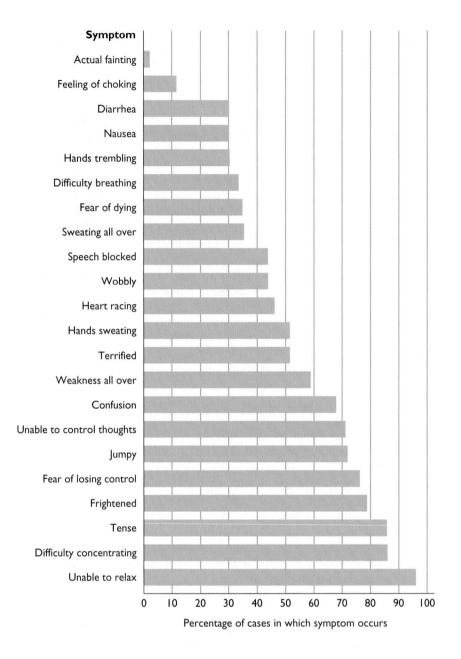

compulsion An irresistible urge to repeatedly carry out some act that seems strange and unreasonable.

As part of an obsessive-compulsive disorder, people may also experience **compulsions,** irresistible urges to repeatedly carry out some act that seems strange and unreasonable even to them. Whatever the compulsive behavior is, people experience extreme anxiety if they cannot carry it out even if it is something they want to stop. The acts may be relatively trivial, such as repeatedly checking the stove to make sure all the burners are turned off, or more unusual, such as washing one's hands so much that they bleed (Frost & Steketee, 2002; Clark, 2007; Moretz & McKay, 2009).

For example, consider this passage from the autobiography of a person with obsessive-compulsive disorder:

I thought my parents would die if I didn't do everything in exactly the right way. When I took my glasses off at night I'd have to place them on the dresser at a particular angle. Sometimes I'd turn on the light and get out of bed seven times until I felt comfortable with the angle. If the angle wasn't right, I felt that my parents would die. The feeling ate up my insides.

If I didn't grab the molding on the wall just the right way as I entered or exited my room; if I didn't hang a shirt in the closet perfectly; if I didn't read a paragraph a certain way; if my hands and nails weren't perfectly clean, I thought my incorrect behavior would kill my parents (Summers, 2000, p. 42).

Although carrying out compulsive rituals may lead to some immediate reduction of anxiety, in the long run the anxiety returns. In fact, people with severe cases lead lives filled with unrelenting tension (Goodman, Rudorfer, & Maser, 2000; Penzel, 2000).

THE CAUSES OF ANXIETY DISORDERS

We've considered the four major types of anxiety disorders, but there are others as well. For instance, *posttraumatic stress disorder* (in which a person re-experiences a stressful event in vivid flashbacks or dreams and which we discussed when we considered stress) is classified as an anxiety disorder.

The variety of anxiety disorders means that no single explanation fits all cases. Genetic factors clearly are part of the picture. For example, if one member of a pair of identical twins has panic disorder, there is a 30% chance that the other twin will have it also. Furthermore, a person's characteristic level of anxiety is related to a specific gene involved in the production of the neurotransmitter serotonin. This is consistent with findings indicating that certain chemical deficiencies in the brain appear to produce some kinds of anxiety disorder (Holmes et al., 2003; Beidel & Turner, 2007; Chamberlain et al., 2008).

Some researchers believe that an overactive autonomic nervous system may be at the root of panic attacks. Specifically, they suggest that poor regulation of the brain's locus ceruleus may lead to panic attacks, which cause the limbic system to become overstimulated. In turn, the overstimulated limbic system produces chronic anxiety, which ultimately leads the locus ceruleus to generate still more panic attacks (Pine et al., 2000; Balaban, 2002; Davies et al., 2008).

There are also biological causes at work in OCD. For example, researchers have found differences in the brains of those with the disorder compared to those without it (see Figure 3; Christian et al., 2008).

"No, I don't need an alarm clock— anxiety is my alarm clock."

Neuroscience in Your Life: One Step Closer to Understanding OCD

FIGURE 3 People with obsessive-compulsive disorder (OCD) have structural differences in their brains. These images show increased levels of grey matter (i.e., more connections or more neurons) in the thalamus (a) and in the left frontal cortex (b) in people with OCD as compared to people without it. These findings help us to understand the potential causes of OCD and may lead to the development of better treatments for the disorder. (Source: Christian et al., 2008, Figure 1.)

(a)

(b)

Psychologists who employ the behavioral perspective have taken a different approach that emphasizes environmental factors. They consider anxiety to be a learned response to stress. For instance, suppose a dog bites a young girl. When the girl next sees a dog, she is frightened and runs away—a behavior that relieves her anxiety and thereby reinforces her avoidance behavior. After repeated encounters with dogs in which she is reinforced for her avoidance behavior, she may develop a full-fledged phobia regarding dogs.

Finally, the cognitive perspective suggests that anxiety disorders grow out of inappropriate and inaccurate thoughts and beliefs about circumstances in a person's world. For example, people with anxiety disorders may view a friendly puppy as a ferocious and savage pit bull, or they may see an air disaster looming every moment they are in the vicinity of an airplane. According to the cognitive perspective, people's maladaptive thoughts about the world are at the root of an anxiety disorder (Frost & Steketee, 2002; Wang & Clark, 2002; Ouimet, Gawronski, & Dozois, 2009).

Somatoform Disorders

somatoform disorders Psychological difficulties that take on a physical (somatic) form, but for which there is no medical cause.

hypochondriasis A disorder in which people have a constant fear of illness and a preoccupation with their health.

conversion disorder A major somatoform disorder that involves an actual physical disturbance, such as the inability to use a sensory organ or the complete or partial inability to move an arm or leg.

Somatoform disorder are psychological difficulties that take on a physical (somatic) form but for which there is no medical cause. Even though an individual with a somatoform disorder reports physical symptoms, no biological cause exists, or if there is a medical problem, the person's reaction is greatly exaggerated.

One type of somatoform disorder is **hypochondriasis** in which people have a constant fear of illness and a preoccupation with their health. These individuals believe that everyday aches and pains are symptoms of a dread disease. The "symptoms" are not faked; rather, they are misinterpreted as evidence of some serious illness—often in the face of inarguable medical evidence to the contrary (Noyes et al., 2003; Fallon & Feinstein, 2001; Abramowitz, Olatunji, & Deacon, 2007; Olatunji, 2008).

Another somatoform disorder is conversion disorder. Unlike hypochondriasis, in which there is no physical problem, **conversion disorders** involve an actual physical disturbance, such as the inability to see or hear or to move an arm or leg. The *cause* of such a physical disturbance is purely psychological; there is no biological reason for the problem. Some of Freud's classic cases involved conversion disorders. For instance, one of Freud's patients suddenly became unable to use her arm without any apparent physiological cause. Later, just as abruptly, the problem disappeared.

Conversion disorders often begin suddenly. People wake up one morning blind or deaf, or they experience numbness that is restricted to a certain part of the body. A hand, for example, may become entirely numb, while an area above the wrist, controlled by the same nerves, remains sensitive to touch—something that is physiologically implausible. Mental health professionals refer to such a condition as "glove anesthesia" because the numb area is the part of the hand covered by a glove and not a region related to pathways of the nervous system (see Figure 4).

Surprisingly, people who experience conversion disorders frequently remain unconcerned about symptoms that most of us would expect to be highly anxiety producing. For instance, a person in good health who wakes up blind may react in a bland, matter-of-fact way. Considering how most of us would feel if we woke up unable to see, this unemotional reaction (called *la belle indifférence,* a French phrase meaning "a beautiful indifference") hardly seems appropriate (Brasic, 2002).

Dissociative Disorders

The classic movie *The Three Faces of Eve* (about a woman with three wildly different personalities) and the book *Sybil* (about a girl who allegedly had 16 personalities) represent a highly dramatic, rare, and controversial class of disorders:

Head band

Neck band

Chest band

Arm band

Waist band

Wrist band

Glove

Knee band

Thigh band

Sock

Ankle band

FIGURE 4 Conversion disorders sometimes produce numbness in specific and isolated areas of the body (indicated by the shaded areas in the figure). For instance, in glove anesthesia, the area of the body covered by a glove feels numb. However, the condition is biologically implausible because of the nerves involved, which suggests that the problem results from a psychological disorder rather than from actual nerve damage.

dissociative disorders. **Dissociative disorders** are characterized by the separation (or dissociation) of different facets of a person's personality that are normally integrated and work together. By dissociating key parts of who they are, people are able to keep disturbing memories or perceptions from reaching conscious awareness and thereby reduce their anxiety (Maldonado & Spiegel, 2003; Houghtalen & Talbot, 2007).

Several dissociative disorders exist, although all of them are rare. A person with a **dissociative identity disorder (DID)** (once called *multiple personality disorder*) displays characteristics of two or more distinct personalities, identities, or personality fragments. Individual personalities often have a unique set of likes and dislikes and their own reactions to situations. Some people with multiple personalities even carry several pairs of glasses because their vision changes with each personality. Moreover, each individual personality can be well adjusted when considered on its own (Ellason & Ross, 2004; Stickley & Nickeas, 2006).

The diagnosis of dissociative identity disorder is controversial. It was rarely diagnosed before 1980, when it was added as a category in the third edition of *DSM* for the first time. At that point, the number of cases increased significantly. Some clinicians suggest the increase was due to more precise identification of the disorder, while others suggest the increase was due to an overreadiness to use the classification. In addition, widespread publicity about cases of DID may have influenced patients to report symptoms of more common personality disorders in ways that made it more likely they would receive a diagnosis of DID. There are also

dissociative disorders Psychological dysfunctions characterized by the separation of different facets of a person's personality that are normally integrated.

dissociative identity disorder (DID) A disorder in which a person displays characteristics of two or more distinct personalities.

dissociative amnesia A disorder in which a significant, selective memory loss occurs.

significant cross-cultural differences in the incidence of DID (Kihlstrom, 2005a; Xiao et al., 2006).

Dissociative amnesia is another dissociative disorder in which a significant, selective memory loss occurs. Dissociative amnesia is unlike simple amnesia, which involves an actual loss of information from memory and typically results from a physiological cause. In contrast, in cases of dissociative amnesia, the "forgotten" material is still present in memory—it simply cannot be recalled. The term *repressed memories* is sometimes used to describe the lost memories of people with dissociative amnesia.

In the most severe form of dissociative amnesia, individuals cannot recall their names, are unable to recognize parents and other relatives, and do not know their addresses. In other respects, though, they may appear quite normal. Apart from an inability to remember certain facts about themselves, they may be able to recall skills and abilities that they developed earlier. For instance, even though a chef may not remember where he grew up and received training, he may still be able to prepare gourmet meals.

In some cases of dissociative amnesia, the memory loss is profound. For example, in one dramatic case, Raymond Power Jr., an attorney, husband, father of two, and Boy Scout leader, left home to go to work one morning. Two days later he was homeless, living a new life a thousand miles away, and had no memory of who he was or how he got there. He was found six months later but still had no recollection of his previous life, including any knowledge of his wife of 30 years or even that he had children (Foderaro, 2006).

dissociative fugue A form of amnesia in which the individual leaves home and sometimes assumes a new identity.

A more unusual form of amnesia is a condition known as **dissociative fugue.** In this state, people take sudden, impulsive trips and sometimes assume a new identity. After a period of time—days, months, or sometimes even years—they suddenly realize that they are in a strange place and completely forget the time they have spent wandering. Their last memories are those from the time just before they entered the fugue state (Hennig-Fast et al, 2008).

The common thread among dissociative disorders is that they allow people to escape from some anxiety-producing situation. Either the person produces a new personality to deal with stress, or the individual forgets or leaves behind the situation that caused the stress as he or she journeys to some new—and perhaps less anxiety-ridden—environment (Putnam, 2000; R. J. Brown, 2006).

Mood Disorders

From the time I woke up in the morning until the time I went to bed at night, I was unbearably miserable and seemingly incapable of any kind of joy or enthusiasm. Everything—every thought, word, movement—was an effort. Everything that once was sparkling now was flat. I seemed to myself to be dull, boring, inadequate, thick brained, unlit, unresponsive, chill skinned, bloodless, and sparrow drab. I doubted, completely, my ability to do anything well. It seemed as though my mind had slowed down and burned out to the point of being virtually useless. (Jamison, 1995a, p. 110)

We all experience mood swings. Sometimes we are happy, perhaps even euphoric; at other times we feel upset, saddened, or depressed. Such changes in mood are a normal part of everyday life. In some people, however, moods are so pronounced and lingering—like the feelings described above by writer (and psychiatrist) Kay Jamison—that they interfere with the ability to function effectively. In extreme cases, a mood may become life threatening; in other cases, it may cause the person to lose touch with reality. Situations such as these represent **mood disorders,** disturbances in emotional experience that are strong enough to intrude on everyday living.

mood disorder A disturbance in emotional experience that is strong enough to intrude on everyday living.

MAJOR DEPRESSION

President Abraham Lincoln. Queen Victoria. Newscaster Mike Wallace.

The common link among these people? Each suffered from periodic attacks of **major depression,** a severe form of depression that interferes with concentration, decision making, and sociability. Major depression is one of the more common forms of mood disorders. Some 15 million people in the United States suffer from major depression, and at any one time, 6–10% of the U.S. population is clinically depressed. Almost one in five people in the United States experiences major depression at some point in life, and 15% of college students have received a diagnosis of depression. The cost of depression is more than $80 billion a year in lost productivity (Winik, 2006; Scelfo, 2007; Simon et al., 2008).

Women are twice as likely to experience major depression as men, with one-fourth of all females apt to encounter it at some point during their lives. Furthermore, although no one is sure why, the rate of depression is going up throughout the world. Results of in-depth interviews conducted in the United States, Puerto Rico, Taiwan, Lebanon, Canada, Italy, Germany, and France indicate that the incidence of depression has increased significantly over previous rates in every area. In fact, in some countries, the likelihood that individuals will have major depression at some point in their lives is three times higher than it was for earlier generations. In addition, people are developing major depression at increasingly younger ages (Miller, 2003; Staley, Sancora, & Tagman, 2006; Kendler et al., 2006a).

When psychologists speak of major depression, they do not mean the sadness that comes from experiencing one of life's disappointments that we all have experienced. Some depression is normal after the breakup of a long-term relationship, the death of a loved one, or the loss of a job. It is normal even after less serious problems, such as doing badly on a test or having a romantic partner forget one's birthday.

People who suffer from major depression experience similar feelings, but the severity tends to be considerably greater. They may feel useless, worthless, and lonely, and they may think the future is hopeless and no one can help them. They may lose their appetite and have no energy. Moreover, they may experience such feelings for months or even years. They may cry uncontrollably, have sleep disturbances, and be at risk for suicide. The depth and duration of such behavior are the hallmarks of major depression. (Figure 5 provides a self-assessment of depression.)

major depression A severe form of depression that interferes with concentration, decision making, and sociability.

> **Study Alert**
> Major depression differs from the normal depression that occasionally occurs during most people's lives; major depression is more intense, lasts longer, and may have no clear trigger.

A Test for Depression

To complete the questionnaire, count the number of statements with which you agree:

1. I feel downhearted, blue, and sad.
2. I don't enjoy the things that I used to.
3. I feel that others would be better off if I were dead.
4. I feel that I am not useful or needed.
5. I notice that I am losing weight.
6. I have trouble sleeping through the night.
7. I am restless and can't keep still.
8. My mind isn't as clear as it used to be.
9. I get tired for no reason.
10. I feel hopeless about the future.

Scoring: If you agree with at least five of the statements, including either item 1 or 2, and if you have had these symptoms for at least two weeks, help from a professional is strongly recommended. If you answer yes to number 3, you should get help immediately.

FIGURE 5 This is a version of a test distributed by mental health organizations during the annual National Depression Screening Day, a nationwide event that seeks to identify people who are suffering from depression that is severe enough to warrant psychological intervention. (Source: National Depression Screening Day, 2003.)

MANIA AND BIPOLAR DISORDER

mania An extended state of intense, wild elation.

While depression leads to the depths of despair, mania leads to emotional heights. **Mania** is an extended state of intense, wild elation. People experiencing mania feel intense happiness, power, invulnerability, and energy. Believing they will succeed at anything they attempt, they may become involved in wild schemes. Consider, for example, the following description of an individual who experienced a manic episode:

> Mr. O'Reilly took a leave of absence from his civil service job. He purchased a large number of cuckoo clocks and then an expensive car, which he planned to use as a mobile showroom for his wares, anticipating that he would make a great deal of money. He proceeded to "tear around town" buying and selling clocks and other merchandise, and when he was not out, he was continuously on the phone making "deals." . . . He was $3,000 in debt and had driven his family to exhaustion with his excessive activity and talkativeness. He said, however, that he felt "on top of the world." (Spitzer et al., 1983, p. 115)

bipolar disorder A disorder in which a person alternates between periods of euphoric feelings of mania and periods of depression.

Typically, people sequentially experience periods of mania and depression. This alternation of mania and depression is called **bipolar disorder** (a condition previously known as manic-depressive disorder). The swings between highs and lows may occur a few days apart or may alternate over a period of years. In addition, in bipolar disorder, periods of depression are usually longer than periods of mania.

Ironically, some of society's most creative individuals may have suffered from bipolar disorder. The imagination, drive, excitement, and energy that they display during manic stages allow them to make unusually creative contributions. For instance, historical analysis of the composer Robert Schumann's music shows that he was most prolific during periods of mania. In contrast, his output dropped off drastically during periods of depression (see Figure 6). On the other hand, the high output associated with mania does not necessarily lead to higher quality: Some of Schumann's greatest works were created outside his periods of mania (Ludwig, 1996; Szegedy Maszak, 2003).

FIGURE 6 The number of pieces written by composer Robert Schumann in a given year is related to his periods of depression and mania (Slater & Meyer, 1959; reprinted in Jamison, 1993). Why do you think mania might be associated with creative productivity in some people?

Despite the creative fires that may be lit by mania, persons who experience this disorder often show a recklessness that produces emotional and sometimes physical self-injury. They may alienate people with their talkativeness, inflated self-esteem, and indifference to the needs of others.

CAUSES OF MOOD DISORDERS

Because they represent a major mental health problem, mood disorders—and, in particular, depression—have received a good deal of study. Several approaches have been used to explain the disorders.

Some mood disorders clearly have genetic and biochemical roots. In fact, most evidence suggests that bipolar disorders are caused primarily by biological factors. For instance, bipolar disorder (and some forms of major depression) clearly runs in some families. Furthermore, researchers have found that several neurotransmitters play a role in depression. For example, alterations in the functioning of serotonin and norepinephrine in the brain are related to the disorder (Plomin & McGuffin, 2003; Kato, 2007; Popa et al., 2008).

Other explanations for depression have also included a focus on psychological causes. For instance, proponents of psychoanalytic approaches see depression as the result of feelings of loss (real or potential) or of anger directed at oneself. One psychoanalytic approach, for instance, suggests that depression is produced by the loss or threatened loss of a parent early in life (Vanheule et al., 2006).

Behavioral theories of depression argue that the stresses of life produce a reduction in positive reinforcers. As a result, people begin to withdraw, which only reduces positive reinforcers further. In addition, people receive attention for their depressive behavior, which further reinforces the depression (Lewinsohn & Essau, 2002; Lewinsohn et al., 2003).

Some explanations for mood disorders attribute them to cognitive factors. For example, psychologist Martin Seligman suggests that depression is largely a response to learned helplessness. *Learned helplessness* is a learned expectation that events in one's life are uncontrollable and that one cannot escape from the situation. As a consequence, people simply give up fighting aversive events and submit to them, which thereby produces depression. Other theorists go a step further and suggest that depression results from hopelessness, a combination of learned helplessness and an expectation that negative outcomes in one's life are inevitable (Kwon & Laurenceau, 2002; Maier & Watkins, 2000; Bjornstad, 2006).

Clinical psychologist Aaron Beck has proposed that faulty cognitions underlie people's depressed feelings. Specifically, his cognitive theory of depression suggests that depressed individuals typically view themselves as life's losers and blame themselves whenever anything goes wrong. By focusing on the negative side of situations, they feel inept and unable to act constructively to change their environment. In sum, their negative cognitions lead to feelings of depression (Newman et al., 2002).

Brain imaging studies suggest that people with depression experience a general blunting of emotional reactions. For example, one study found that the brains of people with depression showed significantly less activation when they viewed photos of human faces displaying strong emotions than did those without the disorder (Gotlib et al., 2004).

Other explanations of depression derive from evolutionary psychology, which considers how our genetic inheritance from our ancestors influences our behavior. In the evolutionary view, depression is an adaptive response to unattainable goals. When people fruitlessly pursue an ever-elusive goal, depression begins, ending pursuit of the goal. Ultimately, when the depression lifts, people can turn to other, more reasonable goals. In this view, depression serves a positive function and in the long run increases the chances of survival for particular individuals, who can then pass the behavior to their offspring. Such reasoning, of course, is highly speculative (Nesse, 2000, Siegert & Ward, 2002; Pfeffer, 2006).

The various theories of depression have not provided a complete answer to an elusive question that has dogged researchers: Why does depression occur in approximately twice as many women as men—a pattern that is similar across a variety of cultures?

One explanation suggests that the stress women experience may be greater than the stress men experience at certain points in their lives—such as when a woman must simultaneously earn a living and be the primary caregiver for her children. In addition, women have a higher risk for physical and sexual abuse, typically earn lower wages than men, report greater unhappiness with their marriages, and generally experience chronic negative circumstances. Furthermore, women and men may respond to stress with different coping mechanisms. For instance, men may abuse drugs, while women respond with depression (Holden, 2005; Nolen-Hoeksema, 2007; Hyde, Mezulis, & Abramson, 2008).

Biological factors may also explain some women's depression. For example, the rate of female depression begins to rise during puberty, so some psychologists believe that hormones make women more vulnerable to the disorder. In addition, 25–50% of women who take oral contraceptives report symptoms of depression, and depression that occurs after the birth of a child is linked to hormonal changes. Finally, structural differences in men's and women's brains that we discussed in the neuroscience and behavior modules may be related to gender differences in depression (Holden, 2005; Graham, Bancroft, & Doll, 2007; Solomon & Herman, 2009).

Ultimately, it is clear that researchers have discovered no definitive solutions to the puzzle of depression, and there are many alternative explanations. Most likely, a complex interaction of several factors causes mood disorders.

Schizophrenia

> Things that relate, the town of Antelope, Oregon, Jonestown, Charlie Manson, the Hillside Strangler, the Zodiac Killer, Watergate, King's trial in L.A., and many more. In the last 7 years alone, over 23 Star Wars scientists committed suicide for no apparent reason. The AIDS cover-up, the conference in South America in 87 had over 1,000 doctors claim that insects can transmit it. To be able to read one's thoughts and place thoughts in one's mind without the person knowing it's being done. Realization is a reality of bioelectromagnetic control, which is thought transfer and emotional control, recording individual brainwave frequencies of thought, sensation, and emotions. (Nolen-Heoksema, 2007, pp. 385–386).

This excerpt illustrates the efforts of a person with schizophrenia, one of the more severe forms of mental disturbance, to communicate. People with schizophrenia account for by far the largest percentage of those hospitalized for psychological disorders. They are also in many respects the least likely to recover from their difficulties.

schizophrenia A class of disorders in which severe distortion of reality occurs.

Schizophrenia refers to a class of disorders in which severe distortion of reality occurs. Thinking, perception, and emotion may deteriorate; the individual may withdraw from social interaction; and the person may display bizarre behavior. Although there are several types of schizophrenia (see Figure 7), the distinctions between them are not always clear. Moreover, the symptoms displayed by persons with schizophrenia may vary considerably over time, and people with schizophrenia show significant differences in the pattern of their symptoms even when they are labeled with the same diagnostic category. Nonetheless, a number of characteristics reliably distinguish schizophrenia from other disorders. They include the following:

- *Decline from a previous level of functioning.* An individual can no longer carry out activities he or she was once able to do.
- *Disturbances of thought and speech.* People with schizophrenia use logic and language in a peculiar way. Their thinking often does not make sense, and

Types of Schizophrenia	
Type	**Symptoms**
Disorganized (hebephrenic) schizophrenia	Inappropriate laughter and giggling, silliness, incoherent speech, infantile behavior, strange and sometimes obscene behavior
Paranoid schizophrenia	Delusions and hallucinations of persecution or of greatness, loss of judgment, erratic and unpredictable behavior
Catatonic schizophrenia	Major disturbances in movement; in some phases, loss of all motion, with patient frozen into a single position, remaining that way for hours and sometimes even days; in other phases, hyperactivity and wild, sometimes violent, movement
Undifferentiated schizophrenia	Variable mixture of major symptoms of schizophrenia; classification used for patients who cannot be typed into any of the more specific categories
Residual schizophrenia	Minor signs of schizophrenia after a more serious episode

FIGURE 7 The distinctions among the different types of schizophrenia are not always clear cut, and symptoms may vary considerably over time.

their logic is frequently faulty, which is referred to as a *formal thought disorder*. They also do not follow conventional linguistic rules (Penn et al., 1997). Consider, for example, the following response to the question "Why do you think people believe in God?"

Uh, let's, I don't know why, let's see, balloon travel. He holds it up for you, the balloon. He don't let you fall out, your little legs sticking down through the clouds. He's down to the smokestack, looking through the smoke trying to get the balloon gassed up you know. Way they're flying on top that way, legs sticking out. I don't know, looking down on the ground, heck, that'd make you so dizzy you just stay and sleep you know, hold down and sleep there. I used to be sleep outdoors, you know, sleep outdoors instead of going home. (Chapman & Chapman, 1973, p. 3)

As this selection illustrates, although the basic grammatical structure may be intact, the substance of thinking characteristic of schizophrenia is often illogical, garbled, and lacking in meaningful content (Holden, 2003; Heinrichs, 2005).

- *Delusions.* People with schizophrenia often have delusions, firmly held, unshakable beliefs with no basis in reality. Among the common delusions people with schizophrenia experience are the beliefs that they are being controlled by someone else, they are being persecuted by others, and their thoughts are being broadcast so that others know what they are thinking (Coltheart, Langdon, & McKay, 2007; Startup, Bucci, & Langdon, 2009).
- *Hallucinations and perceptual disorders.* People with schizophrenia do not perceive the world as most other people do. They also may have *hallucinations,* the experience of perceiving things that do not actually exist. Furthermore, they may see, hear, or smell things differently from others (see Figure 8); they do not even have a sense of their bodies in the way that others do and have difficulty determining where their bodies stop and the rest of the world begins (Copolov et al., 2003; Botvinick, 2004; Thomas et al., 2007).

FIGURE 8 This unusual art was created by an individual suffering from severe mental disturbance.

- *Emotional disturbances*. People with schizophrenia sometimes show a lack of emotion in which even the most dramatic events produce little or no emotional response. Conversely, they may display emotion that is inappropriate to a situation. For example, a person with schizophrenia may laugh uproariously at a funeral or react with anger when being helped by someone.
- *Withdrawal*. People with schizophrenia tend to have little interest in others. They tend not to socialize or hold real conversations with others, although they may talk at another person. In the most extreme cases, they do not even acknowledge the presence of other people and appear to be in their own isolated world.

Usually, the onset of schizophrenia occurs in early adulthood, and the symptoms follow one of two primary courses. In *process schizophrenia,* the symptoms develop slowly and subtly. There may be a gradual withdrawal from the world, excessive daydreaming, and a blunting of emotion until eventually the disorder reaches the point where others cannot overlook it. In other cases, known as *reactive schizophrenia,* the onset of symptoms is sudden and conspicuous. The treatment outlook for reactive schizophrenia is relatively favorable, but process schizophrenia has proved more difficult to treat.

DSM-IV-TR classifies the symptoms of schizophrenia into two types. Positive-symptom schizophrenia is indicated by the presence of disordered behavior such as hallucinations, delusions, and emotional extremes. In contrast, negative-symptom schizophrenia shows an absence or loss of normal functioning, such as social withdrawal or blunted emotions. Schizophrenia researchers sometimes speak of *Type I schizophrenia,* in which positive symptoms are dominant, and *Type II schizophrenia,* in which negative symptoms are more prominent (Buchanan et al., 2007; Levine & Rabinowitz, 2007).

The distinction between Type I and Type II schizophrenia is important because it suggests that two different processes might trigger schizophrenia. Furthermore, it has implications for predicting treatment outcomes.

SOLVING THE PUZZLE OF SCHIZOPHRENIA: BIOLOGICAL CAUSES

Although schizophrenic behavior clearly departs radically from normal behavior, its causes are less apparent. It does appear, however, that schizophrenia has both biological and environmental origins (Sawa & Snyder, 2002).

Let's first consider the evidence pointing to a biological cause. Because schizophrenia is more common in some families than in others, genetic factors seem to

> **Study Alert**
>
> In Type I schizophrenia, positive symptoms (in which hallucinations, delusions, and emotional extremes are present) are dominant; in Type II schizophrenia, negative symptoms (characterized by an absence or loss of normal functioning) are dominant.

Risk of Developing Schizophrenia, Based on Genetic Relatedness to a Person with Schizophrenia		
Relationship	Genetic Relatedness, %	Risk of Developing Schizophrenia, %
Identical twin	100	48
Child of two schizophrenic parents	100	46
Fraternal twin	50	17
Offspring of one schizophrenic parent	50	17
Sibling	50	9
Nephew or niece	25	4
Spouse	0	2
Unrelated person	0	1

FIGURE 9 The closer the genetic links between two people, the greater the likelihood that if one experiences schizophrenia, so will the other sometime during his or her lifetime. However, genetics is not the full story; if it were, the risk of identical twins having schizophrenia would be 100% and not the 48% shown in this figure. (Source: Gottesman, 1991.)

be involved in producing at least a susceptibility to or readiness for developing schizophrenia. For example, the closer the genetic link between a person with schizophrenia and another individual, the greater the likelihood that the other person will experience the disorder (see Figure 9; Brzustowicz et al., 2000; Plomin & McGuffin, 2003; Gottesman & Hanson, 2005).

However, if genetics alone were responsible for schizophrenia, the chance of both of two identical twins having schizophrenia would be 100% instead of just under 50% because identical twins have the same genetic makeup. Moreover, attempts to find a link between schizophrenia and a particular gene have been only partly successful. Apparently, genetic factors alone do not produce schizophrenia (Franzek & Beckmann, 1996; Lenzenweger & Dworkin, 1998).

One intriguing biological hypothesis to explain schizophrenia is that the brains of people with the disorder may harbor either a biochemical imbalance or a structural abnormality. For example, the *dopamine hypothesis* suggests that schizophrenia occurs when there is excess activity in the areas of the brain that use dopamine as a neurotransmitter. This hypothesis came to light after the discovery that drugs that block dopamine action in brain pathways can be highly effective in reducing the symptoms of schizophrenia. Other research suggests that glutamate, another neurotransmitter, may be a major contributor to the disorder (Ohara, 2007; Stone, Morrison, & Pilowsky, 2007; Howes & Kapur, 2009).

Some biological explanations propose that structural abnormalities exist in the brains of people with schizophrenia perhaps as a result of exposure to a virus during prenatal development. For example, some research shows abnormalities in the neural circuits of the cortex and limbic systems of individuals with schizophrenia. Consistent with such research, people with schizophrenia and those without the disorder show different brain functioning (see Figure 10; Bartzokis et al., 2003; Reichenberg & Harvey, 2007; Reichenberg et al., 2009).

Further evidence for the importance of biological factors shows that when people with schizophrenia hear voices during hallucinations, the parts of the brain responsible for hearing and language processing become active. When they have visual hallucinations, the parts of the brain involved in movement and color are active. At the same time, people with schizophrenia often have unusually low activity in the brain's frontal lobes—the parts of the brain involved with emotional regulation, insight, and the evaluation of sensory stimuli (Stern & Silbersweig, 2001).

Neuroscience in Your Life: Brain Changes with Schizophrenia

FIGURE 10 Changes in the brain have been found in people with schizophrenia. In an MRI reconstruction of the brain of a person with schizophrenia (a), the hippocampi (yellow) are shrunken, and the ventricles (gray) are enlarged and fluid-filled. In contrast, an MRI reconstruction of the brain of a person without the disorder (b) is structurally different with larger hippocampi and smaller ventricles. (Source: N.C. Andreasen, University of Iowa.)

(a)   (b)

ENVIRONMENTAL PERSPECTIVES ON SCHIZOPHRENIA

Although biological factors provide important pieces of the puzzle of schizophrenia, we still need to consider past and current experiences in the environments of people who develop the disturbance. For instance, psychoanalytic approaches suggest that schizophrenia is a form of regression to earlier experiences and stages of life. Freud believed that people with schizophrenia lack egos that are strong enough to cope with their unacceptable impulses. They regress to the oral stage—a time when the id and ego are not yet separated. Therefore, individuals with schizophrenia essentially lack an ego and act out impulses without concern for reality.

Although this reasoning is theoretically plausible, little evidence supports psychoanalytic explanations. Somewhat more convincing theories look toward the emotional and communication patterns of the families of people with schizophrenia. For instance, some researchers suggest that schizophrenia results from high levels of expressed emotion. *Expressed emotion* is an interaction style characterized by family members' criticism, hostility, and emotional intrusiveness. Other researchers suggest that faulty communication patterns lie at the heart of schizophrenia (Miklowitz & Thompson, 2003; Lobban, Barrowclough, & Jones, 2006).

Psychologists who take a cognitive perspective on schizophrenia suggest that the problems in thinking that people with the disorder experience point to a cognitive cause. Some suggest that schizophrenia results from *overattention* to stimuli in the environment. Rather than being able to screen out unimportant or inconsequential stimuli and focus on the most important things in the environment, people with schizophrenia may be excessively receptive to virtually everything in their environment. As a consequence, their information-processing capabilities become overloaded and eventually break down. Other cognitive experts argue that schizophrenia results from *underattention* to certain stimuli. According to this explanation, people with schizophrenia fail to focus sufficiently on important stimuli and pay attention to other, less important information in their surroundings (Cadenhead & Braff, 1995).

Although it is plausible that overattention and underattention are related to different forms of schizophrenia, these phenomena do not explain the origins of such information-processing disorders. Consequently, cognitive approaches—like other environmental explanations—do not provide a full explanation of the disorder.

THE MULTIPLE CAUSES OF SCHIZOPHRENIA

The predominant approach used to explain the onset of schizophrenia today, the *predisposition model of schizophrenia,* incorporates a number of biological and environmental factors. This model suggests that individuals may inherit a predisposition or an inborn sensitivity to schizophrenia that makes them particularly vulnerable to stressful factors in the environment, such as social rejection or dysfunctional family communication patterns. The stressors may vary, but if they are strong enough and are coupled with a genetic predisposition, the result will be the onset of schizophrenia. Similarly, a strong genetic predisposition may lead to the onset of schizophrenia even when the environmental stressors are relatively weak.

In short, the models used today associate schizophrenia with several kinds of biological and environmental factors. It is increasingly clear, then, that no single factor but a combination of interrelated variables produces schizophrenia (Meltzer, 2000; McDonald & Murray, 2004; Opler et al., 2008).

> **Study Alert**
>
> Remember that the multiple causes of schizophrenia include biological and environmental factors.

Personality Disorders

I had always wanted lots of things; as a child I can remember wanting a bullet that a friend of mine had brought in to show the class. I took it and put it into my school bag and when my friend noticed it was missing, I was the one who stayed after school with him and searched the room, and I was the one who sat with him and bitched about the other kids and how one of them took his bullet. I even went home with him to help him break the news to his uncle, who had brought it home from the war for him.

But that was petty compared with the stuff I did later. I wanted a Ph.D. very badly, but I didn't want to work very hard—just enough to get by. I never did the experiments I reported; hell, I was smart enough to make up the results. I knew enough about statistics to make anything look plausible. I got my master's degree without even spending one hour in a laboratory. I mean, the professors believed anything. I'd stay out all night drinking and being with my friends, and the next day I'd get in just before them and tell 'em I'd been in the lab all night. They'd actually feel sorry for me. (Duke & Nowicki, 1979, pp. 309–310)

This excerpt provides a graphic first-person account of a person with a personality disorder. A **personality disorder** is characterized by a set of inflexible, maladaptive behavior patterns that keep a person from functioning appropriately in society. Personality disorders differ from the other problems we have discussed because those affected by them often have little sense of personal distress associated with the psychological maladjustment. In fact, people with personality disorders frequently lead seemingly normal lives. However, just below the surface lies a set of inflexible, maladaptive personality traits that do not permit these individuals to function as members of society (Davis & Millon, 1999; Clarkin & Lenzenweger, 2004; Friedman, Oltmanns, & Turkheimer, 2007).

The best-known type of personality disorder, illustrated by the case above, is the **antisocial personality disorder** (sometimes referred to as a sociopathic personality). Individuals with this disturbance show no regard for the moral and ethical rules of society or the rights of others. Although they can appear quite intelligent and likable (at least at first), upon closer examination they turn out to be manipulative and deceptive. Moreover, they lack any guilt or anxiety about their wrongdoing. When those with antisocial personality disorder behave in a way that injures someone else, they understand intellectually that they have caused harm but feel no remorse (Lykken, 1995; Goodwin & Hamilton, 2003; Hilarski, 2007).

People with antisocial personality disorder are often impulsive and lack the ability to withstand frustration. They can be extremely manipulative. They also may have

personality disorder A disorder characterized by a set of inflexible, maladaptive behavior patterns that keep a person from functioning appropriately in society.

antisocial personality disorder A disorder in which individuals show no regard for the moral and ethical rules of society or the rights of others.

> **Study Alert**
>
> Unlike most psychological disorders, personality disorders produce little or no personal distress.

excellent social skills; they can be charming, engaging, and highly persuasive. Some of the best con artists have antisocial personalities.

What causes such an unusual constellation of problem behaviors? A variety of factors have been suggested ranging from an inability to experience emotions appropriately to problems in family relationships. For example, in many cases of antisocial behavior, the individual has come from a home in which a parent has died or left or one in which there is a lack of affection, a lack of consistency in discipline, or outright rejection. Other explanations concentrate on sociocultural factors because an unusually high proportion of people with antisocial personalities come from lower socio-economic groups. Still, no one has been able to pinpoint the specific causes of antisocial personalities, and it is likely that some combination of factors is responsible (Nigg & Goldsmith, 1994; Rosenstein & Horowitz, 1996; Costa & Widiger, 2002).

borderline personality disorder
A disorder in which individuals have difficulty developing a secure sense of who they are.

People with **borderline personality disorder** have difficulty developing a secure sense of who they are. As a consequence, they tend to rely on relationships with others to define their identity. The problem with this strategy is that rejections are devastating. Furthermore, people with this disorder distrust others and have difficulty controlling their anger. Their emotional volatility leads to impulsive and self-destructive behavior. Individuals with borderline personality disorder often feel empty and alone, and they have difficulty cooperating with others. They may form intense, sudden, one-sided relationships in which they demand the attention of another person and then feel angry when they don't receive it. One reason for this behavior is that they may have a background in which others discounted or criticized their emotional reactions, and they may not have learned to regulate their emotions effectively (Links, Eynan, & Heisel, 2007; King-Casas et al., 2008; Hopwood et al., 2009).

narcissistic personality disorder
A personality disturbance characterized by an exaggerated sense of self-importance.

Another example of a personality disturbance is the **narcissistic personality disorder,** which is characterized by an exaggerated sense of self-importance. Those with the disorder expect special treatment from others while at the same time disregarding others' feelings. In some ways, in fact, the main attribute of the narcissistic personality is an inability to experience empathy for other people.

There are several other categories of personality disorder that range in severity from individuals who may simply be regarded by others as eccentric, obnoxious, or difficult to people who act in a manner that is criminal and dangerous to others. Although they are not out of touch with reality like people with schizophrenia, people with personality disorders lead lives that put them on the fringes of society (Millon, Davis, & Millon, 2000; Trull & Widiger, 2003).

Childhood Disorders

We typically view childhood as a time of innocence and relative freedom from stress. In reality, though, almost 20% of children and 40% of adolescents experience significant emotional or behavioral disorders (Romano et al., 2001; Broidy, Nagin, & Tremblay, 2003; Nolen-Hoeksema, 2007).

For example, although major depression is more prevalent in adults, around 2.5% of children and more than 8% of adolescents suffer from the disorder. In fact, by the time they reach age 20, between 15–20% of children and adolescents will experience an episode of major depression (Garber & Horowitz, 2002).

Children do not always display depression the same way adults do. Rather than showing profound sadness or hopelessness, childhood depression may produce the expression of exaggerated fears, clinginess, or avoidance of everyday activities. In older children, the symptoms may be sulking, school problems, and even acts of delinquency (Wenar, 1994; Seroczynski, Jacquez, & Cole, 2003; Koplewicz, 2002).

attention-deficit hyperactivity disorder (ADHD) A disorder marked by inattention, impulsiveness, a low tolerance for frustration, and a great deal of inappropriate activity.

A considerably more common childhood disorder is **attention-deficit hyperactivity disorder,** or **ADHD,** a disorder marked by inattention, impulsiveness, a low tolerance for frustration, and generally a great deal of inappropriate activity. Although all children show such behavior some of the time, it is so common in children diagnosed with ADHD that it interferes with their everyday functioning (Barkley, 2005; Swanson, Harris, & Graham, 2003; Smith, Barkley, & Shapiro, 2006).

ADHD is surprisingly widespread with estimates ranging between 3–5% of the school-age population—or some 3.5 million children under the age of 18 in the United States. Children diagnosed with the disorder are often exhausting to parents and teachers, and even their peers find them difficult to deal with.

The cause of ADHD is not known, although most experts feel that it is produced by dysfunctions in the nervous system. For example, one theory suggests that unusually low levels of arousal in the central nervous system cause ADHD. To compensate, children with ADHD seek out stimulation to increase arousal. Still, such theories are speculative. Furthermore, because many children occasionally show behaviors characteristic of ADHD, it often is misdiagnosed or in some cases overdiagnosed. Only the frequency and persistence of the symptoms of ADHD allow for a correct diagnosis, which only a trained professional can do (Barkley, 2000; Sciutto & Eisenberg, 2007).

Autism, a severe developmental disability that impairs children's ability to communicate and relate to others, is another childhood disorder that usually appears in the first three years and typically continues throughout life. Children with autism have difficulties in both verbal and nonverbal communication, and they may avoid social contact. About one in 110 children are now thought to have the disorder, and its prevalence has risen significantly in the last decade. Whether the increase is the result of an actual rise in the incidence of autism or is due to better reporting is a question of intense debate among researchers (Rice, 2009).

In the most severe cases of autism, children display self-injurious behavior and must wear protective head gear.

Other Disorders

It's important to keep in mind that the various forms of psychological disorders described in *DSM-IV-TR* cover much more ground than we have been able to discuss in this module. Some relate to topics previously considered in other chapters. For example, *psychoactive substance use disorder* relates to problems that arise from the use and abuse of drugs. Furthermore, *alcohol use disorders* are among the most serious and widespread problems. Both psychoactive substance use disorder and alcohol use disorder co-occur with many other psychological disorders such as mood disorders, posttraumatic stress disorder, and schizophrenia, which complicates treatment considerably (Salgado, Quinlan, & Zlotnick, 2007).

Another widespread problem is *eating disorders*. They include such disorders as *anorexia nervosa* and *bulimia*, which we considered in the chapter on motivation and emotion, as well as *binge-eating disorder*, characterized by binge eating without behaviors designed to prevent weight gain. Finally, *sexual disorders*, in which one's sexual activity is unsatisfactory, are another important class of problems. They include *sexual desire disorders*, *sexual arousal disorders*, and *paraphilias*, atypical sexual activities that may include nonhuman objects or nonconsenting partners.

Another important class of disorders is *organic mental disorders*, some of which we touched on previously. These are problems that have a purely biological basis, such as Alzheimer's disease and some types of mental retardation. Remember, there are other disorders that we have not mentioned at all, and each of the classes we have discussed can be divided into several subcategories (Kopelman & Fleminger, 2002; Pratt et al., 2003; Reijonen et al., 2003).

autism A severe developmental disability that impairs children's ability to communicate and relate to others.

RECAP/EVALUATE/RETHINK

RECAP

What are the major psychological disorders?

- Anxiety disorders are present when a person experiences so much anxiety that it affects daily functioning. Specific types of anxiety disorders include phobic disorder, panic disorder, generalized anxiety disorder, and obsessive-compulsive disorder. (p. 453)
- Somatoform disorders are psychological difficulties that take on a physical (somatic) form but for which there is no medical cause. Examples are hypochondriasis and conversion disorders. (p. 458)
- Dissociative disorders are marked by the separation, or dissociation, of different facets of a person's personality that are usually integrated. Major kinds of dissociative disorders include dissociative identity disorder, dissociative amnesia, and dissociative fugue. (p. 458)
- Mood disorders are characterized by emotional states of depression or euphoria so strong that they intrude on everyday living. They include major depression and bipolar disorder. (p. 460)
- Schizophrenia is one of the more severe forms of mental illness. Symptoms of schizophrenia include declines in functioning, thought and language disturbances, perceptual disorders, emotional disturbance, and withdrawal from others. (p. 464)
- Strong evidence links schizophrenia to genetic, biochemical, and environmental factors. According to the predisposition model, an interaction among various factors produces the disorder. (p. 466)
- People with personality disorders experience little or no personal distress, but they do suffer from an inability to function as normal members of society. These disorders include antisocial personality disorder, borderline personality disorder, and narcissistic personality disorder. (p. 469)
- Childhood disorders include major depression, attention-deficit hyperactivity disorder (ADHD), and autism. (p. 470)

EVALUATE

1. Kathy is terrified of elevators. She could be suffering from a(n)
   a. Obsessive-compulsive disorder
   b. Phobic disorder
   c. Panic disorder
   d. Generalized anxiety disorder

2. Carmen described an incident in which her anxiety suddenly rose to a peak, and she felt a sense of impending doom. Carmen experienced a(n) _____ _____.
3. Troubling thoughts that persist for weeks or months are known as
   a. Obsessions
   b. Compulsions
   c. Rituals
   d. Panic attacks
4. An overpowering urge to carry out a strange ritual is called a(n) _____.
5. The separation of the personality, which provides escape from stressful situations, is the key factor in _____ disorders.
6. States of extreme euphoria and energy paired with severe depression characterize _____ disorder.
7. _____ schizophrenia is characterized by symptoms that are sudden and of easily identifiable onset; _____ schizophrenia develops gradually over a person's life span.
8. The _____ _____ states that schizophrenia may be caused by an excess of certain neurotransmitters in the brain.

RETHINK

1. What cultural factors might contribute to the rate of anxiety disorders found in a culture? How might the experience of anxiety differ among people of different cultures?
2. *From the perspective of a social worker:* Personality disorders are often not apparent to others, and many people with these problems seem to live basically normal lives and are not a threat to others. Because these people often appear from the outside to function well in society, why should they be considered psychologically disordered?

Answers to Evaluate Questions

1. b; 2. panic attack; 3. a; 4. compulsion; 5. dissociative; 6. bipolar; 7. reactive, process; 8. dopamine hypothesis

KEY TERMS

anxiety disorder p. 453

phobias p. 454

panic disorder p. 454

generalized anxiety
  disorder p. 455

obsessive-compulsive
  disorder (OCD) p. 455

obsession p. 455

compulsion p. 456

somatoform
  disorders p. 458

hypochondriasis p. 458

conversion disorder p. 458

dissociative
  disorders p. 459

dissociative identity
  disorder (DID) p. 459

dissociative amnesia p. 460

dissociative fugue p. 460

mood disorder p. 460

major depression p. 461

mania p. 462

bipolar disorder p. 462

schizophrenia p. 464

personality disorder p. 469

antisocial personality
  disorder p. 469

borderline personality
  disorder p. 470

narcissistic personality
  disorder p. 470

attention-deficit
  hyperactivity disorder
  (ADHD) p. 470

autism p. 471

Psychological Disorders in Perspective

Key Concepts

How prevalent are psychological disorders?

What indicators signal a need for the help of a mental health practitioner?

How common are the kinds of psychological disorders we've been discussing? Here's one answer: Every second person you meet in the United States is likely to suffer at some point during his or her life from a psychological disorder.

That's the conclusion drawn from a massive study on the prevalence of psychological disorders. In that study, researchers conducted face-to-face interviews with more than 8,000 men and women between the ages of 15 and 54. The sample was designed to be representative of the population of the United States. According to results of the study, 48% of those interviewed had experienced a disorder at some point in their lives. In addition, 30% experienced a disorder in any particular year, and the number of people who experienced simultaneous multiple disorders (known as *comorbidity*) was significant (Welkowitz et al., 2000; Merikangas et al., 2007; Kessler & Wang, 2008).

The most common disorder reported in the study was depression; 17% of those surveyed reported at least one major episode. Ten percent had suffered from depression during the current year. The next most common disorder was alcohol dependence, which occurred at a lifetime incidence rate of 14%. In addition, 7% of those interviewed had experienced alcohol dependence in the last year. Other frequently occurring psychological disorders were drug dependence, disorders involving panic (such as an overwhelming fear of talking to strangers and terror of heights), and posttraumatic stress disorder.

Although some researchers think the estimates of severe disorders may be too high (Narrow et al., 2002), the national findings are consistent with studies of college students and their psychological difficulties. For example, in one study of the problems of students who visited a college counseling center, more than 40% of students reported being depressed (see Figure 1). These figures include only students who sought help from the counseling center and not those who did not seek treatment. Consequently, the figures are not representative of the entire college population (Benton et al., 2003; also see *Applying Psychology in the 21st Century* on page 477).

The significant level of psychological disorders is a problem not only in the United States; according to the World Health Organization, mental health difficulties are also a global concern. Throughout the world, psychological disorders are widespread. Furthermore, there are economic disparities in treatment; more affluent people with mild disorders receive more and better treatment than poor people who have more severe disorders. In fact, psychological disorders make up 14% of global illness, and 90% of people in developing countries receive no care at all for their disorders (see Figure 2 on page 476; The WHO World Mental Health Survey Consortium, 2004; Jacob et al., 2007; Wang et al., 2007).

Also, keep in mind that the incidence of specific disorders varies significantly in other cultures. For instance, cross-cultural surveys show that the incidence of major depression varies significantly from one culture to another. The probability of having at least one episode of depression is only 1.5% in Taiwan and 2.9% in Korea compared with 11.6% in New Zealand and 16.4% in France. Such notable differences underscore the importance of considering the cultural context of psychological disorders (Weissman et al., 1997; Tseng, 2003).

Study Alert

Remember that the incidence of various types of psychological disorders in the general population is surprisingly high.

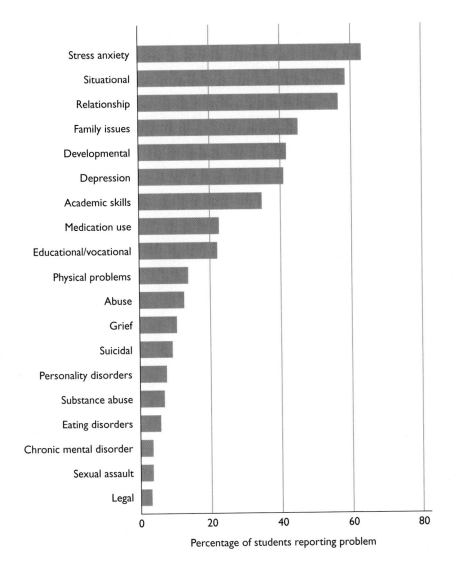

FIGURE 1 The problems reported by students visiting a college counseling center. Would you have predicted this pattern of psychological difficulties? (Source: Benton et al., 2003.)

The Social and Cultural Context of Psychological Disorders

In considering the nature of the psychological disorders described in *DSM-IV-TR*, it's important to keep in mind that the specific disorders reflect Western cultures at the turn of the 21st century. The classification system provides a snapshot of how its authors viewed mental disorder when it was published. In fact, the development of the most recent version of the *DSM* was a source of great debate, which in part reflects issues that divide society.

For example, two disorders caused particular controversy during the revision process. One, known as *self-defeating personality disorde*r, was ultimately removed from the appendix, where it had appeared in the previous revision. The term *self-defeating personality disorder* had been applied to cases in which people who were treated unpleasantly or demeaningly in relationships neither left nor took other action. It was typically used to describe people who remained in abusive relationships.

Although some clinicians argued that it was a valid category they observed in clinical practice, the disorder lacked enough research evidence to support its designation

Study Alert

It is important to understand that the *DSM* is a living document that presents a view of disorders that reflects the culture and historical context of its authors.

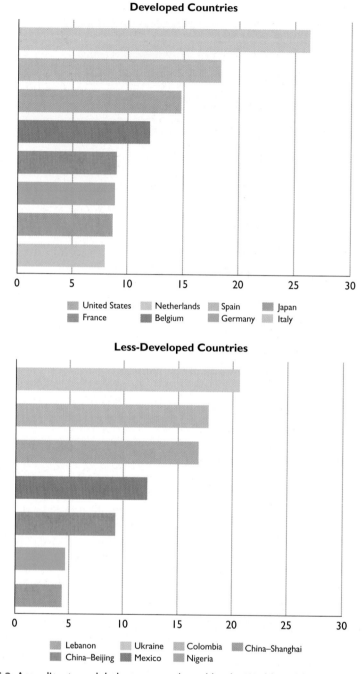

FIGURE 2 According to a global survey conducted by the World Health Organization, the prevalence of psychological disorders is widespread. These figures show the prevalence of any psychological disorder within the last 12 months. (Source: The WHO World Mental Health Survey Consortium, 2004, Table 3.)

as a disorder in *DSM*. Furthermore, some critics complained that use of the label had the effect of condemning targets of abuse for their plight—a blame-the-victim phenomenon—and as a result, the category was removed from the manual.

A second and even more controversial category was *premenstrual dysphoric disorder,* which is characterized by severe, incapacitating mood changes or depression related to a woman's menstrual cycle. Some critics argued that the classification simply labels normal female behavior as a disorder. Former U.S. Surgeon General Antonia

Students Stressed and Depressed

The years spent in college are often thought to be a carefree time filled with growth, intellectual stimulation, and socializing. But a recent survey shows that the opposite may be true: 85% of college students reported feeling stressed in their daily lives and cited such stress factors as grades, school work, finances, family issues, and relationships (Associated Press, 2009).

More troubling is the fact that many students reported mood problems. Forty-two percent said they had felt down, depressed, or hopeless for at least several days during the prior two weeks. More than half reported feeling tired or having sleep problems. More than a third said they felt bad about themselves or that they felt like a failure, and 38% reported having little interest or pleasure in doing things. Eleven percent said they had recently had thoughts that they would be better off dead or that they wanted to hurt themselves in some way.

In all, 9% of college students were judged to be at risk of at least moderate depression. Having a parent who had lost a job during the school year seemed to be an important risk factor: It doubled the chances that a student would be at risk for at least mild depression and would report thoughts of being better off dead.

Another poll found that 55% of undergraduate students had thoughts of suicide at least one time, and 18% had seriously considered it. In addition, the severity of mental health issues among students attending college has been on the rise. One reason is that more people with relatively severe psychological disorders are now at-

In spite of the high percentage of college students reporting mood disorders, few take advantage of available mental health resources.

tending college as a result of better treatment options (Jayson, 2008).

Despite their stress and depression, surprisingly few students report taking advantage of the mental health resources that are available to them. Of those who showed at least moderate symptoms of depression, only a third sought counseling, while fewer than half of those who had suicidal thoughts had done so. Many hadn't even familiarized themselves with the mental health resources that were available on campus.

Part of the problem is that students are reluctant to use counseling services perhaps because they tend to believe that their problems just aren't serious enough to warrant doing so. The survey found that while 84% of students reported having a source of support that they could rely on if they were feeling bad or had suicidal thoughts, most looked to friends or family. Only 20% said that they would consider campus counseling resources (Laven, 2008; Associated Press, 2009; Benac & Tompson, 2009).

RETHINK

- Do you think college students might be at particular risk for developing a psychological disorder? Why?
- Why might having a parent lose a job during the school year lead to an increased risk for depression?

Novello suggested that what "in women is called PMS [premenstrual syndrome, a similar classification] in men is called healthy aggression and initiative" (Cotton, 1993, p. 270). Advocates for including the disorder prevailed, however, and "premenstrual dysphoric disorder" appears in the appendix of *DSM-IV-TR* (Hartung & Widiger, 1998; Pearlstein & Steiner, 2008).

Such controversies underline the fact that our understanding of abnormal behavior reflects the society and culture in which we live. Future revisions of *DSM* may include a different catalog of disorders. Even now, other cultures might include a list of disorders that are very different from the list that appears in the current *DSM*, as we discuss next.

Exploring DIVERSITY

DSM and Culture— and the Culture of *DSM*

In most people's estimation, a person who hears voices of the recently deceased is probably a victim of a psychological disturbance. Yet some Plains Indians routinely hear the voices of the dead calling to them from the afterlife.

This is only one example of the role of culture in labeling behavior as "abnormal." In fact, among all the major adult disorders included in the *DSM* categorization, only four are found across all cultures of the world: schizophrenia, bipolar disorder, major depression, and anxiety disorders. The rest are prevalent primarily in North America and Western Europe (Kleinman, 1996; Cohen, Slomkowski, & Robins, 1999; López & Guarnaccia, 2000).

For instance, take anorexia nervosa, the disorder in which people develop inaccurate views of their body appearance, become obsessed with their weight, and refuse to eat, sometimes starving to death in the process. This disorder typically occurs only in cultures that hold the societal standard that slender female bodies are the most desirable. In most of the world, where such a standard does not exist, anorexia nervosa is rare. Until recently, there was little anorexia nervosa in Asia with some exceptions, such as the upper and upper-middle classes of Japan and Hong Kong, where Western influence is greatest (Watters, 2010).

Similarly, dissociative identity (multiple personality) disorder makes sense as a problem only in societies in which a sense of self is fairly concrete. In India, the self is based more on external factors that are relatively independent of the person. There, when an individual displays symptoms of what people in a Western society would call dissociative identity disorder, Indians assume that that person is possessed either by demons (which they view as a malady) or by gods (which does not require treatment).

Furthermore, even though disorders such as schizophrenia are found throughout the world, cultural factors influence the specific symptoms of the disorder. Hence, catatonic schizophrenia in which unmoving patients appear to be frozen in the same position (sometimes for days), is rare in North America and Western Europe. In contrast, in India, 80% of those with schizophrenia are catatonic.

Other cultures have disorders that do not appear in the West. For example, in Malaysia, a behavior called *amok* is characterized by a wild outburst in which a usually quiet and withdrawn person kills or severely injures another. *Koro* is a condition found in Southeast Asian males who develop an intense panic that the penis is about to withdraw into the abdomen. Some West African men develop a disorder when they first attend college that they call "brain fag"; it includes feelings of heaviness or heat in the head as well as depression and anxiety. Finally, *ataque de nervios* is a disorder found most often among Latinos from the Caribbean. It is characterized by trembling, crying, uncontrollable screams, and incidents of verbal or physical aggression (Cohen, Slomkowski, & Robins, 1999; López & Guarnaccia, 2000; Adams, 2007).

Explanations for psychological disorders also differ among cultures. For example, in China, psychological disorders are commonly viewed as a weakness of the heart, a concept that derives from thousands of years of traditional Chinese medicine. Many terms used to describe emotions and symptoms of psychological disorders make direct reference to the heart—but the association isn't simply a metaphorical one. Chinese people are more likely than people in Western cultures to express their emotional anguish in terms of physical symptoms such as heart pain, "heart panic," or "heart vexed." They may also see their emotional pain as merely a side effect of some underlying physical cause or even focus more on the effects that their symptoms are having on their relationships with friends and family members (Miller, 2006a; Lee, Kleinman, & Kleinman, 2007; Watters, 2010).

In sum, we should not assume that the *DSM* provides the final word on psychological disorders. The disorders it includes are very much a creation and function of Western cultures at a particular moment in time, and its categories should not be seen as universally applicable (Tseng, 2003).

After you've considered the range and variety of psychological disturbances that can afflict people, you may begin to feel that you suffer from one (or more) of the problems we have discussed. In fact, this perception has a name: *medical student's disease*. Although in this case it might more aptly be labeled "psychology student's disease," the basic symptoms are the same: feeling that you suffer from the same sorts of problems you are studying.

BECOMING AN
INFORMED CONSUMER

of Psychology

Deciding When You Need Help

Most often, of course, your concerns will be unwarranted. As we have discussed, the differences between normal and abnormal behavior are often so fuzzy that it is easy to jump to the conclusion that you might have the same symptoms that are involved in serious forms of mental disturbance.

Before coming to such a conclusion, though, keep in mind that from time to time we all experience a wide range of emotions, and it is not unusual to feel deeply unhappy, fantasize about bizarre situations, or feel anxiety about life's circumstances. It is the persistence, depth, and consistency of such behavior that set normal reactions apart from abnormal ones. If you have not previously had serious doubts about the normality of your behavior, it is unlikely that reading about others' psychological disorders will prompt you to re-evaluate your earlier conclusion.

On the other hand, many people do have problems that merit concern, and in such cases, it is important to consider the possibility that professional help is warranted. The following list of symptoms can serve as a guideline to help you determine whether outside intervention might be useful (Engler & Goleman, 1992):

- Long-term feelings of distress that interfere with your sense of well-being, competence, and ability to function effectively in daily activities
- Occasions in which you experience overwhelmingly high stress accompanied by feelings of inability to cope with the situation
- Prolonged depression or feelings of hopelessness, especially when they do not have any clear cause (such as the death of someone close)
- Withdrawal from other people
- Thoughts of inflicting harm on oneself or suicide
- A chronic physical problem for which no physical cause can be determined
- A fear or phobia that prevents you from engaging in everyday activities
- Feelings that other people are out to get you or are talking about and plotting against you
- Inability to interact effectively with others, preventing the development of friendships and loving relationships

This list offers a rough set of guidelines for determining when the normal problems of everyday living have escalated beyond your ability to deal with them by yourself. In such situations, the *least* reasonable approach would be to pore over the psychological disorders we have discussed in an attempt at self-diagnosis. A more reasonable strategy is to consider seeking professional help.

RECAP/EVALUATE/RETHINK

RECAP

How prevalent are psychological disorders?
- About half the people in the United States are likely to experience a psychological disorder at some point in their lives; 30% experience a disorder in any specific year. (p. 474)

What indicators signal a need for the help of a mental health practitioner?
- The signals that indicate a need for professional help include long-term feelings of psychological distress, feelings of inability to cope with stress, withdrawal from other people, thoughts of inflicting harm on oneself or suicide, prolonged feelings of hopelessness, chronic physical problems with no apparent causes, phobias and compulsions, paranoia, and an inability to interact with others. (p. 479)

EVALUATE

1. The latest version of *DSM* is considered to be the conclusive guideline on defining psychological disorders. True or false?

2. _____ _____ _____, characterized by severe, incapacitating mood changes or depression related to a woman's menstrual cycle, was eventually added to the appendix of *DSM-IV-TR* despite controversy surrounding its inclusion.

3. Match the disorder with the culture in which it is most common:

   1. amok
   2. anorexia nervosa
   3. brain fag
   4. catatonic schizophrenia

   a. India
   b. Malaysia
   c. United States
   d. West Africa

RETHINK

1. Why is inclusion in the *DSM-IV-TR* of "borderline" disorders such as self-defeating personality disorder and premenstrual dysphoric disorder so controversial and political? What disadvantages does inclusion bring? Does inclusion bring any benefits?

2. *From the perspective of a college counselor:* What indicators might be most important in determining whether a college student is experiencing a psychological disorder? Do you believe that all students who show signs of a psychological disorder should seek professional help? How might your responses change if the student were from a different culture (e.g., an African society)?

Answers to Evaluate Questions

1. false; the development of the latest version of *DSM* was a source of great controversy, in part reflecting issues that divide society; 2. premenstrual dysphoric disorder; 3. 1-b, 2-c, 3-d, 4-a

Psychology on the Web

1. On the web, research the insanity defense as it is used in U.S. courts of law by consulting at least two sources. Summarize your findings and evaluate them against the perspectives on psychological disorders. Are there differences between legal and psychological interpretations of "sanity"? If so, what are they? Do you think such differences are appropriate?
2. Find information on the web about the controversy surrounding dissociative (or multiple) personality disorder. Summarize both sides of the controversy. Using your knowledge of psychology, state your opinion on the matter.

Epilogue

We've discussed some of the many types of psychological disorders to which people are prone, noted the difficulty psychologists and physicians have in clearly differentiating normal from abnormal behavior, and looked at some of the approaches mental health professionals have taken to explain and treat psychological disorders. We considered today's most commonly used classification scheme, categorized in the *DSM-IV-TR*, and examined some of the more prevalent forms of psychological disorders. To gain a perspective on the topic of psychological disorders, we discussed the surprisingly broad incidence of psychological disorders in U.S. society and the cultural nature of such disorders.

Turn back to the prologue that described the case of Lily. Using the knowledge you've gained about psychological disorders, consider the following questions.

1. Lily was diagnosed as suffering from borderline personality disorder. What elements of her behavior seem to fit the description of the disorder?
2. More generally, what are the symptoms of borderline personality disorder?
3. Which perspective (i.e., medical, psychoanalytic, behavioral, cognitive, humanistic, or sociocultural) provides the most useful explanation for Lily's case, in your opinion? Why?
4. What advantages might there be in using multiple perspectives to address and explain Lily's case?

Treatment of Psychological Disorders

Key Concepts for Chapter 13

Marg MacKrell was just three when her parents noticed the first signs of what turned out to be Tourette syndrome. The blond toddler began sniffing her fingers repeatedly, and over the next six years, her uncontrolled tics came to include clicking, whirring and scrunching her nose. Her condition was manageable until last year, when, at the age of 9, she began to suffer about 60 episodes a day of repeated head jerks that left her sore and spent by nighttime.

So when MacKrell's parents learned about an old but little-used therapy called habit-reversal training (HRT), they decided to try it. Last November, Marg started learning new ways to pre-empt her most severe tics at the Child and Family Study Center at Duke University Medical Center in Durham, N.C. When she felt a head jerk coming on, she was taught to drop her head and stare at the second hand on her watch for a minute. "Soon the head jerking was down by 90 percent," says Marg's mother, Diane MacKrell. "I couldn't believe it." (Skipp & Campo-Flores, 2007, p. 53)

Looking **Ahead**

The therapy that helped young Marg MacKrell start to enjoy a more normal life again is just one of many that have revolutionized the treatment of psychological disorders. Although treatment can take dozens of forms that range from one-meeting informal counseling sessions to long-term drug therapy, all the approaches have a common objective: the relief of psychological disorders with the ultimate aim of enabling individuals to achieve richer, more meaningful, and more fulfilling lives.

Despite their diversity, approaches to treating psychological disorders fall into two main categories: psychologically based and biologically based therapies. Psychologically based therapy, or **psychotherapy,** is treatment in which a trained professional— a therapist—uses psychological techniques to help someone overcome psychological difficulties and disorders, resolve problems in living, or bring about personal growth. In psychotherapy, the goal is to produce psychological change in a person (called a "client" or "patient") through discussions and interactions with the therapist. In contrast, **biomedical therapy** relies on drugs and medical procedures to improve psychological functioning.

As we describe the various approaches to therapy, keep in mind that although the distinctions may seem clear cut, the classifications and procedures overlap a good deal. In fact, many therapists today take an *eclectic approach* to therapy and use a variety of methods with an individual patient. Assuming that both psychological and biological processes often produce psychological disorders, eclectic therapists may draw from several perspectives simultaneously to address both the psychological and the biological aspects of a person's problems (Goin, 2005; Berman, Jobes, & Silverman, 2006).

psychotherapy Treatment in which a trained professional—a therapist—uses psychological techniques to help a person overcome psychological difficulties and disorders, resolve problems in living, or bring about personal growth.

biomedical therapy Therapy that relies on drugs and other medical procedures to improve psychological functioning.

Psychotherapy: Psychodynamic, Behavioral, and Cognitive Approaches to Treatment

Therapists use some 400 different varieties of psychotherapy, approaches to therapy that focus on psychological factors. Although diverse in many respects, all psychological approaches see treatment as a way of solving psychological problems by modifying people's behavior and helping them gain a better understanding of themselves and their past, present, and future.

In light of the variety of psychological approaches, it is not surprising that the people who provide therapy vary considerably in educational background and training (see Figure 1). Many have doctoral degrees in psychology (that is, they have attended graduate school, learned clinical and research techniques, and held an internship). But therapy is also provided by people in fields allied with psychology, such as psychiatry and social work.

Regardless of their specific training, almost all psychotherapists employ one of four major approaches to therapy: psychodynamic, behavioral, cognitive, and humanistic treatments. These approaches are based on the models of personality and psychological disorders developed by psychologists. Here we'll consider the psychodynamic, behavioral, and cognitive approaches in turn. In the next module, we'll explore the humanistic approach as well as interpersonal psychotherapy and group therapy, and we will evaluate the effectiveness of psychotherapy.

Key Concepts

What are the goals of psychologically and biologically based treatment approaches?

What are the psychodynamic, behavioral, and cognitive approaches to treatment?

Getting Help from the Right Person

Clinical Psychologists
Psychologists with a Ph.D. or Psy.D. who have also completed a postgraduate internship. They specialize in assessment and treatment of psychological difficulties, providing psychotherapy and, in some U.S. states, can prescribe drugs.

Counseling Psychologists
Psychologists with a Ph.D. or Ed.D. who typically treat day-to-day adjustment problems, often in a university mental health clinic.

Psychiatrists
M.D.s with postgraduate training in abnormal behavior. Because they can prescribe medication, they often treat the most severe disorders.

Psychoanalysts
Either M.D.s or psychologists who specialize in psychoanalysis, the treatment technique first developed by Freud.

Licensed Professional Counselors or Clinical Mental Health Counselors
Professionals with a master's degree who provide therapy to individuals, couples, and families and who hold a national or state certification.

Clinical or Psychiatric Social Workers
Professionals with a master's degree and specialized training who may provide therapy, usually regarding common family and personal problems.

FIGURE 1 A variety of professionals provide therapy and counseling. Each could be expected to give helpful advice and direction. However, the nature of the problem a person is experiencing may make one or another therapy more appropriate. For example, a person who is suffering from a severe disturbance and who has lost touch with reality will typically require some sort of biologically based drug therapy. In that case, a psychiatrist—who is a physician—would be the professional of choice. In contrast, those suffering from milder disorders, such as difficulty adjusting to the death of a family member, have a broader choice that might include any of the professionals listed in the figure.

"Look, call it denial if you like, but I think what goes on in my personal life is none of my own damn business."

Psychodynamic Approaches to Therapy

psychodynamic therapy Therapy that seeks to bring unresolved past conflicts and unacceptable impulses from the unconscious into the conscious, where patients may deal with the problems more effectively.

Psychodynamic therapy seeks to bring unresolved past conflicts and unacceptable impulses from the unconscious into the conscious, where patients may deal with the problems more effectively. Psychodynamic approaches are based on Freud's psychoanalytic approach to personality, which holds that individuals employ *defense mechanisms*, psychological strategies to protect themselves from unacceptable unconscious impulses.

The most common defense mechanism is repression, which pushes threatening conflicts and impulses back into the unconscious. However, since unacceptable conflicts and impulses can never be completely buried, some of the anxiety associated with them can produce abnormal behavior in the form of what Freud called *neurotic symptoms*.

How do we rid ourselves of the anxiety produced by unconscious, unwanted impulses and drives? To Freud, the answer was to confront the conflicts and impulses by bringing them out of the unconscious part of the mind and into the conscious part. Freud assumed that this technique would reduce anxiety stemming from past conflicts and that the patient could then participate in his or her daily life more effectively.

A psychodynamic therapist, then, faces the challenge of finding a way to assist patients' attempts to explore and understand the unconscious. The technique that has evolved has a number of components, but basically it consists of guiding patients to consider and discuss their past experiences in explicit detail from the time of their first memories. This process assumes that patients will eventually stumble upon long-hidden crises, traumas, and conflicts that are producing anxiety in their adult lives. They will then be able to "work through"—understand and rectify—those difficulties.

PSYCHOANALYSIS: FREUD'S THERAPY

psychoanalysis Freudian psychotherapy in which the goal is to release hidden unconscious thoughts and feelings in order to reduce their power in controlling behavior.

Classic Freudian psychodynamic therapy, called psychoanalysis, tends to be a lengthy and expensive affair. **Psychoanalysis** is Freudian psychotherapy in which the goal is to release hidden unconscious thoughts and feelings in order to reduce their power in controlling behavior.

In psychoanalysis, patients may meet with a therapist with considerable frequency, sometimes as much as 50 minutes a day, four to five days a week, for several years. In their sessions, they often use a technique developed by Freud called *free association*. Psychoanalysts using this technique tell patients to say aloud whatever comes to mind, regardless of its apparent irrelevance or senselessness, and the analysts attempt to recognize and label the connections between what a patient says and the patient's unconscious. Therapists also use *dream interpretation,* examining dreams to find clues to unconscious conflicts and problems. Moving beyond the surface description of a dream (called the *manifest content*), therapists seek its underlying meaning (the *latent content*), which thereby reveals the true unconscious meaning of the dream (Galatzer-Levy & Cohler, 1997; Auld, Hyman, & Rudzinski, 2005; Bodin, 2006).

The processes of free association and dream interpretation do not always move forward easily. The same unconscious forces that initially produced repression may keep past difficulties out of the conscious mind, which produces resistance. *Resistance* is an inability or unwillingness to discuss or reveal particular memories, thoughts, or motivations. Patients can express resistance in many ways. For instance, they may

Study Alert

To better understand how psychodynamic therapy works, review Freud's psychoanalytic theory discussed in the chapter on personality.

be discussing a childhood memory and suddenly forget what they were saying, or they may change the subject completely. It is the therapist's job to pick up instances of resistance and interpret their meaning as well as to ensure that patients return to the subject—which is likely to hold difficult or painful memories for the patients.

Because of the close, almost intimate interaction between patient and psychoanalyst, the relationship between the two often becomes emotionally charged and takes on a complexity unlike most other relationships. Patients may eventually think of the analyst as a symbol of a significant other in their past, perhaps a parent or a lover, and apply some of their feelings for that person to the analyst—a phenomenon known as transference. **Transference** is the transfer to a psychoanalyst feelings of love or anger that had been originally directed to a patient's parents or other authority figures (Van Beekum, 2005; Evans, 2007; Steiner, 2008).

A therapist can use transference to help a patient recreate past relationships that were psychologically difficult. For instance, if a patient undergoing transference views her therapist as a symbol of her father—with whom she had a difficult relationship—the patient and therapist may "redo" an earlier interaction, this time including more positive aspects. Through this process, the patient may resolve conflicts regarding her real father—something that is beginning to happen in the following therapy session:

The close and intense relationship between therapist and patient may become highly complex.

> Sandy: My father . . . never took any interest in any of us. . . . It was my mother—rest her soul—who loved us, not our father. He worked her to death. Lord, I miss her. . . . I must sound angry at my father. Don't you think I have a right to be angry?
>
> Therapist: Do you think you have a right to be angry?
>
> Sandy: Of course, I do! Why are you questioning me? You don't believe me, do you?
>
> Therapist: You want me to believe you.
>
> Sandy: I don't care whether you believe me or not. . . . I know what you're thinking—you think I'm crazy—you must be laughing at me—I'll probably be a case in your next book! You're just sitting there—smirking—making me feel like a bad person—thinking I'm wrong for being mad, that I have no right to be mad.
>
> Therapist: Just like your father.
>
> Sandy: Yes, you're just like my father.—Oh my God! Just now—I—I—thought I was talking to him. (Sue, Sue, & Sue, 1990, pp. 514–515)

transference The transfer of feelings to a psychoanalyst of love or anger that had been originally directed to a patient's parents or other authority figures.

CONTEMPORARY PSYCHODYNAMIC APPROACHES

Few people have the time, money, or patience to participate in years of traditional psychoanalysis. Moreover, no conclusive evidence shows that psychoanalysis, as originally conceived by Freud in the 19th century, works better than other, more recent forms of psychodynamic therapy.

Today, psychodynamic therapy tends to be of shorter duration and usually lasts no longer than 3 months or 20 sessions. The therapist takes a more active role than Freud would have liked by controlling the course of therapy and prodding and advising the patient with considerable directness. Finally, the therapist puts less emphasis on a patient's past history and childhood and concentrates instead on an individual's current relationships and specific complaints (Goode, 2003; Charman, 2004; Wolitzky, 2006).

EVALUATING PSYCHODYNAMIC THERAPY

Even with its current modifications, psychodynamic therapy has its critics. In its longer versions, it can be time consuming and expensive,

"And when did you first realize you weren't like other precipitation?"

especially in comparison with other forms of psychotherapy, such as behavioral and cognitive approaches. Furthermore, less articulate patients may not do as well as more articulate ones.

Ultimately, the most important concern about psychodynamic treatment is whether it actually works, and there is no simple answer to this question. Psychodynamic treatment techniques have been controversial since Freud introduced them. Part of the problem is the difficulty in establishing whether patients have improved after psychodynamic therapy. Determining effectiveness depends on reports from the therapist or the patients themselves—reports that are obviously open to bias and subjective interpretation.

Furthermore, critics have questioned the entire theoretical basis of psychodynamic theory; they maintain that constructs such as the unconscious have not been scientifically confirmed. Despite the criticism, though, the psychodynamic treatment approach has remained viable. For some people, it provides solutions to difficult psychological issues, provides effective treatment for psychological disturbance, and also permits the potential development of an unusual degree of insight into one's life (Clay, 2000; Ablon & Jones, 2005; Bond, 2006).

Behavioral Approaches to Therapy

Perhaps, when you were a child, your parents rewarded you with an ice cream cone when you were especially good . . . or sent you to your room if you misbehaved. Sound principles back up such a child-rearing strategy: Good behavior is maintained by reinforcement, and unwanted behavior can be eliminated by punishment.

behavioral treatment approaches
Treatment approaches that build on the basic processes of learning, such as reinforcement and extinction, and assume that normal and abnormal behavior are both learned.

These principles represent the basic underpinnings of **behavioral treatment approaches.** Building on the basic processes of learning, behavioral treatment approaches make this fundamental assumption: Both abnormal behavior and normal behavior are *learned*. People who act abnormally either have failed to learn the skills they need to cope with the problems of everyday living or have acquired faulty skills and patterns that are being maintained through some form of reinforcement. To modify abnormal behavior, then, proponents of behavioral approaches propose that people must learn new behavior to replace the faulty skills they have developed and unlearn their maladaptive behavior patterns (Krijn et al., 2004; Norton & Price, 2007).

Behavioral psychologists do not need to delve into people's pasts or their psyches. Rather than viewing abnormal behavior as a symptom of an underlying problem, they consider the abnormal behavior as the problem in need of modification. The goal of therapy is to change people's behavior to allow them to function more effectively, such as the treatment that was employed with Marg MacKrell, whose case was discussed in the chapter Prologue. In this view, then, there is no problem other than the maladaptive behavior itself; if you can change that behavior, treatment is successful.

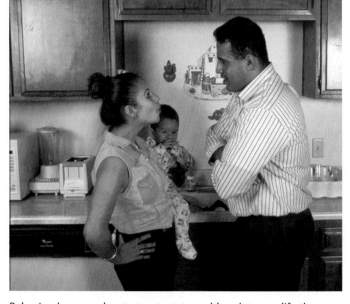

Behavioral approaches to treatment would seek to modify the behavior of this couple rather than to focus on the underlying causes of the behavior.

CLASSICAL CONDITIONING TREATMENTS

Suppose you bite into your favorite candy bar and find that not only is it infested with ants, but you've also swallowed a bunch of them. You immediately become sick to your stomach and throw up. Your long-term reaction? You never eat that kind of candy bar again, and it may be months before you eat

any type of candy. You have learned through the basic process of classical conditioning to avoid candy so that you will not get sick and throw up.

Aversive Conditioning. This simple example illustrates how a person can be classically conditioned to modify behavior. Behavior therapists use this principle when they employ **aversive conditioning,** a form of therapy that reduces the frequency of undesired behavior by pairing an aversive, unpleasant stimulus with undesired behavior. For example, behavior therapists might use aversive conditioning by pairing alcohol with a drug that causes severe nausea and vomiting. After the two have been paired a few times, the person associates the alcohol alone with vomiting and finds alcohol less appealing.

Although aversion therapy works reasonably well in inhibiting substance-abuse problems such as alcoholism and certain kinds of sexual disorders, critics question its long-term effectiveness. Also, important ethical concerns surround aversion techniques that employ such potent stimuli as electric shock, which therapists use only in the most extreme cases, such as patient self-mutilation. Clearly, though, aversion therapy offers an important procedure for eliminating maladaptive responses for some period of time—a respite that provides, even if only temporarily, an opportunity to encourage more adaptive behavior patterns (Bordnick et al., 2004; Delgado, Labouliere, & Phelps, 2006).

Systematic Desensitization. Another treatment that grew out of the classical conditioning is systematic desensitization. In **systematic desensitization,** gradual exposure to an anxiety-producing stimulus is paired with relaxation to extinguish the response of anxiety (Pagoto, Kozak, & Spates, 2006; Choy, Fyer, & Lipsitz, 2007; Dowling, Jackson, & Thomas, 2008).

Suppose, for instance, you were extremely afraid of flying. The very thought of being in an airplane would make you begin to sweat and shake, and you couldn't get yourself near enough to an airport to know how you'd react if you actually had to fly somewhere. Using systematic desensitization to treat your problem, you would first be trained in relaxation techniques by a behavior therapist and learn to relax your body fully—a highly pleasant state, as you might imagine (see Figure 2).

aversive conditioning A form of therapy that reduces the frequency of undesired behavior by pairing an aversive, unpleasant stimulus with undesired behavior.

systematic desensitization A behavioral technique in which gradual exposure to an anxiety-producing stimulus is paired with relaxation to extinguish the response of anxiety.

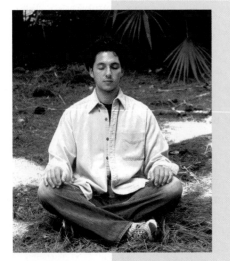

Step 1. Pick a focus word or short phrase that's firmly rooted in your personal belief system. For example, a nonreligious individual might choose a neutral word like *one* or *peace* or *love.* A Christian person desiring to use a prayer could pick the opening words of Psalm 23. *The Lord is my shepherd;* a Jewish person could choose *Shalom.*

Step 2. Sit quietly in a comfortable position.

Step 3. Close your eyes.

Step 4. Relax your muscles.

Step 5. Breathe slowly and naturally, repeating your focus word or phrase silently as you exhale.

Step 6. Throughout, assume a passive attitude. Don't worry about how well you're doing. When other thoughts come to mind, simply say to yourself, "Oh, well," and gently return to the repetition.

Step 7. Continue for 10 to 20 minutes. You may open your eyes to check the time, but do not use an alarm. When you finish, sit quietly for a minute or so, at first with your eyes closed and later with your eyes open. Then do not stand for one or two minutes.

Step 8. Practice the technique once or twice a day.

FIGURE 2 Following these basic steps will help you achieve a sense of calmness by employing the relaxation response.

The next step would involve constructing a *hierarchy of fears*—a list in order of increasing severity of the things you associate with your fears. For instance, your hierarchy might resemble this one:

1. Watching a plane fly overhead
2. Going to an airport
3. Buying a ticket
4. Stepping into the plane
5. Seeing the plane door close
6. Having the plane taxi down the runway
7. Taking off
8. Being in the air

Study Alert

To help remember the concept of hierarchy of fears, think of something that you are afraid of and construct your own hierarchy of fears.

exposure A behavioral treatment for anxiety in which people are confronted either suddenly or gradually with a stimulus that they fear.

Once you had developed this hierarchy and learned relaxation techniques, you would learn to associate the two sets of responses. To do this, your therapist might ask you to put yourself into a relaxed state and then imagine yourself in the first situation identified in your hierarchy. Once you could consider that first step while remaining relaxed, you would move on to the next situation. Eventually you would move up the hierarchy in gradual stages until you could imagine yourself being in the air without experiencing anxiety. Ultimately, you would be asked to make a visit to an airport and later to take a flight.

Exposure Treatments. Although systematic desensitization has proven to be a successful treatment, today it is often replaced with a less complicated form of therapy called exposure. **Exposure** is a behavioral treatment for anxiety in which people are confronted either suddenly or gradually with a stimulus that they fear. However, unlike systematic desensitization, relaxation training is omitted. Exposure allows the maladaptive response of anxiety or avoidance to extinguish, and research shows that this approach is generally as effective as systematic desensitization (Havermans et al., 2007; Hoffmann, 2007; Bush, 2008).

In most cases, therapists use *graded exposure* in which patients are exposed to a feared stimulus in gradual steps. For example, a patient who is afraid of dogs might first view a video of dogs. Gradually the exposure escalates to seeing a live, leashed dog across the room and then actually petting and touching the dog (Berle, 2007; Means & Edinger, 2007).

Exposure has proved to be an effective treatment for a number of problems, including phobias, anxiety disorders, and even impotence and fear of sexual contact. Through this technique, people can learn to enjoy the things they once feared (Choy, Fyer, & Lipsitz, 2007; Franklin, March, & Garcia, 2007; Powers & Emmelkamp, 2008).

OPERANT CONDITIONING TECHNIQUES

Some behavioral approaches make use of the operant conditioning principles that we discussed earlier in the book when considering the topic of learning. These approaches are based on the notion that we should reward people for carrying out desirable behavior and extinguish undesirable behavior by either ignoring it or punishing it.

One example of the systematic application of operant conditioning principles is the *token system,* which rewards a person for desired behavior with a token such as a poker chip or some kind of play money. Although it is most frequently employed in institutional settings for individuals with relatively serious problems and sometimes with children as a classroom management technique, the system resembles what parents do when they give children money for being well behaved—money that the children can later exchange for something they want. The desired behavior may range from simple things such as keeping one's room neat to personal grooming and interacting with other people. In institutions, patients can exchange tokens for some object or activity, such as snacks, new clothes, or, in extreme cases, sleeping in one's own bed rather than in a sleeping bag on the floor.

Contingency contracting, a variant of the token system, has proved quite effective in producing behavior modification. In *contingency contracting,* the therapist and client (or teacher and student or parent and child) draw up a written agreement. The contract states a series of behavioral goals the client hopes to achieve. It also specifies the positive consequences for the client if the client reaches goals—usually an explicit reward such as money or additional privileges. Contracts frequently state negative consequences if the client does not meet the goals. For example, clients who are trying to quit smoking might write out a check to a cause they have no interest in supporting (for instance, the National Rifle Association if they are strong supporters of gun control). If the client smokes on a given day, the therapist will mail the check.

A "Fearless Peer" who models appropriate and effective behavior can help children overcome their fears.

Behavior therapists also use *observational learning,* the process in which the behavior of other people is modeled, to systematically teach people new skills and ways of handling their fears and anxieties. For example, modeling helps when therapists are teaching basic social skills, such as maintaining eye contact during conversation and acting assertively. Similarly, children with dog phobias have been able to overcome their fears by watching another child—called the "Fearless Peer"— repeatedly walk up to a dog, touch it, pet it, and finally play with it. Modeling, then, can play an effective role in resolving some kinds of behavior difficulties, especially if the model receives a reward for his or her behavior (Bandura, Grusec, & Menlove, 1967; Greer, Dudek-Singer, & Gautreaux, 2006; Egliston & Rapee, 2007).

DIALECTICAL BEHAVIOR THERAPY

In **dialectical behavior therapy,** the focus is on getting people to accept who they are regardless of whether it matches their ideal. Even if their childhood has been dysfunctional or they have ruined relationships with others, that's in the past. What matters is who they wish to become (Manning, 2005; Lynch et al., 2007; Wagner, Rizvi, & Hamed, 2007).

dialectical behavior therapy A form of treatment in which the focus is on getting people to accept who they are regardless of whether it matches their ideal.

Like treatment approaches based on the principles of classical and operant conditioning, dialectical behavior therapy is an outgrowth of behavioral approaches, but it also includes components of other perspectives. Therapists using dialectical behavior therapy seek to have patients realize that they basically have two choices: Either they remain unhappy, or they change. Once patients agree that they wish to change, it is up to them to modify their behavior. Patients are taught that even if they experience unhappiness, anger, or any other negative emotion, it doesn't need to rule their behavior. It's their behavior that counts—not their inner life.

Dialectical behavior therapy teaches behavioral skills that help people behave more effectively and keep their emotions in check. Although it is a relatively new form of therapy, increasing evidence supports its effectiveness, particularly with certain personality disorders (Swales & Heard, 2007; Katz, Fotti, & Postl, 2009; Soler et al., 2009).

EVALUATING BEHAVIOR THERAPY

Behavior therapy works especially well for eliminating anxiety disorders, treating phobias and compulsions, establishing control over impulses, and learning complex social skills to replace maladaptive behavior. More than any of the other therapeutic techniques, it provides methods that nonprofessionals can use to change their own behavior. Moreover, it is efficient because it focuses on solving carefully defined problems (Richard & Lauterbach, 2006; Barlow, 2007).

Neuroscience in Your Life: How Behavioral Therapy Changes Your Brain

FIGURE 3 This figure highlights areas of the brain that show a reduced response to highly emotionally arousing pictures after behavioral therapy in patients with borderline personality disorder. The scans on the left (a) show areas of increased activity (in red, yellow, and orange) in those with borderline personality disorder before behavioral therapy as compared to participants who do not have this disorder. The scans on the right (b) show this same comparison after treatment. The scans on the right (b) contain fewer areas of activation, which suggests that after behavioral therapy, the brains of those with borderline personality disorder react more similarly to the brains of those who do not have the disorder. (Source: Schnell & Herpertz, 2007, Figure 3)

(a)   (b)

Critics of behavior therapy believe that because it emphasizes changing external behavior, people do not necessarily gain insight into thoughts and expectations that may be fostering their maladaptive behavior. On the other hand, neuroscientific evidence shows that behavioral treatments can produce actual changes in brain functioning, which suggests that behavioral treatments can produce changes beyond external behavior.

For example, one experiment looked at the neurological reactions of patients with borderline personality disorder who participated in a 12-week dialectical behavioral therapy program. Compared with a control group composed of people who did not have the disorder, the patients showed significant changes in their reactions to highly arousing emotion-evoking stimuli. Following therapy, the patients' neurological functioning was more similar to those without the disorder than it was prior to therapy (see Figure 3).

Cognitive Approaches to Therapy

If you assumed that illogical thoughts and beliefs lie at the heart of psychological disorders, wouldn't the most direct treatment route be to teach people new, more adaptive modes of thinking? The answer is yes, according to psychologists who take a cognitive approach to treatment.

cognitive treatment approaches Treatment approaches that teach people to think in more adaptive ways by changing their dysfunctional cognitions about the world and themselves.

Cognitive treatment approaches teach people to think in more adaptive ways by changing their dysfunctional cognitions about the world and themselves. Unlike behavior therapists, who focus on modifying external behavior, cognitive therapists attempt to change the way people think as well as their behavior. Because they often

FIGURE 4 In the A-B-C model of rational-emotive behavior therapy, negative activating conditions (A) lead to the activation of an irrational belief system (B), which leads to emotional consequences (C). Those emotional consequences then feed back and support the belief system. At what steps in the model could change occur as a result of rational-emotive behavior therapy?

use basic principles of learning, the methods they employ are sometimes referred to as the **cognitive-behavioral approach** (Beck & Rector, 2005; Butler et al., 2006; Friedberg, 2006).

Although cognitive treatment approaches take many forms, they all share the assumption that anxiety, depression, and negative emotions develop from maladaptive thinking. Accordingly, cognitive treatments seek to change the thought patterns that lead to getting "stuck" in dysfunctional ways of thinking. Therapists systematically teach clients to challenge their assumptions and adopt new approaches to old problems.

Cognitive therapy is relatively short term and usually lasts a maximum of 20 sessions. Therapy tends to be highly structured and focused on concrete problems. Therapists often begin by teaching the theory behind the approach and then continue to take an active role throughout the course of therapy by acting as a combination of teacher, coach, and partner.

One good example of cognitive treatment, **rational-emotive behavior therapy,** attempts to restructure a person's belief system into a more realistic, rational, and logical set of views. According to psychologist Albert Ellis (2002, 2004), many people lead unhappy lives and suffer from psychological disorders because they harbor irrational, unrealistic ideas such as these:

- We need the love or approval of virtually every significant other person for everything we do.
- We should be thoroughly competent, adequate, and successful in all possible respects in order to consider ourselves worthwhile.
- It is horrible when things don't turn out the way we want them to.

Such irrational beliefs trigger negative emotions, which in turn support the irrational beliefs and lead to a self-defeating cycle. Ellis calls it the A-B-C model in which negative activating conditions (A) lead to the activation of an irrational belief system (B), which in turn leads to emotional consequences (C). For example, if a person experiences the breakup of a close relationship (A) and holds the irrational belief (B) that "I'll never be loved again," this triggers negative emotions (C) that in turn feed back into support of the irrational belief (see Figure 4).

Rational-emotive behavior therapy aims to help clients eliminate maladaptive thoughts and beliefs and adopt more effective thinking. To accomplish this goal, therapists take an active, directive role during therapy and openly challenge patterns of thought that appear to be dysfunctional. Consider this example:

Martha: The basic problem is that I'm worried about my family. I'm worried about money. And I never seem to be able to relax.

Therapist: Why are you worried about your family? . . .What's to be concerned about? They have certain demands which you don't want to adhere to.

cognitive-behavioral approach
A treatment approach that incorporates basic principles of learning to change the way people think.

rational-emotive behavior therapy
A form of therapy that attempts to restructure a person's belief system into a more realistic, rational, and logical set of views by challenging dysfunctional beliefs that maintain irrational behavior.

Martha: I was brought up to think that I mustn't be selfish.

Therapist: Oh, we'll have to knock that out of your head!

Martha: My mother feels that I shouldn't have left home—that my place is with them. There are nagging doubts about what I should—

Therapist: Why are there doubts? Why should you?

Martha: I think it's a feeling I was brought up with that you always have to give of yourself. If you think of yourself, you're wrong.

Therapist: That's a belief. Why do you have to keep believing that—at your age? You believed a lot of superstitions when you were younger. Why do you have to retain them? Your parents indoctrinated you with this non-sense, because that's their belief. . . . Who needs that philosophy? All it's gotten you, so far, is guilt. (Ellis, 1974, pp. 223–286)

By poking holes in Martha's reasoning, the therapist is attempting to help her adopt a more realistic view of herself and her circumstances (Ellis, 2002; Dryden & David, 2008).

Another influential form of therapy that builds on a cognitive perspective is that of Aaron Beck (Beck, 1995, 2004). Like rational-emotive behavior therapy, Beck's cognitive therapy aims to change people's illogical thoughts about themselves and the world.

However, cognitive therapy is considerably less confrontational and challenging than rational-emotive behavior therapy. Instead of the therapist actively arguing with clients about their dysfunctional cognitions, cognitive therapists more often play the role of teacher. Therapists urge clients to obtain information on their own that will lead them to discard their inaccurate thinking through a process of cognitive appraisal. In *cognitive appraisal,* clients are asked to evaluate situations, themselves, and others in terms of their memories, values, beliefs, thoughts, and expectations. During the course of treatment, therapists help clients discover ways of thinking more appropriately about themselves and others (Rosen, 2000; Beck, Freeman, & Davis, 2004; Moorey, 2007).

EVALUATING COGNITIVE APPROACHES TO THERAPY

Cognitive approaches to therapy have proved successful in dealing with a broad range of disorders, including anxiety disorders, depression, substance abuse, and eating disorders. Furthermore, the willingness of cognitive therapists to incorporate additional treatment approaches (e.g., combining cognitive and behavioral techniques in cognitive behavioral therapy) has made this approach a particularly effective form of treatment (Mitte, 2005; Ishikawa et al., 2007; Bhar et al., 2008).

At the same time, critics have pointed out that the focus on helping people to think more rationally ignores the fact that life is in reality sometimes irrational. Changing one's assumptions to make them more reasonable and logical thus may not always be helpful—even assuming it is possible to bring about true cognitive change. Still, the success of cognitive approaches has made it one of the most frequently employed therapies (Leahy, 2003; Beck & Rector, 2005).

RECAP/EVALUATE/RETHINK

RECAP

What are the goals of psychologically and biologically based treatment approaches?

- Psychotherapy (psychologically based therapy) and bio-medical therapy (biologically based therapy) share the goal of resolving psychological problems by modifying people's thoughts, feelings, expectations, evaluations, and ultimately behavior. (p. 484)

What are the psychodynamic, behavioral, and cognitive approaches to treatment?

- Psychoanalytic approaches seek to bring unresolved past conflicts and unacceptable impulses from the unconscious into the conscious, where patients may deal with the problems more effectively. To do this, therapists use techniques such as free association and dream interpretation. (p. 486)
- Behavioral approaches to treatment view abnormal behavior as the problem rather than viewing that behavior as a symptom of some underlying cause. To bring about a "cure," this view suggests that the outward behavior must be changed by using methods such as aversive conditioning, systematic desensitization, observational learning, token systems, contingency contracting, and dialectical behavior therapy. (p. 488)
- Cognitive approaches to treatment consider that the goal of therapy is to help a person restructure his or her faulty belief system into a more realistic, rational, and logical view of the world. Two examples of cognitive treatments are the rational-emotive behavior therapy and cognitive therapy. (p. 492)

EVALUATE

1. Match the following mental health practitioners with the appropriate description.

   1. Psychiatrist
   2. Clinical psychologist
   3. Counseling psychologist
   4. Psychoanalyst

   a. PhD specializing in the treatment of psychological disorders
   b. Professional specializing in Freudian therapy techniques
   c. MD trained in abnormal behavior
   d. PhD specializing in the adjustment of day-to-day problems

2. According to Freud, people use _____ _____ as a means of preventing unwanted impulses from intruding on conscious thought.
3. In dream interpretation, a psychoanalyst must learn to distinguish between the _____ content of a dream, which is what appears on the surface, and the _____ content, its underlying meaning.
4. Which of the following treatments deals with phobias by gradual exposure to the item producing the fear?
   a. Systematic desensitization
   b. Partial reinforcement
   c. Behavioral self-management
   d. Aversion therapy

RETHINK

1. In what ways are psychoanalysis and cognitive therapy similar, and how do they differ?
2. *From the perspective of a child-care provider:* How might you use systematic desensitization to help children overcome their fears?

Answers to Evaluate Questions

1. 1-c, 2-a, 3-d, 4-b; 2. defense mechanisms; 3. manifest, latent; 4. a

KEY TERMS

psychotherapy p. 484
biomedical therapy p. 484
psychodynamic
   therapy p. 486
psychoanalysis p. 486
transference p. 487

behavioral treatment
   approaches p. 488
aversive
   conditioning p. 489
systematic
   desensitization p. 489

exposure p. 490
dialectical behavior
   therapy p. 491
cognitive treatment
   approaches p. 492

cognitive-behavioral
   approach p. 493
rational-emotive behavior
   therapy p. 493

Psychotherapy: Humanistic, Interpersonal, and Group Approaches to Treatment

Key Concepts

What are the humanistic approaches to treatment?

What is interpersonal therapy?

How does group therapy differ from individual types of therapy?

How effective is psychotherapy, and which kind of psychotherapy works best in a given situation?

humanistic therapy Therapy in which the underlying rationale is that people have control of their behavior, can make choices about their lives, and are essentially responsible for solving their own problems.

Humanistic Therapy

As you know from your own experience, a student cannot master the material covered in a course without some hard work, no matter how good the teacher and the textbook are. *You must* take the time to study, memorize the vocabulary, and learn the concepts. Nobody else can do it for you. If you choose to put in the effort, you'll succeed; if you don't, you'll fail. The responsibility is primarily yours.

Humanistic therapy draws on this philosophical perspective of self-responsibility in developing treatment techniques. The many different types of therapy that fit into this category have a similar rationale: We have control of our own behavior, we can make choices about the kinds of lives we want to live, and it is up to us to solve the difficulties we encounter in our daily lives.

Humanistic therapists believe that people naturally are motivated to strive for self-actualization. As we discussed in the chapter on motivation, *self-actualization* is the term that clinical psychologist Abraham Maslow used to describe the state of self-fulfillment in which people realize their highest potentials in their own unique way.

Instead of acting in the more directive manner of some psychodynamic and behavioral approaches, humanistic therapists view themselves as guides or facilitators. Therapists using humanistic techniques seek to help people understand themselves and find ways to come closer to the ideal they hold for themselves. In this view, psychological disorders result from the inability to find meaning in life and from feelings of loneliness and a lack of connection to others (Cain, 2002).

Humanistic approaches have produced many therapeutic techniques. Among the most important is person-centered therapy.

PERSON-CENTERED THERAPY

Consider the following therapy session excerpt:

Alice: I was thinking about this business of standards. I somehow developed a sort of a knack, I guess, of—well—habit—of trying to make people feel at ease around me, or to make things go along smoothly. . . .

Therapist: In other words, what you did was always in the direction of trying to keep things smooth and to make other people feel better and to smooth the situation.

Alice: Yes. I think that's what it was. Now the reason why I did it probably was—I mean, not that I was a good little Samaritan going around making other people happy, but that was probably the role that felt easiest for me to play. . . .

Therapist: You feel that for a long time you've been playing the role of kind of smoothing out the frictions or differences or what not. . . .

Humanistic therapy focuses on self-responsibility.

Alice: M-hm.

Therapist: Rather than having any opinion or reaction of your own in the situation. Is that it? (Rogers, 1951, pp. 152–153)

The therapist does not interpret or answer the questions the client has raised. Instead, the therapist clarifies or reflects back what the client has said (e.g., "In other words, what you did. . . ."; "You feel that. . . ."; "Is that it?"). This therapeutic technique, known as *nondirective counseling,* is at the heart of person-centered therapy, which was first practiced by Carl Rogers in the mid-20th century (Rogers, 1951, 1980; Raskin & Rogers, 1989).

Person-centered therapy (also called *client-centered therapy*) aims to enable people to reach their potential for self-actualization. By providing a warm and accepting environment, therapists hope to motivate clients to air their problems and feelings. In turn, this enables clients to make realistic and constructive choices and decisions about the things that bother them in their current lives (Bozarth, Zimring, & Tausch, 2002; Kirschenbaum, 2004; Bohart, 2006).

Instead of directing the choices clients make, therapists provide what Rogers calls *unconditional positive regard*—expressing acceptance and understanding, regardless of the feelings and attitudes the client expresses. By doing this, therapists hope to create an atmosphere that enables clients to come to decisions that can improve their lives (Kirschenbaum & Jourdan, 2005; Vieira & Freire, 2006).

Furnishing unconditional positive regard does not mean that therapists must approve of everything their clients say or do. Rather, therapists need to communicate that they are caring, nonjudgmental, and *empathetic*—that is, understanding of a client's emotional experiences (Fearing & Clark, 2000).

Person-centered therapy is rarely used today in its purest form. Contemporary approaches tend to be somewhat more directive with therapists nudging clients toward insights rather than merely reflecting back their statements. However, therapists still view clients' insights as central to the therapeutic process (also see *PsychWork*).

person-centered therapy Therapy in which the goal is to reach one's potential for self-actualization.

Study Alert

To better remember the concept of unconditional positive regard, try offering it to a friend during a conversation by showing your support, acceptance, and understanding no matter what thought or attitude is being offered.

"At the Kansas City Community Center, we help people rebuild their lives."

For Vickie Dickerman, a case manager and substance abuse counselor, this statement is the foundation of her work.

"Treatment is a collaboration between what the client wants from a program and what you, as the professional, see as essential in the treatment planning process. We also assist clients in obtaining their basic needs in order that they may become productive members of society," she said.

Dickerman, who has worked for 20 years in the field of substance abuse with criminal offenders, uses several approaches in helping people rebuild their lives.

"I address 'criminal thinking errors' along with client-centered therapy," she explained. "When clients engage in 'criminal thinking,' they view themselves as victims, focus only their positive attributes, and avoid taking responsibility for their actions." Dickerman seeks to change such thinking and help clients rebuild their self-confidence in their ability to meet their own basic needs.

"Expressing praise to offenders for something that would not appear to be an accomplishment to most of us is of importance since clients' low self-esteem and lack of self-confidence are often the result of lack of reinforcement from family members and their peers," Dickerman added. "Allowing setbacks should be considered a part of the process since individuals with criminal thinking errors experience difficulty with receiving praise and may attempt to sabotage their success."

PsychWork

CASE MANAGER AND
SUBSTANCE ABUSE
COUNSELOR

Name: Vicki Dickerman

Position: Case Manager and Substance Abuse Counselor, Kansas City Community Center

Education: BS in Addiction Studies and Psychology, Park University, Parkville, Missouri; Certified Co-Occurring Disorders Professional

EVALUATING HUMANISTIC APPROACHES TO THERAPY

The notion that psychological disorders result from restricted growth potential appeals philosophically to many people. Furthermore, when humanistic therapists acknowledge that the freedom we possess can lead to psychological difficulties, clients find an unusually supportive environment for therapy. In turn, this atmosphere can help clients discover solutions to difficult psychological problems (Cooper, 2007).

However, humanistic treatments lack specificity, a problem that has troubled their critics. Humanistic approaches are not very precise and are probably the least scientifically and theoretically developed type of treatment. Moreover, this form of treatment works best for the same type of highly verbal client who profits most from psychoanalytic treatment.

Interpersonal Therapy

interpersonal therapy (IPT) Short-term therapy that focuses on the context of current social relationships.

Interpersonal therapy (IPT) considers therapy in the context of social relationships. Although its roots stem from psychodynamic approaches, interpersonal therapy concentrates more on the here and now with the goal of improving a client's current relationships. It typically focuses on interpersonal issues such as conflicts with others, social skills issues, role transitions (such as divorce), or grief (Weissman, Markowitz, & Klerman, 2007).

Interpersonal therapy is more active and directive than traditional psychodynamic approaches, and sessions are more structured. The approach makes no assumptions about the underlying causes of psychological disorders but focuses on the interpersonal context in which a disorder is developed and maintained. It also tends to be shorter than traditional psychodynamic approaches and typically lasts only 12–16 weeks. During those sessions, therapists make concrete suggestions on improving relations with others and offer recommendations and advice.

Because interpersonal therapy is short and structured, researchers have been able to demonstrate its effectiveness more readily than longer-term types of therapy. Evaluations of the approach have shown that interpersonal therapy is especially effective in dealing with depression, anxiety, addictions, and eating disorders (Salsman, 2006; Grigoriadis & Ravitz, 2007; Miller et al., 2008).

Group Therapy, Family Therapy, and Self-Help Groups

group therapy Therapy in which people meet in a group with a therapist to discuss problems.

Although most treatment takes place between a single individual and a therapist, some forms of therapy involve groups of people seeking treatment. In **group therapy,** several unrelated people meet with a therapist to discuss some aspect of their psychological functioning.

People typically discuss with the group their problems, which often center on a common difficulty, such as alcoholism or a lack of social skills. The other members of the group provide emotional support and dispense advice on ways they have coped effectively with similar problems (Alonso, Alonso, & Piper, 2003; Scaturo, 2004; Rigby & Waite, 2007).

Groups vary greatly in terms of the particular model they employ; there are psychoanalytic groups, humanistic groups, and groups corresponding to the other therapeutic approaches. Furthermore, groups also differ with regard to the degree of guidance the therapist provides. In some, the therapist is quite directive; in others, the members of the group

"So, would anyone in the group care to respond to what Clifford has just shared with us?"

set their own agenda and determine how the group will proceed (Beck & Lewis, 2000; Stockton, Morran, & Krieger, 2004).

Because several people are treated simultaneously in group therapy, it is a much more economical means of treatment than individual psychotherapy. On the other hand, critics argue that group settings lack the individual attention inherent in one-to-one therapy and that especially shy and withdrawn individuals may not receive the attention they need in a group setting.

FAMILY THERAPY

One specialized form of group therapy is family therapy. As the name implies, **family therapy** involves two or more family members, one (or more) of whose problems led to treatment. But rather than focusing simply on the members of the family who present the initial problem, family therapists consider the family as a unit to which each member contributes. By meeting with the entire family simultaneously, family therapists try to understand how the family members interact with one another (Cooklin, 2000; Strong & Tomm, 2007).

In group therapy, people with psychological difficulties meet with a therapist to discuss their problems.

Family therapists view the family as a "system" and assume that individuals in the family cannot improve without understanding the conflicts found in interactions among family members. Thus, the therapist expects each member to contribute to the resolution of the problem being addressed.

Many family therapists believe that family members fall into rigid roles or set patterns of behavior with one person acting as the scapegoat, another as a bully, and so forth. In their view, that system of roles perpetuates family disturbances. One goal of this type of therapy, then, is to get the family members to adopt new, more constructive roles and patterns of behavior (Minuchin, 1999; Sprenkle & Moon, 1996; Sori, 2006).

family therapy An approach that focuses on the family and its dynamics.

SELF-HELP THERAPY

In many cases, group therapy does not involve a professional therapist. Instead, people with similar problems get together to discuss their shared feelings and experiences. For example, people who have recently experienced the death of a spouse might meet in a *bereavement support group,* or college students may get together to discuss their adjustment to college.

One of the best-known self-help groups is Alcoholics Anonymous (AA), designed to help members deal with alcohol-related problems. AA prescribes 12 steps that alcoholics must pass through on their road to recovery; they begin with an admission that they are alcoholics and powerless over alcohol. AA provides more treatment for alcoholics than any other therapy; AA and other 12-step programs (such as Narcotics Anonymous) can be as successful in treating alcohol and other substance-abuse problems as traditional types of therapy (Bogenschutz, Geppert, & George, 2006; Galanter, 2007; Gossop, Stewart, & Marsden, 2008).

Evaluating Psychotherapy: Does Therapy Work?

Your best friend, Ben, comes to you because he just hasn't been feeling right about things lately. He's upset because he and his girlfriend aren't getting along, but his difficulties go beyond that. He can't concentrate on his studies, has a lot of trouble getting to sleep, and—this is what really bothers him—has begun to think that people are ganging up on him, talking about him behind his back. It seems that no one really cares about or understands him or makes any effort to see why he's become so miserable.

Ben knows that he ought to get *some* kind of help, but he is not sure where to turn. He is fairly skeptical of psychologists and thinks that a lot of what they say is just mumbo-jumbo, but he's willing to put his doubts aside and try anything to feel better. He also knows there are many different types of therapy, and he doesn't have a clue about which would be best for him. He turns to you for advice because he knows you are taking a psychology course. He asks, "Which kind of therapy works best?"

IS THERAPY EFFECTIVE?

This question requires a complex response. In fact, identifying the single most appropriate form of treatment is a controversial and still unresolved task for psychologists specializing in psychological disorders. In fact, even before considering whether one form of therapy works better than another, we need to determine whether therapy in any form effectively alleviates psychological disturbances.

Until the 1950s, most people simply assumed that therapy was effective. But in 1952 psychologist Hans Eysenck published an influential study challenging that assumption. He claimed that people who received psychodynamic treatment and related therapies were no better off at the end of treatment than were people who were placed on a waiting list for treatment but never received it. Eysenck concluded that people would go into **spontaneous remission**, recovery without treatment, if they were simply left alone—certainly a cheaper and simpler process.

Although other psychologists quickly challenged Eysenck's conclusions, his review stimulated a continuing stream of better controlled, more carefully crafted studies on the effectiveness of psychotherapy. Today most psychologists agree: Therapy does work. Several comprehensive reviews indicate that therapy brings about greater improvement than no treatment at all, with the rate of spontaneous remission being fairly low. In most cases, then, the symptoms of abnormal behavior do not go away by themselves if left untreated—although the issue continues to be hotly debated (Seligman, 1996; Westen, Novotny, & Thompson-Brenner, 2004; Lutz et al., 2006).

WHICH KIND OF THERAPY WORKS BEST?

Although most psychologists feel confident that psychotherapeutic treatment *in general* is more effective than no treatment at all, the question of whether any specific form of treatment is superior to any other has not been answered definitively (Nathan, Stuart, & Dolan, 2000; Westen, Novotny, & Thompson-Brenner, 2004; Abboud, 2005).

For instance, one classic study comparing the effectiveness of various approaches found that although success rates vary somewhat by treatment form, most treatments show fairly equal success rates. As Figure 1 indicates, the rates ranged from about 70–85% greater success for treated compared with untreated individuals. Behavioral and cognitive approaches tended to be slightly more successful, but that result may have been due to differences in the severity of the cases treated (Smith, Glass, & Miller, 1980; Orwin & Condray, 1984).

Other research, which relies on *meta-analysis* in which data from a large number of studies are statistically combined, yields similar general conclusions. Furthermore, a large survey of 186,000 individuals found that respondents felt they had benefited substantially from psychotherapy. However, there was little difference in "consumer satisfaction" on the basis of the specific type of treatment they had received (Seligman, 1995; Malouff, Thorsteinsson, & Schutte, 2007; Cuijpers et al., 2008).

Study Alert

Pay special attention to the discussion of (1) whether therapy is effective in general and (2) what specific types of therapy are effective because it is a key issue for therapists.

spontaneous remission Recovery without treatment.

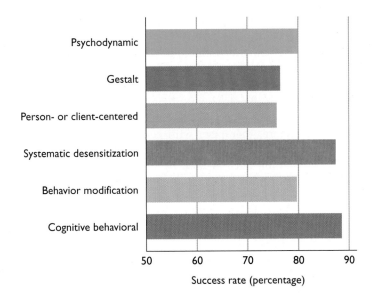

FIGURE 1 Estimates of the effectiveness of different types of treatment, in comparison to control groups of untreated people. The percentile score shows how much more effective a specific type of treatment is for the average patient rather than is no treatment. For example, people given psychodynamic treatment score, on average, more positively on outcome measures than about three-quarters of untreated people. (Source: Adapted from Smith, Glass, & Miller, 1980).

In short, converging evidence allows us to draw several conclusions about the effectiveness of psychotherapy (Strupp & Binder, 1992; Seligman, 1996; Goldfried & Pachankis, 2007):

- *For most people, psychotherapy is effective.* This conclusion holds over different lengths of treatment, specific kinds of psychological disorders, and various types of treatment. Thus, the question, "Does psychotherapy work?" appears to have been answered convincingly: It does (Seligman, 1996; Spiegel, 1999; Westen, Novotny, & Thompson-Brenner, 2004; Payne & Marcus, 2008).
- *On the other hand, psychotherapy doesn't work for everyone.* As many as 10% of people treated show no improvement or actually deteriorated (Boisvert & Faust, 2003; Pretzer & Beck, 2005; Coffman et al., 2007; Lilienfeld, 2007).
- *No single form of therapy works best for every problem, and certain specific types of treatment are better, although not invariably, for specific types of problems.* For example, cognitive therapy works especially well for panic disorders, and exposure therapy relieves specific phobias effectively. However, there are exceptions to these generalizations, and often the differences in success rates for different types of treatment are not substantial (Miller & Magruder, 1999; Westen, Novotny, & Thompson-Brenner, 2004).
- *Most therapies share several basic similar elements.* Despite the fact that the specific methods used in different therapies are very different from one another, there are several common themes that lead them to be effective. These elements include the opportunity for a client to develop a positive relationship with a therapist, an explanation or interpretation of a client's symptoms, and confrontation of negative emotions. The fact that these common elements exist in most therapies makes it difficult to compare one treatment against another (Norcross, 2002; Norcross, Beutler & Levant, 2006).

Consequently, there is no single, definitive answer to the broad question, "Which therapy works best?" because of the complexity in sorting out the various factors that enter into successful therapy. Recently, however, clinicians and researchers have reframed the question by focusing on evidence-based psychotherapy practice. *Evidence-based psychotherapy practice* seeks to use research findings to determine the best practices for treating a specific disorder. To determine best practices, researchers use clinical interviews, client self-reports of improvement in quality of life, reductions in symptoms, observations of behavior, and other outcomes to compare different therapies. By using objective research findings, clinicians are increasingly able to determine the most effective treatment for a specific disorder (APA Presidential Task Force, 2006; Brownlee, 2007; Kazdin, 2008).

Because no single type of psychotherapy is invariably effective for every individual, some therapists use an eclectic approach to therapy. In an *eclectic approach to therapy,* therapists use a variety of techniques, thus integrating several perspectives, to treat a person's problems. By employing more than one approach, therapists can choose the appropriate mix of evidence-based treatments to match the individual's specific needs. Furthermore, therapists with certain personal characteristics may work better with particular individuals and types of treatments, and—as we consider next—even racial and ethnic factors may be related to the success of treatment (Cheston, 2000; Chambless et al., 2006; Hayes, 2008).

Exploring DIVERSITY

Racial and Ethnic Factors in Treatment: Should Therapists Be Color Blind?

Consider the following case report written by a school counselor about Jimmy Jones, a 12-year-old student who was referred to a counselor because of his lack of interest in schoolwork:

> Jimmy does not pay attention, daydreams often, and frequently falls asleep during class. There is a strong possibility that Jimmy is harboring repressed rage that needs to be ventilated and dealt with. His inability to directly express his anger had led him to adopt passive-aggressive means of expressing hostility, i.e., inattentiveness, daydreaming, falling asleep. It is recommended that Jimmy be seen for intensive counseling to discover the basis of the anger. (Sue & Sue, 1990, p. 44)

The counselor was wrong, however. Rather than suffering from "repressed rage," Jimmy lived in a poverty stricken and disorganized home. Because of overcrowding at his house, he did not get enough sleep and consequently was tired the next day. Frequently, he was also hungry. In short, the stresses arising from his environment and not any deep-seated psychological disturbances caused his problems.

This incident underscores the importance of taking people's environmental and cultural backgrounds into account during treatment for psychological disorders. In particular, members of racial and ethnic minority groups, especially those who are also poor, may behave in ways that help them deal with a society that discriminates against them. As a consequence, behavior that may signal psychological disorder in middle-class and upper-class whites may simply be adaptive in people from other racial and socioeconomic groups. For instance, characteristically suspicious and distrustful people may be displaying a survival strategy to protect themselves from psychological and physical injury rather than suffering from a psychological disturbance (Paniagua, 2000; Tseng, 2003; Pottick et al., 2007).

In fact, therapists must question some basic assumptions of psychotherapy when dealing with racial, ethnic, and cultural minority group members. For example, compared with the dominant culture, Asian and Latino cultures typically place much greater emphasis on the group, family, and society. When an Asian or Latino faces a critical decision, the family helps make it—a cultural practice suggesting that family members should also play a role in psychological treatment. Similarly, the traditional Chinese recommendation for dealing with depression or anxiety is to urge people who experience such problems to avoid thinking about whatever is upsetting them. Consider how this advice contrasts with treatment approaches that emphasize the value of insight (Ponterotto, Gretchen, & Chauhan, 2001; McCarthy, 2005; Leitner, 2007).

Clearly, therapists *cannot* be "colorblind." Instead, they must take into account the racial, ethnic, cultural, and social class backgrounds of their clients in determining the nature of a psychological disorder and the course of treatment (Aponte & Wohl, 2000; Pedersen et al., 2002; Hayes, 2008).

Therapists' interpretation of their clients' behavior is influenced by racial, ethnic, cultural, and social class backgrounds of the clients.

RECAP/EVALUATE/RETHINK

RECAP

What are humanistic approaches to treatment?

- Humanistic therapy is based on the premise that people have control of their behavior, that they can make choices about their lives, and that it is up to them to solve their own problems. Humanistic therapies, which take a nondirective approach, include person-centered therapy. (p. 496)

What is interpersonal therapy?

- Interpersonal therapy focuses on interpersonal relationships and strives for immediate improvement during short-term therapy. (p. 498)

How does group therapy differ from individual types of therapy?

- In group therapy, several unrelated people meet with a therapist to discuss some aspect of their psychological functioning and often center on a common problem. (p. 498)

How effective is psychotherapy, and which kind of psychotherapy works best in a given situation?

- Most research suggests that, in general, therapy is more effective than no therapy, although how much more effective is not known. (p. 500)
- The more difficult question of which therapy works best is harder to answer, but it is clear particular kinds of therapy are more appropriate for some problems than for others. (p. 500)
- Because no single type of psychotherapy is invariably effective, eclectic approaches in which a therapist uses a variety of techniques and thus integrates several perspectives are sometimes used. (p. 502)

EVALUATE

1. Match each of the following treatment strategies with the statement you might expect to hear from a therapist using that strategy.
   1. Group therapy
   2. Unconditional positive regard
   3. Behavioral therapy
   4. Nondirective counseling

   a. "In other words, you don't get along with your mother because she hates your girlfriend, is that right?"
   b. "I want you all to take turns talking about why you decided to come and what you hope to gain from therapy."
   c. "I can understand why you wanted to wreck your friend's car after she hurt your feelings. Now tell me more about the accident."
   d. "That's not appropriate behavior. Let's work on replacing it with something else."

2. _____ therapies assume that people should take responsibility for their lives and the decisions they make.
3. One of the major criticisms of humanistic therapies is that
   a. They are too imprecise and unstructured.
   b. They treat only the symptom of the problem.
   c. The therapist dominates the patient-therapist interaction.
   d. They work well only on clients of lower socioeconomic status.
4. In a controversial study, Eysenck found that some people go into _____ _____, or recovery without treatment, if they are simply left alone instead of treated.

RETHINK

1. How can people be successfully treated in group therapy when individuals with the "same" problem are so different? What advantages might group therapy offer over individual therapy?
2. *From the perspective of a social worker:* How might the types of therapies you employ vary depending on a client's cultural and socioeconomic background?

Answers to Evaluate Questions

1. 1-b, 2-c, 3-d, 4-a; 2. humanistic; 3. a; 4. spontaneous remission

KEY TERMS

humanistic therapy p. 496
person-centered therapy p. 497

interpersonal therapy (IPT) p. 498
group therapy p. 498

family therapy p. 499
spontaneous remission p. 500

Biomedical Therapy: Biological Approaches to Treatment

How are drug, electroconvulsive, and psychosurgical techniques used today in the treatment of psychological disorders?

If you get a kidney infection, your doctor gives you an antibiotic; with luck your kidney should be as good as new about a week later. If your appendix becomes inflamed, a surgeon removes it and your body functions normally once more. Could a comparable approach that focuses on the body's physiology be effective for psychological disturbances?

According to biological approaches to treatment, the answer is yes. Therapists routinely use biomedical therapies. This approach suggests that rather than focusing on a patient's psychological conflicts, past traumas, or environmental factors that may produce abnormal behavior, focusing treatment directly on brain chemistry and other neurological factors may be more appropriate. To do this, therapists can provide treatment with drugs, electric shock, or surgery.

Drug Therapy

drug therapy Control of psychological disorders through the use of drugs.

Drug therapy, the control of psychological disorders through drugs, works by altering the operation of neurotransmitters and neurons in the brain. Some drugs operate by inhibiting neurotransmitters or receptor neurons, which reduces activity at particular synapses, the sites where nerve impulses travel from one neuron to another. Other drugs do just the opposite: They increase the activity of certain neurotransmitters or neurons, which allows particular neurons to fire more frequently (see Figure 1).

ANTIPSYCHOTIC DRUGS

antipsychotic drugs Drugs that temporarily reduce psychotic symptoms such as agitation, hallucinations, and delusions.

Probably no greater change has occurred in mental hospitals than the successful introduction in the mid-1950s of **antipsychotic drugs**—drugs used to reduce severe symptoms of disturbance, such as loss of touch with reality and agitation. Previously, the typical mental hospital wasn't very different from the stereotypical 19th-century insane asylum; it gave mainly custodial care to screaming, moaning, clawing patients who displayed bizarre behaviors. However, in just a matter of days after hospital staff members administered antipsychotic drugs, the wards became considerably calmer environments in which professionals could do more than just try to get patients through the day without causing serious harm to themselves or others.

This dramatic change came about through the introduction of the drug *chlorpromazine*. Along with other similar drugs, chlorpromazine rapidly became the most popular and successful treatment for schizophrenia. Today drug therapy is the preferred treatment for most cases of severely abnormal behavior and is used for most patients hospitalized with psychological disorders. The newest generation of antipsychotics, referred to as *atypical antipsychotics,* have fewer side effects; they include *rizperidone, olanzapine,* and *paliperidone* (Lublin, Eberhard, & Levander, 2005; Savas, Yumru, & Kaya, 2007; Nasrallah et al., 2008).

How do antipsychotic drugs work? Most block dopamine receptors at the brain's synapses. Atypical antipsychotics affect both serotonin and dopamine levels in certain parts of the brain, such as those related to planning and goal-directed activity (Sawa & Snyder, 2002; Advokat, 2005).

Drug Treatments			
Class of Drug	**Effects of Drug**	**Primary Action of Drug**	**Examples**
Antipsychotic Drugs, Atypical Antipsychotic Drugs	Reduction in loss of touch with reality, agitation	Block dopamine receptors	Antipsychotic: Chlorpromazine (Thorazine), clozapine (Clozaril), haloperidol (Haldol)
			Atypical Antipsychotic: rizperadine, olanzapine
Antidepressant Drugs			
Tricyclic antidepressants	Reduction in depression	Permit rise in neurotransmitters such as norepinepherine	Trazodone (Desyrel), amitriptyline (Elavil), desipramine (Norpamin)
MAO inhibitors	Reduction in depression	Prevent MAO from breaking down neurotransmitters	Phenelzine (Nardil), tranylcypromine (Parnate)
Selective serotonin reuptake inhibitors (SSRIs)	Reduction in depression	Inhibit reuptake of serotonin	Fluoxetine (Prozac), Luvox, Paxil, Celexa, Zoloft, nefazodone (Serzone)
Mood Stabilizers			
Lithium	Mood stabilization	Can alter transmission of impulses within neurons	Lithium (Lithonate), Depakote, Tegretol
Antianxiety Drugs	Reduction in anxiety	Increase activity of neurotransmitter GABA	Benzodiazepines (Valium, Xanax)

FIGURE 1 The major classes of drugs used to treat psychological disorders have different effects on the brain and nervous system.

Despite the effectiveness of antipsychotic drugs, they do not produce a "cure" in the same way that, say, penicillin cures an infection. Most of the time, the symptoms reappear when the drug is withdrawn. Furthermore, such drugs can have long-term side effects, such as dryness of the mouth and throat, dizziness, and sometimes tremors and loss of muscle control, which may continue after drug treatments are stopped (Voruganti et al., 2007).

ANTIDEPRESSANT DRUGS

As their name suggests, **antidepressant drugs** are a class of medications used in cases of severe depression to improve the patient's mood and feeling of well-being. They are also sometimes used for other disorders, such as anxiety disorders and bulimia (Walsh et al., 2006; Hedges et al., 2007).

Most antidepressant drugs work by changing the concentration of specific neurotransmitters in the brain. For example, *tricyclic drug* increase the availability of norepinephrine at the synapses of neurons, whereas *MAO inhibitors* prevent the enzyme monoamine oxidase (MAO) from breaking down neurotransmitters. Newer antidepressants—such as Lexapro—are *selective serotonin reuptake inhibitors (SSRIs)*. SSRIs target the neurotransmitter serotonin and permit it to linger at the synapse. Some antidepressants produce a combination of effects. For instance, nefazodone (Serzone) blocks serotonin at some receptor sites but not others, while bupropion (Wellbutrin and Zyban) affects the norepinephrine and dopamine systems (see Figure 2; Lucki & O'Leary, 2004; Robinson, 2007; Dhillon, Yang, & Curran, 2008).

Finally, there are some newer drugs on the horizon. For instance, scientists have found that the anesthetic ketamine blocks the neural receptor NMDA, which affects the neurotransmitter glutamate. Glutamate plays an important role in mood regulation and the ability to experience pleasure, and researchers believe that ketamine blockers may prove to be useful in the treatment of depression (Skolnick, Popik, & Trullas, 2009).

antidepressant drugs Medications that improve a severely depressed patient's mood and feeling of well-being.

> **Study Alert**
> To help organize your study of different drugs used in therapy, review Figure 1, which classifies them according to the categories of antipsychotic, atypical antipsychotic, antidepressant, mood-stabilizing, and antianxiety drugs.

FIGURE 2 In (a), selective serotonin reuptake inhibitors (SSRIs) reduce depression by permitting the neurotransmitter serotonin to remain in the synapse. In (b), a newer antidepressant, Nefazodone (Serzone), operates more selectively to block serotonin at some sites but not others, which helps to reduce the side effects of the drug. (Source: Based on Mischoulon, 2000.)

Prozac is a widely prescribed—but still controversial—antidepressant.

The overall success rates of antidepressant drugs is good. Unlike antipsychotic drugs, antidepressants can produce lasting, long-term recovery from depression. In many cases, even after patients stop taking the drugs, their depression does not return. On the other hand, antidepressant drugs may produce side effects such as drowsiness and faintness, and there is evidence that SSRI antidepressants can increase the risk of suicide in children and adolescents (Gibbons et al., 2007; Leckman & King, 2007; Olfson & Marcus, 2008).

Consumers spend billions of dollars each year on antidepressant drugs. In particular, the antidepressant *Fluoxetine*, sold under the trade name *Prozac*, has been highlighted on magazine covers and has been the topic of best-sellers.

Does Prozac deserve its acclaim? In some respects, yes. It is effective and has relatively few side effects. Furthermore, many people who do not respond to other types of antidepressants do well on Prozac. On the other hand, 20–30% of users report experiencing nausea and diarrhea, and a smaller number report sexual dysfunctions (Kramer, 1993; Brambilla et al., 2005; Fenter, 2006).

Another substance that has received a great deal of publicity is *St. John's wort*, an herb that some have called a "natural" antidepressant. Although it is widely used in Europe for the treatment of depression, the U.S. Food and Drug Administration considers it a dietary supplement, and therefore the substance is available here without a prescription.

Despite the popularity of St. John's wort, definitive clinical tests have found that the herb is ineffective in the treatment of depression. However, because some research shows that the herb successfully reduces certain psychological symptoms, some proponents argue that using it is reasonable. In any case, people should not use St. John's wort to medicate themselves without consulting a mental health-care professional (Williams et al., 2000; Shelton et al., 2002; Thachil, Mohan & Bhugra, 2007).

MOOD STABILIZERS

mood stabilizers Drugs used to treat mood disorders that prevent manic episodes of bipolar disorder.

Mood stabilizers are used to treat mood disorders. For example, the drug *lithium*, a form of mineral salts, has been used very successfully in patients with bipolar disorders. Although no one knows definitely why, lithium and other mood stabilizers such as divalproex sodium (*Depakote*) and carbamazepine (*Tegretol*) effectively reduce manic episodes. However, they do not effectively treat depressive phases of bipolar disorder, so antidepressants are usually prescribed during those phases (Abraham & Calabrese, 2007; L. Smith et al., 2007; Salvi et al., 2008).

Lithium and similar drugs have a quality that sets them apart from other drug treatments: They can be a *preventive* treatment that blocks future episodes of manic depression. Often, people who have had episodes of bipolar disorder can take a daily dose of lithium to prevent a recurrence of their symptoms. Most other drugs are useful only when symptoms of psychological disturbance occur.

ANTIANXIETY DRUGS

As the name implies, **antianxiety drugs** reduce the level of anxiety a person experiences and increase feelings of well-being. They are prescribed not only to reduce general tension in people who are experiencing temporary difficulties, but also to aid in the treatment of more serious anxiety disorders (Zito, 1993).

antianxiety drugs Drugs that reduce the level of anxiety a person experiences essentially by reducing excitability and increasing feelings of well-being.

Antianxiety drugs such as Xanax and Valium are among the medications physicians most frequently prescribe. In fact, more than half of all U.S. families have someone who has taken such a drug at one time or another.

Although the popularity of antianxiety drugs suggests that they hold few risks, they can produce a number of potentially serious side effects. For instance, they can cause fatigue, and long-term use can lead to dependence. Moreover, when taken in combination with alcohol, some antianxiety drugs can be lethal. But a more important issue concerns their use to suppress anxiety. Almost every therapeutic approach to psychological disturbance views continuing anxiety as a signal of some other sort of problem. Thus, drugs that mask anxiety may simply be hiding other difficulties. Consequently, rather than confronting their underlying problems, people may be hiding from them through the use of antianxiety drugs.

Electroconvulsive Therapy (ECT)

First introduced in the 1930s, **electroconvulsive therapy (ECT)** is a procedure used in the treatment of severe depression. In the procedure, an electric current of 70–150 volts is briefly administered to a patient's head, which causes a loss of consciousness and often causes seizures. Typically, health-care professionals sedate patients and give them muscle relaxants before administering the current; such preparations help reduce the intensity of muscle contractions produced during ECT. The typical patient receives about 10 ECT treatments in the course of a month, but some patients continue with maintenance treatments for months afterward (Greenberg & Kellner, 2005; Stevens & Harper, 2007).

electroconvulsive therapy (ECT) A procedure used in the treatment of severe depression in which an electric current of 70–150 volts is briefly administered to a patient's head.

ECT is a controversial technique. Apart from the obvious distastefulness of a treatment that evokes images of electrocution, side effects occur frequently. For instance, after treatment patients often experience disorientation, confusion, and sometimes memory loss that may remain for months. Furthermore, ECT often does not produce long-term improvement; one study found that without follow-up medication, depression returned in most patients who had undergone ECT treatments. Finally, even when ECT does work, we do not know why, and some critics believe it may cause permanent brain damage (Sackeim et al., 2001; Gardner & O'Connor, 2008; Kato, 2009).

In light of the drawbacks to ECT, why do therapists use it at all? Basically, they use it because in many severe cases of depression, it offers the only quickly effective treatment. For instance, it may prevent depressed, suicidal individuals from committing suicide, and it can act more quickly than antidepressive medications.

The use of ECT has risen in the last decade with more than 100,000 people undergoing it each year. Still, ECT tends to be used only when other treatments have proved ineffective, and researchers continue to search for alternative treatments (Fink, 2000; Eranti & McLoughlin, 2003; Pandya, Pozuelo, & Malone, 2007).

One new and promising alternative to ECT is **transcranial magnetic stimulation (TMS).** TMS creates a precise magnetic pulse in a specific area of the brain. By activating particular neurons, TMS has been effective in relieving the symptoms of major depression in a number of controlled experiments. However, the therapy can produce side effects, such as seizures and convulsions, and it is still considered experimental (Lefaucheur et al., 2007; Leo & Latif, 2007; Kim, Pesiridou, & O'Reardon, 2009).

transcranial magnetic stimulation (TMS) A depression treatment in which a precise magnetic pulse is directed to a specific area of the brain.

Psychosurgery

psychosurgery Brain surgery once used to reduce the symptoms of mental disorder but rarely used today.

If ECT strikes you as a questionable procedure, the use of **psychosurgery**—brain surgery in which the object is to reduce symptoms of mental disorder—probably appears even more dubious. A technique used only rarely today, psychosurgery was introduced as a "treatment of last resort" in the 1930s.

The initial form of psychosurgery, a *prefrontal lobotomy,* consisted of surgically destroying or removing parts of a patient's frontal lobes, which surgeons thought controlled emotionality. In the 1930s and 1940s, surgeons performed the procedure on thousands of patients often with little precision. For example, in one common technique, a surgeon literally would jab an ice pick under a patient's eyeball and swivel it back and forth (El-Hai, 2005; Ogren & Sandlund, 2007).

Psychosurgery often did improve a patient's behavior—but not without drastic side effects. Along with remission of the symptoms of the mental disorder, patients sometimes experienced personality changes and became bland, colorless, and unemotional. In other cases, patients became aggressive and unable to control their impulses. In the worst cases, treatment resulted in the patient's death.

With the introduction of effective drug treatments—and the obvious ethical questions regarding the appropriateness of forever altering someone's personality—psychosurgery became nearly obsolete. However, it is still used in very rare cases when all other procedures have failed and the patient's behavior presents a high risk to the patient and others. For example, surgeons sometimes use a more precise form of psychosurgery called a *cingulotomy* in rare cases of obsessive-compulsive disorder in which they destroy tissue in the *anterior cignulate* area of the brain. In another technique, *gamma knife surgery,* beams of radiation are used to destroy areas of the brain related to obsessive-compulsive disorder (Shah et al., 2008; Carey, 2009c; Lopes et al, 2009; Wilkinson, 2009).

Occasionally, dying patients with severe, uncontrollable pain also receive psychosurgery. Still, even these cases raise important ethical issues, and psychosurgery remains a highly controversial treatment (Mashour, Walker, & Martuza, 2005; Steele et al., 2007).

Biomedical Therapies in Perspective

In some respects, no greater revolution has occurred in the field of mental health than biological approaches to treatment. As previously violent, uncontrollable patients have been calmed by the use of drugs, mental hospitals have been able to concentrate more on actually helping patients and less on custodial functions. Similarly, patients whose lives have been disrupted by depression or bipolar episodes have been able to function normally, and other forms of drug therapy have also shown remarkable results.

The use of biomedical therapy for everyday problems is rising. For example, one survey of users of a college counseling service found that from 1989 to 2001, the proportion of students receiving treatment who were taking medication for psychological disorders increased from 10% to 25% (Benton et al., 2003).

Furthermore, new forms of biomedical therapy are promising. For example, the newest treatment possibility—which remains experimental at this point—is gene therapy. As we discussed when considering behavioral genetics, specific genes may be introduced to particular regions of the brain. These genes then have the potential to reverse or even prevent biochemical events that give rise to psychological disorders (Sapolsky, 2003; Lymberis et al., 2004; Tuszynski, 2007).

"The drug has, however, proved more effective than traditional psychoanalysis."

Despite their current usefulness and future promise, biomedical therapies do not represent a cure-all for psychological disorders. For one thing, critics charge that such therapies merely provide relief of the *symptoms* of mental disorder; as soon as the drugs are withdrawn, the symptoms return. Although it is considered a major step in the right direction, biomedical treatment may not solve the underlying problems that led a patient to therapy in the first place. Biomedical therapies also can produce side effects that range from minor to serious physical reactions to the development of *new* symptoms of abnormal behavior. Finally, an overreliance on biomedical therapies may lead therapists to overlook alternative forms of treatment that may be helpful.

Still, biomedical therapies—sometimes alone and more often in conjunction with psychotherapy—have permitted millions of people to function more effectively. Furthermore, although biomedical therapy and psychotherapy appear distinct, research shows that biomedical therapies ultimately may not be as different from talk therapies as one might imagine, at least in terms of their consequences.

Specifically, measures of brain functioning as a result of drug therapy compared with psychotherapy show little difference in outcomes. For example, one study compared the reactions of patients with major depression who received either an antidepressant drug or psychotherapy. After six weeks of either therapy, activity in the portion of the brain related to the disorder—the basal ganglia—had changed in similar ways, and that area appeared to function more normally. Although such research is not definitive, it does suggest that at least for some disorders, psychotherapy may be just as effective as biomedical interventions—and vice versa. Research also makes it clear that no single treatment is effective universally and that each type of treatment has both advantages and disadvantages (Hollon, Thase, & Markowitz, 2002; DeRubeis, Hollon, & Shelton, 2003; Pinquart, Duberstein, & Lyness, 2006; Greenberg & Goldman, 2009).

> **Study Alert**
> Remember that biomedical treatments have both benefits and drawbacks.

Community Psychology: Focus on Prevention

While deinstitutionalization has had many successes, it has also contributed to the release of mental patients into the community with little or no support. As a result, many have become homeless.

community psychology A branch of psychology that focuses on the prevention and minimization of psychological disorders in the community.

deinstitutionalization The transfer of former mental patients from institutions to the community.

Each of the treatments we have reviewed has a common element: It is a "restorative" treatment aimed at alleviating psychological difficulties that already exist. However, an approach known as **community psychology** has a different aim: to prevent or minimize the incidence of psychological disorders.

Community psychology came of age in the 1960s, when mental health professionals developed plans for a nationwide network of community mental health centers. The hope was that those centers would provide low-cost mental health services, including short-term therapy and community educational programs. In another development, the population of mental hospitals has plunged as drug treatments made physical restraint of patients unnecessary.

This transfer of former mental patients out of institutions and into the community—a process known as **deinstitutionalization**—was encouraged by the growth of the community psychology movement (see Figure 3). Proponents of deinstitutionalization wanted to ensure not only that deinstitutionalized patients received proper treatment, but also that their civil rights were maintained (Wolff, 2002; St. Dennis et al., 2006).

Unfortunately, the promise of deinstitutionalization has not been met largely because insufficient resources are provided to deinstitutionalized patients. What started as a worthy attempt to move people out of mental institutions and into the community ended, in many cases, with former patients being dumped into the community without any real support. Many became homeless—between 15–35% of all homeless adults are thought to have a major psychological disorder—and some became involved in illegal acts caused by their disorders. In short, many people who

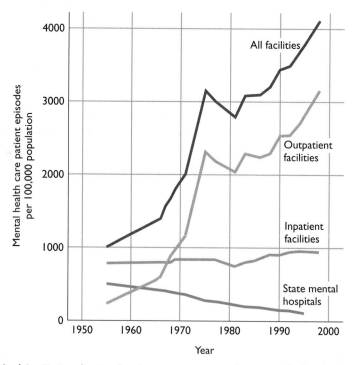

FIGURE 3 As deinstitutionalization has become more prevalent over the last half century, the number of patients being treated in state mental hospitals has declined significantly, while the number of outpatient facilities has increased. (Source: From Rodger Doyle, "Deinstitutionalization," *Scientific American,* December 2002, p. 38. Copyright 2002 Rodger Doyle. Reprinted with permission.)

"Looking good!"

need treatment do not get it, and in some cases care for people with psychological disorders has simply shifted from one type of treatment site to another (Shinn et al., 2007; Dumont & Dumont, 2008; Price, 2009).

On the other hand, the community psychology movement has had some positive outcomes. Its emphasis on prevention has led to new approaches to psychological disorders as we discuss in *Applying Psychology in the 21st Century.* Furthermore, telephone "hot lines" are now common. At any time of the day or night, people experiencing acute stress can call a trained, sympathetic listener who can provide immediate—although obviously limited—treatment (Reese, Conoley, & Brossart, 2002; Paukert, Stagner, & Hope, 2004; Cauce, 2007).

College and high school crisis centers are another innovation that grew out of the community psychology movement. Modeled after suicide prevention hot-line centers (services that enable potential suicide victims to call and speak to someone about their difficulties), crisis centers give callers an opportunity to discuss life crises with a sympathetic listener, who is often a volunteer.

Beating the Odds: Preventing Psychological Disorders Before They Start

When we think about the possibility of contracting physical diseases such as cancer, diabetes, or heart disease, we often think of preventive measures we can take: lose weight, eat nutritious foods, exercise regularly, don't smoke. But when we think of psychological disorders such as depression, anxiety disorders, or schizophrenia, we tend to assume that we are just passive victims and can do nothing to prevent them. But is that assumption really true?

Rather than treating psychological disorders after the symptoms fully appear, some researchers now suggest that an alternative might be to provide appropriate intervention as soon as the initial signs of an impending problem emerge before a disorder fully develops. Taking advantage of opportunities to potentially stop or reduce the progression of psychological disorders would reduce the cost of mental health care as well as lessen the suffering of individual patients. Essentially, these researchers argue, it is cheaper and less painful to prevent a problem from occurring than it is to fix it after the fact (Cloud, 2009; National Research Council and Institute of Medicine of the National Academies, 2009).

But can psychological disorders be prevented, particularly when they have a genetic component? The answer, according to a growing body of research, is yes. The expression of a genetic disposition toward mental illness often depends on environmental factors. Research is finding that young people who are at risk of developing a disorder (because one of their parents suffers from the disorder themselves, for example) benefit from school- and home-based interventions that reduce the environmental stress factors that might trigger the disorder.

Consider, for example, depression. Children of depressed parents are at

Early intervention can prevent psychological disorders from becoming more serious.

increased risk of developing depression themselves. But when these children are active and engaged with others, and when they understand what depression is and that it can be treated, their increased risk of becoming depressed appears to diminish. Specifically, family-based interventions to help children of depressed parents develop resilience have been shown to be effective in reducing the onset of depression. In such programs, parents are taught communication skills, and the children are taught coping skills. In addition, the entire family is educated about depression and how it affects their relationships with one another. Interventions such as this can reduce children's predepressive symptoms and provide better long-term outcomes (Beards-

lee et al., 2007; Riley et al. 2008; Garber et al., 2009).

Other research suggests that early interventions can reduce the onset of additional psychological disorders and related problems, such as substance abuse, conduct disorders, antisocial behavior, aggression, and even schizophrenia. The key is to catch and stop these problems early in life among at-risk children.

The potential benefits in terms of improved quality of life for those individuals as well as potential benefits to society of reducing the cost of care are great, generating increasing interest in approaches to prevention of psychological disorders (National Research Council and Institute of Medicine of the National Academies, 2009).

RETHINK

- Because it is important to catch the symptoms of psychological disorders early on, would you favor routine in-school behavioral screening of children for symptoms of disorders? Why or why not?
- Do you think children of individuals with moderate or severe psychological disorders should receive genetic screening to determine if they carry genes related to the disorder? Why or why not?

If you decide to seek therapy, you're faced with a daunting task. Choosing a therapist is not a simple matter. One place to begin the process of identifying a therapist is at the "Help Center" of the American Psychological Association at http://www.apa .org/helpcenter. And, if you start therapy, several general guidelines can help you determine whether you've made the right choice:

You and your therapist should agree on the goals for treatment. They should be clear, specific, and attainable.

- *You should feel comfortable with your therapist.* You should not be intimidated by or in awe of a therapist. Rather, you should trust the therapist and feel free to discuss the most personal issues without fearing a negative reaction. In sum, the "personal chemistry" should be right.
- *Therapists should have appropriate training and credentials and should be licensed by appropriate state and local agencies.* Check therapists' membership in national and state professional associations. In addition, the cost of therapy, billing practices, and other business matters should be clear. It is not a breach of etiquette to put these matters on the table during an initial consultation.
- *You should feel that you are making progress after therapy has begun, despite occasional setbacks.* If you have no sense of improvement after repeated visits, you and your therapist should discuss this issue frankly. Although there is no set timetable, the most obvious changes resulting from therapy tend to occur relatively early in the course of treatment. For instance, half of patients in psychotherapy improve by the 8th session, and three-fourths by the 26th session. The average number of sessions with college students is just 5 (Crits-Cristoph, 1992; HMHL, 1994; Lazarus, 1997).

Be aware that you will have to put in a great deal of effort in therapy. Although our culture promises quick cures for any problem, in reality, solving difficult problems is not easy. You must be committed to making therapy work and should know that it is you, not the therapist, who must do most of the work to resolve your problems. The effort has the potential to pay off handsomely—as you experience a more positive, fulfilling, and meaningful life.

RECAP/EVALUATE/RETHINK

RECAP

How are drug, electroconvulsive, and psychosurgical techniques used today in the treatment of psychological disorders?

- Biomedical treatment approaches suggest that therapy should focus on the physiological causes of abnormal behavior rather than considering psychological factors. Drug therapy, the best example of biomedical treatments, has brought about dramatic reductions in the symptoms of mental disturbance. (p. 504)
- Antipsychotic drugs such as chlorpromazine very effectively reduce psychotic symptoms. Antidepressant drugs such as Prozac reduce depression so successfully that

they are used very widely. Antianxiety drugs, or minor tranquilizers, are among the most frequently prescribed medications of any sort. (p. 504)
- In electroconvulsive therapy (ECT), used in severe cases of depression, a patient receives a brief electric current of 70 to 150 volts. (p. 507)
- Psychosurgery typically consists of surgically destroying or removing certain parts of a patient's brain. (p. 508)
- The community psychology approach encouraged deinstitutionalization in which previously hospitalized mental patients were released into the community. (p. 510)

EVALUATE

1. Antipsychotic drugs have provided effective, long-term, and complete cures for schizophrenia. True or false?
2. One highly effective biomedical treatment for a psychological disorder that is used mainly to arrest and prevent manic-depressive episodes, is
   a. Chlorpromazine
   b. Lithium
   c. Librium
   d. Valium
3. Psychosurgery has grown in popularity as a method of treatment as surgical techniques have become more precise. True or false?
4. The trend toward releasing more patients from mental hospitals and into the community is known as _____.

RETHINK

1. One of the main criticisms of biological therapies is that they treat the symptoms of mental disorder without uncovering and treating the underlying problems from which people are suffering. Do you agree with this criticism? Why?
2. *From the perspective of a politician:* How would you go about regulating the use of electroconvulsive therapy and psychosurgery? Would you restrict their use or make either one completely illegal? Why?

Answers to Evaluate Questions

1. false; schizophrenia can be controlled but not cured by medication; 2. b; 3. false; psychosurgery is now used only as a treatment of last resort; 4. deinstitutionalization.

KEY TERMS

drug therapy p. 504
antipsychotic drugs p. 504
antidepressant drugs p. 505
mood stabilizers p. 506

antianxiety drugs p. 507
electroconvulsive
   therapy (ECT) p. 507

transcranial magnetic
   stimulation (TMS) p. 507
psychosurgery p. 508

community
   psychology p. 510
deinstitutionalization p. 510

- *The self-serving bias*. When their teams win, coaches usually feel that the success is due to their coaching. But when their teams lose, coaches may think it's due to their players' poor skills. Similarly, if you get an A on a test, you may think it's due to your hard work, but if you get a poor grade, it's due to the professor's inadequacies. The reason is the **self-serving bias,** the tendency to attribute success to personal factors (skill, ability, or effort) and attribute failure to factors outside oneself (Krusemark, Campbell, & Clementz, 2008; Shepperd, Malone, & Sweeny, 2008).

- *The fundamental attribution error*. One of the more common attribution biases is the tendency to overattribute others' behavior to dispositional causes and the corresponding failure to recognize the importance of situational causes. Known as the **fundamental attribution error,** this tendency is prevalent in Western cultures. We tend to exaggerate the importance of personality characteristics (dispositional causes) in producing others' behavior and minimize the influence of the environment (situational factors). For example, we are more likely to jump to the conclusion that someone who is often late to work is too lazy to take an earlier bus (a dispositional cause) than to assume that the lateness is due to situational factors, such as the bus always running behind schedule.

    Why is the fundamental attribution error so common? One reason pertains to the nature of information available to the people making an attribution. When we view another person's behavior in a particular setting, the most conspicuous information is the person's behavior. Because the individual's immediate surroundings remain relatively unchanged and less attention grabbing, we center our attention on the person whose behavior we're considering. Consequently, we are more likely to make attributions based on personal dispositional factors and less likely to make attributions relating to the situation (Follett & Hess, 2002; Langdridge & Butt, 2004; Tal-Or & Papirman, 2007).

Social psychologists' awareness of attribution biases has led, in part, to the development of a new branch of economics called behavioral economics. *Behavioral economics* is concerned with how individuals' biases and irrationally affect economic decisions. Rather than viewing people as rational, thoughtful decision makers who are impartially weighing choices to draw conclusions, behavioral economists focus on the irrationality of judgments (Ariely & Norton, 2009).

> **self-serving bias** The tendency to attribute personal success to personal factors (skill, ability, or effort) and to attribute failure to factors outside oneself.
>
> **fundamental attribution error** A tendency to overattribute others' behavior to dispositional causes and minimize of the importance of situational causes.

Exploring DIVERSITY

Attribution Biases in a Cultural Context: How Fundamental Is the Fundamental Attribution Error?

Attribution biases do not affect all of us in the same way. The culture in which we are raised clearly plays a role in the way we attribute others' behavior.

Take, for example, the fundamental attribution error: the tendency to overestimate the importance of personal, dispositional factors and underattribute situational factors in determining the causes of others' behavior. The error is pervasive in Western cultures and not in Eastern societies. For instance, adults in India were more likely to use situational attributions than dispositional ones in explaining events. These findings are the opposite of those for the United States, and they contradict the fundamental attribution error (Miller, 1984, Lien et al., 2006).

One reason for the difference may lie in the norms and values of Eastern society, which emphasize social responsibility and societal obligations to a greater extent than Western societies. In addition, the language spoken in a culture may lead to different sorts of attributions. For instance, a tardy person using English may say, "I am late"; this suggests a personal, dispositional cause ("I am a tardy person"). In contrast, speakers of Spanish who are late say, "The clock caused me to be late." Clearly, the statement in Spanish implies that the cause is situational (Zebrowitz-McArthur, 1988; Macduff, 2006; Alon & Brett, 2007).

Cultural differences in attributions affect subsequent behavior. For example, parents in Asia tend to attribute good academic performance to effort and hard work (situational factors). In contrast, parents in Western cultures tend to de-emphasize the role of effort and attribute school success to innate ability (a dispositional factor). As a result, Asian students in general may strive harder to achieve and ultimately outperform U.S. students in school (Stevenson, Lee, & Mu, 2000; Lien et al., 2006).

The difference in thinking between people in Asian and Western cultures is a reflection of a broader difference in the way the world is perceived. Asian societies generally have a *collectivistic orientation,* a worldview that promotes the notion of interdependence. People with a collectivistic orientation generally see themselves as parts of a larger, interconnected social network and as responsible to others. In contrast, people in Western cultures are more likely to hold an *individualist orientation* that emphasizes personal identity and the uniqueness of the individual. They focus more on what sets them apart from others and what makes them special (Markus & Kitayama, 2003; Wang, 2004; Markus, 2007).

RECAP/EVALUATE/RETHINK

RECAP

What are attitudes, and how are they formed, maintained, and changed?

- Social psychology is the scientific study of the ways in which people's thoughts, feelings, and actions are affected by others and the nature and causes of individual behavior in social situations. (p. 518)
- Attitudes are evaluations of a particular person, behavior, belief, or concept. (p. 519)
- Cognitive dissonance occurs when an individual simultaneously holds two cognitions—attitudes or thoughts—that contradict each other. To resolve the contradiction, the person may modify one cognition, change its importance, add a cognition, or deny a link between the two cognitions—thus bringing about a reduction in dissonance. (p. 522)

How do people form impressions of what others are like and of the causes of their behavior?

- Social cognition involves the way people understand and make sense of others and themselves. People develop schemas that organize information about people and social experiences in memory and allow them to interpret and categorize information about others. (p. 523)
- People form impressions of others in part through the use of central traits—personality characteristics that receive unusually heavy emphasis when we form an impression. (p. 524)
- Information-processing approaches have found that we tend to average together sets of traits to form an overall impression. (p. 524)

- Attribution theory tries to explain how we understand the causes of behavior, particularly with respect to situational or dispositional factors. (p. 525)

What are the biases that influence the ways in which people view others' behavior?

- Even though logical processes are involved, attribution is prone to error. For instance, people are susceptible to the halo effect, assumed-similarity bias, self-serving bias, and fundamental attribution error (the tendency to over-attribute others' behavior to dispositional causes and the corresponding failure to recognize the importance of situational causes). (p. 526)

EVALUATE

1. An evaluation of a particular person, behavior, belief, or concept is called a(n) _____.
2. One brand of peanut butter advertises its product by describing its taste and nutritional value. It is hoping to persuade customers through _____ route processing. In ads for a competing brand, a popular actor happily eats the product—but does not describe it. This approach hopes to persuade customers through _____ route processing.
3. Cognitive dissonance theory suggests that we commonly change our behavior to keep it consistent with our attitudes. True or false?
4. Sopan was happy to lend his textbook to a fellow student who seemed bright and friendly. He was surprised when his classmate did not return it. His assumption that the bright and friendly student would also be responsible reflects the _____ effect.

RETHINK

1. Joan sees Annette, a new coworker, act in a way that seems abrupt and curt. Joan concludes that Annette is unkind and unsociable. The next day Joan sees Annette acting kindly toward another worker. Is Joan likely to change her impression of Annette? Why or why not? Finally, Joan sees several friends of hers laughing and joking with Annette, treating her in a very friendly fashion. Is Joan likely to change her impression of Annette? Why or why not?

2. *From the perspective of a marketing specialist:* Suppose you were assigned to develop a full advertising campaign for a product, including television, radio, and print ads. How might theories of persuasion guide your strategy to suit the different media?

Answers to Evaluate Questions

1. attitude; 2. central, peripheral; 3. false; we typically change our attitudes and not our behavior to reduce cognitive dissonance; 4. halo

KEY TERMS

social psychology p. 518

attitudes p. 519

central route processing p. 520

peripheral route processing p. 520

cognitive dissonance p. 522

social cognition p. 523

schemas p. 523

central traits p. 524

attribution theory p. 525

situational causes (of behavior) p. 525

dispositional causes (of behavior) p. 526

halo effect p. 526

assumed-similarity bias p. 526

self-serving bias p. 527

fundamental attribution error p. 527

Social Influence and Groups

What are the major sources and tactics of social influence?

social influence The process by which the actions of an individual or group affect the behavior of others.

group Two or more people who interact with one another, perceive themselves as part of a group, and are interdependent.

Study Alert

The distinction between the three types of social pressure—conformity, compliance, and obedience—depends on the nature and strength of the social pressure brought to bear on a person.

conformity A change in behavior or attitudes brought about by a desire to follow the beliefs or standards of other people.

You have just transferred to a new college and are attending your first class. When the professor enters, your fellow classmates instantly rise, bow to the professor, and then stand quietly with their hands behind their backs. You've never encountered such behavior, and it makes no sense to you. Is it more likely that you will (1) jump up to join the rest of the class or (2) remain seated?

On the basis of what research has told us about **social influence,** the process by which the actions of an individual or group affect the behavior of others, a person would almost always choose the first option. As you undoubtedly know from your own experience, pressures to conform can be painfully strong and can bring about changes in behavior that otherwise never would have occurred.

Why can conformity pressures in groups be so strong? For one reason, groups and other people generally play a central role in our lives. As defined by social psychologists, **groups** consist of two or more people who (1) interact with one another; (2) perceive themselves as part of a group; and (3) are interdependent—that is, the events that affect one group member affect other members, and the behavior of members has significant consequences for the success of the group in meeting its goals.

Groups develop and hold *norms,* expectations regarding behavior appropriate to the group. Furthermore, we understand that not adhering to group norms can result in retaliation from other group members, ranging from being ignored to being overtly derided or even being rejected or excluded by the group. Thus, people conform to meet the expectations of the group (Baumeister, Twenge, & Nuss, 2002; Jetten, Hornsey, & Adarves-Yorno, 2006).

Groups exert considerable social influence over individuals that ranges from the mundane, such as the decision to wear a certain kind of jeans, to the extreme, such as the cruelty of guards at the Abu Ghraib prison in Iraq. We'll consider three types of social pressure: conformity, compliance, and obedience.

Conformity: Following What Others Do

Conformity is a change in behavior or attitudes brought about by a desire to follow the beliefs or standards of other people. Subtle or even unspoken social pressure results in conformity.

The classic demonstration of pressure to conform comes from a series of studies carried out in the 1950s by Solomon Asch (Asch, 1951). In the experiments, the participants thought they were taking part in a test of perceptual skills with six other people. The experimenter showed the participants one card with three lines of varying length and a second card that had a fourth line that matched one of the first three (see Figure 1). The task was seemingly straightforward: Each of the participants had to announce aloud which of the first three lines was identical in length to the "standard" line on the second card. Because the correct answer was always obvious, the task seemed easy to the participants.

Indeed, because the participants all agreed on the first few trials, the procedure appeared to be simple. But then something odd began to happen. From the perspective of the participant in the group who answered last on each trial, all the answers of the first six participants seemed to be wrong—in fact, unanimously wrong. And this pattern persisted. Over and over again, the first six participants provided answers that contradicted what the last participant believed to be correct. The last participant faced the dilemma of whether to follow his or her own perceptions or follow the group by repeating the answer everyone else was giving.

As you might have guessed, this experiment was more contrived than it appeared. The first six participants were actually confederates (paid employees of the experimenter) who had been instructed to give unanimously erroneous answers in many of the trials. And the study had nothing to do with perceptual skills. Instead, the issue under investigation was conformity.

Asch found that in about one-third of the trials, the participants conformed to the unanimous but erroneous group answer; about 75% of all participants conformed at least once. However, he found strong individual differences. Some participants conformed nearly all the time, whereas others never did.

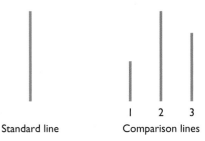

Standard line   Comparison lines

FIGURE 1 Which of the three comparison lines is the same length as the "standard" line?

CONFORMITY CONCLUSIONS

Since Asch's pioneering work, literally hundreds of studies have examined conformity, and we now know a great deal about the phenomenon. Significant findings focus on:

- *The characteristics of the group.* The more attractive a group appears to its members, the greater its ability to produce conformity. Furthermore, a person's relative **status,** the social rank held within a group, is critical: The lower a person's status in the group, the greater groups' power over that person's behavior (Hogg & Hains, 2001).

  status The social rank held within a group.

- *The situation in which the individual is responding.* Conformity is considerably higher when people must respond publicly than it is when they can do so privately, as the founders of the United States noted when they authorized secret ballots in voting.

- *The kind of task.* People working on ambiguous tasks and questions (those with no clear answer) are more susceptible to social pressure. When asked to give an opinion on something, such as what type of clothing is fashionable, a person will more likely yield to conformist pressures than he or she will if asked a question of fact. In addition, tasks at which an individual is less competent than others in the group make conformity more likely. For example, a person who is an infrequent computer user may feel pressure to conform to an opinion about computer brands when in a group of experienced computer users.

- *Unanimity of the group.* Groups that unanimously support a position show the most pronounced conformity pressures. But what about the case in which people with dissenting views have an ally in the group, known as a **social supporter,** who agrees with them? Having just one person present who shares the minority point of view is sufficient to reduce conformity pressures (Prislin, Brewer, & Wilson, 2002; Goodwin, Costa, & Adonu, 2004; Levine & Moreland, 2006).

  social supporter A group member whose dissenting views make nonconformity to the group easier.

GROUPTHINK: CAVING IN TO CONFORMITY

Although we usually think of conformity in terms of our individual relations with others, in some instances conformity pressures in organizations can lead to disastrous effects with long-term consequences. For instance, consider NASA's determination that the falling foam that hit the space shuttle *Columbia* when it took off in 2003 would

Groupthink may explain the poor decision making of NASA engineers that led to the destruction of the space shuttle *Columbia.*

groupthink A type of thinking in which group members share such a strong motivation to achieve consensus that they lose the ability to critically evaluate alternative points of view.

pose no significant danger when it was time for the *Columbia* to land. Despite some engineers' misgivings, a consensus formed that the foam was not dangerous to the shuttle. Ultimately, that consensus proved wrong: The shuttle came apart as it attempted to land, which killed all the astronauts on board (Schwartz & Wald, 2003).

In hindsight, NASA's decision was clearly wrong. How could such a poor decision have been made?

A phenomenon known as groupthink may provide an explanation. **Groupthink** is a type of thinking in which group members share such a strong motivation to achieve consensus that they lose the ability to critically evaluate alternative points of view. Groupthink is most likely to occur when a popular or powerful leader is surrounded by people of lower status—which is obviously the case with any U.S. president and his or her advisers but is also true in a variety of other organizations (Janis, 1997; Kowert, 2002; Baron, 2005; Henningsen, Henningsen, & Eden, 2006).

Groupthink typically leads to poor decisions. Groups limit the list of possible solutions to just a few, and they spend relatively little time considering any alternatives once the leader seems to be leaning toward a particular solution. In addition, groups may fall prey to *entrapment,* a circumstance in which commitments to a failing point of view or course of action are increased to justify investments in time and energy that have already been made (Weiss & Weiss, 2003; Turner, Pratkanis, & Struckman, 2007).

Ultimately, group members may completely ignore information that challenges a developing consensus. Because historical research suggests that many disastrous decisions reflect groupthink, it is important for groups to be on guard (Kowert, 2002; Chapman, 2006; Packer, 2009).

CONFORMITY TO SOCIAL ROLES

Another way in which conformity influences behavior is through social roles. *Social roles* are the behaviors that are associated with people in a given position. For example, the role of "student" comprises behaviors such as studying, listening to an instructor, and attending class. Like a theatrical role, social roles tell us what behavior is associated with a given position.

In some cases, though, social roles influence us so profoundly that we engage in behavior in entirely atypical—and damaging—ways. This fact was brought home in an influential experiment conducted by Philip Zimbardo and colleagues. In the study, the researchers set up a mock prison complete with cells, solitary confinement cubicles, and a small recreation area. The researchers then advertised for participants who were willing to spend 2 weeks in a study of prison life. Once they identified the study participants, a flip of a coin designated who would be a prisoner and who would be a prison guard. Neither prisoners nor guards were told how to fulfill their roles (Zimbardo, Maslach, & Haney, 2000; Zimbardo, 1973, 2007).

After just a few days in this mock prison, the students assigned to be guards became abusive to the prisoners by waking them at odd hours and subjecting them to arbitrary punishment. They withheld food from the prisoners and forced them into hard labor. On the other hand, the students assigned to the prisoner role soon became docile and submissive to the guards. They became extremely demoralized, and one slipped into a depression so severe he was released after just a few days. In fact, after only 6 days of captivity, the remaining prisoners' reactions became so extreme that the study was ended.

The experiment (which, it's important to note, drew criticism on both methodological and ethical grounds) provided a clear lesson: Conforming to a social role can have a powerful consequence on the behavior of even normal, well-adjusted people and induce them to change their behavior in sometimes undesirable ways. This phenomenon may explain how the situation in which U.S. Army guards at the Iraq Abu Ghraib prison found themselves could have led to their abusive behavior toward the prisoners (Zimbardo, 2007; Haney & Zimbardo, 2009).

Compliance: Submitting to Direct Social Pressure

When we refer to conformity, we usually mean a phenomenon in which the social pressure is subtle or indirect. But in some situations social pressure is much more obvious with direct, explicit pressure to endorse a particular point of view or behave in a certain way. Social psychologists call the type of behavior that occurs in response to direct social pressure **compliance.**

Several specific techniques represent attempts to gain compliance. Those frequently employed include:

compliance Behavior that occurs in response to direct social pressure.

- *Foot-in-the-door technique.* A salesperson comes to your door and asks you to accept a small sample. You agree, thinking you have nothing to lose. A little later a larger request comes; because you have already agreed to the first one, you have a hard time turning it down.

   The salesperson in this case is using a tried-and-true strategy that social psychologists call the foot-in-the-door technique. In the *foot-in-the-door technique*, you ask a person to agree to a small request and later ask that person to comply with a more important one. It turns out that compliance with the more important request increases significantly when the person first agrees to the smaller favor.

   Researchers first demonstrated the foot-in-the-door phenomenon in a study in which a number of experimenters went door to door asking residents to sign a petition in favor of safe driving (Freedman & Fraser, 1966). Almost everyone complied with that small, benign request. A few weeks later, different experimenters contacted the residents and made a much larger request for the residents to erect a huge sign on their front lawns that read, "Drive Carefully." The results were clear: 55% of those who had signed the petition agreed to the request to put up a sign, whereas only 17% of the people in a control group who had not been asked to sign the petition agreed to put up a sign.

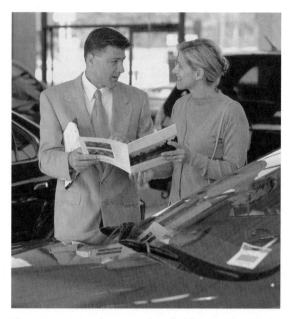

The persuasive techniques identified by social psychologists can be seen in practice at auto dealerships.

Why does the foot-in-the-door technique work? For one reason, involvement with the small request leads to an interest in an issue; taking an action—any action—makes the individual more committed to the issue, which thereby increasing the likelihood of future compliance. Another explanation revolves around people's self-perceptions. By complying with the initial request, individuals may come to see themselves as people who provide help when asked. Then, when confronted with the larger request, they agree in order to maintain the kind of consistency in attitudes and behavior that we described earlier. Although we don't know which of these two explanations is more accurate, it is clear that the foot-in-the-door strategy is effective (Burger & Caldwell, 2003; Bloom, McBride, & Pollak, 2006; Guéguen et al., 2008).

- *Door-in-the-face technique.* A fund-raiser asks for a $500 contribution. You laughingly refuse and tell her that the amount is way out of your league. She then asks for a $10 contribution. What do you do? If you are like most people, you'll probably be a lot more compliant than you would be if she hadn't asked for the huge contribution first. In this tactic, called the *door-in-the-face technique,* someone makes a large request, expects it to be refused, and follows it with a smaller one. This strategy, which is the opposite of the foot-in-the-door approach, has also proved to be effective (Pascual & Guéguen, 2005, 2006; Turner et al., 2007; Ebster & Neumayr, 2008).

In a field experiment that demonstrates the success of this approach, experimenters stopped college students on the street and asked them to agree to a substantial favor—acting as unpaid counselors for juvenile delinquents 2 hours a week for 2 years (Cialdini et al., 1975). Not surprisingly, no one agreed to make such an enormous commitment. But when they were later asked the considerably smaller favor of taking a group of delinquents on a 2-hour trip to the zoo, half the people complied. In comparison, only 17% of a control group of participants who had not first received the larger request agreed.

The use of this technique is widespread. You may have tried it at some point yourself by perhaps by asking your parents for a large increase in your allowance and later settling for less. Similarly, television writers, by sometimes sprinkling their scripts with obscenities that they know network censors will cut out, hope to keep other key phrases intact (Cialdini & Sagarin, 2005).

- *That's-not-all technique.* In this technique, a salesperson offers you a deal at an inflated price. But immediately after the initial offer, the salesperson offers an incentive, discount, or bonus to clinch the deal.

Although it sounds transparent, this practice can be quite effective. In one study, the experimenters set up a booth and sold cupcakes for 75¢ each. In one condition, the experimenters directly told customers that the price was 75¢. In another condition, they told customers that the price was originally $1 but had been reduced to 75¢. As we might predict, more people bought cupcakes at the "reduced" price—even though it was identical to the price in the other experimental condition (Burger, Reed, & DeCesare, 1999; Pratkanis, 2007).

- *Not-so-free* sample. If you ever receive a free sample, keep in mind that it comes with a psychological cost. Although they may not couch it in these terms, salespeople who provide samples to potential customers do so to instigate the norm of reciprocity. The *norm of reciprocity* is the well accepted societal standard dictating that we should treat other people as they treat us. Receiving a *not-so-free sample,* then, suggests the need for reciprocation—in the form of a purchase, of course (Cialdini, 2006; Park & Antonioni, 2007; Burger et al., 2009).

Companies seeking to sell their products to consumers often use the techniques identified by social psychologists for promoting compliance. But employers also use them to bring about compliance and raise employees' productivity in the workplace. In fact, **industrial-organizational (I/O) psychology,** a close cousin to social psychology, considers issues such as worker motivation, satisfaction, safety, and productivity. I/O psychologists also focus on the operation and design of organizations; they ask questions such as how decision making can be improved in large organizations and how the fit between workers and their jobs can be maximized.

industrial-organizational (I/O) psychology The branch of psychology focusing on work- and job-related issues, including worker motivation, satisfaction, safety, and productivity.

Obedience: Following Direct Orders

Compliance techniques are used to gently lead people toward agreement with a request. In some cases, however, requests aim to produce **obedience,** a change in behavior in response to the commands of others. Although obedience is considerably less common than conformity and compliance, it does occur in several specific kinds of relationships. For example, we may show obedience to our bosses, teachers, or parents merely because of the power they hold to reward or punish us.

obedience A change in behavior in response to the commands of others.

To acquire an understanding of obedience, consider for a moment how you might respond if a stranger said to you:

> I've devised a new way of improving memory. All I need is for you to teach people a list of words and then give them a test. The test procedure requires only that you give learners a shock each time they make a mistake on the test. To administer the shocks, you will use a "shock generator" that gives shocks ranging from 15 to 450 volts. You can see that the switches are labeled from "slight shock" through "danger: severe shock" at the top level, where there are three red Xs. But don't worry; although the shocks may be painful, they will cause no permanent damage.

Presented with this situation, you would be likely to think that neither you nor anyone else would go along with the stranger's unusual request. Clearly, it lies outside the bounds of what we consider good sense.

Or does it? Suppose the stranger asking for your help was a psychologist conducting an experiment. Or suppose the request came from your teacher, your employer, or your military commander—all people in authority with a seemingly legitimate reason for the request.

If you still believe it's unlikely that you would comply—think again. The situation presented above describes a classic experiment conducted by social psychologist Stanley Milgram in the 1960s. In the study, an experimenter told participants to give increasingly stronger shocks to another person as part of a study on learning (see Figure 2). In reality, the experiment had nothing to do with learning; the real issue under consideration was the degree to which participants would comply with the experimenter's requests. In fact, the "learner" supposedly receiving the shocks was a confederate who never really received any punishment (Milgram, 2005).

Most people who hear a description of Milgram's experiment feel it is unlikely that *any* participant would give the maximum level of shock—or, for that matter, any shock at all. Even a group of psychiatrists to whom the situation was described predicted that fewer than 2% of the participants would fully comply and administer the strongest shocks.

However, the actual results contradicted both experts' and nonexperts' predictions. Some 65% of the participants eventually used the highest setting on the shock generator—450 volts—to shock the learner. This obedience occurred even though the learner, who had mentioned at the start of the experiment that he had a heart

FIGURE 2 This fearsome "shock generator" led participants to believe they were administering electric shocks to another person, who was connected to the generator by electrodes that were attached to the skin. (Source: Copyright 1965 by Stanley Milgram. From the film *Obedience*, distributed by the New York University Film Library and Pennsylvania State University, PCR.)

condition, demanded to be released, screaming, "Let me out of here! Let me out of here! My heart's bothering me. Let me out of here!" Despite the learner's pleas, most participants continued to administer the shocks.

Why did so many individuals comply with the experimenter's demands? The participants, who were extensively interviewed after the experiment, said they obeyed primarily because they believed that the experimenter would be responsible for any potential ill effects that befell the learner. The participants accepted the experimenter's orders, then, because they thought that they personally could not be held accountable for their actions—they could always blame the experimenter (Blass, 1996, 2004).

Although most participants in the Milgram experiment said later they felt the knowledge gained from the study outweighed the discomfort they may have felt, the experiment has been criticized for creating an extremely trying set of circumstances for the participants and thereby raised serious ethical concerns. Undoubtedly, the same experiment could not be conducted today because of ethical considerations.

Other critics have suggested that Milgram's methods were ineffective in creating a situation that actually mirrored real-world obedience. For example, how often are people placed in a situation in which someone orders them to continue hurting a victim, while the victim's protests are ignored (Blass, 2000, 2004)?

Despite these concerns, Milgram's research remains the strongest laboratory demonstration of obedience. And partial replications of Milgram's work, conducted in an ethically defensible way, find similar results, which adds credence to the original work (Blass, 2009; Burger, 2009).

Furthermore, we need only consider actual instances of obedience to authority to witness some frightening real-life parallels. For instance, after World War II, the major defense that Nazi officers gave to excuse their participation in atrocities during the war was that they were "only following orders." Milgram's experiment, which was motivated in part by his desire to explain the behavior of everyday Germans during World War II, forces us to ask ourselves this question: Would we be able to withstand the intense power of authority?

Study Alert

Because of its graphic demonstration of obedience to authority, the Milgram experiment is one of the most famous and influential studies in social psychology.

RECAP/EVALUATE/RETHINK

RECAP

What are the major sources and tactics of social influence?

- Social influence is the area of social psychology concerned with situations in which the actions of an individual or group affect the behavior of others. (p. 530)
- Conformity refers to changes in behavior or attitudes that result from a desire to follow the beliefs or standards of others. (p. 530)
- Compliance is behavior that results from direct social pressure. Among the ways of eliciting compliance are the foot-in-the-door, door-in-the-face, that's-not-all, and not-so-free-sample techniques. (p. 533)
- Obedience is a change in behavior in response to the commands of others. (p. 535)

EVALUATE

1. A _____ _____, or person who agrees with the dissenting viewpoint, is likely to reduce conformity.
2. Who pioneered the study of conformity?
   a. Skinner
   b. Asch
   c. Milgram
   d. Fiala
3. Which of the following techniques asks a person to comply with a small initial request to enhance the likelihood that the person will later comply with a larger request?
   a. Door-in-the-face
   b. Foot-in-the-door
   c. That's-not-all
   d. Not-so-free sample

4. The _____ _____ _____ _____ technique begins with an outrageous request that makes a subsequent, smaller request seem reasonable.
5. _____ is a change in behavior that is due to another person's orders.

RETHINK

1. Why do you think the Milgram experiment is so controversial? What sorts of effects might the experiment have had on participants? Do you think the experiment would have had similar results if it had not been conducted in a laboratory setting but among members of a social group (such as a fraternity or sorority) with strong pressures to conform?
2. *From the perspective of a sales representative:* Imagine that you have been trained to use the various compliance techniques described in this section. Because these compliance techniques are so powerful, should the use of certain such techniques be forbidden? Should consumers be taught defenses against such techniques? Is the use of such techniques ethically and morally defensible? Why?
3. *From the perspective of an educator:* Student obedience in the elementary and secondary classroom is a major issue for many teachers. How might you promote student obedience in the classroom? What are some of the potentially harmful ways that teachers could use their social influence to elicit student obedience?

Answers to Evaluate Questions

1. social supporter; 2. b; 3. b; 4. door-in-the-face; 5. obedience

KEY TERMS

social influence p. 530
group p. 530
conformity p. 530
status p. 531

social supporter p. 531
groupthink p. 532
compliance p. 533

industrial-organizational
(I/O) psychology p. 535
obedience p. 535

Prejudice and Discrimination

Key Concepts

How do stereotypes, prejudice, and discrimination differ?

How can we reduce prejudice and discrimination?

stereotype A set of generalized beliefs and expectations about a particular group and its members.

prejudice A negative (or positive) evaluation of a particular group and its members.

discrimination Behavior directed toward individuals on the basis of their membership in a particular group.

What do you think when someone says, "He's African American," "She's Chinese," or "That's a woman driver"?

If you're like most people, you'll probably automatically form some sort of impression of what each person is like. Most likely your impression is based on a **stereotype,** a set of generalized beliefs and expectations about a specific group and its members. Stereotypes, which may be negative or positive, grow out of our tendency to categorize and organize the vast amount of information we encounter in our everyday lives. All stereotypes share the common feature of oversimplifying the world: We view individuals not in terms of their unique, personal characteristics, but also in terms of characteristics we attribute to all the members of a particular group.

Stereotypes can lead to **prejudice,** a negative (or positive) evaluation of a group and its members. For instance, racial prejudice occurs when a member of a racial group is evaluated in terms of race and not because of his or her own characteristics or abilities. Although prejudice can be positive ("I love the Irish"), social psychologists have focused on understanding the roots of negative prejudice ("I hate immigrants").

Common stereotypes and forms of prejudice involve race, religion, ethnicity, and gender. Over the years, various groups have been called "lazy" or "shrewd" or "cruel" with varying degrees of regularity by those who are not members of that group. Even today, despite major progress toward reducing legally sanctioned forms of prejudice, such as school segregation, stereotypes remain (Eberhardt et al., 2004; Pettigrew, 2004; Hunt, Seifert, & Armenta, 2006).

Even people who on the surface appear to be unprejudiced may harbor hidden prejudice. For example, when white participants in experiments are shown faces on a computer screen so rapidly that they cannot consciously perceive the faces, they react more negatively to black than to white faces—an example of what has been called *modern racism* (Dovidio, Gaertner, & Pearson, 2005; Liu & Mills, 2006; Pearson, Dovidio, & Pratto, 2007).

Although usually backed by little or no evidence, stereotypes can have harmful consequences. Acting on negative stereotypes results in **discrimination**—behavior directed toward individuals on the basis of their membership in a particular group. Discrimination can lead to exclusion from jobs, neighborhoods, and educational opportunities, and it may result in lower salaries and benefits for members of specific groups. Discrimination can also result in more favorable treatment to favored groups—for example, when an employer hires a job applicant of his or her own racial group because of the applicant's race (Avery, McKay, & Wilson, 2008; Pager & Shepherd, 2008).

Stereotyping not only leads to overt discrimination, but also can cause members of stereotyped groups to behave in ways that reflect the stereotype through a phenomenon known as the *self-fulfilling prophecy.* Self-fulfilling prophecies are expectations about the occurrence of a future event or behavior that act to increase the likelihood the event or behavior will occur. For example, if people think that members of a specific group lack ambition, they may treat them in a way that actually brings about a lack of ambition (Oskamp, 2000; Seibt & Förster, 2005; Madon, Willard, & Guyll, 2006).

Study Alert

Remember that *prejudice* relates to *attitudes* about a group and its members, while *discrimination* relates to *behavior* directed to a group and its members.

The Foundations of Prejudice

No one has ever been born disliking a specific racial, religious, or ethnic group. People learn to hate in much the same way that they learn the alphabet.

According to *observational learning approaches* to stereotyping and prejudice, the behavior of parents, other adults, and peers shapes children's feelings about members of various groups. For instance, bigoted parents may commend their children for expressing prejudiced attitudes. Likewise, young children learn prejudice by imitating the behavior of adult models. Such learning starts at an early age: Children as young as 6 months judge others according to their skin color, and by 3 years of age they begin to show preferences for members of their own race (Ponterotto, Utsey, & Pedersen, 2006; Dovidio & Gaertner, 2006; Bronson & Merryman, 2009).

The mass media also provide information about stereotypes not just for children but for adults as well. Even today, some television shows and movies portray Italians as Mafia-like mobsters, Jews as greedy bankers, and African Americans as promiscuous or lazy. When such inaccurate portrayals are the primary source of information about minority groups, they can lead to the development and maintenance of unfavorable stereotypes (Coltraine & Messineo, 2000; Ward, 2004; Do, 2006).

Other explanations of prejudice and discrimination focus on how being a member of a specific group helps to magnify one's sense of self-esteem. According to *social identity theory*, we use group membership as a source of pride and self-worth. Social identity theory suggests that people tend to be ethnocentric, viewing the world from their own perspective and judging others in terms of their group membership. Slogans such as "gay pride" and "Black is beautiful" illustrate that the groups to which we belong give us a sense of self-respect (Tajfel & Turner, 2004; Hogg, 2006).

However, the use of group membership to provide social respect produces an unfortunate outcome. In an effort to maximize our sense of self-esteem, we may come to think that our own group (our *ingroup*) is better than groups to which we don't belong (our *outgroups*). Consequently, we inflate the positive aspects of our ingroup—and, at the same time, devalue outgroups. Ultimately, we come to view members of

Like father, like son: Social learning approaches to stereotyping and prejudice suggest that attitudes and behaviors toward members of minority groups are learned through the observation of parents and other individuals. How can this cycle be broken?

Neuroscience in Your Life: The Prejudiced Brain

FIGURE 1 Both white and black participants showed greater activity in the amygdala when viewing black faces as compared to viewing white faces in this composite fMRI scan. The researchers hypothesized that negative cultural messages about blacks lead to higher activation of the amygdala while viewing black faces due to its role in negative emotions. What other explanations might have produced the same findings? (Source: Lieberman et al., 2005, Figure 1b.)

outgroups as inferior to members of our ingroup (Tajfel & Turner, 2004). The end result is prejudice toward members of groups of which we are not a part.

Neither the observational learning approach nor the social identity approach provides a full explanation for stereotyping and prejudice. For instance, some psychologists argue that prejudice results when there is perceived competition for scarce societal resources. Thus, when competition exists for jobs or housing, members of majority groups may believe (however unjustly or inaccurately) that minority group members are hindering their efforts to attain their goals; this belief can lead to prejudice. In addition, other explanations for prejudice emphasize human cognitive limitations that lead us to categorize people on the basis of visually conspicuous physical features such as race, sex, and ethnic group. Such categorization can lead to the development of stereotypes and, ultimately, to discriminatory behavior (Mullen & Rice, 2003; Weeks & Lupfer, 2004; Hugenberg & Sacco, 2008).

social neuroscience The subfield of social psychology that seeks to identify the neural basis of social behavior.

The most recent approach to understanding prejudice comes from an increasingly important area in social psychology: social neuroscience. **Social neuroscience** seeks to identify the neural basis of social behavior. It looks at how we can illuminate our understanding of groups, interpersonal relations, and emotions by understanding their neuroscientific underpinnings (Cacioppo, Visser, & Pickett, 2005; Harmon-Jones & Winkielman, 2007).

In one example of the value of social neuroscience approaches, researchers examined activation of the *amygdala,* the structure in the brain that relates to emotion-evoking stimuli and situations, while viewing white and black faces. Because the amygdala is especially responsive to threatening, unusual, or highly arousing stimuli, the researchers hypothesized greater activation of the amygdala during exposure to black faces due to negative cultural associations with racial minorities (Lieberman et al., 2005; Lieberman, 2007).

As you can see in Figure 1, the hypothesis was confirmed: The amygdala showed more activation when participants saw a black face than when they saw a white one. Because both blacks and whites were participants in the study, it is unlikely that the amygdala activation was simply the result of the novelty of viewing members of a racial minority. Instead, the findings suggest that culturally learned societal messages about race led to the brain activation.

Measuring Prejudice and Discrimination: The Implicit Personality Test

Could you be prejudiced and not even know it? The answer, according to the researchers who developed the *Implicit Association Test*, is probably yes. People often fool themselves, and they are very careful about revealing their true attitudes about members of various groups, not only to others but to themselves. However, even though they may truly believe that they are unprejudiced, the reality is that they actually routinely differentiate between people on the basis of race, ethnicity, gender, and sexual orientation.

The Implicit Association Test, or IAT, is an ingenious measure of prejudice that permits a more accurate assessment of people's discrimination between members of different groups. It was developed, in part, as a reaction to the difficulty in finding a questionnaire that would reveal prejudice. Direct questions such as, "Would you prefer interacting with a member of Group X rather than Group Y?" typically identify only the most blatant prejudices, because people try to censor their responses (Rudman & Ashmore, 2007; Schnabel, Asendorpf, & Greenwald, 2008; Greenwald et al., 2009).

In contrast, the IAT makes use of the fact that people's automatic reactions often provide the most valid indicator of what they actually believe. The test asks people a series of questions on a computerized survey that assess the degree to which people associate members of target groups (say, African-Americans versus Whites) with positive stimuli (such as a puppy) versus negative stimuli (such as a funeral). The test is based on the fact that growing up in a particular culture teaches us to unconsciously associate members of particular groups with positive or negative qualities, and we tend to absorb associations about those groups that reflect the culture without even being aware of it (Lane et al., 2007). (If you would like to try out a version of the IAT yourself, there is a demonstration website with a sample test at https://implicit.harvard.edu/implicit. You may well be surprised at the results.)

The results of the IAT show that almost 90% of test-takers have an implicit pro-white bias, and more than two-thirds of non-Arab, non-Muslim volunteers display implicit biases against Arab Muslims. Moreover, more than 80% of heterosexuals display an implicit bias against gays and lesbians (Wittenbrink & Schwarz, 2007).

So, of course, having an implicit bias does not mean that people will overtly discriminate, which is a criticism that has been made of the test. Yet it does mean that the cultural lessons to which we are exposed have a considerable unconscious influence on us. (Interested in how you would perform on the IAT? Go to this website to take the test: https://implicit.harvard.edu/implicit).

> **Study Alert**
> Remember that the IAT allows measurement of attitudes about which people might not be consciously aware as well as attitudes they wish to keep hidden from others.

Reducing the Consequences of Prejudice and Discrimination

How can we diminish the effects of prejudice and discrimination? Psychologists have developed several strategies that have proved effective.

- *Increasing contact between the target of stereotyping and the holder of the stereotype.* Research consistently shows that increasing the amount of interaction between people can reduce negative stereotyping. But only certain kinds of contact are likely to reduce prejudice and discrimination. Situations in which contact is relatively intimate, the individuals are of equal status, or participants must cooperate with one another or are dependent on one another are more likely to reduce stereotyping (Dovidio, Gaertner, & Kawakami, 2003; Tropp & Pettigrew, 2005; Pettigrew & Tropp, 2006).

- *Making values and norms against prejudice more conspicuous.* Sometimes just reminding people about the values they already hold regarding equality and fair treatment of others is enough to reduce discrimination. Similarly, people who hear others making strong, vehement antiracist statements are subsequently more likely to strongly condemn racism (Czopp & Monteith, 2006; Ponterotto, Utsey, & Pedersen, 2006; Tropp & Bianchi, 2006).
- *Providing information about the targets of stereotyping.* Probably the most direct means of changing stereotypical and discriminatory attitudes is education: teaching people to be more aware of the positive characteristics of targets of stereotyping. For instance, when the meaning of puzzling behavior is explained to people who hold stereotypes, they may come to appreciate the actual significance of the behavior (Isbell & Tyler, 2003; Banks, 2006; Nagda, Tropp, & Paluck, 2006).
- *Reducing stereotype threat.* Social psychologist Claude Steele suggests that many African Americans suffer from *stereotype vulnerability,* obstacles to performance that stem from their awareness of society's stereotypes regarding minority group members. He argues that African-American students who receive instruction from teachers who may doubt their abilities and who set up special remedial programs to assist them may come to accept society's stereotypes and believe that they are prone to fail (Aronson & Steele, 2005; Nussbaum & Steele, 2007).

Such beliefs can have devastating effects. When confronted with an academic task, African-American students may fear that their performance will simply confirm society's negative stereotypes. The immediate consequence of this fear is anxiety that hampers performance. But the long-term consequences may be even worse: Doubting their ability to perform successfully in academic environments, African Americans may decide that the risks of failure are so great it is not worth the effort even to attempt to do well. Ultimately, they may "disidentify" with academic success by minimizing the importance of academic endeavors (Steele, 1997; Stone, 2002).

However, Steele's analysis suggests that African Americans may be able to overcome their predicament. Specifically, schools can design intervention programs to train minority group members about their vulnerability to stereotypes and provide them with self-affirmation that reinforces their confidence in their abilities and thereby inoculates them against the fear and doubt triggered by negative stereotypes (Cohen et al., 2006; Wilson, 2006).

RECAP/EVALUATE/RETHINK

RECAP

How do stereotypes, prejudice, and discrimination differ?

- Stereotypes are generalized beliefs and expectations about a specific group and its members. Stereotyping can lead to prejudice and self-fulfilling prophecies. (p. 538)
- Prejudice is the negative (or positive) evaluation of a particular group and its members. (p. 538)
- Stereotyping and prejudice can lead to discrimination, behavior directed toward individuals on the basis of their membership in a particular group. (p. 538)
- According to observational learning approaches, children learn stereotyping and prejudice by observing the behavior of parents, other adults, and peers. Social identity theory suggests that group membership is used as a source of pride and self-worth, and this may lead people to think of their own group as better than others. (p. 539)
- Social neuroscientific approaches to prejudice examine the functioning of the brain and nervous system to understand the basis of prejudice. (p. 540)

How can we reduce prejudice and discrimination?

- Among the ways of reducing prejudice and discrimination are increasing contact, demonstrating positive values against prejudice, and education. (p. 541)

EVALUATE

1. Any expectation—positive or negative—about an individual solely on the basis of that person's membership in a group can be a stereotype. True or false?

KEY TERMS

stereotype p. 538
prejudice p. 538
discrimination p. 538
social neuroscience p. 540

2. The negative (or positive) evaluation of a group and its members is called
   a. Stereotyping
   b. Prejudice
   c. Self-fulfilling prophecy
   d. Discrimination
3. Paul is a store manager who does not expect women to succeed in business. He therefore offers important, high-profile responsibilities only to men. If the female employees fail to move up in the company, it could be an example of a _____ _____ prophecy.

RETHINK

1. Do you think women can be victims of stereotype vulnerability? In what topical areas might this occur? Can men be victims of stereotype vulnerability? Why?
2. *From the perspective of a corrections officer:* How might overt forms of prejudice and discrimination toward disadvantaged groups (such as African Americans) be reduced in a state or federal prison?

Answers to Evaluate Questions

1. true; 2. b; 3. self-fulfilling

Positive and Negative Social Behavior

Why are we attracted to certain people, and what progression do social relationships follow?

What factors underlie aggression and prosocial behavior?

Are people basically good or bad?

Like philosophers and theologians, social psychologists have pondered the basic nature of humanity. Is it represented mainly by the violence and cruelty we see throughout the world, or does something special about human nature permit loving, considerate, unselfish, and even noble behavior as well?

We turn to two routes that social psychologists have followed in seeking answers to these questions. We first consider what they have learned about the sources of our attraction to others, we end with a look at two opposite sides of human behavior: aggression and helping.

Liking and Loving: Interpersonal Attraction and the Development of Relationships

Nothing is more important in most people's lives than their feelings for others. Consequently, it is not surprising that liking and loving have become a major focus of interest for social psychologists. Known more formally as the study of **interpersonal attraction** or **close relationships,** this area addresses the factors that lead to positive feelings for others.

interpersonal attraction (or close relationship) Positive feelings for others; liking and loving.

HOW DO I LIKE THEE? LET ME COUNT THE WAYS

By far the greatest amount of research has focused on liking, probably because it is easier for investigators conducting short-term experiments to produce states of liking in strangers who have just met than to instigate and observe loving relationships over long periods. Consequently, research has given us a good deal of knowledge about the factors that initially attract two people to each other. The important factors social psychologists consider are the following:

- *Proximity.* If you live in a dormitory or an apartment, consider the friends you made when you first moved in. Chances are that you became friendliest with those who lived geographically closest to you. In fact, this is one of the more firmly established findings in the literature on interpersonal attraction: *Proximity* leads to liking (Burgoon et al., 2002; Smith & Weber, 2005).
- *Mere exposure.* Repeated exposure to a person is often sufficient to produce attraction. Interestingly, repeated exposure to *any* stimulus—a person, picture, compact disc, or virtually anything—usually makes us like the stimulus more. Becoming familiar with a person can evoke positive feelings; we then transfer the positive feelings stemming from familiarity to the person him- or herself. There are exceptions, though. In cases of strongly negative initial interactions, repeated exposure is unlikely to cause us to like a person more. Instead, the more we are exposed to him or her, the more we may dislike the individual (Zajonc, 2001; Butler & Berry, 2004).

- *Similarity.* Folk wisdom tells us that birds of a feather flock together. However, it also maintains that opposites attract. Social psychologists have come up with a clear verdict regarding which of the two statements is correct: We tend to like those who are similar to us. Discovering that others have similar attitudes, values, or traits promotes our liking for them. Furthermore, the more similar others are, the more we like them. One reason similarity increases the likelihood of interpersonal attraction is that we assume people with similar attitudes will evaluate us positively. Because we experience a strong **reciprocity-of-liking effect** (a tendency to like those who like us), knowing that someone evaluates us positively promotes our attraction to that person. In addition, we assume that when we like someone else, that person likes us in return (Bates, 2002; Umphress, Smith-Crowe, & Brief, 2007; Montoya & Insko, 2008).

- *Physical attractiveness.* For most people, the equation *beautiful = good* is quite true. As a result, physically attractive people are more popular than physically unattractive ones, if all other factors are equal. This finding, which contradicts the values that most people say they hold, is apparent even in childhood—with children of nursery school age rating their peers' popularity on the basis of attractiveness—and continues into adulthood. Indeed, physical attractiveness may be the single most important element promoting initial liking in college dating situations, although its influence eventually decreases when people get to know each other better (Zebrowitz & Montepare, 2005; Little, Burt, & Perrett, 2006; Luo & Zhang, 2009).

"I'm attracted to you, but then I'm attracted to me, too."

reciprocity-of-liking effect A tendency to like those who like us.

These factors alone, of course, do not account for liking. For example, in one experiment that examined the desired qualities in a friendship, the top-rated qualities in a same-sex friend included sense of humor, warmth and kindness, expressiveness and openness, an exciting personality, and similarity of interests and leisure activities (Sprecher & Regan, 2002). (For more on friendship, see *Applying Psychology in the 21st Century* for a discussion of online social networking.)

HOW DO I LOVE THEE? LET ME COUNT THE WAYS

Whereas our knowledge of what makes people like one another is extensive, our understanding of love is more limited in scope and recently acquired. For some time, many social psychologists believed that love was too difficult to observe and study in a controlled, scientific way. However, love is such a central issue in most people's lives that eventually social psychologists could not resist its allure.

As a first step, researchers tried to identify the characteristics that distinguish between mere liking and full-blown love. They discovered that love is not simply a greater quantity of liking but a qualitatively different psychological state. For instance, at least in its early stages, love includes relatively intense physiological arousal, an all-encompassing interest in another individual, fantasizing about the other, and relatively rapid swings of emotion. Similarly, love, unlike liking, includes elements of passion, closeness, fascination, exclusiveness, sexual desire, and intense caring. We idealize partners by exaggerating their good qualities and minimizing their imperfections (Garza-Guerrero, 2000; Murray, Holmes, & Griffin, 2004).

Other researchers have theorized that there are two main types of love: passionate love and companionate love. **Passionate (or romantic) love** represents a state of intense absorption in someone. It includes intense physiological arousal, psychological interest, and caring for the needs of another. In contrast, **companionate love** is the strong affection we have for those with whom our lives are deeply involved. The love we feel for our parents, other family members, and even some close friends

passionate (or romantic) love A state of intense absorption in someone that includes intense physiological arousal, psychological interest, and caring for the needs of another.

companionate love The strong affection we have for those with whom our lives are deeply involved.

Friends Online: Is Facebook the New Student Union?

If you're a typical college student, you probably use Facebook or some other social networking website. In fact, estimates of usage rates of social networking sites on college campuses run as high as 90%, compared to 33% of older Internet users. When that many people are using a new technology for interpersonal communication, social psychologists take note, and they have begun to examine how college students use social network sites (Lenhart, 2009).

One finding is clear: College students use Facebook primarily to keep in touch with their friends. Few use it to keep in touch with their parents or to meet new people. What seems to interest college students most is the ability to maintain social connections across geographic boundaries efficiently. Specifically, social networking sites allow them to easily keep tabs on old friends from home while at the same time interacting with new friends made at college (Wiley & Sisson, 2006; Pempek, Yermolayeva, & Calvert, 2009; Subrahmanyam et al., 2008).

Another way college students use social network sites is to explore their developing identities. Because users can control how they present themselves to the world on a social network profile, it is easy for college students to "try on" an identity by posting selected photos of themselves, revealing specific tastes and interests, or otherwise presenting themselves in new and different

ways. The feedback they get from others may help them decide which identities and forms of self-presentation suit them best. College students report that religion, political ideology, work, and tastes in media such as music and movies are their most important identity expressions (Pempek, Yermolayeva, & Calvert, 2009).

But how do social network sites affect users' nonvirtual social lives? Maintaining social connections that might otherwise have withered and died seems like a good thing, but it may be detrimental if students spend so much time maintaining online distant or superficial friendships that they sacrifice time spent on intimate, face-to-face interactions with close friends.

New research suggests that social networking sites provide a less intimidating social outlet for students who otherwise have trouble making and keeping friendships, such as those who are introverted or have low self-esteem. One study that tracked college students' Facebook use over time found that those with low self-esteem benefitted the most in terms of building greater social networks through Facebook. Students reported that they found it less awkward to initiate contact with people through Facebook than through other means. They were also better able to learn about social events and other opportunities for face-to-face interaction through Facebook postings than by direct word of mouth, which thereby improved their offline social lives (Steinfeld, Ellison, & Lampe, 2008).

In addition, intensity of Facebook use is positively related to students' life satisfaction, social trust, and civic engagement. In short, research suggests that users of social network sites are not disengaged from the real world and that the benefits of social networking outweigh the costs to students' social lives (Valenzuela, Park, & Kee, 2009).

RETHINK

- Why might college students who use social networking sites more heavily have greater satisfaction in life than those who use it less?
- What aspects of social networking sites allow students to explore their identities? What might be the drawbacks of such experimentation?

falls into the category of companionate love (Masuda, 2003; Regan, 2006; Loving, Crockett, & Paxson, 2009).

Psychologist Robert Sternberg makes an even finer differentiation between types of love. He proposes that love consists of three parts:

- *Decision/commitment,* the initial thoughts that one loves someone and the longer-term feelings of commitment to maintain love.
- *Intimacy component,* feelings of closeness and connectedness.
- *Passion component,* the motivational drives relating to sex, physical closeness, and romance.

According to Sternberg, these three components combine to produce the different types of love. He suggests that different combinations of the three components vary over the course of relationships. For example, in strong, loving relationships, the level of commitment peaks and then remains stable. Passion, on the other hand, peaks quickly and then declines and levels off relatively early in most relationships. In addition, relationships are happiest in which the strength of the various components

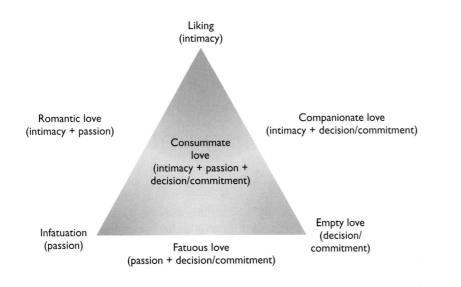

FIGURE 1 According to Sternberg, love has three main components: intimacy, passion, and decision/commitment. Different combinations of these components can create other types of love. Nonlove contains none of the three components.

are similar between the two partners (Sternberg, Hojjat, & Barnes, 2001; Sternberg, 2004a; Sternberg, 2006; see Figure 1).

Is love a necessary ingredient in a good marriage? Yes, if you live in the United States. In contrast, it's considerably less important in other cultures. Although mutual attraction and love are the two most important characteristics men and women in the United States desire in a mate, men in China rated good health as most important, and women there rated emotional stability and maturity as most important. Among the Zulu in South Africa, men rated emotional stability first and women rated dependable character first (Buss, Abbott, & Angleitner, 1990; see Figure 2).

| | Rank Ordering of Desired Characteristics in a Mate | | | | | |
| | United States | | China | | South Africa Zulu | |
	Females	**Males**	**Females**	**Males**	**Females**	**Males**
Mutual attraction—love	1	1	8	4	5	10
Emotional stability and maturity	2	2	1	5	2	1
Dependable character	3	3	7	6	1	3
Pleasing disposition	4	4	16	13	3	4
Education and intelligence	5	5	4	8	6	6
Good health	9	6	3	1	4	5
Good looks	13	7	15	11	16	14
Sociability	8	8	9	12	8	11
Desire for home and children	7	9	2	2	9	9
Refinement, neatness	12	10	10	7	10	7
Ambition and industriousness	6	11	5	10	7	8
Similar education	10	12	12	15	12	12
Good cook and housekeeper	16	13	11	9	15	2
Favorable social status or rating	14	14	13	14	14	17
Similar religious background	15	15	18	18	11	16
Good financial prospect	11	16	14	16	13	18
Chastity (no prior sexual intercourse)	18	17	6	3	18	13
Similar political background	17	18	17	17	17	15

FIGURE 2 Although love may be an important factor in choosing a marriage partner if you live in the United States, other cultures place less importance on it. (Source: Buss, Abbott, & Angleitner, 1990.)

Liking and loving clearly show a positive side of human social behavior. Now we turn to behaviors that are just as much a part of social behavior: aggression and helping behavior.

Aggression and Prosocial Behavior: Hurting and Helping Others

Drive-by shootings, carjackings, and abductions are just a few examples of the violence that seems all too common today. Yet we also find examples of generous, unselfish, thoughtful behavior that suggest a more optimistic view of humankind. Consider, for instance, people such as Mother Teresa, who ministered to the poor in India. Or contemplate the simple kindnesses of life: lending a valued compact disc, stopping to help a child who has fallen off a bicycle, or merely sharing a candy bar with a friend. Such instances of helping are no less characteristic of human behavior than the distasteful examples of aggression.

HURTING OTHERS: AGGRESSION

We need look no further than the daily paper or the nightly news to be bombarded with examples of aggression both on a societal level (war, invasion, assassination) and on an individual level (crime, child abuse, and the many petty cruelties humans are capable of inflicting on one another). Is such aggression an inevitable part of the human condition? Or is aggression primarily a product of particular circumstances that, if changed, could lead to its reduction?

The difficulty of answering such knotty questions becomes apparent as soon as we consider how best to define the term *aggression*. Depending on the way we define the word, many examples of inflicted pain or injury may or may not qualify as aggression (see Figure 3). For instance, a rapist is clearly acting with aggression toward his victim. On the other hand, it is less certain that a physician carrying out an emergency medical procedure without an anesthetic, thereby causing incredible pain to the patient, should be considered aggressive.

aggression The intentional injury of, or harm to, another person.

Most social psychologists define *aggression* in terms of the intent and the purpose behind the behavior. **Aggression** is intentional injury of or harm to another person. By this definition, the rapist is clearly acting aggressively, whereas the physician causing pain during a medical procedure is not (Berkowitz, 2001).

We turn now to several approaches to aggressive behavior developed by social psychologists.

INSTINCT APPROACHES: AGGRESSION AS A RELEASE

If you have ever punched an adversary in the nose, you may have experienced a certain satisfaction despite your better judgment. Instinct theories, which note the prevalence of aggression not only in humans but in animals as well, propose that aggression is primarily the outcome of innate—or inborn—urges.

Sigmund Freud was one of the first to suggest, as part of his theory of personality, that aggression is a primary instinctual drive. Konrad Lorenz, an ethologist (a scientist who studies animal behavior), expanded Freud's notions by arguing that humans, along with members of other species, have a fighting instinct, which in earlier times ensured protection of food supplies and weeded out the weaker of the species (Lorenz, 1966, 1974). Lorenz's instinct approach led to the controversial notion that aggressive energy constantly builds up in an individual until the person finally

Is This Aggression?

To see for yourself the difficulties involved in defining aggression, consider each of the following acts and determine whether it represents aggressive behavior—according to your own definition of aggression.

1. A spider eats a fly. Yes _____ No _____
2. Two wolves fight for the leadership of the pack. Yes _____ No _____
3. A soldier shoots an enemy at the front line. Yes _____ No _____
4. The warden of a prison executes a convicted criminal. Yes _____ No _____
5. A man viciously kicks a cat. Yes _____ No _____
6. A man, while cleaning a window, knocks over a flower pot, which, in falling, injures a pedestrian. Yes _____ No _____
7. Mr. X, a notorious gossip, speaks disparagingly of many people of his acquaintance. Yes _____ No _____
8. A man mentally rehearses a murder he is about to commit. Yes _____ No _____
9. An angry son purposely fails to write to his mother, who is expecting a letter and will be hurt if none arrives. Yes _____ No _____
10. An enraged boy tries with all his might to inflict injury on his antagonist, a bigger boy, but is not successful in doing so. His efforts simply amuse the bigger boy. Yes _____ No _____
11. A senator does not protest the escalation of bombing to which she is normally opposed. Yes _____ No _____
12. A farmer beheads a chicken and prepares it for supper. Yes _____ No _____
13. A hunter kills an animal and mounts it as a trophy. Yes _____ No _____
14. A physician gives a flu shot to a screaming child. Yes _____ No _____
15. A boxer gives his opponent a bloody nose. Yes _____ No _____
16. A Girl Scout tries to assist an elderly woman but trips her by accident. Yes _____ No _____
17. A bank robber is shot in the back while trying to escape. Yes _____ No _____
18. A tennis player smashes her racket after missing a volley. Yes _____ No _____
19. A person commits suicide. Yes _____ No _____
20. A cat kills a mouse, parades around with it, and then discards it. Yes _____ No _____

FIGURE 3 What is aggression? It depends on how the word is defined and in what context it is used. (Source: Adapted from Benjamin, 1985, p. 41.)

discharges it in a process called **catharsis.** The longer the energy builds up, says Lorenz, the greater the amount of the aggression displayed when it is discharged.

Probably the most controversial idea to come out of instinct theories of aggression is Lorenz's proposal that society should provide acceptable ways of permitting catharsis. For example, he suggested that participation in aggressive sports and games would prevent the discharge of aggression in less socially desirable ways. However, little research has found evidence for the existence of a pent-up reservoir of aggression that needs to be released. In fact, some studies flatly contradict the notion of catharsis, which leads psychologists to look for other explanations for aggression (Bushman, Wang, & Anderson, 2005; Scheele & DuBois, 2006; Verona & Sullivan, 2008).

catharsis The process of discharging built-up aggressive energy.

FRUSTRATION-AGGRESSION APPROACHES: AGGRESSION AS A REACTION TO FRUSTRATION

Suppose you've been working on a paper that is due for a class early the next morning, and your computer printer runs out of ink just before you can print out the paper. You rush to the store to buy more ink only to find the sales clerk locking the

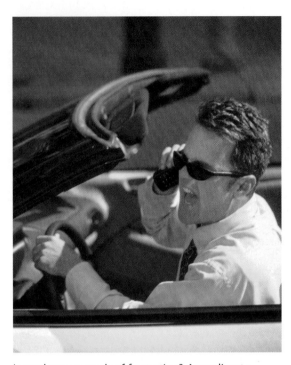

Is road rage a result of frustration? According to frustration-aggression approaches, frustration is a likely cause.

door for the day. Even though the clerk can see you gesturing and begging him to open the door, he refuses, shrugs his shoulders, and points to a sign that indicates when the store will open the next day. At that moment, the feelings you experience toward the sales clerk probably place you on the verge of real aggression, and you are undoubtedly seething inside.

Frustration-aggression theory tries to explain aggression in terms of events like this one. It suggests that *frustration* (the reaction to the thwarting or blocking of goals) produces anger, which leads to a readiness to act aggressively. Whether actual aggression occurs depends on the presence of *aggressive cues*, stimuli that have been associated in the past with actual aggression or violence and that will trigger aggression again (Berkowitz, 2001).

What kinds of stimuli act as aggressive cues? They can range from the most explicit, such as the presence of weapons, to more subtle cues, such as the mere mention of the name of an individual who behaved violently in the past. For example, angered participants in experiments behave significantly more aggressively when in the presence of a gun than in a comparable situation in which no guns are present. Similarly, frustrated participants who view a violent movie are more physically aggressive toward a confederate with the same name as the star of the movie than they are toward a confederate with a different name. It appears, then, that frustration does lead to aggression—at least when aggressive cues are present (Berkowitz, 2001; Marcus-Newhall, Pederson, & Carlson, 2000).

OBSERVATIONAL LEARNING APPROACHES: LEARNING TO HURT OTHERS

Do we learn to be aggressive? The observational learning (sometimes called social learning) approach to aggression says that we do. Taking an almost opposite view from instinct theories, which focus on innate explanations of aggression, observational learning theory emphasizes that social and environmental conditions can teach individuals to be aggressive. The theory sees aggression not as inevitable, but rather as a learned response that can be understood in terms of rewards and punishments.

Observational learning theory pays particular attention not only to direct rewards and punishments that individuals themselves receive, but also to the rewards and punishments that models—individuals who provide a guide to appropriate behavior—receive for their aggressive behavior. According to observational learning theory, people observe the behavior of models and the subsequent consequences of that behavior. If the consequences are positive, the behavior is likely to be imitated when observers find themselves in a similar situation.

Suppose, for instance, a girl hits her younger brother when he damages one of her new toys. Whereas instinct theory would suggest that the aggression had been pent up and was now being discharged, and frustration-aggression theory would examine the girl's frustration at no longer being able to use her new toy, observational learning theory would look to previous situations in which the girl had viewed others being rewarded for their aggression. For example, perhaps she had watched a friend get to play with a toy after he painfully twisted it out of the hand of another child.

Observational learning theory has received wide research support. For example, children of nursery school age who have watched an adult model behave aggressively and then receive reinforcement for it later display similar behavior themselves if they have been angered, insulted, or frustrated after exposure. Furthermore, a significant amount of research links watching television shows containing violence with subsequent viewer aggression (Winerman, 2005; Greer, Dudek-Singer, & Gautreaux, 2006; Carnagey, Anderson, & Bartholow, 2007).

Study Alert

Understand the distinction between the instinctual, frustration-aggression, and observational learning approaches to aggression.

Helping Others: The Brighter Side of Human Nature

Turning away from aggression, we move now to the opposite—and brighter—side of human nature: helping behavior. Helping behavior, or **prosocial behavior** as it is more formally known, has been considered under many different conditions. However, the question that psychologists have looked at most closely relates to bystander intervention in emergency situations. What are the factors that lead someone to help a person in need?

One critical factor is the number of others present. When more than one person witnesses an emergency situation, a sense of **diffusion of responsibility** can arise among the bystanders (as we discussed earlier in the book when we considered research methods). Diffusion of responsibility is the tendency for people to feel that responsibility for acting is shared, or diffused, among those present. The more people who are present in an emergency, the less personally responsible each individual feels—and therefore the less help he or she provides (Blair, Thompson, & Wuensch, 2005 Barron & Yechiam, 2002; Gray, 2006).

For example, think back to the classic case of Kitty Genovese that we described when discussing the topic of research early in the book. Genovese was stabbed multiple times, and—according to some accounts of the event—no one offered help, despite the fact that allegedly close to 40 people who lived in nearby apartments heard her screams for help. The lack of help has been attributed to diffusion of responsibility: The fact that there were so many potential helpers led each individual to feel diminished personal responsibility (Rogers & Eftimiades, 1995; Rosenthal, 2008).

Although most research on helping behavior supports the diffusion-of-responsibility explanation, other factors are clearly involved in helping behavior. According to a model of the helping process, the decision to give aid involves four basic steps (Latané & Darley, 1970; Garcia et al., 2002; see Figure 4):

- *Noticing a person, event, or situation that may require help.*
- *Interpreting the event as one that requires help.* Even if we notice an event, it may be sufficiently ambiguous for us to interpret it as a nonemergency situation. It is here that the presence of others first affects helping behavior. The presence of inactive others may indicate to us that a situation does not require help—a judgment we do not necessarily make if we are alone.
- *Assuming responsibility for helping.* It is at this point that diffusion of responsibility is likely to occur if others are present. Moreover, a bystander's particular expertise is likely to play a role in determining whether he or she helps. For instance, if people with training in medical aid or lifesaving techniques are present, untrained bystanders are less likely to intervene because they feel they have less expertise.
- *Deciding on and implementing the form of helping.* After we assume responsibility for helping, we must decide how to provide assistance. Helping can range from very indirect forms of intervention, such as calling the police, to more direct forms, such as giving first aid or taking the victim to a hospital. Most social psychologists use a *rewards–costs approach* for helping to predict the nature of the assistance a bystander will choose to provide. The general notion is that the bystander's perceived rewards for helping must outweigh the costs if helping is to occur, and most research tends to support this notion (Koper & Jaasma, 2001; Bartlett & DeSteno, 2006; Lin & Lin, 2007).

After determining the nature of the assistance needed, the actual help must be implemented. A rewards–costs analysis suggests that we are most likely to use the

prosocial behavior Helping behavior.

diffusion of responsibility The tendency for people to feel that responsibility for acting is shared, or diffused, among those present.

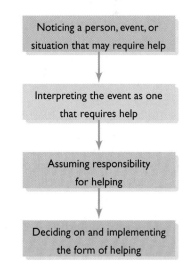

FIGURE 4 The basic steps of helping. (Source: Latané, Bibb; Darley, & John M., *The Unresponsive Bystander: Why Doesn't He Help?*, p. 87–91. Copyright © 1971 Appleton-Century-Crofts. Reproduced by permission of Pearson Education, Inc.)

Altruism is often the only bright side of a natural disaster.

altruism Helping behavior that is beneficial to others but clearly requires self-sacrifice.

least costly form of implementation. However, this is not always the case: In some situations, people behave altruistically. **Altruism** is helping behavior that is beneficial to others but clearly requires self-sacrifice. For example, people who put themselves at mortal risk to help strangers escape from the burning World Trade Center towers during the 9/11 terrorist attack would be considered altruistic (Krueger, Hicks, & McGue, 2001; Batson & Powell, 2003; Manor & Gailliot, 2007).

People who intervene in emergency situations tend to possess certain personality characteristics that differentiate them from nonhelpers. For example, helpers are more self-assured, sympathetic, and emotionally understanding, and they have greater *empathy* (a personality trait in which someone observing another person experiences the emotions of that person) than are nonhelpers (Graziano et al., 2007; Walker & Frimer, 2007; Stocks, Lishner, & Decker, 2009).

Still, most social psychologists agree that no single set of attributes differentiates helpers from nonhelpers. For the most part, temporary situational factors (such as the mood we're in) determine whether we will intervene in a situation requiring aid (Eisenberg, Guthrie, & Cumberland, 2002; Dovidio et al., 2006; Sallquist et al., 2009).

More generally, what leads people to make moral decisions? Clearly, situational factors make a difference. For example, one study asked people to judge the morality of plane crash survivors cannibalizing an injured boy to avoid starvation. Participants in the study were more likely to condemn the behavior if they were placed in an emotional state than if they were less emotional (Schnall et al., 2008).

Other psychologists, using a neuroscience perspective, believe that there's a kind of tug of war between emotion and rationale thinking in the brain. If the rational side wins out, we're more likely to take a logical view of moral situations (if you're at risk for starving, go ahead and eat the injured boy). On the other hand, if the emotional side prevails, we're more likely to condemn the cannibalism, even if it means we may be harmed. In support of such reasoning, researchers have found that different areas of the brain are involved in honest and dishonest moral decisions (Miller, 2008; Greene & Paxton, 2009; see Figure 5).

Neuroscience in Your Life:
Moral Decisions and the Brain

FIGURE 5 Making moral decisions about whether to act honestly or dishonestly results in different areas of the brain being activated. In a study in which people were induced to behave dishonestly, participants showed increased activity in the bilateral dorsolateral prefrontal cortex (DLPFC) area of the brain when they made decisions to lie. (Source: Greene & Paxton, 2009, Figure 3A.)

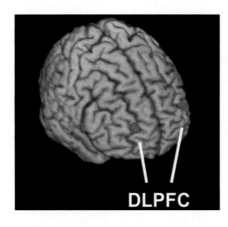

At one time or another, almost everyone feels angry. The anger may result from a frustrating situation, or it may be due to another individual's behavior. The way we deal with anger may determine the difference between a promotion and a lost job or a broken relationship and one that mends itself.

Social psychologists who have studied the topic suggest several good strategies to deal with anger that maximize the potential for positive consequences (Ellis, 2000; Nelson & Finch, 2000). Among the most useful strategies are the following:

BECOMING AN INFORMED CONSUMER

of Psychology

Dealing Effectively with Anger

- *Look again at the anger-provoking situation from the perspective of others*. By taking others' points of view, you may be able to understand the situation better, and with increased understanding you may become more tolerant of the apparent shortcomings of others.
- *Minimize the importance of the situation*. Does it really matter that someone is driving too slowly and that you'll be late to an appointment as a result? Reinterpret the situation in a way that is less bothersome.
- *Fantasize about getting even—but don't act on it*. Fantasy provides a safety valve. In your fantasies, you can yell at that unfair professor all you want and suffer no consequences at all. However, don't spend too much time brooding: Fantasize, but then move on.
- *Relax*. By teaching yourself the relaxation techniques used in systematic desensitization (discussed in the module on treatment of psychological disorders), you can help reduce your reactions to anger. In turn, your anger may dissipate.

No matter which of these strategies you try, above all, don't ignore your anger. People who always try to suppress their anger may experience a variety of consequences, such as self-condemnation, frustration, and even physical illness (Burns, Quartana, & Bruehl, 2007; Quartana & Burns, 2007; Gardner & Moore, 2008).

RECAP/EVALUATE/RETHINK

RECAP

Why are we attracted to certain people, and what progression do social relationships follow?

- The primary determinants of liking include proximity, exposure, similarity, and physical attractiveness. (p. 544)
- Loving is distinguished from liking by the presence of intense physiological arousal, an all-encompassing interest in another, fantasies about the other, rapid swings of emotion, fascination, sexual desire, exclusiveness, and strong feelings of caring. (p. 545)
- Love can be categorized as passionate or companionate. In addition, love has several components: intimacy, passion, and decision/commitment. (p. 545)

What factors underlie aggression and prosocial behavior?

- Aggression is intentional injury of or harm to another person. (p. 548)
- Explanations of aggression include instinct approaches, frustration-aggression theory, and observational learning. (p. 548)
- Helping behavior in emergencies is determined in part by the phenomenon of diffusion of responsibility, which results in a lower likelihood of helping when more people are present. (p. 551)
- Deciding to help is the outcome of a four-stage process that consists of noticing a possible need for help, interpreting the situation as requiring aid, assuming responsibility for taking action, and deciding on and implementing a form of assistance. (p. 551)

EVALUATE

1. We tend to like people who are similar to us. True or false?
2. Which of the following sets are the three components of love proposed by Sternberg?
   a. Passion, closeness, sexuality
   b. Attraction, desire, complementarity
   c. Passion, intimacy, decision/commitment
   d. Commitment, caring, sexuality

3. Based on research evidence, which of the following might be the best way to reduce the amount of fighting a young boy does?
   a. Take him to the gym and let him work out on the boxing equipment.
   b. Make him repeatedly watch violent scenes from the film *The Matrix Reloaded* in the hope that it will provide catharsis.
   c. Reward him if he doesn't fight during a certain period.
   d. Ignore it and let it die out naturally.
4. If a person in a crowd does not help in an apparent emergency situation because many other people are present, that person is falling victim to the phenomenon of _____ _____ _____.

RETHINK

1. Can love be studied scientifically? Is there an elusive quality to love that makes it at least partially unknowable? How would you define "falling in love"? How would you study it?
2. *From the perspective of a criminal justice worker:* How would proponents of the three main approaches to the study of aggression—instinct approaches, frustration-aggression approaches, and observational learning approaches—interpret the aggression of Eric Rudolph, who was convicted of exploding a bomb during the 1996 Summer Olympics in Atlanta and later of attacking several women's clinics? Do you think any of these approaches fits the Rudolph case more closely than the others?

Answers to Evaluate Questions

1. true; 2. c; 3. c; 4. diffusion of responsibility

KEY TERMS

interpersonal attraction (or close relationship) p. 544

reciprocity-of-liking effect p. 545
passionate (or romantic) love p. 545

companionate love p. 545
aggression p. 548
catharsis p. 549
prosocial behavior p. 551

diffusion of responsibility p. 551
altruism p. 552

Psychology on the Web

1. Find examples on the web of advertisements or other persuasive messages that use central route processing and peripheral route processing. What type of persuasion appears to be more prevalent on the web? For what type of persuasion does the web appear to be better suited? Is there a difference between web-based advertising and other forms of advertising?
2. Is "hate crimes legislation" a good idea? Use the web to find at least two discussions of hate crimes legislation—one in favor and one opposed—and summarize in writing the main issues and arguments presented. Using your knowledge of prejudice and aggression, evaluate the arguments for and against hate crimes legislation. State your opinion about whether this type of legislation is advisable.

Epilogue We have touched on some of the major ideas, research topics, and experimental findings of social psychology. We examined how people form, maintain, and change attitudes and how they form impressions of others and assign attributions to them. We also saw how groups, through conformity and tactics of compliance, can influence individuals' actions and attitudes. Finally, we discussed interpersonal relationships, including both liking and loving, and looked at aggression and prosocial behavior, the two sides of a coin that represent the extremes of social behavior.

Turn back to the prologue of this set of modules, which describes Perry Bland's heroism. Use your understanding of social psychology to consider the following questions.

1. What factors would a social psychologist consider in examining why Bland rushed to help two strangers who were trapped in their car?
2. Given what social psychologists know about the factors that lead people to be helpful, do you believe that Bland's helpfulness was caused by situational factors or that it had more to do with his personality? Why?
3. Do you think Bland would have reacted in a similar manner if he had had more time to think about acting? Why or why not?
4. What are some ways in which helping behavior can be encouraged?

Glossary

abnormal behavior Behavior that causes people to experience distress and prevents them from functioning in their daily lives (Module 37).

absolute threshold The smallest intensity of a stimulus that must be present for the stimulus to be detected (Module 8).

action potential An electric nerve impulse that travels through a neuron's axon when it is set off by a "trigger," changing the neuron's charge from negative to positive (Module 5).

activation-synthesis theory Hobson's theory that the brain produces random electrical energy during REM sleep that stimulates memories stored in the brain (Module 12).

activity theory of aging A theory that suggests that the elderly who are most successful while aging are those who maintain the interests and activities they had during middle age (Module 30).

adaptation An adjustment in sensory capacity after prolonged exposure to unchanging stimuli (Module 8).

addictive drugs Drugs that produce a biological or psychological dependence in the user so that withdrawal from them leads to a craving for the drug that, in some cases, may be nearly irresistible (Module 14).

adolescence The developmental stage between childhood and adulthood (Module 29).

age of viability The point at which a fetus can survive if born prematurely (Module 27).

aggression The intentional injury of, or harm to, another person (Module 46).

algorithm A rule that, if applied appropriately, guarantees a solution to a problem (Module 21).

all-or-none law The rule that neurons are either on or off (Module 5).

altruism Helping behavior that is beneficial to others but clearly requires self-sacrifice (Module 46).

Alzheimer's disease A progressive brain disorder that leads to a gradual and irreversible decline in cognitive abilities (Modules 20, 30).

amnesia Memory loss that occurs without other mental difficulties (Module 20).

anal stage According to Freud, a stage from age 12 to 18 months to 3 years of age, in which a child's pleasure is centered on the anus (Module 31).

androgens Male sex hormones secreted by the testes (Module 25).

anorexia nervosa A severe eating disorder in which people may refuse to eat while denying that their behavior and appearance—which can become skeleton-like—are unusual (Module 25).

anterograde amnesia Amnesia in which memory is lost for events that follow an injury (Module 20).

antianxiety drugs Drugs that reduce the level of anxiety a person experiences essentially by reducing excitability and increasing feelings of well-being (Module 42).

antidepressant drugs Medications that improve a severely depressed patient's mood and feeling of well-being (Module 42).

antipsychotic drugs Drugs that temporarily reduce psychotic symptoms such as agitation, hallucinations, and delusions (Module 42).

antisocial personality disorder A disorder in which individuals show no regard for the moral and ethical rules of society or the rights of others (Module 38).

anxiety disorder The occurrence of anxiety without an obvious external cause that affects daily functioning (Module 38).

archetypes According to Jung, universal symbolic representations of a particular person, object, or experience (such as good and evil) (Module 31).

archival research Research in which existing data, such as census documents, college records, and newspaper clippings, are examined to test a hypothesis (Module 5).

arousal approaches to motivation The belief that we try to maintain certain levels of stimulation and activity increasing or reducing them as necessary (Module 24).

association areas One of the major regions of the cerebral cortex; the site of the higher mental processes, such as thought, language, memory, and speech (Module 7).

assumed-similarity bias The tendency to think of people as being similar to oneself even when meeting them for the first time (Module 43).

attachment The positive emotional bond that develops between a child and a particular individual (Module 28).

attention-deficit hyperactivity disorder (ADHD) A disorder marked by inattention, impulsiveness, a low tolerance for frustration, and a great deal of inappropriate activity (Module 38).

attitudes Evaluations of a particular person, behavior, belief, or concept (Module 43).

attribution theory The theory of personality that seeks to explain how we decide, on the basis of samples of an individual's behavior, what the specific causes of that person's behavior are (Module 43).

authoritarian parents Parents who are rigid and punitive and value unquestioning obedience from their children (Module 28).

authoritative parents Parents who are firm, set clear limits, reason with their children, and explain things to them (Module 28).

autism A severe developmental disability that impairs children's ability to communicate and relate to others (Module 38).

autobiographical memories Our recollections of circumstances and episodes from our own lives (Module 19).

autonomic division The part of the peripheral nervous system that controls involuntary movement of the heart, glands, lungs, and other organs (Module 6).

autonomy-versus-shame-and-doubt stage The period during which, according to Erikson, toddlers (ages 1½ to 3 years) develop independence and autonomy if exploration and freedom are encouraged or shame and self-doubt if they are restricted and overprotected (Module 28).

aversive conditioning A form of therapy that reduces the frequency of undesired behavior by pairing an aversive, unpleasant stimulus with undesired behavior (Module 40).

axon The part of the neuron that carries messages destined for other neurons (Module 5).

babble Meaningless speechlike sounds made by children from around the age of 3 months through 1 year (Module 22).

background stressors ("daily hassles") Everyday annoyances, such as being stuck in traffic, that cause minor irritations and may have long-term ill effects if they continue or are compounded by other stressful events (Module 34).

basilar membrane A vibrating structure that runs through the center of the cochlea, dividing it into an upper chamber and a lower chamber and containing sense receptors for sound (Module 10).

behavior modification A formalized technique for promoting the frequency of desirable behaviors and decreasing the incidence of unwanted ones (Module 16).

behavioral assessment Direct measures of an individual's behavior used to describe personality characteristics (Module 33).

behavioral genetics The study of the effects of heredity on behavior (Module 6).

behavioral neuroscientists (or biopsychologists) Psychologists who specialize in considering the ways in which the biological structures and functions of the body affect behavior (Module 5).

behavioral perspective The approach that suggests that observable, measurable behavior should be the focus of study (Modules 2, 37).

behavioral treatment approaches Treatment approaches that build on the basic processes of learning, such as reinforcement and extinction, and assume that normal and abnormal behavior are both learned (Module 40).

biofeedback A procedure in which a person learns to control through conscious thought internal physiological processes such as blood pressure, heart and respiration rate, skin temperature, sweating, and the constriction of particular muscles (Module 7).

biological and evolutionary approaches to personality Theories that suggest that important components of personality are inherited (Module 32).

biomedical therapy Therapy that relies on drugs and other medical procedures to improve psychological functioning (Module 40).

bipolar disorder A disorder in which a person alternates between periods of euphoric feelings of mania and periods of depression (Module 38).

bisexuals Persons who are sexually attracted to people of the same sex and the other sex (Module 25).

borderline personality disorder A disorder in which individuals have difficulty developing a secure sense of who they are (Module 38).

bottom-up processing Perception that consists of the progression of recognizing and processing information from individual components of a stimuli and moving to the perception of the whole (Module 11).

bulimia A disorder in which a person binges on large quantities of food, followed by efforts to purge the food through vomiting or other means (Module 25).

Cannon-Bard theory of emotion The belief that both physiological arousal and emotional experience are produced simultaneously by the same nerve stimulus (Module 26).

case study An in-depth, intensive investigation of an individual or small group of people (Module 3).

cataclysmic events Strong stressors that occur suddenly and typically affect many people at once (e.g., natural disasters) (Module 34).

catharsis The process of discharging built-up aggressive energy (Module 46).

central core The "old brain," which controls basic functions such as eating and sleeping and is common to all vertebrates (Module 7).

central nervous system (CNS) The part of the nervous system that includes the brain and spinal cord (Module 6).

central route processing Message interpretation characterized by thoughtful consideration of the issues and arguments used to persuade (Module 43).

central traits The major traits considered in forming impressions of others (Module 43).

cerebellum (ser-uh-BELL-um) The part of the brain that controls bodily balance (Module 7).

cerebral cortex The "new brain," responsible for the most sophisticated information processing in the brain; contains four lobes (Module 7).

chromosomes Rod-shaped structures that contain all basic hereditary information (Module 27).

chunk A meaningful grouping of stimuli that can be stored as a unit in short-term memory (Module 18).

circadian rhythms Biological processes that occur regularly on approximately a 24-hour cycle (Module 12).

classical conditioning A type of learning in which a neutral stimulus comes to bring about a response after it is paired with a stimulus that naturally brings about that response (Module 15).

cochlea (KOKE-lee-uh) A coiled tube in the ear filled with fluid that vibrates in response to sound (Module 10).

cognitive approaches to motivation Theories suggesting that motivation is a product of people's thoughts, expectations, and goals—their cognitions (Module 24).

cognitive-behavioral approach A treatment approach that incorporates basic principles of learning to change the way people think (Module 40).

cognitive development The process by which a child's understanding of the world changes as a function of age and experience (Module 28).

cognitive dissonance The conflict that occurs when a person holds two contradictory attitudes or thoughts (referred to as cognitions) (Module 43).

cognitive learning theory An approach to the study of learning that focuses on the thought processes that underlie learning (Module 17).

cognitive perspective The approach that focuses on how people think, understand, and know about the world (Module 2).

cognitive perspective on psychological disorders The perspective that suggests that people's thoughts and beliefs are a central component of abnormal behavior (Module 37).

cognitive psychology The branch of psychology that focuses on the study of higher mental processes, including thinking, language, memory, problem solving, knowing, reasoning, judging, and decision making (Module 21).

cognitive treatment approaches Treatment approaches that teach people to think in more adaptive ways by changing their dysfunctional cognitions about the world and themselves (Module 40).

collective unconscious According to Jung, a common set of ideas, feelings, images, and symbols that we inherit from our ancestors, the whole human race, and even animal ancestors from the distant past (Module 31).

community psychology A branch of psychology that focuses on the prevention and minimization of psychological disorders in the community (Module 42).

companionate love The strong affection we have for those with whom our lives are deeply involved (Module 46).

compliance Behavior that occurs in response to direct social pressure (Module 44).

compulsion An irresistible urge to repeatedly carry out some act that seems strange and unreasonable (Module 38).

concepts A mental grouping of similar objects, events, or people (Module 21).

concrete operational stage According to Piaget, the period from 7 to 12 years of age that is characterized by logical thought and a loss of egocentrism (Module 28).

conditioned response (CR) A response that, after conditioning, follows a previously neutral stimulus (e.g., salivation at the ringing of a bell) (Module 15).

conditioned stimulus (CS) A once-neutral stimulus that has been paired with an unconditioned stimulus to bring about a response formerly caused only by the unconditioned stimulus (Module 15).

cones Cone-shaped, light-sensitive receptor cells in the retina that are responsible for sharp focus and color perception, particularly in bright light (Module 9).

confirmation bias The tendency to seek out and weight more heavily information that supports one's initial hypotheses and to ignore contradictory information that supports alternative hypotheses or solutions (Module 21).

conformity A change in behavior or attitudes brought about by a desire to follow the beliefs or standards of other people (Module 44).

consciousness The awareness of the sensations, thoughts, and feelings being experienced at a given moment (Module 12).

constructive processes Processes in which memories are influenced by the meaning we give to events (Module 19).

continuous reinforcement schedule Reinforcing of a behavior every time it occurs (Module 16).

control group A group participating in an experiment that receives no treatment (Module 3).

convergent thinking The ability to produce responses that are based primarily on knowledge and logic (Module 21).

conversion disorder A major somatoform disorder that involves an actual physical disturbance, such as the inability to use a sensory organ or the complete or partial inability to move an arm or leg (Module 38).

coping The efforts to control, reduce, or learn to tolerate the threats that lead to stress (Module 34).

correlational research Research in which the relationship between two sets of variables is examined to determine whether they are associated, or "correlated" (Module 3).

creativity The ability to generate original ideas or solve problems in novel ways (Module 21).

cross-sectional research A research method that compares people of different ages at the same point in time (Module 27).

crystallized intelligence The accumulation of information, skills, and strategies that are learned through experience and can be applied in problem-solving situations (Module 23).

cue-dependent forgetting Forgetting that occurs when there are insufficient retrieval cues to rekindle information that is in memory (Module 20).

culture-fair IQ test A test that does not discriminate against the members of any minority group (Module 23).

daydreams Fantasies that people construct while awake (Module 12).

decay The loss of information in memory through its nonuse (Module 20).

declarative memory Memory for factual information: names, faces, dates, and the like (Module 18).

defense mechanisms In Freudian theory, unconscious strategies that people use to reduce anxiety by concealing the source of it from themselves and others (Module 31).

deinstitutionalization The transfer of former mental patients from institutions to the community (Module 42).

dendrite A cluster of fibers at one end of a neuron that receives messages from other neurons (Module 5).

dependent variable The variable that is measured and is expected to change as a result of changes caused by the experimenter's manipulation of the independent variable (Module 3).

depressants Drugs that slow down the nervous system (Module 14).

depth perception The ability to view the world in three dimensions and to perceive distance (Module 11).

determinism The idea that people's behavior is produced primarily by factors outside of their willful control (Module 2).

developmental psychology The branch of psychology that studies the patterns of growth and change that occur throughout life (Module 27).

***Diagnostic and Statistical Manual of Mental Disorders*, Fourth Edition, Text Revision (*DSM-IV-TR*)** A system, devised by the American Psychiatric Association, used by most professionals to diagnose and classify abnormal behavior (Module 37).

dialectical behavior therapy A form of treatment in which the focus is on getting people to accept who they are regardless of whether it matches their ideal (Module 40).

difference threshold (just noticeable difference) The smallest level of added or reduced stimulation required to sense that a change in stimulation has occurred (Module 8).

diffusion of responsibility The tendency for people to feel that responsibility for acting is shared, or diffused, among those present (Module 46).

discrimination Behavior directed toward individuals on the basis of their membership in a particular group (Module 45).

disengagement theory of aging A theory that suggests that aging produces a gradual withdrawal from the world on physical, psychological, and social levels (Module 30).

dispositional causes (of behavior) Perceived causes of behavior that are based on internal traits or personality factors (Module 43).

dissociative amnesia A disorder in which a significant, selective memory loss occurs (Module 38).

dissociative disorders Psychological dysfunctions characterized by the separation of different facets of a person's personality that are normally integrated (Module 38).

dissociative fugue A form of amnesia in which the individual leaves home and sometimes assumes a new identity (Module 38).

dissociative identity disorder (DID) A disorder in which a person displays characteristics of two or more distinct personalities (Module 38).

divergent thinking The ability to generate unusual, yet nonetheless appropriate, responses to problems or questions (Module 21).

double standard The view that premarital sex is permissible for males but not for females (Module 25).

dreams-for-survival theory The theory suggesting that dreams permit information that is critical for our daily survival to be reconsidered and reprocessed during sleep (Module 12).

drive Motivational tension, or arousal, that energizes behavior to fulfill a need (Module 24).

drive-reduction approaches to motivation Theories suggesting that a lack of a basic biological requirement such as water produces a drive to obtain that requirement (in this case, the thirst drive) (Module 24).

drug therapy Control of psychological disorders through the use of drugs (Module 42).

eardrum The part of the ear that vibrates when sound waves hit it (Module 10).

ego The part of the personality that provides a buffer between the id and the outside world (Module 31).

egocentric thought A way of thinking in which a child views the world entirely from his or her own perspective (Module 28).

ego-integrity-versus-despair stage According to Erikson, a period from late adulthood until death during which we review life's accomplishments and failures (Module 29).

electroconvulsive therapy (ECT) A procedure used in the treatment of severe depression in which an electric current of 70–150 volts is briefly administered to a patient's head (Module 42).

embryo A developed zygote that has a heart, a brain, and other organs (Module 27).

emerging adulthood The period beginning in the late teenage years and extending into the mid-20s (Module 30).

emotional intelligence The set of skills that underlie the accurate assessment, evaluation, expression, and regulation of emotions (Module 23).

emotions Feelings that generally have both physiological and cognitive elements and that influence behavior (Module 26).

endocrine system A chemical communication network that sends messages throughout the body via the bloodstream (Module 6).

episodic memory Memory for events that occur in a particular time, place, or context (Module 18).

estrogens Class of female sex hormones (Module 25).

evolutionary psychology The branch of psychology that seeks to identify behavior patterns that are a result of our genetic inheritance from our ancestors (Module 6).

excitatory message A chemical message that makes it more likely that a receiving neuron will fire and an action potential will travel down its axon (Module 5).

experiment The investigation of the relationship between two (or more) variables by deliberately producing a change in one variable in a situation and observing the effects of that change on other aspects of the situation (Module 3).

experimental bias Factors that distort how the independent variable affects the dependent variable in an experiment (Module 4).

experimental group Any group participating in an experiment that receives a treatment (Module 3).

experimental manipulation The change that an experimenter deliberately produces in a situation (Module 3).

explicit memory Intentional or conscious recollection of information (Module 19).

exposure A behavioral treatment for anxiety in which people are confronted either suddenly or gradually with a stimulus that they fear (Module 40).

extinction A basic phenomenon of learning that occurs when a previously conditioned response decreases in frequency and eventually disappears (Module 15).

extramarital sex Sexual activity between a married person and someone who is not his or her spouse (Module 25).

facial-affect program Activation of a set of nerve impulses that make the face display the appropriate expression (Module 26).

facial-feedback hypothesis The hypothesis that facial expressions not only reflect emotional experience but also help determine how people experience and label emotions (Module 26).

familial retardation Mental retardation in which no apparent biological defect exists but there is a history of retardation in the family (Module 23).

family therapy An approach that focuses on the family and its dynamics (Module 41).

feature detection The activation of neurons in the cortex by visual stimuli of specific shapes or patterns (Module 9).

fetal alcohol syndrome The most common cause of mental retardation in newborns, occurring when the mother uses alcohol during pregnancy (Module 23).

fetus A developing individual from eight weeks after conception until birth (Module 27).

fixations Conflicts or concerns that persist beyond the developmental period in which they first occur (Module 31).

fixed-interval schedule A schedule that provides reinforcement for a response only if a fixed time period has elapsed, making overall rates of response relatively low (Module 16).

fixed-ratio schedule A schedule by which reinforcement is given only after a specific number of responses are made (Module 16).

flashbulb memories Memories centered on a specific, important, or surprising event that are so vivid it is as if they represented a snapshot of the event (Module 19).

fluid intelligence Intelligence that reflects information-processing capabilities, reasoning, and memory (Module 23).

formal operational stage According to Piaget, the period from age 12 to adulthood that is characterized by abstract thought (Module 28).

free will The idea that behavior is caused primarily by choices that are made freely by the individual (Module 2).

frequency theory of hearing The theory that the entire basilar membrane acts like a microphone, vibrating as a whole in response to a sound (Module 10).

functional fixedness The tendency to think of an object only in terms of its typical use (Module 21).

functionalism An early approach to psychology that concentrated on what the mind does—the functions of mental activity—and the role of behavior in allowing people to adapt to their environments (Module 2).

fundamental attribution error A tendency to overattribute others' behavior to dispositional causes and minimize of the importance of situational causes (Module 43).

***g* or *g*-factor** The single, general factor for mental ability assumed to underlie intelligence in some early theories of intelligence (Module 23).

gate-control theory of pain The theory that particular nerve receptors in the spinal cord lead to specific areas of the brain related to pain (Module 10).

general adaptation syndrome (GAS) A theory developed by Selye that suggests that a person's response to a stressor consists of three stages: alarm and mobilization, resistance, and exhaustion (Module 34).

generalized anxiety disorder The experience of long-term, persistent anxiety and worry (Module 38).

generativity-versus-stagnation stage According to Erikson, a period in middle adulthood during which we take stock of our contributions to family and society (Module 29).

genes The parts of the chromosomes through which genetic information is transmitted (Module 27).

genetic preprogramming theories of aging Theories that suggest that human cells have a built-in time limit to their reproduction and that they are no longer able to divide after a certain time (Module 30).

genital stage According to Freud, the period from puberty until death, marked by mature sexual behavior (that is, sexual intercourse) (Module 31).

genitals The male and female sex organs (Module 25).

gestalt laws of organization A series of principles that describe how we organize bits and pieces of information into meaningful wholes (Module 11).

gestalt psychology An approach to psychology that focuses on the organization of perception and thinking in a "whole" sense rather than on the individual elements of perception (Module 2).

grammar The system of rules that determine how our thoughts can be expressed (Module 22).

group Two or more people who interact with one another, perceive themselves as part of a group, and are interdependent (Module 44).

group therapy Therapy in which people meet in a group with a therapist to discuss problems (Module 41).

groupthink A type of thinking in which group members share such a strong motivation to achieve consensus that they lose the ability to critically evaluate alternative points of view (Module 44).

habituation The decrease in the response to a stimulus that occurs after repeated presentations of the same stimulus (Module 28).

hair cells Tiny cells covering the basilar membrane that, when bent by vibrations entering the cochlea, transmit neural messages to the brain (Module 10).

hallucinogen A drug that is capable of producing hallucinations, or changes in the perceptual process (Module 14).

halo effect A phenomenon in which an initial understanding that a person has positive traits is used to infer other uniformly positive characteristics (Module 43).

hardiness A personality characteristic that is associated with a lower rate of stress-related illness and consists of three components: commitment, challenge, and control (Module 34).

health psychology The branch of psychology that investigates the psychological factors related to wellness and illness, including the prevention, diagnosis, and treatment of medical problems (Module 34).

hemispheres Symmetrical left and right halves of the brain that control the side of the body opposite to their location (Module 7).

heritability A measure of the degree to which a characteristic is related to genetic, inherited factors (Module 23).

heterosexuality Sexual attraction and behavior directed to the other sex (Module 25).

heuristic A thinking strategy that may lead us to a solution to a problem or decision, but—unlike algorithms—may sometimes lead to errors (Module 21).

homeostasis The body's tendency to maintain a steady internal state (Module 24).

homosexuals Persons who are sexually attracted to members of their own sex (Module 25).

hormones Chemicals that circulate through the blood and regulate the functioning or growth of the body (Module 6).

humanistic approaches to personality Theories that emphasize people's innate goodness and desire to achieve higher levels of functioning (Module 32).

humanistic perspective The approach that suggests that all individuals naturally strive to grow, develop, and be in control of their lives and behavior (Module 2).

humanistic perspective on psychological disorders The perspective that emphasizes the responsibility people have for their own behavior, even when such behavior is abnormal (Module 37).

humanistic therapy Therapy in which the underlying rationale is that people have control of their behavior, can make choices about their lives, and are essentially responsible for solving their own problems (Module 41).

hypnosis A trancelike state of heightened susceptibility to the suggestions of others (Module 13).

hypochondriasis A disorder in which people have a constant fear of illness and a preoccupation with their health (Module 38).

hypothalamus A tiny part of the brain, located below the thalamus, that maintains homeostasis and produces and regulates vital behavior, such as eating, drinking, and sexual behavior (Module 7).

hypothesis A prediction, stemming from a theory, stated in a way that allows it to be tested (Module 3).

id The raw, unorganized, inborn part of personality whose sole purpose is to reduce tension created by primitive drives related to hunger, sex, aggression, and irrational impulses (Module 31).

identical twins Twins who are genetically identical (Module 27).

identification The process of wanting to be like another person as much as possible, imitating that person's behavior and adopting similar beliefs and values (Module 31).

identity The distinguishing character of the individual: who each of us is, what our roles are, and what we are capable of (Module 29).

identity-versus-role-confusion stage According to Erikson, a time in adolescence of major testing to determine one's unique qualities (Module 29).

implicit memory Memories of which people are not consciously aware but that can affect subsequent performance and behavior (Module 19).

incentive approaches to motivation Theories suggesting that motivation stems from the desire to obtain valued external goals, or incentives (Module 24).

independent variable The variable that is manipulated by an experimenter (Module 3).

industrial-organizational (I/O) psychology The branch of psychology focusing on work- and job-related issues, including worker motivation, satisfaction, safety, and productivity (Module 44).

industry-versus-inferiority stage According to Erikson, the last stage of childhood, during which children age 6 to 12 years may develop positive social interactions with others or may feel inadequate and become less sociable (Module 28).

inferiority complex According to Adler, a problem affecting adults who have not been able to overcome the feelings of inferiority that they developed as children, when they were small and limited in their knowledge about the world (Module 31).

information processing The way in which people take in, use, and store information (Module 28).

informed consent A document signed by participants affirming that they have been told the basic outlines of the study and are aware of what their participation will involve (Module 4).

inhibitory message A chemical message that prevents or decreases the likelihood that a receiving neuron will fire (Module 5).

initiative-versus-guilt stage According to Erikson, the period during which children ages 3 to 6 years experience conflict between independence of action and the sometimes negative results of that action (Module 28).

insight A sudden awareness of the relationships among various elements that had previously appeared to be independent of one another (Module 21).

instincts Inborn patterns of behavior that are biologically determined rather than learned (Module 24).

intellectually gifted The 2%–4% of the population who have IQ scores greater than 130 (Module 23).

intelligence The capacity to understand the world, think rationally, and use resources effectively when faced with challenges (Module 23).

intelligence quotient (IQ) A score that takes into account an individual's mental and chronological ages (Module 23).

intelligence tests Tests devised to quantify a person's level of intelligence (Module 23).

interactionist approach (to language development) The view that language development is produced through a combination of genetically determined predispositions and environmental circumstances that help teach language (Module 22).

interference The phenomenon by which information in memory disrupts the recall of other information (Module 20).

interneurons Neurons that connect sensory and motor neurons, carrying messages between the two (Module 6).

interpersonal attraction (or close relationship) Positive feelings for others; liking and loving (Module 46).

interpersonal therapy (IPT) Short-term therapy that focuses on the context of current social relationships (Module 41).

intimacy-versus-isolation stage According to Erikson, a period during early adulthood that focuses on developing close relationships (Module 29).

introspection A procedure used to study the structure of the mind in which subjects are asked to describe in detail what they are experiencing when they are exposed to a stimulus (Module 2).

James-Lange theory of emotion The belief that emotional experience is a reaction to bodily events occurring as a result of an external situation ("I feel sad because I am crying") (Module 26).

Korsakoff's syndrome A disease that afflicts long-term alcoholics, leaving some abilities intact but including hallucinations and a tendency to repeat the same story (Module 20).

language The communication of information through symbols arranged according to systematic rules (Module 22).

language-acquisition device A neural system of the brain hypothesized by Noam Chomsky to permit understanding of language (Module 22).

latency period According to Freud, the period between the phallic stage and puberty during which children's sexual concerns are temporarily put aside (Module 31).

latent content of dreams According to Freud, the "disguised" meanings of dreams, hidden by more obvious subjects (Module 12).

latent learning Learning in which a new behavior is acquired but is not demonstrated until some incentive is provided for displaying it (Module 17).

lateralization The dominance of one hemisphere of the brain in specific functions, such as language (Module 7).

learned helplessness A state in which people conclude that unpleasant or aversive stimuli cannot be controlled— a view of the world that becomes so ingrained that they cease trying to remedy the aversive circumstances even if they actually can exert some influence on the situation (Module 34).

learning A relatively permanent change in behavior brought about by experience (Module 15).

learning-theory approach (to language development) The theory that language acquisition follows the principles of reinforcement and conditioning (Module 22).

levels-of-processing theory The theory of memory that emphasizes the degree to which new material is mentally analyzed (Module 19).

life review The process by which people examine and evaluate their lives (Module 30).

limbic system The part of the brain that controls eating, aggression, and reproduction (Module 7).

linguistic-relativity hypothesis The notion that language shapes and may determine the way people in a particular culture perceive and understand the world (Module 22).

lobes The four major sections of the cerebral cortex: frontal, parietal, temporal, and occipital (Module 7).

longitudinal research A research method that investigates behavior as participants age (Module 27).

long-term memory Memory that stores information on a relatively permanent basis, although it may be difficult to retrieve (Module 18).

major depression A severe form of depression that interferes with concentration, decision making, and sociability (Module 38).

mania An extended state of intense, wild elation (Module 38).

manifest content of dreams According to Freud, the apparent story line of dreams (Module 12).

masturbation Sexual self-stimulation (Module 25).

means-ends analysis Involves repeated tests for differences between the desired outcome and what currently exists (Module 21).

medical perspective The perspective that suggests that when an individual displays symptoms of abnormal behavior, the root cause will be found in a physical examination of the individual, which may reveal a hormonal imbalance, a chemical deficiency, or a brain injury (Module 37).

meditation A learned technique for refocusing attention that brings about an altered state of consciousness (Module 13).

memory The process by which we encode, store, and retrieve information (Module 18).

menopause The period during which women stop menstruating and are no longer fertile (Module 30).

mental age The age for which a given level of performance is average or typical (Module 23).

mental images Representations in the mind of an object or event (Module 21).

mental retardation (or intellectual disability) A condition characterized by significant limitations both in intellectual functioning and in conceptual, social, and practical adaptive skills (Module 23).

mental set The tendency for old patterns of problem solving to persist (Module 21).

metabolism The rate at which food is converted to energy and expended by the body (Module 25).

metacognition An awareness and understanding of one's own cognitive processes (Module 28).

Minnesota Multiphasic Personality Inventory-2 (MMPI-2) A widely used self-report test that identifies people with psychological difficulties and is employed to predict some everyday behaviors (Module 33).

mirror neurons Specialized neurons that fire not only when a person enacts a particular behavior, but also when a person simply observes *another* individual carrying out the same behavior (Module 5).

mood disorder A disturbance in emotional experience that is strong enough to intrude on everyday living (Module 38).

mood stabilizers Drugs used to treat mood disorders that prevent manic episodes of bipolar disorder (Module 42).

motivation The factors that direct and energize the behavior of humans and other organisms (Module 24).

motor area The part of the cortex that is largely responsible for the body's voluntary movement (Module 7).

motor (efferent) neurons Neurons that communicate information from the nervous system to muscles and glands (Module 6).

myelin sheath A protective coat of fat and protein that wraps around the axon (Module 5).

narcissistic personality disorder A personality disturbance characterized by an exaggerated sense of self-importance (Module 38).

narcotics Drugs that increase relaxation and relieve pain and anxiety (Module 14).

nativist approach (to language development) The theory that a genetically determined, innate mechanism directs language development (Module 22).

naturalistic observation Research in which an investigator simply observes some naturally occurring behavior and does not make a change in the situation (Module 3).

nature–nurture issue The issue of the degree to which environment and heredity influence behavior (Module 27).

need for achievement A stable, learned characteristic in which a person obtains satisfaction by striving for and attaining a level of excellence (Module 25).

need for affiliation An interest in establishing and maintaining relationships with other people (Module 25).

need for power A tendency to seek impact, control, or influence over others and to be seen as a powerful individual (Module 25).

negative reinforcer An unpleasant stimulus whose removal leads to an increase in the probability that a preceding response will be repeated in the future (Module 16).

neo-Freudian psychoanalysts Psychoanalysts who were trained in traditional Freudian theory but who later rejected some of its major points (Module 31).

neonate A newborn child (Module 28).

neurogenesis The creation of new neurons (Module 7).

neurons Nerve cells, the basic elements of the nervous system (Module 5).

neuroplasticity Changes in the brain that occur throughout the life span relating to the addition of new neurons, new interconnections between neurons, and the reorganization of information-processing areas (Module 7).

neuroscience perspective The approach that views behavior from the perspective of the brain, the nervous system, and other biological functions (Module 2).

neurotransmitters Chemicals that carry messages across the synapse to the dendrite (and sometimes the cell body) of a receiver neuron (Module 5).

neutral stimulus A stimulus that, before conditioning, does not naturally bring about the response of interest (Module 15).

norms Standards of test performance that permit the comparison of one person's score on a test with the scores of other individuals who have taken the same test (Module 23).

obedience A change in behavior in response to the commands of others (Module 44).

obesity Body weight that is more than 20% above the average weight for a person of a particular height (Module 25).

object permanence The awareness that objects—and people—continue to exist even if they are out of sight (Module 28).

observational learning Learning by observing the behavior of another person, or model (Module 17).

obsession A persistent, unwanted thought or idea that keeps recurring (Module 38).

obsessive-compulsive disorder A disorder characterized by obsessions or compulsions (Module 38).

Oedipal conflict A child's sexual interest in his or her opposite-sex parent, typically resolved through identification with the same-sex parent (Module 31).

operant conditioning Learning in which a voluntary response is strengthened or weakened, depending on its favorable or unfavorable consequences (Module 16).

operational definition The translation of a hypothesis into specific, testable procedures that can be measured and observed (Module 3).

opponent-process theory of color vision The theory that receptor cells for color are linked in pairs, working in opposition to each other (Module 9).

optic nerve A bundle of ganglion axons that carry visual information to the brain (Module 9).

oral stage According to Freud, a stage from birth to age 12 to 18 months, in which an infant's center of pleasure is the mouth (Module 31).

overgeneralization The phenomenon by which children apply language rules even when the application results in an error (Module 22).

ovulation The point at which an egg is released from the ovaries (Module 25).

panic disorder Anxiety disorder that takes the form of panic attacks lasting from a few seconds to several hours (Module 38).

parasympathetic division The part of the autonomic division of the nervous system that acts to calm the body after an emergency has ended (Module 6).

partial (or intermittent) reinforcement schedule Reinforcing of a behavior some but not all of the time (Module 16).

passionate (or romantic) love A state of intense absorption in someone that includes intense physiological arousal, psychological interest, and caring for the needs of another (Module 46).

perception The sorting out, interpretation, analysis, and integration of stimuli by the sense organs and brain (Module 8).

perceptual constancy The phenomenon in which physical objects are perceived as unvarying and consistent despite changes in their appearance or in the physical environment (Module 11).

peripheral nervous system The part of the nervous system that includes the autonomic and somatic subdivisions; made up of neurons with long axons and dendrites, it branches out from the spinal cord and brain and reaches the extremities of the body (Module 6).

peripheral route processing Message interpretation characterized by consideration of the source and related general information rather than of the message itself (Module 43).

permissive parents Parents who give their children relaxed or inconsistent direction and, although they are warm, require little of them (Module 28).

personal stressors Major life events, such as the death of a family member, that have immediate negative consequences that generally fade with time (Module 34).

personality The pattern of enduring characteristics that produce consistency and individuality in a given person (Module 31).

personality disorder A disorder characterized by a set of inflexible, maladaptive behavior patterns that keep a person from functioning appropriately in society (Module 38).

person-centered therapy Therapy in which the goal is to reach one's potential for self-actualization (Module 41).

phallic stage According to Freud, a period beginning around age 3 during which a child's pleasure focuses on the genitals (Module 31).

phobias Intense, irrational fears of specific objects or situations (Module 38).

phonemes The smallest units of speech (Module 22).

phonology The study of the smallest units of speech, called phonemes (Module 22).

pituitary gland The major component of the endocrine system, or "master gland," which secretes hormones that control growth and other parts of the endocrine system (Module 6).

placebo A false treatment, such as a pill, "drug," or other substance, without any significant chemical properties or active ingredient (Module 4).

place theory of hearing The theory that different areas of the basilar membrane respond to different frequencies (Module 10).

Baraas, R. C., Foster, D. H., & Amano, K. (2006). Anomalous trichromats' judgments of surface color in natural scenes under different daylights. *Neuroscience, 23,* 629–635.

Barandiaran, A. A., Pascual, A. C., & Samaniego, C. M. (2006). A criticism of the Kohlberg theory: The moral development in adults and educative implications. *Revista de Psicología General y Aplicada, 59,* 165–182.

Bargh, J. A., & Chartrand, T. L. (2000). The mind in the middle: A practical guide to priming and automaticity research. In H. T. Reis & C. M. Judd (Eds.), *Handbook of research methods in social and personality psychology.* New York: Cambridge University Press.

Barker, J., & Jones, M. (2008, June). The effects of hypnosis on self-efficacy, affect, and soccer performance: A case study. *Journal of Clinical Sport Psychology, 2,* 127–147.

Barkley, R. (2000). *Taking charge of ADHD* (rev. ed.). New York: Guilford Press.

Barkley, R. (2005). *ADHD and the nature of self-control.* New York: Guildford.

Barlow, D. H. (2007). *Clinical handbook of psychological disorders: A step-by-step treatment manual* (4th ed.). New York: Guilford Press.

Barmeyer, C. I. (2004). Learning styles and their impact on cross-cultural training: An international comparison in France, Germany and Quebec. *International Journal of Intercultural Relations, 28,* 577–594.

Barnes, V. A., Davis, H. C., Murzynowski, J., & Treiber, F. A. (2004). Impact of meditation on resting and ambulatory blood pressure and heart rate in youth. *Medicine, 66,* 909–914.

Barnett, J. E., Wise, E. H., & Johnson-Greene, D. (2007). Informed consent: Too much of a good thing or not enough? *Professional Psychology: Research and Practice, 38,* 179–186.

Baron, R. S. (2005). So right it's wrong: Groupthink and the ubiquitous nature of polarized group decision making. In M. P. Zanna (Ed.), *Advances in experimental social psychology* (Vol. 37). San Diego, CA: Elsevier Academic Press.

Barresi, J. (2007). Consciousness and intentionality. *Journal of Consciousness Studies, 14, Special issue: Concepts of Consciousness: Integrating an Emerging Science,* 77–93.

Barrett, L. F., & Salovey, P. (Eds.). (2002). *The wisdom in feeling: Psychological processes in emotional intelligence.* New York: Guilford Press.

Barrett, L. F., & Wager, T. D. (2006). The structure of emotion: Evidence from neuroimaging studies. *Current Directions in Psychological Science, 15,* 79–83.

Barron, F. (1990). *Creativity and psychological health: Origins of personal vitality and creative freedom.* Buffalo, NY: Creative Education Foundation.

Barron, G., & Yechiam, E. (2002). Private e-mail requests and the diffusion of responsibility. *Computers in Human Behavior, 18,* 507–520.

Bartecchi, C. E., MacKenzie, T. D., & Schrier, R. W. (1995, May). The global tobacco epidemic. *Scientific American,* pp. 44–51.

Bartholow, B. D., Bushman, B. J., & Sestir, M. A. (2005). Chronic violent video game exposure and desensitization to violence: Behavioral and event-related brain potential data. *Journal of Experimental Social Psychology, 42,* 532–539.

Bartlett, F. (1932). *Remembering: A study in experimental and social psychology.* Cambridge, England: Cambridge University Press.

Bartlett, M. Y., & DeSteno, D. (2006). Gratitude and prosocial behavior: Helping when it costs you. *Psychological Science, 17,* 319–325.

Bartocci, G. (2004). Transcendence techniques and psychobiological mechanisms underlying religious experience. *Mental Health, Religion and Culture, 7,* 171–181.

Bartolomeo, J., Cruz, C., Messer, L., Dodd, J., Herndon, J., & Warrick, P. (2009, June 29).

Chastity Bono's sex change: Becoming Chaz. *People,* p. 54.

Bartone, P., Roland, R., Picano, J., & Williams, T. (2008). Psychological hardiness predicts success in U.S. Army Special Forces candidates. *International Journal of Selection and Assessment, 16,* 78–81.

Bartoshuk, L. (2000, July/August). The bitter with the sweet. *APS Observer, 11,* 33.

Bartoshuk, L., & Lucchina, L. (1997, January 13). Are you a supertaster? *U.S. News & World Report,* pp. 58–59.

Bartzokis, G., Nuechterlein, K. H., Lu, P. H., Gitlin, M., Rogers, S., & Mintz, J. (2003). Dysregulated brain development in adult men with schizophrenia: A magnetic resonance imaging study. *Biological Psychiatry, 53,* 412–421.

Baruss, I. (2003). *Alterations of consciousness: An empirical analysis for social scientists.* Washington, DC: American Psychological Association.

Basak, C., Boot, W., Voss, M., & Kramer, A. (2008). Can training in a real-time strategy video game attenuate cognitive decline in older adults? *Psychology and Aging, 23,* 765–777.

Bassottdi, G., Villanacci, V., Fisogni, S., Rossi, E., Baronio, P., Clerici, C., et al. (2007). Enteric glial cells and their role in gastrointestinal motor abnormalities: Introducing the neurogliopathies. *World Journal of Gastroenterology, 14,* 4035–4041.

Bates, E. (2005). Plasticity, localization, and language development. In S. T. Parker & J. Langer (Eds.), *Biology and knowledge revisited: From neurogenesis to psychogenesis.* Mahwah, NJ: Lawrence Erlbaum Associates.

Bates, P. E., Cuvo, T., Miner, C. A., & Korabek, C. A. (2001). Simulated and community-based instruction involving persons with mild and moderate mental retardation. *Research in Developmental Disabilities, 22,* 95–115.

Bates, R. (2002). Liking and similarity as predictors of multi-source ratings. *Personnel Review, 31,* 540–552.

Batson, C. D., & Powell, A. A. (2003). Altruism and prosocial behavior. In T. Millon & M. J. Lerner (Eds.), *Handbook of psychology: Personality and social psychology* (Vol. 5). New York: Wiley.

Bauer, P. (2008). Toward a neuro-developmental account of the development of declarative memory. *Developmental Psychobiology, 50,* 19–31.

Baum, A. (1994). Behavioral, biological, and environmental interactions in disease processes. In S. Blumenthal, K. Matthews, & S. Weiss (Eds.), *New research frontiers in behavioral medicine: Proceedings of the National Conference.* Washington, DC: NIH Publications.

Bauman, S., & Kopp, T. G. (2006). Integrating a humanistic approach in outpatient sex offender groups. *Journal for Specialists in Group Work, 31,* 247–261.

Baumeister, R. F., & Stillman, T. (2006). Erotic plasticity: Nature, culture, gender, and sexuality. In R. D. McAnulty, & M. M. Burnette, *Sex and sexuality, Vol 1: Sexuality today: Trends and controversies.* Westport, CT: Praeger Publishers/Greenwood Publishing.

Baumeister, R. F., Twenge, J. M., & Nuss, C. K. (2002). Effects of social exclusion on cognitive processes: Anticipated aloneness reduces intelligent thought. *Journal of Personality and Social Psychology, 83,* 817–827.

Baumgartner, F. (2002). The effect of hardiness in the choice of coping strategies in stressful situations. *Studia Psychologica, 44,* 69–75.

Baumrind, D. (2005). Patterns of parental authority and adolescent autonomy. *New Directions for Child and Adolescent Development, 108,* 61–69.

Bayliss, D. M., Jarrold, C., Baddeley, A. D., & Gunn, D. M. (2005a). The relationship between short-term memory and working memory: Complex span made simple? *Memory, 13,* 414–421.

Bayliss, D. M., Jarrold, C., Baddeley, A. D., Gunn, D. M., & Leigh, E. (2005b). Mapping the developmental constraints on working memory span

performance. *Developmental Psychology, 41,* 579–597.

Bayne, R. (2005). *Ideas and evidence: Critical reflections on MBTI® theory and practice.* Gainesville, FL: Center for Applications of Psychological Type, CAPT.

Bazalakova, M. H., Wright, J., Schneble, E. J., McDonald, M. P., Heilman, C. J., Levey, A. I., & Blakely, R. D. (2007). Deficits in acetylcholine homeostasis, receptors and behaviors in choline transporter heterozygous mice. *Genes, Brain & Behavior, 6,* 411–424.

Beardslee, W., Wright, E., Gladstone, T., & Forbes, P. (2007). Long-term effects from a randomized trial of two public health preventive interventions for parental depression. *Journal of Family Psychology, 21,* 703–713.

Bearman, C. R., Ball, L. J., & Ormerod, T. C. (2007). The structure and function of spontaneous analogising in domain-based problem solving. *Thinking & Reasoning, 13,* 273–294.

Beatty, J. (2000). *The human brain: Essentials of behavioral neuroscience.* Thousand Oaks, CA: Sage.

Bechara, A., Damasio, A. R., Damasio, H., & Anderson, S. (1994). Insensitivity to future consequences following damage to human prefrontal cortex. *Cognition, 50,* 7–15.

Beck, A. P., & Lewis, C. M. (Eds.). (2000). *The process of group psychotherapy: Systems for analyzing change.* Washington, DC: American Psychological Association.

Beck, A. T. (1995). Cognitive therapy: Past, present, and future. In M. J. Mahoney (Ed.), *Cognitive and constructive psychotherapies: Theory, research, and practice.* New York: Springer.

Beck, A. T. (2004). Cognitive therapy, behavior therapy, psychoanalysis, and pharmacotherapy: A cognitive continuum. In A. Freeman, M. J. Mahoney, P. Devito, & D. Martin (Eds.), *Cognition and Psychotherapy* (2nd ed.). New York: Springer Publishing Co.

Beck, A. T., & Emery, G., with Greenberg, R. L. (1985). *Anxiety disorders and phobias: A cognitive perspective.* New York: Basic Books.

Beck, A. T., Freeman, A., & Davis, D. D. (2004). *Cognitive therapy of personality disorders* (2nd ed.). New York: Guilford Press.

Beck, A. T., & Rector, N. A. (2005). Cognitive approaches to schizophrenia: Theory and therapy. *Annual Review of Clinical Psychology, 1,* 577–606.

Beck, H. P., Levinson, S., & Irons, G. (2009). Finding little Albert: A journey to John B. Watson's infant laboratory. *American Psychologist, 64,* 605–614.

Becker, B. E., & Luthar, S. S. (2007). Peer-perceived admiration and social preference: Contextual correlates of positive peer regard among suburban and urban adolescents. *Journal of Research on Adolescence, 17,* 117–144.

Becker, T. (2003). Is emotional intelligence a viable concept? *Academy of Management Review, 28,* 192–195.

Bedard, W. W., & Parsinger, M. A. (1995). Prednisolone blocks extreme intermale social aggression in seizure-induced, brain-damaged rats: Implications for the amygdaloid central nucleus, corticotrophin-releasing factor, and electrical seizures. *Psychological Reports, 77,* 3–9.

Beersma, D. G. M., & Gordijn, M. C. M. (2007). Circadian control of the sleep-wake cycle. *Physiology & Behavior, 90.*

Begg, D., & Langley, J. (2001). Changes in risky driving behavior from age 21 to 26 years. *Journal of Safety Research, 32,* 491–499.

Begley, S. (2002, September 13). The memory of September 11 is seared in your mind; but is it really true? *The Wall Street Journal,* p. B1.

Begley, S. (2005, April 29). Evolution psychology may not help explain our behavior after all. *The Wall Street Journal,* p. D1.

Begley, S. (2009, February 16). Will the BlackBerry sink the presidency? *Newsweek,* p. 37.

Behrens, M., Lendon, C., & Roe, C. (2009). A common biological mechanism in cancer and Alzheimer's disease? *Current Alzheimer Research, 6,* 196–204.

Beidel, D. C., & Turner, S. M. (2007). Etiology of social anxiety disorder. In D. C. Beidel, & S. M. Turner, *Shy children, phobic adults: Nature and treatment of social anxiety disorders* (2nd ed.). Washington, DC: American Psychological Association.

Beilock, S. L., & Carr, T. H. (2005). When high-powered people fail: Working memory and "choking under pressure" in math. *Psychological Science, 16,* 101–105.

Belar, C. (2008, April). Clinical health psychology: A health care specialty in professional psychology. *Professional Psychology: Research and Practice, 39,* 229–233.

Bellezza, F. S. (2000). Mnemonic devices. In A. E. Kazdin (Ed.), *Encyclopedia of psychology* (Vol. 5). Washington, DC: American Psychological Association.

Belov, D. I., & Armstrong, R. D. (2009). Direct and inverse problems of item pool design for computerized adaptive testing. *Educational and Psychological Measurement, 69,* 533–547.

Belsky, J., & Pluess, M. (2009). The nature (and nurture?) of plasticity in early human development. *Perspectives on Psychological Science, 4,* 345–351.

Bem, D. J. (1996). Exotic becomes erotic: A developmental theory of sexual orientation. *Psychological Review, 103,* 320–335.

Bem, D. J., & Honorton, C. (1994). Does psi exist? Replicable evidence for an anomalous process of information transfer. *Psychological Bulletin, 115,* 4–18.

Benac, N., & Tompson, T. (2009, May 21). AP poll: Most students stressed, some depressed. Retrieved from http://www.denverpost.com/popular/ci_12418610

Benderly, B. L. (2004). Looking beyond the SAT. *American Psychological Society, 17,* 12–18.

Benet-Martinez, V., Lee, F., & Leu, J. (2006). Biculturalism and cognitive complexity: Expertise in cultural representations. *Journal of Cross-Cultural Psychology, 37,* 386–407.

Benham, G., Woody, E. Z., & Wilson, K. S. (2006). Expect the unexpected: Ability, attitude, and responsiveness to hypnosis. *Journal of Personality and Social Psychology, 91,* 342–350.

Benight, C. C. (2004). Collective efficacy following a series of natural disasters. *Stress and Coping: An International Journal, 17,* 401–420.

Benjamin, L. T., Jr. (1985, February). Defining aggression: An exercise for classroom discussion. *Teaching of Psychology, 12*(1), 40–42.

Ben-Porath, Y., & Archer, R. (2008). The MMPI-2 and MMPI-A. *Personality assessment.* New York: Routledge/Taylor & Francis Group.

Benson, E. (2003, April). The science of sexual arousal. *Monitor on Psychology,* pp. 50–56.

Benson, H., Kornhaber, A., Kornhaber, C., LeChanu, M. N., et al. (1994). Increases in positive psychological characteristics with a new relaxation-response curriculum in high school students. *Journal of Research and Development in Education, 27,* 226–231.

Benton, S. A., Robertson, J. M., Tseng, W. C., Newton, F. B., & Benton, S. L. (2003). Changes in counseling center client problems across 13 years. *Professional Psychology: Research and Practice, 34,* 66–72.

Beresneviaté, M., Taylor, G. J., & Bagby, R. M. (2007). Assessing alexithymia and type A behavior in coronary heart disease patients: A multimethod approach. *Psychotherapy and Psychosomatics, 76,* 186–192.

Berk, L. E. (2005). Why parenting matters. In S. Olfman (Ed.), *Childhood lost: How American culture is failing our kids.* Westport, CT: Praeger Publishers/Greenwood Publishing Group.

Berkowitz, L. (2001). On the formation and regulation of anger and aggression: A cognitive-neoassociationistic analysis. In W. G. Parrott (Ed.), *Emotions in social psychology: Essential readings.* New York: Psychology Press.

Berle, D. (2007). Graded exposure therapy for long-standing disgust-related cockroach avoidance in an older male. *Clinical Case Studies, 6,* 339–347.

Berman, A. L.. Jobes, D. A., & Silverman, M. M. (2006). An integrative-eclectic approach to treatment. In A. L. Berman, D. A. Jobes, & M. M. Silverman, *Adolescent suicide: Assessment and intervention* (2nd ed.). Washington, DC: American Psychological Association.

Bernal, G., Trimble, J. E., Burlew, A. K., & Leong, F. T. (Eds.) (2002). *Handbook of racial and ethnic minority psychology.* Thousand Oaks, CA: Sage.

Bernard, L. L. (1924). *Instinct: A study in social psychology.* New York: Holt.

Bernstein, D., & Loftus, E. (2009a). How to tell if a particular memory is true or false. *Perspectives on Psychological Science, 4,* 370–374.

Bernstein, D., & Loftus, E. (2009b). The consequences of false memories for food preferences and choices. *Perspectives on Psychological Science, 4,* 135–139.

Bernstein, D. M., Loftus, G. R., & Meltzoff, A. N. (2005). Object identification in preschool children and adults. *Developmental Science, 8,* 151–161.

Berntsen, D., & Rubin, D. C. (2004). Cultural life scripts structure recall from autobiographical memory. *Memory and Cognition, 32,* 427–442.

Berntsen, D., & Thomsen, D. K. (2005). Personal memories for remote historical events: Accuracy and clarity of flashbulb memories related to World War II. *Journal of Experimental Psychology: General, 134,* 242–257.

Berntson, G. G., Bechara, A., Damasio, H., Tranel, D., & Cacioppo, J. T. (2007). Amygdala contribution to selective dimensions of emotion. *Social Cognitive and Affective Neuroscience, 2,* 123–129.

Berridge, K. C. (2004). Motivation concepts in behavioral neuroscience. *Physiology and Behavior, 81,* 179–209.

Berrios, G. E. (1996). *The history of mental symptoms: Descriptive psychopathology since the 19th century.* Cambridge: Cambridge University Press.

Bertakis, K. (2009). The influence of gender on the doctor–patient interaction. *Patient Education and Counseling, 76,* 356–360.

Bertakis, K., Franks, P., & Epstein, R. (2009). Patient-centered communication in primary care: Physician and patient gender and gender concordance. *Journal of Women's Health, 18,* 539–545.

Berthoud, H. R. (2002). Multiple neural systems controlling food intake and body weight. *Neuroscience and Biobehavioral Reviews, 26,* 393–428.

Betz, N. (2007). Career self-efficacy: Exemplary recent research and emerging directions. *Journal of Career Assessment, 15,* 403–422.

Beyene, Y., Gilliss, C., & Lee, K. (2007). "I take the good with the bad, and I moisturize": Defying middle age in the new millennium. *Menopause, 14,* 734–741.

Bhar, S., Gelfand, L., Schmid, S., Gallop, R., DeRubeis, R., Hollon, S., et al. (2008). Sequence of improvement in depressive symptoms across cognitive therapy and pharmacotherapy. *Journal of Affective Disorders, 110,* 161–166.

Bialystok, E., & Martin, M. M. (2004). Attention and inhibition in bilingual children: Evidence from the dimensional change card sort task. *Developmental Science, 7,* 325–339.

Bianchi, S. M., & Casper, L. M. (2000). American families. *Population Bulletin, 55*(4).

Billiard, M. (2008). Narcolepsy: Current treatment options and future approaches. *Neuropsychiatric Disease and Treatment, 4,* 557–566.

Bindemann, M., Burton, A., Leuthold, H., & Schweinberger, S. (2008, July). Brain potential correlates of face recognition: Geometric distortions and the N250r brain response to stimulus repetitions. *Psychophysiology, 45,* 535–544.

Binet, A., & Simon, T. (1916). *The development of intelligence in children (The Binet-Simon Scale).* Baltimore: Williams & Wilkins.

Bingenheimer, J. B., Brennan, R. T., & Earls, F. J. (2005, May 27). Firearm violence exposure and serious violent behavior. *Science, 308,* 1323–1327.

Binstock, R., & George, L. K. (Eds.). (1996). *Handbook of aging and the social sciences* (4th ed.). San Diego, CA: Academic Press.

Birren, J. E. (Ed.). (1996). *Encyclopedia of gerontology: Age, aging and the aged.* San Diego, CA: Academic Press.

Bishop, M. (2005). Quality of life and psychosocial adaptation to chronic illness and disability: Preliminary analysis of a conceptual and theoretical synthesis. *Rehabilitation Counseling Bulletin, 48,* 219–231.

Bitterman, M. E. (2006). Classical conditioning since Pavlov. *Review of General Psychology, 10,* 365–376.

Bittles, A. H., Bower, C., & Hussain, R. (2007). The four ages of Down syndrome. *European Journal of Public Health, 17,* 121–225.

Bizley, J., Walker, K., Silverman, B., King, A., & Schnupp, J. (2009, February). Interdependent encoding of pitch, timbre, and spatial location in auditory cortex. *Journal of Neuroscience, 29,* 2064–2075.

Bjorklund, D. F., & Ellis, B. J. (2005). *Evolutionary psychology and child development: An emerging synthesis.* New York: Guilford Press.

Bjornstad, R. (2006). Learned helplessness, discouraged workers, and multiple unemployment equilibria. *The Journal of Socio-Economics, 35,* 458–475.

Black, A. L. & McCafferty, D. (1998, July 3–5). The age of contentment. *USA Weekend,* pp. 4–6.

Black, P. (2006). Thrust to wholeness: The nature of self-protection. *Review of General Psychology, 10,* 191–209.

Blair, C. A., Thompson, L. F., & Wuensch, K. L. (2005). Electronic helping behavior: The virtual presence of others makes a difference. *Basic and Applied Social Psychology, 27,* 171–178.

Blakeslee, S. (1991, August 7). Levels of caffeine in various foods. *The New York Times.*

Blakeslee, S. (1992, August 11). Finding a new messenger for the brain's signals to the body. *The New York Times,* p. C3.

Blass, T. (1996). Attribution of responsibility and trust in the Milgram obedience experiment. *Journal of Applied Social Psychology, 26,* 1529–1535.

Blass, T. (2004). *The man who shocked the world: The life and legacy of Stanley Milgram.* New York: Basic Books.

Blass, T. (2009). From New Haven to Santa Clara: A historical perspective on the Milgram obedience experiments. *American Psychologist, 64,* 37–45.

Blass, T. (Ed.) (2000). *Obedience to authority: Current perspectives on the Milgram Paradigm.* Mahwah, NJ: Erlbaum.

Blatter, K., & Cajochen, C. (2007). Circadian rhythms in cognitive performance: Methodological constraints, protocols, theoretical underpinnings. *Physiology & Behavior, 90,* 196–208.

Blixen, C. E., Singh, A., & Xu, M. (2006). What women want: Understanding obesity and preferences for primary care weight reduction interventions among African-American and Caucasian women. *Journal of the National Medical Association, 98,* 1160–1170.

Bloom, P. N., McBride, C. M., & Pollak, K. I. (2006). Recruiting teen smokers in shopping malls to a smoking-cessation program using the foot-in-the-door technique. *Journal of Applied Social Psychology, 36,* 1129–1144.

Blum, D. (2002). *Love at goon park: Harry Harlow and the science of affection.* Cambridge, MA: Perseus.

Boahen, K. (2005, May). Neuromorphic micro-chips. *Scientific American,* pp. 56–64.

Boake, C. (2008, April). Clinical neuropsychology. *Professional Psychology: Research and Practice, 39,* 234–239.

Board of Educational Affairs. (2002). *2002 APA task force report on undergraduate student competencies.* Washington, DC: American Psychological Association.

Bode, C., de Ridder, D. T., Kuijer, R. G., & Bensing, J. M. (2007). Effects of an intervention promoting proactive coping competencies in middle and late adulthood. *Gerontologist, 47,* 42–51.

Boden, J. M., Fergusson, D. M., & Horwood, L. J. (2007). Anxiety disorders and suicidal behaviours in adolescence and young adulthood: Findings from a longitudinal study. *Psychological Medicine, 37,* 431–440.

Bodin, G. (2006). Review of harvesting free association. *Psychoanalytic Quarterly, 75,* 629–632.

Boehm, K. E., & Campbell, N. B. (1995). Suicide: A review of calls to an adolescent peer listening phone service. *Child Psychiatry and Human Development, 26,* 61–66.

Bogart, R. K., McDaniel, R. J., Dunn, W. J., Hunter, C., Peterson, A. L., & Write, E. E. (2007). Efficacy of group cognitive behavior therapy for the treatment of masticatory myofascial pain. *Military Medicine, 172,* 169–174.

Bogenschutz, M. P., Geppert, C. M., & George, J. (2006). The role of twelve-step approaches in dual diagnosis treatment and recovery. *American Journal of Addiction, 15,* 50–60.

Bohart, A. C. (2006). Understanding person-centered therapy: A review of Paul Wilkins' person-centered therapy in focus. *Person-Centered and Experiential Psychotherapies, 5,* 138–143.

Bohn, A., & Berntsen, D. (2007). Pleasantness bias in flashbulb memories: Positive and negative flashbulb memories of the fall of the Berlin Wall among East and West Germans. *Memory and Cognition, 35,* 565–577.

Boisvert, C. M., & Faust, D. (2003). Leading researchers' consensus on psychotherapy research findings: Implications for the teaching and conduct of psychotherapy. *Professional Psychology: Research and Practice, 34,* 508–513.

Boles, D. B. (2005). A large-sample study of sex differences in functional cerebral lateralization. *Journal of Clinical and Experimental Neuropsychology, 27,* 759–768.

Bolger, N., & Amarel, D. (2007). Effects of social support visibility on adjustment to stress: Experimental evidence. *Journal of Personality and Social Psychology, 92,* 458–475.

Boller, F. (2004). Rational basis of rehabilitation following cerebral lesions: A review of the concept of cerebral plasticity. *Functional Neurology: New Trends in Adaptive and Behavioral Disorders, 19,* 65–72.

Bonanni, R., Pasqualetti, P., Caltagirone, C., & Carlesimo, G. (2007). Primacy and recency effects in immediate free recall of sequences of spatial positions. *Perceptual and Motor Skills, 105,* 483–500.

Bonanno, G.A. (2004). Loss, trauma, and human resilience: Have we underestimated the human capacity to thrive after extremely aversive events? *American Psychologist, 59,* 20–28.

Bond, M. (2006).Psychodynamic psychotherapy in the treatment of mood disorders. *Current Opinion in Psychiatry, 19,* 40–43.

Bonnardel, V. (2006). Color naming and categorization in inherited color vision deficiencies. *Visual Neuroscience, 23,* 637–643.

Borbély, A. (1988). *Secrets of sleep* (p. 43, graph). New York: Basic Books.

Bordnick, P. S., Elkins, R. L., Orr, T. E., Walters, P., & Thyer, B. A. (2004). Evaluating the relative effectiveness of three aversion therapies designed to reduce craving among cocaine abusers. *Behavioral Interventions, 19,* 1–24.

Borisenko, J. (2007). Fatherhood as a personality development factor in men. *The Spanish Journal of Psychology, 10,* 82–90.

Bornstein, R. F. (2003). Psychodynamic models of personality. In T. Millon & M. J. Lerner (Eds.), *Handbook of psychology: Personality and social psychology* (Vol. 5). New York: Wiley.

Bosma, H., van Boxtel, M. P. J., Ponds, R. W. H. M., Houx, P. J. H., & Jolles, J. (2003). Education and age-related cognitive decline: The contribution of mental workload. *Educational Gerontology, 29,* 165–173.

Botvinick, M. (2004, August 6). Probing the neural basis of body ownership. *Science, 305,* 782–783.

Bouchard, C., & Bray, G. A. (Eds.). (1996). *Regulation of body weight: Biological and behavioral mechanisms.* New York: Wiley.

Bouchard, T. J., Jr. (2004). Genetic influence on human psychological traits: A survey. *Current Directions in Psychological Science, 13,* 148–151.

Bouchard, T. J., Jr., Segal, N. L., Tellegen, A., McGue, M., Keyes, M. & Krueger, R. (2004). Genetic influence on social attitudes: Another challenge to psychology from behavior genetics. In L. F. DiLalla (Ed.), *Behavior genetics principles: Perspectives in development, personality, and psychopathology.* Washington, DC: American Psychological Association.

Bourne, L. E., & Dominowski, R. L. (1979). *Cognitive processes.* Upper Saddle River, NJ: Pearson Education.

Bourne, L. E., Dominowski, R. L., Loftus, E. F., & Healy, A. F. (1986). *Cognitive processes* (2nd ed.). Englewood Cliffs, NJ: Prentice Hall.

Bower, G. H., Thompson, S. S., & Tulving, E. (1994). Reducing retroactive interference: An interference analysis. *Journal of Experimental Psychology Learning, Memory, and Cognition, 20,* 51–66.

Bower, J. M., & Parsons, L. M. (2003, August). Rethinking the "lesser brain." *Scientific American,* pp. 51–57.

Boxer, P., Huesmann, L., Bushman, B., O'Brien, M., & Moceri, D. (2009). The role of violent media preference in cumulative developmental risk for violence and general aggression. *Journal of Youth and Adolescence, 38,* 417–428.

Boyce, W. T., & Ellis, B. J. (2005). Biological sensitivity to context: An evolutionary-developmental theory of the origins and functions of stress reactivity. *Development and Psychopathology, 17,* 271–301.

Boyd-Wilson, B. M., McClure, J., & Walkey, F. H. (2004). Are well-being and illusory perceptions linked? The answer may be yes, but. . . . *Australian Journal of Psychology, 56,* 1–9.

Boyle, S. H., Williams, R. B., Mark, D. B., Brummett, B. H., Siegler, I. C., & Barefoot, J. C. (2005). Hostility, age, and mortality in a sample of cardiac patients. *American Journal of Cardiology, 96,* 64–72.

Bozarth, J. D., Zimring, F. M., & Tausch, R. (2002). Client-centered therapy: The evolution of a revolution. In D. J. Cain (Ed.), *Humanistic psychotherapies: Handbook of research and practice.* Washington, DC: American Psychological Association.

Brambilla, P., Cipriani, A., Hotopf, M., & Barbui, C. (2005). Side-effect profile of fluoxetine in comparison with other SSRIs, tricyclic and newer antidepressants: A meta-analysis of clinical trial data. *Pharmacopsychiatry, 38,* 69–77.

Brasic, J. R. (2002). Conversion disorder in childhood. *German Journal of Psychiatry, 5,* 54–61.

Braun, A. R., Balkin, T. J., Wesensten, N. J., Gwadry, F., Carson, R. E., Varga, M., et al. (1998). Dissociated pattern of activity in visual cortices and their projections during human rapid eye movement sleep. *Science, 279,* pp. 91–95.

Brausch, A. M. & Gutierrez, P. M. (2009). Differences in non-suicidal self-injury and suicide attempts in adolescents. *Journal of Youth and Adolescence, 21,* 46–51.

Brazelton, T. B. (1969). *Infants and mothers: Differences in development.* New York: Dell.

Breland, K., & Breland, M. (1966). *Animal behavior.* New York: Macmillan.

Brennen, T., Vikan, A., & Dybdahl, R. (2007). Are tip-of-the-tongue states universal? Evidence from speakers of an unwritten language. *Memory, 15,* 167–176.

Brewer, J. B., Zhao, Z., Desmond, J. E., Glover, G. H., & Gabrieli, J. D. E. (1998, August 21). Making memories: Brain activity that predicts how well visual experience will be remembered. *Science, 281,* 1185–1187.

Brewer, M. B., & Hewstone, M. (Eds.). (2003). *Social cognition.* Malden, MA: Blackwell Publishers.

Bright, P., Buckman, J., & Fradera, A. (2006). Retrograde amnesia in patients with hippo-campal, medial temporal, temporal lobe, or frontal pathology. *Learning & Memory, 13,* 545–557.

Brislin, R., Worthley, R., & MacNab, B. (2006). Cultural intelligence: Understanding behaviors that serve people's goals. *Group & Organization Management, 31,* 40–55.

Brock, T. C., & Green, M. C. (Eds.). (2005). *Persuasion: Psychological insights and perspectives* (2nd ed.). Thousand Oaks, CA: Sage Publications.

Bröder, A., & Schiffer, S. (2006). Stimulus format and working memory in fast and frugal strategy selection. *Journal of Behavioral Decision Making, 19,* 361–380.

Brody, J. (2008, May 20). Trying to break nicotine's grip. *The New York Times,* p. E9.

Broidy, L. M., Nagin, D. S., & Tremblay, R. E. (2003). Developmental trajectories of childhood disruptive behaviors and adolescent delinquency: A six-site, cross-national study. *Developmental Psychology, 39,* 222–245.

Broman, C. L. (2005). Stress, race and substance use in college. *College Student Journal, 39,* 340–352.

Bronson, P., & Merryman, A. (2009). *NurtureShock.* New York: Twelve.

Brooker, R. J., Widmaier, E. P., Graham, L., & Stiling, P. (2008). *Biology.* New York: McGraw-Hill.

Brown, E. (2001, September 17). The World Health Organization takes on big tobacco (but don't hold your breath): Anti-smoking advocates are mounting a global campaign: It's going to be a long, hard fight. *Forbes,* pp. 37–41.

Brown, J. (2006). Attribution: Theories, affect and evolution. *Dissertation Abstracts International: Section B: The Sciences and Engineering, 67*(2-B), 1201.

Brown, L. S., & Pope, K. S. (1996). *Recovered memories of abuse: Assessment, therapy, forensics.* Washington, DC: American Psychological Association.

Brown, P. K., & Wald, G. (1964). Visual pigments in single rod and cones of the human retina. *Science, 144,* 45–52.

Brown, R. (1958). How shall a thing be called? *Psychological Review, 65,* 14–21.

Brown, R. J. (2006). Different types of "dissociation" have different psychological mechanisms. *Journal of Trauma Dissociation, 6,* 7–28.

Brown, R., & Robertson, E. (2007). Off-line processing: Reciprocal interactions between declarative and procedural memories. *The Journal of Neuroscience, 27*(39), 10468–10475.

Brown, S., & Martinez, M. J. (2007). Activation of premotor vocal areas during musical discrimination. *Brain and Cognition, 63,* 9–69.

Brown, S., Martinez, M. J., & Parson, L. M. (2006). Music and language side by side in the brain: A PET study of the generation of melodies and sentences. *European Journal of Neuroscience, 23,* 2791–2803.

Brownlee, K. (2007). What works for whom? A critical review of psychotherapy research. *Psychiatric Rehabilitation Journal, 30,* 239–240.

Bruce, V., Green, P. R., & Georgeson, M. (1997). *Visual perception: Physiology, psychology and ecology* (3rd ed.). Mahwah, NJ: Erlbaum.

Bruggeman, H., Yonas, A., & Konczak, J. (2007). The processing of linear perspective and binocular information for action and perception. *Neuropsychologia, 45,* 1420–1426.

Brunet, A., Orr, S., Tremblay, J., Robertson, K., Nader, K., & Pitman, R. (2008). Effect of post-retrieval propranolol on psychophysiologic responding during subsequent script-driven traumatic imagery in post-traumatic stress. *Journal of Psychiatric Research, 42,* 503–506.

Brunet, A., Orr, S. P., Tremblay, J., Robertson, K., Nader, K., & Pitman, R. K. (2007). Effect of post-retrieval propranolol on psychophysio-logic responding during subsequent script-driven traumatic imagery in post-traumatic stress disorder. *Journal of Psychiatric Research, 22,* 301–315.

Bryant, R. M., Coker, A. D., Durodoye, B. A., McCollum, V. J., Pack-Brown, S. P., Constantine, M. G., &

O'Bryant, B. J. (2005). Having our say: African American women, diversity, and counseling. *Journal of Counseling and Development, 83,* 313–319.

Brydon, L., Edwards, S., Mohamed-Ali, V., & Steptoe, A. (2004). Socioeconomic status and stress-induced increases in interleukin-6. *Brain, Behavior, and Immunity, 18,* 281–290.

Brzustowicz, L. M., Hodgkinson, K. A., Chow, E. W. C., Honer, W. G., & Bassett, A. S. (2000, April 28). Location of major susceptibility locus for familial schizophrenia on chromosome 1q21–q22. *Science, 288,* 678–682.

Buchanan, R. W., Javitt, D. C., Marder, S. R., Schooler, N. R., Gold, J. M., McMahon, R. P., et al. (2007). The Cognitive and Negative Symptoms in Schizophrenia Trial (CONSIST): The efficacy of glutamatergic agents for negative symptoms and cognitive impairments. *American Journal of Psychiatry, 164,* 1593–1602.

Buchanan, T., & Selmon, N. (2008). Race and gender differences in self-efficacy: Assessing the role of gender role attitudes and family background. *Sex Roles, 58,* 822–836.

Buchanan, T. W., & Adolphs, R. (2004). The neuroanatomy of emotional memory in humans. In D. Reisberg & P. Hertel (Eds.), *Memory and emotion.* London: Oxford University Press.

Buchert, R., Thomasius, R., Wilke, F., Petersen, K., Nebeling, B., Obrocki, J., Schulze, O., Schmidt, U., & Clausen, M. (2004). A voxel-based PET investigation of the long-term effects of "ecstasy" consumption on brain serotonin transporters. *American Journal of Psychiatry, 161,* 1181–1189.

Buehner, M., Krumm, S., & Ziegler, M. (2006). Cognitive abilities and their interplay: Reasoning, crystallized intelligence, working memory components, and sustained attention. *Journal of Individual Differences, 27,* 57–72.

Bukobza, G. (2009). Relations between rebelliousness, risk-taking behavior, and identity status during emerging adulthood. *Identity, 9,* 159–177.

Bulik, C. M., Tozzi, F., Anderson, C., Mazzeo, S. E., Aggen, S., & Sullivan, P. F. (2003). The relation between eating disorders and components of perfectionism. *American Journal of Psychiatry, 160,* 366–368.

Bunge, S. A., & Wallis, J. D. (2008). *Neuroscience of rule-guided behavior.* New York: Oxford University Press.

Bunting, M. (2006). Proactive interference and item similarity in working memory. *Journal of Experimental Psychology: Learning, Memory, and Cognition, 32,* 183–196.

Burbach, M. E., Matkin, G. S., & Fritz, S. M. (2004). Teaching critical thinking in an introductory leadership course utilizing active learning strategies: A confirmatory study. *College Student Journal, 38,* 482–493.

Burchinal, M. R., Roberts, J. E., & Riggins, R., Jr. (2000). Relating quality of center-based child care to early cognitive and language development longitudinally. *Child Development, 71,* 338–357.

Bureau of Labor Statistics. (2007). *American time use survey.* Washington, DC: Bureau of Labor Statistics.

Burger, J. M. (2009). Replicating Milgram: Would people still obey today? *American Psychologist, 64,* 1–11.

Burger, J. M., & Caldwell, D. F. (2003). The effects of monetary incentives and labeling on the foot-in-the-door effect: Evidence for a self-perception process. *Basic and Applied Social Psychology, 25,* 235–241.

Burger, J. M., Reed, M., & DeCesare, K. (1999). The effects of initial request size on compliance: More about the that's-not-all technique. *Basic and Applied Social Psychology, 21,* 243–249.

Burgoon, J. K., & Bacue, A. E. (2003). Nonverbal communication skills. In J. O. Greene & B. R. Burleson (Eds.), *Handbook of communication and social interaction skills.* Mahwah, NJ: Lawrence Erlbaum.

Burke, C., & McDaniel, J. (2001). *A special kind of hero.* Lincoln, NE: Doubleday.

Burns, J. W., Quartana, P. J., & Bruehl, S. (2007). Anger management style moderates effects of emotion suppression during initial stress on pain and cardiovascular responses during subsequent pain-induction. *Annals of Behavioral Medicine, 34,* 154–165.

Burns, N. R., Bryan, J., & Nettelbeck, T. (2006). Ginkgo biloba: No robust effect on cognitive abilities or mood in healthy young or older adults. *Human Psychopharmacology: Clinical and Experimental, 21,* 27–37.

Busey, T. A., & Loftus, G. R. (2007). Cognitive science and the law. *Trends in Cognitive Science, 11,* 111–117.

Bush, J. (2008). Viability of virtual reality exposure therapy as a treatment alternative. *Computers in Human Behavior, 24,* 1032–1040.

Bushman, B. J., & Anderson, C. (2001). Media violence and the American public: Scientific facts versus media misinformation. *American Psychologist, 56,* 477–489.

Bushman, B. J., Wang, M. C., & Anderson, C. (2005). Is the curve relating temperature to aggression linear or curvilinear? Assaults and temperature in Minneapolis reexamined. *Journal of Personality and Social Psychology, 89,* 62–66.

Buss, D. (2009). How can evolutionary psychology successfully explain personality and individual differences? *Perspectives on Psychological Science, 4,* 359–366.

Buss, D. M. (2001). Human nature and culture: An evolutionary psychological perspective. *Journal of Personality, 69,* 955–978.

Buss, D. M. (2003a). *The evolution of desire: Strategies of human mating.* New York: Basic Books.

Buss, D. M. (2004). Sex differences in human mate preferences: Evolutionary hypotheses tested in 37 cultures. In H. T. Reis & C. E. Rusbult (Eds.), *Close relationships: Key readings.* Philadelphia: Taylor & Francis.

Buss, D. M., Abbott, M., & Angleitner, A. (1990). International preferences in selecting mates: A study of 37 cultures. *Journal of Cross-Cultural Psychology, 21,* 5–47.

Butcher, J. N. (2005). *A beginner's guide to the MMPI-2* (2nd ed.). Washington, DC: American Psychological Association.

Butler, A. C., Chapman, J. E., Forman, E. M., & Beck, A. T. (2006). The empirical status of cognitive-behavioral therapy: A review of meta-analyses. *Clinical Psychology Review, 26,* 17–31.

Butler, L. D., Koopman, C., Neri, E., Giese-Davis, J., Palesh, O., Thorne-Yocam, K. A., et al. (2009). Effects of supportive-expressive group therapy on pain in women with metastatic breast cancer. *Health Psychology, 28,* 579–587.

Butler, L. T., & Berry, D. C. (2004). Understanding the relationship between repetition priming and mere exposure. *British Journal of Psychology, 95,* 467–487.

Byne, W. (1996). Biology and homosexuality: Implications of neuroendocrinological and neuroanatomical studies. In R. P. Cabaj & T. S. Stein (Eds.), *Textbook of homosexuality and mental health.* Washington, DC: American Psychiatric Press.

Byrne-Davis, L., & Vedhara, K. (2008). Psychoneuroimmunology. *Social and Personality Psychology Compass, 2,* 751–764.

Cabanac, M., & Frankham, P. (2002). Evidence that transient nicotine lowers the body weight set point. *Physiology & Behavior, 76,* 539–542.

Cabioglu, M., Ergene, N., & Tan, Ü. (2007, May). Smoking cessation after acupuncture treatment. *International Journal of Neuroscience, 117,* 571–578.

Cachelin, F. M., & Regan, P. C. (2006). Prevalence and correlates of chronic dieting in a multi-ethnic U.S. community sample. *Eating and Weight Disorders, 11,* 91–99.

Cacioppo, J. T., Berntson, G. G., & Crites, S. L., Jr. (1996). Social neuroscience: Principles of psycho-physiological arousal and response. In E. T. Higgins & A. W. Kruglanski (Eds.), *Social psychology: Handbook of basic principles.* New York: Guilford.

Cacioppo, J. T., & Decety, J. (2009). What are the brain mechanisms on which psychological processes are based? *Perspectives on Psychological Science, 4,* 10–18.

Cacioppo, J. T., Visser, P. S., & Pickett, C. L. (2005). *Social neuroscience: People thinking about thinking people.* Cambridge, MA: MIT Press.

Cadenhead, K. & Braff, D. L. (1995). Neurophysiology of schizophrenia: Attention, information processing, and inhibitory processes in schizophrenia. In J. A. Den Boer., H. G. M. Westenberg & H. M. van Praag (Eds.), *Advances in the neurobiology of schizophrenia.* Oxford, England: John Wiley & Sons.

Caelian, C. F. (2006).The role of perfectionism and stress in the suicidal behaviour of depressed adolescents. *Dissertation Abstracts International: Section B: The Sciences and Engineering, 66*(12-B), 6915.

Cahill, L. (2005, May). His brain, her brain. *Scientific American,* pp. 40–47.

Cai, D., Shuman, T., Gorman, M., Sage, J., & Anagnostaras, S. (2009). Sleep selectively enhances hippocampus-dependent memory in mice. *Behavioral Neuroscience, 123,* 713–719.

Cain, D. J. (Ed.). (2002). *Humanistic psychotherapies: Handbook of research and practice.* Washington, DC: American Psychological Association.

Calin-Jageman, R. J., & Fischer, T. M. (2007). Behavioral adaptation of the aplysia siphon-withdrawal response is accompanied by sensory adaptation. *Behavioral Neuroscience, 121,* 200–211.

Cameron, O. G. (2002). *Visceral sensory neuroscience: Interoception.* London: Oxford University Press.

Campbell, T. S., & Ditto, B. (2002). Exaggeration of blood pressure–related hypoalgesia and reduction of blood pressure with low frequency transcutaneous electrical nerve stimulation. *Psychophysiology, 39,* 473–481.

Cannon, W. B. (1929). Organization for physiological homeostatics. *Physiological Review, 9,* 280–289.

Cantwell, R. H., & Andrews, B. (2002). Cognitive and psychological factors underlying secondary school students' feelings towards group work. *Educational Psychology, 22,* 75–91.

Capaldi, E. D. (Ed.). (1996). *Why we eat what we eat: The psychology of eating.* Washington, DC: American Psychological Association.

Caplan, D., Waters, G., & Dede, G. (2007). A study of syntactic processing in aphasia I: Behavioral (psycholinguistic) aspects. *Brain and Language, 101,* 103–150.

Carey, B. (2004, December 21). When pressure is on, good students suffer. *The New York Times,* p. D7.

Carey, B. (2008, May 29). Monkeys think, moving artificial arm as own. *The New York Times,* p. A1.

Carey, B. (2009a, April 6). So you just want to forget? Science is working on an eraser. *The New York Times,* p. A1.

Carey, B. (2009b, July 28). In battle, hunches prove to be valuable assets. *The New York Times,* p. A1.

Carey, B. (2009c, November 27). Surgery for mental ills offers hope and risk. *The New York Times,* p. A1

Carhart-Harris, R., (2007). Speed > Ecstasy > Ritalin: The science of amphetamines. *Journal of Psychopharmacology, 21,* 225.

Carnagey, N., Anderson, C., & Bartholow, B. (2007). Media violence and social neuroscience: New questions and new opportunities. *Current Directions in Psychological Science, 16,* 178–182.

Carnagey, N., Anderson, C. A., & Bushman, B. J. (2007). The effect of video game violence on physiological desensitization to real-life violence. *Journal of Experimental Social Psychology, 43,* 489–496.

Carney, D., Colvin, C., & Hall, J. (2007). A thin slice perspective on the accuracy of first impressions. *Journal of Research in Personality, 41,* 1054–1072.

Carney, R. N., & Levin, J. R. (1998). Coming to terms with the keyword method in introductory psychology: A "neuromnemonic" example. *Teaching of Psychology, 25*, 132–135.

Carney, R. N., & Levin, J. R. (2003). Promoting higher-order learning benefits by building lower-order mnemonic connections. *Applied Cognitive Psychology, 17*, 563–575.

Carpenter, S. (2002, April). What can resolve the paradox of mental health disparities? *APA Monitor, 33*, 18.

Carrillo, M., Ricci, L., Coppersmith, G., & Melloni, R. (2009, August). The effect of increased serotonergic neurotransmission on aggression: A critical meta-analytical review of preclinical studies. *Psychopharmacology, 205*, 349–368.

Carter, R. T. (2003). Becoming racially and culturally competent: The racial-cultural counseling laboratory. *Journal of Multicultural Counseling and Development, 31*, 20–30.

Cartwright, R. (2006). A neuroscientist looks at how the brain makes up our minds. *PsycCRITIQUES, 51*, 35–41.

Cartwright, R., Agargum, M. Y., & Kirkby, J. (2006). Relation of dreams to waking concerns. *Psychiatry Research, 141*, 261–270.

Caruso, E. (2008). Use of experienced retrieval ease in self and social judgments. *Journal of Experimental Social Psychology, 44*, 148–155.

Carvalho, F. M., Pereira, S. R. C., Pires, R. G. W., Ferraz, V. P., Romano-Silva, M. A., Oliveira-Silva, I. F., & Ribeiro, A. M. (2006). Thiamine deficiency decreases glutamate uptake in the prefrontal cortex and impairs spatial memory performance in a water maze test. *Pharmacology, Biochemistry and Behavior, 83*, 481–489.

Carver, C., & Scheier, M. (2002). Coping processes and adjustment to chronic illness. In A. Christensen & M. Antoni (Eds.), *Chronic physical disorders: Behavioral medicine's perspective*. Malden: Blackwell Publishers.

Cary, P. (2007). A brief history of the concept of free will: Issues that are and are not germane to legal reasoning. *Behavioral Sciences & the Law, 25, Special issue: Free will*, 165–181.

Casasanto, D. (2008). Who's afraid of the big bad whorf? Crosslinguistic differences in temporal language and thought. *Language Learning, 58*, 63–79.

Case, R., & Okamoto, Y. (1996). The role of central conceptual structures in the development of children's thought. *Monographs of the Society for Research in Child Development, 61*, v–265.

Casey, S. D., Cooper-Brown, L. J., & Wacher, D. P. (2006). The use of descriptive analysis to identify and manipulate schedules of reinforcement in the treatment of food refusal. *Journal of Behavioral Education, 15*, 41–52.

Cashon, C. H., & Cohen, L. B. (2004). Beyond U-shaped development in infants' processing of faces: An information-processing account. *Journal of Cognition and Development, 5*, 59–80.

Cassells, J. V. S. (2007). The virtuous roles of truth and justice in integral dialogue: Research, theory, and model practice of the evolution of collective consciousness. *Dissertation Abstracts International Section A: Humanities and Social Sciences, 67*(10-A), 4005.

Cattell, R. B., Cattell, A. K., & Catell, H. E. P. (1993). *Sixteen personality factor questionnaire (16PF)* (5th ed.). San Antonio, TX: Harcourt Brace.

Cattell, R. B., Cattell, A. K., & Cattell, H. E. P. (2000). *The sixteen personality factor™ (16PF®) questionnaire*. Champaign, IL: Institute for Personality and Ability Testing.

Cauce, A. M. (2007). Bringing community psychology home: The leadership, community and values initiative. *American Journal of Community Psychology, 39*, 1–11.

Cavallini, E., Pagnin, A., & Vecchi, T. (2003). Aging and everyday memory: The beneficial effect of memory training. *Archives of Gerontology & Geriatrics, 37*, 241–257.

Cavenett, T., & Nixon, R. D. V. (2006). The effect of arousal on memory for emotionally-relevant information: A study of skydivers. *Behaviour Research and Therapy, 44*, 1461–1469.

Centers for Disease Control and Prevention (CDC). (2000). *Suicide prevention fact sheet*. Atlanta: National Center for Injury Prevention and Control.

Centers for Disease Control and Prevention (CDC). (2004b, June 11). Suicide and attempted suicide. *MMWR, 53*, 471.

Chamberlain, K., & Zika, S. (1990). The minor events approach to stress: Support for the use of daily hassles. *British Journal of Psychology, 81*, 469–481.

Chamberlain, S. R., Menzies, L., Hampshire, A., Suckling, J., Fineberg, N. A., del Campo, N., et al. (2008, July 18). Orbitofrontal dysfunction in patients with obsessive-compulsive disorder and their unaffected relatives. *Science, 321*, 421–422.

Chambless, D. L., Crits-Christoph, P., Wampold, B. E., Norcross, J. C., Lambert, M. J., Bohart, A. C., et al. (2006). What should be validated? In J. C. Norcross, L. E. Beutler, & R. F. Levant, (Eds.). *Evidence-based practices in mental health: Debate and dialogue on the fundamental questions*. Washington, DC: American Psychological Association.

Chandra, P. (2007). Review of Language, mind, and brain: Some psychological and neurological constraints on theories of grammar. *Cognitive Systems Research, 8*, 53–56.

Chandran, S., & Menon, G. (2004). When a day means more than a year: Effects of temporal framing on judgments of health risk. *Journal of Consumer Research, 31*, 375–389.

Chang, J., & Sue, S. (2005). Culturally sensitive research: Where have we gone wrong and what do we need to do now? In M. G. Constantine, *Strategies for building multicultural competence in mental health and educational settings*. Hoboken, NJ: John Wiley & Sons.

Chang, S. W., & Ansley, T. N. (2003). A comparative study of item exposure control methods in computerized adaptive testing. *Journal of Educational Measurement, 40*, 71–103.

Chapkis, W., & Webb, R. (2008). *Dying to get high: Marijuana as medicine*. New York: New York University Press.

Chapman, J. (2006). Anxiety and defective decision making: An elaboration of the group-think model. *Management Decision, 44*, 1391–1404.

Chapman, L. J., & Chapman, J. P. (1973). *Disordered thought in schizophrenia*. New York: Appleton-Century-Crofts.

Charlton, S. (2009, January). Driving while conversing: Cell phones that distract and passengers who react. *Accident Analysis & Prevention, 41*, 160–173.

Charman, D. P. (2004). *Core processes in brief psychodynamic psychotherapy: Advancing effective practice*. Mahwah, NJ: Lawrence Erlbaum Associates.

Chechile, R. A. (2003). Review of 'Elements of Psychophysical Theory.' *Journal of Mathematical Psychology, 47*, 385.

Chen, A., Zhou, Y., & Gong, H. (2004). Firing rates and dynamic correlated activities of ganglion cells both contribute to retinal information processing. *Brain Research, 1017*, 13–20.

Cheney, C. D. (1996). Medical non adherence: A behavior analysis. In J. R. Cautela & W. Ishaq (Eds.), *Contemporary issues in behavior therapy: Improving the human condition: Applied Clinical Psychology*. New York: Plenum Press.

Cheng, C., & Cheung, M. L. (2005). Cognitive processes underlying coping flexibility: Differentiation and integration. *Journal of Personality, 73*, 859–886.

Cheng, S., & Kwan, K. (2008). Attachment dimensions and contingencies of self-worth: The moderating role of culture. *Personality and Individual Differences, 45*, 509–514.

Cheston, S. E. (2000). A new paradigm for teaching counseling theory and practice. *Counselor Education & Supervision, 39*, 254–269.

Cho, A. (2000, June 16). What's shakin' in the ear? *Science, 288*, 1954–1955.

Cho, S., Holyoak, K. J., & Cannon, T. D. (2007). Analogical reasoning in working memory: Resources shared among relational integration, interference resolution, and maintenance. *Memory & Cognition, 35*, 1445–1455.

Chomsky, N. (1968). *Language and mind*. New York: Harcourt Brace Jovanovich.

Chomsky, N. (1978). On the biological basis of language capacities. In G. A. Miller & E. Lennenberg (Eds.), *Psychology and biology of language and thought*. New York: Academic Press.

Chomsky, N. (1991). Linguistics and cognitive science: Problems and mysteries. In A. Kasher (Ed.), *The Chomskyan turn*. Cambridge, MA: Blackwell.

Chou, K. (2005). Everyday competence and depressive symptoms: Social support and sense of control as mediators or moderators? *Aging and Mental Health, 9*, 177–183.

Choy, Y., Fyer, A. J., & Lipsitz, J. D. (2007). Treatment of specific phobia in adults. *Clinical Psychology Review, 27*, 266–286.

Christ, S. E., Steiner, R. D., & Grange, D. K. (2006). Inhibitory control in children with phenylketonuria. *Developmental Neuropsychology, 30*, 845–864.

Christakis, A., & Fowler, J. (2007). The spread of obesity in a large social network over 32 years. *The New England Journal of Medicine, 357*, 370–379.

Christakis, N. A., & Fowler, J. H. (2008). The collective dynamics of smoking in a large social network. *The New England Journal of Medicine, 358*, 2249–2258.

Christensen, A. J., & Johnson, J. A. (2002). Patient adherence with medical treatment regimens: An interactive approach. *Current Directions in Psychological Science, 11*, 94–101.

Christian, C. J., Lencz, T., Robinson, D. G., Burdick, K. E., Ashtari, M., Malhotra, A. K., et al. (2008). Gray matter structural alterations in obsessive-compulsive disorder: Relationship to neuropsychological functions. *Neuroimaging, 164*, 123–131.

Chronicle, E. P., MacGregor, J. N., & Ormerod, T. C. (2004). What makes an insight problem? The roles of heuristics, goal conception, and solution recoding in knowledge-lean problems. *Journal of Experimental Psychology: Learning, Memory, and Cognition, 30*, 14–27.

Chrysikou, E. G. (2006). When a shoe becomes a hammer: Problem solving as goal-derived, ad hoc categorization. *Dissertation Abstracts International: Section B: The Sciences and Engineering, 67*(1-B), 569.

Cialdini, R. B. (2006). *Influence: The psychology of persuasion*. New York: Collins.

Cialdini, R. B., & Sagarin, B. J. (2005). Principles of interpersonal influence. In T. C. Brock & M. C. Green (Eds.), *Persuasion: Psychological insights and perspectives* (2nd ed.). Thousand Oaks, CA: Sage Publications.

Cialdini, R. B., Schaller, M., Houlihan, D., Arps, K., Fultz, J., & Beaman, A. L. (1975). Reciprocal concessions procedure for inducing compliance: The door-in-the-face technique. *Journal of Personality and Social Psychology, 31*, 206–215.

Clark, D. A. (2004). *Cognitive-behavioral therapy for OCD*. New York: Guilford.

Clark, D. A. (2007). Obsessions and compulsions. In N. Kazantzis & L. L'Abate, *Handbook of homework assignments in psychotherapy: Research, practice, prevention*. New York: Springer Science + Business Media.

Clark, L., Bechara, A., Damasio, H., Sahakian, B., Robbins, T., & Aitken, M. (2008). Differential effects of insular and ventromedial prefrontal cortex lesions on risky decision-making. *Brain: A Journal of Neurology, 131*, 1311–1322.

Clarke-Stewart, K. A., Vandell, D. L., McCartney, K., Owen, M. T., & Booth, C. (2000). Effects of parental separation and divorce on very young children. *Journal of Family Psychology, 14*, 304–326.

Clarkin, J. F., & Lenzenweger, M. F. (Eds.) (2004). *Major theories of personality disorders* (2nd ed.). New York: Guilford.

Clay D. L. (2000). Commentary: Rethinking our interventions in pediatric chronic pain and treatment research. *Journal of Pediatric Psychology, 25,* 53–55.

Clayton, K., & Lundberg-Love, P. (2009). Caffeine: Pharmacology and effects of the world's most popular drug. *The Praeger international collection on addictions, Vol 2: Psychobiological profiles.* Santa Barbara, CA: Praeger/ABC-CLIO.

Cleary, A. M. (2006). Relating familiarity-based recognition and the tip-of-the-tongue phenomenon: Detecting a word's recency in the absence of access to the word. *Memory & Cognition, 34,* 804–816.

Clements, A. M., Rimrodt, S. L., & Abel, J. R. (2006). Sex differences in cerebral laterality of language and visuospatial processing. *Brain and Language, 98,* 150–158.

Clements, M. (1994, August 7). Making love, how old, how often. *Parade,* p. 18.

Clemons, T. L. (2006). Underachieving gifted students: A social cognitive model. *Dissertation Abstracts International Section A: Humanities and Social Sciences, 66*(9-A), 3208.

Cloud, J. (2000, June 5). The lure of ecstasy. *Time,* pp. 60–68.

Cloud, J. (2009, January 19). Minds on the Edge. *Time,* pp. 40–46.

Cloud, J. (2009, June 22). Staying sane may be easier than you think. *Time,* p. 72.

Coan, J. A., Schaefer, H. S., & Davidson, R. J. (2006). Lending a hand: Social regulation of the neural response to threat. *Psychological Science, 17*(12), 1032–1039.

Coates, S. L., Butler, L. T., & Berry, D. C. (2006). Implicit memory and consumer choice: The mediating role of brand familiarity. *Applied Cognitive Psychology, 20,* 1101–1116.

Cobos, P., Sanchez, M., Garcia, C., Vera, M. N., & Vila, J. (2002). Revisiting the James versus Cannon debate on emotion: Startle and autonomic modulation in patients with spinal cord injuries. *Biological Psychology, 61,* 251–269.

Cochran, S. D. (2000). Emerging issues in research on lesbians' and gay men's mental health: Does sexual orientation really matter? *American Psychologist, 56,* 33–41.

Coffman, S. J., Martell, C. R., Dimidjian, S., Gallop, R., & Holon, S. D. (2007). Extreme nonresponse in cognitive therapy: Can behavioral activation succeed where cognitive therapy fails? *Journal of Consulting Clinical Psychology, 75,* 531–545.

Cohen, B. H. (2002). *Explaining psychological statistics* (2nd ed.). New York: Wiley.

Cohen, G. L., Garcia, J., Apfel, N., & Master, A. (2006). Reducing the racial achievement gap: A social-psychological intervention. *Science, 313,* 1307–1310.

Cohen, J. (2003). Things I have learned (so far). In A. E. Kazdin (Ed.), *Methodological issues and strategies in clinical research* (3rd ed.). Washington, DC: American Psychological Association.

Cohen, L., & Cashon, C. (2003). Infant perception and cognition. In R. Lerner & M. Easterbrooks (Eds.), *Handbook of psychology: Developmental psychology* (Vol. 6). New York: Wiley.

Cohen, P. (2009). Medical marijuana: The conflict between scientific evidence and political ideology. Part one of two. *Journal of Pain & Palliative Care Pharmacotherapy, 23,* 4–25.

Cohen, P., Slomkowski, C., & Robins, L. N. (Eds.). (1999). *Historical and geographical influences on psychopathology.* Mahwah, NJ: Erlbaum.

Cohen, S. (2004, November). Social relationships and health. *American Psychologist,* 676–684.

Cohen, S., Doyle, W. J., Turner, R., Alper, C. M., & Skoner, D. P. (2003). Sociability and susceptibility to the common cold. *Psychological Science, 14,* 389–395.

Cohen, S., Hamrick, N., & Rodriguez, M. (2002). Reactivity and vulnerability to stress-associated risk for upper respiratory illness. *Psychosomatic Medicine, 64,* 302–310.

Cohen, S., Kamarck, T., & Mermelstein, R. (1983). A global measure of perceived stress. *Journal of Health and Social Behavior, 24,* 385–396.

Coleman, E. (2002). Masturbation as a means of achieving sexual health. *Journal of Psychology and Human Sexuality, 14,* 5–16.

Coles, R. (1997). *The moral intelligence of children.* New York: Random House.

Colland, V. T., Van Essen-Zandvliet, L. E. M., Lans, C., Denteneer, A., Westers, P., & Brackel, H. J. L. (2004). Poor adherence to self-medication instructions in children with asthma and their parents. *Patient Education and Counseling, 55,* 416–421.

Collins, A. M., & Loftus, E. F. (1975). A spreading-activation theory of semantic processing. *Psychological Review, 82,* 407–428.

Collins, A. M., & Quillian, M. R. (1969). Retrieval times from semantic memory. *Journal of Verbal Learning and Verbal Behavior, 8,* 240–247.

Colom, R., Jung, R. E., & Haier, R. J. (2006). Finding the g-factor in brain structure using the method of correlated vectors. *Intelligence, 34,* 561–570.

Coltheart, M., Langdon, R., & McKay, R. (2007). Schizophrenia and monothematic delusions. *Schizophrenia Bulletin, 33,* 642–647.

Coltraine, S., & Messineo, M. (2000). The perpetuation of subtle prejudice: Race and gender imagery in 1990s television advertising. *Sex Roles, 42,* 363–389.

Colwell, M. J., & Lindsey, E. W. (2005). Preschool children's pretend and physical play and sex of play partner: Connections to peer competence. *Sex Roles, 52,* 497–509.

Combrink-Graham, L., & McKenna, S. B. (2006). Families with children with disrupted attachments. In L. Combrink-Graham, *Children in family contexts: Perspectives on treatment.* New York: Guilford Press.

Compagni, A., & Manderscheid, R. W. (2006). A neuro-scientist-consumer alliance to transform mental health care, *Journal of Behavioral Health Services & Research, 33,* 265–274.

Comuzzie, A. G., & Allison, D. B. (1998, May 29). The search for human obesity genes. *Science, 280,* 1374–1377.

Conduit, R., Crewther, S. G., & Coleman, G. (2004). Spontaneous eyelid movements (ELMS) during sleep are related to dream recall on awakening. *Journal of Sleep Research, 13,* 137–144.

Conger, R., & Donnellan, M. (2007). An interactionist perspective on the socioeconomic context of human development. *Annual Review of Psychology, 58,* 175–199.

Conger, R. D., Wallace, L. E., Sun, Y., Simons, R. L., McLoyd, V. C., & Brody, G. H. (2002). Economic pressure in African American families: A replication and extension of the family stress model. *Developmental Psychology, 38,* 179–193.

Conner, M., Povey, R., Sparks, P., James, R., & Shepherd, R. (2003). Moderating role of attitudinal ambivalence within the theory of planned behaviour. *British Journal of Social Psychology, 42,* 75–94.

Connolly, A. C. (2007). Concepts and their features: Can cognitive science make good on the promises of concept empiricism? *Dissertation Abstracts International: Section B: The Sciences and Engineering, 67*(7-B), 4125.

Conte, H. R., Plutchik, R., & Draguns, J. G. (2004). The measurement of ego defenses in clinical research. In U. Hentschel, G. Smith, J. G. Draguns, & W. Ehlers (Eds.), *Defense mechanisms: Theoretical, research and clinical perspectives.* Oxford, England: Elsevier Science Ltd.

Conway, M. A. (Ed.) (2002). *Levels of processing 30 years on special issue of memory.* Hove, UK: Psychology Press.

Cooke, J. R., & Ancoli-Israel, S. (2006). Sleep and its disorders in older adults. *Psychiatric Clinics of North America, 29,* 1077–1093.

Cooklin, A. (2000). Therapy, the family and others. In H. Maxwell, *Clinical psychotherapy for health professionals.* Philadelphia: Whurr Publishers.

Cooper, H., & Patall, E. (2009, June). The relative benefits of meta-analysis conducted with individual participant data versus aggregated data. *Psychological Methods, 14,* 165–176.

Cooper, J. (2007). *Cognitive dissonance: Fifty years of a classic theory.* Thousand Oaks, CA: Sage Publications.

Cooper, J., Mirabile, R., & Scher, S. J. (2005). Actions and attitudes: The theory of cognitive dissonance. In T. C. Brock & M. C. Green (Eds.), *Persuasion: Psychological insights and perspectives* (2nd ed.). Thousand Oaks, CA: Sage Publications.

Cooper, J., & Strayer, D. (2008). Effects of simulator practice and real world experience on cell-phone-related driver distraction. *Human Factors, 50,* 893–902.

Cooper, M. (2007). Humanizing psychotherapy. *Journal of Contemporary Psychotherapy, 37,* 11–16.

Cooper, Z., & Shafran, R. (2008). Cognitive behaviour therapy for eating disorders. *Behavioural and Cognitive Psychotherapy, 36,* 713–722.

Coplan, R., Reichel, M., & Rowan, K. (2009). Exploring the associations between maternal personality, child temperament, and parenting: A focus on emotions. *Personality and Individual Differences, 46,* 241–246.

Copolov, D. L., Seal, M. L., Maruff, P., Ulusoy, R., Wong, M. T. H., TochonDanguy, et al. (2003). Cortical activation associated with the human experience of auditory hallucinations and perception of human speech in schizophrenia: A PET correlation study. *Psychiatry Research: Neuroimaging, 123,* 139–152.

Cordnoldi, C., De Beni, R., & Helstrup, T. (2007). Memory sensitivity in autobiographical memory. In S. Magnussen, & T. Helstrup, *Everyday memory.* New York: Psychology Press.

Coren, S. (1992). The moon illusion: A different view through the legs. *Perceptual and Motor Skills, 75,* 827–831.

Coren, S. (2004). Sensation and perception. In I. B. Weiner. *Handbook of Psychology* (Vol. 1). Hoboken, NJ: John Wiley & Sons.

Coren, S., & Ward, L. M. (1989). *Sensation and perception* (3rd ed.). San Diego, CA: Harcourt Brace Jovanovich.

Cornelius, M. D., Taylor, P. M., Geva, D., & Day, N. L. (1995). Prenatal tobacco and marijuana use among adolescents: Effects on offspring gestational age, growth, and morphology. *Pediatrics, 95,* 57–68.

Cornell, C. B. (2006). A graduated scale for determining mental age. *Dissertation Abstracts International: Section B: The Sciences and Engineering, 66*(9-B), 5121.

Corsello, A. (2005). The wronged man. In *The best American magazine writing, 2005.* New York: Columbia University Press.

Cosmides, L., & Tooby, J. (2004). Social exchange: The evolutionary design of a neurocognitive system. In M. S. Gazzaniga (Ed.), *Cognitive neurosciences* (3rd ed.). Cambridge, MA: MIT.

Costa, P. T., Jr., & Widiger, T. A. (Eds.). (2002). *Personality disorders and the Five-Factor Model of personality* (2nd ed.). Washington, DC: American Psychological Association.

Cotton, P. (1993, July 7). Psychiatrists set to approve DSM-IV. *Journal of the American Medical Association, 270,* 13–15.

Couturier, J., & Lock, J. (2006). Eating disorders: Anorexia nervosa, bulimia nervosa, and binge eating disorder. In T. G. Plante, *Mental disorders of the new millennium: Biology and function* (Vol 3). Westport, CT: Praeger Publishers/Greenwood Publishing.

Coventry, K. R., Venn, S. F., Smith, G. D., & Morley, A. M. (2003). Spatial problem solving and functional relations. *European Journal of Cognitive Psychology, 15,* 71–99.

Cowan, N., Towse, J. N., Hamilton, Z., Saults, J. S., Elliott, E. M., Lacey, J. F., et al. (2003). Children's working-memory processes: A response-timing analysis. *Journal of Experimental Psychology: General, 132,* 113–132.

Cowley, G. (2000, January 31). Alzheimer's: Unlocking the mystery. *Time,* pp. 46–54.

Cowley, G. (2003, February 24). Our bodies, our fears. *Newsweek,* pp. 43–44.

Cox, J. (2003, May 6). How far would you go to save your life? *Denver Post,* p. F1.

Cox, R., Baker, S. E., Macdonald, D. W., & Berdoy, M. (2004). Protecting egg prey from carrion crows: The potential of aversive conditioning. *Applied Animal Behaviour Science, 87,* 325–342.

Coyle, N. (2006). The hard work of living in the face of death. *Journal of Pain and Symptom Management, 32,* 266–274.

Coyle, T. R. (2006). Test-retest changes on scholastic aptitude tests are not related to g. *Intelligence, 34,* 15–27.

Craik, F. I. M. (1990). Levels of processing. In M. E. Eysenck (Ed.), *The Blackwell dictionary of cognitive psychology.* London: Blackwell.

Craik, F., & Lockhart, R. (2008). Levels of processing and Zinchenko's approach to memory research. *Journal of Russian & East European Psychology, 46,* 52–60.

Cramer, P. (2007). Longitudinal study of defense mechanisms: Late childhood to late adolescence. *Journal of Personality, 75,* 1–23.

Creasey, G. L. (2005). *Research methods in lifespan development* (6th ed.). Boston: Allyn & Bacon.

Creswell, J., & Landon, T. (2009, January 25). The talented Mr. Madoff. *The New York Times,* p. 1.

Crews, F. (1996). The verdict on Freud. *Psychological Science, 7,* 63–68.

Criswell, H., Ming, Z., Kelm, M., & Breese, G. (2008, August). Brain regional differences in the effect of ethanol on GABA release from presynaptic terminals. *Journal of Pharmacology and Experimental Therapeutics, 326,* 596–603.

Crits-Christoph, P. (1992). The efficacy of brief dynamic psychotherapy: A meta-analysis. *American Journal of Psychiatry, 149,* 151–158.

Crombag, H. S., & Robinson, R. E. (2004). Drugs, environment, brain, and behavior. *Current Directions in Psychological Science, 13,* 107–111.

Cropley, A. (2006). In praise of convergent thinking. *Creativity Research Journal, 18,* 391–404.

Crosnoe, R., & Elder, G. H., Jr. (2002). Successful adaptation in the later years: A life course approach to aging. *Social Psychology Quarterly, 65,* 309–328.

Crum, A. J., & Langer, E. J. (2007). Mind-set matters: Exercise and the placebo effect. *Psychological Science, 18,* 165–171.

Cruz, A., & Green, B. G. (2000). Thermal stimulation of taste. *Nature, 403,* 889–892.

Cuijpers, P., van Straten, A., Andersson, G., & van Oppen, P. (2008). Psychotherapy for depression in adults: A meta-analysis of comparative outcome studies. *Journal of Consulting and Clinical Psychology, 76,* 909–922.

Culhane-Pera, K. A., Borkan, J. M., & Patten, S. (2007). Culture and ethnicity. In O. J. Z. Sahler & J. E. Carr, *The behavioral sciences and health care* (2nd rev. and updated ed.). Ashland, OH: Hogrefe & Huber Publishers.

Cullinane, C. A., Chu, D. Z. J., & Mamelak, A. N. (2002). Current surgical options in the control of cancer pain. *Cancer Practice, 10,* s21–s26.

Cummings, A., Ceponiene, R., & Koyama, A. (2006). Auditory semantic networks for words and natural sounds. *Brain Research, 1115,* 92–107.

Cunningham, P. (2006). Early years teachers and the influence of Piaget: Evidence from oral history. *Early Years An International Journal of Research and Development, 26,* 5–16.

Cynkar, A. (2007). The changing gender composition of psychology. *Monitor on Psychology, 38,* 46–48.

Cwikel, J., Behar, L., & Rabson-Hare, J. (2000). A comparison of a vote count and a meta-analysis review of intervention research with adult cancer patients. *Research on Social Work Practice, 10,* 139–158.

Czopp, A. M., & Monteith, M. J. (2006). Thinking well of African Americans: Measuring complimentary stereotypes and negative prejudice. *Basic and Applied Social Psychology, 28,* 233–250.

Daftary, F., & Meri, J. W. (2002). *Culture and memory in medieval Islam.* London: I. B. Tauris.

Dai, D. Y., & Wang, X. (2007). The role of need for cognition and reader beliefs in text comprehension and interest development. *Contemporary Educational Psychology, 32,* 332–347.

Daines, B. (2006). Violations of agreed and implicit sexual and emotional boundaries in couple relationships—some thoughts arising from Levine's 'A clinical perspective on couple infidelity.' *Sexual and Relationship Therapy, 21,* 45–53.

Dalal, A. K., & Misra, G. (2006). Psychology of health and well-being: Some emerging perspectives [Special issue: Psychology of health and well-being]. *Psychological Studies, 51,* 91–104.

Dale, A. (2006). Quality issues with survey research. *International Journal of Social Research Methodology: Theory & Practice, 9, Special issue: Quality in Social Research,* 143–158.

Dale, J. W., & von Schantz, M. (2007). *From genes to genomes: Concepts and applications of DNA technology.* New York: John Wiley & Sons.

Daley, E. M., McDermott, R. J., Brown, K. R. M., & Kittleson, M. J. (2003). Conducting Web-based survey research: A lesson in Internet designs. *American Journal of Health Behavior, 27,* 116–124.

Damasio, A. (2003, May 15). Mental self: The person within. *Nature, 423,* 227.

Damon, W. (1999, August). The moral development of children. *Scientific American,* pp. 72–78.

Danaei, G., Vender Hoorn, S., Lopez, A. D., Murray, C. J. L. & Ezzati, M. (2005). Causes of cancer in the world: Comparative risk assessment of nine behavioural and environmental risk factors. Comparative Risk Assessment collaborating group (Cancers). *Lancet, 366,* 1784–1793.

Dani, J. A., & Montague, P. (2007). Disrupting addiction through the loss of drug-associated internal states. *Nature Neuroscience, 10,* 403–404.

D'Arcy, R., C. N., Bolster, R., B., & Ryner, L. (2007). A site directed fMRI approach for evaluating functional status in the anterolateral temporal lobes. *Neuroscience Research, 57,* 120–128.

Darley, J. M., & Latané, B. (1968). Bystanders' intervention in emergencies: Diffusion of responsibility. *Journal of Personality and Social Psychology, 8,* 377–383.

Darwin, C. J., Turvey, M. T., & Crowder, R. G. (1972). An auditory analogue of the Sperling partial-report procedure: Evidence for brief auditory storage. *Cognitive Psychology, 3,* 255–267.

Das, A. (2007). Masturbation in the United States. *Journal of Sex & Marital Therapy, 33,* 301–317.

Das, A., Parish, W., & Laumann, E. (2009). Masturbation in urban China. *Archives of Sexual Behavior, 38,* 108–120.

Davidson, R. J., Gray, J. A., LeDoux, J. E., Levenson, R. W., Panksepp, J., & Ekman, P. (1994). Is there emotion-specific physiology? In P. Ekman & R. J. Davidson (Eds.), *The nature of emotion.* New York: Oxford University Press.

Davies, S., Jackson, P., Lewis, G., Hood, S., Nutt, D., & Potokar, J. (2008). Is the association of hypertension and panic disorder explained by clustering of autonomic panic symptoms in hypertensive patients? *Journal of Affective Disorders, 111,* 344–350.

Davis, J., Senghas, A., & Ochsner, K. (2009). How does facial feedback modulate emotional experience? *Journal of Research in Personality, 43,* 822–829.

Davis, L. J. (2009, June 15). Sotomayor and the New Haven firefighters case: More myths than facts. *The Washington Times,* p. A04.

Davis, O., Haworth, C., & Plomin, R. (2009, January). Learning abilities and disabilities: Generalist genes in early adolescence. *Cognitive Neuropsychiatry, 14,* 312–331.

Davis, R. D., & Millon, T. (1999). Models of personality and its disorders. In T. Millon, P. H. Blaney, & R. D. Davis, (Eds), *Oxford textbook of psychopathology.* New York: Oxford University Press.

Davis, S. F. (2007). The nose knows best. *PsycCRITIQUES, 52,* 22–31.

Day, A. L., & Livingstone, H. A. (2003). Gender differences in perceptions of stressors and utilization of social support among university students. *Canadian Journal of Behavioural Science, 35,* 73–83.

Day, R. D., & Lamb, M. E. (2004). *Conceptualizing and measuring father involvement.* Mahwah, NJ: Lawrence Erlbaum Associates.

DeAngelis, D., & Monahan, J. (2008). Professional credentials and professional regulations: Social work professional development. In B. W. White, K. M. Sowers, & C. N. Dulmus, (Eds.), *Comprehensive handbook of social work and social welfare, Vol. 1: The profession of social work.* Hoboken, NJ: John Wiley & Sons.

De Bini, R., Pazzaglia, F., & Gardini, S. (2007). The generation and maintenance of visual mental images: Evidence from image type and aging. *Brain and Cognition, 63,* 271–278.

Dean, C., & Dresbach, T. (2006). Neuroligins and neurexins: Linking cell adhesion, synapse formation and cognitive function. *International Journal of Psychiatry in Clinical Practice, 10 (Suppl.),* 5–11.

Dean-Borenstein, M. T. (2007). The long-term psychosocial effects of trauma on survivors of human-caused extreme stress situations. *Dissertation Abstracts International: Section B: The Sciences and Engineering, 67*(11-B), 6733.

Dearing, E., McCartney, K., & Taylor, B. (2009). Does higher quality early child care promote low-income children's math and reading achievement in middle childhood? *Child Development, 80,* 1329–1349.

Deary, I. J., & Der, G. (2005). Reaction time, age, and cognitive ability: Longitudinal findings from age 16 to 63 years in representative population samples. *Aging, Neuropsychology, & Cognition, 12,* 187–215.

Deater-Deckard, K., Ivy, L., & Smith, J. (2005). Resilience in gene-environment transactions. In S. Goldstein & R. B. Brooks (Eds.), *Handbook of resilience in children.* New York: Kluwer Academic/Plenum Publishers.

Deci, E. L., & Ryan, R. M. (2008). Facilitating optimal motivation and psychological well-being across life's domains. *Canadian Psychology/Psychologie Canadienne, 49,* 14–23.

Dediu, D., & Ladd, D. R. (2007). From the Cover: Linguistic tone is related to the population frequency of the adaptive haplogroups of two brain size genes, ASPM and microcephalin. *Proceedings of the National Academy of Sciences, 104,* 10944–10949.

DeGaton, J. F., Weed, S., & Jensen, L. (1996). Understanding gender differences in adolescent sexuality. *Adolescence, 31,* 217–231.

de Gelder, B. (2000). More to seeing than meets the eye. *Science, 289,* 1148–1149.

deGroot, A. (1978). *Thought and choice in chess.* Paris: Mouton de Gruyter.

deGroot, A. D. (1966). Perception and memory versus thought: Some old ideas and recent findings. In B. Kleinmuntz (Ed.), *Problem solving: Research, method, and theory.* New York: Wiley.

DeLamater, J. D., & Sill, M. (2005). Sexual desire in later life. *Journal of Sex Research, 42,* 138–149.

Delgado, M. R., Labouliere, C. D., & Phelps, E. A. (2006). Fear of losing money? Aversive conditioning with secondary reinforcers [Special issue: Genetic, comparative and cognitive studies of social behavior]. *Social Cognitive and Affective Neuroscience, 1,* 250–259.

Delinsky, S. S., Latner, J. D., & Wilson, G. T. (2006). Binge eating and weight loss in a self-help behavior modification program. *Obesity, 14*, 1244–1249.

DeLoache, J., & LoBue, V. (2009). The narrow fellow in the grass: Human infants associate snakes and fear. *Developmental Science, 12*, 201–207.

del Rosal, E., Alonso, L., & Moreno, R. (2006). Simulation of habituation to simple and multiple stimuli. *Behavioural Processes, 73*, 272–277.

Demaree, H. A., & Everhart, D. E. (2004). Healthy high-hostiles: Reduced para-sympathetic activity and decreased sympathovagal flexibility during negative emotional processing. *Personality and Individual Differences, 36*, 457–469.

Dement, W. C., & Wolpert, E. A. (1958). The relation of eye movements, body mobility, and external stimuli to dream content. *Journal of Experimental Psychology, 55*, 543–553.

Dempster, F. N. (1981). Memory span: Sources for individual and developmental differences. *Psychological Bulletin, 89*, 63–100.

Denmark, G. L., & Fernandez, L. C. (1993). Historical development of the psychology of women. In F. L. Denmark & M. A. Paludi (Eds.), *A handbook of issues and theories*. Westport, CT: Greenwood Press.

Dennett, D. C. (2003). *Freedom evolves*. New York: Viking.

Dennis, I. (2007). Halo effects in grading student projects. *Journal of Applied Psychology, 92*, 1169–1176.

Dennis, T. A., Cole, P. M., Zahn-Waxler, C., & Mizuta, I. (2002). Self in context: Autonomy and relatedness in Japanese and U.S. mother-preschooler dyads. *Child Development, 73*, 1803–1817.

Denollet, J. (2005). DS14: Standard assessment of negative affectivity, social inhibition, and Type D personality. *Psychosomatic Medicine, 67*, 89–97.

Deouell, L. Y., Parnes, A., & Pickard, J. (2006). Spatial location is accurately tracked by human auditory sensory memory: Evidence from the mismatch negativity. *European Journal of Neuroscience, 24*, 1488–1494.

Deregowski, J. B. (1973). Illusion and culture. In R. L. Gregory & G. H. Combrich (Eds.), *Illusion in nature and art*. New York: Scribner.

Derryberry, W. P. (2006). Review of social motivation: Conscious and unconscious processes. *Journal of Moral Education, 35*, 276–278.

DeRubeis, R., Hollon, S., & Shelton, R. (2003, May 23). Presentation, American Psychiatric Association meeting, Philadelphia.

Deshields, T., Tibbs, T., Fan, M. Y., & Taylor, M. (2006). Differences in patterns of depression after treatment for breast cancer [Electronic article published August 12, 2005]. *Psycho-Oncology, 15(5)*, 398–406.

Des Jarlais, D. C., Sloboda, A., Friedman, S. R., Tempakski, B., McKnight, C., & Braine, N. (2006). Diffusion of the *D.A.R.E* and Syringe Exchange Programs. *American Journal of Public Health, 96*, 1354–1357.

Desimone, R. (1992, October 9). The physiology of memory: Recordings of things past. *Science, 258*, 245–255.

Dessing, J. C., Peper, C. E., Bullock, D., & Beek, P. J. (2005). How position, velocity, and temporal information combine in the prospective control of catching: Data and model. *Journal of Cognitive Neuroscience, 17*, 668–686.

Detoledo-Morrell, L., Stoub, T. R., & Wang, C. (2007). Hippocampal atrophy and disconnection in incipient and mild Alzheimer's disease. *Progressive Brain Research, 163C*, 741–823.

Detterman, D. K., Gabriel, L. T., & Ruthsatz, J. M. (2000). Intelligence and mental retardation. In R. J. Sternberg et al. (Eds.), *Handbook of intelligence*. New York: Cambridge University Press.

Devonport, J. J., & Lane, A. M. (2006). Relationships between self-efficacy, coping and student retention. *Social Behavior and Personality, 34*, 127–138.

Dey, E. L., Astin, A. W., Korn, W. S., & Berz, E. R. (2004). *The American freshman: National norms for fall, 1990*. Los Angeles: Higher Education Research Institute, Graduate School of Education, UCLA.

Dhillon, S., Yang, L., & Curran, M. (2008). Spotlight on bupropion in major depressive disorder. *CNS Drugs, 22*, 613–617.

Diamond, M. (2009). Human intersexuality: Difference or disorder? *Archives of Sexual Behavior, 38*, 172.

DiCano, P., & Everitt, B. J. (2002). Reinstatement and spontaneous recovery of cocaine-seeking following extinction and different durations of withdrawal. *Behavioural Pharmacology, 13*, 397–406.

Dickerson, S. S., Kemeny, M. E., Aziz, N., Kim, K. H., & Fahey, J. L. (2004). Immunological effects of induced shame and guilt. *Psychosomatic Medicine, 66*, 124–131.

Diener, E., & Biswas-Diener, R. (2002). Will money increase subjective well-being? *Social Indicators Research, 57*, 119–169.

Diener, E., & Clifton, D. (2002). Life satisfaction and religiosity in broad probability samples. *Psychological Inquiry, 13*, 206–209.

Diener, E., Lucas, R. E., & Oishi, S. (2002). Subjective well-being: The science of happiness and life satisfaction. In C. R. Snyder & S. J. Lopez (Eds.), *Handbook of positive psychology*. London: Oxford University Press.

Diener, E., Lucas, R. E., & Scollon, C. N. (2006). Beyond the hedonic treadmill: Revising the adaptation theory of well-being. *American Psychologist, 61*, 305–314.

Diener, E., & Seligman, M. E. P. (2002). Very happy people. *Psychological Science, 18*, 81–84.

Diener, E., & Seligman, M. E. P. (2004). Beyond money: Toward an economy of well-being. *Psychological Science in the Public Interest, 5*, 1–31.

Diener, M., Isabella, R., Behunin, M., & Wong, M. (2008). Attachment to mothers and fathers during middle childhood: Associations with child gender, grade, and competence. *Social Development, 17*, 84–101.

Di Fabio, A., & Palazzeschi, L. (2009). An in-depth look at scholastic success: Fluid intelligence, personality traits or emotional intelligence? *Personality and Individual Differences, 46*, 581–585.

Di Forti, M., Lappin, J., & Murray, R. (2007, March). Risk factors for schizophrenia—All roads lead to dopamine. *European Neuropsychopharmacology, 17*, S101–SS107.

DiGiovanna, A. G. (1994). *Human aging: Biological perspectives*. New York: McGraw-Hill.

Dijksterhuis, A., Chartrand, T. L., & Aarts, H. (2007). Effects of Priming and Perception on Social Behavior and Goal Pursuit. *Frontiers of Social Psychology, 17*, 33–40.

Dillard, J. P., & Shen, L. (2004). On the nature of reactance and its role in persuasive health communication. *Communication Monographs, 72*, 144–168.

Dillard, J. P., & Shen, L. (2007). Self-report measures of discrete emotions. In R. A. Reynolds, R. Woods, & J. D. Baker, *Handbook of research on electronic surveys and measurements*. Hershey, PA: Idea Group Reference/IGI Global, 2007.

Dillon, J. (2008, April). Reclaiming humanistic psychology from modernity: Problems and solutions. *Journal of Humanistic Psychology, 48*, 221–242.

DiLorenzo, P. M., & Yougentob, S. L. (2003). Olfaction and taste. In M. Gallagher & R. J. Nelson, *Handbook of psychology: Biological psychology (Vol 3)*. New York: Wiley.

Dixon, R. A., & Cohen, A. L. (2003). Cognitive development in adulthood. In R. M. Lerner, M. A. Easterbrooks, et al. (Eds.), *Handbook of psychology: Developmental psychology (Vol. 6)*. New York: Wiley.

Dixon, R. A., Rust, T. B., & Feltmate, S. E. (2007). Memory and aging: Selected research directions and application issues. *Canadian Psychology Psychologie Canadienne, 48*, 67–76.

Do, V. T. (2006). Asian American men and the media: The relationship between ethnic identity, self-esteem, and the endorsement of stereotypes. *Dissertation Abstracts International: Section B: The Sciences and Engineering, 67*(6-B), 3446.

Dobbins, A. C., Jeo, R. M., Fiser, J., & Allman, J. M. (1998, July 24). Distance modulation of neural activity in the visual cortex. *Science, 281*, 552–555.

Dodge, K. A. (2004). The nature-nurture debate and public policy [Special issue: 50th anniversary issue, part 2: The maturing of the human development sciences—Appraising past, present, and prospective agendas]. *Merrill-Palmer Quarterly: Journal of Developmental Psychology, 50*, 418–427.

Doi, T. (1990). The cultural assumptions of psychoanalysis. In J. W. Stigler, R. A. Shweder, & G. Herdt (Eds.), *Cultural psychology: Essays on comparative human development*. New York: Cambridge University Press.

Dolan, P., & White, M. P. (2007). How can measures of subjective well-being be used to inform public policy? *Perspectives on Psychological Science, 2*, 71–85.

Dolan, R. J. (2002, November 8). Emotion, cognition, and behavior. *Science, 298*, 1191–1194.

Dolbier, C. L., Smith, S. E., & Steinhardt, M. A. (2007). Relationships of protective factors to stress and symptoms of illness. *American Journal of Health Behavior, 31*, 423–433.

Dollinger, S. J. (2003). Need for uniqueness, need for cognition and creativity. *Journal of Creative Behavior, 37*, 99–116.

Domhoff, G. W. (1996). *Finding meaning in dreams: A quantitative approach*. New York: Plenum Press.

Donahoe, J. W. (2003). Selectionism. In K. A. Lattal, & P. N. Chase (Eds.), *Behavior theory and philosophy*. New York: Kluwer Academic/Plenum Publishers.

Donahoe, J. W., & Vegas, R. (2004). Pavlovian Conditioning: The CSUR Relation. *Journal of Experimental Psychology: Animal Behavior Processes, 30*, 17–33.

Doty, R. L., Green, P. A., Ram, C., & Yankell, S. L. (1982). Communication of gender from human breath odors: Relationship to perceived intensity and pleasantness. *Hormones and Behavior, 16*, 13–22.

Dougall, A. L., & Baum, A. (2004). Psychoneuroimmunology and trauma. In P. P. Schnurr & B. L. Green (Eds.), *Trauma and health: Physical health consequences of exposure to extreme stress*. Washington, DC: American Psychological Association.

Douglas Brown, R., Goldstein, E., & Bjorklund, D. F. (2000). The history and zeitgeist of the repressed-false-memory debate: Scientific and sociological perspectives on suggestibility and childhood memory. In D. F. Bjorklund (Ed.), *False-memory creation in children and adults: Theory, research, and implications*. Mahwah, NJ: Lawrence Erlbaum.

Douglas, O., Burton, K. S., & Reese-Durham, N. (2008). The effects of the multiple intelligence teaching strategy on the academic achievement of eighth grade math students. *Journal of Instructional Psychology, 35*, 182–187.

Dovidio, J. F., & Gaertner, S. L. (2006). A multilevel perspective on prejudice: Crossing disciplinary boundaries. In P. A. M. Van Lange, *Bridging social psychology: Benefits of transdisciplinary approaches*. Mahwah, NJ: Lawrence Erlbaum Associates.

Dovidio, J. F., Gaertner, S. L., & Kawakami, K. (2003). Intergroup contact: The past, present, and the future. *Group Processes and Intergroup Relations, 6*, 5–20.

Dovidio, J. F., Gaertner, S. L., & Pearson, A. R. (2005). On the nature of prejudice: The psychological foundations of hate. In R. J. Sternberg (Ed.), *Psychology of hate*. Washington, DC: American Psychological Association.

Dovidio, J. F., Piliavin, J. A., Schroeder, D. A., & Penner, L. A. (2006). *The social psychology of prosocial behavior*. Mahwah, NJ: Lawrence Erlbaum Associates.

Dowling, N., Jackson, A., & Thomas, S. (2008). Behavioral interventions in the treatment of pathological gambling: A review of activity scheduling and desensitization. *International Journal of Behavioral Consultation and Therapy, 4,* 172–187.

Doyle, R. (2002, December). Deinstitutionalization. *Scientific American,* 38.

Drewes, A. A. (2005). Play in selected cultures: Diversity and universality. In E. Gil & A. A. Drewes, *Cultural issues in play therapy.* New York: Guilford Press.

Drews, F., Pasupathi, M., & Strayer, D. (2008, December). Passenger and cell phone conversations in simulated driving. *Journal of Experimental Psychology: Applied, 14,* 392–400.

Drob, S. (2005). The mystical symbol: Some comments on Ankor, Giegerich, Scholem, and Jung. *Journal of Jungian Theory & Practice, 7,* 25–29.

Dryden, W., & David, D. (2008). Rational emotive behavior therapy: Current status. *Journal of Cognitive Psychotherapy, 22,* 195–209.

Ducharme, J. M., Sanjuan, E., & Drain, T. (2007). Errorless compliance training: Success-focused behavioral treatment of children with Asperger syndrome. *Behavior Modification, 31,* 329–344.

Duffy, M., Gillig, S. E., Tureen, R. M., & Ybarra, M. A. (2002). A critical look at the DSM-IV. *Journal of Individual Psychology, 58,* 363–373.

Duke, M., & Nowicki, S., Jr. (1979). *Abnormal psychology: Perspectives on being different.* Monterey, CA: Brooks/Cole.

Dumont, M., & Dumont, D. (2008). Deinstitutionalization in the United States and Italy: A historical survey. *International Journal of Mental Health, 37,* 61–70.

Duncker, K. (1945). On problem solving. *Psychological Monographs, 58* (5, whole no. 270).

Durik, A. M., Hyde, J. S., & Marks, A. C. (2006). Ethnicity and gender stereotypes of emotion. *Sex Roles, 54,* 429–445.

Eagly, A., & Chaiken, S. (1998). Attitude structure and function. In D. T. Gilbert & S. T. Fiske (Eds.), *Handbook of social psychology* (Vol. 1, 4th ed.). New York: McGraw-Hill.

Eaker, E. D., Sullivan, L. M., Kelly-Hayes, M., D'Agostino, R. B., Sr., & Benjamin, E. J. (2004). Anger and hostility predict the development of atrial fibrillation in men in the Framingham Offspring Study. *Circulation, 109,* 1267–1271.

Ebbinghaus, H. (1885/1913). *Memory: A contribution to experimental psychology* (H. A. Roger & C. E. Bussenius, Trans.). New York: Columbia University Press.

Eberhard, K. M., Cutting, J. C., & Bock, K. (2005). Making syntax of sense: Number agreement in sentence production. *Psychological Review, 112,* 531–559.

Eberhardt, J. L., Goff, P. A., Purdie, V. J., & Davies, P. G. (2004). Seeing black: Race, crime, and visual processing. *Journal of Personality and Social Psychology, 87,* 876–893.

Eberling, J., Jagust, W., Christine, C., Starr, P., Larson, P., Bankiewicz, K., et al. (2008, May). Results from a phase I safety trial of hAADC gene therapy for Parkinson disease. *Neurology, 70*(21), 1980–1983.

Ebstein, R. P., Benjamin, J., & Belmaker, R. H. (2003). Behavioral genetics, genomics, and personality. In R. Plomin & J. C. DeFries (Eds.), *Behavioral genetics in the postgenomic era.* Washington, DC: American Psychological Association.

Ebster, C., & Neumayr, B. (2008). Applying the door-in-the-face compliance technique to retailing. *The International Review of Retail, Distribution and Consumer Research, 18,* 121–128.

Ecenbarger, W. (1993, April 1). America's new merchants of death. *The Reader's Digest,* p. 50.

Eckardt, M. H. (2005). Karen Horney: A portrait: The 120th anniversary, Karen Horney, September 16, 1885. *American Journal of Psychoanalysis, 65,* 95–101.

Edwards, R. R., & Fillingim, R. B. (2007). Self-reported pain sensitivity: Lack of correlation with pain threshold and tolerance. *European Journal of Pain, 11,* 594–598.

Egan, K. (2005). Students' development in theory and practice: The doubtful role of research. *Harvard Educational Review, 75,* 25–41.

Egliston, K., & Rapee, R. (2007). Inhibition of fear acquisition in toddlers following positive modelling by their mothers. *Behaviour Research and Therapy, 45,* 1871–1882.

Eisch, A., Cameron, H., Encinas, J., Meltzer, L., Ming, G., & Overstreet-Wadiche, L. (2008, November). Adult neurogenesis, mental health, and mental illness: Hope or hype? *Journal of Neuroscience, 28*(46), 1785–1791.

Eisenberg, N., Guthrie, I. K., & Cumberland, A. (2002). Prosocial development in early adulthood: A longitudinal study. *Journal of Personality and Social Psychology, 82,* 993–1006.

Eizenberg, M. M., & Zaslavsky, O. (2004). Students' verification strategies for combinatorial problems. *Mathematical Thinking and Learning, 6,* 15–36.

Ekman, P. (1972). Universals and cultural differences in facial expressions of emotion. In J. Cole (Ed.), *Darwin and facial expression: A century of research in review.* New York: Academic Press.

Ekman, P. (1994a). All emotions are basic. In P. Ekman & R. J. Davidson (Eds.), *The nature of emotion: Fundamental questions.* New York: Oxford University Press.

Ekman, P. (1994b). Strong evidence for universals in facial expressions: A reply to Russell's mistaken critique. *Psychological Bulletin, 115,* 268–287.

Ekman, P. (2003). *Emotions revealed: Recognizing faces and feelings to improve communication and emotional life.* New York: Times Books.

Ekman, P., Levenson, R. W., & Friesen, W. V. (1983, September 16). Autonomic nervous system activity distinguishes among emotions. *Science, 223,* 1208–1210.

Ekman, P., & O'Sullivan, M. (1991). Facial expression: Methods, means, and moues. In R. S. Feldman & B. Rimé (Eds.), *Fundamentals of nonverbal behavior.* Cambridge, England: Cambridge University Press.

Ekroll, V., & Scherzer, T. R. (2009). Apparent visual motion of the observer's own limbs. *Perception, 38,* 778–780.

Elfhag, K., Tynelius, P., & Rasmussen, F. (2007). Sugar-sweetened and artificially sweetened soft drinks in association to restrained, external and emotional eating. *Physiology & Behavior, 91,* 191–195.

El-Hai, J. (2005). *The lobotomist: A maverick medical genius and his tragic quest to rid the world of mental illness.* New York: Wiley.

Elkins, D. (2009). Why humanistic psychology lost its power and influence in American psychology: Implications for advancing humanistic psychology. *Journal of Humanistic Psychology, 49,* 267–291.

Elkins, G., Marcus, J., Bates, J., Hasan, R. M., & Cook, T. (2006). Intensive hypnotherapy for smoking cessation: a prospective study. *International Journal of Clinical Experimental Hypnosis, 54,* 303–315.

Ellason, J. W., & Ross, C. A. (2004). SCL-90-R norms for dissociative identity disorder. *Journal of Trauma and Dissociation, 5,* 85–91.

Ellins, E., Halcox, J., Donald, A., Field, B., Brydon, L., Deanfield, J., et al. (2008). Arterial stiffness and inflammatory response to psychophysiological stress. *Brain, Behavior, and Immunity, 22,* 941–948.

Elliott, A. (2002). *Psychoanalytic theory: An introduction* (2nd ed.). Durham, NC: Duke University Press.

Elliott, J., Berman, H., & Kim, S. (2002). Critical ethnography of Korean Canadian women's menopause experience. *Health Care for Women International, 23,* 377–388.

Ellis, A. (1974). *Growth through reason.* Hollywood, CA: Wilshire Books.

Ellis, A. (2000). *How to control your anger before it controls you.* New York: Citadel.

Ellis, A. (2002). *Overcoming resistance: A rational emotive behavior therapy integrated approach* (2nd ed.). New York: Springer.

Ellis, A. (2004). Expanding the ABCs of rational emotive behavior therapy. In A. Freeman,

M. J. Mahoney, P. Devito, & D. Martin (Eds.), *Cognition and psychotherapy* (2nd ed.). New York: Springer Publishing Co.

El-Mallakh, R. S., & Abraham, H. D. (2007). MDMA (Ecstasy). *Annals of Clinical Psychiatry, 19,* 45–52.

Emick, J., & Welsh, M. (2005). Association between formal operational thought and executive function as measured by the Tower of Hanoi-Revised. *Learning and Individual Differences, 15,* 177–188.

Endres, T., & Fendt, M. (2007). Conditioned behavioral responses to a context paired with the predator odor trimethylthiazoline. *Behavioral Neuroscience, 121,* 594–601.

Engen, T. (1987). Remembering odors and their names. *American Scientist, 75,* 497–503.

Engler, J., & Goleman, D. (1992). *The consumer's guide to psychotherapy.* New York: Simon & Schuster.

Epstein, R. (1996). *Cognition, creativity, and behavior: Selected essays.* Westport, CT: Praeger/Greenwood.

Eranti, S. V., & McLoughlin, D. M. (2003). Electroconvulsive therapy: State of the art. *British Journal of Psychiatry, 182,* 8–9.

Erickson, R. (2008, February). A study of the science of taste: On the origins and influence of the core ideas. *Behavioral and Brain Sciences, 31,* 59–75.

Erikson, E. H. (1963). *Childhood and society.* New York: Norton.

Ervik, S., Abdelnoor, M., & Heier, M. S. (2006). Health-related quality of life in narcolepsy. *Acta Neurologica Scandinavica, 114,* 198–204.

Etchegary, H. (2004). Psychological aspects of predictive genetic-test decision: What do we know so far? *Analyses of Social Issues and Public Policy, 4,* 13–31.

Evans, A. M. (2007). Transference in the nurse-patient relationship. *Journal of Psychiatric and Mental Health Nursing, 14,* 189–195.

Evans, D. E., & Rothbart, M. K. (2007). Developing a model for adult temperament. *Journal of Research in Personality, 41,* 868–888.

Evans, D., & Rothbart, M. (2009). A two-factor model of temperament. *Personality and Individual Differences, 47,* 565–570.

Evans, J. B. T. (2004). Informal reasoning: Theory and method. *Canadian Journal of Experimental Psychology, 58,* 69–74.

Evans, J. B. T., & Feeney, A. (2004). The role of prior belief in reasoning. In J. P. Leighton (Ed.), *Nature of reasoning.* New York: Cambridge University Press.

Evcik, D., Kavuncu, V., Cakir, T., Subasi, V., & Yaman, M. (2007). Laser therapy in the treatment of carpal tunnel syndrome: A randomized controlled trial. *Photomedical Laser Surgery, 25,* 34–39.

Everette, M. (2008). Gestational weight and dietary intake during pregnancy: Perspectives of African American women. *Maternal & Child Health Journal, 12,* 718–724.

Everly, G. S., Jr., & Lating, J. M. (2007). Psychotherapy: A cognitive perspective. In A. Monat, R. S. Lazarus, & G. Reevy, *The Praeger handbook on stress and coping* (Vol. 2). Westport, CT: Praeger Publishers/Greenwood Publishing.

Eysenck, H. J. (1990). Biological dimensions of personality. In L. A. Pervin (Ed.), *Handbook of personality: Theory and research.* New York: Guilford Press.

Eysenck, H. J. (1995). *Eysenck on extraversion.* New York: Wiley.

Fagan, J. F., & Holland, C. R. (2002). Equal opportunity and racial differences in IQ. *Intelligence, 30,* 361–387.

Fagan, J. F., & Holland, C. R. (2007). Racial equality in intelligence: Predictions from a theory of intelligence as processing. *Intelligence, 35,* 319–334.

Fagan, J. F., & Holland, C. R. (2009). Culture-fair prediction of academic achievement. *Intelligence, 37,* 62–67.

Fagan, J., & Press, J. (2008). Father influences on employed mothers' work-family balance. *Journal of Family Issues, 29,* 1136–1160.

Falck-Ytter, T., & Gredebäck, G. (2006). Infants predict other people's action goals. *Nature Neuroscience, 9,* 878–879.

Fallon, A. (2006). Informed consent in the practice of group psychotherapy. *International Journal of Group Psychotherapy, 56,* 431–453.

Fallon, B. A., & Feinstein, S. (2001). Hypochondriasis. In K. A. Phillips (Ed.), *Somatoform and factitious disorders.* Washington, DC: American Psychiatric Association.

Fanselow, M. S., & Poulos, A. M. (2005). The neuroscience of mammalian associative learning. *Annual Review of Psychology, 56,* 207–234.

Fearing, V. G., & Clark, J. (Eds.). (2000). *Individuals in context: A practical guide to client-centered practice.* Chicago: Slack Publishing.

Fedeli, A., Braconi, S., Economidou, D., Cannella, N., Kallupi, M., Guerrini, R., et al. (2009). The paraventricular nucleus of the hypothalamus is a neuroanatomical substrate for the inhibition of palatable food intake by neuropeptide S. *European Journal of Neuroscience, 30,* 1594–1602.

Fee, E., Brown, T. M., Lazarus, J., & Theerman, P. (2002). Exploring acupuncture: Ancient ideas, modern techniques. *American Journal of Public Health, 92,* 1592.

Feinberg, A. W. (2002, April). Homo-cysteine may raise Alzheimer's risk: A physician's perspective. *HealthNews,* p. 4.

Feldhusen, J. F., (2006). The role of the knowledge base in creative thinking. In J. C. Kaufman, & J. Baer, *Creativity and reason in cognitive development.* New York: Cambridge University Press.

Feldman, D. H. (2003). Cognitive development in childhood. In R. M. Lerner, M. A. Easterbrooks, et al. (Eds.), *Handbook of psychology: Developmental psychology* (Vol. 6.). New York: Wiley.

Feldman, D. H. (2004). Piaget's stages: The unfinished symphony of cognitive development. *New Ideas in Psychology, 22,* 175–231.

Feldman, R. S. (Ed.). (1993). *Applications of non-verbal behavioral theories and research.* Hillsdale, NJ: Erlbaum.

Feldt, L. S. (2005). Estimating the reliability of cichotomous or trichotomous scores. *Educational and Psychological Measurement, 65,* 28–41.

Fenter, V. L. (2006). Concerns about Prozac and direct-to-consumer advertising of prescription drugs. *International Journal of Risk & Safety in Medicine, 18,* 1–7.

Feret, A., Steinweg, S., Griffin, H. C., & Glover, S. (2007). Macular degeneration: types, causes, and possible interventions. *Geriatric Nursing, 28,* 387–392.

Feshbach, S., & Tangney, J. (2008, September). Television viewing and aggression: Some alternative perspectives. *Perspectives on Psychological Science, 3,* 387–389.

Festinger, D., Marlowe, D., Croft, J., Dugosh, K., Arabia, P., & Benasutti, K. (2009). Monetary incentives improve recall of research consent information: It pays to remember. *Experimental and Clinical Psychopharmacology, 17,* 99–104.

Festinger, L. (1957). *A theory of cognitive dissonance.* Stanford, CA: Stanford University Press.

Festinger, L., & Carlsmith, J. M. (1959). Cognitive consequences of forced compliance. *Journal of Abnormal and Social Psychology, 58,* 203–210.

Fichtenberg, C. M., & Glantz, S. A. (2006). Association of the California tobacco control program with declines in cigarette consumption and mortality from heart disease. In K. E. Warner, *Tobacco control policy.* San Francisco, CA: Jossey-Bass.

Fields, R. D. (2004, April). The other half of the brain. *Scientific American,* pp. 55–61.

Fields-Meyer, T. (1995, September 25). Having their say. *People,* pp. 50–60.

Fine, R., & Fine, L. (2003). *Basic chess endings.* New York: Random House.

Fingelkurts, A., Fingelkurts, A. A., & Kallio, S. (2007). Hypnosis induces a changed composition of brain oscillations in EEG: A case study. *Contemporary Hypnosis, 24,* 3–18.

Fink, G. (Ed.). (2000). *Encyclopedia of stress.* New York: Academic Press.

Finkelhor, D. (2002). *Sexual abuse in the United States.* Durham, NH: University of New Hampshire.

Finkelstein, M. (2009). Intrinsic vs. extrinsic motivational orientations and the volunteer process. *Personality and Individual Differences, 46,* 653–658.

Finkler, K. (2004). Traditional healers in Mexico: The effectiveness of spiritual practices. In U. P. Gielen, J. M. Fish, & J. G. Draguns (Eds.), *Handbook of culture, therapy, and healing.* Mahwah, NJ: Lawrence Erlbaum Associates.

Finlay, F. O., Jones, R., & Coleman, J. (2002). Is puberty getting earlier? The views of doctors and teachers. *Child: Care, Health and Development, 28,* 205–209.

Finley, C. L., & Cowley, B. J. (2005). The effects of a consistent sleep schedule on time taken to achieve sleep. *Clinical Case Studies, 4,* 304–311.

Firestein, B. A. (Ed.). (1996). *Bisexuality: The psychology and politics of an invisible minority.* Thousand Oaks, CA: Sage.

First, M. B., Frances, A., & Pincus, H. A. (2002). *DSM-IV-TR handbook of differential diagnosis.* Arlington, VA: American Psychiatric Publishing.

Fischer, K. W., Shaver, P. R., & Carnochan, P. (1990). How emotions develop and how they organize development. *Cognition and Emotion, 4,* 81–127.

Fishbach, A., Dhar, R., & Zhang, Y. (2006). Subgoals as substitutes or complements: The role of goal accessibility. *Journal of Personality and Social Psychology, 91,* 232–242.

Fisher, C. B. (2003). *Decoding the ethics code: A practical guide for psychologists.* Thousand Oaks, CA: Sage.

Fisher, C. B., Hoagwood, K., Boyce, C., Duster, T., Frank, D. A., Grisso, T., et al. (2002). Research ethics for mental health science involving ethnic minority children and youths. *American Psychologist, 57,* 1024–1040.

Fisk, J. E., Bury, A. S., & Holden, R. (2006). Reasoning about complex probabilistic concepts in childhood. *Scandinavian Journal of Psychology, 47,* 497–504.

Fitzgerald, P., & Daskalakis, Z. (2008, January). The use of repetitive transcranial magnetic stimulation and vagal nerve stimulation in the treatment of depression. *Current Opinion in Psychiatry, 21,* 25–29.

Flam, F. (1991, June 14). Queasy riders. *Science, 252,* 1488.

Flavell, S. W., Cowan, C. W., Kim, T., Greer, P. L., Lin, Y., Paradis, S., et al. (2006, February 17). Activity-dependent regulation of MEF2 transcription factors suppresses excitatory synapse number. *Science, 311,* 1008–1010.

Fleck, J. I., Green, D. L., Payne, L., Stevenson, J. L., Bowden, E. M., Jung-Beeman, M., et al. (2008). The transliminal brain at rest: Baseline EEG, unusual experiences, and access to unconscious mental activity. *Cortex, 44,* 1353–1363.

Fleischman, D. A., Wilson, R. S., Gabrieli, J. D. E., Bienias, J. L., & Bennett, D. A. (2004). A longitudinal study of implicit and explicit memory in old persons. *Psychology and Aging, 19,* 617–625.

Fleming, J. (2000). Affirmative action and standardized test scores. *Journal of Negro Education, 69,* 27–37.

Foderaro, L. W. (2006, February 16). Westchester lawyer, his memory lost, is found in Chicago shelter after 6 months. *The New York Times,* p. B3.

Fogarty, J. S., & Young, G. A., Jr. (2000). Patient-physician communication. *Journal of the American Medical Association, 289,* 92.

Folk, C., & Remington, R. (2008, January). Bottom-up priming of top-down attentional control settings. *Visual Cognition, 16,* 215–231.

Folkman, S., & Moskowitz, J. T. (2000). Stress, positive emotion, and coping. *Current Directions in Psychological Science, 9,* 115–118.

Folkman, S., & Moskowitz, J. T. (2004). Coping: Pitfalls and promise. *Annual Review of Psychology, 55,* 745–774.

Follett, K., & Hess, T. M. (2002). Aging, cognitive complexity, and the fundamental attribution error. *Journal of Gerontology: Series B: Psy-chological Sciences and Social Sciences, 57B,* P312–P323.

Forbey, J., & Ben-Porath, Y. (2007). Computerized adaptive personality testing: A review and illustration with the MMPI-2 computerized adaptive version. *Psychological Assessment, 19,* 14–24.

Forer, B. (1949). The fallacy of personal validation: A classroom demonstration of gullibility. *Journal of Abnormal and Social Psychology, 44,* 118–123.

Forgas, J. P., & Laham, S. M. (2005). The interaction between affect and motivation in social judgments and behavior. In J. P. Forgas, K. P. Williams, & S. M. Laham (Eds.), *Social motivation: Conscious and unconscious processes.* New York: Cambridge University Press.

Forlenza, M. J., & Baum, M. J. (2004). Psycho-neuroimmunology. In T. J. Boll, R. G. Frank, A. Baum, & J. L. Wallander (Eds.) *Handbook of clinical health psychology, Vol. 3: Models and perspectives in health psychology.* Washington, DC: American Psychological Association 81–114.

Foster, K. M. (2005). Introduction: John Uzo Ogbu (1939–2003): How do you ensure the fair consideration of a complex ancestor? Multiple approaches to assessing the work and legacy of John Uzo Ogbu. *International Journal of Qualitative Studies in Education, 18,* 559–564.

Foster, P., Drago, V., FitzGerald, D., Skoblar, B., Crucian, G., & Heilman, K. (2008). Spreading activation of lexical-semantic networks in Parkinson's disease. *Neuropsychologia, 46,* 1908–1914.

Foulds, J., Gandhi, K. K., Steinberg, M. B., Richardson, D. L., Williams, J. M., Burke, M. V., et al. (2006). Factors associated with quitting smoking at a tobacco dependence treatment clinic. *American Journal of Health Behavior, 30,* 400–412.

Fountas, K. N., & Smith, J. R. (2007). Historical evolution of stereotactic amygdalotomy for the management of severe aggression. *Journal of Neurosurgery, 106,* 716–713.

Fournier, J., Deremaux, S., & Bernier, M. (2008). Content, characteristics and function of mental images. *Psychology of Sport and Exercise, 9,* 734–748.

Fowler, C. A., & Galantucci, B. (2008). The relation of speech perception and speech production. In Pisoni, D. B. & Remez, R. E. (Eds)., *The handbook of speech perception.* Malden, MA: Blackwell Publishing.

Fowler, J., & Christakis, N. (2009). Dynamic spread of happiness in a large social network: Longitudinal analysis over 20 years in the Framingham Heart Study. *British Medical Journal, 338,* 1–13.

Fox, C. R. (2006). The availability heuristic in the classroom: How soliciting more criticism can boost your course ratings. *Judgment and Decision Making, 1,* 86–90.

Fox, S., & Spector, P. E. (2000). Relations of emotional intelligence, practical intelligence, general intelligence, and trait affectivity with interview outcomes: It's not all just "G." *Journal of Organizational Behavior, 21,* 203–220.

Frankenberg, W. K., et al. (1992). *Denver II training manual.* Denver, CO: Denver Developmental Materials.

Franklin, A., Pilling, M., & Davies, I. (2005). The nature of infant color categorization: Evidence from eye movements on a target decision task. *Journal of Experimental Child Psychology, 91,* 227–248.

Franklin, M. E., March, J. S., & Garcia, A. (2007). Treating obsessive-compulsive disorder in children and adolescents. In C. Purdon, M. M. Antony, & L. J. Summerfeldt, (Eds.), *Psychological treatment of obsessive-compulsive disorder: Fundamentals and beyond.* Washington, DC: American Psychological Association.

Franko, D., & Striegel-Moore, R. (2002). The role of body dissatisfaction as a risk factor for depression in adolescent girls: Are the differences black and white? *Journal of Psychosomatic Research, 53,* 975–983.

Franks, D. D., & Smith, T. S. (1999) (Eds.). *Mind, brain, and society: Toward a neuro-sociology of emotion.* Stamford, CT: JAI Press.

Franzek, E., & Beckmann, H. (1996). Gene-environment interaction in schizophrenia: Season-of-birth effect reveals etiologically different subgroups. *Psychopathology, 29,* 14–26.

Frasure-Smith, N., Lesperance, F., & Talajic, M. (2000). The prognostic importance of depression, anxiety, anger, and social support following myocardial infarction: Opportunities for improving survival. In P. M. McCabe, N. Schneiderman, T. M. Field, & A. R. Wellens (Eds.), *Stress, coping, and cardiovascular disease.* Mahwah, NJ: Erlbaum.

Fredrickson, B. L., & Branigan, C. (2005). Positive emotions broaden the scope of attention and thought-action repertoires. *Cognition and Emotion, 19,* 313–332.

Freedman, D. S. (1995). The importance of body fat distribution in early life. *American Journal of the Medical Sciences, 310,* S72–S76.

Freedman, J. L., & Fraser, S. C. (1966). Compliance without pressure: The foot-in-the-door technique. *Journal of Personality and Social Psychology, 4,* 195–202.

Frensch, P. A., & Rünger, D. (2003). Implicit learning. *Current Directions in Psychological Science, 12,* 13–18.

Freud, S. (1922/1959). *Group psychology and the analysis of the ego.* London: Hogarth.

Friborg, O., Barlaug, D., Martinussen, M., Rosenvinge, J. H., & Hjemdal, O. (2005). Resilience in relation to personality and intelligence. *International Journal of Methods in Psychiatric Research, 14,* 29–42.

Friborg, O., Hjemdal, O., & Rosenvinge, J. H. (2006). Resilience as a moderator of pain and stress. *Journal of Psychosomatic Research, 61,* 213–219.

Friedberg, R. D. (2006). A cognitive-behavioral approach to family therapy. *Journal of Contemporary Psychotherapy, 36,* 159–165.

Friedman, J. N. W., Oltmanns, T. F., & Turkheimer, E. (2007). Interpersonal perception and personality disorders: Utilization of a thin slice approach. *Journal of Research in Personality, 41,* 667–688.

Friedman, M. J. (2006). Posttraumatic stress disorder among military returnees from Afghanistan and Iraq. *American Journal of Psychiatry, 163,* 586–593.

Frijda, N. H. (2005). Emotion experience. *Cognition and Emotion, 19,* 473–497.

Frincke, J. L., & Pate, W. E., II. (2004, March). *Yesterday, today, and tomorrow. Careers in Psychology 2004, what students need to know.* Paper presented at the Annual Convention of the Southeastern Psychological Association, Atlanta, GA.

Frings, L., Wagner, K., Unterrainer, J., Spreer, J., Halsband, U., & Schulze-Bonhage, A. (2006). Gender-related differences in lateralization of hippocampal activation and cognitive strategy. *Neuroreport, 17,* 417–421.

Fritsch, T., McClendon, M. J., Smyth, K. A., Lerner, A. J., Friedland, R. P., & Larsen, J. D. (2007). Cognitive functioning in healthy aging: The role of reserve and lifestyle factors early in life. *Gerontologist, 47,* 307–322.

Frost, L. E., & Bonnie, R. J. (Eds.). (2001). *The evolution of mental health law.* Washington, DC: American Psychological Association.

Frost, R. O., & Steketee, G. (Eds.). (2002). *Cognitive approaches to obsessions and compulsions: Theory, assessment, and treatment.* New York: Pergamon Press.

Fuller, A. (2006). Hypnosis and ideomotor compliance in the treatment of smoking tobacco and cannabis. *Australian Journal of Clinical Hypnotherapy and Hypnosis, 27,* 14–18.

Funder, D. C. (1991). Global traits: A neo-Allportian approach to personality. *Psychological Science, 2,* 31–39.

Furnham, A., & Crump, J. (2005). Personality traits, types, and disorders: An examination of the relationship between three self-report measures. *European Journal of Personality, 19,* 167–184.

Furumoto, L., & Scarborough, E. (2002). Placing women in the history of psychology: The first American women psychologists. In W. E. Pickren (Ed.), *Evolving perspectives on the history of psychology.* Washington, DC: American Psychological Association.

Fusari, A., & Ballesteros, S. (2008, August). Identification of odors of edible and nonedible stimuli as affected by age and gender. *Behavior Research Methods, 40,* 752–759.

Gaab, J., Rohleder, N., Nater, U. M., & Ehlert, U. (2005). Psychological determinants of the cortisol stress response: The role of anticipatory cognitive appraisal. *Psychoneuroendocrinology, 30,* 599–610.

Gaffney, K. F., & Henry, L. L. (2007). Identifying risk factors for postpartum tobacco use. *Journal of Nursing Scholarship, 39,* 126–132.

Galanter, E. (1962). Contemporary psychophysics. In R. Brown, E. Galanter, E. Hess, & G. Maroler (Eds.), *New directions in psychology.* New York: Holt.

Galanter, M. (2007). Spirituality and recovery in 12-step programs: An empirical model. *Journal of Substance Abuse Treatment, 33,* 265–272.

Galatzer-Levy, R. M., & Cohler, B. J. (1997). *Essential psychoanalysis: A contemporary introduction.* New York: Basic Books.

Galef, D. (2001, April 27). The information you provide is anonymous, but what was your name again? *The Chronicle of Higher Education, 47,* p. B5.

Gallup News Service (1998). *Adults who find that premarital sex is not wrong.* Washington, DC: Gallup News Service.

Gallup Poll. (2001, June 8). *Americans' belief in psychic and paranormal phenomena is up over last decade.* Washington, DC: The Gallup Organization.

Gami, A. S., Howard, D. E., Olson, E. J., & Somers, V. K. (2005). Day-night pattern of sudden death in obstructive sleep apnea. *New England Journal of Medicine, 353,* 1206–1214.

Gangestad, S. W., Simpson, J. A., Cousins, A. J., Garver-Apgar, C. E., & Christensen, P. N. (2004). Women's preferences for male behavioral displays change across the menstrual cycle. *Psychological Science, 15,* 203–207.

Ganong, L. H., & Coleman, M. (1999). *Changing families, changing responsibilities: Family obligations following divorce and remarriage.* Mahwah, NJ: Erlbaum.

Garb, H. N., Wood, J. M., Lilenfeld, S. O., & Nezworski, M. T. (2005). Roots of the Rorschach controversy. *Clinical Psychology Review, 25,* 97–118.

Garber, J., Clarke, G., Weersing, V., Beardslee, W., Brent, D., Gladstone, T., et al. (2009). Prevention of depression in at-risk adolescents: A randomized controlled trial. *Journal of the American Medical Association, 301,* 2215–2224.

Garber, J., & Horowitz, J. L. (2002). Depression in children. In I. H. Gotlib & C. L. Hammen (Eds.), *Handbook of depression.* New York: Guilford Press.

Garcia, J. (1990). Learning without memory. *Journal of Cognitive Neuroscience, 2,* 287–305.

Garcia, J. (2003). Psychology is not an enclave. In R. J. Sternberg (Ed.), *Psychologists defying the crowd: Stories of those who battled the establishment and won.* Washington, DC: American Psychological Association.

Garcia, S. M., Weaver, K., Moskowitz, G. B., & Darley, J. M. (2002). Crowded minds: The implicit bystander effect. *Journal of Personality and Social Psychology, 83,* 843–853.

Garcia-Andrade, C., Wall, T. L. & Ehlers, C. L. (1997). The firewater myth and response to alcohol in Mission Indians. *Journal of Psychiatry, 154,* 983–988.

Garcia-Palacios, A., Hoffman, H., & Carlin, A. (2002). Virtual reality in the treatment of spider phobia: A controlled study. *Behavior Research & Therapy, 40,* 983–993.

Gardini, S., Cornoldi, C., De Beni, R., & Venneri, A. (2009). Cognitive and neuronal processes involved in sequential generation of general and specific mental images. *Psychological Research/Psychologische Forschung, 73,* 633–643.

Gardner, B., & O'Connor, D. (2008). A review of the cognitive effects of electroconvulsive therapy in older adults. *The Journal of ECT, 24,* 68–80.

Gardner, E. P., & Kandel, E. R. (2000). Touch. In E. R. Kandel, J. H. Schwartz, & T. M. Jessell (Eds.), *Principles of neural science* (4th ed.). New York: McGraw-Hill.

Gardner, F., & Moore, Z. (2008). Understanding clinical anger and violence: The anger avoidance model. *Behavior Modification, 32,* 897–912.

Gardner, H. (1975). *The shattered mind: The person after brain damage.* New York: Knopf.

Gardner, H. (1999). *Intelligence reframed: Multiple intelligences for the 21st century.* New York: Basic Books.

Gardner, H. (2000). The giftedness matrix: A developmental perspective. In R. C. Friedman & B. M. Shore (Eds.). *Talents unfolding: Cognition and development.* Washington, DC: American Psychological Association.

Gardner, H. (2005). Scientific psychology: Should we bury it or praise it? In R. J. Sternberg (Ed.), *Unity in psychology: Possibility or pipe dream?* Washington, DC: American Psychological Association.

Gardner, H. (2006). *Multiple intelligences: New horizons in theory and practice* by New York: Basic Books.

Garlow, S. J., Purselle, D. C., & Heninger, M. (2007). Cocaine and alcohol use preceding suicide in African American and White adolescents. *Journal of Psychiatric Research, 41,* 530–536.

Garn, C. L., Allen, M. D., Larsen, J. D., & Cortex, A. (2009). An fMRI study of sex differences in brain activation during object naming. *Journal Devoted to the Study of the Nervous System and Behavior, 45,* 610–618.

Garrigan, P., & Kellman, P. (2008, February). Perceptual learning depends on perceptual constancy. PNAS *Proceedings of the National Academy of Sciences of the United States of America, 105,* 2248–2253.

Garwick, G. B. (2007). Intelligence-related terms in mental retardation, learning disability, and gifted/talented professional usage, 1983–2001: The 1992 mental retardation redefinition as natural experiment. *Dissertation Abstracts International Section A: Humanities and Social Sciences, 67*(9-A), 3296.

Garwood, C. L., & Potts, L. A. (2007). Emerging pharmacotherapies for smoking cessation. *American Journal of Health Systems Pharmacology, 64,* 1693–1698.

Garza-Guerrero, C. (2000). Idealization and mourning in love relationships: Normal and pathological spectra. *Psychoanalytic Quarterly, 69,* 121–150.

Gass, C. S., Luis, C. A., Meyers, T. L., & Kuljis, R. O. (2000). Familial Creutzfeldt-Jakob disease: A neuropsychological case study. *Archives of Clinical Neuropsychology, 15,* 165–175.

Gatchel, R. J., & Oordt. M. S. (2003). Obesity. In R. J. Gatchel & M. S. Oordt, *Clinical health psychology and primary care: Practical advice and clinical guidance for successful collaboration.* Washington, DC: American Psychological Association.

Gatchel, R. J. & Weisberg, J. N. (2000). *Personality characteristics of patients with pain.* Washington, DC: APA Books.

Gathercole, S. E., & Baddeley, A.D. (1993). *Working memory and language processing.* Hillsdale, NJ: Erlbaum.

Gazzaniga, M. S. (1998, July). The split brain revisited. *Scientific American,* pp. 50–55.

Gazzaniga, M. S., Ivry, R. B., & Mangun, G. R. (2002). *Cognitive neuroscience: The biology of the mind* (2nd ed.). New York: W. W. Norton.

Ge, X., Kim, I. J., Brody, G. H., Conger, R. D., Simons, R. L., Gibbons, F. X., et al. (2003). It's about timing and change: Pubertal transition effects on symptoms of major depression among African American youths. *Developmental Psychology, 39,* 430–439.

Gegenfurtner, K. R. (2003). Color vision. *Annual Review of Neuroscience, 26,* 181–206.

Gelbard-Sagiv, H., Mukamel, R., Harel, M., Malach, R., & Fried, I. (March 2008). Internally generated reactivation of single neurons in human hippocampus during free recall. *Science, 322,* 96–101.

Gelfand, M. M. (2000). Sexuality among older women. *Journal of Women's Health and Gender Based Medicine, 9*(Suppl. 1), S15–S20.

Gelman, R., & Baillargeon, R. (1983). A review of some Piagetian concepts. In J. H. Flavell & E. M. Markman (Eds.), *Handbook of child psychology, Vol. 3: Cognitive development* (4th ed.). New York: Wiley.

Gelman, R., & Kit-Fong Au, T. (Eds.). (1996). *Perceptual and cognitive development.* New York: Academic Press.

Gennaro, R. J. (2004). *Higher-order theories of consciousness: An anthology.* Amsterdam, Netherlands: John Benjamins.

Genovese, J. E. C. (2006). Piaget, pedagogy, and evolutionary psychology. *Evolutionary Psychology, 4,* 2127–2137.

Gentner, D., Goldin, S., & Goldin-Meadow, S. (Eds.). (2003). *Language in mind: Advances in the study of language and cognition.* Cambridge, MA: MIT.

George, M. S., Wassermann, E. M., Williams, W. A., Callahan, A., Ketter, T. A., Baser, P., et al. (1995). Daily repetitive transcranial magnetic stimulations (rTMS) improves mood in depression. *Neuroreport: An International Journal for the Rapid Communication of Research in Neuroscience, 6,* 1853–1856.

George, S., & Moselhy, H. (2005). Cocaine-induced trichotillomania. *Addiction, 100,* 255–256.

George, T. P. (1999). Design, measurement, and analysis in developmental research. In M. Bornstein & M. Lamb, *Developmental psychology.* Mahwah, NJ: Erlbaum.

Georgiou, G. A., Bleakley, C., Hayward, J., Russo, R., Dutton, K., Eltiti, S., et al. (2005). Focusing on fear: Attentional disengagement from emotional faces. *Visual Cognition, 12,* 145–158.

Gerdes, A., Uhl, G., & Alpers, G. (2009). Spiders are special: Fear and disgust evoked by pictures of arthropods. *Evolution and Human Behavior, 30,* 66–73.

Gershkoff-Stowe, L., Connell, B., & Smith, L. (2006). Priming overgeneralizations in two- and four-year-old children. *Journal of Child Language, 33,* 461–486.

Gerstel, N. (2005, April 8). In search of time. *Science, 308,* 204–205.

Getner, D., & Holyoak, K. J. (1997, January). Reasoning and learning by analogy. *American Psychologist, 52,* 32–34.

Giacobbi, P. R., Jr., Lynn, T. K., Wetherington, J. M., Jenkins, J., Bodendorf, M., & Langley, B. (2004). Stress and coping during the transition to university for first-year female athletes. *Sports Psychologist, 18,* 1–20.

Giacomini, M., Baylis, F., & Robert, J. (2007). Banking on it: Public policy and the ethics of stem cell research and development. *Social Sciences Medicine, 22,* 88–84.

Gibb, K., Tunbridge, D., Chua, A., & Frederickson, N. (2007). Pathways to inclusion: Moving from special school to mainstream. *Educational Psychology in Practice, 23,* 109–127.

Gibbons, R. D., Brown, C. H., Hur, K., Marcus, S. M., Bhamik, D. K., Erkens, J. A., et al. (2007). Early evidence on the effects of regulators' suicidal warnings on SSRI prescriptions and suicide in children and adolescents. *American Journal of Psychiatry, 164,* 1356–1363.

Gibbs, N. (2005, August 8). Being 13. *Time,* pp. 41–55.

Gibbs, W. W. (2002, August.) From mouth to mind. *Scientific American,* p. 26.

Gigerenzer, G. (2007). *Gut feelings: The intelligence of the unconscious.* Penguin Group: New York.

Gilbert, D. T., McNulty, S. E., Guiliano, T. A., & Benson, J. E. (1992). Blurry words and fuzzy deeds: The attribution of obscure behavior. *Journal of Personality and Social Psychology, 62,* 18–25.

Gilbert, D. T., Miller, A. G., & Ross, L. (1998). Speeding with Ned: A personal view of the correspondence bias. In J. M. Darley & J. Cooper (Eds.), *Attribution and social interaction: The legacy of Edward E. Jones.* Washington, DC: American Psychological Association.

Gilbert, P. D. (2007). Spirituality and mental health: A very preliminary overview. *Current Opinions in Psychiatry, 20,* 594–598.

Gilboa, A., Winocur, G., & Rosenbaum, R. S. (2006). Hippocampal contributions to recollection in retrograde and anterograde amnesia. *Hippocampus, 16,* 966–980.

Gilchrist, A., Cowan, N., & Naveh-Benjamin, M. (2009). Investigating the childhood development of working memory using sentences: New evidence for the growth of chunk capacity. *Journal of Experimental Child Psychology, 104,* 252–265.

Gilestro, G. F., Tononi, G., & Cirelli, C. (2009, April 3). Widespread changes in synaptic markers as a function of sleep and wakefulness in Drosophila. *Science, 324,* 109–112.

Gilligan, C. (1996). The centrality of relationships in psychological development: A puzzle, some evidence, and a theory. In G. G. Noam & K. W. Fischer (Eds.), *Development and vulnerability in close relationships.* Hillsdale, NJ: Erlbaum.

Gilligan, C. (2004). Recovering psyche: Reflections on life-history and history. *Annual of Psychoanalysis, 32,* 131–147.

Gladwell, M. (2004, September 20). Annals of psychology: Personality, plus how corporations figure out who you are. *The New Yorker,* 42–45.

Gladwin, T. (1964). Culture and logical process. In N. Goodenough (Ed.), *Explorations in cultural anthropology: Essays in honor of George Peter Murdoch.* New York: McGraw-Hill.

Glass, K., Flory, K., Hankin, B., Kloos, B., & Turecki, G. (2009). Are coping strategies, social support, and hope associated with psychological distress among Hurricane Katrina survivors? *Journal of Social and Clinical Psychology, 28,* 779–795.

Glickler, J. (2006). Advancing in advancement: A self-efficacy study of development practitioners in higher education. *Dissertation Abstracts International: Section B: The Sciences and Engineering, 67*(2-B), 1190.

Glicksohn, J., & Nahari, G. (2007). Interacting personality traits? Smoking as a test case. *European Journal of Personality, 21,* 225–234.

Glisky, E. L. (2007). Changes in cognitive function in human aging. In D. R. Riddle, *Brain aging: Models, methods, and mechanisms.* Boca Raton, FL: CRC Press.

Goffin, R. D., Jelley, R. B., & Wagner, S. H. (2003). Is halo helpful? Effects of inducing halo on performance rating accuracy. *Social Behavior and Personality, 31,* 625–636.

Goin, M. K. (2005). A current perspective on the psychotherapies. *Psychiatric Services, 56,* 255–257.

Gold, P. E., Cahill, L., & Wenk, G. L. (2002). Ginkgo biloba: A cognitive enhancer? *Psychological Science in the Public Interest, 3,* 2–7.

Golden, R. N., Gaynes, B. N., Ekstsrom, R. D., Hamer, R. M., Jacobsen, F. M., Suppes, T., et al. (2005). The efficacy of light therapy in the treatment of mood disorders: A review and meta-analysis of the evidence. *The American Journal of Psychiatry, 162,* 656–662.

Golden, W. L. (2006). Hypnotherapy for anxiety, phobias and psychophysiological disorders. In R. A. Chapman, *The clinical use of hypnosis in cognitive behavior therapy: A practitioner's casebook.* New York: Springer Publishing.

Goldfried, M. R., & Pachankis, J. E. (2007). On the next generation of process research. *Clinical Psychology Review, 27,* 760–768.

Goldstein, S. N. (2006). The exploration of spirituality and identity status in adolescence. *Dissertation Abstracts International: Section B: The Sciences and Engineering, 67*(6-B), 3481.

Goldstone, R. L., & Kersten, A. (2003). Concepts and categorization. In A. F. Healy & R. W. Proctor (Eds.), *Handbook of psychology: Experimental psychology* (Vol. 4). New York: Wiley.

Goleman, D. (1988, January 21). Doctor and patient; physicians may bungle key part of treatment: The medical interview. *The New York Times,* p. B16.

Goleman, D. (1993, July 21). "Expert" babies found to teach others. *The New York Times,* p. C10.

Golimbet, V. E., Alfimova, M. V., Gritsenko, I. K., & Ebstein, R. P. (2007). Relationship between dopamine system genes and extraversion and novelty seeking. *Neuroscience Behavior and Physiology, 37,* 601–606.

Golombok, S., Cook, R., Bish, A., & Murray, C. (1995). Families created by the new reproductive technologies: Quality of parenting and social and emotional development of the children. *Child Development, 66,* 285–298.

Gontier, N. (2008). Genes, brains, and language: An epistemological examination of how genes can underlie human cognitive behavior. *Review of General Psychology, 12,* 170–180.

Gontkovsky, S. T. (2005). Neurobiological bases and neuropsychological correlates of aggression and violence. In J. P. Morgan (Ed.), *Psychology of aggression.* Hauppauge, NY: Nova Science Publishers.

Gontkovsky, S. T., & Beatty, W. W. (2006). Practical methods for the clinical assessment of information processing speed. *International Journal of Neuroscience, 116,* 1317–1325.

Goode, E. (1999, April 13). If things taste bad, "phantoms" may be at work. *The New York Times,* pp. D1–D2.

Goode, E. (2003, January 28). Even in the age of Prozac, some still prefer the couch. *The New York Times,* Section F, p. 1.

Goodman, G., & Quas, J. (2008). Repeated interviews and children's memory: It's more than just how many. *Current Directions in Psychological Science, 17,* 386–390.

Goodman, W. K., Rudorfer, M. V., & Maser, J. D. (2000). *Obsessive-compulsive disorder: Contemporary issues in treatment.* Mahwah, NJ: Lawrence Erlbaum Associates.

Goodwin, R., Costa, P., & Adonu, J. (2004). Social support and its consequences: 'Positive' and 'deficiency' values and their implications for support and self-esteem. *British Journal of Social Psychology, 43,* 465–474.

Goodwin, R. D., & Hamilton, S. P. (2003). Lifetime comorbidity of antisocial personality disorder and anxiety disorders among adults in the community. *Psychiatry Research, 117,* 159–166.

Gooren, L. (2006). The biology of human psychosexual differentiation. *Hormones and Behavior, 50,* 589–601.

Gossop, M., Stewart, D., & Marsden, J. (2008). Attendance at Narcotics Anonymous and Alcoholics Anonymous meetings, frequency of attendance and substance use outcomes after residential treatment for drug dependence: A 5-year follow-up study. *Addiction, 103,* 119–125.

Gotlib, I. H., Krasnoperova, E., Yue, D. N., & Joorman, J. (2004). Attentional biases for negative interpersonal stimuli in clinical depression. *Journal of Abnormal Psychology, 113,* 127–135.

Gottesman, I. I. (1991). *Schizophrenia genesis: The origins of madness.* New York: Freeman.

Gottesman, I. I., & Hanson, D. R. (2005). Human development: Biological and genetic processes. *Annual Review of Psychology, 56,* 263–286.

Gottlieb, D. A. (2004). Acquisition with partial and continuous reinforcement in pigeon autoshaping. *Learning and Behavior, 32,* 321–334.

Gottlieb, D. A. (2006). Effects of partial reinforcement and time between reinforced trials on terminal response rate in pigeon autoshaping. *Behavioural Processes, 72,* 6–13.

Gould, E., Reeves, A. J., Graziano, M. S. A., & Gross, C. G. (1999, October 15). Neurogenesis in the neocortex of adult primates. *Science,* 548–552.

Gould, R. L. (1978). *Transformations.* New York: Simon & Schuster.

Govindarajan, A., Kelleher, R. J., & Tonegawa, S. (2006). A clustered plasticity model of long-term memory engrams. *Nature Reviews Neuroscience, 7,* 575–583.

Gowaty, P. A. (2003). Power asymmetries between the sexes, mate preferences, and components of fitness. In C. B. Travis (Ed.), *Evolution, gender, and rape.* Cambridge, MA: MIT.

Gradinaru, V., Mogri, M., Thompson, K. R., Henderson, J. M., & Deisseroth, K. (2009). Optical deconstruction of Parkinsonian neural circuitry. *Science, 324,* 354–359.

Grady, D., & Altman, L. K. (2008, December 29). Lessons for other smokers in Obama's efforts to quit. *The New York Times,* p. A12.

Graham, C. A., Bancroft, J., & Doll, H. A. (2007). Does oral contraceptive-induced reduction in free testosterone adversely affect the sexuality or mood of women? *Psychoneuroendocrinology, 32,* 246–255.

Graham, S. (1992). Most of the subjects were white and middle class. *American Psychologist 47*(5), 629–639.

Grahek, N. (2007). *Feeling pain and being in pain* (2nd ed.). Cambridge, MA: MIT Press.

Granic, I., Hollenstein, T., & Dishion, T. (2003). Longitudinal analysis of flexibility and reorganization in early adolescence: A dynamic systems study of family interactions. *Developmental Psychology, 39,* 606–617.

Grann, J. D. (2007). Confidence in knowledge past: An empirical basis for a differential decay theory of very long-term memory monitoring. *Dissertation Abstracts International Section A: Humanities and Social Sciences, 67,* 2462.

Grant, A. (2008). Does intrinsic motivation fuel the prosocial fire? Motivational synergy in predicting persistence, performance, and productivity. *Journal of Applied Psychology, 93,* 48–58.

Gray, G. C. (2006). The regulation of corporate violations: Punishment, compliance, and the blurring of responsibility. *British Journal of Criminology, 46,* 875–892.

Graziano, M. S., Taylor, C. S., & Moore, T. (2002). Complex movements evolved by microstimulation of precentral cortex. *Neuron, 34,* 841–851.

Graziano, W. G., Habashi, M. M., Sheese, B. E., & Tobin, R. M. (2007). Agreeableness, empathy, and helping: A person situation perspective. *Journal of Personality and Social Psychology, 93,* 583–599.

Green, B. G., & George, P. (2004). Thermal taste predicts higher responsiveness to chemical taste and flavor. *Chemical Senses, 29,* 617–628.

Green, J., Lynn, S., & Montgomery, G. (2008, January). Gender-related differences in hypnosis-based treatments for smoking: A follow-up meta-analysis. *American Journal of Clinical Hypnosis, 50,* 259–271.

Green, J. S., Henderson, F. R., & Collinge, M. D. (2003). *Prevention and control of wildlife damage: Coyotes.* Lincoln: University of Nebraska, Institute of Agriculture and Natural Resources. Retrieved from http://wildlifedamage.unl.edu/handbook/handbook/carnivor/ca_c51.pdf

Greenberg, G., & Rosenheck, R. (2008). Jail incarceration, homelessness, and mental health: A national study. *Psychiatric Services, 59,* 170–177.

Greenberg, R., & Goldman, E. (2009). Antidepressants, psychotherapy or their combination: Weighing options for depression treatments. *Journal of Contemporary Psychotherapy, 39,* 83–91.

Greenberg, R. M., & Kellner, C. H. (2005). Electroconvulsive therapy: A selected review. *The American Journal of Geriatric Psychiatry, 13,* 268–281.

Greene, J. D., & Paxton, J. M. (2009). Patterns of neural activity associated with honest and dishonest moral decisions. *PNAS Proceedings of the National Academy of Sciences of the United States of America, 106*(30), 12506–12511.

Greene, J. D., Sommerville, R. B., Nystrom, L. E., Darley, J. M., & Cohen, J. D. (2001, September 14). An fMRI investigation of emotional engagement in moral judgment. *Science, 293,* 2105–2108.

Greenfield, S. (2002). Mind, brain and consciousness. *British Journal of Psychiatry, 181,* 91–93.

Greenspan, S. (2006). Functional concepts in mental retardation: Finding the natural essence of an artificial category. *Exceptionality, 14,* 205–224.

Greenwald, A. G., Draine S. C., & Abrams, R. L. (1996, September 20). Three cognitive markers of unconscious semantic activation. *Science, 272,* 1699–1702.

Greenwald, A. G., Nosek, B. A., & Banaji, M. R. (2003). Understanding and using the Implicit Association Test: 1. An improved scoring algorithm. *Journal of Personality and Social Psychology 85,* 197–216.

Greenwald, A. G., Nosek, B. A., & Sriram, N. (2006). Consequential validity of the implicit association test: Comment on Blanton and Jaccard. *American Psychologist, 61,* 56–61.

Greenwald, A., Poehlman, T., Uhlmann, E., & Banaji, M. (2009). Understanding and using the Implicit Association Test: III. Meta-analysis of predictive validity. *Journal of Personality and Social Psychology, 97,* 17–41.

Greer, R. D., Dudek-Singer, J., & Gautreaux, G. (2006). Observational learning. *International Journal of Psychology, 41,* 486–499.

Gregg, J. P., Lit, L., Baron, C. A., Hertz-Picciotto, I., Walker, W., Davis, R. A., et al. (2007). Gene expression changes in children with autism. *Genomics, 12,* 88–97.

Gregory, R. L. (1978). *The psychology of seeing* (3rd ed.). New York: McGraw-Hill.

Gregory, R. L. (2008). Emmert's Law and the moon illusion. *Spatial Vision, 21,* 407–720.

Gregory, S. (1856). *Facts for young women.* Boston.

Grigorenko, E. (2009). Speaking genes or genes for speaking? Deciphering the genetics of speech and language. *Journal of Child Psychology and Psychiatry, 50,* 116–125.

Grigoriadis, S., & Ravitz, P. (2007). An approach to interpersonal psychotherapy for postpartum depression: Focusing on interpersonal changes. *Canadian Family Physician, 53,* 1469–1475.

Grimes, T., & Bergen, L. (2008, April). The epistemological argument against a causal relationship between media violence and sociopathic behavior among psychologically well viewers. *American Behavioral Scientist, 51,* 1137–1154.

Grindstaff, J. S., & Fisher, L. A. (2006). Sport psychology consultants' experience of using hypnosis in their practice: An exploratory investigation. *The Sport Psychologist, 20,* 368–386.

Gronholm, P., Rinne, J. O., Vorobyev, V., & Laine, M. (2005). Naming of newly learned objects: A PET activation study. *Brain Research and Cognitive Brain Research, 14,* 22–28.

Gross, D. M. (2006). *The secret history of emotion: From Aristotle's rhetoric to modern brain science.* Chicago: University of Chicago Press.

Grossmann, T., Striano, T., & Friederici, A. D. (2007). Developmental changes in infants' processing of happy and angry facial expressions: A neurobehavioral study. *Brain and Cognition, 64,* 30–41.

Groves, R. M., Singer, E., Lepkowski, J. M., Heeringa, S. G., & Alwin, D. F. In S. J. House, F. T. Juster, R. L. Kahn, H. Schuman, & E. Singer. (2004). *A telescope on society: Survey research and social science at the University of Michigan and beyond.* Ann Arbor, MI: University of Michigan Press.

Grucza, R., Norberg, K., & Bierut, L. (2009). Binge drinking among youths and young adults in the United States: 1979–2006. *Journal of the American Academy of Child & Adolescent Psychiatry, 48,* 692–702.

Grunwald, T., Boutros, N. N., Pezer, N., von Oertzen, J., Fernandez, G., Schaller, C., & Elger, C. E. (2003). Neuronal substrates of sensory gating within the human brain. *Biological Psychiatry, 15,* 511–519.

Guadagno, R. E., & Cialdini, R. B. (2002). Online persuasion: An examination of gender differences in computer-mediated interpersonal influence [Special issue: Groups and Internet]. *Group Dynamics, 6,* 38–51.

Guastella, A., Mitchell, P., & Dadds, M. (2008, January). Oxytocin increases gaze to the eye region of human faces. *Biological Psychiatry, 63,* 3–5.

Guéguen, N., Marchand, M., Pascual, A., & Lourel, M. (2008). Foot-in-the-door technique using a courtship request: A field experiment. *Psychological Reports, 103,* 529–534.

Guerrero, L., La Valley, A., & Farinelli, L. (2008, October). The experience and expression of anger, guilt, and sadness in marriage: An equity theory explanation. *Journal of Social and Personal Relationships, 25,* 699–724.

Guilleminault, C., Kirisoglu, C., Bao, G., Arias, V., Chan, A., & Li, K. K. (2005). Adult chronic sleepwalking and its treatment based on polysomnography. *Brain, 128* (Pt. 5), 1062–1069.

Guldemond, H., Bosker, R., Kuyper, H., & van der Werf, G. (2007). Do highly gifted students really have problems? [Special issue: Current research on giftedness: International perspectives]. *Educational Research and Evaluation, 13,* 555–568.

Gurin, P. (2006). Informing theory from practice and applied research. *Journal of Social Issues, 62,* 621–628.

Guthrie, R. V. (1998). *Even the rat was white: A historical view of psychology* (2nd ed.). Needham Heights, MA: Allyn & Bacon.

Gutierrez, P. M., Muehlenkamp, J. L., Konick, L. C., & Osman, A. (2005). What role does race play in adolescent suicidal ideation? *Archives of Suicide Research, 9,* 177–192.

Gwynn, M. I., & Spanos, N. P. (1996). Hypnotic responsiveness, nonhypnotic suggestibility, and responsiveness to social influence. In R. G. Kunzendorf, N. P. Spahos, & B. Wallace (Eds.), *Hypnosis and imagination.* Amityville, NY: Baywood.

Haberstick, B. C., Schmitz, S., Young, S. E., & Hewitt, J. K. (2005).Contributions of genes and environments to stability and change in externalizing and internalizing problems during elementary and middle school. *Behavior Genetics, 35,* 381–396.

Hackam, D. G. (2007). Translating animal research into clinical benefit. *British Medical Journal, 334,* 163–1644.

Hadjistavropoulos, T., Craig, K. D., & Fuchs-Lacelle, S. (2004). *Social influences and the communication of pain.* Mahwah, NJ: Lawrence Erlbaum Associates.

Haier, R. J., Colom, R., Schroeder, D. H., Condon, C. A., Tang, C., Eaves, E., et al. (2009). Gray matter and intelligence factors: Is there a neuro-g? *Intelligence, 37,* 136–144.

Haley, W. E., Clair, J. M., & Saulsberry, K. (1992). Family caregiver satisfaction with medical care of their demented relatives. *Gerontologist, 32,* 219–226.

Halford, S. (2006). Collapsing the boundaries? Fatherhood, organization and home-working. *Gender, Work & Organization, 13,* 383–402.

Halkitis, P. (2009). *Methamphetamine addiction: Biological foundations, psychological factors, and social consequences.* Washington, DC: American Psychological Association.

Hall, R. E. (2002). *The Bell Curve*: Implications for the performance of black/white athletes. *Social Science Journal, 39,* 113–118.

Halle, M, (2009, August 4). Can drilling electrodes into your brain help you lose weight? *Daily Mail* (London).

Hallschmid, M., Benedict, C., Born, J., Fehm, H., & Kern, W. (2004). Manipulating central nervous mechanisms of food intake and body weight regulation by intranasal administration of neuropeptides in man. *Physiology and Behavior, 83,* 55–64.

Halpern, D. F. (2005). Psychology at the intersection of work and family: Recommendations for employers, working families, and policy-makers. *American Psychologist, 60,* 397–409.

Halpert, J. (2003, April 28). What do patients want? *Newsweek,* pp. 63–64.

Hamani, Y., Sciaki-Tamir, Y., Deri-Hasid, R., Miller-Pogrund, T., Milwidsky, A., & Haimov-Kochman, R. (2007). Misconceptions about oral contraception pills among adolescents and physicians. *Human Reproduction, 22,* 3078–3083.

Hamann, S. (2001). Cognitive and neural mechanisms of emotional memory. *Trends in Cognitive Sciences, 5,* 394–400.

Hamann, S. B., Ely, T. D., Hoffman, J. M., & Kilts, C. D. (2002). Ecstasy and agony: Activation of human amygdala in positive and negative emotion. *Psychological Science, 13,* 135–141.

Hambleton, R. K. (2006). Psychometric models, test designs and item types for the next generation of educational and psychological tests. In D. Bartram, & R. K. Hambleton, *Computer-based testing and the Internet: Issues and advances.* New York: John Wiley & Sons.

Hamer, D. H., Hu, S., Magnuson, V. L., Hu, N., & Pattatucci, A. M. L. (1993, July 16). A linkage between DNA markers on the X chromo-some and male sexual orientation. *Science, 261,* 321–327.

Hamer, M., Taylor, A., & Steptoe, A. (2006). The effect of acute aerobic exercise on stress related blood pressure responses: A systematic review and meta-analysis. *Biological Psychology, 71,* 183–190.

Hamilton, A. (2009, July 11). Can gaming slow mental decline in the elderly? *Time.* Retrieved from http://www.time.com/time/health/article/0,8599,1909852,00.html

Hamilton, A. C., & Martin, R. C. (2007). Semantic short-term memory deficits and resolution of interference: A case for inhibition? In D. S. Gorfein & C. M. Macleod, *Inhibition in cognition.* Washington, DC: American Psychological Association.

Hamilton, W. L., Biener, L., & Brennan, R. T. (2008). Do local tobacco regulations influence perceived smoking norms? Evidence from adult and youth surveys in Massachusetts. *Health Education Research, 23,* 709–722.

Hammond, C., & Gold, M. (2008). Caffeine dependence, withdrawal, overdose and treatment: A review. *Directions in Psychiatry, 28,* 177–190.

Hammond, D. C. (2007, April). Review of the efficacy of clinical hypnosis with headaches and migraines [Special issue: Evidence-based practice clinical hypnosis—part 1]. *International Journal of Clinical and Experimental Hypnosis 55,* 207–219.

Haney, C., & Zimbardo, P. (2009). Persistent dispositionalism in interactionist clothing: Fundamental attribution error in explaining prison abuse. *Personality and Social Psychology Bulletin, 35,* 807–814.

Hanley, S. J., & Abell, S. C. (2002). Maslow and relatedness: Creating an interpersonal model of self-actualization. *Journal of Humanistic Psychology, 42,* 37–56.

Hannon, E. E., & Johnson, S. P. (2005). Infants use meter to categorize rhythms and melodies: Implications for musical structure learning. *Cognitive Psychology, 50,* 354–377.

Harding, D.J., & Jencks, C. (2003). Changing Attitudes toward premarital sex: Cohort, period, and aging effects. *The Public Opinion Quarterly, 67,* 211–226.

Hardison, D. M. (2006). Review of phonetics and phonology in language comprehension and production: Differences and similarities. *Studies in Second Language Acquisition, 28,* 138–140.

Hardt, J., Sidor, A., Nickel, R., Kappis, B., Petrak, P., & Egle, U. (2008). Childhood adversities and suicide attempts: A retrospective study. *Journal of Family Violence, 23,* 713–718.

Hardy, L. T., (2007). Attachment theory and reactive attachment disorder: theoretical perspectives and treatment implications. *Journal of Child and Adolescent Psychiatric Nursing, 20,* 27–39.

Harlow, H. F., & Zimmerman, R. R. (1959). Affectional responses in the infant monkey. *Science, 130,* 421–432.

Harlow, J. M. (1869). Recovery from the passage of an iron bar through the head. *Massachusetts Medical Society Publication, 2,* 329–347.

Harmon-Jones, E., & Winkielman, P. (2007). *Social neuroscience: Integrating biological and psychological explanations of social behavior.* New York, NY: Guilford Press.

Harold, G. T., Fincham, F. D., Osborne, L. N., & Conger, R. D. (1997). Mom and dad are at it again: Adolescent perceptions of marital conflict and adolescent psychological distress. *Developmental Psychology, 33,* 333–350.

Harper, T. (1978, November 15). It's not true about people 65 or over. *Green Bay Press-Gazette* (Wisconsin), p. D-1.

Hart, B., & Risley, T. R. (1997). Use of language by three-year-old children. Courtesy of Drs.Betty Hart and Todd Risley, University of Kansas.

Hartmann, E. (1967). *The biology of dreaming.* Springfield, IL: Charles C. Thomas Publisher.

Hartung, C. M., & Widiger, T. A. (1998). Gender differences in the diagnosis of mental disorders: Conclusions and controversies of the DSM-IV. *Psychological Bulletin, 123,* 260–278.

Harvard Mental Health Letter (HMHL). (1994, March). Brief psychodynamic therapy—Part I. *Harvard Mental Health Letter,* p. 10.

Harvey, J. H., Wenzel, A., & Sprecher, S. (Eds.). (2004). *The handbook of sexuality in close relationships.* Mahwah, NJ: Lawrence Erlbaum Associates.

Haslam, A., O'Brien, A., Jetten, J., Penna, S., & Vormedal, K. (2005). Taking the strain: Social identity, social support, and the experience of stress. *British Journal of Social Psychology, 44,* 355–370.

Haslam, C., & Lawrence, W. (2004). Health-related behavior and beliefs of pregnant smokers. *Health Psychology, 23,* 486–491.

Hassold, T. J., & Patterson, D. (1999). *Down syndrome: A promising future, together.* New York, NY: Wiley-Liss.

Hastings, R. P., & Oakford, S. (2003). Student teachers' attitudes towards the inclusion of children with special needs. *Educational Psychology, 23,* 87–94.

Hatsopoulos, N. G., & Donoghue, J. P. (2009). The Science of Neural Interface Systems. *Annual Review of Neuroscience, 19,* 245–251.

Hauke, C. (2006). The unconscious: Personal and collective. In R. K. Papadopoulos, *The handbook of Jungian psychology: Theory, practice and applications.* New York: Routledge.

Hauser, M. D. (2000). The sound and the fury: Primate vocalizations as reflections of emotion and thought. In N. L. Wallin & B. Merker (Eds.), *The origins of music.* Cambridge, MA: MIT.

Hauser, M. D., Chomsky, N., & Fitch, W. T. (2002, November, 22). The faculty for language: What is it, who has it, and how did it evolve? *Science, 298,* 1569–1579.

Hausmann, R., Tyson, L. D., & Zahidi, S. (2009). *The Global Gender Gap Report, 2009.* Geneva, Switzerland: World Economic Forum.

Havermans, R. C., Mulkens, S., Nederkoorn, C., & Jansen, A. (2007). The efficacy of cue exposure with response prevention in extinguishing drug and alcohol cue reactivity. *Behavioral Interventions, 22,* 121–135.

Haviland-Jones, J., & Chen, D. (1999, April 17). *Human olfactory perception.* Paper presented at the Association for Chemoreception Sciences, Sarasota, Florida.

Haviland-Jones, J. M., & Wilson, P. J. (2008). A 'nose' for emotion: Emotional information and challenges in odors and semiochemicals. In M. Lewis, J. M. Haviland-Jones, & L. G. Barrett (Eds.), *Handbook of emotions* (3rd ed.). New York: Guilford Press.

Hawkes, Christopher H., & Doty, R. L. (2009). *The neurology of olfaction.* Cambridge, UK: Cambridge University Press.

Hayflick, L. (2007). Biological aging is no longer an unsolved problem. *Annals of the New York Academy of Sciences, 1100,* 1–13.

Haynes, P., Nixon, J. C., & West, J. F. (1990). Time perception and consumer behaviour: Some cross-cultural implications. *International Journal of Consumer Studies, 14,* 14–27.

Hays, P. A. (2008). *Addressing cultural complexities in practice: Assessment, diagnosis, and therapy* (2nd ed.). Washington, DC: American Psychological Association.

Health Pages. (2003, March 13). Just what the doctor ordered. Retrieved from http://www.thehealthpages.com/articles/ar-drord.html

Heath, R. A. (2006). *The Praeger handbook of transsexuality: Changing gender to match mindset.* Westport, CT: Praeger Publishers/ Greenwood Publishing.

Heatherton, T., & Sargent, J. (2009). Does watching smoking in movies promote teenage smoking? *Current Directions in Psychological Science, 18,* 63–67.

Hecht, J. M. (2007). *The happiness myth: Why what we think is right is wrong. A history of what really makes us happy.* New York: HarperSanFrancisco/ HarperCollins.

Hedgepeth, E. (2005). Different lenses, different vision. *School Administrator, 62,* 36–39.

Hedges, D. W., Brown, B. L., Shwalk, D. A., Godfrey, K., & Larcher, A. M. (2007). The efficacy of selective serotonin reuptake inhibitors in adult social anxiety disorder: A meta-analysis of double-blind, placebo-controlled trials. *Journal of Psychopharmacology, 21,* 102–111.

Hegarty, P. (2007). From genius inverts to gendered intelligence: Lewis Terman and the power of the norm [Special issue: Power matters: Knowledge politics in the history of psychology]. *History of Psychology, 10,* 132–155.

Hegarty, P., & Massey, S. (2007). Anti-homosexual prejudice . . . as opposed to what? Queer theory and the social psychology of anti-homosexual attitudes. *Journal of Homosexuality, 52,* 47–71.

Heilman, K. M. (2005). *Creativity and the brain.* New York: Psychology Press.

Heinrichs, R. W. (2005). The primacy of cognition in schizophrenia. *American Psychologist, 60,* 229–242.

Heller, S. (2005). *Freud A to Z.* New York: Wiley.

Helmbold, N., Troche, S. & Rammsayer, T. (2007). Processing of temporal and nontemporal information as predictors of psychometric intelligence: A structural-equation-modeling approach. *Journal of Personality, 75,* 985–1006.

Helmuth, L. (2000, August 25). Synapses shout to overcome distance. *Science, 289,* 1273.

Henderlong, J., & Lepper, M. R. (2002). The effects of praise on children's intrinsic motivation: A review and synthesis. *Psychological Bulletin, 128,* 774–795.

Henderson, J., Kesmodel, U., & Gray, R. (2007). Systematic review of the fetal effects of prenatal binge-drinking. *Journal of Epidemiology and Community Health, 61,* 1069–1073.

Henderson, N. D. (1982). Correlations in IQ for pairs of people with varying degrees of genetic relatedness and shared environment. *Annual Review of Psychology, 33,* 219–243.

Hennig-Fast, K., Meister, F., Frodl, T., Beraldi, A., Padberg, F., Engel, R., et al. (2008). The case of persistent retrograde amnesia following a dissociative fugue: Neuropsychological and neurofunctional underpinnings of loss of autobiographical memory and self-awareness. *Neuropsychologia, 46*(12), 2993–3005.

Henningsen, D. D., Henningsen, M. L., & Eden, J. (2006). Examining the symptoms of group-think and retrospective sensemaking. *Small Group Research, 37,* 36–64.

Henry, D., McClellen, D., Rosenthal, L., Dedrick, D., & Gosdin, M. (2008, February). Is sleep really for sissies? Understanding the role of work in insomnia in the US. *Social Science & Medicine, 66,* 715–726.

Hentschel, U., Smith, G., Draguns, J. G., & Elhers, W. (2004). *Defense mechanisms: Theoretical, research and clinical perspectives.* Oxford, England: Elsevier Science.

Herbenick, D., Reece, M., Sanders, S., Dodge, B., Ghassemi, A., & Fortenberry, J. (2009). Prevalence and characteristics of vibrator use by women in the United States: Results from a nationally representative study. *Journal of Sexual Medicine, 6,* 1857–1866.

Herrán, A., Carrera, M., & Sierra-Biddle, D. (2006). Panic disorder and the onset of agoraphobia. *Psychiatry and Clinical Neurosciences, 60,* 395–396.

Herrington, D. M., & Howard, T. D. (2003). From presumed benefit to potential harm— Hormone therapy and heart disease. *New England Journal of Medicine, 349,* 519–521.

Herrnstein, R. J., & Murray, D. (1994). *The bell curve.* New York: Free Press.

Hertzog, C., Kramer, A., Wilson, R., & Lindenberger, U. (2008). Enrichment effects on adult cognitive development: Can the functional capacity of older adults be preserved and enhanced? *Psychological Science in the Public Interest, 9,* 1–65.

Herzberg, L. (2009). Direction, causation, and appraisal theories of emotion. *Philosophical Psychology, 22,* 167–186.

Heshka, S., Anderson, J. W., Atkinson, R. L., Greenway, F. L., Hill, J. O., Phinney, S. D., et al. (2003). Weight loss with self-help compared with a structured commercial program: A randomized trial. *Journal of the American Medical Association, 289,* 1792–1798.

Hess, M. J., Houg, S., & Tammaro, E. (2007). The experience of four individuals with paraplegia enrolled in an outpatient interdisciplinary sexuality program. *Sexuality and Disability, 25,* 189–195.

Hess, T. M., Hinson, J. T., & Statham, J. A. (2004). Explicit and implicit stereotype activation effects on memory: Do age and awareness moderate the impact of priming? *Psychology and Aging, 19,* 495–505.

Hewitt, B., & Egan, H. W. (2009, February 23). Flight 1549: The right stuff. *People, 71,* pp. 10–14.

Heyman, G. D., & Diesendruck, G. (2002). The Spanish *ser/estar* distinction in bilingual children's reasoning about human psychological characteristics. *Developmental Psychology, 38,* 407–417.

Hibbard, P. (2007, February). A statistical model of binocular disparity. *Visual Cognition, 15,* 149–165.

Hiby, E. F., Rooney, N. J., & Bradshaw, J. W. S. (2004). Dog training methods: Their use, effectiveness and interaction with behaviour and welfare. *Animal Welfare, 13,* 63–69.

Hilarski, C. (2007). Antisocial personality disorder. In B. A. Thyer & J. S. Wodarski, *Social work in mental health: An evidence-based approach.* Hoboken, NJ: John Wiley & Sons.

Hilgard, E. (1992). Disassociation and theories of hypnosis. In E. Fromm & M. E. Nash (Eds.), *Contemporary hypnosis research.* New York: Guilford.

Hill, J. O., Catenacci, V., & Wyatt, H. R. (2005). Obesity: Overview of an epidemic. *Psychiatric Clinics of North America, 28,* 1–23.

Hillix, W. A. (2007). The past, present, and possible futures of animal language research. In D. A. Washburn, *Primate perspectives on behavior and cognition.* Washington, DC: American Psychological Association.

Hirschler, B. (2007, May 1). Doctors test gene therapy to treat blindness. *Reuters,* p. 9.

Hirsh, I. J., & Watson, C. S. (1996). Auditory psychophysics and perception. *Annual Review of Psychology, 47,* 461–484.

Ho, S. M. Y., Saltel, P., Machavoine, J., Rapoport-Hubschman, N., & Spiegel, D. (2004). Cross-cultural aspects of cancer care. In National Institutes of Health and Stanford University School of Medicine, *Cancer, culture, and communication.* New York: Kluwer Academic/Plenum Publishers.

Hobfoll, S. E., Freedy, J. R., Green B. L., & Solomon, S. D. (1996). Coping in reaction to extreme stress: The roles of resource loss and resource availability. In M. Zeidner & N. S. Endler (Eds.), *Handbook of coping: Theory, research, applications.* New York: Wiley.

Hobfoll, S. E., Hall, B. J., & Canetti-Nisim, D. (2007). Refining our understanding of traumatic growth in the face of terrorism: Moving from meaning cognitions to doing what is meaningful. *Applied Psychology: An International Review, 56,* 345–366.

Hobson, J. A. Sleep. (1989) by J. Allan Hobson. New York: W. H. Freeman.

Hobson, J. A. (2005). In bed with Mark Solms? What a nightmare! A reply to Domhoff (2005). *Dreaming, 15,* 21–29.

Hochschild, A. (2001, February). A generation without public passion. *Atlantic Monthly,* pp. 33–42.

Hock, H. S., & Ploeger, A. (2006). Linking dynamical perceptual decisions at different levels of description in motion pattern formation: Psychophysics. *Perception & Psychophysics, 68,* 505–514.

Hoff, E. (2003). Language development in childhood. In R. M. Lerner et al. (Eds.), *Handbook of psychology: Developmental psychology* (Vol. 6). New York: Wiley.

Hoff, E. (2008). *Language development.* New York: Wadsworth.

Hoffer, T. B., Selfa, L., Welch, V., Jr., Williams, K., Hess, M., Friedman, J., et al. (2005, March 8). *Doctorate recipients from United States universities: Summary report 2003.* Chicago: NORC at the University of Chicago.

Hofmann, S. G. (2007). Enhancing exposure-based therapy from a translational research perspective. *Behaviour Research and Therapy, 45,* 1987–2001.

Hofmann, W., Gschwendner, T., Castelli, L., & Schmitt, M. (2008). Implicit and explicit attitudes and interracial interaction: The moderating role of situationally available control resources. *Group Processes & Intergroup Relations, 11,* 69–87.

Hogan, J., Davies, S., & Hogan, R. (2007). Generalizing personality-based validity evidence. In S. M. McPhail, *Alternative validation strategies: Developing new and leveraging existing validity evidence.* Hoboken, NJ: John Wiley & Sons.

Hoge, C. W., & Castro, C. A. (2006, September 2). Post-traumatic stress disorder in UK and US forces deployed to Iraq. *Lancet, 368,* 837.

Hogg, M. A. (2006). Social identity theory. In P. J. Burke, *Contemporary social psychological theories.* Palo Alto, CA: Stanford University Press.

Hogg, M. A., & Hains, S. C. (2001). Intergroup relations and group solidarity: Effects of group identification and social beliefs on depersonalized attraction. In M. A. Hogg & D. Abrams (Eds.), *Intergroup relations: Essential readings.* New York: Psychology Press.

Holden, C. (2003, January 17). Deconstructing schizophrenia. *Science, 299,* 333–335.

Holden, C. (2007, June 29). Embryonic stem cells. Stem cell science advances as politics stall. *Science, 316,* 1825.

Holden, L. M. (2005). Complex adaptive systems: Concept analysis. *Journal of Advanced Nursing, 52,* 651–657.

Holland, J. C., & Lewis, S. (2001). *The human side of cancer: Living with hope, coping with uncertainty.* New York: Quill.

Holler, G. D. (2006). Relations of hypnotic susceptibility, absorption, imagery, sexual fantasy, sexual daydreaming, and social desirability to sexual satisfaction. *Dissertation Abstracts International: Section B: The Sciences and Engineering, 67,* 3453.

Holleran, S., Mehl, M., & Levitt, S. (2009). Eavesdropping on social life: The accuracy of stranger ratings of daily behavior from thin slices of natural conversations. *Journal of Research in Personality, 43,* 660–672.

Hollingworth, H. L. (1943/1990). *Leta Stetter Hollingworth: A biography.* Boston: Anker.

Hollins, K. (2007). Consequences of antenatal mental health problems for child health and development. *Current Opinions on Obstetric Gynecology, 19,* 568–573.

Hollis, K. L. (1997, September). Contemporary research on Pavlovian conditioning: A "new" functional analysis. *American Psychologist, 52,* 956–965.

Hollon, S. D., Thase, M. E., & Markowitz, J. C. (2002). Treatment and prevention of depression. *Psychological Science in the Public Interest, 3,* 39–77.

Holloway, L. (2000, December 16). Chief of New York City schools plans to revamp bilingual study. *The New York Times,* p. A1.

Holmes, A., Yang, R. J., Lesch, K. P., Crawley, J. N., & Murphy, D. L. (2003). Mice lacking the Serotonin Transporter Exhibit 5-HT-sub(1A) receptor-mediated abnormalities in tests for anxiety-like behavior. *Neuropsychopharmacology, 28,* 2077–2088.

Holowka, S., & Pettito, L. A. (2002, August 30). Left hemisphere cerebral specialization for babies while babbling. *Science, 297,* 1515.

Holt, M., & Jahn, R. (2004, March, 26). Synaptic vesicles in the fast lane. *Science, 303,* 1986–1987.

Holy, T. E., Dulac, C., & Meister, M. (2000, September 1). Responses of vomeronasal neurons to natural stimuli. *Science, 289,* 1569–1572.

Hongchun, W., & Ming, L. (2006). About the research on suggestibility and false memory. *Psychological Science (China), 29,* 905–908.

Hopkins, W., & Cantalupo, C. (2008, June). Theoretical speculations on the evolutionary origins of hemispheric specialization. *Current Directions in Psychological Science, 17,* 233–237.

Hopwood, C., Newman, D., Donnellan, M., Markowitz, J., Grilo, C., Sanislow, C., et al. (2009). The stability of personality traits in individuals with borderline personality disorder. *Journal of Abnormal Psychology, 118,* 806–815.

Horinek, D., Varjassyová, A., & Hort, J. (2007). Magnetic resonance analysis of amygdalar volume in Alzheimer's disease. *Current Opinion in Psychiatry, 20,* 273–277.

Horn, J. L. (2002). Selections of evidence, misleading assumptions, and over-simplifications: The political message of *The Bell Curve.* In J. M. Fish (Ed.), *Race and intelligence: Separating science from myth.* Mahwah, NJ: Erlbaum.

Horney, K. (1937). *Neurotic personality of our times.* New York: Norton.

Horton, K. D., Wilson, D. E., Vonk, J., Kirby, S. L., & Nielsen, L. (2005). Measuring automatic retrieval: A comparison of implicit memory, process dissociation, and speeded response procedures. *Acta Psychologica, 119,* 235–263.

Houghtalen, R. P., & Talbot, N. (2007). Dissociative disorders and cognitive disorders. In O. J. Z. Sahler & J. E. Carr, *The behavioral sciences and health care* (2nd rev. and updated ed.). Ashland, OH: Hogrefe & Huber Publishers, 2007.

Howe, C. J. (2002). The countering of overgeneralization. *Journal of Child Language, 29,* 875–895.

Howes, O., & Kapur, S. (2009). The dopamine hypothesis of schizophrenia: Version III—The final common pathway. *Schizophrenia Bulletin, 35,* 549–562.

Howitt, D., & Cramer, D. (2000). *First steps in research and statistics: A practical workbook for psychology students.* Philadelphia: Psychology Press.

Hu, F. B., Li, T. Y., Colditz, G. A., Willett, W. C., & Manson, J. E. (2003). Television watching and other sedentary behaviors in relation to risk of obesity and type 2 diabetes mellitus in women.

Journal of the American Medical Association, 289, 1785–1791.

Hubbard, K., O'Neill, A., & Cheakalos, C. (1999, April 12). Out of control. *People,* pp. 52–72.

Hubel, D. H., & Wiesel, T. N. (2004). *Brain and visual perception: The story of a 25-year collaboration.* New York: Oxford University Press.

Huber, F., Beckmann, S. C., & Herrmann, A. (2004). Means-end analysis: Does the affective state influence information processing style? *Psychology and Marketing, 21,* 715–737.

Hudson, W. (1960). Pictorial depth perception in subcultural groups in Africa. *Journal of Social Psychology, 52,* 183–208.

Hudspeth, A. J. (2000). Hearing. In E. R. Kandel, J. H. Schwartz, & T. M. Jessell (Eds.), *Principles of neural science* (4th ed.). New York: McGraw-Hill.

Hugdahl, K., Thomsen, T., & Ersland, L. (2006). Sex differences in visuo-spatial processing: An fMRI study of mental rotation. *Neuropsychologia, 44,* 1575–1583.

Hugenberg, K., & Sacco, D. (2008). Social categorization and stereotyping: How social categorization biases person perception and face memory. *Social and Personality Psychology Compass, 2,* 1052–1072.

Huijie, T. (2006). The measurement and assessment of mental health: A longitudinal and cross-sectional research on undergraduates, adults and patients. *Psychological Science (China), 29,* 419–422.

Hull, C. L. (1943). *Principles of behavior.* New York: Appleton-Century-Crofts.

Hummer, T. A., & McClintock, M. K. (2009). Putative human pheromone and rostadienone attunes the mind specifically to emotional information. *Hormones and Behavior, 55,* 548–559.

Humphrey, N., Curran, A., & Morris, E. (2007). Emotional intelligence and education: A critical review. *Educational Psychology, 27,* 235–254.

Humphreys, G. W., & Müller, H. (2000). A search asymmetry reversed by figure-ground assignment. *Psychological Science, 11,* 196–200.

Hunt, E. (1994). Problem solving. In R. J. Sternberg (Ed.), *Thinking and problem solving: Handbook of perception and cognition* (2nd ed.). San Diego, CA: Academic Press.

Hunt, E. (2005). Information processing and intelligence: Where we are and where we are going. In R. J. Sternberg & J. E. Pretz, *Cognition and intelligence: Identifying the mechanisms of the mind.* New York: Cambridge University Press.

Hunt, J. S., Seifert, A. L., & Armenta, B. E. (2006). Stereotypes and prejudice as dynamic constructs: Reminders about the nature of intergroup bias from the hurricane Katrina relief efforts. *Analyses of Social Issues and Public Policy (ASAP), 6,* 237–253.

Hunt, M. (1974). *Sexual behaviors in the 1970s.* New York: Dell.

Hurt, C. S., Ganerjee, S., Tunnard, C., Whitehead, D. L., Tsolaki, M., Mecocci, P., et al. (2005). Insight, cognition and quality of life in Alzheimer's disease. *NeuroMed Consortium, Journal of Neurology, Neurosurgery & Psychiatry, 81,* 331–336.

Huston, A. C., Donnerstein, E., Fairchild, H. H., Feshback, N. D., Katz, P., Murray, J. P., et al. (1992). *Big world, small screen: The role of television in American society.* Omaha, NE: University of Nebraska Press.

Hutchinson, S. L., Baldwin, C. K., & Oh, S-S. (2006). Adolescent coping: Exploring adolescents' leisure-based responses to stress. *Leisure Sciences, 28,* 115–131.

Hyde, J. S., Lindberg, S. M., Linn, M. C., Ellis, A. B., & Williams, C. C. (2008). Gender similarities characterize math performance. *Science, 321,* 494–495.

Hyman, R. (1994). Anomaly or artifact? Comments on Bem and Honorton. *Psychological Bulletin, 115,* 19–24.

Hyman, S. E. (2003, September). Diagnosing disorders. *Scientific American,* pp. 96–103.

Iachini, T., & Giusberti, F. (2004). Metric properties of spatial images generated from locomotion: The effect of absolute size on mental scanning. *European Journal of Cognitive Psychology, 16,* 573–596.

Iacoboni, M. (2009, January). Imitation, empathy, and mirror neurons. *Annual Review of Psychology, 60,* 653–670.

Iaria, G., Palermo, L., Committeri, G., & Barton, J. (2009). Age differences in the formation and use of cognitive maps. *Behavioural Brain Research, 196,* 187–191.

Ievers-Landis, C. E., Hoff, A. L., Brez, C., Cancilliere, M. K., McConnell, J., & Kerr, D. (2005). Situational analysis of dietary challenges of the treatment regimen for children and adolescents with phenylketonuria and their primary caregivers. *Journal of Developmental and Behavioral Pediatrics, 26,* 186–193.

Iglesias, A. (2005). Awake-alert hypnosis in the treatment of panic disorder: A case report. *American Journal of Clinical Hypnosis, 47,* 249–257.

Igo, S. E. (2006). Review of A telescope on society: Survey research and social science at the University of Michigan and beyond. *Journal of the History of the Behavioral Sciences, 42,* 95–96.

Ihler, E. (2003). Patient-physician communication. *Journal of the American Medical Association, 289,* 92.

Ikonomidou, C., Bittigau, P., Ishimaru, M. J., Wozniak, D. F., Koch, C., Genz, K., et al. (2000, February 11). Ethanol-induced apoptotic neurodegeneration and fetal alcohol syndrome. *Science, 287,* 1056–1060.

Ilies, R., Arvey, R. D., & Bouchard, T. J., Jr. (2006). Darwinism, behavioral genetics, and organizational behavior: A review and agenda for future research [Special issue: Darwinian perspectives on behavior in organizations]. *Journal of Organizational Behavior, 27,* 96–141.

Imamura, M., & Nakamizo, S. (2006). An empirical test of formal equivalence between Emmert's Law and the size-distance invariance hypothesis. *The Spanish Journal of Psychology, 9*(2), 295–299.

Innocenti, G. M. (2007). Subcortical regulation of cortical development: Some effects of early, selective deprivations. *Progressive Brain Research, 164,* 23–37.

Interlandi, J. (2008, March 3). What addicts need. *Newsweek,* p. 31–16.

International Human Genome Sequencing Consortium (2003). *International Consortium completes Human Genome Project.* Bethesda, MD: National Human Genome Research Institute.

Irwin, M. (2008). Human psychoneuroimmunology: 20 years of discovery. *Brain, Behavior, and Immunity, 22,* 129–139.

Irwin, R. R. (2006). Spiritual development in adulthood: Key concepts and models. In C. Hoare, *Handbook of adult development and learning.* New York: Oxford University Press.

Isacson, O., & Kordower, J. (2008). Future of cell and gene therapies for Parkinson's disease. *Annals of Neurology, 64,* S122–SS138.

Isay, R. A. (1994). *Being homosexual: Gay men and their development.* Lanham, MD: Jason Aronson.

Isbell, L. M., & Tyler, J. M. (2003). Teaching students about in-group favoritism and the minimal groups paradigm. *Teaching of Psychology, 30,* 127–130.

Ishikawa, S., Okajima, I., Matsuoka, H., & Sakano, Y. (2007). Cognitive behavioural therapy for anxiety disorders in children and adolescents: A meta-analysis. *Child and Adolescent Mental Health, 12,* 164–172.

Iversen, S., & Iversen, L. (2007). Dopamine: 50 years in perspective. *Trends in Neurosciences, 30,* 188–193.

Iverson, L. (2000). *The science of marijuana.* Oxford, England: Oxford University Press.

Iverson, P., Kuhl, P. K., Reiko, A. Y., Diesch, E., Tohkura, Y., Ketterman, A., et al. (2003). A perceptual interference account of acquisition difficulties for non-native phonemes. *Cognition, 87,* B47–B57.

Izard, C. E. (1990). Facial expressions and the regulation of emotions. *Journal of Personality and Social Psychology, 58,* 487–498.

Izard, C. E. (1994). Innate and universal facial expressions: Evidence from developmental and cross-

cultural research. *Psychological Bulletin, 115,* 288–299.

Izard, C. E., & Abe, J. A. (2004). Developmental changes in facial expressions of emotions in the strange situation during the second year of life. *Emotion, 4,* 251–265.

Jackson, J. D. (2006). Trauma, attachment, and coping: Pathways to resilience. *Dissertation Abstracts International: Section B: The Sciences and Engineering, 67*(1-B), 547.

Jacob, K. S., Kumar, P. S., Gayathri, K., Abraham, S., & Prince, M. J. (2007). *The diagnosis of dementia in the community* [Special issue: Focus on psychogeriatrics in the developing world]. *International Psychogeriatrics, 19,* 669–678.

Jacobs, J. A., & Gerson, K. (2004). *The time divide: Work, family, and gender inequality.* Cambridge, MA: Harvard University Press.

Jacobs, M., Roesch, S., Wonderlich, S., Crosby, R., Thornton, L., Wilfley, D., et al. (2009). Anorexia nervosa trios: Behavioral profiles of individuals with anorexia nervosa and their parents. *Psychological Medicine, 39,* 451–461.

Jacoby, L. L., Bishara, A. J., Hessels, S., & Hughes, A. (2007). Probabilistic retroactive interference: The role of accessibility bias in interference effects. *Journal of Experimental Psychology: General, 136,* 200–216.

Jaffé, A., Prasad, S. A., & Larcher, V. (2006). Gene therapy for children with cystic fibrosis— Who has the right to choose? *Journal of Medical Ethics, 32,* 361–364.

Jain, S., Mills, P. J., & Von Känel, R. (2007). Effects of perceived stress and uplifts on inflammation and coagulability. *Psychophysiology, 44,* 154–160.

James, H. S., Jr. (2005). Why did you do that? An economic examination of the effect of extrinsic compensation on intrinsic motivation and performance. *Journal of Economic Psychology, 26,* 549–566.

James, W. (1890). *The principles of psychology.* New York: Holt.

Jamieson, G. A. (2007). *Hypnosis and conscious states: The cognitive neuroscience perspective.* New York: Oxford University Press.

Jamison, K. R. (1995a). *An unquiet mind: A memoir of moods and madness.* New York: Knopf.

Janes, A. C., Frederick, B. deB., Merlo-Pich, E., Renshaw, P. F., Evins, A. E., Fava, M., et al. (2009). Brain fMRI reactivity to smoking-related images before and during extended smoking abstinence. *Experimental and Clinical Psychopharmacology, 17*(6), 365–373.

Jang, H., Reeve, J., Ryan, R. M., & Kim, A. (2009, August). Can self-determination theory explain what underlies the productive, satisfying learning experiences of collectivistically oriented Korean students? *Journal of Educational Psychology, 101,* pp. 644–661.

Jang, S. J., You, S. H., & Ahn, S. H. (2007). Neurorehabilitation-induced cortical reorganization in brain injury: A 14-month longitudinal follow-up study. *NeuroRehabilitation, 22,* 117–122.

Janis, I. L. (1997). Groupthink. In R. P. Vecchio, *Leadership: Understanding the dynamics of power and influence in organizations.* Notre Dame, IN: University of Notre Dame Press.

Jarlais, D. C. D., Arasteh, K., & Perlis, T. (2007). The transition from injection to non-injection drug use: Long-term outcomes among heroin and cocaine users in New York City. *Addiction, 102,* 778–785.

Jayson, S. (2008, August 18). More than 50% of college students felt suicidal. *USA Today,* p. 10B.

Jenkins, A. M., Albee, G. W., Paster, V. S., Sue, S., Baker, D. B., Comas-Diaz, L., et al. (2003). Ethnic minorities. In D. K. Freedheim, *Handbook of psychology: History of psychology* (Vol. 1). Hoboken, NJ: John Wiley & Sons.

Jenkins, S. R. (1994). Need for power and women's careers over 14 years: Structural power, job satisfaction, and motive change. *Journal of Personality and Social Psychology, 66,* 155–165.

Jensen, A. R. (2002). Galton's legacy to research on intelligence. *Journal of Biosocial Science, 34,* 145–172.

Jensen, A. R. (2005). Psychometric g and mental chronometry. *Cortex, 41,* 230–231.

Jequier, E. (2002). Pathways to obesity. *International Journal of Obesity and Related Metabolic Disorders, 26,* S12–S17.

Jetten, J., Hornsey, M. J., & Adarves-Yorno, I. (2006). When group members admit to being conformist: The role of relative intragroup status in conformity self-reports. *Personality and Social Psychology Bulletin, 32,* 162–173.

Jha, A. (2006, February 3). Pill could make painful memories a thing of past: Common drug may help to fight post traumatic stress. *The Guardian* (London), p. 15.

Joe, G. W., Flynn, P. M., & Broome, K. M. (2007). Patterns of drug use and expectations in methadone patients. *Addictive Behaviors, 32,* 1640–1656.

Johnson, G. B. (2000). *The living world* (p. 600), Boston: McGraw-Hill.

Johnson, H. D. (2004). Gender, grade and relationship differences in emotional closeness within adolescent friendships. *Adolescence, 39,* 243–255.

Johnson, J. G., Cohen, P., Smailes, E. M., Kasen, S., & Brook, J. S. (2002, March 29). Television viewing and aggressive behavior during adolescence and adulthood. *Science, 295,* 2468–2471.

Johnson, S. P. (2004). Development of perceptual completion in infancy. *Psychological Science, 15,* 769–775.

John-Steiner, V., & Mahn, H. (2003). Sociocultural contexts for teaching and learning. In W. M. Reynolds & G. E. Miller (Eds.), *Handbook of psychology: Educational psychology* (Vol. 7). New York: Wiley.

Johnston, L. D., O'Malley, P. M., & Bachman, J. G. (2003). *Monitoring the future: National results on adolescent drug use: Overview of key findings, 2002.* Bethesda MD: National Institute on Drug Abuse.

Johnston, L. D., O'Malley, P. M., Bachman, J. G., & Schulenberg, J. E. (2007). *Monitoring the future national results on adolescent drug use: Overview of key findings, 2006* (NIH Publication No. 07-6202). Bethesda, MD: National Institute on Drug Abuse.

Johnston, L. D., O'Malley, P. M., Bachman, J. G., & Schulenberg, J. E. (2009). *Monitoring the future national results on adolescent drug use; overview of key findings, 2008* (NIH Publication No. 09-7401). Bethesda, MD: National Institute on Drug Abuse.

Johnston, L. D., O'Malley, P. M., Bachman, J. G., & Schulenberg, J. E. (2009). *Monitoring the future national survey results on drug use: 1975–2008. Volume I: Secondary school students* (NIH Publication No. 09-7402). Bethesda, MD: National Institute on Drug Abuse.

Johnston, M. V. (2004). Clinical disorders of brain plasticity. *Brain and Development, 26,* 73–80.

Jones, A. L. (2006). The contemporary psychoanalyst: Karen Horney's theory applied in today's culture. *PsycCRITIQUES, 51,* 127–134.

Jones, J. E., & Corp, E. S. (2003). Effect of naltrexone on food intake and body weight in Syrian hamsters depends on metabolic status. *Physiology and Behavior, 78,* 67–72.

Jones, J. M. (2007). Exposure to chronic community violence: Resilience in African American children. *Journal of Black Psychology, 33,* 125–149.

Jones, K., Callen, F., Blagrove, M., & Parrott, A. (2008). Sleep, energy and self rated cognition across 7 nights following recreational ecstasy/MDMA use. *Sleep and Hypnosis, 10,* 2–38.

Jones, R. K., Darroch, J. E., & Singh, S. (2005). Religious differentials in the sexual and reproductive behaviors of young women in the United States. *Journal of Adolescent Health, 36,* 279–288.

Jorgensen, G. (2006). Kohlberg and Gilligan: Duet or duel? *Journal of Moral Education, 35,* 179–196.

Joyce, J. (1934). *Ulysses.* New York: Random House.

Julien, R. M (2001). *A primer of drug action* (9th ed.). New York: Freeman.

Jung, C. G. (1961). *Freud and psychoanalysis.* New York: Pantheon.

Jung, J. (2002). *Psychology of alcohol and other drugs: A research perspective.* Thousand Oaks, CA: Sage.

Juster, F. T., Ono, H., & Stafford, F. (2002). *Report on housework and division of labor.* Ann Arbor, MI: Institute for Social Research.

Jylha, M. (2004). Old age and loneliness: Cross-sectional and longitudinal analyses in the Tampere longitudinal study on aging. *Canadian Journal on Aging/La Revue Canadienne du Vieillissement, 23,* 157–168.

Kadosh, R., Henik, A., & Walsh, V. (2009, May). Synaesthesia: Learned or lost? *Developmental Science, 12,* 484–491.

Kagan, J., Snidman, N., Kahn, V., & Towsley, S. (2007). The preservation of two infant temperaments into adolescence. *Monographs of the Society for Research in Child Development, 72,* 1–75.

Kahneman, D., Diener, E., & Schwarz, N. (1998). *Wellbeing: The foundations of hedonic psychology.* New York: Russell Sage Foundation.

Kalb, C. (2001, February 26). DARE checks into rehab. *Newsweek,* pp. 56.

Kalb, C. (2003, May 19). Taking a new look at pain. *Newsweek,* pp. 51–52.

Kaller, C. P., Unterrainer, J. M., Rahm, B., & Halsband, U. (2004). The impact of problem structure on planning: Insights from the Tower of London task. *Cognitive Brain Research, 20,* 462–472.

Kallio, S., & Revonsuo, A. (2003). Hypnotic phenomena and altered states of consciousness: A multilevel framework of description and explanation. *Contemporary Hypnosis, 20,* 111–164.

Kaminski, P., Chapman, B. P., Haynes, S. D., & Own, L. (2005). Body image, eating behaviors, and attitudes toward exercise among gay and straight men. *Eating Behaviors, 6,* 179–187.

Kandel, E. R., Schwartz, J. H., & Jessell, T. M. (Eds.) (2000). *Principles of neural science* (4th ed.). New York: McGraw-Hill.

Kane, M. J., & Engle, R. W. (2002). The role of prefrontal cortex in working-memory capacity, executive attention, and general fluid intelligence: An individual-differences perspective. *Psychonomic Bulletin and Review, 9,* 637–671.

Kanner, A. D., Coyne, J. C., Schaefer, C., & Lazarus, R. S. (1981). Comparison of two modes of stress measurement: Daily hassles and uplifts versus major life events. *Journal of Behavioral Medicine, 4,* 14.

Kantrowitz, B., & Underswood, A. (2007, June 25). The teen drinking dilemma. *Newsweek,* pp. 36–37.

Kaplan, J. R., & Manuck, S. B. (1989). The effect of propranolol on behavioral interactions among adult male cynomolgus monkeys (*Macaca fascicularis*) housed in disrupted social groupings. *Psychosomatic Medicine, 51,* 449–462.

Kaplan, M. S., Huguer, N., McFarland, B. H., & Newsom, J. T. (2007). Suicide among male veterans: A prospective population-based study. *Journal of Epidemiological Community Health, 61,* 619–624.

Kaplan, R .M., & Saccuzzo, D. P. (2001). *Psychological testing: Principles, applications, and issues* (5th ed.). Belmont, CA: Wadsworth/Thomson Learning.

Kara, P., & Boyd, J. (2009, April). A micro-architecture for binocular disparity and ocular dominance in visual cortex. *Nature, 458*(7238), 627–631.

Karaszewski, B. (2008). Sub-neocortical brain: A mechanical tool for creative generation? *Trends in Cognitive Sciences, 12,* 171–172.

Karni, A., Tanne, D., Rubenstein, B. S., Askenasy, J. J. M., & Sagi, D. (1994, July 29). Dependence on REM sleep of overnight improvement of a perceptual skill. *Science, 265,* 679–682.

Kasof, J. (2009, May). Cultural variation in seasonal depression: Cross-national differences in winter versus summer patterns of seasonal affective disorder. *Journal of Affective Disorders, 115,* 79–86.

Kassam, K. S., Gilbert, D. T., Swencionis, J. K., & Wilson, T. D. (2009). Misconceptions of memory: The Scooter Libby effect. *Psychological Science, 20,* 551–552.

Kassel, J. D., Evatt, D. P., Greenstein, J. E., Wardle, M. C., Yates, M. C., & Veilleux, J. C. (2007). The acute effects of nicotine on positive and negative affect in adolescent smokers. *Journal of Abnormal Psychology, 116,* 543–553.

Kassin, S. M. (2005). On the psychology of confessions: Does innocence put innocents at risk? *American Psychologist, 60,* 215–228.

Kaštelan, A., Franciškovic, A., Tanja, M., & Moro, L. (2007). Psychotic symptoms in combat-related post-traumatic stress disorder. *Military Medicine, 172,* 273–277.

Kato, K., & Pedersen, N. L. (2005). Personality and coping: A study of twins reared apart and twins reared together. *Behavior Genetics, 35,* 147–158.

Kato, N. (2009). Neurophysiological mechanisms of electroconvulsive therapy for depression. *Neuroscience Research, 64,* 3–11.

Kato, R., Yokoi, H., Arieta, A. H., Yu, W., & Arai, T. (2009). Mutual adaptation among man and machine by using f-MRI analysis. *Robotics and Autonomous Systems,* 161–166.

Kato, T. (2007). Molecular genetics of bipolar disorder and depression. *Psychiatry and Clinical Neurosciences, 61,* 3–19.

Katsiyannis, A., Zhang, D., & Woodruff, N. (2005). Transition supports to students with mental retardation: An examination of data from the national longitudinal transition study 2. *Education and Training in Developmental Disabilities, 40,* 109–116.

Katz, L., Fotti, S., & Postl, L. (2009). Cognitive-behavioral therapy and dialectical behavior therapy: Adaptations required to treat adolescents. *Psychiatric Clinics of North America, 32,* 95–109.

Katz, M. (2001). The implications of revising Freud's empiricism for drive theory. *Psychoanalysis and Contemporary Thought, 24,* 253–272.

Kaufman, A., Johnson, C., & Liu, X. (2008). A CHC theory-based analysis of age differences on cognitive abilities and academic skills at ages 22 to 90 years. *Journal of Psychoeducational Assessment, 26,* 350–381.

Kaufman, J. C., & Baer, J. (2006). *Creativity and reason in cognitive development.* New York: Cambridge University Press.

Kawasaki, C., Nugent, J. K., Miyashita, H., Miyahara, H., & Brazelton, T. B. (1994). The cultural organization of infants' sleep [Special issue: Environments of birth and infancy]. *Children's Environment, 11,* 135–141.

Kawashima, H., Izaki, Y., & Grace, A. A. (2006). Cooperativity between hippocampal-pre-frontal short-term plasticity through associative long-term potentiation. *Brain Research, 1109,* 37–44.

Kazar, D. B. (2006). Forensic psychology: Did we leave anything out? *PsycCRITIQUES, 51,* 88–97.

Kazdin, A. (2008). Evidence-based treatment and practice: New opportunities to bridge clinical research and practice, enhance the knowledge base, and improve patient care. *American Psychologist, 63,* 146–159.

Kearns, K. P. (2005). Broca's aphasia. In L. L. LaPointe (Ed.), *Aphasia and related neurogenic language disorders* (3rd ed.). New York: Thieme New York.

Keating, D. P., & Clark, L. V. (1980). Development of physical and social reasoning in adolescence. *Developmental Psychology, 16,* 23–30.

Keehn, J. D. (1996). *Master builders of modern psychology: From Freud to Skinner.* New York: New York University Press.

Keillor, J. M., Barrett, A. M., Crucian, G. P., Kortenkamp, S., & Heilman, K. M. (2002). Emotional experience and perception in the absence of facial feedback. *Journal of the International Neuropsychological Society, 8,* 130–135.

Kelley, H. (1950). The warm-cold variable in first impressions of persons. *Journal of Personality and Social Psychology, 18,* 431–439.

Kelly, D., & Tangney, B. (2006). Adapting to intelligence profile in an adaptive educational system. *Interacting with Computers, 18,* pp. 385–409.

Kelly, J. B. (2000). Children's adjustment in conflicted marriage and divorce: A decade review of research. *Journal of the American Academy of Child & Adolescent Psychiatry, 39,* 963–973.

Keltikangas-Järvinen, L., Räikkönen, K., Ekelund, J., & Peltonen, L. (2004). Nature and nurture in novelty seeking. *Molecular Psychiatry, 9,* 308–311.

Kemeny, M. E. (2007). Psychoneuroimmunology. In H. S. Friedman & R. C. Silver, *Foundations of health psychology.* New York: Oxford University Press.

Kempermann, G., & Gage, F. H. (1999, May). New nerve cells for the adult brain. *Scientific American,* pp. 48–53.

Kemps, E., & Tiggemann, M. (2007). Reducing the vividness and emotional impact of distressing autobiographical memories: The importance of modality-specific interference. *Memory, 15,* 412–422.

Kendler, K., Halberstadt, L., Butera, F., Myers, J., Bouchard, T., & Ekman, P. (2008). The similarity of facial expressions in response to emotion-inducing films in reared-apart twins. *Psychological Medicine, 38*(10), 1475–1483.

Kendler, K. S., Gatz, M., & Gardner, C. O. (2006). Personality and major depression. *Archives of General Psychiatry, 63,* 1113–1120.

Kendler, K. S., Gatz, M., & Gardner, C. O. (2006a). Personality and major depression. *Archives of General Psychiatry, 63,* 1113–1120.

Kennedy, J. E. (2004). A proposal and challenge for proponents and skeptics of psi. *Journal of Parapsychology, 68,* 157–167.

Kensinger, E. (2007). Negative emotion enhances memory accuracy: Behavioral and neuroimaging evidence. *Current Directions in Psychological Science, 16,* 213–218.

Kenway, L., & Wilson, M. A. (2001). Temporally structured replay of awake hippocampal ensemble activity during rapid eye movement sleep. *Neuron, 29,* 145–156.

Kesebir, P., & Diener, E. (2008). In pursuit of happiness: Empirical answers to philosophical questions. *Perspectives on Psychological Science, 3,* 117–125.

Kess, J. F., & Miyamoto, T. (1994). *Japanese psycholinguistics.* Amsterdam, Netherlands: John Benjamins.

Kessler, R. C., & Wang, P. S. (2008). The descriptive epidemiology of commonly occurring mental disorders in the United States. *Annual Review of Public Health, 29,* 115–129.

Kettenmann, H., & Ransom, B. R. (2005). *Neuroglia* (2nd ed.). New York: Oxford University Press.

Key, W. B. (2003). Subliminal sexuality: The fountainhead for America's obsession. In T. Reichert & J. Lambaiase (Eds.), *Sex in advertising: Perspectives on the erotic appeal. LEA's communication series.* Mahwah, NJ: Lawrence Erlbaum.

Khazaal, Y., Chatton, A., Claeys, F., Ribordy, F., Zullino, D., & Cabanac, M. (2008). Antipsychotic drug and body weight set-point. *Physiology & Behavior, 95,* 157–160.

Kidd, E., & Lum, J. (2008). Sex differences in past tense overregularization. *Developmental Science, 11,* 882–889.

Kiecolt, J. K. (2003). Satisfaction with work and family life: No evidence of a cultural reversal. *Journal of Marriage and Family, 65,* 23–35.

Kihlstrom, J. F. (2005a). Dissociative disorders. *Annual Review of Clinical Psychology, 1,* 227–253.

Kihlstrom, J. F. (2005b). Is hypnosis an altered state of consciousness or what? Comment. *Contemporary Hypnosis, 22,* 34–38.

Kihlstrom, J. F., Schacter, D. L., Cork, R. C., Hurt, C. A., & Behr, S. E. (1990). Implicit and explicit memory following surgical anesthesia. *Psychological Science, 1,* 303–306.

Kim, D. R., Pesiridou, A., & O'Reardon, J. P. (2009). Transcranial magnetic stimulation in the treatment of psychiatric disorders. *Current Psychiatry Reports, 11,* 447–52.

Kim, H., Clark, D., & Dionne, R. (2009, July). Genetic contributions to clinical pain and analgesia: Avoiding pitfalls in genetic research. *The Journal of Pain, 10,* 663–693.

Kim, K. H., Relkin, N. R., Lee, K. M., & Hirsch, J. (1997, July 10). Distinct cortical areas associated with native and second languages. *Nature, 388,* 171–174.

Kim, N. (2008). The moon illusion and the size-distance paradox. In Cummins-Sebree, S., Riley, M. A., & Shockley, K. (Eds.) *Studies in perception and action IX: Fourteenth International Conference on Perception and Action.* Mahwah, NJ: Lawrence Erlbaum Associates.

Kim, S-E., Kim, J-W, & Kim, J-J. (2007). The neural mechanism of imagining facial affective expression. *Brain Research, 1145,* 128–137.

Kimbrel, N. A. (2007). A model of the development and maintenance of generalized social phobia. *Clinical Psychological Review, 8,* 69–75.

Kim-Cohen, J., Caspi, A., & Moffitt, T. E. (2003). Prior juvenile diagnoses in adults with mental disorder: Developmental follow-back of a prospective-longitudinal cohort. *Archives of General Psychiatry, 60,* 709–717.

Kim-Cohen, J., Moffitt, T. E., Taylor, A., Pawlby, S. J., & Caspi, A. (2005). Maternal depression and children's antisocial behavior: Nature and nurture effects. *Archives of General Psychiatry, 62,* 173–181.

King-Casas, B., Sharp, C., Lomax-Bream, L., Lohrenz, T., Fonagy, P., & Montague, P. R. (2008, August, 8). The rupture and repair of cooperation in borderline personality disorder. *Science, 321,* 806–810.

Kirk, E. P., Jacobsen, D. J., Gibson, C., Hill, J. O., & Donnelly, J. E. (2003). Time course for changes in aerobic capacity and body composition in overweight men and women in response to long-term exercise: The Midwest exercise trial (MET). *International Journal of Obesity, 27,* 912–919.

Kirk, K. M., Bailey, J. M., & Martin, N. G. (2000). Etiology of male sexual orientation in an Australian twin sample. *Psychology, Evolution & Gender, 2,* 301–311.

Kirsch, I., & Braffman, W. (2001). Imaginative suggestibility and hypnotizability. *Current Directions in Psychological Science, 10,* 57–61.

Kirsch, I., Lynn, S. J., Vigorito, M., & Miller, R. R. (2004). The role of cognition in classical and operant conditioning. *Journal of Clinical Psychology, 60,* 369–392.

Kirschenbaum, H. (2004). Carl Rogers's life and work: An assessment on the 100th anniversary of his birth. *Journal of Counseling and Development, 82,* 116–124.

Kirschenbaum, H., & Jourdan, A. (2005). The current status of Carl Rogers and the person-centered approach. *Psychotherapy: Theory, Research, Practice, Training, 42,* 37–51.

Kish, S., Fitzmaurice, P., Boileau, I., Schmunk, G., Ang, L., Furukawa, Y., et al. (2009). Brain serotonin transporter in human methamphetamine users. *Psychopharmacology, 202,* 649–661.

Kiss, A. (2004). Does gender have an influence on the patient-physician communication? *Journal of Men's Health and Gender, 1,* 77–82.

Kleinman, A. (1996). How is culture important for DSM-IV? In J. E Mezzich, A. Kleinman, H. Fabrega, Jr., & D. L. Parron (Eds.), *Culture and psychiatric diagnosis: A DSM-IV perspective.* Washington, DC: American Psychiatric Press.

Klötz, F., Garle, M., & Granath, F. (2006). Criminality among individuals testing positive for the presence of anabolic androgenic steroids. *Archives of General Psychiatry, 63,* 1274–1279.

Kluck, A. (2008). Family factors in the development of disordered eating: Integrating dynamic and behavioral explanations. *Eating Behaviors, 9,* 471–483.

Kluger, J. (2001, April 2). Fear not! *Time,* pp. 51–62.

Kluger, J. (2006, December 4). Why we worry about the things we shouldn't and ignore the things we should. *Time,* pp. 64–71.

Klump, K., & Culbert, K. (2007). Molecular genetic studies of eating disorders: Current status and future directions. *Current Directions in Psychological Science, 16,* 37–41.

Knight, S. C., & Meyer, R. G. (2007). Forensic hypnosis. In A. M. Goldstein, *Forensic psychology: Emerging topics and expanding roles.* Hoboken, NJ: John Wiley & Sons.

Knoblich, G., & Sebanz, N. (2006). The social nature of perception and action. *Current Directions in Psychological Science, 15,* 99–111.

Kobayashi, F., Schallert, D. L., & Ogren, H. A. (2003). Japanese and American folk vocabularies for emotions. *Journal of Social Psychology, 143,* 451–478.

Koch, C., & Greenfield, S. (2007, October.) How does consciousness happen? *Scientific American,* pp. 76–83.

Kohlberg, L. (1984). *The psychology of moral development: Essays on moral development* (Vol. 2). San Francisco: Harper & Row.

Kohlberg, L., & Ryncarz, R. A. (1990). Beyond justice reasoning: Moral development and consideration of a seventh stage. In C. N. Alexander & E. J. Langer (Eds.), *Higher stages of human development: Perspectives on adult growth.* New York: Oxford University Press.

Kohler, C. G., Turner, T., Stolar, N. M., Bilker, W. B., Brensinger, C. M., Gur, R. E., et al. (2004). Differences in facial expressions of four universal emotions. *Psychiatry Research, 128,* 235–244.

Köhler, W. (1927). *The mentality of apes.* London: Routledge & Kegan Paul.

Kojima, M., & Kangawa, K. (2008). Structure and function of ghrelin. *Results & Problems in Cell Differentiation, 46,* 89–115.

Kolata, G. (2002, December 2). With no answers on risks, steroid users still say "yes." *The New York Times,* p. 1A.

Kolb, B., Gibb, R., & Robinson, T. E. (2003). Brain plasticity and behavior. *Current Directions in Psychological Science, 12,* 1–5.

Konig, R. (2005). Introduction: Plasticity, learning, and cognition. In R. Konig., P. Heil., E. Budinger & H. Scheich (Eds.), *The auditory cortex: A synthesis of human and animal research.* Mahwah, NJ: Lawrence Erlbaum Associates.

Koocher, G. P., Norcross, J. C., & Hill, S. S. (2005). *Psychologists' desk reference* (2nd ed.). New York: Oxford University Press.

Kopelman, M. D., & Fleminger, S. (2002). Experience and perspectives on the classification of organic mental disorders. *Psychopathology, 35,* 76–81.

Koper, R. J., & Jaasma, M. A. (2001). Interpersonal style: Are human social orientations guided by generalized interpersonal needs? *Communications Reports, 14,* 117–129.

Koplewicz, H. (2002). *More than moody: Recognizing and treating adolescent depression.* New York: Putnam.

Korecka, J. A., Verhaagen, J., & Hol, E. M. (2007). Cell-replacement and gene-therapy strategies for Parkinson's and Alzheimer's disease. *Regenerative Medicine, 2,* 425–426.

Kosambi, D. D. (1967). The Vedic "Five Tribes." *American Oriental Society, 14,* 5–12.

Kosfeld, M., Heinrich, M., Zak, P. J., Fischbacher, U., & Fehr, E. (2005, June 2). Oxytocin increases trust in humans. *Nature, 435,* 673–676.

Kosslyn, S. M. (2005). Mental images and the brain. *Cognitive Neuropsychology, 22,* 333–347.

Kosslyn, S. M., Cacioppo, J. T., Davidson, R. J., Hugdahl, K., Lovallo, W. R., Spiegel, D., et al. (2002). Bridging psychology and biology. *American Psychologist, 57,* 341–351.

Kotre, J., & Hall, E. (1990). *Seasons of life.* Boston: Little, Brown.

Kounios, J., Fleck, J. I., Green, D. L., Payne, L., Stevenson, J. L., Bowden, E. M., et al. (2008). The origins of insight in resting-state brain activity. *Neuropsychologia, 46,* 281–291.

Kovacs, A. M., & Mehler, J. (2009, July 31). Flexible learning of multiple speech structures in bilingual infants. *Science, 325,* 611–612.

Kovelman, I., Baker, S .A., & Petitto, L. A. (2008). Bilingual and monolingual brains compared: A functional magnetic resonance imaging investigation of synatictic processing and a possible "neural signature" of bilingualism. *Journal of Cognitive Neuroscience, 20*(1), 153–169.

Kovelman, I., Shalinsky, M.H., Berens, M.S., &, Petitto, L.A. (2008). Shining new light on the brain's "bilingual signature": A functional Near Infrared Spectroscopy investigation of semantic processing. *Neuroimage, 39,* 1457–1471.

Kowert, P. A. (2002). *Groupthink or deadlock: When do leaders learn from their advisors? SUNY Series on the presidency.* Albany: State University of New York Press.

Kozaric-Kovacic, D., & Borovecki, A. (2005). Prevalence of psychotic comorbidity in combat-related post- traumatic stress disorder. *Military Medicine, 170,* 223–226.

Kozulin, A., Gindis, B., Ageyev, V. S., & Miller, S. M. (2003). *Vygotsky's educational theory in cultural context.* New York: Cambridge University Press.

Kramer, P. (1993). *Listening to Prozac.* New York: Viking.

Kreher, D., Holcomb, P., Goff, D., & Kuper-berg, G. (2008). Neural evidence for faster and further automatic spreading activation in schizophrenic thought disorder. *Schizophrenia Bulletin, 34,* 473–482.

Kreuger, A. (2007). Are we having fun yet? Categorizing and evaluating changes in time allocation. *Brookings Papers on Economic Activity* (Vol. 2), *38,* 193–218.

Krijn, M., Emmelkamp, P. M. G., Olafsson, R. P., & Biemond, R. (2004). Virtual reality exposure therapy of anxiety disorders: A review. *Clinical Psychology Review, 24,* 259–281.

Krueger, K., & Dayan, P. (2009). Flexible shaping: How learning in small steps helps. *Cognition, 110,* 380–394.

Krueger, R. G., Hicks, B. M., & McGue, M. (2001). Altruism and antisocial behavior: Independent tendencies, unique personality correlates, distinct etiologies. *Psychological Science, 12,* 397–402.

Krull, D. S., & Anderson, C. A. (1997). The process of explanation. *Current Directions in Psychological Science, 6,* 1–5.

Krusemark, E., Campbell, W., & Clementz, B. (2008). Attributions, deception, and event related potentials: An investigation of the self-serving bias. *Psychophysiology, 45,* 511–515.

Kübler-Ross, E. (1969). *On death and dying.* New York: Macmillan.

Kubovy, M., Epstein, W., & Gepshtein, S. (2003). Foundations of visual perception. In A. F. Healy, & R. W. Proctor (Eds.). *Handbook of psychology: Experimental psychology* (Vol. 4). New York: Wiley.

Kuo, L. J. (2007). Effects of bilingualism on development of facets of phonological competence (China). *Dissertation Abstracts International Section A: Humanities and Social Sciences, 67* (11-A), 4095.

Kuppens, P., Ceulemans, E., Timmerman, M. E., Diener, E., & Kim-Prieto, C. (2006). Universal intracultural and intercultural dimensions of the recalled frequency of emotional experience. *Journal of Cross Cultural Psychology, 37,* 491–515.

Kuriyama, K., Stickgold, R., & Walker, M. P. (2004). Sleep-dependent learning and motor-skill complexity. *Learning and Memory, 11,* 705–713.

Kuther, T. L. (2003). *Your career in psychology: Psychology and the law.* New York: Wadsworth.

Kvavilashvili, L., & Fisher, L. (2007). Is time-based prospective remembering mediated by self-initiated rehearsals? Role of incidental cues, ongoing activity, age, and motivation. *Journal of Experimental Psychology: General, 136,* 112–132.

Kwon, P., & Laurenceau, J. P. (2002). A longitudinal study of the hopelessness theory of depression: Testing the diathesis-stress model within a differential reactivity and exposure framework [Special issue: Reprioritizing the role of science in a realistic version of the scientist-practitioner model]. *Journal of Clinical Psychology, 50,* 1305–1321.

Laas, I. (2006). Self-actualization and society: A new application for an old theory. *Journal of Humanistic Psychology, 46,* 77–91.

LaBar, K. (2007). Beyond fear: Emotional memory mechanisms in the human brain. *Current Directions in Psychological Science, 16,* 173–177.

Lacerda, F., von Hofsten, C., & Heimann, M. (2001). *Emerging cognitive abilities in early infancy.* Mahwah, NJ: Lawrence Erlbaum Associates.

Laederach-Hofmann, K., & Messerli-Buergy, N. (2007). Chest pain, angina pectoris, panic disorder, and Syndrome X. In J. Jordan, B. Barde & A. M. Zeiher, *Contributions toward evidence-based psychocardiology: A systematic review of the literature.* Washington, DC: American Psychological Association.

Lagacé-Séguin, D. G., & d'Entremont, M. L. (2006). The role of child negative affect in the relations between parenting styles and play. *Early Child Development and Care, 176,* 461–477.

Lahti, J., Räikkönen, K., Ekelund, J., Peltonen, L., Raitakari, O. T., & Keltikangas-Järvinen, L. (2005). Novelty seeking: Interaction between parental alcohol use and dopamine D4 receptor gene exon III polymorphism over 17 years. *Psychiatric Genetics, 15,* 133–139.

Laing, R. D., & Szasz, T. (2004). "Knowing what ain't so." *Psychoanalytic Review, 91,* 331–346.

Laird, J. D., & Bressler, C. (1990). William James and the mechanisms of emotional experience. *Personality and Social Psychology Bulletin, 16,* 636–651.

Lakhan, S., & Vieira, K. (2009, May 15). Schizophrenia pathophysiology: Are we any closer to a complete model? *Annals of General Psychiatry, 8.*

Lal, S. (2002). Giving children security: Mamie Phipps Clark and the racialization of child psychology. *American Psychologist, 57,* 20–28.

Lamal, P. A. (1979). College students' common beliefs about psychology. *Teaching of Psychology, 6,* 155–158.

Lamb, M. E., & Garretson, M. E. (2003). The effects of interviewer gender and child gender on the informativeness of alleged child sexual abuse victims in forensic interviews. *Law and Human Behavior, 27,* 157–171.

Lamborn, S. D., & Groh, K. (2009). A four-part model of autonomy during emerging adulthood: Associations with adjustment. *International Journal of Behavioral Development, 33,* 393–401.

Lane, K. A., Banaji, M. R., Nosek, B. A., & Greenwald, A. G. (Eds.). (2007). Understanding and using the implicit association test: IV: What we know (so far) about the method. In B. Wittenbrink & N. Schwarz, *Implicit measures of attitudes.* New York: Guilford Press.

Lane, S. D., Cherek, D. R., & Tcheremissine, O. V. (2007). Response perseveration and adaptation in heavy marijuana-smoking adolescents. *Addictive Behaviors, 32,* 977–990.

Lang, A. J., Sorrell, J. T., & Rodgers, C. S. (2006). Anxiety sensitivity as a predictor of labor pain. *European Journal of Pain, 10,* 263–270.

Langan-Fox, J., & Grant, S. (2006). The Thematic Apperception Test: Toward a standard measure of the big three motives. *Journal of Personality Assessment, 87,* 277–291.

Langdridge, D., & Butt, T. (2004). The fundamental attribution error: A phenomenological critique. *British Journal of Social Psychology, 43,* 357–369.

Langreth, R. (2000, May 1). Every little bit helps: How even moderate exercise can have a big impact on your health. *The Wall Street Journal,* p. R5.

Lankov, A. (2004). The dawn of modern Korea: Changes for better or worse. *The Korea Times,* p. A1.

Lanza, S. T., & Collins, L. M. (2002). Pubertal timing and the onset of substance use in females during early adolescence. *Prevention Science, 3,* 69–82.

Laqueur, T. W. (2003). *Solitary sex: A cultural history of masturbation.* New York: Zone.

Larsen, R. J., & Buss, D. M. (2006). *Personality psychology: Domains of knowledge about human nature with PowerWeb* (2nd ed.). New York: McGraw-Hill.

Lascaratos, G., Ji, D., & Wood, J. P. (2007). Visible light affects mitochondrial function and induces neuronal death in retinal cell cultures. *Vision Research, 47,* 1191–1201.

Latané, B., & Darley, J. M. (1970). *The unresponsive bystander: Why doesn't he help?* New York: Appleton-Century-Crofts.

Laugharne, J., Janca, A., & Widiger, T. (2007). Posttraumatic stress disorder and terrorism: 5 years after 9/11. *Current Opinion in Psychiatry, 20,* 36–41.

Lavelli, M., & Fogel, A. (2005). Developmental changes in the relationship between the infant's attention and emotion during early face-to-face communication. *Developmental Psychology, 41,* 265–280.

Laven, A. (2008). Freshmen college student mental health and their resource usage. *Dissertation Abstracts International Section A: Humanities and Social Sciences, 69,* 136.

Lavenex, P., & Lavenex, P. (2009). Spatial memory and the monkey hippocampus: Not all space is created equal. *Hippocampus, 19,* 8–19.

Lazarus, A. A. (1997). *Brief but comprehensive psychotherapy: The multimodal way.* New York: Springer.

Lazarus, R. S. (1995). Emotions express a social relationship, but it is an individual mind that creates them. *Psychological Inquiry, 6,* 253–265.

Leahy, R. L. (2003). *Roadblocks in cognitive-behavioral therapy: Transforming challenges into opportunities for change.* New York: Guilford Press.

Leary, C., Kelley, M., Morrow, J., & Mikulka, P. (2008). Parental use of physical punishment as related to family environment, psychological well-being, and personality in undergraduates. *Journal of Family Violence, 23,* 1–7.

Leckman, J. F., & King, R. A. (2007). A developmental perspective on the controversy surrounding the use of SSRIs to treat pediatric depression. *American Journal of Psychiatry, 164,* 1304–1306.

Lee, A., Isaac, M. & Janca, A. (2007). Posttraumatic stress disorder and terrorism. In A. Monat, R. S. Lazarus & G. Reevy (Eds.), *The Praeger handbook on stress and coping* (Vol. 1). Westport, CT: Praeger Publishers/Greenwood Publishing Group.

Lee, A. Y., & Aaker, J. L. (2004). Bringing the frame into focus: The influence of regulatory fit on processing fluency and persuasion. *Journal of Personality and Social Psychology, 86,* 205–218.

Lee, D., Kleinman, J., & Kleinman, A. (2007). Rethinking depression: An ethnographic study of the experiences of depression among Chinese. *Harvard Review of Psychiatry, 15,* 1–8.

Lee, H. J., & Kwon, S. M. (2003). Two different types of obsession: Autogenous obsessions and reactive obsessions. *Behaviour Research & Therapy, 41,* 11–29.

Lee, H. J., Kwon, S. M., Kwon, J. S., & Telch, M. J. (2005). Testing the autogenous reactive model of obsessions. *Depress Anxiety, 21,* 118–129.

Lee-Chai, A. Y., & Bargh, J. A. (Eds.). (2001). *The use and abuse of power: Multiple perspectives on the causes of corruption.* Philadelphia, PA: Psychology Press.

Lee-Chiong, T. L. (2006). *Sleep: A comprehensive handbook.* New York: Wiley-Liss.

Lefaucheur, J. P., Brugieres, P., Menard-Lefaucheur, I., Wendling, S., Pommier, M., & Bellivier, F. (2007). The value of navigation-guided rTMS for the treatment of depression: An illustrative case. *Neurophysiologic Clinics, 37,* 265–271.

Lehar, S. (2003). *The world in your head: A gestalt view of the mechanism of conscious experience.* Mahwah, NJ: Lawrence Erlbaum Associates.

Lehman, D. R., & Taylor, S. E. (1988). Date with an earthquake: Coping with a probable, unpredictable disaster. *Personality and Social Psychology Bulletin, 13,* 546–555.

Lehrman, S. (2007). Going beyond X and Y. *Scientific American,* pp. 40–41.

Leib, J. R., Gollust, S. E., Hull, S. C., & Wilfond, B. S. (2005). Carrier screening panels for Ashkenazi Jews: Is more better? *Genetic Medicine, 7,* 185–190.

Leibel, R. L., Rosenbaum, M., & Hirsch, J. (1995, March 9). Changes in energy expenditure resulting from altered body. *New England Journal of Medicine, 332,* 621–628.

Leiblum, S. R., & Chivers, M. L. (2007). Normal and persistent genital arousal in women: New perspectives. *Journal of Sex & Marital Therapy, 33,* 357–373.

Leigh, J. H., Zinkhan, G. M. & Swaminathan, V. (2006). Dimensional relationships of recall and recognition measures with selected cognitive and affective aspects of print ads. *Journal of Advertising, 35,* 105–122.

Leiter, S., & Leiter, W. M. (2003). *Affirmative action in antidiscrimination law and policy: An overview and synthesis. SUNY series in American constitutionalism.* Albany: State University of New York Press.

Leitner, L. M. (2007). Diversity issues, postmodernism, and psychodynamic therapy. *PsycCRITIQUES, 52,* no pagination specified.

Lemay, E., & Clark, M. (2008). How the head liberates the heart: Projection of communal responsiveness guides relationship promotion. *Journal of Personality and Social Psychology, 94,* 647–671.

Lemay, E. P., Jr., Clark, M. S., & Feeney, B. C. (2007). Projection of responsiveness to needs and the construction of satisfying communal relationships. *Journal of Personality and Social Psychology, 92,* 834–853.

Lemonick, M. D. (2000, December 11). Downey's downfall. *Time,* p. 97.

Lenhart, A. (2009, January 14). *Adults and social network websites.* Washington, DC: Pew Internet & American Life Project.

Lenzenweger, M. F., & Dworkin, R. H. (Eds.). (1998). *The origins and development of schizophrenia: Advances in experimental psychopathology.* Washington, DC: American Psychological Association.

Leo, R. J., & Latif, T. (2007). Repetitive transcranial magnetic stimulation (rTMS) in experimentally induced and chronic neuropathic pain: A review. *The Journal of Pain, 8,* 453–459.

Leonard, E. (2009, May 18). Kirstie Alley: I've let myself go. *People,* p. 50.

Lepage, J. F., & Theoret, H. (2007). The mirror neuron system: grasping others' actions from birth? *Developmental Science, 10,* 513–523.

Leppänen, J. M., Moulson, M. C., Vogel-Farley, V. K. & Nelson, C. A. (2007). An ERP study of emotional face processing in the adult and infant brain. *Child Development, 78,* 232–245.

Lepper, M. R., Corpus, J. H., & Iyengar, S. S. (2005). Intrinsic and extrinsic motivational orientations in the classroom: Age differences and academic correlates. *Journal of Educational Psychology, 97,* 184–196.

Leung, F. K. S. (2002). Behind the high achievement of East Asian students [Special issue: Achievements in mathematics and science in an international context]. *Education Research and Evaluation, 8,* 87–108.

LeVay, S. (1993). *The sexual brain.* Cambridge, MA: MIT.

Levi, A., Chan, K. K., & Pence, D. (2006). Real men do not read labels: The effects of masculinity and involvement on college students' food decisions. *Journal of American College Health, 55,* 91–98.

Levin, B. E., (2006). Metabolic sensing neurons and the control of energy homeostasis. *Physiology & Behavior, 89,* 486–489.

Levin, R. J. (2007). Sexual activity, health and well-being—the beneficial roles of coitus and masturbation. *Sexual and Relationship Therapy, 22,* 135–148.

Levin, R., & Nielsen, T. (2009, April). Nightmares, bad dreams, and emotion dysregulation: A review and new neurocognitive model of dreaming. *Current Directions in Psychological Science, 18,* 84–88.

Levine, J. M., & Moreland, R. L. (2006). Small groups: An overview. In J. M. Levine & R. L. Moreland (Eds.), *Small groups.* New York: Psychology Press.

Levine, S. Z., & Rabinowitz, J. (2007). Revisiting the 5 dimensions of the Positive and Negative Syndrome Scale. *Journal of Clinical Psychopharmacology, 27,* 431–436.

Levinson, D. (1992). *The seasons of a woman's life.* New York: Knopf.

Levinson, D. J. (1990). A theory of life structure development in adulthood. In C. N. Alexander & E. J. Langer (Eds.), *Higher stages of human development: Perspectives on adult growth.* New York: Oxford University Press.

Levy, B. (1996). Improving memory in old age through implicit self-stereotyping. *Journal of Personality and Social Psychology, 71,* 1092–1107.

Levy, B. R., & Myers, L. M. (2004). Preventive health behaviors influenced by self-perceptions of aging. *Preventive Medicine: An International Journal Devoted to Practice and Theory, 39,* 625–629.

Levy, B. R., Slade, M. D., Kunkel, S. R., & Kasl, S. V. (2002). Longevity increased by positive self-perceptions of aging. *Journal of Personality & Social Psychology, 83,* 261–270.

Lewin, T. (2003, December 22). For more people in their 20s and 30s, going home is easier because they never left. *The New York Times,* p. A27.

Lewinsohn, P. M., & Essau, C. A. (2002). Depression in adolescents. In I. H. Gotlib & C. L. Hammen (Eds.), *Handbook of depression.* New York: Guilford Press.

Lewinsohn, P. M., Petit, J. W., Joiner, T. E., Jr., & Seeley, J. R. (2003). The symptomatic expression of major depressive disorder in adolescents and young adults. *Journal of Abnormal Psychology, 112,* 244–252.

Li, J. (2005). Mind or virtue: Western and Chinese beliefs about learning. *Current Directions in Psychological Science, 14,* 190–194.

Li, J., Wang, L., & Fischer, K. W. (2004). The organization of Chinese shame concepts. *Cognition and Emotion, 18,* 767–797.

Li, M. D., Cheng, R., Ma, J. Z., & Swan, G. E. (2003). A meta-analysis of estimated genetic and environmental effects on smoking behavior in male and female adult twins. *Addiction, 98,* 23–31.

Li, M. D., Lou, X., Chen, G., Ma, J. Z., & Elston, R. C. (2008). Gene-gene interactions among CHRNA4, CHRNB2, BDNF, and NTRK2 in nicotine dependence. *Biological Psychiatry, 64,* 951–957.

Li, T-K., Volkow, N. D., & Baler, R. D. (2007). The biological bases of nicotine and alcohol co-addiction. *Biological Psychiatry, 61,* 1–3.

Li, X., Wang, M., Poliakoff, E., & Luo, Y. (2007). Attention to threat in high and low trait-anxious individuals: A study using extremely threatening pictorial cues. *Perceptual and Motor Skills, 104,* 1097–1106.

Liang, K. A. (2007). Acculturation, ambivalent sexism, and attitudes toward women who engage in premarital sex among Chinese American young adults. *Dissertation Abstracts International: Section B: The Sciences and Engineering, 67*(10-B), 6065.

Lidz, J., & Gleitman, L. R. (2004). Argument structure and the child's contribution to language learning. *Trends in Cognitive Sciences, 8,* 157–161.

Lieberman, M. D. (2007). Social cognitive neuroscience: A review of core processes. *Annual Review of Psychology, 58,* 259–289.

Lieberman, M. D., Hariri, A., Jarcho, J. M., Eisenberger, N. I., & Bookheimer, S. Y. (2005). An fMRI investigation of race-related amygdala activity in African-American and Caucasian-American individuals. *Nature Neuroscience, 8,* 720–722.

Lien, Y-W., Chu, R-L., Jen, C-H., & Wu, C-H. (2006). Do Chinese commit neither fundamental attribution error nor ultimate attribution error? *Chinese Journal of Psychology, 48,* 163–181.

Lilienfeld, S. O. (2007). Psychological treatments that cause harm. *Perspectives on Psychological Science, 2,* 53–58.

Lin, C-H., & Lin, H-M. (2007). What price do you ask for the 'extra one'? A social value orientation perspective. *Social Behavior and Personality, 35,* 9–18.

Lin, Y. Y., Chen, W. T., Liao, K. K., Yeh, T. C., Wu, Z. Z., & Ho, L. T. (2005). Hemispheric balance in coding speech and non-speech sounds in Chinese participants. *Neuroreport, 16,* 469–473.

Lindblad, F., Lindahl, M., & Theorell, T. (2006). Physiological stress reactions in 6th and 9th graders during test performance. *Stress and Health: Journal of the International Society for the Investigation of Stress, 22,* 189–195.

Lindemann, O., & Bekkering, H. (2009). Object manipulation and motion perception: Evidence of an influence of action planning on visual processing. *Journal of Experimental Psychology: Human Perception and Performance, 35,* 1062–1071.

Lindh-Astrand, L., Brynhildsen, J., & Hoffmann, M. (2007). Attitudes towards the menopause and hormone therapy over the turn of the century. *Maturitas, 56,* 12–20.

Lindley, L. D. (2006). The paradox of self-efficacy: Research with diverse populations. *Journal of Career Assessment, 14,* 143–160.

Lindorff, M. (2005). Determinants of received social support: Who gives what to managers? *Journal of Social and Personal Relationships, 22,* 323–337.

Lindsay, P. H., & Norman, D. A. (1977). *Human information processing* (2nd ed.). New York: Academic Press.

Lindsay, P., Maynard, I., & Thomas, O. (2005). Effects of hypnosis on flow states and cycling performance. *Sport Psychologist, 19,* 164–177.

Lindsey, E., & Colwell, M. (2003). Preschoolers' emotional competence: Links to pretend and physical play. *Child Study Journal, 33,* 39–52.

Links, P. S., Eynan, R., & Heisel, M. J. (2007). Affective instability and suicidal ideation and behavior in patients with borderline personality disorder. *Journal of Personality Disorders, 21,* 72–86.

Liszkowski, U., Schäfer, M., Carpenter, M., & Tomasello, M. (2009). Prelinguistic infants, but not chimpanzees, communicate about absent entities. *Psychological Science, 20,* 654–660.

Litowitz, B. E. (2007). Unconscious fantasy: A once and future concept. *Journal of the American Psychoanalytic Association, 55,* 199–228.

Little, A., Burt, D. M., & Perrett, D. I. (2006). What is good is beautiful: Face preference reflects desired personality. *Personality and Individual Differences, 41,* 1107–1118.

Little, K., Ramssen, E., Welchko, R., Volberg, V., Roland, C., & Cassin, B. (2009). Decreased brain dopamine cell numbers in human cocaine users. *Psychiatry Research, 168,* 173–180.

Liu, J. H., & Mills, D. (2006). Modern racism and neo-liberal globalization: The discourses of plausible deniability and their multiple functions. *Journal of Community & Applied Social Psychology, 16,* 83–99.

Liu, L., He, S-Z., & Wu, Y. (2007). An analysis of the characteristics of single parent families with different structures and their children. *Chinese Journal of Clinical Psychology, 15,* 68–70.

Livesley, W., & Jang, K. (2008). The behavioral genetics of personality disorder. *Annual Review of Clinical Psychology, 4,* 247–274.

Lobato, M. I., Koff, W. J., & Manenti, C. (2006). Follow-up of sex reassignment surgery in transsexuals: A Brazilian cohort. *Archives of Sexual Behavior, 35,* 711–715.

Lobban, F., Barrowclough, C., & Jones, S. (2006). Does expressed emotion need to be understood within a more systemic framework? An examination of discrepancies in appraisals between patients diagnosed with schizophrenia and their relatives. *Social Psychiatry and Psychiatric Epidemiology, 41,* 50–55.

Lobo, I., & Harris, R. (2008, July). GABA$_a$ receptors and alcohol. *Pharmacology, Biochemistry and Behavior, 90,* 90–94.

Locicero, A., & Sinclair, S. (2008, March). Terrorism and terrorist leaders: Insights from developmental and ecological psychology. *Studies in Conflict & Terrorism, 31,* 227–250.

Locke, J. L. (2006). Parental selection of vocal behavior: Crying, cooking, babbling, and the evolution of language. *Human Nature, 17,* 155–168.

Lockl, K., & Schneider, W. (2007). Knowledge about the mind: Links between theory of mind and later metamemory. *Child Development, 78,* 148–167.

Lofholm, N. (2003, May 6). Climber's kin share relief: Ralston saw 4 options, they say; death wasn't one of them. *Denver Post,* p. A1.

Loftus, E. F. (1993). Psychologists in the eyewitness world. *American Psychologist, 48,* 550–552.

Loftus, E. F. (2004). Memories of things unseen. *Current Directions in Psychological Science, 13,* 145–147.

Loftus, E. F., & Bernstein, D. M. (2005). Rich false memories: The royal road to success. In A. F. Healy, *Experimental cognitive psychology and its applications.* Washington, DC: American Psychological Association.

Loftus, E. F., & Palmer, J. C. (1974). Reconstruction of automobile destruction: An example of the interface between language and memory. *Journal of Verbal Learning and Verbal Behavior, 13,* 585–589.

Long, G. M., & Beaton, R. J. (1982). The case for peripheral persistence: Effects of target and background luminance on a partial-report task. *Journal of Experimental Psychology: Human Perception and Performance, 8,* 383–391.

Lopes, A. C., Greenberg, B. D., Noren, G., Canteras, M. M., Busatto, G. F. de Mathis, et al. (2009). Treatment of resistant obsessive-compulsive disorder with ventral capsular/ventral striatal gamma capsulotomy: A pilot prospective study. *The Journal of Neuropsychiatry and Clinical Neurosciences, 21,* 381–392.

López, S. R., & Guarnaccia, P. J. (2005). Cultural dimensions of psychopathology: The social world's impact on mental illness. In J. E. Maddux & B. A. Winstead (Eds.), *Foundations for a contemporary understanding.* Mahwah, NJ: Lawrence Erlbaum Associates.

López, S. R., & Guarnaccia, P. J. J. (2000). Cultural psychopathology: Uncovering the social world of mental illness. *Annual Review of Psychology, 51,* 571–598.

Lorenz, K. (1966). *On aggression.* New York: Harcourt Brace Jovanovich.

Lorenz, K. (1974). *Civilized man's eight deadly sins.* New York: Harcourt Brace Jovanovich.

Lothane, Z. (2005). Jung, A biography. *Journal of the American Psychoanalytic Association, 53,* 317–324.

Loving, T., Crockett, E., & Paxson, A. (2009). Passionate love and relationship thinkers: Experimental evidence for acute cortisol elevations in women. *Psychoneuroendocrinology, 34,* 939–946.

Lowe, P., Humphreys, C., & Williams, S. J. (2007). Night terrors: Women's experiences of (not) sleeping where there is domestic violence. *Violence against Women, 13,* 549–561.

Lowery, D., Fillingim, R. B., & Wright, R. A. (2003). Sex differences and incentive effects on perceptual and cardiovascular responses to cold pressor pain. *Psychosomatic Medicine, 65,* 284–291.

Lu, J., Sherman, D., Devor, M., & Saper, C. B. (2006). A putative flip-flop switch for control of REM sleep. *Nature, 441,* 589–594.

Lubell, K. M., Swahn, M. H., Crosby, A. E., & Kegler, S. R. (2004). Methods of suicide among persons aged 10–19 years—United States, 1992–2001. *MMWR, 53,* 471–473. Retrieved from http://www.cdc.gov/mmwr/PDF/wk/mm5322.pdf.

Lublin, H., Eberhard, J., & Levander, S. (2005). Current therapy issues and unmet clinical needs in the

treatment of schizophrenia: A review of the new generation antipsychotics. *International Clinical Psychopharmacology, 20,* 183–198.

Lucas, W. (2008). Parents' perceptions of the Drug Abuse Resistance Education program (DARE). *Journal of Child & Adolescent Substance Abuse, 17,* 99–114.

Luchins, A. S. (1946). Classroom experiments on mental set. *American Journal of Psychology, 59,* 295–298.

Lucki, I., & O'Leary, O. F. (2004). Distinguishing roles for norepinephrine and serotonin in the behavioral effects of antidepressant drugs. *Journal of Clinical Psychiatry, 65,* 11–24.

Luders, E., Narr, K. L., Zaidel, E., Thompson, P. M., & Toga, A. W. (2006). Gender effects on callosal thickness in scaled and unscaled space. *Neuroreport, 17,* 1103–1106.

Ludwig, A. M. (1996, March). Mental disturbances and creative achievement. *The Harvard Mental Health Letter,* pp. 4–6.

Lun, V. M., & Bond, M. H. (2006). Achieving relationship harmony in groups and its consequence for group performance. *Asian Journal of Social Psychology, 9,* 195–202.

Luo, S., & Zhang, G. (2009). What leads to romantic attraction: Similarity, reciprocity, security, or beauty? Evidence from a speed-dating study. *Journal of Personality, 77,* 933–964.

Luria, A. R. (1968). *The mind of a mnemonist.* Cambridge, MA: Basic Books.

Luthar, S. S., Cicchetti, D., & Becker, B. (2000). The construct of resilience: A critical evaluation and guidelines for future work. *Child Development, 71,* 543–562.

Lutz, C. K. & Novak, M. A. (2005) Environmental enrichment for nonhuman primates: theory and application. *ILAR Journal, 46,* 178–191.

Lutz, W., Lambert, M. J., Harmon, S. C., Tschitsaz, A., Schurch, E., & Stulz, N (2006). The probability of treatment success, failure and duration—What can be learned from empirical data to support decision making in clinical practice? *Clinical Psychology & Psychotherapy, 13,* 223–232.

Ly, D. H., Lockhart, D. J., Lerner, R. A., & Schultz, P. G. (2000, March 31). Mitotic misregulation and human aging. *Science, 287,* 2486–2492.

Lykken, D. T. (1995). *The antisocial personalities.* Mahwah, NJ: Erlbaum.

Lymberis, S. C., Parhar, P. K., Katsoulakis, E., & Formenti, S. C. (2004). Pharmacogenomics and breast cancer. *Pharmacogenomics, 5,* 31–55.

Lynch, T. R., Trost, W. T, Salsman, N., & Linehan, M. M. (2007). Dialectical behavior therapy for borderline personality disorder. *Annual Review of Clinical Psychology, 3,* 181–205.

Lynn, S. J., Fassler, O., & Knox, J. (2005). Hypnosis and the altered state debate: Something more or nothing more? Comment. *Contemporary Hypnosis, 22,* 39–45.

Lynn, S. J., Kirsch, I., Barabasz, A., Cardena, E., & Patterson, D. (2000). Hypnosis as an empirically supported clinical intervention: The state of the evidence and a look to the future. *International Journal of Clinical and Experimental Hypnosis, 48,* 239–259.

Lynn, S. J., Lock, T., Loftus, E. F., Krackow, E., & Lilienfeld, S. O. (2003). The remembrance of things past: Problematic memory recovery techniques in psychotherapy. In S. O. Lilienfeld, S. J. Lynn & J. M. Lohr (Eds.), *Science and pseudoscience in clinical psychology.* New York: Guilford Press.

Lynn, S. J., Neufeld, V., Green, J. P., Sandberg, D., et al. (1996). Daydreaming, fantasy, and psychopathology. In R. G. Kunzendorf, N. P. Spanos, & B. Wallace (Eds.), *Hypnosis and imagination. Imagery and human development series.* Amityville, NY: Baywood.

Macaluso, E., & Driver, J. (2005). Multisensory spatial interactions: a window onto functional integration in the human brain. *Trends in Neurosciences, 28,* Issue 5, 264–271.

Macaluso, E., Frith, C. D., & Driver, J. (2000, August 18). Modulation of human visual cortex by cross-modal spatial attention. *Science, 289,* 1206–1208.

Macduff, I. (2006). Your pace or mine? Culture, time and negotiation. *Negotiation Journal, 22,* 31–45.

Mackay, J., & Eriksen, M. (2002). *The tobacco atlas.* Geneva, Switzerland: World Health Organization.

Mack, J. (2003). *The museum of the mind.* London: British Museum Publications.

MacLean, L., Edwards, N., Garrard, M., Sims-Jones, N., Clinton, K., & Ashley, L. (2009, March). Obesity, stigma and public health planning. *Health Promotion International, 24,* 88–93.

MacLennan, A. (2009). Evidence-based review of therapies at the menopause. *International Journal of Evidence-Based Healthcare, 7,* 112–123.

Macmillan, M. (1996). *Freud evaluated: The completed arc.* Cambridge, MA: MIT.

MacNeilage, P. F., Rogers, L. J., & Vallortigara, G. (2009, July). Origins of the left & right brain. *Scientific American,* pp. 60–67.

MacPherson, K. (2002, March 17). Unfilled pink-collar jobs threaten service cuts. *Pittsburgh Post-Gazette,* p. 7.

Madden, D. J. (2007). Aging and visual attention. *Current Directions in Psychological Science, 16,* 70–74.

Maddi, S. R. (2007). The story of hardiness: Twenty years of theorizing, research, and practice. In A. Monat, R. S. Lazarus, & G. Reevy, *The Praeger handbook on stress and coping* (Vol. 2). Westport, CT: Praeger Publishers/ Greenwood Publishing.

Mader, S. S. (2000). *Biology* (6th ed.). Boston: McGraw-Hill.

Madon, S., Willard, J., & Guyll, M. (2006). Self-fulfilling prophecy effects of mothers' beliefs on children's alcohol use: Accumulation, dissipation, and stability over time. *Journal of Personality and Social Psychology, 90,* 911–926.

Magida, A. J. (2006). *Opening the doors of wonder: Reflections on religious rites of passage.* Berkeley, CA: University of California Press.

Magoni, M., Bassani, L., Okong, P., Kituuka, P., Germinario, E. P., Giuliano, M., et al. (2005). Mode of infant feeding and HIV infection in children in a program for prevention of mother-to-child transmission in Uganda. *AIDS, 19,* 433–437.

Magoon, M., & Critchfield, T. (2008). Concurrent schedules of positive and negative reinforcement: Differential-impact and differential-outcomes hypotheses. *Journal of the Experimental Analysis of Behavior, 90,* 1–22.

Magruder, K., & Yeager, D. (2009). The prevalence of PTSD across war eras and the effect of deployment on PTSD: A systematic review and meta-analysis. *Psychiatric Annals, 39,* 778–788.

Maguire, E. A., Kumaran, D., Hassabis, D., & Kopelman, M.D. (2010). Autobiographical memory in semantic dementia: A longitudinal fMRI study. *Neuropsychologia, 48,* 123–136.

Maguire, E. A., Woollett, K., & Spiers, H. J. (2006). London taxi drivers and bus drivers: A structural MRI and neuropsychological analysis. *Hippocampus, 16,* 1091–1101.

Mahmood, M., & Black, J. (2005). Narcolepsycataplexy: How does recent understanding help in evaluation and treatment. *Current Treatment Options in Neurology, 7,* 363–371.

Maier, S. F., & Watkins, L. R. (2000). Learned helplessness. In A. E. Kazdin, *Encyclopedia of psychology* (Vol. 4). Washington, DC: American Psychological Association.

Majdandzic, M., & van den Boom, D. C. (2007). Multimethod longitudinal assessment of temperament in early childhood. *Journal of Personality, 75,* 121–167.

Majeres, R. L. (2007). Sex differences in phono-logical coding: Alphabet transformation speed. *Intelligence, 35,* 335–346.

Maldonado, J. R., & Spiegel, D. (2003). Dissociative disorders. In R. E. Hales & S. C. Yudofsky, *The American*

Psychiatric Publishing textbook of clinical psychiatry (4th ed.). Washington, DC: American Psychiatric Publishing.

Malle, B. F. (2004). *How the mind explains behavior: Folk explanations, meaning, and social interaction.* Cambridge, MA: MIT.

Malouff, J. M., Thorsteinsson, E. B., & Schutte, N. S. (2007). The efficacy of problem solving therapy in reducing mental and physical health problems: A meta-analysis. *Clinical Psychology Review, 27,* 46–57.

Malpas, P. (2008, April). Predictive genetic testing of children for adult-onset diseases and psychological harm. *Journal of Medical Ethics, 34,* 275–278.

Mamassis, G., & Doganis, G. (2004). The effects of a mental training program on juniors pre-competitive anxiety, self-confidence, and tennis performance. *Journal of Applied Sport Psychology, 16,* 118–137.

Mancinelli, R., Binetti, R., & Ceccanti, M. (2007). Woman, alcohol and environment: Emerging risks for health. *Neuroscience & Biobehavioral Reviews, 31,* 246–253.

Manly, J., & Echemendia, R. (2007). Race-specific norms: Using the model of hypertension to understand issues of race, culture, and education in neuropsychology. *Archives of Clinical Neuropsychology, 22,* 319–325.

Manly, J. J. (2005). Advantages and disadvantages of separate norms for African Americans. *Clinical Neuropsychologist, 19,* 270–275.

Manly, J. J. (2006). Deconstructing race and ethnicity: Implications for measurement of health outcomes [Special issue: Measurement in a multi-ethnic society]. *Medical Care, 44,* S10–S16.

Mann, K., Ackermann, K., Croissant, B., Mundle, G., Nakovics, H., & Diehl, A. (2005). Neuroimaging of gender differences in alcohol dependence: are women more vulnerable? *Alcoholism: Clinical & Experimental Research, 29,* 896–901.

Manning, M. A., & Hoyme, E. H. (2007). Fetal alcohol spectrum disorders: A practical clinical approach to diagnosis. *Neuroscience & Biobehavioral Reviews, 31,* 230–238.

Manning, S. Y. (2005). Dialectical behavior therapy of severe and chronic problems. In L. VandeCreek (Ed.), *Innovations in clinical practice: Focus on adults.* Sarasota, FL: Professional Resource Press/Professional Resource Exchange.

Manor, J. K., & Gailliot, M. T. (2007). Altruism and egoism: Prosocial motivations for helping depend on relationship context. *European Journal of Social Psychology, 37,* 347–358.

Manstead, A. S. R., Frijda, N., & Fischer, A. H. (Eds.). (2003). *Feelings and emotions: The Amsterdam Symposium.* Cambridge, England: Cambridge University Press.

Manstead, A. S. R., & Wagner, H. L. (2004). *Experience emotion.* Cambridge, England: Cambridge University Press.

Marcaurelle, R., Bélanger, C., & Marchand, A. (2005). Marital predictors of symptom severity in panic disorder with agoraphobia. *Journal of Anxiety Disorders, 19,* 211–232.

Marcus-Newhall, A., Pedersen, W. C., & Carlson, M. (2000). Displaced aggression is alive and well: A meta-analytic review. *Journal of Personality and Social Psychology, 78,* 670–689.

Marks, I. M. (2004). The Nobel prize award in physiology to Ivan Petrovich Pavlov–1904. *Australian and New Zealand Journal of Psychiatry, 38,* 674–677.

Markus, H. R. (2007). Sociocultural psychology: The dynamic interdependence among self systems and social systems. In S. Kitayama, & D. Cohen, (Eds.), *Handbook of cultural psychology.* New York: Guilford Press.

Markus, H. R., & Kitayama, S. (2003). Models of agency: Sociocultural diversity in the construction of action. In V. Murphy-Berman & J. J. Berman (Eds.), *Cross-cultural differences in perspectives on the self.* Lincoln, NE: University of Nebraska Press.

Marmar, C. (2009). Mental health impact of Afghanistan and Iraq deployment: Meeting the challenge of a new generation of veterans. *Depression and Anxiety, 26,* 493–497.

Maroda, K. J. (2004). A relational perspective on women and power. *Psychoanalytic Psychology, 21,* 428–435.

Marsh, B. (2008, February 24). A growing cloud over the planet. *The New York Times,* p. WK4.

Marsh, H. W., Hau, K. T., & Sung, R. Y. T. (2007). Childhood obesity, gender, actual-ideal body image discrepancies, and physical self-concept in Hong Kong children: Cultural differences in the value of moderation. *Developmental Psychology, 43,* 647–662.

Marshall, K., Laing, D. G., & Jinks, A. L. (2006). The capacity of humans to identify components in complex odor-taste mixtures. *Chemical Senses, 31,* 539–545.

Marshall, L., & Born, J. (2007, October). The contribution of sleep to hippocampus-dependent memory consolidation. *Trends in Cognitive Sciences, 11*(10), 442–450.

Marshall, M. K. (2007). The critical factors of coaching practice leading to successful coaching outcomes. *Dissertation Abstracts International: Section B: The Sciences and Engineering, 67*(7-B), 4092.

Marshall, R. D., Bryant, R. A, & Amsel, L. (2007). The psychology of ongoing threat: Relative risk appraisal, the September 11 attacks, and terrorism-related fears. *American Psychologist, 62,* 304–316.

Marshall, R. D., Bryant, R. A., Amsel, L., Suh, E. J., Cook, J. M., & Neria, Y. (2007). The psychology of ongoing threat: Relative risk appraisal, the September 11 attacks and terrorism-related fears. *American Psychologist, 62,* 304–316.

Marszalek, J. (2007). Computerized adaptive testing and the experience of flow in examinees. *Dissertation Abstracts International Section A: Humanities and Social Sciences, 67*(7-A), 2465.

Martelle, S., Hanley, C., & Yoshino K. (2003, January 28). "Sopranos" scenario in slaying? *Los Angeles Times,* p. B1.

Martin, A. J., & Marsh, H. W. (2002). Fear of failure: Friend or foe? *Australian Psychologist, 38,* 31–38.

Martin, L., & Pullum, G. K. (1991). *The great Eskimo vocabulary hoax.* Chicago: University of Chicago Press.

Martin, P. D., & Brantley, P. J. (2004). Stress, coping, and social support in health and behavior. In J. M. Raczynski & L. C. Leviton (Eds.), *Handbook of clinical health psychology, Vol. 2: Disorders of behavior and health.* Washington, DC: American Psychological Association.

Martindale, C. (1981). *Cognition and consciousness.* Homewood, IL: Dorsey.

Mascia, K., & Servis, R. (2009, August 24). Mail carriers to the rescue. *People,* p. 108–110.

Mashour, G. A., Walker, E. E., & Martuza, R. L. (2005). Psychosurgery: Past, present, and future. *Brain Research Reviews, 48,* 409–419.

Maslow, A. H. (1970). *Motivation and personality.* New York: Harper & Row.

Maslow, A. H. (1987). *Motivation and personality* (3rd ed.). New York: Harper & Row.

Massaro, D. W., & Chen, T. H. (2008). The motor theory of speech perception revisited. *Psychonomic Bulletin & Review, 15,* 453–457.

Mast, F. W., & Kosslyn, S. M. (2002). Visual mental images can be ambiguous: Insights from individual differences in spatial transformation abilities. *Cognition, 86,* 57–70.

Masters, W., & Johnson, V. (1994). *Heterosexuality.* New York: Harper Collins.

Masuda, M. (2003). Meta-analyses of love scales: Do various love scales measure the same psychological constructs? *Japanese Psychological Research, 45,* 25–37.

Mataix-Cols, D., & Bartres-Faz, D. (2002). Is the use of the wooden and computerized versions of the Tower of Hanoi Puzzle equivalent? *Applied Neuropsychology, 9,* 117–120.

Maton, K. I., Kohout, J. L., Wicherski, M., Leary, G. E., & Vinokurov, A. (2006). Minority students of color and the psychology graduate pipeline. *American Psychologist, 61,* 117–131.

Matson, J., & LoVullo, S. (2008). A review of behavioral treatments for self-injurious behaviors of persons with autism spectrum disorders. *Behavior Modification, 32,* 61–76.

Matsumoto, D. (2002). Methodological requirements to test a possible in-group advantage in judging emotions across cultures: Comment on Elfenbein and Ambady (2002) and evidence. *Psychological Bulletin, 128,* 236–242.

Matsumoto, D., & Willingham, B. (2009). Spontaneous facial expressions of emotion of congenitally and noncongenitally blind individuals. *Journal of Personality and Social Psychology, 96,* 1–10.

Matthews, G., & Funke, G. J. (2006). Worry and information-processing. In G. C. L. Davey & A. Wells, *Worry and its psychological disorders: Theory, assessment and treatment.* Hoboken, NJ: Wiley Publishing.

Maurer, D., Lewis, T. L., Brent, H. P., & Levin, A. V. (1999, October 1). Rapid improvement in the acuity of infants after visual input. *Science, 286,* 108–110.

Mayer, J. D., Salovey, P., & Caruso, D. R. (2004). Emotional intelligence: Theory, findings, and implications. *Psychological Inquiry, 15,* 197–215.

Mayer, J. D., Salovey, P., & Caruso, D. R. (2008). Emotional intelligence: New ability or eclectic traits? *American Psychologist, 63,* 503–517.

Maynard, A. E., & Martini, M. I. (2005). *Learning in cultural context: Family, peers, and school.* New York: Kluwer Academic/Plenum Publishers.

Mazard, A., Laou, L., Joliot, M., & Mellet, E. (2005). Neural impact of the semantic content of visual mental images and visual percepts. *Brain Research and Cognitive Brain Research, 24,* 423–435.

McAdams, D. P., Diamond, A., de St. Aubin, E., & Mansfield, E. (1997). Stories of commitment: The psychosocial construction of generative lives. *Journal of Personality and Social Psychology, 72,* 678–694.

McCabe, C., & Rolls, E. T. (2007). Umami: A delicious flavor formed by convergence of taste and olfactory pathways in the human brain. *European Journal of Neuroscience, 25,* 1855–1864.

McCabe, M. (2009). Anorgasmia in women. *Journal of Family Psychotherapy, 20,* 177–197.

McCarthy, J. (2005). Individualism and collectivism: What do they have to do with counseling? *Journal of Multicultural Counseling and Development, 33,* 108–117.

McCaul, K. D., Johnson, R. J., & Rothman, A. J. (2002). The effects of framing and action instructions on whether older adults obtain flu shots. *Health Psychology, 21,* 624–628.

McCauley, R. N., & Henrich, J. (2006), Susceptibility to the Müller-Lyer illusion, theory-neutral observation, and the diachronic penetrability of the visual input. *Philosophical Psychology, 19,* 79–101.

McClelland, D. C. (1985). How motives, skills, and values determine what people do. *American Psychologist, 40,* 812–825.

McClelland, D. C. (1993). Intelligence is not the best predictor of job performance. *Current Directions in Psychological Research, 2,* 5–8.

McClelland, D. C., Atkinson, J. W., Clark, R. A., & Lowell, E. L. (1953). *The achievement motive.* New York: Appleton-Century-Crofts.

McClure, J., Sutton, R. M., & Sibley, C. G. (2007). Listening to reporters or engineers? How instance-based messages about building design affect earthquake fatalism. *Journal of Applied Social Sciences, 37,* 1956–1973.

McCrae, R. R., & Costa, P. T., Jr. (1986). A five-factor theory of personality. In L. A. Pervin & O. P. John (Eds.), *Handbook of personality: Theory and research* (2nd ed.). New York: Guilford.

McCrae, R. R., Terracciano A., & 78 Members of the Personality Profiles of Cultures Project. (2005). Universal features of personality traits from the observer's perspective: Data from 50 cultures. *Journal of Personality and Social Psychology, 88,* 547–561.

McCrink, K., & Wynn, K. (2007). Ratio abstraction by 6-month-old infants. *Psychological Science, 18,* 740–745.

McDaniel, M. A., Maier, S. F., & Einstein, G. O. (2002). "Brain specific" nutrients: A memory cure? *Psychological Science in the Public Interest, 3,* 12–18.

McDonald, C., & Murray, R. M. (2004). Can structural magnetic resonance imaging provide an alternative phenotype for genetic studies of schizophrenia? In M. S. Keshavan, J. L. Kennedy, & R. M. Murray (Eds.), *Neurodevelopment and schizophrenia.* New York: Cambridge University Press.

McDonald, H. E., & Hirt, E. R. (1997). When expectancy meets desire: Motivational effects in reconstructive memory. *Journal of Personality and Social Psychology, 72,* 5–23.

McDougall, W. (1908). *Introduction to social psychology.* London: Methuen.

McDowell, D. M., & Spitz, H. I. (1999). *Substance abuse.* New York: Brunner/ Mazel.

McEwen, B. S. (1998, January 15). Protective and damaging effects of stress mediators [Review article]. *New England Journal of Medicine, 338,* 171–179.

McGaugh, J. L. (2003). *Memory and emotion: The making of lasting memories.* New York: Columbia University Press.

McGilvray, J. (Ed.). (2004). *The Cambridge companion to Chomsky.* Oxford, England: Cambridge University Press.

McGinn, D. (2003, June 9). Testing, testing: The new job search. *Time,* pp. 36–38.

McGregor, K. K., & Capone, N. C. (2004). Genetic and environmental interactions in determining the early lexicon: Evidence from a set of tri-zygotic quadruplets. *Journal of Child Language, 31,* 311–337.

McIntyre, K., Korn, J., & Matsuo, H. (2008). Sweating the small stuff: How different types of hassles result in the experience of stress. *Stress and Health: Journal of the International Society for the Investigation of Stress, 24,* 383–392.

McKinley, M. J., Cairns, M. J., Denton, D. A., Egan, G., Mathai, M. L., Uschakov, A., et al. (2004). Physiological and pathophysiological influences on thirst. *Physiology and Behavior, 81,* 795–803.

McMurtray, A. M., Licht, E., Yeo, T., Krisztal, E., Saul, R. E., & Mendez, M. F. (2007). Positron emission tomography facilitates diagnosis of early-onset Alzheimer's disease. *European Neurology, 59,* 31–37.

McNamara, P. (2004). *An evolutionary psychology of sleep and dreams.* Westport, CT: Praeger Publishers/ Greenwood Publishing Group.

Mead, M. (1949). *Male and female.* New York: Morrow.

Means, M. K., & Edinger, J. D. (2007). Graded exposure therapy for addressing claustrophobic reactions to continuous positive airway pressure: A case series report. *Behavioral Sleep Medicine, 5,* 105–116.

Medeiros, R., Prediger, R. D. S., Passos, G. F., Pandolfo, P., et al. (2007). Connecting TNF-α signaling pathways to iNOS expression in a mouse model of Alzheimer's disease: Relevance for the behavioral and synaptic deficits induced by amyloid β protein. *Journal of Neuroscience, 27,* 5394–5404.

Meeter, M., & Murre, J. M. J. (2004). Consolidation of long-term memory: Evidence and alternatives. *Psychological Bulletin, 130,* 843–857.

Mehl-Madrona, L. E. (2004). Hypnosis to facilitate uncomplicated birth. *American Journal of Clinical Hypnosis, 46,* 299–312.

Meinlschmidt, G., & Heim, C. (2007). Sensitivity to intranasal oxytocin in adult men with early parental separation. *Biological Psychiatry, 61,* 1109–1111.

Mel, B. W. (2002, March 8). What the synapse tells the neuron. *Science, 295,* 1845–1846.

Mel'nikov, K. S. (1993, October–December). On some aspects of the mechanistic approach to the study of processes of forgetting. *Vestnik Moskovskogo Universiteta Seriya 14 Psikhologiya,* pp. 64–67.

Meltzer, H. Y. (2000). Genetics and etiology of schizophrenia and bipolar disorder. *Biological Psychiatry, 47,* 171–173.

Meltzoff, A. N. (1996). The human infant as imitative generalist: A 20-year progress report on infant imitation with implications for comparative psychology. In C. M. Heyes & B. G. Galef, Jr. (Eds.), *Social learning in animals: The roots of culture.* San Diego, CA: Academic Press.

Melzack, R., & Katz, J. (2001). The McGill Pain Questionnaire: Appraisal and current status. In D. Turk & R. Melzack, (Eds.). *Handbook of pain assessment* (2nd ed.). New York: Guilford Press.

Melzack, R., & Katz, J. (2004). *The gate control theory: Reaching for the brain.* Mahwah, NJ: Lawrence Erlbaum Associates.

Mental Health Information Center, U.S. Department of Health and Human Services. (2002, December). Deinstitutionalization. *Scientific American,* p. 38.

Merikangas, K. R., Ames, M., Cui, L., Stang, P. E., Ustun, T. B., VonKorff, M., et al. (2007). The impact of comorbidity of mental and physical conditions on role disability in the US adult household population. *Archives of General Psychiatry, 64,* 1180–1188.

Messer, S. B., & McWilliams, N. (2003). The impact of Sigmund Freud and *The Interpretation of Dreams.* In R. J. Sternberg (Ed.), *The anatomy of impact: What makes the great works of psychology great.* Washington, DC: American Psychological Association.

Messner, M., Reinhard, M., & Sporer, S. (2008). Compliance through direct persuasive appeals: The moderating role of communicator's attractiveness in interpersonal persuasion. *Social Influence, 3,* 67–83.

Meyer-Bahlburg, H. (1997). The role of prenatal estrogens in sexual orientation. In L. Ellis & L. Ebertz (Eds.), *Sexual orientation: Toward biological understanding.* Westport, CT: Praeger.

Meyer, I., & Ladewig, J. (2008). The relationship between number of training sessions per week and learning in dogs. *Applied Animal Behaviour Science, 111,* 311–320.

Meyerowitz, J. (2004). *How sex changed: A history of transsexuality in the United States.* Cambridge, MA: Harvard University Press.

Michael, R. T., Gagnon, J. H., Laumann, E. O., & Kolata, G. (1994). *Sex in America: A definitive survey.* Boston: Little, Brown.

Midanik, L. T., Tam, T. W., & Weisner, C. (2007). Concurrent and simultaneous drug and alcohol use: Results of the 2000 national alcohol survey. *Drug and Alcohol Dependence, 90,* 72–80.

Middlebrooks, J. C., Furukawa, S., Stecker, G. C., & Mickey, B. J. (2005). Distributed representation of sound-source location in the auditory cortex. In R. König, P. Heil, E. Budinger, & H. Scheich (Eds.), *Auditory cortex: A synthesis of human and animal research.* Mahwah, NJ: Lawrence Erlbaum Associates.

Miesenbock, G. (2008, October). Lighting up the brain. *Scientific American,* pp. 52–59.

Mifflin, L. (1998, January 14). Study finds a decline in TV network violence. *The New York Times,* p. A14.

Mignon, A., & Mollaret, P. (2002). Applying the affordance conception of traits: A person perception study. *Personality and Social Psychology Bulletin, 28,* 1327–1334.

Mika, V. S., Wood, P. R., Weiss, B. D., & Trevino, L. (2007). Ask Me 3: Improving communication in a Hispanic pediatric outpatient practice. *American Journal of Behavioral Health, 31,* S115–S121.

Miklowitz, D. J., & Thompson, M. C. (2003). Family variables and interventions in schizophrenia. In G. Sholevar & G. Pirooz (Eds.), *Textbook of family and couples therapy: Clinical applications.* Washington, DC: American Psychiatric Publishing.

Mikulincer, M., & Shaver, P. R. (2005). Attachment security, compassion, and altruism. *Current Directions in Psychological Science, 14,* 34–38.

Miletic, M. P. (2002). The introduction of a feminine psychology to psychoanalysis: Karen Horney's legacy [Special issue: Interpersonal psychoanalysis and feminism]. *Contemporary Psychoanalysis, 38,* 287–299.

Milgram, S. (1965). *Obedience* [film]. New York University Film Library and Pennsylvania State University, PCR.

Milgram, S. (2005). *Obedience to authority.* Pinter & Martin: New York.

Miller, G. (2006). A spoonful of medicine—and a steady diet of normalcy. *Science, 311,* 464–465.

Miller, G. (2008, May 9). The roots of morality. *Science, 320,* 734–737.

Miller, G. A. (1956). The magical number seven, plus or minus two: Some limits on our capacity for processing information. *Psychology Review, 63,* 81–97.

Miller, G. F., & Penke, L. (2007). The evolution of human intelligence and the coefficient of additive genetic variance in human brain size. *Intelligence, 35,* 97–114.

Miller, J. A., & Leffard, S. A. (2007). Behavioral assessment. In S. R. Smith & L. Handler, *The clinical assessment of children and adolescents: A practitioner's handbook.* Mahwah, NJ: Lawrence Erlbaum Associates.

Miller, J. (1984). Culture and the development of everyday social explanation. *Journal of Personality and Social Psychology, 46,* 961–978.

Miller, L. A., Taber, K. H., Gabbard, G. O., & Hurley, R. A. (2005). Neural underpinnings of fear and its modulation: Implications for anxiety disorders. *The Journal of Neuropsychiatry and Clinical Neurosciences, 17,* 1–6.

Miller, L., Gur, M., Shanok, A., & Weissman, M. (2008). Interpersonal psychotherapy with pregnant adolescents: Two pilot studies. *Journal of Child Psychology and Psychiatry, 49,* 733–742.

Miller, M. N., & Pumariega, A. J. (2001). Culture and eating disorders: A historical and cross-cultural review. *Psychiatry: Interpersonal and Biological Processes, 64,* 93–110.

Miller, N. E., & Magruder, K. M. (Eds.). (1999). *Cost-effectiveness of psychotherapy: A guide for practitioners, researchers, and policymakers.* New York: Oxford University Press.

Miller, W. R., & Thoresen, C. E. (2003). Spirituality, religion, and health: An emerging research field. *American Psychologist, 58,* 24–35.

Miller-Jones, D. (1991). Informal reasoning in inner-city children. In J. F. Voss & D. N. Perkins (Eds.), *Informal reasoning and education.* Hillsdale, NJ: Lawrence Erlbaum.

Miller-Perrin, C., Perrin, R., & Kocur, J. (2009). Parental physical and psychological aggression: Psychological symptoms in young adults. *Child Abuse & Neglect, 33,* 1–11.

Millon, T., Davis, R., & Millon, C. (2000). *Personality disorders in modern life.* New York: Wiley.

Milner, B. (1966). Amnesia following operation on temporal lobes. In C. W. M. Whitty & P. Zangwill (Eds.), *Amnesia.* London: Butterworth.

Milner, B. (2005). The medial temporal-lobe amnesic syndrome. *Psychiatric Clinics of North America, 28,* 599–611.

Milton, J., & Wiseman, R. (1999). Does psi exist? Lack of replication of an anomalous process of information transfer. *Psychological Bulletin, 125,* 387–391.

Miner, J., & Clarke-Stewart, K. (2008). Trajectories of externalizing behavior from age 2 to age 9: Relations with gender, temperament, ethnicity, parenting, and rater. *Developmental Psychology, 44,* 771–786.

Miner-Rubino, K., Winter, D. G., & Stewart, A. J. (2004). Gender, social class, and the subjective experience of aging: Self-perceived personality change from early adulthood to late midlife. *Personality and Social Psychology Bulletin, 30,* 1599–1610.

Minnesota Multiphasic Personality Inventory-2 (1989). Regents of the University of Minnesota.

Mintz, A., & Brule, D. (2009). Methodological issues in studying suicide terrorism. *Political Psychology, 30,* 361–367.

Minuchin, S. (1999). Retelling, reimagining, and re-searching: A continuing conversation. *Journal of Marital and Family Therapy, 25,* 9–14.

Miquel, J., (2006). Integración de teorías del envejeci-miento (parte I). Integration of theories of ageing. *Revista Espanola de Geriatria y Gerontologia, 41,* 55–63.

Mischel, W. (2004). Toward an integrative science of the person. *Annual Review of Psychology, 55,* 1–22.

Mischel, W. (2009). From Personality and Assessment (1968) to Personality Science, 2009. *Journal of Research in Personality, 43,* 282–290.

Mischel, W., & Shoda, Y. (2008). Toward a unified theory of personality: Integrating dispositions and process-ing dynamics within the cognitive-affective process-ing system. In O. P. Oliver, R. W. Robins, & L. A. Pervin (Eds.) *Handbook of personality psychology: Theory and research* (3rd ed). New York: Guilford Press.

Mischoulon, D. (2000, June). Anti-depressants: Choices and controversy. *HealthNews,* p. 4.

Miserando, M. (1991). Memory and the seven dwarfs. *Teaching of Psychology, 18,* 169–171.

Mitchell, D. B., & Schmitt, F. A. (2006). Short- and long-term implicit memory in aging and Alzheimer's disease. *Neuropsychological Development and Cognition, B, Aging and Neuropsychological Cognition, 13,* 611–635.

Mitte, K. (2005). Meta-analysis of cognitive-behavioral treatments for generalized anxiety disorder: A com-parison with pharmacotherapy. *Psychological Bulletin, 131,* 785–795.

MLA (2005). MLA Language Map; all languages other than English combined. Retrieved from http://www.mla.org/census_map&source=county (based on 2000 U.S. Census Bureau figures).

Moffitt, T. E., & Caspi, A. (2007). Evidence from behav-ioral genetics for environmental contributions to antisocial conduct. In J. E. Grusec & P. D. Hastings, *Handbook of socialization: Theory and research.* New York: Guilford Press.

Moffitt, T. E., Caspi, A., & Rutter, M. (2006). Measured gene-environment interactions in psychopathol-ogy: Concepts, research strategies, and implica-tions for research, intervention, and public understanding of genetics. *Perspectives on Psychological Science, 1,* 5–27.

Mograss, M., Guillem, F., Brazzini-Poisson, V., & Godbout, R. (2009, May). The effects of total sleep deprivation on recognition memory processes: A study of event-related potential. *Neurobiology of Learning and Memory, 91,* 343–352.

Mohapel, P., Leanza, G., Kokaia, M., & Lindvall, O. (2005). Forebrain acetylcholine regulates adult hippo-campal neurogenesis and learning. *Neurobiology of Aging, 26,* 939–946.

Moher, C., Gould, D., Hegg, E., & Mahoney, A. (2008). Non-generalized and generalized conditioned reinforcers: Establishment and validation. *Behavioral Interventions, 23,* 13–38.

Mokdad, A. H., Brewer, R. D., & Naimi, T. (2007). Binge drinking is a problem that cannot be ignored. *Preventive Medicine: An International Journal Devoted to Practice and Theory, 44,* 303–304.

Montgomery, K. J., Isenberg, N., & Haxby, J.V. (2007). Communicative hand gestures and object-directed hand movements activated the mirror neuron sys-tem. *Social, Cognitive and Affective Neuroscience, 2,* 114–122.

Montgomery, S. (2006). Serotonin noradrenaline reup-take inhibitors: Logical evolution of antidepressant development. *International Journal of Psychiatry in Clinical Practice, 10,* 5–11.

Montgomery, S. A., Nil, R., Dürr-Pal, N., Loft, H., & Boulenger, J. P. (2005). A 24-week randomized, double-blind, placebo-controlled study of escitalo-pram for the prevention of generalized social anxi-ety disorder. *Journal of Clinical Psychiatry, 66,* 1270–1278.

Montoya, R., & Insko, C. (2008). Toward a more com-plete understanding of the reciprocity of liking effect. *European Journal of Social Psychology, 38,* 477–498.

Moody, H. R. (2000). *Aging: Concepts and controversies.* Thousand Oaks, CA: Sage.

Moore, D. G., Goodwin, J. E., & George, R. (2007). Infants perceive human point-light displays as solid forms. *Cognition, 104,* 377–396.

Moore, M. M. (2002). Behavioral observation. In M. W. Wiederman & B. E. Whitley (Eds.), *Handbook for conducting research on human sexuality.* Mahwah, NJ: Lawrence Erlbaum.

Moorey, S. (2007). Cognitive therapy. In W. Dryden, *Dryden's handbook of individual therapy* (5th ed.). Thousand Oaks, CA: Sage Publications.

Morad, Y., Barkana, Y., Zadok, D., Hartstein, M., Pras, E., & Bar-Dayan, Y. (2009, July). Ocular parame-ters as an objective tool for the assessment of truck drivers fatigue. *Accident Analysis and Prevention, 41,* 856–860.

Mora-Giral, M., Raich-Escursell, R. M., Segues, C.V., Torras-Claras, A. J., & Huon, G. (2004). Bulimia symptoms and risk factors in university students. *Eating and Weight Disorders, 9,* 163–169.

Moran, A. (2009). Cognitive psychology in sport: Progress and prospects. *Psychology of Sport and Exercise, 10,* 420–426.

Moretz, M., & McKay, D. (2009). The role of perfectionism in obsessive-compulsive symptoms: 'Not just right' experiences and checking compul-sions. *Journal of Anxiety Disorders, 23,* 640–644.

Morgan, A. A., Marsiske, M., & Whitfield, K. E. (2008). Characterizing and explaining differences in cog-nitive test performance between African American and European American older adults. *Experimental Aging Research, 34,* 80–100.

Morone, N. E., & Greco, C. M. (2007). Mind-body interventions for chronic pain in older adults: A structured review. *Pain Medicine, 8,* 359–375.

Morris, J. F., Waldo, C. R., & Rothblum, E. D. (2001). A model of predictors and outcomes of outness among lesbian and bisexual women. *American Journal of Orthopsychiatry, 71,* 61–71.

Morrone, A. S., & Pintrich, P. R. (2006). Achievement motivation. In G. G. Bear & K. M. Minke, *Children's needs III: Development, prevention, and intervention.* Washington, DC: National Association of School Psychologists.

Morrow, J., & Wolff, R. (1991, May). Wired for a mira-cle. *Health,* pp. 64–84.

Mosher, C. J., & Akins, S. (2007). *Drugs and drug policy: The control of consciousness alteration.* Thousand Oaks, CA: Sage Publications.

Moskowitz, G. B. (2004). *Social cognition: Understanding self and others.* New York: Guilford Press.

Motley, M. T. (1987, February). What I meant to say. *Psychology Today,* pp. 25–28.

Muammar, O. M. (2007). An integration of two com-peting models to explain practical intelligence. *Dissertation Abstracts International: Section B: The Sciences and Engineering, 67(7-B),* 4128.

Mueller, C. E. (2009). Protective factors as barriers to depression in gifted and nongifted adolescents. *Gifted Child Quarterly, 53,* 3–14.

Mullen, B., & Rice, D. R. (2003). Ethnophaulisms and exclusion: The behavioral consequences of cogni-tive representation of ethnic immigrant groups. *Personality and Social Psychology Bulletin, 29,* 1056–1067.

Munakata, Y. (2006). Information processing approaches to development. In D. Kuhn, R. S. Siegler, W. Damon, & R. M. Lerner, *Handbook of child psychology: Vol 2, Cognition, perception, and language* (6th ed.) Hoboken, NJ: John Wiley & Sons.

Munger, D. (2009, April 20). Super-recognizers: people with an amazing ability to recognize faces. Retrieved from http://scienceblogs.com/cognitive-daily/2009/04/super-recognizers_people_with.php

Murphy, D., et al. (2008, November). How the serotonin story is being rewritten by new gene-based discov-eries principally related to SLC6A4, the serotonin transporter gene, which functions to influence all cellular serotonin systems. *Neuropharmacology, 55,* 932–960.

Murphy, G. J., Glickfield, L. L., Balsen, Z., & Isaacson, J. S. (2004). Sensory neuron signaling to the brain: Properties of transmitter release from olfactory nerve terminals. *Journal of Neuroscience, 24,* 3023–3030.

Murphy, G. L. (2005). The study of concepts inside and outside the laboratory: Medin versus Medin. In W. Ahn, R. L. Goldstone, B. C. Love, A. B. Markman, & P. Wolff (Eds.), *Categorization inside and outside the laboratory: Essays in honor of Douglas L. Medin.* Washington, DC: American Psychological Association.

Murphy, R. T., Wismar, K., & Freeman, K. (2003). Stress symptoms among African-American college stu-dents after the September 11, 2001 terrorist attacks. *Journal of Nervous and Mental Disease, 191,* 108–114.

Murphy, S., et al. (1998). Interference under the influ-ence. *Personality and Social Psychology Bulletin, 24,* 517–528.

Murphy, S. T., & Zajonc, R. B. (1993). Affect, cognition, and awareness: Affective priming with optimal and suboptimal stimulus exposures. *Journal of Personality and Social Psychology, 64,* 723–739.

Murray, B. (June 2002). Good news for bachelor's grads. *Monitor on Psychology,* pp. 30–32.

Murray, R., Lappin, J., & Di Forti, M. (2008, August). Schizophrenia: From developmental deviance to dopamine dysregulation. *European Neuropsychopharmacology, 18,* S129–SS134.

Murray, S. L., Holmes, J. G., & Griffin, D. W. (2004). The benefits of positive illusions: Idealization and the construction of satisfaction in close relationships. In H. T. Reis & C. E. Rusbult (Eds.), *Close relation-ships: Key readings.* Philadelphia, PA: Taylor & Francis.

Murthy, P., Kudlur, S., George, S., & Mathew, G. (2009). A clinical overview of fetal alcohol syndrome. *Addictive Disorders & Their Treatment, 8,* 1–12.

Myers, D. G. (2000). The funds, friends, and faith of happy people. *American Psychologist, 55,* 56–67.

Myers, L. L. (2007). Anorexia nervosa, bulimia ner-vosa, and binge eating disorder. In B. A. Thyer, & J. S. Wodarski. *Social work in mental health: An evidence-based approach.* Hoboken, NJ: John Wiley & Sons.

Myerson, J., Adams, D. R., Hale, S., & Jenkins, L. (2003). Analysis of group differences in processing speed: Brinley plots, Q-Q plots, and other conspir-acies. *Psychonomic Bulletin and Review, 10,* 224–237.

Myrtek, M. (2007). Type a behavior and hostility as independent risk factors for coronary heart dis-ease. In J. Jordan, B. Barde & A. M. Zeiher, *Contributions toward evidence-based psychocardiology: A systematic review of the literature.* Washington, DC: American Psychological Association.

Mytinger, C. (2001). *Headhunting in the Solomon Islands: Around the Coral Sea.* Santa Barbara, CA: Narrative Press.

Nadeem, E., & Graham, S. (2005). Early puberty, peer victimization, and internalizing symptoms in eth-nic minority adolescents. *Journal of Early Adolescence, 25,* 197–222.

Nagai, Y., Goldstein, L. H., Fenwick, P. B. C., & Trimble, M. R. (2004). Clinical efficacy of galvanic skin response biofeedback training in reducing sei-zures in adult epilepsy: A preliminary randomized controlled trial. *Epilepsy and Behavior, 5,* 216–223.

Nagda, B. A., Tropp, L. R., & Paluck, E. L. (2006). Looking back as we look ahead: Integrating research, theory, and practice on intergroup rela-tions. *Journal of Social Research, 62,* 439–451.

Naik, G. (2004, December 29). New obesity boom in Arab countries has old ancestry. *The Wall Street Journal,* p. A1.

Naik, G. (2009, February 3). Parents agonize over treatment in the womb. *Wall Street Journal*, p. D1.

Najman, J. M., Aird, R., Bor, W., O'Callaghan, M., Williams, G. M., & Shuttlewood, G. J. (2004). The generational transmission of socioeconomic inequalities in child cognitive development and emotional health. *Social Science and Medicine, 58*, 1147–1158.

Nakamura, Y. (2004). Isolation of p53-target genes and their functional analysis. *Cancer Science, 95*, 7–11.

Naldini, L. (2009, November 6). A comeback for gene therapy. *Science, 326*, 805–806.

Narrow, W. E., Rae, D. S., Robins, L. N., & Regier, D. A. (2002). Revised prevalence estimates of mental disorders in the United States: Using a clinical significance criterion to reconcile 2 surveys' estimates. *Archives of General Psychiatry, 59*, 115–123.

Nasir, N. S., & Hand, V. (2006). From the court to the classroom: Opportunities for engagement, learning, and identity in basketball and classroom mathematics. *Journal of the Learning Sciences, 17*, 143–179.

Nasrallah, H., Black, D., Goldberg, J., Muzina, D., & Pariser, S. (2008). Issues associated with the use of atypical antipsychotic medications. *Annals of Clinical Psychiatry, 20*, S24-S29.

Nathan, P. E., Stuart, S. P., & Dolan, S. L. (2000). Research on psychotherapy efficacy and effectiveness: Between Scylla and Charybdis? *Psychological Bulletin, 126*, 964–981.

National Adolescent Health Information Center. (2003). *Fact Sheet on Demographics: Adolescents.* San Francisco: University of California, San Francisco.

National Association for the Education of Young Children. (2005). *Position statements of the NAEYC.* Retrieved from http://www.naeyc.org/about/positions.asp#where.

National Center for Health Statistics. (2000). *Health United States, 2000 with adolescent health chartbook.* National Center for Health Statistics, Hyattsville, MD.

National Depression Screening Day. (2003, March 26). Questionnaire on website. Retrieved from http://www.mentalhealthscreening.org/dep/depsample.htm#sampletest

National Institute of Child Health and Human Development (NICHD) Early Child Care Research Network. (1999). Child care and mother–child interaction in the first 3 years of life. *Psychology, 35*, 1399–1413.

National Institute of Child Health and Human Development (NICHD) Early Child Care Research Network. (2000). The relation of child care to cognitive and language development. *Child Development, 71*, 960–980.

National Institute of Child Health and Human Development (NICHD) Early Child Care Research Network. (2001). Child-care and family predictors of preschool attachment and stability from infancy. *Development Psychology, 37*, 847–862.

National Institute of Child Health and Human Development (NICHD) Early Child Care Research Network. (2002). Child-care structure—process—outcome: Direct and indirect effects of child-care quality on young children's development. *Psychological Science, 13*, 199–206.

National Institute of Child Health and Human Development (NICHD) Early Child Care Research Network. (2006). Child-care effect sizes for the NICHD study of early child care and youth development. *American Psychologist, 61*, 99–116.

National Research Council (2001). *Eager to learn: Educating our preschoolers.* Washington, DC: National Academy Press.

National Research Council and Institute of Medicine of the National Academies. (2009). *Preventing mental, emotional, and behavioral disorders among young people: Progress and possibilities.* Washington, DC: National Academies Press.

Natvig, G. K., Albrektsen, G., & Ovarnstrom, U. (2003). Methods of teaching and class participation in relation to perceived social support and stress: Modifiable factors for improving health and well-being among students. *Educational Psychology, 23*, 261–274.

Naveh-Benjamin, M., Craik, F. I. M., Gavrilescu, D., & Anderson, N. D. (2000). Asymmetry between encoding and retrieval processes: Evidence from divided attention and a calibration analysis. *Memory & Cognition, 28*, 965–967.

Naveh-Benjamin, M., Guez, J., & Sorek, S. (2007). The effects of divided attention on encoding processes in memory: Mapping the locus of interference. *Canadian Journal of Experimental Psychology, 61*, 1–12.

Neher, A. (2006). Evolutionary psychology: Its programs, prospects, and pitfalls. *American Journal of Psychology, 119*, 517–566.

Neitz, J., Neitz, M., & Kainz, P. M. (1996, November 1). Visual pigment gene structure and the severity of color vision defects. *Science, 274*, 801–804.

Nelson, P. D. (2007). The globalization of psychology: What does it mean? *The Educator, 5*, 1–4.

Nelson, W. M., III, & Finch, A. J., Jr. (2000). Managing anger in youth: A cognitive-behavioral intervention approach. In P. C. Kendall, *Child & adolescent therapy: Cognitive-behavioral procedures* (2nd ed.). New York: Guilford Press.

Neron, S., & Stephenson, R. (2007). Effectiveness of hypnotherapy with cancer patients' trajectory: Emesis, acute pain, and analgesia and anxiolysis in procedures. *International Journal of Clinical Experimental Hypnosis, 55*, 336–354.

Nesdale, D., Maass, A., & Durkin, K. (2005). Group norms, threat, and children's racial prejudice. *Child Development, 76*, 652–663.

Nesheim, S., Henderson, S., Lindsay, M., Zuberi, J., Grimes, V., Buehler, J., et al. (2004). *Prenatal HIV testing and antiretroviral prophylaxis at an urban hospital—Atlanta, Georgia, 1997–2000.* Atlanta, GA: Centers for Disease Control.

Nesse, R. M. (2000). Is depression an adaptation? *Archives of General Psychiatry, 57*, 14–20.

Nestler, E. J., & Malenka, R. C. (2004, March). The addicted brain. *Scientific American*, pp. 78–83.

Nestoriuc, Y., & Martin, A. (2007, March). Efficacy of biofeedback for migraine: A meta-analysis. *Pain, 128*, 111–127.

Nestoriuc, Y., Martin, A., Rief, W., & Andrasik, F. (2008, September). Biofeedback treatment for headache disorders: A comprehensive efficacy review. *Applied Psychophysiology and Biofeedback, 33*, 125–140.

Neubauer, A. C., & Fink, A. (2005). Basic information processing and the psychophysiology of intelligence. In R. J. Sternberg & J. E. Pretz, *Cognition and intelligence: Identifying the mechanisms of the mind.* New York: Cambridge University Press, 2005.

Neumann, N., & Birbaumer, N. (2004, December). Thinking out loud. *Scientific American: Mind*, pp. 37–45.

Neumark-Sztainer, D. (2009, March). Preventing obesity and eating disorders in adolescents: What can health care providers do? *Journal of Adolescent Health, 44*, 206–213.

Newby-Clark, I. R., & Ross, M. (2003). Conceiving the past and future. *Personality and Social Psychology Bulletin, 29*, 807–818.

Newell, A., & Simon, H. (1972). *Human problem solving.* Englewood Cliffs, NJ: Prentice Hall.

Newman, C. F., Leahy, R. L., Beck, A. T., Reilly-Harrington, N. A., & Gyulai, L. (2002). *Bipolar disorder: A cognitive therapy approach.* Washington, DC: American Psychological Association.

Newman, M., & Bakay, R. (2008, April). Therapeutic potentials of human embryonic stem cells in Parkinson's disease. *Neurotherapeutics, 5*, 237–251.

Newport, F., & Carroll, J. (2002, November 27). Battle of the bulge: Majority of Americans want to lose weight. *Gallup News Service*, pp. 1–9.

The New York Times. (1993, November 15). No. 2 pencil fades as graduate exam moves to computer. *The New York Times*, p. B9.

Niccols, A. (2007). Fetal alcohol syndrome and the developing socio-emotional brain. *Brain Cognition, 65*, 135–142.

Nicholson, I. A. M. (2003). *Inventing personality: Gordon Allport and the science of selfhood.* Washington, DC: American Psychological Association.

Nickerson, R. S., & Adams, M. J. (1979). *Cognitive Psychology, 11*, 297.

Niedenthal, P. M. (2007, May 18). Embodying emotion. *Science, 316*, 1002–1005.

Nielsen, C., Staud, R., & Price, D. (2009, March). Individual differences in pain sensitivity: Measurement, causation, and consequences. *The Journal of Pain, 10*, 231–237.

Nielsen, C., Stubhaug, A., Price, D., Vassend, O., Czajkowski, N., & Harris, J. (2008, May). Individual differences in pain sensitivity: Genetic and environmental contributions. *Pain, 136*, 21–29.

Nielson, T. A., Stenstrom, P., & Levin, R. (2006). Nightmare frequency as a function of age, gender, and September 11, 2001: Findings from an internet questionnaire. *Dreaming, 16*, 145–158.

Nigg, J. T., & Goldsmith, H. H. (1994). Genetics of personality disorders: Perspectives from personality and psychopathology research. *Psychological Bulletin, 115*, 346–380.

Nilsson, H., Juslin, P., & Olsson, H. (2008). Exemplars in the mist: The cognitive substrate of the representativeness heuristic. *Scandinavian Journal of Psychology, 49*, 201–212.

Nimrod, G., & Kleiber, D. A. (2007). Reconsidering change and continuity in later life: Toward an innovation theory of successful aging. *International Journal of Human Development, 65*, 1–22.

Nisbett, R. (2003). *The geography of thought.* New York: Free Press.

Nisbett, R. E. (2007, December 9). All brains are the same color. *The New York Times*, p. E11.

Nisbett, R.E. (2009, February). All brains are the same color. *Association for Psychological Science Observer, 22*(3), 20–21.

Nishida, M., Pearsall, J., Buckner, R., & Walker, M. (2009, May). REM sleep, prefrontal theta, and the consolidation of human emotional memory. *Cerebral Cortex, 19*, 1158–1166.

Nishino, S. (2007, June). Clinical and neurobiological aspects of narcolepsy. *Sleep Medicine, 8*, 373–399.

Nissle, S., & Bschor, T. (2002). Winning the jackpot and depression: Money cannot buy happiness. *International Journal of Psychiatry in Clinical Practice, 6*, 183–186.

Nittrouer, S., & Lowenstein, J. H. (2007). Children's weighting strategies for word-final stop voicing are not explained by auditory sensitivities. *Journal of Speech, Language, and Hearing Research, 50*, 58–73.

Noble, H. B. (1999, March 12). New from the smoking wars: Success. *The New York Times*, pp. D1–D2.

Nolen-Hoeksema, S. (2007). *Abnormal psychology* (4th ed.). New York: McGraw-Hill.

Norcia, A. M., Pei, F., Bonneh, Y., Hou, C., Sampath, V., & Petter, M. W. (2005). Development of sensitivity to texture and contour information in the human infant. *Journal of Cognitive Neuroscience, 17*, 569–579.

Norcross, J. C. (2002). Empirically supported therapy relationships. In J. C. Norcross, *Psychotherapy relationships that work: Therapist contributions and responsiveness to patients.* New York: Oxford University Press.

Norcross, J. C., Beutler, L. E., & Levant, R. F. (2006). *Evidence-based practices in mental health: Debate and dialogue on the fundamental questions.* Washington, DC: American Psychological Association.

Norlander, T., Von Schedvin, H., & Archer, T. (2005). Thriving as a function of affective personality: Relation to personality factors, coping strategies and stress. *Anxiety, Stress & Coping: An International Journal, 18*, 105–116.

Norton, P. J., & Price, E. C. (2007). A meta-analytic review of adult cognitive-behavioral treatment outcome across the anxiety disorders. *Journal of Nervous and Mental Disease, 195*, 521–531.

Noy, V. M. (2006). A psychoneuroimmunology program for Hispanic women with stage I–II breast cancer. *Dissertation Abstracts International: Section B: The Sciences and Engineering, 66*(11–B), 6287.

Noyes, R., Jr., Stuart, S. P., Langbehn, D. R., Happel, R. L., Longley, S. L., Muller, B. A., et al. (2003). Test of an interpersonal model of hypochondriasis. *Psychosomatic Medicine, 65,* 292–300.

Ntinas, K. M. (2007). Behavior modification and the principle of normalization: Clash or synthesis? *Behavioral Interventions, 22,* 165–177.

Nucci, L. P. (2002). The development of moral reasoning. In U. Goswami (Ed.), *Blackwell handbook of childhood cognitive development. Blackwell Handbooks of developmental psychology.* Malden, MA: Blackwell.

Nunes, A., & Kramer, A. F. (2009). Experience-based mitigation of age-related performance declines: Evidence from air traffic control. *Journal of Experimental Psychology: Applied, 15,* 12–24.

Nurnberger, J. I., Jr., & Bierut, L. J. (2007, April). Seeking the connections: Alcoholism and our genes. *Scientific American,* pp. 46–53.

Nussbaum, A.D. & Steele, C. M. (2007). Situational disengagement and persistence in the face of adversity. *Journal of Experimental Social Psychology, 43,* 127–134.

Nyberg, L., & Tulving, E. (1996). Classifying human long-term memory: Evidence from converging dissociations. *European Journal of Cognitive Psychology, 8,* 163–183.

Oatley, K., Keltner, D., & Jenkins, J. M. (2006). *Understanding emotions.* Oxford, England: Blackwell.

Oberauer, K. (2007). In search of the magic number. *Experimental Psychology, 54,* 245–246.

O'Brien, K. M., & LeBow, M. D. (2007). Reducing maladaptive weight management practices: Developing a psychoeducational intervention program. *Eating Behaviors, 8,* 195–210.

Occhionero, M. (2004). Mental processes and the brain during dreams. *Dreaming, 14,* 54–64.

O'Connor, D. B., & O'Connor, R. C. (2004). Perceived changes in food intake in response to stress: The role of conscientiousness. *Stress and Health: Journal of the International Society for the Investigation of Stress, 20,* 279–291.

Oehman, A., & Mineka, S. (2003). The malicious serpent: Snakes as a prototypical stimulus for an evolved module of fear. *Current Directions in Psychological Science, 12,* 5–9.

Offer, D., Kaiz, M., Howard, K. I., & Bennett, E. S. (2000). The altering of reported experiences. *Journal of the American Academy of Child & Adolescent Psychiatry, 39,* 735–742.

Ogbu, J. (1992). Understanding cultural diversity and learning. *Educational Researcher, 21,* 5–14.

O'Grady, W. D., & Dobrovolsky, M. (Eds.). (1996). *Contemporary linguistic analysis: An introduction* (3rd ed.). Toronto: Copp Clark Pitman.

Ogren, K., & Sandlund, M. (2007). Lobotomy at a state mental hospital in Sweden. A survey of patients operated on during the period 1947–1958. *Nordic Journal of Psychiatry, 61,* 355–362.

Ohara, K. (2007). The n-3 polyunsaturated fatty acid/dopamine hypothesis of schizophrenia. *Progress in Neuro-Psychopharmacology & Biological Psychiatry, 31,* 469–474.

Ohira, T., Hozawa, A., Iribarren, C., Daviglus, M. L., Matthews, K. A., Gross, M. D., et al. (2007). Longitudinal association of serum carotenoids and tocopherols with hostility: The CARDIA study. *American Journal of Epidemiology, 18,* 235–241.

Ojha, H., & Pramanick, M. (2009). Effects of age on intensity and priority of life needs. *Journal of the Indian Academy of Applied Psychology, 35,* 131–136.

O'Keefe, T., & Fox, K. (Eds.). (2003). *Finding the real me: True tales of sex and gender diversity.* San Francisco: Jossey-Bass.

Olatunji, B. (2008). New directions in research on health anxiety and hypochondriasis: Commentary on a timely special series. *Journal of Cognitive Psychotherapy, 22,* 183–190.

Olds, M. E., & Fobes, J. L. (1981). The central basis of motivation: Intracranial self-stimulation studies. *Annual Review of Psychology, 32,* 123–129.

Olfson, M., & Marcus, S. (2008). A case-control study of antidepressants and attempted suicide during early phase treatment of major depressive episodes. *Journal of Clinical Psychiatry, 69,* 425–432.

Olivardia, R., & Pope, H. (2002). Body image disturbance in childhood and adolescence. In D. Castle & K. Phillips (Eds.), *Disorders of body image.* Petersfield, England: Wrightson Biomedical Publishing.

Oliver, M. B., & Hyde, J. S. (1993). Gender differences in sexuality: A meta-analysis. *Psychological Bulletin, 114,* 29–51.

Olson, D. H., & DeFrain, J. (2005). *Marriages and families: Intimacy, diversity, and strengths with PowerWeb.* New York: McGraw-Hill.

Oosterhof, N. N., & Todorov, A. (2008). The functional basis of face evaluation. *Proceedings of the National Academy of Sciences of the United States of America, 105,* 11087–11092.

Ophir, E., Nass, C., & Wagner, A. D. (2009). Cognitive control in media multitaskers. *PNAS Proceedings of the National Academy of Sciences of the United States of America, 106,* 15583–15587.

Opler, M., Perrin, M., Kleinhaus, K., & Malaspina, D. (2008). Factors in the etiology of schizophrenia: Genes, parental age, and environment. *Primary Psychiatry, 15,* 37–45.

Oppenheimer, D. M. (2004). Spontaneous discounting of availability in frequency judgment tasks. *Psychological Science, 15,* 100–105.

OpportunityNYC.org. (2009). *About Opportunity NYC family rewards.* Retrieved from http://opportunitynyc.org/about

Ornat, S. L., & Gallo, P. (2004). Acquisition, learning, or development of language? Skinner's "Verbal behavior" revisited. *Spanish Journal of Psychology, 7,* 161–170.

Orwin, R. G., & Condray, D. S. (1984). Smith and Glass' psychotherapy conclusions need further probing: On Landman and Dawes' re-analysis. *American Psychologist, 39,* 71–72.

Oskamp, S. (Ed.). (2000). *Reducing prejudice and discrimination.* Mahwah, NJ: Erlbaum.

Otake, K., Shimai, S., & Tanaka-Matsumi, J. (2006). Happy people become happier through kindness: A counting kindnesses intervention. *Journal of Happiness Studies, 7,* 361–375.

Ouimet, A., Gawronski, B., & Dozois, D. (2009). Cognitive vulnerability to anxiety: A review and an integrative model. *Clinical Psychology Review, 29,* 459–470.

Oveis, C., Gruber, J., Keltner, D., Stamper, J., & Boyce, W. (2009). Smile intensity and warm touch as thin slices of child and family affective style. *Emotion, 9,* 544–548.

Oviedo-Jokes, E., et al. (2009). Diacetylmorphine versus methadone for the treatment of opioid addiction. *The New England Journal of Medicine, 361,* 777–786.

Packer, D. (2009). Avoiding groupthink: Whereas weakly identified members remain silent, strongly identified members dissent about collective problems. *Psychological Science, 20,* 546–548.

Pager, D., & Shepherd, H. (2008). The sociology of discrimination: Racial discrimination in employment, housing, credit, and consumer markets. *Annual Review of Sociology, 34,* 181–209.

Pagonis, T. A., Angelopoulos, N., & Koukoulis, G. N. (2006). Psychiatric side effects induced by supraphysiological doses of combinations of anabolic steroids correlate to the severity of abuse. *European Psychiatry, 21,* 551–562.

Pagoto, S. L., Kozak, A. T., & Spates, C. R. (2006). Systematic desensitization for an older woman with a severe specific phobia: An application of evidenced-based practice. *Clinical Gerontologist, 30,* 89–98.

Pallanti, S., & Bernardi, S. (2009, July). Neurobiology of repeated transcranial magnetic stimulation in the treatment of anxiety: A critical review. *International Clinical Psychopharmacology, 24,* 163–173.

Pandya, M., Pozuelo, L., & Malone, D. (2007). Electroconvulsive therapy: What the internist needs to know. *Cleveland Clinic Journal of Medicine, 74,* 679–685.

Paniagua, F. A. (2000). *Diagnosis in a multicultural context: A casebook for mental health professionals.* Thousand Oaks, CA: Sage.

Paquier, P. F., & Mariën, P. (2005). A synthesis of the role of the cerebellum in cognition. *Aphasiology, 19,* 3–19.

Parish, C. L., & Arenas, E. (2007). Stem-cell-based strategies for the treatment of Parkinson's disease. *Neurodegenerative Disease, 4,* 339–347.

Park, A. (2008, December 22). The happiness effect: How emotions and even behaviors can spread like an epidemic. *Time,* p. 40.

Park, D. C. (2007). Eating disorders: A call to arms. *American Psychologist, 62,* 158.

Park, H., & Antonioni, D. (2007). Personality, reciprocity, and strength of conflict resolution strategy. *Journal of Research in Personality, 41,* 110–125.

Parke, R. D. (2004). Development in the family. *Annual Review of Psychology, 55,* 365–399.

Parker, E. S., Cahill, L., & McGaugh, J. L. (2006). A case of unusual autobiographical remembering. *Neurocase, 12,* 35–49.

Parker-Pope, T. (2003, April 22). The diet that works. *The Wall Street Journal,* pp. R1, R5.

Parmley, M. C. (2007). The effects of the confirmation bias on diagnostic decision making. *Dissertation Abstracts International: Section B: The Sciences and Engineering, 67*(8-B), 4719.

Parra, A., & Argibay, J. C. (2007). Comparing psychics and non-psychics through a 'token-object' forced-choice ESP test. *Journal of the Society for Psychical Research, 71,* 80–90.

Pascual, A., & Guéguen, N. (2005). Foot-in-the-door and door-in-the-face: A comparative meta-analytic study. *Psychological Reports, 96,* 122–128.

Pascual, A., & Guéguen, N. (2006). Door-in-the-face technique and monetary solicitation: An evaluation in a field setting. *Perceptual and Motor Skills, 103,* 974–978.

Pascual, M. A., & Rodriguez, M. A. (2006). Learning by operant conditioning as a nonlinear self-organized process. *Nonlinear Dynamics, Psychology, and Life Sciences, 10,* 341–364.

Pastalkova, E., Serrano, P., Pinkhasova, D., Wallace, E., Fenton, A., & Sacktor, T. (2006). Storage of Spatial Information by the Maintenance Mechanism of LTP. *Science, 313,* 1141–1144.

Pauk, W., & Owens, R. (2007). *How to study in college.* Florence, KY: Cengage Press.

Paukert, A., Stagner, B., & Hope, K. (2004). The assessment of active listening skills in helpline volunteers. *Stress, Trauma, and Crisis: An International Journal, 7,* 61–76.

Paul, A. M. (2004). *Cult of personality: How personality tests are leading us to miseducate our children, mismanage our companies and misunderstand ourselves.* New York: Free Press.

Paulmann, S., Jessen, S., & Kotz, S. A. (2009). Investigating the multimodal nature of human communication: Insights from ERPs. *Journal of Psychophysiology, 23,* 63–76.

Paulozzi, L. J. (2006). Opioid analgesic involvement in drug abuse deaths in American metropolitan areas. *American Journal of Public Health, 96,* 1755–1757.

Pavitt, C. (2007). Impression formation. In B. B. Whaley & W. Samter, *Explaining communication: Contemporary theories and exemplars.* Mahwah, NJ: Lawrence Erlbaum Associates.

Payne, D. G. (1986). Hyperamnesia for pictures and words: Testing the recall level hypothesis. *Journal of Experimental Psychology: Learning, Memory, and Cognition, 12,* 16–29.

Payne, K., & Marcus, D. (2008). The efficacy of group psychotherapy for older adult clients: A meta-analysis. *Group Dynamics: Theory, Research, and Practice, 12,* 268–278.

Pearce, J. M. S. (2007). Synaesthesia. *European Neurology, 57,* 120–124.

Pearce, R. R., & Lin, Z. (2007). Chinese American post-secondary achievement and attainment: A cultural and structural analysis. *Educational Review, 59,* 19–36.

Pearlstein, T., & Steiner, M. (2008). Premenstrual dysphoric disorder: Burden of illness and treatment update. *Journal of Psychiatry & Neuroscience, 33,* 291–301.

Pearson, A. R., Dovidio, J. F., & Pratto, F. (2007). Racial prejudice, intergroup hate, and blatant and subtle bias of whites toward blacks in legal decision making in the United States. *International Journal of Psychology & Psychological Therapy, 7,* 125–134.

Pearson, J., & Clifford, C. W. G. (2005). When your brain decides what you see: Grouping across monocular, binocular, and stimulus rivalry. *Psychological Science, 16,* 516–519.

Pedersen, P. B., Draguns, J. G., Lonner, W. J., & Trimble, J. E. (Eds.). (2002). *Counseling across cultures* (5th ed.). Thousand Oaks, CA: Sage.

Pedraza, O., & Mungas, D. (2008). Measurement in cross-cultural neuropsychology. *Neuropsychology Review, 18,* 184–193.

Peiro, J. M., & Lunt, I. (2002). The context for a European framework for psychologists' training. *European Psychologist, 7,* 169–179.

Pell, M. D., Monetta, L., Paulmann, S., & Kotz, S. A. (2009). Recognizing emotions in a foreign language. *Journal of Nonverbal Behavior, 33,* 107–120.

Pellegrini, S., Muzio, R. N., Mustaca, A. E., & Papini, M. R. (2004). Successive negative contrast after partial reinforcement in the consummatory behavior of rats. *Learning and Motivation, 35,* 303–321.

Pelli, D. G., Burns, C. W., & Farell, B. (2006). Feature detection and letter identification. *Vision Research, 46,* 4646–4674.

Pellis, S. M., & Pellis, V. C. (2007). Rough-and-tumble play and the development of the social brain. *Current Directions in Psychological Science, 16,* 95–97.

Pempek, T., Yermolayeva, Y., & Calvert, S. (2009). College students' social networking experiences on Facebook. *Journal of Applied Developmental Psychology, 30,* 227–238.

Penley, J. A., Tomaka, J., & Wiebe, J. S. (2002). The association of coping to physical and psychological health outcomes: A meta-analytic review. *Journal of Behavioral Medicine, 25,* 551–603.

Penn, D. L., Corrigan, P. W., Bentall, R. P., Racenstein, J. M., & Newman, L. (1997). Social cognition in schizophrenia. *Psychological Bulletin, 121,* 114–132.

Penney, J. B., Jr. (2000). Neurochemistry. In B. S. Fogel, et al. (Eds.), *Synopsis of neuropsychiatry.* New York: Lippincott Williams & Wilkins.

Penzel, F. (2000). *Obsessive-compulsive disorders: A complete guide to getting well and staying well.* New York: Oxford University Press.

Perez, R. M., DeBord, K. A., & Bieschke, K. J. (Eds). (2000). *Handbook of counseling and psychotherapy with lesbian, gay, and bisexual clients.*

Washington, DC: American Psychological Association.

Perloff, R. M. (2003). *The dynamics of persuasion: Communication and attitudes in the 21st century* (2nd ed.). Mahwah, NJ: Erlbaum.

Perry, B. (2008, May 19) 'I don't know how to forget.' *People,* p. 143.

Pert, C. B. (2002). The wisdom of the receptors: Neuropeptides, the emotions, and body-mind. *Advances in Mind-Body Medicine, 18,* 30–35.

Pervin, L. A. (1990). *Handbook of personality: Theory and research.* New York: Guilford Press.

Pervin, L. A. (2003). *The science of personality* (2nd ed.). London: Oxford University Press.

Pesmen, C. (2006). Health and wealth techniques to help keep chronic pain from taking over. *Money Builder, 35,* 48.

Peterfi, Z., McGinty, D., Sarai, E., & Szymusiak, R. (2010). Growth hormone-releasing hormone activates sleep regulatory neurons of the rat preoptic hypothalamus. *American Journal of Physiology: Regulatory, Integrative and Comparative Physiology, 298,* R147–R156.

Peters, E., Hess, T. M., Västfjäll, D., & Auman, C. (2007). Adult age differences in dual information processes. *Perspectives on Psychological Science, 2,* 1–23.

Peters, J., Suchan, B., Koster, O., & Daum, I. (2007). Domain-specific retrieval of source information in the medial temporal lobe. *European Journal of Neuroscience, 26,* 1333–1343.

Peterson, C. (2000). The future of optimism. *American Psychologist, 55,* 44–55.

Peterson, L. R., & Peterson, M. J. (1959). Short-term retention of individual items. *Journal of Experimental Psychology, 58,* 193–198.

Petersson, K. M., Silva, C., Castro-Caldas, A., Ingvar, M., & Reis, A. (2007). Literacy: A cultural influence on functional left-right differences in the inferior parietal cortex. *European Journal of Neuroscience, 26,* 791–799.

Petrill, S. A. (2005). Introduction to this special issue: Genes, environment, and the development of reading skills. *Scientific Studies of Reading, 9,* 189–196.

Petrill, S. A., & Deater-Deckard, K. (2004). The heritability of general cognitive ability: A within-family adoption design. *Intelligence, 32,* 403–409.

Pettigrew, T. F. (2004). Justice deferred: A half century after *Brown v. Board of Education. American Psychologist, 59,* 521–529.

Pettigrew, T. F., & Tropp, L. R. (2006). A meta-analytic test of intergroup contact theory. *Journal of Personality and Social Psychology, 90,* 751–783.

Pettito, L. A. (1993). On the ontogenetic requirements for early language acquisition. In B. de Boysson-Bardies, S. de Schonen, P. W. Jusczyk, P. McNeilage, & J. Morton (Eds.), *Developmental neurocognition: Speech and face processing in the first year of life. NATO ASI series D: Behavioural and social sciences* (Vol. 69). Dordrecht, Netherlands: Kluwer Academic.

Petty, R. E., Cacioppo, J. T., Strathman, A. J., & Priester, J. R. (2005). To think or not to think: Exploring two routes to persuasion. In T. C. Brock & M. C. Green (Eds.), *Persuasion: Psychological insights and perspectives* (2nd ed.). Thousand Oaks, CA: Sage Publications.

Pfeffer, C. R. (2006). An evolutionary perspective on childhood depression. In P. S. Jensen, P. Knapp, & D. A. Mrazek, *Toward a new diagnostic system for child psychopathology: Moving beyond the DSM.* New York: Guilford Press.

Phelps, R. P. (2005). *Defending standardized testing.* Mahwah, NJ: Lawrence Erlbaum Associates.

Philip, P., Sagaspe, P., Moore, N., Taillard, J., Charles, A., Guilleminault, C., et al. (2005). Fatigue, sleep restriction and driving performance. *Accident Analysis and Prevention, 37,* 473–478.

Piaget, J. (1970). Piaget's theory. In P. H. Mussen (Ed.), *Carmichael's manual of child psychology* (3rd ed., Vol. I). New York: Wiley.

Piaget, J., & Inhelder, B. (1958). *The growth of logical thinking from childhood to adolescence* (A. Parsons & S. Seagrin, Trans.). New York: Basic Books.

Picchioni, D., Goeltzenleucher, B., Green, D. N., Convento, M. J., Crittenden, R., Hallgren, M., et al. (2002). Nightmares as a coping mechanism for stress. *Dreaming: Journal of the Association for the Study of Dreams, 12,* 155–169.

Pickel, K. (2009). The weapon focus effect on memory for female versus male perpetrators. *Memory, 17,* 664–678.

Pickering, G. J., & Gordon, R. (2006). Perception of mouthfeel sensations elicited by red wine are associated with sensitivity to 6-N-propylthiouracil. *Journal of Sensory Studies, 21,* 249–265.

Piechowski, M. M. (2003). From William James to Maslow and Dabrowski: Excitability of character and self-actualization. In D. Ambrose, L. M. Cohen, et al. (Eds.), *Creative intelligence: Toward theoretic integration: Perspectives on creativity.* Cresskill, NJ: Hampton Press.

Pietarinen, A.-V. (2006). The evolution of semantics and language-games for meaning. *Interaction Studies: Social Behaviour and Communication in Biological and Artificial Systems, 7,* 79–104.

Pillay, S. S., Gruber, S. A., Rogowska, J., Simpson, N., & Yurgelun-Todd, D. A. (2006). fMRI of fearful facial affect recognition in panic disorder: the cingulate gyrus-amygdala connection. *Journal of Affective Disorders, 94,* 173–181.

Pillay, S. S., Rogowska, J., Gruber, S. A., Simpson, N., & Yurgelun-Todd, D. A. (2007). Recognition of happy facial affect in panic disorder: an fMRI study. *Journal of Anxiety Disorders, 21,* 381–393.

Pilotti, M., Chodorow, M., & Shono, Y. (2009). The benefits and costs of prior exposure: A large-scale study of interference effects in stimulus identification. *American Journal of Psychology, 122,* 191–208.

Pincus, T., & Morley, S. (2001). Cognitive-processing bias in chronic pain: A review and integration. *Psychological Bulletin, 127,* 599–617.

Pine, D. S., Klein, R. G., Coplan, J. D., Papp, L. A., Hoven, C. W., Martinez, J., et al. Differential carbon dioxide sensitivity in childhood anxiety disorders and nonill comparison group. *Archives of General Psychiatry, 57,* 960–967.

Pinel, J. P. J., Assanand, S., & Lehman, D. R. (2000). Hunger, eating and ill health. *American Psychologist, 55,* 1105–1116.

Pinker, S. (1994). *The language instinct.* New York: William Morrow.

Pinker, S. (2004). Clarifying the logical problem of language acquisition. *Journal of Child Language, 31,* 949–953.

Pinker, S., & Jackendoff, R. (2005). The faculty of language: What's special about it? *Cognition, 96,* 201–236.

Pinkerton, S. D., Bogart, L. M., Cecil, H., & Abramson, P. R. (2002). Factors associated with masturbation in a collegiate sample. *Journal of Psychology and Human Sexuality, 14,* 103–121.

Pinkerton, S. D., Cecil, H., Bogart, L. M., & Abramson, P. R. (2003). The pleasures of sex: An empirical investigation. *Cognition and Emotion, 17,* 341–353.

Pinquart, M., Duberstein, P. R., & Lyness J. M. (2006). Treatments for later-life depressive conditions: A meta-analytic comparison of pharmacotherapy and psychotherapy. *American Journal of Psychiatry, 163,* 1493–1501.

Pi-Sunyer, X. (2003). A clinical view of the obesity problem. *Science, 299,* 859–860.

Pitman, R. K., & Delahanty, D. L. (2005). Conceptually driven pharmacologic approaches to acute trauma. *CNS Spectrums, 10,* 99–106.

Platek, S., & Kemp, S. (2009, February). Is family special to the brain? An event-related fMRI study of familiar, familial, and self-face recognition. *Neuropsychologia, 47,* 849–858.

Plomin, R. (2003). 50 years of DNA: What it has meant to psychological science. *American Psychological Society, 16,* 7–8.

Plomin, R. (2005). Finding genes in child psychology and psychiatry: When are we going to be there? *Journal of Child Psychology and Psychiatry, 46,* 1030–1038.

Plomin, R. (2009). The nature of nurture. In K. McCartney & R. A. Weinberg, (Eds.). *Experience and development: A festschrift in honor of Sandra Wood Scarr.* New York: Psychology Press.

Plomin, R., & Caspi, R. (1999). Behavioral genetics and personality. In L. A. Pervin & O. P. John (Eds.), *Handbook of personality: Theory and research.* (2nd ed.). New York: Guilford.

Plomin, R., & Davis, O. (2009, January). The future of genetics in psychology and psychiatry: Microarrays, genome-wide association, and non-coding RNA. *Journal of Child Psychology and Psychiatry, 50,* 63–71.

Plomin, R., & McGuffin, P. (2003). Psychopathology in the postgenomic era. *Annual Review of Psychology, 54,* 205–228.

Plowright, C. M. S., Simonds, V. M., & Butler, M. A. (2006). How bumblebees first find flowers: Habituation of visual pattern preferences, spontaneous recovery, and dishabituation. *Learning and Motivation, 37,* 66–78.

Pluess, M., & Belsky, J. (2009). Differential susceptibility to rearing experience: The case of childcare. *Journal of Child Psychology and Psychiatry, 50,* 396–404.

Pogarksy, G., & Piquero, A. R. (2003). Can punishment encourage offending? Investigating the 'resetting' effect. *Journal of Research in Crime and Delinquency, 40,* 95–120.

Pole, N. (2007).The psychophysiology of post-traumatic stress disorder: A meta-analysis. *Psychological Bulletin, 133,* 34–45.

Polivy, J., & Herman, C. P. (2002). Causes of eating disorders. *Annual Review of Psychology, 53,* 187–213.

Polivy, J., Herman, C. P., & Boivin, M. (2005). Eating disorders. In J. E. Maddux and B. A. Winstead, *Psychopathology: Foundations for a contemporary understanding.* Mahwah, NJ: Lawrence Erlbaum Associates.

Pollack, A. (2006, July 13). Paralyzed man uses thoughts to move a cursor. *The New York Times,* p. B5.

Polonsky, D. C. (2006). Review of the big book of masturbation: From angst to zeal. *Journal of Sex & Marital Therapy, 32,* 75–78.

Pomerlau, O. F. (1995). Individual differences in sensitivity to nicotine: Implications of genetic research on nicotine dependence [Special issue: Genetic, environmental, and situational factors mediating the effects of nicotine]. *Behavior Genetics, 25,* 161–177.

Ponterotto, J. G., Gretchen, D., Chauhan, R. V. (2001). Cultural identity and multicultural assessment: Quantitative and qualitative tools for the clinician. In L. A. Suzuki, & J. G. Ponterotto (Eds.), *Handbook of multicultural assessment: Clinical, psychological, and educational applications* (2nd ed.). San Francisco: Jossey-Bass/Pfeiffer.

Ponterotto, J. G., Utsey, S. O., & Pedersen, P. B. (2006). *Preventing prejudice: A guide for counselors, educators, and parents.* Thousand Oaks, CA: Sage Publications.

Poo, C. & Isaacson, J. S. (2007). An early critical period for long-term plasticity and structural modification of sensory synapses in olfactory cortex. *Journal of Neuroscience, 27,* 7553–7558.

Popa, D., Léna, C., Alexandre, C., & Adrien, J. (2008). Lasting syndrome of depression produced by reduction in serotonin uptake during postnatal development: Evidence from sleep, stress, and behavior. *The Journal of Neuroscience, 28,* 88–97.

Porte, H. S., & Hobson, J. A. (1996). Physical motion in dreams: One measure of three theories. *Journal of Abnormal Psychology, 105,* 329–335.

Posner, M. I., & DiGirolamo, G. J. (2000). Cognitive neuroscience: Origins and promise. *Psychological Bulletin, 126,* 873–889.

Post, J., Ali, F., Henderson, S., Shanfield, S., Victoroff, J., & Weine, S. (2009, Spring). The psychology of suicide terrorism. *Psychiatry: Interpersonal and Biological Processes, 72,* 13–31.

Poteat, V. P., & Espelage, D. L., (2007, May). Predicting psychosocial consequences of homophobic victimization in middle school students. *Journal of Early Adolescence, 27*(2), 175–191.

Pottick, K. J., Kirk, S. A., Hsieh, D. K., & Tian, X. (2007). Judging mental disorder in youths: Effects of client, clinician, and contextual differences. *Journal of Consulting Clinical Psychology, 75,* 1–8.

Powell, L. H. (2006). Review of marital and sexual lifestyles in the United States: Attitudes, behaviors, and relationships in social context. *Family Relations, 55,* 149.

Powell, L. H, Shahabi, L, & Thoresen, C. E. (2003). Religion and spirituality: Linkages to physical health. *American Psychology, 58,* 36–52.

Powers, K. D. (2006). An analysis of Kohlbergian moral development in relationship to biblical factors of morality in seminary students (Lawrence Kohlberg). *Dissertation Abstracts International: Section B: The Sciences and Engineering, 67*(6-B), 3485.

Powers, M., & Emmelkamp, P. (2008). Virtual reality exposure therapy for anxiety disorders: A meta-analysis. *Journal of Anxiety Disorders, 22,* 561–569.

Pratkanis, A. R. (2007). Social influence analysis: An index of tactics. In A. R. Pratkanis, *The science of social influence: Advances and future progress.* New York: Psychology Press.

Pratkanis, A. R., Epley, N., & Savitsky, K. (2007). Issue 12: Is subliminal persuasion a myth? In J. A. Nier, *Taking sides: Clashing views in social psychology* (2nd ed.) New York: McGraw-Hill.

Pratt, H. D., Phillips, E. L., Greydanus, D. E., & Patel, D. R. (2003). Eating disorders in the adolescent population: Future directions [Special issue: Eating disorders in adolescents]. *Journal of Adolescent Research, 18,* 297–317.

Pressley, M. P., & Harris., K. R. (2006). Cognitive strategies instruction: From basic research to classroom instruction. In P. A. Alexander & P. H. Winne, *Handbook of educational psychology.* Mahwah, NJ: Lawrence Erlbaum Associates.

Pretzer, J. L., & Beck, A. T. (2005). A cognitive theory of personality disorders. In M. F. Lenzenweger & J. F. Clarkin (Eds.), *Major theories of personality disorder* (2nd ed.). New York: Guilford Press.

Price, D. D. (2000, June 9). Psychological and neural mechanisms of the affective dimension of pain. *Science, 288,* 1769–1772.

Price, M. (2008. September). Against doctors' orders. *Monitor on Psychology,* pp. 34–36.

Prince, C. V. (2005). Homosexuality, transvestism and transsexuality: Reflections on their etymology and differentiation. *International Journal of Transgenderism, 8,* 15–18.

Prinz, J. (2007). Emotion: Competing theories and philosophical issues. In P. Thagard, *Philosophy of psychology and cognitive science.* Amsterdam, Netherlands: North Holland/ Elsevier.

Prislin, R., Brewer, M., & Wilson, D. J. (2002). Changing majority and minority positions within a group versus an aggregate. *Personality and Social Psychology Bulletin, 28,* 640–647.

Proffitt, D. R. (2006). Distance perception. *Current Directions in Psychological Science, 15,* 131–139.

Prohovnik, I., Skudlarski, P., Fulbright, R. K., Gore, J. C., & Wexler, B. E. (2004). Functional MRI changes before and after onset of reported emotions. *Psychiatry Research: Neuroimaging, 132,* 239–250.

Proudfoot, D. (2009). Meaning and mind: Wittgenstein's relevance for the 'does language

shape thought?' debate. *New Ideas in Psychology, 27,* 163–183.

Puca, R. M. (2005). The influence of the achievement motive on probability estimates in pre- and post-decisional action phases. *Journal of Research in Personality, 39,* 245–262.

Puhl, R., & Latner, J. (2007). Stigma, obesity, and the health of the nation's children. *Psychological Bulletin, 133,* 557–580.

Putnam, F. W. (2000). Dissociative disorders. In A. J. Sameroff & M. Lewis (Eds.), *Handbook of developmental psychopathology* (2nd ed.). Dordrecht, Netherlands: Kluwer Academic Publishers.

Quartana, P. J., & Burns, J. W. (2007). Painful consequences of anger suppression. *Emotion, 7,* 400–414.

Quas, J. A., Malloy, L. C., & Melinder, A. (2007). Developmental differences in the effects of repeated interviews and interviewer bias on young children's event memory and false reports. *Developmental Psychology, 43,* 823–837.

Quenot, J. P., Boichot, C., Petit, A., Falcon-Eicher, S., d'Athis, P., Bonnet, C., et al. (2005). Usefulness of MRI in the follow-up of patients with repaired aortic coarctation and bicuspid aortic valve. *International Journal of Cardiology, 103,* 312–316.

Quinn, D. M., Kahng, S. K., & Crocker, J. (2004). Discreditable: Stigma effects of revealing a mental illness history on test performance. *Personality and Social Psychology Bulletin, 30,* 803–815.

Quintana, S. M., Aboud, F. E., & Chao, R. K. (2006). Race, ethnicity, and culture in child development: Contemporary research and future directions. *Child Development, 77,* 1129–1141.

Rabin, J. (2004). Quantification of color vision with cone contrast sensitivity. *Visual Neuroscience, 21,* 483–485.

Rachman, S. (1990). Learned resourcefulness in the performance of hazardous tasks. In Rosenbaum, M. (Ed.), *Learned resourcefulness: On coping skills, self-control, and adaptive behavior.* New York: Springer.

Rachman, S., & deSilva, P. (2004). *Panic disorders: The facts.* Oxford, England: Oxford University Press.

Rado, J., Dowd, S., & Janicak, P. (2008). The emerging role of transcranial magnetic stimulation (TMS) for treatment of psychiatric disorders. *Directions in Psychiatry, 28,* 315–332.

Raffaele, P. (2006, November). Speaking Bonobo. *Smithsonian Magazine.*

Rahman, Q., Kumari, V., & Wilson, G. D. (2003). Sexual orientation-related differences in pre-pulse inhibition of the human startle response. *Behavioral Neuroscience, 117,* 1096–1102.

Rajagopal, S. (2006). The placebo effect. *Psychiatric Bulletin, 30,* 185–188.

Ramachandra, V. (2009, February). On whether mirror neurons play a significant role in processing affective prosody. *Perceptual and Motor Skills, 108,* 30–36.

Ramachandran, V. S. (2004). *A brief tour of human consciousness: From impostor poodles to purple numbers.* New York: Pi Press.

Ramachandran, V. S., & Hubbard, E. M. (2001). Synesthesia—a window into perception, thought and language. *Journal of Consciousness Studies, 8,* 3–34.

Ramos, R. T. (2006). Antidepressants and dizziness. *Journal of Psychopharmacology, 20,* 708–713.

Ramsay, M. C., Reynolds, C. R., & Kamphaus, R. W. (2002). *Essentials of behavioral assessment.* New York: Wiley.

Ramus, F. (2006). Genes, brain, and cognition: A roadmap for the cognitive scientist. *Cognition, 101,* 247–249.

Randolph-Seng, B., & Nielsen, M. E. (2009). Opening the doors of perception: Priming altered states of consciousness outside of conscious awareness. *Archiv für Religionspsychologie/Archive for the Psychology of Religions, 31,* 237–260.

Rangell, L. (2007). *The road to unity in psychoanalytic theory.* Lanham, MD: Jason Aronson.

Rapport, R. L. (2005). *Nerve endings: The discovery of the synapse.* New York: W. W. Norton.

Raskin, N. J., & Rogers, C. R. (1989). Person-centered therapy. In R. J. Corsini & D. Wedding (Eds.), *Current psychotherapies* (4th ed.). Itasca, IL: F. E. Peacock.

Rassin, E. (2008). Individual differences in the susceptibility to confirmation bias. *Netherlands Journal of Psychology, 64,* 87–93.

Rassin, E., & Muris, P. (2007). Abnormal and normal obsessions: A reconsideration. *Behaviour Research and Therapy, 45,* 1065–1070.

Ravindran, A. V., Matheson, K., Griffiths, J., Merali, Z., & Anisman, H. (2002). Stress, coping, uplifts, and quality of life in subtypes of depression: A conceptual framework and emerging data. *Journal of Affective Disorders, 71,* 121–130.

Ray, L., Bryan, A., MacKillop, J., McGeary, J., Hesterberg, K., & Hutchison, K. (2009). The dopamine D4 receptor gene exon III polymorphism, problematic alcohol use and novelty seeking: Direct and mediated genetic effects. *Addiction Biology, 14,* 238–244.

Ray, L. A., & Hutchison, K. E. (2007). Effects of naltrexone on alcohol sensitivity and genetic moderators of medication response: a double-blind placebo-controlled study. *Archives of General Psychiatry, 64,* 1069–1077.

Ray, R., et al. (2008). Neuroimaging, genetics and the treatment of nicotine addiction. *Behavioural Brain Research, 193,* 159–169.

Raz, A. (2007). Suggestibility and hypnotizability: Mind the gap. *American Journal of Clinical Hypnosis, 49,* 205–210.

Read, J., Beattie, M., Chamberlain, R., & Merrill, J. (2008). Beyond the 'binge' threshold: Heavy drinking patterns and their association with alcohol involvement indices in college students. *Addictive Behaviors, 33,* 225–234.

Redding, G. M. (2002). A test of size-scaling and relative-size hypotheses for the moon illusion. *Perception and Psychophysics, 64,* 1281–1289.

Redding, G. M., & Hawley, E. (1993). Length illusion in fractional MüllerLyer stimuli: An object-perception approach. *Perception, 22,* 819–828.

Redish, A. D. (2004). Addiction as a computational process gone awry. *Science, 306,* 1944–1947.

Reece, M., Herbenick, D., Sanders, S., Dodge, B., Ghassemi, A., & Fortenberry, J. (2009, July). Prevalence and characteristics of vibrator use by men in the United States. *Journal of Sexual Medicine, 6,* 1867–1874.

Reed, P. (2007). Response rate and sensitivity to the molar feedback function relating response and reinforcement rate on VI+ schedules of reinforcement. *Journal of Experimental Psychology: Animal Behavior Processes, 33,* 428–439.

Reed, P., & Morgan, T. (2008). Effect on subsequent fixed-interval schedule performance of prior exposure to ratio and interval schedules of reinforcement. *Learning & Behavior, 36,* 82–91.

Reed, S. K. (1996). *Cognition: Theory and applications* (4th ed.). Pacific Grove, CA: Brooks/ Cole.

Reese, R. J., Conoley, C. W., & Brossart, D. F. (2002). Effectiveness of telephone counseling: A field-based investigation. *Journal of Counseling Psychology, 49,* 233–242.

Regan, P. C. (2006). Love. In R. D. McAnulty, & M. M. Burnette, *Sex and sexuality, Vol 2: Sexual function and dysfunction.* Westport, CT: Praeger Publishers/ Greenwood Publishing.

Reichenberg, A., & Harvey, P. D. (2007). Neuropsychological impairments in schizophrenia: Integration of performance-based and brain imaging findings. *Psychological Bulletin, 133,* 212–223.

Reichenberg, A., Harvey, P., Bowie, C., Mojtabai, R., Rabinowitz, J., Heaton, R., et al. (2009).

Neuropsychological function and dysfunction in schizophrenia and psychotic affective disorders. *Schizophrenia Bulletin, 35,* 1022–1029.

Reif, A., & Lesch, K. P. (2003). Toward a molecular architecture of personality. *Behavioural Brain Research, 139,* 1–20.

Reijonen, J. H., Pratt, H. D., Patel, D. R., & Greydanus, D. E. (2003). Eating disorders in the adolescent population: An overview [Special issue: Eating disorders in adolescents]. *Journal of Adolescent Research, 18,* 209–222.

Reilly, T., & Waterhouse, J. (2007). Altered sleep-wake cycles and food intake: The Ramadan model. *Physiology & Behavior, 90,* 219–228.

Reiner, R. (2008, March). Integrating a portable biofeedback device into clinical practice for patients with anxiety disorders: Results of a pilot study. *Applied Psychophysiology and Biofeedback, 33,* 55–61.

Reisberg, D. (1997). *Cognition: Exploring the science of the mind.* New York: Norton.

Reisberg, D. (2009). *Cognition: Exploring the science of the mind.* New York: Norton.

Reiss, S., & Havercamp, S. M. (2005). Motivation in developmental context: A new method for studying self-actualization. *Journal of Humanistic Psychology, 45,* 41–53.

Relier, J. P. (2001). Influence of maternal stress on fetal behavior and brain development. *Biology of the Neonate, 79,* 168–171.

Rende, R. (2007). Thinking inside and outside the (black) box: Behavioral genetics and human development. *Human Development, 49,* 343–346.

Repp, B. H., & Knoblich, G. (2007). Action can affect auditory perception. *Psychological Science, 18,* 6–7.

Rescorla, R. A. (1988). Pavlovian conditioning: It's not what you think it is. *American Psychologist, 43,* 151–160.

Reynolds, C. R., & Ramsay, M. C. (2003). Bias in psychological assessment: An empirical review and recommendations. In J. R. Graham & J. A. Naglieri (Eds.), *Handbook of psychology: Assessment psychology* (Vol. 10). New York: Wiley.

Reynolds, R. I., & Takooshian, H. (1988, January). Where were you August 8, 1985? *Bulletin of the Psychonomic Society, 26,* 23–25.

Rice, C. (2009, December 18). Prevalence of Autism Spectrum Disorders—Autism and Developmental Disabilities Monitoring Network, United States, 2006. *MMWR, 58*(SS10), 1–20.

Rice, M. L., Tomblin, J. B., Hoffman, L., Richman, W. A., & Marquis, J. (2004). Grammatical tense deficits in children with SLI and nonspecific language impairment: Relationships with non-verbal IQ over time. *Journal of Speech, Language, and Hearing Research, 47,* 816–834.

Rich, E. L., & Shapiro, M. L. (2007). Prelimbic/ infralimbic inactivation impairs memory for multiple task switches, but not flexible selection of familiar tasks. *Journal of Neuroscience, 27,* 4747–4755.

Richard, D. C. S., & Lauterbach, D. (Eds). (2006). *Handbook of exposure therapies.* New York: Academic Press.

Richards, R. (2006). Frank Barron and the study of creativity: A voice that lives on. *Journal of Humanistic Psychology, 46,* 352–370.

Richardson, A. S., Bergen, H. A., Martin, G., Roeger, L., & Allison, S. (2005). Perceived academic performance as an indicator of risk of attempted suicide in young adolescents. *Archives of Suicide Research, 9,* 163–176.

Richardson, B. (2002, September 30). Light-bulb moments. *The Wall Street Journal,* p. R7.

Richgels, D. J. (2004). Paying attention to language. *Reading Research Quarterly, 39,* 470–477.

Riedel, G., Platt, B., & Micheau, J. (2003). Glutamate receptor function in learning and memory. *Behavioural Brain Research, 140,* 1–47.

Rieber, R. W., & Robinson, D. K. (2006). Review of the essential Vygotsky. *Journal of the History of the Behavioral Sciences, 42,* 178–180.

Rigby, L., & Waite, S. (2007). Group therapy for self-esteem: Using creative approaches and metaphor as clinical tools. *Behavioural and Cognitive Psychotherapy, 35,* 361–364.

Riley, A., Valdez, C, Barrueco, S., Mills, C., Beardslee, W., Sandler, I., et al. (2008). Development of a family-based program to reduce risk and promote resilience among families affected by maternal depression: Theoretical basis and program description. *Clinical Child and Family Psychology Review, 11,* 12–29.

Riniolo, T. C., Koledin, M., Drakulic, G. M., & Payne, R. A. (2003). An archival study of eyewitness memory of the Titanic's final plunge. *Journal of General Psychology, 130,* 89–95.

Rinn, W. E. (1984). The neuropsychology of facial expression: A review of neurological and psychological mechanisms for producing facial expressions. *Psychological Bulletin, 95,* 52–77.

Rinn, W. E. (1991). Neuropsychology of facial expression. In R. S. Feldman & B. Rimé (Eds.), *Fundamentals of non-verbal behavior.* Cambridge, England: Cambridge University Press.

Riolo, F. (2007). Ricordare, ripetere e rielaborare: Un lascito di Freud alia psicoanalisi futura. Remembering, repeating, and working through: Freud's legacy to the psychoanalysis of the future. *Rivista di Psicoanalisi, 53,* 439–446.

Rivera-Gaxiola, M., Klarman, L., Garcia-Sierra, A., & Kuhl, P. K. (2005). Neural patterns to speech and vocabulary growth in American infants. *Neuroreport: For Rapid Communication of Neuroscience Research, 16,* 495–498.

Robbins, B. (2008). What is the good life? Positive psychology and the renaissance of humanistic psychology. *The Humanistic Psychologist, 36,* 96–112.

Robert, S. (2006). Deictic space in Wolof: Discourse, syntax and the importance of absence. In M. Hickman & S. Robert (Eds.), *Space in languages: Linguistic systems and cognitive categories.* Amsterdam, Netherlands: John Benjamins.

Roberts, M. E., Moore, S. D., & Beckham, J. C. (2007). Post-traumatic stress disorder and substance use disorders. In M. Al'bsi, *Stress and addiction: Biological and psychological mechanisms.* San Diego, CA: Elsevier Academic Press.

Robins, R. W. (2005, October 7). The nature of personality: Genes, culture, and national character. *Science, 310,* 62–63.

Robinson, D. N. (2007). Theoretical psychology: What is it and who needs it? *Theory & Psychology, 17,* 187–198.

Rock, A. (1999, January). Quitting time for smokers. *Money,* pp. 139–141.

Rodd, Z. A., Bell, R. L., Sable, H. J. K., Murphy, J. M., & McBride, W. J. (2004). Recent advances in animal models of alcohol craving and relapse. *Pharmacology, Biochemistry and Behavior, 79,* 439–450.

Roesch, S. C., Adams, L., Hines, A., Palmores, A., Vyas, P., Tran, C., et al. (2005). Coping with prostate cancer: A meta-analytic review. *Journal of Behavioral Medicine, 28,* 281–293.

Rogers, C. (1980). *A way of being.* Boston: Houghton Mifflin.

Rogers, C. R. (1951). *Client-centered therapy.* Boston: Houghton-Mifflin.

Rogers, C. R. (1971). A theory of personality. In S. Maddi (Ed.), *Perspectives on personality.* Boston: Little, Brown.

Rogers, C. R. (1995). *A way of being.* Boston: Houghton Mifflin.

Rogers, J. M. (2009). Tobacco and pregnancy: Overview of exposures and effects. *Birth Defects Res. C. Embryo Today, 84,* 152–160.

Rogers, P. (2002, August 2). Too much, too soon. *People,* pp. 79–82.

Rogers, P., & Eftimiades, M. (1995, July 24). Bearing witness. *People Weekly,* pp. 42–43.

Rogers, S. (2007). The underlying mechanisms of semantic memory loss in Alzheimer's disease and semantic dementia. *Dissertation Abstracts International: Section B: The Sciences and Engineering, 67*(10-B), 5591.

Rohan, K. J., Roecklein, K. A., & Tierney Lindsey, K. (2007). A randomized controlled trial of cognitive-behavioral therapy, light therapy, and their combination for seasonal affective disorder. *Journal of Consulting and Clinical Psychology, 75*, 489–500.

Roid, G., Nellis, L. & McLellan, M. (2003). Assessment with the Leiter International Performance Scale—Revised and the S-BIT. In R. S. McCallum & R. Steve (Eds.), *Handbook of nonverbal assessment.* New York: Kluwer Academic/Plenum Publishers.

Roisman, G. I., Collins, W. A. Sroufe, L. A., & Egeland, B. (2005). Predictors of young adults' representations of and behavior in their current romantic relationship: Prospective tests of the prototype hypothesis. *Attachment and Human Development, 7,* 105–121.

Roizen, N. J., & Patterson, D. (2003). Down's syndrome. *Lancet, 361,* 1281–1289.

Rollman, G. B. (2004). *Ethnocultural variations in the experience of pain.* Mahwah, NJ: Lawrence Erlbaum Associates.

Rom, S. A., Miller, L., & Peluso, J. (2009). Playing the game: Psychological factors in surviving cancer. *International Journal of Emergency Mental Health, 11,* 25–36.

Romano, E., Tremblay, R. E., Vitaro, E., Zoccolillo, M., & Pagani, L. (2001.) Prevalence of psychiatric diagnoses and the role of perceived impairment: Findings from an adolescent community sample. *Journal of Child Psychology and Psychiatry and Allied Disciplines, 42,* 451–461.

Romeu, P. F. (2006). Memories of the terrorist attacks of September 11, 2001: A study of the consistency and phenomenal characteristics of flashbulb memories. *The Spanish Journal of Psychology, 9,* 52–60.

Rorschach, H. (1924). *Psychodiagnosis: A diagnostic test based on perception.* New York: Grune & Stratton.

Rose, N., & Blackmore, S. (2002). Horses for courses: Tests of a psychic claimant. *Journal of the Society for Psychical Research, 66,* 29–40.

Rosen, H. (2000). The creative evolution of the theoretical foundations for cognitive therapy [Special issue: Creativity in the context of cognitive therapy]. *Journal of Cognitive Psychotherapy, 14,* 123–134.

Rosen, J. (2005, August 28.) The future v. Roberts. *The New York Times Magazine,* pp. 24–29, 44, 50–51.

Rosenbloom, T., & Wolf, Y. (2002). Sensation seeking and detection of risky road signals: A developmental perspective. *Accident Analysis and Prevention, 34,* 569–580.

Rosenhan, D. L. (1973). On being sane in insane places. *Science, 179,* 250–258.

Rosenman, R. H., Grand R. J., Jenkins, C. D., Friedman, M, Straus, R., & Wurm, M. (1994). Coronary heart disease in the Western Collaborative Group Study: Final follow-up experience of 8½ years. In A. Steptoe & J. Wardle, (Eds), *Psychosocial processes and health: A reader.* New York: Cambridge University Press.

Rosenstein, D. S., & Horowitz, H. A. (1996). Adolescent attachment and psychopathology. *Journal of Consulting and Clinical Psychology, 64,* 244–253.

Rosenthal, A. M. (2008) *Thirty-eight witnesses: The Kitty Genovese case.* Hoboken, NJ: Melville House Publishing.

Rosenthal, R. (2002). Covert communication in classrooms, clinics, courtrooms and cubicles. *American Psychologist, 57,* 838–849.

Rosenthal, R. (2003). Covert communication in laboratories, classrooms, and the truly real world. *Current Directions in Psychological Science, 12,* 151–154.

Ross, H. E. (2000). Sensation and perception. In D. S. Gupta, et al. (Eds.), *Psychology for psychiatrists.* London: Whurr Publishers.

Ross, H. E., & Plug, C. (2002). *The mystery of the moon illusion: Exploring size perception.* Oxford: University Press.

Ross, J. (2006). Sleep on a problem . . . It works like a dream. *The Psychologist, 19,* 738–740.

Ross, P. E. (2004, April). Draining the language out of color. *Scientific American,* pp. 46–51.

Rossato, M., Pagano, C., & Vettor, R. (2008). The cannabinoid system and male reproductive functions. *Journal of Neuroendocrinology, 20,* 90–93.

Rossell, S. L., Bullmore, E. T., Williams, S. C. R., & David, A. S. (2002). Sex differences in functional brain activation during a lexical visual field task. *Brain and Language, 80,* 97–105.

Rossi, J. J., June, C. H., & Kohn, D. B. (2007). Genetic therapies against HIV. *Natural Biotechnology, 25,* 1444–1454.

Rossouw, J. E., Prentice, R. L., Manson, J. E., Wu, L., Barad, D., Barnabei, V. M., et al. (2007). Postmenopausal hormone therapy and risk of cardiovascular disease by age and years since menopause. *Journal of the American Medical Association, 297,* 1465–1477.

Rotan, L. W., & Ospina-Kammerer, V. (2007). *Mindbody medicine: Foundations and practical applications.* New York: Routledge/Taylor & Francis Group.

Roter, D. L., Hall, J. A., & Aoki, Y. (2002). Physician gender effects in medical communication: A meta-analytic review. *Journal of the American Medical Association, 288,* 756–764.

Rothblum, E. D. (1990). Women and weight: Fad and fiction. *Journal of Psychology, 124,* 5–24.

Roughton, R. E. (2002). Rethinking homosexuality: What it teaches us about psychoanalysis. *Journal of the American Psychoanalytic Association, 50,* 733–763.

Routtenberg, A., & Lindy, J. (1965). Effects of the availability of rewarding septal and hypothalamic stimulation on bar pressing for food under conditions of deprivation. *Journal of Comparative and Physiological Psychology, 60,* 158–161.

Rowe, J., Toni, I., Josephs, O., Frackowiak, R. S. J., & Passingham, R. E. (2000, June 2). The prefrontal cortex: Response selection or maintenance within working memory? *Science, 288,* 1656–1660.

Royzman, E. B., Cassidy, K. W., & Baron, J. (2003). "I know, you know": Epistemic egocentrism in children and adults. *Review of General Psychology, 7,* 38–65.

Rozencwajg, P., Cherfi, M., Ferrandez, A. M., Lautrey, J., Lemoine, C., & Loarer, E. (2005). Age-related differences in the strategies used by middle aged adults to solve a block design task. *International Journal of Aging and Human Development, 60,* 159–182.

Rozin, P., Kabnick, K., Pete, E., Fischler, C., & Shields, C. (2003). The ecology of eating: Smaller portion sizes in France than in the United States help explain the French paradox. *Psychological Science, 14,* 450–454.

Rubichi, S., Ricci, F., Padovani, R., & Scaglietti, L. (2005). Hypnotic susceptibility, baseline attentional functioning, and the Stroop task. *Consciousness and Cognition: An International Journal, 14,* 296–303.

Rubin, B. D., & Katz, L. C. (1999). Optical imaging of odorant representations in the mammalian olfactory bulb. *Neuron 23,* 499–511.

Rubin, D. C. (1985, September). The subtle deceiver: Recalling our past. *Psychology Today,* pp. 39–46.

Rubin, D. C., Schrauf, R. W., Gulgoz, S., & Naka, M. (2007). Cross-cultural variability of component processes in autobiographical remembering: Japan, Turkey, and the USA. *Memory, 15,* 536–547.

Rudman, L. A. & Ashmore, R. D. (2007). Discrimination and the Implicit Association Test. *Group Processes & Intergroup Relations, 10,* 359–372.

Rudner, M., & Rönnberg, J. (2008). The role of the episodic buffer in working memory for language processing. *Cognitive Processing, 9,* 19–28.

Rule, N. O., Ambady, N., & Hallett, K. C. (2009). Female sexual orientation is perceived accurately, rapidly, and automatically from the face and its features. *Journal of Experimental Social Psychology, 45,* 1245–1251.

Runco, M. A. (2006). Introduction to the special issue: Divergent thinking. *Creativity Research Journal, 18,* 249–250.

Rusche, B. (2003) The 3Rs and animal welfare—conflict or the way forward? *ALTEX, 20, (Suppl. 1),* 63–76.

Ruscher, J. B., Fiske, S. T., & Schnake, S. B. (2000). The motivated tactician's juggling act: Compatible vs. incompatible impression goals. *British Journal of Social Psychology, 39,* 241–256.

Rushton, J.P. & Jensen, A.R. (2006). The totality of available evidence shows the race IQ gap still remains. *Psychological Science, 17,* 921–922.

Russell, J. A., & Sato, K. (1995). Comparing emotion words between languages. *Journal of Cross Cultural Psychology, 26,* 384–391.

Russell, R., Duchaine, B., & Nakayama, K. (2009). Super-recognizers: People with extraordinary face recognition ability. *Psychonomic Bulletin & Review, 16,* 252–257.

Russo, N. (1981). Women in psychology. In L. T. Benjamin, Jr. & K. D. Lowman (Eds.), *Activities handbook for the teaching of psychology.* Washington, DC: American Psychological Association.

Rustin, M. (2006). Infant observation research: What have we learned so far? *Infant Observation, 9,* 35–52.

Rutherford, B., Rose, S., Sneed, J., & Roose, S. (2009, April). Study design affects participant expectations: A survey. *Journal of Clinical Psychopharmacology, 29,* 179–181.

Rutter, M. (2002). Nature, nurture, and development: From evangelism through science toward policy and practice. *Child Development, 73,* 1–21.

Rutter, M. (2006). *Genes and behavior: Nature-nurture interplay explained.* Malden, MA: Blackwell Publishing.

Rychlak, J. (1997). *In defense of human consciousness.* Washington, DC: American Psychological Association.

Rydell, R., McConnell, A., & Mackie, D. (2008). Consequences of discrepant explicit and implicit attitudes: Cognitive dissonance and increased information processing. *Journal of Experimental Social Psychology, 44,* 1526–1532.

Rymer, R. (1994). *Genie: A scientific tragedy.* New York: Penguin.

Saarni, C. (1999). *Developing emotional competence.* New York: Guilford.

Sachs-Ericsson, N., Joiner, T., Plant, E. A., & Blazer, D. G. (2005). The influence of depression on cognitive decline in community-dwelling elderly persons. *American Journal of Geriatric Psychiatry, 13,* 402–408.

Sackeim, H. A., Haskett, R. F., Mulsant, B. H., Thase, M. E., Mann, J. J., Pettinati, H. M., et al. (2001). Continuation pharmaco-therapy in the prevention of relapse following electroconvulsive therapy: A randomized controlled trial. *Journal of the American Medical Association, 285,* 1299–1307.

Sacks, O. (2003, July 28). The mind's eye. *The New Yorker,* pp. 48–59.

Saczynski, J., Willis, S., & Schaie, K. (2002). Strategy use in reasoning training with older adults. *Aging, Neuropsychology, & Cognition, 9,* 48–60.

Sadker, M., & Sadker, D. (1994). *Failing at fairness: How America's schools cheat girls.* New York: Scribners.

Saggino, A., Perfetti, B., & Spitoni, G. (2006). Fluid intelligence and executive functions: New perspectives. In L. V. Wesley, *Intelligence: New research.* Hauppauge, NY: Nova Science Publishers.

Sahin, N. T., Pinker, S., & Halgren, E. (2006). Abstract grammatical processing of nouns and verbs in Broca's area: Evidence from fMRI. *Cortex, 42,* 540–562.

Sakai, K. L. (2005, November 4). Language acquisition and brain development. *Science, 310,* 815–817.

Salgado, D. M., Quinlin, K. J., & Zlotnick, C. (2007). The relationship of lifetime polysubstance dependence to trauma exposure, symptomatology, and psychosocial functioning in incarcerated women with comorbid PTSD and substance use disorder. *Journal of Trauma Dissociation, 8*, 9–26.

Sallquist, J., Eisenberg, N., Spinrad, T. L., Eggum, N. D., & Gaertner, B. (2009). Assessment of pre-schoolers' positive empathy: Concurrent and longitudinal relations with positive emotion, social competence, and sympathy. *The Journal of Positive Psychology, 4*, 223–233.

Salmela-Aro, K., & Nurmi, J-E. (2007). Self-esteem during university studies predicts career characteristics 10 years later. *Journal of Vocational Behavior, 70*, 463–477.

Salsman, N. L. (2006). Interpersonal change as an outcome of Time-Limited Interpersonal Therapy. *Dissertation Abstracts International: Section B: The Sciences and Engineering, 66*(9-B), 5103.

Salvi, V., Fagiolini, A., Swartz, H., Maina, G., & Frank, E. (2008). The use of antidepressants in bipolar disorder. *Journal of Clinical Psychiatry, 69*, 1307–1318.

Samantaray, S. K., Srivastava, M., & Mishra, P. K. (2002). Fostering self concept and self actualization as bases for empowering women in national development: A challenge for the new millennium. *Social Science International, 18*, 58–63.

Samoilov, V., & Zayas, V. (2007). Ivan Petrovich Pavlov (1849–1936). *Journal of the History of the Neurosciences, 16*, 74–89.

Sams, M., Hari, R., Rif, J., & Knuutila, J. (1993). The human auditory memory trace persists about 10 sec: Neuromagnetic evidence. *Journal of Cognitive Neuroscience, 5*, 363–370.

Samuel, D. B., & Widiger, T. A. (2006). Differentiating normal and abnormal personality from the perspective of the DSM. In S. Strack, *Differentiating normal and abnormal personality* (2nd ed.). New York: Springer Publishing.

Sanderson, M. (2007). Assessment of manic symptoms in different cultures. *British Journal of Psychiatry, 190*, 178.

Sandomir, R. (2007, July 17). W. W. E.'s testing is examined after Bennoit murder-suicide. *The New York Times*, p. S3.

Sandoval, J., Frisby, C. L., Geisinger, K. F., Scheuneman, J. D., & Grenier, J. R. (Eds.). (1998). *Test interpretation and diversity: Achieving equity in assessment.* Washington, DC: American Psychological Association.

Santel, S., Baving, L., Krauel, K., Munte, T. F. & Rotte, M. (2006, October 9). Hunger and satiety in anorexia nervosa: fMRI during cognitive processing of food pictures. *Brain Research, 1114*, 138–148.

Santelli, J., Carter, M., Orr, M., & Dittus, P. (2009, April). Trends in sexual risk behaviors, by nonsexual risk behavior involvement, U.S. high school students, 1991–2007. *Journal of Adolescent Health, 44*, 372–379.

Saper, C. B., Lu, J., Chou, T. C., & Gooley, J. (2005). The hypothalamic integrator for circadian rhythms. *Trends in Neuroscience, 28*, 152–157.

Sapolsky, R. M. (2003). Gene therapy for psychiatric disorders. *American Journal of Psychiatry, 160*, 208–220.

Sargent, J. D., Stoolmiller, M., Worth, K. A., Cal, C. S., Wills, T. A., Gibbons, F. X., et al. (2007). Exposure to smoking depictions in movies: Its association with established adolescent smoking. *Archives of Pediatric Adolescent Medicine, 161*, 849–856.

Sato, N., Shimamura, M., & Takeuchi, D. (2007). Gene therapy for ischemic brain disease with special reference to vascular dementia. *Geriatrics & Gerontology International, 7*, 1–14.

Saucier, D. A., & Cain, M. E. (2006). The foundations of attitudes about animal research. *Ethics & Behavior, 16*, 117–133.

Savage, J., & Yancey, C. (2008). The effects of media violence exposure on criminal aggression: A meta-analysis. *Criminal Justice and Behavior, 35*, 772–791.

Savage-Rumbaugh, E. S., Toth, N., & Schick, K. (2007). Kanzi learns to knap stone tools. In

D. A. Washburn, *Primate perspectives on behavior and cognition.* Washington, DC: American Psychological Association.

Savas, H. A., Yumru, M., & Kaya, M. C. (2007). Atypical antipsychotics as 'mood stabilizers': A retrospective chart review. *Progress in Neuro-Psychopharmacology & Biological Psychiatry, 31*, 1064–1067.

Savazzi, S., Fabri, M., Rubboli, G., Paggi, A., Tassinari, C. A., & Marzi, C. A. (2007). Interhemispheric transfer following callosotomy in humans: Role of the superior colliculus. *Neuropsychologia, 45*, 2417–2427.

Saville, B. (2009). Performance under competitive and self-competitive fixed-interval schedules of reinforcement. *The Psychological Record, 59*, 21–38.

Sawa, A., & Snyder, S. H. (2002, April 26). Schizophrenia: Diverse approaches to a complex disease. *Science, 296*, 692–695.

Sayette, M. A. (1993). An appraisal disruption model of alcohol's effects on stress responses in social drinkers. *Psychological Bulletin, 114*, 459–476.

Saywitz, K., & Goodman, G. (1990). Unpublished study reported in Goleman, D. (1990, November 6). Doubts rise on children as witnesses. *The New York Times*, pp. C1, C6.

Scarr, S. (1998). American child care today. *American Psychologist, 53*, 95–108.

Scarr, S., & Weinberg, R. A. (1976). I.Q. test performance of black children adopted by white families. *American Psychologist, 31*, 726–739.

Scaturo, D. J. (2004). Fundamental clinical dilemmas in contemporary group psychotherapy. *Group Analysis, 37*, 201–217.

Scelfo, J. (2007, February 26). Men & depression: Facing darkness. *Newsweek*, p. 43–50.

Schachter, S., & Singer, J. E. (1962). Cognitive, social, and physiological determinants of emotional state. *Psychological Review, 69*, 379–399.

Schacter, D. L., & Badgaiyan, R. D. (2001). Neuroimaging of priming: New perspectives on implicit and explicit memory. *Current Directions in Psychological Science, 10*, 1–4.

Schacter, D. L., Dobbins, I. G., & Schnyer, D. M. (2004). Specificity of priming: A cognitive neuroscience perspective. *Nature Reviews Neuroscience, 5*, 853–862.

Schaefer, R. T. (2000). *Sociology: A brief introduction* (3rd ed.). Boston: McGraw-Hill.

Schaie, K. W. (2005a). Longitudinal studies. In *Developmental influences on adult intelligence: The Seattle Longitudinal Study.* New York: Oxford University Press.

Schaie, K. W. (2005b). What can we learn from longitudinal studies of adult development? *Research in Human Development, 2*, 133–158.

Schaller, M., & Crandall, C. S. (Eds.) (2004). *The psychological foundations of culture.* Mahwah, NJ: Lawrence Erlbaum Associates.

Schechter, T., Finkelstein, Y., & Koren, G. (2005). Pregnant "DES daughters" and their offspring. *Canadian Family Physician, 51*, 493–494.

Schedlowski, M., & Tewes, U. (Eds.) (1999). *Psychoneuroimmunology: An interdisciplinary introduction.* New York: Plenum.

Scheele, B., & DuBois, F. (2006). Catharsis as a moral form of entertainment. In J. Bryant, & P. Vorderer, *Psychology of entertainment.* Mahwah, NJ: Lawrence Erlbaum Associates Publishers.

Scheff, T. J. (1998). Shame in the labeling of mental illness. In P. Gilbert & B Andrews, (Eds.), *Shame: Interpersonal behavior, psychopathology, and culture.* New York: Oxford University Press.

Scheier, M. F., Carver, C. S., & Bridges, M. W. (1994). Distinguishing optimism from neuroticism (and trait anxiety, self-mastery, and self-esteem): A reevaluation of the Life Orientation Test. *Journal of Personality and Social Psychology, 67*, 1063–1078.

Schenone, M. H., Aquin, E., Li, Y., Lee, C., Kruger, M., & Bahado-Singh, R. O. (2010). Prenatal prediction of neonatal survival at the borderline viability.

Journal of Maternal-Fetal Neonatal Medicine, 12, 31–38.

Schepers, P., & van den Berg, P. T. (2007). Social factors of work-environment creativity. *Journal of Business and Psychology, 21*, 407–428.

Schieber, F. (2006). Vision and aging. In J. E. Birren & K. W. Schaire, *Handbook of the psychology of aging* (6th ed.). Amsterdam, Netherlands: Elsevier.

Schiffer, A. A., Pedersen, S. S., Widdershoven, J. W., Hendriks, E. H., Winter, J. B., & Denollet, J. (2005). The distressed (type D) personality is independently associated with impaired health status and increased depressive symptoms in chronic heart failure. *European Journal of Cardiovascular Prevention and Rehabilitation, 12*, 341–346.

Schillinger, D., Bindman, A., Wang, F., Stewart, A., & Piette, J. (2004). Functional health literacy and the quality of physician-patient communication among diabetes patients. *Patient Education and Counseling, 52*, 315–323.

Schmidt, J. P. (2006). The Discovery of neurotransmitters: A fascinating story and a scientific object lesson. *PsycCRITIQUES, 61*, 101–115.

Schmidt, N. B., Kotov, R., & Joiner, T. E., Jr. (2004). *Taxometrics: Toward a new diagnostic scheme for psychopathology.* Washington, DC: American Psychological Association.

Schmitt, D. P., Allik, J., & Mccrae, R. R. (2007). The geographic distribution of Big Five personality traits: Patterns and profiles of human self-description across 56 nations. *Journal of Cross-Cultural Psychology, 38*, 173–212.

Schmitt, D., Realo, A., Voracek, M., & Allik, J. (2008). Why can't a man be more like a woman? Sex differences in Big Five personality traits across 55 cultures. *Journal of Personality and Social Psychology, 94*, 168–182.

Schnabel, K., Asendorpf, J., & Greenwald, A. (2008). Assessment of individual differences in implicit cognition: A review of IAT measures. *European Journal of Psychological Assessment, 24*, 210–217.

Schnall, S., Haidt, J., Clore, G. L., & Jordan, A. H. (2008). Disgust as embodied moral judgment. *Personality and Social Psychology Bulletin, 34*, 1096–1109.

Schnatz, P. F., Murphy, J. L., O'Sullivan, D. M., & Sorosky, J. I. (2007). Patient choice: Comparing criteria for selecting an obstetrician-gynecologist based on image, gender, and professional attributes. *American Journal of Obstetrics and Gynecology, 197*, 548–561.

Schneider, A. & Domhoff, G. W. (2002). *The quantitative study of dreams.* www.dreamresearch.net.

Schnell, K., & Herpertz, S. C. (2007). Effects of dialectic-behavioral-therapy on the neural correlates of affective hyperarousal in borderline personality disorder. *Journal of Psychiatric Research, 41*, 837–847.

Schredl, M., Fricke-Oerkermann, L., Mitschke, A., Wiater, A., & Lehmkuhl, G. (2009, September). Longitudinal study of nightmares in children: Stability and effect of emotional symptoms. *Child Psychiatry and Human Development, 40*, 439–449.

Schredl, M., & Piel, E. (2005). Gender differences in dreaming: Are they stable over time? *Personality and Individual Differences, 39*, 309–316.

Schroers, M., Prigot, J., & Fagen, J. (2007, December). The effect of a salient odor context on memory retrieval in young infants. *Infant Behavior & Development, 30*, 685–689.

Schubert, T., & Koole, S. (2009). The embodied self: Making a fist enhances men's power-related self-conceptions. *Journal of Experimental Social Psychology, 45*, 828–834.

Schulte-Ruther, M., Markowitsch, J. J., Fink, G. R., & Piefke, M. (2007). Mirror neuron and theory of mind mechanisms involved in face-to-face interactions: A functional magnetic resonance imaging approach to empathy. *Journal of Cognitive Neuroscience, 19*, 1354–1372.

Schutt, R. K. (2001). *Investigating the social world: The process and practice of research.* Thousand Oaks, CA: Sage.

Schwartz, B. (2008). Working memory load differentially affects tip-of-the-tongue states and feeling-of-knowing judgments. *Memory & Cognition, 36,* 9–19.

Schwartz, B. L. (2001). The relation of tip-of-the-tongue states and retrieval time. *Memory & Cognition, 29,* 117–126.

Schwartz, B. L. (2002). The phenomenology of naturally-occurring tip-of-the-tongue states: A diary study. In S. P. Shohov (Ed.), *Advances in psychology research* (Vol. 8). Huntington, NY: Nova.

Schwartz, J. M., & Begley, S. (2002). *The mind and the brain: Neuroplasticity and the power of mental force.* (2002). New York: Regan Books/Harper Collins.

Schwartz, J., & Wald, M. L. (2003). NASA's curse? "Groupthink" is 30 years old, and still going strong. *The New York Times,* p. C1.

Schwartz, P., Maynard, A., & Uzelac, S. (2008). Adolescent egocentrism: A contemporary view. *Adolescence, 43*(171), 441–448.

Schwartz, S. J., Côté, J. E., & Arnett, J. J. (2005). Identity and agency in emerging adulthood: Two developmental routes in the individualization process. *Youth & Society, 37,* 201–229.

Schwenkreis, P., El Tom, S., Ragert, P., Pleger, B., Tegenthoff, M., & Dinse, H. (2007, December). Assessment of sensorimotor cortical representation asymmetries and motor skills in violin players. *European Journal of Neuroscience, 26,* 3291–3302.

Sciutto, M., & Eisenberg, M. (2007). Evaluating the evidence for and against the overdiagnosis of ADHD. *Journal of Attention Disorders, 11,* 106–113.

Scullin, M. H., Kanaya, T., & Ceci, S. J. (2002). Measurement of individual differences in children's suggestibility across situations. *Journal of Experimental Psychology: Applied, 8,* 233–246.

Seamon, M. J., Fass, J. A., Maniscalco-Feichtl, M., & Abu-Shraie, N. A. (2007). Medical marijuana and the developing role of the pharmacist. *American Journal of Health System Pharmacy, 64,* 1037–1044.

Sears, D. O. (1986). College sophomores in the laboratory: Influences of a narrow data base on social psychology's view of human nature. *Journal of Personality and Social Psychology, 51,* 515–530.

Sebel, P. S., Bonke, B., & Winograd, E. (Eds.). (1993). *Memory and awareness in anesthesia.* Englewood Cliffs, NJ: Prentice-Hall.

Sebire, S. J., Standage, M., & Vansteenkiste, M. (2009). Examining intrinsic versus extrinsic exercise goals: cognitive, affective, and behavioral outcomes. *Journal of Sport Exercise Psychology, 31,* 189–210.

Seeley, R., Stephens, T., & Tate, P. (2000). *Anatomy & Physiology* (5th ed.). Boston: McGraw-Hill.

Sefcek, J. A., Brumbach, B. H., & Vasquez, G. (2007). The evolutionary psychology of human mate choice: How ecology, genes, fertility, and fashion influence mating strategies. *Journal of Psychology & Human Sexuality, 18,* 125–182.

Segall, M. H., Campbell, D. T., & Herskovits, M. J. (1966). *The influence of culture on visual perception.* New York: Bobbs-Merrill.

Segerstrom, S. C., & Miller, G. E. (2004). Psychological stress and the human immune system: A meta-analytic study of 30 years of inquiry. *Psychological Bulletin, 130,* 601–630.

Seibt, B., & Förster, J. (2005). Stereotype threat and performance: How self-stereotypes influence processing by inducing regulatory foci. *Journal of Personality and Social Psychology, 87,* 38–56.

Seli, H. (2007). Self in self-worth protection: The relationship of possible selves to achievement motives and self-worth protective strategies. *Dissertation Abstracts International Section A: Humanities and Social Sciences, 67*(9-A), 3302.

Seligman, M. E. (2007). *What you can change . . . and what you can't: The complete guide to successful self-improvement.* New York: Vintage.

Seligman, M. E. P. (1975). *Helplessness: On depression, development, and death.* San Francisco: Freeman.

Seligman, M. E. P. (1995, December). The effectiveness of psychotherapy: The *Consumer Reports* study. *American Psychologist, 50,* 965–974.

Seligman, M. E. P. (1996, October). Science as an ally of practice. *American Psychologist, 51,* 1072–1079.

Selkoe, D. (2008). Soluble oligomers of the amyloid β-protein impair synaptic plasticity and behavior. *Behavioural Brain Research, 192,* 106–113.

Selkoe, D. J. (1997, January 31). Alzheimer's disease: Genotypes, phenotype, and treatments. *Science, 275,* 630–631.

Selkoe, D. J. (2002). Alzheimer's disease is a synaptic failure. *Science, 298,* 789–791.

Sellbom, M., & Ben-Porath, Y. S. (2006). The Minnesota Multiphasic Personality Inventory-2. In R. P. Archer, *Forensic uses of clinical assessment instruments.* Mahwah, NJ: Lawrence Erlbaum Associates.

Sellbom, M., Fischler, G., & Ben-Porath, Y. (2007). Identifying MMPI-2 Predictors of police officer integrity and misconduct. *Criminal Justice and Behavior, 34,* 985–1004.

Sells, R. (1994, August). *Homosexuality study.* Paper presented at the annual meeting of the American Statistical Association, Toronto.

Selove, R. (2007). The glass is half full: Current knowledge about pediatric cancer and sickle cell anemia. *PsycCRITIQUES, 52,* 88–99.

Selsky, A. (1997, February 16). African males face circumcision rite. *The Boston Globe,* p. C7.

Selye, H. (1976). *The stress of life.* New York: McGraw-Hill.

Selye, H. (1993). History of the stress concept. In L. Goldberger & S. Breznitz (Eds.), *Handbook of stress: Theoretical and clinical aspects* (2nd ed.). New York: Free Press.

Semler, C. N., & Harvey, A. G. (2005). Misperception of sleep can adversely affect daytime functioning in insomnia. *Behaviour Research and Therapy, 43,* 843–856.

Semykina, A., & Linz, S. J. (2007). Gender differences in personality and earnings: Evidence from Russia. *Journal of Economic Psychology, 28,* 387–410.

Sen, B., Sinha, S., Ahmed, S., Ghosh, S. Gangopadhyay, P. K., & Usha, R. (2007). Lack of association of HOXA1 and HOXB1 variants with autism in the Indian population. *Psychiatric Genetics, 17,* 22–36.

Seroczynski, A. D., Jacquez, F. M., & Cole, D. A. (2003). Depression and suicide during adolescence. In G. R. Adams & M. D. Berzonsky (Eds.), *Blackwell handbook of adolescence.* Malden, MA: Blackwell Publishers.

Serpell, R. (2000). Intelligence and culture. In R. Sternberg (Ed.), *Handbook of intelligence.* Cambridge, England: Cambridge University Press.

Seymour, B. (2006). Carry on eating: Neural pathways mediating conditioned potentiation of feeding. *Journal of Neuroscience, 26,* 1061–1062.

Shafer, V. L. & Garrido-Nag, K. (2007). The neurodevelopmental bases of language. In E. Hoff & M. Shatz, *Blackwell handbook of language development.* Malden, MA: Blackwell Publishing.

Shah, D. B., Pesiridou, A., Baltuch, G. H., Malone, D. A. & O'Reardon, J. P. (2008). Functional neurosurgery in the treatment of severe obsessive compulsive disorder and major depression: Overview of disease circuits and therapeutic targeting for the clinician. *Psychiatry, 5,* 24–33.

Shaikholeslami, R., & Khayyer, M. (2006). Intrinsic motivation, extrinsic motivation, and learning English as a foreign language. *Psychological Reports, 99,* 813–818.

Shankar, G., & Simmons, A. (2009, January). Understanding ethics guidelines using an internet-based expert system. *Journal of Medical Ethics, 35,* 65–68.

Shapiro, L. R. (2006). Remembering September 11th: The role of retention interval and rehearsal on flashbulb and event memory. *Memory, 14,* 129–147.

Sharma, H. S., Sjoquist, P. O., & Ali, S. F. (2007). Drugs of abuse-induced hyperthermia, blood-brain barrier dysfunction and neurotoxicity: neuroprotective effects of a new antioxidant compound h-290/51. *Current Pharmaceutical Design, 13,* 1903–1923.

Shea, A., & Steiner, M. (2008). Cigarette smoking during pregnancy. *Nicotine & Tobacco Research, 10,* 267–278.

Shelton, R. C., Keller, M. B., Gelenberg, A., Dunner, D. L., Hirschfeld, R. M. A., Thase, M. E., et al. (2002). The effectiveness of St. John's wort in major depression: A multi-center, randomized placebo-controlled trial. *Journal of the American Medical Association, 285,* 1978–1986.

Shepard, R. N., & Metzler, J. (1971). Mental rotation of three-dimensional objects. *Science, 171*(3972), 701–703.

Sheppard, L. D., & Vernon, P. A. (2008). Intelligence and speed of information-processing: A review of 50 years of research. *Personality and Individual Differences, 44,* 535–551.

Shepperd, J., Malone, W., & Sweeny, K. (2008). Exploring causes of the self-serving bias. *Social and Personality Psychology Compass, 2,* 895–908.

Sherblom, S. (2008). The legacy of the 'care challenge': Re-envisioning the outcome of the justice-care debate. *Journal of Moral Education, 37,* 81–98.

Sherman, S. L., Allen, E. G., Bean, L. H., & Freeman, S. B. (2007). Epidemiology of Down syndrome [Special issue: Down syndrome]. *Mental Retardation and Developmental Disabilities Research Reviews, 13,* 221–227.

Shier, D., Butler, J., & Lewis, R. (2000). *Hole's essentials of human anatomy and physiology* (7th ed.). Boston: McGraw-Hill.

Shiffman, S. (2007). Use of more nicotine lozenges leads to better success in quitting smoking. *Addiction, 102,* 809–814.

Shimono, K., & Wade N. J. (2002). Monocular alignment in different depth planes. *Vision Research, 42,* 1127–1135.

Shin, A., Zheng, H., & Berthoud, H. (2009). An expanded view of energy homeostasis: Neural integration of metabolic, cognitive, and emotional drives to eat. *Physiology & Behavior, 97,* 572–580.

Shinn, M., Gottlieb, J., Wett, J. L., Bahl, A., Cohen, A., & Baron, E. D. (2007). Predictors of homelessness among older adults in New York City: Disability, economic, human and social capital and stressful events. *Journal of Health Psychology, 12,* 696–708.

Shmuel, A., Chaimow, D., Raddatz, G., Ugurbil, K., & Yacoub, E. (2010). Mechanisms underlying decoding at 7 T: Ocular dominance columns, broad structures, and macroscopic blood vessels in V1 convey information on the stimulated eye. *NeuroImage, 49,* 1957–1964.

Shoda, Y., & Mischel, W. (2006). Applying meta-theory to achieve generalisability and precision in personality science. *Applied Psychology: An International Review, 55,* 439–452.

Shors, T. J. (2009, March). Saving new brain cells. *Scientific American,* pp. 47–54.

Shurkin, J. N. (1992). *Terman's kids: The ground-breaking study of how the gifted grow up.* Boston: Little, Brown.

Shweder, R. A. (1994). You're not sick, you're just in love: Emotion as an interpretive system. In P. Ekman & R. J. Davidson (Eds.), *The nature of emotion: Fundamental questions.* New York: Oxford.

Sidman, M. (2006). The distinction between positive and negative reinforcement: Some additional considerations. *Behavior Analyst, 29,* 135–139.

Siegel, J. M. (2003, November). Why we sleep. *Scientific American,* pp. 92–97.

Siegel, R. K. (1989). *Intoxication: Life in pursuit of artificial paradise.* New York: E. P. Dutton.

Siegert, R. J., & Ward, T. (2002). Clinical psychology and evolutionary psychology: Toward a dialogue. *Review of General Psychology, 6,* 235–259.

Siemer, M., Mauss I., & Gross, J. J. (2007). Same situation—different emotions: How appraisals shape our emotions. *Emotion, 7,* 592–600.

Sifrit, K. J. (2006). The effects of aging and cognitive decrements on simulated driving performance. *Dissertation abstracts international: Section B: The sciences and engineering, 67*, 2863.

Silva, M. T. A., Gonçalves, F. L., & Garcia-Mijares, M. (2007). Neural events in the reinforcement contingency. *Behavior Analyst, 30*, 17–30.

Silverman, K., Roll, J., & Higgins, S. (2008). Introduction to the special issue on the behavior analysis and treatment of drug addiction. *Journal of Applied Behavior Analysis, 41*, 471–480.

Silverstein, M. L. (2007). Rorschach test findings at the beginning of treatment and 2 years later, with a 30-year follow-up. *Journal of Personality Assessment, 88*, 131–143.

Simcock, G., & Hayne, H. (2002). Breaking the barrier? Children fail to translate their pre-verbal memories into language. *Psychological Science, 13*, 225–231.

Simon, G., Ludman, E., Unützer, J., Operskalski, B., & Bauer, M. (2008). Severity of mood symptoms and work productivity in people treated for bipolar disorder. *Bipolar Disorders, 10*, 718–725.

Simon, S., & Hoyt, C. (2008). Exploring the gender gap in support for a woman for president. *Analyses of Social Issues and Public Policy (ASAP), 8*, 157–181.

Simonton, D. K. (2000). Archival research. In A. E. Kazdin (Ed.), *Encyclopedia of psychology* (Vol. 1). Washington, DC: American Psychological Association.

Simonton, D. K. (2009). Varieties of (scientific) creativity: A hierarchical model of domain-specific disposition, development, and achievement. *Perspectives on Psychological Science, 4*, 441–452.

Singer, J. L. (2006). Why imagery, personal memories, and daydreams matter. In J. L. Singer, *Imagery in psychotherapy*. Washington, DC: American Psychological Association.

Singh, S., Wulf, D., Samara, R, & Cuca, Y. P. (2000). Gender differences in the timing of first intercourse: Data from 14 countries. *International Family Planning Perspectives, 26*, 21–28, 43.

Sininger, Y. S., & Cone-Wesson, B. (2004, September 10). Asymmetric cochlear processing mimics hemispheric specialization. *Science, 305*, 1581.

Sininger, Y. S., & Cone-Wesson, B. (2006). Lateral asymmetry in the ABR of neonates: evidence and mechanisms. *Hearing Research, 212*, 203–211.

Skinner, B. F. (1957). *Verbal behavior*. New York: Appleton-Century-Crofts.

Skinner, B. F. (1975). The steep and thorny road to a science of behavior. *American Psychologist, 30*, 42–49.

Skipp, C., & Campo-Flores, A. (2007, September 3). Taking on Tourette's. *Newsweek*, p. 53.

Skolnick, P., Popik, P., Trullas, R. (2009). Glutamate-based antidepressants: 20 years on. *Trends in Pharmacological Science, 30*, 563–569.

Slater, E., & Meyer, A. (1959). Contributions to a pathography of the musicians: Robert Schumann. *Confinia Psychiatrica*. Reprinted in K. R. Jamison, *Touched with fire: Manic-depressive illness and the artistic temperament*. New York: Free Press.

Sleek, S. (1997 June). Can "emotional intelligence" be taught in today's schools? *APA Monitor*, p. 25.

Sloan, E. P., et al. (1993). The nuts and bolts of behavioral therapy for insomnia. *Journal of Psychosomatic Research, 37* (Suppl.), 19–37.

Smart, R. G. (2007). Review of introduction to addictive behaviours. *Addiction, 102*, 831.

Smetana, J. B. (2007). Strategies for understanding archetypes and the collective unconscious of an organization. *Dissertation Abstracts International Section A: Humanities and Social Sciences, 67*(12-A), 4714.

Smetana, J., Daddis, C., & Chuang, S. (2003). "Clean your room!" A longitudinal investigation of adolescent-parent conflict and conflict resolution in middle-class African American families. *Journal of Adolescent Research, 18*, 631–650.

Smetana, J. G. (2005). Adolescent-parent conflict: Resistance and subversion as developmental process. In L. Nucci (Ed.), *Conflict, contradiction, and contrarian elements in moral development and education*. Mahwah, NJ: Lawrence Erlbaum Associates.

Smith, B. H., Barkley, R. A., & Shapiro, C. J. (2006). Attention-Deficit/Hyperactivity Disorder. In E. J. Mash & R. A. Barkley, *Treatment of childhood disorders* (3rd. ed). New York: Guilford Press.

Smith, C. (2006). Symposium V—Sleep and learning: New developments [Special issue: Methods and learning in functional MRI]. *Brain and Cognition, 60*, 331–332.

Smith, C. A., & Lazarus, R. S. (2001). Appraisal components, core relational themes, and the emotions. In W. G. Parrott (Ed.), *Emotions in social psychology: Essential readings* (pp. 94–114). Philadelphia: Psychology Press.

Smith, C. D., Chebrolu, J., Wekstein, D. R., Schmitt, F. A., & Markesbery, W. R. (2007). Age and gender effects on human brain anatomy: a voxel-based morphometric study in healthy elderly. *Neurobiology of Aging, 28*, 1057–1087.

Smith, E. (1988, May). Fighting cancerous feelings. *Psychology Today*, pp. 22–23.

Smith, E. R., & Semin, G. R. (2007). Situated social cognition. *Current Directions in Psychological Science, 16*, 132–135.

Smith, L., Cornelius, V., Warnock, A., Bell, A., & Young, A. (2007). Effectiveness of mood stabilizers and antipsychotics in the maintenance phase of bipolar disorder: A systematic review of randomized controlled trials. *Bipolar Disorders, 9*, 394–412.

Smith, M. B. (2003). Moral foundations in research with human participants. In A. E. Kazdin (Ed.), *Methodological issues & strategies in clinical research* (3rd ed.). Washington, DC: American Psychological Association.

Smith, M. L., Glass, G. V., & Miller, T. I. (1980). *The benefits of psychotherapy*. Baltimore: The Johns Hopkins University Press.

Smith, R. A., & Weber, A. L. (2005). Applying social psychology in everyday life. In F. W. Schneider, J. A. Gruman & L. M. Coutts, *Applied social psychology: Understanding and addressing social and practical*. Thousand Oaks, CA: Sage Publications.

Smith, W. B. (2007). Karen Horney and psychotherapy in the 21st century. *Clinical Social Work Journal, 35*, 57–66.

Smolowe, J. (2008, June 23). Medical miracle surgery for an unborn child. *People*, p. 96.

Snyder, D. J., Fast, K., & Bartoshuk, L. M. (2004). Valid comparisons of suprathreshold sensations. *Journal of Consciousness Studies, 11*, 96–112.

Snyder, J., Cramer, A., & Afrank, J. (2005). The contributions of ineffective discipline and parental hostile attributions of child misbehavior to the development of conduct problems at home and school. *Developmental Psychology, 41*, 30–41.

Snyder, M. (2002). Applications of Carl Rogers' theory and practice to couple and family therapy: A response to Harlene Anderson and David Bott. *Journal of Family Therapy, 24*, 317–325.

Sobel, K., Gerrie, M., Poole, B., & Kane, M. (2007, October). Individual differences in working memory capacity and visual search: The roles of top-down and bottom-up processing. *Psychonomic Bulletin & Review, 14*, 840–845.

Society for Personality Assessment. (2005). The status of Rorschach in clinical and forensic practice: An official statement by the board of trustees of the Society for Personality Assessment. *Journal of Personality Assessment, 85*, 219–237.

Sohr-Preston, S. L., & Scaramella, L. V. (2006). Implications of timing of maternal depressive symptoms for early cognitive and language development. *Clinical Child and Family Psychology Review, 9*, 65–83.

Sokolove, M. (2003, November 16). Should John Hinckley go free? *The New York Times Magazine*, pp. 52–54, 92.

Soler, J., Pascual, J., Tiana, T., Cebrià, A., Barrachina, J., Campins, M., et al. (2009). Dialectical behav-

iour therapy skills training compared to standard group therapy in borderline personality disorder: A 3-month randomised controlled clinical trial. *Behaviour Research and Therapy, 47*, 353–358.

Solomon, M., & Herman, J. (2009). Sex differences in psychopathology: Of gonads, adrenals and mental illness. *Physiology & Behavior, 97*, 250–258.

Sommer, R., & Sommer, B. (2001). *A practical guide to behavioral research: Tools and techniques* (5th ed.). New York: Oxford University Press.

Sori, C. F. (Ed.). (2006). *Engaging children in family therapy: Creative approaches to integrating theory and research in clinical practice*. New York: Routledge/ Taylor & Francis Group.

Soussignan, R. (2002). Duchenne smile, emotional experience, and automatic reactivity: A test of the facial feedback hypothesis. *Emotion, 2*, 52–74.

South, S., & Krueger, R. (2008). An interactionist perspective on genetic and environmental contributions to personality. *Social and Personality Psychology Compass, 2*, 929–948.

Spackman, M. P., Fujiki, M., & Brinton, B. (2006). Understanding emotions in context: The effects of language impairment on children's ability to infer emotional reactions. *International Journal of Language & Communication Disorders, 41*, 173–188.

Spangler, W. D. (1992). Validity of questionnaire and TAT measures of need for achievement: Two meta-analyses. *Psychological Bulletin, 112*, 140–154.

Spanos, N. P., Barber, T. X., & Lang, G. (2005). Cognition and self-control: Cognitive control of painful sensory input. *Integrative Physiological & Behavioral Science, 40*, 119–128.

Spearman, C. (1927). *The abilities of man*. London: Macmillan.

Speirs-Neumeister, K. L., & Finch, H. (2006). Perfectionism in high-ability students: Relational precursors and influences on achievement motivation. *Gifted Child Quarterly, 50*, 238–251.

Spence, M. J., & DeCasper, A. J. (1982, March). *Human fetuses perceive maternal speech*. Paper presented at the meeting of the International Conference on Infant Studies, Austin, TX.

Spencer, S. J., Fein, S., Zanna, M. P., & Olson, J. M. (Eds.) (2003). *Motivated social perception: The Ontario Symposium* (Vol. 9). Mahwah, NJ: Erlbaum.

Spencer-Rodgers, J., Peng, K., Wang, L., & Hou, Y. (2004). Dialectical self-esteem and East-West differences in psychological well-being. *Personality and Social Psychology Bulletin, 30*, 1416–1432.

Sperling, G. (1960). The information available in brief visual presentation. *Psychological Monographs, 74*, pp. 29.

Sperry, R. (1982). Some effects of disconnecting the cerebral hemispheres. *Science, 217*, 1223–1226.

Spiegel, D. (1996). Hypnosis. In R. E. Hales & S. C. Yudofsky (Eds.), *The American Psychiatric Press synopsis of psychiatry*. Washington, DC: American Psychiatric Press.

Spiegel, D. (Ed.). (1999). *Efficacy and cost-effectiveness of psychotherapy*. New York: American Psychiatric Press.

Spielberger, C. D. (2006). Cross-cultural assessment of emotional states and personality traits. *European Psychologist, 11*, 297–303.

Spiers, H. J., & Maguire, E. A. (2007). Decoding human brain activity during real-world experiences. *Trends in Cognitive Science, 11*, 356–365.

Spindler, H., Kruse, C., Zwisler, A., & Pedersen, S. (2009). Increased anxiety and depression in Danish cardiac patients with a type D personality: Cross-validation of the Type D Scale (DS14). *International Journal of Behavioral Medicine, 16*, 98–107.

Spinella, M., & Lester, D. (2006). Can money buy happiness? *Psychological Reports, 99*, 992.

Spitz, H. H. (1987). Problem-solving processes in special populations. In J. G. Borkowski & J. D. Day (Eds.), *Cognition in special children: Comparative approaches to retardation, learning disabilities, and gift-edness.* Norwood, NJ: Ablex.

Spitzer, R. L., Skodol, A. E., Gibbon, M., & Williams, J. B. W. (1983). *Psychopathology: A case book.* New York: McGraw-Hill.

Sprecher, S., & Hatfield, E. (1996). Premarital sexual standards among U.S. college students: Comparison with Russian and Japanese students. *Archives of Sexual Behavior, 25,* 261–288.

Sprecher, S., & Regan, P. C. (2002). Liking some things (in some people) more than others: Partner preferences in romantic relationships and friendships. *Journal of Social and Personal Relationships, 19,* 436–481.

Sprenger, M. (2007). *Memory 101 for educators.* Thousand Oaks, CA: Corwin Press.

Sprenkle, D. H., & Moon, S. M. (Eds.). (1996). *Research methods in family therapy.* New York: Guilford Press.

Springen, K. (2004, August 9). Anxiety: Sweet and elusive sleep. *Newsweek,* p. 21.

Squire, L. R., Clark, R. E., & Bayley, P. J. (2004). Medial temporal lobe function and memory. In M. S. Gazzaniga (Ed.), *Cognitive neurosciences* (3rd ed.). Cambridge, MA: MIT.

Staddon, J. E. R., & Cerutti, D. T. (2003). Operant conditioning. *Annual Review of Psychology, 54,* 115–144.

Staley, J. K., & Sanacora, G., & Tamagnan, G. (2006). Sex differences in diencephalon serotonin transporter availability in major depression. *Biological Psychiatry, 59,* 40–47.

Stankov, L. (2003). Complexity in human intelligence. In R. J. Sternberg, J. Lautrey, et al. (Eds.), *Models of intelligence: International perspectives.* Washington, DC: American Psychological Association.

Stanojevic, S., Mitic, K., & Vujic, V. (2007). Exposure to acute physical and psychological stress alters the response of rat macrophages to corticosterone, neuropeptide Y and beta-endorphin. *International Journal on the Biology of Stress, 10,* 65–73.

Stanton, A. L., Danoff-Burg, S., Cameron, C. L., Bishop, M., Collins, C. A., Kirk, S. B., et al. (2000). Emotionally expressive coping predicts psychological and physical adjustment to breast cancer. *Journal of Consulting and Clinical Psychology, 68,* 875–882.

Stapel, D. A., & Semin, G. R. (2007). The magic spell of language: Linguistic categories and their perceptual consequences. *Journal of Personality and Social Psychology, 93,* 23–33.

Starcevic, V., Berle, D., Milicevic, D., Hannan, A., Pamplugh, C., & Eslick, G. D. (2007). Pathological worry, anxiety disorders and the impact of co-occurrence with depressive and other anxiety disorders. *Journal of Anxiety Disorders, 21,* 1016–1027.

Startup, M., Bucci, S., & Langdon, R. (2009). Delusions of reference: A new theoretical model. *Cognitive Neuropsychiatry, 14,* 110–126.

St. Dennis, C., Hendryx, M., Henriksen, A. L., Setter, S. M., & Singer, B. (2006). Postdischarge treatment costs following closure of a state geropsychiatric ward: Comparison of 2 levels of community care. *Primary Care Companion Journal of Clinical Psychiatry, 8,* 279–284.

Steblay, N., Dysart, J., Fulero, S., & Lindsay, R. C. L. (2003). Eyewitness accuracy rates in police showup and lineup presentations: A meta-analytic comparison. *Law & Human Behavior, 27,* 523–540.

Steele, C. M. (1997). A threat in the air: How stereotypes shape intellectual identity and performance. *American Psychologist, 52,* 613–629.

Steele, C. M., & Josephs, R. A. (1990). Alcohol myopia: Its prized and dangerous effects. *American Psychologist, 45,* 921–933.

Steele, J. D., Christmas, D., Eljamel, M. S., & Matthews, K. (2007). Anterior cingulotomy for major depression: clinical outcome and relationship to lesion characteristics. *Biological Psychiatry, 12,* 127–134.

Stegerwald, F., & Janson, G. R. (2003). Conversion therapy: Ethical considerations in family counseling. *Family Journal—Counseling and Therapy for Couples and Families, 11,* 55–59.

Steiger, A. (2007). Neurochemical regulation of sleep. *Journal of Psychiatric Research, 41,* 537–552.

Stein, L. A. R., & Graham, J. R. (2005). Ability of substance abusers to escape detection on the Minnesota Multiphasic Personality Inventory-Adolescent (MMPI-A) in a juvenile correctional facility. *Assessment, 12,* 28–39.

Steinberg, L. (2007). Risk taking in adolescence: New perspectives from brain and behavioral science. *Current Directions in Psychological Science, 16,* 55–59.

Steiner, J. (2008). Transference to the analyst as an excluded observer. *The International Journal of Psychoanalysis, 89,* 39–54.

Steinfeld, C., Ellison, N., & Lampe, C. (2008). Social capital, self-esteem, and use of online social network sites: A longitudinal analysis. *Journal of Applied Developmental Psychology, 29,* 434–445.

Stemler, S. E., & Sternberg, R. J. (2006). Using situational judgment tests to measure practical intelligence. In J. A. Weekley & R. E. Ployhart (Eds.), *Situational judgment tests: Theory, measurement, and application.* Mahwah, NJ: Lawrence Erlbaum Associates.

Stemler, S. E., Sternberg, R. J., Grigorenko, E. L., Jarvin, L., & Sharpes, K. (2009). Using the theory of successful intelligence as a framework for developing assessments in AP physics. *Contemporary Educational Psychology, 34,* 195–209.

Stenbacka, L., & Vanni, S. (2007). fMRI of peripheral visual field representation. *Clinical Neurophysiology, 108,* 1303–1314.

Stenklev, N. C., & Laukli, E. (2004). Cortical cognitive potentials in elderly persons. *Journal of the American Academy of Audiology, 15,* 401–413.

Stephenson, R. H., & Banet-Weiser, S. (2007). Supersized kids: Obesity, children, moral panic, and the media. In J. A. Bryant, *The children's television community.* Mahwah, NJ: Lawrence Erlbaum Associates.

Stern, E., & Silbersweig, D. A. (2001). Advances in functional neuroimaging methodology for the study of brain systems underlying human neuropsychological function and dysfunction. In D. A. Silbersweig & E. Stern (Eds.), *Neuropsychology and functional neuroimaging: Convergence, advances and new directions.* Amsterdam, Netherlands: Swets and Zeitlinger.

Stern, R. M., & Koch, K. L. (1996). Motion sickness and differential susceptibility. *Current Directions in Psychological Science, 5,* 115–120.

Sternberg, R. J. (1990). *Metaphors of mind: Conceptions of the nature of intelligence.* New York: Cambridge University Press.

Sternberg, R. J. (1998). *Successful intelligence: How practical and creative intelligence determine success in life.* New York: Plume.

Sternberg, R. J. (2000). Intelligence and wisdom. In R. J. Sternberg et al. (Eds.), *Handbook of intelligence.* New York: Cambridge University Press.

Sternberg, R. J. (2000). The Holey Grail of general intelligence. *Science, 289,* 399–401.

Sternberg, R. J. (2002). Individual differences in cognitive development. In U. Goswami (Ed.), *Blackwell handbook of childhood cognitive development. Blackwell handbooks of developmental psychology.* Malden, MA: Blackwell.

Sternberg, R. J. (2004). A triangular theory of love. In H. T. Reis & C. E. Rusbult (Eds.), *Close relationships: Key readings.* Philadelphia, PA: Taylor & Francis.

Sternberg, R. J. (2005). Culture and measurement. *Measurement: Interdisciplinary Research and Perspectives, 3,* 108–113.

Sternberg, R. J. (2006). A duplex theory of love. In R. J. Sternberg, Ed., *The new psychology of love.* New Haven, CT: Yale University Press.

Sternberg, R. J. (2007). Who are the bright children? The cultural context of being and acting intelligent. *Educational Researcher, 36,* 148–155.

Sternberg, R. J., & Beall, A. E. (1991). How can we know what love is? An epistemological analysis. In

G. J. O. Fletcher & F. D. Fincham (Eds.), *Cognition in close relationships.* Hillsdale, NJ: Erlbaum.

Sternberg, R. J., Grigorenko, E. L., & Kidd, K. K. (2005). Intelligence, race, and genetics. *American Psychologist, 60,* 46–59.

Sternberg, R. J., & Hedlund, J. (2002). Practical intelligence, "g," and work psychology. *Human Performance, 15,* 143–160.

Sternberg, R. J., Hojjat, M., & Barnes, M. L. (2001). Empirical aspects of a theory of love as a story. *European Journal of Personality, 15,* 1–20.

Sternberg, R. J., & Jarvin, L. (2003). Alfred Binet's contributions as a paradigm for impact in psychology. In R. J. Sternberg (Ed.), *The anatomy of impact: What makes the great works of psychology great.* Washington, DC: American Psychological Association.

Sternberg, R. J., Kaufman, J. C., & Pretz, J. E. (2004). A propulsion model of creative leadership [Special issue: Creativity in the workplace]. *Creativity and Innovation Management, 13,* 145–153.

Sternberg, R. J., & O'Hara, L. A. (2000). Intelligence and creativity. In R. Sternberg et al. (Eds.), *Handbook of intelligence.* New York: Cambridge University Press.

Sternberg, R. J., & Pretz, J. E. (2005). *Cognition and intelligence: Identifying the mechanisms of the mind.* New York: Cambridge University Press.

Stettler, N., Stallings, V. A., Troxel, A. B., Zhao, J. Z., Schinnar, R., Nelson, S. E., et al. (2005). Weight gain in the first week of life and overweight in adulthood. *Circulation, 111,* 1897–1903.

Stevens, C., Lauinger, B., Neville, H. (2009). Differences in the neural mechanisms of selective attention in children from different socioeconomic backgrounds: An event-related brain potential study. *Developmental Science, 12,* 634–646.

Stevens, C. F. (1979, September). The neuron. *Scientific American,* p. 56.

Stevens, G., & Gardner, S. (1982). *The women of psychology: Pioneers and innovators* (Vol. 1). Cambridge, MA: Schenkman.

Stevens, M. C., Skudlarski, P., Pearlson, G. D., & Calhoun, V. D. (2009). Age-related cognitive gains are mediated by the effects of white matter development on brain network integration. *Neuroimage, 48,* 738–746.

Stevens, M. J., & Gielen, U.P. (Eds.). (2007). *Toward a global psychology: Theory, research, intervention, and pedagogy.* Mahwah, NJ: Lawrence Erlbaum.

Stevens, P., & Harper, D. J. (2007). Professional accounts of electroconvulsive therapy: A discourse analysis. *Social Science & Medicine, 64,* 1475–1486.

Stevens, S. S., & Pashler, H. E. (2002). *Steven's handbook of experimental psychology: Learning, motivation, and emotion.* New York: Wiley.

Stevenson, H. W., Lee, S., & Mu, X. (2000). Successful achievement in mathematics: China and the United States. In C. F. M. van Lieshout & P. G. Heymans (Eds.), *Developing talent across the life span.* New York: Psychology Press.

Stevenson, R. J., & Case, T. I. (2005). Olfactory imagery: A review. *Psychonomic Bulletin and Review, 12,* 244–264.

Stickgold, R., Hobson, J. A., Fosse, R., & Fosse, M. (2001, November 2). Sleep, learning, and dreams: Off-line memory reprocessing. *Science, 294,* 1052–1057.

Stickgold, R., & Wehrwein, P. (2009, April 27). Sleep now, remember later. *Newsweek,* pp. 56–57.

Stickley, T., & Nickeas, R. (2006). Becoming one person: Living with dissociative identity disorder. *Journal of Psychiatric and Mental Health Nursing, 13,* 180–187.

Stix, G. (2008, November). Jacking into the brain. *Scientific American,* pp. 56–61.

St. Jacques, P. L., & Levine, B. (2007). Ageing and autobiographical memory for emotional and neutral events. *Memory, 15,* 129–144.

Stocks, E., Lishner, D., & Decker, S. (2009). Altruism or psychological escape: Why does empathy promote prosocial behavior? *European Journal of Social Psychology, 39,* 649–665.

Stockton, R., Morran, D. K., & Krieger, K. (2004). An overview of current research and best practices for training beginning group leaders. In J. L. DeLucia-Waack, D. A. Gerrity, C. R. Kalodner, & M. T. Riva (Eds.), *Handbook of group counseling and psychotherapy.* Thousand Oaks, CA: Sage Publications.

Stone, J. (2002). Battling doubt by avoiding practice: The effects of stereotype threat on self-handicapping in white athletes. *Personality and Social Psychology Bulletin, 28,* 1667–1678.

Stone, J., Morrison, P., & Pilowsky, L. (2007). Glutamate and dopamine dysregulation in schizophrenia—A synthesis and selective review. *Journal of Psychopharmacology, 21,* 440–452.

Storm, L., & Ertel, S. (2001). Does psi exist? Comments on Milton and Wiseman's (1999) meta-analysis of Ganzfeld's research. *Psychological Bulletin, 127,* 424–433.

Stouffer, E. M., & White, N. M. (2006). Neural circuits mediating latent learning and conditioning for salt in the rat. *Neurobiology of Learning and Memory, 86,* 91–99.

Strange, D., Clifasefi, S., & Garry, M. (2007). False memories. In M. Garry & H. Hayne, *Do justice and let the sky fall: Elizabeth Loftus and her contributions to science, law, and academic freedom.* Mahwah, NJ: Lawrence Erlbaum Associates.

Strathern, A., & Stewart, P. J. (2003). *Landscape, memory and history: Anthropological perspectives.* London: Pluto Press.

Strauss, E. (1998, May 8). Writing, speech separated in split brain. *Science, 280,* 287.

Strayer, D. L., & Drews, F. A. (2007). Cell-phone-induced driver distraction. *Current Directions in Psychological Science, 16,* 128–131.

Strayer, D. L., Drews, F. A., Crouch, D. J., & Johnston, W. A. (2005). Why do cell phone conversations interfere with driving? In W. R. Walker and D. Herrmann (Eds.), *Cognitive technology: Transforming thought and society.* Jefferson, NC: McFarland & Company.

Striano, T., & Vaish, A. (2006). Seven- to 9-month-old infants use facial expressions to interpret others' actions. *British Journal of Developmental Psychology, 24,* 753–760.

Striegel-Moore, R., & Bulik, C. M. (2007). Risk factors for eating disorders. *American Psychologist, 62,* 181–198.

Stroink, M. (2007). Processes and preconditions underlying terrorism in second-generation immigrants. *Peace and Conflict: Journal of Peace Psychology, 13,* 293–312.

Strong, T., & Tomm, K. (2007). Family therapy as re-coordinating and moving on together. *Journal of Systemic Therapies, 26,* 42–54.

Strupp, H. H., & Binder, J. L. (1992). Current developments in psychotherapy. *The Independent Practitioner, 12,* 119–124.

Subrahmanyam, K., Reich, S., Waechter, N., & Espinoza, G. (2008). Online and offline social networks: Use of social networking sites by emerging adults. *Journal of Applied Developmental Psychology, 29,* 420–433.

Sue, D. W., & Sue, D. (1990). Counseling the culturally different: Theory and practice (2nd ed.). Oxford, England: John Wiley & Sons.

Sue, D. W., Sue, D., & Sue, S. (1990). *Understanding abnormal behavior* (3rd ed.). Boston: Houghton-Mifflin.

Suh, E. M. (2002). Culture, identity consistency, and subjective well-being. *Journal of Personality & Social Psychology, 83,* 1378–1391.

Suhail, K., & Chaudhry, H. R. (2004). Predictors of subjective well-being in an Eastern Muslim culture. *Journal of Social and Clinical Psychology, 23,* 359–376.

Suizzo, M-A., & Bornstein, M. H. (2006). French and European American child-mother play: Culture and gender considerations. *International Journal of Behavioral Development, 30,* 498–508.

Sullivan, J., Riccio, C., & Reynolds, C. (2008, September). Variations in students' school- and teacher-related attitudes across gender, ethnicity, and age. *Journal of Instructional Psychology, 35,* 296–305.

Summers, M. (2000) *Everything in its place.* New York: Putnam.

Super, C. M. (1980). Cognitive development: Looking across at growing up. In C. M. Super & S. Harakness (Eds.), *New directions for child development: Anthropological perspectives on child development.* San Francisco: Jossey-Bass.

Surette, R. (2002). Self-reported copycat crime among a population of serious and violent juvenile offenders. *Crime & Delinquency, 48,* 46–69.

Susser, E. S., Herman, D. B., & Aaron, B. (2002, August). Combating the terror of terrorism. *Scientific American,* pp. 70–77.

Sutin, A. R., & Robins, R. W. (2007). Phenomenology of autobiographical memories: The Memory Experiences Questionnaire. *Memory, 15,* 390–411.

Svarstad, B. (1976). Physician-patient communication and patient conformity with medical advice. In D. Mechanic (Ed.), *The growth of bureaucratic medicine.* New York: Wiley.

Svartdal, F. (2003). Extinction after partial reinforcement: Predicted vs. judged persistence. *Scandinavian Journal of Psychology, 44,* 55–64.

Swain, P. I. (2006). *New developments in eating disorders research.* Hauppauge, NY: Nova Science Publishers.

Swales, M. A., & Heard, H. L. (2007). The therapy relationship in dialectical behaviour therapy. In P. Gilbert & R. L. Leahy, *The therapeutic relationship in the cognitive behavioral psychotherapies.* New York: Routledge/ Taylor & Francis.

Swann, W. B., Jr., Chang-Schneider, C., & Larsen McClarty, K. (2007). Do people's self-views matter? Self-concept and self-esteem in everyday life. *American Psychologist, 62,* 84–94.

Swanson, H. L., Harris, K. R., & Graham, S. (Eds.). (2003). *Handbook of learning disabilities.* New York: Guilford Press.

Swets, J. A., & Bjork, R.A. (1990). Enhancing human performance: An evaluation of "new age" techniques considered by the U.S. Army. *Psychological Science, 1,* 85–96.

Swing, E., & Anderson, C. (2007). The unintended negative consequences of exposure to violent video games. *International Journal of Cognitive Technology, 12,* 3–13.

Szasz, T. (2006). The pretense of psychology as science: The myth of mental illness in statu nascendi. *Current Psychology: Developmental, Learning, Personality, Social, 25,* 42–49.

Szasz, T. S. (1994). *Cruel compassion: Psychiatric control of society's unwanted.* New York: Wiley.

Szegedy Maszak, M. (2003, January 13). The sound of unsound minds. *U.S. News & World Report,* pp. 45–46.

Tadmor, C., T. (2007). Biculturalism: The plus side of leaving home? The effects of second-culture exposure on integrative complexity and its consequences for overseas performance. *Dissertation Abstracts International Section A: Humanities and Social Sciences, 67*(8-A), 3068.

Taggi, F., Crenca, A., Cedri, C., Giustini, M., Dosi, G., & Marturano, P. (2007). Road safety and the tsunami of cell phones. *Ann Ig, 19,* 269–274.

Tajfel, H., & Turner, J. C. (2004). The social identity theory of intergroup behavior. In J. T. Jost & J. Sidanius (Eds.), *Political psychology: Key readings.* New York: Psychology Press.

Takahashi, M., Nakata, A., Haratani, T., Ogawa, Y., & Arito, H. (2004). Post-lunch nap as a worksite intervention to promote alertness on the job. *Ergonomics, 47,* 1003–1013.

Takizawa, T., Kondo, T., & Sakihara, S. (2007). Stress buffering effects of social support on depressive symptoms in middle age: Reciprocity and community mental health: Corrigendum. *Psychiatry and Clinical Neurosciences, 61,* 336–337.

Talarico, J. (2009). Freshman flashbulbs: Memories of unique and first-time events in starting college. *Memory, 17,* 256–265.

Talarico, J., & Rubin, D. (2007). Flashbulb memories are special after all; in phenomenology, not accuracy. *Applied Cognitive Psychology, 21,* 557–578.

Talmi, D., Anderson, A., Riggs, L., Caplan, J., & Moscovitch, M. (2008). Immediate memory consequences of the effect of emotion on attention to pictures. *Learning & Memory, 15,* 172–182.

Tal-Or, N., & Papirman, Y. (2007). The fundamental attribution error in attributing fictional figures' characteristics to the actors. *Media Psychology, 9,* 331–345.

Talukdar, S., & Shastri, J. (2006). Contributory and adverse factors in social development of young children. *Psychological Studies, 51,* 294–303.

Tan, L., Chan, A., Kay, P., Khong, P., Yip, L., & Luke, K. (2008). Language affects patterns of brain activation associated with perceptual decision. *PNAS Proceedings of the National Academy of Sciences of the United States of America, 105*(10), 4004–4009.

Tan, L., & Ward, G. (2008). Rehearsal in immediate serial recall. *Psychonomic Bulletin & Review, 15,* 535–542.

Tanner, J. M. (1978). *Education and physical growth* (2nd ed.). New York: International Universities Press.

Tanner, J. M. (1990). *Foetus into man: Physical growth from conception to maturity* (rev. ed.). Cambridge, MA: Harvard University Press.

Taras, H., & Potts-Datema, W. (2005). Chronic health conditions and student performance at school. *Journal of School Health, 75,* 255–266.

Tasker, F. (2005). Lesbian mothers, gay fathers, and their children: A review. *Journal of Developmental and Behavioral Pediatrics, 26,* 224–240.

Taylor, F., & Bryant, R. A. (2007). The tendency to suppress, inhibiting thoughts, and dream rebound. *Behaviour Research and Therapy, 45,* 163–168.

Taylor, S. (2003). Anxiety sensitivity and its implications for understanding and treating PTSD. *Journal of Cognitive Psychotherapy, 17,* 179–186.

Taylor, S. E. (1995). Quandary at the crossroads: Paternalism versus advocacy surrounding end-of-treatment decisions. *American Journal of Hospital Palliatory Care, 12,* 43–46.

Taylor, S. E., Kemeny, M. E., Reed, G. M., Bower, J. E., & Gruenewald, T. L. (2000). Psychological resources, positive illusions, and health. *American Psychologist, 55,* 99–109.

Teff, K. L., Petrova, M., & Havel, P. J. (2007). 48-h Glucose infusion in humans: Effect on hormonal responses, hunger and food intake. *Physiology & Behavior, 90,* 733–743.

Tellegen, A., Lykken, D. T., Bouchard, T. J., Jr., Wilcox, K. J., Segal, N. L., & Rich, S. (1988). Personality similarity in twins reared apart and together. *Journal of Personality and Social Psychology, 54,* 1031–1039.

Templer, D. I., & Arkawa, H. (2006). Association of race and color with mean IQ across nations. *Psychological Reports, 99,* 191–196.

Tenenbaum, H. R., & Leaper, C. (2002). Are parents' gender schemas related to their children's gender-related cognitions? A meta-analysis. *Developmental Psychology, 38,* 615–630.

Tenopyr, M. L. (2002). Theory versus reality: Evaluation of 'g' in the workplace. *Human Performance, 15,* 107–122.

Teodorov, E., Salzgerber, S. A., Felicio, L. F., Varolli, F. M. F., & Bernardi, M. M. (2002). Effects of perinatal picrotoxin and sexual experience on heterosexual and homosexual behavior in male rats. *Neurotoxicology and Teratology, 24,* 235–245.

Terry, W. S. (2003). *Learning and memory: Basic principles, processes, and procedures* (2nd ed.). Boston: Allyn & Bacon.

Thachil, A. F., Mohan, R., & Bhugra, D. (2007). The evidence base of complementary and alternative therapies in depression. *Journal of Affective Disorders, 97,* 23–35.

Tharp, R. G. (1989). Psychocultural variables and constants: Effects on teaching and learning in schools [Special issue: Children and their development: Knowledge base, research agenda, and social policy application]. *American Psychologist, 44,* 349–359.

Thatcher, D. L., & Clark, D. B. (2006). Adolescent alcohol abuse and dependence: Development, diagnosis, treatment and outcomes. *Current Psychiatry Reviews, 2,* 159–177.

Thomas, P., Mathur, P., Gottesman, I. I., Nagpal, R., Nimgaonkar, V. L., & Deshpande, S. N. (2007). Correlates of hallucinations in schizophrenia: A cross-cultural evaluation. *Schizophrenia Research, 92,* 41–49.

Thompson, J. (2000, June 18). "I was certain, but I was wrong." *The New York Times,* p. E14.

Thorkildsen, T. A. (2006). An empirical exploration of language and thought. *PsycCRITIQUES, 51,* no pagination specified.

Thorndike, E. L. (1932). *The fundamentals of learning.* New York: Teachers College.

Thornton, A., & McAuliffe, K. (2006, July 14). Teaching in wild meerkats. *Science, 313,* 227–229.

Thornton, A., & Young-DeMarco, L. (2001). Four decades of trends in attitudes toward family issues in the United States: The 1960s through the 1990s. *Journal of Marriage and the Family, 63,* 1009–1017.

Thrash, T. M., & Elliot, A. J. (2002). Implicit and self-attributed achievement motives: Concordance and predictive validity. *Journal of Personality, 70,* 729–755.

Time. (1966, July 22). Less pain, more gain. *Time.*

Tippin, J., Sparks, J., & Rizzo, M. (2009, August). Visual vigilance in drivers with obstructive sleep apnea. *Journal of Psychosomatic Research, 67,* 143–151.

Tirri, K., & Nokelainen, P. (2008). Identification of multiple intelligences with the Multiple Intelligence Profiling Questionnaire III [Special issue: High-ability assessment]. *Psychology Science, 50,* 206–221.

Titone, D. A. (2002). Memories bound: The neuroscience of dreams. *Trends in Cognitive Science, 6,* 4–5.

Todorov, A., & Duchaine, B. (2008). Reading trustworthiness in faces without recognizing faces. *Cognitive Neuropsychology, 25,* 1–16.

Tolman, E. C., & Honzik, C. H. (1930). Introduction and removal of reward and maze performance in rats. *University of California Publications in Psychology, 4,* 257–275.

Tommasi, L. (2009). Mechanisms and functions of brain and behavioural asymmetries. *Philosophical Transactions of the Royal Society B, 364,* 855–859.

Tononi, G., & Koch, C. (2008). The neural correlates of consciousness: An update. In A. Kingstone & M. B. Miller (Eds.), *The year in cognitive neuroscience.* Malden, MA: Blackwell Publishing.

Toole, L. M., DeLeon, I. G., Kahng, S., Ruffin, G. E., Pletcher, C. A., & Bowman, L. G. (2004). Re-evaluation of constant versus varied punishers using empirically derived consequences. *Research in Developmental Disabilities, 25,* 577–586.

Toth, J. P., & Daniels, K. A. (2002). Effects of prior experience on judgments of normative word frequency: Automatic bias and correction. *Journal of Memory and Language, 46,* 845–874.

Touhara, K. (2007). Molecular biology of peptide pheromone production and reception in mice. *Advanced Genetics, 59,* 147–171.

Tracy, J. L., & Robins, R. W. (2004). Show your pride: Evidence for a discrete emotion expression. *Psychological Science, 15,* 194–197.

Tranter, L. J., Koutstaal, W. (2008). Age and flexible thinking: An experimental demonstration of the beneficial effects of increased cognitively stimulating activity on fluid intelligence in healthy older adults. *Neuropsychology and Cognition, 15,* 184–207.

Travis, F. (2006). From I to I: Concepts of self on a object-referral/self-referral continuum. In A. P. Prescott, *The concept of self in psychology.* Hauppauge, NY: Nova Science Publishers.

Travis, F., et al. (2009, February). Effects of transcendental meditation practice on brain functioning and stress reactivity in college students. *International Journal of Psychophysiology, 71,* 170–176.

Tremblay, A. (2004). Dietary fat and body weight set point. *Nutrition Review, 62*(7, Pt 2), S75–S77.

Triesch, J., Jasso, H., & Deák, G. O. (2007). Emergence of mirror neurons in a model of gaze following. *Adaptive Behavior, 15,* 149–165.

Tropp, L. R., & Bianchi, R. A. (2006). Valuing diversity and interest in intergroup contact. *Journal of Social Issues, 62,* 533–551.

Tropp, L. R., & Pettigrew, T. F. (2005). Differential relationships between intergroup contact and affective and cognitive dimensions of prejudice. *Personality and Social Psychology Bulletin, 31,* 1145–1158.

Troyer, A. K., Häfliger, A., & Cadieux, M. J. (2006). Name and face learning in older adults: Effects of level of processing, self-generation, and intention to learn. *Journals of Gerontology: Series B: Psychological Sciences and Social Sciences, 61,* P67–P74.

Trull, T. J., & Widiger, T. A. (2003). Personality disorders. In G. Stricker, T. A. Widiger, et al. (Eds.), *Handbook of psychology: Clinical psychology* (Vol. 8). New York: Wiley.

Tsai, A., Yang, M., Lan, C., & Chen, C. (2008). Evaluation of effect of cognitive intervention programs for the community-dwelling elderly with subjective memory complaints. *International Journal of Geriatric Psychiatry, 23,* 1172–1174.

Tsai, K. J., Tsai, Y. C., & Shen, C. K. (2007). GCSF rescues the memory impairment of animal models of Alzheimer's disease. *Journal of Experimental Medicine, 11,* 1273–1289.

Tsaousis, I., Nikolaou, I., & Serdaris, N. (2007). Do the core self-evaluations moderate the relationship between subjective well-being and physical and psychological health? *Personality and Individual Differences, 42,* 1441–1452.

Tseng, W. S. (2003). *Clinician's guide to cultural psychiatry.* San Diego, CA: Elsevier Publishing.

Tsukasaki, T., & Ishii, K. (2004). Linguistic-cultural relativity of cognition: Rethinking the Sapir-Whorf hypothesis. *Japanese Psychological Review, 47,* 173–186.

Tsunoda, T. (1985). *The Japanese brain: Uniqueness and universality.* Tokyo: Taishukan Publishing.

Tucker Blackwell, V.G. (2006). Factors which influence the academic motivation and disengagement of adolescent, African American males within a social-historical and psychological context. *Dissertation Abstracts International, 67,* 1654A.

Tuerlinckx, F., De Boeck, P., & Lens, W. (2002). Measuring needs with the Thematic Apperception Test: A psychometric study. *Journal of Personality and Social Psychology, 82,* 448–461.

Tugay, N., et al. (2007). Effectiveness of transcutaneous electrical nerve stimulation and interferential current in primary dysmenorrhea. *Pain Medicine, 8,* 295–300.

Tulving, E. (2000). Concepts of memory. In E. Tulving, F. I. M. Craik, et al. (Eds.). *The Oxford handbook of memory.* New York: Oxford University Press.

Tulving, E. (2002). Episodic memory and common sense: How far apart? In A. Baddeley & J. P. Aggleton (Eds.), *Episodic memory: New directions in research.* London: Oxford University Press.

Tulving, E., & Psotka, J. (1971). Retroactive inhibition in free recall: Inaccessibility of information available in the memory store. *Journal of Experimental Psychology, 87,* 1–8.

Tulving, E., & Thompson, D. M. (1983). Encoding specificity and retrieval processes in episodic memory. *Psychological Review, 80,* 352–373.

Turk, D. C. (1994). Perspectives on chronic pain: The role of psychological factors. *Current Directions in Psychological Science, 3,* 45–49.

Turkewitz, G. (1993). The origins of differential hemispheric strategies for information processing in the relationships between voice and face perception. In B. de Boysson-Bardies, S. de Schonen, P. W. Jusczyk, P. McNeilage, & J. Morton (Eds.), *Developmental neurocognition: Speech and face processing in the first year of life. NATO ASI series D: Behavioural and social sciences* (Vol. 69). Dordrecht, Netherlands: Kluwer Academic.

Turnbull, O., & Solms, M. (2007). Awareness, desire, and false beliefs: Freud in the light of modern neuropsychology. *Cortex, 43,* 1083–1090.

Turner, M. E., Pratkanis, A. R., & Struckman, C. K. (2007). Groupthink as social identity maintenance. In C. K. Struckman, *The science of social influence: Advances and future progress.* New York: Psychology Press.

Turner, M., Tamborini, R., Limon, M., & Zuckerman-Hyman, C. (2007). The moderators and mediators of door-in-the-face requests: Is it a negotiation or a helping experience? *Communication Monographs, 74,* 333–356.

Turner, W. J. (1995). Homosexuality, Type 1: An Xq28 phenomenon. *Archives of Sexual Behavior, 24,* 109–134.

Tuszynski, M. H. (2007). Nerve growth factor gene therapy in Alzheimer's disease. *Alzheimer's Disease and Associated Disorders, 21,* 179–189.

Tversky, A., & Kahneman, D. (1987). Rational choice and the framing of decisions. In R. Hogarth & M. Reder (Eds.), *Rational choice: The contrast between economics and psychology.* Chicago: University of Chicago Press.

Tydgat, I., & Grainger, J. (2009). Serial position effects in the identification of letters, digits, and symbols. *Journal of Experimental Psychology: Human Perception and Performance, 35,* 480–498.

Ubell, E. (1993, January 10). Could you use more sleep? *Parade,* pp. 16–18.

Umphress, E. E., Smith-Crowe, K., & Brief, A. P. (2007). When birds of a feather flock together and when they do not: Status composition, social dominance orientation, and organizational attractiveness. *Journal of Applied Psychology, 92,* 396–409.

Ünal-Karagüven, M. (2009). Psychological impact of an economic crisis: A Conservation of Resources approach. *International Journal of Stress Management, 16,* 177–194.

Underwood, A. (2005, October 3). The good heart. *Newsweek,* p. 49.

Unsworth, N., & Engle, R. W. (2005). Individual differences in working memory capacity and learning: Evidence from the serial reaction time task. *Memory and Cognition, 33,* 213–220.

Updegraff, K. A., Helms, H. M., McHale, S. M., Crouter, A. C., Thayer, S. M., & Sales, L. H. (2004). Who's the boss? Patterns of perceived control in adolescents' friendships. *Journal of Youth & Adolescence, 33,* 403–420.

Ursprung, W. W., Sanouri, A., & DiFranza, J. R. (2009). The loss of autonomy over smoking in relation to lifetime cigarette consumption. *Addictive Behaviors, 22,* 12–19.

U.S. Bureau of the Census. (2000). *Census 2000.* Retrieved from American Fact Finder http://factfinder.census.gov/servlet/BasicFactsServlet

U.S. Bureau of the Census. (2001). *Living arrangements of children.* Washington, DC: Author.

U.S. Senate Select Committee on Intelligence (2004, July 9). *Report of the U.S. intelligence community's prewar intelligence assessments on Iraq.* Retrieved from http://www.gpoaccess.gov/serialset/creports/iraq.html

Uttl, B., Graf, P., & Cosentino, S. (2003). Implicit memory for new associations: Types of conceptual representations. In J. S. Bowers & C. J. Marsolek (Eds.), *Rethinking implicit memory.* London: Oxford University Press.

Uylings, H. B. M. (2006). Development of the human cortex and the concept of 'critical' or 'sensitive' periods. *Language Learning, 56,* 59–90.

Vaillant, G. E., & Vaillant, C. O. (1990). Natural history of male psychological health: XII. A 46-year study of predictors of successful aging at age 65. *American Journal of Psychiatry, 147,* 31–37.

Vaitl, D., Schienle, A., & Stark, R. (2005). Neurobiology of fear and disgust. *International Journal of Psychophysiology, 57,* 1–4.

Valencia, R. R., & Suzuki, L. A. (2003). *Intelligence testing and minority students: Foundations, performance factors, and assessment issues.* Thousand Oaks, CA: Sage.

Valenzuela, S., Park, N., & Kee, K. F. (2009). Is there social capital in a social network site? Facebook use and college students' life satisfaction, trust, and participation. *Journal of Computer-Mediated Communications, 14,* 875–901.

Valsiner, J., Diriwächter, R., & Sauck, C. (2005). Diversity in unity: Standard questions and nonstandard interpretations. In *Science and medicine in dialogue: Thinking through particulars and universals.* Westport, CT: Praeger Publishers/Greenwood Publishing Group.

Vanasse, A., Niyonsenga, T., & Courteau, J. (2004). Smoking cessation within the context of family medicine: Which smokers take action? *Preventive Medicine: An International Journal Devoted to Practice and Theory, 38,* 330–337.

Van Beekum, S. (2005). The therapist as a new object. *Transactional Analysis Journal, 35,* 187–191.

Van De Graaff, K. (2000). *Human anatomy* (5th ed.). Boston: McGraw-Hill.

Vandell, D. L., Burchinal, M. R., Belsky, J., Owen, M. T., Friedman, S. L., Clarke-Stewart, et al. (2005). *Early child care and children's development in the primary grades: Follow-up results from the NICHD Study of Early Child Care.* Paper presented at the biennial meeting of the Society for Research in Child Development, Atlanta, GA.

Van den Wildenberg, W. P. M., & Van der Molen, M. W. (2004). Developmental trends in simple and selective inhibition of compatible and incompatible responses. *Journal of Experimental Child Psychology, 87,* 201–220.

van der Helm, P. A. (2006). Review of perceptual dynamics: Theoretical foundations and philosophical implications of gestalt psychology. *Philosophical Psychology, 19,* 274–279.

Vandervert, L. R., Schimpf, P. H., & Liu, H. (2007). How working memory and the cerebellum collaborate to produce creativity and innovation. *Creativity Research Journal, 19,* 1–18.

Vanheule, S., Desmet, M., Rosseel, Y., & Meganck, R. (2006). Core transference themes in depression. *Journal of Affective Disorders, 91,* 71–75.

van Hooren, S. A. H., Valentijn, A. M., & Bosma, H. (2007). Cognitive functioning in healthy older adults aged 64–81: A cohort study into the effects of age, sex, and education. *Aging, Neuropsychology, and Cognition, 14,* 40–54.

van Marle, K., & Wynn, K. (2009). Infants' auditory enumeration: Evidence for analog magnitudes in the small number range. *Cognition, 111,* 302–316.

van Oort, R., & Kessels, R. (2009). Executive dysfunction in Korsakoff's syndrome: Time to revise the DSM criteria for alcohol-induced persisting amnestic disorder? *International Journal of Psychiatry in Clinical Practice, 13,* 78–81.

Van Overwalle, F., & Siebler, F. (2005). A connectionist model of attitude formation and change. *Personality and Social Psychology Review, 9,* 231–274.

Vansteenkiste, M., Simons, J., Lens, W., Soenens, B., & Matos, L. (2005). Examining the motivational impact of intrinsic versus extrinsic goal framing and autonomy-supportive versus internally controlling communication style on early adolescents' academic achievement. *Child Development, 76,* 483–501.

van Wel, F., Linssen, H., & Abma, R. (2000). The parental bond and the well-being of adolescents and young adults. *Journal of Youth & Adolescence, 29,* 307–318.

Varma, S. (2007). A computational model of Tower of Hanoi problem solving. *Dissertation Abstracts International: Section B: The Sciences and Engineering, 67*(8-B), 4736.

Vartanian, O. (2009). Variable attention facilitates creative problem solving. *Psychology of Aesthetics, Creativity, and the Arts, 3,* 57–59.

Vassalli, A., & Dijk, D. (2009). Sleep function: Current questions and new approaches. *European Journal of Neuroscience, 29,* 1830–1841.

Vedantam, S. (2005, January 23). See no bias. *Washington Post,* p. W12.

Vega, C. P. (2006). The effects of therapeutic components on at-risk middle school children's grades and attendance: An archival study of an after-school prevention program. *Dissertation Abstracts International: Section B: The Sciences and Engineering, 66,* 4504.

Vellacott, J. (2007). Resilience: A psychoanalytic exploration. *British Journal of Psychotherapy, 23,* 163–170.

Velliste, M., Perel, S., Spalding, M., Whitford, S., & Schwartz, A. (2008). Cortical control of a prosthetic arm for self-feeding. *Nature, 453,* 1098–1101.

Veltman, M. W. M., & Browne, K. D. (2001). Three decades of child mal-treatment research: Implications for the school years. *Trauma Violence and Abuse, 2,* 215–239.

Veniegas, R. C. (2000). Biological research on women's sexual orientations: Evaluating the scientific evidence. *Journal of Social Issues, 56,* 267–282.

Verdejo, A., Toribio, I., & Orozco, C. (2005). Neuropsychological functioning in methadone maintenance patients versus abstinent heroin abusers. *Drug and Alcohol Dependence, 78,* 283–288.

Verfaellie, M., & Keane, M. M. (2002). Impaired and preserved memory processes in amnesia. In L. R. Squire & D. L. Schacter (Eds.), *Neuropsychology of memory* (3rd ed.). New York: Guilford Press.

Verleger, R., Schuknecht, S., Jaskowski, P., & Wagner, U. (2008). Changes in processing of masked stimuli across early- and late-night sleep: A study on behavior and brain potentials. *Brain and Cognition, 68,* 180–192.

Vernon, P., Villani, V., Vickers, L., & Harris, J. (2008, January). A behavioral genetic investigation of the Dark Triad and the Big 5. *Personality and Individual Differences, 44,* 445–452.

Verona, E., & Sullivan, E. (2008). Emotional catharsis and aggression revisited: Heart rate reduction following aggressive responding. *Emotion, 8,* 331–340.

Victor, S. B., & Fish, M. C. (1995). Lesbian mothers and the children: A review for school psychologists. *School Psychology Review, 24,* 456–479.

Vieira, E. M., & Freire, J. C. (2006). Alteridade e psicologia humanista: Uma leitura ética da abordagem centrada na pessoa. Alterity and humanistic psychology: An ethical reading of the person-centered approach. *Estudos de Psicologia, 23,* 425–432.

Villemure, C., Slotnick, B. M., & Bushnell, M. C. (2003). Effects of odors on pain perception: Deciphering the roles of emotion and attention. *Pain, 106,* 101–108.

Virginia Tech Transportation Institute. (2009). New data from VTTI provides insight into cell phone use and driving distraction. Retrieved from http://www.vtti.vt.edu/PDF/7-22-09-VTTI-Press_Release_Cell_phones_and_Driver_Distraction.pdf

Vitaro, F., Brendgen, M., & Arseneault, L. (2009). Methods and measures: The discordant MZ-twin method: One step closer to the holy grail of causality. *International Journal of Behavioral Development, 33,* 376–382.

Vitiello, A. L., Bonello, R. P., & Pollard, H. P. (2007). The effectiveness of ENAR® for the treatment of chronic neck pain in Australian adults: A preliminary single-blind, randomised controlled trial. *Chiropractic Osteopathology, 9,* 9.

Vitello, P. (2006, June 12). A ring tone meant to fall on deaf ears. *The New York Times,* A1.

Vleioras, G., & Bosma, H. A. (2005). Are identity styles important for psychological well-being? *Journal of Adolescence, 28,* 397–409.

Vogt, D., Rizvi, S., Shipherd, J., & Resick, P. (2008). Longitudinal investigation of reciprocal relationship between stress reactions and hardiness. *Personality and Social Psychology Bulletin, 34,* 61–73.

Volterra, V., Caselli, M. C., Capirci, O., Tonucci, F., & Vicari, S. (2003). Early linguistic abilities of Italian children with Williams syndrome [Special issue: Williams syndrome]. *Developmental Neuropsychology, 23,* 33–58.

Voruganti, L. P., Awad, A. G., Parker, B., Forrest, C., Usmani, Y., Fernando, M. L. D., et al. (2007). Cognition, functioning and quality of life in schizophrenia treatment: Results of a one-year randomized controlled trial of olanzapine and quetiapine. *Schizophrenia Research, 96,* 146–155.

Voss, J., & Paller, K. (2008). Brain substrates of implicit and explicit memory: The importance of concurrently acquired neural signals of both memory types. *Neuropsychologia, 46*(13), 3021–3029.

Vygotsky, L. S. (1926/1997). *Educational psychology.* Delray Beach, FL: St. Lucie Press.

Wachs, T. D., Pollitt, E., Cueto, S., & Jacoby, E. (2004). Structure and cross-contextual stability of neonatal temperament. *Infant Behavior and Development, 27,* 382–396.

Waddell, J., & Shors, T.J. (2008). Neurogenesis, learning and associative strength. *European Journal of Neurosciences, 27,* 3020–3028.

Wadden, T. A., Crerand, C. E., & Brock, J. (2005). Behavioral treatment of obesity. *Psychiatric Clinics of North America, 28,* 151–170.

Wade, K. A., Sharman, S. J., & Garry, M. (2007). False claims about false memory research. *Consciousness and Cognition: An International Journal, 16,* 18–28.

Wager, T. D (2005). The neural bases of placebo effects in pain. *Current Directions in Psychological Science, 14,* 175–180.

Wagner, A. W., Rizvi, S. L., & Hamed, M. S. (2007). Applications of dialectical behavior therapy to the treatment of complex trauma-related problems: When one case formulation does not fit all. *Journal of Trauma Stress, 20,* 391–400.

Wagner, H. J., et al. (2004). A strategy for treatment of Epstein Barr virus-positive Hodgkin's disease by targeting interleukin 12 to the tumor environment using tumor antigen-specific T cells. *Cancer Gene Therapy, 2,* 81–91.

Wagner, R. K. (2002). Smart people doing dumb things: The case of managerial incompetence. In R. J. Sternberg (Ed.), *Why smart people can be so stupid.* New Haven, CT: Yale University Press.

Wagstaff, G. (2009, January). Is there a future for investigative hypnosis? *Journal of Investigative Psychology and Offender Profiling, 6,* 43–57.

Wain, H. J., Grammer, G. G., & Stasinos, J. (2006). Psychiatric intervention for medical and surgical patients following traumatic injuries. In E. C. Ritchie, P. J. Watson, & M. J. Friedman, *Interventions following mass violence and disasters: Strategies for mental health practice.* New York: Guilford Press.

Walker, L., & Frimer, J. (2009). The song remains the same: Rebuttal to Sherblom's re-envisioning of the legacy of the care challenge. *Journal of Moral Education, 38,* 53–68.

Walker, L. J., & Frimer, J. A. (2007). Moral personality of brave and caring exemplars. *Journal of Personality and Social Psychology, 93,* 845–860.

Walker, M. P., & van der Helm, E. (2009). Overnight therapy? The role of sleep in emotional brain processing. *Psychological Bulletin, 135,* 731–748.

Walker, W. (2008, May). Introducing hypnosis for pain management to your practice. *Australian Journal of Clinical & Experimental Hypnosis, 36,* 23–29.

Walker, W. R., Skowronski, J. J., & Thompson, C. P. (2003). Consolidation of long-term memory: Evidence and alternatives. *Review of General Psychology, 7,* 203–210.

Waller, B., Cray, J., & Burrows, A. (2008, June). Selection for universal facial emotion. *Emotion, 8,* 435–439.

Wallerstein, J. S., Lewis, J., Blakeslee, S., & Lewis, J. (2000). *The unexpected legacy of divorce.* New York: Hyperion.

Walsh, B. T., Kaplan, A. S., Attia, E., Olmstead, M., Parides, M., Carter, J. C., et al. (2006). Fluoxetine after weight restoration in anorexia nervosa: A randomized controlled trial. *JAMA: Journal of the American Medical Association, 295,* 2605–2612.

Walsh, R., & Shapiro, S. L. (2006). The meeting of meditative disciplines and western psychology. *American Psychologist, 61,* 227–239.

Wang, A., & Clark, D. A. (2002). Haunting thoughts: The problem of obsessive mental intrusions [Special issue: Intrusions in cognitive behavioral therapy]. *Journal of Cognitive Psychotherapy, 16,* 193–208.

Wang, Q. (2003). Infantile amnesia reconsidered: A cross-cultural analysis. *Memory, 11,* 65–80.

Wang, P. S., Aguilar-Gaxiola, S., Alonso, J., Angermeyer, M. C., Borges, G., Bromet, E. J., et al. (2007, September 8). Use of mental health services for anxiety, mood, and substance disorders in 17 countries in the WHO world mental health surveys. *Lancet, 370,* 841–850.

Wang, Q. (2004). The emergence of cultural self-constructs: Autobiographical memory and self-description in European American and Chinese children. *Developmental Psychology, 40,* 3–15.

Wang, Q., & Conway, M. A. (2006). Autobiographical memory, self, and culture. In L-G. Nilsson & N. Ohta, *Memory and society: Psychological perspectives.* New York: Psychology Press.

Wang, X., Lu, T., Snider, R. K., & Liang, L. (2005). Sustained firing in auditory cortex evoked by preferred stimuli. *Nature, 435,* 341–346.

Ward, L. M. (2004). Wading through the stereotypes: Positive and negative associations between media use and Black adolescents' conceptions of self. *Developmental Psychology, 40,* 284–294.

Ward-Baker, P. D. (2007). The remarkable oldest old: A new vision of aging. *Dissertation Abstracts International Section A: Humanities and Social Sciences, 67*(8-A), 3115.

Warden, C. A., Wu, W-Y., & Tsai, D. (2006). Online shopping interface components: Relative importance as peripheral and central cues. *CyberPsychology & Behavior, 9,* 285–296.

Ward, W. C., Kogan, N., & Pankove, E. (1972). Incentive effects in children's creativity. *Child Development, 43,* 669–677.

Wark, B., Lundstrom, B., & Fairhall, A. (2007, August). Sensory adaptation. *Current Opinion in Neurobiology, 17,* 423–429.

Wasserman, E. A., & Miller, R. R. (1997). What's elementary about associative learning? *Annual Review of Psychology, 48,* 573–607.

Watson, J. B. (1924). *Behaviorism.* New York: Norton.

Watson, M., Haviland, J. S., Greer, S., Davidson, J., & Bliss, J. M. (1999). Influence of psychological response on survival in breast cancer: A population-based cohort study. *Lancet, 354,* 1331–1336.

Watters, E. (2010, January 10). The Americanization of mental illness. *The New York Times,* p. C2.

Waxman, S. (2009). Learning from infants' first verbs. *Monographs of the Society for Research in Child Development, 74,* 127–132.

Weber, R., Ritterfeld, U., & Kostygina, A. (2006). Aggression and violence as effects of playing violent video games? In P. Vorderer, & J. Bryant, (Eds.), *Playing video games: Motives, responses, and consequences.* Mahwah, NJ: Lawrence Erlbaum Associates.

Wechsler, H., Kuo, M., Lee, H., & Dowdall, G. W. (2000). *Environmental correlates of underage alcohol use and related problems of college students.* Cambridge, MA: Harvard School of Public Health.

Wechsler, H., Lee, J. E., Nelson, T. F., & Kuo, M. (2002). Underage college students' drinking behavior, access to alcohol, and the influence of deterrence policies. *Journal of American College Health, 50,* 223–236.

Weeks, M., & Lupfer, M. B. (2004). Complicating race: The relationship between prejudice, race, and social class categorizations. *Personality and Social Psychology Bulletin, 30,* 972–984.

Wegener, D. T., Petty, R. E., Smoak, N. D., & Fabrigar, L. R. (2004). Multiple routes to resisting attitude change. In E. S. Knowles & J. A. Linn (Eds.), *Resistance and persuasion.* Mahwah, NJ: Lawrence Erlbaum Associates.

Wehrle, R., Kaufmann, C., Wetter, T. C., Holsboer, F., Auer, D. P., Pollmacher, T., & Czisch, M. (2007). Functional microstates within human REM sleep: First evidence from fMRI of a thalamocortical network specific for phasic REM periods. *European Journal of Neuroscience, 25,* 863–871.

Weinberg, M. S., Williams, C. J., & Pryor, D. W. (1991, February 27). Personal communication. Indiana University, Bloomington.

Weiner, B. A., & Wettstein, R. (1993). *Legal issues in mental health care.* New York: Plenum Press.

Weiner, I. B. (2004a). Monitoring psychotherapy with performance-based measures of personality functioning. *Journal of Personality Assessment, 83,* 323–331.

Weiner, I. B. (2004b). Rorschach Inkblot method. In M. E. Maruish (Ed.), *Use of psychological testing for treatment planning and outcomes assessment, Vol. 3: Instruments for adults* (3rd ed.). Mahwah, NJ: Lawrence Erlbaum Associates.

Weinstein, L. (2007). Selected genetic disorders affecting Ashkenazi Jewish families. *Family & Community Health, 30,* 50–62.

Weinstein, M., Glei, D. A., Yamazaki, A., & Ming-Cheng, C. (2004). The role of intergenerational relations in the association between life stressors and depressive symptoms. *Research on Aging, 26,* 511–530.

Weiss, A., Bates, T., & Luciano, M. (2008). Happiness is a personal(ity) thing: The genetics of personality and well-being in a representative sample. *Psychological Science, 19,* 205–210.

Weiss, W. M., & Weiss, M. R. (2003). Attraction-and entrapment-based commitment among competitive female gymnasts. *Journal of Sport & Exercise Psychology, 25,* 229–247.

Weissman, M., Markowitz, J., & Klerman, G. L. (2007). *Clinician's quick guide to interpersonal psychotherapy.* New York: Oxford University Press.

Weissman, M. M., Bland, R. C., Canino, G. J., Faravelli, C., Greenwald, S., Hwu, H. G., et al. (1997, July 24–31). Cross-national epidemiology of major depression and bipolar disorder. *Journal of the American Medical Association, 276,* 293–299.

Welkowitz, L. A., Struening, E. L., Pittman, J., Guardino, M., & Welkowitz, J. (2000). Obsessive-compulsive disorder and comorbid anxiety problems in a national anxiety screening sample. *Journal of Anxiety Disorders, 14,* 471–482.

Wells, G. L., Olson, E. A., & Charman, S. D. (2002). The confidence of eyewitnesses in their identifications from lineups. *Current Directions in Psychological Science, 11,* 151–154.

Wenar, C. (1994). *Developmental psychopathology: From infancy through adolescence* (3rd ed.). New York: McGraw-Hill.

Wensley, D., & King, M. (2008, June). Scientific responsibility for the dissemination and interpretation of genetic research: Lessons from the 'warrior gene' controversy. *Journal of Medical Ethics, 34,* 507–509.

Wenzel, A., Zetocha, K., & Ferraro, R. F. (2007). Depth of processing and recall of threat material in fearful and nonfearful individuals. *Anxiety, Stress & Coping: An International Journal, 20,* 223–237.

Werblin, F., & Roska, B. (2007, April). The movies in our eyes. *Scientific American,* pp. 73–77.

Werker, J. F., & Tees, R. C. (2005). Speech perception as a window for understanding plasticity and commitment in language systems of the brain. *Developmental Psychobiology, 46,* 233–234.

Werner, J. S., Pinna, B., & Spillmann, L. (2007, March). Illusory color and the brain. *Scientific American,* 90–96.

Wertheimer, M. (1923). Untersuchungen zur Lehre von der Gestalt, II. *Psychol. Forsch., 5,* 301–350. In R. Beardsley & M. Wertheimer (Eds.). (1958), *Readings in perception.* New York: Van Nostrand.

West, D. S., Harvey-Berino, J., & Raczynski, J. M. (2004). Behavioral aspects of obesity, dietary intake, and chronic disease. In J. M. Raczynski and L. C. Leviton (Eds.), *Handbook of clinical health psychology: Vol. 2. Disorders of behavior and health.* Washington, DC: American Psychological Association.

West, J. R., & Blake, C. A. (2005). Fetal alcohol syndrome: An assessment of the field. *Experimental Biological Medicine, 6,* 354–356.

West, R. L., Bagwell, D. K., & Dark-Freudeman, A. (2007). Self-efficacy and memory aging: The impact of a memory intervention based on self-efficacy. *Neuropsychological Development and Cognition, B, Aging and Neuropsychological Cognition, 14,* 1–28.

West, S. L., & O'Neal, K. K. (2004). Project D.A.R.E. outcome effectiveness revisited. *American Journal of Public Health, 94,* 1027–1029.

Westen, D., Novotny, C. M., & Thompson-Brenner, H. (2004). The empirical status of empirically supported psychotherapies: Assumptions, findings, and reporting in controlled clinical trials. *Psychological Bulletin, 130,* 631–663.

Westerberg, H., Brehmer, Y., D'Hondt, N., Söderman, D., & Bäckman, L. (2008, April). *Computerized training of working memory: A controlled, randomized trial.* Paper presented at the 2008 annual meeting of the Cognitive Neuroscience Society.

Westerhausen, R., Moosmann, M., Alho, K., Medvedev, S., Hämäläinen, H., & Hugdahl, K. (2009, January). Top-down and bottom-up interaction: Manipulating the dichotic listening ear advantage. *Brain Research, 1250,* 183–189.

Westerterp, K. R. (2006). Perception, passive overfeeding and energy metabolism. *Physiology & Behavior, 89,* 62–65.

Wetter, D. W., Fiore, M. C., Gritz, E. R., Lando, H. A., Stitzer, M. L., Hasselblad, V., et al. (1998). The Agency for Health Care Policy and Research. Smoking cessation clinical practice guideline: Findings and implications for psychologists. *American Psychologist, 53,* 657–669.

Whaley, B. B. (Ed.). (2000). *Explaining illness: Research, theory, and strategies.* Mahwah, NJ: Erlbaum.

Whisman, M., & Snyder, D. (2007). Sexual infidelity in a national survey of American women: Differences in prevalence and correlates as a function of method of assessment. *Journal of Family Psychology, 21,* 14–154.

Whitbourne, S. (2010). *The search for fulfillment.* New York: Ballantine.

Whitbourne, S. K. (2000). The normal aging process. In S. K. Whitbourne & S. Krauss (Eds.), *Psychopathology in later adulthood.* New York: Wiley.

Whitbourne, S. K., & Wills, K (1993). Psychological issues in institutional care of the aged. In S. B. Goldsmith (Ed.), *Long-term care.* Gaithersburg, MD: Aspen Press.

Whitbourne, S. K., Zuschlag, M. K., Elliot, L. B., & Waterman, A. S. (1992). Psychosocial development in adulthood: A 22-year sequential study. *Journal of Personality and Social Psychology, 63,* 260–271.

Whitebread, D., Coltman, P., Jameson, H., & Lander, R. (2009). Play, cognition and self-regulation: What exactly are children learning when they learn through play? *Educational and Child Psychology, 26,* 40–52.

Whitehouse, W. G., Orne, E. C., Dinges, D. F., Bates, B. L., Nadon, R., & Orne, M. T. (2005). The cognitive interview: Does it successfully avoid the dangers of forensic hypnosis? *American Journal of Psychology, 118,* 213–234.

White, L. (2007). Linguistic theory, universal grammar, and second language acquisition. In B. Van Patten & J. Williams, *Theories in second language acquisition: An introduction.* Mahwah, NJ: Lawrence Erlbaum Associates.

Whitfield, J. B., Zhu, G., Madden, P. A., Neale, M. C., Heath, A. C., & Martin, N. G. (2004). The genetics of alcohol intake and of alcohol dependence. *Alcoholism: Clinical and Experimental Research, 28,* 1153–1160.

WHO World Mental Health Survey Consortium. (2004). Prevalence, severity, and unmet need for treatment of mental disorders in the World Health Organization World Mental Health Surveys. *Journal of the American Medical Association, 291,* 2581–2590.

Whorf, B. L. (1956). *Language, thought, and reality.* New York: Wiley.

Wickelgren, E. A. (2004). Perspective distortion of trajectory forms and perceptual constancy in visual event identification. *Perception and Psychophysics, 66,* 629–641.

Widaman, K. (2009). Phenylketonuria in children and mothers: Genes, environments, behavior. *Current Directions in Psychological Science, 18,* 48–52.

Widiger, T. A., & Clark, L. A. (2000). Toward *DSM-V* and the classification of psychopathology. *Psychological Bulletin, 126,* 946–963.

Widmeyer, W. N., & Loy, J. W. (1988). When you're hot, you're hot! Warm-cold effects in first impressions of persons and teaching effectiveness. *Journal of Educational Psychology, 80,* 118–121.

Wielgosz, A. T., & Nolan, R. P. (2000). Biobehavioral factors in the context of ischemic cardiovascular disease. *Journal of Psychosomatic Research, 48,* 339–345.

Wiggins, J. S. (2003). *Paradigms of personality assessment.* New York: Guilford Press.

Wildavsky, B. (2000, September 4). A blow to bilingual education. *U.S. News & World Report,* pp. 22–28.

Wiley, C., & Sisson, M. (2006, November). *Ethics, accuracy, and assumption: The use of Facebook by students and employers.* Paper presented at the Southwestern Ohio Council for Higher Education Special Topics Forum, Dayton, OH.

Wilgoren, J. (1999, October 22). Quality day care, early, is tied to achievements as an adult. *The New York Times,* p. A16.

Wilkinson, H. A. (2009). Cingulotomy. *Journal of Neurosurgery, 110,* 607–611.

Wilkinson, L., & Olliver-Gray, Y. (2006). The significance of silence: Differences in meaning, learning styles, and teaching strategies in cross-cultural settings [Special issue: Child language]. *Psychologia: An International Journal of Psychology in the Orient, 49,* 74–88.

Willander, J., & Larsson, M. (2006). Smell your way back to childhood: Autobiographical odor memory. *Psychonomic Bulletin & Review, 13,* 240–244.

Willems, R. M., & Hagoort, P. (2007). Neural evidence for the interplay between language, gesture, and action: a review. *Brain Language, 101,* 278–289.

Williams, J. E., & Bennett, S. M. (1975). The definition of sex stereotypes via the Adjective Check List. *Sex Roles, 1,* 327–337.

Williams, J. E., Paton, C. C., Siegler, I. C., Eigenbrodt, M. L., Nieto, F. J., & Tyroler, H. A. (2000). Anger proneness predicts coronary heart disease risk: Prospective analysis from the Atherosclerosis Risk in Communities (ARIC) Study. *Circulation, 101,* 2034–2039.

Williams, J. W., Mulrow, C. D., Chiquette, E., Noel, P. H., Aguilar, C., & Cornell, J. (2000). A systematic review of newer pharmacotherapies for depression in adults: Evidence report summary. *Annals of Internal Medicine, 132,* 743–756.

Williamson, P., McLeskey, J., & Hoppey, D. (2006). Educating students with mental retardation in general education classrooms. *Exceptional Children, 72,* 347–361.

Willis, G. (2008, June). Intraocular microinjections repair experimental Parkinson's disease. *Brain Research, 1217,* 119–131.

Willis, G. L. (2005). The therapeutic effects of dopamine replacement therapy and its psychiatric side effects are mediated by pineal function. *Behavioural Brain Research, 160,* 148–160.

Willis, J., & Todorov, A. (2006). First impressions: Making up your mind after a 100-ms exposure to a face. *Psychological Science, 17,* 592–598.

Willis, S. L., & Schaie, K. W. (1994). In C. B. Fisher & R. M. Lerner (Eds.), *Applied developmental psychology.* New York: McGraw-Hill.

Wills, T., Sargent, J., Stoolmiller, M., Gibbons, F., & Gerrard, M. (2008). Movie smoking exposure and smoking onset: A longitudinal study of mediation processes in a representative sample of U.S. adolescents. *Psychology of Addictive Behaviors, 22,* 269–277.

Wilson, T. D. (2006, September 1). The power of social psychological interventions. *Science, 313,* 1251–1252.

Wilson, T. G., Grilo, C. M., & Vitousek, K. M. (2007). Psychological treatment of eating disorders [Special issue: Eating disorders]. *American Psychologist, 62,* 199–216.

Windholz, G., & Lamal, P. A. (2002). Koehler's insight revisited. In R. A. Griggs (Ed.), *Handbook for teaching introductory psychology, Vol. 3: With an emphasis on assessment.* Mahwah, NJ: Erlbaum.

Winerman, L. (2005, June). ACTing up. *Monitor on Psychology,* pp. 44–45.

Winik, L. W. (2006, October 1). The true cost of depression. *Parade,* p. 7.

Winner, E. (2003). Creativity and talent. In M. H. Bornstein & L. Davidson (Eds.), *Well-being: Positive development across the life course.* Mahwah, NJ: Lawrence Erlbaum.

Winsler, A., Madigan, A. L., & Aquilino, S. A. (2005). Correspondence between maternal and paternal parenting styles in early childhood. *Early Childhood Research Quarterly, 20,* 1–12.

Winson, J. (1990, November). The meaning of dreams. *Scientific American,* pp. 86–96.

Winstead, B. A., & Sanchez, A. (2005). Gender and psychopathology. In J. E. Maddux & B. A. Winstead, *Psychopathology: Foundations for a contemporary understanding.* Mahwah, NJ: Lawrence Erlbaum Associates.

Winston, J. S., O'Doherty, J., & Kilner, J. M. (2006). Brain systems for assessing facial attractiveness. *Neuropsychologia, 45,* 195–206.

Winter, D. G. (1988). The power motive in women— and men. *Journal of Personality and Social Psychology, 54,* 510–519.

Winter, D. G. (1995). *Personality: Analysis and interpretation of lives.* New York: McGraw-Hill.

Winter, D. G. (2007). The role of motivation, responsibility, and integrative complexity in crisis escalation: Comparative studies of war and peace crises. *Journal of Personality and Social Psychology, 92,* 920–937.

Winters, B. D., & Bussey, T. J. (2005). Glutamate receptors in perirhinal cortex mediate encoding, retrieval, and consolidation of object recognition memory. *Journal of Neuroscience, 25,* 4243–4251.

Wiseman, R., & Greening, E. (2002). The mind machine: A mass participation experiment into the possible existence of extra-sensory perception. *British Journal of Psychology, 93,* 487–499.

Witelson, S., Kigar, D., Scamvougeras, A., Kideckel, D., Buck, B., Stanchev, P., et al. (2008). Corpus callosum anatomy in right-handed homosexual and heterosexual men. *Archives of Sexual Behavior, 37,* 857–863.

Witt, C. M., Jena, S., & Brinkhaus, B. (2006). Acupuncture for patients with chronic neck pain. *Pain, 125,* 98–106.

Wittchen, H., Nocon, A., Beesdo, K., Pine, D., Höfler, M., Lieb, R., et al. (2008). Agoraphobia and panic. *Psychotherapy and Psychosomatics, 77,* 147–157.

Wittenbrink, B., & Schwarz, N. (Eds.). (2007). *Implicit measures of attitudes.* New York: Guilford Press.

Wixted, J. T., & Carpenter, S. K. (2007). The Wickelgren Power Law and the Ebbinghaus Savings Function. *Psychological Science, 18,* 133–134.

Wolfe, M. S. (2006, May). Shutting down Alzheimer's. *Scientific American,* 73–79.

Wolff, N. (2002). Risk, response, and mental health policy: Learning from the experience of the United Kingdom. *Journal of Health Politic and Policy Law, 27,* 801–802.

Wolitzky, D. L. (2006). Psychodynamic theories. In J. C. Thomas, D. L. Segal, & M. Hersen, *Comprehensive handbook of personality and psychopathology, Vol. 1: Personality and everyday functioning.* Hoboken, NJ: John Wiley & Sons.

Woller, K., Buboltz, W., & Loveland, J. (2007). Psychological reactance: Examination across age, ethnicity, and gender. *American Journal of Psychology, 120,* 15–24.

Wood, J. M., Nezworski, M. T., Lilienfeld, S. O., & Garb, H. N. (2003). *What's wrong with the Rorschach? Science confronts the controversial inkblot test.* New York: Wiley.

Wood, W. (2000). Attitude change: Persuasion and social influence. *Annual Review of Psychology, 51,* 539–570.

Woodruff, S. I., Conway, T. L., & Edwards, C. C. (2007). Sociodemographic and smoking- related psychosocial predictors of smoking behavior change among high school smokers. *Addictive Behaviors, 33,* 354–358.

Woods, S. C., Schwartz, M. W., Baskin, D. G., & Seeley, R. J. (2000). Food intake and the regulation of body weight. *Annual Review of Psychology, 51,* 255–277.

Woods, S. C., & Seeley, R. J. (2002). Hunger and energy homeostasis. In H. Pashler & R. Gallistel (Eds.). *Steven's handbook of experimental psychology* (3rd ed.), *Vol. 3: Learning, motivation, and emotion.* New York: Wiley.

Woodson, S. R. J. (2006). Relationships between sleepiness and emotion experience: An experimental investigation of the role of subjective sleepiness in the generation of positive and negative emotions. *Dissertation Abstracts International: Section B: The Sciences and Engineering, 67(5–B),* 2849.

Woollett, K., & Maguire, E. (2009). Navigational expertise may compromise anterograde associative memory. *Neuropsychologia, 47,* 1088–1095.

Wren, A. M., & Bloom, S. R. (2007). Gut hormones and appetite control. *Gastroenterology, 132,* 2116–2130.

Wright, K. (2002, September). Times of our lives. *Scientific American,* pp. 59–65.

Wrosch, C., Bauer, I., & Scheier, M. (2005, December). Regret and quality of life across the adult life span: The influence of disengagement and available future goals. *Psychology and Aging, 20,* 657–670.

Wrzesniewski, K., & Chylinska, J. (2007). Assessment of coping styles and strategies with school-related stress. *School Psychology International, 28,* 179–194.

Wu, L-T., Schlenger, W. E., & Galvin, D. M. (2006). Concurrent use of methamphetamine, MDMA, LSD, ketamine, GHB, and flunitrazepam among American youths. *Drug and Alcohol Dependence, 84,* 102–113.

Wuethrich, B. (2001, March 16). Does alcohol damage female brains more? *Science, 291,* 2077–2079.

Wurtz, R. H., & Kandel, E. R. (2000). Central visual pathways. In E. R. Kandel, J. H. Schwartz, & T. M.

Jessell (Eds.), *Principles of neural science* (4th ed.). New York: McGraw-Hill.

Wynn, K., Bloom, P., & Chiang, W. C. (2002). Enumeration of collective entities by 5-month-old infants. *Cognition, 83,* B55–B62.

Wyra, M., Lawson, M. J., & Hungi, N. (2007). The mnemonic keyword method: The effects of bidirectional retrieval training and of ability to image on foreign language vocabulary recall. *Learning and Instruction, 17,* 360–371.

Xiao, Z., Yan, H., Wang, Z., Zou, Z., Xu, Y., Chen, J., et al. (2006). Trauma and dissociation in China. *American Journal of Psychiatry, 163,* 1388–1391.

Yao, S-Q., Zhour, Y-H., & Jiang, L. (2006). The intelligence scale for Chinese adults: Item analysis, reliability and validity. *Chinese Journal of Clinical Psychology, 14,* 441–445.

Yao, Y., Kelly, M., Sajikumar, S., Serrano, P., Tian, D., Bergold, P., et al. (2008). PKMζ maintains late long-term potentiation by *n*-ethylmaleimide-sensitive factor/gluR2-dependent trafficking of postsynaptic AMPA receptors. *Journal of Neuroscience, 28,* 7820–7827.

Yapko, M. D. (2006). Utilizing hypnosis in addressing ruminative depression-related insomnia. In M. D. Yapko, *Hypnosis and treating depression: Applications in clinical practice.* New York: Routledge/Taylor & Francis Group.

Yardley, L., & Moss-Morris, R. (2009, January). Current issues and new directions in psychology and health: Increasing the quantity and quality of health psychology research. *Psychology & Health, 24,* 1–4.

Yeomans, M. R., Tepper, B. J., & Ritezschel, J. (2007). Human hedonic responses to sweetness: Role of taste genetics and anatomy. *Physiology & Behavior, 91,* 264–273.

Yesilyaprak, B., Kisac, I., & Sanlier, N. (2007). Stress symptoms and nutritional status among survivors of the Marmara region earthquakes in Turkey. *Journal of Loss & Trauma, 12,* 1–8.

Yordanova, J., Kolev, V., Verleger, R., Bataghva, Z., Born, J., & Wagner, U. (2008). Shifting from implicit to explicit knowledge: Different roles of early- and late-night sleep. *Learning & Memory, 15,* 508–515.

Zacks, J. (2008). Neuroimaging studies of mental rotation: A meta-analysis and review. *Journal of Cognitive Neuroscience, 20,* 1–19.

Zaitsu, W. (2007). The effect of fear on eyewitness' retrieval in recognition memory. *Japanese Journal of Psychology, 77,* 504–511.

Zajonc, R. B. (2001). Mere exposure: A gateway to the subliminal. *Current Directions in Psychological Science, 10,* 224–228.

Zaragoza, M. S., Belli, R. F., & Payment, K. E. (2007). Misinformation effects and the suggestibility of eyewitness memory. In M. Garry & H. Hayne, *Do justice and let the sky fall: Elizabeth Loftus and her contributions to science, law, and academic freedom.* Mahwah, NJ: Lawrence Erlbaum Associates.

Zarren, J. I., & Eimer, B. N. (2002). *Brief cognitive hypnosis: Facilitating the change of dysfunctional behavior.* New York: Springer.

Zaslow, M., Halle, T., & Martin, L. (2006). Child outcome measures in the study of child care quality. *Evaluation Review, 30,* 577–610.

Zebrowitz, L. A., & Montepare, J. M. (2005, June 10). Appearance DOES matter. *Science, 308,* 1565–1566.

Zebrowitz-McArthur, L. (1988). Person perception in cross-cultural perspective. In M. H. Bond (Ed.), *The cross-cultural challenge to social psychology.* Newbury Park, CA: Sage.

Zeigler, D. W., et al. (2005). The neurocognitive effects of alcohol on adolescents and college students. *Preventive Medicine: An International Journal Devoted to Practice and Theory, 40,* 23–32.

Zevon, M., & Corn, B. (1990). Paper presented at the annual meeting of the American Psychological Association, Boston, MA.

Zhang, F., Chen, Y., Heiman, M., & Dimarchi, R. (2005). Leptin: Structure, function and biology. *Vitamins and Hormones: Advances in Research and Applications, 71,* 345–372.

Zhou, Z., & Buck, L. B. (2006, March 10). Combinatorial effects of odorant mixes in olfactory cortex. *Science, 1477–1481.*

Zhou, Z., Liu, Q., & Davis, R. L. (2005). Complex regulation of spiral ganglion neuron firing patterns by neurotrophin-3. *Journal of Neuroscience, 25,* 7558–7566.

Zians, J. (2007). A comparison of trait anger and depression on several variables: Attribution style, dominance, submissiveness, need for power, efficacy and dependency. *Dissertation Abstracts International: Section B: The Sciences and Engineering, 67(7-B),* 4124.

Zigler, E., Bennett-Gates, D., Hodapp, R., & Henrich, C. (2002). Assessing personality traits of individuals with mental retardation. *American Journal on Mental Retardation, 107,* 181–193.

Zigler, E. F., Finn-Stevenson, M., & Hall, N. W. (2002). The first three years and beyond: Brain development and social policy. In E. F. Zigler, M. Finn-Stevenson, & N. W. Hall, *Current perspectives in psychology.* New Haven, CT: Yale University Press.

Zimbardo, P. (2007). *The Lucifer effect: Understanding how good people turn evil.* New York: Random House.

Zimbardo, P. G. (1973). On the ethics of intervention in human psychological research: With special reference to the Stanford Prison *Experiment. Cognition, 2,* 243–256.

Zimbardo, P. G. (2004). Does psychology make a significant difference in our lives? *American Psychologist, 59,* 339–351.

Zimbardo, P. G., Maslach, C., & Haney, C. (2000). Reflections on the Stanford Prison Experiment: Genesis, transformations, consequences. In T. Blass (Ed.), *Obedience to authority: Current perspectives on the Milgram Paradigm.* Mahwah, NJ: Lawrence Erlbaum Associates.

Zimmerman, U. S., Blomeyer, D., & Laucht, M. (2007). How gene-stress-behavior interactions can promote adolescent alcohol use: The roles of predrinking allostatic load and childhood behavior disorders [Special issue: Adolescents, drug abuse and mental disorders]. *Pharmacology, Biochemistry and Behavior, 86,* 246–262.

Zito, J. M. (1993). *Psychotherapeutic drug manual* (3rd ed., rev.). New York: Wiley.

Zolotor, A., Theodore, A., Chang, J., Berkoff, M., & Runyan, D. (2008). Speak softly—and forget the stick: Corporal punishment and child physical abuse. *American Journal of Preventive Medicine, 35,* 364–369.

Zuckerman, M. (1978, February). The search for high sensation. *Psychology Today,* pp. 30–46.

Zuckerman, M. (2002). Genetics of sensation seeking. In J. Benjamin, R. P. Ebstein, et al. (Eds.), *Molecular genetics and the human personality.* Washington, DC: American Psychiatric Publishing.

Zuckerman, M., & Kuhlman, D. M. (2000). Personality and risk-taking: Common biosocial factors [Special issue: Personality processes and problem behavior]. *Journal of Personality, 68,* 999–1029.

Zuger, A. (2005, November 10). Doctors learn how to say what no one wants to hear. *The New York Times,* p. S1.

Credits

Text and Line Art Credits

Chapter 1

Module 1: Figure 4: From Tara L. Kuther, *The Psychology Major's Handbook*, 1st ed., p. 114. © 2003 Wadsworth, a part of Cengage Learning, Inc. Reproduced by permission. www.cenage.com/permissions. **Module 3: Figure 5:** From Darley, J. M., & Latané, B. (1968). Bystander intervention in emergencies: Diffusion of responsibility. *Journal of Personality and Social Psychology, 8,* 377–383. Published by The American Psychological Association, adapted with permission. **Module 4: Figure 1:** From Stevens, C., Lauinger, B., Neville, H. (2009). Differences in the neural mechanisms of selective attention in children from different socioeconomic backgrounds: An event-related brain potential study. *Developmental Science* 12(4): 634–646. Reprinted by permission of John Wiley & Sons, Inc.

Chapter 2

Module 5: Figure 1: Line art from Kent Van De Graaff, *Human Anatomy*, updated 5th ed. Copyright © 2000 by The McGraw-Hill Companies, Inc. Reprinted with permission. **Figure 3:** From Sylvia S. Mader, *Human Biology*, 6th ed., p. 250. Copyright © 2000 by The McGraw-Hill Companies, Inc. Reprinted with permission of The McGraw-Hill Companies. **Figure 4a:** From Sylvia S. Mader, *Human Biology*, 6th ed., p. 250. Copyright © 2000 by The McGraw-Hill Companies, Inc. Reprinted with permission of The McGraw-Hill Companies. **Figure 4b:** From George B. Johnson, *The Living World*, 2nd ed., p. 600. Copyright © 2000 by The McGraw-Hill Companies, Inc. Reprinted with permission of The McGraw-Hill Companies. **Module 6: Figure 2:** From Michael W. Passer and Ronald E. Smith, *Psychology*. Copyright © 2001 by The McGraw-Hill Companies, Inc. Reprinted with permission of The McGraw-Hill Companies. **Figure 3:** From Michael W. Passer and Ronald E. Smith, *Psychology*, p. 91. Copyright © 2001 by The McGraw-Hill Companies, Inc. Reprinted with permission of The McGraw-Hill Companies. **Figure 4:** Adapted from Robert J. Brooker, Eric P. Widmaier, Linda Graham, and Peter Stiling, *Biology*, p. 1062. Copyright © 2008 by The McGraw-Hill Companies, Inc. Reprinted with permission of The McGraw-Hill Companies. **Module 7: Figure 2:** From Rod R. Seeley, Trent D. Stephens, and Philip Tate, *Anatomy & Physiology*, 5th ed., p. 384. Copyright © 2000 by The McGraw-Hill Companies, Inc. Reprinted with permission of The McGraw-Hill Companies. **Figure 3:** Adapted from Robert J. Brooker, Eric P. Widmaier, Linda Graham, and Peter Stiling, *Biology*, p. 940. Copyright © 2008 by The McGraw-Hill Companies, Inc. Reprinted with permission of The McGraw-Hill Companies. **Figure 4:** Adapted from Allen M. Schneider and Barry Tarshis, *Elements of Physiological Psychology*, p. 87. Copyright © 1995 by The McGraw-Hill Companies, Inc. Reprinted with permission of The McGraw-Hill Companies. **Figure 8:** From Robert J. Brooker, Eric P. Widmaier, Linda Graham, and Peter Stiling, *Biology*, p. 943. Copyright © 2008 by The McGraw-Hill Companies, Inc. Reprinted with permission of The McGraw-Hill Companies.

Chapter 3

Module 9: Figure 1: From Camille B. Wortman, Elizabeth F. Loftus, and Charles Weaver, *Psychology*, 5th ed., p. 113. Copyright © 1999 by The McGraw-Hill Companies, Inc. Reprinted with permission of The McGraw-Hill Companies. **Figure 3:** From David Shier, Jackie Butler, and Ricki Lewis, *Hole's Essentials of Human Anatomy and Physiology*, 7th ed., p. 283. Copyright © 2000 by The McGraw-Hill Companies, Inc. Reprinted with permission of The McGraw-Hill Companies. **Figure 5:** From Sylvia S. Mader, *Human Biology*, 6th ed., p. 250. Copyright © 2000 by The McGraw-Hill Companies, Inc. Reprinted with permission of The McGraw-Hill Companies. **Module 10: Figure 1:** From Robert J. Brooker, Eric P. Widmaier, Linda Graham, and Peter Stiling, *Biology*, p. 956. Copyright © 2008 by The McGraw-Hill Companies, Inc. Reprinted with permission of The McGraw-Hill Companies. **Figure 2:** From Rod R. Seeley, Trent D. Stephens, and Philip Tate, *Anatomy & Physiology*, 5th ed., p. 384. Copyright © 2000 by The McGraw-Hill Companies, Inc. Reprinted with permission of The McGraw-Hill Companies. **Figure 3:** From Paul Vitello, "A Ring Tone Meant to Fall on Deaf Ears," New York Times, June 12, 2006, p. A1. Copyright © 2006 New York Times. All rights reserved. Reprinted by permission. **Figure 4:** Adapted from Bartoshuk, L., & Lucchina, L., "Take a taste test" from Brownlee, S., & Watson, T. (1997, January 13). The senses. *U.S. News & World Report*, pp. 51–59. Reprinted by permission of Linda Bartoshuk. **Figure 6:** From "Hearing Colors, Tasting Shapes" by Vilayanur S. Ramachandran and Edward M. Hubbard. Copyright © 2003 by Scientific American, Inc. All rights reserved. **Module 11: Figure 4:** From Stanley Coren and Lawrence M. Ward, *Sensation & Perception*, 3rd ed. (1989), p. 329. Reprinted with permission of John Wiley & Sons, Inc. **Figure 5 (b, c):** From Stanley Coren and Lawrence M. Ward, *Sensation & Perception*, 3rd ed. (1989), p. 5. Reprinted with permission of John Wiley & Sons, Inc. **Figure 8:** Adapted from Picture 2 from Figure 1 (p. 186) from Hudson, W. (1960). Pictorial depth perception in sub-cultural groups in Africa. *Journal of Social Psychology, 52,* 183–208. Reprinted by permission of the publisher (Taylor & Francis, http://www.informaworld.com).

Chapter 4

Module 12: Figure 1: From Palladino, J. J., & Carducci, B. J. (1984). Students' knowledge of sleep and dreams. *Teaching of Psychology, 11,* 189–191. Reprinted by permission of the publisher (Taylor & Francis, http://www.informaworld.com). **Figure 2:** Figure on p. 16 from the book *Sleep* by J. Allan Hobson. Copyright © 1989 by J. Allan Hobson. Reprinted by permission of Henry Holt and Company, LLC. **Figure 4:** From *Secrets of Sleep* by Alexander Borbély, p. 43. Copyright © 1988 Alexander Borbély. Reprinted by permission of Basic Books, a member of the Perseus Books Group. **Figure 6:** From Adam Schneider and G. William Domhoff, *The Quantitative Study of Dreams* (2002). Reprinted by permission of G. William Domhoff, www.dreamresearch.net. **Module 14: Figure 1:** From Johnston, L. D., O'Malley, P. M., Bachman, J. G., & Schulenberg, J. E. (2009). *Monitoring the future national survey results on drug use: 1975–2008. Volume I: Secondary school students* (NIH Publication No. 09-7402). Bethesda, MD: National Institute on Drug Abuse. **Figure 2:** From Sylvia S. Mader, *Human Biology*, 6th ed., p. 250. Copyright © 2000 by The McGraw-Hill Companies, Inc. Reprinted with permission of The McGraw-Hill Companies. **Figure 3:** *The New York Times* graphic "Levels of caffeine in various foods" from Blakeslee, S. (1991, August 7). The secrets of caffeine: America's favorite drug. *The New York Times.* Copyright © 1991 by The New York Times Co. Reprinted with permission. **Figure 7:** From Johnston, L. D., O'Malley, P. M., Bachman, J. G., & Schulenberg, J. E. (2007). *Monitoring the Future national results on adolescent drug use: Overview of key findings, 2006* (NIH Publication No. 07-6202). Bethesda, MD: National Institute on Drug Abuse.

Chapter 5

Module 17: Figure 1: From Tolman, E. C., & Honzik, C. H. (1930). Introduction and removal of reward and maze performance in rats. *University of California Publications in Psychology, 4,* 257–275. **Figure 3:** From Anderson, J. A., & Adams, M. (1992). Acknowledging the learning styles of diverse student populations: Implications for instructional design. *New Directions for Teaching and Learning, 49,* 19–33. Reprinted with permission of John Wiley & Sons, Inc.

Chapter 6

Module 18: Figure 6: From Collins, A. M., & Loftus, E. F. (1975). A spreading-activation theory of semantic processing. *Psychological Review, 82,* 407–428. Published by The American Psychological Association, adapted with permission. **Figure 7:** From Kent Van De Graaff, *Human Anatomy*, updated 5th ed. Copyright © 2000 by The McGraw-Hill Companies, Inc. Reprinted with permission of The McGraw-Hill Companies. **Figure 8:** Graphs from Maguire, E. A., Woollett, K., and Spiers, H. J. (2006). London Tax Drivers and Bus Drivers: A Structural MRI and Neuropsychological Analysis. *Hippocampus, 16,* 1091–1101. Reprinted by permission of John Wiley & Sons, Inc. **Module 19: Figure 3:** From David C. Rubin, "The Subtle

Deceiver: Recalling Our Past," *Psychology Today*, September 1985, pp. 39–46. Reprinted with permission from *Psychology Today* magazine. (Copyright © 1985 Sussex Publishers, LLC.). **Figure 4:** Reprinted from *Journal of Verbal Learning and Verbal Behavior*, vol. 13, Loftus, E. F., & Palmer, J. C., "Reconstruction of automobile destruction: An example of the interface between language and memory," pp. 585–589, Copyright 1974, with permission from Elsevier. **Figure 5:** Data from Table 2 (p. 266) from Bahrick, H. P., Hall, L. K., & Berger, S. A. (1996). Accuracy and distortion in memory for high school grades. *Psychological Science*, 7, 265–269. Copyright © 1996, Association for Psychological Science. Reprinted by permission of Sage Publications, Inc. **Module 20: Figure 2:** Reprinted from *Cognitive Psychology*, vol. 11, Nickerson, R. S., & Adams, M. J., "Long-term memory for a common object," pp. 287–307. Copyright 1979, with permission from Elsevier.

Chapter 7

Module 22: Figure 1: MLA Language Map, 2005. Reprinted by permission of the Modern Language Association. © 2005 Modern Language Association. **Module 23: Figure 1:** Text from *Multiple Intelligences: New Horizons in Theory and Practice* by Howard Gardner. Copyright © 2006 by Howard Gardner. Reprinted by permission of Basic Books, a member of the Perseus Books Group. **Figure 6:** Adapted from Table 1 (p. 410) from Henderson, N. D. (1982). Human behavior genetics. Reprinted, with permission, from the *Annual Review of Psychology*, Volume 33 © 1982 by Annual Reviews. www.annualreviews.org.

Chapter 8

Module 24: Figure 1: "Do You Seek Out Sensation?" questionnaire from Marvin Zuckerman, "The Search for High Sensation?" *Psychology Today*, February 1978, pp. 30–46. Reprinted with permission from *Psychology Today* magazine. (Copyright © 1978 Sussex Publishers, LLC.). **Module 26: Figure 1:** Adapted from Figure 1 (p. 1067) from Shaver, P., Schwartz, J., Kirson, D., & O'Connor, C. (1987). Emotion knowledge: Further exploration of a prototype approach. *Journal of Personality and Social Psychology*, 52, 1061–1086. Published by The American Psychological Association, adapted with permission. **Figure 3:** Line art of brain: From Dolan, R. J. (2002). Emotion, cognition, and behavior. *Science*, 298, no. 5596, 1191–1194 (Figure 1, p. 1192). Drawing of brain reprinted with permission from AAAS.

Chapter 9

Module 28: Figure 3: Figure 2 (p. 239) from Leppänen, J. M., Moulson, M. C., Vogel-Farley, V. K., & Nelson, C. A. (2007). An ERP study of emotional face processing in the adult and infant brain. *Child Development*, 78, 232–245. Reprinted by permission of John Wiley & Sons, Inc. **Figure 10:** Judith A. Schickedanz, et al., *Understanding Children and Adolescents*, 4th edition, p. 440, Figure 13.1, © 2001 Pearson Education, Inc. Reproduced by permission of Pearson Education, Inc. All rights reserved. **Figure 11:** From Dempster, F. N. (1981). Memory span: Sources for individual and developmental differences. *Psychological Bulletin*, 89, 63–100. Published by The American Psychological Association, adapted with permission. **Module 29: Figure 2:** Rest, J. (1968). *Developmental hierarchy in preference and comprehension of moral judgment.* Unpublished doctoral dissertation, University of Chicago. **Figure 4:** Graph adapted from Table 2

(p. 64) from Boehm, K. E., & Campbell, N. B. (1995). Suicide: A review of calls to an adolescent peer listening phone service. *Child Psychiatry and Human Development*, 26, 61–66. Copyright © 1995 Springer Netherlands. With kind permission of Springer Science and Business Media. **Module 30: Figure 1:** From Arnett, S. (2001). Conceptions of the transitions to adulthood: Perspectives from adolescence to midlife. *Journal of Adult Development*, 8, 133–144. Reprinted by permission of Springer Science and Business Media.

Chapter 10

Module 32: Figure 1: From Eysenck, H. J. (1990). Biological dimensions of personality. In L. A. Pervin (Ed.), *Handbook of personality: Theory and research* (p. 246). New York: Guilford. Reprinted by permission of Guilford Press. **Figure 2:** From Pervin, L. A. (Ed.). (1990). *Handbook of personality: Theory and research* (chapter 3). New York: Guilford. Reprinted by permission of Guilford Press. **Figure 4:** From Tellegen, A., Lykken, D. T., Bouchard, T. J., Jr., Wilcox, K. J., Segal, N. L., & Rich, S. (1988). Personality similarity in twins reared apart and together. *Journal of Personality and Social Psychology*, 54, 1031–1039. Published by The American Psychological Association, reprinted with permission.

Chapter 11

Module 34: Figure 1: Map by Cleo Vilett, from Susser, E. S., Herman, D. B., & Aaron, B. (2002, August). Combating the terror of terrorism. *Scientific American*, p. 74. Reprinted by permission of Cleo Vilett. **Figure 2 top:** Adapted from Table 2 (p. 475) from Chamberlain, K., & Zika, S. (1990). The minor events approach to stress: Support for the use of daily hassles. Reproduced with permission from the *British Journal of Psychology*, 81, 469–481, © The British Psychological Society. **Figure 2 bottom:** Adapted from Table III (p. 14) from Kanner, A. D., Coyne, J. C., Schaefer, C., & Lazarus, R. S. (1981). Comparison of two modes of stress measurement: Daily hassles and uplifts versus major life events. *Journal of Behavioral Medicine*, 4, 1–39. © 1981 Plenum Publishing Corporation. With kind permission of Springer Science and Business Media. **Figure 3:** "Perceived Stress Scale" (pp. 394–395) adapted from Cohen, S., Kamarck, T., & Mermelstein, R. (1983). A global measure of perceived stress. *Journal of Health and Social Behavior*, 24, 385–396. Reprinted by permission of the American Sociological Association. **Figure 4:** From Hans Selye, *The Stress of Life.* Copyright © 1976 by The McGraw-Hill Companies, Inc. Reprinted with permission of The McGraw-Hill Companies. **Module 36: Figure 1:** From Daniel Goleman, "Doctor and Patient; Physicians May Bungle Key Part of Treatment: The Medical Interview." From *The New York Times*, January 21, 1988, p. B16. © 1988 The New York Times. All rights reserved. Used by permission and protected by the Copyright Laws of the United States. The printing, copying, redistribution, or retransmission of the material without express written permission is prohibited. www.nytimes.com. **Figure 2:** From Andrews, F. M., & Withey, S. B. (1976). *Social indicators of well-being: Americans' perceptions of life quality*, p. 376. © 1976 Plenum Press, New York. With kind permission of Springer Science and Business Media.

Chapter 12

Module 38: Figure 1: Adapted from Susan Nolen-Hoeksema, *Abnormal Psychology*, 4th ed., p. 232. Copyright © 2007 by The McGraw-Hill Companies,

Inc. Reprinted with permission of The McGraw-Hill Companies. **Figure 2:** From *Anxiety Disorders and Phobias: A Cognitive Perspective* by Aaron T. Beck and Gary Emery, with Ruth L. Greenberg, Tables 6.1 and 6.2 (pp. 87–88). Copyright © 1985 by Aaron T. Beck, Gary Emery, Ruth L. Greenberg. Reprinted by permission of Basic Books, a member of Perseus Books Group. **Figure 5:** From Table 3 (p. 65) from Zung, W. W. K. (1965). A self-rating depression scale. *Archives of General Psychiatry*, 12, 63–70. Copyright © 1965, American Medical Association. All rights reserved. Reprinted with permission. **Figure 6:** Adapted from Slater, E., & Meyer, A. (1959). Contributions to a pathography of the musicians: Robert Schumann. *Confinia Psychiatrica*, 2, 65–94, Table II. Reprinted by permission of S. Karger AG, Basel. **Figure 9:** Table showing genetic probability of inheriting schizophrenia from the book *Schizophrenia Genesis* by Irving I. Gottesman. Copyright © 1990 by Irving I. Gottesman. Reprinted by permission of Henry Holt and Company, LLC. **Module 39: Figure 1:** From Benton, S. A., et al. (2003). Changes in counseling center client problems across 13 years. *Professional Psychology: Research and Practice*, 34, 66–72. Published by The American Psychological Association, adapted with permission.

Chapter 13

Module 40: Figure 2: Text reprinted by permission of Herbert Benson, M.D., Benson-Henry Institute for Mind Body Medicine, Massachusetts General Hospital, Chestnut Hill, MA. **Module 41: Figure 1:** Smith, Mary Lee, Gene V. Glass, and Thomas I. Miller. *The Benefits of Psychotherapy*, p. 89, Table 5-1. © 1980 The Johns Hopkins University Press. Reprinted with permission of The Johns Hopkins University Press. **Module 42: Figure 3:** From Rodger Doyle, "Deinstitutionalization," *Scientific American*, December 2002, p. 38. Copyright 2002 Rodger Doyle. Reprinted with permission.

Chapter 14

Module 43: Figure 2: From Cacioppo, J. T., Berntson, G. G., & Crites, S. L., Jr. (1996). Social neuroscience: Principles of psychophysiological arousal and response. In E. T. Higgins & A. W. Kruglanski (Eds.), *Social psychology: Handbook of basic principles*. © 1996 The Guilford Press. Reprinted by permission of the publisher. **Figure 4:** Adapted from Anderson, C. A., Krull, D. S., & Weiner, B. (1996). Explanations: Processes and consequences. In E. T. Higgins & A. W. Kruglanski (Eds.), *Social psychology: Handbook of basic principles* (p. 274). © 1996 The Guilford Press. Reprinted by permission of the publisher. **Module 46: Figure 1:** From Sternberg, R. J. (1986). A triangular theory of love. *Psychological Review*, 93, 119–135. Published by The American Psychological Association, adapted with permission. **Figure 2:** From Buss, D. M., et al. (1990). International preferences in selecting mates: A study of 37 cultures. *Journal of Cross-Cultural Psychology*, 21(1), 5–47, copyright © 1990 by Sage Publications. Reprinted by permission of Sage Publications, Inc. **Figure 3:** From Table 1 (p. 41) from Benjamin, L. T., Jr. (1985). Defining aggression. An exercise for classroom discussion. *Teaching of Psychology*, 12, 40–42. Reprinted by permission of the publisher. **Figure 4:** Latané, Bibb; Darley, John M.; *The Unresponsive Bystander: Why Doesn't He Help?*, p. 87–91. Copyright © 1971 Appleton-Century-Crofts. Reproduced by permission of Pearson Education, Inc.

Photo Credits

Front Matter

p. xiii: © Comstock/PictureQuest; **p. xiv (top):** © Alexander Tsiaras/Stock Boston; **p. xiv (bottom):** © Studio Photogram/Alamy RF; **p. xv:** © Nicholas Devore III/Photographers/Aspen/Still Media; **p. xvi (top):** © Getty Images; **p. xvi (bottom):** © Steve Raymer/Corbis; **p. xvii:** © Ariel Skelley/Blend Images/Alamy; **p. xviii (top):** © Michael Schwarz; **p. xviii (bottom):** © Image Source/Superstock; **p. xix:** © Inspirestock Inc./Alamy; **p. xx (top):** © Orbit/Masterfile; **p. xx (bottom):** © Zave Smith/Corbis; **p. xxi (top):** © Blend Images/Superstock RF; **p. xxii:** © AFP/Getty Images; **p. xxxviii:** © Comstock/PunchStock; **p. xl:** ©Stockbyte/Getty Images; **p. xli:** © Photodisc/PunchStock; **p. xlii:** © Digital Vision/Getty Images; **p. xliii:** © Photodisc; **p. xliv:** © Stockbyte/Getty Images; **p. xlvii:** ©Stockbyte/PunchStock

Chapter 1

Opener: © Comstock/PictureQuest; **p. 3 (top):** © David Buffington/Getty Images; **p. 3 (center left):** © Bettmann/Corbis; **p. 3 (center right):** © Thomas Pflaum/Visum/The Image Works; **p. 3 (bottom):** © Douglas Faulkner/Photo Researchers; **p. 4 (top):** © AP Images/Bill Haber; **p. 4 (center):** © Comstock/PictureQuest; **p. 7 (top):** © Jeff Greenberg/Photo Researchers; **p. 7 (center):** © Chuck Keeler/Getty Images; **p. 7 (bottom):** © David Buffington/Getty Images; **p. 10:** © Veronique Burger/Photo Researchers; **p. 15:** © Bettmann/Corbis; **p. 16 (top left):** © Corbis; **p. 16 (top right):** Courtesy, Wellesley College Archives. Photographed by Notman; **p. 16 (center):** © The Granger Collection; **p. 16 (bottom left):** © Photo Researchers; **p. 16 (bottom right):** © Bettmann/Corbis; **p. 17 (top left):** © Culver Pictures; **p. 17 (top right):** © The Granger Collection; **p. 17 (bottom left):** © The Granger Collection; **p. 17 (bottom right):** Courtesy, Elizabeth Loftus; **p. 19:** © Bettmann/Corbis; **p. 21:** © AP Images/Hadi Mizban **p. 29:** © Robert I. M. Campbell/National Geographic Image Collection; **p. 31:** © Bill Aron/PhotoEdit; **p. 33:** © James Wilson/Woodfin Camp; **p. 36 (top):** © Bill Aron/PhotoEdit; **p. 36 (bottom):** © Marc Steinmetz/VISUM/The Image Works; **p. 41:** © Thomas Pflaum/Visum/The Image Works; **p. 43:** © Douglas Faulkner/Photo Researchers; **p. 47:** © Comstock/PictureQuest

Chapter 2

Opener: © Alexander Tsiaras/Stock Boston; **p. 49 (top):** © Dennis Kunkel/Visuals Unlimited; **p. 49 (center):** © Passieka/SPL/Photo Researchers; **p. 49 (bottom):** © Martin Rotker/Photo Researchers; **p. 50 (top):** © Living Art Enterprises, LLC/Photo Researchers; **p. 50 (center):** © Alexander Tsiaras/Stock Boston; **p. 52:** © Dennis Kunkel/Visuals Unlimited; **p. 57 (top, center):** © Moonrunner Design Ltd.; **p. 57 (bottom):** © Michael Buckner/Getty Images for Michael J. Fox Foundation for Parkinson's Research; **p. 67:** © AP Images/Jeff Roberson; **p. 69:** © Martin Rotker/Photo Researchers; **p. 70(a):** © SPL/Photo Researchers; **p. 70(b):** © Volker Steger/Peter Arnold; **p. 70(c):** © Roger Ressmeyer/Corbis; **p. 70(d):** © Bryan Christie Design; **p. 72:** © Stephane de Sakutin/AFP/Getty Images; **p. 76:** © AP Images/Chris O'Meara; **p. 77:** Courtesy, Trustees of the British Museum, Natural History; **p. 79(a–c):** From Kato, R., Yokoi, H., Arieta, A.H., Yu, W., Arai, T. (2009). Mutual adaptation among man and machine by using f-MRI analysis. *Robotics and Autonomous Systems, 57,* 161–166

Chapter 3

Opener: © Studio Photogram/Alamy RF; **p. 87 (top):** © Curtis Myers/Stock Connection; **p. 87 (center left):** © Joe Epstein/Design Conceptions; **p. 87 (center right):** © Digital Vision/Getty; **p. 88:** © Studio Photogram/Alamy RF; **p. 90:** © Curtis Myers/Stock Connection; **p. 91:** © Marty Heitner/The Image Works; **p. 95 (both):** © Biophoto Associates/Photo Researchers; **p. 100(1–3):** Shmuel, A., Chaimow, D., Raddatz, G., Ugerbil, K., Yacoub, E. (2010). Mechanisms underlying decoding at 7T: Ocular dominance columns, broad structures, and macroscopic blood vessels in V1 convey information on the stimulated eye. *NeuroImage, 49,* 1957–1964. © 2010 with permission from Elsevier; **p. 101(a–c):** © Joe Epstein/Design Conceptions; **p. 108 (top):** © NASA; **p. 108 (bottom):** © Prof. P. Motta/Deptartment of Anatomy/University "La Sapienza", Rome/SPL/Photo Researchers; **p. 109:** © Omikron/Photo Researchers; **p. 112:** © Liu Yang/Redlinek/Corbis RF; **p. 119:** © Jeff Greenberg/Stock Boston; **p. 120:** © Cary Wolinsky/Stock Boston; **p. 122:** © John G. Ross/Photo Researchers; **p. 127:** © Studio Photogram/Alamy RF

Chapter 4

Opener: © Nicholas Devore III/Photographers/Aspen/Still Media; **p. 129 (top):** © Ted Spagna/Photo Researchers; **p. 129 (center):** © Liquidlibrary/PictureQuest; **p. 129 (bottom):** © Bob Daemmrich/The Image Works; **p. 130:** © Nicholas Devore III/Photographers/Aspen/Still Media; **p. 133 (all):** © Ted Spagna/Photo Researchers; **p. 134:** © CC Studio/Photo Researchers; **p. 136:** Walker, M. P., van der Helm, E. (2009). Overnight therapy? The role of sleep in emotional brain processing. *Psychological Bulletin, 135*(5), 731–748. Reprinted with permission from the American Psychological Association; **p. 138:** © PhotoDisc/Getty Images; **p. 140 (top):** © Philippe Garo/Photo Researchers; **p. 140 (bottom):** © Don Smith/Alamy; **p. 141 (top):** © B. Boissonnet/BSIP/Corbis; **p. 141 (bottom):** © Jose Carrillo/Stock Boston; **p. 145:** © AP Images/Midland Daily News/Erin Painter; **p. 147:** © Liquidlibrary/PictureQuest; **p. 149:** © Suzanne Opton; **p. 155 (left):** © Bob Daemmrich/The Image Works; **p. 155 (right):** © Jim Arbogast/Getty Images; **p. 157:** © Andrew Brookes/Corbis; **p. 161:** © Nicholas Devore III/Photographers/Aspen/Still Media

Chapter 5

Opener: © Getty Images; **p. 163 (top):** © Scott T. Baxter/Getty Images; **p. 163 (bottom):** © Spencer Grant/Stock Boston; **p. 164:** © Getty Images; **p. 166:** © Culver Pictures; **p. 168:** © Scott T. Baxter/Getty Images; **p. 175:** © Nina Leen/Time & Life Pictures/Getty Images; **p. 177 (top left):** © PhotoDisc/Getty Images; **p. 177 (top right):** © Stockbyte/Corbis; **p. 177 (bottom left):** © BananaStock/PunchStock; **p. 177 (bottom right):** © Amy Etra/PhotoEdit; **p. 178:** © NYC Center for Economic Opportunity, Office of the Mayor, City of New York; **p. 182:** © Stephen Chernin/Getty Images; **p. 183:** Courtesy, Dr. Marian Bailey; **p. 184 (left):** © The McGraw-Hill Companies, Inc./Jill Braaten, photographer; **p. 184 (right):** © Robin Nelson/PhotoEdit; **p. 190 (top):** Courtesy, Albert Bandura; **p. 190 (bottom):** © Spencer Grant/Stock Boston; **p. 191(a–d):** From Montgomery, K. J. Isenberg, N., Haxby, J. V. (2007). Communicative hand gestures and object-directed hand movements activated the mirror neuron system. *Social, Cognitive and Affective Neuroscience, 2,* 114–122 by permission of Oxford University Press; **p. 192 (both):** From Meltzoff, A. N. (1988). Imitation of Televised Models by Infants. *Child Development, 59,* 1221–1229. Photo Courtesy of A. N. Meltzoff & M. Hanak; **p. 193:** © Design Pics Inc./Alamy; **p. 195:** © Getty Images

Chapter 6

Opener: © Steve Raymer/Corbis; **p. 197 (top):** © Bob Wallace/Stock Boston; **p. 197 (center):** © Disney Enterprises, Inc; **p. 197 (bottom):** © Paul Thompson, UCLA Laboratory of Neuroimaging, 2003; **p. 198:** © Steve Raymer/Corbis; **p. 201:** © Bob Wallace/Stock Boston; **p. 209(a-b):** Maguire, E. A., Woollett, K., Spiers, H. J. (2006). London Taxi Drivers and Bus Drivers: A Structural MRI and Neuropsychological Analysis, *Hippocampus 16*:1091–1101. Reproduced with permission from John Wiley and Sons; **p. 210:** © Marty Bahamonde/FEMA; **p. 212:** © Disney Enterprises, Inc; **p. 216 (top):** © St Petersburg Times/Steve J. Coddington/The Image Works; **p. 216 (center):** © Syracuse Newspapers/H. Bragman/The Image Works; **p. 216 (bottom):** © David Young-Wolff/PhotoEdit; **p. 218:** © AP Images/Paul Sakuma; **p. 220:** © Albert Moldvay/National Geographic/Getty Images; **p. 226(a–c):** Reprinted from Maguire, E. A., et al. Autobiographical memory in semantic dementia: A longitudinal fMRI study. *Neuropsychologia.* 2010 Jan; 48(1):123–136. © 2010 with permission from Elsevier; **p. 229:** © Steve Raymer/Corbis

Chapter 7

Opener: © Ariel Skelley/Blend Images/Alamy; **p. 231 (top):** © Paul Souders/Corbis; **p. 231 (center):** Courtesy, Dr. Laura Ann Petitto @1991/photo by Robert LaMarche; **p. 231 (bottom):** © Harold Holt/Hulton Archive/Getty Images; **p. 232:** © Ariel Skelley/Blend Images/Alamy; **p. 233:** © Kevin C. Cox/Getty Images; **p. 239 (left):** © Hoby Finn/Getty Images; **p. 239 (right):** © Stockbyte/PunchStock; **p. 241(a–c):** © Superstock; **p. 246:** © Roberto Otero/Black Star; **p. 250:** Courtesy, Dr. Laura Ann Petitto @1991/photo by Robert LaMarche; **p. 252:** © AP Images; **p. 254:** Courtesy, The Language Research Center, Georgia State University; **p. 256:** From Kovelman, I., Shalinsky, M. H., Berens, M. S., &, Petitto, L. A. (2008). Shining new light on the brain's "bilingual signature": A functional Near Infrared Spectroscopy investigation of semantic processing. *Neuroimage, 39,* 1457–1471. © 2008 with permission from Elsevier. Photo: © Laura Ann Petitto, University of Toronto; **p. 259:** © David Hiser/Photographers/Aspen/Still Media; **p. 260:** © Paul Souders/Corbis; **p. 262(1):** © Harold Holt/Hulton Archive/Getty Images; **p. 262(2):** © Bettmann/Corbis; **p. 262(3):** © Cold Spring Harbor Laboratory; **p. 262(4):** © Bettmann/Corbis; **p. 262(5):** © David Hiser/Photographers/Aspen/Still Media; **p. 262(6):** © Bettmann/Corbis; **p. 262(7):** © George C. Beresford/Getty Images; **p. 262(8):** © Royalty-Free/Corbis; **p. 266:** © Roger Viollet/The Image Works; **p. 269:** © M. Siluk/The Image Works; **p. 272:** © Ingram Publishing/Alamy; **p. 279:** © Ariel Skelley/Blend Images/Alamy

Chapter 8

Opener: © Michael Schwarz; **p. 281 (center):** © Ryan McVay/Getty Images; **p. 281 (bottom):** Used by permission of Dr. Don Dutton; **p. 282:** © Michael Schwarz; **p. 283:** © AP Images/E. Pablo Kosmicki; **p. 293 (center):** © Jupiterimages/ImageSource; **p. 293 (bottom):** © Karen Kasmauski/Corbis; **p. 294:** © Ed Quinn/Corbis; **p. 295(a, b):** Santel, S., Baving, L., Krauel, K., Muente, T. F., Rotte, M. Hunger and satiety in anorexia nervosa: fMRI during cognitive processing of food pictures. *Brain Research, V.1114,*(1) 9 Oct. 2006, pp. 138–148. Figure 4. © 2006 with permission from Elsevier; **p. 300:** © Rachel Epstein/The Image Works; **p. 303:** Reprinted by permission of the publishers from Henry A. Murray, *Thematic Apperception Test,* Plate 12F, Cambridge, Mass.: Harvard University Press, Copyright © 1943 by the Presidents and Fellows of Harvard College, © 1971 by Henry A. Murray; **p. 310:** © Eric Fowke/PhotoEdit; **p. 312:** © Art Resource, NYC; **p. 313 (all):** Matsumoto & Ekman, 1988; **p. 315:** © AP Images/Petros Karadjias; **p. 317:** © Michael Schwarz

Chapter 9

Opener: © Look GMBH/eStock Photography; **p. 319 (top):** © Lennart Nilsson/Albert Bonniers Forlag AB/A Child Is Born/Dell Publishing; **p. 319 (center left):** © Laura Dwight/Peter Arnold; **p. 319 (center right):** © Purestock/Punchstock; **p. 319 (bottom):** © Deborah Davis/PhotoEdit; **p. 320:** © Look GMBH/eStock Photography; **p. 321:** © Peter Byron; **p. 325(a):** © D. W. Fawcett/Photo Researchers; **p. 325(b):** © L. Willatt, East Anglian Regional Genetics Service/SPL/Photo Researchers; **p. 325(c):** © Kenneth Eward/Photo Researchers; **p. 325(d):** © Biophoto Associates/Science Source/Photo Researchers; **p. 326:** © Peter Menzel/Photo Researchers; **p. 327 (top):** © Lennart Nilsson/Albert Bonniers Forlag AB/A Child Is Born/Dell Publishing; **p. 327 (bottom):** © Petit Format/Science Source/Photo Researchers; **p. 332:** © Charles Gupton/Stock Boston; **p. 334 (all):** From: A. N. Meltzoff & M. K. Moore. 1977. "Imitation of facial and manual gestures by human neonates." *Science, 198:* 75–78. © 1977 American Association for the Advancement of Science; **p. 338:** Harlow Primate Laboratory, University of Wisconsin; **p. 341:** © SW Productions/Getty Images; **p. 342:** © Banana Stock/Punchstock; **p. 344:** © Farrell Grehan/Corbis; **p. 345:** © Laura Dwight/Peter Arnold, **p. 353:** © Purestock/Punchstock; **p. 354:** © David Young Wolff/Getty Images; **p. 356:** © Olive Pierce/Black Star; **p. 358:** © Photodisc/Superstock; **p. 359:** © Mary Kate Denny/PhotoEdit; **p. 364:** © image100/Corbis; **p. 365:** © Robert Houser/UpperCut Images/Getty Images; **p. 368:** © Deborah Davis/PhotoEdit; **p. 370:** © AP Images/Gary Malerba; **p. 371:** © Bob Daemmrich/Stock Boston; **p. 375:** © Look GMBH/eStock Photography

Chapter 10

Opener: © Inspirestock Inc./Alamy; **p. 377 (top):** © Guy Gillette/Photo Researchers; **p. 377 (center):** © Meritt Vincent/PhotoEdit; **p. 377 (bottom):** © Hogrefe Publishing; **p. 378:** © Inspirestock Inc./Alamy; **p. 380:** © Corbis Premium RF/Alamy; **p. 381:** © Bettmann/Corbis; **p. 382:** © Guy Gillette/Photo Researchers; **p. 384:** © Andy Sacks/Getty Images; **p. 385 (left):** © Warner Brothers Pictures/PhotoFest; **p. 385 (right):** © Warner Brothers Pictures/PhotoFest; **p. 386:** © Bettmann/Corbis; **p. 391:** © Bob Daemmrich/The Image Works; **p. 392:** © The McGraw-Hill Companies, Inc./Lars A. Niki, photographer; **p. 394:** © BananaStock/

Punchstock; **p. 396:** © Brand X Pictures/Punchstock; **p. 397:** Gardini, S., Cloninger, C. R., Venneri, A. (2009). Individual differences in personality traits re?ect structural variance in specific brain regions, *Brain Research Bulletin, 79*(5), 265–270. © 2009 with permission from Elsevier; **p. 405:** © Hogrefe Publishing; **p. 407 (top):** © BananaStock; **p. 409:** © Inspirestock Inc./Alamy

Chapter 11

Opener: © Orbit/Masterfile; **p. 411 (top):** © Ariel Skelley/Blend Images/Corbis; **p. 411 (center):** © Reza/Webistan/Corbis; **p. 411 (bottom):** © Jose Luis Pelaez/Corbis; **p. 412:** © Orbit/Masterfile; **p. 413:** © Ariel Skelley/Blend Images/Corbis; **p. 415:** © Royalty-Free/Corbis; **p. 420:** © Dr. David Phillips/Visuals Unlimited; **p. 422:** From Coan, J., Schaefer, H. S., Davidson, R. J. Lending a Hand: Social Regulation of the Neural Response to Threat. *Psychological Science, 17,* 1032–1039. Reprinted with permission from John Wiley and Sons; **p. 427:** © Lucas Jackson/Reuters; **p. 428:** Janes, A. C., et al. (2009). Brain fMRI Reactivity to Smoking-Related Images Before and During Extended Smoking Abstinence. *Experimental and Clinical Psychopharmacology, 6,* 365–373. Reprinted with permission from the American Psychological Association; **p. 430:** © Reza/Webistan/Corbis; **p. 435:** © Jose Luis Pelaez/Corbis; **p. 436:** © Kevin Dodge/Corbis; **p. 439:** © Orbit/Masterfile

Chapter 12

Opener: © Zave Smith/Corbis; **p. 441 (top):** © AP Images/Brett Coomer; **p. 441 (center):** © Victoria and Albert Museum; **p. 441 (bottom):** © Phyllis Picardi; **p. 442:** © Zave Smith/Corbis; **p. 444:** © AP Images/Brett Coomer; **p. 449:** Reprinted with permission from the *Diagnostic and Statistical Manual of Mental Disorders,* Text Revision, Copyright 2000. American Psychiatric Association; **p. 455:** © Owen Franken/Corbis; **p. 457 (both):** Christian, C. J., et al. (2008). Gray matter structural alterations in obsessive–compulsive disorder: Relationship to neuropsychological functions. *Journal of Neuroimaging,164*(2), 123–131. © 2008 with permission from Elsevier; **p. 466 (all):** © Victoria and Albert Museum; **p. 468 (both):** Courtesy, Nancy Andreasen, University of Iowa Hospitals & Clinics; **p. 471:** © Tony Freeman/PhotoEdit; **p. 477:** © Sharon Gekoski-Kimmel/MCT/Landov; **p. 481:** © Zave Smith/Corbis

Chapter 13

Opener: © Blend Images/Superstock RF; **p. 483 (top):** © Bruce Ayres/Getty Images; **p. 483 (center):** © Jon Bradley/Getty Images; **p. 483 (bottom):** © Will & Deni McIntyre/Photo Researchers; **p. 484:** © Blend Images/Superstock RF; **p. 487:** © Getty RF; **p. 488:** © Jonathan Nourok/PhotoEdit; **p. 489:** © Bill Aron/PhotoEdit; **p. 491:** © Michael Newman/PhotoEdit; **p. 492 (both):** Schnell, K., Herpertz, S. C. (2007). Effects of dialectic-behavioral-therapy on the neural correlates of affective hyperarousal in borderline personality disorder. *Journal of Psychiatric Research, 41,* 837–847, Figure 3. © 2007 with permission from Elsevier; **p. 496:** © Don Hammond/Design Pics/Royalty-Free/Corbis; **p. 497:** © Royalty-Free/Corbis; **p. 499:** © Jon Bradley/Getty Images; **p. 502:** © Image Source/Alamy RF; **p. 506:** © Custom Medical Stock Photo; **p. 510:** © Phyllis Picardi; **p. 512:** © Michael Newman/PhotoEdit; **p. 515:** © Blend Images/Superstock RF

Chapter 14

Opener: © AFP/Getty Images; **p. 517 (top):** © Paul Barton/Corbis; **p. 517 (center left):** © Superstock/PictureQuest/JupiterImages; **p. 517 (center right):** © Barbara Burnes/Photo Researchers; **p. 517 (bottom):** © Bob Daemmrich/The Image Works; **p. 518:** © AFP/Getty Images; **p. 519:** © AP Images/Elise Amendola; **p. 521:** © Michael Peuckert/Imagebroker/Alamy; **p. 526:** © Paul Barton/Corbis; **p. 532:** © Jim Sugar/Corbis; **p. 534:** © Superstock/PictureQuest/JupiterImages; **p. 536 (both):** From the film *Obedience* © 1965 by Stanley Milgram and distributed by Penn. State Media Sales. Permission granted by Alexandra Milgram; **p. 539:** © Barbara Burnes/Photo Researchers; **p. 540:** Lieberman, M. D., et al. (2005) An fMRI investigation of race-related amygdala activity in African-American and Caucasian-American individuals. *Nature Neuroscience, 8*(6), 720–722. Reprinted by permission from Macmillan Publishers Ltd.; **p. 546:** © E. D. Torial/Alamy; **p. 550:** © Bob Daemmrich/The Image Works; **p. 552:** © Reuters NewMedia Inc./Corbis; **p. 553:** Greene, Joshua D., Paxton, Joseph M. (2009). Patterns of neural activity associated with honest and dishonest moral decisions. *PNAS, 106* (30), 12506–12511; **p. 555:** © AFP/Getty Images.

Name Index

Subject Index